# THE APPLICATION OF EU LAW
# IN THE NEW MEMBER STATES

*Brave New World*

# THE APPLICATION OF EU LAW
# IN THE NEW MEMBER STATES

*Brave New World*

*Edited by*

Adam Łazowski

T·M·C· ASSER PRESS

Cover design: Teresa Bubak-Mitela. Courtesy of the Artist.

ISBN 978-90-6704-274-1

# ACKNOWLEDGEMENTS

This book would not be possible without hard work and kind assistance of several people. Primarily the Editor is very grateful to all authors who submitted their contributions and managed to cope with the Editor's endless requests for clarifications and updates. Special thanks goes to the Asser Press team, who made conversion of the manuscript into a book possible. The Editor is very grateful to Dr. Steven Blockmans, who despite his very busy schedule, was always ready to assist, read critically parts of the manuscript and take the photo of *Nový Svet* for the cover. The photo of *Új világ* was kindly taken by Petra Várbíró. However, it wouldn't be possible without the assistance of Dr. Tamara Takács to whom I am very grateful. The cover was designed by Mrs. Teresa Bubak- Mitela (http://www.bubak-mitela.com) who patiently survived the Editor's ever changing ideas. I owe special thanks to my father Wojciech Łazowski who offered tremendous help and made the book cover possible. Last but not least, special thanks goes to my wife Anna, who read critically my own contributions to the book, helped me tremendously with editing, sub-editing, indexing and remained ever so patient when I was loosing faith in this project. Dziękuję z całego serca!

# SUMMARY OF CONTENTS

# TABLE OF CONTENTS

*Chapter 9*
**Poland: Constitutional Drama and Business as Usual**                                         277
Adam Łazowski and Aleksandra Wentkowska

## Chapter 12
**The Application of EU Law in Hungary: Challenges and Emerging Practices**     379
Tamara Takács

*Chapter 13*
**The Application of the EU Law in Slovenia: Teething Troubles of the Blue-eyed Boy**                                                421
Saša Zagorc and Samo Bardutzky

# LIST OF ABBREVIATIONS

| | |
|---|---|
| AFSJ | Area of Freedom, Security and Justice |
| AJCL | American Journal of Comparative Law |
| ALCSC | Administrative Law Chamber of the Estonian Supreme Court |
| ANI | National Integrity Agency |
| APL | Administrative Procedure Law |
| ARIB | Agricultural Registers and Information Board |
| CAA | Constitution of the Republic of Estonia Amendment Act |
| CAP | Common Agricultural Policy |
| CCC | Czech Constitutional Court |
| CDE | Cahiers de Droit Européen |
| CEE | Central and Eastern Europe |
| CEEC | Central and Eastern European Countries |
| CFI | Court of First Instance of the European Communities |
| CFSP | Common Foreign and Security Policy |
| CivCSC | Civil Chamber of the Supreme Court |
| CJQ | Civil Justice Quarterly |
| C.M.L.R. | Common Market Law Reports |
| CMLRev. | Common Market Law Review |
| COMECON | Council for Mutual Economic Assistance |
| CoR | Committee of the Regions |
| CPL | Criminal Procedure Law |
| CPR | Civil Procedure Rules |
| CRA | Communications Regulatory Authority (Lithuania) |
| CRCSC | Constitutional Review Chamber of the Supreme Court (Estonia) |
| CRE | Constitution of the Republic of Estonia |
| CRIA | Cambridge Review of International Affairs |
| CrimCSC | Criminal Chamber of the Supreme Court (Estonia) |
| CSC | Czech Supreme Court |
| CTM | Community trademark |
| CYELP | Croatian Yearbook of European Law and Policy |
| CYELS | Cambridge Yearbook of European Legal Studies |
| DNA | National Anti-Corruption Directorate (Romania) |
| DPC | Droit Polonais Contemporain |
| E.C.C. | European Commercial Cases |
| E.Eur.Case Rep. of Const. L. | East European Case Reporter of Constitutional Law |
| EA | Europe Agreements |
| EAEC | European Atomic Energy Community |

| | |
|---|---|
| EAW | European Arrest Warrant |
| EBLR | European Business Law Review |
| EC | European Community |
| ECB | European Central Bank |
| ECHR | Convention for the Protection of Human Rights and Fundamental Freedoms |
| ECJ | European Court of Justice |
| ECLR | European Competition Law Review |
| ECR | European Court Reports |
| ECT | European Constitutional Treaty |
| ECtHR | European Court of Human Rights |
| EEA | European Economic Areas |
| EEC | European Economic Community |
| EESC | European Economic and Social Committee |
| EFA Rev. | European Foreign Affairs Review |
| EFTA | European Free Trade Association |
| EJLS | European Journal of Legal Studies |
| ELJ | European Law Journal |
| ELRev. | European Law Review |
| ENP | European Neighbourhood Policy |
| EP | European Parliament |
| EPL | European Public Law |
| ESDI | European Security and Defence Identity |
| EU | European Union |
| EUBAM | European Union Border Assistance Mission |
| EuConst | European Constitutional Law Review |
| Euro.C.L.Y. | European Current Law Yearbook |
| EUSR | European Union Special Representative |
| EuZW | Europäische Zeitschrift für Wirtschaftsrecht |
| Evro PP | Evro Pravna Praksa |
| FTA | free trade agreement |
| GAERC | General Affairs and External Relations Council |
| GATT 1947 | General Agreement on Tariffs and Trade |
| GLJ | German Law Journal |
| GSR | Geneva Convention on the Status of Refugees |
| GYIL | German Yearbook of International Law |
| Harv. ILJ | Harvard International Law Journal |
| HRLJ | Human Rights Law Journal |
| I.L.Pr. | International Litigation Procedure |
| I·CON | International Journal of Constitutional Law |
| ICLQ | International and Comparative Law Quarterly |
| ILA | International Law Association |
| ILJ | Industrial Law Journal |
| Int'l J. Refugee L. | International Journal of Refugee Law |
| JCMS | Journal of Common Market Studies |
| JEPP | Journal of European Public Policy |
| JHA | Justice and Home Affairs |

| | |
|---|---|
| JLE | Journal of Legal Education |
| JLP | Journal of Legal Pluralism |
| LQR | Law Quarterly Review |
| NRC | Državna revizijska komisija za revizijo postopkov javnih naročil [National Review Commission for Reviewing Public Procurement Award Procedures] |
| OHIM | The Office of Harmonization for the Internal Market |
| OJLS | Oxford Journal of Legal Studies |
| OPOCE | EU Publications Office |
| PJCC | Police and Judicial Co-operation in Criminal Matters |
| PolYBIL | Polish Yearbook of International Law |
| RDP | Revue du Droit Public |
| RELEX | European Commission Directorate for External Relations |
| RT | Riigi Teataja (State Gazette, Estonian Official Journal) |
| SAC | Supreme Administrative Court |
| SC | Supreme Court |
| SCC | Slovak Constitutional Court |
| SCI | Site of Community Importance |
| SIS | Schengen Information System |
| SSC | Slovak Supreme Court |
| TAIEX | Technical Assistance and Information Exchange instrument |
| TEU | Treaty on European Union |
| TFEU | Treaty on the Functioning of the European Union |
| TI | Transparency International |
| TRIPS | Agreement on Trade Related Aspects of Intellectual Property Rights |
| UChLRev. | The University of Chicago Law Review |
| UN | United Nations |
| UNMIK | Interim Administration Mission in Kosovo |
| US | United States of America |
| VAT | Value Added Tax |
| VDSSL | Višje delovno in socialno sodišče v Ljubljani [Higher Labour and Social Court in Ljubljana] |
| YEL (sometimes YBEL) | Yearbook of European Law |
| YPES | Yearbook of Polish European Studies |
| ZSE | Zeitschrift für Staats- und Europawissenschaften |

*On the day the wall came down*
*They threw the locks onto the ground*
*And with glasses high we raised a cry for freedom had arrived*

David Gilmour (Pink Floyd)
Gdańsk Shipyard
August 2006

# INTRODUCTION

Five years after the fifth enlargement and more than two years after the sixth expansion of the European Union (EU), an attempt is being made to give those two groundbreaking events a reality check.[1] Arguably, the time has come to subject the triumphant political discourse, praising the unprecedented endeavor of expanding the European Union from fifteen to twenty-seven Member States against the test of effectiveness. The crucial question is: has the patient survived the operation and is it still alive and breathing normally?[2] On the one hand, we may hear that the European Union is in crisis and the fundamental questions of *finalité* remain unanswered. We also hear of the constitutional drama and post-enlargement blues undermining the effectiveness of the integration enterprise. On the other hand, some argue that the two recent waves of enlargement have been the EU's most successful foreign policy projects, which proved their purpose and justified the political and economic sacrifices. To evaluate all pertinent factors underpinning the fifth and sixth enlargements of the European Union would go beyond the scope of one book. That would require a multi-volume, interdisciplinary study of enormous proportions.

The focus of this study is on the application of EU law in the twelve new Member States of the European Union. It is not a matter of professional chauvinism of the authors but rather a method of introducing critical analysis of legal issues into the equation of post-accession political and academic discourse. The recent two enlargements are often perceived as *par excellence* political processes of reunification of Europe. Undoubtedly, such an approach has merits. However, it should be remembered that the Community Treaties established a new legal order, for which the Member States passed sovereign competences for joint governance and – what is equally important – the subjects of that

---

[1] The accession of Bulgaria and Romania is considered by many as the second wave of the fifth enlargement of the European Union. Although politically the 2004 and 2007 enlargements are part of the same project, they are not in legal terms. The accession of ten countries on 1 May 2004 and the remaining two on 1 January 2007 is governed by separate Accession Treaties, which provide for similar but not the same entry conditions. As explained later in this book, both Bulgaria and Romania have been special cases due to domestic problems with compliance with EU *acquis*. Almost three years after the accession, Bulgaria and Romania are still covered by a tailor-made post-accession monitoring mechanism and, to much regret, are still underperforming. Bearing in mind the above, we refer to fifth and sixth enlargements of the European Union.

[2] One of the early analyses clearly suggests that this is the case. See further P. Settembri, 'The surgery succeeded. Has the patient died? The impact of enlargement on the European Union', *Jean Monnet Working Paper* No. 4/07.

*A. Łazowski (ed.), The Application of EU Law in the New Member States*
© 2010, T·M·C·Asser press, *The Hague, The Netherlands and the Authors*

legal order are not only the States themselves but also individuals.[3] These fundamentals were established by the European Court of Justice at the very early stages of the integration exercise and remain equally valid in 2009. The legal aspects of the recent enlargements have already received a fair degree of attention in the academic writing; however, the focus was mainly on the constitutional challenges of membership in the European Union. The scope of this volume is much broader. The authors aimed at an in-depth and comprehensive analysis of national legal orders and reception of EU law by national authorities, with particular emphasis on domestic judiciaries. All chapters grouped in Part Three of the book follow the same structure, allowing readers to appreciate a comparative analysis of crucial legal issues related to the recent enlargements of the European Union. Parts One and Two were tailored to create a proper systemic background and tackle several horizontal matters, including the impact of the enlargements on the European Union (Part One – West meets East) and on the newcomers (Part Two – East meets West).

Before inviting readers to dwell into this "Brave New World", it is fitting to explain the symbolic title of this book, its leitmotif and the photographs on the cover. One may ask if the new Member States are a Brave New World, and, if so, are they the Huxley's world or rather something different. The editor of this volume argued recently that Poland – the biggest newcomer – is on its way from Ismail Kadare's 'Palace of Dreams'[4] to Europe.[5] Similarly in this volume, together with the contributors from both sides of the late Iron Curtain, the editor argues that the new Member States have gone during the past twenty years from Huxley's vision of the world to a rather new environment. It may still be considered as "work in progress"; however the progress has been tremendous. By the same token, the title term "Brave New World" has received a new meaning. Although criticism of legal developments is clearly *en vogue* these days, it is only fair to take into account the unprecedented breadth of the legal reforms the Central and Eastern European countries have had to go through during the past two decades.

When one appreciates the negative impact of Communist brain-drain on law-makers and judiciary as well as the mentality of its members, the perception of the last twenty years of legal *rapprochement* towards Europe changes considerably. From that perspective a glass filled with water looks half full, not half empty. In this context we are facing the Brave New World – countries in transition, which as a part of the integration exercise, had to reform their legal orders totally and in a very short time get ready to deal with this new legal order (as proclaimed by the European Court of Justice). This book demonstrates that the change has come, and EU law is paving its way – sometimes against all odds – in the new Member States. This process is clearly far from over and will take decades to complete. Yet, the first five years (in the case of eight countries which joined in 2004) is instructive enough to demonstrate the limits and potential of

---

[3] ECJ, Case 26/62 *NV Algemene Transport- en Expeditie Onderneming van Gend & Loos v. Netherlands Inland Revenue Administration* [1963] *ECR* 1.

[4] I. Kadare, *The Palace of Dreams* (Random House, Vintage Classics 2008).

[5] A. Łazowski, 'From Palace of Dreams to Europe', paper presented at a conference '"Legacies and Prospects" Poland 1989: 20 Years On', St. Antony's College, Oxford University, 8 June 2009. Text available at http://westminster.academia.edu/AdamLazowski/Talks.

the enlargement project. Arguably, the legal order of the European Union has survived this important test; however, it has also demonstrated the challenges to the EU's absorption capacity. The latter is usually understood in a very political fashion as the ability of the European Union to function properly and maintain its effectiveness. It should also be understood as covering the ability of the legal order underpinning the integration endeavor to remain effective and efficient. Following the accession of Romania and Bulgaria, an interesting rule of thumb emerges. The legal absorption capacity of the European Union decreases proportionally to the gravity of domestic problems with human rights standards, corruption, independence of judiciary, etc. EU conditionality employed thus far *vis-à-vis* countries aspiring for membership has worked relatively well with countries to which the first verse of Pink Floyd's 'Great Day for Freedom' applies. A number of countries that emerged on the ashes of Communism engaged in absurdities and atrocities depicted in the remaining verses of this very moving tune. This book is about the ten countries that raised the glasses high as freedom arrived and passed on peaceful, albeit turbulent at times, multidimensional transition. It all started with three Visegrad countries – Czechoslovakia, Hungary and Poland. Prague, Budapest and Warsaw – capitals of the trio – have their new world streets, and this symbolic fact is reflected on the cover of this book. For those countries who turned to far rockier paths, there is a long way to go; however, as this book proves, the Brave New World is a possible and feasible scenario.

*Tempus edax rerum* said Ovid a long time ago. This very acute observation applies to all things in life, including books. With a rapidly changing legal landscape it is almost impossible to publish a book on EU law which by the time it reaches readers is still up-to-date. Alas, this book is no exception. Since the material was submitted in June 2009 a number of developments has taken place. Not only a plethora of new case law has emerged but also the Treaty of Lisbon entered into force on 1 December 2009. The cut off date for this volume was 1 June 2009 and the authors aimed to reflect the law as it stood then. As always with edited volumes some chapters were submitted early, some late. Every effort was made to update them all so that the book gives readers a comprehensive overview of the legal developments which took place since the European Union enlarged in 2004 and 2007. In several chapters the centre of gravity is on the first years of membership with a view of demonstrating the emerging practices of national courts undergoing a fast track Copernican revolution. However, a brief account of major subsequent developments was also made where necessary.

Adam Łazowski

*Chapter 1*

# IT WORKS! THE EUROPEAN UNION IN THE WAKE OF 2004 AND 2007 ENLARGEMENTS

Adam Łazowski*

## 1.   INTRODUCTION

The fifth and sixth enlargements of the European Union are generally considered to be unprecedented historical events, leading to the unification of Europe. At the same time, it is argued that the accession of ten countries from Central and Eastern Europe as well as the Mediterranean islands of Malta and Cyprus have changed for good the shape and functioning of the European Union. By the same token, some say that the "big bang" expansion has undermined the ability of the EU to function properly, and the EU is suffering from enlargement fatigue or blues. Clearly the dynamics of the European Union have changed. With twenty-seven Member States on board, the European Union has had to go through several adjustments; yet it proved to be flexible enough to operate fairly successfully in this new environment. The purpose of the first part of this book is to look at how the West met the East, and how that has changed the European Union. This will lay the systemic foundations for the analysis of application of EU law in the new Member States. This chapter will pinpoint several issues that are discussed throughout the book. It will serve as an introduction to contributions contained in Parts Two and Three. In order to make the picture more or less complete, Chapter 2 will look at the geopolitical implications of the accession of the Central and Eastern European countries as well as Malta and Cyprus.[1]

---

* Reader in Law, School of Law, University of Westminster, London.
[1]  See further, *inter alia*, A. Mayhew, *Recreating Europe. The European Union's Policy towards Central and Eastern Europe* (Cambridge, Cambridge University Press 1999); A. Ott and K. Inglis, eds., *Handbook on European Enlargement. A Commentary on the Enlargement Process* (The Hague, T.M.C. Asser Press 2002); C. Hillion, ed., *EU Enlargement. A Legal Approach* (Oxford-Portland, Oregon, Hart Publishing 2004); W. Jacoby, *The Enlargement of the European Union and NATO. Ordering from the Menu in Central and Eastern Europe* (Cambridge, Cambridge University Press 2004); N. Nugent, ed., *European Union Enlargement* (London, Palgrave Macmillan 2004); A.L. Dimitrova, ed., *Driven to Change. The European Union's Enlargement Viewed from the East* (Manchester, Manchester University Press 2004); E. Brimmer and S. Fröhlich, eds., *The Strategic Implications of European Union Enlargement* (Washington, Center for Transatlantic Relations 2005); A.F. Tatham, *Enlargement of the European Union* (The Hague, Wolters Kluwer 2009).

*A. Łazowski (ed.), The Application of EU Law in the New Member States*
© 2010, T·M·C·ASSER PRESS, *The Hague, The Netherlands and the Authors*

## 2.    FIFTH AND SIXTH ENLARGEMENTS IN A NUTSHELL

### 2.1.    From six to fifteen – previous enlargement rounds

It is not accidental that the fifth wave of accession is often referred to as the "big bang" enlargement. As supplemented by the *petit* sixth enlargement, it has led to almost doubling of the number of Member States of the European Union. This fact in itself makes the recent developments unique and unprecedented. Never before had the European Communities/European Union engaged in such a complex political, economic and legal exercise. It already had the experience of letting in much poorer countries undergoing economic transition. However, to invite Greece, Spain and Portugal to join had been one thing; to let in ten ex-Communist countries was another. Therefore, a short reminder of previous accession rounds seems fitting.[2] The first enlargement took place in 1973 when Denmark, Ireland and the United Kingdom joined the club.[3] This was followed by two Mediterranean enlargements. First Greece joined the European Communities in 1981; then Spain and Portugal followed in 1986. Both waves proved to be quite a challenge as all three countries were freshly freed from authoritarian regimes and undergoing a painful political and economic transition. One should not forget that by the time of the third enlargement, the European Communities were undergoing the first major treaty revision[4] and laying foundations for the ambitious internal market program.[5] The fourth round of accessions was in fact the first enlargement of the European Union (which was established in 1993 following the entry into force of the Treaty of Maastricht).[6] The EFTA enlargement[7] (as it is often referred to) was just a taste of what was to come with the emerging democracies of Central and Eastern Europe.[8] Already at that time the European Union had Cyprus and Malta knocking on its door and quite a rocky relationship with Turkey and its membership aspirations.

### 2.2.    From fifteen to twenty-seven

In political terms, the membership of Central and Eastern European countries is a logical consequence of historical events and decisions taken in the early 1990s. In a

---

[2] For an in-depth analysis, see, *inter alia*, Tatham, *op. cit.* n. 1, at pp. 7-69; Ch. Preston, *Enlargement and Integration in the European Union* (London and New York, Routledge 1997).

[3] At that time Norway nearly joined the European Communities; however the results of a nationwide referendum stopped the *rapprochement*.

[4] Single European Act, *OJ* 1987 L 169/1. Single European Act was signed in February 1986 and entered into force on 1 July 1987.

[5] See further, *inter alia*, P. Craig, 'The Evolution of the Single Market', in C. Barnard and J. Scott, eds., *The Law of the Single European Market. Unpacking the Premises* (Oxford and Portland, Oregon, Hart Publishing 2002) pp. 1-40.

[6] Treaty on European Union, *OJ* 1992 C 191/1. See further, *inter alia*, D. O'Keeffe, P. Twomey, eds., *Legal Issues of the Treaty of Maastricht* (London-New York-Chichester-Brisbane-Toronto-Singapore, Wiley Chancery Law 1994).

[7] It merits attention that it was the second attempt of Norway to become a member of the European Communities/European Union. Again, the nation rejected the membership bid in a nationwide referendum. See further C. Archer, *Norway outside the European Union. Norway ad European integration from 1994 to 2004* (London and New York, Routledge 2005).

[8] For more on the EFTA enlargement, see, *inter alia*, Tatham, *op. cit.* n. 1, pp. 57-69.

way it closes the loop of dramatic changes that started with the partly free Polish elections on 4 June 1989 and fairly peaceful revolutions in Czechoslovakia, Hungary and the rest of the region.[9] All those countries had been victims of the post-World War II settlement, that is, under brutal dominance of the Soviet Union, with no chance of participation in the integration endeavor. The accession to the European Union brings to an end the phase of an unprecedented drive towards Europe, expressed by membership in the Council of Europe, the OECD and NATO. Accession to the EU is not icing on the cake but rather the most complex and far reaching exercise. The membership of Cyprus and Malta is rather a different story. In the case of the former, it was an idiosyncratic process where the division of the island and constant tensions between Greece and Turkey played an important role. The accession of Malta was determined by swings of mood and, at some point in time, freezing of the application for membership (and subsequent resubmission).

### 2.2.1. *Countries of Central and Eastern Europe*

The starting point for European *rapprochement* of the former Communist countries of Central and Eastern Europe was establishing diplomatic relations in late 1980s.[10] On the one hand, it was a clear sign of a demise of the Communist regimes established in close "co-operation" with the Soviet Union. On the other hand, it was a catalyst for closer co-operation with the European Communities, which, in the short run, led to the conclusion of trade agreements. Prior to democratic reforms of the 1990s, there had been very limited co-operation between the EC and COMECON countries.[11] The basic platform for co-operation was the GATT 1947 framework; however some of those countries had sectoral trade agreements with the European Economic Community.[12] An important quality change came in the late 1980s when comprehensive trade agreements were concluded,[13] *inter alia,* with Hungary,[14]

---

[9] This was not the case in former Yugoslavia, where the collapse of the country can be called anything but amicable. However, in all ten countries that joined the European Union in 2004 and 2007, the transition was not accompanied by bloodshed.

[10] For a detailed account, see, *inter alia*, Mayhew, *op. cit.* n. 1.

[11] Council for Mutual Economic Assistance was an economic co-operation endeavor for the Soviet Union and satellite countries. The assistance was one sided and ultimately the only beneficiary remained the Soviet Union itself. See further, *inter alia*, J. Brine, *Comecon: the rise and fall of an international socialist organization* (New Brunswick, Transaction Publishers 1992).

[12] For example, the following agreements were concluded with Bulgaria: Agreement between the European Economic Community and the People's Republic of Bulgaria on trade in textile products, *OJ* 1982 L 330/2; Exchange of Letters between the European Economic Community and the People's Republic of Bulgaria on trade in the sheepmeat and goatmeat sector, *OJ* 1982 L 43/13; Agreement between the European Economic Community and the People's Republic of Bulgaria on trade in textile products, *OJ* 1986 L 293/2.

[13] For an overview, see D. Horovitz, 'EC-Central/East European relations: New principles for a new era', 27 *CMLRev.* (1990) pp. 259-284.

[14] Council Decision of 21 November 1988 concerning the conclusion of an Agreement between the European Economic Community and the Hungarian People's Republic on trade and commercial and economic co-operation, *OJ* 1988 L 327/1.

Czechoslovakia,[15] Poland[16] and Bulgaria.[17] With the drastic economic reforms in full
swing combined with a drive of new political elites towards Europe, the European
Communities and its Member States had no choice but to offer a path for gradual
*rapprochement*.[18]

While the fall of Communism was met with widespread enthusiasm in Western
Europe, the membership aspirations of its Eastern neighbors were quite a different
matter. The initial reaction of the twelve Member States of the European Communities
was rather reserved, proving that the time had yet to come for this kind of commitment.
In many ways, the Western European countries were taken by surprise by the rapid and
unexpectedly peaceful developments behind the Iron Curtain. There was no strategy
or clear plan for rearranging the relations of the European Communities with their close
neighbors to the East. Since to offer membership at that stage was unthinkable, the
decision was made to offer association to the new democracies of Central and Eastern
Europe.[19] Shortly afterwards the negotiations of Europe Agreements (EA) with the first
group of countries (Poland, Hungary and Czechoslovakia) commenced. This was followed by negotiations with Bulgaria and Romania (1992-1993) as well as with the three
Baltic states (Lithuania, Latvia and Estonia) and Slovenia (1995). In terms of contents
and structure, all Europe Agreements were quite similar if not exactly the same.[20] They
were a new generation of comprehensive association agreements covering political and
economic co-operation, provisions on movement of goods, right of establishment,
movement of services, competition law, approximation of laws as well as cultural and
financial co-operation.[21] The Europe Agreements provided a legal basis for creation of
joint institutions – association councils, association committees as well as parliamen-

---

[15] Agreement between the European Economic Community and the European Atomic Energy Community and the Czech and Slovak Federal Republic on trade and commercial and economic co-operation,
*OJ* 1990 L 291/29.

[16] Agreement between the European Economic Community and the Polish People's Republic on trade
and commercial and economic co-operation, *OJ* 1989, L 339/2.

[17] Agreement between the European Economic Community and the People's Republic of Bulgaria on
trade and commercial and economic co-operation, *OJ* 1990 L 291/9.

[18] See, *inter alia*, Communication from the Commission to the Council, Implications of recent changes in central and eastern Europe for the Community's relations with the countries concerned, SEC (90) 111
final; Communication from the Commission to the Council and the Parliament, The development of Community's relations with the countries of central and eastern Europe, SEC (90) 196 final; Communication
from the Commission, The development of Community's relations with the countries of central and eastern Europe, SEC (90) 717 final; Communication from the Commission to the Council and Parliament, Association agreements with countries of central and eastern Europe: a general outline, COM (90) 398 final.

[19] For a detailed account, see, *inter alia*, M. Maresceau, '"Europe Agreements": A New Form of Co-
operation between the European Community and Central and Eastern Europe', in P.-Ch. Müller-Graff, ed.,
*East Central European States and the European Communities: Legal Adaptation to the Market Economy*
(Baden-Baden, Nomos 1993) pp. 209 et seq.; M. Maresceau and E. Montaguti, 'The relations between the
European Union and Central and Eastern Europe: A legal appraisal', 32 *CMLRev.* (1995) pp. 1327-1367.

[20] For a very comprehensive overview, see Ott and Inglis, *op. cit.* n. 1.

[21] Europe Agreements fell under the category of mixed agreements, thus requiring lengthy ratification
by all Member States of the European Communities/European Union. Therefore, separate interim trade
agreements were concluded to facilitate entry into force of trade-related provisions of EAs at the earliest
possibility.

tary association committees. Following their ratification, the Europe Agreements entered into force.[22] The first two to do so were EAs with Poland and Hungary on 1 February 1994. The last one was EA Slovenia, which entered into force on 1 February 1999.

As already noted, the question of membership in the European Communities/ European Union was a priority for the Central and Eastern European countries almost from the start of economic and political reforms. This was not the case on the other side of the diminishing Iron Curtain. It is only fair to mention that, in the years following the White Paper of 1985[23] and the Single European Act, the European Communities were preoccupied with the implementation of the internal market programme. At the same time, the next IGC, filled with ambitious dossiers, was emerging on the horizon, and the creation of the European Economic Area was pending.[24] This, together with the complex transformation that the newly born democracies had to face, meant that the EC Member States were quite reluctant to discuss the prospect of eastern enlargement. It should be stressed that 'originally, Europe Agreements were perceived by the EU more as an alternative to, rather than a preparatory instrument for, accession.'[25] Yet, the EU membership ambitions of the newly associated countries were, in the case of the early Europe Agreements, mirrored in unilateral declarations inserted into the preambles of the Europe Agreements.

---

[22] Europe Agreement establishing an association between the European Communities and their Member States, of the one part, and the Republic of Poland, of the other part, *OJ* 1993 L 348/2; Europe Agreement establishing an association between the European Communities and their Member States, of the one part, and the Republic of Hungary, of the other part, *OJ* 1993 L 347/2; Europe Agreement establishing an association between the European Communities and their Member States, of the one part, and the Czech Republic, of the other part, *OJ* 1994 L 360/2; Europe Agreement establishing an association between the European Communities and their Member States, of the one part, and the Slovak Republic, of the other part, *OJ* 1994 L 359/2; Europe Agreement establishing an association between the European Communities and their Member States, of the one part, and Romania, of the other part, *OJ* 1994 L 357/2; Europe Agreement establishing an association between the European Communities and their Member States, of the one part, and the Republic of Bulgaria, of the other part, *OJ* 1994 L 358/3; Europe Agreement establishing an association between the European Communities and their Member States, of the one part, and the Republic of Lithuania, of the other part, *OJ* 1998 L 51/2; Europe Agreement establishing an association between the European Communities and their Member States, of the one part, and the Republic of Latvia, of the other part, *OJ* 1998 L 26/3; Europe Agreement establishing an association between the European Communities and their Member States, of the one part, and the Republic of Estonia, of the other part, *OJ* 1998 L 68/3; Europe Agreement establishing an association between the European Communities and their Member States, acting within the framework of the European Union, of the one part, and the Republic of Slovenia, of the other part, *OJ* 1999 L 51/3.

[23] Completing the Internal Market. White Paper from the Commission to the European Council, COM (85) 310 final.

[24] It is notable that Central and Eastern European countries rejected the idea of joining the European Economic Area and stuck to their EC/EU aspirations. At that time, Peers argued that 'Although the EAs may serve well as an interim measure while the EA States become familiar with the EU legal system, a comparison of the EEA with EAs will demonstrate that membership of the EEA is the best way of preparing EA States for EU membership.' See S. Peers, 'An ever closer waiting room?: The case for Eastern European accession to the European Economic Area', 32 *CMLRev.* (1995) pp. 187-213, at p. 189.

[25] M. Maresceau, 'Pre-accession', in M. Cremona, ed., *The Enlargement of the European Union* (Oxford, Oxford University Press 2003) pp. 9-42, at p. 15.

For instance, EA Bulgaria read

> 'that Bulgaria's ultimate objective is to become a member of the Community, and that this
> association, in the view of the Parties, will help Bulgaria to achieve this objective.'

As the pressure was mounting – even before the entry into force of the first Europe Agreement – the Member States decided to react to calls coming from Warsaw, Prague, Budapest and other capitals in Central and Eastern Europe. The European Communities were ready to announce that the new democracies would have a chance to accede provided they fulfilled the membership criteria. This landmark decision was taken during the Copenhagen European Council in June 1993,[26] and the applications for membership followed.[27]

The first major step was the European Commission's White Paper on the preparation of the CEECs for integration into the internal market, which identified the internal market *acquis* that the aspiring countries were supposed to transpose and implement.[28] At the end of 1995, the European Council requested the European Commission to present its opinion on the membership applications that had by then been submitted by most countries of Central and Eastern Europe. The batch of opinions was presented on 15 July 1997, together with a policy document entitled Agenda 2000.[29] Following the recommendations of the European Commission, during a summit in December 1997 in Luxembourg, the European Council decided on opening accession negotiations with the first group of countries (Poland, Czech Republic, Hungary, Estonia, Slovenia and Cyprus). Two years later the European Council in Helsinki decided to open negotiations with the remaining group of countries.[30]

The developments initiated by the Copenhagen European Council paved the way for adoption of an unprecedented pre-accession strategy. Another important boost came from the Essen European Council in December 1994. Due to the complexity of the process and the level of development of the applicant countries, the previous enlargements could not serve as a model. As noted by Kirstyn Inglis, 'No other enlargement has focused on so many and such a diversity of countries, nor indeed on countries so dramatically different from the Union in political and economic terms.'[31] A number of tools have been used as a part of this strategy. The main legal instruments were the Europe Agreements, reoriented from mere association treaties into pivotal pre-accession vehicles. A patchwork of other instruments has included various policy instruments and, at a later stage, accession partnerships. The latter were the main policy instruments

---

[26] *Bull. EU* 6-1993, point 13.

[27] Hungary (31 March 1994), Poland (5 April 1994), Romania (22 June 1995), Slovakia (27 June 1995), Latvia (13 October 1995), Estonia (24 November 1995), Lithuania (8 December 1995), Bulgaria (14 December 1995), Czech Republic (17 January 1996), Slovenia (10 June 1996).

[28] White Paper – Preparation of the candidate countries of Central and Eastern Europe for integration into the Internal Market of the Union, COM (95) 163 final.

[29] European Commission. Agenda 2000, For a stronger and wider Union, COM (1997) 2000 final.

[30] At that time Malta was back on board, following the reactivation of its membership application.

[31] K. Inglis, 'The Europe Agreements compared in the light of their pre-accession reorientation', 37 *CMLRev.* (2000) pp. 1173-1210, at p. 1176.

of this strategy. They were based on Council Regulation 622/98/EC[32] and updated regularly, allowing the candidate countries to respond with updates and adjustments of their own national plans for the adoption of the *acquis* (NPAA). An important role was also played by the European Commission's annual progress reports.

The negotiations were completed quite symbolically during the European Council meeting in Copenhagen in December 2002.[33] This was followed by an intense period of finalising the Accession Treaty and its signature at Acropolis on 16 April 2003.[34] Following a series of referenda in nine out of ten acceding countries and completion of ratification procedures by all parties, the Accession Treaty entered into force on 1 May 2004.[35] It should be noted that by the time of the European Council in Copenhagen in 2002 neither Bulgaria nor Romania managed to fulfill the necessary criteria. This forced the European Union to develop even further its pre-accession strategy and new set of instruments supporting the necessary reforms.[36] Despite continuing efforts and growing doubts as to the level of preparedness of both countries, the Accession Treaty was signed on 25 April 2005.[37] Following the ratification procedures in both acceding

---

[32] Council Regulation (EC) No 622/98 of 16 March 1998 on assistance to the applicant States in the framework of the pre-accession strategy, and in particular on the establishment of Accession Partnerships, *OJ* 1998 L 85/1.

[33] See further, *inter alia*, C. Banasiński, 'The Negotiations Decision-Making Machinery', 25 *PolYBIL* (2001) pp. 69-84.

[34] Treaty between the Kingdom of Belgium, the Kingdom of Denmark, the Federal Republic of Germany, the Hellenic Republic, the Kingdom of Spain, the French Republic, Ireland, the Italian Republic, the Grand Duchy of Luxembourg, the Kingdom of the Netherlands, the Republic of Austria, the Portuguese Republic, the Republic of Finland, the Kingdom of Sweden, the United Kingdom of Great Britain and Northern Ireland (Member States of the European Union) and the Czech Republic, the Republic of Estonia, the Republic of Cyprus, the Republic of Latvia, the Republic of Lithuania, the Republic of Hungary, the Republic of Malta, the Republic of Poland, the Republic of Slovenia, the Slovak Republic, concerning the accession of the Czech Republic, the Republic of Estonia, the Republic of Cyprus, the Republic of Latvia, the Republic of Lithuania, the Republic of Hungary, the Republic of Malta, the Republic of Poland, the Republic of Slovenia and the Slovak Republic to the European Union, *OJ* 2003 L 236/17. For a legal appraisal see, *inter alia*, K. Inglis, 'The Union's fifth Accession Treaty: New means to make enlargement possible', 41 *CMLRev.* (2004) pp. 937-973; Ch. Hillion, 'The European Union is dead. Long live the European Union... a commentary on the Treaty of Accession 2003', 29 *ELRev.* (2004) pp. 583-612.

[35] The only newcomer not to hold an accession referendum was Cyprus. See further, A. Albi, 'Referendums in the CEE Candidate Countries: Implications for the EU Treaty Amendment Procedure', in Hillion, ed., *op. cit.* n. 1, pp. 57-75.

[36] See further, K. Inglis, 'EU enlargement: Membership conditions applied to future and potential Member States', in S. Blockmans and A. Łazowski, eds., *The European Union and Its Neighbours. A Legal appraisal of the EU's policies of stablisation, partnership and integration* (The Hague, T.M.C. Asser Press 2006) pp. 61-92.

[37] Treaty between the Kingdom of Belgium, the Czech Republic, the Kingdom of Denmark, the Federal Republic of Germany, the Republic of Estonia, the Hellenic Republic, the Kingdom of Spain, the French Republic, Ireland, the Italian Republic, the Republic of Cyprus, the Republic of Latvia, the Republic of Lithuania, the Grand Duchy of Luxembourg, the Republic of Hungary, the Republic of Malta, the Kingdom of the Netherlands, the Republic of Austria, the Republic of Poland, the Portuguese Republic, the Republic of Slovenia, the Slovak Republic, the Republic of Finland, the Kingdom of Sweden, the United Kingdom of Great Britain and Northern Ireland (Member States of the European Union) and the Republic of Bulgaria and Romania, concerning the accession of the Republic of Bulgaria and Romania to the European Union, *OJ* 2005 L 157/11. For a legal appraisal see, *inter alia*, A. Łazowski, 'And Then They Were Twenty-Seven... A Legal Appraisal of the Sixth Accession Treaty', 44 *CMLRev.* (2007) pp. 401-430.

countries and twenty five EU Member States, both countries joined the European Union on 1 January 2007. As explained later in this chapter, the European Union decided not to employ an unprecedented membership postponement safeguard clause.

## 2.2.2. *Cyprus*

The accession of Cyprus to the European Union has been particularly complex due to the division of the island and the ongoing dispute as to its future.[38] The relationship between the European Communities and Cyprus dates back to the early 1970s when an association agreement was concluded.[39] It entered into force on 1 June 1973. A membership application was formally submitted on 3 July 1990; however *avis* was only published three years later on 30 June 1993.[40] The European Commission declared willingness to give the application a green light, subject to resolution of the conflict between Greece and Turkey. Consequentially, Cyprus did not become a part of the fourth enlargement (together with EFTA countries). A political decision to start accession negotiations during the next enlargement round was taken by the European Council meeting in Corfu in 1994. A formal decision in this respect was approved by the European Council in 1997, and Cyprus was invited, together with a group of the most advanced countries of Central and Eastern Europe, to start negotiations in the spring of 1998. Despite lack of progress in the resolution of the conflict about Northern Cyprus (failure of the so called Annan Plan), accession to the European Union took place on 1 May 2004.[41] In order to tackle the legal issues surrounding the division of the island, a special Protocol No 10 was annexed to the Act of Accession,[42] and a so-called green line regulation was adopted by the Council.[43]

## 2.2.3. *Malta*

The accession of Malta to the European Union on 1 May 2004 followed an idiosyncratic *rapprochement* that lasted for several years and was a victim of a changing domestic political climate in Valetta.[44] Before joining the EU, Malta had been associ-

---

[38] See further, *inter alia*, G. Vassiliou, 'The Accession of Cyprus to the EU', in G. Vassiliou, ed., *The Accession Story. The EU from 15 to 25 Countries* (Oxford, Oxford University Press 2007) pp. 117-143, Tatham, *op. cit.* n. 1, pp. 127-141.

[39] Agreement establishing an association between the European Economic Community and the Republic of Cyprus, *OJ* 1973 L 133/2.

[40] Commission Opinion on the Application of the Republic of Cyprus for Membership, COM (93) 313 final.

[41] See further, *inter alia*, F. Hoffmeister, *Legal aspects of the Cyprus problem: Annan plan and EU accession* (Leiden, Martinus Nijhoff Publishers 2006).

[42] Protocol No 10 on Cyprus of the Act of Accession, *OJ* 2003 L 236/955. See also ECJ, Case C-420/07 *Meletis Apostolides v. David Charles Orams, Linda Elizabeth Orams* [2009] *ECR* I-00000.

[43] Council Regulation 866/2004/EC of 29 April 2004 on a regime under Art. 2 of Protocol No 10 of the Act of Accession, *OJ* 2004 L 206/51. For an academic appraisal, see N. Skoutaris, 'The application of the acquis communautaire in the areas not under the effective control of the Republic of Cyprus: the Green Line Regulation', 45 *CMLRev.* (2008) pp. 727-755.

[44] For a detailed account see, *inter alia*, R.C. Caruana, 'The accession of Malta to the EU', in Vassiliou, *op. cit.* n. 38, pp. 259-296; Tatham, *op. cit.* n. 1, pp. 118-127.

ated with the European Community for a period of more than 30 years. An association agreement was signed already in 1970 and entered into force on 1 April 1971.[45] It provided for an ambitious plan of creating a customs union during a ten-year period (divided into two phases); however, due to political reasons, this objective was not achieved under the association framework. As noted by Alan Tatham, following the change of power in 1987, the 'new government did not attempt to resuscitate the dormant customs union between Malta and the EEC. Instead it determined to seek membership.'[46] A formal application for the membership in the European Communities was submitted on 16 July 1990. *Avis* of the European Commission followed in 1993.[47] For several reasons, mainly economic, the opinion was negative. As already noted, the membership application for political reasons was frozen in 1996 and reactivated following parliamentary elections in 1998. A subsequent positive opinion of the European Commission allowed Malta to join the second group of countries negotiating the terms of accession. Malta eventually became part of the "big bang" enlargement of the European Union and joined on 1 May 2004.

## 2.3.    The Accession Treaties 2003 and 2005

### 2.3.1.    *The legal character and structure of Accession Treaties*

Before turning to a brief overview of the two Accession Treaties, it is worth noting their legal character and structure. Being concluded between existing Member States and acceding countries, Accession Treaties are part of primary law; thus, they contain, *inter alia*, amendments to the Founding Treaties of the European Union.[48] Their main and rather obvious purpose is to regulate the terms of accession of new countries. For practical reasons all six enlargements to date have been governed by one treaty each; irrespective of the number of acceding countries, there has always been one Accession Treaty. With the "big bang" enlargement of 2004, this practice resulted in a bulky and voluminous legal act composed of several parts divided in the academic writing into the Accession Treaty *sensu stricto* and the Accession Treaty *sensu largo*. The first encompassed the Accession Treaty itself – a very short legal act composed of a handful of provisions. The latter, the Accession Treaty *sensu largo,* is supplemented by the Act on Conditions of Accession and numerous protocols annexed to it. This is where the heart of the matter is as the protocols regulate transitional periods, granting waivers from application of EU law for both the old and new Member States. The Accession Treaties are supplemented by final acts, which do not have a binding force, yet may be of relevance for the interpretation of the treaties.

---

[45] Agreement establishing an association between the European Economic Community and Malta, *OJ* 1971 L 61/2.

[46] Tatham, *op. cit.* n. 1, at p. 119.

[47] Commission Opinion on Malta's Application for Membership, COM (93) 312 final.

[48] Being part of primary law Accession Treaties fall *ex definitio* under the jurisdiction of the European Court of Justice. See, *inter alia*, ECJ, Case C-161/07 *Commission of the European Communities v. Republic of Austria* [2008] *ECR* nyr.

The Accession Treaty for Bulgaria and Romania is even more complex than this. Its complexity is directly linked to the constitutional reform of the European Union and arrangements set forth by the Treaty establishing a Constitution for Europe.[49] At the time of drafting the Accession Treaty, the reform was still underway; thus it had been necessary to take into account two alternative scenarios of a sequence in which both treaties would enter into force. To this end, the Accession Treaty *sensu stricto* is supplemented by the equally worded Protocol on Conditions for Accession and the Act on Conditions for Accession. The Protocol would have served as the legal basis for the enlargement had the Constitution entered into force.[50]

### 2.3.2. *Transitional periods*

The Accession Treaties 2003 and 2005 provided for similarly worded transitional periods.[51] For the European Union and its Member States, waiving free movement of workers and transitional periods for the Common Agriculture Policy seemed to be a key priority. For some of the acceding countries, ownership of real estate, falling under free movement of capital, was a major issue. Moreover, for economic reasons these countries requested long transitional periods for some parts of the environmental *acquis*. When it comes to the ten countries that joined the European Union in 2004, the majority of transitional periods have either already expired or are about to end. Free movement of workers is – at the time of writing – governed almost fully by Article 39 EC and secondary legislation adopted to give it effect.[52] Several arrangements applied in the first five years, when the old Member States were free to restrict movement of workers from the eight Central and Eastern European countries, led in some cases to litigation reaching the highest judicial authorities.[53] The only exceptions are Germany and Austria, which decided to employ the transitional periods for the last two years available under the Accession Treaty 2003.[54] As expected, immigration from the newcomers was quite substantial in the first years upon the accession and led to controversies and debates on

---

[49]  Treaty establishing a Constitution for Europe, *OJ* 2004 C 310/1.

[50]  The latter provided for protocols on Conditions of Accessions annexed to the EU Constitution instead of separate Accession Treaties supplemented by acts on conditions for accession.

[51]  In relation to the Accession Treaty 2003 see, *inter alia*, K. Inglis, 'The Accession Treaty and its Transitional Arrangements: A Twilight Zone for the New Members of the Union', in Hillion, ed., *op. cit.* n. 1, pp. 77-109. For the analysis of the Accession Treaty for Bulgaria and Romania, see, *inter alia*, Łazowski, *loc. cit.* n. 37, pp. 419-427.

[52]  Regulation (EEC) No 1612/68 of the Council of 15 October 1968 on freedom of movement for workers within the Community, *OJ* 1968 p. 475.

[53]  This was the case in the United Kingdom, where a system of workers registration scheme applied. See, *inter alia*, S. Currie, '"Free" movers? The post-accession experience of accession-8 migrant workers in the United Kingdom', 31 *ELRev.* (2006) pp. 207-229. For a major judicial development, see House of Lords, *Zalewska (AP) (Appellant) v. Department for Social Development (Respondents) (Northern Ireland)* [2009] 1 C.M.L.R. 24.

[54]  See more, M. Dougan, 'A Spectre is Haunting Europe... Free Movement of Persons and the Eastern Enlargement', in Hillion, ed., *op. cit.* n. 1, pp. 111-141; K. Kowalik-Bańczyk, 'Polish Transitional Periods Relating to Four Freedoms – Temporary Derogations', 27 *PolYBIL* (2004-2005) pp. 184-198.

the negative impact of the "Polish plumber" syndrome.[55] It is notable that neither free movement of services nor right of establishment was generally exempted in the first five years of the enlarged European Union.[56] Because of considerable differences in the GDP between the old and new Member States, it was only a question of time when accusations of social dumping would be raised.[57] This led to a heated political debate (ultimately affecting the shape of the Directive on Movement of Services)[58] and land-mark judgments of the European Court of Justice in cases C-438/05 *Viking Line*,[59] C-341/05 *Laval un Partneri*[60] and C-346/06 *Rüffert*.[61]

Transitional arrangements for Bulgaria and Romania are, as a matter of principle, similar to the ones provided in the Accession Treaty 2003.[62] However, in the wake of considerable migration of workers from Central and Eastern Europe that followed the "big bang" enlargement, most of the old Member States decided to use fully the pos-sibility provided in the Accession Treaty 2005. Thus, nationals of the two countries are still covered by transitional periods with very limited access to labour markets of most of the old Member States.

### 2.3.3. *Safeguard clauses*

Both Accession Treaties provided for tailor-made safeguard clauses allowing for the suspension of certain membership rights in cases of non-compliance with the terms of accession. This included an economic safeguard clause as well as internal market and JHA clauses.[63] In the case of the "big bang" enlargement, none of the clauses was employed in practice, and the system expired three years after accession.[64]

A very similar set of clauses was also used in the Accession Treaty 2005, and this time the internal market clause was used once to suspend the application of parts of air

---

[55] Communication from the Commission to the European Parliament, the Council, the European Eco-nomic and Social Committee and the Committee of the Regions – The impact of free movement of workers in the context of EU enlargement – Report on the first phase (1 January 2007-31 December 2008) of the transitional arrangements set out in the 2005 Accession Treaty and as requested according to the transi-tional arrangement set out in the 2003 Accession Treaty, COM (2008) 765 final.

[56] The only exceptions were transitional periods for posting of workers in several sectors available to Germany and Austria.

[57] Communication from the Commission to the European Parliament, the Council, the European Eco-nomic and Social Committee, the Committee of the Regions and the European Central Bank. Five years of an enlarged EU – Economic achievements and challenges, COM (2009) 79 final.

[58] Directive 2006/123/EC of the European Parliament and of the Council of 12 December 2006 on services in the internal market, *OJ* 2006 L 376/36.

[59] ECJ, Case C-438/05 *International Transport Workers' Federation and Finnish Seamen's Union v. Viking Line ABP and OÜ Viking Line Eesti* [2007] *ECR* I-10779.

[60] ECJ, Case C-341/05 *Laval un Partneri Ltd v. Svenska Byggnadsarbetareförbundet, Svenska Byggnadsarbetareförbundets avdelning 1, Byggettan and Svenska Elektrikerförbundet* [2007] *ECR* I-11767.

[61] ECJ, Case C-346/06 *Dirk Rüffert v. Land Niedersachsen* [2008] *ECR* I-1989.

[62] See further Łazowski, *loc. cit.* n. 37, pp. 419-427.

[63] Arts. 37-39 Act on Conditions of Accession 2005.

[64] See K. Inglis, 'The Accession Treaty and its Transitional Arrangements: A Twilight Zone for the New Members of the Union', in Hillion, *op. cit.* n. 1, pp. 77-109, at pp. 100-107.

transport *acquis* to Bulgaria.[65] Under the terms of Regulation 1962/2006/EC, air wor-
thiness and maintenance certificates issued by the Bulgarian authorities were not
recognised in the European Union. Moreover, air carriers having Bulgarian licenses
were not granted unlimited access to the EU aviation market and were treated as if they
were third-country carriers. It is fitting to note that alleged non-compliance with some
of the entry conditions resulted in adoption of a special post-accession scrutiny mechanism. In December 2006, the European Commission adopted two decisions outlining
the mechanics of the verification mechanism.[66]

Concerns regarding the preparedness (or rather lack of it) of Bulgaria and Romania
led the Member States to an unprecedented move. The sixth Accession Treaty is the
first to contain a clause giving the power to the European Union to delay the membership of a country with which an Accession Treaty has already been signed.[67] Not only
does it differentiate the two countries from the ones that acceded in 2004, but it also
sets different standards for Bulgaria and Romania. The legal basis for the safeguard
clause is Article 4.2. of the Accession Treaty in conjunction with Article 39 of the Act.
Annex IX to the Act is of particular importance, when it comes to the commitments
undertaken by Romania.[68] In September 2006, the European Commission recommended the accession of both countries on 1 January 2007, subject to very strict scrutiny of both newcomers. The membership postponement safeguard clause wasn't used;
however, it can be argued that its existence *per se* played an important political role. It
served as a stick to discipline the forthcoming members in their last minute pre-accession efforts. Had it been used, its potential benefits would have been rather limited. The
postponement of membership by 12 months would not have saved the European Union
from admitting the two countries struggling with their accession commitments. Twelve
months in an antechamber would probably not be enough for the newcomers to meet
their challenges. At the same time, such a political decision to delay the membership
could have seriously undermined the political momentum of the enlargement, without-

---

[65] Commission Regulation 1962/2006 of 21 December 2006 on application of Art. 37 of the Act of
Accession of Bulgaria to the European Union, *OJ* 2006 L 408/8. See also Commission Regulation (EC)
No 875/2008 of 8 September 2008 repealing Regulation (EC) No 1962/2006, *OJ* 2008 L 240/3.

[66] Commission Decision 2006/928/EC of 13 December 2006 establishing a mechanism for co-operation and verification of progress in Romania to address specific benchmarks in the areas of judicial reform
and the fight against corruption, *OJ* 2006 L 354/56; Commission Decision 2006/929/EC of 13 December
2006 establishing a mechanism for co-operation and verification of progress in Bulgaria to address specific
benchmarks in the areas of judicial reform and the fight against corruption and organised crime, *OJ* 2006
L 354/58. See further, Chapters 16 and 17 in this volume.

[67] The conditions for the delay of membership are spelled out in Art. 39.1 of the Act. The Council
could have used the safeguard clause if there was 'clear evidence that the state of preparations or adoption
and implementation of the acquis in Bulgaria or Romania is such that there is a serious risk of either of
those States being manifestly unprepared to meet the requirements of membership by the date of accession
of 1 January 2007 in a number of important areas.' In order to adopt a decision in this respect, the unanimity in Council would have been required.

[68] The list includes the implementation of the Schengen Action Plan, combat of illegal immigration,
reform of the judiciary, rigorous enforcement of anti-corruption legislation and strategy, enforcement of
multi-annual anti-crime strategy, enforcement of anti-trust and state aid rules. Failure to meet those commitments could have resulted in the application of safeguard clause. In such case, the decision of Council
would have required qualified majority only.

giving the European Union legal instruments to enforce its demanding conditionality. Such a move could have potentially alienated the two countries and their public opinion. In political and legal terms, the decision to open the doors on 1 January 2007 gave the European Union more chances to influence the necessary alignment with *acquis* and all EU policies. Whether those chances have been used is another story. As argued in Chapters 16 and 17, practice demonstrates several drawbacks of the post-accession bridging policy employed by the European Union. This triggers questions as to the potential and limits of EU's pre-accession policy.[69]

## 3.     THE IMPACT OF THE FIFTH AND SIXTH ENLARGEMENTS ON THE INSTITUTIONAL STRUCTURE OF THE EUROPEAN UNION

### 3.1.     The fourth accession criterion

According to the European Commission:

> 'The institutions and organs of the present Community cannot ensure that the progress of integration will continue in an enlarged Community: on the contrary, there is a reason to fear that the Community decision making procedures will deteriorate. If this happened, it would be difficult or even impossible to create a Community based on the rule of law, which is the foundation of the Community and the sole means of recognizing in law that to equal rights correspond equal obligations. The institutions and organs of the enlarged Community must accordingly be decisively strengthened.'[70]

Readers may be surprised to learn that this argument was made by the Commission already in 1978, that is, five years after the first enlargement. This has shortly become a standard argument, used like a mantra by policy-makers and politicians alike. The ability of the European Communities/European Union to operate with an ever-growing number of Member States has turned into a discourse on the absorption capacity of the club and became the fourth criterion in the set developed by the European Council in Copenhagen in 1993.[71] The question is whether the European Union itself complied with the fourth accession criterion. It is striking to note that the first version of the Preamble to the Reform Treaty (later rebranded into the Treaty of Lisbon) contained the following statement:

> 'Desiring to complete the process started by the Treaty of Amsterdam and by the Treaty of Nice of adapting the institutions of the European Union to function in an enlarged Union.'[72]

---

[69]   See further, Chapters 16 and 17 in this volume.

[70]   Communication sent by the Commission to the Council on 20 April 1978. General considerations on the problems of enlargement, COM (78) 120 final, p. 15.

[71]   See further, G. Edwards, 'Reforming the Union's Institutional Framework: A New EU Obligation?', in Hillion, *op. cit.* n. 1, pp. 23-43.

[72]   Draft Treaty amending the Treaty on European Union and the Treaty establishing the European Community. Draft Preamble, Brussels 24 July 2007, CIG 4/07.

If one reads this proviso in a cynical way, the only conclusion possible is that the European Union admits openly to have failed to do the homework. It doesn't come as a surprise that the final version of the Lisbon Treaty[73] contains a slightly different recital in the Preamble.[74]

Much has been written about the impact of the fifth and sixth enlargements on the EU institutions.[75] With this in mind, this section of the chapter will only highlight the most important developments. No doubt the "big bang" enlargement of 2004 has exposed the EU institutional apparatus to a serious risk of turning into an ineffective Tower of Babel, incapable of governing the European Union in a productive fashion. The practice so far has proven that the enlarged EU is able to deliver and no major institutional drama has taken place. As argued in the title of this chapter – it works! It is obvious that it works in a different way from what it had done before 1 May 2004; however the system proved to be flexible enough to survive twelve more Member States.[76] This must not create false impressions that the EU can go without a far-reaching reform of its institutional set-up. The accession of Bulgaria and Romania only strengthens the need. As the European Commission notes in its Enlargement Strategy paper, 'The EU does not need new institutional arrangements simply for the sake of enlargement; it also needs them so that the current Union can function better.'[77]

The history of the institutional reform goes back to the late 1990s when the Member States took the first attempt to revamp the organisational chart of the European Union so that it can function successfully with – at that time – an unspecified number of new countries on board. The Treaty of Amsterdam, despite its many good qualities, turned out to be a missed opportunity.[78] The negotiations focused on several fundamental issues, including strengthening of the second and third pillars of the European Union, yet failed short of reforming the institutional framework.[79] By the time of signature of the Treaty of Amsterdam, it was clear that another intergovernmental conference was necessary in order to prepare the Union for the forthcoming enlargement. This time, however, the mandate of the IGC was very narrow, limited mainly to 'Amsterdam leftovers' and reform of the EU's court system. This allowed a more focused IGC. Interestingly enough, the negotiations leading up to the Treaty of Nice were conducted in parallel to – and under pressure of – accession negotiations with twelve aspiring countries. The final outcome was probably less ambitious than expected; yet it pro-

---

[73] Treaty of Lisbon amending the Treaty on European Union and the Treaty establishing the European Community, *OJ* 2007 C 306/1.

[74] 'Desiring to complete the process started by the Treaty of Amsterdam and by the Treaty of Nice with a view to enhancing the efficiency and democratic legitimacy of the Union and to improving the coherence of its action.'

[75] See, *inter alia*, Tatham, *op. cit.* n. 1, pp. 339-432.

[76] See H. Wallace, *Adapting to Enlargement of the European Union: Institutional Practice since May 2004*, Trans European Policy Studies Association, available at http://www.tepsa.be.

[77] Communication from the Commission to the European Parliament and the Council. Enlargement Strategy and Main Challenges 2006-2007, COM (2006) 649, p. 18.

[78] Treaty of Amsterdam amending the Treaty on European Union, the Treaties establishing the European Communities and certain related acts, *OJ* 1997 C 340/1.

[79] See further, D. O'Keeffe, P. Twomey, eds., *Legal Issues of the Amsterdam Treaty* (Oxford-Portland, Oregon, Hart Publishing 1999).

vided the European Union with an arrangement for the accession of all countries with which negotiations were pending at the time. A declaration and a protocol annexed to the Treaty of Nice contained a blueprint which was later followed in both Accession Treaties. At the same time, an indication was made as to the further institutional reforms necessary to enhance the EU's capacity to operate in the post-enlargement environment. This was a clear sign of fundamental problems undermining the political consensus in the EU and arguable lack of vision as to the future of the integration project. It is only fair to note here that by that time, the European Union was clearly suffering from "treaty revision fatigue." The Treaty of Nice was the fourth major reform of the Founding Treaties in less than fifteen years. Considering the milestone character of the Single European Act and Treaty of Maastricht as well as the legislative effort that followed, it is not surprising that yet another round of negotiations proved difficult. At the same time, the mid-1990s were characterised by a generation change among the political circles. The likes of Tony Blair in the United Kingdom or Gerhard Schröder in Germany belong to a post-war generation that perceives the European integration in a more technocratic way. Thus, the Treaty of Nice prepared the European Union for the accession of new states, yet failed to provide a long-term arrangement and left the institutional reform incomplete. The demise of the Treaty establishing a Constitution for Europe and the uncertain future of the Treaty of Lisbon may mean that the Nice arrangement will remain in operation for the years to come.[80]

The involvement of the new Member States in the work of the European Union had started already before the accession to the EU. On the one hand, the future members were fully involved in the work of the European Convention preparing the EU Constitution; on the other, as of the date of accession, they were covered by the information and consultation procedure in the Council. Moreover, nominees from national parliaments were allowed to participate in some of the works of the European Parliament. All those developments, as well as the impact of the enlargement on key players in the EU decision making, are analysed in the sections of this chapter that follow.

## 3.2.    The European Council

During the years since the first meeting of the heads of states/governments, the European Council has developed into a key political player in EU decision making.[81] In the European Union of twenty-seven Member States, it is the source of ultimate political approval of key decisions taken at EU level. As of the date of accession, the new Member States have been fully involved in the work of the European Council, and during the Slovene and Czech Presidencies (respectively the first six months of 2008 and 2009), chaired the meetings. With enlargement on the horizon, the European Council has

---

[80] Further on the absorption capacity, institutional reform and future enlargements, see, *inter alia*, F. Amtenbrink, 'On the European Union's institutional capacity to cope with further enlargement', in S. Blockmans and S. Prechal, eds., *Reconciling the Deepening and Widening of the European Union* (The Hague, T.M.C. Asser Press 2007) pp. 111-131.

[81] J. Werts, *The European Council* (London, John Harper Publishing 2008).

become more formalised as of the Seville Summit in 2002[82] and now meets – as a matter of principle – in Brussels only.[83] Interestingly enough, participation in European Council meetings has led to a major conflict in Poland, one of the newcomers. Disagreements between the President and Prime Minister led to a series of diplomatic scandals at the EU level. At the domestic level, they resulted in a competence struggle and judgment of the Constitutional Tribunal.[84] In the future functioning of the European Council, a big and major change will come with the entry into force of the Treaty of Lisbon. It gives the European Council a formal status of an EU institution and formalises its powers in the EU decision-making procedures.[85]

## 3.3.    The Council of the European Union

As already indicated, the institutional engagement of the new Member States had already started with the signature of respective Accession Treaties. From that moment, acceding countries had an observer status in the Council of the European Union and, at the same time, had been covered by the information and consultation procedure.[86] This exercise had a twofold purpose. At the EU level, it allowed representatives of the future members to participate in the work of the Council and, by the same token, influence the shape of EU legislation. This aspect of the information and consultation procedure has been recently analysed by the European Court of Justice. The Court held:

> 'in the framework of that procedure and by making use of the observer status, which they have in the Council, with the opportunities for dialogue and cooperation which those special mechanisms afford them, that the future Member States may, once informed of the future adoption of new Community acts, assert their interest in obtaining the necessary transitional derogations; these might be needed, for example, because it would be impossible to ensure immediate application of those acts on accession, or because of major socio-economic problems to which such application might give rise.'[87]

---

[82]  See further, Werts, *op. cit.* n. 81, at pp. 63-67.

[83]  The latter provided by the Treaty of Nice.

[84]  Postanowienie z dnia 20 maja 2009 r. Sygn. Akt Kpt 2/08 (not yet reported, on file with the author). See further, Chapter 9 in this volume.

[85]  See, *inter alia*, M. Dougan, 'The Treaty of Lisbon 2007: Winning Minds, not Hearts', 45 *CMLRev.* (2008) pp. 617-703, at pp. 627-630.

[86]  Exchange of Letters between the European Union and the Czech Republic, the Republic of Estonia, the Republic of Cyprus, the Republic of Latvia, the Republic of Lithuania, the Republic of Hungary, the Republic of Malta, the Republic of Poland, the Republic of Slovenia and the Slovak Republic on an information and consultation procedure for the adoption of certain decisions and other measures to be taken during the period preceding accession, *OJ* 2003 L 236/986; Exchange of Letters between the European Union and the Republic of Bulgaria and Romania on an information and consultation procedure for the adoption of certain decisions and other measures to be taken during the period preceding accession, *OJ* 2005 L 157/393.

[87]  ECJ, Case C-413/04, *European Parliament v. Council of the European Union* [2006] *ECR* I-11221, para. 67; Case C-414/04 *European Parliament v. Council of the European Union* [2006] *ECR* I-11279, para. 44.

Although the Court's comments refer to the procedure set forth in the Accession Treaty 2003, they are fully applicable to the one which also covered Bulgaria and Romania. The information and consultation procedure also had a pivotal internal effect. It gave the newcomers a unique opportunity to set up internal procedures for the co-ordination of EU matters and the necessary testing well ahead of the accession. Naturally, the extent to which the procedures have been successfully used is a different matter.

With the accession to the European Union, all new Member States became fully engaged in the work of the Council. Following a few months of a transitional period provided for in Article 26 of the Act on Conditions of Accession, the voting system designed in the Treaty of Nice and incorporated into the Accession Treaty 2003 entered into force on 1 November 2004.[88] As empirical studies prove, the worries and concerns, which had been expressed prior to the enlargement, have not materialised. Since 1 May 2004, the European Union has not suffered from a political paralysis comparable to the empty-chair crisis inspired by France. Decision-making procedures proved to be flexible enough to accommodate a big number of new players, without undermining the ability of the European Union to act. Some patterns have changed, and increasing the role of COREPER is growing.[89] It is only natural that increased diversity within the block makes negotiations more difficult; however the general evaluation of the work of the Council seems to be positive. This does not mean that there is no space for improvement. An attempt in this respect is made in the Treaty of Lisbon, which provides for new voting rules in the Council and revision of the current system of rotating presidencies.[90] As briefly mentioned, two out of twelve new Member States have so far held presidencies in the European Union. The Slovenian six months at the driving seat of the European Union is generally considered a successful effort.[91] The same cannot be said about the Czech Presidency in the first six months of 2009. It was run in a very difficult international and domestic political environment and most likely will be remembered as a disappointment.

### 3.4. The European Parliament

Representatives of the new Member States became involved in the work of the European Parliament even before the enlargements of the European Union. During the period preceding the accession, national parliaments of the acceding countries were invited to nominate observers to the European Parliament (in numbers equal to the number of seats allocated in the respective Accession Treaties).[92] As of the date of accession and until the general elections were held, national parliaments also nominated members of

---

[88] See Art. 12 of the Act on Conditions of Accession.

[89] See further on the idiosyncrasies of the Council, *inter alia*, F. Hayes-Renshaw, H. Wallace, *The Council of Ministers*, 2nd edn. (Basingstoke, Palgrave Macmillan 2006).

[90] See further, *inter alia*, Dougan, *loc. cit.* n. 85, pp. 633-635.

[91] For an evaluation see S. Kajnč, 'The Slovenian Presidency: Meeting Symbolic and Substantive Challenge', 47 *JCMS (JCMS Annual Review of the European Union in 2008)* (2009), pp. 89-98.

[92] For political reasons only there was a rather shameful delay in inviting Bulgarian and Romanian observers. See further, Łazowski, *loc. cit.* n. 37, p. 407.

the European Parliament. In the case of the 2004 enlargement, it was a very short-term solution as the EU-wide elections for the assembly were scheduled for 10-13 June 2004. In the case of Bulgaria and Romania, the elections, pursuant to Article 24(2) of the Act on Conditions of Accession, had to take place before the end of 2007. Until that happened, MEPs from Bulgaria and Romania were nominated by national parliaments.[93] It is fitting to note that as of the date of the sixth enlargement until the beginning of the 2009-2014 term, the number of MEPs exceeded the limit of 736 laid down in Article 189 EC.[94] This exception was allowed under the terms of the Accession Treaty 2005, and as of the new term of the European Parliament, the number of MEPs is reduced to numbers agreed upon during the negotiations leading up to the Treaty of Nice.

With the first full term of the enlarged European Parliament over, several conclusions can be drawn. First, the European Parliament is functioning in a successful fashion, despite the increase of its membership. As empirical research proves, MEPs from the new Member States have become gradually involved in the work of the assembly. The second part of the 2004-2009 term has proved particularly instructive.[95] The appointment of Jerzy Buzek, former Polish Prime Minister, for the President of the European Parliament for the first two-and-a-half years of the 2009-2014 term is very symbolic in this context. Second, the elections in 2004 and 2009 had a very low turnout, demonstrating quite limited interest of EU citizens in the work of the only democratically elected EU institution. Particularly worrying is extremely low turnout in the new Member States, with Slovakia at the very bottom of the list (20%).[96] Third, following the pattern well known from previous treaties reforming the European Communities/European Union, the Parliament is again the winner in the case of the Treaty of Lisbon. If the latter enters into force, the European Parliament will have even more powers than under the current framework. Considering the average turnout in the last few elections, an interesting rule of thumb emerges. The more powers the European Parliament gets, the less interested are the voters. Last but not least, the discourse about the feasibility of multiple seats of the European Parliament has regained thrust. The accession of twelve new Member States has definitely increased the costs of the entire ordeal.

## 3.5. The European Commission

*Modus operandi* for the enlargement of the European Commission was laid down in the Treaty of Nice and the Accession Treaties 2003 and 2005. With the accession of Bulgaria and Romania, the number of members of the European Commission has increased to 27.[97] This factor in itself has given strength to arguments supporting the

---

[93] The elections took place on 20 May 2007 (Bulgaria) and 25 November 2007 (Romania).

[94] During that period, the European Parliament was composed of 785 members.

[95] See, *inter alia*, J. De Clerck-Sachsse and P.M. Kaczyński, *The European Parliament – More powerful, less legitimate? An outlook for the 7th term*, CEPS Working Document No 314/May 2009.

[96] See further, House of Commons, European Parliament Elections 2009, Research Paper 09/53, p. 23.

[97] In the period between the "big bang" enlargement and the appointment of the Barroso Commission, the European Commission was composed of 30 members. This was due to the fact that the previous

abolition of the "one commissioner per state" rule.[98] With the appointment of Bulgarian and Romanian commissioners in early 2007, the allocation of portfolios became a major issue. Giving the consumer protection dossier to M. Kuneva was justified by the importance of that policy area, the "multilingualism" portfolio given to L. Obran seemed artificial (to say the least). The Treaty of Lisbon provides a partial solution, allowing creation of a rotation system. This, however, will be subject to decisions of the European Council. The situation following the negative referendum on the Treaty in Ireland demonstrates that the reduction of size of the European Commission will remain an issue for the years to come.

In the period following the last two waves of enlargements, the European Commission played an enormous role in policing breaches of EU law in the new Member States. In the case of the countries that joined in the big wave of 2004, the Commission has the traditional set of tools based on Articles 226 and 228 EC. As practice proves, after a very short honeymoon, the European Commission has been engaged in a robust scrutiny of the newcomers' performance. As explained earlier in this chapter, it also plays a special role under the verification mechanism employed *vis-à-vis* Bulgaria and Romania.[99]

### 3.6.  The European Court of Justice and the Court of First Instance

The European Court of Justice and the Court of First Instance seem to be, at least for the time being, the only EU institutions that benefited directly from the fifth and sixth waves of enlargement. The caseload of the courts has remained roughly at the same level; however the capacity has increased as a result of appointment of new judges. This, together with the positive effects of the reform introduced by the Treaty of Nice, has facilitated a reduction of case backlog and speeding up of the procedures. Unfortunately, this has not had a positive impact on the quality of judgments. As often argued in the academic writing, the quality of case law remains a major issue.[100] The question is whether the European Court of Justice will be able to cope with the workload when the initial shyness of courts from the new Member States disappears[101] and infractions against the new Member States become more frequent. Potential entry into force of the Treaty of Lisbon will have an impact as the jurisdiction of the ECJ in Justice and Home Affairs will become full and compulsory.[102] It is certain that the language regime

---

European Commission was appointed pursuant to an old rule allowing the five biggest Member States to have two commissioners.

[98]   The discussion in this respect has been going on for years now. See, *inter alia*, A. Bar Cendón, 'The Number of Members of the Commission: A Possible Reform?', in E. Best et al., eds., *Rethinking the European Union. IGC 2000 and Beyond* (Maastricht, European Institute of Public Administration 2000) p. 77.

[99]   See further, Chapters 16 and 17 in this volume.

[100]   See, for instance, J. Komarek, 'In the Court(s) we Trust? On the Need for Hierarchy and Differentiation in the Preliminary Ruling Procedure', 32 *ELRev.* (2007) pp. 467-491.

[101]   See M. Bobek, 'Learning to talk: Preliminary rulings, the courts of the new Member States and the Court of Justice' 45 *CMLRev.* (2008) pp. 1611-1643.

[102]   For a comprehensive overview, see, *inter alia*, A. Hinarejos, *Judicial Control in the European Union. Reforming Jurisdiction in the Intergovernmental Pillars* (Oxford, Oxford University Press 2010).

at the ECJ is another major issue.[103] On the one hand, it is fully understandable that the current arrangement allowing references and submissions in all official languages is only appropriate. On the other hand translation of various procedural documents is a tedious and time-consuming job. As proved by the debate that preceded the introduction of the urgent preliminary ruling procedure for JHA references, the Member States are not willing to reform the current system.[104] Arguably, a potential reform of the European Court of Justice and the Court of First Instance is inevitable.

4.       THE IMPACT OF THE FIFTH AND SIXTH ENLARGEMENTS ON
         THE LEGAL ORDER OF THE EUROPEAN UNION –
         PRELIMINARY REMARKS

One of the aims of the pre-accession policy employed by the European Union is to guarantee that any state joining the club complies with the threshold conditions and is capable of complying with the obligations stemming from membership upon the accession. Even very general analysis of the Copenhagen criteria proves that some of the criteria are formulated in a very general fashion and are based on EU and Council of Europe *acquis* jointly. This makes the scrutiny as well as verification of compliance very difficult and moves the centre of gravity from legal to political tools. The capacity of traditional infraction procedures based on Articles 226 and 228 EC Treaty is quite limited in this respect.[105] Such generally formulated conditions like the respect for the rule of law and independence of judiciary are absolutely fundamental for smooth functioning of the European Union. The accession of Bulgaria and Romania and the troubles that have followed only substantiate this argument. One should remember that the EU's absorption capacity (as explained earlier) is not only limited to matters of institutional framework and decision-making procedures. Unlike other international organisations, the European Union is based on an internal legal order, which is directly applicable in national legal systems of its Member States. Thus, the ability of the newcomers to apply EU law in practice of administrative authorities and domestic courts is absolutely pivotal for the success of integration endeavor. Accession of states which are not capable of guaranteeing the effectiveness of EU law may ultimately undermine the very foundations of the legal order of the European Union. The experience of all six enlargements demonstrates the kind of challenge application of EU law is.

---

[103] See L. Mulders, 'Translation at the Court of Justice of the European Communities' in S. Prechal and B. Van Roermund, eds., *The Coherence of EU Law. The Search for Unity in Divergent Concepts* (Oxford, Oxford University Press 2008) pp. 45-59; K. McAuliffe, 'Enlargement at the European Court of Justice: Law, Language and Translation', 14 *ELJ* (2008) pp. 806-818.

[104] See further, A. Łazowski, 'Towards the reform of the preliminary ruling procedure in JHA Area', in S. Braum and A. Weyembergh, eds., *Le contrôle juridictionnel dans l'espace pénal européen* (Bruxelles, Editions de l'Université de Bruxelles 2009) pp. 211-226.

[105] On failure of EU conditionality in this respect, see D. Kochenov, *EU Enlargement and the Failure of Conditionality. Pre-accession Conditionality in the Fields of Democracy and the Rule of Law* (Austin-Boston-Chicago-New York-The Netherlands, Wolters Kluwer 2008).

The first five years of the enlarged European Union (almost three in the case of Bulgaria and Romania) show that no catastrophic events with the transposition of *acquis* (mainly directives) followed the accession. The new Member States follow the steps of the older colleagues and stay within the general limits of the transposition deficit. Surprisingly, one of the recent scoreboards of the European Commission puts Bulgaria on the top of the list with 0% transposition deficit.[106] This, of course, is an indication only, and the challenges of implementation are definitely far more daunting. As argued by Michal Bobek, the performance of public administration in the new Member States is far from perfect, and much remains to be done in the coming years.[107] Poland may serve as an excellent example in this respect.[108] The first wave of EU-related cases dealt with taxation of second-hand cars. This ultimately led to a first-ever reference for a preliminary ruling from a Polish court. As clear from the court's order on reference as well as the final judgment in this case,[109] the customs authorities refused to apply EC law and follow the principle established by the ECJ in case 103/88 *Fratelli Constanzo*.[110] It simply held that administrative authorities were not bound by EC law and to apply it was the domain of national courts. This decision of the customs authorities was not an accident but regrettably part of everyday practice.

The first major challenge to the effectiveness of EU law in the new Member States was the "lost in translation syndrome." Considerable delays with the publication of the Special Edition of the Official Journal in the languages of the new Member States triggered countless practical problems and divergent case law of national courts. The European Court of Justice held in case C-161/06 *Skoma-Lux*[111] that such legislation could not have been enforced against individuals.[112] This principle, in relation to the 2007 accessions, was confirmed by the Bulgarian Supreme Administrative Court in the *Ilcheva v. AEMD Plovdiv* case.[113] The quality of available translation was another matter. Differences among different language versions became a standard feature of EU law. This, as argued by Michal Bobek in Chapter 5, has undermined the effectiveness of EU law in the new Member States.

Another major issue which should be pinpointed at the outset is the controversial case law of the European Court of Justice in so-called pre-accession cases. Following

---

[106]  The European Commission. Internal Market Scoreboard No. 17, p. 11.

[107]  M. Bobek, 'Thou Shall Have Two Masters: the Application of European Law by Administrative Authorities in the New Member States', 1 *REALaw* (2008) pp. 51-63.

[108]  See further, Chapter 9 in this volume.

[109]  Voivod Administrative Court in Warsaw, Case III SA/Wa 254/07 *Brzeziński v. Dyrektor Izby Celnej* [2008] 3 C.M.L.R. 28.

[110]  ECJ, Case 103/88 *Fratelli Costanzo SpA v. Comune di Milano* [1988] *ECR* 1838.

[111]  ECJ, Case C-161/06 *Skoma-Lux sro v. Celní ředitelství Olomouc* [2007] *ECR* I-10841.

[112]  For an academic appraisal, see, *inter alia*, K. Lasiński-Sulecki and W. Morawski, 'Late Publication of EC Law in Languages of New Member States and its Effects: Obligations on Individuals Following the Court's Judgment in Skoma-Lux', 45 *CMLRev.* (2008) pp. 705-725; M. Bobek, 'The Binding Force of Babel: The Enforcement of EC Law Unpublished in the Languages of the New Member States', 9 *CYELS* (2007) pp. 43-80. See also Chapters 4 and 5 in this volume.

[113]  Supreme Administrative Court of Bulgaria, judgment of 15 April 2008 in Case *Ilcheva v. AEMD Plovdiv*, not reported (on file with the author). See further, Chapter 17 in this volume.

the judgment in case C-302/04 *Ynos kft v. János Varga,*[114] the ECJ consistently holds that it has no jurisdiction to deal with references for the preliminary ruling if facts took place before the enlargement.[115] This happens at the time when references in the *Dzodzi* line of cases are gladly considered by the ECJ.[116] Such an approach has discouraged at least some new European judges from referring and left them alone with daunting problems of interpretation of EU law. Moreover, the fact that only a few new Member States have recognised the jurisdiction of the ECJ in the Third Pillar has undermined the effectiveness of EU law in this respect.[117]

The biggest challenge, however, is the ability of judges from the new Member States to apply effectively EU law in their courts. This is exactly the focus of this volume. It demonstrates various tendencies and patterns followed by courts of the new Member States. It gives lots of reasons for satisfaction and as many reasons for concern. EU law definitely works in the twelve new countries; however, the key question is how. Chapters contained in Part Three of the book provide the readers with an overview of all twelve legal orders of the newcomers and the application of EU law therein.

## 5.    CONCLUSIONS

It works! That is a simple conclusion that can be drawn. The European Union has survived the fifth and sixth enlargements, and, despite suffering from the post-accession blues, it is gradually adjusting to this new environment. The European Union has clearly evolved in the past five years, and certain things will never be the same. As rightly noted by Hillion in 2004, 'The European Union is dead. Long live the European Union.'[118] Clearly the dynamics of the European Union have changed, and new challenges have been created by the historical enlargements. One can easily see it in the EU domestic arena.[119] Dilemmas of the alleged social dumping, increased protectionism of the old Member States in the wake of the financial crisis, tensions associated with the movement of Eastern workers towards the West are just a selection of examples. A major issue that remains is the constitutional reform. It is paradoxical that the first attempt to give the European Union a Constitution (although in the garment of an international treaty) failed in the two founding Member States. The latter factor is usu-

---

[114] ECJ, Case C-302/04 *Ynos kft v. János Varga* [2006] *ECR* I-371.

[115] See N. Półtorak, 'Ratione temporis application of the preliminary rulings procedure', 45 *CMLRev.* (2008) pp. 1357-1381.

[116] In the recent case law, see ECJ Case C-170/03 *Staatssecretaris van Financiën v. J.H.M. Feron* [2005] *ECR* I-2299, para. 11. See also para. 22 of the Opinion of Advocate General Kokott in Case C-280/06 *Autorità Garante della Concorrenza e del Mercato v. Ente tabacchi italiani – ETI SpA and Others and Philip Morris Products SA and Others v. Autorità Garante della Concorrenza e del Mercato and Others* [2007] *ECR* I-893. See further, Chapter 4 in this volume.

[117] See Information concerning the declarations by the Republic of Hungary, the Republic of Latvia, the Republic of Lithuania and the Republic of Slovenia on their acceptance of the jurisdiction of the Court of Justice to give preliminary rulings on the acts referred to in Art. 35 of the Treaty on European Union, *OJ* 2008 C 69/1.

[118] *Loc. cit.* n. 34.

[119] The external dimension is discussed in the next chapter of this volume.

ally referred to as demonstration of post-accession fatigue. True or not, it has made, at least in political terms, the life of the European Union more difficult than expected.

In legal terms, the European Union is still alive, despite gloomy early predictions. As argued in the introduction to this volume, it is a Brave New World slowly coming to terms with the unique legal order of the European Union. The path to membership outlined in the first sections of this chapter shows a tremendous effort the new Member States took before the accession. On the one hand, one can argue that the judicial culture of the West and East are still worlds apart.[120] On the other hand, one has to appreciate that judiciaries and public administration of those countries have had to undergo a change of minds and hearts during the past two decades. It is not a desperate search for excuses but rather a reality check.

---

[120] Z. Kühn, 'Worlds Apart: Western and Central European Judicial Culture at the Onset of the European Enlargement', 52 *AJCL* (2004) pp. 531-568.

*Chapter 2*

# LA NOUVELLE VAGUE:
# THE INTRODUCTION OF A MORE SIGNIFICANT
# OST-POLITIK IN THE EU'S SECURITY POLICIES

Steven Blockmans*

## 1.    INTRODUCTION

The European Union's leap from fifteen to twenty-seven members has consigned the Cold War legacy of separate and hostile camps in Eastern and Western Europe to the shelves of history. For those states not already members of NATO and the EC/EU, the effects of the fall of the Iron Curtain were particularly urgent as they all had to deal with the insecurities of internal transition, some even with disintegration and war. For many Central and Eastern European states, the practical response to these security predicaments has been a movement toward NATO, thereby affirming the transatlantic link to the "hard" power of the US – and the EU – as the best method to address myriad "soft" security challenges. The 2004/7 enlargements of the EU have widened the European security community by incorporating twelve new Member States and thereby contributing to the stability of a large swath of Central and Eastern Europe. However, security concerns remain and, in some cases, have been heightened. By the southeastward push of its borders, the Union has imported "hard" security threats (e.g., the unresolved dispute over Cyprus)[1] and has confronted more directly threats in its (new) neighbourhoods (e.g., tensions over Kosovo's independence, bursts of violence in the simmering conflicts in the Southern Caucasus, the standoff in the Middle East conflict). Moreover, the EU's "big bang" enlargement coincided with a period of international tensions over the war in Iraq, the Bush administration's War on Terror and "softer" security challenges such as mass illegal immigration, organised crime and the disruption of the flow of energy resources, to name just a few. In parallel, within the EU, there has been a sense of transition and political tension over the failed Constitutional Treaty;[2] the future of the

---

* Senior research fellow in EU law and Deputy Head of Research at T.M.C. Asser Institute, The Hague, The Netherlands.

[1] The security aspects related to the Cyprus issue will remain outside the scope of this contribution. For historical and political backgrounds and a legal analysis, see M. Brus, M. Akgün, S. Blockmans, et al., *A Promise to Keep: Time to End the International Isolation of the Turkish Cypriots* (Istanbul, TESEV 2008).

[2] Treaty establishing a Constitution for Europe, *OJ* 2004 C 310/1.

*A. Łazowski (ed.), The Application of EU Law in the New Member States*
© 2010, T·M·C·ASSER PRESS, *The Hague, The Netherlands and the Authors*

Lisbon Treaty;[3] the direction and extent of future EU enlargement; economic and budgetary difficulties; the shape of the Area of Freedom Security and Justice, especially the
nature of border security and the direction of Police and Judicial Co-operation in
Criminal Matters; and differing visions of the Common Foreign and Security Policy, in
particular the European Security and Defence Policy. The addition of twelve new
Member States has impacted on how the EU perceives and tackles these tensions and
transitions, thereby shaping the European Union's security role overall.

This chapter explores how the widening of security interests, agendas and capabilities has affected the deepening of security integration. In doing so, the chapter
employs a rather artificial distinction between issues of external security (CFSP/ESDP)
and matters of internal security (AFSJ/PJCC). A theme which will emerge is the merging of the concepts of internal and external security (both are trans-boundary in nature)
and the shifting emphasis between "hard" and "soft" security (while the EU is equip-
ping itself for harder security missions, the more pressing types of security issues which
it has to deal with often on a daily basis have a softer security character). This chapter
also examines the impact of enlargements on leadership within the European Union, a
prerequisite for internal cohesion and external projection. Internal cohesion (coherence)
refers to the level of unity of institutional and policy co-ordination on which the EU's
*acquis sécuritaire* rests, while external projection relates to how (consistent) the enlarged
EU behaves both within its immediate neighbourhoods and farther afield. Can the
European Union numbering 27 Member States (hereafter EU-27) or more achieve
consensus on any issue, let alone topics as sensitive as security policies? While it may
be a little early to pass definitive judgment, the 15 Member States of the EU prior to
the 2004 enlargement (hereafter EU-15) have already encountered difficulties reaching
consensus on security issues. What will become clear from this chapter is that the latest round of enlargement has not just created new security problems but has also com-
pounded crucial challenges that the EU-15 have been avoiding.

Before considering the impact of the fifth and sixth waves of enlargement on the EU's
external (section 3) and internal security policies (section 4), it is worth sketching out
the general contours of coherence and consistency (section 2). The institutional aspects
thereof will be revisited towards the end of this chapter, when the impact of the recent
two waves of enlargement on decision-making on the EU's security policies is discussed
(section 5). Some concluding remarks will wrap up this contribution (section 6).


2.        COHERENCE AND CONSISTENCY IN EU SECURITY POLICIES

The issue of size affects both coherence and consistency in EU security policies, as
both the CFSP/ESDP and the AFSJ/PJCC, the main mechanisms for external projection,
are potentially constrained by the existing levels of internal cohesion. There is a linger-
ing concern that the seemingly perpetual accession of new Member States, each with
its own interests and agendas, will result in greater difficulties in attaining the necessary
level of consensus. While in a veto system such increases do not seem to really matter,

---

[3] Treaty of Lisbon amending the Treaty on European Union and the Treaty establishing the European
Community, *OJ* 2007 C 306/1.

as it only takes one state to block a proposal,[4] the chances of disagreement and delay increase exponentially as the numbers of participants rise, particularly on issues that touch on sensitive national security concerns. Although the increase in numbers has not, as yet, overtly affected the process of deepening (integration), particularly in the sphere of internal security, it would be unwise to downplay this quantitative element too much. In this case, size does matter.

Internal cohesion refers to the impact that widening the membership has had and will continue to have on pre-existing policies across the security spectrum, both internal and external. Thus, this relates not only to how pre-existing policy proposals *per se* are affected, where the impact has not been even, but also how the EU's institutional structures adapt to manage the wider membership base and ensure that necessary leadership is provided. Given the issues that dominate the security agenda, it may not be possible, in the longer term, to maintain such a clear distinction between the internal and external conceptions. To a certain extent, this has been recognised by the Member States when signing the Reform Treaty in Lisbon in December 2007: the pillar structure of the Union is set to be partly abolished with the "communitarisation" of the Third Pillar.[5] The CFSP and the newly called "Common Security and Defence Policy", however, remain covered by the intergovernmental method of the EU Treaty.

External projection is more concerned with the challenges that confront the EU as its borders are pushed outwards. These challenges are not necessarily new. Defining relations with Russia, for instance, has been an issue on the external relations agenda since its inception. However, the Union's new geographical and geopolitical position has brought such relations into sharper focus. The EU has already attempted to delineate its roles and responsibilities within what it has termed its "neighbourhood", consisting of "European" states of the post-Soviet space (Belarus, Moldova and Ukraine), countries of the Southern Caucasus (Armenia, Azerbaijan and Georgia) and the countries on the eastern and southern shores of the Mediterranean (from Syria to Morocco).[6] The EU has also defined policies applicable to other clusters of neighbouring states: the pre-accession process for Turkey, Croatia and Macedonia (FYROM);[7] the Stabilisation and Association Process for the other countries of the Western Balkans

---

[4] See T. Valášek, 'New EU Members in Europe's Security Policy', 18 *CRIA* (2005) pp. 217-228, at p. 217. See, more generally, T. Valášek, *The 'Easternization' of Europe's Security Policy* (Brussels, IVO-CDI 2004).

[5] The provisions on AFSJ/PJCC have been regrouped under the TFEU. Throughout this chapter, references to provisions of the Lisbon Treaty have been based on the consolidated versions of the Treaty on European Union (hereafter new TEU) and the Treaty on the functioning of the European Union (hereafter TFEU), as published in *OJ* 2008 C 115/1.

[6] For details on the European Neighbourhood Policy, see http://ec.europa.eu/world/enp/index_ en.htm. For an academic analysis, see, e.g., S. Blockmans and A. Łazowski, eds., *The European Union and Its Neighbours: A Legal Appraisal of the EU's Policies of Stabilisation, Partnership and Integration* (The Hague, T.M.C. Asser Press 2006); M. Cremona and C. Hillion, 'L'Union fait la force? Potential and Limitations of the European Neighbourhood Policy as an Integrated EU Foreign and Security Policy', *EUI Working Papers*, LAW No. 2006/39.

[7] See S. Blockmans, 'Consolidating the Enlargement Agenda for Southeastern Europe', in S. Blockmans and S. Prechal, eds., *Reconciling the Deepening and Widening of the European Union* (The Hague, T.M.C. Asser Press 2007) pp. 59-86.

(Albania, Bosnia-Herzegovina, Kosovo, Montenegro, Serbia);[8] the European Economic Area (Iceland, Liechtenstein, Norway)[9] and the countries bordering the Black Sea.[10] Furthermore, it operates complicated sets of bilateral relations with Switzerland[11] and Russia.[12]

The EU will have to ensure that the enlargements do not (further) disrupt the internal cohesion and add to, instead of detract from, the ability to externally project security and stability. Donald Rumsfeld's conceptualisation of "old" and "new" Europe must not be set in stone, nor must the EU allow its perception of security to remain static.

## 3.       EXTERNAL SECURITY

### 3.1.    **Common Foreign and Security Policy**

#### 3.1.1.   *New sensitivities, new horizons*

The fault lines that opened up across Europe in 2003 over the war in Iraq were ominous signs for the development of a cohesive CFSP and led to Rumsfeld's evocation of "old" and "new" Europe. All Central and Eastern European EU candidate countries signed letters supporting the US policy on the enforcement of UN Security Council Resolution 1441 (2002). The Czech Republic, Hungary, Poland and Slovakia appended their names to a letter signed by the leaders of five EU Member States (Denmark, Italy, Portugal, Spain and the UK) supporting the US campaign to "disarm" Iraq.[13] A more strongly formulated statement followed from the "Vilnius Ten": Albania, Bulgaria, Croatia, Estonia, Latvia, Lithuania, Macedonia, Romania, Slovakia and Slovenia. In their joint statement, they declared that 'we are prepared to contribute to an international coalition to enforce its provisions and the disarmament of Iraq.'[14] The importance of these letters is that they provide a clear political statement in favour of US leadership and, therefore,

---

[8] See S. Blockmans, *Tough Love: The European Union's Relations with the Western Balkans* (The Hague, T.M.C. Asser Press 2007) at pp. 241-307.

[9] See A. Łazowski, 'Box of Chocolates Integration: the European Economic Area and Switzerland Revisited', in Blockmans and Prechal, eds., *op. cit.* n. 7, pp. 87-110.

[10] See F. Tazzariani, *A Synergy for Black Sea Cooperation: Guidelines for an EU Initiative*, CEPS Policy Brief No. 105 (Brussels, CEPS 2006).

[11] See Łazowski, *loc. cit.* n. 9.

[12] See C. Hillion, *The European Union and its East-European Neighbours: A Laboratory for the Organisation of EU External Relations* (Oxford, Hart Publishing forthcoming in 2010).

[13] Statement to international newspapers by José Maria Aznar, José Manuel Barroso, Silvio Berlusconi, Tony Blair, Vaclav Havel, Peter Medgyessy, Leszek Miller and Anders Fogh Rasmussen, 'United We Stand', *The Wall Street Journal*, 30 January 2003. See E. Pond, 'The Dynamics of Alliance Diplomacy over Iraq', *EUI Working Papers RSCA* No. 2004/26 (Florence, EUI 2004).

[14] 'Statement of the Vilnius Group of Countries in response to the presentation by the United States Secretary of State to the United Nations Security Council concerning Iraq', Statement by the Foreign Ministers of Albania, Bulgaria, Croatia, Estonia, Latvia, Lithuania, Macedonia, Romania, Slovakia, Slovenia, 5 February 2003, available at http://www.am.gov.lv/en/news/press-releases/2003/feb/2868/.

in favour of an Atlanticist CFSP/ESDP. The position of the majority of "old" Member States, Germany and France in particular, was one of 'emphatically reject[ing] the impending war.'[15] The French position was hardened by the perceived "with us or against us" attitude of US policy. By March 2003, there were clear for and against camps within Europe, with the Central and Eastern European countries of "new" Europe strongly supporting the US. Divisions were further exacerbated by French President Chirac, who demanded that the candidate countries adopt the Franco-German position. He noted that the countries of Central and Eastern Europe had 'lost a good opportunity to keep quiet', calling their support for the US 'infantile' and 'reckless'.[16] There was even an implicit threat that they might have their EU accession blocked by a French referendum. Although the other EU Member States and the European Commission rejected Chirac's criticism, the incident further reinforced the notion of "old" and "new" Europe. It should not be surprising that such divisions developed over Iraq, raising fundamental issues of war and peace, the legitimacy of the use of force, the role of the United Nations, the future of the Middle East and the nature of the transatlantic relationship. But, as will be shown, these are not the only sensitivities which put the cohesion and effectiveness of the EU's security policies immediately before and after the fifth enlargement to the test.

For historical as well as geographical reasons, none of the twelve new Member States has overseas interests or extensions, let alone a colonial past. Unlike previous enlargements, therefore, the enlargements of 2004/7 did not entail a significant widening of the horizons of the Union's external policies. However, the new Member States have a strong interest in the formulation of those external policies of the European Union that might affect their immediate vicinity. This should not come as a surprise, as most of them have become the new external frontier of the EU. The permeability and safety of the eastern borders and all common neighbourhood policies touch upon their vital interests and shape their behaviour on foreign policy and security issues. The fate of national minorities, cross-border trade and visa regulations, energy and environmental issues, Balkan stability, relations with Belarus, Ukraine, Moldova, the Southern Caucasus and, of course, Russia are cases in point. In this sense, the new Member States' impact on CFSP (and ESDP) has been geographically limited but intensely focused.[17] Yet, this does not necessarily mean that there is a sort of Central European "bloc" on, for instance, relations with Russia or Belarus. Countries like Slovakia and Bulgaria have different historical and cultural sensitivities from the Baltic

---

[15] See the speech by Federal Foreign Minister of Germany Joschka Fisher to the UN Security Council, 19 March 2003, available at http://www.auswaertiges-amt.de/www/en/archiv_print?archiv_id=4224.

[16] As reported by I. Traynor and I. Black, 'Eastern Europe dismayed at Chirac snub', *The Guardian*, 19 February 2003.

[17] See already the projections made by S. Duke, *Beyond the Chapter: Enlargement Challenges for CFSP and ESDP* (Maastricht, EIPA 2003) and in the contributions to H. Neuhold and E. Sucharipa, eds., *The CFSP/ESDP After Enlargement: A Bigger EU = A Stronger EU?* (Vienna School of International Studies, Favorita Papers 2003). See also G. Müller-Brandeck-Bocquet, *The Future of the European Foreign, Security and Defence Policy after Enlargement* (Baden-Baden, Nomos 2006). For a legal analysis, see M. Cremona, 'The Impact of Enlargement: External Policy and External Relations', in M. Cremona, ed., *The Enlargement of the European Union* (Oxford, Oxford University Press 2003) pp. 161-208.

States or Poland, while geographical proximity and cross-border trade or minority issues may condition the approach to Russia, Ukraine or the Western Balkans in several and diverse ways.

### 3.1.2.  *Aligning to the* acquis

Like the Acceding States in the enlargement wave before them, the prospective members from Central and Eastern Europe participated in the Common Foreign and Security Policy of the Union even before they acceded to the EU.[18] Arguably, it is thanks to this preparation that enlarging the CFSP *acquis* has hardly raised any problems. Another explanation lies in the fact that thanks to the CFSP's largely declaratory nature, its incorporation into the national legal system required few domestic adjustments and did not impose substantial budgetary burdens. Moreover, conditionality did not play a significant role in this domain. The process of legal adaptation and policy convergence, therefore, went relatively well. The pre-accession negotiations on the RELEX and CFSP chapters of the *acquis* (Chapters 26 and 27 respectively) went rather smoothly and were quickly brought to an end in all cases.[19] The only issues that stirred up some controversy – through requests for transitional periods (Chapter 26) or through non-alignment with CFSP common positions or *démarches* (Chapter 27) – were those that involved relations with fellow applicants and/or neighbours. As long as the enlargement process appeared to proceed in different gears for the two main groups invited to the negotiating table – the Luxembourg Six (1997) and the Helsinki Six (1999) – the most advanced candidates were afraid of dismantling bilateral or sub-regional arrangements that had proved effective in improving relations and security at all levels. Once it became clear that almost all countries under consideration would accede to the European Union at roughly the same time, that worry disappeared.[20] As noted in the previous section, similar fears were aired with respect to relations with the eastern neighbours.

### 3.2.  **European Security and Defence Policy**

#### 3.2.1.  *Dual enlargement*

In the early 1990s, the general expectation was that "Europe" would eventually be reunited under the aegis of both NATO and the European Union. The process would take some time, due to, *inter alia*, the differences in membership criteria of the two

---

[18] In 1994, Austria, Finland, Sweden and Norway had finalised their Accession Treaty and were expected to join the EU on 1 January 1995. In anticipation of that, they were invited to participate in CFSP activities from the spring of 1994, i.e., before the ratification referenda in the following months. Norway, therefore, was a partner in CFSP for a few months although it did not become an EU member: in November 1994, the "No" to accession was to prevail (as it had already done in 1972).

[19] See the country reports in A. Missiroli, ed., *Bigger EU, Wider CFSP, Stronger ESDP? The View from Central Europe*, Occasional Papers No. 34 (Paris, EUISS 2002).

[20] The applicants' attitude is well analysed in J.-L. Dehaene and P. Dunay, *Boxes: Why CFSP and ESDP Do Not Matter Much to EU Candidate Countries*, RSC Policy Papers No. 01/5 (San Domenico di Fiesole, EUI 2001).

organisations,[21] but both integration tracks would be completed in the time span of a decade or so. In 1997, however, the two enlargement processes took divergent paths: a relatively quick but selective enlargement of NATO and a slower and more inclusive pre-accession process of the EU. For the former, the driving factors were of a quintessentially geopolitical nature, for the latter of a typically functional, administrative character.[22] Yet, the fact that the US and NATO "delivered" security and stability to Europe throughout the 1990s, while the EU and its big Member States did not, has played an important role in the perceptions of the Central European public until this day. As a result, the Atlantic Alliance is more popular than the European Union among applicants, although the social and economic benefits from NATO membership are disproportionally lower than those of the EU. Needless to say that all candidates from Central and Eastern Europe were pushing for a clear understanding between NATO and the EU: they did not want to be forced to choose between Washington and Brussels on security matters.

### 3.2.2.    *Aligning to the* acquis

Going from the above, it hardly comes as a surprise that all applicants from Central Europe reacted late and rather defensively to the launch of the European Security and Defence Policy in 1999.[23] On the one hand, they seemed not to understand its rationale and, above all, feared that it could undermine NATO's internal cohesion because of driving the US out of Europe. On the other hand, some of the applicants suspected that involvement in the ESDP might come as an alternative to NATO membership, which was their main security goal. By contrast, for those candidate countries that were already full-fledged NATO members, the key issue was notably the establishment of a clearly defined relationship with the Alliance, whereby all relevant decisions would be taken at 15+6 (EU Member States plus other European allies). In many ways, and with varying emphasis, Warsaw, Prague and Budapest considered the ESDP acceptable only as

---

[21] Enlargement of NATO is based upon Art. 10 of the Washington Treaty, which states that membership is open to any 'European State in a position to further the principles of this Treaty and to contribute to the security of the North Atlantic area.' In addition, countries seeking NATO membership are also expected to meet certain political, economic and military requirements, which are laid out in Chapter 5 (paras. 68-78) of the 1995 'Study on NATO Enlargement', available at http://www.nato.int/docu/basictxt/enl-9501. htm. See also S. Larrabee, *NATO Enlargement: Prague and Beyond* (Brussels, CEPS 2001). On the development of EU membership criteria, see F. Hoffmeister, 'Changing Requirements for Membership', in A. Ott and K. Inglis, eds., *Handbook on European Enlargement – A Commentary on the Enlargement Process* (The Hague, T.M.C. Asser Press 2002) pp. 90-102; K. Smith, 'The Evolution and Application of EU Membership Conditionality', in Cremona, ed., *op. cit.* n. 17, pp. 105-139; C. Hillion, 'The Copenhagen Criteria and their Progeny', in C. Hillion, ed., *EU Enlargement: A Legal Approach* (Oxford, Hart Publishing 2004) pp. 1-22; and S. Blockmans, 'Raising the Threshold for Further EU Enlargement: Process, Problems and Prospects', in A. Ott and E. Vos, eds., *50 Years of European Integration: Foundations and Perspectives* (The Hague, T.M.C. Asser Press 2009) pp. 203-219.
[22] Among the few studies that compare the two dynamics, see M. Smith and G. Timmins, *Building a Bigger Europe: EU and NATO Enlargement in Comparative Perspective* (Aldershot, Ashgate 2000); and A. Hyde-Price, 'The Antinomies of European Security: Dual Enlargement and the Reshaping of the European Order', 21 *Contemporary Security Policy* (2000) pp. 139-167.
[23] See the contributions to Missiroli, ed., *op. cit.* n. 19.

a European Security and Defence Identity (ESDI) within or under the supervision of NATO.[24] Over time, however, such attitudes evolved towards a warmer acceptance of the ESDP blueprint as eventually spelt out in the Treaty of Nice[25] and in the so-called "Berlin Plus" Agreement.[26] As with the CFSP, aligning to the *acquis sécuritaire* of the European Union posed no significant problems.

### 3.2.3.  *Impact of enlargement on the ESDP*

In spite of their relatively short record of freedom of action (and – for some – independence) on the international scene, during the past few years, all ten new Member States from Central Europe[27] have been increasingly engaged in civilian and military crisis-management operations, under UN, NATO and EU flags. As a rule, they have done so as modular components of bigger multinational units and under foreign command. Much as their contributions have been limited in absolute numbers and their functions, they have proved the willingness and ability of the new Member States to participate and perform in Article 17 TEU-type (aka "Petersberg") operations, especially in the Western Balkans and in the eastern neighbourhood, but also farther afield.[28]

Also, the ten countries committed forces and capabilities to the so-called "Headline Goal 2010."[29] Modest as they are, the "voluntary" contributions by the new Member States display a remarkable degree of political goodwill.[30] What is worth noting is not only the fact that all the forces earmarked for the Headline Goal 2010 are "double-hatted" (i.e., answerable to both NATO and the EU), but also that in most newly acceded countries, participation in NATO-led or EU-led missions is seen as a driving factor towards some sort of functional role specialisation. Such specialisation, of course, is the result of making virtue out of necessity: financial, technical and human resourc-

---

[24] See R. Trzaskowski, 'Poland', in Missiroli, ed., *op. cit.* n. 19, pp. 19-25; R. Khol, 'Czech Republic', *ibidem*, pp. 26-30; and E. Nagyne Rózsa, 'Hungary', *ibidem*, pp. 36-41.

[25] Treaty of Nice amending the Treaty on European Union, the Treaties establishing the European Communities and certain related acts, *OJ* 2001 C 80/1.

[26] See J.W. de Zwaan, 'Foreign Policy and Defence Cooperation in the European Union: Legal Foundations', in S. Blockmans, ed., *The European Union and Crisis Management: Policy and Legal Aspects* (The Hague, T.M.C. Asser Press 2008) pp. 17-36. However, acceding Cyprus and Malta were excluded from participating in future EU-led operations using NATO assets, the price to be paid by the EU to strike a deal struck with Turkey over the "Berlin Plus" arrangements. See M. Reichard, 'The EU-NATO "Berlin Plus" Agreement: The Silent Eye of the Storm', in Blockmans, ed., *ibidem*, pp. 233-253.

[27] For the significantly different issues raised by the two Mediterranean countries (Cyprus and Malta), see M. Maresceau and E. Lannon, eds., *The EU's Enlargement and Mediterranean Strategies: A Comparative Analysis* (Basingstoke, Palgrave 2001).

[28] For troop contributions, see the Factsheets on ESDP Operations, available on the website of the Council of the EU, at http://www.consilium.europa.eu/cms3_fo/showPage.asp?id=268&lang=en&mode=g. See also A. Shepherd, 'The Implications of EU Enlargement for the European Security and Defence Policy', in D. Brown and A. Shepherd, eds., *The Security Dimensions of EU Enlargement: Wider Europe, Weaker Europe?* (Manchester, Manchester University Press 2007) pp. 20-37, at pp. 28-31.

[29] See J.-Y. Haine, 'Assessing the Union's Military Capabilities: ESDP and the European Crisis of Liberal Internationalism', in Blockmans, ed., *op. cit.* n. 26, pp. 107-134.

[30] See also L. Kubosova, 'Poland indicates support for boosting EU's military role', *EU Observer*, 25 April 2008.

es are scarce and have to be concentrated and focused on viable objectives – all the more so since all the countries under consideration are in the process of overhauling and modernising their military forces. Nonetheless, this role specialisation falls neatly in line with the development at the EU level of the so-called "Battlegroups" – small, integrated, national or multi-national force packages of about 1,500 troops, two of them on stand-by for a period of six months, that can be deployed rapidly to restore order and prevent further aggravation in a civil conflict.[31]

Similar constraints on resources apply to the ten new Member States' defence- procurement policies. While most countries are still substituting or upgrading old equipment from the Soviet era, the need to become more interoperable with NATO allies and EU partners is putting additional pressure on public budgets and decision-makers.[32] What is worth noting, though, is that, here too, some evolution has occurred throughout Central Europe. Whilst in the late 1990s, tenders were almost systematically won by American firms (partly as a side effect of the candidates' willingness to gain Washington's support in their bids for NATO membership), officials seem to have gradually adopted a more balanced attitude. As a result, European companies have more chances now, for reasons that are linked in part to the EU membership but also to the more credible offset programmes they may be able to offer. Procurement policy, in other words, remains largely driven by political considerations (the two enlargements – NATO and EU) but increasingly takes into account the added value of domestic job creation in high-tech sectors that may prove crucial in the future.[33]

### 3.3.    Common neighbourhood policies

As noted before, the southeastward push of its borders has confronted the European Union more directly with a number of hard security threats (simmering and explosive

---

[31] See R. Hamelink, 'The Battlegroups Concept: A Versatile Force Package', *Impetus* (Brussels, Council of the EU 2006) at p. 12; EU Council Secretariat, 'Factsheet EU Battlegroups', EU BG 02, November 2006; G. Lindstrom, *Enter the EU Battlegroups*, Chaillot Paper No. 97 (Paris, EUISS 2007). The Poles will form the bulk of a Battlegroup developed with Germany, Latvia, Lithuania and Slovakia, in the first half of 2010. The Czechs are forming a unit with the Germans and Austrians. Italy, Hungary and Slovenia were already on stand-by in the second half of 2007. The Czech Republic will also be part of a Czech-Slovak Battlegroup in the second half of 2009. Estonia co-operated with Sweden, Finland, Ireland and Norway in the so-called "Nordic Battlegroup", on stand-by in the first half of 2008. The "Balkan Battlegroup" consists of Greece, Bulgaria, Cyprus and Romania. Romania will also form part of an Italian-Romanian-Turkish Battlegroup, on stand-by in the second half of 2010.
[32] See A. Georgopoulos, 'The European Armaments Policy: A *Conditio Sine Qua Non* for the European Security and Defence Policy?', in M. Trybus and N. White, eds., *European Security Law* (Oxford, Oxford University Press 2007) pp. 198-222, at pp. 203-204. For a more comprehensive overview, see the contributions to H.J. Giesmann and G.E. Gustenau, eds., *Security Handbook 2001 – Security and Military in Central and Eastern Europe* (Baden-Baden, Nomos 2001).
[33] For backgrounds and analysis, see M. Trybus, 'The new European Defence Agency: A Contribution to a Common European Security and Defence Policy and a Challenge to the Community *Acquis*?', 43 *CMLRev.* (2006) pp. 1964-2003; M. Trybus, *European Union Law and Defence Integration* (Oxford, Portland-Oregon Hart Publishing 2005) and M. Trybus, *European Defence Procurement Law: International and National Procurement Systems as Models for a Liberalised Defence Procurement Market in Europe* (The Hague, Kluwer Law International 1999).

conflicts in the Balkans, the Southern Caucasus and the Middle East) and softer security challenges (e.g., mass illegal migration, organised crime and the disruption of the
flow of energy resources) in its (new) neighbourhoods. Rather out of self-interest and
a sense of moral duty than out of sheer altruism has the EU launched attempts at sta-
bilising its immediate environs by engaging its neighbouring countries, so as to persuade
them to adopt an outlook similar to its own. In fact, the European Union's long-term
stability – as well as the credibility of its external security policies – will depend, to a
large extent, on how it manages this task.

Attention in this chapter will be limited to an analysis of the impact of enlargement
on the development of the European Neighbourhood Policy (ENP) and on EU-Russia
relations. While other case studies might have been pursued (e.g., Turkey and the
countries of the Western Balkans), these are excluded from the analysis because the
impact of the fifth and sixth rounds of enlargement on relations with those states has
been less spectacular than that on relations with Russia and the eastern ENP countries.

### 3.3.1.   *Impact of the fifth enlargement on the ENP*

The creation of the European Neighbourhood Policy, launched in 2003 with the publication of the "Wider Europe" initiative,[34] was the European Commission's response
to the wish of some of the EU-15 to develop a new strategy ahead of the Union's 2004
enlargement to mitigate the exclusion effects for countries like Ukraine, Belarus and
Moldova,[35] and to prevent the Mediterranean countries pooled together in the "Barcelona
Process" from being disadvantaged by the new initiative.[36] A detailed plan was published
a year later in a strategy paper on the ENP.[37] That is also when the geographical scope
of the policy was further widened to include three countries from the Southern Caucasus
(Armenia, Azerbaijan and Georgia). Shortly thereafter, the ENP entered into its phase
of implementation with the conclusion of the first batch of country-specific Action
Plans.[38]

---

[34] Communication from the Commission to the Council and the European Parliament. Wider Eu-
rope-Neighbourhood: A New Framework for Relations with our Eastern and Southern Neighbours, COM
(2003) 104 final. This communication was preceded by a highly influential Joint letter of 7 August 2002
by Commissioner Chris Patten and the EU High Representative for the CFSP on Wider Europe, available
at http://www.europa.eu.int/comm/world/enp/pdf/_0130163334_001_en.pdf and a speech by Commission
President Romano Prodi, entitled 'A Wider Europe – A Proximity Policy as the Key to Stability', for the
Sixth ECSA-World Conference, Brussels, 5-6 December 2002, SPEECH/02/619.

[35] Jack Straw, then Minister of Foreign Affairs of the UK, was reported to have sent a letter to his
Spanish colleague Josep Pique, holder of the Presidency of the EU at the time, calling for "special neigh-
bour status" for Ukraine, Belarus and Moldova, 'including free trade rights with the EU, and a close relationship on border, justice, home affairs, security and defence issues.' See S. Castle, 'Straw looks to EU's
future frontiers', *The Independent*, 16 April 2002.

[36] On the origins of the ENP, see M. Emerson, *The European Neighbourhood Policy: Strategy or
Placebo?*, CEPS Working Document No. 215 (Brussels, CEPS 2004). On the legal and institutional is-
sues of the ENP, see M. Cremona, 'The European Neighbourhood Policy: Legal and Institutional Issues',
*CDDRL Working Paper* No. 2004/25.

[37] Communication from the Commission. European Neighbourhood Policy. Strategy Paper, COM
(2004) 373 final.

[38] See Communication from the Commission to the Council on the Commission proposals for Action Plans under the European Neighbourhood Policy (ENP), COM (2004) 795 final. The Action Plans

The ENP is an EU foreign and security policy tool aimed at better accommodating the Union's interests and desires with the (economic) opportunities raised and security threats (illegal migration and trafficking, terrorism, violent or "frozen conflicts", etc.) posed by the neighbouring countries.[39] As such, the ENP is a unilaterally defined regional implementation of the European Security Strategy (ESS),[40] based on a security concept which embraces all three pillars of the EU.[41] One of the main problems of the ENP is that the countries that have been offered enhanced relationships under the policy are not only geographically but also politically and economically miles apart. Arguably, gathering such a heterogeneous group of countries under the umbrella of one single foreign and security policy may not be the most effective way to seize the opportunities and tackle the challenges in the Mediterranean region, Eastern Europe and the Southern Caucasus. Moreover, the whole package of *quid pro quo* hardly looks like a credible balance of obligations and incentives.[42] For all the comprehensive lists of would-be obligations laid down in the Action Plans, the ENP does not appear as a particularly strong leverage for securing a sustained process of all-encompassing transformation of the EU's outer periphery. On the one hand, this is due to the fact that the ENP does not offer the incentives expected by the neighbouring countries, e.g., the financial and technical assistance to support and/or reward reforms, a significant degree of integration in EU policies and programmes and the prospect of EU membership, the "pull" needed in "European" countries like Ukraine and Moldova that could one day fulfil the conditions set in Article 49 EU. On the other hand, the ENP is perceived as weak because the disincentives which the Union can apply are not strong enough to force long-ruling political elites into the tracks of progressive democratic reform (e.g., Belarus, Egypt and Syria). For these and other reasons, it should come as no surprise that the ENP has received a fair degree of criticism.[43] The Commission itself admitted as much in its 2007 Communication on 'A Strong European Neighbourhood Policy', when it proposed further action to make the ENP fully effective: 'a great deal remains to be done.'[44] The question remains, however, whether the European Union can go

---

are "benchmarked roadmaps" in bringing about needed reforms to bring the neighbours closer to the EU. See Address by Javier Solana, 'The role of the EU in promoting and consolidating democracy in Europe's East', at the Common Vision for a Common Neighbourhood Conference, Vilnius, 4 May 2006. For a list of ENP reference documents, including the action plans, see http://ec.europa.eu/world/enp/documents_en.htm.

[39] See B. Ferrero-Waldner, 'The European Neighbourhood Policy: The EU's Newest Foreign Policy Instrument', 11 *EFA Rev.* (2006) pp. 139-142; and S. Blockmans and A. Łazowski, 'The EU and Its Neighbours: Questioning Identity and Relationships', in Blockmans and Łazowski, eds., *op. cit.* n. 6, pp. 3-18, at pp. 7-8.

[40] *A Secure Europe in a Better world – The European Security Strategy*, drafted under the responsibility of the High Representative for the CFSP and approved by the Brussels European Council on 12 December 2003, available at http://ue.eu.int/uedocs/cmsUpload/78367.pdf.

[41] See Cremona and Hillion, *op. cit.* n. 6, at pp. 5-8 and p. 21.

[42] See also J. Kelley, 'New Wine in Old Wineskins: Policy Adaptation in the European Neighbourhood Policy', 44 *JCMS* (2006) pp. 29-55, at p. 36.

[43] See, e.g., S. Blockmans and A. Łazowski, 'Conclusions: Squaring the Ring of Friends', in Blockmans and Łazowski, eds., *op. cit.* n. 6, pp. 613-639; and Cremona and Hillion, *op. cit.* n. 6.

[44] Communication from the Commission to the European Parliament and the Council. A Strong European Neighbourhood Policy, COM (2007) 774 final, at p. 2.

further in developing links with its partners that go beyond the current ENP yet fall short of accession agreements. According to the Commission, the ENP is expected to enter into a new era with the conclusion of the next generation of 'deep and comprehensive free trade agreements (FTAs)' with all ENP countries – like the one which the EU is currently negotiating with Ukraine – to create a common regulatory framework.[45] However, such aspirations are best kept for the longer term. The Commission itself has indicated that, in the short- to medium-term, deep and comprehensive FTAs would have too negative an impact on the structure of the weak economies of, e.g., Georgia, Armenia and Azerbaijan, and would go even further than what is already in place for the neighbouring countries on the southern shores of the Mediterranean. Thus, the scope and breadth of the new FTAs are to be based on an evaluation of the performance based on an individual Action Plan and may in most cases amount to nothing more than a minor update.

The policy of pooling the Mediterranean, the Eastern European and the South Caucasian countries together in a one-size-fits-all framework has not only been criticised by "European" countries like Ukraine and Moldova as unattractive and in need of revision (i.e., differentiation).[46] The Southern Mediterranean countries have regarded the ENP as diminishing the spirit of "partnership" underpinning the Euro-Med relations since the Barcelona declaration.[47] After their accession to the EU, Poland and the Baltic states have been the most vocal in their support for a separate eastern dimension of the ENP.[48] It has been reported that the German Presidency of the EU in the first half of 2007 toyed with the idea of following up on the idea by separating the ENP countries eligible and non-eligible for EU membership.[49] But it took the boldness of French President Sarkozy to come up with a plan of such sorts. On 13 July 2008, at the beginning of the French EU Presidency, Sarkozy unveiled his long-anticipated plan for a Union of the Mediterranean to reinforce the Barcelona Process.[50] In a parallel move, but prior to the media circus at the Paris Summit of leaders from all but one (Libya) of the 43 countries involved in the French initiative, Poland and Sweden officially tabled a proposal for an Eastern Partnership between the EU and its neighbours Armenia, Azerbaijan, Georgia, Moldova and Ukraine – with Poland presenting the deal as a path

---

[45] Communication from the Commission to the Council and the European Parliament on strengthening the European Neighbourhood Policy, COM (2006) 726 final, at pp. 4-5. On the new agreement with Ukraine, see C. Hillion, 'Mapping-Out the New Contractual Relations between the European Union and Its Neighbours: Learning from the EU-Ukraine "Enhanced Agreement"', 12 *EFA Rev.* (2007) pp. 169-182.

[46] See Cremona and Hillion, *op. cit.* n. 6, at p. 16.

[47] See E. Lannon and P. van Elsuwege, 'The EU's Emerging Neighbourhood Policy and its Potential Impact on the Euro-Mediterranean Partnership', in P. Xuereb, ed., *Euro-Med Integration and the "Ring of Friends": The Mediterranean's Europe Challenge* (Valetta, European Documentation and Research Centre 2003).

[48] See, e.g., E. Piontek, 'Ukraine', in Blockmans and Łazowski, eds., *op. cit.* n. 6, pp. 499-529.

[49] See A. Balzan, 'Berlin in plans to split EU neighbourhood states', *EU Observer*, 17 July 2006.

[50] See the twenty-page Joint Declaration of the Paris Summit of the Mediterranean, Paris 13 July 2008; and E. Vucheva, 'Sarkozy beaming at birth of Mediterranean Union', *EU Observer*, 14 July 2008. See also the Communication of the Commission to the European Parliament and the Council, 'Barcelona Process: Union for the Mediterranean', COM (2008) 319 final.

toward EU membership.[51] While this initiative immediately saw some criticism from Bulgaria and Romania, countries which do not want to see the Union's Black Sea Synergy undermined, both the Commission and the Czech Republic, which took over the EU's Presidency from France in the first half of 2009, have thrown their weight behind the Polish-Swedish plan.[52] In December 2008 the European Commission published a communication outlining key features of the new framework.[53] This was followed by a formal launch of the new endeavour during the Eastern Partnership summit in Prague. The summit adopted a joint declaration on the Eastern Partnership.[54]

### 3.3.2.   Impact of enlargements on EU-Russia relations

Russia merits special attention because of its geostrategic location, its sheer territorial, political, economic and military size, and the fact that it is dealing with a broad range of security issues which have a direct bearing on the EU. The relationship with Russia is a key factor for the EU's security and, given their recent history, even more so for the new Member States from Central and Eastern Europe, in terms of realising the objective of creating a stable neighbourhood. EU-Russia relations colour a wide array of EU activities, from energy security to counter-terrorism, from the advancement of the CFSP/ESDP to the future of the EU's enlargement process in relation to Ukraine, Moldova and potentially even Belarus. Wherever the EU turns, Russia seems to be there. As a result, the way this relationship develops in the longer term will affect the effectiveness of the EU's entire security agenda.

   With that situation in mind, the prospects for productive partnership are rather bleak. Ahead of the eastern enlargements of the European Union, Moscow concluded that pursuing "enhanced bilateralism" would be the best way for developing its relations with the EU.[55] It favoured the development of a strategic partnership with the European Union, based on a relationship between equals.[56] Understandably, Russia excluded itself

---

[51] A 2,5 page proposal was presented on 23 May 2008. See R. Goldirova, 'Eastern Partnership could lead to enlargement, Poland says', *EU Observer*, 27 May 2008.

[52] *Ibidem*: "'It goes in the same direction that we want. And we see that the next year, we need to balance. This year, it is a Mediterranean year. So, the next year would be the eastern year", the [Czech Republic's] deputy prime minister, Alexandr Vondra, told journalists.' This observation is supported by the fact that Sweden took over the EU Presidency from the Czech Republic in the second half of 2009.

[53] Communication from the Commission to the European Parliament and the Council. Eastern Partnership, COM (2008) 823 final; Commission Staff Working Paper accompanying the Communication from the Commission to the European Parliament and the Council. Eastern Partnership, SEC (2008) 2974/3.

[54] Joint Declaration of the Prague Eastern Partnership Summit, Prague 7 May 2009, Council Doc. 8435/09.

[55] The term is used by the editor of this volume in a similar context of the EU's external relations. See A. Łazowski, 'Enhanced Bilateralism and Multilateralism: Integration without Membership', 45 *CMLRev.* (2008) pp. 1433-1458.

[56] Four so-called "common spaces" (a Common European Economic Space, a Common Space of Freedom, Security and Justice, a Common Space of External Security and a Common Space on Research and Education, including cultural aspects) were conceptualised and launched by both parties to the relationship, in the context of the EU-Russia High Level Group (consisting of equal numbers of Russian and EU representatives (Art. 93 PCA)) and the May 2003 EU-Russia Summit in Saint Petersburg, to breathe new life into the 1997 Partnership and Cooperation Agreement (PCA). See 11th EU-Russia Summit con-

from the scope of the ENP because it regarded the policy as too condescending – inso-far as the EU had tried to apply it to Russia like to any other neighbouring country – and as too competitive with its own security interests in the shared neighbourhood, espe-cially *vis-à-vis* Ukraine, Georgia, Moldova and the disputed areas of Transnistria, South Ossetia and Abkhazia.[57] Russia effectively sees those parts of the EU's "neighbourhood" as its own 'sphere of vitally important interests.'[58] The development of the ENP, a direct consequence of the EU's borders shifting further eastwards, has therefore been viewed by elements of the Russian political elite as a challenge and an incentive for them to be more, not less, active in the region. This attitude represents a new challenge to find-ing cohesion in EU decision-making. Following the Orange Revolution of December 2004, for instance, Ukraine has moved up the enlargement agenda, helped along by encouraging words from the likes of Poland.[59] While the EU has not rushed to for-mally embrace Ukraine within the accession process – a move held back by Germany and France, in particular – as that would not be well received by Russia, the Union cannot distance itself too much either. Nonetheless, if the democratic process in Ukraine is to be stabilised and consolidated, some indication of a long-term perspective on EU membership may be necessary because the ENP process and an association agreement are not sufficient to meet Kiev's expectations.[60] Once again, a difficult balance will have to be struck between competing security objectives, with certain of the new Member States lobbying in favour of Ukrainian inclusion.

The situation is complicated further because of the scale of potential Russian lever-age. In the field of energy security, the ongoing gas dispute between Russia and Ukraine, which erupted during the ice-cold New Year's period of 2006, has raised fears in the EU regarding the levels of Russian energy dependence. The gravity of the situation became even clearer during another winter gas crisis in the early months of 2009. However, the possibility of energy as an effective bargaining chip in wider relations needs to be put in context. While Ukraine, Moldova, Belarus and certain EU Member States rely to a large extent on Russian supplies, Russia equally relies on the demand for natural gas to fuel its steady economic revival. If the ability to turn gas taps on and off is a strong card, it also is one of the very few cards which Russia holds. Perched between the two new Member States – Lithuania and Poland – the Russian exclave of Kaliningrad is another example where continued good neighbourly relations are essen-tial.

In the mid- to longer term, the ability to overcome some of the difficulties in EU-Russia relations will depend, in part, on the attitudes of the new Member States. Given their history, they have more reason than most to be wary of Russian intentions

clusions, 31 May 2003, Press Release No. 9937/03. At the EU-Russia Summit of 10 May 2005 four "Road Maps" were adopted, establishing long lists of actions to further the development of the common spaces and – indirectly – the PCA.

[57] See, e.g., A. Zagorski, 'Russia and the Shared Neighbourhood', in D. Lynch, ed., *What Russia Sees*, Chaillot Paper No. 74 (Paris, EUISS 2005) pp. 61-77.

[58] Andrei Kozyrev cited in J. Bugajiski, 'Russia's New Europe', *The National Interest* (2003-4) at p. 85.

[59] See Piontek, *loc. cit.* n. 48.

[60] See 'EU keeps door half-open for Ukraine', *Euractiv.com*, 10 September 2008.

and actions. Former Polish President Aleksander Kwasniewski has noted that 'Russia is not ready to propose a new chapter in its relations with all of us.'[61] However, there is a danger in placing too much emphasis on such words, at the expense of actions on the ground, at least in the initial phase after the accession of the Central and Eastern European countries to the EU. For instance, even when relations between the Baltic States and Russia were tense over the treatment of the Russian diasporas and the delineation of borders, the arms trade continued.[62] An even more significant example can be found in relation to the human rights situation in Chechnya, suggesting that the desire for smoother relations effectively outweighed the legitimate concerns of the new Member States – at least in the short term. In May 2005, one year after the "big bang" enlargement of the EU, the following statement was issued at the end of the annual EU-Russia Summit: 'the leaders of the EU and Russia addressed in a constructive spirit, internal developments in the EU and Russia, including the situation in Chechnya.'[63]

But gradually, some new Member States have hardened their positions and have led the EU to take a more robust approach towards Russia. A spat between Russia and Poland over Russia's decision in November 2005 to ban the import of meat originating from or transiting through Poland over alleged health concerns even led Warsaw to veto the opening of talks about a "PCA *bis*" after the expiry of the first period of validity of the PCA in 2007. Concerned at the lack of EU solidarity on issues such as the German-Russian plan to build a gas pipeline bypassing Poland and Lithuania, Warsaw was supported by Vilnius in its threats to widen the veto to encompass the EU's internal negotiations on a new common energy policy. In addition, Lithuania threatened to add a veto of its own in order to get the EU to help break Russia's oil-supply blockade on Mazeikiu Nafta, the only petrol refinery in the Baltic States.[64] The shooting of journalist Anna Politkovskaya in Moscow in October 2006 and the mysterious poisoning of ex-KGB agent Alexander Litvinenko in London one month later added to the souring of EU-Russia relations.[65]

In another show of newly found confidence to look the bear in the eyes, the Estonian authorities ordered the removal of a Soviet-era war memorial from the centre of Tallinn in April 2007.[66] This move sparked violent demonstrations which left one dead and several wounded, provoked angry condemnation from Russia and led to a cyber-attack on Estonian authorities and businesses, allegedly orchestrated from Russia.[67] The Prime

---

[61] Cited in Valášek, *op. cit.* n. 4, at p. 220.

[62] See P. Holtom, 'An Assessment of the Baltic States Contribution to EU Efforts to Prevent Proliferation and Combat Illicit Arms Trafficking', in Brown and Shepherd, eds., *op. cit.* n. 28, pp. 99-114.

[63] 15th EU-Russia summit conclusions, Press Release No. 8799/05 (Presse 110), 10 May 2005, at p. 3.

[64] See E. Vucheva, 'Poland and Lithuania to coordinate positions on Russia', *EU Observer*, 9 May 2008.

[65] These events are still producing aftershocks. For instance, the closing of British Council cultural offices in Russia in January 2008 was part of the row about the UK's attempts to extradite a Russian businessman over the death of Litvinenko.

[66] Meanwhile, Estonia set itself on a new collision course with Russia over the trial of an elderly Soviet war hero, Arnold Meri, on a charge of genocide over deportations of Estonians to Siberia in 1949. See 'Estonia tries Soviet war figure', *BBC News*, 20 May 2008.

[67] As reported by I. Traynor, 'Russia accused of unleashing cyberwar to disable Estonia', *The Guardian*, 17 May 2007.

Minister's website was attacked on 27 April, the day the country was mired in protest and violence. The President's site also went down as did those of several departments. In a wired country that touts its paperless government and likes to call itself E-stonia, the attacks prompted officials to declare Estonia the first country to fall victim to a virtual war. The Estonian Defence Minister Jaak Aaviksoo raised the issue at a meeting of NATO, saying that the Alliance, which Estonia joined in 2004, needed to urgently debate the question – once seemingly a distant threat – of whether mass computer attacks posed a threat to national security. As a result, NATO leaders, at their Summit in Bucharest on 4 April 2008, agreed to a common Policy on Cyber Defence and setting up a Cyber Defence Management Authority (CDMA) in Brussels.[68] On 14 May 2008, seven NATO members – Estonia, Germany, Italy, Latvia, Lithuania, Slovakia and Spain – signed a pact formally establishing a so-called Cooperative Cyber Defence Centre of Excellence, to be set up in Tallinn.[69] Despite strong pressure from some Eastern European members, and in particular Estonia, the competences of the new authority will fall exclusively on Article 4 of the North Atlantic Treaty. In other words, members will "consult together" in case of cyber attacks, but will not be bound to "assist" each other as foreseen in Article 5 of the Treaty.[70]

In December 2007, Russia ended the two-year-old meat ban after the government of the nationalist Jarosław Kaczyński was replaced by a coalition led by the liberal Prime Minister Donald Tusk who showed his reservations towards co-operation with the US on a missile shield, distrusted and opposed by Moscow as an attempt to neutralise, whether immediately or in the future, its nuclear arsenal. However, NATO's agreement at the Bucharest Summit to sign up to much of America's plans for missile defence in Europe, supposedly to counter a threat emanating from Iran,[71] was a blow for Moscow. The allies agreed that a proliferation of missiles poses an increasing threat and welcomed the planned deployment of defence systems in Poland and the Czech Republic as a substantial contribution to their security. In reaction, Russia demanded that the missile interceptors should not be deployed in Poland until the threat is real and wanted the planned tracking radar in the Czech Republic to be cemented into the ground so that it could not be moved. As none of these demands were taken into account when the US and the Czech Republic signed an agreement on the missile shield on 8 July 2008, Russia warned that the accord might lead to a military response and turned off the oil tap on the Czech Republic.[72] When the US and Poland signed their agreement

---

[68] Point 47 of the Bucharest Summit Declaration Issued by the Heads of State and Government participating in the meeting of the North Atlantic Council in Bucharest on 3 April 2008, Press Release (2008)049 of 3 April 2008, available at http://www.nato.int/docu/pr/2008/p08-049e.html.

[69] As reported by R. Goldirova, 'NATO picks Estonia for high-tech crime centre', *EU Observer*, 15 May 2008. The signatories will all provide staff and funding for the Centre; the US will send an observer.

[70] As reported in 'NATO agrees common approach to cyber defence', *EurActiv.com*, 4 April 2008.

[71] Bucharest Summit Declaration, *loc. cit.* n. 68, points 27, 29, 37-38 and 41.

[72] See J. Dempsey and D. Bilefsky, 'U.S. and Czech Republic sign agreement on missile shield', *International Herald Tribune*, 8 July 2008; 'Russia vows to react to U.S. missile shield', *International Herald Tribune*, 15 July 2008; J. Dempsey, 'Russia denies that politics lie behind halted oil deliveries', *International Herald Tribune*, 14 July 2008; and J. Dempsey, 'Russia further cuts its oil deliveries to Czech

on 14 August 2008, Russia responded with a chilling warning that Warsaw had made itself a legitimate target for an attack by agreeing to host an anti-missile system.[73]

Much to the dismay of the other Member States, especially France and Germany, Lithuania in April 2008 blocked a Council decision on the opening of new PCA negotiations with Russia. This beating of the drums pushed the Council to include in the Commission's negotiating mandate three items to which Lithuania had been calling attention: Russia's effective co-operation in the field of justice and law enforcement, Lithuania's standpoint on energy relations and Russia's attitude to the so-called "frozen conflicts" in Abkhazia and Transnistria, with emphasis on the territorial integrity of Georgia and Moldova.[74] On 21 May 2008, the EU finally reached an agreement at the level of ambassadors (COREPER) on negotiating directives for the new PCA with Russia, which was endorsed by the foreign ministers at the GAERC meeting in Brussels on 26 May 2008.[75]

Dominated by meat, murder, monuments, missiles and energy relations, the political climate in the EU-Russia relationship saw a dramatic drop in temperature, which was to a considerable extent the result of a more assertive attitude adopted by the European Union after the accession of new Member States from Central and Eastern Europe. Meanwhile, a new and much more dangerous dispute has erupted over the meddling by Moscow in the previously called "frozen conflicts" in the shared neighbourhood, in particular over the Georgian breakaway republics of Abkhazia and South Ossetia. The diverging attitudes over these conflicts deserve separate attention before some conclusions are drawn on the future of the EU's common eastern neighbourhood policies, EU-Russia relations in particular.

### 3.3.3.   Impact of enlargements on the (not so) "frozen" conflicts

The long-time "frozen conflicts" on the eastern borders of the European Union (Transnistria, Abkhazia, Nagorno-Karabakh, South Ossetia) have belatedly emerged on the EU's radar, helped to prominence by the enlargements of the Union with countries from Central and Eastern Europe, in particular the Baltic States and Romania. In fact, the conflicts over Transnistria, Abkhazia, South Ossetia and Nagorno-Karabakh can no longer be considered "frozen."[76] All are in motion or risk the outbreak of new

Republic', *International Herald Tribune*, 30 July 2008. The case of the Czech Republic shows, however, that some new Member States have learned to spread their energy security risks. See J. Dempsey, 'Czechs dealing with Russian oil cutback', *International Herald Tribune*, 17 July 2008.

[73] See T. Shanker and N. Kulish, 'Russia lashes out on missile deal', *New York Times*, 15 September 2008.

[74] See the EU Presidency's Press Release, 'Agreement on start of negotiations for new Partnership and Cooperation Agreement with Russian Federation', 11 May 2008.

[75] See Council Press Release 9866/08 (Presse 140).

[76] The dispute between Azerbaijan and Armenia over Nagorno-Karabakh will remain outside the scope of this chapter as, at least here, Russia, the US and France as co-chairs of the so-called "Minsk Group" (EU Member States Germany, Italy, Portugal, the Netherlands, Sweden and Finland are also participating in the process) are relatively united and have advanced proposals to resolve the conflict. But both the Armenian and Azeri sides seem to believe that time is on their side with a status quo. Renewed fighting should be understood in this context. See 'Karabakh casualty toll disputed', *BBC News*, 3 March 2008.

violence. The term "simmering" conflicts thus seems more appropriate to describe the current situation.[77]

For Moldova, whose aspiration for future EU membership is strongly supported by neighbouring Romania, accession negotiations will not begin until the situation regarding Transnistria has been fully resolved.[78] However, such a resolution is impossible without the acquiescence of the Russian government, given its political, diplomatic, economic and military ties with that region.[79] Yet, the 2005 Road Map for a Common Space of External Security is not very detailed as far as it concerns 'the settlement of regional conflicts, *inter alia*, in regions adjacent to EU and Russian borders.'[80] Despite the EU's insistence, Russia was not ready to engage in a more concrete plan for common action in the shared – and troubled – security space.

Transnistria, which is located within the internationally recognised borders of Moldova, between the river Dniester and the border with Ukraine, violently split from Moldova in 1992. Since then, the standoff between Chişinau and Tiraspol continues. The EU supports the Moldovan interpretation of the principle of territorial integrity. While the EU claims to be increasingly involved in the resolution of the conflict over Transnistria, its impact remains rather limited due to the conflict's own dynamics and in view of Moscow's opposition. In March 2005, the Council of the EU appointed Adriaan Jacobovits de Szeged as EU Special Representative for Moldova.[81] He had been a Special Envoy for the Transnistrian conflict for the OSCE Chairman-in-Office under the Dutch Presidency in 2003 and was mandated by the EU to (continue to) assist in the resolution of the conflict. One of his tasks is to oversee the activities of the EU Border Assistance Mission (EUBAM) Ukraine/Moldova.[82] This EUBAM was deployed on the Ukrainian/Moldovan border in November 2005, after the Commission's President Barroso and the High Representative for the CFSP Solana received a joint letter by the Ukrainian and Moldovan Presidents inviting the EU to support their efforts in fighting smuggling and trafficking through Transnistria.[83] Since 2005, the EU is also an observer to the so-called "5+2" mediation process for Transnistria.[84] Recent developments in Moldova have been quite discouraging for the EU's efforts to resolve the conflict in a

---

[77] See M. Emerson, *Time to Think of a Strategic Bargain with Russia*, CEPS Policy Brief No. 160 (Brussels, CEPS 2008).

[78] See, e.g., O. Schmidtke and C. Chira-Pascanut, 'The Promise of Europe: Moldova and the Process of Europeanization', in O. Schmidtke and S. Yekelchyk, eds., *Europe's Last Frontier? Belarus, Moldova, and Ukraine between Russia and the European Union* (New York/Basingstoke, Palgrave Macmillan 2008) pp. 133-156.

[79] See S. Yekelchyk, 'Out of Russia's Long Shadow: The Making of Modern Ukraine, Belarus, and Moldova', in Schmidtke and Yekelchyk, eds., *op. cit.* n. 78, pp. 9-30.

[80] 15th EU-Russia Summit, 10 May 2005, *loc. cit.* n. 63, at p. 39.

[81] Council Joint Action 2005/265/CFSP appointing a Special representative of the European Union for the Republic of Moldova, *OJ* 2005 L 81/50. *Nota bene*: the EUSR is Dutch, not Hungarian.

[82] Council Joint Action 2005/776/CFSP, amending the mandate of the European Union Special Representative for Moldova, *OJ* 2005 L 292/13.

[83] See A. Skvortova, 'Moldova', in Blockmans and Łazowski, eds., *op. cit.* n. 6, pp. 549-574, at pp. 563-564.

[84] The "five" being Russia, Ukraine, OSCE, the EU and the US, the "two" being Moldova and Transnistria.

"European" way. In a declaration signed jointly by the Moldovan President Vladimir Voronin and the Transnistrian leader Igor Smirnov in April 2007, Moldova for the first time recognised the political leadership of the breakaway province as a legitimate entity.[85] And despite the EU's claims to the contrary, Russia tends to consider Kosovo's independence as a precedent for the breakaway region of Transnistria.[86] In fact, Moscow has been consistently devious in evading any serious peace and reconciliation negotiations, either under UN or OSCE auspices.

The latter applies to Abkhazia and South Ossetia as well, the two secessionist regions located within the internationally recognised borders of Georgia.[87] In the last months, tensions have soared over the two breakaway republics and briefly led to a war between Russia and Georgia in August 2008. This small war was preceded by a consistent policy under President Putin, most notably since the Rose Revolution of 2003, to undermine Georgia and its leadership.[88] Russia not only protected the secessionist entities with so-called "peacekeepers", it also engaged in policies of creeping annexation, notably through issuing Russian passports to these populations and installing Russian officials in key positions. Russia tolerated or encouraged pin-prick provocations by the separatists, as typified by the shelling of villages of South Ossetia in the year leading up to its invasion in Georgia-proper. In August 2007, a Russian air force fighter dropped a missile near a Georgian radar facility in South Ossetia, and in April 2008, an unmanned Georgian drone was shot down when flying over Abkhazia.[89] On 16 April 2008, President Putin announced Russia's intention to expand support for the two separatist regions and to establish legal connections with the regions' *de facto* governments.[90] These instances led NATO to accuse Russia of stirring tensions in Georgia,[91] and five Ministers

---

[85] Voronin allegedly acted under pressure of the Kremlin. See 'A thaw in the river', *The Economist*, 19 April 2007.

[86] Kosovo, which declared its independence from Serbia on 17 February 2008, has (as of 15 October 2008) been recognised as a sovereign state by 50 (out of 192 UN member) states, including a majority of EU Member States (22 out of 27), and all neighbouring countries minus Bosnia-Herzegovina. Greece, the Republic of Cyprus, Romania, Spain and the Slovak Republic have either indicated that they will not officially recognise Kosovo or that they will wait for the appropriate moment to do so. On the final status talks for Kosovo, the legal fall-out of the decision of the US and other countries to recognise Kosovo as a sovereign state and the legal imbroglio with UNMIK after the EU's biggest civilian ESDP operation to date was launched (EULEX Kosovo), see Blockmans, *op. cit.* n. 8, at pp. 210-220; C.J. Borgen, 'Kosovo's Declaration of Independence: Self-determination, Secession and Recognition', 12 *ASIL Insight* (2008), available at http://www.asil.org/insights/2008/02/insights080229.html; and the legal commentaries available online at http://www.kosovocompromise.com.

[87] For backgrounds and analysis, see A. Łabędzka, 'The Southern Caucasus (Armenia, Azerbaijan and Georgia)', in Blockmans and Łazowski, eds., *op. cit.* n. 6, pp. 575-612, at p. 603.

[88] For instance, by imposing a wine embargo and (air and road) transport blockades.

[89] See C.J. Chivers, 'Georgia-Russia tension escalates over downed drone', *New York Times*, 22 April 2008; and C.J. Chivers, 'U.N. blames Russia for downed drone', *New York Times*, 26 May 2008.

[90] While the announcement fell short of offering official recognition to Abkhazia and South Ossetia, it signalled a comprehensive deepening of ties between the enclaves and Russia, including in trade, agriculture, education, diplomacy and social support. See C.J. Chivers, 'Russia Expands Support for Breakaway Regions in Georgia', *New York Times*, 17 April 2008.

[91] See Statement by the NATO Secretary General on Abkhazia and South Ossetia, Press Release (2008)056, 16 April 2008.

of Foreign Affairs – almost all from new Member States (Latvia, Lithuania, Poland, Slovenia and Sweden) – visited Tbilisi to reiterate the European Union's backing for Georgia's sovereignty and territorial integrity.[92]

EU support for the strengthening of the Georgian state has been a long-term objective for some time, but it received a fresh impetus after the accession of the Baltic States to the EU.[93] Estonia, Latvia and Lithuania perceive themselves as being in the frontline with Russia and fear that if Russia gets away with its meddling in the internal affairs (including invasion and occupation) of Georgia, they may be next. In this context, it is not difficult to understand why Estonia urged other EU Member States to decide on sending an ESDP peacekeeping mission to Georgia shortly before the conflict in South Ossetia spiralled out of control at the beginning of August 2008.[94]

### 3.3.4. *The future of the EU's eastern neighbourhood policies:* quo vadis?

With its invasion, bombardment and occupation of strategic towns and posts throughout Georgia, Russia forced the rest of Europe to think of the Soviet tanks that invaded Prague exactly forty years earlier,[95] and Moscow's appeasement policies towards Hitler, first by allowing the annexation of Sudetenland and then by agreeing to divide Poland, Finland, Estonia, Lithuania and Romania in Nazi and Soviet spheres of influence. With the crisis in Georgia, relations between the EU and Russia have reached a crossroads. It has been noted that the 21st century's first war has seen Russia acting in line with the European *realpolitik* models of the 19th and early 20th centuries.[96] Presumably, inaction by the EU and the US will be taken by Russia's zero-sum politicising leadership as an encouragement to move on from "success" in Georgia to pursue comparable objectives, tactics and methods in Ukraine and Moldova. Moscow's neo-imperialist/neo-Soviet strategy seems intent on using all political, diplomatic, economic and military means to regain lost ground with the collapse of the Soviet Union and the decline during Yeltsin's chaotic presidential years to redraw the strategic map of Europe and to oppose the hegemony of the US in an attempt to create a bipolar world order. In the classic manner of nationalist-authoritarian regimes, Russia's leaders propagate the idea that the country is surrounded by enemies, warranting speeches that Russia will defend its citizens anywhere with crushing force;[97] that the states on the Black Sea (including

---

[92] See the EU Presidency's Press Release, 'EU ministers in Georgia for a peaceful resolution of conflicts and endorsement of its territorial integrity and sovereignty', 12 May 2008.

[93] See 'The European Union and Russia. Divide, rule or waffle?', *The Economist*, 1 May 2008.

[94] See 'Georgia accused of lethal attack', *BBC News*, 1 August 2008; 'Russia vows to defend S Ossetia', *BBC News*, 5 August 2008; P. Runner, 'Estonia urges EU peacekeepers for Georgia', *EU Observer*, 5 August 2008; R. Olearchyk and C. Clover, 'Fighting intensifies in South Ossetia', *Financial Times*, 7 August 2008; and M. Schwirtz, A. Barnard and C.J. Chivers, 'Fighting escalates in Caucasus', *International Herald Tribune*, 9 August 2008.

[95] See the stunning monograph with searing photographs by J. Koudelka, *Prague Invasion 68* (New York, Aperture 2008).

[96] See I. Krastev, 'Russia and the Georgian War: the Great-Power Trap', *Open Democracy*, 21 August 2008.

[97] In the aftermath of the August 2008 Russo-Georgian war, President Medvedev laid down five principles that would guide Russian foreign policy: the primacy of international law; the quest for a multi-polar

Bulgaria and Romania) should be very careful about what they are doing and what they allow others to do in their territorial waters;[98] and that Bulgaria (and Romania, for that matter) joining any other club – be it NATO or the EU – has been a historical mistake which would later need to be corrected.[99] By that rationale, the eastern advance by NATO and the European Union (and of the democratic political regimes that these international organisations favour) must be stopped and the "near abroad" firmly brought back under Moscow's influence. The statement of Vladimir Chizhov, Russia's Ambassador to the European Union, that Bulgaria, Cyprus and Greece are Russia's "Trojan horses" in the EU is particularly revealing.[100] Whether deliberate or not, the silence on the part of the EU and its Member States sends a clear signal to Moscow that Russia can bully its neighbours freely and position itself as an alternative power in the region. The proof of this was delivered when Russia's diplomatic discourse sank to a new depth of *realpolitik* arrogance when Dmitri Rogozin, Russia's Ambassador to NATO, challenged the West by saying that it is not willing to defend countries like Georgia and Ukraine with military action, at least until and unless they were NATO members.[101] While this may be true, Russia's leadership is wrongly assuming that, with its petro-power, it is immune from economic and political sanctions which the West may employ.[102] Russia's economy is extremely weak and vulnerable beyond its natural resources sectors. The negative impact of Russia's escapade in Georgia, aggravated by the global financial crisis, hit home hard on Moscow's stock market.[103]

---

world; no isolation of Russia; the protection of its citizens; and – last but not least – spheres of influence: 'Russia, just like other countries in the world, has regions where it has its privileged interests.' When asked what these priority regions were, he replied: 'Certainly the regions bordering [on Russia], but not only them.' See P. Reynolds, 'New Russian world order: the five principles', *BBC News*, 1 September 2008.

[98] See V. Tcherneva, 'Where does Russia's 'sphere of influence' end?', available at http://www.ecfr.eu/content/entry/commentary_tcherneva_where_does_russias_sphere_of_influence_end.

[99] *Ibidem.*

[100] *Ibidem.* For the conceptualisation and categorisation of EU Member States' positions on Russia-related topics, see M. Leonard and N. Popescu, *A Power Audit of EU-Russia Relations*, ECFR Policy Paper (ECFR, London 2007) at p. 2: 'We have identified five distinct policy approaches to Russia shared by old and new members alike: 'Trojan Horses' (Cyprus and Greece) who often defend Russian interests in the EU system, and are willing to veto common EU positions; 'Strategic Partners' (France, Germany, Italy and Spain) who enjoy a 'special relationship' with Russia which occasionally undermines common EU policies; 'Friendly Pragmatists' (Austria, Belgium, Bulgaria, Finland, Hungary, Luxembourg, Malta, Portugal, Slovakia and Slovenia) who maintain a close relationship with Russia and tend to put their business interests above political goals; 'Frosty Pragmatists' (Czech Republic, Denmark, Estonia, Ireland, Latvia, the Netherlands, Romania, Sweden and the United Kingdom) who also focus on business interests but are less afraid than others to speak out against Russian behaviour on human rights or other issues; and 'New Cold Warriors' (Lithuania and Poland) who have an overtly hostile relationship with Moscow and are willing to use the veto to block EU negotiations with Russia.' For backgrounds and analysis on the "Trojan Horses", see pp. 27-30 of the policy paper.

[101] See M. Evans, 'Russia dismisses Nato's "empty words" as it stands firm in Georgia', *The Times*, 20 August 2008.

[102] One can think of Russia's expulsion from the G8, refusing Russia to enter the WTO, advancing Ukraine's and Georgia's NATO membership and building up NATO's forward deployment of military resources in the new Member States close to Russia.

[103] See R. Wingfield Hayes, 'Russian invasion spooks investors', *BBC News*, 5 September 2008; and 'Russia and its neighbours: bang, crash', *The Economist*, 18 September 2008.

The hypothetical list of punitive measures which could be adopted by the EU is testimony to the huge progress which Russia has made in the last 18 years in normalising its place in Europe. These countermeasures proceed from declarations publicly condemning Russian actions (already done) to the revoking of visa facilitation, the freezing of assets of Russian companies and individuals in the EU and the suspension of numerous financial and operating programmes.[104] In a rare sign of unity, but at the instigation of some of the new Member States, the European Union suspended negotiations of a new PCA until Russia redeployed its forces to positions held prior to 7 August 2008, with a view to full application of the six-point peace plan of 12 August 2008 negotiated by "EU President" Sarkozy.[105] Furthermore, the European Council tasked the Council of Ministers and the Commission to conduct a 'careful in-depth examination of the situation and of the various aspects of EU-Russia relations' in the run-up of the EU-Russia summit, which took place in Nice on 14 November 2008.[106] Whether this study will form the first step towards the adoption of a new "Common Strategy" towards Russia remains to be seen.[107] Not much progress has been achieved during the most recent EU-Russia summit in Khabarovsk on 21-22 May 2009. With the sense of urgency over the Georgian crisis dissipating, the divisions among EU Member States of how to deal with Russia are slowly reappearing. Regrettably, the differences in positions among EU Member States – from the "new cold warriors" (e.g., Lithuania and Poland) to Russia's "Trojan horses" in the EU (e.g., Bulgaria and Cyprus) – are so far apart, that building a common framework on EU-Russia relations might provide the ultimate example in defining the lowest common denominator in EU external relations policies and law. Finally, the EU may have to redevelop principles of solidarity for its close neighbours in response to Russia's bullying. It is hoped that the new Eastern Partnership proposed by Poland and Sweden will provide the way forward.

## 4.      INTERNAL SECURITY

### 4.1.      Towards an area of freedom, security and justice

Central to the EU's role in meeting security challenges is the policy area of Justice and Home Affairs, developed under the Third Pillar of the EU created by the Treaty of Maastricht. JHA activities encompass a considerable array of activities, but their core purpose is clearly set out in Article 29 TEU, namely 'to provide citizens with a high level of safety within an area of freedom, security and justice by developing common

---

[104] See S. Blockmans, 'EU-Russia Relations through the Prism of the European Neighbourhood and Partnership Instrument', 13 *EFA Rev.* (2008) pp. 167-187.

[105] Presidency Conclusions, Extraordinary European Council, Brussels, 1 September 2008, doc. 12594/08, at 11.

[106] *Ibidem.*

[107] The application of the first and so far only Common Strategy of 1999 was extended only once until 24 June 2004. See Common Strategy 2003/471/CFSP of the European Council of 20 June 2003 amending Common Strategy 1999/414/CFSP on Russia in order to extend the period of its application, *OJ* 2003 L 157/68.

action among the Member States.' That objective, the provision continues, 'shall be achieved by preventing and combating crime, organised or otherwise, in particular terrorism, trafficking in persons and offences against children, illicit drugs trafficking and illicit arms trafficking, corruption and fraud' through co-operation by police, customs and judicial authorities.

Even before the recent two waves of enlargement, the amount of work that had been done in the field of migration, security and anti-terrorism looked impressive, at least when taking the number of legal instruments that have been adopted as a point of departure. The JHA record has been one of extensive deepening, with a strong development of its *acquis* and a noticeable emphasis on the creation of several agencies, ranging from Europol and Eurojust to the European Drugs Monitoring Agency for Drugs Addiction and FRONTEX, the agency which co-ordinates operational co-operation among Member States in the field of external border control.[108]

The development of the JHA reflects two important processes. The first is the "securisation" of new dangers other than the conventional military threat to the state. These threats emanate both from within the EU but also, significantly, from outside. Hence, the JHA has been driven by post-Cold War security challenges such as transnational crime and drug trafficking, terrorism, immigration and refugees. The second is the interrelationship between the concepts of "freedom" and "security." The Area of Freedom, Security and Justice is premised on a notion of freedom that entails unhindered movement by citizens of EU Member States across internal borders and, in addition, the ability of these same citizens 'to live in a law-abiding environment' guaranteed by actions of national and EU authorities aimed at effective law enforcement and access to justice.[109] The latter is a profound development. The disappearance of internal borders is not only significant for European economic and social integration but also goes to the very heart of the EU's status as part of the European security community. The removal of internal borders has been taken a step further by the development of cross-border communities. For those living and working within the European Union, the internal borders have increasingly obtained a virtual quality. For those outside the EU, however, things appear rather different. As one observer has pointed out, the EU's internal preoccupation has a major external consequence, for '[i]t implies a fundamental distinction between a "safe(r) inside" and an "unsafe(r) outside" with the EU's frontiers as the dividing line and law enforcement as the key instrument to maintain and further enhance this distinction.'[110]

---

[108] Council Regulation (EC) No 2007/2004 of 26 October 2004 establishing a European Agency for the Management of Operational Cooperation at the External Borders of the Member States of the European Union, *OJ* 2004 L 349/1.

[109] 'Action Plan of the Council and the Commission on How Best to Implement the Provisions of the Treaty of Amsterdam on the Area of Freedom, Security and Justice', *OJ* 1999 C 19/4.

[110] J. Monar, 'Justice and Home Affairs in a Wider Europe: The Dynamics of Inclusion and Exclusion', *Working Paper* 07/00 (Economic and Social Research Council 'One Europe or Several?' Programme) at pp. 4-5.

## 4.2.     Border security

### 4.2.1.  *Enlarging the borderless zone in Europe*

The single-most important instrument in policing the EU's borders is the Schengen system. "Schengen" dates from 14 June 1985, when the governments of Belgium, Germany, France, Luxembourg and the Netherlands signed an agreement in the small town in Luxembourg, which gave its name to the accord, with a view to enabling 'all nationals of the Member States to cross internal borders freely' and to enable the 'free circulation of goods and services.'[111] The five founding countries signed the Convention implementing the Schengen Agreement on 19 June 1990,[112] and were later joined by Italy (1990), Spain and Portugal (1991), Greece (1992), Austria (1995) and Denmark, Sweden and Finland (1996). On 19 December 1996, Norway and Iceland concluded an association agreement with the Schengen states in order to join the Schengen zone.[113] The UK and Ireland have "opted out" of the zone, but they have signed up to agreements on security.[114] The Schengen *acquis* was incorporated into the legal framework of the European Union in 1999 by way of protocols attached to the Treaty of Amsterdam.[115] Council Decision 1999/435/EC was adopted on 20 May 1999, determining the legal basis for each of the provisions or decisions, which constitute the Schengen *acquis*, in conformity with the relevant provisions of the EC and EU Treaties.[116]

---

[111] Agreement signed in Schengen on 14 June 1985 between the Governments of the States of the Benelux Economic Union, the Federal Republic of Germany and the French Republic on the gradual abolition of checks at their common borders, *OJ* 2000 L 239/13.

[112] Convention signed in Schengen on 19 June 1990 between the Kingdom of Belgium, the Federal Republic of Germany, the French Republic, the Grand Duchy of Luxembourg and the Kingdom of the Netherlands, implementing the Schengen Agreement of 14 June 1985, *OJ* 2000 L 239/19.

[113] Agreement concluded by the Council of the European Union and the Republic of Iceland and the Kingdom of Norway concerning the latter's association with the implementation, application and development of the Schengen *acquis*, *OJ* 1999 L 176/36. See N. Wichmann, 'The Participation of the Schengen Associates: Inside or Outside?', 11 *EFA Rev.* (2006) pp. 87-107.

[114] Treaty establishing the European Community (consolidated version) – B. Protocols annexed to the Treaty on European Union and the Treaty establishing the European Community – Protocol (No 3) on the application of certain aspects of Art. 14 of the Treaty establishing the European Community to the United Kingdom and to Ireland (1997), *OJ* 2006 C 321 E/196; and Protocol (No 4) on the position of the United Kingdom and Ireland (1997), *OJ* 2006 C 321 E/198; Council Decision 2000/365/EC of 29 May 2000 concerning the request of the United Kingdom of Great Britain and Northern Ireland to take part in some of the provisions of the Schengen *acquis*, *OJ* 2000 L 131/43; Council Decision 2002/192/EC of 28 February 2002 concerning Ireland's request to take part in some of the provisions of the Schengen *acquis*, *OJ* 2002 L 64/20; and Council Decision 2004/926/EC of 22 December 2004 on the putting into effect of parts of the Schengen *acquis* by the United Kingdom of Great Britain and Northern Ireland, *OJ* 2004 L 395/70.

[115] Treaty of Amsterdam amending the Treaty on European Union, the Treaties establishing the European Communities and Related Acts, *OJ* 1997 C 340/1.

[116] Council Decision 1999/435/EC of 20 May 1999 concerning the definition of the Schengen *acquis* for the purpose of determining, in conformity with the relevant provisions of the Treaty establishing the European Community and the Treaty on European Union, the legal basis for each of the provisions or decisions which constitute the acquis, *OJ* 1999 L 176/1.

Nine of the ten states which joined the European Union in 2004 became members of the Schengen area at the end of 2007.[117] Switzerland, which already implements and applies parts of the Schengen *acquis* listed in Annex 1 to the EC/EU-Swiss Agreement on Schengen,[118] as well as the decisions of the Executive Committee and directives and regulations listed in Annex B,[119] became a member of the Schengen area in late 2008 as a result of the positive outcome of a referendum organised on the matter on 5 June 2005.[120] Three new EU Member States – Cyprus, Bulgaria and Romania – have still to meet the necessary requirements. It is not yet known when they will join the borderless zone, but Cyprus is expected to do so around 2009.[121] Bulgaria and Romania are hoping to follow suit by 2011, but this expectation has been thrown into doubt when the European Commission in July 2008 found the two states to be too slow on implementing change to combat fraud and corruption.[122]

### 4.2.2.   *Aligning to the* acquis

Lifting internal border control is a question of trust among the Member States. It is through a rigorous peer evaluation process that the Schengen countries have ensured that each state is equipped to guard the external borders on behalf of all other members and issue visas valid for the whole Schengen area. The new Member States were com-

---

[117] Council Decision 2007/801/EC of 6 December 2007 on the full application of the provisions of the Schengen *acquis* in the Czech Republic, the Republic of Estonia, the Republic of Latvia, the Republic of Lithuania, the Republic of Hungary, the Republic of Malta, the Republic of Poland, the Republic of Slovenia and the Slovak Republic, *OJ* 2007 L 323/34. Controls at internal land and sea borders among Estonia, the Czech Republic, Lithuania, Hungary, Latvia, Malta, Poland, Slovakia and Slovenia and the 15 existing Schengen members were lifted on 21 December 2007. Airports followed suit on 30 March 2008, thereby extending the free movement area by 4,278 km² and bringing the total population in the Schengen area to almost 405 million.

[118] Agreement between the European Union, the European Community and the Swiss Confederation on the Swiss Confederation's association with the implementation, application and development of the Schengen *acquis*, *OJ* 2008 L 53/52. See also Protocol between the European Community, the Swiss Confederation and the Principality of Liechtenstein to the Agreement between the European Community and the Swiss Confederation concerning the criteria and mechanisms for establishing the State responsible for examining a request for asylum lodged in a Member State or in Switzerland, *OJ* 2009 L 161/8. The Protocol will formally extend the Schengen zone also to Liechtenstein.

[119] *Inter alia*, Council Regulation (EC) No 1683/95 of 29 May 1995 laying down a uniform format for visas, *OJ* 1995 L 164/1 (as amended); Council Regulation (EC) No 539/2001 of 15 March 2001 listing the third countries whose nationals must be in possession of visas when crossing the external borders and those whose nationals are exempt from that requirement, *OJ* 1991 L 81/1 (as amended); Council Regulation (EC) No 1091/2001 of 28 May 2001 on freedom of movement with a long-stay visa, *OJ* 2001 L 150/4.

[120] On the nature of the EC/EU-Swiss Agreement on Schengen, see Łazowski, *loc. cit.* n. 9, at pp. 101-102.

[121] Cyprus confirmed its readiness for the evaluation process for police co-operation and data protection (as of 1 May 2006) and these areas of Schengen co-operation were evaluated in 2006. Cyprus also informed the Council that it would only be prepared to determine the dates of its readiness in other areas of Schengen co-operation once the Schengen Information System II is ready at the end of 2008.

[122] See Report from the Commission to the European Parliament and the Council, 'On Progress in Bulgaria under the Co-operation and Verification Mechanism', COM (2008) 495 final; and Report from the Commission to the European Parliament and the Council, 'On Progress in Romania under the Co-operation and Verification Mechanism', COM (2008) 494 final. See further Chapters 16 and 17 in this volume.

pelled to adopt and implement the full Schengen *acquis* without the possibility to renegotiate its terms.[123] Meeting the tough demands imposed on the candidate countries when it concerns the quality of external border controls, implying a systematic surveillance of each individual passing the external border as well as exercising effective border surveillance at authorised border-crossing points, has not been easy.[124] The eight members from Central and Eastern Europe which joined the Schengen zone at the end of 2007 have worked hard to improve their handling of external border controls, visa policy, data protection and police co-operation. During the two preceding years, experts from the Member States carried out the so-called "Schengen evaluation" of the candidate members. Although experts from the European Commission also participated in these evaluations, the responsibility for the evaluation remained with the Council. The evaluation consisted in particular of verifying that the accompanying measures allowing for the lifting of internal border controls are correctly and efficiently applied by the new Member States. In total 58 evaluation missions covering data protection, police co-operation, external border controls at land, sea and air borders, and visa policy were undertaken in 2006.[125] In 2007, 15 re-evaluation visits were carried out, together with a new sea and air border evaluation.[126] Nine Schengen Information System (SIS) evaluation visits were also conducted.[127] The connection of the 9 new members to the SIS – which shares information on wanted and missing people, those refused entry, and lost and stolen property – was assured before membership could be agreed to. Justice and Home Affairs Ministers concluded on 8 November 2007 that the Schengen *acquis* criteria had been met by all candidate countries.[128] This feat would not have been possible without financial solidarity. According to the European Commission, EUR 1 billion was spent between 2004 and 2006 through the Schengen Facility on beefing up security on the new EU frontiers, including the establishing of missions along the Polish and Slovak borders.[129]

### 4.2.3. *Impact of Schengen enlargement for EU citizens*

For three-and-a-half years, the EU remained segregated in two parts as the external border still ran between the old and the new Member States for as long as the Schengen

---

[123] See M. den Boer, 'Mirror, Mirror on the Wall…Who's the Fairest of Them All? The Double Logic in the Imposition of JHA Instruments of Control on Candidate Countries', *EUI Working Paper* (Florence, EUI 2001). The same demand was not imposed on Switzerland, which negotiated an opt-out clause on the anti-money laundering measures before its accession to Schengen.

[124] See S. Lavenex, 'EU External Governance in "Wider Europe"', 11 *JEPP* (2004) pp. 680-700.

[125] See the programme of the Schengen evaluation of the 10 new Member States in doc. 7638/2/05 REV 2, SCH-EVAL 20, COMIX 200.

[126] See the updated programme in doc. 16025/06, SCH-EVAL 191, COMIX 1014.

[127] *Ibidem.*

[128] See Council Conclusions on Schengen Evaluation on New Member States, reprinted in *Bulletin EU* 11-2007, point 1.37.3.

[129] See European Commission, MEMO/07/619, 31 March 2008. The Schengen Facility, which was created under Art. 35(1) of the Act of Accession 2003 will also be applied for implementation of the Schengen *acquis* in Bulgaria and Romania. Ultimately, considerable financial assistance is provided by the European External Borders Fund (EUR 1.82 billion for the period 2007-2013).

*acquis* had not been fully operational. The historical enlargement of the Schengen area with nine new Member States has resulted in a very tangible expression of the free movement ideal of the European integration process.[130] In principle, all citizens of the enlarged Schengen space can now benefit from quicker and easier travelling: a citizen can travel from Faro to Tallinn and from Košice to Cork without border checks. This is symbolic of a united Europe and underlines the basic right of EU citizens to move freely. Perhaps more tangibly, it will be easier for families, relatives and friends living on different sides of a border to visit each other. Long queues at busy border crossing points will no longer exist. Border regions will develop together as it will be easier to travel from one region to another. Also, an increase in tourism is expected, with a positive impact on infrastructure.

EU citizens are allowed to enter the territory of EU Member States on presentation of a valid passport or ID card unless the person constitutes a genuine, present and sufficiently serious threat to public policy or public security. All persons who enter the Schengen area legally are allowed to cross internal borders with, and between, the new Schengen Member States without border checks. Internal borders are land borders between the Member States, airports for flight connections among the Schengen states and seaports for regular ferry connections among the Schengen states. It should be noted, however, that the abolition of internal border checks does not affect the exercise of police powers, even within internal border zones.

While the enlargement of the Schengen area means that some 405 million people will now be able to travel more easily within it, it also constitutes a new burden for some EU neighbours.

### 4.2.4.   *Impact of Schengen enlargement on the EU's neighbours*

Third-country nationals submitted to the visa obligation can travel with one Schengen visa within the enlarged Schengen area and no longer need to apply for a national visa for the nine new Schengen states. As far as the entry conditions are concerned, there are no changes involved for third-country nationals when they cross the external border of one of the new Schengen states, except that they will be checked not only against national systems but also against the SIS. In reality, however, the nine new Schengen members have been applying the Schengen rules on checks at external borders from the date of accession, i.e., 1 May 2004. It should be noted that the Member States can request persons to hold or carry documents while on their territory. Also, the abolition of internal border checks does not affect the exercise of security checks on persons carried out at ports and airports.

Third-country nationals need to be in possession of (i) a valid passport or travel document; (ii) a valid Schengen visa (a residence permit issued by a Schengen state has an equivalent effect to a Schengen visa);[131] (iii) sufficient means for the intended

---

[130] Dixit Franco Frattini, 'Enlargement of the Schengen area: achieving the European goal of free movement of persons', Commission Press Release, IP/07/1968, 20 December 2007. See also E. Vucheva, 'EU marks "historical" enlargement of borderless zone', *EU Observer*, 21 December 2007.

[131] See *OJ* 2006 C 247; as updated in *OJ* 2007 C 153.

stay; and should not be (iv) designated for the purpose of refusing entry; and (v) considered as a threat to public policy, internal security, public health or international relations.[132] The short-stay Schengen visa for third-country nationals currently costs EUR 60, which is a significant increase for some non-EU citizens. Belarusians, for instance, used to pay EUR 5 for a trip to neighbouring Lithuania. They are now further restricted in their movement (including visits to relatives and chances for better education and trade) by the new Schengen visa wall. In an effort to prevent new dividing lines from taking hold, the European Community has concluded visa-facilitation agreements with other EU neighbours – Ukraine, Moldova, Bosnia-Herzegovina, Serbia, Montenegro, Macedonia and Albania, which have entered into force on 1 January 2008.[133] Russian citizens are also covered by such an agreement, which entered into force in June of 2007.[134] These agreements have been complemented by readmission agreements, binding the contracting states to readmit people who are illegally residing in the EU.[135] Under the visa facilitation agreements, citizens of these countries can obtain a Schengen visa for EUR 35 while certain categories of citizens (e.g., holders of diplomatic passports) are exempted from the fee. The agreements set time-limits for issuing a visa (normally 10 days). In addition, they simplify and clarify the procedures for issuing visas to certain categories of persons (e.g., business people, students, journalists). Frequent travellers will be granted multi-entry visas with long periods of validity. In individual cases, the price may be reduced or waived in accordance with national law when this measure serves to promote cultural interests, in the field of foreign policy, development policy or other area of vital public interest. The Commission has recently started a dialogue on a visa-free regime with the countries of the Western Balkans,[136] and it is intent on realising a similar deal with other neighbouring countries, including Russia.

## 4.3.    Counter-terrorism

Counter-terrorism has emerged from the shadows of the Third Pillar, propelled into the limelight by the events of 11 September 2001 in the US and maintained by terrorist attacks in Madrid (11 March 2004) and London (7 July 2005). Given the relative symmetry of the development of the EU's counter-terrorism policy with the enlargement process, it is worth considering what bearing the latter has had on the former.[137]

---

[132] See the European Commission's website 'Your Europe, Citizens, Travelling in Europe: Schengen', available at http://ec.europa.eu/youreurope/nav/en/citizens/travelling/schengen-area/index_en.html.
[133] See, e.g., Agreement between the European Community and Ukraine on the facilitation of the issuance of visas, *OJ* 2007 L 332/68, and Agreement between the European Community and the Republic of Serbia on the facilitation of the issuance of visas, *OJ* 2007 L 334/137.
[134] Agreement between the European Community and the Russian Federation on the facilitation of the issuance of visas to the citizens of the European Union and the Russian Federation, *OJ* 2007 L 129/27.
[135] See, e.g., Agreement between the European Community and the Republic of Albania on the readmission of persons residing without authorisation, *OJ* 2005 L 124/22, and Agreement between the European Community and the Russian Federation on readmission, *OJ* 2007 L 129/40.
[136] See European Commission, MEMO/08/142, 5 March 2008.
[137] See also D. Brown, 'The Impact of Enlargement on the EU's Counter-Terrorist Framework', in Brown and Shepherd, eds., *op. cit.* n. 28, pp. 38-53.

The terrorist attacks that took place on 11 September 2001 had a firm impact on the number of legal instruments announced by the European Council and the speed of their adoption.[138] These instruments generally intended to support the convergence among criminal law systems. However, long as Europe's regulatory list in the area of law enforcement co-operation may seem, it is interesting to observe that the Member States have not yet established deep institutional co-operation in the law enforcement area, thereby indicating that they prefer to stay in the driving seat when it concerns the governance of internal security.[139] This "implementation gap" is partly the consequence of the 2004/7 enlargements of the European Union. This is not to say that the new Member States are the worst offenders here, but it is an observation which reflects the tendency of the EU Presidencies to look for new horizons and launch a lot of initiatives in a sexy policy field that are designed as "press stunts", but in fact have "little value" and even less follow-up.[140] Unfortunately, this observation applies to the whole AFSJ. As the pace of regulatory activity speeds up, the level of implementation drops due to poor implementation of agreed objectives and measures by an increasing body of Member States.[141]

5.     IMPACT OF ENLARGEMENT ON LEADERSHIP AND DECISION-
       MAKING

Regardless of efforts to converge security policies, without efficient decision-making and/or clear leadership, such efforts may be futile. Clear leadership is needed to ensure that decisions on counter-terrorism or launching ESDP missions are made swiftly and to ensure clear direction during operations. With increasingly diverse interests and approaches to dealing with external and internal security issues, the fifth and sixth waves of enlargement have stretched the sense of solidarity and commonality to the maximum. This is best illustrated in the Area of Freedom, Security and Justice. As a direct result of enlargements, initiatives by old Member States – such as the G5 meet-

---

[138] See M. Den Boer, 'The EU Counter-Terrorism Wave: Window of Opportunity or Profound Policy Transformation?', in M. van Leeuwen, ed., *Confronting Terrorism: European Experiences, Threat Perceptions and Policies* (The Hague, Kluwer Law International 2003) pp. 185-206.

[139] See J. Monar, 'The EU's Approach Post-September 11: Global Terrorism as a Multidimensional Law Enforcement Challenge', 20 *CRIA* (2007) pp. 267-283.

[140] See S. Ludford, 'An EU Justice and Home Affairs Policy: What Should it Comprise?', in J. Apap, ed., *Justice and Home Affairs in the European Union* (Northampton, Edward Elgar 2004) at p. 29.

[141] See Communication from the Commission to the Council and the European Parliament, Scoreboard to review progress on the area of "Freedom, Security and Justice" in the European Union, COM (2000) 167 final/2. For academic analyses, see, e.g., N. Walker, 'In Search of the Area of Freedom, Security and Justice: A Constitutional Odyssey', in N. Walker, ed., *Europe's Area of Freedom, Security and Justice* (Oxford, Oxford University Press 2004) pp. 3-37; A. Sorel, 'Asylum, Migration and Border Controls in the Hague Programme', in J.W. de Zwaan and F. Goudappel, eds., *Freedom, Security and Justice in the European Union: Implementation of the Hague Programme* (The Hague, T.M.C. Asser Press 2006) pp. 11-16; and M. den Boer, 'A Diagnosis of the Area of Freedom, Security and Justice: Remedies and Reforms in the Domains of Immigration, Terrorism and Security, in Blockmans and Prechal, eds., *op. cit.* n. 7, pp. 13-28.

ings of the JHA Ministers of France, Germany, Italy, Spain and the UK and the conclusion on 27 July 2005 of the Treaty of Prüm by seven Member States – (briefly)
heralded the renaissance of conducting business among smaller groupings of like-
minded states outside the framework of the EU Treaties.[142] Yet, leadership and decision-
making within the European Union are potentially the hardest issues to resolve, with
already extremely sensitive areas further complicated by enlargement. In particular, the
rise in the number of small states (all new EU Member States except Poland and
Romania) spells greater opposition to large state dominance.

Leadership is required at three levels: (i) the political drive to crystallise the idea of
a security policy; (ii) the institutional responsibility within EU structures; and (iii) the
practical administration of EU policy. The lack of leadership at these levels makes it
difficult to decide whether a crisis exists, then to determine the scale of the crisis and
to achieve a consensus on the response. This failure was clearly illustrated by the arguments over a military intervention in Iraq. In addition, without leadership, it will be
harder to achieve the reforms needed to close the infamous "capabilities-expectations
gap" in the field of CFSP/ESDP and AFSJ/PJCC.[143] However, talk of leadership immediately raises concerns about the emergence of *directoires*.[144] This form of enhanced
co-operation consists of a small number of EU Member States, usually the largest or
most powerful, constituting the core decision-making body. The primary concern is
that such a move will marginalise other/smaller Member States. Such sensitivities were
evident in late 2001, when UK Prime Minister Blair called an informal meeting with
his French and German counterparts to discuss terrorism.[145] When news of the meeting
spread, several leaders of other EU Member States demanded to attend. Those that were
not invited or found out too late took great offence at what they saw as a deliberate
snub. They feared that the big three EU states were deciding policy without them and
would then present them with a *fait accompli*. This example helps to demonstrate the

---

[142] Convention between the Kingdom of Belgium, the Federal Republic of Germany, the Kingdom of
Spain, the French Republic, the Grand Duchy of Luxembourg, the Kingdom of the Netherlands and the
Republic of Austria on the stepping up of cross-border co-operation particularly in combating terrorism,
cross-border crime and illegal migration, Prüm (Germany), 27 May 2005, Council Secretariat, Brussels,
7 July 2005, 10900/05. The Treaty of Prüm has in the meantime been incorporated in the EU's *acquis*.
See Initiative of the Kingdom of Belgium, the Republic of Bulgaria, the Federal Republic of Germany,
the Kingdom of Spain, the French Republic, the Grand Duchy of Luxembourg, the Kingdom of the Netherlands, the Republic of Austria, the Republic of Slovenia, the Slovak Republic, the Italian Republic,
the Republic of Finland, the Portuguese Republic, Romania and the Kingdom of Sweden, with a view to
adopting a Council Decision on the stepping up of cross-border co-operation, particularly in combating
terrorism and cross-border crime, *OJ* 2007 C 71/35.

[143] See C. Hill, 'The Capability-Expectations Gap, or Conceptualising Europe's International Role',
31 *JCMS* (1993) pp. 305-328; and C. Hill, 'Closing the Capabilities-Expectations Gap?', in J. Peterson
and H. Sjursen, eds., *A Common Foreign Policy for Europe: Competing Visions of the CFSP* (London,
Routledge 1998) pp. 18-38.

[144] See, e.g., S. Keukeleire, 'Directorates in the CFSP/CESDP of the European Union: A Plea for
"Restricted Crisis Management Group"', 6 *EFA Rev.* (2001) pp. 75-101; T. Jäger, 'Enhanced Cooperation
in the Treaty of Nice and Flexibility in the Common Foreign and Security Policy', 7 *EFA Rev.* (2002) pp.
297-316.

[145] As reported by S. Castle, 'Campaign against Terrorism: Policy – Blair will urge Bush to accept',
*The Independent*, 6 November 2001.

improbability of a fixed membership *directoire* becoming a permanent feature, at least within the EU framework.

The fifth and sixth enlargements of the EU with twelve new Member States have complicated the Union's political balance. The three biggest EU Member States – France, Germany and the UK – continue to be crucial to the EU's security policy formulation, as their efforts to spearhead a resolution of the nuclear dispute with Iran demonstrates. At the next level down, Italy and Spain have been joined by Poland and Romania as other "large states", demanding a seat at the top table. However, as the majority of new Member States can be classified as "small states", their sensitivities within CFSP/ESDP and AFSJ/PJCC decision-making have become an even greater issue.[146] Due to their markedly Atlanticist orientation, the new Member States have tipped the internal balance of the EU in that direction. But because, here also, there is no talk of a Central European "bloc", they will not want any form of *directoire* to emerge for decision-making on security policies, regardless of what combination of large states that *directoire* may entail.

There is also the issue of unanimity-based decision-making procedures in the largely intergovernmental security policies of the EU, the outcome of which has been made more difficult by the eastern enlargements. The arguments in the European Convention on the Future of Europe between medium-sized states, such as Poland and Spain, and the largest states, particularly Germany, over the number of weighted votes in the Council and a double-majority voting system exemplify the sensitivities of the issue. This argument also illustrates how wary some of the entrants are about being dominated by the older and larger Member States. The intergovernmental nature of decision-making does not foster a sense of commonality. Member States may wield their veto whenever they disapprove, when the position taken is contrary to their interests, when external pressure is exerted upon them or when domestic opposition pressurises the government.

Arguably, the Lisbon Treaty will improve both leadership and decision-making in the areas of CFSP/ESDP and AFSJ/PJCC. The introduction of a High Representative of the Union for Foreign Affairs and Security (Art. 18 new TEU), while initially controversial,[147] may improve leadership, especially when duly assisted by the European Commission, of which s/he will be one of the Vice-Presidents, and the future European External Action Service (Art. 27 new TEU).[148] Then again, much will depend on the High Representative's *rapport* with the newly created President of the European Council (Art. 15 new TEU), who will also be responsible for the external representation of the EU on issues concerning the Common Foreign and Security Policy. The delimitation

---

[146] See A. Wivel, 'The Security Challenge of Small EU Member States: Interests, Identity and the Development of the EU as a Security Actor', 43 *JCMS* (2005) pp. 393-412.

[147] For an analysis of the proposal to create an EU Minister of Foreign Affairs, as included in the botched Treaty establishing a Constitution for Europe, see J. Wouters, 'The Union Minister of Foreign Affairs: Europe's Single Voice or Trojan Horse?', in J.W. de Zwaan, J.H. Jans, F.A. Nelissen and S. Blockmans, eds., *The European Union, An Ongoing Process of Integration – Liber Amicorum Alfred E. Kellermann* (The Hague, T.M.C. Asser Press 2004) pp. 77-86.

[148] See de Zwaan, *loc. cit.* n. 26, at pp. 28-34.

of responsibilities of both personalities is far from clear, at least on the basis of the Treaty text. In addition, there are two other authorities responsible for representing the European Union to the outside world: the rotating Presidency of the Council in con-figurations other than that of Foreign Affairs (Arts. 16(9) new TEU and 236 TFEU) and the President of the Commission. Future practice will have to show how the new arrangements will work out. One may wonder in all honesty whether the new arrange-ments will really contribute to enhancing the Union's visibility and to demonstrating greater unity to the outside world.[149] While the same reservations should apply to the enhanced co-operation provisions, the introduction of "permanent structured co-operation" in the Lisbon Treaty (on the model of the Battlegroup concept) may allow for a more flexible (and – the hope is – a more effective) development of CFSP/ESDP in the future.[150]

As a result of the complete "communitarisation" of AFSJ/PJCC, there will be a more uniform decision-making regime: more impetus will be given to qualified majority voting and the application of the co-decision procedure with the European Parliament. Apart from an adaptation of the so-called "constructive abstention" provision,[151] the unanimity principle for decision-making with regard to CFSP/ESDP has been main-tained. This means that consensus-building among twenty seven (or more) Member States will become easier in the field of internal security but remain elusive in the field of external security.

Finally, the Lisbon Treaty prescribes that the Council may entrust the execution of a task, within the Union framework, to a group of Member States in order to protect the Union's values and serve its interests.[152] This principle is referred to as the "Group of the willing" clause and allows for greater flexibility in decision-making and action-taking. The same applies for the new concept of "permanent structured co-operation": 'Those Member States whose military capabilities fulfil higher criteria and which have made more binding commitments to one another in this area with a view to the most demanding missions shall establish permanent structured cooperation within the Union framework.'[153]

## 6.     CONCLUDING REMARKS

The fifth and sixths enlargements of the European Union are a security policy *an sich*. It is a security policy "by other means" and a security policy "in its own right", so to

---

[149] See S. Duke, 'Peculiarities in the Institutionalisation of CFSP and ESDP', in Blockmans, ed., *op. cit.* n. 26, pp. 75-105, at p. 100.

[150] Art. 42(6) new TEU. Further modalities concerning this new concept of "permanent structured co-operation" can be found in Art. 46 new TEU.

[151] The changes in Art. 31 new TEU notably concern the situation where one-third of the Member States comprising at least one-third of the population of the EU abstains from voting. In such a situation the decision shall not be adopted. This is a variant of the present text of Art. 23(1) and (2) TEU, which refer to 'one third of the votes' weighted in accordance with Art. 205(2) TEC.

[152] Art. 42(5) new TEU. Further details about this option are to be found in Art. 44 new TEU.

[153] Art. 42(6) new TEU. Further modalities about this option are to be found in Art. 46 new TEU.

speak. It is a security policy "by other means" because extending the Union's values, rules, opportunities *and* constraints to (potential) candidate countries makes instability and conflict in the region much less likely. And although such adjustment may entail elements of risk, it could be argued that hitherto enlargement is a more successful security policy than CFSP and ESDP.[154] EU enlargement is a security policy "in its own right" because the new Member States bring interests and skills that broaden the scope of the common external policies.[155] This was the case with the first enlargement of the European Communities in 1973 due to the British and Danish outreach overseas. It was even more so with the southern enlargements of the 1980s, which paved the way for the successful completion of post-authoritarian transitions, a significant reinforcement of the Communities' presence in the Mediterranean basin and an equally significant extension of "Europe's" influence in Central and South America. The 1995 northern enlargement brought more stability to the Baltic rim and strengthened the Union's drive to co-operate through the OSCE on a northern security dimension. It also marginally altered the internal balance between allied and non-allied Member States.

The "big bang" enlargement of 2004 was nothing like the previous accession waves and is unlikely to be anything similar to those in the future. It was fundamentally different in size, scope and character. The sixth enlargement that followed was much smaller in scale. It is clear that the twelve new Member States have brought their own preferences and interests to bear, thereby complicating the already contentious security policies of the EU. The European rift over the war in Iraq and relations with Russia suggest that, when their own interests are strong, the new Member States will not be as compliant as some of the older Member States would perhaps want them to be. Fortunately, the security strategies and policies of the new Member States demonstrate significant overlap with the European Security Strategy, thereby consolidating EU priorities and adding weight to its initiatives. Despite the nuances which persist among the new Member States, due to their different historical trajectories, geopolitical situation, size and available resources,[156] the fifth and sixth enlargements have introduced an undisputedly new eastern dimension to the EU's security policies, a more encompassing and at the same time more assertive *Ost-politik* than the one sought by Willy Brandt in the 1970s. It is more significant because the European Union of today does not operate in the stalemate security situation of the Cold War. Instead, the EU has to deal with a wide variety of trans-border security challenges that it had more or less ignored until May 2004. The merging of the concepts of internal and external security and the blurring distinctions between hard and soft security demand a more holistic and inclusive approach in tackling them if the EU wants to realise some of the objec-

---

[154] See, more generally, M. Cremona, 'Enlargement: A Successful Instrument of EU Foreign Policy?', in T. Tridimas and P. Nebbia, eds., *EU Law for the Twenty-First Century: Volume I* (Oxford, Hart Publishing 2004) pp. 397-413.

[155] See A. Missiroli, ed., *Coherence for European Security Policy: Debates–Cases–Assessments*, Occasional Paper No. 27 (Paris, EUISS 2001) at pp. 6-7. On EU enlargement as "risk management", see P. Cecchini, E. Jones and J. Lorentzen, 'Europe and the Concept of Enlargement', 42 *Survival* (2001) pp. 155-165.

[156] For the significantly different issues raised by the two Mediterranean countries (Cyprus and Malta), see the contributions to Maresceau and Lannon, eds., *op. cit.* n. 27.

tives listed in its 2003 European Security Strategy. In this respect, the experience and expertise of the new Member States will be indispensable for the Union.[157]

---

[157] See A. Agh, *Eastern Enlargement and the Future of the EU27: EU Foreign Policy in a Global World* (Budapest, Together for Europe Research Centre of the Hungarian Academy of Sciences 2006).

*Part Two*
*East Meets West*

*Chapter 3*

# CONSTITUTIONAL CHANGES AND CHALLENGES IN THE NEW MEMBER STATES

Anneli Albi*

1.    INTRODUCTION: AMENDMENT OF CONSTITUTIONS
      AS A PREREQUISITE FOR SMOOTH APPLICATION OF EU LAW
      BY COURTS

The book at hand seeks to gauge the application of EC/EU law by courts of the new Member States that joined the EU in 2004 and 2007. The picture that emerges from the country-specific contributions is that national courts of the new Member States in general have readily embarked on the application of EU law, doing so with a considerable measure of EU-enthusiasm at times. Nonetheless, a limited number of judgments have drawn disapproving comments, in particular, the Polish Constitutional Tribunal's judgment in the *European Arrest Warrant* case[1] where national provisions implementing EU law were declared unconstitutional, the *Accession Treaty* judgment[2] where a strong statement was delivered with regard to the supremacy of the Polish Constitution and the Hungarian Constitutional Court's *Sugar Stocks* case where a national act implementing an EC Regulation was annulled on the grounds of incompatibility with constitutional rights.[3] The critical notes regarding these judgments have their origin in a theme that has come to permeate much of the debate on the Constitutional Court's approach to the supremacy of EC law: whether or not the national courts are co-operative and friendly towards EC/EU law. This rather one-dimensional spectrum, however, suffers from a key weakness, in that it is ill-equipped to capture the sheer complexity of the legal, political, administrative and other factors that may pose genuine challenges to the forthright granting of supremacy to EC law in certain cases. In particular, difficulties have arisen in situations where a direct conflict has been identi-

---

\* Senior Lecturer in EU Law, University of Kent, Canterbury, United Kingdom.
[1] Constitutional Tribunal, 27 April 2005, Case P 1/05 (*re Conformity of provisions on EAW with the Constitution*) [2006] 1 C.M.L.R. 36.
[2] Constitutional Tribunal, 11 May 2005, Case K 18/04 (*re Conformity of the Accession Treaty 2003 with the Polish Constitution*) OTK Z.U. 2005/5A/49; an English summary of the judgment is available at the Constitutional Tribunal website http://www.trybunal.gov.pl/eng/summaries/documents/K_18_04_GB.pdf.
[3] Decision 17/2004 (V. 25) AB.

*A. Łazowski (ed.), The Application of EU Law in the New Member States*
© 2010, T·M·C·Asser press, *The Hague, The Netherlands and the Authors*

fied between a norm of a national constitution and a norm of EC/EU law, precisely the sort of scenario that led to annulments in the above cases. As a matter of fact, the courts in question went to great lengths to eliminate any harmful consequences to EC/EU law, e.g., by granting a transitional period of eighteen months for constitutional amendment in Poland.[4] Against this background, this chapter seeks to broaden the supremacy equation by assessing whether suitable constitutional frameworks have been put in place by political actors in the new Member States in order to enable smooth application of EC/EU law by the courts.

The EU-related constitutional amendments in the new Member States were predominantly introduced in 2001-2003, with the exception of Poland, which joined on the basis of the new Constitution adopted in 1997, and Cyprus, where no amendment was deemed necessary prior to the accession. As regards the countries of Central and Eastern Europe, the historical background of the adoption of the constitutional amendments, along with the legal and political context, has been provided by the author elsewhere.[5] The story of amendments contained a considerable element of drama: the solemn, heartfelt declarations on sovereignty and national identity in the constitutional texts and the political rhetoric of the early 1990s quickly gave way to a transfer of state powers to what Euro sceptics often likened to a European superstate; cunning plots in devising constitutional amendments and shrewd procedural manoeuvring in staging the referenda succeeded in warding off any public perception on loss of sovereignty; and constitutional arguments regarding the proper content and amendment procedure invariably paled in significance in the face of (geo-)political imperatives. The amendments that were adopted in the CEE prior to accession were broadly characterised as minimalist, on the following grounds:[6] (a) the amendments were predominantly addressed to international organisations in general rather than specifically to the European Union; (b) in a number of countries manifest conflicts with EU law were left unresolved within the constitutions contrary to the advice of legal experts; and (c) in some countries (mainly the Baltic states), the amendments appeared to sidestep the rigid constitutional amendment procedures which included the requirement of a referendum for changes regarding sovereignty.

In the subsequent years, however, the balance sheet has considerably changed, with a number of further amendments having been adopted in a more relaxed political climate that followed the successful holding of accession referenda. For example, in Lithuania, the Constitutional Act on Membership in the European Union was adopted in July 2004 and entered into force on 13 August 2004, three months after accession.[7] Additionally, Article 125(2) of the Lithuanian Constitution was amended in April 2006 to ensure conformity with the requirements of the Economic and Monetary Union.[8] In Latvia,

---

[4] This is the maximum the Constitutional Tribunal is allowed to grant pursuant to Art. 190(3) of the Polish Constitution.

[5] See A. Albi, *EU Enlargement and the Constitutions of Central and Eastern Europe* (Cambridge, Cambridge University Press 2005) pp. 67-121.

[6] For details, see Albi, *op. cit.* n. 5, at pp. 78-121.

[7] See further Chapter 7 in this volume.

[8] *Ibidem.*

EU-amendments were resumed on 23 September 2004, removing conflicts from Article 101 (voting rights of EU citizens in local elections) and Article 98 (extradition of citizens). The amendments entered into force on 21 October 2004. In Poland, Article 55 of the Constitution was amended on 8 September 2006, in order to allow for extradition of Polish citizens in the wake of the aforementioned declaration of unconstitutionality by the Polish Constitutional Tribunal.[9] A Supreme Court decision on the same matter also prompted on 28 July 2006 an amendment in Cyprus, where the Constitution had not been amended prior to accession.[10] Slovakia supplemented its fairly extensive set of EU-amendments by adopting on 14 May 2004 constitutional provisions regarding the European Parliament elections.[11] These amendments will be referred to as "post-accession amendments" in the remaining parts of this chapter. In addition to these post-accession amendments, the above-mentioned trend of minimalism has additionally been countered by the rather exemplary EU-provisions that can be showcased by Romania and Bulgaria that joined in 2007.[12]

Against this background, this chapter seeks to offer a systematic comparative account of the issues that have hitherto led to amendment in the new Member States or have prompted calls to that effect. Where the matter has been subject to a Constitutional Court or Supreme Court scrutiny, a brief introduction to relevant cases will be provided. The analysis will commence by exploring the provisions on delegation of sovereignty, turning the focus then to the supremacy and direct effect of EC/EU law. This will be followed by parts exploring the constitutional issues arising from the separation of powers, the free movement rights of EU citizens and the adoption of the common currency. The final section will flag some further areas that warrant discussion, such as the ratification of the Lisbon Treaty,[13] the position of the national languages and issues arising from the protection of fundamental rights. In terms of the geographical scope of the study, the focus will predominantly be on the new Member States from Central and Eastern Europe and on some overarching trends that stem from their historical past under Soviet domination; however the constitutional developments in Cyprus and Malta will also be included. In terms of the substantive scope, this chapter will focus on the content of the EU-amendments; broader issues such as amendment procedures, constitutional review procedures, amendments on other issues (such as NATO) will not be addressed here as an extensive account with comparative tables has been provided elsewhere.[14] A word of caution is in order: given the geographical and substantive scope of this comparative study, it is probably inevitable that some amendments and developments may have been overlooked or misrepresented.

---

[9]  See further Chapter 9 in this volume.
[10]  Supreme Court of Cyprus, 7 November 2005, Judgment in case *Attorney General of the Republic v. Konstantinou*, [2007] 3 C.M.L.R. 42. See further Chapter 15 in this volume.
[11]  See further Chapter 11 in this volume.
[12]  See further Chapters 16 and 17 in this volume (respectively).
[13]  Treaty of Lisbon amending the Treaty on European Union and the Treaty establishing the European Community, *OJ* 2007 C 306/1.
[14]  See Albi, *op. cit.* n. 5, at pp. 78-121.

A final introductory remark concerns ambiguity of the requirement to bring constitutions in conformity with EU law, and the comparative state of play in the older Member States. While it is incumbent upon the accession countries to align their legislation with the requirements of the wide-ranging *acquis communautaire*, it is less straightforward whether the harmonisation requirement extends to national constitutions. As a fundamental expression of state sovereignty, constitutions establish the foundational rules on the distribution of powers and decision-making within a state, and states thus hold the prerogative of determining whether and to what extent participation in the EU receives a mention in their national constitutions. It will be seen, though, that the latest expansions offer some evidence of nascent inroads by the EU into the national autonomy in this respect, for example, by virtue of the European Commission's requests to amend the constitutional provisions on the judiciary in Slovakia, Romania and Bulgaria and to adjust the rules on the national currency in Estonia.[15] However, the core constitutional provisions on the organisation of powers and their transfer to the EU remain firmly within the remit of the Member States. In the absence of unified EU requirements, national constitutions represent an area of law that, intriguingly, appears to be rather poorly adjusted for EU membership. Amongst the constitutions of the 15 old Member States,[16] four offer no mention of the EU – the constitutions of the Netherlands, Luxembourg, Denmark and Spain. Indeed it has been noted that were an alien to land in these countries and read their constitutions, he may well miss their membership of the EU altogether.[17] Three other constitutions – those of Finland, Belgium and Italy – accommodate the transfer of powers under a broader clause on international organisations, but make explicit references to the EU in relation to a limited number of specific issues. The third group consists of those constitutions that contain explicit provisions on the delegation of powers to the European Union: the constitutions of France, Germany, Portugal, Ireland, Austria, Sweden and, after a 2001 reform, Greece. Besides the transfer clauses, most constitutions in this group contain further provisions dealing with various specific aspects of EU membership.[18] Overall, considerable diversity exists within the constitutional landscape of the old Member States, with no standard model being available for accession countries. However, for reasons which will be considered in the final part of this chapter, the third group is recommended as a model for the other countries, and provisions from these constitutions in particular will form the point of reference in the comparative account that follows. While at the pre-accession stage of amendment, this model hardly resonated with the constitutional drafters of accession countries, a rather different picture has emerged in result of the

---

[15] See, *inter alia*, Council Decision 2003/396/EC of 19 May 2003 on the principles, priorities, intermediate objectives and conditions contained in the Accession Partnership with Bulgaria, *OJ* 2003 L 145/1. One of the priority areas was the revision of the Bulgarian Constitution to guarantee the voting rights stemming from Art. 19 EC.

[16] For a comparative overview, see M. Claes, 'Constitutionalizing Europe at its Source: The "European Clauses" in the National Constitutions: Evolution and Typology', 24 *YBEL* (2005) pp. 81-125. For accounts on individual countries, see contributions published in A.E. Kellermann, et al., eds., *EU Enlargement: The Constitutional Impact at EU and National Level* (The Hague, T.M.C. Asser Press 2001).

[17] Claes, *loc. cit.* n. 16, at p. 107.

[18] For details, see, e.g., Claes, *loc. cit.* n. 16, at p. 81 and Albi, *op.cit.* n. 5, at pp. 9-17.

additional post-accession amendments and the entry of Romania and Bulgaria; indeed in constitutional terms, the majority of the new Member States would now seem better prepared for EU membership than the older Member States.

## 2.      DELEGATION OF SOVEREIGNTY

Constitutions have been portrayed as a reflection of a society's soul,[19] that is 'a characteristic way of life, the national character of a people, their ethos or fundamental nature as a people, a product of their particular history and social conditions.'[20] This statement could not apply better to the constitutions of Central and Eastern Europe: they embody a historical quest for sovereign governance which, regained after the breakdown of the Communist regime, is protected in markedly stronger terms than in the Western European constitutions. Indeed, the author has earlier explored various elements in the CEE constitutions which led to their characterisation as "souverainist" constitutions;[21] such features included the absence of provisions on delegation of powers to international organisations in virtually all CEE constitutions (with the exception of Lithuania). Accession to the EU posed what Wojciech Sadurski has tellingly characterised as the "sovereignty conundrum": '[c]ountries with a proud national history, which have only just emerged from several decades of … oppressive domination by the Soviet Union' now embarked upon 'the surrender [of] their sovereignty again, this time for an admittedly benign foreign body, but a foreign nevertheless.'[22] Delegation of powers to the European Union therefore warrants an inquiry as to how the constitutions were adjusted to allow for a transfer of powers.

As noted in the introductory section, the EU has set virtually no requirements to the constitutional basis for participation in the EU within national constitutions, and a great deal of diversity has thus emerged on the comparative landscape. One classic issue to resolve has been the question whether the amendments ought to be addressed to international organisations in general or to the EU specifically. Here the older Member States broadly fall into two groups.[23] France, Germany, Portugal, Ireland and Sweden have addressed the delegation of powers clause explicitly to the European Union besides a general clause on international organisations. Although in the Austrian Constitution, the delegation clause is addressed to "intergovernmental organisations" rather than expressly to the EU, the symbolic importance of placing an extensive section on the

---

[19] W. Sadurski, 'Conclusions: On the Relevance of Institutions and the Centrality of Constitutions in Post-Communist Transitions', in J. Zielonka and A. Pravda, eds., *Democratic Consolidation in Eastern Europe. Volume 1: Institutional Engineering* (Oxford, Oxford University Press 2001) pp. 455-493, at p. 461.

[20] F. Pitkin, 'The Idea of a Constitution', 37 *JLE* (1987) pp. 167-169, at p. 167, cited in Sadurski, *loc. cit.* n. 19, at p. 462.

[21] Albi, *op. cit.* n. 5, pp. 18-35.

[22] W. Sadurski, 'The Role of the EU Charter of Rights in the Process of Enlargement', in G. Bermann and K. Pistor, eds., *Law and Governance in an Enlarged European Union* (Oxford-Portland, Oregon, Hart Publishing 2004) pp. 61-95, at p. 71.

[23] For details, see, *inter alia*, Claes, *loc. cit.* n. 16, at p. 81, and Albi, *op. cit.* n. 5, pp. 9-17.

European Union into the very first chapter of the Constitution (Chapter 1B, Arts. 23a-23f) justifies its addition to the first group. On the other hand, the constitutions of Italy, Spain, Denmark, Luxembourg, the Netherlands, Belgium and Finland contain a broader clause on international organisations. Greece has opted for a solution of its own: Article 28 of the Constitution, which provides that powers may be vested in international organisations, was complemented in 2001 by a so-called "interpretative clause", according to which Article 28 equally constitutes the foundation for participation in the European integration process.

By way of illustration of the delegation clauses, Article 88(1) of the French Constitution, which forms part of Title XV on the European Union, provides that France shall participate 'in the European Union constituted by States that have freely chosen ... to exercise some of their powers in common.'[24] Article 23(1) of the German Constitution provides for participation in the EU to 'realize a unified Europe', and allows the country to 'delegate sovereign powers' to this end. As regards the issue of how the delegation or transfer of competences is formulated in the constitutions, no standard formulation appears to be available. On the contrary, a plethora of formulations has been deployed, such as "delegation", "transfer", "vesting in" or "attribution", of "powers" or "sovereign rights", and "limitation" or "restriction" of "(exercise) of sovereignty"; indeed different formulations can even be found within the same constitution.

For the countries that joined in the course of the latest enlargements, scholarly commentators recommended the first model where the delegation of powers clause would have been addressed to the European Union directly. This rested primarily on the assumption that such clauses would better reflect the *sui generis* nature of the EU, which entails rather more extensive delegation of powers than international organisations. The absence of such a clause would prompt questions about a "European deficit" in the national constitutions and a degree of obsoleteness of the constitutional provisions with regard to the realities in the exercise of state powers. However, in the course of the first stage of amendments, these concerns did not resonate with the constitutional drafters in CEE countries; in the initial draft amendments, the "international organisation" approach had been taken almost universally across the CEE, although some countries opted for explicit EU-amendments at a later stage. The reasons behind the "international organisations" approach have been explored elsewhere in greater detail. They included the prevalence of the traditional theoretical views to sovereignty which fed into the amendments,[25] the quest to resolve several issues at once given the absence of constitutional provisions on delegation of powers to international organisations[26] and the quest to downplay the impact of the EU upon sovereignty in the public perception

---

[24] For details, see, *inter alia*, A. Bonnie, 'The Constitutionality of Transfers of Sovereignty: the French Approach', 4 *EPL* (1998) pp. 517-532.

[25] See Albi, *op. cit.* n. 5, at p. 409. See also A. Sajó, 'Accession's Impact on Constitutionalism in the New Member States', in Bermann and Pistor, *op. cit* n. 22, pp. 415-435, at p. 417.

[26] For example, in the Czech Republic the formula of "international organisations" reflected the aim to simultaneously accommodate membership in the EU and other organisations, such as NATO and the International Criminal Court. See I. Šlosarčík, 'The Reform of the Constitutional Systems of Czechoslovakia and the Czech Republic in 1990-2000', 7 *EPL* (2001) pp. 529-547, at p. 544.

prior to accession referenda. The result in some cases is a rather clumsy formulation whereby the constitutional provisions draw a distinction between international organisations which involve a "transfer of powers" and those which do not, whether in relation to the ratification of treaties, application of law or participation of national parliaments.

Some examples of the "international organisation" approach include: the Czech Republic Constitution, in which the new Article 10a provides that '[s]ome powers of the Czech Republic may be transferred to an international organization or institution' by an international agreement. Article 90(1) of the Polish Constitution provides that Poland may 'delegate to an international organization or international institution the competence of organs of State authority in relation to certain matters.'[27] The Constitution of Slovenia allows the country to 'transfer the exercise of part of its sovereign rights to international organisations which are based on respect for human rights and fundamental freedoms, democracy and the principles of the rule of law' (Art. 3a(1)).

Lithuania's case is evocative in terms of the change that has occurred in the perception of the constitutional significance of the EU. Lithuania joined the EU under a pre-existing clause – Article 136 of the Constitution – on international organisations, on the basis of a 1998 expert group report that portrayed the EU as an ordinary international organisation without any considerable impact on sovereignty.[28] However, a few months after accession (July 2004), a free-standing Constitutional Act on Membership of Lithuania in the EU was additionally adopted, authorising the delegation of state competences to the EU.[29] Article 1 of the Act provides that:

'The Republic of Lithuania as a Member State of the European Union shall share with or delegate to the European Union competences of its State institutions in the spheres provided for in the founding Treaties of the European Union and to the extent that, together with the other Member States of the European Union, it could jointly meet its commitments in those spheres and could also enjoy the rights accorded by membership.'

As shown by I. Jarukaitis in Chapter 7 of this volume, the addition of this provision resulted from a realisation in the governmental and parliamentary circles that the description "international organisation" in Article 136 of the Lithuanian Constitution was inadequate and artificial for membership of the EU, which is a *sui generis* organ-

---

[27] See further, *inter alia*, S. Biernat, 'The Openness of the Constitution of the Republic of Poland Towards European Integration', in G. Amato, et al., eds., *The Constitutional Revision in Today's Europe* (London, Esperia Publications 2002) pp. 439-451; K. Wójtowicz, 'Proposed Changes in the Polish Constitution of 1997 ahead of Poland's Accession to the European Union', 25 *PolYBIL* (2001) pp. 27-44; A. Łazowski, 'International Agreements in the Legal Orders of the Candidate Countries. Poland', in A. Ott and K. Inglis, eds., *Handbook on European Enlargement* (The Hague, T.M.C. Asser Press 2002) pp. 299-308, at pp. 305-307.
[28] 'Republic of Lithuania Constitutional Law on the Amendment of Articles 136 and 138 of the Constitution of the Republic of Lithuania. Draft of the Working Group established under the Seimas Chancellery', in *Stojimas I Europos Sajunga Ir Konstitucija. Seminaro Medziaga 29-30.06.1999* (Vilnius, Eugrimas 2000) at p. 142.
[29] See further Chapter 7 in this volume.

isation in nature, and the provision in question would have been insufficient to reinterpret the Constitution.[30]

Amongst the 2004 countries, only Slovakia and Hungary chose to address the delegation of powers' provisions in a straightforward manner to the European Union prior to accession. In Slovakia, new paragraph 2 of Article 7 of the Slovakian Constitution provides that:

> 'the Slovak Republic may, by an international treaty ratified and promulgated as stipulated by law, or on the basis of such treaty, transfer the execution of a part of its rights to the European Communities and European Union.'

In Hungary, the first paragraph of Article 2A of the Constitution provides that:

> 'By virtue of treaty, the Republic of Hungary, in its capacity as a Member State of the European Union, may exercise certain constitutional powers jointly with other Member States to the extent necessary in connection with the rights and obligations conferred by the treaties on the foundation of the European Union and the European Communities ...; these powers may be exercised independently and by way of the institutions of the European Union.'

Additionally, Article 6(4) of the Constitution contains a reference to the objectives of European integration, stating that 'Hungary shall participate in establishing European unity for the accomplishment of the freedom, welfare and safety of European peoples.'

This welcome trend in terms of addressing the provisions directly to the EU was followed by Romania and Bulgaria, which acceded on 1 January 2007. In Romania, a rather extensive package of altogether seventy-nine amendments was approved in a referendum on 18-19 October 2003.[31] The first paragraph of Article 148 of the Constitution provides that:

> 'Romania's accession to the constituent treaties of the European Union, with a view to transferring certain powers to Community institutions, as well as to exercising in common with the other member states the abilities stipulated in such treaties, shall be carried out by means of a law adopted in the joint session of the Chamber of Deputies and the Senate, with a majority of two thirds of the number of deputies and senators.'

In Bulgaria, the amendments were introduced in 2005; Article 4 of the Constitution provides that the 'Republic of Bulgaria shall participate in the construction and development of the European Union.'[32]

---

[30] *Ibidem.*
[31] See further Chapter 16 in this volume.
[32] See further E. Tanchev, M. Belov, 'Constitutional Gradualism: Adapting to EU Membership and Improving the Judiciary in the Bulgarian Constitution', 14 *EPL* (2008) pp. 3-19, at p. 10. See also Chapter 17 in this volume.

In Malta and Cyprus, the amendment provisions do not contain a formulation referring to the delegation or transfer of powers, although both make a reference to the
Accession Treaty.[33] In Malta, the amended Section 65 of the Constitution provides:

> 'Subject to the provisions of this Constitution, Parliament may make laws for the peace, order
> and good government of Malta in conformity with full respect of human rights, generally
> accepted principles of international law and Malta's international and regional obligations
> in particular those assumed by the Treaty of Accession to the European Union signed in
> Athens on the 16th of April 2003.'[34]

In Cyprus, a provision on the application of EC/EU law was introduced well after
accession in 2006; it will be considered later in this chapter.[35] In both countries, these
provisions remain virtually the only EU-amendments.

The solutions chosen in Estonia and Latvia are worthy of a separate mention because
of the number of cases brought to the highest courts to contest the procedural correctness of the accession and amendment process. In all three Baltic states, the rigid constitutional amendment procedures include a referendum for amending the provisions
on sovereignty, with elevated procedural requirements (e.g., higher turnout). These
procedures proved too challenging to comply with strictly in the process of EU accession, against the background where public support for EU membership was consistently low; the question of delegation of sovereignty was rather sensitive due to the
recent reinstatement of independence. There had been calls from various quarters in
Estonia and Latvia to amend several provisions of their national constitutions prior to
accession. In Estonia, an authoritative expert committee had explicitly called for amendment of Article 1 (on the inalienability of sovereignty).[36] In Estonia, the Constitution
was, strictly speaking, not amended but "supplemented" instead by an independently
standing Act Supplementing the Constitution. In a laconic wording, it authorises
Estonia's membership in the EU (Art. 1), with the Constitution being 'applied, taking
into consideration the rights and obligations deriving from the Accession Treaty' (Art.
2). The Act was approved in a referendum on 14 September 2003, where two referenda – on accession and on the "supplementing" of the Constitution – were fused into
one, following an amendment to the Referendum Act. Such steps led to nine cases being

---

[33] Treaty between the Kingdom of Belgium, the Kingdom of Denmark, the Federal Republic of Ger-
many, the Hellenic Republic, the Kingdom of Spain, the French Republic, Ireland, the Italian Republic, the
Grand Duchy of Luxembourg, the Kingdom of the Netherlands, the Republic of Austria, the Portuguese
Republic, the Republic of Finland, the Kingdom of Sweden, the United Kingdom of Great Britain and
Northern Ireland (Member States of the European Union) and the Czech Republic, the Republic of Estonia, the Republic of Cyprus, the Republic of Latvia, the Republic of Lithuania, the Republic of Hungary,
the Republic of Malta, the Republic of Poland, the Republic of Slovenia, the Slovak Republic, concerning
the accession of the Czech Republic, the Republic of Estonia, the Republic of Cyprus, the Republic of
Latvia, the Republic of Lithuania, the Republic of Hungary, the Republic of Malta, the Republic of Poland,
the Republic of Slovenia and the Slovak Republic to the European Union, *OJ* 2003 L 236/17.

[34] See further Chapter 14 in this volume.

[35] See also Chapter 15 in this volume.

[36] 'Potential Accession to the European Union and its Consequences to Estonian Constitutional Law'
[in Estonian], Report of the Constitutional Expert Commission' (Tallinn, 1998, on file with the author).

brought to the Supreme Court after the accession referendum,[37] contesting the following: the constitutionality of "supplementing" the Constitution rather than inserting
amendments into its text, the constitutionality of the ratification of the Accession Treaty
without a prior amendment of Article 1 of the Constitution and the constitutionality of
the merger of the different types of referenda. All claims were rejected by the Supreme
Court on procedural grounds, reflecting the pragmatic efforts of the judges of a very
small Member State not to "rock the boat", given their new role as European as well
as national judges. However, since the meaning of the Act Supplementing the
Constitution has caused considerable controversy and uncertainty, there are plans
underway to draft a new constitution at a later stage.

In Latvia, the amendments were put in place by way of parliamentary procedure in
2003. A new paragraph was added to Article 68 of the Constitution, providing that:

> 'Upon entering into international agreements, Latvia, with the purpose of strengthening
> democracy, may delegate a part of its State institution competences to international institu-
> tions.'

The second new paragraph provides that membership in the European Union is subject
to a referendum; a referendum may also be held on 'substantial changes in the terms
regarding the membership of Latvia', where requested by at least half of all members
of Parliament. For EU referenda, the minimum turnout requirement was reduced from
50% (as required for constitutional amendment referenda under Art. 79 of the
Constitution) to half the turnout rate of the previous parliamentary elections. Such steps
rested on the argument that no harm ensues from EU accession to the principles of
sovereignty and independence as established in Articles 1 and 2 of the Constitution.[38]
This mode of constitutional amendment prompted the submission of five petitions to
the Constitutional Court in November 2003,[39] claiming that Parliament was not authorised to adopt the amendments without a prior amendment of Articles 1 and 2 of the
Constitution. The petitions contested the constitutionality of both the amendments and
the accession referendum as well as the Accession Treaty. Similarly to the pragmatic
approach of the Estonian Supreme Court, the Latvian Constitutional Court declared the
petitions inadmissible on the grounds that the applicants had failed to substantiate the
violation of their fundamental rights under the Constitution. The Court also noted that
the choice of the constitutional amendment procedure falls to the Parliament, with the
Constitutional Court having no competence to assess the conformity of one norm of
the Constitution with another or with the Constitution as a whole. Where a norm has

---

[37] See Decision No. 3-4-1-11-03 of 24 September 2003, *Vilu and Estonian Voters Union*, and Decision No. 3-4-1-12-03 of 29 September 2003, *Kulbok*, available at the website of the Supreme Court, http://
www.nc.ee.

[38] *The Theoretical Foundation of the Amendments to Satversme proposed by the Working Group*
(Ministry of Justice of the Republic of Latvia, Riga 2001) p. 6.

[39] The registration numbers of these cases are 119-123/2003; the decisions of inadmissibility are not
available in English. The decisions are summarised in A. Endzins, 'Constitutional Court of the Republic
of Latvia', in *The Position of Constitutional Courts Following Integration into the European Union, Proceedings of the Conference held in Bled, Slovenia, 30.09.-02.10.2004*, at pp. 214-215.

been incorporated into the Constitution, it forms an integral part of it and enjoys a corresponding legal force.[40] It may be of interest to add that in Lithuania, where the above-mentioned free-standing Act on EU was adopted a few months after the EU accession, the Constitutional Court sought to foreclose any potential legal challenges to the constitutionality of the application of EU law between 1 May 2004 and 13 August 2004 by stating that Lithuania's EU membership 'is constitutionally confirmed' by the Constitutional Act on EU Membership, which is 'a constituent part of the Constitution.'[41]

The transfer of powers to the EU was also contested in Poland, where the constitutionality of the Accession Treaty was questioned on the grounds of fourteen alleged conflicts between the Accession Treaty and the Constitution.[42] The Constitutional Tribunal held that Article 90 of the Constitution formed a legitimate basis for accession and dismissed all other claims on the grounds of various arguments, which will be considered in different parts of this chapter.

The account on the sovereignty provisions could not be drawn to a close without mentioning that the constitutional amendments additionally established higher thresholds for the majorities required for the ratification of treaties involving a transfer of powers, and that the amendments were accompanied by referenda on accession to the EU in all countries with the exception of Cyprus, Bulgaria and Romania. The details surrounding the accession procedures and the organisation of referenda have been provided elsewhere.[43]

3.        SUPREMACY AND DIRECT EFFECT OF EC LAW

3.1.        **The position of EC law in relation to ordinary national law**

While the issue of delegation of sovereignty received a hesitant response in the national constitutional texts of the new Member States, the application of EC law represents an area where the new Member States appear to go noticeably further than the older Member States. Amongst the old Member States, the Irish Constitution was until recently the only one to expressly establish the supremacy of Community law (Art. 29(4) of the Constitution); Portugal also introduced a clause to this effect in 2005 (Art. 8 para. 4 of the Constitution). In the other constitutions of the older Member States, this important issue is accommodated under general clauses on the delegation of powers or under provisions regarding the application of international law, which on some occasions (e.g., the Netherlands) were introduced in view of application of EC law.

By way of an introductory synopsis of the main changes in the new Member States, the following could be noted. The provisions addressing the supremacy of EC/EU law have been put in place in Slovakia, Romania, Lithuania, Malta, Cyprus, Poland, the

---

[40]  For a summary of the decisions, see Endzins, *loc. cit.* n. 39, at pp. 214-215.
[41]  See I. Jarukaitis in Chapter 7 of this volume, referring to a judgment of 13 December 2004.
[42]  Judgment of 11 May 2005 in Case K 18/04, *loc. cit.* n. 2.
[43]  See Albi, *op. cit.* n. 5, pp. 67-121 and pp. 138-162.

Czech Republic and Slovenia. In the last three, the relevant provisions are addressed to international organisations but were primarily aimed at accommodating EC law. In Estonia, a general interpretative provision was introduced; no provisions regarding the application of EC law can be found in the constitutions of Latvia, Bulgaria and Hungary. It may be worthy to note that a dualist approach to international law had previously been taken by Hungary, the Czech Republic, Slovakia, Romania and Malta, whereas the other countries broadly adhered to the monist approach. By virtue of the amendments, the Czech Republic and Slovakia were transformed to monist countries, with the others establishing the supremacy of EC law but remaining dualist with regard to international treaties. In Hungary, the status of EC law remained conspicuously unresolved within the text of the Constitution. The subsequent sections will provide further details regarding the amendments. In the second part of this chapter, it will be seen that courts of the new Member States have set certain limits to the supremacy of EC law regarding the national constitutions, along the lines of their counterparts in the older Member States.

The supremacy clause deals expressly with EC/EU law in Lithuania, Slovakia, Romania, Cyprus and Malta. It may be of interest to note that in Lithuania and Slovakia, the scope of the provisions, which refer to EU law rather than EC law, appears to be wider than that under the case law of the European Court of Justice. Lithuania has been a monist country where under Article 138(3) of the Constitution, ratified treaties are granted the position of a "constituent part" of Lithuania's legal system. Nonetheless, a special clause on EU law was added in paragraph 2 of the 2004 Constitutional Act, which provides:

'The norms of acquis of the European Union shall be an integral part of the legal order of the Republic of Lithuania. Where these arise from the founding Treaties of the European Union, the norms of acquis shall apply directly, while in the event of a collision between legal norms, the norms of acquis shall prevail over the laws and other legal acts of the Republic of Lithuania.'

According to a Lithuanian commentator,[44] such a formulation had been inspired by Article I-6 of the EU Constitutional Treaty.[45] Additionally, the indirect effect of the Third Pillar law following the ECJ judgment in *Pupino*[46] appears to add weight to speaking about the application of EU law rather than EC law. In Slovakia, Article 11 previously granted direct applicability and precedence to (ratified and promulgated) human rights treaties in the event of a conflict with domestic acts. Other treaties were applied "by reference" through a national law; they ranked the same as statutes and were subject to the *lex posterior* rule.[47] The amendments deal separately with the supremacy of EC/EU law and with that of international treaties; the former is addressed

---

[44] See I. Jarukaitis in Chapter 7 in this volume.

[45] Treaty establishing a Constitution for Europe, *OJ* 2004 C 310/1.

[46] ECJ, Case C-105/03 *Criminal proceedings against Maria Pupino* [2005] *ECR* I-5285.

[47] See, *inter alia*, M. Hoskova, 'Legal Aspects of the Integration of the Czech Republic and Slovakia into European Security and Economic Structures', 37 *GYIL* (1994) pp. 68-92, at p. 84.

in the second sentence of Article 7(2): 'Legally binding acts of the European Communities and European Union shall take precedence over the laws of the Slovak Republic.' Supremacy of international agreements is established in the new paragraph 5 of Article 7, which accords precedence to certain categories of treaties, and the new Article 1(2), according to which Slovakia honours its obligations arising from treaties and the general rules of international law. The position of EC law and international law is further strengthened by provisions on the role of courts. Article 144 of the Constitution provides that judges are bound, along with the Constitution and constitutional laws, by EU law and directly applicable treaties, and the courts have to initiate constitutional review proceedings should they deem an act incompatible with the Constitution, EU law or with a directly applicable treaty provision.

In Romania, paragraph 2 of Article 148 of the Constitution establishes that the provisions of the treaties and of mandatory Community regulations 'shall take precedence over the opposite provisions of the national laws, in compliance with the provisions of the accession act.' This provision is also to be applied to acts that revise the EU's constituent treaties in the future (para. 3). These provisions are reinforced by paragraph 4, which obliges the Parliament, the President, the Government and judicial authorities to guarantee the implementation of the obligations arising under EU law. These provisions are significant because Romania is a partially dualist country, where only human rights treaties have enjoyed precedence. In Cyprus, the constitutional amendment on the position of EU law was put in place in July 2006 after the Supreme Court's judgment of 7 November 2005 on the unconstitutionality of surrender pursuant to EAW.[48] The new Article 1A of the Constitution provides that:

> '[N]o constitutional provision shall be construed as invalidating laws enacted, acts resolved or measures taken by the Republic, which become necessary as a result of the obligations undertaken by Cyprus as a European Union member state, nor shall they hinder from Regulations, Directives or other acts or binding legislative measures enacted by the European Union or European Communities or their institutional organs or competent authorities on the basis of the founding Treaties of the European Union or the European Communities, from producing legal effect in the Republic.'

In terms of application of international treaties, Cyprus has been a monist country where Article 169 of the 1960 Constitution provides that treaties – which are ratified by the Parliament and published – acquire superior force in relation to any municipal law.[49] Malta had previously been a dualist country where the Constitution prior to 2003 contained no references either to the international legal order in general or to the EU.[50] The supremacy of EC law is accommodated under the general EU clause in Section 65 of the Maltese Constitution, which was considered above.[51]

---

[48] *Loc. cit.* n. 10.

[49] On the position of international treaties in Cyprus, see N. Emiliou, 'Cyprus', in A. Kellermann, et al., eds., *The Impact of EU Accession on the Legal Orders of New Member States and (Pre-) Candidate Countries* (The Hague, T.M.C. Asser Press 2006) pp. 303-311, at p. 304.

[50] See P. Xuereb, 'Malta', in Kellermann, et al., *op. cit.* n. 49, at p. 409.

[51] See also Xuereb, *loc. cit.* n. 50 at p. 411.

The "international organisations" approach was used in Poland, Slovenia and the Czech Republic. In Slovenia, however, the provisions were essentially addressed to EC law and enjoy a privileged position in comparison with other international treaties. In terms of application of public international law, Slovenia has been a monist country where, under Article 8, laws and regulations are to comply with the generally accepted principles of international law and binding international agreements, and ratified and published international treaties are applied directly. Still, a special clause was added to secure the position of EC law (para. 3 of Art. 3a of the Constitution):

> 'Legal acts and decisions adopted within international organisations to which Slovenia has transferred the exercise of part of its sovereign rights shall be applied in Slovenia in accordance with the legal regulation of these organisations.'[52]

The Czech Republic moved by virtue of the 2001 amendments from a dualist to a monist approach towards international law. Previously direct applicability and precedence were accorded solely to human rights treaties, provided that these were ratified and promulgated (the then Art. 10). Other treaties were applied "by reference" through a national law, and their rank equalled to statutes, being subject to the *lex posterior* rule.[53] The amendments considerably strengthen the position of treaties: the reworded Article 10 provides that promulgated, ratified and binding international agreements 'constitute part of legislation' and are applied in the event of a conflict with domestic statutes; Article 1(2) of the Constitution declares that the Republic observes obligations arising from international law. These provisions are reinforced by amendments concerning the role of the judiciary: judges are bound by those international agreements that constitute a part of legislation, and they are entitled to assess the conformity of legal acts with such international agreements (Art. 95 of the Constitution). Where a conflict is found, the matter is referred to the Constitutional Court.

In Poland, the status of international law had not been regulated in the constitutional acts prior to the adoption of the 1997 Constitution, but a monist approach had been taken by the Constitutional Tribunal.[54] According to Article 91 of the 1997 Constitution,[55] a ratified and promulgated international agreement:

> 'shall constitute part of the domestic legal order and shall be applied directly, unless its application depends on the enactment of a statute' (para. 1), and it takes 'precedence over statutes if such an agreement cannot be reconciled with the provisions of such statutes' (para. 2).

The third paragraph of Article 91 of the Constitution prepares Poland for the application of EU secondary legislation, granting direct applicability and precedence to laws established by the above-mentioned international organisations, where so provided by the

---

[52] See further Chapter 13 in this volume.

[53] See Šlosarčík, *loc. cit.* n. 26, at p. 539; Hoskova, *loc. cit.* n. 47, at p. 84.

[54] W. Czapliński, 'The Relationship between International Law and Polish Municipal Law in the Light of the 1997 Constitution and Jurisprudence', 121-124 *DPC* (1999) pp. 19-26, at p. 21.

[55] See Czapliński, *loc. cit.* n. 54, at pp. 19-20; Łazowski, *loc. cit.* n. 27, at pp. 299-305.

agreement establishing the organisation. Further, Article 9 provides that Poland shall respect international law binding upon it, and Article 87 provides that ratified international agreements form part of the sources of universally binding law in Poland. Unlike direct applicability, supremacy is granted only to those treaties that have been ratified by parliamentary statute (Arts. 89 and 91 of the Constitution).

A distinctly specific approach was adopted in Estonia, where the Constitutional Act on EU Membership provides that the Constitution is 'applied, taking into consideration the rights and obligations deriving from the Accession Treaty' (Art. 2). The meaning of this provision was clarified in two successive judgments of the Constitutional Review Chamber of the Supreme Court. In April 2005, in a case regarding the electoral rights of EU citizens,[56] the Court pointed out, with reference to the ECJ's decision in *IN.CO. GE. '90*,[57] that a national act which conflicts with EC law could simply be set aside in a concrete dispute. A stronger position to EC law was granted in May 2006,[58] when the Court delivered its opinion on the compatibility with EU law of Article 111 of the Constitution, according to which the Bank of Estonia has the exclusive right to issue the Estonian currency. The Constitutional Chamber stated that the text of the Constitution is to be read together with the Act Supplementing the Constitution, and, consequently, those parts of the Constitution that are incompatible with EU law are not to be applied.

No special amendment on the position of EC law was put in place in Latvia, Bulgaria and Hungary. In Bulgaria, supremacy and direct effect of EC law can be accommodated under the pre-existing Article 5(4), which provides that:

> 'Any international instruments which have been ratified by the constitutionally established procedure, promulgated, and come into force with respect to the Republic of Bulgaria, shall be considered part of the domestic legislation of the country. They shall supersede any domestic legislation stipulating otherwise.'

It may be worthy of mention though that commentators earlier considered this provision to form an insufficient basis to ensure the supremacy of EC secondary law.[59] It can be presumed that in Latvia and Hungary, the application of EC law is ensured under the general provisions on the delegation of powers; the Constitution of the former contains no special provisions on international law. Hungary's situation is intriguing because it adheres to dualism, and the norms of international law have not had precedence;[60] this issue had deliberately been left unresolved prior to accession.[61] Article 7(1) of the

---

[56] Decision No. 3-4-1-1-05 of 19 April 2005, available at http://www.nc.ee.

[57] ECJ, Joined Cases C-10/97 to C-22/97 Ministero delle *Finanze v. IN.CO.GE.*'90 Srl [1998] *ECR* I-6307.

[58] Opinion No. 3-4-1-3-06 on the interpretation of Art. 111 (on the Bank of Estonia), available at http://www.nc.ee.

[59] E. Tanchev, 'National Constitutions and EU Law: Adapting the 1991 Bulgarian Constitution in the Accession to the European Union', 6 *EPL* (2000) pp. 229-241, at pp. 233-234 and p. 241.

[60] A. Harmathy, 'Constitutional Questions of the Preparation of Hungary to Accession to the European Union', in Kellermann, et al., *op. cit.* n. 16, pp. 315-320, at p. 324.

[61] A. Sajó, 'Learning Co-operative Constitutionalism the Hard Way: the Hungarian Constitutional Court Shying Away from EU Supremacy', 2 *ZSE* (2004) pp. 351-371, at p. 353.

Constitution provides that the legal system of Hungary accepts the generally recognised principles of international law, and that the country's domestic law shall be harmonised with the obligations assumed under international law.

## 3.2.    Supremacy of EC law and national constitutions

While solid constitutional bases for the application of EC law have been put in place in general, question marks remain as to whether the supremacy extends to the national constitutions, which is required by EC law according to the ECJ cases such as *Internationale Handelsgesellschaft*.[62] To this end, an important issue to note is that unlike the constitutions of the old Member States, most Central and Eastern European constitutions, as well as the Cypriot and Maltese constitutions, expressly establish the principle that the constitution is the highest legal source in the country.[63] This rule is often reinforced by the prohibition to ratify treaties that are in conflict with the constitution and the requirement to amend the constitution when such a conflict is identified. To this end, preliminary review of treaties has been present in the constitutions of Slovenia (Art. 160(2)), Poland (Arts. 133(1.2) and 188(1)), Bulgaria (Art. 149(4) and, since 2005, Art. 85(4)). Additionally, the system of preliminary review of treaties was introduced as part of the EU amendments in Slovakia (Art. 125a) and the Czech Republic (Arts. 89(3) and 87(2)), and relevant provisions were strengthened in Romania (Arts. 11(3) and 145(3)).

For all these constitutional provisions, it appears that none of the Constitutional or Supreme Courts carried out a substantive review of the constitutionality of a relevant Accession Treaty prior to the accession. Only the Polish Constitutional Tribunal reviewed it after accession, and the Estonian Supreme Court and Latvian Constitutional Court were asked to review the accession and amendment procedure. As already explained, in the latter two cases, the applications were dismissed on procedural grounds.

In cases where the position of EC law *vis-à-vis* the national constitution has been addressed, a mixed picture has emerged. While on the one hand, it was seen above that the Estonian Supreme Court granted full supremacy to EU law, in the main, supremacy appears to be granted to the national constitution with the proviso that the constitution has to be amended to remove obstacles to application of EU law. This occurred in the Polish and Cypriot judgments regarding extradition of the nationals under the EAW and in the Polish judgment on the Accession Treaty. In addition, the Polish and the Czech Constitutional Courts have subjected the application of EC law to the requirement that fundamental rights and the principle of rule of law and democracy are sufficiently respected by the EU.[64] In line with the above cases, the general view in the

---

[62]  ECJ, Case 11/70 *Internationale Handelsgesellschaft mbH v. Einfuhr- und Vorratsstelle für Getreide und Futtermittel* [1970] *ECR* 1125, at 1134.

[63]  E.g., Art. 8 of the Polish Constitution; Art. 153(1) of the Slovene Constitution; Art. 7 of the Lithuanian Constitution; Art. 5 of the Bulgarian Constitution; Art. 2(2) of the Slovak Constitution; Art. 77(1) of the Hungarian Constitution; new Art. 1(5) of the Romanian Constitution (Art. 51 prior to 2003); Art. 179(1) of the Cypriot Constitution; Art. 6 of the Maltese Constitution.

[64]  See also W. Sadurski, "'Solange, chapter 3": Constitutional Courts in Central Europe – Democracy – European Union', 14 *ELJ* (2008) pp. 1-35; A. Albi, 'Constitutional Rights *versus* Supremacy of EC law

new Member States appears to be that the supremacy of EC law stems from the national constitutions rather than from the special nature of EC law.[65]

## 4.     SEPARATION OF POWERS

The previous sections considered the broader foundations created within the national constitutions for the delegation of powers and application of EC law. The remaining parts will provide a shorter synopsis of specific areas where developments in EU law have prompted constitutional revision or calls to that effect, commencing with the role of the national parliaments in the EU decision-making mechanisms.

One of the central concepts in the Western constitutions is the idea that power belongs to the people who exercise it via representative democracy. Consequently, most constitutions contain a version of a provision declaring that a parliament is the supreme legislative power in the country. In the process of European integration, the national parliaments have seen their power and stature eroded in a twofold way: first, powers have increasingly been transferred from the national to the supranational level, and, second, the decision-making process in the EU is heavily dominated by the executive branch, even though the European Parliament's role has gradually been strengthened by successive treaties.

Amongst the older Member States, eight countries have deemed it necessary to secure in the constitution the control of the national parliaments over the governments in the EU decision-making process.[66] The relevant provisions typically set out the parliaments' right to receive information regarding proposals for legislative acts in the EU, and their right to issue positions to the national governments in their decision-making activity in the Council. Such provisions can be found in the constitutions of Germany (Arts. 23(2-3), 52(3a)), Finland (Arts. 93(2), 96-97, 50(3)), Portugal (Arts. 161n, 163f and 197(1i)), Austria (Art. 23e), Sweden (Parliament Act Chapter 10), France (Art. 88(4)), Belgium (Art. 168) and Greece (Art. 70(8)). In addition, some constitutions acknowledge the role of the European Parliament. For example, Austria has introduced amendments concerning some organisational issues pertaining to the work and elections of the European Parliament members (Arts. 10(1), 23b, 30(3), 151(11), 141). The Constitution of Belgium has a provision on the election date of the European Parliament (Art. 117(2)). The constitutions of Italy, Finland and Austria contain the prohibition of parallel powers in the European Parliament and in state institutions. In terms of other issues arising in connection with the separation of powers, the constitutions of Germany,

---

in the New Member States: Ironies in the Light of the Pre-accession Conditionality', in U. Bernitz and J. Nergelius, eds., *The General Principles of European Community Law* (The Hague, Kluwer Law International 2008) pp. 281-301.

[65] See, e.g., Xuereb, *loc. cit.* n. 50, at p. 412 with regard to Malta, and the contribution by I. Jarukaitis in the present volume with regard to Lithuania.

[66] For a comparative overview of scrutiny mechanisms, see P. Kiiver, *The National Parliaments in the European Union: A Critical View on EU Constitution-Building* (The Hague, Kluwer Law International 2006).

Austria, Belgium, Portugal and Italy have introduced provisions on the participation of federal subdivisions, autonomous regions and/or local municipalities in EU affairs. The constitutions of Austria (Art. 23c) and Portugal (Art. 164p) regulate the national nomination of EU officials. The Constitution of Finland assigns EU issues to the Government's competence, while representation in foreign affairs had hitherto fallen under the President's responsibility (Art. 93). The German Constitution contains a provision on the administration of EC taxes at the federal level (Art. 108(1)).

Amongst the new Member States, the issue of parliamentary control prompted amendments in a substantial number of countries: Lithuania (Constitutional Act of 2004, para. 3), the Czech Republic (Art. 10b), Romania (Art. 148(5)), Bulgaria (Art. 105), Slovenia (Art. 3a(4)) and Hungary (Arts. 35(1) and 35A). The provisions are similar in content and will not be reproduced here. In broad lines, they confer on the parliaments the right to be informed and consulted by the Government, often providing that a more detailed relationship is to be regulated by a special law. The European Parliament finds mention in Hungary and Slovakia. In Hungary, Article 30A(1) provides that the President shall announce the general elections of the members of Parliament as well as European parliamentary elections, and contains some other provisions on the European Parliament, which will be considered in the next section. In Slovakia, the post-accession amendments of 14 May 2005 prohibit simultaneous membership in the European Parliament and the Slovak Parliament, and enable the Constitutional Court to decide whether elections to the European Parliament were legitimate. No provisions within the text of the constitutions on these important aspects of exercise of powers can be found in Poland, Estonia, Latvia, Malta and Cyprus.

Amongst other issues, the need to facilitate implementation of EU measures has prompted amendments in some countries, as the constitutions typically reserve certain areas of regulation for parliamentary legislation. The importance of the provisions facilitating implementation by governmental decrees was clearly demonstrated by the Hungarian Constitutional Court's *Sugar Stocks* case, where the constitutional requirement that tax obligations can be imposed by parliamentary legislation only led to a delay in implementing an EU measure and to the consequent annulment of the implementing measure on the grounds of the principle of non-retroactivity.[67] Thus far only Slovakia, Lithuania and Romania have such provisions in place. In Slovakia, Article 120(2) of the Constitution facilitates the implementation of EU obligations, authorising the Government to issue decrees in order to execute obligations under EU Treaties. In addition, Article 13(1) permits the imposition of duties on citizens by government decrees under the above-mentioned Article 120(2), as well as by international treaties under Article 7(4). A provision on implementation of EU obligations was also introduced in Lithuania's Constitutional Act on EU Membership. In Romania, Article 148(4) provides that the Parliament, the President of Romania, the Government, and the judicial authorities should guarantee that the obligations resulting from the Accession Act and the provisions of Article 148(2) are implemented. In the Czech Republic and Hungary, provisions to this effect were under consideration, but their adoption did not succeed.

---

[67] See Sajó, *loc. cit.* n. 61.

5.        FREE MOVEMENT OF EU CITIZENS

5.1.        **Voting rights of EU citizens**

In constitutional law textbooks, voting rights have traditionally been presented as an inextricable bond between citizens and the sovereign nation-state, and it is typical for constitutions to reserve voting rights for national citizens only. The Treaty of Maastricht, which introduced the concept of EU citizenship, opened the voting rights up to transnational levels. Article 19 EC Treaty provides that every citizen of the Union residing in a Member State of which he is not a national shall have the right to vote and stand as a candidate in municipal elections and elections to the European Parliament.[68] It comes as no surprise that such an unprecedented move prompted amendments in a considerable number of countries. Indeed in France, the Constitutional Council held in the *Maastricht* decision[69] that EU citizens' electoral rights in local elections encroach upon the essential conditions of national sovereignty and are incompatible with Article 3 of the Constitution, which provides that national sovereignty belongs to the people and that only French nationals form the electorate. This led to a corresponding amendment of the French Constitution (Art. 88(3)). A similar scenario unfolded in Spain: Article 13(2) of the Constitution of Spain was amended prior to the ratification of the Treaty of Maastricht to allow the citizens of other states to vote and stand in the elections, under the conditions provided in the treaties.[70] The right to participate in local elections also necessitated an amendment in Germany (Art. 28(1)), Portugal (Art. 15(5)), Austria (Arts. 23a and 117(2)) and Belgium (Art. 8(3)). Additionally, the Portuguese and Austrian constitutions stipulate the EU citizens' right to stand and vote in the elections to the European Parliament.

The opening up of voting rights to citizens from other countries also prompted amendments in a number of new Member States and led to judicial litigation in some of the countries that failed to do so. By way of an introductory synopsis, provisions on the voting rights of EU citizens in local elections were introduced in Hungary (Art. 70(2)), Romania (Art. 16(4)), Bulgaria (Art. 42(3)) and Latvia (Art. 101), with Slovakia (Art. 30(1)) and Lithuania (Art. 119) extending the voting rights not only to EU citizens but to all permanent residents. The participation in the European Parliament elections of resident EU citizens received explicit mention in the amendments in Bulgaria (Art. 42(3)) and Hungary (Art. 70(4)).

The most far-reaching provisions regarding electoral rights were put in place in Hungary. Article 70(2) of the Hungarian Constitution grants EU citizens the right to be elected and to vote in local elections and notably extends the right to participation in referenda and popular initiatives; however only Hungarian citizens are allowed to stand

---

[68]  See further J. Shaw, *The Transformation of Citizenship in the European Union Electoral Rights and the Restructuring of Political Space* (Cambridge, Cambridge University Press 2007).

[69]  Decision No. 92-308 DC, 09 April 1992, available at http://www.conseil-constitutionnel.fr/decision/1992/92308dc.htm. For comment, see, *inter alia*, Bonnie, *loc. cit.* n. 24, pp. 517-532.

[70]  Despite this provision, the Spanish Constitution was placed into the first group of constitutions in section 1 of this chapter because its text contains no explicit mention of the EU.

as candidates for mayors. Unlike other new Member States' constitutions, several provisions address issues surrounding elections to the European Parliament. Article 70(4) grants voting rights to this end to both Hungarian nationals and resident EU citizens; Article 71(1) provides that members of the European Parliament 'are elected by direct, secret ballot by voting citizens, based on their universal and equal right to vote'; and Article 71(3) envisages the adoption of a separate law on elections to the European Parliament.

In Latvia, Article 101 was amended to allow EU citizens to vote in local elections; the amendment entered into force after accession in October 2004. This amendment is of broader interest for the reason that no such rights are enjoyed by a sizeable body of so-called non-citizens, mainly the Russian-speaking persons who have not acquired Latvian citizenship despite having lived in the country for a long time. By contrast, the voting rights in local elections were extended to all foreigners with permanent residence in Lithuania (Art. 119) and Slovakia (Art. 30(1) but without the right to stand for elected offices (Art. 30(4)).[71]

In Bulgaria and Romania, the adoption of a special law on voting rights of EU citizens is envisaged under the amendments. In addition, in Romania, Article 38 provides that 'After Romania's accession to the European Union, Romanian citizens shall have the right to elect and be elected for the European Parliament', with EU citizens somewhat curiously receiving no separate mention.

No amendments on electoral rights were put in place in the constitutions of Poland, Estonia, Slovenia, the Czech Republic, Cyprus and Malta; in these countries, the constitutions afford some room for interpretation. For example, the Constitution of Slovenia permits determining by a statute the voting rights of foreigners, containing thereby an exception to the general rule that the right to active and passive suffrage belongs to the citizens (Arts. 43 and 44). In the Czech Constitution, Article 100(1) defines the units of territorial self-administration as 'territorial communities of citizens', which leaves room for interpretation. Nonetheless, given the constitutional importance of voting rights, the rights of EU citizens would have merited recognition at the constitutional level; in particular, the countries which introduced amendments on the issue of the voting rights of EU citizens in the European Parliament elections remained very limited in number.

The absence of amendments on these issues led to legal challenges in Poland and Estonia. Prior to accession, both had seen unsuccessful calls for amendment; in Poland Article 62(1) provides that voting rights in local elections are the preserve of the Polish citizens.[72] This led to a case, decided on 31 May 2004, where a group of members of the *Sejm* (lower house of Parliament) argued that the Elections to the European Parliament Act 2004 was unconstitutional, on the grounds that the participation of foreign nationals was in conflict with the principle of the sovereignty of the Polish people (Art. 4(1) of the Constitution), as well as with the clauses that grant the right to

---

[71] In Estonia, non-citizens who have permanent residence have the right to vote in local elections under ordinary legislation.

[72] See, *inter alia*, Wójtowicz, *loc. cit.* n. 27, at pp. 40-44, and Biernat, *loc. cit.* n. 27, at p. 445. See also Chapter 9 in this volume.

vote to Polish citizens only. The Constitutional Tribunal rejected the claim, underlining the importance of the constitutional principle mandating an EU-friendly interpretation of national law.[73] Subsequently, the constitutionality of the right of EU citizens to participate in local elections was tested in the *Accession Treaty* case.[74] Here the Court dismissed the claim on the grounds that the above-mentioned Article 4 (on the sovereignty of the Polish people) does not encompass local elections, and Article 62(1), which guarantees to the Polish citizens the right to elect, *inter alia*, their representatives to local self-government bodies, does not preclude the possibility of also granting the right to the citizens of other states.

In Estonia, the legal challenge concerned the ambiguity surrounding the right to belong to political parties: Article 48 of the Constitution confines the membership of political parties to Estonian citizens only. An equivalent rule is in place in Slovakia (Art. 29(2)) and Lithuania (Art. 35). Such provisions may diminish the practical effectiveness of the right of EU citizens to vote and stand in the elections to the European Parliament and local councils. Such a claim was put to the Constitutional Review Chamber of the Estonian Supreme Court in 2005 by the Chancellor of Justice,[75] who argued that a provision of the Political Parties Act 1994, which confines the eligibility for membership in political parties to Estonian citizens only, was unconstitutional when reading the above-mentioned Article 48 of the Constitution together with the Act Supplementing the Constitution, as well as being in conflict with Article 19 EC. That is because the contested provision would not, in effect, ensure equal opportunities for an EU citizen who stands as a candidate in local elections. The petition was dismissed on procedural grounds: no legal basis existed for declaring a national law invalid *in abstracto* on the grounds of a conflict with EC law. Nonetheless, this area may well be in need of further clarification; a dissenting opinion expressed the view that a preliminary ruling to this end ought to have been requested from the European Court of Justice.

## 5.2.    The sale of real estate

The requirement to remove the ban on the sale of real estate for non-nationals appears to be an area where virtually no amendments have been prompted in the old Member States but which has affected a considerable number of new Member States. This requirement, which has its origin in the ECJ case law on freedom of establishment under Article 43 EC and free movement of capital under Article 56 EC,[76] was explicitly put to Bulgaria and Romania by the European Commission in its *Avis* and annual Progress Reports.[77]

---

[73] Constitutional Tribunal, 31 May 2004, Case K 15/04 (*re Conformity of the Law on Elections to the European Parliament with the Constitution*), OTK Z.U. 2004/5A/47. See further Chapter 9 in this volume.

[74] Judgment of 11 May 2005 in Case K 18/04, *loc. cit.* n. 2.

[75] Decision No. 3-4-1-1-05 of 19 April 2005, available at http://www.nc.ee. The Chancellor of Justice is an institution similar to ombudsman; he has the right to initiate constitutional review proceedings in the Constitutional Chamber of the Supreme Court.

[76] ECJ, Case C-305/97 *Commission of the European Communities v. Greece* [1989] *ECR* 1461; Case C-302/97 *Klaus Konle v. Republik Österreich* [1999] *ECR* I-3099.

[77] European Commission, Opinion on Romania's Application for EU Membership, Brussels, July 1997, at p. 81.

Consequently, this issue led to amendments in Slovenia, Lithuania, Romania and Bulgaria; the texts of the other constitutions contained no direct conflict in this respect. In Slovenia and Lithuania, the issue came up first in the context of ratification of the respective Europe Agreements.[78] In order to be able to ratify the Europe Agreement, Slovenia revised in 1997 Article 68 of the Constitution, which at the time provided that foreigners may not acquire land except by inheritance in circumstances where reciprocity of such rights is recognised. The amendment provided that foreigners may acquire ownership rights to real estate under the condition of reciprocity. On the eve of EU membership, the amendment of this Article came up again, with Slovenia having to abolish the principle of reciprocity from Article 68 of the Constitution.[79] In Lithuania, Article 47 of the Constitution was first reformulated in June 1996 so as to allow foreigners to acquire non-agricultural land. In January 2003, this provision was further amended to also enable the sale of agricultural land to EU citizens. However, the land sale will effectively become possible as of 2011, due to the seven-year transitional period pursuant to the Accession Treaty 2003. Romania and Bulgaria had been granted under the Europe Agreements transitional periods for the sale of land to EU citizens. Prior to EU accession, Bulgaria amended Article 22 of the Constitution, by providing that:

> 'Foreigners and foreign legal persons may acquire property over land under the conditions ensuing from Bulgaria's accession to the European Union, or by virtue of an international treaty that has been ratified, published and entered into force for the Republic of Bulgaria, as well as through inheritance by operation of the law.'

In Romania, Article 41(2) of the Constitution introduces the possibility for foreigners to acquire land 'under the terms resulting from Romania's accession to the European Union and other international treaties Romania is party to, on a mutual basis, as well as a result of lawful inheritance.' Despite these amendments, both countries are able to retain transitional periods for certain types of real estate under the Accession Treaty 2005.[80]

---

[78] Europe Agreement establishing an Association between the European Communities and their Member States, of the one part, and the Republic of Lithuania, of the other part, *OJ* 1998 L 51/3; Europe Agreement establishing an association between the European Communities and their Member States, acting within the framework of the European Union, of the one part, and the Republic of Slovenia, of the other part, *OJ* 1999 L 51/3.

[79] See further Chapter 13 in this volume.

[80] Treaty between the Kingdom of Belgium, the Czech Republic, the Kingdom of Denmark, the Federal Republic of Germany, the Republic of Estonia, the Hellenic Republic, the Kingdom of Spain, the French Republic, Ireland, the Italian Republic, the Republic of Cyprus, the Republic of Latvia, the Republic of Lithuania, the Grand Duchy of Luxembourg, the Republic of Hungary, the Republic of Malta, the Kingdom of the Netherlands, the Republic of Austria, the Republic of Poland, the Portuguese Republic, the Republic of Slovenia, the Slovak Republic, the Republic of Finland, the Kingdom of Sweden, the United Kingdom of Great Britain and Northern Ireland (Member States of the European Union) and the Republic of Bulgaria and Romania, concerning the accession of the Republic of Bulgaria and Romania to the European Union, *OJ* 2005 L 157/11. For details, see, *inter alia*, A. Łazowski and S. Yosifova, 'Bulgaria', in S. Blockmans and A. Łazowski, eds., *The European Union and its Neighbours. A Legal Appraisal of*

## 5.3.    Public service and social rights

This subsection will briefly flag some issues surrounding work in public service and the social rights of migrant EU citizens, which have prompted no amendments but may need consideration in the future. The effectiveness of the EU citizens' right to non-discrimination when exercising free movement may necessitate revision or broad interpretation of constitutional provisions that entitle only citizens to work in public service[81] and to the social security rights, such as state assistance in the case of old age, unemployment, disability and medical aid.[82] Regarding work in public service, which can be exempted from the equal treatment rules under Article 39(4) EC, ECJ case law shows that the scope of public service is interpreted narrowly. It includes only positions involving the exercise of public powers, and the exemption from equal treatment only applies to the admission to a post, without extending to subsequent employment.[83] As far as the entitlement to social welfare is concerned, Article 7(2) of Regulation 1612/68/EEC provides for equal treatment of migrant EU workers in all social and tax advantages,[84] and Article 24(1) of Directive 2004/38/EC provides for equal treatment of migrant EU citizens as long as the person does not become an unreasonable burden on the host state's social security system.[85] These rules may thus necessitate adjustment of some constitutional provisions of the new Member States.

## 5.4.    Extradition of own citizens

One area where the incompatibility between national constitutional provisions and EU law has led to a number of high-profile clashes is the extradition of national citizens under the Framework Decision on the European Arrest Warrant.[86] This area has seen Constitutional Court judgments in a number of countries; the judgments are considered

---

the EU's Policies of Stabilisation, Partnership and Integration (The Hague, T.M.C. Asser Press 2006) pp. 207-246, at p. 237.

[81] For example, work in public service is confined to citizens in the Constitutions of Slovakia (Art. 30(4)), Hungary (Art. 70(4)), Latvia (Art. 101), Lithuania (Art. 33) and Poland (Art. 60).

[82] See provisions in constitutions of Slovenia Art. 50(1); Slovakia (Arts. 35(3) and 39(1)), Hungary (Art. 70/E(1)); Lithuania (Art. 52); Bulgaria (Arts. 51(1), 52 and 58(1); Poland (Arts. 67(1)) and 67(2)).

[83] See, inter alia, ECJ, Case 149/79 Commission of the European Communities v. Belgium [1980] ECR 3881; ECJ, Case 152/73 Giovanni Maria Sotgiu v. Deutsche Bundespost [1979] ECR 153.

[84] Regulation (EEC) No 1612/68 of the Council of 15 October 1968 on freedom of movement for workers within the Community, OJ 1968 L 257/2.

[85] Directive 2004/38/EC of the European Parliament and of the Council of 29 April 2004 on the right of citizens of the Union and their family members to move and reside freely within the territory of the Member States amending Regulation (EEC) No 1612/68 and repealing Directives 64/221/EEC, 68/360/EEC, 72/194/EEC, 73/148/EEC, 75/34/EEC, 75/35/EEC, 90/364/EEC, 90/365/EEC and 93/96/EEC, OJ 2004 L 158/77. See also ECJ, Case C-184/99 Rudy Grzelczyk v. Centre public d'aide sociale d'Ottignies-Louvain-la-Neuve [2001] ECR I-6193.

[86] Council Framework Decision 2002/584/JHA of 13 June 2002 on the European arrest warrant and the surrender procedures between Member States, OJ 2002 L 190/1. For an academic appraisal see, inter alia, N. Keizer and E. van Sliedregt, eds., The European Arrest Warrant in Practice (The Hague, T.M.C. Asser Press 2009).

in greater detail in other contributions to this volume.[87] In broad lines, four highest courts identified incompatibilities between the requirement to surrender own nationals and the domestic Constitutions: the Polish and Cypriot courts did so on the grounds that their Constitutions did not allow extradition, while in France and Germany, a breach of fundamental rights was established. This led to amendments of extradition provisions in Poland and Cyprus and to the creation of a general basis for extradition pursuant to EAW in France (Art. 88(2) of the Constitution).

Poland had seen prior to accession several calls for amending Articles 52(4) and 55 of the Constitution.[88] The latter provided in an explicit and unconditional manner that 'The extradition of a Polish citizen shall be forbidden.' As already noted, the amendment eventually occurred after accession following the Constitutional Tribunal's European Arrest Warrant judgment.[89] While the Tribunal declared the national implementing provisions unconstitutional, it did not put an end to extradition, granting instead an 18-month transitional period to Parliament, during which the Constitution was to be amended and the surrender of the Polish nationals was to continue. Thus Article 55 was amended on 8 September 2006, maintaining the ban on extradition subject, however, to exceptions set forth in international treaties.[90] A similar scenario unfolded in Cyprus: the Supreme Court annulled on 7 November 2005 the national implementing law on the basis of reasoning that closely followed the Polish judgment. Consequently, the Cypriot Constitution, which had not hitherto been amended in relation to EU membership, underwent a revision on 1 July 2006, with the introduction of Article 1A on supremacy of EU law as seen earlier in this Chapter.[91] Additionally, Article 11 of the Constitution was amended in order to allow for surrender of citizens under the European Arrest Warrant.

The issue of constitutionality of extradition was also considered by the Czech Constitutional Court. In the Czech Charter of Fundamental Rights, which forms a part of the Czech constitutional order, Article 14(4) prohibits forcing a citizen to leave his or her country, and it had earlier been commented that there is a conflict in this respect

---

[87] See also, *inter alia*, E. Guild, ed., *Constitutional Challenges to the European Arrest Warrant* (Nijmegen, Wolf Legal Publishers 2006)

[88] See, *inter alia*, Wójtowicz, *loc. cit.* n. 27, at pp. 40-44, and Biernat, *loc. cit.* n. 27, at p. 455.

[89] A. Nußberger, 'Poland: The Constitutional Tribunal on the implementation of the European Arrest Warrant', 6 *I·CON* (2008) pp. 162-170; A. Łazowski, 'Constitutional Tribunal on the Surrender of Polish Citizens Under the European Arrest Warrant. Decision of 27 April 2005', 1 *EuConst* (2005) pp. 569-581; A. Wyrozumska, 'Some Comments on the Judgments of the Polish Constitutional Tribunal on the EU Accession Treaty and on the Implementation of the European Arrest Warrant', 27 *PolYBIL* (2004-2005) pp. 5-31; D. Leczykiewicz, 'Trybunal Konstytucyjny (Polish Constitutional Tribunal), Judgment of 27 April 2005, No. P 1/05', 43 *CMLRev.* (2006) pp. 1181-1192.

[90] For an in-depth analysis of this constitutional development, see A. Łazowski, 'From EU with Trust: the Potential and Limits of the Mutual Recognition in the Third Pillar from the Polish Perspective', in G. Vernimmen-Van Tiggelen, L. Surano, A. Weyembergh, eds., *The future of mutual recognition in criminal matters in the European Union / L'avenir de la reconnaissance mutuelle en matière pénale dans l'Union européenne* (Bruxelles, Editions de l'Université de Bruxelles 2009) pp. 419-444, at pp. 432-434.

[91] See further Chapter 15 in this volume.

with the European Arrest Warrant Framework Decision.[92] The Czech Constitutional Court decided the case on 3 May 2006, finding that Article 14(4) of the Charter does not preclude a temporary surrender of the Czech citizens under the European Arrest Warrant, when interpreting the provision in conformity with EU obligations.[93]

Several other new Member States had decided to amend the provisions on extradition prior to accession. While retaining the general ban on extradition, the amendments to the constitutions of Slovenia (Art. 47), Romania (Art. 19(1)) and Bulgaria (Art. 25(4)) provide an exception where so required by a ratified international treaty. In Slovakia, Article 23(4) earlier provided that a citizen 'must not be forced to leave his homeland and he must not be deported or extradited'; Constitutional Act No. 90/2001 repealed the word "extradite" so as to enable the implementation of the Framework Decision on the European Arrest Warrant. In Latvia, the prohibition to extradite Latvian citizens in Article 98 was amended after accession on 23 September 2004, providing that:

> 'A citizen of Latvia may not be extradited to a foreign country, except in the cases provided for in international agreements ratified by the Saeima if by the extradition the basic human rights specified in the Constitution are not violated.'

Amongst the remaining countries (Estonia, Hungary, Malta, Lithuania), the potential for a constitutional conflict has been alluded to in Hungary and Estonia. In Hungary, Article 69(1) of the Constitution stipulates that a Hungarian national cannot be expelled from the country.[94] Although the Estonian Constitution allows extradition of citizens under the conditions prescribed by international treaties, it has been pointed out that Article 36 of the Constitution subjects extradition to the Government's decision, whereas a judicial decision is required under the European Arrest Warrant system.[95] The Lithuanian Constitution does not appear to be incompatible with the European Arrest Warrant because Article 13(2), albeit generally prohibiting the extradition of citizens, does allow for the extradition of citizens where so provided by international treaties concluded by Lithuania.[96]

---

[92] I. Šlosarčík and S. Klouckova, 'Czech Republic', in *Criminal Law in the European Union: A Giant Leap or A Small Step? – FIDE 2004 National Reports*, http://www.fide2004.org/reports/mc/mc04b.pdf, at p. 46.

[93] Constitutional Court of the Czech Republic, 3 May 2006 (*Re Constitutionality of Framework Decision on the European Arrest Warrant*) [2007] 3 C.M.L.R. 24.

[94] For a view according to which this provision may be in need of amendment, see J. Czuczai, 'Hungary', in Kellermann et al., *op. cit.* n. 49, at p. 348.

[95] K. Raba, 'Estonia', in *Criminal Law in the European Union: A Giant Leap or A Small Step? – FIDE 2004 National Reports*, http://www.fide2004.org/reports/mc/mc06b.pdf, pp. 89-90.

[96] V. Vadapalas, 'Lithuania' in *Criminal Law in the European Union: A Giant Leap or A Small Step? – FIDE* 2004, http://www.fide2004.org/reports/mc/mc13b.pdf, at p. 197.

6.        ECONOMIC AND MONETARY UNION

Associated with a state's authority and national identity, the control over national currency has traditionally formed yet another core area of sovereignty,[97] and it is regulated in some form in most constitutions. In comparison with many other policy areas
where the Member States have delegated to the EU some prerogatives, the entrance
into the Economic and Monetary Union means a complete, albeit progressive, surrender of monetary competences.[98] As with the voting rights of EU citizens, the French
*Conseil Constitutionnel* spelled out in the *Maastricht* decision that the EMU affects the
'essential conditions of exercise of national sovereignty' and therefore necessitates a
constitutional amendment prior to ratifying the Treaty. Amongst other old Member
States,[99] the UK and Denmark have negotiated an opt-out from the single currency,
while Sweden has a formal obligation to join the Eurozone although this has been put
on hold following its 2003 referendum. Of the twelve participating old Member States,
provisions to this effect are found in the constitutions of Germany, France, Portugal
and Greece. By way of example, Article 88(2) of the French Constitution provides that
'France consents to the transfers of competences necessary for the establishment of the
Economic and Monetary Union.' In Germany, Article 88, which was equally amended
prior to the ratification of the Maastricht Treaty, provides that the Federal Bank's 'tasks
and powers can ... be transferred to the European Central Bank which is independent
and primarily bound by the purpose of securing the stability of prices.'
      For the new Member States, the adoption of the euro constitutes an obligation
rather than an option once the criteria are fulfilled. The criteria have indeed been fulfilled
by Slovenia, which adopted the common currency on 1 January 2007, Cyprus and Malta
(1 January 2008) and Slovakia (1 January 2009), bringing the number of Eurozone
countries to sixteen. None of the above countries has introduced special EMU-related
amendments. The only countries to have hitherto amended their constitutions are
Lithuania, Hungary and Romania. In Lithuania, the second paragraph of Article 125,
which provided that 'the right of issue of currency shall belong exclusively to the Bank
of Lithuania', was abrogated on 25 April 2006. In Hungary, Article 32D(1), which
previously provided that the National Bank 'is responsible for issuing legal tender,
protecting the stability of the national currency and regulating the circulation of
money', was reformulated regarding the role of the National Bank and provides for the
adoption of a special law. In Romania, the amended version of Article 136(2) provides
that:

      'Under the circumstances of Romania's accession to the European Union, the circulation and
      replacement of the national currency by that of the European Union may be acknowledged,
      by means of an organic law.'

---

[97] A. Chirico, *La soveranita monetaria tra ordine giuridico e processo economico* (Padova, CEDAM
2003) at p. 139.
[98] Chirico, *op. cit.* n. 97, at p. 144.
[99] On the national constitutional ramifications of EMU, see A. Albi, 'Common Currency and National
Constitutions,' in F. Torres, et al., eds., *EMU Rules: The Political and Legal Consequences of European
Monetary Integration* (Baden-Baden, Nomos 2006) pp. 69-80.

In Poland and Estonia, which had seen calls for amendment of the monetary provisions, the decision not to amend prompted litigation. In Poland, Article 227(1) of the Constitution bestows upon the National Bank of Poland the exclusive right to issue the Polish currency, to formulate the monetary policy and to safeguard the value of the Polish currency. The compatibility of this provision with the Accession Treaty 2003 was contested by the applicants in the *Accession Treaty* case. While rejecting the applicants' claim on the ground that Article 105 EC that deals with EMU matters is not of a self-executing nature, the Tribunal stated that once Poland adopts the common currency in the future, a decision may well be required to amend the Polish Constitution in this respect. In Estonia, the European Commission requested the revision of Article 111, which sets out the Bank of Estonia's exclusive right to issue Estonia's currency; however, the Government insisted that Article 111 does not preclude the adoption of the common currency when read together with the Act Supplementing the Constitution. Consequently, Parliament requested the opinion of the Constitutional Chamber of the Estonian Supreme Court on this matter. The Constitutional Chamber, in already mentioned case No. 3-4-1-3-06, held on 11 May 2006 that Article 111 indeed posed no obstacles to the adoption of the euro, since the text of the Constitution is to be read together with the Act Supplementing the Constitution; as a result, those parts of the Constitution that are incompatible with EC law are not to be applied. Some commentators pointed out that in this case, the Court was placed under considerable political pressure, with the Chairman of Parliament openly indicating that a result favourable to the adoption of the euro was expected from the Supreme Court.[100]

The monetary provisions in the constitutions of the Czech Republic, Slovakia and Slovenia are worded broadly enough as to leave a sufficient margin for interpretation and expressly allow making changes by laws rather than requiring amendment of the constitutions. For instance, in Slovakia, Article 56 provides that the Republic 'establishes a bank of issue'. The Czech Constitution provides that the Czech National Bank 'is the central bank of the State', and '[i]ts activities are primarily oriented towards currency stability' (Art. 98(1)). However, as with Poland and Estonia, the obligation to safeguard "currency stability" in the Czech Constitution may need revision so as to replace this obligation with the safeguarding of price stability. This could, however, be put into effect by means of a law rather than requiring a constitutional amendment. In Latvia, the rather laconically worded Constitution does not regulate monetary issues.

## 7.    OTHER SELECTED ISSUES

In this section, a handful of other areas which hold the potential for conflict will be flagged for a more detailed discussion in the future.

---

[100] U. Lõhmus, 'Euroopa Liidu õigussüsteem ja põhiseaduslikkuse kontroll pärast 1. maid 2004' ['European Union Legal System and Constitutional Supervision after 1 May 2004'], 1 *Juridica* (2006) pp. 3-16, at p. 13.

The first remark concerns the ratification of the Lisbon Treaty. Space will not allow us to consider this area in greater detail. However, it appears striking that of the twenty-seven Member States, only France has amended its Constitution in view of ratification (doing so prior to the ratification of both the Constitutional Treaty and the Lisbon Treaty), with Ireland set to do.[101] Additionally, it would be in order to note that in the case of Romania and Bulgaria, the Accession Treaty[102] formally referred to the Constitutional Treaty, providing that '[i]n the event that the Treaty establishing a Constitution for Europe is not in force on the date of accession', these countries 'become Parties to the Treaties on which the Union is founded, as amended or supplemented' (Art. 1.2 of the Accession Treaty 2005). In addition, the Romanian Constitution could also be regarded as containing a clear basis for ratification, as paragraphs 1 and 2 of Article 148 on the transfer of powers to the EU and on the precedence of EC law 'shall also apply ... for the accession to the acts revising the constituent treaties of the European Union' (Art. 148(3)).

The second area worth flagging concerns the independence of the judiciary, a new area where the European Commission has actively called for amendment in some countries, in particular Bulgaria, Romania and Slovakia.[103] This requirement formed part of the broader Copenhagen political criteria and was partly mandated by the concerns surrounding the mutual recognition and trust in enforcement of EU law.

Third, intricate issues have arisen with regard to the constitutional provisions which proclaim the status of the national language as the official language and provide that only published laws are binding. For example, a preliminary ruling was sought from the Czech Republic for clarification about the status of those parts of EU legislation that were not published in the national language in time for accession.[104] In addition, Estonia has seen domestic litigation as to whether private parties could be expected to be aware of certain EU legislation prior to accession, under the Accession Treaty alone.[105] Here it may be pertinent to note that the Czech Republic and Slovakia introduced amendments that envisage the adoption of a special law on the publication of EU law (Art. 87(4) of the Slovak Constitution) and of international agreements (Art. 52 of the Czech Constitution). The importance attached to the protection of the national languages by some new Member States is demonstrated by developments in Latvia, where

---

[101] For a more detailed discussion, see A. Albi, 'Introduction: The European Constitution and National Constitutions in the Context of "Post-national Constitutionalism"', in A. Albi and J. Ziller, eds., *The European Constitution and National Constitutions: Ratification and Beyond* (The Hague, Kluwer Law International 2006) pp. 1-14.

[102] For a legal appraisal see A. Łazowski, 'And Then They Were Twenty-Seven... A Legal Appraisal of the Sixth Accession Treaty', 44 *CMLRev.* (2007) pp. 401-430.

[103] For a detailed analysis of the European Commission's Annual Opinions regarding the reform of the judiciary, see D. Kochenov, *EU Enlargement and the Failure of Conditionality. Pre-accession Conditionality in the Fields of Democracy and the Rule of Law* (Austin, Boston, Chicago, New York, The Netherlands, Wolters Kluwer 2008).

[104] See M. Bobek, 'The Binding Force of Babel: The Enforcement of EC Law Unpublished in the Languages of the New Member States', 9 *CYELS* (2006-2007), pp. 43-80. See also Chapters 4 and 5 in this volume.

[105] For details, see A. Albi, 'Supremacy of EC Law in the New Member States: Bringing Parliaments into the Equation of "Co-operative constitutionalism"', 3 *EuConst* (2007) pp. 25-67.

the position of the national language was strengthened by virtue of two constitutional amendments in 1998 and 2001, and Estonia, where an amendment to the Preamble of the Constitution was adopted in April 2007 to add to the list of the State's obligations the duty to protect the Estonian language, besides the pre-existing obligation to protect the Estonian culture and identity.

The fourth area that merits flagging is the protection of fundamental rights. One characteristic of the CEE constitutions lies in detailed, extensive catalogues of fundamental rights, which have been vigorously protected by the Constitutional Courts, with a high ratio of annulment of legislative acts. In this respect, areas where the national legislation implements EU law may pose considerable difficulties, as the level of protection by the European Court of Justice is notoriously low; some early cases where the contrast has become conspicuous have been explored by the author elsewhere.[106] As noted above in section 3.2, the Constitutional Courts of Poland and the Czech Republic have made the acceptance of supremacy of EC law over their national constitutions conditional upon the adequate protection of fundamental rights and the principles of rule of law and democracy.

## 8.    CONCLUDING REMARKS: WHY DO EU AMENDMENTS MATTER?

This chapter sought to identify areas where there appears to be crystallising practice in terms of potential need for amendment of the national constitutions, depending on different circumstances surrounding individual constitutions and the general constitutional culture in the individual Member States. It was seen that the initially unsatisfactory picture in the new Member States has shown considerable improvement after accession, partly in result of judgments of the Constitutional and Supreme Courts. This raises the question that is often posed, especially by those more attuned to political realities surrounding the amendment of constitutions, as to "why fix it if it ain't broken", i.e., why embark on a cumbersome amendment process if the constitution has proved generally to work well in practice. While the shortcomings in the adaptation of the constitutions are, as seen above, a matter of national discretion and will trigger no sanctions from the EU, they do have important ramifications for the states' internal legal system, which will subsequently be briefly outlined.

First and foremost, this chapter began by considering the implications for the judiciary. It is hoped that the different sections of the chapter showed that an inadequate constitutional framework may place an excessive burden upon the Constitutional Courts in adjudicating conflicts between national law and EU law and shift their framework of reference from the legal and constitutional requirements to considerations of political and European expediency. It was seen that on some occasions, genuine limits may well exist to EU-friendly interpretation, and that the courts have instead engaged in a dialogue with national parliaments with regard to the need to remove manifest conflicts with EU law from the national constitutions. With the hands of the courts thus being

---

[106] *Ibidem.*

tied by the constraints of EU membership, the role of political institutions, especially parliaments, assumes particular importance in the European "cooperative constitutionalism" in terms of exercising self-control and extra prudence when drafting constitutional amendments.[107]

Second, the spectre of devaluation of national constitutions looms in the case of inadequate amendments. Are constitutions taken seriously in the context of the ever-increasing Europeanisation of governance, or have they perhaps in part been reduced to paper tigers? Bruno De Witte coined the notion of "European deficit" in the national constitutions, pointing to the fact that constitutions might be gradually becoming somewhat obsolete with regard to the realities in the exercise of powers.[108] In Denmark, where the Constitution in 2009 still contains no explicit mention of the EU, and the courts rarely exercise constitutional review, Hjalte Rasmussen has noted a trend towards "waning constitutionalism" and "constitutional amorphousness."[109]

In terms of the extent of the amendment, it should be borne in mind that constitutions in general have been classified into two main types – "historic" and "revolutionary."[110] The former, which include, for example, the UK and Dutch Constitutions, have developed incrementally over a long-term period, being non-formalistic and at least as much political in nature as legal. By contrast, the latter group of constitutions, which include, for instance, those of Germany, Italy, France and Ireland, tend to have their origin in a political or social cataclysm, which forms the "moving myth" that inspires the constitution. These constitutions create the political reality and tend to have a distinctly legal character, being enforced by Constitutional Courts.[111] The constitutions of Central and Eastern Europe clearly belong in the second group: as a reaction to the Communist period marked by nihilism to constitutional rules, they have a distinctly legal character, are relatively lengthy and detailed and their observance is rigorously policed by powerful Constitutional Courts, with a high ratio of annulment of legislative acts.[112] It is clear that adequate EU amendments assume greater importance in the case of those countries whose constitutions are revolutionary in nature, if the constitutional culture is to be preserved.

Third, adequate EU amendments simply enhance legal certainty and clarity for the citizens and provide a greater legitimacy for the transfers of powers to the supranational level.

---

[107] *Ibidem.*

[108] B. De Witte, 'Constitutional Aspects of European Union Membership in the Original Six Member States: Model Solutions for the Applicant Countries?', in Kellermann, et al., *op. cit.* n. 16, pp. 65-79, at p. 73; see also Claes, *loc. cit.* n. 16.

[109] H. Rasmussen, 'Denmark's Waning Constitutionalism and Article 20 of the Constitution on Transfer of Sovereignty', in Albi and Ziller, eds., *op. cit.* n. 101, pp. 149-156.

[110] See L. Besselink, 'The Dutch Constitution, the European Constitution and the Referendum in the Netherlands', in Albi and Ziller, eds., *op. cit.* n. 101, pp. 113-123.

[111] *Ibidem.*

[112] This argument has been developed in more detail in Albi, *op. cit.* n. 5, at p. 22. See also E. Smith, 'The Constitution as an Instrument of Change: Introduction', in E. Smith, ed., *The Constitution as an Instrument of Change* (Stockholm, SNS Förlag 2003) p. 15.

Finally, the EU amendments have an important channelling effect on legal education and on discourse on constitutionalism. Ample evidence of the importance of constitutional amendments was on offer for anyone observing the amendment process during the last few years in CEE. Whereas much of the constitutional commentary in the 1990s was marked by cherishing the absolute and inalienable sovereignty, a distinct change occurred in the wake of the EU amendments. The talk of transnational governance and supranational democracy markedly entered into the discourse of constitutional lawyers. Crucially, the idea of supranational governance also became part of legal education and modules of constitutional law; this has a fundamental effect on the mindset and framework of thinking for national lawyers and judges.

Against this background, countries which are considering various routes for constitutional amendment, whether as Member States or in the capacity as countries hoping to join in the future, would be well advised to exercise their discretion in favour of those models where constitutions contain a wider set of provisions addressing specifically the EU rather than membership of international organisations in general. The constitutions of Germany, France, Portugal and, amongst the new Member States, those of Slovakia and Romania are particularly well-placed to offer suitable examples to this end. It is worth bearing in mind that the broader nature and credibility of the constitution may well be at stake in choosing the course of action.

*Chapter 4*

# INTERTEMPORAL LEGAL ISSUES IN THE EUROPEAN UNION CASE LAW RELATING TO THE 2004 AND 2007 ACCESSIONS

Saulius Lukas Kalėda*

## 1. INTRODUCTION

Intertemporal law denotes a set of principles relating to the application of law in time, derived from the rule *tempus regit actum*, according to which an act must be assessed in the light of the legal rules contemporaneous with it.[1] The principles guiding the temporal application of successive legal norms gain a particular importance in the context of an extensive legal change.

Accession of states to the European Union and the ensuing extension of EU law to new Member States bring about a very important legal transformation. Its consequences are broadly addressed in the case law of the European Court of Justice, enriched and developed on the occasion of each enlargement of the EC and the EU. The recent accessions added a number of new developments to that case law, which may be systemised around two main areas concerning the legal issues relating, on the one hand, to the period immediately preceding accession and, on the other, to the application of European Union law in the new Member States after their accession.

## 2. LEGAL ISSUES CONCERNING THE PERIOD PRECEDING ACCESSION

### 2.1. "Interim period"

Accession of a state to the EU is based on an international agreement concluded pursuant to Article 49(2) TEU. An accession treaty, which includes an act of accession, its annexes and protocols, is a complex document setting the basic principles of accession, containing adaptations to European Union primary and secondary law, as well as tran-

---

* Legal secretary at the Court of First Instance of the European Communities. The views expressed in this article are those of the author alone.

[1] See, with regard to international law, the resolutions adopted by the Institute of International Law in 1975, 'Intertemporal Problem in Public International Law', and 1981, 'The Problem of Choice of Time in Private International Law', available at http://www.idi-iil.org. Regarding Community law, see T. Heukels, *Intertemporales Gemeinschaftsrecht* (Baden-Baden, Nomos Verlag 1990).

*A. Łazowski (ed.), The Application of EU Law in the New Member States*
© 2010, T·M·C·ASSER PRESS, *The Hague, The Netherlands and the Authors*

sitional arrangements agreed in the course of accession negotiations.[2] An accession treaty enters into force on the date of accession.[3] The period immediately preceding that date is of extreme importance, since a number of preparatory measures have to be taken by the EU institutions in order to ensure the immediate integration of new Member States into the EU legal order. Those measures are addressed by specific arrangements relating to the "interim period", stretching between the date of formal conclusion of accession negotiations and the date of accession.[4]

According to the established practice, at the end of accession negotiations, parties agree that EU acts adopted after a specific date (the "cut-off date") would no longer be considered in the negotiations.[5] EU legal acts taken after that date are subject to an information and consultation procedure, a mechanism for consulting Acceding States with regard to EU legislation, which begins to apply upon the completion of negotia-

---

[2] See, in relation to the 2004 enlargement: Treaty between the Kingdom of Belgium, the Kingdom of Denmark, the Federal Republic of Germany, the Hellenic Republic, the Kingdom of Spain, the French Republic, Ireland, the Italian Republic, the Grand Duchy of Luxembourg, the Kingdom of the Netherlands, the Republic of Austria, the Portuguese Republic, the Republic of Finland, the Kingdom of Sweden, the United Kingdom of Great Britain and Northern Ireland (Member States of the European Union) and the Czech Republic, the Republic of Estonia, the Republic of Cyprus, the Republic of Latvia, the Republic of Lithuania, the Republic of Hungary, the Republic of Malta, the Republic of Poland, the Republic of Slovenia, the Slovak Republic, concerning the accession of the Czech Republic, the Republic of Estonia, the Republic of Cyprus, the Republic of Latvia, the Republic of Lithuania, the Republic of Hungary, the Republic of Malta, the Republic of Poland, the Republic of Slovenia and the Slovak Republic to the European Union, *OJ* 2003 L 236/17 (hereafter the Accession Treaty 2003) and Act concerning the Conditions of Accession of the Czech Republic, the Republic of Estonia, the Republic of Cyprus, the Republic of Latvia, the Republic of Lithuania, the Republic of Hungary, the Republic of Malta, the Republic of Poland, the Republic of Slovenia and the Slovak Republic and the adjustments to the Treaties on which the European Union is founded, *OJ* 2003 L 236/33 (the Act of Accession 2003). With regard to the 2007 accession, see Treaty between the Kingdom of Belgium, the Czech Republic, the Kingdom of Denmark, the Federal Republic of Germany, the Republic of Estonia, the Hellenic Republic, the Kingdom of Spain, the French Republic, Ireland, the Italian Republic, the Republic of Cyprus, the Republic of Latvia, the Republic of Lithuania, the Grand Duchy of Luxembourg, the Republic of Hungary, the Republic of Malta, the Kingdom of the Netherlands, the Republic of Austria, the Republic of Poland, the Portuguese Republic, the Republic of Slovenia, the Slovak Republic, the Republic of Finland, the Kingdom of Sweden, the United Kingdom of Great Britain and Northern Ireland (Member States of the European Union) and the Republic of Bulgaria and Romania, concerning the accession of the Republic of Bulgaria and Romania to the European Union, *OJ* 2005 L 157/11 and Act concerning the Conditions of Accession of the Republic of Bulgaria and Romania and the adjustments to the treaties on which the European Union is founded, *OJ* 2005 L 157/203 (hereafter the Accession Treaty 2005 and the Act of Accession 2005). For a legal appraisal of these legal acts see, *inter alia*, K. Inglis, 'The Union's fifth Accession Treaty: New means to make enlargement possible', 41 *CMLRev.* (2004) pp. 937-973; Ch. Hillion, 'The European Union is dead. Long live the European Union... a commentary on the Treaty of Accession 2003', 29 *ELRev.* (2004) pp. 583-612; A. Łazowski, 'And Then They Were Twenty-Seven... A Legal Appraisal of the Sixth Accession Treaty', 44 *CMLRev.* (2007) pp. 401-430.

[3] The discussed Accession Treaties entered into force, respectively, on 1 May 2004 (Art. 2(2) of the Accession Treaty 2003) and 1 January 2007 (Art. 4(2) of the Accession Treaty 2005).

[4] See, for Council interim arrangements related to the 2004 accession, documents Nos. 13569/02 of 4 November 2002, 14303/02 14 of November 2002 and 5171/02 of 10 December 2002, available at the Public register of Council documents, http://register.consilium.europa.eu/.

[5] In the 2004 accession, such cut-off date was 1 November 2002; in the 2007 accession – 1 October 2004. See Art. 55 of the Act of Accession 2003 and Art. 55 of the Act of Accession 2005.

tions. From the date of signature of an accession treaty,[6] certain provisions contained therein become applicable, such as the clauses enabling the EU institutions to implement accession instruments and Acceding Countries to present their requests for transitional measures with regard to new EU legal acts (Art. 2(3) of the Accession Treaty 2003).

Insofar as those arrangements are linked to an accession treaty, disputes concerning them pertain to EU law and may be brought before the European Court of Justice.[7] In particular, after the 2004 accession, the ECJ delivered several judgments concerning the powers of the EU institutions to adopt acts concerning acceding countries and to adapt the Accession Treaty 2003, as well as the corresponding rights of acceding countries to interact in the EU legislative procedures and to challenge Community acts adopted before accession.

## 2.2.    Adoption of EU acts in the "interim period"

In principle, an accession treaty already includes modifications of EU legislation necessitated by accession. However, those modifications have to be supplemented before accession in order to implement an accession treaty, to take into account new EU legislation and, possibly, to introduce adjustments overlooked during accession negotiations.

Formally, an accession treaty constitutes the legal basis for amendments of EU legislation required by accession. During the 1973 and 1981 accessions, it was therefore considered that such acts could be adopted only upon the entry into force of the respective Accession Treaties.[8] That solution proved to be highly impractical, as it required a large body of legislation to be formally adopted, published and entered into force on the date of accession. A clause expressly envisaged in later accession instruments allowed the acts based on an accession treaty to be adopted after its signature.[9]

---

[6] The Accession Treaty 2003 was signed in Athens on 16 April 2003; the Accession Treaty 2005 was signed in Luxembourg on 25 April 2005.

[7] As of 1 June 2004, the Court of First Instance has the jurisdiction in actions brought by a Member State against an act of, or failure to act by, the European Commission (with the exception of acts concerning enhanced co-operation under the EC Treaty).

[8] Treaty of 22 January 1972 between the Member States of the EC, the Kingdom of Denmark, the Republic of Ireland, the Kingdom of Norway and the United Kingdom of Great Britain and Northern Ireland, *OJ* 1972 L 73/4; Treaty of 28 May 1979 between the Member States of the EC and the Hellenic Republic concerning the accession of the Hellenistic Republic to the EC, *OJ* 1979 L 291/5.

[9] Treaty of 12 June 1985 between the Member States of the EC and the Kingdom of Spain and the Portuguese Republic to the EEC and the EAEC, *OJ* 1985 L 302/9; Treaty of 24 June 1994 between the Member States of the EC and the Kingdom of Norway, the Republic of Austria, the Republic of Finland and the Kingdom of Sweden concerning accession to the EU, *OJ* 1994 C 241/1; Act concerning the Conditions of Accession of the Kingdom of Norway, the Republic of Austria, the Republic of Finland and the Kingdom of Sweden and the adjustments to the Treaties on which the European Union is founded, *OJ* 1994 C 241/8. See M. Sohier, 'Observations comparatives sur les conditions d'adhésion de l'Espagne et du Portugal', 21 *CDE* (1985) pp. 584-608, at p. 606; D. Booß and J. Forman, 'Enlargement: Legal and Procedural Aspects', 32 *CMLRev.* (1995) pp. 95-130, at p. 110. See also the Opinions of the Advocates General in Cases 337/88 *Società agricola fattoria alimentare SpA (SAFA) v. Amministrazione delle finanze*

The Accession Treaty 2003 and the Act of Accession 2003 contain several provisions in that regard. Particularly important are two general clauses allowing EU institutions to introduce "temporary derogations" from EU legal acts adopted in the period between the cut-off date and the date of signature of the Accession Treaty (Art. 55 AA) and to make "necessary adaptations" to EU legislation not provided in the accession instruments (Art. 57 AA). Thus, Article 55 AA is a tool for taking into account the situation of the Acceding Countries with regard to new EU legislation, which could no longer have been considered in the negotiations, while Article 57 AA constitutes a stand-by mechanism for making adjustments which escaped notice during negotiations.[10] Both clauses are modelled on similar provisions in the Act of Accession 1995, Articles 151(2) and 169, which envisaged a simplified legislative procedure without participation of the European Parliament, even with regard to the amendment of EU acts adopted under the co-decision procedure. Unsurprisingly therefore, already after accession in 1995, the European Parliament sought to ensure that those provisions were interpreted strictly. In the case C-259/95 *European Parliament v. Council*, the ECJ confirmed that the intention underlying the provisions in question was to set up a flexible procedure for the adaptation of Community acts by reason of accession, which justified derogating from the rule of co-decision.

In the context of the 2004 accession, the European Parliament brought two somewhat similar challenges to Council acts adopted on the basis of Article 57 AA.[11] The contested acts provided for certain temporary derogations, with regard to Estonia and Slovenia, from the legislation adopted jointly by the European Parliament and the Council after conclusion of the accession negotiations.[12] The European Parliament argued that the Council could have relied neither on Article 57 AA, as that provision enabled it only to "adapt" Community legislation, nor on Article 55 AA, since the latter only applied to measures enacted before the signature of the Accession Treaty 2003. Thus, according to the European Parliament, both derogations should have been adopted under the usual co-decision procedure. The Court easily confirmed that Article 57 AA does not permit the adoption of temporary derogations, dismissing as irrelevant the Council's argument that similar provision had been used to adopt derogations in the case of previous enlargements. This finding was based on a long-standing legal formula drawing the difference between "derogating" from Community acts and their "adaptation", the latter term being limited to the provisions "designed merely to render [Community] measures applicable in the new Member States, to the exclusion of all

---

*dello Stato* [1990] *ECR* I-1, para. 8, and C-259/95 *European Parliament v. Council of the European Union* [1997] *ECR* I-5303, para. 6.

[10] Opinion of Advocate General La Pergola in Case C-259/95 *Parliament v. Council, loc. cit.* n. 9, paras. 5-9.

[11] ECJ, Case C-413/04 *European Parliament v. Council of the European Union* [2006] *ECR* I-11221 and Case C-414/04 *European Parliament v. Council of the European Union* [2006] *ECR* I-11279. See further D. Simon, 'Base juridique et droit transitoire', 41 *Europe* (2007) pp. 7-8.

[12] Respectively, Regulation No 1228/2003 of the European Parliament and of the Council of 26 June 2003 on conditions for access to the network for cross-border exchanges in electricity, *OJ* 2003 L 176/1; Directive 2003/54/EC of the European Parliament and of the Council of 26 June 2003 concerning common rules for the internal market in electricity, *OJ* 2003 L 176/37.

other amendments."[13] While drawing this terminological distinction, the ECJ has also referred to the structure of the Act of Accession, which contains separate parts devoted to "Adaptations" and "Transitional Measures."[14] As a consequence, the acts had to be annulled due to their incorrect legal basis. In the Estonian case, the annulment was limited to the provisions of the challenged directive introducing new derogations and did not affect those which simply repeated the measures already provided for in the Act of Accession 2003.[15]

The interpretation given by the ECJ to Article 57 AA revealed an apparent imperfection of the accession instruments, which contained no provision whatsoever allowing the adoption of derogations in favour of the Acceding Countries as regards EU legislation enacted after the signature of the Accession Treaty 2003. The Council, supported by the intervening governments, relied on that practical argument in its defence, indicating that, in the absence of explicit provisions in the Accession Treaty 2003, the EU cannot legislate in respect of the Acceding States until they become members of the EU. That argument allowed the ECJ to clarify for the first time that, following the signature of the Accession Treaty 2003, 'there is no objection in principle' to Community measures addressing the future Member States being adopted directly on the basis of the EC Treaty, rather than under the Accession Treaty 2003. This rather far-reaching interpretation is followed by a more carefully worded statement, according to which the provisional application of the Accession Treaty 2003 'does not affect the possibility of provision being made, in acts adopted not under that Treaty but on the basis of the EC Treaty itself, for the conditions under which such acts ... will apply to the future Member States once accession has taken place.'[16] The pronouncement in question put an end to an old discussion relating to the provisional application of Community legislative powers in the context of accession. A possibility of such anticipatory legislation was first debated in 1973 on the occasion of the first enlargement of the European Communities. The issue was regarded as highly controversial, as it seemed disputable that the European Communities might legislate with regard to the Acceding States before the Accession Treaty 1972 entered into force.[17] In the context of subsequent accessions, it was accepted that some provisions of the Accession Treaties would apply provisionally, enabling the Community institutions to adopt certain acts concerning the

---

[13] *Loc. cit.* n. 11; paras. 32-38 (Case C-413/04) and paras. 30-36 (Case C-414/04).

[14] That indication must be taken with caution, as the structure of the Act of Accession 2003 is not clear-cut: its part on "adaptations" includes a number of measures derived from the negotiating arrangements, which can hardly be described as mere adjustments of legislation. See further – in relation to Act of Accession 1994 – Booß and Forman, *loc. cit.* n. 9, at n. 30.

[15] *Loc. cit.* n. 11, paras. 51-52 (Case C-413/04). In the case relating to Slovenia, the Court acceded to the defendant's request to maintain the effects of the annulled Regulation until the adoption of a new regulation (Case C-414/04, para. 59).

[16] *Loc. cit.* n. 11, para. 62 (Case C-413/04) and para. 65 (Case C-414/04). The Court followed the suggestion of Advocate General Geelhoed, who observed that 'there is no inherent restriction on the Community legislature to anticipate the accession of new Member States in legislation adopted under the EC Treaty prior to accession'; see Opinion of Advocate General Geelhoed in Case C-414/04, para. 56.

[17] See J-P. Puissochet, *L'élargissement des Communautés européennes: présentation et commentaire du Traité et des Actes relatifs à l'adhésion du Royaume-Uni, du Danemark et de l'Irlande* (Paris, Éditions Techniques et Économiques 1973) p. 437.

Acceding States. Thus, Article 2(3) of the Accession Treaty 2003 provides that the EU institutions may adopt before accession a number of measures which enter into force only on the date of accession, including those envisaged by Articles 55 and 57 AA. By allowing the same measures to be adopted directly under the EC Treaty in anticipation of accession, the two mentioned judgments of the European Court of Justice reduce to some extent the importance of those clauses. More generally, the ECJ seems to confirm that the simplified legislative procedures envisaged in the Accession Treaties have to be interpreted strictly, and the measures required by accession should preferably be addressed pursuant to usual legislative powers provided for in the EC Treaty.

The existence of such provisional legislative powers with regard to the Acceding States may be justified both under international law[18] and Community case law relating to the implementation of international agreements.[19] However, the concise reasoning of the ECJ does not indicate whether the Community power to legislate with regard to the states which are still, formally, third countries, follows from the provisional application of the Accession Treaty 2003 or rather directly from Article 49 TEU. It may also be noted that the affirmation of the Community power to legislate in anticipation of accession was not strictly necessary in the context of the two mentioned cases, which were anyway decided after accession. Regarding its value as a precedent, the regulatory gap invoked by the Council had already been addressed at the time of the judgments, by the 2005 Act concerning the accession of Bulgaria and Romania.[20]

## 2.3.    Information and consultation procedure

Insofar as some EU measures concerning the future Member States may be adopted before accession, it seems justified to ask how those states participate in the EU legislative procedure before their accession. The Accession Treaty 2003 did not provide for any measures in that regard, with the exception of Article 55 AA, allowing a future Member State to request temporary derogations from EU legal acts adopted during the "interim period". In the absence of formal arrangements in the Accession Treaty 2003, the issue was addressed by separate bilateral agreements establishing the information and consultation procedure, concluded at the end of the accession negotiations between each of the Acceding States and the EU, and later annexed to the Final Act to the Accession Treaty 2003.[21] From the date of signature of the Accession Treaty 2003, that

---

[18] Art. 25 of the 1969 Vienna Convention on the Law of Treaties allows for a provisional application of a treaty before its entry into force.
[19] See ECJ, Joined Cases C-63/90 and C-67/90 *Portuguese Republic and Kingdom of Spain v. Council of the European Communities* [1992] *ECR* I-5073, para. 19. The European Court of Justice confirmed the legality of a Council regulation implementing an international agreement on fishery resources, adopted before the entry into force of that agreement (Council Regulation (EEC) No 4054/89 of 19 December 1989 allocating for 1990 Community catch quotas in Greenland waters, *OJ* 1989 L 389/65).
[20] See Art. 55 of the Act of Accession 2005, allowing the Council to introduce temporary derogations from EU acts adopted before the date of accession. See also Łazowski, *loc. cit.* n. 2, at pp. 421-422.
[21] Exchange of Letters between the European Union and the Czech Republic, the Republic of Estonia, the Republic of Cyprus, the Republic of Latvia, the Republic of Lithuania, the Republic of Hungary, the Republic of Malta, the Republic of Poland, the Republic of Slovenia and the Slovak Republic on an in-

procedure was supplemented by unilateral Council measures allowing the Acceding States to take part in COREPER and Council meetings as "active observers", which gave them a possibility to present their position but no voting rights.[22]

The information and consultation procedure dates back to the first enlargement of the European Communities,[23] and remained virtually unchanged during the enlargements that followed. It allows the Acceding State to request "consultations" with regard to the proposals for EC/EU legislation transmitted to the Council. The consultations take place in the Interim Committee, composed on the EU side of COREPER members. Should serious difficulties remain, the Acceding State may request a discussion at the ministerial level. Thus, the procedure in question does not lead to any formal involvement of Acceding States in the EU legislative process but rather constitutes a prolongation of the arrangements applicable during the accession negotiations. Its provisions are not integrated in the accession treaty, which, however, does not mean that they are denied all formal significance, particularly in respect of the interpretation of that Treaty.[24]

It is disputable whether or not a violation of the information and consultation procedure could constitute the legal ground for annulment of EU acts adopted before accession. In Joined cases 39/81, 43/81, 85/81 and 88/81 *Halyvourgiki* dealing with the 1981 accession, Advocate General Verloren van Themaat dismissed such possibility, relying on the fact that the information and consultation procedure was not incorporated into the Accession Treaty 1979. The ECJ did however examine the substance of the argument, concluding that, in any event, the procedure had been duly followed in the case at hand.[25]

That issue was raised again in the two cases discussed above.[26] In those cases, Poland argued that the Community institutions could not adopt Community acts concerning the Acceding States, since there was no formal arrangement concerning these states' involvement in the Community legislative procedure. The ECJ dismissed that argument remarking that the Acceding States had the benefit of the "active observer" status and of the information and consultation procedure, which 'could lead to the grant of possible transitional derogations in favour of an acceding State' even before accession. The ECJ further noted, making a parallel to its *Halyvourgiki* judgment, that it had no evidence suggesting that the information and consultation procedure had not been properly followed with regard to the acts in question. Therefore, the new Member States had been given the opportunity to assert their interests with regard to the Community

---

formation and consultation procedure for the adoption of certain decisions and other measures to be taken during the period preceding accession, *OJ* 2003 L 236/986.

[22] See Council document No 5171/02 of 10 December 2002, at http://register.consilium.europa.eu.

[23] See Puissochet, *op. cit.* n. 17, at pp. 527-528.

[24] According to Art. 31(2) of the 1969 Vienna Convention on the Law of Treaties, the terms of a treaty are interpreted in the context of any agreement made between the parties in connection with its conclusion, as well as any instrument accepted by the other parties as an instrument related to the treaty.

[25] See ECJ, Joined Cases 39/81, 43/81, 85/81 and 88/81 *Halyvourgiki Inc. and Helliniki Halyvourgia SA v. Commission of the European Communities* [1982] *ECR* 593, para. 15, and the Opinion of Advocate General Verloren Van Themaat, at pp. 624-625.

[26] *Loc. cit.* n. 11.

acts adopted before accession, even though they did not formally participate in their adoption.[27]

The ECJ made another passing reference to the Acceding States' participation in the Community legislative process in case C-460/05 *Poland v. Council*, noting, in the description of the facts of the dispute, that from the date of signature of the Accession Treaty 2003, Poland benefited from the right to be heard in the legislative process leading to the adoption of Community directives. Moreover, since Poland was 'closely associated' in the 'consultations preceding the adoption of the directive' in question and was in a position to know the reasons for its adoption, the rejection of its observations did not need to be specifically addressed in the text.[28]

Remarkably, the information and consultation procedure and the "observer" status were relied on by the ECJ to justify the statement that the EU institutions may legislate in respect of acceding countries even before their accession. Implicitly in this interpretation, the arrangements in question are considered as necessary steps in the adoption of Community acts, which may be subject to judicial control. That interpretation may seem overstretching the significance of both mechanisms, which have their basis in neither the accession treaty nor the EC Treaty, but only derive from separate bilateral arrangements or even unilateral measures. Overall, however, it remains important that the ECJ has confirmed the formal requirement to consult the Acceding States with regard to Community measures adopted before accession, even though the Accession Treaty 2003 did not contain any arrangements in that regard. A similar procedure applicable for the purposes of accession of Bulgaria and Romania does not appear to have led to any significant legal disputes.[29]

## 2.4.    Modification of the Act of Accession

Accession treaties and acts on conditions of accession constitute EU primary law and – as a general rule – cannot be modified by the EU institutions. This rule is subject to exceptions reflecting the dual nature of an act of accession, which largely contain provisions amending EU secondary law. Thus, while Article 7 of the Act of Accession 2003 stipulates that its provisions are subject to the same amendment procedures as the original Treaties, Article 9 AA establishes a wide limitation to this rule: the provisions of the Act relating to EU secondary acts, with the exception of transitional measures, have the same status as these acts and are subject to the same rules regarding their amendment.

Transitional measures provided for in the Act of Accession 2003, including those relating to secondary law, continue to be safeguarded as EU primary law. That solution seems justified by the fact that such measures normally result from a negotiating compromise reached between the Member States and acceding countries. This safeguard

---

[27] *Loc. cit.* n. 11 (Case C-413/04 *Parliament v. Council*) at paras. 71-72.

[28] See ECJ, Case C-460/05 *Republic of Poland v. European Parliament and Council of the European Union* [2007] *ECR* I-102, paras. 13 and 20.

[29] For a legal appraisal of this procedure in the context of the 2007 accession, see Łazowski, *loc. cit.* n. 2, at p. 406.

is however attenuated by the provision of Article 8 AA, confirming that EU acts to which the transitional measures relate retain their status in law, and the EU institutions retain power to modify or repeal EU acts concerned by transitional arrangements. The function of that provision is delicate, as modification of an EU act which lies at the basis of a transitional arrangement may affect the arrangement itself.[30]

The ECJ was asked to interpret the latter provision in case C-460/05 *Poland v. the European Parliament and Council*, which was a challenge to the legality of a new directive on the recognition of professional qualifications, which consolidated and repealed previous legal acts in this sector.[31] Some of the acts repealed contained transitional arrangements introduced by the Act of Accession 2003, in particular, regarding the recognition of formal qualifications of nurses and midwifes in Poland before accession. In the consolidation exercise, the EU institutions reintroduced the transitional arrangements in the new legislation, in virtually identical terms. Poland challenged the legality of that measure arguing that the institutions were not allowed to readopt the arrangements contained in the Accession Treaty 2003. The ECJ confirmed that the institutions retained their power to repeal secondary legislation affected by transitional arrangements provided for in the Act of Accession 2003, but only insofar as this did not undermine the arrangement itself. Since the references in the Act of Accession 2003 became obsolete after the repeal of legislation, the EU institutions not only acted in compliance with EU law, but also were obliged to reintroduce the provisions of the Act of Accession 2003 in the new legislation.[32]

In case C-273/04 *Poland v. Council*,[33] the European Court of Justice addressed a related situation in the agricultural sector. Regarding the Common Agricultural Policy (CAP), Article 23 AA explicitly allows the Council – acting unanimously – to adapt transitional arrangements agreed upon in the Accession Treaty 2003, in case of modification of the relevant Community rules. This provision, justified by frequent changes of the rules in the agricultural sector, follows the practice developed since the 1973 enlargement,[34] which so far had remained unchallenged. Its scope was addressed by an action introduced by Poland several weeks after the accession.

The Act of Accession 2003 provided for a gradual introduction of direct payments from the CAP with regard to the new Member States. Since – in the meantime – the CAP reform introduced some new payments for nuts and energy crops and supplementary payments in the dairy sector, the Council adapted the Act of Accession 2003 in order to include the reference to this new legislation. The decision was taken pursuant to Article 23 AA before the entry into force of the Accession Treaty 2003. Poland chal-

---

[30] For instance, J-P. Puissochet observes that the Community institutions can repeal secondary acts affected by a transitional arrangement agreed in an accession treaty, even if this rendered the whole arrangement obsolete; see Puissochet, *op. cit.* n. 17, at pp. 199-200.

[31] Directive 2005/36/EC of the European Parliament and of the Council of 7 September 2005 on the recognition of professional qualifications, *OJ* 2005 L 255/22.

[32] *Loc. cit.* n. 28, para. 18.

[33] ECJ, Case C-273/04 *Republic of Poland v. Council of the European Union* [2007] *ECR* I-8925.

[34] See Puissochet, *op. cit.* n. 17, p. 328. See, with regard to a similar provision in Art. 148(2) of the Act of Accession 1994, the Opinion of Advocate General Elmer in Joined Cases C-71/95, C-155/95 and C-271/95 *Kingdom of Belgium v. Commission of the European Communities* [1997] *ECR* I-687, para. 37.

lenged that decision, arguing that the Council misused its powers by unilaterally extending the scope of a transitional measure agreed upon in the accession negotiations. The parties agreed that Article 23 AA was limited to "adaptations" and could not be used to enlarge the scope of measures envisaged in the Act of Accession 2003. Thus, the main question before the European Court of Justice was whether the transitional arrangement in question, as originally agreed in the Act of Accession 2003, concerned direct payments in general or only those in place at the time of negotiations. The Advocate General and the European Court of Justice concluded that it was clear, under a literal, systematic and teleological interpretation of the Act of Accession 2003, that the arrangement at hand was of general application and included future direct payments.[35] That interpretation was supported by the *travaux préparatoires* of the Accession Treaty 2003, which showed that gradual introduction of direct payments was intended as a general measure, and that no compromise has been reached to limit its scope to any particular sectors.[36] Accordingly, the Council could lawfully adapt the Act of Accession 2003 to include references to the new direct payments resulting from the CAP reform, insofar as it did not alter in any way the scope of the original measure.

That reasoning, otherwise uncontroversial, contains an apparent difficulty: if the Council did not in any way alter the scope of the Act of Accession 2003, why was it necessary to adapt it? According to the interpretation of the Act given by the ECJ, its original provisions already applied to potential new direct payments. Thus, it is not evident why the introduction of new payments would have led to a 'conflict between the provisions of the Act of Accession and the new body of rules', requiring adaptation of the Act.[37] In that regard, the commented case may be compared to the judgment in case C-460/05 *Poland v. European Parliament and Council* as well as the judgment in case C-413/04 *Parliament v. Council*, discussed above.[38] According to that case law, where a reference contained in the Act of Accession 2003 is rendered obsolete by the adoption of new Community legislation, the Council may reintroduce the arrangement made in the Act of Accession 2003 exercising its general legislative powers, without it being necessary to adapt the Act of Accession 2003 itself. If that case law were applied to the case at hand, the Council could have introduced a transitional arrangement in the new CAP regulations without adapting the Act of Accession 2003. Thus, there appears to be some inconsistency between the conditions of amendment of transitional arrangements in the agricultural sector and other domains.

---

[35] *Loc. cit.* n. 33, paras. 52-71; Opinion of Advocate General Maduro, paras. 68-73.

[36] Generally, the ECJ is reluctant to admit preparatory documents even as subsidiary means of interpretation: 'neither individual statements of position nor joint declarations of the Member States may be used for the purpose of interpreting a provision where ... their content is not reflected in its wording and therefore has no legal significance'. See ECJ, Case C-329/95 *Administrative proceedings brought by VAG Sverige AB* [1997] *ECR* I-2675, para. 23, and Case C-233/97 *KappAhl Oy* [1998] *ECR* I-8069, para. 23.

[37] *Loc. cit.* n. 33, para. 49.

[38] Para. 52 and para. 18 (respectively).

## 2.5. Conditions for annulment of Community acts adopted before accession

Accession treaties constitutes EU primary law and, as such, are not subject to the judicial review under the law of the European Union. This also applies to adaptations to EU secondary legislation contained in acts of accession,[39] and may even extend to some aspects of legislation implementing acts of accession.[40] Otherwise accession treaties do not affect the conditions of judicial review of EU secondary law.[41]

In the light of those principles, a new Member State cannot challenge its obligation to implement EU acts adopted before accession, an obligation stemming directly from an Accession Treaty,[42] but is not precluded from challenging the legality of EU acts at the basis of this obligation. From a practical perspective, it is, however, unlikely that a Member State could successfully challenge an act adopted some time before its accession, since Article 230(5) EC provides for a two-month time limit for bringing an action. In that regard, a new Member State cannot rely on the fact that it did not have an opportunity to challenge the validity of an EU act adopted before its accession, since that would amount to challenging the obligations that it freely entered by concluding an Accession Treaty.[43]

It is not evident that the same considerations apply with regard to EU acts adopted before accession, but upon the completion of accession negotiations. It might seem dishonest to consider that a new Member State freely entered the obligation to comply with such acts. The issue is even more urgent, as EU acts in question are often adopted with a forthcoming accession in mind, but without formal participation of Acceding States, for which the judicial challenge may constitute the only effective means to defend their interests. Exactly this issue was raised in the first action brought by Poland after its accession in case C-273/04 against the Council (the substance of the case is discussed above). In this case, Poland challenged the Council's decision adapting the Act of Accession 2003, adopted and published in the Official Journal of the European Union just over a month before the 2004 enlargement. The decision entered into force on the date of accession. The time limit for bringing an action expired on 24 June 2004,

---

[39] ECJ, Joined Cases 31 and 35/86 *Levantina Agricola Industrial SA (LAISA) and CPC España SA v. Council of the European Communities* [1988] *ECR* 2285.

[40] ECJ, Case 119/86 *Kingdom of Spain v. Council and Commission of the European Communities* [1987] *ECR* 4121, paras. 15, 20-21.

[41] In *König*, the Council argued that new Member States had accepted to implement Community law as it stood on the date of their accession, thus, the legislation forming the basis of this obligation was no longer open to challenge. The ECJ rejected this argument stating that 'no provisions in the Treaty of Accession … can be construed as validating measures, whatever their form, which are incompatible with the Treaties establishing the Communities .' See ECJ, Case 185/73 *Hauptzollamt Bielefeld v. Offene Handelsgesellschaft in Firma H.C. König* [1974] *ECR* 607, para. 3.

[42] ECJ, Case C-313/89 *Commission of the European Communities v. Kingdom of Spain* [1991] *ECR* I-5231, paras. 9-10.

[43] ECJ, Case C-194/01 *Commission of the European Communities v. Republic of Austria* [2004] *ECR* I-4579, para. 41; and paras. 50-51 of the Opinion of the Advocate General. See also para. 57 of the Opinion of the Advocate General in Case C-290/98 *Commission of the European Communities v. Republic of Austria* [2000] *ECR* I-7835.

and Poland missed this deadline by several days. The provisions relating to time limits are of strict application and would otherwise suffice to dismiss the action. However, Poland argued that, in this case, *dies a quo* for calculating the procedural time limit should be set at the date of accession, since only from that date Poland could rely on Article 230(2) EC allowing the Member States to bring actions against Community acts. The Council objected arguing that Poland could have challenged its decision, even before accession, on the basis of Article 230(4) EC, which applies to the annulment actions brought by applicants other than the Member States and the EU institutions.

Advocate General Poiares Maduro delivered a detailed analysis of the judicial protection afforded to new Member States against the acts adopted before their accession. His principal suggestion was that the action should be admissible in the light of the principle of effective judicial protection. Before the accession, Poland could not bring annulment actions as a Member State. Even though it could have relied on 230(4) EC, it was not evident that the action directed against the measure of general application would have been admissible under the *Plaumann* test,[44] since Poland could have failed to show that it was individually concerned by the regulation addressed to all Member States. Thus, setting the *dies a quo* as the date of accession was, according to the Advocate General, the only solution that would enable Poland to effectively defend its rights in the context of such a Community measure. That reasoning, however, could not be extended to all EU acts, but would have to be limited, temporally, to the acts adopted in the interval between the date of signature of the Accession Treaty 2003 and the date of its entry into force and, materially, to those affecting the balance of the rights and obligations enshrined in the Accession Treaty 2003.[45]

The suggestion of Advocate General Maduro, albeit largely based on the ECJ's case law relating to the effective judicial protection, is not short of controversies. First, even disregarding political delicacy, it seems difficult to examine the admissibility of an action raised by a future Member State from a perspective of a non-privileged applicant. Thus, under the proposed reasoning, the ECJ would have to admit, even if implicitly, that a challenge brought by an Acceding State to a Community regulation would not satisfy the *Plaumann* test, even though such regulation is expressly addressed to it in its future status as a Member State.[46] Moreover, such action under Article 230(4) would fall within the jurisdiction of the Court of First Instance. Second, the limitations proposed by the Advocate General seem excessively rigid. Since all Community acts adopted after the cut-off date of the negotiations and applicable after accession may affect the future Member States, it is not evident why their right to effective judicial protection should be restricted to the acts adopted after the signature of an Accession Treaty and concerning the arrangements agreed therein.

A different solution to this issue was proposed in the literature on the subject. It starts from a premise that a prospective Member State cannot be expected to challenge

---

[44] ECJ, Case 25/62 *Plaumann & Co. v. Commission of the European Economic Community* [1963] *ECR* 95, at p. 107.

[45] See paras. 27-48 and 53 of the Opinion of Advocate General Maduro in Case C-273/04, *loc. cit.* n. 33.

[46] *Ibidem*, paras. 43-44.

EU measures on the basis of Article 230(4) EC, as that would lead to inequality among the Member States and infringe upon their privileged status in controlling the balance of powers within the European Union. Consequently, regarding the acts explicitly addressed to acceding countries and entering into force on the date of their accession, the procedural time limits should start to be counted from the date of accession, when new Member States can effectively rely on Article 230(2) EC.[47]

Yet another, and radically different, approach could be deduced from the considerations relating to the provisional application of the accession treaty. The law of treaties allows a signed treaty to be applied in some respects even before its entry into force. Thus, even in the absence of explicit provisions, there is – in principle – no obstacle preventing an acceding country from invoking Article 230(2) EC as soon as it has signed an accession treaty, insofar as such provisional application of Article 230(2) EC were necessary to ensure its effective application after accession.

The latter interpretation could provide a uniform approach to the institutional powers in the period preceding an accession. The ECJ has recognised that, as soon as an Accession Treaty is signed, the EU institutions may adopt acts concerning an acceding country on the basis of the EC Treaty, thus applying the treaty provisionally in anticipation of accession. Arguably, this power of the institutions should lead to the corresponding competence of the European Court of Justice, admitting challenges brought by an Acceding State directly under Article 230(2) EC, even before accession. Thus, the case law relating to the anticipated application of the EC Treaty by the EU legislature, with regard to acceding countries, would be extended to include the anticipated application of Article 230(2) EC. Evidently, since this interpretation is a novelty, it would have been inappropriate to apply it to the application at hand, which could have been declared admissible on account of the principle of legal certainty.

In the judgment, the ECJ did not decide the issue in question, briefly stating that it was necessary 'to rule at the outset on the substance of the case.'[48] It might seem striking that the ECJ turned directly to the substance of the case, without first deciding if it was admissible. However, such solution is not unusual in the case law, which contains numerous instances in which the ECJ or the CFI decided that it was not necessary to rule on the admissibility, since the form of order sought by the applicant in any event had to be dismissed on the substance.[49] That practice has recently been criticised by Advocate General Ruiz-Jarabo Colomer, but the criticism has not been shared by the

---

[47] See S. Biernat, 'Kwestia dopuszczalności pierwszych skarg Polski do sądów wspólnotowych' [On the question of admissibility of Poland's first applications before the Community courts], in W. Popiołek, et al., eds., *Rozprawy prawnicze. Księga Pamiątkowa Profesora Maksymiliana Pazdana* [Essays in Law. Liber Amicorum Maksymilian Pazdan] (Kraków, Kantor Wydawniczy Zakamycze 2005) pp. 569-584.

[48] *Loc. cit.* n. 33, para. 33.

[49] ECJ, Case 189/73 *Gijsbertus van Reenen v. Commission of the European Communities* [1975] *ECR* 445, para. 8. For some recent examples, see ECJ, Case C-23/00P *Council of the European Union v. Boehringer Ingelheim Vetmedica GmbH and C. H. Boehringer Sohn* [2002] *ECR* I-1873, paras. 51-52; Case C-233/02 *French Republic v. Commission of the European Communities* [2004] *ECR* I-2759, para. 26; Joined Cases T-217/99, T-321/00 and T-222/01 *Sociedade de Indústrias Agrícolas Açoreanas (Sinaga) SA v. Commission of the European Communities* [2006] *ECR* II-67, para. 68; T-171/02 *Regione autonoma della Sardegna v. Commission of the European Communities* [2005] *ECR* II-2123, para. 155.

ECJ.[50] The views of the Advocate General and of the ECJ diverged also regarding the consequences of the pronouncement in question. The Advocate General considered that, insofar as the ECJ ruled on the substance, it must have accepted implicitly that the action was admissible.[51] However, the ECJ ruled out such interpretation stating that the proper administration of justice could justify the dismissal of the action on the merits without any decision on admissibility.[52]

It may be deduced from the latter pronouncement that, in case C-273/04 *Poland v. Council*, the Court did not rule on the admissibility of the action, even implicitly, thus leaving the issue open. This approach could be explained by the fact that there was probably no need to establish a clear precedent, as no similar dispute has been brought in the context of the accession of Bulgaria and Romania. The same issue relating to the admissibility of direct actions by a new Member State was however raised in two cases before the CFI.[53]

3.       TEMPORAL SCOPE OF EU LAW WITH REGARD TO THE NEW
         MEMBER STATES

3.1.     **The principle of "immediate effect" of EU law**

As a leading principle accepted in all accessions to the EC and the EU, EU law becomes fully and immediately applicable in respect to a new member state on the date of its accession. This consideration underlies the provision of Article 2 AA, according to which, 'from the date of accession, the provisions of the original Treaties and the acts adopted by the institutions and the European Central Bank before accession shall be binding on the new Member States and shall apply in those States under the conditions laid down in those Treaties and in the [Act of Accession].'[54]

The provision in question is, certainly, only a starting point in defining the temporal application of EU law in the new Member States, which is subject to further rules

---

[50] See paras. 31-35 of the Opinion of Advocate General Ruiz-Jarabo Colomer in Case C-23/00P *Council of the European Union v. Boehringer Ingelheim Vetmedica GmbH and C.H. Boehringer Sohn*. See also the Opinion of Advocate General Mayras in Case 189/73 *Gijsbertus van Reenen v. Commission of the European Communities*.

[51] See para. 22 of the Opinion of Advocate General Ruiz-Jarabo Colomer in Case C-23/00P *Council of the European Union v. Boehringer Ingelheim Vetmedica GmbH and C.H. Boehringer Sohn*. See also the Opinion of Advocate General Mischo in Case C-73/97P *French Republic v. Comafrica SpA and Dole Fresh Fruit Europe Ltd & Co. and Commission of the European Communities* [1999] *ECR* I-185.

[52] See ECJ, Case C-23/00P *Council of the European Union v. Boehringer Ingelheim Vetmedica GmbH and C.H. Boehringer Sohn*, para. 51.

[53] CFI, Case T-257/04 *Republic of Poland v. Commission of the European Communities*, [2009] *ECR* II-0000; Case T-258/04 *Republic of Poland v. Commission of the European Communities*, [2009] *ECR* II-0000.

[54] See, with regard to a similar provision in the context of the 1981 accession, ECJ, Case 258/81 *Metallurgiki Halyps A.E. v. Commission of the European Communities* [1982] *ECR* 4261, paras. 7-8, and, on the occasion of the 1995 accession, paras. 52-53 of the Opinion of Advocate General Léger in Case C-194/01 *Commission of the European Communities v. Republic of Austria* [2004] *ECR* I-4579.

governing the application of EU law in time. In that regard, the rules applied in the context of accession are similar to those concerning, generally, the temporal application of EU law. The ECJ has early accepted the principle of "immediate effect" (*l'effet immédiat*)[55] of new law, originally derived from the French legal doctrine.[56] According to that principle, new substantive legal rules immediately apply to the "current" or "pending" situations, including the future effects of situations that came about under the previous rules, but do not affect the situations permanently "fixed" or "established" before their entry into force.[57] Similarly, in the context of accession, EU law 'must be regarded as being immediately applicable and binding on the new Member States from the date of its accession, with the result that it applies to the future effects of situations arising prior to that new Member State's accession to the Communities.'[58]

Application of the above principle to a given legal situation depends, essentially, on the assessment of its effects in time: whether, at the date of accession, the situation was still pending or has already been definitely established. This, in turn, requires a case-by-case approach strongly reliant on the interpretation of the legal rules involved. In that regard, case law developed in the context of subsequent accessions contains various examples of intertemporal solutions depending on the nature of the Community rules at hand.[59]

In a number of cases relating to the 1995 enlargement, the ECJ adopted a remarkably wide approach regarding the temporal scope of Community law, often disagreeing with solutions suggested by national judges or by the Advocates General.[60] Those examples

---

[55] For the use of this term, see para. 57 of the Opinion of Advocate General Cosmas in Case C-321/97 *Ulla-Brith Andersson and Susannne Wåkerås-Andersson v. Svenska staten (Swedish State)* [1999] *ECR* I-3551. See also paras. 57 and 64 of the Opinion of Advocate General Jacobs in Case C-162/00 *Land Nordrhein-Westfalen and Beata Pokrzeptowicz-Meyer* [2002] *ECR* I-1049, and para. 144 of his opinion in Case C-195/98 *Österreichischer Gewerkschaftsbund, Gewerkschaft öffentlicher Dienst and Republik Österreich* [2000] *ECR* I-10497.

[56] P. Roubier, *Les conflits de lois dans le temps* (Paris, Daloz-Sirey 1960).

[57] In particular, ECJ, Cases 1/73 *Westzucker GmbH v. Einfuhr- und Vorratsstelle für Zucker* [1973] *ECR* 723, para. 5; 270/84 *Assunta Licata v. Economic and Social Committee* [1986] *ECR* 2305, para. 31; C-162/00 *Land Nordrhein-Westfalen and Beata Pokrzeptowicz-Meyer, loc. cit.* n. 55, paras. 49-52. More recently, see CFI, Case T-25/04 *González y Díez, SA v. Commission of the European Communities* [2007] *ECR* II-3121, para. 70, referring to a 'principle ... according to which a new rule applies immediately to the future effects of a situation which came about under the old rule', that is, 'to situations which are current at the time of entry into force of the new rule, and not in respect of situations which ... were definitively established under the old rule .' Different considerations apply to the entry into force of new procedural rules, which immediately apply to all pending disputes; see ECJ, Joined Cases 212/80 to 217/80 *Amministrazione delle finanze dello Stato v. Srl Meridionale Industria Salumi and others; Ditta Italo Orlandi & Figlio and Ditta Vincenzo Divella v. Amministrazione delle finanze dello Stato* [1981] *ECR* 2735, para. 9, and the Opinion of Advocate General Warner in Case 7/76 *Société IRCA (Industria romana carni e affini SpA) v. Amministrazione delle finanze dello Stato* [1976] *ECR* 1213, at p. 1238.

[58] ECJ, Case C-122/96 *Stephen Austin Saldanha and MTS Securities Corporation v. Hiross Holding AG* [1997] *ECR* I-5325, para. 14.

[59] See S. Kalėda, 'Immediate Effect of Community Law in the New Member States', 10 *ELJ* (2004) pp. 102-122.

[60] ECJ, Case C-43/95 *Data Delecta Aktiebolag and Ronny Forsberg v. MSL Dynamics Ltd* [1996] *ECR* I-4661; Case C-122/96 *Stephen Austin Saldanha and MTS Securities Corporation v. Hiross Holding AG, loc. cit.* n. 58; Case C-275/96 *Anne Kuusijärvi v. Riksförsäkringsverket* [1998] *ECR* I-3419; Case

show that temporal interpretation of Community law in the accession-related context is a complicated legal exercise, in which the European Court of Justice accepts its overall guiding role.

Several cases brought in the aftermath of the 2004 enlargement and already decided by the ECJ did not involve any wider disputes concerning the temporal scope of specific EU rules. This seems surprising since, apparently, courts in the new Member States were confronted with a large number of intertemporal issues, which have not been referred to the ECJ and largely remained in the domain of the national judiciary.[61] The preliminary references addressed to the ECJ by the judiciary in the new Member States raised, however, at least two broader issues: first, the temporal scope of the ECJ's jurisdiction to decide on preliminary references and, second, the consequences of the late publication of EU acts in the new official languages.[62]

### 3.2.    Temporal scope of the preliminary rulings' jurisdiction

The ten new Member States of the EU were obliged to fully integrate the EU legal order on the date of their accession on 1 May 2004. Bulgaria and Romania joined the EU in the next wave of enlargement on 1 January 2007, and, as of that date, both countries had the obligation to apply EU law. However, the process of approximation of law started in the early 1990s and continued in parallel with the accession negotiations. This process also included national courts, which long before accession began to interpret national rules in the light of EU law. In some instances, national courts have even decided that they are bound to ensure the *interprétation conforme*, due to the obligations arising under their domestic law or under the Europe Agreements concluded with the EC and its Member States.[63]

The accession opened for the national courts in the new Member States a possibility of referring their questions relating to validity and interpretation of EU law to the ECJ pursuant to Articles 234 EC, 68 EC and Article 150 EAEC. Only a few Member States recognised the jurisdiction of the ECJ to handle preliminary rulings in the Third Pillar matters (Art. 35 TEU).[64] Initially, it was uncertain if the preliminary ruling pro-

---

C-389/99 *Sulo Rundgren* [2001] *ECR* I-3731; Case C-28/00 *Liselotte Kauer and Pensionsversicherungsanstalt der Angestellten* [2002] *ECR* I-1343; Case C-290/00 *Johann Franz Duchon and Pensionsversicherungsanstalt der Angestellten* [2002] *ECR* I-3567. In these cases the national courts considered that Community law applied only because of a reference made in their national law. In *Saldanha* and *Kauer* the Advocates General suggested that Community law did not apply *ratione temporis*.

[61] See, regarding Polish courts, Chapter 9 in this volume. Regarding Lithuanian courts, see Y. Goldammer, E. Matulionytė, 'The application of European Union law in Lithuania', 31 *ELRev.* (2006) pp. 260-270.

[62] For an overview see, *inter alia*, M. Bobek, 'Learning to talk: Preliminary rulings, the courts of the new Member States and the Court of Justice', 45 *CMLRev.* (2008) pp. 1611-1643.

[63] See, with regard to Polish courts, S. Biernat, '"European" Rulings of Polish Courts Prior to Accession to the European Union', 1 *The Polish Foreign Affairs Digest* (2005) pp. 127-150.

[64] The first to recognise the jurisdiction of the ECJ was the Czech Republic in a declaration annexed to the 2003 Accession Treaty. It was shortly followed by Hungary, and at the later stage by Latvia, Lithuania and Slovenia (see Information concerning the declarations by the Republic of Hungary, the Republic of Latvia, the Republic of Lithuania and the Republic of Slovenia on their acceptance of the jurisdiction

cedure could be employed with regard to all disputes pending at the date of accession. Given that a number of EU acts had already been transposed and applied in the new Member States before accession, it might seem consequent to invoke the preliminary rulings mechanism with regard to all pending disputes requiring the interpretation of EU rules, even those relating to their indirect application before accession.

Moreover, at least for the disputes that came about after the signature of the Accession Treaty 2003, such extension of the preliminary rulings mechanism could find its formal justification in that Treaty. Under the Accession Treaty 2003, the new Member States were obliged to apply Community directives from the date of accession (Art. 54 AA). Evidently, in order to comply with that obligation, the future Member States were obliged to transpose directives already before their accession. In that regard, Article 54 AA may be viewed as provisionally imposing certain accession obligations even before accession[65] and containing a hidden transposition period starting, at the latest, from the date of signature of the Accession Treaty 2003 and ending on the date of accession. Since the Member States' courts may be obliged to interpret national law in conformity with a directive even before the expiry of its transposition period,[66] it is possible to consider that the courts in the new Member States were bound to take into account the provisions of a transposed directive even before accession, as a matter of Community law, and, accordingly, should be allowed to address preliminary references to the European Court of Justice.

The European Court of Justice seems to have ruled out such interpretation in several cases concerning the 1995 accession. On that occasion, the ECJ admitted that Community law could produce effects in a new Member State even before accession, on the basis of domestic law or of the international agreements concluded with the Community, but declared that the existence of such effects did not bring the situations that take place before accession within the proper scope of the Community legal order. Therefore, such situations were not covered by the Court's jurisdiction under Article 234 EC, which only concerned the interpretation of Community law 'as regards its application in the new Member States with effect from the date of their accession .'[67]

---

of the Court of Justice to give preliminary rulings on the acts referred to in Art. 35 of the Treaty on European Union, *OJ* 2008 L 70/23). Following the judgment of the Constitutional Tribunal, also Poland was expected to recognise the jurisdiction of the ECJ in 2009. Further on the latter development, see Chapter 9 in this volume.

[65] Puissochet, *op. cit.* n. 17, at p. 434, interpreting a similar provision in the Act of Accession 1972 as 'faisant un appel discret à la théorie de l'application provisoire des traités internationaux avant leur ratification .'

[66] ECJ, Case C-212/04 *Konstantinos Adeneler, Pandora Kosa-Valdirka, Nikolaos Markou, Agapi Pantelidou, Christina Topalidou, Apostolos Alexopoulos, Konstantinos Vasiniotis, Vasiliki Karagianni, Apostolos Tsitsionis, Aristidis Andreou, Evangelia Vasila, Kalliopi Peristeri, Spiridon Sklivanitis, Dimosthenis Tselefis, Theopisti Patsidou, Dimitrios Vogiatzis, Rousas Voskakis, Vasilios Giatakis v. Ellinikos Organismos Galaktos (ELOG)* [2006] *ECR* I-60, para. 123.

[67] See ECJ, Case C-27/96 *Danisco Sugar AB v. Allmänna ombudet* [1997] *ECR* I-6653, para. 25; Case C-140/97 *Walter Rechberger, Renate Greindl, Hermann Hofmeister and Others v. Republik Österreich* [1999] *ECR* I-3499, paras. 38-40; Case C-321/97 *Ulla-Brith Andersson and Susannne Wåkerås-Andersson v. Svenska staten (Swedish State)*, *loc. cit.* n. 55, paras. 30-32.

Despite the existence of those precedents, the issue came back in the context of the 2004 accession in case C-302/04 *Ynos*,[68] the first reference submitted by the new Member States' judiciary.[69] The facts of the dispute in the main proceedings concerned the application of the Council Directive 93/13/EEC on unfair terms in consumer contracts, to the contractual obligations entered into by a consumer before the date of accession.[70] That situation was manifestly restricted to the pre-accession period.[71] Nevertheless, several intervening Member States suggested that the ECJ should give a preliminary ruling, since, under the pre-accession obligations, the national court was bound to interpret its national law in conformity with the Directive. The ECJ disagreed and declared, making a brief reference to the judgment in case C-321/97 *Andersson*, that it did not have the jurisdiction to give interpretation of Community law with regard to the dispute which occurred prior to the date of accession.[72] Thus, the ECJ established a strict parallel between the temporal scope of Community law in a new Member State and the temporal scope of the preliminary rulings' jurisdiction. Remarkably, despite the reliance on a precedent, the judgment was delivered in the Grand Chamber, reserved for settling important legal debates.[73]

There was, arguably, a need for such an authoritative pronouncement, given the very particular nature of the preliminary rulings' mechanism. This procedure enables the ECJ to interpret EU rules and to rule on their validity, but not to apply them directly. Such interpretative exercise does not necessarily require that the dispute before the national court fell directly within the scope of application of EU law. Thus, for instance, in its "*Dzodzi* case law", the ECJ declared that it 'has jurisdiction to give preliminary rulings on questions concerning Community provisions in situations where the facts of the cases being considered by the national courts are outside the scope of Community law but where those provisions had been rendered applicable by domestic law.'[74] Moreover the ECJ has accepted to rule in a number of "purely internal" cases, which fell outside of the proper scope of Community law due to the lack of any foreign element, but which nevertheless involved a real dispute concerning the interpretation of

---

[68] ECJ, Case C-302/04 *Ynos kft v. János Varga* [2006] *ECR* I-371. See further Chapter 12 in this volume.

[69] The reference was submitted by the Hungarian Court (Szombathelyi Városi Bíróság) by Order of that court of 10 June 2004.

[70] Council Directive 93/13/EEC of 5 April 1993 on unfair terms in consumer contracts, *OJ* 1993 L 95/29.

[71] According to the intertemporal solution in Art. 10 of Directive 93/13, the Member States are obliged to transpose the directive only with regard to the contracts concluded after the expiry of the transposition period; thus, for the new Member States, only with regard to the contracts concluded after accession.

[72] ECJ, Case C-321/97 *Ulla-Brith Andersson and Susannne Wåkerås-Andersson v. Svenska staten (Swedish State)*, *loc. cit.* n. 55, paras. 37-38.

[73] For critical assessment see N. Półtorak, 'Ratione temporis application of the preliminary rulings procedure' 45 *CMLRev.* (2008) pp. 1357-1381.

[74] In the recent case law, see ECJ, Case C-170/03 *Staatssecretaris van Financiën v. J.H.M. Feron* [2005] *ECR* I-2299, para. 11. See also para. 22 of the Opinion of Advocate General Kokott in Case C-280/06 *Autorità Garante della Concorrenza e del Mercato v. Ente tabacchi italiani – ETI SpA and Others and Philip Morris Products SA and Others v. Autorità Garante della Concorrenza e del Mercato and Others* [2007] *ECR* I-893.

Community rules made applicable by virtue of national law.[75] The effects produced by Community law in a new Member State before its accession might be regarded as a similar situation, since, in that situation, the Community provisions are also invoked outside their proper context. Thus, the judgment in *Ynos* dispersed any doubts as to the fact that the ECJ is not willing to extend its jurisdiction to such new situations.[76]

The ECJ's reluctance to rule on the interpretation of Community law in a pre-accession situation seems to be fully justified by the fact that the interpretation given by the ECJ might be relied upon by the national court to conclude that its pre-accession domestic law was not in compliance with the Community rules. That result would be inappropriate, since the ECJ has clearly no jurisdiction to address a new Member State's failure to apply Community law prior to its accession.[77] Thus, the court might have been exposed to criticism for overstepping its powers under the Founding Treaties, had it decided to use its interpretative jurisdiction in the situations outside the temporal scope of Community law.

This caveat does not equally apply to all situations, which is evidenced by two cases decided in a follow-up to the *Ynos* judgment. In those cases, the ECJ rejected as inadmissible, by reasoned orders, two references for preliminary ruling coming from the courts in the new Member States, both concerning the interpretation of the Sixth VAT Directive with regard to the taxation periods antedating the accession to the EU.[78] The first case – C-261/05 *Lákep* – dealt with the conformity of a municipal tax applied in Hungary with the Sixth VAT Directive.[79] The ECJ observed that the dispute before the national judge concerned the application of the tax before accession and, therefore, declined its jurisdiction, referring to the *Ynos* judgment.

The situation in the second case was quite different. In case C-168/06 *Ceramika Paradyż*, the referring court from Poland asked if an administrative sanction envisaged in its domestic VAT legislation, which entered into force on the date of accession, could

---

[75]  ECJ, Case C-281/98 *Roman Angonese v. Cassa di Risparmio di Bolzano SpA* [2000] *ECR* I-4139, para. 18; Case C-448/98 *Criminal proceedings against Jean-Pierre Guimont* [2000] *ECR* I-10663, para. 22; Joined Cases *Hans Reisch and Others (joined cases C-515/99 and C-527/99 to C-540/99) v. Bürgermeister der Landeshauptstadt Salzburg and Grundverkehrsbeauftragter des Landes Salzburg and Anton Lassacher and Others (joined cases C-519/99 to C-524/99 and C-526/99) v. Grundverkehrsbeauftragter des Landes Salzburg and Grundverkehrslandeskommission des Landes Salzburg* [2002] *ECR* I-2157, para. 26.

[76]  After the *Ynos* judgment, a doubt was raised, if the Court had not abandoned its *Dzodzi* case law; see Opinion of Advocate General Kokott in Case C-280/06 *ETI SpA and Others, loc. cit.* n. 74, at para. 63.

[77]  See, for instance, paras. 35-36 of the Opinion of Advocate General Saggio in Case C-290/98 *Commission of the European Communities v. Republic of Austria* [2000] *ECR* I-7835. The Commission argued that the unlawful conduct constituting the subject matter of the infringement action began one year before the accession of Austria, due to its obligations under the EEA Agreement. The Advocate General rejected this argument, reminding that from the point of view of Community law, only actions of a Member State subsequent to its accession to the EU may be subject to a ruling of the European Court of Justice.

[78]  Sixth Council Directive 77/388/EEC of 17 May 1977 on the harmonisation of the laws of the Member States relating to turnover taxes – Common system of value added tax: uniform basis of assessment, *OJ* 1977 L 145/1.

[79]  ECJ, Case C-261/05 *Lakép kft, Pár-Bau kft and Rottelma kft v. Komáron-Esztergom Megyei Közigazgatási Hivatal* [2006] *ECR* I-20.

be justified in light of the Sixth VAT Directive.[80] The European Court of Justice dismissed the question as inadmissible, on the ground that the imposition of the sanction
related to the taxation period before accession. The ECJ's decision put the national
court in an ambiguous situation, since it still had to decide, without the benefit of a
binding interpretation of Community law, if the Polish legislation enforced already
after accession was compliant with the Sixth VAT Directive.[81]

This solution may be explained by the difficulties inherent in ascertaining the material date for application of the rules imposing administrative sanctions. According to
Polish administrative law, a violation can only be sanctioned if the sanction continues
to be envisaged by the legal rules applicable at the time of the decision. Thus, the
national court was obliged to ascertain that it still had a legal basis to impose a sanction
after accession, even though it related to the events before accession. This would not
be the case if the legislation enacted after accession were found contrary to Community
law and inapplicable. If the same situation were framed from a different angle, the
national court was essentially applying the principle of retroactivity *in mitius* with
regard to coercive administrative measures. Since similar temporal principles are
accepted in Community law,[82] it would seem possible to admit that the dispute fell
within the proper scope of Community law, regardless of the fact that the tax violation
took place before accession.

Further indication of the fact that the *Ynos* principle cannot be applied automatically was given in *Telefónica O2 Czech Republic*.[83] The case concerned consecutive
administrative decisions adopted in the context of administrative proceedings commenced before accession, compelling Telefónica 02 to connect its network with that of
Czech On Line. This obligation has been addressed by decisions adopted before accession, which were, however, annulled by the courts. The decision in question was
adopted after accession, and the obligation imposed concerned future behaviour of the
undertaking concerned. Advocate General Ruiz-Jarabo Colomer summarised the *Ynos*
case law as concerning exclusively the events which 'were completed in a Member
State prior to its entry into the Communities', remarking that this case law should not
prevent the ECJ from ruling in the context of pending situations, which began before
accession.[84] The view of the Advocate General was shared by the ECJ, which con-

---

[80] ECJ, Case C-168/06 *Ceramika Paradyż sp. z oo v. Dyrektor Izby Skarbowej w Łodzi* [2007] *ECR* I-29.

[81] This was followed by a reference from the Supreme Administrative Court of Poland dealing with the same rules with regard to the post-accession taxation periods. On 15 January 2009, the European Court of Justice delivered the judgment and held that the EC VAT legislation did not preclude the Polish law in question. ECJ, Case C-502/07 *K-1 sp. z o.o. v. Dyrektor Izby Skarbowej w Bydgoszczy* [2009] *ECR* I-00000.

[82] Community law recognises the principle of the retroactive application of the more lenient penalty, which is 'based on the idea that a defendant should not be convicted for behaviour that is no longer pun-ishable at the time of the conviction based on the modified view of the legislature'; see the Opinion of Advocate General Kokott in Case C-142/05 *Mickelsson and Roos*, pending, para. 26 and the case law cited.

[83] ECJ, Case C-64/06 *Telefónica O2 Czech Republic as, formerly Český Telecom as, v. Czech On Line as* [2007] *ECR* I-4887.

[84] See the Opinion of Advocate General Ruiz-Jarabo Colomer in Case C-64/06 *Telefónica O2 Czech Republic as, formerly Český Telecom as, v. Czech On Line as*, *loc. cit.* n. 83, para. 32.

cluded that it had jurisdiction to rule in the case, insofar as the situation was still pending at the date of accession, regardless of the fact that the dispute before the national administration and the judiciary commenced before accession.[85]

Overall, the fact that the European Court of Justice put a strict temporal limitation on its preliminary rulings' jurisdiction does not seem striking. Indeed, the *Ynos* case law has been anticipated by several decisions of the new Member States' courts, declaring that Article 234 EC could not be invoked in the context of the pre-accession disputes.[86] Accordingly, first preliminary references introduced after accession mostly concerned the facts that took place exclusively after accession.[87] It is still remarkable that, in *Ynos* and the two subsequent orders based on this precedent, the ECJ has almost automatically accepted that it lacks competence to rule in the context of the disputes arisen before accession. This approach may be contrasted with the judgments delivered after the 1995 accession, in which the ECJ engaged in a detailed temporal analysis of the Community rules in issue, cautiously considering whether the situation at hand had already been established on the date of accession or could be regarded as still pending.[88]

Similar problems did not arise in relation to the accession of Bulgaria and Romania. So far a handful of references from those states have reached the European Court of Justice, with intertemporal issues briefly mentioned only in the Romanian case C-33/07 *Jipa*.[89]

### 3.3.    Publication of EU law in the new official languages

Accession of new Member States brings about a modification to the EU language regime. Thus, the texts of the Founding Treaties in the new languages are annexed to acts of accession and become authentic under the same conditions as the texts drawn up in the original languages (in relation to the recent two waves of enlargement, see Art. 61(2) of the Act of Accession 2003 and Art. 60(2) of the Act of Accession 2005). Regarding Community secondary law, the Acts of Accession modified the two Council Regulations determining the languages used by the EEC and the EAEC[90] to include the new languages, thus requiring Community legislation to be adopted and published

---

[85] ECJ, Case C-64/06 *Telefónica O2 Czech Republic as, formerly Český Telecom as, v. Czech On Line as, loc. cit.* n. 83, paras. 21 and 28.

[86] With regard to Polish administrative courts, see Chapter 9 in this volume.

[87] See, for instance, ECJ, Case C-437/05 *Jan Vorel v. Nemocnice Český Krumlov* [2007] *ECR* I-331, concerning the interpretation of the concept of working time with regard to a situation of a Czech doctor required to perform on-call duty starting from 1 May 2004, or Case C-313/05 *Maciej Brzeziński v. Dyrektor Izby Celnej w Warszawie* [2007] *ECR* I-513, brought in the context of the taxation of a vehicle imported into Poland in June 2004.

[88] See, in particular, cases concerning the 1995 accession, *loc. cit.* n. 60.

[89] ECJ, Case C-33/07 *Ministerul Administrației și Internelor – Direcția Generală de Pașapoarte București v. Gheorghe Jipa* [2008] *ECR* I-5157. The reference was submitted on 17 January 2007, literally a few weeks after the accession. For an academic appraisal of this development, see Chapter 16 in this volume. The first Bulgarian reference did not raise intertemporal issues (ECJ, Case C-545/07 *Apis-Hristovich EOOD v. Lakorda AD* [2009] *ECR* I-00000).

[90] In the context of the 2004 accession, see Annex II, points 22.1 and 22.2 of the Act of Accession 2003 (*OJ* 2003 L 236/791), amending Council Regulation No 1 of 15 April 1958, determining the languages to

from the date of accession in new official languages.[91] The consequences of that modification were reflected in Community case law; for instance, the European Court of Justice consistently uses the new linguistic versions in order to solve any divergences in the Community texts.[92]

Special arrangements were necessary for the translation and publication of EU legal acts pre-dating the accession. According to Article 58 of the Act of Accession 2003 (and similar Art. 58 in the Act of Accession 2005), the texts of EU legislation in the new languages are equally authentic as the adopted texts and have to be published in the Official Journal, if the original texts were so published. It is notorious that Special Editions of the Official Journal[93] containing existing EU legislation in the new languages had not been available on the date of accession, but were gradually published afterwards.[94] In the meantime, the texts authenticated by the Commission and the Council have been provided, on a provisional basis, on an Internet page accessible from the EUR-LEX.[95] Pending the finalisation of the ongoing works related to electronic publication of EU acts,[96] the availability of EU legal texts on the Internet does not, however, equal their formal publication.[97] Although some delays in publication of

---

be used by the EEC (*JO* 1958 L 17/385), and Council Regulation No 1 of 15 April 1958, determining the languages to be used by the EAEC (*JO* 1958 L 17/401).

[91] An exception was provided for a period of three years from accession with regard to drafting of EU acts in Maltese, (regulations adopted pursuant to the co-decision procedure were not covered by the transitional regime thus published accordingly). These acts were expected to be published in Maltese by 31 December 2008. See Council Regulation (EC) No 930/2004 of 1 May 2004 on temporary derogation measures relating to the drafting in Maltese of the acts of the institutions of the European Union, *OJ* 2004 L 169/1; Council Regulation (EC) No 1738/2006 of 23 November 2006 amending Regulation (EC) No 930/2004 on temporary derogation measures relating to the drafting in Maltese of the acts of the institutions of the European Union, *OJ* 2006 L 329/1. Since 1 January 2007, that is, after the accession of Bulgaria and Romania as well as introduction of Gallic as the official language, the total number of languages has increased to twenty-three; thus the Official Journal of the EU is published in all those languages. See Council Regulation (EC) No 920/2005 of 13 June 2005 amending Regulation No 1 of 15 April 1958, determining the language to be used by the European Economic Community, and Regulation No 1 of 15 April 1958, determining the language to be used by the European Atomic Energy Community and introducing temporary derogation measures from those Regulations, *OJ* 2005 L 156/3.

[92] See ECJ, Case C-174/05 *Stichting Zuid-Hollandse Milieufederatie and Stichting Natuur en Milieu v. College voor de toelating van bestrijdingsmiddelen* [2006] *ECR* I-2443, para. 23.

[93] See, with regard to the 1973 enlargement, Council Regulation No 857/72 of 25 April 1972 providing for special editions of the Official Journal of the European Communities, *OJ* 1972 L 101/1.

[94] See also Chapter 5 in this volume.

[95] See the documents of the EU Publications Office (OPOCE) 'Enlargement and electronic publication of the *acquis* in the new languages' and 'EUR-Lex taking enlargements into account', Nos 8744/03 of 13 May 2003 and 8738/05 of 7 June 2005, available at the public register of Council documents, at http://register.consilium.europa.eu/.

[96] According to the OPOCE report to the Council, the audit of technical conditions ensuring equal status of electronic and paper editions of the *Official Journal* should have been concluded by September 2007; see document No 10645/07 of 2 June 2007. The conditions allowing to 'propose the change' of the status of the electronic edition should have been met by the end of 2008, but further necessary adaptations are foreseen to be carried out by 2009-2010; see document No 16295/07 of 14 December 2007, both documents available at http://register.consilium.europa.eu/.

[97] A limited exception is provided by the case law only as regards the 'publication' triggering the count of time limits for bringing annulment proceedings (Art. 230(5) EC) with regard to certain European

EU acts adopted before accession have also been reported in the context of previous accessions,[98] with the exception of the first enlargement of the European Communities in 1973,[99] it is only the 2004 accession and also the subsequent accession of Bulgaria and Romania that led to a more extensive legal discussion as to the consequences of such late publication with regard to the validity of EU acts and their application in the new Member States.[100]

It is not evident that the lack of publication in a new official language should affect the validity of EU legislation. Certainly, under Article 254 EC, a publication in the Official Journal of the European Union is a pre-condition for the entry into force of Community measures of general application.[101] Moreover, even though the legislator is in principle free to fix a date of entry into force, a measure which takes effect from a point in time before its publication is retroactive and may be declared invalid.[102] In the light of those principles, a publication in the Official Journal might be regarded as a condition of validity of those Community acts, for which such publication is obligatory.[103] However, Community acts adopted before accession have been duly published at the time of their adoption. Accession of new Member States does not lead to a re-

---

Commission decisions in state aid and competition law, where the fact that the European Commission gives third parties full access to the text of a decision placed on its website, combined with publication of a summary notice in the *Official Journal of the European Union*, is considered as proper publication. See CFI, Case T-17/02 *Fred Olsen v. Commission of the European Communities* [2005] *ECR* II-2031, para. 80. See also orders of CFI in Cases T-321/04 *Air Bourbon SAS v. Commission of the European Communities* [2005] *ECR* II-3469; T-426/04 *Tramarin Snc di Tramarin Andrea e Sergio v. Commission of the European Communities* [2005] *ECR* II-4765; T-98/04 *Nuova Agricast Srl and Others v. Commission of the European Communities*, *OJ* 2005 C 229/22; T-274/06 *Estaser El Mareny, SL, v. Commission of the European Communities* [2007] *ECR* II-143.

[98] See X. Yataganas, 'Main legal problems arising during the interim period and immediately after Greece's accession to the European Communities', 20 *JCMS* (1982) pp. 348-349. See also ECJ, Case 160/84 *Oryzomyli Kavallas OEE and others v. Commission of the European Communities* [1986] *ECR* 1633, para. 14.

[99] All relevant Community texts in English and Danish had been published before 1 January 1973; see Puissochet, *op. cit.* n. 17, at p. 440.

[100] For a detailed analysis, see M. Bobek, 'The Binding Force of Babel. The Enforcement of EC Law Unpublished in the Languages of the New Member States', 6 *EUI Working Paper* (2007) and 9 *CYELS* (2006-2007) pp. 43-80.

[101] See also Art. 163 EAEC that deals with the publication requirements in relation to Euratom secondary legislation. There is no provision in the EU Treaty dealing with the publication regime of acts adopted in the second and third pillars of the EU. This lacuna is filled by the Council Regulation 1049/2001/EC Regulation (EC) No 1049/2001 of the European Parliament and of the Council of 30 May 2001 regarding public access to European Parliament, Council and Commission documents, *OJ* 2001 L 145/43. See also Council Decision 2006/683/EC, Euratom of 15 September 2006 adopting the Council's Rules of Procedure (as amended), *OJ* 2006 L 285/47.

[102] See ECJ, Case 98/78 *A. Racke v. Hauptzollamt Mainz* [1979] *ECR* 69, para. 20; Case 99/78 *Weingut Gustav Decker KG v. Hauptzollamt Landau* [1979] *ECR* 101, para. 8; Case 224/82 *Meiko-Konservenfabrik v. Federal Republic of Germany* [1983] *ECR* 2539, paras. 12 and 20.

[103] The Court has stated, *in passim*, that the publication of a regulation has constitutive effect. See ECJ, Case 185/73 *Hauptzollamt Bielefeld v. Offene Handelsgesellschaft in Firma H.C. König* [1974] *ECR* 607, para. 5. See also para. 64 of the Opinion of Advocate General Lenz in Case C-91/92 *Paola Faccini Dori v. Recreb Srl.* [1994] *ECR* I-3325, and para. 24 of the Opinion of Advocate General Kokott in Case C-161/06 *Skoma-Lux sro v. Celní ředitelství Olomouc* [2007] *ECR* I-10841.

enactment of the existing legislation, but only to the modification of its scope, which moreover stems directly from primary law.

Application of such EU acts seems to be a different issue. According to Article 2 AA (identically worded in the Acts of Accession of 2003 and 2005), EU acts adopted before accession are binding on the new Member States from the date of accession and apply in those states under the conditions laid down in Community law. Thus, the provision in question draws a distinction between the binding character of such acts with respect to the new Member States and their application in those Member States.[104]

According to the first part of that provision, the new Member States accept to be bound by the existing EU acts as a matter of primary law. According to a legal fiction employed in Article 53 AA, they are considered as having received, upon accession, notification of the existing directives and decisions addressed to all Member States and are obliged, under Article 54 AA, to comply with such acts by the date of accession. That obligation is not subject to the publication of EU acts in the new languages. Moreover, as primary law, it is not open to challenge before the ECJ. That interpretation appears to have been accepted in the existing accession practice: for instance, in the context of the 1981 accession, the Greek State Council considered that the national authorities were bound to adopt the legislation implementing Community acts even before they were published in Greek, although such acts could not produce their effects directly.[105]

Under this construction, delays in publication of EU acts in new languages do not affect their application with regard to new Member States or their indirect application in those states. Similar construction seems to have been accepted by the new Member States acceding in 2004, insofar as they agreed to transpose Community directives and EU framework decisions even before accession took place, on the basis of their unofficial translations. Moreover, after accession, the issue of publication has not been raised in the infringement proceedings or in the context of preliminary references concerning the application of directives. For all practical reasons, the lack of authentic publication of a directive in a given language may also be attenuated by the fact that the national courts may in any case be obliged to consider the text in other language versions.[106]

According to the second part of the provision of Article 2 AA, the application of EU acts in the new Member States is subject to the conditions laid down in EU law. Those conditions include Article 254 EC, making the publication of certain Community acts compulsory.[107] In this regard, the ECJ has recognised that a 'fundamental principle of Community law requires that a measure adopted by the public authorities shall not be applicable to those concerned before they have the opportunity to make themselves acquainted with it .'[108] The modification of Regulation 1 of 1958 introducing the new

---

[104] See also para. 20 of the Opinion of Advocate General Kokott in Case C-161/06 *Skoma-Lux sro v. Celní ředitelství Olomouc, loc. cit.* n. 103.

[105] See Yataganas, *loc. cit.* n. 98, at p. 349.

[106] ECJ, Case C-63/06 *UAB Profisa v. Muitinės departamentas prie Lietuvos Respublikos finansų ministerijos,* [2007] *ECR* I-3239, paras. 13-14.

[107] See Puissochet, *op. cit.* n. 17, at p. 180.

[108] See ECJ, Case 98/78 *A. Racke v. Hauptzollamt Mainz, loc. cit.* n. 102, para. 15.

official languages of Community acts is guided by similar legal requirements: at least for the texts directly applicable in the Member States, it is indispensable for the administration and individuals to have a possibility to become acquainted with such texts in their language.[109] Thus, Community acts cannot be applied directly in the new Member States before they are officially published in the relevant language.

Although the solution resulting from those considerations seems to present the best practical approach in the accession-related context,[110] it remains obviously unusual, as some Community acts would be binding on the new Member States but could not be applied directly by their administration and judiciary. The case law of the Court existing at the time of the 2004 accession did not provide much guidance in this regard. In case 160/84 *Oryzomyli Kavallas*, a case concerning the accession of Greece in 1981, the European Court of Justice considered that a failure to comply with a requirement imposed by the Community legislation, which was not available in Greek, could not be imputed to the negligence of an individual trader. The ECJ did not address the question of direct application of the Regulations in question in Greece, even though it appeared that they were not published until several months after accession, and that the customs authorities used the texts in foreign languages or manuscript translations.[111] In more recent cases C-108/01 *Consorzio del Prosciutto di Parma*[112] and C-469/00 *Ravil SARL and Bellon import SARL*[113] concerning unpublished specifications relating to the protected designations of origin, the ECJ decided that a specification determining the scope of protection resulting from a Community regulation could not be relied upon against individuals until adequately published, but could nevertheless be applied with regard to those who, before the entry into force of the Community regulation, had been aware of the specification in question by virtue of previous national rules.[114]

Given the existence of those doubts, it is not surprising that the national courts addressing this issue after the 2004 accession reached different conclusions. In Poland, the Voivod Adminstrative Court in Bydgoszcz annulled a decision of customs authorities adopted on the basis of the Community Customs Code, which had not at the time of facts been published in Polish.[115] The Administrative Court stated that the administration could not directly apply unpublished Community legislation since that would violate the principle of legal certainty. A different approach was taken by the Estonian Supreme Court, which considered that a professional customs agent was supposed to

---

[109] See Puissochet, *op. cit.* n. 17, at p. 58 and p. 440.

[110] See Bobek, *loc. cit.* n. 100, at pp. 18-19.

[111] See ECJ, Case 160/84 *Oryzomyli Kavallas OEE and others v. Commission of the European Communities, loc. cit.* n. 98. It appears from para. 3 of the Opinion of Advocate General Mischo, that the relevant regulation wasn't published on 15 October 1981, over ten months after the accession of Greece to the European Communities.

[112] ECJ, Case C-108/01 *Consorzio del Prosciutto di Parma, Salumificio S. Rita SpA and Asda Stores Ltd, Hygrade Foods Ltd.* [2003] *ECR* I-5121.

[113] ECJ, Case C-469/00 *Ravil SARL and Bellon import SARL, Biraghi SpA.* [2003] *ECR* I-5053.

[114] For a critical appraisal see S. Enchelmaier, 41 *CMLRev.* (2004) pp. 825-838. See also ECJ, Case C-158/06 *Stichting ROM-projecten v. Staatssecretaris van Economische Zaken* [2007] *ECR* I-5103; Case C-345/06 *Gottfried Heinrich*, [2009] *ECR* nyr.

[115] Wyrok Wojewódzkiego Sądu Administracyjnego w Bydgoszczy, sygn. akt. I SA/Bd275/05 (not reported, on file with the Author).

be acquainted with the Community customs legislation irrespective of whether or not it was published in Estonian.[116]

The issue was settled by the European Court of Justice case C-161/06 *Skoma-Lux,*[117] a case concerning a fine imposed by the Czech customs authorities on a wine importer who had made inexact customs declarations. Some of the declarations in question had been submitted after accession, and the authorities imposing a fine relied in part on the Commission Regulation implementing the Community Customs Code, which had not yet been promulgated in the Czech language.[118] The Czech judge, selected for the appeal against the decision, referred the matter to the ECJ, asking, first, if the Community regulation could be directly relied upon against an individual before it was published in the relevant official language and, second, if the lack of publication in the Official Journal of the European Union affected its validity in terms of *Foto-Frost* judgment.[119]

The Advocate General has suggested that the absence of publication in the new languages did not render Community acts adopted before accession invalid, but that such acts could not be directly invoked against the individuals in the new Member States.[120] In the judgment – delivered by the ECJ in the composition of the Grand Chamber – the ECJ essentially confirmed that analysis. Thus, on the one hand, the ECJ recalled that, under Article 254(2) EC, a Community regulation can only enter into force if it is published in the Official Journal of the European Union. The same condition also applies, on the basis of Articles 2 and 58 AA, with regard to the enforcement of the existing Community legislation in the new Member States after their accession. According to this interpretation, which is guided by the principles of legal certainty and non-discrimination, Community legislation which has not been published in the Official Journal of the European Union in the language of a new Member State cannot be imposed on individuals in that state.[121] On the other hand, the ECJ confirmed that such unpublished Community legislation remained valid and was binding on the new Member States from the date of their accession, as the lack of publication only delayed its application with regard to individuals. The ECJ also found it necessary to state clearly that its judgment did not lead to the annulment of the unpublished legislation, but only concerned its "enforceability".[122]

---

[116]  The text of the judgment available on the website of the Supreme Court of Estonia at http://www. riigikohus.ee. See further Bobek, *loc. cit.* n. 100 and Chapter 6 in this volume.

[117]  ECJ, Case C-161/06 *Skoma-Lux sro v. Celní ředitelství Olomouc, loc. cit.* n. 103.

[118]  Commission Regulation (EEC) No 2454/93 of 2 July 1993 laying down provisions for the implementation of Council Regulation (EEC) No 2913/92 establishing the Community Customs Code, *OJ* 1993 L 253/1.

[119]  ECJ, Case 314/85 *Foto-Frost v. Hauptzollamt Lübeck-Ost* [1987] *ECR* 4199.

[120]  See the Opinion of the Advocate General in *Skoma-Lux*, paras. 26-33 and 41-43. Interestingly, the Advocate General also examined if the regulation, which has been published in the meantime, could be applied retroactively to the time of the events (paras. 62-63). That analysis might seem unnecessary, as such retroactive application could not, in any case, re-establish the legality of administrative decisions adopted on the basis of the unpublished legislation.

[121]  See ECJ, Case C-161/06 *Skoma-Lux sro v. Celní ředitelství Olomouc, loc. cit.* n. 103, paras. 33-35 and 51.

[122]  *Ibidem*, paras. 58-61 and 68. This solution was recently invoked by Advocate General Ruiz-Jarabo Colomer in his Opinion of 17 January 2009 in case C-560/07 *Balbiino AS v. Põllumajandusminister and Maksu- ja Tolliameti Põhja maksu- ja tollikeskus*, at paras. 36-41.

In that regard, it is interesting to note that, although the regulation was not annulled, the European Court of Justice relied on Article 231 EC to limit the effects of its judgment. Under that provision, when the CFI or ECJ annul a piece of Community secondary legislation, they may preserve some of its legal consequences. Similarly, in case C-161/06 *Skoma-Lux*, the ECJ indicated that national decisions taken pursuant to unpublished and, thus unenforceable, provisions of Community law retain their legal effect, with the exception of the decisions subject to the pending challenge at the date of the judgment, as well as the situations in which the preservation of legal effects of the existing administrative or judicial decisions, in particular of a coercive nature, would compromise fundamental rights.[123]

## 4.    CONCLUDING REMARKS

The fifth and sixth enlargements of the European Union, given their unprecedented extent, constituted a unique occasion to clarify a number of temporal legal issues linked to the accession of new Member States. Importantly, the ECJ used this opportunity not only to expand its existing jurisprudence relating to new accessions, but also to tread on new grounds.

Thus, with regard to the pre-accession arrangements, the European Court of Justice affirmed that the EU institutions can lawfully adopt, before accession, certain provisions concerning acceding countries using the general legislative powers under the EC Treaty, and not only the specific procedures envisaged in an accession treaty. The ECJ also admitted that, starting from the date of signature of an accession treaty, Member States to be have the right to interact in the pre-accession legislation, and that right may be taken into account in the context of judicial review of EU acts adopted shortly before accession. Regarding the application of EU law after accession, the ECJ set a clear limit to the scope of its preliminary rulings jurisdiction in the context of pre-accession disputes pending before courts in new Member States and, more recently, clarified the consequences of the absence of publication of EU acts in new official languages.

In the latter regard, the decision of the European Court of Justice is explicitly founded on the considerations relating to the equal treatment of individuals in the old and the new Member States.[124] This reminds us that that technical distinction should remain just a catch-phrase employed for practical reasons, while the EU Member States face the same world, always old and always new, as the 'light about the moon is always new and always old ... for the sun in his revolution always adds new light, and there is the old light of the previous month.'[125]

---

[123]  *Ibidem*, paras. 69-73.

[124]  *Ibidem*, para. 39.

[125]  Plato, *Cratylus* (translation by B. Jowett, 1999, quoted from Project Gutenberg http://www.gutenberg.org).

*Chapter 5*

# THE NEW EUROPEAN JUDGES AND THE LIMITS OF THE POSSIBLE

Michal Bobek*

## 1.    INTRODUCTION

In classical narratives of the story called the European integration, national judges are said to have "mandate" under EC law; they are "empowered" by EC law, or, in the less thrilling versions of the story, they just become "Community judges." With power come duties and responsibility. Not only are national judges obliged to apply substantive EC law, they are also requested to apply it in the way required by the European Court of Justice. How precisely national judges are supposed to do it has traditionally been portrayed exclusively through the case law of the ECJ. Not much attention has been paid to the reality in the Member States´ courts. Throughout the years, the ECJ's case law has created an image of a veritable European judicial Hercules, who reads in many official languages of the European Union. He not only knows all national and EU law, which he applies *ex officio*, but also engages in comparative interpretation of law; he is a judge who has identified himself with the European *telos*, which he is applying on the national level.

In every legal system, there is a difference between the normative requirements of the law and the reality of day-to-day application. The question generally asked is how wide is the gap. The wider the gap, the less efficient is the activity of the norms-setting body, as it is itself driving further and further away from the application reality. This chapter outlines some of the areas in which the gap between, on the one hand, the requirements of the European Court of Justice as far as the "correct" methodology of the application of EC law by national courts is concerned, and, on the other hand, the practice and the realistic capacities of the national courts, which have become very wide. Our primary focus (and the source of experience) is the judicial potential in the courts of new Member States; however, most of the conclusions made in this chapter can be fairly extended to courts and judges of the "old" Member States as well.

* Researcher, European University Institute, Department of Law, Florence, Italy. I am obliged to Jan Komárek and Petr Bříza for their valuable comments. This is a shorter version of the contribution 'On the Application of European Law in (Not Only) the Courts of the New Member States: "Don't Do as I Say"?', 10 *CYEL* (2007-2008) pp. 1-34. All opinions expressed are strictly personal to the author.

*A. Łazowski (ed.), The Application of EU Law in the New Member States*
© 2010, T·M·C·ASSER PRESS, *The Hague, The Netherlands and the Authors*

The structure of this chapter is dialectic: first, it summarises some of the requirements the ECJ's case law lays on the national courts' judges when applying EC law.
Second, a sober assessment of the judicial capacity in these areas is provided with, if
possible, some examples from case law from the new Member States. Finally, broader
conclusions as far as national judges' capacities and incentives for the domestic application of EU law and their interaction with the ECJ are made, including inspirations
the European Union legal order may draw from the game theory.

## 2.    THE EUROPEAN JUDICIAL HERCULES IN ACTION

### 2.1.    The linguist

The European Union currently has 23 official languages.[1] All those languages are
equally authentic. When interpreting EU law, national judges are asked to consider
other language versions of EU legislation as well, in order to arrive at the correct interpretation thereof. Comparing various language versions[2] of EU law is governed by
three basic principles:

(i)    the prohibition of reading one language version in isolation;
(ii)   the prohibition of majoritisation;
(iii)  overcoming the discrepancy by taking into account other methods of interpreta-
       tion, especially the logical, systematic and purposive reading of the normative
       text.

The prohibition of reading one language version in isolation from the others[3] is an
extension of the principle of equal authenticity of all the official languages of the
European Union. By establishing this principle, the European Court of Justice tries

---

[1] With respect to primary law, see Art. 314 EC or Art. 53 TEU (and the respective final provisions
in other European Union Treaties); with respect to secondary law, see Art. 1 of the Regulation 1/58/EEC
determining the languages to be used by the European Economic Community, *JO* 1958 17/390, English
special edition: Series I, Chapter 1952-1958, p. 59. There are, however, temporal derogations in respect of
Irish (Gaelic) and Maltese – see Council Regulation (EC) No 930/2004 of 1 May 2004 on temporary derogation measures relating to the drafting in Maltese of the acts of the institutions of the European Union,
*OJ* 2004 L 169/1 and Council Regulation (EC) No 920/2005 of 13 June 2005 amending Regulation No 1 of
15 April 1958 determining the language to be used by the European Economic Community and Regulation
No 1 of 15 April 1958 determining the language to be used by the European Atomic Energy Community
and introducing temporary derogation measures from those Regulations, *OJ* 2005 L 156/3.
[2] Generally on the topic, see, e.g., G. Van Calster, 'The EU's Tower of Babel. The Interpretation by
the European Court of Justice of Equally Authentic Texts Drafted in more than one Official Language',
17 *YEL* (1997) pp. 363-393; C. Luttermann, 'Rechtssprachenvergleich in der Europäischen Union', *EuZW*
(1999) p. 154; B. Pozzo and V. Jacometti, eds., *Multilingualism and the Harmonisation of European Law*
(Alphen aan den Rijn, Kluwer Law International 2006).
[3] Most recently, ECJ, Case C-63/06 *UAB Profisa v. Muitinės departamentas prie Lietuvos Respublikos finansų ministerijos* [2007] *ECR* I-3239, para. 13. Further, *inter alia*, ECJ, Case 26/69 *Stauder v. Stadt
Ulm* [1969] *ECR* 419, para. 3; Case 55/87 *Alexander Moksel Import und Export GmbH & Co. Handels-KG
v. Bundesanstalt für landwirtschaftliche Marktordnung* [1988] *ECR* 3845, para. 15 or Case C-296/95 *The*

above all to prevent the situation in which, for instance, an English court would seek to "solve" the discrepancy between, for example, English and French versions of an EU legal measure by declaring that only the English version is relevant and binding on the territory of the United Kingdom.

The prohibition of majoritisation, or the prevailing of the majority of language versions over the minority,[4] is again a logical consequence of the equality of all the official languages. If all the versions are equally authentic, then the meaning which the minority of them or just one of them gives cannot be automatically outvoted by the majoritarian meaning.

The *Anglo-Polish Fishing* case[5] is a classical account of this rule. The case concerned the determination of a precise moment when fish become goods for the purposes of customs. Whereas the French, Italian, Greek, Danish and Dutch texts of the relevant Community legislation on the origin of goods referred to the decisive moment as "extraction from the sea" (*extraits de la mer*), i.e., the act of physical separation of the fish from its natural environment, the German version was satisfied with the moment when the fish is caught (*gefangen*). The English "taken from the sea" appeared to be somewhere in the midway. The European Court of Justice noted that the comparative examination of the various language versions does not enable a conclusion to be reached in favour of any of the language versions, despite the fact that a clear majority of the language versions would hint in the direction of determining as the relevant factor the moment in which the fish is genuinely separated from its natural environment.[6]

The prohibition of majoritisation is absolute. It is applicable not only in situations like that one described above, i.e., where there is a genuine divergence in the meaning of an EU rule in various languages, but also in cases of evident shortcomings or mistakes in translation of EU legislation. After the 2004 enlargement (and presumably also after the 2007 one), both instances are numerous. Shortcomings in translation are typically caused by the disregard for the established legal terms already existent in the legal language or by disregard for the already established EU terminology in the language into which the text is being translated.[7] Translation mistakes were caused by the hasty translation of tens of thousands of items of EU secondary legislation.[8] However, even

*Queen and Commissioners of Customs and Excise,* ex parte *EMU Tabac SARL, The Man in Black Limited and John Cunningham* [1998] *ECR* I-1605, para. 36.

[4] *Ibidem,* see also instructive opinions of Advocates General in Case C-227/01 *Commission of the European Communities v. Kingdom of Spain* [2004] *ECR* I-8253, paras. 22-28 or Case C-371/02 *Björnekulla Fruktindustrier AB v. Procordia Food AB* [2004] *ECR* I-5791, paras. 34-43.

[5] ECJ, Case 100/84 *Commission of the European Communities v. United Kingdom of Great Britain and Northern Ireland* [1985] *ECR* 1169. See also the very helpful and literarily rich Opinion of the AG Mancini at pp. 1170-1176.

[6] *Ibidem,* at p. 1182 (para. 16).

[7] See, e.g., ECJ, Case 55/87 *Alexander Moksel Import und Export GmbH & Co. Handels-KG v. Bundesanstalt für landwirtschaftliche Marktordnung* [1988] *ECR* 3845, in which a similar problem arose because of a divergence in terminology in German translations of Community regulations and the introduction of a new term "*Werktag*" without clarifying its relationship to the already existent "*Arbeitstag.*"

[8] And not only secondary law. For instance, the Czech version of Art. 254(1) and (2) EC does not operate with the notion of "entry into force", as all the other language versions (e.g., "*entrent en vigueur*", "*treten in Kraft*", "*wchodzą w życie*"), but just with "validity" resulting from the publication of a legal act.

in cases of blunt mistakes in translation of secondary legislation, there is the prohibition of majoritisation.

The *UAB Profisa* case[9] provides the latest example. The case concerned the Lithuanian transposition of the Council Directive 92/83/EEC excise duty on alcohol and alcoholic beverages.[10] An erroneous translation of the Directive into Lithuanian considerably restricted the grounds on which an importer of chocolate products containing ethyl alcohol could be exempted from excise duty. The national implementing law simply copied the narrow definition from the wrongly translated directive and denied the importer in question the possibility of duty exemption. It appears that in the particular case, the meaning in all other languages was clear,[11] demonstrating that a translation mistake occurred only in the Lithuanian version. However, even in this case, the European Court of Justice maintained that one language version cannot be outvoted by the contrary and clear meaning of the other 19.

The preceding two principles are only capable of detecting problems among the various language versions of the text. They are not, however, able to solve the problem. In reality, they work quite to the contrary: after considering other language versions, a difference in various texts is detected. This divergence cannot be solved on the basis of simple reassertion of how many languages hint in one direction and how many in the other, i.e., by a language "voting". If the two preceding principles were to be left on their own, they would create an impasse. The divergence is thus bridged by resorting to a third principle, which allows for overcoming the stalemate. One is allowed to disregard the conflicting language versions in favour of the systematic or purposive reading of the statute, which is independent of the conflicting text. In the words of the European Court of Justice, 'Where there is divergence between the various language versions of a Community text, the provision in question must be interpreted by reference to the purpose and general scheme of the rules of which it forms part.'[12]

This particular approach meant, for instance, in the already discussed case of *Anglo-Polish Fishing*, resorting to the intention of the Community legislature and to system-

---

Last sentence of Art. 254(1) EC in Czech reads 'They shall become valid on the date specified in them or, in the absence thereof, on the twentieth day following that of their publication.' If interpreted literally, this would mean that according to the Czech version of the Treaty, Community regulations or directives never enter into force.

[9] ECJ, Case C-63/06 *UAB Profisa v. Muitinės departamentas prie Lietuvos Respublikos finansų ministerijos* [2007] *ECR* I-3239.

[10] Council Directive 92/83/EEC of 19 October 1992 on the harmonisation of the structures of excise duties on alcohol and alcoholic beverages, *OJ* 1992 L 316/21.

[11] As was argued by the European Commission, which was perhaps the only entity that was genuinely able to compare, in its submission, all the then equally authentic 20 versions of the provision in question (written observations submitted on behalf of the European Commission of 22 May 2006 in the Case C-63/06, *UAB Profisa*, ref. JURM(2006)3084-FR, pp. 5-8).

[12] ECJ, Case C-1/02 *Privat-Molkerei Borgmann GmbH & Co. KG v. Hauptzollamt Dortmund* [2004] *ECR* I-3219 para. 25; Case C-437/97 *Evangelischer Krankenhausverein Wien v. Abgabenberufungskommission Wien and Wein & Co. HandelsgesmbH v. Oberösterreichische Landesregierung* [2000] *ECR* I-1157, para. 42 or Case C-372/88 *Milk Marketing Board of England and Wales v. Cricket St Thomas Estate* [1990] *ECR* I-1345, para. 19.

atic interpretation (analogy) of the rules on origin of goods in Community law.[13] In the *UAB Profisa* case, the decisive aspect was the objective pursued by the exemptions and the systematic reading of the Directive,[14] which meant that the exemption of products from the excise duty covered by the provision is the rule and refusal is the exception.

Theoretically, the principles of comparative linguistic interpretation together with the principle of equal authenticity of all the linguistic versions could be interpreted, if taken to the extreme, as meaning that the content of a Community legal norm is not contained in, for example, its French or English version but only in the aggregate of all the authentic language versions. Correct literal interpretation[15] of any single piece of Community legislation which is drafted in more languages[16] must thus involve the parallel reading of all of the language versions.

## 2.2.    Knowledge of the law

Most of the continental civil law systems are based on the assumption expressed in the old Roman maxim *iura novit curia* – the court knows the law. It means that a judge is obliged to apply valid laws *ex officio*, i.e., of his/her own motion. If s/he disregards this obligation, a decision may be quashed on appeal or/and the state may incur liability. The correlative privilege of the parties to the dispute is not to have to argue points of law but just to deliver the facts of the case before the judge.

This maxim is still present in the Central European legal systems and the legal theory of most new Member States. For instance, the Czech as well as the Slovak fundamental code of procedure, the Code of Civil Procedure, is based on the assumption that parties to a dispute are only obliged to prove their factual statements. Conversely, they are not obliged to prove the valid law published in the official collection of laws.[17]

The European Court of Justice's case law regarding the knowledge of a national judge in respect to Community legislation is basically an extension of the national principles. When assessing the duty of a national judge to apply Community law *ex officio*, the European Court of Justice cross-referred the issue and sent it back to the national level. National courts are not obliged to raise issues concerning a breach of Community law of their own motion, provided that national regulations do not require

---

[13] *Loc. cit.* n. 5, paras. 18 and 19.

[14] *Loc. cit.* n. 9, paras. 17 and 18.

[15] It serves to be mindful that the comparison of the various language versions of the Community legislation forms a part of literal interpretation of the rule. It is not, as commonly mistaken, for comparative reasoning as such.

[16] But not necessarily all; there are, by now, linguistic regimes in Community law which reduce the amount of official languages to, for instance, five. See Art. 115 of the Council Regulation (EC) No 40/94 of 20 December 1993 on the Community trade mark, *OJ* 1994 L 11/1, which limits languages of the OHIM to English, French, German, Italian and Spanish. See also ECJ, Case C-361/01 P *Kik v. OHIM* [2003] *ECR* I-8283, especially paras. 88-94.

[17] Art. 121 *zákon č. 99/1963 Sb., soudní řád správní* [Code of Civil Procedure]. The Czech version of the provision, which remained the same for both countries from the times of the Czech and Slovak Federation, refers only to the Czech Collection of Laws, whereas the Slovak provision, which has been in the meantime amended, expressly includes also the Official Journal of the European Communities.

them to do so with respect to national law.[18] If the question were to be returned to the national level, and the principle of equality applied, the conclusion would be that judges in most new Member States are obliged to raise points of EC law on their own motion and to actively seek and apply relevant EC law.

## 2.3.    The comparative lawyer

Comparative methodology plays, at least again in the official narrative, an important role in the development of the Community legal order, not only before the European Court of Justice itself[19] but also in national courts. There is no doubt that a reference to the decisions of the courts of other Member States interpreting and applying Community law can be a valuable source of inspiration. Moreover, Article 10 EC and the duty of sincere and loyal co-operation entail not only diagonal dimension (the Community institutions – the Member States) but also horizontal dimension, which involves the authorities of the Member States, inclusive of courts. The reference in Member States' courts to the decisions of the courts of other Member States applying EC law would thus border on the advisable use of comparative legal reasoning before national courts.[20]

The duty of national judges in matters of comparative methodology does not stop, however, at the level of the "advisable." At least for the courts of last instance, there is the duty to use comparative reasoning and to compare their interpretation of Community law with the interpretation reached in the courts of other Member States. In the words of the European Court of Justice, national courts of last instance shall make sure that a matter of interpretation of Community law 'is equally obvious to the courts of the other Member States and to the Court of Justice.'[21]

The European Court of Justice never specified how precisely the national courts have to make sure that their interpretation is equally obvious to their counterparts in other Member States: by a detailed comparative study of the decisions of other European courts (of last instance) or by considering at least some of them? Advocate General

---

[18] See ECJ, Joined Cases C-430/93 and C-431/93 *Jeroen Van Schijndel and Johannes Nicolaas Cornelis van Veen v. Stichting Pensioenfonds voor Fysiotherapeuten* [1995] *ECR* I-4705, paras. 13-15; Case C-312/93 *Peterbroeck, Van Campenhout & Cie SCS v. Belgian State* [1995] *ECR* I-4599, paras. 12 and 14; Case C-72/95 *Aannemersbedrijf P.K. Kraaijeveld BV e.a. v. Gedeputeerde Staten van Zuid-Holland* [1996] *ECR* I-5403, paras. 58 and 60, or, most recently, Case C-2/06 *Willy Kempter KG v. Hauptzollamt Hamburg-Jonas* [2008] *ECR* I-411, para. 45. See further, *inter alia*, S. Prechal, 'Community Law in National Courts: The Lessons from Van Schijndel', 35 *CMLRev.* (1998) pp. 681-706.

[19] Further see K. Lenaerts, 'Interlocking Legal Orders in the European Union and Comparative Law', 52 *ICLQ* (2003) pp. 873-906.

[20] See, e.g., U. Drobnig, S. Van Erp, eds., *The Use of Comparative Law by Courts. XIVth International Coungress of Comparative Law, Athens 1997* (The Hague – London – Boston, Kluwer Law International 1999) or U. Uyterhoeven, *Richterliche Rechtsfindung und Rechtsvergleichung. Eine Vorstudie über die Rechtsvergleichung als Hilfsmittel der richterlichen Rechtsfindung im Privatrecht* (Bern, Verlag Stämpfli 1959). In Drobnig's classification this type of use of comparative argument would fall into the "advisable" category.

[21] ECJ, Case 283/81 *Srl CILFIT and Lanificio di Gavardo SpA v. Ministry of Health* [1982] *ECR* 3415, para. 16.

Miguel Poiares Maduro, writing extra-judicially, recently offered a "milder" interpretation of this particular obligation imposed upon national courts by the European Court of Justice. In his view, the core of the *CILFIT* doctrine is the obligation of the national judicial body to justify its decisions in a universal manner by reference to the EU context. Furthermore, the decision must be grounded in an interpretation that could be applied by any other national court in similar situations.[22]

The latest opportunity for the European Court of Justice to clarify – or perhaps to substantially reformulate – this aspect of the *CILFIT* decision came in the *Intermodal Transports* case.[23] In this case, the European Court of Justice was asked by the Dutch *Hoge Raad* [the Council of State] what argumentative value a national court of last instance shall accord to an administrative decision concerning the same issue but originating from another Member State, which runs contrary to the interpretation the national court is about to adopt. In the case at hand, a Dutch company was involved in a dispute before national customs authorities regarding the classification of tractors in the combined nomenclature of the common customs tariff. In the course of the judicial proceedings regarding the argument about the proper sub-heading under which the tractors were to be put, the Dutch company submitted to the Dutch court binding tariff information issued by Finnish authorities regarding the same type of tractor, but issued to a third party, a Finnish company. The question asked by the *Hoge Raad* in respect to this document was whether or not producing such a document in the course of judicial proceedings before a national court of last instance, which wants to adopt a decision running counter to that document, automatically triggers the *CILFIT* scenario and thus means that the issue is not equally clear to the courts of other Member States, with the ensuing duty to refer the question to the European Court of Justice.

The decision of the European Court of Justice stated two things. First, it restated the *CILFIT* criteria. Second, it noted that the *CILFIT* criteria do not apply in respect to decisions of administrative authorities of other Member States. The ECJ held that 'a court cannot be required to ensure that, in addition, the matter is equally obvious to bodies of a non-judicial nature such as administrative authorities.'[24]

It would thus appear that, as far as the requirements of the European Court of Justice are concerned, lower courts would be well advised to use the argumentative help and inspiration from the decision of their colleagues in other Member States, whereas Member States' courts of last instance are under a duty to consider the decisions on the same matters issued by their counterparts in other Member States.

## 2.4.     The guardian of the European telos

Much has been written about teleological reasoning in EU law; from praising it as the key method in the interpretation, characteristic of the treaties establishing the Com-

---

[22] M. Poiares Maduro, 'Interpreting European Law: Judicial Adjudication in a Context of Constitutional Pluralism', 1 *EJLS* (2007) p. 18.

[23] ECJ, Case C-495/03 *Intermodal Transports BV v. Staatssecretaris van Financiën* [2005] *ECR* I-8151.

[24] *Ibidem*, para. 39.

munities/Union,[25] to calling it the cause for the European Court of Justice running wild and engaging in revolting judicial behaviour.[26]

Teleological reasoning in (not only) EU law is a sort of consequentialist reasoning, i.e., reasoning out of a positive or a negative consequence.[27] The extensive use of teleological reasoning in EU law is a necessary consequence of the systematic nature of the EU legal order; not much textual exegesis is possible in a lacunae system of legal norms, most of them by their nature objectives-stating or finality norms, which do not specify the way the aim is to be achieved. Moreover, as was shown above, the multilingual character of EU norms also fosters the need for greater recourse to purposive or systematic reasoning which helps to bridge the discrepancies between the respective language versions.

While there is a very close link between the teleological reasoning and the "*effet utile*" argument, they are not the same.[28] The rule of effectiveness constitutes a value choice within the teleological reasoning itself; the identified purpose ("telos") is the effective functioning of Community institutions and the exercise of their powers. The argument of *effet utile* thus constitutes a certain type of teleological reasoning.

In interpreting and applying EU law, judges should consider EU objectives and the purpose the interpreted piece of EU legislation seeks to attain. This requirement is strongly visible in many areas of the case law of the European Court of Justice, most notably perhaps as far as the principle of effective protection of individual rights derived from Community law on the national level. Following this purpose (and seeking to achieve this consequence), national judges are entitled to do pretty much anything, including setting aside the provisions of the national constitution.

3.      NATIONAL COURTS: MISSION IMPOSSIBLE?

Now let us turn back to the national level and try to paint perhaps a more realistic picture of what national judges do and what they can reasonably be expected to do.

---

[25] P. Pescatore, 'Les objectifs de la Communauté européenne comme principes de l´interprétation dans la jurisprudence de la Cour de justice', quoted after F. Dumon, 'La jurisprudence de la Cour de justice – Examen critique des methods d´interprétation', in *Rencontre judiciaire et universitaire 27-28 septembre 1976* (Luxembourg, Office for Official Publications 1976) pp. III-80.

[26] H. Rasmussen, *On Law and Policy in the European Court of Justice* (Dordrecht, Martinus Nijhoff Publisher 1986).

[27] The reasoning employed by the European Court of Justice provides ample examples of both. For the reasoning out of positive consequence see, e.g., ECJ, Case 26/62 *NV Algemene Transport- en Expeditie Onderneming van Gend & Loos v. Netherlands Inland Revenue Administration* [1963] *ECR* 1 ('The Community is a new legal order of international law and it thus must have the following characteristics'), for the example of reasoning out of a negative consequence, see, e.g., ECJ, Case C-453/99 *Courage Ltd and Others v. Bernard Crehan* [2001] *ECR* I-6297 ( 'If we do not allow for damages for private breaches of Community competition rules, the effective enforcement of EC competition rules on the national level will be compromised').

[28] See H. Kutscher, 'Méthodes d´interprétation vues par un juge à la Cour', in *Rencontre judiciaire et universitaire 27-28 septembre 1976* (Luxembourg, Office for Official Publications 1976) pp. I-39 et seq.

## 3.1. Resolved to create an even less and less comprehensible union?

Following the 2004 enlargement, the language of EU legislation has become partially a nightmare, partially a rich source of cynic amusement and – above all – the reason for considerable legal uncertainty. Already in 1985, Advocate General Mancini famously noted, with respect to the style of drafting of Community legislation and its linguistic clarity, that 'I doubt whether Marguerite Yourcenar or Graham Green would be prepared to read each morning a piece or two of Community legislation "pour prendre le ton", as Stendhal used to read articles of the Code Civil.'[29] It is, however, submitted that following hasty translations of tens of thousands of EU primary and secondary laws into the languages of new Member States, the language problems reached a completely new dimension.

To start with, there were no official translations of EU legislation available at the moment of the accession.[30] The failure to publish EU legislation has, however, generated surprisingly little litigation. The European Court of Justice has so far addressed this issue in two decisions,[31] in both admitting, directly or indirectly, that there actually were no binding and duly published versions of European Union legislation in the languages of the new Member States.

The *Skoma-Lux* case concerned enforcement of EC legislation unpublished in the Czech language, in the particular case a regulation, by the Czech administrative authorities. The reference was submitted by the Regional Court in Ostrava [*Krajký soud v Ostravě*] in course of proceedings between the company Skoma-Lux, s.r.o. and the Customs Authority, regarding a fine imposed on Skoma-Lux in respect to customs infringements which it was alleged to have committed between March and May 2004. One of the grounds raised by the company for the fine to be annulled was that the Customs Authority could not enforce against it the Community legislation which had not yet been published in the Czech language in the Official Journal of the EU.

Assessing the issue, the Grand Chamber of the European Court of Justice observed that, as far as the position of individuals in a similar situation was concerned, Community law:

'precludes the obligations contained in Community legislation which has not been published in the Official Journal of the European Union in the language of a new Member State, where that language is an official language of the European Union, from being imposed on individuals in that State.'[32]

---

[29] AG Mancini's opinion in Case 100/84 *Commission of the European Communities v. United Kingdom of Great Britain and Northern Ireland* [1985] *ECR* 1169, at p. 1173.

[30] Further see M. Bobek, 'The Binding Force of Babel: The Enforcement of EC Law Unpublished in the Languages of the New Member States', 9 *CYELS* (2007) pp. 43-80.

[31] ECJ, Case C-161/06 *Skoma Lux sro v. Celní ředitelství Olomouc* [2007] *ECR* I-10841; Case C-273/04 *Republic of Poland v. Council of the European Union* [2007] *ECR* I-8925.

[32] ECJ, Case C-161/06 *Skoma Lux sro v. Celní ředitelství Olomouc*, *loc. cit.* n. 31, para. 74. Further on the implications of the *Skoma-Lux* decision, see K. Lasiński-Sulecki and W. Morawski, 'Late Publication of EC Law in Languages of New Member States and its Effects: Obligations on Individuals Following the Court's Judgment in Skoma-Lux', 45 *CML Rev.* (2008) pp. 705-725.

Taking into account the considerable impact the decision could have on the already adopted decisions on the national level, it appears that the Court sought to limit the temporal effects of its decision. It stated that its decision should not be applicable to national decisions adopted prior to the decision, with the exception of 'decisions which had been the subject of administrative or judicial proceedings at the date of this judgment.'[33] It added that the Member States are not, under Community law, obliged to call into question already adopted decisions.

However, this approach of an "already closed chapter" is in fact negated in the following paragraph, where the ECJ reopens the door to the potential litigants by stating that there still remains a possibility of reopening final decisions on the national level in cases of:

> 'exceptional circumstances where ... there have been administrative measures or judicial decisions, in particular of a coercive nature, which would compromise fundamental rights: it is for the competent national authorities to ascertain this within those limits.'[34]

It remains to be seen what the domestic practice makes out of this. The exception is framed very broadly: any decision by which national authorities have imposed financial penalties for disregarding unpublished Community legislation could be said to be an administrative measure of coercive nature, which touches upon a fundamental right – the right to property. The first direct application of the *Skoma-Lux* holding was, apart from the decision in the original case itself, probably a decision of the Slovak Supreme Court [*Najvyšší súd*].[35] The factual circumstances in the case at hand were similar to the *Skoma-Lux* litigation: an importer had been fined by the customs authorities for wrongful declarations. The court annulled the administrative decision, following the Court's decision in *Skoma-Lux* and the express motion in the pleading of the applicant concerning the lack of application of the relevant customs legislation in the Slovak version of the Official Journal of the European Union.

A further step in the application of the *Skoma-Lux* holding was made by the Czech Supreme Administrative Court. In the original *Skoma-Lux* case, as well as in the Slovak decision, the fact that Community legislation was not duly published at the material time was invoked in the pleading of the parties. Another question was whether the issue of publication was to be considered only following an express motion in this respect made by a party or whether the national courts ought to examine this on their own motion. The answer of the Supreme Administrative Court upheld the latter approach: by a decision of 18 June 2008, the Court started reviewing, on its own motion, whether in the cases that were pending before the administrative courts or administrative authorities at the date of the *Skoma-Lux* decision,[36] the administrative decision which imposed obligations upon individuals was based on a duly published regulation. If not,

---

[33]  *Ibidem*, para. 71.
[34]  *Ibidem*, para. 73.
[35]  Judgment of 18 March 2008, 5 Sžf 59/2007, accessible via the JuriFast database at http://www.juradmin.eu.
[36]  ECJ, Case C-161/06 *Skoma Lux sro v. Celní ředitelství Olomouc*, *loc. cit.* n. 31, para. 72.

the decisions of the administrative authorities were annulled; these decisions concerned above all customs[37] disputes but also general sanctions imposed in other areas of administrative law, such as a fine imposed on a lorry driver for the disregard of compulsory rest periods.[38]

Another lasting language problem in the courts of the new Member States is the quality of translation of EU legislation – inconsistency in terminology, blatant mistakes in translation, parts of legislation which are incomprehensible. These problems, unfortunately, do not concern only the pre-accession *acquis*, which had to be translated *en bloc*. They also involve secondary legislation published after the "big bang" enlargement.

Mistakes and inconsistencies are gradually being detected and removed by corrigenda published in the Official Journal of the European Union. One would nonetheless assume that the issue of a corrigendum is designed for correcting typing or type-setting mistakes, not substantively changing or, in fact, rewriting the content of the legal measure. This is often not the case. For instance, the Commission Regulation (EC) No 865/2006 of 4 May 2006 laying down detailed rules concerning the implementation of Council Regulation (EC) No 338/97 on the protection of species of wild fauna and flora was published in the Czech version of the Official Journal on 19 June 2006.[39] It entered into force 20 days later, and the administrative authorities started applying it.

More than a year later, in August 2007, a corrigendum of the Czech version of the Regulation was published in the Official Journal of the EU.[40] The corrigendum contains no less than 122 corrections to the Regulation, which is composed of 75 articles, i.e., more or less every article is amended twice, including the title of the Regulation itself. The corrections are not mere typing mistakes, but *de facto* substantive amendments of the entire Regulation. They include the change of singular forms into plural, turning positive statements into negative ones or changing the nature of a list of conditions to be fulfilled (from requiring at least one of the criteria to be met into the requirement of all the criteria to be met). What now of the tens or perhaps already hundreds of administrative decisions which have been issued by the Czech authorities in reliance on the text of the Regulation published in the Official Journal and which are now not in conformity with the "corrected" version of the Regulation?

These and other instances of language incomprehensibility create an overall (perhaps not just) sentiment of considerable legislative instability and chaos of EU legislation in the new Member States. But let us return to the original motive of this section – the judicial interpretation of EU law by consulting more (or perhaps all) language versions

---

[37] Judgment of the SAC of 18 June 2008, 1 Afs 21/2008, http://www.nssoud.cz.

[38] As provided for in Council Regulation (EEC) No 3820/85 of 20 December 1985 on the harmonisation of certain social legislation relating to road transport, *OJ* 1985 L 370/1 – see judgment of the Supreme Adminstrative Court of 24 January 2008, 9 As 36/2007, published as no 1533/2008 Coll. of the SAC.

[39] Commission Regulation (EC) No 865/2006 of 4 May 2006 laying down detailed rules concerning the implementation of Council Regulation (EC) No 338/97 on the protection of species of wild fauna and flora by regulating trade therein, *OJ* 2006 L 166/1.

[40] Oprava nařízení Komise (ES) č. 865/2006 ze dne 4. května 2006 o prováděcích pravidlech k nařízení Rady (ES) č. 338/97 o ochraně druhů volně žijících živočichů a planě rostoucích rostlin regulováním obchodu s těmito druhy, *OJ* 2007 L 211/30.

of the EU legislation. What is the reasonable potential of a national judge in such situations?

Of course, the national judges do not normally read any language versions other than their own; not even (or perhaps especially not) versions from the judges of last instance courts, upon whom the European Court of Justice laid a specific requirement in this respect.[41] One can only reasonably expect a judge to look into another language version of a piece of EU legislation when the degree of incomprehension of the national version reaches the stage in which the interpretation of the piece of legislation in the national language alone would lead to absurd results. Comparing language versions could thus be conceived of as an alternative to a certain "mischief rule" or protection against absurdity rule.

Conventionally, one understands methods or "canons" of legal interpretation as the way of eliminating uncertainties in the interpretation of a legal provision. In other words, the methods of interpretation are there to help the interpreter to arrive at a reasonable reading of the norm, not to create additional problems. The requirement of a comparative linguistic exercise in 23 languages, or even in whatever lower, more manageable number of languages, does nothing but create problems. Considered from this perspective, the comparative language exercise is not a "method of interpretation", but typically a "method of obfuscation" of a legal provision.

The effect of the comparison of various language versions typically is just more confusion and legal uncertainty. Its impact is to untie the interpreter from the text of the rule itself; the interpreter detects, with the reference to divergence among the various language versions, an inconsistency in various language versions. The only way of overcoming the inconsistency is by setting aside the wording and, by relying on systematic or purposive reading of the text of the law, reformulating the rule. The requirement of the comparative language exercise may thus be perceived as a universal means for bringing into the game purposive reasoning in defiance of the text of the legal provision.

This may be one of the main reasons, obviously apart from the linguistic competence itself,[42] why national judges virtually never follow the European Court of Justice's guidance as far as the comparison of the various language versions is concerned. On the rare occasions the national courts actually attempt to conduct anything which could be called a comparison of various language versions, they first limit themselves to one or only a few of the more significant languages within the EU (English, French and German, occasionally also Italian or Spanish), and second, the reference to the other language versions is used in the form of a confirming argument to the conclusion already

---

[41] *Loc. cit.* n. 21, para. 18.

[42] Which is more assumed than real; the proof of knowledge of at least one foreign language is not a condition for the appointment to the judicial office neither in the Czech Republic, nor in Slovakia, nor, to the knowledge of the author, in any other of the new Member States. On the other hand, this is not anything in which the new Member States would deviate from the practice in the old Member States; let us imagine that the knowledge of a foreign language would be made a compulsory condition for the appointment to a judicial office in say the United Kingdom or France.

reached within the interpretation of the text of the norm in the national language.[43] Additionally, the depth of the argument tends to be quite far from genuine language comparison; the practice is just to put two or three notions in the foreign language into brackets next to the word or notion in the original language.[44] The argumentative value of such enterprise is questionable.

What can be a realistic role of the comparison of the various language versions of the Community legislation in a national court?[45] Its role should perhaps be limited to a "mistake verification point", i.e., to instances in which the judge or an attorney detects an obvious error in the national version of the EU provision and needs to verify whether or not it is a mistake in translation (or, euphemistically put, "co-drafting"). Realistically, the comparative study will be limited to one, two or three major languages, typically English, French or German.[46]

## 3.2.    The limits of knowledge

Of all the requirements of the European Court of Justice regarding the application of EU law in national courts examined in this chapter, this one is perhaps the least problematic. In cross-referring the issue back to the national procedural law, the ECJ appears to have genuinely remained faithful to the often more verbal than real procedural

---

[43] For instance, in a series of recent decisions concerning the interpretation of the Protocol on Asylum for Nationals of Member States of the European Union (*OJ* 1997 C 340/103), the Czech *Nejvyšší správní soud* [Supreme Administrative Court] used the reference to the English, German and French version of a provision of Art. 1 of the Protocol just to confirm that the meaning of the provision was equally vague in the other languages as well. See judgment of 19 July 2006, Case no 3 Azs 259/2005, no 977/2006 Coll. SAC. In another recent decision, *Krajský soud v. Ostravě* [Regional Court in Ostrava] confirmed by reference to the English, French, German and Slovak versions of the Council Regulation (EEC) No 2658/87 of 23 July 1987 on the tariff and statistical nomenclature and on the Common Customs Tariff (*OJ* 1987 L 256/1) that a list of conditions which appeared in a provision is indeed supposed to be a non-closed list – judgment of 4 December 2007, Case no 22 Ca 167/2007, unpublished. See also a recent order of the Czech Supreme Court of 31 January 2008, Case no 29 Odo 164/2006, no 84/2008 in *Soudní judikatura* [the Collection of Decisions of the Czech Courts].

[44] Or, more typically, not to mention the foreign version at all: an example is a recent decision of the Czech Supreme Administrative Court, in which the court uttered a passing remark that the clear wording (in the sense of *CILFIT acte clair*) of the Czech version of a provision of a Community directive is not called into question by neither English, nor German, French, Italian, Polish or Slovak wording of the same text. The court, however, did not analyse the wordings of the other version in any detail (or at least did not put it into the reasoning itself). See judgment of 29 August 2007, case no 1 As 13/2007, published as no 1461/2008 Coll. SAC.

[45] Or perhaps in the European Court of Justice itself? See a surprisingly frank remark by AG Jacobs in Case C-338/95 *Wiener v. Hauptzollamt Emmerich* [1997] *ECR* I-6518 (para. 65 of the opinion), in which he noted, with respect to the *CILFIT* requirements as far as comparing various language versions are concerned, that it is somehow exaggerated to require from Member States' courts something that even the European Court of Justice does not normally do.

[46] Which does make sense also because as far as EU legislation of the last years is concerned, more than 70% of it is drafted in English, about 15% in French and the rest (15%) in other languages, out of which German is the strongest of the "small" drafting languages. This means that if consulting these language versions, there is a high chance that one is actually reading the "original" text. Figures originating from DG Translation Information Booklet *Translating for a Multilingual Community* (Luxembourg, Office for Official Publications 2007) p. 6.

autonomy of the legal orders of the Member States. EU law is to be applied in the same manner as national law; if the judge is obliged to know the national law and raise it on his/her own motion, so must EU law. The principle of equivalence seems not (yet?) to have been pushed to the side by the requirement of effectiveness.

The problem with the national knowledge of EU law is, at least in the judicial context of the new Member States brought in by the last two waves of EU enlargement, of a different nature; the assumption that judges know the law has been gradually eroded from within the national legal system without, however, the necessary adjustment of the rules of procedure. The legislative frenzy of the past two decades, caused first by the fall of the Communist rule and the need of reshaping the entire legal system and later by the approximation of laws and the complete renewal of the legal order, resulted into what one justice of the Czech Constitutional Court called "deconstruction"[47] of the legal order. Avalanches of amendments and new legislation cannot leave even the greatest legislative optimist with the conviction that judges still know the law. It is clear that the *iura novit curia* maxim is not tenable with respect not only to Community law, but also to national law as well. What might have been a workable procedural solution in the era of centuries-old legal codes and legislative and judicial stability is no longer possible, given today's tens of thousands of pages of EU and national legislation and case law.

This has clear impact on the judicial behaviour and the appearance of EU law issues before national courts. In the initial stage of the application of EU law in the new Member States, EU law arguments have been raised solely or primarily by the parties' legal representatives. This is perhaps no surprise to the legal systems of the old Member States, especially those where the judicial procedure is more adversarial. To require, however, greater activity on the part of the legal representatives in the new Member States is quite a novelty as far as the position of the parties and the conduct of proceedings are concerned, since *iura novit curia* has bred inertia among legal representatives. It remains to be seen whether such novelty may eventually spill over into purely domestic cases, where quality legal representation will no longer be a matter of simply reiterating the facts and leaving the court to determine the law.

There is little point in asking the frequent question of domestic (non)application of EU law, trying to speculate how big a percentage of cases passes through the entire national judicial system without the EU law angles in it being detected. In this respect, it serves to be mindful that, with the exception of a few specialised (mostly administrative) jurisdictions, for a national judge, EU law is just the proverbial "cherry on the cake", which appears in perhaps few per cents (or even per mille) of total cases the judge regularly disposes of. For these reasons, and taking into account the special post-

---

[47] In this context, Justice Holländer was referring to the Czech Code of Civil Procedure, which, within one year, had undergone 18 direct and indirect amendments. P Holländer, *Ústavněprávní argumentace* [Constitutional Legal Reasoning] (Prague, Linde Publishing 2003) p. 11.

accession situation in the new Member States,[48] one can hardly expect that judges will know European Union law.[49]

The remaining question is whether the absence of knowledge is only temporal or whether the maxim that "judge knows the law" begs the question what is the reasonable knowledge of EU law one may expect from a national judge to have?

The national case law of some of the older Member States could provide certain guidance as to what might be a reasonable standard of knowledge of EU law for national judges. For instance, the German *Bundesverfassungsgericht* has declared itself ready to assess, via the individual constitutional complaint, whether or not ordinary courts of last instance did not violate their duty to make a preliminary reference to the European Court of Justice.[50] In doing so, it also indirectly examines whether or not the courts of last instance did apply EC law correctly. The standard the *Bundesverfassungsgericht* applies when reviewing the decisions of the ordinary courts is, perhaps, somewhat lighter than a categorical obligation that judges should know all EU law. For instance, a 2001 decision[51] of the *Bundesverfassungsgericht* concerned a surgeon in Hamburg who wished to apply for the qualification of self-employed practitioner. For that, she had to have at least 12 months of full-time practice. Because of maternity leave, the surgeon sought to replace a part of the full-time practice requirement with a part-time one. Her requests in this respect were rejected, and applications to the administrative courts, including the *Bundesverwaltungsgericht* acting as the court of last instance, unsuccessful.

The *Bundesverfassungsgericht* quashed the final decision of the *Bundesverwaltungsgericht,* holding that the approach taken by the administrative court was unacceptable for two reasons. Firstly, the *Bundesverwaltungsgericht* failed to deal with the recognised conflict between the national law and Community directives and did not identify or apply any case law of the European Court of Justice. Secondly, it did not take into account a fundamental principle of Community law, namely the prohibition of discrimination on the basis of sex.[52]

It may be submitted that the view taken by the *Bundesverfassungsgericht* represents a more realistic view about what knowledge of EC law may be reasonably expected from national judges. They should be aware of the basic principles of EC law, including the prohibition of discrimination on the basis of nationality, sex, basic rules of consumer protection, the duty of loyal and sincere co-operation. If raised by the parties, national judges are, of course, obliged to deal with more detailed regulatory issues.

---

[48] Especially the above-sketched linguistic factors, which do not comprise only the absence or wrong translations of EU legislation. For instance, the entire pre-accession case law of the European Court of Justice, which could provide some guidance, is inaccessible in the languages of the new Member States.

[49] As far as the varying degree of knowledge of EU Law in the new Member States is concerned, see the example of the Slovak legal system, which provides for the experts on EU Law before national courts. See further Chapter 11 in this volume.

[50] BVerfGE 73, 339 (366); BVerfGE 82, 159 (194); Order of 21 May 1996 – 1 BvR 866/96 -, NVwZ 1997, p. 481; Order of 5 August 1998 – 1 BvR 264/98 -, DB 1998, p. 1919.

[51] BVerfG, 1 BvR 1036/99 vom 9 January 2001, Absatz-Nr. (1-25), available online at http://www. bverfg.de/entscheidungen/rk20010109_1bvr103699.htm.

[52] *Ibidem*, para. 20.

This is perhaps what might be (one day) reasonably required of domestic judges – to be aware of principles and, if asked, to be able to navigate within the system of EU law.

## 3.3.    Why compare?

Despite the numerous recent doctrinal calls for judicial dialogues, judicial conversations or even a global community of courts,[53] national judges are not comparative lawyers and never will be. From all the requirements on the methodology of national courts presented in this chapter, this one is perhaps the most distant from reality. There are no good examples in which a national court of last instance would at least try to ascertain what may be the opinion of other national courts. With only slight exaggeration, there is no European Community of courts; there are just 27 national clusters, each rooted in its own national system and methodology.

This is not to say that there is no comparative law exchange. This exchange, however, is typically indirect, i.e., through the doctrine and doctrinal writings, which do take into account the issues and practices of the implementation and application of EU law in other Member States. The rather rare instances of any direct and express comparative argument in higher judicial decisions[54] tend to follow the already established historical patterns of comparative authority. For instance, the Central European states have traditionally been, as far as legal theory and comparative law are concerned, under a strong German influence.[55] If any comparative argument is attempted, the traditional point of inspiration has been German law and especially the case law of the *Bundesverfassungsgericht* and the respective German supreme federal courts.

It is highly unlikely that any of the decisions of national courts would satisfy even the comparative core of the *CILFIT* doctrine; i.e., last instance decisions of national courts are to be placed in an EU law context, so that they could be applied by any other national court in similar situations.[56] National courts follow their particular interests and national methodology; it is hard to see, for example, how the holding of a Slovak Supreme Court decision could be freely transferable to an English Court of Appeal reasoning. Not only is there a striking difference in the form of reasoning and the decision itself, but each of the courts follows a different aim, tailored to the particular needs of the national system.

---

[53] From the vast literature, see, *inter alia*, A.-M. Slaughter, 'A Global Community of Courts', 44 *Harv. ILJ* (2003) pp. 191-219; Ch. McCrudden, 'A Common Law of Human Rights? Transnational Judicial Conversations on Constitutional Rights', 20 *OJLS* (2000) pp. 499-532; V.C. Jackson, 'Comparative Constitutional Federalism and Transnational Judicial Discourse', 2 *I•CON* (2004) pp. 91-138.

[54] In the Czech Republic, for instance, one has to mention the plenary decision of the Czech Constitutional Court on the European Arrest Warrant, in which the court considered in its reasoning case law on the EAW from Poland and Germany. Constitutional Court of the Czech Republic, 3 May 2006, (*Re Constitutionality of Framework Decision on the European Arrest Warrant*), [2007] 3 C.M.L.R. 24.

[55] For the description of the situation in 1990s, see, e.g., J.A. Frowein and T. Marauhn, eds., *Grundfragen der Verfassungsgerichtsbarkeit in Mittel- und Osteuropa. Beiträge zum ausländischen öffentlichen Recht und Völkerrecht. Band 130* (Berlin-Heidelberg-New York, Springer Verlag 1998). More particularly on Hungary, see L. Sólyom and G. Brunner, *Constitutional Judiciary in a New Democracy. The Hungarian Constitutional Court* (Ann Arbor, The University of Michigan Press 1999).

[56] See Maduro, *loc. cit.* n. 22.

The reasons why national courts do not engage in any comparative exercise in the interpretation of EU law on the national level are multiple. For a great part, they overlap with the reasons why municipal courts use comparative reasoning only very rarely – from the practical constraints (including time, resources, accessibility of materials, language barriers, limited utility of the comparative exercise) through the procedural ones (such as rules of procedure, absence of party intervention, absence of third party briefs) to political or economic ones.[57] As aptly captured by Sir Konrad Schiemann, when reflecting on the academic calls for greater use of comparative methodology by national courts: 'I have the impression that academics tend not to be sufficiently conscious of the unremitting pressure a judge is under to produce an adequate judgment soon rather than a better judgment later. The lower down the judicial ladder a judge finds himself the greater that pressure is in general. But I was very conscious of it even in the Court of Appeal in England.'[58]

There would perhaps be a realistic way to make national judges aware of parallel decisions rendered in application of EU law in other Member States – by delegating to the legal representatives of the parties the task of identifying the cases from other Member States and bringing them to the attention of the national judge. This approach may already function in the jurisdictions where parties are to argue points of law as well; however, in the inquisitorial systems of procedure present in most continental countries,[59] the legal representatives of the parties tend to limit themselves to restatements of facts.

In this perspective, the above-described decision of the European Court of Justice in the *Intermodal Transports* case[60] is not to be welcomed; it may actually act as dissuasion to the parties to become active and look for cases in other Member States on their own. After *Intermodal Transports*, why should an individual or his/her legal representative invest any time or energy into identifying the relevant decisions from other Member States if the national court of last instance is not obliged to submit a request for a preliminary ruling if it wishes to deviate from the approach already taken elsewhere? On the other hand, it should be stressed that *Intermodal Transports* only concerned the argumentative value of administrative decisions in the courts of other Member States; the argumentative weight of judicial decisions should and perhaps would be assessed differently.

---

[57] For an introduction to this debate, see, *inter alia,* B. Markesinis and J. Fedtke, *Judicial Recourse to Foreign Law. A New Source of Inspiration?* (Abingdon, UCL Press and Taylor & Francis Group 2006) or G. Canivet, M. Andenas, D. Fairgrieve eds., *Comparative Law before the Courts* (London, British Institute of International and Comparative Law 2004).

[58] K. Schiemann, 'The Judge as Comparativist', in B. Markesinis, J. Fedtke, *Judicial Recourse to Foreign Law. A New Source of Inspiration?* (Abingdon, UCL Press and Taylor & Francis Group 2006) pp. 358-372, at p. 369.

[59] See R.G. Fentiman, 'Foreign Law in National Courts', in Canivet, Andenas, Fairgrieve, *op. cit.* n. 57, pp. 13-31, at p. 15.

[60] *Loc. cit.* n. 23.

## 3.4.    Whose telos?

There is no reason to think that national judges would not be able to employ purposive reasoning in their decision-making. As a matter of fact, they sometimes do. The key question is whether the national "telos" overlaps with the European one. As this chapter will examine further,[61] the purposes and values of Union and national judges in a particular case may be identical. They may, however, also differ. The question then becomes whether or not the values and purposes put forward by EU law are still within the realm of an acceptable compromise or whether they are outside it. Should the latter be the case, the rejection of the purposive reasoning and the positivist exegesis of the (typically national) law serves as a useful and diplomatic way of saying "no".

The classical objection against the use of purposive reasoning is its unpredictability and lack of democratic legitimacy; judges are not called to place their normative preferences or values into the law that is the task of the legislator.[62] In the Community guise, the problem with the use of purposive reasoning is not that much unpredictability of the value choice of the judge; quite to the contrary, recourse to teleological reasoning by the ECJ is almost always a journey to a known destination called *effet utile*. The problem with the case law of the European Court of Justice for a substantive number of national judges might be the fact that purposive reasoning is reduced to one and only one purpose – the full effectiveness of Community law, which is turned into the crucial principle not allowing for any balancing or opposition.[63]

Before and shortly after the 2004 enlargement, considerable scepticism has been expressed as far as the argumentative abilities of the "new European judges" were concerned, *inter alia,* their (in)ability to use purposive reasoning. The judges in the new Member States were said to be trapped in the realms of mechanical jurisprudence and textual positivism, unable to apply abstract legal principles, with a negative attitude towards teleological (purposive) argumentation, and incapable of using comparative legal arguments.[64]

Although the judicial standards in the new Member States could always be improved, the above outlined fears were perhaps too pessimistic. As is evident from the practice of Czech or Polish courts, the courts are very well able to work with persuasive authority and employ purposive reasoning. As a matter of fact, the vast majority of judicial applications of EC law has so far been within the framework of the persuasive, non-binding authority. As is described elsewhere in this volume,[65] the area of greatest judicial application of EU law in the first years following the accession has been the

---

[61]   See sections 4 and 5 of this chapter.

[62]   For a classic account, see A. Scalia, *A Matter of Interpretation* (Princeton, New Jersey, Princeton University Press 1997) pp. 3-48.

[63]   See R. Procházka, 'Prekážka rozhodnutej veci – judikatúra Súdného dvora ES a jej dopad na konanie vnútroštátnych súdov' [Res iudicata – the Case law of the Court of Justice and its Impact on the Procedure before National Courts], 10 *Justičná Revue* (2007) pp. 1240-1248, at p. 1248.

[64]   See Z. Kühn, 'The Application of European Law in the New Member States: Several (Early) Predictions', 6 *GLJ* (2005) pp. 565-582. Similar remarks have been made in relation to Croatia in T. Ćapeta, 'Courts, Legal Culture and EU Enlargement', 1 *CYELP* (2005) pp. 23-53.

[65]   See, *inter alia*, Chapter 10 in this volume.

use of European Union law in the voluntary interpretation of national law conforming with EU law.

Equally, as is evidenced in the handful of requests for preliminary rulings from the new Member States, some of them have rapidly learned how to use the new procedural tool in order to get rid of problematic or obsolete national legislation.[66]

However, it is true that there are still considerable reservations as far as purposive interpretation is concerned. Central and Eastern European judges appear to display scepticism towards the teleological and *effet utile* style of reasoning used by the European Court of Justice. This might be caused by their negative historical experience. Heretical though it may sound, there are some striking similarities between the communist/Marxist and EU approaches to legal reasoning and the requirements of judicial activism placed on national judges.[67] Marxist law required, at least in its early (Stalinist) phase, that judges disregard the remnants of the old bourgeois legal system in the interest of the victory of the working class and the communist revolution. Judges were supposed to apply the law in an anti-formalistic, teleological way, always directing their aim towards the victory of the working class and the dialectic approach.[68]

EC law requires national judges to set aside all national law which is incompatible with the full effectiveness of Community law, i.e., with such open-ended principles and aims as the full effectiveness of EC law enforcement, or the unity of EC law across the entire Union. In a way, both approaches are very similar; open-ended clauses take precedence over a textual interpretation of the written law. Often the desired result comes first, with a backward style of reasoning being used to arrive at it. The only visible difference is that the universal "all-use" argument has changed – from the victory of the working class to the full effectiveness of EC law.

This comparison is, of course, exaggerated. Yet there is a grain of truth in it. The scepticism towards a teleological style of reasoning shown by post-communist judiciaries in the new Member States has its historical roots. During the last decades of communist rule in Central Europe, legal formalism and strict textual interpretation of the law become a natural line of defence against the anti-formalistic teleological style of judicial reasoning officially required by Party policy.[69] After the Velvet Revolution, a slow, timid emancipation of the judiciary began, but the historical distrust remains.

---

[66] The second-hand car importation cases from Hungary and Poland being a prime example. See, ECJ Case C-313/05 *Maciej Brzeziński v. Dyrektor Izby Celnej w Warszawie* [2007] *ECR* I-513 and joined cases C-290/05 and C-333/05 *Ákos Nádasdi v. Vám- és Pénzügyőrség Észak-Alföldi Regionális Parancsnoksága and Ilona Németh v. Vám- és Pénzügyőrség Dél-Alföldi Regionális Parancsnoksága* [2006] *ECR* I-10115.

[67] Or, moreover, any freshly established dictatorial system, which, in its first stage, seeks to eliminate the remnants of the previous legal order via interpretation – see, with respect to the situation in the Nazi Germany, B. Rüthers, *Die unbegrenzte Auslegung: Zum Wandel der Privatrechtsordnung im Nationalsozialismus* (Thübingen, Mohr Siebeck 1968).

[68] See, *inter alia*, F. Boura, 'K otázce výkladu zákonů' [On the Question of Interpretation of Laws], 88 *Právník* (1949) p. 292 at p. 297, who argues, shortly after the Communist take-over in the former Czechoslovakia, that '... the fundamental canon of interpretation is that the interpretation of any legal provision must be in conformity with the nature and aims of the peoples' democratic order.' On the formalistic and purposive reasoning in Communist law, see Z. Kühn, 'Worlds Apart: Western and Central European Judicial Culture at the Onset of the European Enlargement', 52 *AJCL* (2004) pp. 531-568.

[69] See Z. Kühn, *Aplikace práva soudcem v. éře středoevropského komunismu a transformace. Analýza příčin postkomunistické právní krize* [Judicial Application of Law in Central Europe in the Communist

For these reasons, teleological reasoning might not be overwhelmingly welcomed in the new Member States' courts. Whether it is good or bad is open to question; there might be, however, some positives for the European Court of Justice itself in having national judges stick to a reasonable degree of positivistic reasoning, especially if the purpose (telos) pursued by Community law conflicts with the national one. Somewhat cynically put, in these scenarios, the aim of the Community is better served if national judges are limited positivists, who, on the one hand, accept the normative value of Community law and ECJ case law but, at the same time, refuse to have recourse to purposive reasoning. Provided that there is case law on the matter in question, they are more likely to follow it instead of questioning it and starting to look for their own "telos".

The reservations of the new Member States' judges with respect to purposive reasoning are often also age-related; older, higher court judges appear to be more positivistic than their younger first-instance colleagues. However, the approach might also differ within one single institution. A vivid example of a diverging opinion on the role of purposive reasoning was the internal split of the Czech Supreme Administrative Court in the question of the possibility of judicial review of town and country plans. A question which arose in a case before the Court was whether or not town and country plans can be reviewed before administrative courts. The first chamber of the Court held that they could.[70] In doing so, it extensively relied on the indirect effect of the Århus Convention[71] and the relevant Community directives,[72] one of the main grounds being the reasoning against a negative consequence and the purpose of the public participation in environment matters. The legal opinion of the other chambers diverged; the issue was eventually submitted to the Grand Chamber of the Court, which is called to arbitrate in cases of conflicts between the chambers of the Court. The Grand Chamber, composed of the more senior members of the Court, reversed.[73] Its reasoning follows the classical Central European bi-polar logic of binding/non-binding sources of law, neglecting any

---

and Transformation Eras. An Analysis of the Post-Communist Legal Crisis] (Prague, C.H. Beck 2005) p. 86. The same patterns and tensions concerning methodology were also discernable in Fascist Italy. See G. Calabresi, 'Two Functions of Formalism', 67 *UChLRev.* (2000) pp. 479-488.

[70] Judgment of the SAC of 18 July 2006, case no 1 Ao 1/2006, published as no 968/2006 Coll. SAC.

[71] (United Nations) Convention on Access to Information, Public Participation in Decision-Making and Access to Justice in Environmental Matters, done at Århus, Denmark, on 25 June 1998, which is a "mixed" treaty, as the European Community and the Member States are parties to it (see Council Decision 2005/370/EC of 17 February 2005 on the conclusion, on behalf of the European Community, of the Convention on access to information, public participation in decision-making and access to justice in environmental matters, *OJ* 2005 L 124/1).

[72] Directive 2001/42/EC of the European Parliament and of the Council of 27 June 2001 on the assessment of the effects of certain plans and programmes on the environment, *OJ* 2001 L 197/30; Directive 2003/4/EC of the European Parliament and of the Council of 28 January 2003 on public access to environmental information and repealing Council Directive 90/313/EEC, *OJ* 2003 L 41/26; Directive 2003/35/EC of the European Parliament and of the Council of 26 May 2003 providing for public participation in respect of the drawing up of certain plans and programmes relating to the environment, *OJ* 2003 L 156/17.

[73] Judgment of the SAC (Grand Chamber) of 13 March 2007, case no 3 Ao 1/2007, available at http://www.nssoud.cz.

possible indirect effect and disregarding the purpose of the legislation on public participation in decision-making and access to justice in environmental matters.[74]

## 4.        THE GENUINE FUNCTIONING OF THE EUROPEAN LEGAL ORDER – "DO NOT DO AS I SAY?"

The above-sketched contrasts reveal enigmas of the day-to-day functioning of EU law in national courts. The entire system functions only because the national judges disregard most of what the European Court of Justice requires of them. To be more precise, most of them are blissfully ignorant of the genuine requirements the ECJ set on their methodology in the application of EU law. The few who actually do know soon become resigned and resilient. If the national judges were genuinely to start following the Luxembourg guidance, the entire EU judicial system would collapse within months.[75]

For instance, let us imagine that all national courts, which are in functional terms[76] courts of last instance, would genuinely start following the *CILFIT* guidelines and refer all the non- *acte éclairé* or *acte clair* cases to the European Court of Justice. As no national court is able to meet the *CILFIT* guidelines, especially as far as the requirements for the existence of *acte clair* are currently set, national courts of last instance would turn themselves into post offices just sending cases to Luxembourg. The amount of cases referred to the European Court of Justice would also be quite different if national judges really started to raise EU law issues of their own motion and not only if forced by the parties to do so. Equally, the number of problems in the interpretation of EU law would rise exponentially should judges start reading the legislation in several languages and compare the various language versions and so on.

Apart from the methodological differences and the natural constraints of the activity of national judges examined above, additional reasons for the resistance *vis-à-vis* the European Court of Justice's case law are typically twofold – ambiguity of the case law and value unacceptability.

### 4.1.    **Ambiguity**

Absent any real enforcement mechanism, European case law functions as *de facto* precedents due to various factors, the most important ones being, apart from value compatibility, which will be assessed below, the persuasive force and quality of reasoning, which is able to deliver a clear line of case law, to the maximum degree possible

---

[74] The case is – at the time of writing – pending before the Czech Constitutional Court, where it was submitted as a constitutional complaint – case no Pl. ÚS 14/07.

[75] An intriguing literary inspiration here would be the behaviour of a Czech classic icon, the brave soldier Švejk, who disrupted the functioning of the Austro-Hungarian Army by exactly following the orders issued by his superiors – see J. Hašek, *The Good Soldier Švejk and His Fortunes in the World War* (London, Penguin Classics 2005).

[76] See F. Jacobs, 'Which courts and tribunals are bound to refer to the European Court', 2 *ELRev.* (1977) pp. 119-121.

free of internal contradiction. This is of course an ideal, which all Supreme Courts, being the precedent-setting courts, seek to approach. It is, however, also clear that the more complex and contradictory the case law gets, the ability to follow decreases, and there develops a greater space for disregard and an increase in the cases being referred to the court.[77]

There are areas of EU law in which even specialised EU lawyers get lost. For example: the doctrines of (in)direct effect are a mess;[78] the European Court of Justice does not appear to have a clear vision on the notion of discrimination; hardly anyone is able to maintain the difference between Article 30 EC exceptions and the mandatory requirements exceptions in the area of free movement of goods; what precisely are national courts supposed to do with respect to final decisions which turn out to be incompatible with EC law is a puzzle to everyone. If viewed in connection with the judicial liability for disregard of the European Court of Justice's case law, one cannot but agree that the European Court of Justice 'sometimes entertains a very optimistic view on the clarity of its case law.'[79] It is obvious that if in these and other areas, not even the experts are able to ascertain what the law is, how could one ask the same from national judges, who have not but a fraction of the time experts and academics can spend in the study of the case law of the European Court of Justice.

Obviously, some areas of law are "fresh", and, as such, they are still being created; others need an "update" and perhaps a change of the case law. There is, nonetheless, only a certain degree of change national courts are able to register and to follow. A prime example of an area of law where (not only) national courts have considerable difficulties to follow is the already mentioned duty to reopen final national decisions which are incompatible with EC law. In 2004, this duty seemed to mean to set aside national decisions incompatible with EC law.[80] Later in 2004, Article 10 EC and the requirement of effective protection of individual rights amounted to the duty to reopen final national decisions provided that the administrative authority had such powers under national law.[81] In 2006, the principle was interpreted as not requiring national courts to reopen final judicial decisions incompatible with EC law.[82] Just a year later,

---

[77] Statistically, there appears to be an inverse proportion between the amount of decisions a supreme jurisdiction renders and the amount of cases it receives from lower courts; the more decisions and case law a precedent- setting jurisdiction produces, the less predictable its case law gets and the greater demand for new decisions from lower courts. See M. Bobek, 'Quantity or Quality? Re-Assessing the Role of Supreme Jurisdictions in Central Europe', *EUI LAW Working Paper* No 2007/36; for similar reflections in the context of the work of the European Court of Justice, see J. Komárek, '"In the Court(s) We Trust?" On the need for hierarchy and differentiation in the preliminary ruling procedure', 32 *ELRev.* (2007) pp. 467-491.

[78] Recently, see A. Dashwood, 'From Van Duyn to Mangold via Marshall: Reducing Direct Effect to Absurdity?', 9 *CYELS* (2007) pp. 81-109.

[79] P.J. Wattel, 'Köbler, CILFIT and Welthgrove: We Can't Go on Meeting Like This', 41 *CMLRev.* (2004) pp. 177-190.

[80] See, e.g., ECJ, Case C-224/97 *Erich Ciola and Land Vorarlberg* [1999] *ECR* I-2517; Case C-201/02 *The Queen on the application of Delena Wells and Secretary of State for Transport, Local Government and the Regions* [2004] *ECR* I-723.

[81] ECJ, Case C-453/00 *Kühne & Heitz NV and Productschap voor Pluimvee en Eieren* [2004] *ECR* I-837.

[82] ECJ, Case C-234/04 *Rosmarie Kapferer v. Schlank & Schick GmbH* [2006] *ECR* I-258.

in 2007, the same principle meant the opposite.[83] In 2008, the European Court of Justice appears to be retreating somewhat, perhaps heading back to the equivalence principle originally announced in 2004.[84] Some commentators have aptly called such areas of case law "instruments of disorientation".[85] In the face of such "guidance" from the European Court of Justice, the most common (and hardly surprising) reaction from the national courts is to ignore EU law angles to the domestic dispute altogether.

There is perhaps another reason why the decisions of the European Court of Justice are losing some of their persuasive force. In an understandable need to cut down the length and the cost of the translation of the decisions at the European Court of Justice, several measures have been taken. One of them is the return of the magisterial style of the judgments, which now tend to be shorter and shorter, especially as far as the summary of the arguments of the parties is concerned, which are cut considerably or sometimes missing altogether. The quality of the reasoning and their persuasive force suffer.[86]

Finally, it remains to be seen whether the situation in respect of these lasting problems will get any better with the current European Court of Justice composed of 27 justices.[87] A judicial body of such size is no longer able to genuinely meet and discuss as a body; it turns into a classical civilian Supreme Court with small chambers deciding the bulk of cases and the Grand Chamber (which is not the full court) being summoned only occasionally to adjudicate on the contentious disputes and unify the case law. If one is to draw the lesson from the functioning of continental Supreme Courts composed of tens of judges, the predictability and a clear line of case law tends not to be one of the virtues of such a model.[88]

## 4.2.    Value unacceptability

In a pluralistic Community, the systematic compatibility of the values of the national and Union legal orders is generally presumed.[89] However, every presumption constitutes certain generalisation about the reality. Our aim at this stage is not to define precisely whether or not the instances of conflicts are value conflicts as such or conflicts in the realisation of a shared value, to which either of the players in the particular game accords

---

[83]   ECJ, Case C-119/05 *Ministero dell'Industria, del Commercio e dell'Artigianato v. Lucchini SpA* [2007] *ECR* I-I-6199.

[84]   ECJ, Case C-2/06 *Willy Kempter KG v. Hauptzollamt Hamburg-Jonas* [2008] *ECR* I-411.

[85]   See Procházka, *loc. cit.* n. 63.

[86]   An extreme example of lack of any reasoning is the recent decision in Case C-273/04 *Republic of Poland v. Council of the European Union, ECR* [2007] I-8925, where the European Court of Justice, instead of dealing with the hotly debated issue of the admissibility of the action just stated in one sentence (para. 33) 'In the present case, the Court considers it necessary to rule at the outset on the substance of the case.' If such a decision were to be appealed in any of the national judicial systems, it would have been instantly annulled for lack of reasoning. For further examples, see Komárek, *loc. cit.* n. 77 at pp. 482-483.

[87]   A (traditionally) sceptic view is offered by H. Rasmussen, 'Present and Future European Judicial Problems After Enlargement and the Post-2005 Ideological Revolt', 44 *CMLRev.* (2007) pp. 1661–1687.

[88]   See Bobek, *loc. cit.* n. 77.

[89]   See M. Poiares Maduro, 'Contrapunctual Law: Europe's Constitutional Pluralism in Action' in N. Walker (ed.) *Sovereignty in Transition* (Oxford, Portland-Oregon, Hart Publishing 2003) pp. 501-537, at p. 504.

different weight. In practical terms of an individual case, the conflict boils down to the same disagreement, irrespective of the fact whether the conflict is described as one of values or one of realisation of the shared values. Our assumption simply is that in concrete individual cases, national and Union interests may clash. Out of this collision, instances of intentional disregard of EU law by national courts come about. This typically happens in areas where requirements of the European Court of Justice go too far and create what one may call areas of "virtual case law." "Virtual" because these requirements or principles find their reflection only in a few references from national courts and in the case law of the ECJ but no real application in the practice of the national courts. Areas of virtual case law are typically born out of an unreserved and sweeping assertion of *effet utile* of EU law over any other interests and values. Other interests are sacrificed for the greater veneration of the golden calf of full effectiveness of Community law. The only problem is, as was already mentioned above in the context of teleological reasoning by the European Court of Justice, that the idol of national courts might be a different one.

A recent example of this approach might be the European Court of Justice's decision in the *Lucchini* case. The case concerned the duty of a national court to reopen final judicial decisions which granted state aid incompatible with Community law. Lucchini SpA was awarded – in breach of EC law – state aid by Italian authorities. The award was confirmed and enforced by Italian civil courts, who ordered the aid to be paid. The conflict the ECJ was asked to resolve was between the national provisions, which precluded any new examination of a final judicial decision and the principle of full effectiveness of Community law. The European Court of Justice gave a clear preference to the latter and opined that:

> 'Community law precludes the application of a provision of national law ... which seeks to lay down the principle of *res judicata* in so far as the application of that provision prevents the recovery of State aid granted in breach of Community law which has been found to be incompatible with the common market in a decision of the Commission of the European Communities which has become final.'[90]

The decision is a matter of considerable controversy.[91] It is clear, however, that its structure is quite one-sided: the interest of the Community dominates, while the interest of the national judge and the sound administration of justice on the national level, which would also entail the need to finish litigation at some stage, even if the decision is flawed, are discarded. It is hard to imagine that national judges would be inclined to follow a similar decision of the European Court of Justice; not because they would not respect the ECJ, but because the tenet of the decision does not serve other than Community purposes, completely disregarding the interests of national systems.[92]

---

[90] *Loc. cit.* n. 83, para. 63.

[91] From the first few case notes, see, *inter alia*, P. Bříza 'ECJ case Lucchini SpA – is there anything left of res judicata principle?', 27 *CJQ* (2008) pp. 40-50; X. Groussot and T. Minssen, 'Res Judicata in the Court of Justice Case-Law: Balancing Legal Certainty with Legality?', 3 *EUConst* (2007) pp. 385-417.

[92] The issue of Consequences of incompatibility with EC law for final administrative decisions and final judgments of administrative courts in the Member States was actually one of the topics of the 21st Col-

5.    THE RELATIONSHIP BETWEEN THE EUROPEAN COURT OF
      JUSTICE AND THE NATIONAL COURTS – THE STRATEGY OF THE
      SECOND BEST CHOICE?

With a series of considerable simplifications, the latter example of value conflicts between national courts and the European Court of Justice could be reduced to a matrix of a non-cooperative game, which is one of the basic models in the game theory.[93] The players of the game are a national court and the European Court of Justice. The game called preliminary rulings is an infinite non-cooperative game; "non-cooperative" is not because one would call into question the classical statements of the European Court of Justice concerning the "relationship of co-operation" established between the ECJ and the national courts,[94] but because by definition provided by the game theory, a non-cooperative game is one in which the actors are not able to agree in advance on a joint plan of action for the individual game; i.e., there is no communication prior to the individual game on the rules of it.[95]

Naturally, players choose strategies that maximise their own playoffs. One of the key assumptions of the game theory is that a player will always choose a dominant strategy, if possible a strictly dominant one, i.e., the best choice for a player for every possible choice by the other player. To overcome the one-sided, often binary dominance of one player over the other, the core concept of solving games in the post-WWII game theory became the so-called *Nash equilibrium*. The Nash solution concept to the non-cooperative games was to make the strategy chosen by one player subject to the choice of the other; the equilibrium point is one in which neither player can do better by choosing a different strategy than the other chooses.[96]

Now what can be potential playoffs for the European Court of Justice and a national court in a preliminary ruling game? If viewed through the lenses of the already discussed principle of full effectiveness of Community law, the playoff in an individual case might be asserting full and unconditional effectiveness of Community law, asserting some of it or asserting none. The dominant strategy for the European Court of Justice might be to assert full and unconditional effectiveness of Community law. However, if the full effectiveness in an individual case conflicts with values pursued by a national court, the greatest playoff for the national court would be precisely the

---

loquium of the Association of the Councils of State and the Supreme Administrative Jurisdictions of the European Union, which was held in May 2008 at the Supreme Administrative Court of Poland, Warsaw.

    [93] For an introduction see, *inter alia*, S.P. Hargreaves Heap and Y. Varoufakis, *Game Theory, A Critical Text*, 2nd edn. (London-New York, Routledge 2004) or D.G. Baird, R.H. Gertner, R.C. Picker, *Game Theory and the Law* (Cambridge, Harvard University Press 1994).

    [94] See, *inter alia*, ECJ, Case C-99/00 *Criminal proceedings against Kenny Roland Lyckeskog* [2002] *ECR* I-4839, para. 14; Case C-337/95 *Parfums Christian Dior SA and Parfums Christian Dior BV v. Evora BV* [1997] *ECR* I-6013, para. 25; Case 283/81, *loc. cit.* n. 21, para. 7 or Case 244/80 *Foglia v. Novello* [1981] *ECR* 3045, para. 16.

    [95] See the classical definition by J.F. Nash, 'Two-person Cooperative Games' and J.F. Nash, 'Non-Cooperative Games', both reprinted in J.F. Nash, *Essays on Game Theory* (Cheltenham, Edward Elgar Publishing 1996).

    [96] First put forward in J.F. Nash, 'Non-Cooperative Games', 54 *Annals of Mathematics* (1951) pp. 286-295.

opposite strategy – no assertion of the *effet utile*, which would basically mean not to refer the case to the ECJ at all. The equilibrium point in this game would thus be asserting some effectiveness and primacy of EC law, but still leaving some strategic space for the conflicting interest of the other party. Only if such strategy is adopted, both parties will be induced to play and later continue in the repetition of the game. The *Nash equilibrium* would thus rest with the limited assertion of the full effectiveness, which would partially satisfy both players, and they would be happy settling for the particular strategy, not feeling the need of changing it.

An example of a strategy which would perhaps come close to the equilibrium point between the conflicting interests of a national court and the ECJ would be the recent decision in the already discussed *Skoma-Lux* case.[97] In the scenarios open in this case, the greatest playoff for the ECJ in terms of full effectiveness of Community law would be to assert the full application of Community law on the territories of the new Member States irrespective of whether or not the legislation in question was or was not translated and duly published in the languages of the new Member States. Conversely, the greatest playoff for a national constitutional system, based on the assumption of the exclusivity of a national language as the means of communicating the content of a legal rule, would be to state that Community norms not available in the national language have no effect on the territory of that Member State. The compromise equilibrium position was to state that decisions adopted on the basis of non-translated Community legislation could not be enforced against individuals in those Member States and, at the same time, to limit the temporal effects of the decision. Such decision awards playoffs to both parties and induces them to continue the game.

The opposite example would be the already mentioned *Lucchini* decision. Here the playoff of the national court is negative (the interest of *res iudicata*) and the only (dominant) strategy is the full effectiveness of Community law. It may be submitted that such a decision induces the national court to exit the game in the future due to negative playoffs. An alternative solution to the game presented by that case, which would come closer to the *Nash equilibrium*, might perhaps be to uphold the value of both interests in question (full effectiveness as well as *res iudicata*), thus downgrading the playoffs of either party, and seek a compromise solution, for example, via the state liability regime.

By its nature, preliminary rulings are a repetitive game; the strategy and playoffs of previous rounds are reflected in the subsequent ones. Typically, the short term gains in one round are insufficient to compensate for future losses, especially if the costs from non-cooperation or the complete refusal to further participate in the game on the parts of national courts are very low or non-existent. One may only recall the example of the *Bundesverfassungsgericht,* which, although it declared itself to be entitled[98] (and perhaps even obliged) to participate in the preliminary rulings game, never actually did so. The costs of the refusal to play for the *Bundesverfassungsgericht* are, apart from occasional doctrinal critique, none. Similarly, the probability of other negative conse-

---

[97] *Loc. cit.* n. 31, paras. 31-34.
[98] BVerfGE 52, 187 (201) – "*Vielleicht-Beschluss.*"

quences for the refusal to play the preliminary ruling game, be it in the form of Article 226 EC proceedings[99] or a national action for damages caused by the individual by incorrect application of Community law by a national court,[100] are negligible.

There would be, of course, also games in which the interests of both players do not conflict and the Nash equilibrium is one of co-operation – the classical example[101] here would be of stag/hare hunt, which involves two hunters, who each have only two strategies – either hunt independently for a hare or together for a stag. A hunter can catch a hare alone. But they will only catch stag if they hunt together. Sharing a stag is always a better strategy than getting a single hare.

Examples of overlapping interests of the submitting national court and the European Court of Justice are numerous; one may even hope that they are more numerous than the instances of conflicts. One recent example involving the courts of the new Member States might be the Polish case of national tax on imported second-hand cars. From the wording of the request for the preliminary rulings, submitted by the *Wojewódzki Sąd Administracyjny* in Warsaw, it was quite apparent that the submitting court already made up its mind, and its aim was to get rid of the weed of national legislation acting as an obstacle to the free movement of goods. In similar situations, the requests for preliminary rulings are rather requests for posterior approval for a legal opinion already adopted by the national court. The interests of both parties overlap.

Our goal at this stage is not to design a true model for the game of preliminary rulings. That would be extremely difficult, also taking into account the number of players involved (the plurality of national courts), the potential divergence of interests among national courts themselves, the difference in the rather long-term strategy of case law development, followed by the European Court of Justice, and the strategy of national courts, functioning more like trial courts in the individual case. The above-outlined ideas remain rather in the realm of inspiration. The inspiration is, nonetheless, instructive; the interaction between the European Court of Justice and the national courts should seek (Nash) equilibrium points, not strict dominance.

This would mean, in practical terms, the willingness on both sides to look for and to accept "second best choices". If we skip the game theory lingo, we arrive at a simple call for compromise solutions. This requires, on the part of national judges, to honestly try to become "Community judges" and, on the part of the European Court of Justice, to realise reasonable limits on the part of national courts in their activity as the Community judiciary. The above- described areas of the requirements on the methodology in the application of European Union law by national courts is a prime place to start.

---

[99] For one of the few instances, see ECJ, Case C-129/00 *Commission of the European Communities v. Italian Republic* [2003] *ECR* I-14637.

[100] ECJ, Case C-224/01 *Gerhard Köbler v. Republik Österreich* [2003] *ECR* I-10239.

[101] Further see Baird, Gertner, Picker, *op. cit.* n. 93, at pp. 35 et seq.

*Part Three*
*From Estonia to Bulgaria ...  the Application of EU Law*

*Chapter 6*

## "COMMUNITY, IDENTITY, STABILITY": IDEALS AND PRACTICE IN BUILDING A BRIDGE BETWEEN THE LEGAL SYSTEMS OF THE EUROPEAN UNION AND ONE OF THE SMALLEST OF THE "BRAVE NEW WORLD"

Julia Laffranque*

> 'O wonder!
> How many goodly creatures are there here!
> How beauteous mankind is!
> O brave new world
> That has such people in't!'
>
> *Miranda's speech in Shakespeare's*
> *'The Tempest', Act V, Scene I*

1.    INTRODUCTION – "COMMUNITY, IDENTITY, STABILITY" AND LEGAL SYSTEM(S)

"Community, Identity, Stability" is the motto of Aldous Huxley's utopian World State in his novel, called "Brave New World", influenced slightly by the above-cited writing of Shakespeare. In turn, that novel has inspired the editor of this book to make use of Huxley's title and denote the Central and Eastern European Member States of the European Union (EU) as a Brave New World, however, in a positive meaning. For the author of this chapter, stimulated by Huxley's work, without wishing in any way to compare the EU with the English author's World State, employing the slogan "Community, Identity, Stability", also in a positive sense, seems tempting in describing some of the important principles of the EU.

* Judge at the Supreme Court of Estonia, docent of EU law at Faculty of Law, University of Tartu, Estonia. This chapter does not reflect any official position of the State or its jurisdictions, including the Supreme Court and expresses purely personal views of the author, who has tried to respect the self restraint of a judge as much as possible. The focus of the analysis is on the first years of membership in the European Union; however, a selection of recent developments is also included to reflect the law as it stood in July 2009.

*A. Łazowski (ed.), The Application of EU Law in the New Member States*
© 2010, T·M·C·ASSER PRESS, *The Hague, The Netherlands and the Authors*

Common values and general principles should build a solid base in the relationship between the European Community law[1] and the laws of the Member States.[2] Depending on the division of competences between the EU and its members,[3] this does not necessarily mean losing the identities of national legal culture and legislation of the Member States.[4] At the same time, it is important for the European Community to ensure that its law is applied effectively and in a uniform manner which will strengthen the identity of Community law, as well as preserve stability in the relationship between the EC and Member States.[5] If collisions take place, the principle of supremacy of EC law will be decisive.[6]

But is it ever possible to achieve it all – community, identity and stability – at the same time, while applying EC law in the legal system of a Member State or when Community institutions are faced with a situation where EC law is interacting with the national law? This chapter will demonstrate that sometimes even conflicting ideals are not always easily transferable to the practice. The first experiences of the countries of the "Brave New World" in applying EC law show that the practice can very much differ from the theory. This, as such, is not new, if we take into account that there are similar discrepancies between legal doctrine and legal practice in "pure" national cases. Nevertheless, it is even more complicated when legal systems vary. Are there perhaps hidden values behind the ideal values, and are these hidden values in practice valued more than others? Are there values that remain ideals, and others that are applied to justify the practice?

Despite this author's antipathy against contrasts, such as "old *versus* new", "big *versus* small", "they *versus* us", "legal system of the EC *versus* national legal system" – distinctions, which unfortunately, seem to be quite a trend these days – one has to admit that differences still exist. This is also why the contrasts are used in the title of this chapter with a hope that the "new" along with the "old", as well as the EU itself,

---

[1] In spite of the desire to follow the competences of the EC/EU and its legal development, the terms EC law/EU law are used somewhat in a tangle in this chapter, as a strict distinction between them is not always made in Estonia.

[2] See, e.g., Art. 6 TEU, Arts. 5 and 10 EC.

[3] See, e.g., the principle of subsidiarity in Art. 5 para. 2 EC.

[4] It is even truer, if we consider the motto of the EU – "United in diversity"– which has been removed from the Treaty of Lisbon, but probably continues to play an important role in the EU regardless of the tragic fate of its first formal "home to be", the Treaty establishing a Constitution for Europe.

[5] See the principle of loyal co-operation in the Art. 10 EC, as well as the case law of the ECJ on the procedural autonomy of the Member States, however, with the requirement to respect the principles of *effet utile* and equivalence/equal treatment. See also ECJ, Joined Cases 205 to 215/82 *Deutsche Milchkontor GmbH and others v. Federal Republic of Germany* [1983] *ECR* 2633; as well as some recent trends of the ECJ defining the limits of the procedural autonomy of the Member States, such as ECJ, Case C-453/00 *Kühne & Heitz NV v. Produktschap voor Pluimvee en Eieren* [2004] *ECR* I-837; ECJ, Case C-234/04 *Rosmarie Kapferer v. Schlank & Schick GmbH* [2006] *ECR* I-2585; ECJ, Joined Cases C-392/04 and C-422/04 *i-21 Germany GmbH (C-392/04) and Arcor AG & Co. KG (C-422/04) v. Bundesrepublik Deutschland* [2006] *ECR* I-8559.

[6] ECJ, Case 6/64 *Flaminio Costa v. ENEL* [1964] *ECR*, English special edition p. 585; supremacy of EC law over national constitutions of the Member States, see ECJ, Case 11/70 *Internationale Handelsgesellschaft mbH v. Einfuhr- und Vorratsstelle für Getreide und Futtermittel* [1970] *ECR* 1125.

will in the future be stable, co-operating identities in one community, rather than con-flicting controversies.

Although a legal system, as we know it, is typical to a state, the EU has its unique legal system which operates continually alongside the laws of the Member States.[7] The Community legal system, a term which seems to be confidently used by the European Court of Justice, appears as essentially a unified one whilst being characterised by the simultaneous application of provisions of diverse origins (international, EC and national).[8]

This chapter will illustrate that for the "Brave New World", a distinction between the legal systems of EC/EU and its Member States is still relevant, and finding the best method in building a solid bridge among these systems seems to be one of the key ele-ments. To exemplify an intriguing dilemma, the following question can be asked: is the Estonian legal system from 1 May 2004, the day Estonia joined the EU, part of the Community legal system or *vice versa* – is the EC legal system now part of our legal system? At first, this seems like an abstract problem, but it has turned out to be a crucial issue in applying EC law by national authorities and courts in Estonia. Of course, an answer depends on which angle the matters are looked upon, and sometimes the systems are desperately blurred.

First in this chapter, the aspects concerning the application and implementation of EC/EU law within the Estonian legal system will be analysed. The chapter then con-tinues to examine the matters where the EC/EU is faced with questions concerning Estonian law. Since after the EU-accession, the centre of gravity of EU law contacts with Estonia has switched from the approximation of Estonian law with *acquis* done by law-makers to the application and interpretation by the judiciary; therefore, empha-sis will be given to court practice. The material leans mainly on relevant Estonian case law enriched with some comparative law elements, but it is limited mostly to decisions of the Supreme Court of Estonia. Obviously, it is possible to reflect only a selection of different situations where the two legal systems have come to close relationship.

Even if one agrees that complete harmonisation of legal systems of the EU and its Member States cannot be the goal and admits that for the old Member States, the prob-lems of accommodation have been a long-lasting process as well, it must be noted that from the point of view of the last enlargements, the approaching of legal systems in practice will take time, especially since the twist in mentality in the "Brave New World" requires a certain period. And the other way round; it will take some time before the importance and contribution of, e.g., the national courts and individual litigants of the new Member States in constructing the EC legal system from the ground up, will be noticed and, as well, encouraged by the others, including the Community institutions.

---

[7] For different approaches concerning the construction of Community legal system see, *inter alia*, W. Mattli and A-M. Slaughter, 'Constructing The European Community Legal System From The Ground Up: The Role Of Individual Litigants And National Courts', *Jean Monnet Working Paper* 1996; I. Weyland, 'The Application of Kelsen's Theory of the Legal System to European Community Law – The Supremacy Puzzle Resolved', 21 *JLP* (2002) pp. 1-37.

[8] See the Opinion of Advocate General Tesauro of 13 November 1997 in ECJ, Case C-53/96 *Hermès International (a partnership limited by shares) v. FHT Marketing Choice BV* [1998] *ECR* I-3603.

Therefore, the foundations of a firm bridge among the legal systems relentlessly merit consideration.


2.      THE APPLICATION OF EUROPEAN COMMUNITY/UNION LAW
        IN THE ESTONIAN LEGAL SYSTEM

The cornerstone of the bridge between EU law and the Estonian legal system can be found in addition to the Accession Treaty[9] in the Constitution of the Republic of Estonia Amendment Act (CAA),[10] approved by the people in a referendum on 14 September 2003. The main text of the Constitution remained intact. The CAA has only four articles; however, their meaning is far-reaching. The core of the Act consists of its first two articles, which provide for a "protective clause" (called also "defence clause") stating that Estonia may belong to a European Union which respects the fundamental principles of the Estonian Constitution (Art. 1) and stipulate that the Estonian Constitution shall be applied taking into account the EU *acquis* transposed by the Accession Treaty (Art. 2). Article 2 essentially, although without an *expressis verbis* confirmation, covers the principles of supremacy and direct effect of EC law. The fundamental principles of the Constitution, underlined in Article 1 of the CAA are the central values without which the Estonian state loses its essence. Neither the Constitution nor the CAA defines these fundamental principles. Experts who have derived them from the preamble, Chapter I: "General Provisions" and Articles 10 and 11 of Chapter II: "Fundamental Rights, Freedoms and Duties" of the Constitution, have concluded that the fundamental principles should be defined in the form of an open catalogue. This covers, above all: national sovereignty, the state's foundations of liberty, justice and law, protection of internal and external peace, preservation of the Estonian nation and culture through the ages, human dignity, social statehood, democracy, the rule of law, respect for fundamental rights and freedoms, proportionate exercise of state authority.[11]

Starting from 1 May 2004 everybody in Estonia had to adjust to the above-mentioned cornerstones and their implications which might not immediately have had an obvious effect on everyday life. Some of the consequences of the accession are only beginning

---

[9] Treaty between the Kingdom of Belgium, the Kingdom of Denmark, the Federal Republic of Germany, the Hellenic Republic, the Kingdom of Spain, the French Republic, Ireland, the Italian Republic, the Grand Duchy of Luxembourg, the Kingdom of the Netherlands, the Republic of Austria, the Portuguese Republic, the Republic of Finland, the Kingdom of Sweden, the United Kingdom of Great Britain and Northern Ireland (Member States of the European Union) and the Czech Republic, the Republic of Estonia, the Republic of Cyprus, the Republic of Latvia, the Republic of Lithuania, the Republic of Hungary, the Republic of Malta, the Republic of Poland, the Republic of Slovenia, the Slovak Republic, concerning the accession of the Czech Republic, the Republic of Estonia, the Republic of Cyprus, the Republic of Latvia, the Republic of Lithuania, the Republic of Hungary, the Republic of Malta, the Republic of Poland, the Republic of Slovenia and the Slovak Republic to the European Union, *OJ* 2003 L 236/17.

[10] *RT* (Riigi Teataja = State Gazette, Estonian Official Journal) I 2003, 64, 429. Available in English at http://www.legaltext.ee/et/andmebaas/ava.asp?m=022.

[11] Positions of the Working Group formed by the Estonian Parliament on the Constitutional Analysis of the Ratification of the Treaty establishing a Constitution for Europe. Summary, pp. 5-6. Available at http://www.riigikogu.ee/public/Riigikogu/epsl_20051211_ee.pdf (in Estonian).

to reveal themselves. Few of them are of a transitional nature. Nevertheless, ever since Estonia's accession to the EU, all Estonian courts have become courts of the EU; therefore, their responsibilities have grown tremendously. These tasks demand from a judge not only additional homework – to read and analyse EC law, including ECJ case law – but also something even more important – a change in mentality. This does not arrive overnight. Therefore, the opening up towards EC law in Estonia has taken place gradually (at first cautious, later much more active) under the leadership of the Supreme Court (SC) of Estonia [*Riigikohus*].[12] The Administrative Law Chamber (ALCSC) of the latter has taken the initiative in beginning the judicial dialogue with the ECJ.

### 2.1.   Supremacy of European Union law over Estonian law: from cautious modesty to provocative EU friendliness

The other chambers of the Supreme Court and the lower courts have been at first waiting anxiously for some guidelines from the SC *en banc* (General Assembly) and the Constitutional Review Chamber of the Supreme Court (CRCSC) about the relationship to Community law and the interpretation of the CAA. Before this section of the chapter goes into details of the ground-breaking Supreme Court judgments concerning the supremacy and application of Community law in Estonia, the evolution of the Supreme Court practice in EC law matters is discussed.

### 2.1.1.   *Respect and silence in the pre-accession phase. Continuous restraint in the judgment of 19 April 2005 of the Supreme Court en banc in the Elections Coalitions II case*

The pre-accession case law of the Supreme Court can be described as quite eclectic. Respect for the general principles of EC law was established at an early stage; yet there are regrettably no judgments interpreting the different agreements between Estonia and the EC.

It is of interest that some ten years before Estonia's EU membership, the Supreme Court stated in a judgment concerning the review of the constitutionality of Article 25 paragraph 3 of the Property Law Enforcement Act, that the general principles of Community law form part of the sources of Estonian law.[13] The Supreme Court repeated this idea in a later ruling of 24 March 1997 of the Administrative Law Chamber, where it recognised the principle of equal treatment, regarded by the ECJ as one of the general principles of Community law, also as a general principle of Estonian law.[14]

---

[12] The Supreme Court of Estonia is the highest court of the country, also fulfilling the functions of a Constitutional Court (Art. 149 of the Constitution of the Republic of Estonia (CRE)). The SC comprises of 19 justices and 4 chambers: Civil Chamber, Criminal Chamber, Administrative Law Chamber and Constitutional Review Chamber. Constitutional review cases are adjudicated either at the sessions of the CRC or sitting en banc (General Assembly of the SC). More information is available at http://www.riigikohus.ee/?id=142 (in English).

[13] Decision of 30 September 1994 of the CRCSC, Case No. III-4/A-5/94 (*RT* 1 1994, 80, 1159). In English available at the home page of the SC at http://www.nc.ee/?id=482.

[14] Case No. 3-3-1-5-97 (*RT* III 1997, 12, 136) (in Estonian only, henceforth it will be only indicated if a text in English is available; if this is not the case only a reference to Estonian Riigi Teataja will be given).

However, the highest court of the country kept quiet as far as the Europe Agreement[15] and later the Accession Treaty were concerned and made no statements about the pre-accession application of EC law, interpretation of national law in accordance with EC law before the accession, etc. Only some dissenting opinions[16] of two Supreme Court justices (both at the time of writing their dissents, respectively, chief justices of the Court and experienced in working with *acquis* of the Council of Europe) looked for references and examples in EC law.[17] The silence cannot be justified by lack of complaints.[18] For instance, the Supreme Court was seized in 12 matters in which the ratification of the Accession Treaty and/or the referendum about Estonia's accession to the EU, including constitutional amendments, was contested. Conversely, the Supreme Court dismissed all claims on procedural grounds (e.g., the deadline to challenge was not respected, there was no right for individuals to contest, etc.) and did not discuss the issue in its substance.[19] As opposed to the claims of individuals, some of whom were eurosceptically oriented, neither the Chancellor of Justice[20] nor the President of the Republic questioned the constitutionality of the ratification of the Accession Treaty.

In contrast to the above-described restraint, it is remarkable that the decisions of the Supreme Court refer to the EU's Charter of Fundamental Rights (the Charter). In three cases, this happened even before Estonia's accession to the EU (at that time, the ECJ did not yet dare to refer to the Charter, only some Advocates General did!). Moreover, the Charter is not legally binding, and even if it will be one day, this will affect the Member States mostly in cases when they apply EU law. Summarising the practice of *Riigikohus* referring to the Charter, two features can be brought out: 1) the Supreme Court has used the Charter in "domestic cases" (however, not as the only source/argument of interpretation), i.e., in matters which did not have a direct link to EC law.

---

[15] Europe Agreement establishing an association between the European Communities and their Member States, on the one part, and the Republic of Estonia, on the other part, *OJ* 1998 L 68/3.

[16] Estonian judicial system recognises the right to dissenting opinion. See in detail J. Laffranque, 'Dissenting Opinion and Judicial Independence', 8 *Juridica International* (2003) pp. 162-172.

[17] Dissent of R. Maruste on the CRCSC judgment of 27 May 1998, Case No. III/4-1-4/98 (*RT* I 1998, 49, 752), where he referred, in interpreting Estonian labour law, to the former Art. 3(c) and 48(2) EC and to Art. 68 EA Estonia, where under approximation of laws was required. Dissent of R. Maruste on the CRCSC judgment of 6 October 1997, Case No. III/4-1-3/97 (*RT* I 1997, 74, 1268), where he points out the legal force of the ECJ rulings. Dissent of U. Lõhmus on the CRCSC judgment of 5 October 2000, Case No. 3-4-1-8-00 (*RT* III 2000, 21, 232; available in English at the home page of the SC at http://www.nc.ee/?id=445), where he discusses the legal clarity and refers to the resolution of EU Council of Ministers of 8 June 1993 according to which the wording of legal acts has to be clear and simple.

[18] E.g., the President of the Republic contested that the Non-profit Associations Act was, *inter alia*, in conflict with EA Estonia. The SC, however, did not analyse this aspect, also because the Europe Agreement was at that time not yet in force. See J. Laffranque, 'Co-existence of the Estonian Constitution and European Law', 7 *Juridica International* (2002) pp. 17-27, at p. 23.

[19] See, e.g., Order of 26 February 2004 of the CRCSC, Case No. 3-4-1-6-04, not published, available at the home page of the SC at http://www.nc.ee/klr/lahendid/tekst/RK/3-4-1-6-04.html (in Estonian). About similar claims, see A. Albi, 'Supremacy of EC Law in the New Member States. Bringing parliaments into the Equation of "Co-operative Constitutionalism"', 3 *EuConst* (2007) pp. 25-67, at p. 43.

[20] An independent official responsible for reviewing the legislation of the legislative and executive powers and of local governments for conformity with the Constitution and the laws (Art. 139 of the CRE). The Chancellor of Justice also carries out the tasks of an ombudsman.

Exceptions here are the case of distributing EU structural aid[21] and the dissenting opinion concerning the right of a citizen of one Member State to belong to a political party in another member country;[22] in these cases the relevance of EC law was present. 2) The Supreme Court has used the Charter in very important and sensitive areas, such as, human dignity,[23] right to good administration,[24] justice (procedural fundamental rights),[25] solidarity[26] and also the right to bequeath one's property.[27] These examples indicate the areas where the Charter could be necessary as a supplementary source of law in Estonia.

On the above-described background, it almost seems as if the Supreme Court has with utmost diplomatic skills selected carefully the EC law aspects it considered "safe" and "noble" to touch upon – the general principles, the Charter – and has tried to escape from interpreting the constitutionality of the transfer of Estonia's sovereign competences to the EU. This tactic was easier to pursue prior to Estonia's accession to the EU when it was still possible to hide behind the lack of procedural possibilities for reaching a decision in European integration matters. Regrettably, the modesty, which could to an outsider even give an impression of ignorance, continued for a considerable while after Estonia joined the EU.

In the so-called *Election coalitions II* case,[28] the Chancellor of Justice raised, *inter alia*, the issue of the conformity of Estonian law with Community law in the course of an abstract constitutionality review of Estonian legislation. According to the opinion of the Chancellor of Justice, Article 5, paragraph 1 of the Political Parties Act, which allowed only Estonian citizens to belong to a political party, restricted the rights of citizens of other EU Member States to set up their candidacies for municipal elections.[29]

---

[21] Art. 41 of the Charter; judgment of 19 December 2006 of the ALCSC, Case No. 3-3-1-80-06 (*RT* III 2007, 1, 10). Summary of the judgment in English and French in the Information System Jurifast at the home page of the Association of the Councils of State and Supreme Administrative Jurisdictions of the EU: http://www.juradmin.eu/docs/EE01/EE01000011.pdf and at the home page of the SC at http://www.nc.ee/?id=719.

[22] Art. 12 para.1 of the Charter; dissenting opinion of justice J. Laffranque (the author of this chapter acting in her judicial capacity) to the judgment of the SC *en banc* of 19 April 2005, Case No. 3-4-1-1-05 joined by justices T. Anton, P. Jerofejev, H. Kiris, I. Koolmeister and H. Salmann (*RT* III 2005, 13, 128). Available in English at http://www.nc.ee/?id=391.

[23] Art. 1 of the Charter; judgment of 28 March 2006 of the ALCSC, Case No. 3-3-1-14-06 (*RT* III 2006, 11, 108).

[24] Judgment of 17 February 2003 of the CRCSC, Case No. 3-4-1-1-03 (*RT* III 2003, 5, 48). Available in English at http://www.nc.ee/?id=418 and judgment of 19 December 2006 of the ALCSC, *loc. cit.* n. 21.

[25] Reference to the Charter in general and to the principle according to which a heavier penalty shall not be imposed than that which was applicable at the time a criminal offence was committed. See judgment of 17 March 2003 of the SC *en banc*, Case No. 3-1-3-10-02 (*RT* III 2003, 10, 95). Available in English at http://www.nc.ee/?id=419.

[26] Art. 34 of the Charter; judgment of 21 January 2004 of the CRCSC, Case No. 3-4-1-7-03 (*RT* III 2004, 5, 45). Available in English at http://www.nc.ee/?id=412.

[27] Art. 17 of the Charter; judgment of 23 February 2005 of the SC *en banc*, Case No. 3-2-1-73-04 (*RT* III 2005, 8, 73). Available in English at http://www.nc.ee/?id=394.

[28] Judgment of 19 April 2005 of the SC *en banc*, Case No. 3-4-1-1-0 (*RT* III 2005, 13,128). Available in English at http://www.nc.ee/?id=391.

[29] The Political Parties Act has been amended by now, and it does allow citizens of other EU Member States to belong to Estonian parties. See *RT* I 2006, 52, 384 (in Estonian).

The Chancellor of Justice found this to be contrary to Community law and, *via* the CAA, also contrary to the Estonian Constitution. However, the Supreme Court in its judgment did not answer this question and did not analyse the CAA. The majority of the Court took the view that neither the Chancellor of Justice Act nor the Constitutional Review Proceedings Act (CRPA) gives the Chancellor of Justice the authority to ask the Supreme Court to repeal an act because it is contrary to Community law. 'There are many ways how to bring domestic law into conformity with Community law; neither the Constitution nor the Community law requires a constitutional review process for this purpose.'[30] The Supreme Court found that it is up to the legislature to decide to allow for a review. Neither did a majority of the Supreme Court relate the issue of conformity with EC/EU law with the issue of the conformity of national law with the CAA.

It may be asked whether such a position was adopted because of the limited competence of the Supreme Court, or rather the lack of competence of the Chancellor of Justice, according to the Court, to initiate a review of the conformity of Estonian law with Community law, or in fact, the Court's cautiousness in handling the CAA and the EC law aspects. Delving into EC law could have led to asking for a preliminary ruling from the ECJ and, considering the short time left till the elections of local government councils, would have been unreasonable in the opinion of a majority.[31] The Supreme Court *en banc* did, however, briefly discuss the relations between Estonian law and EU law, noting as follows:

> 'European Union law does indeed have supremacy over Estonian law, but taking into account the case-law of the ECJ, this means supremacy upon application. ... The national act, which is in conflict with European Union law, should be set aside in a specific dispute. ... This does not mean that such an abstract review procedure over national law should exist on the national level.'[32]

The Supreme Court *en banc* did not say whether the Community law can have supremacy over the Estonian Constitution.

In a dissenting opinion it was concluded that the Chancellor of Justice essentially contested the conformity of the Political Parties Act to the Constitution, the substance of which had been renewed by the CAA, and the Supreme Court *en banc* should have answered this question in the framework of constitutional review, using the help of EC law for interpretation purposes and even asking the ECJ for a preliminary ruling, if necessary.[33]

---

[30] Judgment of 19 April 2005 of the SC *en banc*, *loc. cit.* n. 28, para. 49.
[31] See critically C. Ginter, 'Constitutional Review and EC Law in Estonia', 31 *ELRev.* (2006) pp. 912-923.
[32] Judgment of 19 April 2005 of the SC *en banc*, *loc. cit.* n. 28. para. 49.
[33] Dissenting opinion of Justice J. Laffranque, *loc. cit.* n. 22.

2.1.2.   *In the opinion of 11 May 2006, the Constitutional Review Chamber of the Supreme Court favours EU law over the Estonian Constitution. Conflicts about the euro instead of the European Arrest Warrant*

An unexpected setback to the reserve attitude of the Supreme Court occurred when the Constitutional Review Chamber of the Supreme Court was asked by the Estonian Parliament [*Riigikogu*] whether the Bank of Estonia could have the sole right to issue Estonian currency upon the introduction of the euro, and how the provision of the Constitution setting out such a right should be interpreted in conjunction with the CAA and EC law. The *Riigikogu* seemed to wish to receive an answer to the following question unsolved in the judgment of the Supreme Court in *Elections Coalitions II* case: what is the character of the modifications made to Estonian constitutional law due to the country's EU accession? The problem was acute because of the European Commission's doubts that there is a conflict between Article 111 of the Estonian Constitution and Article 106 EC. This could have been an obstacle to the introduction of the euro in Estonia.[34]

It should be noted that Lithuania has, in order to become a full member of the Economic and Monetary Union and to introduce the euro, preferred to amend its Constitution to ensure clarity and avoid conflicts. Lithuania had also already previously adopted a constitutional act affirming the constitutionality of EU-accession and building a bridge between Lithuanian law and Community law.[35] Nevertheless, Lithuania additionally modified Article 125 of its Constitution in April 2006, by deleting the sentence according to which the Bank of Lithuania had the sole right to issue Lithuanian currency and by supplementing the paragraph about the legal bases of the Bank of Lithuania.[36] As seen below, Estonia chose a different path and the potential conflict was – in the opinion of the Supreme Court – overcome with the help of the CAA, so that the Constitution did not need to be amended.

In response to the question about the euro, the CRCSC stated in its opinion of 11 May 2006, that under the conditions of full membership of the Economic and Monetary Union, the Bank of Estonia shall not have the sole right to issue Estonian currency

---

[34]  Art. 111 of the CRE reads as follows: 'The Bank of Estonia has the sole right to issue Estonian currency. The Bank of Estonia shall regulate currency circulation and shall uphold the stability of the national currency.' However, at the same time, the CAA states in Art. 2 that as of Estonia's accession to the EU, the Constitution of Estonia applies taking account of the rights and obligations arising from the Accession Treaty. The opinion of the European Commission was in 2005 available at: http://europa.eu.int/comm/economy_finance/publications/european_economy/convergencereports2004_en.htm. According to the Commission, Art. 111 of the CRE is in conflict with EC law; the opinion does not mention the CAA. The European Central Bank (ECB), however, refers in its assessment to both the Constitution and the CAA but urges that Art. 111 should be amended with regard to legal certainty. The ECB's position is available at http://www.ecb.int/pub/pdf/conrep/cr2004en.pdf.

[35]  See I. Jarukaitis, 'Ratification of European Constitution in Lithuania and its Impact on the National Constitutional System', in A. Albi and J. Ziller, eds., *The European Constitution and National Constitutions: Ratification and Beyond* (The Hague, Kluwer International Law 2007) pp. 17-24. See also Chapters 3 and 7 in this volume.

[36]  See Valstybes žinos (Lithuanian State Gazette) 2006, No. 48-1701, published on 29 April 2006.

anymore.[37] However, the grounds and *obiter dicta* of this opinion are more important than the wording of the operative part. Namely, the Supreme Court expressly admitted the supremacy of EU law over the Estonian Constitution. There are no counterparts to this bold expression of EU-fondness in other Member States. The behaviour of the CRCSC as a "Constitutional Court" of Estonia demonstrates the unprecedented submissiveness to the EU, because a constitutional jurisdiction is traditionally seen as the last resort of sovereignty. The supremacy of EU law, as stated by the Supreme Court's opinion of 11 May 2006, was at the time laid down only in Article I-6 of the Treaty establishing a Constitution for Europe, which will not enter into force. The Lisbon Treaty does not envisage a similar statement about the primacy of EU law and contains only a declaration to the relevant case law of the ECJ.[38] As is well-known, the ECJ has so far only admitted the supremacy of Community law, the First Pillar of the EU, even if it is moving towards extending the supremacy to legal acts of the Third Pillar.[39]

The Estonian Supreme Court's opinion is also remarkable for the fact that it has not attempted to overcome the conflicts by way of interpretation, not even by application of the Constitution *via* the CAA. The latter was suggested by the explanatory memorandum to the draft CAA.[40] It has been the position of the authors of the CAA; the Chancellor of Justice, the Minister of Justice and the *Riigikogu*. Even in the judgment of the ALCSC delivered on 10 May 2006, one day prior to the opinion, the ALCSC settled a matter based on the fact that according to the CAA, as to Estonia's accession to the EU, the Estonian Constitution applies, taking account of the rights and obligations arising from the Accession Treaty, and added that the principle also concerns application of Article 113 (taxes) of the Constitution in the context of EU law.[41] In its opinion of 11 May 2006, however, the CRCSC instead "deactivated" the provisions of the Constitution that were contrary to the CAA and EU law. The Supreme Court's opinion does not specify how to ascertain in each separate case which provisions of the Constitution are "dormant" and are not applicable, or if "sleeping beauty" should wake up one day (for example, if Estonia withdraws from the EU). The opinion of 11 May 2006 of the CRCSC settled the matter as follows:

> 'The Constitution must be read together with the CAA, applying only the part of the Constitution that is not amended by the CAA. ... As such, only that part of the Constitution is applicable, which is in conformity with EU law or which regulates the relationships that are not regulated by EU law. The effect of those provisions of the Constitution that are not compatible with EU law and thus inapplicable is suspended. This means that within the

---

[37] Case No. 3-4-1-3-06 (*RT* III 2006, 19, 176); available in English at http://www.nc.ee/?id=377.

[38] Treaty of Lisbon amending the Treaty on European Union and the Treaty establishing the European Community, *OJ* 2007 C 306/1.

[39] See ECJ, Case C-105/03 *Criminal proceedings against Maria Pupino* [2005] *ECR* I-5285.

[40] Explanatory Memorandum to the CAA. (1067 SE, 9th composition of the Riigikogu). Available at http://web.riigikogu.ee/ems/saros- n/mgetdoc?itemid=021360008&login=proov&password=&system=ems&server=ragne11 (in Estonian).

[41] Judgment of the ALCSC of 10 May 2006, Case No. 3-3-1-66-05 (*RT* III 2006, 19, 180), para. 9. A summary in English and French available at the Information System Jurifast at http://www.juradmin.eu/docs/EE01/EE01000003.pdf and at http://www.riigikohus.ee/?id=719.

spheres of exclusive competence of the EU or where there is a shared competence with the EU, in the case of a conflict between Estonian legislation, including the Constitution and the EU law, the EU law shall apply.'[42]

For the sake of correctness, it must be noted that at least in one case, the Tallinn Administrative Court has, as early as 28 December 2005, admitted the supremacy of the legal acts of the EU institutions over Estonian legal acts, including the Constitution.[43] This stunning statement has nevertheless not been debated at all, probably out of ignorance and limited interest in a judgment of a first instance court.

The Supreme Court opinion, however, was dissented by Justices Eerik Kergandberg and Villu Kõve. They believed that the Supreme Court only spoke half the truth, i.e., it spoke about the supremacy of EU law over the Estonian Constitution but did not specify the limits of the supremacy and failed to interpret the fundamental principles of the Constitution, which are stated in the protective clause of the CAA.[44] Justice Kõve was of the opinion that the principle of supremacy of EU law has been "overestimated."[45] It is difficult not to agree with him.

However, it should be admitted that non-recognition by the Member States and their jurisdictions of the supremacy of EU law over the constitutions is becoming a facade, while the influence of EC law, including the well-established case law of the ECJ, is constantly growing. This does not preclude, but instead deepens, the need for clarification of the conditions and limits of supremacy which the CRCSC unfortunately failed to do. Therefore, it appears as if the Supreme Court was intentionally provocative in its EU friendliness, perhaps in order to give the legislator some thoughts about the future of the constitutionality review and the review of EU law conformity of national law. Although the opinion of the Supreme Court is not formally mandatory to the Parliament, nevertheless *Riigikogu* chose to be guided by the Supreme Court's opinion.

Compared to the case law of the Supreme Courts/Constitutional Courts of other new EU Member States,[46] two distinctions can be made: 1) the Supreme Court of Estonia has *expressis verbis* accepted the supremacy of the "whole" EU law, even over the Estonian Constitution and 2) the issues which have caused constitutional arguments tend to be selective.

The selectiveness can be illustrated by the fact that unlike in many other EU Member States, there has been no dispute in Estonia concerning the compliance of the European Arrest Warrant with the Constitution. Although the Constitution does not completely exclude extradition of Estonian citizens, as Article 36, paragraph 2 of the Constitution

---

[42]  See opinion of 11 May 2006 of the CRCSC *loc. cit.* n. 37, paras. 14-16.

[43]  Judgment of 28 December of 2005 of the Tallinn Administrative Court, Case No. 3-562/2004 (3-04-406), para. 2 of the reasoning.

[44]  See the dissenting opinion of E. Kergandberg and the dissenting opinion of V. Kõve to the opinion of 11 May 2006 of the CRCSC, *loc. cit.* n. 37. The English text of the dissents is available at http://www.nc.ee/?id=663.

[45]  The dissenting opinion of V. Kõve, para. 3.

[46]  Even when the higher jurisdictions of the other new Member States have principally accepted the supremacy of EC law, they have not expressed this with regard to their national constitutions. See Chapters 9, 12 and 15 in this volume (Poland, Hungary and Cyprus respectively).

stipulates that an Estonian citizen can be extradited to a foreign state only under the conditions prescribed by an international treaty; an EU framework decision cannot be regarded as a traditional international treaty. However, in this case, the potential conflict was overcome without court dispute and with the help of the CAA (as was, in fact, also the question about the euro; however concerning the euro, at least, the *Riigikogu* asked for the opinion of the Supreme Court).

In practice, the European Arrest Warrant was mentioned in a judgment of the Criminal Chamber of the Supreme Court (CrimCSC) of 4 May 2006. In this case, one of the accused was a Latvian citizen who after committing the offence, returned to Latvia. During the proceedings in the Estonian lower level courts in 2003, it was found that neither the Latvian Constitution nor the agreement between Estonia, Latvia and Lithuania on legal assistance and judicial co-operation provided a possibility to extradite a Latvian citizen to Estonia. However, at a later stage, the situation changed because of the enforcement of the European Arrest Warrant. Therefore, the Supreme Court affirmed, speaking on Latvia's behalf and without any constitutional remorse, that the surrender procedure based on the Council Framework Decision on the European Arrest Warrant prevails upon the legal assistance and judicial cooperation agreement between the Baltic states and obliges Latvia to extradite its citizen, transfer him/her for trial and allow the proceedings to take place in Estonia.[47]

In a decision of 26 June 2008[48] of the CRCSC, the Supreme Court admited that it has no competence to decide whether a piece of EC secondary legislation is in conformity with the primary Community law and/or with the Estonian Constitution. The Supreme Court can only review modifications of the primary Community law with the Estonian Constitution before the ratification of treaties changing the foundations of the EU. The Supreme Court refered in its decision to an order of the ALCSC from 7 May 2008 in the case No. 3-3-1-85-07[49] and confirmed that if there is a possible collision between Estonian law and EC law and/or Estonian law and the Estonian Constitution, a deciding judge(s) should first check the compatibility of an Estonian act with EC law. The CRCSC emphasised the following:

> 'The Chamber shall set out a non-exhaustive list of the cases when the Supreme Court is competent to adjudicate petitions for the review the constitutionality of a provision relating to the EU law. First the Supreme Court is competent to review the constitutionality of a provision relating to the EU law if formal constitutionality of the provision is contested – this is so for the reason that the EU law does not regulate either the requirements concerning the competence, procedure and form established for the issue of legislation of general application in Estonia, or the observance of the requirement that laws be enacted solely by the parliaments and the requirement of legal clarity. Secondly the Supreme Court is competent to review the constitutionality of such provisions relating to the EU law which regulate also the situations not regulated by the EU law and the constitutional review is petitioned in regard to those situations only. Thirdly the Supreme Court has this competence in a situation where

---

[47] Judgment of 4 May 2006 of the CrimCSC, Case No. 3-1-1-5-06 (*RT* III 2006, 20, 181), para. 12.

[48] Order of 26 June 2008 of the CRCSC, Case No. 3-4-1-5-08 (*RT* III 2008, 33, 222).

[49] Order of 7 May 2008 of the ALCSC, Case No. 3-3-1-85-07, available at the home page of the SC.

the EU law including the case law of the ECJ gives the Member States the rights of discretion upon the transposition and implementation of the EU law in the exercise of which the Member States are bound by their constitutions and principles arising from the constitutions. When the EU law sets an objective to the Member States that leaves the measures for the achievement to the Member States, the measures should be in conformity with the EU law and Estonian constitution.'

## 2.2.  Running smoothly: considerable referrals to European Community law in Estonian courts

The majority of the burden of Community law-based cases in Estonia lies within the administrative jurisdiction. There are already countless cases in Estonian courts where EC law plays a certain part – from plain referral to application and interpretation, leading even to a situation where provisions of national law which were contrary to a Community measure had to be set aside. In this connection, topics such as transitional measures; customs and tax law; subsidies from structural funds, especially in the agricultural sector; environmental law and to a certain, still very modest extent, also competition law, are worth mentioning.

However, there has been EC law contact in court cases concerning private law as well, e.g., in fields of trademark law, cross-border insolvency proceedings, co-operation between courts of the Member States in taking of evidence in civil or commercial matters, accounting standards, rights of custody, equal treatment of women and men in labour cases.

In criminal jurisdiction, EU matters have been discussed in connection with the misdemeanours in the field of customs; the European Arrest Warrant and the Council Framework Decision on the standing of victims in criminal proceedings.

Most of the referrals take place in cases where Community regulations are applied because they are largely directly applicable (e.g., customs law, agricultural issues and the cases concerning the support from structural funds). Nevertheless, without going into very much detail about the relationship between national law and EC law, we can see that this kind of application is somehow mechanical, and the referrals are more or less automatic. More "creative" referrals can be found in fields where EC law is mostly in the form of directives, and, therefore, it can be necessary to interpret the national legislation looking at the Community norms (e.g., tax issues, environmental law, trademark matters, etc.).

There have not been considerable cases about the application of fundamental freedoms of the EU, such as free movement of persons, services, goods and capital. Equally, the fundamental freedoms have, therefore, not often constituted parts of reasoning of judgments. In fact, there are not so many cases concerning the fundamental freedoms in Estonian courts partly because some of the work is done by the so called SOLVIT-system,[50] the national contact point of which is the Ministry of Economic Affairs and Communication. Maybe it is also because the movement of persons from other Member States to Estonia is not very vibrant, and finally, because natural persons

---

[50]  See SOLVIT home page http://europa.eu.int/solvit/site/index_et.htm.

in Estonia, including even some of their legal advisers, are still in a familiarising process with EC law. On the other hand, sometimes the complainants tend to exaggerate EC law arguments. The main problem is that the litigants do not always differentiate between a situation when only national law applies and circumstances where there is an EC law contact. As far as the procedural rights are concerned, unawareness seems to exist as to the possibilities to access the national courts in EU matters and get help from the Court of First Instance of the European Communities (CFI) as well as from the ECJ.

Concerning the practice of the Supreme Court, the Administrative Law Chamber recognised the approximation of Estonian legislation with EC law as a purpose for changes in national legislation[51] and harmonised its own practice to EC law to a certain extent even before Estonia joined the Union.[52] On numerous occasions, the ALCSC interpreted the Council Sixth VAT Directive.[53] In a case about turnover taxes, the ALCSC applied *expressis verbis* the reasoning of the ECJ judgment of 21 February 2006,[54] stating that EC law precludes any right of a taxable person to deduct input VAT, where the transactions, from which that right derives, constitute an abusive practice.[55] Similar conclusions of the Supreme Administrative Court of Lithuania in its judgment of 27 October 2004 in the case No. A1-355-2004[56] confirm that the uniform application of Community VAT law in the new Member States can, nevertheless, be quite successful. Fortunately, Estonia has so far no such problems like the questions concerning the registration duty on used motor vehicles (taxes on second-hand vehicles).[57]

In Estonia, ECJ case law has also effectively been referred to in customs cases concerning, e.g., the nature of acceptance of customs declarations, the application of Article 220, paragraph 2b of the Community Customs Code (CCC), the interpretation of a "mistake" of the customs authority, etc.[58] Furthermore, the CCC has also been successfully applied in criminal cases concerning the customs offences.[59]

---

[51] Judgment of the ALCSC of 7 April 2005, Case No. 3-3-1-5-05 (*RT* III 2005, 12, 117).

[52] E.g., the ALCSC has said that the Estonian nomenclature of goods needs to be in accordance with the combined nomenclature used in the EU. Judgments of the ALCSC of 15 March 2004, Case No. 3-3-1-7-04 (*RT* III 2004, 9, 103) and of 15 March 2004, Case No. 3-3-1-6-04 (*RT* 2004, 9, 102).

[53] Case No. 3-3-1-90-06 (*RT* III 2007, 6, 52).

[54] ECJ, Case C-255/02 *Halifax plc, Leeds Permanent Development Services Ltd and County Wide Property Investments Ltd v. Commissioners of Customs & Excise* [2006] *ECR* I-1609.

[55] Judgment of 7 December of 2006 of the ALCSC, Case No. 3-3-1-63-06 (*RT* III 2006, 46, 392).

[56] Summary in English and French available in the Information System Jurifast at http://www.juradmin.eu/docs/LT01/LT01000003.pdf. Judgment of the Lithuanian Supreme Court of 6 April 2006 in the Case No. A1-794/2006, available at http://www.juradmin.eu/docs/BE02/BE02000405.pdf. See also the judgment of the Administrative Senate of the Supreme Court of Latvia in a Case KA208, which can be considered as a milestone decision applying duly ECJ case law, as the Latvian court practice in tax matters has been previously criticized for differing completely from the established case law of the ECJ. Available at: http://www.lt-v.lv/pdf/Saldo%20Nr.17_10_2006_SN.pdf.

[57] Compare ECJ, Case C-313/05 *Maciej Brzeziński v. Dyrektor Izby Celnej w Warszawie* [2007] *ECR* I-513; Joined Cases C-290/05 and C-333/05 *Ákos Nádasdi v. Vám- és Pénzügyőrség Észak-Alföldi Regionális Parancsnoksága (C-290/05) and Ilona Németh v. Vám- és Pénzügyőrség Dél-Alföldi Regionális Parancsnoksága (C-333/05)* [2006] *ECR* I-10115.

[58] Judgment of 10 May 2006 of the ALCSC, Case No. 3-3-1-66-05, *loc.cit.* n. 41.

[59] Judgment of 3 March 2006 of the CrimCSC, Case No. 3-1-1-155-05 (*RT* III 2006, 9, 80).

However, the Estonian courts have been chary in implementing EC competition law. This deficiency is probably due to the restricted amount of competition cases in general. First steps in opening up Estonian case law based on principles of EC competition law have been taken in matters regarding the distribution of structural aid[60] and concerning telecommunications networks and services (in this case, however, the EC directives were not used as grounds for argumentation in the Court's findings).[61] At least the courts have encouraged administrative bodies in general to make use of competition law, which so far has been mostly a monopoly of the Estonian Competition Board.

Case law in environmental matters, traditionally, has courageously referred to EC law.[62] Supposedly, the EC law context in environmental law cases will grow even more because of the NATURA 2000 networking programme.

### 2.2.1.   Community law conform interpretation of Estonian law and its limits

The same positive approach as taken by the administrative jurisdiction, as far as interpretation of national law in conformity with EC law is concerned, can also be noticed in the practice of the Civil Chamber of the Supreme Court (CivCSC).[63]

The CivCSC found it possible to interpret national law in line with an EC directive even before the deadline for Member States to transpose the directive into national legislation.[64] Of course, this does not necessarily mean a direct application of the directive.[65] As a comparison, the Supreme Court of Cyprus decided that Council Directive 2003/109/EC could not be applied before the deadline for its transposition.[66]

---

[60]   Judgment of 19 December 2006 of the ALCSC, *loc. cit.* n. 21.

[61]   Judgment of 20 September 2007 of the ALCSC, Case No. 3-3-1-33-07, nyr.

[62]   E.g., judgment of 9 March 2005 of the ALCSC, Case No. 3-3-1-88-04 (*RT* III 2005, 10, 90) emphasised the importance of the evaluation of alternatives in planning a landfill waste. Council Directive 1999/31/EC of 26 April 1999 on the landfill of waste (*OJ* 1999 L 182/1) and Directive 2001/42/EC of the European Parliament and of the Council of 27 June 2001 on the assessment of the effects of certain plans and programmes on the environment (*OJ* 2001 L 197/30), were taken into account.

[63]   E.g., in a case concerning combating late payment in commercial transactions, judgment of 14 June 2005 of the CivCSC, Case No. 3-2-1-66-05 (*RT* III 2005, 23, 245). The Estonian courts have also bravely interpreted the Council Directive 93/13/EEC on unfair terms in consumer contracts (*OJ* 1993 L 95/29) (see Order of 7 February 2005 of the Tartu County Court in the case AS Balti Investereingute Grupp). The interpretation of the same Directive was subject of the Hungarian city court's preliminary reference to the ECJ (Case C-302/04 *Ynos kft v. János Varga* [2006] *ECR* I-371); however, the ECJ did not interpret the Directive, since it found that it had no jurisdiction because the dispute in the main proceedings had taken place prior to Hungary's accession to the EU.

[64]   Judgment of 21 December 2004, Case No. 3-2-1-145-04 (*RT* III 2005, 3, 27).

[65]   See, e.g., ECJ, Case 80/86 *Criminal proceedings against Kolpinghuis Nijmegen BV.* [1987] *ECR* 3969.

[66]   Judgments of the Supreme Court of Cyprus Cases No. 1652/05 and No. 1653/05, see Bulletin 'Reflets.' Informations rapides sur les développements juridiques présentant un intérêt communautaire No. 2, 2006. Available at http://curia.europa.eu/et/coopju/apercu_reflets/lang/index.htm. These cases concerned a delicate matter – transposition of the Council Directive 2003/109/EC concerning the status of third-country nationals who are long-term residents (*OJ* 2003 L 16/44). The same Directive has been pointed out in several occasions in residence permit cases in Estonia as well, but the courts have not applied it prior to the transposition deadline.

An exemplary case in Estonia, where the conflict between national law and Community law was overcome by EC law conform interpretation, is the judgment of 30 March 2006 of the CivCSC concerning the trademark law.[67] It is even called in the literature a "landmark decision."[68] The Court concluded that the legislator had no conscious or deliberate wish to establish a regulation different from that of the First Council Directive 89/104/EEC to approximate the laws of the Member States relating to trademarks[69] and added that when interpreting a national regulation based on the Directive, the principles of the Directive have to be taken into account as much as possible.

Other examples concerning the EC law conform application of Estonian law, as well as its limits, take us back to customs law cases. Here the ALCSC has created two characteristics worth noticing. First, the limited availability of Community law in Estonian resulting from the late publication of the Official Journal of the EU was never seen as a real/acute problem in Estonia, neither by the applicants nor by the courts. Second, according to the ALCSC, the Community law conform application does not necessarily extend to cases which had occurred prior to Estonia's accession to the EU.[70]

As far as the publication of EC law and its availability is concerned, the ALCSC found in the judgment of 10 May 2006[71] that amendments to legislation and the lack of application practice of these do not justify the submission of incorrect data. It held:

'Estonia's accession to the EU was a process that lasted for years. All pertinent legal acts had been published either in the OJ of the European Union or in the *Riigi Teataja* (Estonian Official Gazette). As of the day of publication in the OJ, the community legal acts become a positive law, which everyone must know and take into account and nobody can invoke the fact that he or she was ignorant of the existence of a certain tax.'[72]

Furthermore, the ALCSC referred to the ECJ judgment in the *Kavallas* case[73] and held that upon the accession of a state to the EU, pursuant to the Accession Treaty, the state's enterpreneurs immediately become the subjects of and have to take into account Community law. Although the amounts at stake in this case were much higher than in

---

[67] Judgment of 30 March 2006 of the CivCSC, Case No. 3-2-1-4-06 (*RT* III 2006, 12, 118).

[68] See C. Ginter, 'Effective Implementation of the Trade Mark Directive in Estonia', 6 *ECLR* (2007) pp. 337-345.

[69] First Council Directive 89/104/EEC of 21 December 1988 to approximate the laws of the Member States relating to trademarks, *OJ* 1989 L 40/1.

[70] Judgment of 23 October 2006 of the ALCSC in the Case No. 3-3-1-57-06 (*RT* III 2006, 39, 335). A summary in English and French available in the Information System Jurifast at http://www.juradmin.eu/docs/EE01/EE01000009.pdf and at http://www.riigikohus.ee/?id=719.

[71] *Loc. cit.* n. 41. In this case, an Estonian company bought foodstuffs from Poland which were loaded on a transport vehicle before and reached Estonia after Estonia's accession to the EU. The customs official accepted the customs declaration and made few amendments to it. Later it was discovered that the tax had been wrongly calculated. The Tax Authority ordered the payment of tax arrears (275,565 EEK = 17 607 EUR). The dispute was whether the declarant had a reason to assume that as the Customs Authority had accepted the declaration, the taxes had been calculated correctly and could not be amended *ex post facto*.

[72] Judgment of 10 May 2006 of the ALCSC, *loc. cit.* n. 41, para. 12 of the judgment.

[73] ECJ, Case 160/84 *Oryzomyli Kavallas OEE and others v. Commission of the European Communities* [1986] *ECR* 1633.

the case in which a Czech court made a reference for preliminary ruling to the ECJ,[74] the ALCSC of Estonia seemed not to be interested in making a question of principle out of this unlike its Polish and Czech colleagues.[75] Even though the conduct of the ALCSC does not correspond to the later opinion of Advocate General J. Kokott[76] and the ECJ ruling in the *Skoma-Lux* case, it seems to have been pragmatic at the moment it occurred. Later on, the ALCSC has in its case law followed the ECJ judgment and correctly applied the principles elaborated in the *Skoma-Lux* case.[77] This attitude was founded on the fact that in the Estonian case, the company acted through a professional agent[78] and perhaps also because the applicants did not pursue the arguments of non-publication very persistently. They did not plead for a preliminary reference but rather in their counter-arguments referred to Community law which was also unpublished in Estonian in a legally binding version at the time of accession.

In another case, the ALCSC continued its strict position and provided as follows: 'In the current case there is no dispute as to the availability of the Commission regulation and that there were linguistic problems in understanding the regulation, even if the official publication of the regulation in Estonian was delayed.'[79]

The Supreme Court is quite flexible regarding the EC law conform interpretation of national legislation in cases that had occurred prior to the EU-accession and draws certain limits. Therefore, the changes in the Estonian legal order caused by the EU-accession cannot automatically be applicable to events which had taken place before Estonia joined the EU. The ALCSC accepts that the substantive customs law could have been more favourable to customs declarants before the accession to the EU. It held that 'Estonia was under the obligation to bring its law into conformity with the EU law even before the accession and it was recommendable that Estonia applied and interpreted its law accordingly. Furthermore, the relevant Estonian norms were modelled after the Community Customs Code. Nevertheless, the national law valid before the accession to the EU cannot automatically be interpreted on the basis of the EU law, without taking into account the facts of a concrete case and the treaties regulating the relations between Estonia and the EU at the time (e.g., Association Agreement). It is after the accession that the EU law conforming interpretation of national law became

---

[74] ECJ, Case C-161/06 *Skoma Lux sro v. Celní ředitelství Olomouc* [2007] *ECR* I-10841.

[75] The Estonian approach can be seen as the other extreme – a firm position, compared to the Polish one, in which the Administrative Court in Bydgoszcz annulled the national Customs Authority's decisions based on EC legislation not available in Polish, whereas the Czech reference for preliminary ruling is regarded as a middle course. See M. Bobek, 'The Binding Force of Babel: The Enforcement of EC Law Unpublished in the Languages of the New Member States', 9 *CYELS* (2006-2007) pp. 43-80.

[76] Opinion of 18 September 2007 of Advocate General J. Kokott in the Case C-161/06 *Skoma Lux sro v. Celní ředitelství Olomouc*.

[77] See judgment of 13 October 2008 of the ALCSC, Case No. 3-3-1-36-08.

[78] Judgment of 10 May 2006 of the ALCSC, *loc. cit.* n. 41, para. 12: 'Whether the European legal acts were available in Estonian at the time of completing customs formalities is irrelevant, as the company acted through a professional customs agent.'

[79] Judgment of 5 October 2006 of the ALCSC, Case No. 3-3-1-33-06 (*RT* III 2006, 35, 301), para. 20. A summary in English and French available in the Information System Jurifast at http://www.juradmin. eu/docs/EE01/EE01000007.pdf. Also available at the home page of the SC at http://www.nc.ee/?id=719.

legally binding.'[80] The Estonian Supreme Court made in this connection a reference to
the judgment of the ECJ of 10 January 2006 in the Hungarian court reference in case
*János Varga*.[81] It seems that the Administrative Law Chamber, in order to justify a more
flexible national regulation shortly before the country joined the EU, skilfully used the
non-willingness of the ECJ to increase its workload and admit cases concerning pre-
accession circumstances. Certain parallels can be made to the judgment of the Polish
Supreme Administrative Court in the case No. II GSK 168/05,[82] in which the Court
noted that the obligation put down in Article 68 EA Poland, to approximate Polish law
with the Community legislation during the period of association, cannot be seen as
identical to the obligations of Polish administrative bodies and courts after the accession
date. The CivCSC, in a judgment of 8 November 2006, also disregarded the litigants'
arguments about the applicability of Council Directive 2001/23/EC on the safeguarding
of employees' rights in the event of transfers of undertakings[83] because the facts of the
case had taken place before Estonia's accession to the EU.[84]

### 2.2.2.   The Supreme Court as European (administrative) law professor. Reactions to the ECJ Pupino judgment: interpreting the interpretation

As we have seen above, on several occasions, especially in administrative law, the
Supreme Court of Estonia has explained the consequences of the influence of Community
law on Estonian legislation and given guidelines to other courts how to apply EC law.
For instance, the ALCSC clarified in its order of 26 April 2006 in what cases and under
which conditions an Estonian judge could doubt the validity of Community law. The
Administrative Law Chamber stated, *inter alia*, that the relationship between Estonia
and the EU is determined in the CAA adopted by a referendum. According to the
ALCSC, an Estonian judge cannot doubt the legality of the primary law of the EC but
can, in exceptional cases, question the validity of secondary Community law. However,
it is the ECJ that exercises the review of compatibility of the secondary legislation of
the EC to the primary one. In the case of an act implementing Community law, a judge,
if in doubt, has to ascertain whether the implementing act is in conformity with EC law.
If it is, the pertinent Estonian legislation shall be applied. If there is an incompatibility,
it has to be found if EC law could be applied directly, irrespective of the inapplicable
implementation act.[85]

---

[80]   Judgment of the ALCSC of 23 October 2006, *loc. cit.* n. 70, para. 16.
[81]   ECJ, Case C-302/04 *Ynos kft v. Janos Varga* [2006] *ECR* I-371; see also ECJ, Case C-261/05 *Lakép
kft, Pár-Bau kft and Rottelma kft v. Komáron-Esztergom Megyei Közigazgatási Hivatal* [2006] *ECR* I-20.
[82]   Summary in English and French available in the Information System Jurifast at http://www.juradmin.
eu/docs/BE02/BE02000293.pdf.
[83]   Council Directive 2001/23/EC on the approximation of the laws of the Member States relating
to the safeguarding of employees' rights in the event of transfers of undertakings, businesses or parts of
undertakings or businesses, *OJ* 2001 L 82/16.
[84]   Case No. 3-2-1-103-06 (*RT* III 2006, 41, 349); judgment, para. 12.
[85]   Order of 25 April 2006 of the ALCSC, Case No. 3-3-1-74-05 (*RT* III 2006, 17, 154). Summary in
English and French available at the Information System Jurifast at http://www.juradmin.eu/docs/BE02/
BE02000423.pdf. Also available at the home page of the SC at http://www.nc.ee/?id=719.

In a way, the Supreme Court could be regarded as professor of European (Administrative) law. In the initial phase of EU membership, the teaching task of the Supreme Court is to be evaluated as positive. However, there is a growing tendency, especially in administrative cases, that the judgments of all courts are increasing in length, and that their wording becomes complicated and difficult to understand due to the use of the terminology of EC legislation. At the same time, it is good that the quality of the reasoning has improved, the judgments have become more substantial and the general principles of law have been increasingly valued. The references to well-established ECJ case law have frequently become self-evident,[86] and the judgments, in particular of the Supreme Court, have influenced the legislator to consider carefully EC law and have contributed to the general evolution of law.

Whereas the administrative judges feel more at home in interpreting national law in the light of Community measures (including ECJ case law), the Criminal Chamber of the Supreme Court was faced with a difficult challenge to "interpret the interpretation" and decode the ECJ judgment in the *Pupino* case.[87] The question was, if, and when, under what conditions, can a court build its decision on the testimony of a minor given during the preliminary enquiries instead of at the hearing in the court. The Estonian Code of Criminal Procedure does not provide such an opportunity. However, the courts of lower levels admitted this kind of possibility relying on the judgment of the ECJ in the *Pupino* case. The CrimCSC started its evaluation of the practice of first and second instance courts by explaining the nature of an EU framework decision.[88] The CrimCSC was of the opinion that a framework decision cannot replace valid national law. The latter is autonomous and open for modifications in the light of the purposes given by a framework decision only by the intermediation of the national legislator. According to the CrimCSC, although the ECJ extended the Community conform interpretation of national laws to framework decisions, the *Pupino* judgment can by no means be understood as giving a framework decision direct effect in Member States. The national law must be interpreted as far as possible in the light and in accordance with a framework decision; however, it must be done so that fundamental rights, including in particular the right to a fair trial, are respected. The interpretation cannot exceed the borders of the national law and must not lead to an injustice trial of the accused.[89] The CrimCSC found that the courts of first and second instance have interpreted the *Pupino* judgment wrongly by drawing their conclusions not from national law but, instead, from a legal act that does not have a direct effect in Estonia. Furthermore, the CrimCSC somehow short-sightedly distinguishes between the right of the lower courts to rely upon the

---

[86] Despite the frequent references to the well-established case law of the ECJ, the Supreme Court of Estonia has not – differently from the Czech Constitutional Court (see its decision of 8 March 2006, Pl. US 50/04) – admitted judicial borrowing from decisions of courts of other Member States (at least not publicly).

[87] *Loc. cit.* n. 39.

[88] Judgment of 7 March 2007 of the CrimCSC, Case No. 3-1-1-125-06 (*RT* III 2007, 11, 85).

[89] *Ibidem*, para. 10. Later, theCrimCSC repeated the reasoning of its judgment of 7 March 2007 and referred to the ECJ judgment in *Pupino* case; see judgment of 15 October 20007 of the CrimCSC, Case No. 3-1-1-45-07, nyr, para. 16.2.

framework decision and the ECJ judgment, giving the latter lesser importance. It is also questionable if, after the *Pupino* case law, limitations to the autonomy of national criminal procedure are continually ruled out, as understood by the CrimCSC in its reading of the ECJ judgment.

2.3.     **Problems in application of European Community law in Estonia: the morning after [the accession] – bittersweet sugar affairs and disappointed farmers**

Similarly to some of the other new Member States, Estonia had to face the problem of illegal surplus stocks of sugar and other food stuffs on the day of accession. In this context, two Commission Regulations are relevant – 1972/2003/EC, establishing transitional measures to be adopted in new Member States in respect to trade in agricultural products[90] and 60/2004/EC of January 2004, establishing transitional measures in respect to the sugar sector.[91] Both of them urged the Member States to determine their surpluses of sugar and other agricultural products stocked at the time of the accession. These overstocks were, if exceeding the permissible amount, penalised by fines. The Member States could, however, under certain circumstances, collect the necessary payments of the Member State fine from the entrepreneurs who have caused this excess. The aim of the two above-mentioned regulations was to prevent purchase of these products for speculative ends. Estonia, unlike Poland,[92] did not challenge the above-mentioned Community measures. Virtually at the last minute, on 7 April 2004, Estonia adopted its Overstock Charge Act, which entered into force on 1 May 2004.[93] Based on this Act, the Ministry of Agriculture began to determine the surplus stocks of companies. Relying on the findings of the Ministry of Agriculture, the Tax and Customs Board issued administrative decisions about payments of overstock charges. The acts of the Ministry of Agriculture and the Tax and Customs Board were contested in Estonian administrative courts as the holders of the overstocks found this to be contrary to the principle of legitimate expectations and did not agree with the way the stocks were determined. Some thirty cases were brought before the courts, the first one reaching the Supreme Court at the beginning of 2006.

In the meantime, the European Commission determined with its Regulation 832/2005/ EC of May 2005 the concrete surplus quantities of sugar, isoglucose and fructose for the Czech Republic, Estonia, Cyprus, Latvia, Lithuania, Hungary, Malta, Poland,

---

[90] Commission Regulation 1972/2003/EC of 10 November 2003 on transitional measures to be adopted in respect of trade in agricultural products on account of the accession of the Czech Republic, Estonia, Cyprus, Latvia, Lithuania, Hungary, Malta, Poland, Slovenia and Slovakia, *OJ* 2003 L 293/3.

[91] Commission Regulation 60/2004/EC of 14 January 2004 laying down transitional measures in the sugar sector by reason of the accession of the Czech Republic, Estonia, Cyprus, Latvia, Lithuania, Hungary, Malta, Poland, Slovenia and Slovakia, *OJ* 2004 L 9/8.

[92] CFI, Case T-257/04 *Republic of Poland v. Commission of the European Communities* [2009] *ECR* nyr.

[93] *RT* I 2004, 30, 203.

Slovenia and Slovakia.[94] The biggest amount was for Estonia – 91,464 tons of sugar! This bitterness of the usually sweet sugar caused Estonia to bring action before the CFI (Estonia did not agree that sugar stocked in private households for non-speculative purposes was included in the 91,464 tons; see in detail below). Thus, parallel court cases on different motives and of diverse jurisdictions were launched. The CFI has not yet responded. In turn, the ALCSC delivered its judgment on 5 October 2006, which marked a milestone in many ways in the Estonian legal order. Not only have the orders of payments and fines caused disputes, but also the other way around; the statements of non-payments may cause trouble, if these payments are not fines but instead supports from the structural funds of the EU! Here again, the applicants claim that their legitimate expectations are at stake, due to the frequent changes in legislation about the criteria of eligibility for aid. In Estonia, the implementing body in charge of distributing the structural support of the EU in the agricultural sector and of inspection thereof is the Agricultural Registers and Information Board (ARIB) based in Tartu. Tartu Administrative and Circuit Courts are, therefore, overburdened with approximately 50 cases only on agricultural support. Nevertheless, this number is not more than 0.5% of all the applications filed in the ARIB for structural aid.[95] Community legislation in this matter is complicated: stipulations of structural aid, agricultural policy and competition law have to be understood and sometimes applied together, and the Estonian norms do not always necessarily help to bring clarity in this situation; therefore, the ALCSC has been asked to have a say as a court of cassation. Here again, the ALCSC did something the Estonian courts had not practiced before, but this time, very confidently making up its mind independently, the Court turned in one of the structural aid cases to the ECJ (explained in detail below). In other cases, it has helped lower jurisdictions to interpret Estonian law in conformity with EC law and apply the principles of administrative procedure in this context, at the same time assuring the principles of EC law: *effet utile* and equivalency. Subsequently, some core elements of the legal construction of the ALCSC judgment on surplus stocks and of judicial review of the distribution of structural aid of the EU in agriculture policy are reflected.

2.3.1.   *Judgment of 5 October 2006 of the Administrative Law Chamber of the Supreme Court in the Hadler case: setting aside national norms which were found to be in non-conformity with EC law*

In this case, on the basis of administrative acts issued by the Ministry of Agriculture and the Tax and Customs Board, a company called Hadler was obliged to pay a charge for the surplus stocks of maltose. The charge was around 2,000 Estonian crowns

---

[94] Regulation 832/2005/EC of May 2005 the concrete surplus quantities of sugar, isoglucose and fructose for the Czech Republic, Estonia, Cyprus, Latvia, Lithuania, Hungary, Malta, Poland, Slovenia and Slovakia, *OJ* 2005 L 138/3.

[95] The director of the Agricultural Registers and Information Board, J. Kallas, at a seminar on agricultural support related cases of 21 September 2007 organised by Estonian Law Centre. See L. Kanger, 'Analyse of the practice of Community law application in Estonian administrative court practice on example of agricultural subsidies and overstock charge cases', p. 4, on file with the author.

(approximately 165 euros), a ridiculous sum compared to amounts in other cases pending in lower courts on similar issues where the fines amounted to millions of Estonian crowns. However, often the numbers are not important if it comes to creating precedents in matters of principle. The ALCSC annulled the judgments of lower courts, satisfied the appeal of the company for the repeal of the referred acts and did not apply Article 6, paragraph 1 of the Overstock Charge Act due to the conflict thereof with the EC law.[96] Article 6, paragraph 1 of the mentioned Act established the method of calculation of carryover stock. According to the Overstock Charge Act, Estonian authorities were told to use an automatic system for all handlers: a multiple of 1.2 of the average of the stocks available as of 1 May 2004 and of the four previous years. The ALCSC found this to be contrary to Article 4, paragraph 2 of Commission Regulation 1972/2003/EC, according to which to determine the surplus stock of each holder, the circumstances in which stocks were built up should be taken into account. The Supreme Court was of the opinion that the use of the criterion (multiplier 1.2) established in Estonian law does not allow taking into account the circumstances due to which an individual company has acquired surplus stocks. Furthermore, the Supreme Court equally criticised the legislature for passing the relevant Estonian law too late, thus giving the companies very little time, if any at all, to adjust to the renewed circumstances. Nevertheless, the ALCSC once again stressed that a professional was aware of possible changes in the sugar sector at the time the EC Regulation was passed and had an opportunity to make necessary adjustments. However, with the exception that all details, such as, e.g., the multiple 1.2, were not foreseen in Community law and came as last minute stipulations with the Estonian implementing act. At the same time, the ALCSC did not question the validity of the Community regulations and cited in this context the ECJ judgments in *Weidacher*[97] and *Hinton*.[98] In another case, where the accordance of a Commission Regulation with the Estonian Constitution was questioned, the Tallinn Administrative Court stated that it did not have the competence to question the conformity of the Commission Regulation with the Estonian Constitution.[99] The ALCSC found that although the Regulation of the European Commission is, as a rule, directly applicable to the Member States and its individuals, in this case, it did not produce direct effect since it did not specify its implementation in detail.[100] Although the Czech Constitutional Court under similar circumstances, by declaring the relevant national law invalid, stated that due to the direct applicability of the EC Regulation, the Czech Government was no longer entitled to adopt a national implementing act,[101] it seems a mission

---

[96] Judgment of 5 October 2006 of the ALCSC, *loc. cit.* n. 79.

[97] ECJ, Case C-179/00 *Gerald Weidacher (as administrator of the insolvent company Thakis Vertriebs- und Handels GmbH) v. Bundesminister für Land- und Forstwirtschaft* [2002] *ECR* I-501.

[98] ECJ, Case C-30/00 *William Hinton & Sons L^{da} v. Fazenda Pública* [2001] *ECR* I-7511.

[99] Judgment of 14 June 2006 of Tallinn Administrative Court, Case No. 3-05-272, para. 4.

[100] This manoeuvre of the ALCSC has been criticised by the Estonian judge at the ECJ, arguing that the EC Regulation should have been applied directly, or that at least a preliminary reference should have been asked. See U. Lõhmus, 'Kuidas liikmesriigi kohtusüsteem tagab Euroopa Liidu õiguse tõhusa toime (How Do the Court Systems of Member States Ensure the Efficient Functioning of European Union Law)?', 3 *Juridica* (2007) p. 151.

[101] Judgment of 8 March 2006, *loc. cit.* n. 86.

impossible to determine the carryover and surplus stocks and the concrete fines there-of based only on the wording of the Commission Regulation. Therefore, the ALCSC suggested that the national legislator should change the relevant Article of the Overstock Charge Act in order to assure its compliance with EC law. The more flexible regula-tory framework that would be more favourable to the companies can also be enacted retroactively.

The judgment of 5 October 2006 of the ALCSC has been called in the literature a remarkable expression of judicial inventiveness.[102] Indeed, the Estonian Supreme Court proficiently avoided the conflicts between Estonian law and the Estonian Constitution, as well as Community law and the Constitution. This was unlike, e.g., the Hungarian Constitutional Court, which, in its decision of 25 May 2004 No. 17/2004, found that the issue was neither about the conflict between relevant EC law and domestic law nor about the validity or interpretation of EC law, but about compliance with the national constitution of the domestic legislation implementing EC law, that was adopted prior to the EU accession.[103] The ALCSC judgment in the *Hadler* case was ground-breaking in many ways: it constructed a model according to which, despite the claims of the applicants that the Estonian law was also contrary to the Constitution, the Court con-centrated first on whether there is a controversy with EC law. The ALCSC had experi-ence to analyse Community law quite confidently, even *ex officio*, if needed. Moreover, the ALCSC used the *acte clair* doctrine by interpreting the Commission Regulation (this will be explained later on in this chapter). This was also the first time an Estonian court had not applied a national norm because it was judged to be in conflict with EC law. However, by setting the national norm aside, the ALCSC found it difficult to apply the relevant Commission Regulation directly. Therefore, the ALCSC gave the legisla-ture guidelines how to come out of this situation and finally, by doing all the above-mentioned, created a precedent, which in these cases is quite original.

The Estonian lower administrative courts followed literally the practice of the ALCSC. The Tax and Customs Board annulled immediately after the Supreme Court judgment its previous decisions, contested in similar cases in administrative courts. The legislature changed the law, which, nevertheless, continued to apply the multiple 1.2 in determining the carryover stocks.[104] This led to further litigation in Estonian courts and a reference for preliminary ruling to the European Court of Justice on the interpretation of EC law (leading to verification of conformity of Estonian law with EC legislation).

2.3.2.  *Problems with distribution of structural aid of the EU in agricultural matters and the review by Estonian courts*

Estonian farmers expected a great deal from the country's accession to the EU. However, just like the companies in charge of sweets and ice cream, who, looking in the mirror

---

[102]  See Albi, *loc. cit.* n. 19, at p. 50.

[103]  *Loc. cit.* n. 46.

[104]  Modifications of 25 January 2007, *RT* I 2007, 12, 65.

the day after Estonia's EU-inauguration celebrations, faced a reflection of a speculator, the agriculturists cannot always realise the profits they dreamt of, relying on the EU-related pre-accession myths. Most of the court disputes concerning the distribution of structural aid for farmers were caused by the quite opposite understanding between the applicants for payments and the administrative body responsible for structural aid of what is an eligible land and whether the parcel is in good condition to qualify for the support. These disagreements are connected with the inspection competence of the responsible Estonian body, ARIB. They deal with, e.g., the control reports of on-the-spot checks: their content and character, whether they can be unilaterally changed by ARIB at a later stage and, therefore, contested by the farmers in the courts; the issue of burden of proof; the question in which circumstances the case of *force majeure* occurs (the Estonian courts have used this in *stricto sensu* and only in very limited cases),[105] etc. Therefore, the conflicts concern not only the rejection of applications to grant aid, but also the reductions and exclusions of a support which can lead to considerable repayments. Some allegations made against ARIB assert that the decisions of ARIB are not at all or very poorly motivated. For example, a standard electronic form with only references to articles of relevant laws has been used to reject the requests; thus, for an individual applicant to find out the reason why his/her application has been turned down can become a game of *Sudoku*. Furthermore, the right to be heard has been subject to claims filed against ARIB.

Whereas other courts have concentrated mainly on formalistic procedural issues and have been somewhat reluctant to express their views about the possible relationship between Estonian law and EC law, as well as to discuss general principles of law and have followed quite firmly the arguments presented in the governmental documents, such as the National Development Plan for the use of EU Structural Funds, the above-indicated problems and their possible solutions have been reflected in several important judgments of the ALCSC. First of all, the ALCSC has confirmed that the rules of administrative procedure, especially its fundamental principles, apply to the procedures concerning the distribution of structural aid and of their inspection and that in this connection, the principle of good administration familiar both to Estonian and EC law needs to be respected.[106] Furthermore, the ALCSC has underlined the importance of granting the applicant the right to be heard, which – according to the ECJ – constitutes a general principle of EC law, and referred to the relevant ECJ case law.[107] In this context, the Court also explained the burden of proof and found that if an administrative authority responsible for the award of structural aid has doubts as to the conformity of an aid application to the objectives of EC law, it has a responsibility to prove it.[108] In the case under discussion, the Supreme Court was of the opinion that ARIB had cor-

---

[105] See the analysis of Kanger, *loc. cit.* n. 95, pp. 15-17.

[106] See judgment of 15 February 2005 of the ALCSC, Case No. 3-3-1-90-04, para. 14, *RT* III 2005, 7, 61 and judgment of 19 December 2006, *loc. cit.* n. 21, para. 16.

[107] *Ibidem*, para. 20; ECJ case law referred: ECJ, Case C-142/87 *Kingdom of Belgium v. Commission of the European Communities* [1990] *ECR* I-959; Case C-269/90 *Technische Universität München v. Hauptzollamt München-Mitte* [1991] *ECR* I-5469.

[108] Judgment of 19 December 2006 of the ALCSC, *loc. cit.* n. 21, para. 21.

rectly applied the competition law, but it had failed to guarantee the applicant the right to be heard in order to explain whether the two parties under discussion could be deemed to be considered one applicant.

In another case, the ALCSC was not pleased with the motivation of ARIB which refused to satisfy an application for investment support simply because there were no more budgetary means available. The Court repealed the decision of ARIB and urged the board to motivate substantially the refusal to grant aid.[109]

A fascinating case concerned the specific conditions of Estonia's biggest island – Saaremaa, where, due to the natural/geographical particularities and according to the local farming practices, bovine animals and sheep are grazed in brush woody pasture land. However, ARIB refused to satisfy an area aid application of an agricultural producer from Saaremaa and reclaimed already granted aid, because on-the-spot check revealed that the parcel was partly covered with forest. The ALCSC invalidated the contested decision, since ARIB had failed to motivate why the authorities came to the conclusion that irrespective of the trees growing on the pasture, it was not possible to graze animals in a similar way as on the parcels without trees in the same area. The Court based its finding on the Council Regulation 1782/2003/EC[110] (establishing common rules for direct support schemes under the Common Agricultural Policy and establishing certain support schemes for farmers), as well as on the Commission Regulation 796/2004/EC[111] and an advisory working document of the European Commission (AGRI/60363/2005) – both implementing the Regulation 1782/2003/EC. The ALCSC stated that the purpose of the category of aid and the activity for which aid is applied have to be taken into account.[112] The Supreme Court also pointed out that when granting area aids within the EU Common Agricultural Policy, the Member States can consider standards of particular areas. The EC law does not provide expressly that such standards be established as norms; however, the standards must be unambiguous both for the applicant and the authority granting aid and must take into account the principles of legal certainty and clarity. Unfortunately this had not been the case.

With this background, it is possible to conclude that the Estonian legal system has increasingly come to a close contact with the foundations of Community law. Despite the fact that these relations have been sometimes accidental and the case law of Estonian courts is not always constant, the general principles of EC law – supremacy, direct

---

[109]   Judgment of 27 February 2007 of the ALCSC, Case No. 3-3-1-93-06 (*RT* III 2007, 9, 77).

[110]   Council Regulation 1782/2003/EC of 29 September 2003 establishing common rules for direct support schemes under the Common Agricultural Policy and establishing certain support schemes for farmers and amending Regulations (EEC) No 2019/93, (EC) No 1452/2001, (EC) No 1453/2001, (EC) No 1454/2001, (EC) No 1868/94, (EC) No 1251/1999, (EC) No 1254/1999, (EC) No 1673/2000, (EEC) No 2358/71 and (EC) No 2529/2001, *OJ* 2003 L 270/1.

[111]   Commission Regulation 796/2004/EC of 21 April 2004 laying down detailed rules for the implementation of cross-compliance, modulation and the integrated administration and control system provided for in Council Regulation (EC) No 1782/2003 establishing common rules for direct support schemes under the Common Agricultural Policy and establishing certain support schemes for farmers, *OJ* 2004 L 141/18.

[112]   Judgment of 20 June 2007 of the ALCSC, Case No. 3-3-1-26-07 (*RT* III 2007, 27, 228). Summary in English and French available at the Information System Jurifast at http://www.juradmin.eu/docs/EE01/EE01000015.pdf and at http://www.riigikohus.ee/?id=719.

effect, EC law conform interpretation of national law, equivalency, *effet utile* – have been courageously applied in Estonia. Although a judgment of the Tallinn Administrative Court took the position that starting from 1 May 2004, one can no longer speak about the legal space of Estonia, but instead of a legal space of the European Union,[113] it would be too early to arrange farewell services for the Estonian legal order (especially since there remain, although very few, areas with no EC competence). On the contrary, this should not be the purpose of the EC/EU legal system. Instead, Estonia, especially Estonian state authorities, administrative bodies and courts need to apply Estonian law in a creative harmony with EU law (why not also in the spheres not involving EU competence or EU law aspect, if it is necessary for uniform application of law), but not to try too enthusiastically to forget its own legal traditions and not to be, on the other hand, too cautious to dig into the complicated world of EU law. A proof of existence of at least two different legal systems exists in cases involving fundamental principles and rights, including rule of law, legitimate expectations and legal certainty. To solve these problems, intervention in the system of judicial review might be necessary as seen below. Nonetheless, the Estonian legal system has reached out for the EU legal order and is waiting for a friendly handshake.

3.    ESTONIAN LAW FINDING ITS PLACE IN THE EUROPEAN
      COMMUNITY/UNION LEGAL SYSTEM

The third part of this chapter concentrates to a paramount degree on direct actions to the ECJ/CFI which have been submitted by the European Commission, by the Estonian Government and by individuals. In addition, a digest of the most important cases where Estonia has acted as intervener will be given. Due to the dynamics of those developments, it is quite difficult to keep the balance between the analyses of the second and third part of this chapter. Nevertheless, the simple fact that the ECJ is, to a certain extent, involved with the issues of Estonian law, gives hope that the Estonian legal system will not only be of negative influence, thus being considered as not respecting the Community law, but also can contribute to the creation of certain models, e.g., dealing with how to prevent and solve conflicts between EC law and national law. Hopefully, this can be done *via* preliminary references from Estonian courts, the significance of which is covered in the second section of the third part of this chapter, and in introducing some innovations to the procedural laws of the both systems, which will be discussed at the end of the third part.

---

[113] Judgment of 28 December 2005 of Tallinn Administrative Court Case No. 3-2562/2004(=3-04-406), para. 2 of the grounds of the decision. Available in the Estonian database of courts decisions (in Estonian) at http://www.kohus.ee/kohtulahendid/index.aspx.

3.1.    **Getting to know each other in a not-so-friendly way:
Commission against Estonia. Defending the honor and joining the
others: Estonian jam in Luxembourg.**

As of September 2009, the European Commission had submitted six infringement
actions against Estonia to the ECJ. Fortunately for Estonia, four of them have been
removed from the register of the ECJ due to Estonia's efforts to adopt the necessary
national legislation needed in order to transpose the relevant EC directives. In one case
the Court found Estonia to be in breach of EC law,[114] and one case is pending at the
time of writing. However, this does not exclude the amounts of disputes pending in a
pre-trial phase as a "sword of Damocles" above the Estonian administration. The legal
proceedings involving Estonia constitute a veritable challenge for the small Member
State to ensure a well-coordinated and thoroughly analysed legal policy in the EU.
Unfortunately, the practice tends to be more or less a work of a "fire department"
rather than preventative occupation. Estonia itself has challenged Community measures
twice. Whilst defending itself and/or its honor in the Community courts is a minimum
'must' for a Member State, then the situations where Estonia is involved as a third
party in other proceedings, including supporting the protection of the rights of natural
and legal persons of Estonia, shows in real terms how well the country is prepared in
finding its way in the judicial system of the EC. In the first years of EU membership,
Estonia has intervened in more than 10 cases.

3.1.1.   *Happy unhappiness: resolving most of the problems at early stage*

The four infringement cases, as of today removed from the ECJ register, concerned the
dissatisfaction of the European Commission of Estonia's progress in the following
sectors: internal market in natural gas (in essence problems with opening up for the
competition), free movement of services, competition in postal services, rights of the
employees and ship waste. However, the latter (non transposition of a directive regulating ship generated waste and cargo residues)[115] has been re-activated and is pending as
case C-46/09.

Estonia was lucky to have been given a little over a year *post*-EU accession as a sort
of "adjustment time" before the first action against the new Member State was brought
by the European Commission 22 September 2005.[116] However, the first "pre-trial"
proceedings started quite soon after the country joined the European Union, as the first
letter of formal notice dated 13 October 2004 and considered the insufficient transposition of 3 directives. Based on this letter, the Estonian Government decided on 9

---

[114]  ECJ, Case C-464/08 *Commission of the European Communities v. Republic of Estonia* [2009] *ECR*
nyr.
   [115]  Directive 2005/65/EC of the European Parliament and of the Council of 26 October 2005 on enhancing port security, *OJ* 2005 L 310/28.
   [116]  Case C-351/05 *Commission of the European Communities v. Republic of Estonia, OJ* 2005
C 281/12. See also *re removal from the Register Order of the President of the Court of 31 May 2006 –
Commission of the European Communities v. Republic of Estonia* (Case C-351/05), *OJ* 2006 C 224/33.

December 2004 to prepare draft law concerning modifications of Natural Gas and Electricity Market Acts.[117] Therefore, the situation was already undergoing mending at the time the first action was brought to the ECJ accusing Estonia of failing to comply with the obligation under Directive 2003/55/EC, concerning common rules for the internal market in natural gas.[118] Estonia had failed to notify the laws, regulations and administrative provisions necessary to transpose that Directive into national law, because the national law was not yet adopted by the *Riigikogu*. The prescribed period for transposition of the Directive expired on 1 July 2004. Estonia had had a hard time to liberalise the gas market, because in the Baltic States natural gas is imported from Russia, and there it can only be bought from one company. Therefore, real competition does not exist, and it is difficult to ensure that the transmission and distribution systems are operated through legally separate entities, required by the EU. In practice, this could only raise administrative costs for the one Russian company, including, in the end effect, a considerable price increase for Estonian consumers.[119] Nevertheless, Estonia modified its law, and the necessary amendments of the Estonian Natural Gas Act entered into force on 11 December 2005.[120] Therefore, the infringement no longer existed, and the application of the European Commission was withdrawn.

A similar scenario took place in the case of transposition of European Parliament and Council Directive 2002/39/EC on further opening to competition of Community postal services,[121] European Parliament and Council Directive 2002/14/EC establishing a general framework for informing and consulting employees in the EC[122] and Directive 2000/59/EC of the European Parliament and of the Council of 27 November 2000 on port reception facilities for ship-generated waste and cargo residues.[123] In all these cases the Commission's initial actions were withdrawn due to adoption of required legislation in Estonia.[124] In all four cases, Estonia had to pay the costs of the court (ECJ)

---

[117] See the minutes of Estonian Government meeting of 9 December 2004, agenda p. 23. Available in Estonian at http://www.valitsus.ee/brf/index.php?id=1152.

[118] Directive 2003/55/EC of the European Parliament and of the Council of 26 June 2003 concerning common rules for the internal market in natural gas and repealing Directive 98/30/EC, *OJ* 2003 L 176/57.

[119] See E. Kisel from Estonian Ministry of Economic Affairs and Communication in his interview for Estonian daily newspaper *Postimees* of 7 July 2005.

[120] *RT* I 2005, 64, 483.

[121] Directive 2002/39/EC of the European Parliament and of the Council of 10 June 2002 amending Directive 97/67/EC with regard to the further opening to competition of Community postal services, *OJ* 2002 L 176/21.

[122] Directive 2002/14/EC of the European Parliament and of the Council of 11 March 2002 establishing a general framework for informing and consulting employees in the European Community, *OJ* 2002 L 80/29.

[123] Directive 2000/59/EC of the European Parliament and of the Council of 27 November 2000 on port reception facilities for ship-generated waste and cargo residues, *OJ* 2000 L 332/81.

[124] Case C-397/06 *Commission of the European Communities v. Republic of Estonia*, *OJ* 2006 C 281/26; removal from the Register pursuant to Order of the President of the Court of 24 April 2007 – *Commission of the European Communities v. Republic of Estonia* (Case C-397/06), *OJ* 2007 C 183/29; Case C-178/06 *Commission of the European Communities v. Republic of Estonia*, *OJ* 2006 C 143/26; removal from the Register pursuant to Order of the President of the Court of 21 March 2007 – *Commission of the European Communities v. Republic of Estonia* (Case C-178/06), *OJ* 2007 C 96/28; Case C-68/08 *Commission of the European Communities v. Republic of Estonia*, *OJ* 2008 C 92/21; removal from the

because Estonia repaired the violations of EC law only after the actions of the Commission were brought. As mentioned above, unfortunately the matter concerning ship waste has once again found its way to the European Court of Justice as the European Commission questions the adoption of necessary legislation transposing the Directive into Estonian law.

Indirectly another dispute affected the energy policy of Estonia. This happened in case C-413/04, where the European Parliament contested the legal basis of the Council Directive which, in essence, prolonged for another 4 years the transitional period given to Estonia to open its electricity market (compared to the agreements made in accession documents). Estonia was allowed to open its electricity market on 31 December 2012 instead of 31 December 2008 as initially agreed.[125] Another parallel case C-414/04 concerned similar temporary derogations in favor of Slovenia.[126] The Government of Estonia, accompanied by the Government of Poland, intervened in both cases; however, those interventions were unsuccessful. The granting of a further derogation for the period 2009 to 2012 would have guaranteed security of investments in generating oil shale plants and security of energy supply in Estonia while allowing the serious environmental problems created by those plants to be resolved. As oil shale is the only indigenous energy resource in Estonia and around 90% of the electricity produced in Estonia is from this solid fuel, to secure its supply was and is, therefore, of great strategic importance. The action of the European Parliament focused skillfully on whether the Act concerning the Conditions of Accession of Estonia and nine other new Member States to the EU and the adjustments to the treaties on which the EU is founded (Act of Accession 2003)[127] make up a correct legal basis for the contested Directive. However, the actual substance of the case was the protection of common rules for the internal market in electricity and the fear of opening up easy and unlimited possibilities for new Member States to prolong their derogations from EC law. The ECJ, by partly annulling the contested Directive[128] tactfully stressed in its judgment that its action does not concern the substantive justification for Estonia's request for derogation, but solely the legal basis on which the contested Directive was adopted. Nevertheless, the ECJ pointed out that, while the contested Directive 2004/85/EC was intended to delay temporarily the effective application of certain provisions of initial electricity market Directive 2003/54/EC[129] regarding Estonia, some of the measures which it contained are also measures of adaptation necessary to ensure the full appli-

---

Register pursuant to Order of the President of the Court of 16 October 2008 – *Commission of the European Communities v. Republic of Estonia* (Case C-68/08), *OJ* 2009 C 6/18.

[125]   ECJ, Case C-413/04 *European Parliament v. Council of the European Union* [2006] *ECR* I-11221.

[126]   ECJ, Case C-414/04 *European Parliament v. Council of the European Union* [2006] *ECR* I-11279.

[127]   Act concerning the Conditions of Accession of the Czech Republic, the Republic of Estonia, the Republic of Cyprus, the Republic of Latvia, the Republic of Lithuania, the Republic of Hungary, the Republic of Malta, the Republic of Poland, the Republic of Slovenia and the Slovak Republic and the adjustments to the Treaties on which the European Union is founded, *OJ* 2003 L 236/33.

[128]   Council Directive 2004/85/EC amending Directive 2003/54/EC of the European Parliament and of the Council as regards the application of certain provisions to Estonia, *OJ* 2004 L 236/10.

[129]   Directive 2003/54/EC of the European Parliament and of the Council of 26 June 2003 concerning common rules for the internal market in electricity and repealing Directive 96/92/EC, *OJ* 2003 L 176/37.

cability of the Directive 2003/54/EC regarding that Member State. The transitional derogation contained in the Act of Accession 2003 did not lapse as a result of amendments to the old Directive by the new, contested Directive. However, according to the ECJ, any further derogations do not come within the meaning of "adaptation" as the term is used in Article 57 of the Act of Accession 2003. The ECJ held:

> 'The further derogations introduced by the contested directive constitute measures whose sole object and purpose, like most temporary derogations, is to postpone temporarily the effective application of the Community act concerned, and whose adoption therefore involves a political assessment.'[130]

Without going into the substance of the derogation but concentrating on its analysis concerning the legal basis, the ECJ concluded that the contested Directive must be annulled insofar as it grants Estonia a derogation beyond the initial 31 December 2008. At least the ECJ acknowledged the need to avoid a situation of uncertainty for the economic operators and investors in the electricity sector in Estonia and for the workers concerned, as expressed by the Estonian Government, and therefore maintained the effects of the annulled parts of the Directive until a new directive is adopted.

The above-mentioned cases are testing the limits of the Estonian capacity to ensure sound and co-ordinated legal policy in the EU and at the same time also to inform its people as well as economic operators about the rules of the game in the legal system of the European Union. This includes involving the national Parliament at an early stage in the issues regarding EU policies.

### 3.1.2. *Matters of principles: Estonia versus the European Commission. Other ways to influence: Estonia as intervener*

As mentioned above, Estonia has not contested the Commission Regulations concerning the surplus stocks of sugar and other agricultural products in general; instead it has brought an action against a Commission Regulation determining the quantities of overstocked sugar for Estonia. In this action (as of September 2009 still pending before the CFI), Estonia essentially challenges the inclusion, in determining the excess quantity of sugar, the quantity of sugar held in private households.[131] The Estonian Government blames the Commission for not taking into account the specific circumstances of stockpiling in Estonia. This constitutes an infringement of right to property of companies and/or private households, since any measures implementing the EC Regulation would impose a restriction on them which could not be justified by a legitimate aim and would be a disproportionate interference with their rights.[132] In its

---

[130] ECJ, Case C-413/04, *loc. cit.* n. 125, para. 60.

[131] Case T-324/05 *Republic of Estonia v. Commission of the European Communities*, OJ 2005 C 271/24.

[132] In its application, the Estonian Government seems to be willing to fight also for the rights of companies which were not speculators. This can, however, not be deduced from the conduct of state authorities towards Estonian companies in the so-called "sugar cases" in national courts discussed above.

arguments, the Government seeks support from a wide range of general principles of law, such as the principle to state reasons laid down in Article 253 EC and the principles of sound administration, good faith, non-discrimination and proportionality. Furthermore, Estonia finds the Regulation to be in breach of the principle of joint responsibility of the Commission. Indeed, Estonia is (at least was for a long time) a country of traditional agricultural production where more or less every household has its own little vegetable and/or fruit garden. Making jam is popular even today, as it was essential during the Soviet occupation since purchasing (eatable) marmalade in the shops at that time was almost impossible. However, whether the Estonian jam will have any success in Luxembourg remains to be seen.

Besides defending its honor and traditions about the jam, Estonia has initiated another action against the European Commission. This time the Estonian Government is suing the European Commission for cutting its greenhouse gas allocation and seeks to annul the Decision of the Commission of 4 May 2007 concerning the national greenhouse gas allocation plan submitted by Estonia in accordance with Directive 2003/87/EC.[133] In the Estonian application, the following grounds for the annulment of the Decision are stated: excess of competence of the Commission; manifest errors of assessment, since the Commission did not take into account correct information available to it; infringement of Article 175(2)(c) EC, since under the EC Treaty, the Commission does not have competence to adopt measures which significantly affect a Member State's choice between different energy sources and the general structure of its energy supply; as well as the traditional grounds: violation of the obligation to state reasons and infringement of the principle of good administration.[134]

On this background, it is evident that both – agricultural issues (also the first preliminary reference from Estonia dealt with this topic) and supply of energy are at the heart of Estonia's concern both internally as well as in the EU. It also shows that in these areas, at least as far as the agricultural matters are concerned, the weaknesses of a sound approximation of Estonian legislation to EC law, and, even more, the coherent implementation are self-evident. The issues of energy supply are of a politically sensitive nature.

The balance of direct actions of the Estonian Government is not remarkable. However, there are other ways to protect one's interests and perhaps also to influence the EC legal system, such as, e.g., interventions in other cases.[135] Naturally, a fellow sufferer should be supported, as occurred when Estonia intervened in the case T-316/05 *Cyprus v. Commission,* where Cyprus challenged the same EC Regulation, on concrete quantities

---

[133] Directive 2003/87/EC of the European Parliament and of the Council of 13 October 2003 establishing a scheme for greenhouse gas emission allowance trading within the Community and amending Council Directive 96/61/EC, *OJ* 2003 L 275/32.

[134] Case T-263/07 *Republic of Estonia v. Commission of the European Communities, OJ* 2007 C 223/17.

[135] As far as the information on Estonia's interventions is concerned, the author is thankful to L. Uibo from the Ministry of Foreign Affairs of Estonia, agent of Estonian government before the ECJ, for the outline of his paper at the conference organised by FIDE Estonia and Estonian Academic Law Society: 'EU Law in 50 years from Rome to Tartu', 18 April 2007, Tartu. Available in Estonian at http://www.oigusselts.ee/leht.php?pgID=4&lang=est.

of surplus sugar stocks, that was contested by Estonia.[136] At the same time, solidarity was not shown in the case where Poland challenged the validity of Commission Regulation 1972/2003/EC.[137] It is not clear whether Estonia remained ignorant because Poland brought the action quite soon after the EU accession of the 10 new Member States, and Estonia was not yet accustomed to intervene, or Estonia kept the distance out of political reasons and preferred not to contest at this stage and to agree with the principles of the EC Regulation on the fight against speculation so that the eventual fines could be collected from the companies and a consecutive, not proportional, Community measure could be challenged at a later stage. Naturally, Estonia has intervened in a case where the applicant was an Estonian company and in the first Estonian reference for preliminary ruling.

In the context of other interventions, the freedom to provide services and right of establishment have also attracted Estonia's attention. This includes two landmark judgments C-341/05 *Laval*[138] and C-438/05 *Viking.*[139] Another case, which Estonia joined, concerning, *inter alia,* shipping issues is C-308/06 *Intertanko.*[140] Estonian intervention was deemed to be necessary since Estonia as a coastal state has also faced similar problems due to the considerable pollution of the Baltic Sea. Furthermore, Estonia has intervened in the *Skoma Lux* case, concerning the unavailability of EU legal acts in the languages of most of the "Brave New World" on the date of their accession. Although, as seen above, this issue has not caused real problems in Estonia, and the Estonian courts have tried to prevent any further legal disputes on this matter, the Estonian Government considered it important to express its views.

If most of the cases where Estonia has been involved appear to more or less affect Estonia directly and/or concern the transitional measures regarding the new Member States, then there is also an intervention of Estonia in a case C-440/05 *Commission v. Council* about more "global EU law issues."[141]

Of course, the quality of the interventions should outweigh the number of interventions. Nonetheless, the relative reluctance of Estonia to join in the pending cases before the ECJ and the CFI, compared, e.g., with Poland, has its reasons in the limited administrative capacity of Estonia. In the pre-accession phase, the Ministry of Justice lost the battle over the right to represent the government in the ECJ to the Ministry of Foreign Affairs. This decision, which reflects the prevailing view in Estonia to look at the court cases in the ECJ as part of the country's foreign policy, might not have been necessarily constructive, considering the growing importance of judicial co-operation in criminal law and civil matters. However, in the end, what counts is the expertise of the

---

[136] Case T-316/05 *Republic of Cyprus v. Commission of the European Communities, OJ* 2005 C 271/23.
[137] *Loc. cit.* n. 92.
[138] ECJ, Case C-341/05 *Laval un Partneri Ltd v. Svenska Byggnadsarbetareförbundet, Svenska Byggnadsarbetareförbundets avdelning 1, Byggettan and Svenska Elektrikerförbundet* [2007] *ECR* I-11767.
[139] ECJ, Case C-438/05 *International Transport Workers' Federation and Finnish Seamen's Union v. Viking Line ABP and OÜ Viking Line Eesti* [2007] *ECR* I-10779.
[140] ECJ, Case C-308/06 *The Queen, on the application of International Association of Independent Tanker Owners (Intertanko) and Others v. Secretary of State for Transport* [2008] *ECR* I-4057.
[141] ECJ, Case C-440/05 *Commission of the European Communities v. Council of the European Union* [2007] *ECR* I-9097.

people and the manpower, instead of the formal division of competences among the ministries. It is true that despite the rather competitive qualifications of the Estonian civil servants, not enough attention is paid to increase the number of people analysing ECJ case law in order to create a centre of competence. This shortsightedness is distressing because it is from the litigations and preliminary references of others that one could learn to prevent its own conflicts. Also, the co-ordination among different ministries should be strengthened, and the know-how of external experts should be increased.

### 3.2.   Loosing the battle: failure of an Estonian company to be admitted to the "playground". To ask or not to ask a question to the ECJ – that is a question

Unfortunately it is quite difficult for private persons to get access to the Community courts in Luxembourg – to "knock on Heaven's door".[142] Nevertheless, it is important to note that the first failure of an Estonian company in this respect started a debate on how to find alternative solutions to protect the rights of individuals, both on the EC and the national levels. These discussions must involve the preliminary ruling procedures. As to the latter, the following keywords used by national judges are worth mentioning: time-consuming, complicated, expensive, confusing answers and authoritarian attitude of the ECJ. Furthermore, the use of preliminary references by Estonian courts is hampered because Estonia has so far regrettably failed to adopt a declaration concerning the jurisdiction of the ECJ under Article 35 TEU.

### 3.2.1.   *Fishing in wrong waters: order of the Court of First Instance of the EC of 9 January 2007 in the case of Lootus Teine OÜ*

The first direct action for annulment brought by an Estonian company – Lootus Teine OÜ – contested annexes of Council Regulations concerning fishing opportunities for deep-sea species for the new Member States and fishing opportunities for 2005 and 2006 for Community fishing vessels for certain deep-sea fish stocks.[143] Lootus Teine OÜ is an Estonian fishing company which practices deep-sea fishing in the area administered by the North East Atlantic Fisheries Commission (NEAFC)[144] and enjoys in Estonia historic fishing rights for deep-sea fish. Lootus Teine OÜ is the only entrepreneur to have obtained a fishing permit for deep-sea species in 2004 and the only one to

---

[142]  An expression used by T. Tridimas; however, in the context of access of national courts to the ECJ via preliminary references, see T. Tridimas, 'Knocking on Heaven's Door: Fragmentation, Efficiency and Defiance in the Preliminary Reference Procedure', 40 *CMLRev.* (2003) pp. 9-50.

[143]  Annex to Council Regulation 2269/2004/EC of 20 December 2004 amending Regulations (EC) Nos 2340/2002 and 2347/2002 as concerns fishing opportunities for deep-sea species for the new Member States which acceded in 2004, *OJ* 2004 L 396/1, and, second, Part 2 of the Annex to Council Regulation 2270/2004/EC of 22 December 2004 fixing for 2005 and 2006 the fishing opportunities for Community fishing vessels for certain deep-sea fish stocks, *OJ* 2004 L 396/4. See CFI, Case T-127/05 *Lootus Teine Osaühing (Lootus) v. Council of the European Union* [2007] *ECR* I-1.

[144]  Established by the Convention on Future Multilateral Co-Operation in North-East Atlantic Fisheries.

have applied for one for 2005 in Estonia. Article 6(9) of the Act of Accession 2003 provides that, as from the date of accession, fisheries' agreements concluded by the new Member States shall be managed by the Community, and that the rights and obligations resulting for the new Member States from those agreements are not affected during the period in which the provisions of those agreements are provisionally maintained. It is in this context that the contested measures were issued, allocating Estonia fishing opportunities, measured in metric tons of allowable catch of certain stocks in 2004, 2005 and 2006. According to Lootus Teine OÜ, these allocations constituted only a fraction of what Estonia legally harvested before the EU accession. On this basis, the company contended that the challenged measures violated Article 6(9) of the Act of Accession 2003 as well as the principle of proportionality and should therefore be annulled.

The application of the company was supported by the Estonian Government. The Estonian Government stated that Estonian historic fishing rights do not allow the Estonian authorities to grant a fishing permit to a new undertaking.

The CFI, however, dismissed by its order the action as inadmissible. According to the CFI, first, the contested provisions cannot, by themselves, directly affect the applicant's legal situation, and second, the Estonian Government did have considerable discretion as to their implementation. The CFI was of the opinion that it is for the Member States to manage the fishing opportunities allocated to them, and the application of Community provisions is not purely automatic.[145]

If one is to follow the lines of numerous case law examples of the CFI/ECJ concerning the application of Article 230, paragraph 4 EC and *locus standi* of natural and legal persons, including the *Plaumann* test[146] and the strict position of ECJ in *Jégo-Quéré*[147] case law, the order of dismissal of the CFI came as no surprise. The failure of Lootus Teine OÜ to be admitted to discuss the substantial arguments of its application in the CFI is just another sad demonstration of the unwillingness of the CFI/ECJ to open up an improved access for individuals. Whether it is an artificially and purposely created obstacle due to the workload of the CFI/ECJ or whether it is for different reasons, unfortunately this does not necessarily encourage other Estonian companies and private persons to seek protection of their rights in the CFI. This discouragement was reflected by the fact that Lootus Teine OÜ did not appeal the CFI order. One might even say that Community law, compared to Estonian law, does not provide equal opportunities to challenge legal acts of general application. Moreover, the EC equivalency principle is, unfortunately, not applicable in this direction. However, on this background, one starts to search other/better ways to protect the rights of natural and legal persons, such as Lootus Teine OÜ. The Council, defendant in the *Lootus Teine OÜ* case, suggested that the correct approach would be to bring an action before the national courts against the

---

[145] *Loc. cit.* n. 143, para. 42.
[146] ECJ, Case 25/62 *Plaumann & Co. v. Commission of the European Economic Community* [1963] *ECR* 199.
[147] ECJ, Case C-263/02P *Commission of the European Communities v. Jégo-Quéré* [2004] *ECR* I-3425 as opposed to the wish of the CFI to open up the access of individuals in granting them the right from Art. 47 of the Charter, CFI, Case T-177/01 *Jégo- Quére v. Commission of the European Communities* [2002] *ECR* II-2365.

national measures applying the contested provisions since the national measures are the only ones which directly affect the applicant. However, this would not help Lootus Teine OÜ, because the national authorities cannot by themselves increase the fishing opportunities allocated by the EC. It would have made little sense to question the historic fishing rights provided by national law, which were, in fact, favorable to the company, as Lootus Teine OÜ was the only company from Estonia fishing in these deep-sea waters and having also the historic fishing rights *de jure*. The only light at the end of the tunnel would have been to question the amount of quotas allocated by national authorities, which, in turn, were allocated to Estonia by the Council. This could have led to the issue of validity of the Community measure, and the company could have urged an Estonian administrative court to refer the question to the ECJ. Even though an administrative court is not bound by an applicant's request for preliminary reference, this could have had more perspectives than the action before the CFI eventually did. Besides, this way the admissibility issue could have been avoided and the Community court could have gone directly to the substance of the matter.

Another possibility would have been that the Estonian Government would bring via Article 230, paragraph 2 EC an action against the annexes of the contested Council Regulations. According to the representative of the company,[148] Lootus Teine OÜ had turned with a respective request to the Estonian ministries of environment and foreign affairs; however the government did not manage to file an application in due time (according to Art. 230 para. 5, two months after the publication of the contested measure). This unfortunate experience gave the Estonian Government a topic for reflection on how to improve its administrative capacity and the co-operation between the ministries in the interests of its individuals and companies if the latter would benefit from contesting and eventually annulling a Community measure, in the event that this idea is in essence also supported by the national authorities.

As of September 2009, another case initiated by the Estonian Author's Union was pending at the Court of First Instance.[149] The plaintiff challenged the validity of a competition law decision of the European Commission.[150]

3.2.2.   *Application of the acte éclairé and acte claire doctrine. Reasons behind the non-asking and finally getting there...*

Estonian courts have come across different thinkable situations concerning the preliminary reference procedure. It is remarkable that the Supreme Court has in its practice used all doctrines concerning the question: 'To ask or not to ask a preliminary ruling from the ECJ.'

---

[148]   See outline of the paper of T. Sild from Lextal Law Office at the conference organised by FIDE Estonia and Estonian Academic Law Society: 'EU Law in 50 years from Rome to Tartu', 18 April 2007 Tartu. Available in Estonian at http://www.oigus-selts.ee/leht.php?pgID=4&lang=est.

[149]   Case T-416/08 *Eesti Autorite Ühing v. Commission of the European Communities*, OJ 2008 C 313/40.

[150]   Commission Decision C (2008) 3435 final of 16 July 2008 (Case COMP/C2/38.698 – CISAC) relating to a proceeding under Art. 81 EC and Art. 53 EEA.

The CivCSC stated in its judgment of 30 March 2006 concerning the EC/Estonian trademark law, where one of the parties had asked for a reference, that the case constituted an *acte éclairé* situation.[151] The questions proposed by the plaintiff were either not significant in order to solve the case or had already been answered by the ECJ in its previous, well-established case law. The Supreme Court admitted that the national law was in contradiction with EC law; however, the CivCSC interpreted the national law in conformity with the Community law and referred the case back to the court of first instance. By doing so, the Supreme Court was confident that there exists no reason to turn to the ECJ; however, it did not exclude the possibility that the question may rise again, when the first instance civil court in Estonia will start rediscussing the case.[152]

The ALCSC was even bolder, using in its judgment of 5 October 2006 in the above-described *Hadler* case,[153] the *acte clair* doctrine. The Supreme Court found that it was obvious in this matter that the Overstock Charge Act did not guarantee taking into consideration the circumstances established in Article 4 paragraph 2 of the Commission Regulation 1972/2003/EC, and that this amounted to an *acte claire* situation. Upon the purposive interpretation of Commission Regulation 1972/2003/EC, especially its Article 4, paragraph 2, the Chamber had no doubts which would have prompted the need to ask for a preliminary ruling from the ECJ. In this case, the parties did not, at any stage of the proceedings, ask for a preliminary reference. The Court considered it on its own initiative and then decided not to refer. However, even after the legislative amendments – which were partly inspired by the ALCSC judgment, but did not apply it in all aspects – the complaints regarding the overstock problems found once again its way to the Estonian administrative courts. Therefore, in order to clarify the "sugar saga", the Administrative Court of Tallinn submitted a reference for a preliminary ruling. In its response in the judgment in the *Balbiino* case, differently from the ALCSC in the *Hadler* judgment, the ECJ accepted the multiple (coefficient) 1.2 as EC law conform, because it found that EC law leaves to the Member States enough discretion to determine the methods of calculating surplus stocks. Nevertheless in this context it is interesting to note that the Commission shared in the beginning of the litigation the opinion of the ALCSC and changed its view during the oral procedure. Furthermore, according to the view of the Advocate General in the *Balbiino* case,[154] the application of the coefficient 1.2 does not undermine the objectives of the Community legislation. The Advocate General considered that there is no objection to the application of this coefficient from the perspective of the principle of equal treatment because it is just one factor in the complex methods of calculating the surplus stocks. Now it is for the national courts to determine whether the coefficient 1.2 is in real circumstances really only one factor in the complex methods of calculating the surplus stocks or the only factor; from the *Hadler* case in the ALCSC judgment it seems that the coefficient 1.2 was used as

---

[151] Judgment of 30 March 2006 of the CivCSC, *loc. cit.* n. 67.

[152] *Ibidem*, para. 59.

[153] Judgment of 5 October 2006 of the ALCSC, *loc. cit.* n. 79.

[154] Opinion of Advocate General Ruiz-Jarabo Colomer, ECJ, Case C-560/07 *Balbiino AS v. Põlluma-jandusminister and Maksu- ja Tolliameti Põhja maksu- ja tollikeskus* [2009] *ECR* nyr.

primary or even the only method to determine the surplus stock and this is why the ALCSC did not find it EC law conform.

Earlier, in a case, also discussed above, concerning the municipal elections and, *inter alia*, the review of constitutionality of the Political Parties Act, the Supreme Court *en banc* had already avoided opening up the dialog with the ECJ.[155]

Further contacts of the ALCSC with the issues of preliminary references have led to teaching the other courts as to when and how they could ask the ECJ for a preliminary ruling. According to the ALCSC, an Estonian court is entitled to request a preliminary ruling from the ECJ on the interpretation of an EC regulation, and on the basis of the ruling, it can decide whether the Estonian legislation implementing the EC regulation is compatible with the latter.[156] The Supreme Court cited, *inter alia,* the ECJ judgment in *CILFIT* case.[157]

But the question "whether to ask a question" has not only occurred during the interpretation of EC law. In another case concerning the overstock charges, the Tallinn Administrative Court stayed its proceedings because Poland had challenged before the CFI the same articles of the same Commission Regulation that were relevant in the case at hand before the Estonian court. The case reached the ALCSC, which quoted the ECJ judgments in cases C-143/88 & C-92/89 *Zuckerfabrik,*[158] 314/85 *Foto-Frost*[159] and C-461/03 *Gaston Schul*[160] and argued that an administrative court must analyse and substantiate whether and why it is of the opinion that the validity of EC legislation is to be doubted. In this case, the court of first instance had failed to do so. The mere fact that another Member State has brought an action for annulment does not constitute a ground for questioning the validity of EC legislation and for the stay of proceedings in Estonia. If the Administrative Court had sufficiently substantiated why it questioned the validity of the EC Regulation, the Court itself should have, in addition to the stay of proceedings, asked for a preliminary ruling from the ECJ, irrespective of the fact that Poland had already contested the Regulation.[161]

Another problem present in this very same case was the absence at that time of a national procedural provision which would enable a court to stay proceedings because there are other cases pending in the CFI/ECJ, and the court would like to wait for their outcome, or because the court would like to make a reference to the ECJ. The ALCSC didn't mind the lacuna in the Estonian procedural law and constructed a right of an Estonian court to refer to the ECJ based directly on Article 234 EC. It did, however, point to a relevant Estonian draft law trying to introduce a procedural ground and urged

---

[155] See judgment of 19 April 2005 of SC *en banc, loc. cit.* n. 28 and dissenting opinion of justice Laffranque, *loc. cit.* n. 22.

[156] Order of 25 April 2006 the ALCSC, Case No. 3-3-1-74-05, *loc. cit.* n. 85, para. 13.

[157] ECJ, Case 283/81 *Srl CILFIT and Lanificio di Gavardo SpA v. Ministry of Health* [1982] *ECR* 3415.

[158] ECJ, Joined Cases C-143/88 and C-92/89 *Zuckerfabrik Süderdithmarschen AG v. Hauptzollamt Itzehoe and Zuckerfabrik Soest GmbH v. Hauptzollamt Paderborn* [1991] *ECR* I-415.

[159] ECJ, Case 314/85 *Foto-Frost v. Hauptzollamt Lübeck-Ost* [1987] *ECR* 4199.

[160] ECJ, Case C-461/03 *Gaston Schul Douane-expediteur BV v. Minister van Landbouw, Natuur en Voedselkwaliteit* [2005] *ECR* I-10513.

[161] Order of 25 April 2006 the ALCSC, Case No. 3-3-1-74-05, *loc. cit.* n. 85, paras. 21 and 22.

the legislator to adopt such a provision, which the latter later did. Presently, Article 356, paragraph 3 of the Civil Procedure Code (in this respect also applicable to administrative procedure) stipulates that a court may suspend a proceeding until a decision of the ECJ takes force, if it makes a reference for a preliminary ruling to the ECJ, and the reference is relevant in order to decide the case at hand.[162]

The reaction of the Supreme Court to a demand made by a party to ask for a preliminary reference does merit a closer look. In the previously discussed case concerning the trademark law, the representative of the plaintiff, *Gulf International Ltd.*, had asked the CivCSC to make a preliminary reference to the ECJ concerning the interpretation of the trademark Directive. The CivCSC pointed out that the exclusive right to ask for a preliminary reference lies within the Court, and that a demand for a reference to ECJ cannot be regarded as an independent procedural demand which must be decided by a court order.[163] Instead, it is an opinion of the respective party as to the substance: application and interpretation of law, to which the Court is not bound. However, as noted above, the CivCSC considered it important to explain in the grounds of its judgment why it did not find it necessary to refer a question to the ECJ. The Supreme Court has continued this practice and has always reasoned the refusal to refer.

In this connection, another problem should be explained. Namely, the Supreme Court of Estonia has in its Civil and Criminal Chambers and in the Administrative Law Chamber a system of leave to appeal. An appeal is admitted to be heard only if it refers to the improper application of norms of substantive law, essential infringements of provisions of the court procedure law; and/or a decision of the Supreme Court is considered to be of importance from the point of view of the uniform application of law or of creating a precedent.[164] The orders not to take a matter to be decided are not reasoned. The question, therefore, is: what should be done if the applicant has in proceedings in previous court levels asked for a preliminary reference to the ECJ and the courts, however, have not satisfied this request. The order of first and second level courts to stay a proceeding due to a preliminary reference can be appealed; however, a request to refer is not considered to be an independent procedural demand. The Supreme Court has considered itself as a court in the meaning of Article 234, paragraph 3 EC. This is derived from the ECJ judgment in the *Lyckeskog*[165] case, which stated that where the decisions of a national court or tribunal can be appealed to a Supreme Court, despite the fact that a Supreme Court will examine an appeal as to its substance only if it has declared it admissible, that national court or tribunal is not under the obligation to refer but a Supreme Court is. Thus, if the Estonian Supreme Court agrees with decisions made in the same proceeding previously and does not find a reference to the ECJ necessary, there is no need to give a leave to appeal, unless there are other reasons for it. On the contrary, if the Supreme Court does not agree with the courts of first and second

---

[162] See amendments to the Civil Procedure Code, in force since 1 September 2006, *RT* I 2006, 31, 235.

[163] Judgment of 30 March 2006 of CivCSC, Case No. 3-2-1-4-06, *loc. cit.* n. 67, para. 56.

[164] See also K. Merusk, 'The constitutional law of the Republic of Estonia', in C. Kortmann, J. Fleuren, W. Voermans, eds., *Constitutional Law of the 10 EU Member States* (Alphen aan den Rijn, Wolters Kluwer 2006), p. III-1-III-72, at p. III-59.

[165] ECJ, Case C-99/00 *Criminal proceedings against Kenny Roland Lyckeskog* [2002] *ECR* I-4839.

instance and a request for a preliminary reference has been made by the party, the Supreme Court must, in any case, give the respective appeal a leave and examine the case in substance. In practice, the Community law aspect can, therefore, constitute a solid ground for leave to appeal as a ground of its own, although this is not mentioned in the relevant Estonian procedural laws. This might be because wrong application of EC law automatically constitutes improper application of substantive law or any of the other reason stated above used by the Supreme Court to admit the matters.

In practice there are quite a few demands from the parties to refer a case to the ECJ. Sometimes it is obvious that even no relevance to EC law exists; in other cases there is mostly well-established case law of the ECJ.[166]

Therefore, we can see that Estonian courts have made good use of the ECJ case law concerning the preliminary references and are orienting quite well in this matter. However, they have been very reluctant to ask a question of their own. Despite a special handbook written by an Estonian judge to guide her colleagues in coping with Article 234 EC and drafting preliminary references,[167] only four references from lower instance courts have been submitted to the European Court of Justice.[168] Supposedly, this cannot be only due to the excellent knowledge of EC law of the Estonian judges! There are several factors mentioned briefly above which have caused this kind of restraint: no similar procedural possibility in national law, e.g., to stay proceedings for constitution-ality review in the Supreme Court, therefore, no experience in drafting questions; lack of time to prepare the questions due to heavy workload; fear to make a fool out of oneself in Luxembourg; reluctance of some of the parties because of the amount of time and money which a preliminary reference "adventure" consumes; no obligation to refer in interpretation issues. In addition, there are cases which have legal policy importance and/or could have severe consequences to parties and therefore cannot possibly wait another two years. Articles 68 EC and 35 EU are, anyhow, an untouched territory in the Estonian court practice, the latter, as mentioned due to Estonia's failure to declare the ECJ jurisdiction. Since the courts of lower levels have comfortably waited for the Supreme Court to do the "dirty job", the highest court of the country has been the first in Estonia to ask a preliminary reference. This situation is perhaps com-parable to Lithuania, as there it was also the Supreme Administrative Court which

---

[166] E.g., in its judgment of 10 May 2007 the Tallinn Administrative Court, Case No. 3-06-389, para. 24 has not satisfied the request of the applicant to ask for a preliminary ruling from the ECJ. The case involved interpretation of Arts. 56 and 58 EC. The Court stated that first, the lower level court does not have an obligation to refer as there are judicial remedies available against its decision in national law, and second, as far as the case at hand is concerned, the legal situation is clear enough to establish that there is no contradiction between the Income Tax Act of Estonia and the EC Treaty.

[167] J. Laffranque 'Õppematerjal kohtunikele 2005: Eelotsuse küsimine Euroopa Kohtult' [Study ma-terials for judges 2005: References to the European Court of Justice] (Tartu, Eesti Õiguskeskus 2005).

[168] See, ECJ, Case C-560/07 *Balbiino AS v. Põllumajandusminister and Maksu- ja Tolliameti Põhja maksu- ja tollikeskus* [2009] *ECR* nyr; Case C-56/08 *Pärlitigu OÜ v. Maksu- ja Tolliameti Põhja maksu- ja tollikeskus* [2009] *ECR* nyr. See also two pending Cases C-140/08 *Rakvere Lihakombinaat AS v. Põlluma-jandusministeerium et Maksu- ja Tolliameti Ida maksu- ja tollikeskus*, *OJ* 2008 C 171/13; C-249/09 *Novo Nordisk AS v. Ravimiamet*, *OJ* 2009 C 220/22.

opened up the dialogue,[169] followed by the Constitutional Court. However, in most of the new Member States, the courts of lower level have been the active ones.[170]

The first reference from Estonia was sent on 14 May 2007, and the European Court of Justice rendered its judgment on 4 June 2009.[171] It concerns structural aid in agricultural policy. In essence, the case involves the legitimate expectations of a farming unit JK Otsa Talu which wanted to apply for agri-environmental support and would have qualified for this support under the conditions laid down in a Minister of Agriculture Regulation in 2004 for the period of 2004-2006. However, JK Otsa Talu decided to apply for support in 2005 in order to prepare its massive area for agri-environmental production. Yet, in 2005, the requirements of the Estonian Regulation had been changed, apparently because of the scarcity of budgetary resources necessary for satisfying relevant applications for support. Therefore, the ALCSC had doubts whether additional requirements resulting from the amendment of the Minister of Agriculture Regulation were in conformity with the objectives of EC law, including with the spirit of the agri-environmental support established in Council Regulation 1257/1999/EC on support for rural development from the European Agricultural Guidance and Guarantee Fund (EAGGF).[172] The ALCSC formulated two questions, both with two alternatives, and described at the end of the reference a vision of its own answers to the questions. In this respect, the Estonian court seems to have followed the trend of some German courts, e.g., the German Federal Administrative Court, which explains in its references how it would itself answer the question sent to the ECJ.[173] The ECJ held that the Council Regulation in question did not preclude national legislation of that type. The answer of the ECJ to the ALCSC reference shows that there might be slight differences between the two jurisdictions as how to interpret the general principles of law such as equal treatment and legitimate expectations. This can be due to the diverse viewpoints and the necessity for the ECJ to safeguard a more general interest of the agricultural policy of the European Union. Nevertheless, the ALCSC has followed the ECJ guidelines as how to interpret the EC law and on 9 September 2009 rendered a final judgment in the *JK Otsa Talu* case not entertaining the plaintiff's claim.[174]

From a more general perspective, it is fitting to note that on the one hand, Estonian courts waited a while to proceed with their references, while, on the other hand, at the same time the subject matter of first referral did not fall into the category of early dis-

---

[169] ECJ, Case C-63/06 UAB *Profisa v. Muitinės departamentas prie Lietuvos Respublikos finansų ministerijos* [2007] *ECR* I-3239.

[170] See, *inter alia*, Chapter 9 in this volume.

[171] ECJ, Case C-241/07 *JK Otsa Talu OÜ v. Põllumajanduse Registrite ja Informatsiooni Amet (PRIA)* [2009] *ECR* nyr.

[172] Council Regulation 1257/1999/EC of 17 May 1999 on support for rural development from the European Agricultural Guidance and Guarantee Fund (EAGGF) and amending and repealing certain Regulations, *OJ* 1999 L 160/80.

[173] See M. Groepper, 'The Preliminary Ruling Proceeding before the CJ according to Article 234 EC Treaty', at the seminar of 24 April 2006 in Tallinn organised by TAIEX-Office and Estonian Law Centre, 'Seminar on the Preliminary Ruling Procedure Article 234 EC Treaty'. Paper on file with the author.

[174] See Judgment of 9 September 2009 of ALCSC, Case No. 3-3-1-95-06.

appointments as was the case with the Hungarian courts.[175] Finally, it should be noted that here again, the ALCSC raised the "question about asking the question" out of its own initiative; however, the non-conformity of the national law with the one of the EC had been pointed out by the applicant.

Soon after the first preliminary reference, in another case before the ALCSC, again concerning agricultural support, ARIB asked for a reference. It seems as if the first reference had opened up the "Pandora's box" and gave the parties an impulse to make more use of the preliminary references. The ALCSC proposed that the other party of the case should express its opinion about the reference; the other litigant did not oppose the suspension of the proceedings due to a reference. However, the ALCSC did not continue the structural support for agriculture saga in the ECJ and did not ask for another preliminary ruling. The ALCSC denied the need to refer by using a working document of the European Commission in order to interpret the EC law and stated that ARIB had not applied the EC law correctly. Furthermore, Estonia had failed to stipulate exemptions allowed by the Community measures. Therefore, the question of interpretation of EC law was in the opinion of the ALCSC irrelevant to solve the case.[176]

In order to sum up the first experiences of Estonian courts with the preliminary ruling procedure, one has to say that after the ALCSC has opened up the referrals to the ECJ, four other references of other Estonian courts have been made as of September/October 2009 to the ECJ. Three of them come from the Tallinn Administrative Court, which serves as a court of first instance and one from the Tartu District Court (second instance court). Thus all three court levels of Estonia are represented among those asking preliminary references from the ECJ. Estonian courts including the Supreme Court have used both *acte éclairé* and *acte claire* doctrine, but also referred questions concerning both – the interpretation and validity of EC law. The areas covered in the references included mostly EC tax and customs law; however they also included the distribution of agricultural subsidies and free movement of goods. Three judgments of the ECJ in Estonian references were rendered thus far, and in one of those cases a final judgment of the Estonian court was delivered. Although the distance between the first and the second reference from Estonia was around 7 months, interestingly the ECJ rendered the judgments in both cases on the same day (4 June 2009). Thus the first reference from Estonia waited for an answer approximately two years. The Estonian judge at the ECJ who was in a chamber handling one of those cases described both first references of the Estonian courts as well and skilfully drafted. The good quality and the importance of topics of these references can also be taken from the fact that in both cases the ECJ proceeded in a chamber of five instead of three judges.[177]

---

[175] See, in particular, ECJ, Case C-328/04 *Criminal proceedings against Attila Vajnai* [2005] *ECR* I-8577; ECJ, Case C-302/04 *Ynos kft v. János Varga* [2006] *ECR* I-371.

[176] Judgment of 20 June 2007 of the ALCSC, Case No. 3-3-1-26-07, *loc. cit.* n. 112.

[177] See U. Lõhmus, 'Eesti kohtute esimesed eelotsusetaotlused said lahenduse: Euroopa Kohtu 4. juuni 2009 aasta otsused asjades C-241/07 (JK Otsa Talu) ja C-560/07 (Balbiino)' ['The first requests by the Estonian courts for a preliminary ruling have been answered'], 5 *Juridica* (2009) pp. 321-327, at p. 327.

### 3.3.    Call for improvements of judicial review

From the above analysis, we can see that a common area of concern, where the bridge between two legal systems needs to get better, is the tendency in both – Estonia and the EC – especially in their respective jurisdictions, to hide behind insufficient procedural norms, in order to avoid taking a stand in substantial matters. However, where conflicts of law arise, they need to be solved, and this requires appropriate resolution mechanisms. This needs to be done both ways – in Estonia and in the Community legal order *sensu stricto* – in order to ensure better protection of rights of individuals in the EU, including Estonia, to improve the application of EC law in Estonia and at the same time enhance the possibilities of Estonia to influence the creation of Community law, including precedents.

The Working Group of recognised legal experts formed by the Constitutional Committee of the *Riigikogu* on the constitutional analysis of the ratification of the Treaty establishing a Constitution for Europe, which also analysed the Estonian CAA, emphasised the need for the legislator to include additional legal control mechanisms into the Estonian constitutional review system. As an example, the extension of competences of the Constitutional Court of the Czech Republic with the right to carry out the constitutional review of agreements dealing with the EU accessions and Founding Treaties of the EU was pointed out.[178]

Two amendments since Estonia's membership in the EU have been made into the national system of constitutional review:

1)  The amendment to the State Liability Act supplemented judicial constitutional review with the possibility to decide on the inactivity (failure to issue legislation of general application) of the legislature. This amendment was motivated by the concept that a Member State is liable for failure to transpose EC law correctly and in due course.[179]

2)  The competence of the Supreme Court was also expanded by the function of giving opinions. Namely, the CRPA and the *Riigikogu* Rules of Procedure Act Amendment Act, which entered into force on 23 December 2005, provide for the preliminary review of Estonian draft laws that are required for meeting the commitments of an EU Member State. In its opinion the Supreme Court has to clarify how to interpret the Constitution in conjunction with EC law, if interpretation of the Constitution is decisive in passing the draft law.

The question is whether the two above-described amendments of the system of constitutional review are enough for finding the right procedural framework in matters

---

[178]  Positions of the Working Group, *op. cit.* n. 11. Summary p. 8.

[179]  See the explanatory memorandum to the draft State Liability Act and Constitutional Review Proceedings Act Amendment Act 357 SE. Available at http://web.riigikogu.ee/ems/saros-in/mgetdoc?itemid=041130026&login=proov&password=&system=ems&server=ragne11 (in Estonian) referring to the ECJ, Cases C-479/93 *Andrea Francovich v. Italian Republic* [1995] *ECR* I-3843; ECJ, Joined Cases C-46/93 and C-48/93 *Brasserie du Pêcheur SA v. Bundesrepublik Deutschland and The Queen v. Secretary of State for Transport,* ex parte: *Factortame Ltd and others* [1996] *ECR* I-1029.

related to EC law and the Estonian Constitution or whether additional improvement is needed?

Further improvements might be handy not only in constitutional review, but also as far as the role of administration, the liability of courts and the administrative court procedure as such are concerned. However, too little attention in Estonian legal policy is given to how to participate in improving the judicial review in the ECJ.

### 3.3.1.   *Challenges of serving two Gods in the constitutional review*

The CRCSC has, in its first opinion of 11 May 2006 (discussed in substance above), also explained the procedural aspects of its new competence to give opinions. The Supreme Court noted that, in order for the interpretation of the Constitution in conjunction with EC law to be crucial for the adoption of a draft, the draft or its provision must be directly related to the provision or principle cited by the *Riigikogu*. The interpretation of such provision or principle must not be blatantly obvious. An opinion is justified only if the meaning of a provision or principle of the Constitution, when interpreted in conjunction with the CAA and EC law, is unclear or arguable and makes the legislative proceeding in the *Riigikogu* difficult. These guidelines help to avoid the *Riigikogu's* abuse of the right to ask for the Supreme Court's opinion in the future.

However, it seems that insufficient forethought was given to the extension of the competence of the Supreme Court. It was not preceded by an analysis of, e.g., the question of whether and in what form a body that administrates justice can simultaneously give opinions.[180] It is not sure either whether the Supreme Court may take a view on amendments to the EU Founding Treaties, should this become necessary. It cannot be precluded that as the EU develops, a question may arise about the possible conflict of proposed changes to the primary law of the EC with the fundamental principles of the Estonian Constitution. To identify the latter, an additional control mechanism is needed. For example, in France and Spain, the constitutional council/court conducted a preliminary review of the conformity of the constitutions of their respective countries to the Treaty establishing a Constitution for Europe.[181] The same was done in certain Member States in connection with the Lisbon Treaty (see, e.g., the judgment of 7 April 2009 of the Latvian Constitutional Court[182] and the decision of 30 June 2009 of the Federal Constitutional Court of Germany).[183] The Supreme Court's opinion should have

---

[180] See, e.g., judgment of 28 September 1995 of the European Court of Human Rights in the Case No. 14570/89 *Procola v. Luxembourg*, available at http://cmiskp.echr.coe.int/tkp197/search.asp?sessionid =1471248&skin=hudoc-en. However, giving opinions is quite a common practice for international courts and the ECJ.

[181] Decision of the French Constitutional Council [Conseil Constitutionnel] of 19 November 2004, matter No. 2004-505. – DC, *JO* 24.11.2004, p. 19885. Available at http://www.conseil-constitutionnel.fr/. Declaration of the Spanish Constitutional Court of 13 December 2004 DTC 1/2004. Available at http:// www.tribunalconstitucional.es/Stc2004/DTC2004-001.htm.

[182] Constitutional Court of Latvia, 7 April 2009, Case 2008-35-01 (*re Conformity of the Treaty of Lisbon with the Latvian Constitution*) nyr (on file with the author).

[183] Federal Constitutional Court of Germany, 30 June 2009, Case 2 BvE 2/08 (*re Conformity of the Treaty of Lisbon with the German Constitution*) nyr (on file with the author).

also been asked in Estonia; an opinion by the *ad hoc* group of experts in the Constitutional Committee of the Parliament cannot replace the position of a "constitutional jurisdiction."

Moreover, one should avoid, in the light of ECJ case law,[184] a mechanism proposed by the Chancellor of Justice[185] that would be able to screen conformity of secondary EC legislation with the Estonian Constitution. In this context, also another important question arises, namely, where to draw the line between conflicts of national law with the Constitution including the CAA and conflicts of national law with the EC law.[186] Equalising a conflict of national law with EC law with a conflict with the Constitution might not be the best solution for Estonia. It may be necessary only in principal issues (such as the protection of fundamental rights and freedoms). In the Order of 26 June 2008, the CRCSC made an attempt to specify its competences to engage in a constitutionality review of EC secondary and primary legislation. As noted above, it limited the jurisdiction to very few cases and gave a non-exhaustive list of the cases when it is competent to deal with petitions for the review of constitutionality of a provision relating to EU law. The possibility to rely on a conflict with EC law in any proceedings, if this is relevant and necessary in order to ensure equal protection of the rights of persons in situations of contesting domestic law and EC law, should not be precluded. Otherwise, Estonia would not comply with its loyal co-operation commitment under Article 10 EC. One should also consider giving the Chancellor of Justice the competence to contest Estonian legislation which is contrary to EC law. As discussed above, at present the Supreme Court denied this competence due to lack of legal basis.

Which "God" must be served first – the Constitution or EC law? Thus, which issue must be verified first – possible non-conformity with the Constitution or with Community law? The situation is less problematic if the result is the same because national law is, in fact, in contradiction with both EC law and the Constitution. Theoretically, this has to be the only possible outcome, since the Constitution has been transformed "Community law conform" with the help of the CAA. However, in practice, the circumstances can be much more complicated.[187] The ALCSC tends to create a custom

---

[184] ECJ, Cases *Foto-Frost* and *Gaston Schul, loc. cit.* nn. 159 and 160. See the same cautiousness expressed towards Polish Constitutional Tribunal's ambitions in Chapter 9 of this volume.

[185] See its speech at the Riigikogu on 27 September 2007. Available in Estonian at http://www.oigus-kantsler.ee/?menuID=17.

[186] The division of competences with the ECJ seems to be a problem elsewhere in the jurisdictions of the new Member States as well (not considering the saga of some founding and older Member States' Constitutional Courts, headed by the German Federal Constitutional Court case law, on this problem). E.g., the Polish Constitutional Court declined by its Order of 19 December 2006 its jurisdiction to answer a question on the conformity of Polish law with EC law because such matters fall within the jurisdiction of the ECJ. However, it made a vague and flexible reservation for its jurisdiction to handle EU-related matters with constitutional implications; see Chapter 9 in this volume. Compare the judgment of 16 June 2006 of the Hungarian Constitutional Court, Case No. 1053/E/2005, which dismissed a request to declare domestic legislation to be in contravention of the Constitution, because the legislation was also and mainly seen to be in contradiction with EC law.

[187] There could be situations when there is no conflict of national law with EC law, but still a conflict of national law with the Constitution since it may protect certain values more than EC law. Regarding the question of whether in such a case it is still possible, as a next step, for an administrative court to initiate

which starts in EU-related issues with proving conformity of a national provision with EC law, and, thus, if a contradiction is found, the additional constitutionality review in this case is no longer needed.[188] Nevertheless, sometimes cases occur where a lower level court fails to notice the non-compliance with EC law and seeks a constitutional review, which will end up at the CRCSC.[189] It is hard to discover what the reasons behind this kind of behaviour are; it appears as if the judges do not yet feel as comfortable in EC law as in constitutional law and choose the easiest way. For example, in a case concerning the value added tax (VAT) of theatre admissions and differentiation in the percentage thereof, the CRCSC faced a question whether a differentiation among theatres (allowing some theatres to benefit from a lower percentage of the taxable amount of 5% of admissions) based on the percentage of the state support of their income is justified by EC law or not. The Tallinn Administrative Court dealt with this issue only very broadly and reasoned the non-application of relevant article of Estonian law with its non-conformity with the principle of equal treatment laid down in the Estonian Constitution. The Supreme Court, acting as Constitutional Court, did not take a stand on whether in such a case, because of the doubts that Estonia has failed to transpose correctly the Sixth VAT Directive,[190] it would be wiser to concentrate on EC law issues only. Hence, the CRCSC did not yet sense the responsibility as an EU court as strongly as it could have[191] and rather concentrated on "safe" constitutional matters.[192] Nevertheless, the CRCSC declared the relevant article of Estonian Value Added Tax Act unconstitutional and invalid and admitted in the reasoning of its judgment that problems might exist also in terms of EC law conformity by pointing out to the legislator the relevant Community measures that must be supported.[193] In a later case concerning state aid, the CRCSC advised courts to start with checks of conformity of Estonian law with EC law and only when there is no EC law relevance verify the compatibility with the Estonian Constitution (Order of 16 June 2008 in the case *Aspen* discussed above).

---

constitutional review in order to check the compliance of domestic provision with the Constitution, the newest trends in old Member States in this respect can be seen in the decision of French Conseil d'État, which considered on 8 February 2007 that insofar as the contested domestic provision is based on legitimate EC law, the national provision cannot be repealed, since this would essentially invalidate the EC law (Case No. 287110 Arcelor. Available at http://www.conseil-etat.fr/ce/jurispd/index_ac_ld0706.shtml).

[188] See Judgment of 5 October 2006 of the ALCSC, *loc. cit.* n. 79.

[189] In Estonia, the concrete constitutionality review is conducted on a decentralized manner; thus, all courts can declare laws unconstitutional. However, only the SC can declare laws invalid. Therefore, the other courts must initiate a constitutionality review to declare a norm invalid, if they have not applied the norm because they found it to be unconstitutional. (See Art. 15 para. 2 and Art. 152 of the CRE).

[190] Sixth Council Directive 77/388/EEC of 17 May 1977 on the harmonisation of the laws of the Member States relating to turnover taxes – Common system of value added tax: uniform basis of assessment, *OJ* 1977 L 145/1.

[191] Compare with the Lithuanian Constitutional Court which has asked by its decision of 8 May 2007 in a Case No. 47/04 a preliminary reference from the ECJ. In English available at http://www.lrkt.lt/dokumentai/2007/d070508.doc.

[192] Similarly to the Hungarian Constitutional Court in its decision of 25 May 2004 No. 17/2004, *loc. cit.* n. 46.

[193] Judgment of 26 September 2007 of the CRCSC, Case No. 3-4-1-12-07, nyr.

Considering the above-treated problems, notwithstanding the EU (law) friendliness of the opinion of 11 May 2006 of the CRCSC, the first preliminary reference of the Supreme Court in deciding constitutional matters will probably not take place tomorrow, unless the system of constitutionality review will be further improved. This is even truer since the two amendments made so far to the constitutionality review – state liability for failure to transpose Community law and the Supreme Court's competence to give opinions on the interpretation of the Constitution/CAA with conjunction of EC law – have been made of very limited use. The procedural restrictions may, however, have a crucial impact on the possibilities of the Supreme Court in constitutional issues to influence the legal system of the EU.

3.3.2.    *Judicial remedies and discordant perplexity of legal certainty, loyal*
          *co-operation and responsibility*

Considering the above-described cases concerning, e.g., surplus stocks of agricultural products, structural support for farmers, official publication of EU legal acts in Estonian, knowledge of importers and customs declarants about EC law following the EU accession, etc., the principles of legal certainty and legitimate expectations do not always fit into the scheme of loyal co-operation of Estonia towards the EU. And yet, the same ideals and values are appreciated in the legal systems of both the EU and Estonia. However, in practice, quite often a weighting needs to take place between the ideals of protecting identity and the ideals of protecting community in order to reach stability between two legal orders. And as we know, it is no secret that on the Community level, Community values, including uniform application of EC law, securing the competition in the internal market and/or the loyal co-operation between the EU and its Member States, seem over and over again to prevail. If it is sometimes difficult even for a Supreme Court to decide how to serve the two Gods, the Estonian administrative bodies and courts of lower level have much more difficulty in a more limited time to juggle in the discordant perplexity of legal certainty loyal co-operation and their own responsibility.

Therefore, the ALCSC has underlined the importance of an administrative body to preserve the effective impact of EC law upon implementing national procedural law.[194] The Tallinn Administrative Court has, in turn, considered that an administrative body has to decide itself whether a national norm is in accordance with EC law, and, if not, set a national norm aside.[195] In this case, the court criticised the position of the Tax and Customs Board which had argued that it was obliged to apply an Estonian Act as long as it was declared constitutional and valid, despite its possible contradiction with Community law. This matter illustrates again the difficulties for administrative bodies to apply in practice the ECJ- developed principles of effectiveness and equivalency, limiting the national procedural autonomy. A problem is that first, the administrative

---

[194]   Judgment of 19 December 2006 of the ALCSC, *loc. cit.* n. 21, paras. 20 and 21.
[195]   Judgment of 10 May 2007 of Tallinn Administrative Court Case No. 3-06-389, *loc. cit.* n. 166, para. 9.

bodies hesitate to take the responsibility to act as Community watchdogs out of fear for the national legislature; second, the supremacy of the application of EC law may leave the fate of Estonian law, which has been set aside due to a conflict, unresolved, which, in turn, may lead to problems of legal clarity and legal certainty. Which law is to be applied in a new case when Estonian law, already set aside by an administrative body or a court, continues to be formally in force? Specific cases may, of course, be solved based on the supremacy of application. Administrative acts (decisions) relying on domestic law that is contrary to EC law can be revoked by an administrative court. As a minimum, an Estonian court should be allowed to declare Estonian law to be contrary to EC law in the operative part of its decision, as did the ALCSC in the *Hadler* case, discussed above. However, it is currently impossible to request a court to repeal a law or regulation that is contrary to EC law. The only hope is that the legislature will make the necessary amendments based on the court's decision. Unfortunately, experience shows that one cannot always rely on this. Neither is it clear whether a complaint about the legislature's inactivity is a feasible and efficient legal remedy in such cases. Although the case law of the ECJ is limited to the supremacy of EC law on application and does not consider a separate mechanism repealing domestic law contrary to Community law necessary, and most Member States have taken the same path, the lack of a requirement in Estonian law under which a request could be submitted for repeal of a domestic legal provision which is contrary to EC law, in the same way as constitutional review proceedings can be initiated, may result in a weaker protection of persons' rights under Community law compared to the protection that individuals have of their rights under domestic law.

In Estonia, there are not yet court cases inspired by the ECJ judgments in cases such as *Kühne & Heitz*,[196] *Kempter*,[197] *i-21 Germany*,[198] *Kapferer*,[199] *Lucchini*.[200] However, the possibility of resumption of the administrative proceedings exists in Estonia; it is the discretion of an administrative authority. Nonetheless, there are no special provisions allowing reopening proceedings and repealing an administrative act because it is in conflict with EC law. But even if the Estonian legislator does not amend the Administrative Procedure Act in the light of the *Kühne & Heitz* precedent, and if the ECJ case law continues to underline the principles developed in *Kühne & Heitz*, inventiveness and courage to act in the interest of EC law by administrative authorities and courts needs to be expected. Nevertheless, despite the responsibilities of legislative and executive powers under the Estonian State Liability Act, as far as courts are concerned, the responsibility of courts is limited and occurs only if a judge committed a criminal offence in course of proceedings (Art. 15 of State Liability Act). But again, even here, one might be able to find a remedy in EC law, relying on case law of the ECJ in cases

---

[196] *Loc. cit.* n. 5.
[197] ECJ Case C-2/06 *Willy Kempter KG v. Hauptzollamt Hamburg-Jonas* [2008] *ECR* I-411.
[198] *Loc. cit.* n. 5.
[199] *Loc. cit.* n. 5.
[200] ECJ, Case C-119/05 *Ministero dell'Industria, del Commercio e dell'Artigianato v. Lucchini SpA.* [2007] *ECR* I-6199.

*Köbler*[201] and *Traghetti,*[202] which sooner or later, will probably need to be reflected in Estonian written law as well, unless, of course, Estonia, including its courts, wishes to influence EU/ECJ to develop case law in a different direction from, e.g., *Kühne & Heitz* and *Köbler.*

Regrettably, the issues of protection of fundamental rights, *locus standi* and better access to Community courts, improved awareness of EU citizens about their rights, new methods how to reduce the workload of the ECJ and at the same time enable protection of rights stemming from Community legislation, as well as co-operation between the ECJ and courts of the Member States and reforms of the EC judicial system are barely, if not at all, discussed in Estonian Government's European Union Policy papers.[203] However, the importance of these subjects should not be underestimated, especially since the time, which the proceedings in the ECJ and the CFI nowadays take, is unsatisfactory, and the role of national courts in the interpretation of EC law needs to be redefined. Instead, the Estonian Government's European Union Policy seems to value more the economic aspects of the European integration than the democratic functioning of the Union and protection of fundamental rights. Fortunately, the Member State has in its official statements, nevertheless, supported the Charter of Fundamental Rights to be given legally binding value,[204] as well as called for the simplification of legal instruments of the EU and democratisation of the decision-making process in the EU. Additional proposals of Estonia in shaping the legal system of the EU would nevertheless be welcome.


4.      CONCLUSIONS


Regardless of the initial reluctance in making statements concerning the relationship between Estonian legislation and EC law, the Estonian Supreme Court has, after two years of Estonia's EU membership, overwhelmingly advocated for "Community" in acknowledging the supremacy of EU law even over the Estonian Constitution. However, the possible limits of supremacy, as expressed in the Constitution Amendment Act, are not elaborated in the opinion of the CRCSC. A year later, the ALCSC made the first Estonian reference for a preliminary ruling to the ECJ, after the Supreme Court had in previous relevant cases exhausted all different doctrines concerning the obligation to

---

[201]  ECJ, Case C-224/01 *Gerhard Köbler v. Republik Österreich* [2003] *ECR* I-10239.

[202]  ECJ, Case C-173/03 *Traghetti del Mediterraneo SpA v. Repubblica italiana* [2006] *ECR* I- 5177.

[203]  The Estonian Government's European Union Policy for 2004-2006, approved by the Estonian Government on 22 April 2004, available in English at http://www.riigikantselei.ee/failid/The_Government_s_European_Policy_for_2004_2006_FINAL.pdf; Draft of the Estonian Government's European Union Policy for 2007-2011 open for comments in the public, provisionally adopted by the Estonian Government on 28 June 2007, available at http://www.osale.ee/files/consult/1_ELPOL%202007-2011%20eeln%F5u.pdf (in Estonian).

[204]  See Information and Position of Estonia at the European Council on 21-22 June 2007, p. 2. Available at the home page of the State Chancellery of the Estonian Government at http://www.riigikantselei.ee/failid/2007_06_11_VV_seisukohad__K.pdf (in Estonian).

refer, such as *acte éclairé* and *acte claire*. The first reference was followed by references in other cases and by different courts as well.

While in the rest of the legal fields, the contacts of Estonian jurisdictions with EC law have been mostly accidental, adjudication of Estonian administrative courts, especially in dealing with the transitional measures and structural support of the EU in the agricultural sector, has a constant Community law influence. EC law has been mainly invoked by parties; the ALCSC, however, has applied EC law also *ex officio*, as well as set aside national norms that were in conflict with EC measures. Similarly to other new Member States, EC law has played an important role in Estonia, besides the surplus stock affairs, in customs and tax cases but not in the framework of taxes on second-hand vehicles. In the CFI/ECJ, the cases directly or indirectly involving Estonia concern mainly, besides the agricultural issues, also the delicate aspects of energy policy.

Nevertheless, in Estonia, EU/EC law has been more or less applied, referred to and respected, in all of three major areas: public law, private law and criminal law. Good examples here are the EC law conform interpretation of Estonian Trade Mark Act, as well as the interpretation by the CrimCSC of the ECJ judgment in *Pupino* case.

The non-availability of officially binding versions of EU legislation in Estonian at the time of the accession did not cause any serious problems, and according to the Supreme Court, the pre-accession Estonian law does not necessarily need to be interpreted in line with EC law with the same intensity as after accession.

The integration of legal systems has been intensively undertaken by the judiciaries, which have switched places with the legislator and law-making competences of the executive, who both played a far more important role in the pre-accession phase by approximating Estonian legislation to the law of the EC. The current passivity and partial ignorance of the legislature have been compensated by judicial activism. The weakest link appears to be the administrative bodies. While implementing the Community norms, they are not always well informed about the purposes of EC law and the intentions of national law-makers and, therefore, balance between the two, without daring, e.g., not to apply a national norm violating EC law. This is why enhanced co-operation among all state powers in understanding EC law is still necessary.

As far as "identity" is concerned, if bringing Estonian jam to Luxembourg can be to a certain extent even funny, then one must be careful that the protection of one's identity does not transform into turning the back to the common ideals. Instead, identity can be preserved of its best by contributing one's positive experiences to the others. Although Estonia has been successful in repairing its defaults and the four initial cases brought by the European Commission against Estonia have been removed from the register of the ECJ, the weakness of Estonia's ability to give considerable input to the Community legal and judicial system is characterised by the small number of considerable interventions in other ECJ proceedings. Original ideas shared with others are only visible in Estonia's attempt to increase the availability of consolidated electronic versions of EC legal acts and in proposal making them legally binding. However, the legal questions in general are not the strongest part of Estonia's EU policy. The country tends to concentrate on the economic side of the Community, which was perhaps one of the key features of the EC of six back in the 1950s. But even ever since the beginning, the

EC has been a strong Community of law, where the common values have a legal frame-work, and measures are taken respecting the rule of law. This is especially important for a small Member State, and, therefore, Estonia needs to put more emphasis on its legal policy in the EU. Especially, since one cannot deny a certain reluctance and mis-trust from the "big" towards the "small" and even more from the "old" towards the "new." Active and knowledgeable participation in EU legal policy is important also in order to inform Estonian citizens, the Parliament, economic operators and the public in general about the developments in the EU legal system. To achieve this, impact analysis of the effects of EU law on Estonian law should be made parallel to the par-ticipation in Community law-making; co-operation among different ministries and other administrative bodies should be improved; involvement of the public, the *Riigikogu* and third sector in the decision-making process concerning EU issues should be strength-ened; administrative capacity in analysing ECJ case law *via* a competence centre should be increased. This would also help the EC legal system as a whole to be more demo-cratic and transparent in its decision-making, simpler and easily understandable to the people.

Unlike "Community" and "Identity", "Stability" in relations between the Estonian legal system and the one of the EC seems to be missing the most. Perhaps this will only come with time when the cases in Estonian courts will not primarily involve transi-tional and support measures of the EU, but rather also entail other domains of law, such as social and environmental law.

Unfortunately, ideals and practice in building the bridge between the Estonian and the EU legal systems do diverge, especially as far as general principles and protection of fundamental rights and freedoms are concerned. On the one hand, although the Estonian written law *prima facie* has well been approximated with EC law and taken over the European values, the implementation of these norms in everyday life can be quite difficult and, therefore, varies from ideals. In this context, the issue of change of mentality is crucial, and all relevant fundamental principles including the principles of EC law must be respected throughout the course of the implementation. The implement-ers and interpreters of law should feel in EC law as comfortable as in Estonian law. On the other hand, even if the principles of EC law are, e.g., effectively applied in Estonian courts and even though the general principles appreciated by EC law are equally famil-iar to the Estonian Constitution, the paradox is that they still can come to a conflict with each other if the interests of private persons and of the EU need to be weighed. This weighing can differ from the weighing between the interests of the individual and the public used in national law. In cases having the EC law contact, sometimes one cannot stop feeling that both – the interests of the EU at large in securing uniform application of Community law and the interests of Estonia in fulfilling its duties as a Member State of the EU – selfishly and with disproportional injustice prevail over the legitimate expectations and other fundamental rights of individuals. And yet, as ideal, the main interests of the EU should, of course, serve the people of the Union.

For that reason, in this respect, both legal systems – the one of the EU/EC and the one of Estonia – need to improve the mechanisms of legal remedies and judicial review. As unpopular as this may sound, much more attention in building the bridge between the two legal systems should indeed be paid to the development of procedural law. Various, at first look "formalities", such as, issues of legal basis and standing, tend to serve often as a purpose, instead of a measure, and/or create obstacles to the concordance between the effective protection of rights of individuals and uniform application as well as effectiveness of EC law. The EU should enlarge the possibilities for individuals to challenge legal acts of general application in the CFI/ECJ, but on the other hand, search the ways to decrease the workload of the CFI/ECJ, e.g., in enabling the ECJ to concentrate on fundamental, constitutional issues and in increasing the trust in national judges. In Estonia, besides the two amendments made so far to the constitutionality review – introducing state liability for failure to transpose EC law and extending the Supreme Court's competence to give opinions on the interpretation of the Constitution with conjunction of EC law – further improvements might be beneficial, not only in constitutional review, but also in the administrative procedure and introducing the liability of courts for failure to apply correctly EC law and ask for preliminary references in accordance with the ECJ's case law.

Isaac Newton once said: 'We build too many walls and not enough bridges.' Naturally, it will not be easy to build a stable bridge of community and identity between the legal systems, including judicial systems, of the EC and one of the smallest of the "Brave New World." Besides the constitutional amendments and procedural norms, the most important cornerstones of this bridge are the people, including the politicians, civil servants and judges who will need to maintain this link. However, a failure is not permitted. To find a right balance between EU law and national law, between the ideals and practice, between the effectiveness of EC law and the protection of the rights of individuals is definitely very important. Especially, when we consider that the EU has unfortunately distanced itself from a common person and that the overall future of the Union faces crises, or to put it bolder – to a certain extent existential threats, which even the Treaty of Lisbon may not entirely disperse.

*Chapter 7*

# LITHUANIA'S MEMBERSHIP IN THE EUROPEAN UNION AND APPLICATION OF EU LAW AT NATIONAL LEVEL

Irmantas Jarukaitis*

## 1.     INTRODUCTION

Lithuania is one of those Member States of the European Union in which support for the European integration process had been constantly high among the public and main political parties before the accession to the EU. This remains the case five years after the "big bang" enlargement, of which Lithuania was a part. Arguably, it is one of the reasons why Lithuania managed to avoid various constitutional shake-ups after the accession, comparable to those seen in some other new EU Member States. Thus, although the membership triggered some very interesting legal developments at the national level, in general, the first five years of Lithuania's participation in the EU endeavour proved to be rather calm. At the same time, emphasis should be placed on the fact that accession to the EU and incorporation of EU law into the national legal system is only part of a bigger transformation process which started once Lithuania regained independence. The total revision of national law (some authors speak about a gradual change of the whole "legal tradition") started back in the 1990s, and it could be argued that the process is far from over. Thus, the accession negotiations and approximation of national law with EU law went hand in hand with the (re)formation of the national legal system. Lithuania's accession to the EU was another huge transformation from a legal perspective since both political institutions and courts had to get used to their new role. Although it would be too daring to state that Lithuania has already found its place within the European Union, one could say that it is in an active (and successful) search of its new identity after becoming an EU Member State.

This chapter aims at providing some general description of various legal developments related to Lithuania's accession to the EU, its involvement in EU matters as well as transposition and application of EU law at the national level. It is composed of two major parts. The first briefly describes the constitutional framework which was laid down in order to establish a clear constitutional basis for Lithuania's accession to

* Lecturer at the Faculty of Law, Vilnius University. Deputy Director General of the European Law Department, Ministry of Justice, Vilnius. The usual disclaimer applies. The chapter reflects the law as it stood on 31 January 2009. Brief acknowledgements of subsequent developments were made in a few places.

*A. Łazowski (ed.), The Application of EU Law in the New Member States*
© 2010, T·M·C·ASSER PRESS, *The Hague, The Netherlands and the Authors*

the EU and provides some insight about the involvement of Lithuanian political institutions in EU matters. The second is devoted to the analysis of national court practice, dealing with interpretation and application of EU law. It mainly focuses on the jurisprudence of the Constitutional Court of Lithuania performing abstract constitutional review; however, some tendencies in the practice of other courts (courts of general competence and administrative courts) are highlighted as well.

2.      CONSTITUTIONAL BASIS OF LITHUANIA'S MEMBERSHIP IN THE EU AND INVOLVEMENT OF NATIONAL POLITICAL INSTITUTIONS IN EU MATTERS

2.1.    **The Constitutional Act on Lithuania's Membership in the European Union**

With the entry into force of the Europe Agreement,[1] Lithuania, along with other candidate states from Central and Eastern Europe, started wider deliberations on the impact of future EU membership on the national constitution. The question was whether the Lithuanian Constitution should be amended, and, if so, how, in order to reflect the fact that membership in the EU has a profound impact on some core national constitutional principles. Views within the academic community and political circles were very diverse, and discussions concerning the necessity, content and form of constitutional amendments related to membership in the EU lasted for several years.[2] Finally, a consensus was reached among major political parties represented in the *Seimas* (the Parliament) that constitutional amendments were necessary. Therefore, the Constitutional Act on Membership of the Republic of Lithuania in the European Union (hereafter the Constitutional Act) was adopted on 13 July 2004 and entered into force one month later.[3] Comparing the content of the Constitutional Act with EU-related constitutional

---

[1] Europe Agreement establishing an association between the European Communities and their Member States, of the one part, and the Republic of Lithuania of the other part, *OJ* 1998 L 51/3.
[2] For more details about the process of drafting of constitutional amendments, see, in particular V. Vadapalas and I. Jarukaitis, 'Constitution of the Republic of Lithuania, International Law and Accession to the European Union', in F.F. Segado, ed., *The Spanish Constitution in the European Constitutional Context/La Constitución Española en el Contexto del Constitucionalismo Europeo* (Madrid, Dykinson S.L. 2003) pp. 473-488; I. Jarukaitis, 'Lithuania', in A.E. Kellermann, J. Czuczai, S. Blockmans, A. Albi, W.Th. Douma, eds., *The Impact of EU Accession on the Legal Orders of New Member States and (Pre-) Candidate Countries. Hopes and Fears* (The Hague, T.M.C. Asser Press 2006) pp. 385-390.
[3] The Constitutional Act on Membership of the Republic of Lithuania in the European Union provides:
'The Seimas of the Republic of Lithuania,
executing the will of the citizens of the Republic of Lithuania expressed during the referendum held on 10-11 of May 2003 on the membership of the Republic of Lithuania in the European Union,
expressing its conviction that the European Union respects human rights and fundamental freedoms and that membership in the European Union will contribute to a more effective safeguarding of human rights and freedoms,
noting that the European Union respects national identity and constitutional traditions of its Member States,

provisions adopted in other EU Member States, one may conclude that it represents one of the most complex solutions and covers a broad range of issues. First of all, it defines some deeper values and assumptions on which Lithuania's membership in the EU is based. Further, it provides the constitutional basis for a vertical transfer of public powers to the supranational level (powers which had been exercised at the national level prior to the accession). It defines the relationship between the EU and the national legal order. Finally, it establishes the constitutional basis for a special co-operation mechanism between the *Seimas* and the Government in EU matters and envisages a specific procedure for adoption of EU-related decisions within the Government.

A few general remarks about the provisions of the Constitutional Act are fitting. First, it is clear that by adoption of the Act, the *Seimas* recognised the *sui generis*

---

seeking to ensure full participation of the Republic of Lithuania in European integration as well as the security of the Republic of Lithuania and welfare of its citizens,

on 16 September 2003 ratified the Treaty between the Kingdom of Belgium, the Kingdom of Denmark, the Federal Republic of Germany, the Hellenic Republic, the Kingdom of Spain, the French Republic, Ireland, the Italian Republic, the Grand Duchy of Luxembourg, the Kingdom of the Netherlands, the Republic of Austria, the Portuguese Republic, the Republic of Finland, the Kingdom of Sweden, the United Kingdom of Great Britain and Northern Ireland (Member States of the European Union) and the Czech Republic, the Republic of Estonia, the Republic of Cyprus, the Republic of Latvia, the Republic of Lithuania, the Republic of Hungary, the Republic of Malta, the Republic of Poland, the Republic of Slovenia, the Slovak Republic concerning the Accession of the Czech Republic, the Republic of Estonia, the Republic of Cyprus, the Republic of Latvia, the Republic of Lithuania, the Republic of Hungary, the Republic of Malta, the Republic of Poland, the Republic of Slovenia, the Slovak Republic to the European Union signed on 16 April 2003 in Athens,

adopts and promulgates this Constitutional Act:

1. The Republic of Lithuania as a Member State of the European Union shall share with or entrust to the European Union competencies of its State institutions in the spheres provided for in the founding Treaties of the European Union and to the extent that, together with the other Member States of the European Union, it could jointly meet its commitments in those spheres and could also enjoy the rights accorded by membership.

2. The norms of *acquis* of the European Union shall be an integral part of the legal order of the Republic of Lithuania. Where it follows from the founding Treaties of the European Union, the norms of *acquis* shall apply directly, while in the event of a conflict between legal norms, the norms of *acquis* shall prevail over the laws and other legal acts of the Republic of Lithuania.

3. The Government shall inform the Seimas about the proposals to adopt legal acts of the European Union. As regards the proposals to adopt the legal acts of the European Union regulating the spheres which, under the Constitution of the Republic of Lithuania, are related to the competences of the Seimas, the Government shall consult the Seimas. The Seimas may recommend to the Government a position of the Republic of Lithuania in respect of these proposals. The Seimas European Affairs Committee and the Foreign Affairs Committee, in accordance with the procedure set forth in the Statute of the Seimas, may submit to the Government the opinion of the Seimas concerning the proposals concerning the adoption of legal acts of the European Union. The Government shall assess the recommendations or opinions submitted by the Seimas or its Committees and shall duly inform the Seimas about their execution following the procedure prescribed by legal acts.

4. The Government shall consider the proposals related to the adoption of the legal acts of the European Union following the procedure prescribed by legal acts. The Government may adopt decisions or resolutions concerning those proposals and their adoption shall not be subject to the provisions of Article 95 of the Constitution' (*Valstybės žinios*, 2004, No. 111-4123).

The English version of the Act is available at http://www3.lrs.lt/cgi-bin/preps2?Condition1=23787 6&Condition2.

nature of the EU and its legal system. Several facts confirm such a conclusion. Article 136 of the Constitution establishes the basis for Lithuania's membership in international organisations.[4] However, that provision was considered to be inadequate or not voluminous enough for membership in the EU. The description of "international", given its features, was considered artificial and would not allow for reinterpretation of the Constitution, which in some cases is inevitable given Lithuania's membership in the EU. Besides, such a conclusion is supported by positions expressed by the *Seimas* and the Government at the European Convention.[5] Those proceedings coincided with drafting of EU-related national constitutional amendments. An explanatory memorandum to the draft Constitutional Act explicitly recognised the *sui generis* nature of the EU and stated, among other things, that when acceding to the EU, Lithuania becomes a member of a broader political community, whose members are not only states but EU citizens as well.[6] Further, the Preamble to the Constitutional Act recognises that, on the one hand, the EU is built on the same core values which are enshrined in the Lithuanian Constitution and clearly spells out willingness of Lithuania to participate in the process of integration and by doing this, to develop and promote these constitutional ideals and ensure they are materialised throughout the whole of Europe.[7] On the other hand, it recognises that Lithuania's membership in the EU creates preconditions for a better attainment of some national constitutional ideals, especially security and high-level living standards.[8]

Given the wide scope and nature of public powers that the EU possesses and the particularities of their exercise, it could be stated that one of the aims of EU-related constitutional amendments is the reconstruction of a system of public powers, defined by the national constitution. In that sense, the whole Constitutional Act and paragraph 1 in particular are related to the rationalisation and organisation functions performed by the Constitution. It reflects the fact that while retaining the status of a state political community, Lithuania became a part of the broader European political community. Such participation in a wider political community triggers different changes with regard to the exercise of public powers. Among other things, it modifies the principle of democracy,[9] which is at the heart of the Lithuanian Constitution. From that point

---

[4] Art. 136 of the Constitution provides: 'the Republic of Lithuania shall participate in international organizations provided that this does not contradict the interests and independence of the State.'

[5] See, for example, Resolution of 19 December 2001 of the *Seimas* on the negotiations of Lithuania's membership in the European Union available at http://www3.lrs.lt/owa-bin/owarepl/inter/owa/U0113594. doc; Resolution of 29 May 2003 of the *Seimas* on discussion concerning the future of Europe, available at http://www3.lrs.lt/owa-bin/owarepl/inter/owa/U0113597.doc as well as Decree of the Government of 25 September 2003 on the Governments' position with regard to the draft EU Constitutional Treaty (*Valstybės žinios*, 2003, No. 42-9159).

[6] Text of the explanatory memorandum of the draft Constitutional Act is available at http://www3.lrs. lt/pls/inter3/dokpaieska.showdoc_l?p_id=223996.

[7] 'expressing its conviction that the European Union respects human rights and fundamental freedoms and that membership in the European Union will contribute to a more effective safeguarding of human rights and freedoms' and 'seeking to ensure full participation of the Republic of Lithuania in European integration.'

[8] 'seeking to ensure ... the security of the Republic of Lithuania and welfare of its citizens.'

[9] Here the principle of democracy is understood in its narrow sense – as participation and representation in decision-making.

of view, the modification is twofold. First of all, paragraph 1 of the Act recognises that alongside the horizontal division of public powers among state institutions, there is a vertical division, which was envisaged before the adoption of the Constitutional Act and emerged after accession to the EU. Thus, the accession to the EU triggered a redrawing of political boundaries; Lithuania became part of a broader European political community, which is, among other things, based on the principle of majoritarian decision-making, whereas the legitimacy of the exercise of public powers is secured both through national and supranational "channels". On the one hand, by becoming part of the European political community, Lithuanian citizens acquired the right to participate directly or indirectly in adoption of decisions, which makes a direct impact on their lives and thus secures their interests more effectively. Their participation and representation in decision-making is secured through national, as well as supranational institutions, including the European Parliament. On the other hand, it means that certain decisions, adopted within the wider political community, are taken not only by members of the Lithuanian political community ("national majority"), but by members of other national political communities as well (or the "European majority"). Accordingly, in areas of EU competence, Lithuanian citizens and European citizens/ nationals of other EU Member States form the common European community, within which political/value decisions are being made, but at the same time, in certain cases the whole national community may become "a minority" (e.g., in cases where it is outvoted in the EU Council). Of course, such a political community is in part based on principles other than state community, since the creation of the wider European community does not mean the end of national/state political communities or their identities.[10] However, one may argue that there is a common minimum value affinity among the members of such a community, ensuring its (relative) stability and development. Thus, it could be concluded that paragraph 1 of the Constitutional Act opens up the national constitutional order and "stretches" the limits of public powers which are sanctioned by the Constitution (and thus, the limits of the Constitution itself), since after adoption of the Constitutional Act, the Constitution embraces not only public powers, exercised by the state institutions,[11] but by supranational institutions as well.[12]

In this context it should be noted that the jurisprudence of the Constitutional Court of Lithuania shows its implicit recognition of the expansion of the boundaries of political community prompted by Lithuania's accession to the EU, since in some rulings, the Court makes a recourse to the principle of democracy when describing the

---

[10] In this context, attention should be drawn to the careful language of the Constitutional Act, since the Preamble expressly refers to the duty of the EU to respect the national identity and constitutional traditions of its Member States, while para. 1 of the Act speaks of "trust of competences," but not their ultimate surrender/renouncement.

[11] Art. 4 of the Constitution stipulates: 'the People shall exercise the supreme sovereign power vested in them either directly or through their democratically elected representatives,' whereas Art. 5 provides that 'in Lithuania, the powers of the State shall be exercised by the Seimas, the President of the Republic and Government, and the Judiciary. The scope of powers shall be defined by the Constitution.'

[12] E. Šileikis, *Alternatyvi konstitucinė teisė* [The Alternative Constitutional Law] (Vilnius, Teisinės informacijos centras 2005) at p. 149.

exercise of public powers not only by state institutions and not only by nationals of Lithuania.[13]

Further, the accession to the EU and the Constitutional Act modifies the principle of (horizontal) separation of powers. First of all, a new balance is established between the Parliament and the Government. Although, as will be seen later in this chapter, the *Seimas* actively participates in EU decision-making, the Governments' powers, given its legislative role in the EU Council, are substantially enhanced.[14] Moreover, a balance of powers between national courts is redefined as well. Considering the principles the ECJ pronounced in the *Simmenthal II* decision,[15] powers of review of some national legal acts concerning their compatibility with Lithuania's ratified international agreements shift from the Constitutional Court[16] to ordinary courts as far as primary and secondary EU law is concerned. At the same time, it means that ordinary courts acquire more powers, since after accession, they have the power to set aside national legal acts which are not in conformity with EU law.

Paragraph 2 of the Constitutional Act deserves a comment as well. It describes the way in which the consequences of transferred public powers – adopted EU legal acts "flow" back to the national level and become part of the national legal system.

---

[13] Thus, the Court in *obiter dictum* of the ruling of 21 December 2006 *re Lithuanian Radio and Television Funding and Radio Frequencies* (full text of the ruling available at http://www.lrkt.lt/dokumentai/2006/r061221.htm) when defining duties of the public broadcaster noted that '*[t]he principle of democracy* entrenched in the Constitution *inter alia* implies that the law must establish the legal regulation where, at the time of election campaigns, the public broadcaster gives air-time to the political parties and political organisations, *the candidates to the Seimas*, *to the European Parliament*, to the post of the President of the Republic and to municipal councils who participate in the election' [emphasis added]. Clearly, the European Parliament is mentioned on equal footing with the national parliament when speaking about the principle of democracy, thus – democratic legitimacy. Further, in the ruling of 9 February 2007 on Elections of Municipal Councils (full text of the ruling available at http://www.lrkt.lt/dokumentai/2007/r070209.htm), the Constitutional Court stated that 'the right to self-government is implemented through *democratic* representation; municipal councils, through which the right to self-government is implemented, may not be formed in a way so that there might arise doubts as to their *legitimacy and legality*, *inter alia*, as to the fact whether the principles of a democratic state under the rule of law were not violated in the course of election of *persons* to political representative institutions' [emphasis added]. Here, the Court doesn't use the term "citizens" but "persons" instead, since after revision of Art. 119 of the Constitution (see further in this chapter) the right to participate in municipal elections is conferred not only to Lithuanian citizens, but to all persons permanently living in Lithuania. Again, for the Court, democratic participation and legitimacy of adopted decisions are not confined solely to community based on national citizenship.

[14] Before the accession to the EU, the Constitutional Court was very clear about the fact that the Constitution doesn't provide a basis for delegated legislative powers of the Government. See, for example, the ruling of 26 October 1995 *re the Restoration of Citizen's Ownership Rights to Land* (full text of the ruling available at http://www.lrkt.lt/dokumentai/1995/n5a1026a.htm).

[15] ECJ, Case 106/77 *Amministrazione delle Finanze dello Stato v. Simmenthal Spa.* [1978] *ECR* 629.

[16] For example, in the ruling of 25 April 2002 *re the Refusal to Investigate Part of a Petition* (full text of the ruling available at http://www.lrkt.lt/dokumentai/2002/d020425.htm), the Constitutional Court just hinted that it has powers to review the compatibility of decrees of the Government with Lithuania's ratified international agreements, whereas in its ruling of 16 January 2007 on the decree of the President of the Republic by which Judges D. Japertas, P. Linkevičienė and A. Gudas were dismissed from office (full text of the ruling available at http://www.lrkt.lt/dokumentai/2007/r070116.htm), the Court actually performed such kind of review and ruled that a particular decree of the President of the Republic did not contravene the Constitution of Lithuania or Art. 6 para. 2 of the European Convention on Human Rights.

Again, it may be concluded that the *sui generis* nature, and thus, the relative autonomy of the EU legal system, is recognised, since the Constitution makes a clear distinction between public international law and EU law.[17] Attention should be drawn to the fact that when incorporating the EU legal system into a national one and spelling out its specific features, paragraph 2 of the Constitutional Act explicitly covers not only European Community law but also European Union law, thus going even further than the ECJ has done so far.[18] Such a broad provision was drafted taking into account results of the European Convention, namely Article I-6 of the EU Constitutional Treaty.[19] Thus, differently from the German constitutional jurisprudence, for example, it is not possible – from the point of view of Lithuanian constitutional law – to treat "deliberately" legal acts of the Third Pillar as acts of public international law.[20] On the other hand, the mere adoption of paragraph 2 of the Constitutional Act means that one of the core tenets of ECJ practice – the absolute autonomy of EC law and its self-referentiality – is rejected, since from the domestic point of view, the basis of validity of EU law in Lithuania and its primacy over national law emanate from the Constitution and not from EU law. Using terminology proposed by Professor Hart,[21] one can say that the rule of recognition remains at the national level – paragraph 2 of the Constitutional Act simply adjusts the criteria of validity in order to embrace EU law and ensure its validity/effectiveness at the national level. Thus, the Constitution demonstrates its normative insularity but also shows its cognitive openness,[22] taking into account the changed social reality – Lithuania's membership in the EU. Accordingly, both paragraph 2 of the Constitutional Act[23] and the Constitutional Court are entirely explicit about the fact that paragraph 2 of the Act establishes only a collision rule in case of a difference between two legal rules belonging to different legal systems; there was no intention on the part of the Parliament to shift the rule of recognition from Article 7 paragraph 1 of

---

[17] Attention should be drawn to the fact that Art. 138 para. 3 of the Constitution serves as the basis for incorporation of international treaties into the national legal system. It reads: 'International treaties ratified by the Seimas of the Republic of Lithuania shall be a constituent part of the legal system of the Republic of Lithuania.'

[18] As far as Third Pillar legislation is concerned the ECJ has so far developed the principle of indirect effect, although it might be argued that in effect the principle of indirect effect is a different (not so intensive) form of manifestation of the principle of primacy, especially taking into account the practical impact of the ECJ ruling in *Pupino* on national proceedings in this case. See Case C-105/03 *Criminal Proceedings against Maria Pupino* [2005] *ECR* I-5285.

[19] Treaty establishing a Constitution for Europe, *OJ* 2004 C 310/1. The same is true for the Treaty of Lisbon, since after its entry into force, the current pillar structure would disappear and there would be no difference between secondary EU legal acts in terms of material spheres of their regulation. See Treaty of Lisbon amending the Treaty on European Union and the Treaty establishing the European Community, signed at Lisbon, *OJ* 2007 C 306/1.

[20] This is the view of the German Federal Constitutional Court. See Federal Constitutional Court of Germany, 18 July 2005, Case 2 BVR 2236/04 (*re Constitutionality of German Law Implementing the Framework Decision on a European Arrest Warrant*) [2006] 1 C.M.L.R. 16.

[21] H.L.A. Hart, *Teisės samprata* [The Concept of Law] (Vilnius, Pradai 1997).

[22] G. Teubner, *Law as an Autopoietic System* (Oxford, Blackwell 1993).

[23] Para. 2 of the Constitutional Act provides for priority of EU legal rule over national provision 'in case of conflict.'

the Constitution[24] to paragraph 2 of the Constitutional Act. Such an opinion is shared by the academic community[25] and the Constitutional Court.[26]

Nevertheless, the consequences of such a provision clearly go beyond being a mere rule of conflict. The substance of paragraph 2 of the Constitutional Act can be summarised as follows. First, as *expressis verbis* provided in paragraph 2 of the Act, EU law becomes "law of the land" in Lithuania. It means that Lithuanian courts and other state institutions have a constitutional duty to apply EU law and interpret national law in conformity with EU law, ensure its effectiveness and safeguard its primacy in case of conflict. Accordingly, private persons have the constitutional right to rely on provisions of EU law and require a reference of the issue to the ECJ where EU law is involved, whereas national courts have the constitutional right and duty to refer questions concerning validity and interpretation of EU law[27] to the ECJ. Thus, Lithuanian courts become European courts, whereas the ECJ becomes "a court" within the meaning of the Constitution of Lithuania as well.[28] Further, national legislative and other institutions have the *constitutional obligation* to ensure timely and effective implementation of EU law[29] and to set necessary preconditions for its effective functioning at the national level.

---

[24] Art. 7 para. 1 of the Constitution provides: 'Any law or other statute which contradicts the Constitution shall be invalid.'

[25] E. Kūris, 'Lietuvos Respublikos Konstitucija ir Europos teisės iššūkiai' [The Constitution of the Republic of Lithuania and Challenges of European Law], 6(54) *Justitia* (2004) pp. 36 et seq.; A. Abramavičius, 'Narystė Europos Sąjungoje ir Lietuvos Respublikos Konstitucinio Teismo įgaliojimai' [Membership in the European Union and Authority of the Constitutional Court of Lithuania], 2 *Konstitucinė Jurisprudencija. Lietuvos Respublikos Konstitucinio Teismo biuletenis* (2006) pp. 313 et seq.; I. Jarukaitis, 'Adoption of the Third Constitutional Act and its Impact on the National Constitutional System', 60 *Teisė/Mokslo darbai* (2006) pp. 29-30.

[26] See further in this chapter.

[27] The *Seimas* has recognised the jurisdiction of the ECJ in the Third Pillar under Art. 35 para. 3(b) EU by Law of 22 March 2007 (*Valstybės žinios*, 2007, No. 39-1436).

[28] For example, under Art. 12 para. 2 of the Law on the Bank of Lithuania 'a decision regarding the dismissal of the Chairperson of the Board of the Bank of Lithuania on the grounds provided for in Paragraph 1 of this Article shall be made by the Seimas of the Republic of Lithuania on the recommendation of the President of the Republic.' According to Art. 105 para. 1 of the Constitution of Lithuania, a constitutionality of decisions of the *Seimas* may be questioned before the Constitutional Court of Lithuania. At the same time, Art. 12 para. 4 of the Law on the Bank of Lithuania, which was amended in the light of EU law, provides, that '[t]he Chairperson of the Board of the Bank of Lithuania shall have the right to refer to the European Court of Justice a decision regarding his dismissal prior to the expiration of his term of office within two months from the announcement of the decision or from the receipt of the notification thereof or, if the above has not occurred, from the date when the decision became known to the plaintiff on the grounds that the decision was in breach of the Treaty establishing the European Community or any other legal provision related to the application of the above Treaty.'

[29] Interestingly enough, one of the parties argued before the Supreme Administrative Court of Lithuania that certain provisions of the Insurance Law are incompatible with Directive 2002/87/EC (Directive 2002/87/EC of the European Parliament and of the Council of 16 December 2002 on the supplementary supervision of credit institutions, insurance undertakings and investment firms in a financial conglomerate and amending Council Directives 73/239/EEC, 79/267/EEC, 92/49/EEC, 92/96/EEC, 93/6/EEC and 93/22/EEC, and Directives 98/78/EC and 2000/12/EC of the European Parliament and of the Council, *OJ* 2003 L 35/1) and that the *Seimas* (the legislature) has a constitutional duty, stemming from the Constitutional Act, to implement directives correctly. The Court rejected the argument about incompatibility

Several other issues related to the constitutional basis of Lithuania's accession to the EU should be noted. First, as has already been mentioned, the Constitutional Act was adopted upon Lithuania's accession to the EU and came into force on 14 August 2004. The reasons for such lateness are not clear, since the voting results in the *Seimas* show that political support for the Constitutional Act was high.[30] Realising the risk of uncertainty and understatement of the value of the Constitutional Act, the Constitutional Court pre-empted the probable doubts about the constitutionality of, for example, the application of EC regulations between 1 May 2004 and 14 August 2004 and decided to correct the faults of the political process by stating that Lithuania's membership in the EU 'is *constitutionally confirmed* by the Constitutional Act of the Republic of Lithuania "On Membership of the Republic of Lithuania in the European Union", a constituent part of the Constitution' [emphasis added].[31] Thus, the Court clearly indicated to likely applicants that it will reject any constitutional complaints about unconstitutionality of (application of) EU legislation based on the arguments about the belated adoption of the constitutional basis for the membership.

Further, once the Constitutional Act was adopted, the Constitutional Court, recognising (presumably) its extensive impact on contents of the Constitution, hinted about the possibility of reinterpretation of the Constitution once certain constitutional amendments were adopted.[32] As some examples of pre-accession jurisprudence of

---

by simply stating that it found none, and that in any case at the time of proceedings, the implementation period, prescribed by the Directive, still had not expired. Because of that, it (understandably) expressed no view as regards a constitutional duty of the legislature and hasn't referred the issue to the Constitutional Court. See Decision of the Court of 27 September 2005 in case A15-626/2005.

[30] During the first voting concerning the adoption of the Constitutional Act on 30 March 2004, out of 141 MPs, 117 voted "for", 4 – "against", 0 – "abstained". During the second voting on 13 July 2004, 115 voted "for", 5 – "against", 0 – "abstained".

[31] See, for example, ruling of 13 December 2004 *re the State Service* (full text of the ruling available at http://www.lrkt.lt/dokumentai/2004/r041213.htm).

[32] Thus, in the ruling of 14 March 2006 *re the Limitation of Rights of Ownership in Areas of Particular Value and in Forest Land* (full text of the ruling available at http://www.lrkt.lt/dokumentai/2006/r060314. htm), although not referring to the Constitutional Act, the Court noted that 'The principle of a state under the rule of law implies continuity of the jurisprudence' (Constitutional Court rulings of 12 July 2001, 30 May 2003, decision of 13 February 2004 and ruling of 13 December 2004). This can also be said as regards the jurisprudence of the Constitutional Court: '[t]he continuity of the constitutional jurisprudence *does not mean that the constitutional doctrine cannot be corrected, or that its provisions cannot be reinterpreted.* In the constitutional justice case at issue it needs to be noted that it is necessary to reinterpret official provisions of the constitutional doctrine (to correct the official constitutional doctrine), it is (or might be) necessary inter alia *in the cases when amendments are made to corresponding articles (parts thereof) of the Constitution.* After an amendment of the Constitution comes into force, whereby a certain provision of the Constitution is altered (or abrogated) on the basis of which (i.e. in the course of construction of which) the previous constitutional doctrine was formed (as regards the corresponding issue of the constitutional legal regulation), the Constitutional Court, under the Constitution, enjoys exceptional powers to hold whether it is possible (and to what extent) to invoke the official constitutional doctrine formulated by the Constitutional Court on the basis of previous provisions of the Constitution, or whether it is no longer possible to invoke it (and to what extent) ... In its acts the Constitutional Court has held many times that *the provisions of the Constitution, which is an integral act ... are interrelated and constitute a harmonious system,* that there is a balance among the values entrenched in the Constitution, that it is not permitted to construe any provision of the Constitution in a way so that the content of any other provision of the Constitution would be distorted or denied, since thus the essence of the entire constitutional legal regulation and the balance

the Constitution Court reveal, such reinterpretation of the Constitution may be neces-sary.[33] Finally, it should be mentioned that accession to the EU prompted not only adoption of the Constitutional Act. In addition, provisions of the Constitution, which

---

of values entrenched in the Constitution would be disturbed. Taking account of this, one is to hold that *reinterpretation of the official constitutional doctrinal statements* (correction of the official constitutional doctrine) *could be necessary also* <u>*when such amendment to the Constitution is made*</u> (a certain provision of the Constitution is amended or abrogated, or a new provision is entrenched in the Constitution) <u>*whereby the content of the entire constitutional legal regulation is corrected in essence*</u>, *even though the constitu-tional provision in question*, on the grounds of which (i.e. in the course of the construction of which) the previous official constitutional doctrine with respect to a certain issue of the constitutional regulation was formulated, *is not formally altered*' [emphasis added].

[33] For example, on 6 October 1999, the Constitutional Court rendered a ruling on the compliance of Parts 1, 2 and 3 of Art. 8 and Parts 7, 8 and 9 of Art. 16 of Lithuanian Law on Telecommunications with the Lithuanian Constitution (full text of the ruling available at http://www.lrkt.lt/dokumentai/1999/n9a1006a. htm). It decided that temporary restrictions of the competition in a fixed telecommunications service mar-ket were not in breach of Art. 46 of the Constitution. Thus, it confirmed that the Parliament had the right to grant temporary exclusive rights to certain economic entities in the telecommunications sector on the basis of the Lithuanian Constitution. Although fully supporting conclusions reached by the Constitutional Court (once interpreting the Constitution, the Court relied extensively on EC law, mentioned further), one may wonder, what would be a decision of the Court, if Lithuania were an EU Member State at the time of adop-tion of a decision (or, if to look from a different angle, such a constitutional dispute would arise now)? At that time, these issues were regulated by the European Commission Directive 90/388/EC on competition in the markets for telecommunications services (*OJ* 1990 L 192/10). Art. 2 of the Directive provided that the telecom sector should have been *de jure* free for competition as of 1 January 1998. The only possibility for the Member States to delay the opening of telecom markets was to apply to the European Commission for a transitional period (Art. 1 of the Directive 96/19/EC, amending the Directive 90/388/EC). Thus, in such a legal environment, the *Seimas* would have no legal ground to grant the transitional period on its own initiative and it wouldn't be possible to interpret Art. 46 of the Constitution as allowing a temporary grant of exclusive rights in telecoms sector, since the competence to decide on these issues was transferred to the EU level. Even more, the constitutional doctrine in this area is already impacted by Lithuania's accession to the EU in a sense, given the existence of the new Directive 2002/77/EC, which completely prohibits the grant of any exclusive or special rights in electronic communications sector. Currently it is not possible to interpret Art. 46 of the Constitution of Lithuania as allowing the *Seimas* to grant temporary or permanent exclusive or special rights in the electronic communications sector. Such developments prompt speaking about the transformation of the content of Art. 46 of the Constitution triggered by EU law without its formal amendment.

    The ruling of 21 October 1999 concerning writing of names and family names in passports may serve as another example (full text of the ruling available at http://www.lrkt.lt/dokumentai/1999/n9a1021a.htm). The Court held: 'taking account of the fact that the passport ... is an official document certifying a perma-nent legal link between an individual and the state, i.e. the citizenship of an individual, and the fact that cit-izenship relations belong to the sphere of public life of the state, the *name and family name of an individual must be written in the state language*' [emphasis added]. It means that only letters of Lithuanian language are allowed in Lithuanian passports. After Lithuania's accession to the EU, that part of the Court's *obiter dictum* should be seen in the light of the ECJ's practice (e.g., ECJ, Case C-168/91 *Christos Konstantinidis v. Stadt Altensteig – Standesamt and Landratsamt Calw – Ordnungsamt* [1993] *ECR* I-1191 and Case C-148/02 *Carlos Garcia Avello v. Belgian State* [2003] *ECR* I-11613). The same is true with regard to the ruling of 2 September 2004 on VAT payers (full text of the ruling available at http://www.lrkt.lt/dokumen-tai/2004/r040902.htm) where the Court stated that 'under the Constitution *taxes may be established only by the Seimas and only by law*' [emphasis added]. It's quite obvious that once Lithuania acceded to the EU, taxes (e.g., VAT, excise duty, sugar tax) may be established and regulated at the EU level as well.

were considered to be not in line with requirements of EU law, were amended both before and after Lithuania's accession to the EU.[34]

## 2.2.  Involvement of national political institutions in EU decision-making

As already mentioned, the general attitude of the public to Lithuania's membership in the EU remains highly positive. The same conclusion applies to the attitude of Lithuanian political institutions to EU integration.[35] It is more evident when one makes a comparison with national court practice, which – to some extent – is more reserved. In part it's natural, since national political institutions had been intensively involved in the European integration process (in the form of negotiations) long before states' accession to the EU; therefore, they are more experienced when dealing with EU issues, whereas national courts, with some reservations, were formally confronted with EU law only after the accession to the EU.

Some adaptations of the regulatory system, tailoring the national legal system to European needs, were made. Alongside paragraphs 3 and 4 of the Constitutional Act, some other pieces of national legislation were either amended or adapted in order to make reforms both in the legislative and executive fields of competence. The Statute of the *Seimas*[36] was amended to expand the role of the European Affairs Committee of the *Seimas*, to establish procedures allowing the Parliament to execute supervision of compliance with the principle of subsidiarity and to define the relationship with the Government in the EU decision-making process. In addition, the Law of the Government was amended, and the Regulations of the Government on the co-ordination of EU affairs were adopted.[37]

After five years of membership in the EU, a conclusion could be drawn that state institutions regard EU matters as priority. Practice shows that the Parliament took a proactive stance and continually submits its positions to the Government regarding drafts of EU secondary legislation. Like some national parliaments of other EU Member States, the *Seimas* (the European Affairs Committee) is active in supervising whether a particular piece of draft EU legislation is compatible with the principle of subsidiarity and once even adopted a declaration that the Commission's proposal for

---

[34] In order to secure the right of foreign nationals to acquire land in Lithuania, Art. 47 of the Constitution was amended twice before the accession. The first amendment was adopted in 1996 in order to secure the entry into force of the Europe Agreement; the second in 2003 to secure the accession to the EU. The same was done with regard to the right of EU citizens to participate in municipal elections. For that purpose, Art. 119 of the Constitution was amended. It should be noted that the right to participate in municipal elections was extended further than required by EU law, since it was granted not only to EU citizens, but to 'all persons, permanently residing in Lithuania'. For more details see Jarukaitis, *loc. cit.* n. 2, at pp. 396-397. Furthermore, taking into account Lithuania's prospective accession to the Eurozone, Art. 125 para. 2 of the Constitution (which before amendments provided that 'the right of issue of currency shall belong exclusively to the Bank of Lithuania') was repealed on 25 April 2006.

[35] Here the term "political" is used to distinguish national courts from other state institutions.

[36] *Valstybės žinios,* 1999, No. 5-97.

[37] Decree of the Government of 9 January 2004, No. 21 (*Valstybės žinios*, 2004, No. 8-184). See further Jarukaitis, *loc. cit.* n. 2, at pp. 402-404.

a directive on criminal measures to ensure the enforcement of intellectual property rights was not in line with that principle.[38] Moreover, the *Seimas* adopted a special fast-track procedure, ensuring more speedy adoption of EU related laws. All these measures, as well as a structured and co-ordinated approach to EU matters at the governmental level, ensure a constantly high level of transposition of EU acts at the national level,[39] which in turn secures a sound legal environment for investments and has a direct impact on the fast growth of states' GDP. In part, it may be assumed that because of these measures, Lithuania was one of the last of new EU Member States which were brought to the ECJ by the Commission for infringements of EC law. Up to now, the European Commission initiated only two infringement actions before the ECJ,[40] and they were related not to transposition of EU law but to securing that certain adopted measures are applied in practice.[41]

At the same time, a degree of criticism is raised from time to time about the quality of national legislation transposing EU law (allegedly being a mere rewriting of directives) and, more generally, about the capabilities of state institutions to form and effectively safeguard national positions at the EU level. Arguably, the full potential of state institutions is far from being exhausted. These problems may be due to a number of reasons. In this author's opinion, one of the main issues is a self-perception of the state after its accession to the EU, the search for its new place, identity and definition of its priorities within the EU. Being an EU Member State results in new "rules of the game" when it comes to reconciling different interests and finding solutions which would be acceptable not only inside the state but to other states as well. Of course, it could take some time to get used to these new rules of the game. The pace of EU legislative procedures combined with tight deadlines for transposition of legislation and lack of experience of public-service officials when dealing with EU issues as well as lack of tradition of consultation with private partners may be identified as causes of

---

[38] *Valstybės žinios*, 2006, No. 121-4590. See also: I. Jarukaitis, 'Bendrieji parlamentinės ir teisminės subsidiarumo principo kontrolės aspektai' [General Aspects of Political and Judicial Control of the Subsidiarity Principle], 3(65) *Justitia* (2007) pp. 17-30.

[39] Regular Scoreboards published by the European Commission demonstrate that Lithuania is capable of performing really well in terms of transposition. See European Commission, Scoreboard, July 2009, No. 19, at p. 13.

[40] The first action was brought by the Commission on 7 June 2007. The case concerned the effective operation of a system facilitating identification of callers' location when an emergency number 112 is dialled. On 11 September 2008 the ECJ rendered a judgment and declared Lithuania to be in breach of EC law (ECJ, Case C-274/07 *Commission of the European Communities v. Republic of Lithuania* [2008] *ECR* I-7117). The Commission lodged a second action on 29 July 2008 (Case C-350/08 *Commission of the European Communities v. Republic of Lithuania*, OJ 2008 C 247/16). It deals with the anti-cancer drug "Grasalva", produced by a Lithuanian company. The European Commission started the infringement proceedings claiming that registration of the drug was not in conformity with EU law, although it had been registered before Lithuania's accession to the EU. The case raises interesting issues of (possible) application of EU law to pre-accession situations. The case is pending at the time of writing.

[41] Statistics on the administrative stage of infringement proceedings reveal that until December 2007, the European Commission initiated 93 infringement proceedings against Lithuania, six of which reached the stage of reasoned opinion. In the majority of cases, these relate not to transposition, but to actual implementation/application of certain requirements imposed by EU law.

such problems. However, these problems should not be exaggerated. Selected examples show that Lithuania sees itself as an active promoter of the European ideals and has the vision of a strong European Union. In this context, the nomination of Lithuania's President Mr. Valdas Adamkus for the title of the "European of the Year", thus recognising his efforts to find a compromise over the Reform Treaty at the European Council meeting in June 2007, merits attention. Lithuania is active in encouraging the European Neighbourhood Policy with other states, forming the common EU energy security policy[42] and promoting the effective functioning of a dynamic internal market.[43] Moreover, Lithuania is quite active in using judicial tools when it comes to expression of its interests at the EU level and setting directions for development of EU law. This concerns interventions in preliminary ruling procedures initiated by national courts of other EU Member States[44] and in direct actions submitted by various applicants. To date, the Government of Lithuania initiated or intervened in more than 60 cases decided by or pending before the Court of First Instance or the European Court of Justice.[45] Some of these cases attracted the attention of the Government not (only) because of particular national interest, but also because they were considered as being important for development of EU law in general.[46]

---

[42] See further Chapter 2 in this volume.

[43] In this context, note should be taken of Lithuania's efforts to adopt a more open/liberal version of the so-called Services Directive (Directive 2006/123/EC of the European Parliament and of the Council of 12 December 2006 on services in the internal market, *OJ* 2006 L 376/36).

[44] Intervention of the Government in preliminary ruling proceedings initiated by Lithuanian courts is compulsory under national legislation.

[45] Lithuania lodged two actions for annulment challenging the legality of decisions of the European Commission. The first concerns the European Commission's Decision 2007/361/EC on surplus stocks of agricultural products (Case T-262/07 *Republic of Lithuania v. Commission of the European Communities*, *OJ* 2007 C 211/53). In the second action, Lithuania is challenging the Commission's Decision K(2007)3407 on a national allocation plan of permissions for emission of $CO^2$ gases (Case T-368/07 *Republic of Lithuania v. Commission of the European Communities*, *OJ* 2007 C 283/35). In other instances, the Government of Lithuania intervened in direct actions brought by other EU Member States or the Commission as well as preliminary ruling procedures or requests for an opinion of the ECJ (Art. 300(6) EC).

[46] This includes, *inter alia*, ECJ, Case C-303/05 *Advocaten voor de Wereld VZW v. Leden van de Ministerraad* [2007] *ECR* I-3633; Case C-440/05 *Commission of the European Communities v. Council of the European Union* [2007] *ECR* I-9097; Case C-341/05 *Laval un Partneri Ltd v. Svenska Byggnadsarbetareförbundet, Svenska Byggnadsarbetareförbundets avdelning 1, Byggettan and Svenska Elektrikerförbundet* [2007] *ECR* I-11767; Case C-303/06 *S. Coleman v. Attridge Law and Steve La* [2008] *ECR* I-5603; Case C-353/06 *Stefan Grunkin and Dorothee Regina Paul* [2008] *ECR* I-7639; Case C-239/07 *Julius Sabatauskas and Others* [2008] *ECR* I-7523; Case C-195/08PPU *Inga Rinau* [2008] *ECR* I-5271; Case 1/08, request of an opinion concerning division of competence with regard to GATS, submitted by the Commission (*OJ* 2008 C 183/6), pending at the time of writing.

3. THE APPLICATION AND INTERPRETATION OF EU LAW IN LITHUANIAN COURTS

3.1. **Jurisprudence of the Constitutional Court of Lithuania: from EU law as a doctrinal tool for interpretation of the Constitution to a recognition of the impact of EU law on the Constitution and co-operation with the ECJ**

3.1.1. *Introduction*

In contrast to some other new EU Member States (e.g., Cyprus, Poland), there were no direct constitutional challenges to Lithuania's membership in the EU or requirements stemming from EU law to date. Despite the belated adoption of the Constitutional Act, neither the Accession Treaty[47]/ratifying law, nor some other pieces of national legislation dealing with EU-related issues (e.g., elections to the European Parliament, the European Arrest Warrant,[48] the issue of non-publication of some pieces of EU leg-

---

[47] Treaty between the Kingdom of Belgium, the Kingdom of Denmark, the Federal Republic of Germany, the Hellenic Republic, the Kingdom of Spain, the French Republic, Ireland, the Italian Republic, the Grand Duchy of Luxembourg, the Kingdom of the Netherlands, the Republic of Austria, the Portuguese Republic, the Republic of Finland, the Kingdom of Sweden, the United Kingdom of Great Britain and Northern Ireland (Member States of the European Union) and the Czech Republic, the Republic of Estonia, the Republic of Cyprus, the Republic of Latvia, the Republic of Lithuania, the Republic of Hungary, the Republic of Malta, the Republic of Poland, the Republic of Slovenia, the Slovak Republic, concerning the accession of the Czech Republic, the Republic of Estonia, the Republic of Cyprus, the Republic of Latvia, the Republic of Lithuania, the Republic of Hungary, the Republic of Malta, the Republic of Poland, the Republic of Slovenia and the Slovak Republic to the European Union , *OJ* 2003 L 236/17.

[48] Council Framework Decision 2002/584/JHA of 13 June 2002 on the European arrest warrant and the surrender procedures between Member States, *OJ* 2002 L 190/1. It should be noted that Art. 13 para. 2 of the Constitution provides: 'it shall be prohibited to extradite a citizen of the Republic of Lithuania to another state unless an international treaty of the Republic of Lithuania establishes otherwise.' There had been some discussions before the accession to the EU whether provisions of the Framework Decision (to be more precise, national implementing law) establishing the requirement to surrender own nationals were in line with above-mentioned constitutional prohibition. In the opinion of some Lithuanian constitutional lawyers, Art. 13 para. 2 of the Constitution (or more generally, a self-understanding of a state community) embraces the principled impossibility of extradition of own nationals (Šileikis*, op. cit.* n. 12, at pp. 136-137). However, discussions haven't led to any constitutional amendments, since it was decided that Art. 13 para. 2 of the Constitution doesn't establish an absolute prohibition to extradite Lithuanian nationals; therefore it is broad enough to sanction the surrender of nationals both under the European Arrest Warrant or to the International Criminal Court (detailed rules are established in the Code of Criminal Proceedings of Lithuania, and, at least, the Lithuanian statutory law does make a distinction between extradition (*ekstradicija*) and surrender (*perdavimas*)). It seems that thus far Lithuanian courts share such opinion, since they reject pleas of Lithuanian citizens about the illegality of surrender to other EU Member States only on the basis of Lithuanian nationality. For example, in the Order of 30 November 2004, No. 1S-281, the Court of Appeal (which is the court of last instance in surrender cases) dismissed such arguments by simply pointing to Lithuania's obligations to apply the *acquis* under the Accession Treaty (thus basically saying that there is an international treaty (at least indirectly) "establishing otherwise"). Besides, it didn't stay the proceedings and didn't refer the issue to the Constitutional Court. In this author's opinion, Art. 13 para. 2 of the Constitution should be interpreted in conjunction with the Preamble of the Constitutional Act, acknowledging among the other things that 'the European Union respects human rights and

islation in the Lithuanian language, the constitutionality of ratification of the EU Constitutional Treaty or the Lisbon Treaty[49]) were challenged before the Constitutional
Court. However, regarding the application or interpretation of EU law at the national
level, the Constitutional Court is not the ordinary judicial body in a sense that it,
strictly speaking, doesn't *apply* EU law.[50] At the same time, it would be hard to argue
that EU law and the ECJ practice are irrelevant when it comes to the interpretation
of the Constitution, especially taking into account the existence of the Constitutional
Act. Arguably, at least in general terms, the jurisprudence of the Constitutional Court
shows its consistent positive approach towards the European integration process and
EU law, although such openness is not boundless.

For the sake of convenience, the analysis of EU law related practice of the Constitutional Court is divided into pre- and post-accession periods. In case of the latter the
analysis is presented in a number of subparagraphs.

---

fundamental freedoms and that membership in the European Union will contribute to a more effective
safeguarding of human rights and freedoms.' Thus, if a constitutional presumption of the adequate protection of human rights in other EU Member States exists, it would be incumbent upon a defendant to prove
that it's not the case in a particular EU Member State. Besides, it could be argued that the European Arrest
Warrant system sets preconditions for more effective safeguarding of rights of victims of crimes (not only
Lithuanian nationals, but nationals of other EU Member States) within the meaning of the cited passage
of the Preamble of the Constitutional Act. It should be noted as well that the Government of the Republic
of Lithuania in its intervention to *Advocaten voor de Wereld* case argued that the case did not reveal any
doubts concerning the legality of the EAW Framework Decision.

Finally, the fact that on 23 October 2001, the Extradition Treaty between the Government of the Republic of Lithuania and the Government of the United States of America was concluded (*Valstybės žinios*,
2002, No. 15-559) merits attention in this context. Art. 3 of the Treaty provides that an '[e]xtradition shall
not be refused based on the nationality of the person sought.' Thus, it would be difficult to argue that an
extradition is allowed under the Constitution, whereas surrender within the EU, which is based on much
more close co-operation among its members, is unconstitutional.

[49] Several non-governmental organisations called for ratification of the EU Constitutional Treaty by
referendum, arguing that it established radical changes to the EU, thus it deserved approval by the people.
The Society of Lawyers of Lithuania suggested referring the issue to the Constitutional Court, requesting
an opinion on compatibility of the EU Constitutional Treaty with the Constitution of Lithuania. However,
neither the referendum was organised, nor the Constitutional Court was consulted. The EU Constitutional
Treaty was ratified by the law of the *Seimas*. The same course of affairs was with the Treaty of Lisbon.
There were calls from some political parties and non-governmental organisations to hold a referendum
or to refer the issue to the Constitutional Court. However, the *Seimas* decided that there was no need for
a referendum or a reference to the Constitutional Court and ratified the Treaty on 8 May 2008 (*Valstybės
žinios*, 2008, No. 56-2123). As a matter of fact, the Petition Commission of the *Seimas* was confronted
with a request from a group of persons asking the *Seimas* to refer the issue of constitutionality of ratification of the Treaty of Lisbon to the Constitutional Court even after adoption of the ratifying law. However,
such request was rejected on the ground that the Treaty doesn't alter the nature of the EU; therefore, the
Constitutional Act would still serve as a suitable constitutional basis for Lithuania's membership in the EU
after entry into force of the Treaty of Lisbon. It should be noted that under Art. 106 of the Constitution, the
*Seimas* and the President of Republic have the right, but not a duty, to ask *an opinion* of the Constitutional
Court concerning constitutionality of international agreements.

[50] Here one significant reservation should be made, since, as will be noted further, the Constitutional
Court relied on Art. 234 EC when deciding to proceed with a request for preliminary ruling to the European
Court of Justice. Thus, it relied on an EU legal rule (applied it) in order to justify its procedural decision.

### 3.1.2.    Pre-accession jurisprudence of the Constitutional Court

The Constitutional Court started referring to EU law well before the accession to the European Union. One of the first rulings where the Court made a reference to EU legal acts, among other sources of doctrinal interpretation, was delivered in December 1998, when the Court held that the death penalty established in the Criminal Code was contrary to the Constitution. Here the Court took note of the Resolution adopted by the European Parliament on 13 June 1997, where the Parliament made a strong statement against the death penalty. The Court also took into account the Declaration on the Abolition of the Death Penalty of 10 November 1997 of the Conference of the Representatives of the Governments of the EU Member States, in which the Treaty of Amsterdam was adopted.[51]

Further, in one of its rulings concerning the constitutionality of temporary exclusive rights granted by the law to a particular telecommunications operator, the Constitutional Court extensively relied on EU law, including various directives and decisions adopted by the European Commission. In this author's opinion, this ruling deserves particular attention, since the main arguments of the Court were based on provisions of EU law.[52] Apart from these two rulings, the Constitutional Court also referred to EU law in other decisions.[53] Interestingly enough, some pre-accession rulings of the

---

[51]  Ruling of 9 December 1998 *re on the compliance of the death penalty provided for in Art. 105 of the Criminal Code with the Constitution of the Republic of Lithuania* (full text of the ruling available at http://www.lrkt.lt/dokumentai/1998/n8a1209a.htm).

[52]  Ruling of 6 October 1999 *re on the compliance of Parts 1, 2 and 3 of Art. 8 and Parts 7, 8 and 9 of Art. 16 of the Republic of Lithuania Law on Telecommunications with the Constitution of the Republic of Lithuania* (full text of the ruling available at http://www.lrkt.lt/dokumentai/1999/n9a1006a.htm). See further I. Jarukaitis, 'Implementation of the New EU Regulatory Framework for Electronic Communications in Lithuania', in J. Taeger, A. Wiebe, eds., *Informatik-Wirtschaft-Recht Regulierung in der Wissensgesellschaft. Festschrift für Wolfgang Kilian* (Baden-Baden, Nomos Verlag 2004) pp. 464-466.

[53]  Ruling of 13 February 1997 on the compliance of Arts. 1 and 30 of the Law on Alcohol Control of the Republic of Lithuania, Arts. 1, 3 and 11 of the Law on Tobacco Control of the Republic of Lithuania. See also Ruling of 2 February 1996 on Resolution of the Government of the Republic of Lithuania No. 179 'On the Control of Advertising for Alcohol' with the Constitution of the Republic of Lithuania (full text of the ruling available at http://www.lrkt.lt/dokumentai/1997/n7a0213a.htm); Ruling of 11 November 1998 on the compliance of Part 4 of Art. 38 of the Republic of Lithuania Law on Elections to the *Seimas* and Part 4 of Art. 36 of the Republic of Lithuania Law on Elections to Local Government Councils with the Constitution of the Republic of Lithuania (full text of the ruling available at http://www.lrkt.lt/dokumentai/1998/n8a1111a.htm); Ruling of 23 October 2002 on the compliance of Art. 8 and para. 3 of Art. 14 of the Republic of Lithuania Law on the Provision of Information to the Public with the Constitution of the Republic of Lithuania (full text of the ruling available at http://www.lrkt.lt/dokumentai/2002/r021023. htm); Ruling of 26 January 2004 on the Law on Alcohol Control and the Rules for Licensing the Production of Alcohol Products (full text of the ruling available at http://www.lrkt.lt/dokumentai/2004/r040126. htm); Ruling of 5 March 2004 regarding the Regulations on Granting the Social Allowance and Payment Thereof (full text of the ruling available at http://www.lrkt.lt/dokumentai/2004/r040305.htm). For more details, see also E. Kūris, 'Ekstranacionaliniai veiksniai Lietuvos Respublikos Konstituciniam Teismui aiškinant Konstituciją' [Extra-national Factors Influencing Interpretation of the Constitution by the Constitutional Court] 50 *Teisė. Mokslo darbai* (2004) pp. 87-91; E. Kūris, 'The Constitutional Court of Lithuania and Lithuania's Membership in the European Union', in *The Position of Constitutional Courts Following Integration into the European Union* (Ljubljana 2005) pp. 195-197. Text available at http://www.us-rs.si/media/zbornik.pdf.

Court reveal not only positive, but also negative references to EU law, meaning that the absence of legislation at EU level was used as a doctrinal source of interpretation of the Constitution.[54] Before Lithuania's accession to the EU, the Constitutional Court used EU law simply as one of many (doctrinal) sources of inspiration for interpretation of the Constitution. Decisions of the ECJ were never cited; however, some rulings heavily relied on EU law (e.g., the ruling on Telecommunications Law) or hinted to the readiness of the Court to follow the European line of interpretation in cases where several ways of interpretation of relevant constitutional provisions were possible (e.g., the ruling on Pharmaceutical Activities).[55]

### 3.1.3.   *Post-accession jurisprudence of the Constitutional Court*

When Lithuania acceded to the EU, the status of EU law at the national level changed completely, since, according to the Constitutional Act, it became an integral part of national law. The approach of the Constitutional Court to EU law as a doctrinal source of interpretation of the Constitution remained unchanged for some time. In some early post-accession rulings, the Court simply kept mentioning EU legal provisions along with other sources of interpretation without going deeper into their content or describing its general attitude towards EU law or ECJ practice. For example, in one of the rulings concerning the constitutionality of certain provisions of the Lithuanian Customs Code, it stressed that the provisions in question were almost identical to those of the EC Customs Code and (providing some other arguments as well) ruled that there was no conflict with the Constitution.[56] Some other cases were more complex and interest-

---

[54] Thus, in the ruling of 14 March 2002 on the compliance of Art. 11 para. 2 of the Law on Pharmaceuticals with the Constitution of the Republic of Lithuania (full text of the ruling available at http://www.lrkt.lt/dokumentai/2002/r020314.htm), the Court held, *inter alia*, that '[i]t needs to be noted that *European Union law does not regulate particular issues of ownership of pharmacies and permits the member states to decide by themselves the questions concerning regulation of relations of ownership of pharmacies*. As regards regulation of pharmaceutical activities, it is established in many states of the European Union that only individuals who have had pharmaceutical education may set up pharmacies and that they may belong by right of ownership to such individuals only. In some states of the European Union pharmacies may be owned not only by individuals who have had pharmaceutical education but by other natural persons as well' [emphasis added]. Thus, although the Court uses the absence of EU legislation as an argument along with other arguments based on regulatory traditions of other foreign states in rulings' *obiter dictum*, it kind of implicitly creates an impression that had EU law regulated the issue in a particular way, the Court would have followed such line in its judgment.

[55] Note should be taken of the fact that in cases involving an EU law element, the Constitutional Court developed a practice to ask an expert opinion about a regulation of certain issues at the EU level from the European Law Department at the Ministry of Justice. It is a special expert institution, which has the competence to verify compliance of draft national legislation with EU law. It also represents the Government of the Republic of Lithuania before the CFI and the ECJ.

[56] See the ruling of 27 January 2005 on the compliance of Item 2 of para. 1 of Art. 30 of the Customs Code with the Constitution of the Republic of Lithuania (full text of the ruling available at http://www.lrkt.lt/dokumentai/2005/r050127.htm). This was one of the shortest rulings ever delivered by the Court. It is not entirely clear from the Court's reasoning whether such identity between national and EU legal provisions *per se* was a basis for rejection of doubts concerning unconstitutionality. The ruling does not provide an answer to this question.

ing; however, the Court followed the same approach.[57] Arguably, these cases were a good opportunity for the Court to express its more generalised position towards the status of EU law in Lithuania after its accession to the EU.[58]

Nevertheless, later rulings of the Court reveal its gradual change of attitude. First, the ruling of 14 March 2006 is of particular importance.[59] Here, the Court stated that 'the Constitution consolidates not only the principle that in cases when national legal acts establish a legal norm which competes *with that established in an international treaty*, then *the international treaty* is to be applied, but also, *in regard of European Union law*, establishes explicitly *the collision rule*, which consolidates *the priority of application* of European Union legal acts in the cases where the provisions of the

---

[57] The questions referred to the Constitutional Court were raised by the County Administrative Court which had to decide on the guilt of a person who, acting as an Internet services provider (ISP), provided services to persons allegedly disseminating information inciting national and racial hatred. The Administrative Court had doubts about the compatibility of provisions of the governmental decree dealing with the issues of ISP's liability with the freedom of expression and information as well as the principle that activities of the producer and/or disseminator of public information may be temporarily suspended or terminated only by a decision of a court. In its ruling of 19 September 2005 on the procedure for dissemination of information not to be divulged to the public (full text of the ruling: http://www.lrkt.lt/dokumentai/2005/r050919.htm), the Constitutional Court ruled that the above-mentioned provisions did not contravene either the Constitution or the Law on the Provision of Information to the Public. It should be noted that as regards various aspects of ISP's liability, the E-commerce Directive (Directive 2000/31/EC of the European Parliament and of the Council of 8 June 2000 on certain legal aspects of information society services, in particular electronic commerce, in the Internal Market, *OJ* 2000 L 178/1) regulates these issues at the EU level. In its ruling, the Constitutional Court simply cited provisions of the E-commerce Directive without going into further analysis of these provisions or referring questions for preliminary ruling to the ECJ on the content of the E-commerce Directive. The Constitutional Court followed the same approach in the ruling of 17 January 2006 concerning the constitutionality of provisions of the Law on Securities Market (full text of the ruling available at http://www.lrkt.lt/dokumentai/2006/n060117.htm). Here the constitutionality of the institute of the submission of an official offer to buy up the remaining securities (in case a person already acquired more than 40% of votes of the issuer at the general meeting of the shareholders) was questioned. It should be noted that at the EU level, relevant provisions are established in the Directive 2004/25/EC of the European Parliament and of the Council of 21 April 2004 on takeover bids (*OJ* 2004 L 142/12).

[58] First question is whether there is a need to scrutinise the issue at all if it is regulated in detail in EU law. It could be argued that if the Constitutional Court had no doubts concerning the legality of the EU secondary legislation in question and there were no other grounds (which were not covered by EU law) to question the constitutionality of national implementing law, then there were no grounds for constitutional review at all, since EU law is interpreted by the ECJ. If the Constitutional Court had its doubts about the legality of a particular piece of legislation, it might admit the issue for review and refer questions to the ECJ concerning validity of the EU legal act in question. Such practice shows that at that time the Constitutional Court had the EU dimension in mind when reaching decisions and was willing to take it into account. On the other hand, the Court's approach to EU law was still rather cautious, since in case there is no ECJ practice interpreting a particular provision of EU law, the mere text of a particular directive usually doesn't show a complete picture. In such cases, one may wonder what is the exact meaning of those provisions, to what extent a directive harmonises certain issues and to what extent the Member States have discretion after implementing a directive and accommodating it to particular national needs. All in all, it means that once there is a reference to a particular legal provision, there is a need to understand its contents, its meaning. For that reason, provisions of a particular directive have to be interpreted, and that's where the ECJ should play its part. Of course, it doesn't mean that when the Constitutional Court has doubts about the legality of a particular provision of EU secondary legislation, it may not share such doubts with the ECJ.

[59] Ruling of 14 March 2006 on the Limitation of the Rights of Ownership in Areas of Particular Value and in Forest Land (full text of the ruling available at http://www.lrkt.lt/dokumentai/2006/r060314.htm).

European Union arising from the founding Treaties of the European Union *compete with* the legal regulation established in Lithuanian national legal acts (regardless of what their legal power is), *save the Constitution itself* [emphasis added].

Such *obiter dictum* stimulates some thoughts. First, it could be claimed that it apparently reflects the Court's desire to reassess the constitutional reality after Lithuania's accession to the EU and adoption of the Constitutional Act and to reaffirm that the ultimate source of authority rests within the Constitution despite the existence of the Constitutional Act. Such a conclusion is supported by the fact that the cited part of the ruling was not, strictly speaking, necessary to reach its *ratio decidendi*.[60] Thus, the Court clearly indicates that it regards paragraph 2 of the Constitutional Act as a collision rule, not as an amendment to Article 7 of the Constitution. Further, the Court makes it clear that even as a collision rule, it does not extend automatically to the Constitution of Lithuania. On the other hand, the Court does not negate the impact of EU law on the Lithuanian Constitution, but simply does not specify its precise vision about the interaction of EU law and the Lithuanian Constitution, leaving this issue for the future. Emphasis should be placed on the fact that the Court makes a clear distinction between public international law and the EU legal system. Thus, it might be argued that the Court recognises the *sui generis* nature of EU law and indirectly suggests that it is ready to acknowledge a relative autonomy of EU law.[61] Yet, while earlier jurisprudence shows the Court's willingness to take the European dimension into account, this ruling might be understood as an implicit hint that should there be *an expressed conflict* between EU law and the Lithuanian Constitution, resolution of which is impossible through the use of the principle of consistent interpretation, the Constitution would prevail.[62]

---

[60] Neither the question of hierarchy between national (constitutional) law and EU law nor the content of certain EU legal acts was at issue. The Court simply cited para. 2 of the Constitutional Act and added the ending 'save the Constitution itself.'

[61] It may sound as a truism, because as was mentioned above, such distinction *expressis verbis* flows from the Constitution. However, earlier practice of the Court reveals that its approach to EU law is not entirely consistent. For example, in the ruling of 13 December 2004 on the State Service (full text of the ruling available at http://www.lrkt.lt/dokumentai/2004/r041213.htm), the Court stated among other things that 'it needs to be noted that *respective international obligations* of the Republic of Lithuania originate from *the membership of this country in the European Union*, which is constitutionally confirmed by the Constitutional Act of the Republic of Lithuania "On Membership of the Republic of Lithuania in the European Union", a constituent part of the Constitution' [emphasis added]. Thus, it seems that in this case, the Court is inclined to treat EU law more as public international law rather than the *sui generis* legal system. However, this is the only manifestation of such an approach because the Court never used that expression in its subsequent practice.

[62] As is well-known, some national constitutional courts of other EU Member States expressed similar opinions. See, for example, decisions No. 2004-496 DC; No. 2004-497 DC; No. 2004-498 DC; No. 2004-499 DC (text of decisions available at http://www.conseil-constitutionnel.fr/tableau/tab04.htm) adopted by the French *Conseil Constitutionnel* in June and July 2004 and judgment of 27 April 2005 of the Polish Constitutional Tribunal concerning constitutionality of the European Arrest Warrant (reported in [2006] 1 C.M.L.R. 36). Further, attention should be drawn to the fact that the former President of the Constitutional Court of Lithuania Prof. E. Kūris has noted that *ad hoc* constitutional amendments could be regarded as a proper form for removal of constitutional conflicts between EU law and national constitutions: Kūris, *op. cit.* n. 53, at p. 203. Furthermore, attention should be drawn to the fact that in 1995, before Lithuania's

However, recent practice of the Constitutional Court shows that such a scenario is highly unlikely. First, in its ruling of 21 December 2006, the Court made a step forward and citing for the first time numerous decisions of the Court of First Instance and the European Court of Justice,[63] noted that '[t]he Constitutional Court has stated several times that the jurisprudence of the European Court of Human Rights, as source of legal interpretation, *is important for interpretation and application of Lithuanian law. The same should be said about the jurisprudence of the Court of First Instance and the European Court of Justice*'[64] [emphasis added]. Such a statement, according to the former President of the Court means 'a silent commitment of the Constitutional Court in each case, where the issue falls within the regulation of [EU law] and where a relevant jurisprudence of [CFI and ECJ] exists, to take into account that jurisprudence, but that should not be reflected every time in the text of the ruling.'[65] Without any doubt, such a statement may be treated as an explicit recognition of the impact EU law has on national law, including the Lithuanian Constitution. Of course, it doesn't eliminate all grounds for conflict but it does indicate the Court's willingness to do its best to avoid it.

A further step in developing a coherent approach to EU law was taken on 8 May 2007 when the Court made a reference to the ECJ for a preliminary ruling concerning the interpretation of Article 20 of Directive 2000/54/EC.[66] In this author's opinion,

---

accession to the ECHR, the Constitutional Court delivered an opinion concerning the compatibility of the ECHR with the Constitution of Lithuania (Opinion of 24 January 1995 on the European Convention for the Protection of Human Rights and Fundamental Freedoms) (full text of the ruling available at http://www.lrkt.lt/dokumentai/1995/i5a0124a.htm) where the Court stated, *inter alia*, that '[t]he provisions of the convention *might be recognized as contradicting the Constitution if*: (1) the Constitution established a complete and final list of rights and freedoms and the Convention set forth some other rights and freedoms; (2) *the Constitution prohibited some actions and the Convention defined them as one or another right or freedom*; (3) *some provision of the Convention could not be applied in the legal system of the Republic of Lithuania because it was not consistent with some provision of the Constitution*' [emphasis added].

[63] Recently, in the ruling of 15 May 2007 on the provisions of the Law on State Secrets and Official Secrets and the Law on the Proceedings of Administrative Cases (full text of the ruling available at http://www.lrkt.lt/dokumentai/2007/r070515.htm), the Court took note of several decisions of the CFI (Joint Cases T-110/03, T-150/03 and T-405/03 *Jose Maria Sison v. the Council of the European Union* [2005] *ECR* II-1429) and the ECJ (C-266/05P *Jose Maria Sison v. the Council of the European Union,* [2007] *ECR* I-1233) where both Courts were dealing with limits of access to secret information. In the ruling of 29 November 2007 on the Law on Profit Tax of Legal Persons (not yet reported), the Court again made a reference to the ECJ practice – this time to *Stichting 'Goed Wonen'* case (ECJ, C-376/02 *Stichting 'Goed Wonen' v. Staatssecretaris van Financiën* [2005] *ECR* I-3445). In the latter, the ECJ applied the principles of legitimate expectations (the principle, which is still rather new in the jurisprudence of the Constitutional Court) and legal certainty.

[64] Ruling of 21 December 2006 on Lithuanian Radio and Television funding and radio frequencies (full text of the ruling available at http://www.lrkt.lt/dokumentai/2006/r061221.htm). That formula in itself is not entirely new in the Court's practice, since it was coined to describe an influence of the practice of the European Court of Human Rights on the Lithuanian Constitution in earlier jurisprudence of the Court. In the above-mentioned ruling, it simply adapted the formula to the practice of the CFI and the ECJ.

[65] Kūris, *op. cit.* n. 53, at pp. 85-86.

[66] Decision of 8 May 2007 on applying to the Court of Justice of the European Communities (full text of decision available at http://www.lrkt.lt/dokumentai/2007/d070508.htm). The reference was submitted against the following factual and legal background. On 1 July 2004, the *Seimas* adopted the law amending the Law on Electricity which came into force on 10 July 2004. Art. 15 para. 2 of the Law (wording of 1

such a decision is extraordinary from various perspectives. First of all, looking at it from the perspective of the practice of national Constitutional Courts of other EU Member States and EU law itself, one may note that national Constitutional Courts usually treat themselves as outside the scope of preliminary rulings procedure.[67] Thus, the Constitutional Court of Lithuania is one among few national Constitutional Courts that ever used the preliminary rulings procedure and referred questions on content or validity of EU law to the ECJ.[68] Moreover, attention should be drawn to the fact that proceedings in cases before the Constitutional Court are not traditional *inter partes*

---

July 2004) provides: 'The transmission system operator shall be responsible for ensuring that conditions for the connection of equipment of electricity producers, distribution system operators and customers are in conformity with the requirements laid down in legal acts and that discriminatory conduct is excluded. *Customer's equipment may be connected to the transmission grid only when the distribution system operator refuses to connect consumer's equipment located in the territory indicated in the distribution system operator's license to the distribution network due to established technical and operational requirements*' [emphasis added]. A group of MPs of the *Seimas* referred the complaint to the Constitutional Court claiming that such provisions are not in line with, *inter alia,* Art. 46 paras. 1, 2, 4 and 5 of the Constitution ('1. Lithuania's economy shall be based on the right of private ownership, freedom of individual economic activity and initiative. 2. The State shall support economic efforts and initiative that are useful to society … 4. The law shall prohibit monopolisation of production and the market and shall protect freedom of fair competition. 5. The State shall defend the interests of the consumer'). At the EU level, the European Parliament and the Council Directive 2003/54/EC concerning common rules for the internal market in electricity and repealing Directive 96/92/EC (*OJ* 2003 L 176/37) was adopted on 26 June 2003. Abovementioned amendments to the Law on Electricity were adopted with the aim to implement provisions of Directive 2003/54/EC. Art. 20 of Directive 2003/54/EC provides: '1. Member States shall ensure the implementation of a system of third party access to the transmission and distribution systems based on published tariffs, applicable to all eligible customers and applied objectively and without discrimination between system users. Member States shall ensure that these tariffs, or the methodologies underlying their calculation, are approved prior to their entry into force in accordance with Article 23 and that these tariffs, and the methodologies – where only methodologies are approved – are published prior to their entry into force. 2. *The operator of a transmission or distribution system may refuse access where it lacks the necessary capacity*. Duly substantiated reasons must be given for such refusal, in particular having regard to Article 3. Member States shall ensure, where appropriate and when refusal of access takes place, that the *transmission or distribution system operator* provides relevant information on measures that would be necessary to reinforce the network. The party requesting such information may be charged a reasonable fee reflecting the cost of providing such information' [emphasis added]. Considering provisions of both national and EU law, it's not surprising that the precise content of Art. 20 of the Directive was of particular relevance before making a decision concerning the legality of Art. 15 para. 2 of the Law on Electricity. Thus, the Constitutional Court decided to refer the following question to the ECJ: 'Is Article 20 of Directive 2003/54/EC of the European Parliament and of the Council of 26 June 2003 concerning common rules for the internal market in electricity and repealing Directive 96/92/EC to be interpreted as obliging Member States to establish legal rules whereby any third party has the right, at his discretion, provided that the electricity system has 'the necessary capacity' , to choose the system – electricity transmission system or electricity distribution system – to which he wishes to be connected, and the operator of that system has an obligation to grant access to the network?'

[67] For more details, see, for example: F. Mayer, *The European Constitution and the Courts. Adjudicating European Constitutional Law in a Multilevel System*, Jean Monnet Working Paper 9/03.

[68] So far the Austrian *Verfassungsgerichtshof*, the Belgian *Cour d'Arbitrage* (as of May 2007 – *Cour Constitutionnelle*) and, recently, the Italian *Corte Constituzionale* made several references to the ECJ. Several other national Constitutional Courts (notably, the German Federal Constitutional Court and the Polish Constitutional Court) hinted about the possibility of making a reference to the ECJ but haven't done so to date.

disputeswithin the meaning of the ECJ practice,[69] but cases of *abstract constitutional review* of constitutionality of national legal acts. The Constitutional Court is not an ordinary judicial dispute settlement body but rather the institution exercising the constitutional supervision of national legislation. Thus, the reference of the Constitutional Court may to some extent require a liberal approach of the ECJ with regard to admissibility of reference.[70] Moreover, once referring the question to the ECJ, the Constitutional Court has implicitly recognised the ECJ's powers to rule on the issue of division of competence between the EU and national levels. This, as is well-known, is a rather delicate matter because the question submitted to the ECJ may be reframed as follows: "who is competent to regulate a disputed issue". Of course, it doesn't mean that the Constitutional Court made an irrevocable decision on this issue. It is clear that in this particular case, the issue of competence was not a sensitive one, but theoretically it might arise in the future.

The reference of the Constitutional Court is nonetheless also interesting from the perspective of national (constitutional) law. First, it merits attention that unlike other pieces of national legislation governing procedural issues of courts' proceedings, the Law on the Constitutional Court[71] was not supplemented with provisions on references to the ECJ. With this in mind, one may argue that the *Seimas* didn't project that the Constitutional Court would be willing to use the preliminary ruling procedure at all. Therefore, it is interesting to look at the legal basis for the Constitutional Court's

---

[69] For criteria of admissibility of references, see, *inter alia*, ECJ, Joined Cases C-110/98 to C-147/98 *Gabalfrisa SL and Others v. Agencia Estatal de Administración Tributaria (AEAT)* [2000] *ECR* I-1577; Case C-54/96 *Dorsch Consult Ingenieurgesellschaft mbH v. Bundesbaugesellschaft Berlin mbH* [1997] *ECR* I-4961; Case 14/86 *Pretore di Salò v. Persons unknown* [1987] *ECR* 2545.

[70] Several remarks on admissibility are fitting. First, the ECJ practice shows that the requirement of existence of *inter partes* proceedings at the national level is not an absolute one (e.g., para. 31 of judgment in *Dorsch Consult* case). Basically, the ECJ requires that national proceedings have to lead to a decision *of a judicial nature* (see, for example, ECJ, Case C-111/94 *Job Centre Coop. ARL* [1995] *ECR* I-3361, para. 9). Moreover, a recent referral of the Belgian *Cour d'Arbitrage* in *Advocaten voor de Wereld* case is to some extent similar to that of the Constitutional Court of Lithuania (there is one difference though, because in *Advocaten voor de Wereld* a constitutional complaint was lodged by a non-profit organisation instead of group of MP's), and there the issue of admissibility because of lack of *inter partes* proceedings was not raised. One may say that there was a dispute in the case at issue (between the "minority" – namely, the group of MP's, who lodged a constitutional complaint, and the "majority" – the *Seimas*), the process was adversarial (both the applicant and the representatives of the *Seimas* were allowed to submit their observations) and it was obvious that the Constitutional Court would render a decision of judicial nature. The case was named *Sabatauskas and Others v. Lietuvos Respublikos Seimas*, thus making an indirect hint to an adversarial nature of national proceedings. Attention should be drawn to the fact that there was no other way to ask for a preliminary ruling from the ECJ, since decisions of the Constitutional Court are final. Thus, the Constitutional Court had either to refer the question to the ECJ or to interpret provisions of the Directive on its own and to take the responsibility that later on the ECJ could potentially rule otherwise. Such a scenario could then lead to the necessity of amendments of the Lithuanian Constitution. Finally, it should be noted that in its written observations submitted in the case, the European Commission discussed the issue of admissibility and expressed the view that the reference was admissible. The ECJ delivered a ruling in this case on 9 October 2008 (ECJ, Case C-239/07 *Sabatauskas and Others v. Lietuvos Respublikos Seimas* , *loc. cit.* n. 46). The ECJ did not discuss the issue of admissibility but delivered a ruling on the merits (see further in this chapter). Thus, it treated the reference as admissible.

[71] English translation of the Law available at http://www.lrkt.lt/Documents3_e.html.

decision to refer[72] and its arguments explaining the necessity to seek assistance of the ECJ.[73] Given the fact that the Constitutional Court expressly recognised the ECJs' role in ensuring the principle of rule of law and its statement that 'it is necessary to construe the disputed provision ... in the context of the legal regulation established in the said directive', one may argue that the Court derived the constitutional right (or even a duty) to refer questions on EU law to the ECJ from paragraph 2 of the Constitutional Act (which is applicable both to the Constitutional Court itself and also to other national courts). Such a statement is related to another striking fact. The Constitutional Court referred to the ECJ even before any Lithuanian courts of general competence did.[74] Therefore, one may speculate that by such reference, the Court wanted to encourage other national courts to use the preliminary ruling procedure in cases where an EU law element is present as well. From a theoretical point of view, the most interesting scenario would be the ECJ's answer to the preliminary question that EU law *requires* to grant the access to transmission network. Would in such case the Constitutional Court rule that incompatibility of national provision with EU legal provision is *per se* a ground for a declaration that cited national provision contravenes the Constitution? One could think that such a line of reasoning would be a logical development of jurisprudence given Constitutional Court's earlier-mentioned state-

---

[72] The Court based its decision on Art. 102 of the Constitution (Art. 102 provides that '[t]he Constitutional Court shall decide whether the laws and other acts of the Seimas are not in conflict with the Constitution and whether the acts of the President of the Republic and the Government are not in conflict with the Constitution or laws. The status of the Constitutional Court and the procedure for the execution of its powers shall be established by the Law on the Constitutional Court of the Republic of Lithuania'), Art. 234 EC and Art. 1 and 28 of the Law on the Constitutional Court (Art. 1 of the Law provides: 'The Constitutional Court of the Republic of Lithuania shall guarantee the supremacy of the Constitution of the Republic of Lithuania in the legal system as well as constitutional legality by deciding, according to the established procedure, whether the laws and other acts adopted by the *Seimas* are not in conflict with the Constitution and whether acts of the President of the Republic and the Government are not in conflict with the Constitution or laws. In cases established in the Constitution and this Law, the Constitutional Court shall present conclusions to the Seimas and the President of the Republic. The Constitutional Court shall be a free and independent court which implements judicial power according to the procedure established by the Constitution of the Republic of Lithuania and this Law.' Art. 28 establishes some interim procedural steps to be taken by the Court, but it doesn't establish an express basis for referral to the ECJ. Thus, the only *express* legal basis for the reference mentioned by the Constitutional Court was Art. 234 EC. Besides, whereas in its earlier practice, the Constitutional Court stressed its paramount place in ensuring and developing the principle of rule of law in the national legal system, here the Court referred to Art. 220 EC and recognised the role of the ECJ in ensuring the principle of rule of law ('under Article 220 of the Treaty Establishing the European Community, the Court of Justice of European Communities shall ensure that in the interpretation and application of this Treaty the law is observed'). Of course, looking at this issue from the point of view of EU law, the situation is very simple, because the national court may directly rely on Art. 234 EC.

[73] First, the Court reiterated its exclusive role in the national constitutional system in guaranteeing the supremacy of the Constitution and constitutional legality. Further, it noted that the Law on Electricity was adopted, *inter alia*, with the aim to implement the Directive 2003/54/EC. Then it referred to para. 2 of the Constitutional Act, reiterated the *obiter dictum* of above-mentioned ruling ('save the Constitution itself') and added that '*it is necessary to construe the disputed provision of the Law* which, as mentioned, was passed while implementing *inter alia* Directive 2003/54/EC, *in the context of the legal regulation established in the said directive*' [emphasis added].

[74] This was the second reference made by Lithuanian courts to the ECJ. The first was made by the Supreme Administrative Court, whereas courts of general competence had not done that at that time.

ments about the impact of the ECJ practice on the interpretation of national law and would confirm the argument that paragraph 2 of the Constitutional Act establishes a constitutional duty to adopt national acts which are compatible with EU law. However, it seems that such a scenario must be postponed for the future. The ECJ rendered the judgment on 9 October 2008 and held that national law may establish rules such as those whose constitutionality is questioned before the Constitutional Court.[75] Thus, the Constitutional Court in principle retained its full discretion to rule on the consti- tutionality of disputed provisions. The Constitutional Court rendered its decision on 4 December 2008 and held that the challenged legislation was in compliance with the Lithuanian Constitution.[76]

A note should be taken of the fact that such referral to the ECJ opens a door to other possible references.[77] In addition, it creates preconditions for more active participation of national Constitutional Courts in development of the ECJ practice. Such participa- tion would ensure a more horizontal dialogue between national and EU constitutional

---

[75] The ECJ ruled that 'Article 20 of Directive 2003/54/EC of the European Parliament and of the Council of 26 June 2003 concerning common rules for the internal market in electricity and repealing Directive 96/92/EC is to be interpreted as defining the Member States' obligations only in respect of the access and not the connection of third parties to the electricity transmission and distribution systems and as not laying down that the system of network access that the Member States are required to establish must allow an eligible customer to choose, at his discretion, the type of system to which he wishes to connect. Article 20 must also be interpreted as not precluding national legislation which lays down that an eligible customer's equipment may be connected to a transmission system only where the distribution system operator refuses, on account of established technical or operating requirements, to connect to its system the equipment of the eligible customer which is on the territory included in its licence. It is, however, for national courts to verify that the implementation and application of that access system takes place in accordance with objective and non-discriminatory criteria between the users of the transmission and distribution systems.'

[76] Case No. 47/04, for the text of the judgment in English see http://www.lrkt.lt/dokumentai/2008/ r081204.htm).

[77] One of the most recent and interesting issues – the petition of a group of MPs submitted to the Constitutional Court in September 2007 concerning the constitutionality of Art. 2 para. 6 of the Law on Implementation of the Council Regulation 2201/2003/EC of 27 November 2003 concerning jurisdiction and the recognition and enforcement of judgments in matrimonial matters and the matters of parental responsibility, repealing Regulation 1347/2000/EC (*Valstybės žinios*, 2005, No. 58-2004). Art. 2 para. 6 of the Law provides '[a] special complaint may be brought to the Court of Appeal concerning a court decision to return a child or to refuse to return a child. *In cases concerning a return of a child a cassation shall not be allowed*' [emphasis added] and implements Art. 11 para. 3 of the said regulation which provides that '[a] court to which an application for return of a child is made as mentioned in paragraph 1 *shall act ex- peditiously in proceedings on the application, using the most expeditious procedures available in national law*. Without prejudice to the first subparagraph, *the court shall, except where exceptional circumstances make this impossible, issue its judgment no later than six weeks after the application is lodged*' [emphasis added]. Such reference of MPs to the Constitutional Court was prompted by the Rinau case, whereas the access to the Supreme Court by way of cassation complaint is forbidden in this kind of cases. Accord- ing to the complaint of a group of MPs, the above-mentioned provision contravenes the Preamble of the Constitution of Lithuania and the principle of rule of law. It's obvious that there is a direct link between Art. 2 para. 6 of the Law and Art. 11 para. 3 of the Regulation. On the other hand, it should be noted that the existence of such a link doesn't mean automatically that a reference to the ECJ is inevitable, since the Constitutional Court may simply rule that, for example, the Constitution doesn't guarantee the right to cassation in every case.

levels, minimisation of the danger of constitutional conflicts and, among other things, the respect for national identities of the EU Member States which are 'inherent in their fundamental structures, political and constitutional.'[78]

Finally, attention should be drawn to the fact that the Constitutional Court has already started re-evaluation of its own practice formed before accession to the EU and identifies areas in which reinterpretation of the Constitution is needed.[79]

Thus, it can be argued that the approach of the Constitutional Court of Lithuania is truly pro-European. The Court is (in this author's opinion) successful in establishing a delicate balance between, on the one hand, the supremacy of the Constitution, the exclusive role it plays in the national constitutional system, the mechanism of national constitutional supervision, based on the idea of national constitutional law as a "higher law" and the needs of European integration on the other. In contrast to some Constitutional Courts of other EU Member States, the Constitutional Court of Lithuania has never expressed any claims concerning, for example, the possibility of review of sec-

---

[78] Art. I-5 of the EU Constitutional Treaty; Art. 3a para. 2 EU (as amended by the Treaty of Lisbon).

[79] For example, in its ruling of 26 September 2006 on the powers of the Minister of Finance to establish the amount of fines (*Valstybės žinios*, 2006, No.104-3985), the Court stated that '[i]t needs to be noted that the Constitutional Court has formed the official constitutional doctrine of taxes and other obligatory payments in *inter alia* the constitutional justice cases in which one investigated the constitutionality of legal acts (parts thereof) *which had been passed before 14 August 2004*, when the Constitutional Act of the Republic of Lithuania "On Membership of the Republic of Lithuania in the European Union", which, under Article 150 of the Constitution, is a constituent part of the Constitution, came into force ... *Upon entry into force of the Constitutional Act of the Republic of Lithuania "On Membership of the Republic of Lithuania in the European Union"*, the official constitutional doctrine of taxes and other obligatory payments, which had been formed until then, *is developed by taking account of the said amendment to the Constitution*' [emphasis added]. Further, in the ruling of 27 June 2007 on the Compliance of the Republic of Lithuania Law on the Procedure of Publication and Coming Into Force of Laws and Other Legal Acts of the Republic of Lithuania (wording of 6 April 1993) and Government of the Republic of Lithuania Resolution No. 1269 on the Planning Scheme (General Plan) of Curonian Spit National Park of 19 December 1994 (wording of 19 December 1994) with the Constitution of the Republic of Lithuania (*Valstybės žinios*, 2007, No.72-2865), the Court pointed to the necessity to reinterpret its earlier practice with regard to the form in which the Government adopts its decisions and adoption of the Constitutional Act. The Court stated among other things that 'the provisions of the official constitutional doctrine that the Government, while resolving the affairs of state governance, must always adopt resolutions and that they have to be officially published irrespective of the fact whether the legal acts adopted by the Government are normative or individual, as well as irrespective of the fact for what subject or circle of subjects they are designed, were formulated in the Constitutional Court jurisprudence, *inter alia* the constitutional justice cases in which it was investigated whether the legal acts (paragraphs thereof) which had been issued yet before 14 August 2004, when the Republic of Lithuania Constitutional Act "On the Membership of the Republic of Lithuania in the European Union" ... whereby the membership of the Republic of Lithuania in the European Union was approved in a constitutional manner. ... Upon coming into force of the Constitutional Act ... the formerly formulated official constitutional doctrine of the Government acts is developed in the Constitutional Court jurisprudence while taking account of the fact that Paragraph 4 of this Constitutional Act established that the Government shall consider the proposals to adopt the acts of European Union law following the procedure established by legal acts. As regards these proposals, the Government may adopt decisions or resolutions for the adoption of which the provisions of Article 95 of the Constitution are not applicable.' Of course, this example is elementary, since para. 4 of the Constitutional Act *expressis verbis* indicates its purpose to establish a derogation from Art. 95 of the Constitution (and was drafted namely having in mind the earlier formed practice of the Constitutional Court).

ondary EU law[80] and, as a recently submitted review of the jurisprudence of the Court reveals, its approach to EU law is positive. Such practice of the Court without any doubt has an integrative influence and at the same time stabilises both EU and national legal systems. It could be argued that jurisprudence of the Court confirms the pluralistic understanding of the relationship between the EU and national legal systems where a relative autonomy but also the influence of the "other"/EU legal system is recognised without renouncing the identity of the national legal system.

### 3.2. The interpretation and application of EU law by Lithuanian courts of general competence and administrative courts: a reserved approach

Similarly to the Constitutional Court, Lithuanian courts of general competence and administrative courts had already faced EU law before Lithuania's accession to the EU. One should note that during the Soviet times, the role of a judge was strictly that of *la bouche de la loi* or, to put it differently, an approach to law when exercising justice was rather positivistic (or even texto-centristic). Courts were reluctant to invoke general principles of law, whereas international law was almost non-existent in the judicial discourse. Such a tendency remained for some time once Lithuania re-established its independence. Nevertheless, the last years bear witness to a gradual change in self-perception of courts in general and their attitude towards international law in particular.[81] The same is true with regard to EU law. Once the process of accession to the EU started, courts were confronted with a huge flow of national legislation which was a direct product of approximation of national law with EU law. Therefore, the necessity to take into account EU law once interpreting and applying national law was inevitable before the accession. The Supreme Court of Lithuania and the Supreme Administrative Court of Lithuania started referring to EU law several years before the accession, using the intentions of the legislature to approximate particular pieces of legislation with EU law as their point of reference.[82] Therefore, the principle of indirect effect of EU law became a tool for national courts already at the pre-accession

---

[80] So far, the Lithuanian academic community agrees that constitutional review of secondary EU legal acts is not permitted: Kūris, *op. cit.* n. 53, at pp. 200-201; Z. Namavičius, 'Suverenitetas ir Europos Sąjunga' [Sovereignty and the European Union] in *Konstitucinių teismų vaidmuo Europos Sąjungos narystės kontekste* (Vilnius, Lietuvos Respublikos Konstitucinis Teismas 2004) at pp. 17-18; Abramavičius, *op. cit.* n. 25, at pp. 313-314; E. Jarašiūnas, 'Lietuvos Respublikos Konstitucija ir Europos integracija' [The Constitution of Lithuania and the European Integation] in *Konstitucija, Nacionalinė teisė ir Europos teisė* (Vilnius 2004) at p. 27; I. Jarukaitis, 'Europos Sąjungos teisės inkorporavimo ir taikymo Lietuvos Respublikoje konstituciniai pagrindai' [The Constitutional Basis of the Republic of Lithuania for Incorporation and Application of EU Law], 4(62) *Justitia* (2006) at pp. 46-47. On the other hand, opinions differ as to what extent and how the Constitutional Court could perform the constitutional review of national legal acts implementing EU law.

[81] In this author's opinion, the jurisprudence of the Constitutional Court, stressing the independence judiciary and its responsibilities in ensuring the rule of law was one of the factors which influenced such changes.

[82] Regarding the position of international law and application of EU law in Lithuania before the accession, see, in particular: Jarukaitis, *loc. cit.* n. 2, at pp. 385-390 and pp. 398-401; V. Vadapalas and I. Jarukaitis, 'Lithuania', in A. Ott and K. Inglis, eds., *Handbook on European Enlargement. A Commentary on the Enlargement Process* (The Hague, T.M.C. Asser Press 2002) pp. 281-289.

stage, although, in this author's opinion, not all judicial decisions can be considered as successful examples of such indirect reliance on EU law.[83] Moreover, shortly before the accession, amendments of the Law on Courts,[84] the Law on Administrative Proceedings[85] and the Code of Civil Proceedings[86] were made. One of the aims of these amendments was to create legal preconditions for proper functioning of the preliminary ruling procedure (e.g., by establishing that one of the grounds for suspension of national proceedings is a reference of questions to the ECJ concerning interpretation or validity of EU law).

The natural limits of this chapter do not permit a very detailed and precise analysis of Lithuanian court practice after accession to the EU. However, several years of the membership in the EU reveal some tendencies in interpretation and application of EU law by national courts. First of all, just as before the accession, the application of EU law mainly remains the privilege of the highest courts. Although it is possible to find examples of application of EU law by lower courts, it is too early to conclude that the application of EU law is a routine issue for ordinary Lithuanian courts. Several objective and subjective factors contribute to such a state of affairs. Accession to the EU and the impact of EU law on the national legal system are only pieces of a bigger picture, since in the period following re-establishment of independence, the total transformation of the national legal system took place. Courts were faced with new laws in almost all areas: new criminal, civil, procedural codes came into force in 2001-2003; other fields of regulation have been all but stable in the past decade. Thus, courts had to get accustomed to a new legal environment to which EU law adds yet another dimension. Furthermore, a heavy workload of courts should be mentioned. Without any doubt, such a workload has an impact on the quality of judicial decisions in general and the courts' willingness to devote their time to EU law in particular.[87] This factor is related

---

[83] For example, just before Lithuania's accession to the EU, the Telecommunications Law implementing the old EU regulatory framework for telecommunications was adopted (at that time the EU had already adopted the "new" EU electronic communications framework, but the European Commission made it very clear that Acceding States had first to implement the "old" regulatory framework, whereas the "new" framework had to come into effect at the day of accession). The Communications Regulatory Authority adopted several decisions imposing certain *ex ante* obligations on some telecoms operators. Several complaints were submitted to administrative courts. The Supreme Administrative Court annulled decisions of the CRA partly because of the fact that the CRA had not provided reasons why certain obligations were imposed, although such practice was a direct outcome of transposed provisions of the "old" EU regulatory framework, and the Parliament clearly indicated its will to transpose the "old" framework. The Court noted that although the Telecommunications Law transposed the "old" framework, it was necessary to interpret the Law in the context of the "new" EU regulatory framework, although regarding a dispute at issue, it established entirely different principles. In principle, that meant that the Court required the CRA not to apply provisions of the Telecommunications Law once conducting a market analysis procedure and based its decision on provisions of EU law which at that time were not implemented in national law and could not be relied on simply because of the fact that at that time Lithuania was not an EU Member State. See, for example, decision of 12 January 2004 in case P1-12/2004.

[84] *Valstybės žinios*, 1994, No. 46-841.

[85] *Valstybės žinios*, 1999, No. 13-308.

[86] *Valstybės žinios*, 2002, No. 36-1340.

[87] For example, 5 regional administrative courts (43 judges in total) acting as the first instance courts delivered decisions in more than 20,000 cases in 2006. Source http://www.teismai.lt/teismai/Informacija%20apie%20Lietuvos%20Respublikos%20teismu%20darba%202006%20metais.pdf.

to another issue – the knowledge of EU law. Although the situation is improving, judges of lower courts still lack adequate training in EU law, and because of that, the question still remains as to what extent EU law has already become "their" law.[88]

When it comes to the EU related practice of Lithuanian courts several issues merit attention. First, the tendency remains that in a majority of cases, courts rely on the principle of consistent interpretation – i.e., they interpret and apply national law in the light of EU law. Moreover, a reliance on the principle of consistent interpretation was supplemented with direct application of regulations after the accession, which is especially evident in customs cases.[89] However, although not in numerous cases, national court practice relying on the principle of primacy of EU law already exists. In some cases, the Supreme Administrative Court, referring to the earlier-mentioned practice of the Constitutional Court of Lithuania,[90] explicitly recognises the duty to take into account EU law, not excepting the practice of the CFI and the ECJ in a rather abstract manner,[91] whereas some decisions demonstrate its willingness to apply the principle of primacy of EU law in practice.[92] For its part, the Supreme Court of Lithuania has overruled decisions of lower courts stating that they incorrectly applied national and EU law and ignored the principle of primacy of EU law.[93] Even more, some authors

---

[88] Although, for example, the Supreme Administrative Court has a separate section analysing the practice of international courts, lower courts do not have such resources.

[89] See, for example, decision of 11 May 2007 in case No. A17-1137/2007.

[90] Rulings of 14 March 2006 (*loc. cit.* n. 59) and 21 December 2006 (*loc. cit.* n. 64).

[91] Decision of 28 May 2007 in case No. A6-238/2007. The Court noted in the *obiter dictum* of its decision that national law establishes a duty to apply EU law and take into account rulings of the ECJ. Although this decision is an example of application of the principle of consistent interpretation, it is of interest because of creative application of the ECJ decision to particular circumstances. The Supreme Administrative Court was confronted with a question as to whether illegally produced alcohol should be subjected to the excise duty. Referring to the ECJ's decision in *Tullihallitus* case (ECJ, Case C-455/98 *Tullihallitus v. Kaupo Salumets and other* [2000] *ECR* I-4993), which related to taxation of alcohol smuggled into the Community territory, the Court decided that the Directive 92/12/EC doesn't provide that a smuggled alcohol could be exempted from the excise duty. The same reasoning was followed in the decision of 5 July 2007 in case A3-689-07.

[92] Thus, the Court in decision No. A8-207/2007 of 26 February 2007 referred to para. 2 of the Constitutional Act, took note of the duty to apply EU law stemming from it and ruled that some provisions of the Order of the Minister of Finance establishing different rules with regard to taxation of dividends received from Lithuanian and Estonian companies are incompatible with the principle of free movement of capital established in Art. 56 EC as developed by the ECJ (e.g., ECJ, Case C-35/98 *Staatssecretaris van Financiën v. B.G.M. Verkooijen* [2000] *ECR* I-4071).

[93] Decision of 29 December 2006 of the Supreme Court of Lithuania in case 3K-3-690/2006, which concerned the application of provisions of the Code of Civil Procedure of Lithuania and Regulation 1348/2000/EC. The Court explicitly referred to the principle of primacy of EU law and noted that in this particular case, a lower court disregarded its duty to apply the Regulation and not to apply provisions of the Code of Civil Procedure. Further, in decision No. 3K-3-91/2008 of 7 January 2008, the Supreme Court referred to *obiter dictum* of the decision of 14 March 2006 of the Constitutional Court and explicitly stated that 'the principle of primacy of EU law means that courts *have a constitutional duty* to interpret national law in a way consistent with EU law in order to ensure effectiveness of EU law.' Yet, attention should be drawn to the fact that in this case the Court itself interpreted provisions of the Regulation 2201/2003/EC, although at that time the ECJ had yet to express its opinion concerning provisions of the Regulation, which were of particular importance in this case (the main issue was the meaning of Art. 11 para. 3 of the Regulation which read: 'a court to which an application for return of a child is made ... *shall act expeditiously* in proceedings on the application, *using the most expeditious procedures available in national law*' [empha-

state that some influence of Lithuanian court practice on the ECJ practice could be detected.[94]

The impact of EU law is mostly visible in the following areas: taxation (including customs),[95] aid from structural funds,[96] agriculture,[97] competition,[98] electronic communications[99] and intellectual property.[100, 101] Thus, it might be concluded that at least Supreme Courts of Lithuania are rather active when it comes to the application of EU law.

---

sis added]. All this raises a question if 'the correct application of Community law [was] so obvious as to leave no scope for any reasonable doubt as to the manner in which the question raised is to be resolved' and recalls that 'before it comes to the conclusion that such is the case, the national court or tribunal must be convinced that the matter is equally obvious to the courts of other member states and to the Court of Justice. Only if those conditions are satisfied, may the national court or tribunal refrain from submitting the question to the Court of Justice and to take upon itself the responsibility for resolving it' (ECJ, Case 283/81 *Srl CILFIT* [1982] *ECR* 3415, para. 16).

[94] For example, on 27 October 2004 the Supreme Administrative Court rendered a judgment in case No. A1-355/2004 concerning the VAT carousel fraud in which it established certain principles with regard to the right of VAT deduction. The ECJ took an analogous approach to the issue in its later practice (e.g., ECJ, Joined Cases C-354/03, C-355/03 and C-484/03, *Optigen Ltd (C-354/03), Fulcrum Electronics Ltd (C-355/03) and Bond House Systems Ltd (C-484/03) v. Commissioners of Customs & Excise* [2006] *ECR* I-483). See also V. Valančius, 'Europos Sajungos teisės poveikis Lietuvos administracinei justicijai: tendencijų kontūrai. Pirma dalis' ['The Impact of European Union Law on Administrative Justice in Lithuania: Contours of Tendencies. First Part'], 7(97) *Jurisprudencija* (2007) pp. 36-37.

[95] See, for example, decision of the Supreme Administrative Court of 21 September 2004 in case No. A7-745-04; decision of 27 October 2004 in case A1-355/2004 (the application of the principle of fiscal neutrality).

[96] See, for example, decision of the Supreme Administrative Court of 11 December 2007 in case No. A11-1125/2007 (application of Regulation No 796/2004).

[97] See, for example, decision of the Supreme Administrative Court of 31 May 2006 in case No. A16-995/2006 (forfeiture of bananas import licence security pursuant to Regulation 896/2001/EC of 7 May 2001 laying down detailed rules for applying Council Regulation (EEC) No 404/93 regarding the arrangements for importing bananas into the Community, *OJ* 2001 L 126/6).

[98] See, for example, decision of the Supreme Administrative Court of 11 May 2006 in case No. A1-686/2006 (the notion of concerted practice and criteria determining whether a particular behaviour could be qualified as concerted practice); decision of 22 December 2006 in case No. A2-2207/2006 (the application of competition law to a postal sector).

[99] These cases usually involve complaints against decisions of the Communications Regulatory Authority designating certain undertakings as having significant market power within defined electronic communications markets and imposing certain *ex ante* obligations according to national acts implementing the new EU electronic communications regulatory framework. See, for example, decision of the Supreme Administrative Court of 7 June 2007 in case No. A17-589/2007 (in particular, the question of the scope of judicial revision of administrative acts was at issue. Here the Court made numerous references to practice of both the CFI and the ECJ); decision of 18 December 2006 in case No. A7-2203-06; decision of 18 December 2006 in case No. A6-2202/2006.

[100] See, for example, decision of the Supreme Court of 27 March 2006 in case No. 3K-3-209/2006 (a relation between a company name and well-known trademark); decision of 2 May 2006 in case No. 3K-3-275/2006 (three-dimensional trademarks and absolute grounds for refusal of registration of a trademark). For more detailed analysis concerning the application of EU law by Lithuanian courts in competition and intellectual property cases, see in particular Y. Goldammer and E. Matulionyte, 'Towards an Improved Application of European Union Law in Lithuania: The Examples of Competition Law and Intellectual Property Law', 3 *CYELP* (2007) pp. 307-330.

[101] See also Valančius, *loc. cit.* n. 94, at pp. 33-38.

On the other hand, similarly to national courts of other new EU Member States, Lithuanian courts still are not that eager to participate in the judicial dialogue with the ECJ. Apart from the already discussed references from the Constitutional Court, to date only four references to the ECJ have been submitted by Lithuanian administrative courts and courts of general competence. Two of those were submitted by the Supreme Administrative Court,[102] while the other two were submitted by Panevėžys District Court[103] and the Supreme Court of Lithuania.

---

[102] The first case (decision of 20 December 2005 in case No. A15-1292/2005) in which the Supreme Administrative Court decided to refer a question concerning the interpretation of Art. 27 of the Council Directive 92/83/EEC was rather trivial (Council Directive 92/83/EEC of 19 October 1992 on the harmonisation of the structures of excise duties on alcohol and alcoholic beverages, *OJ* 1992 L 316/21). The main concern of the Court was differences between the Lithuanian version of the Directive and other language versions. The ECJ rendered its judgment on 19 April 2007 (Case C-63/06 *UAB Profisa v. Muitinės departamentas prie Lietuvos Respublikos finansų ministerijos* [2007] *ECR* I-3239). The ECJ confirmed that the issue was not very sophisticated. It proceeded without an opinion of the Advocate General and – when providing the answer to the referred question – simply used a linguistic method of interpretation of the Directive. The second reference was more interesting and dealt with the concept of turnover tax in EU law. In 2005, the *Seimas* decided to adopt the Law on Temporary Social Tax (*Valstybės žinios*, 2005, No. 76-2739), introducing a tax which was – to some extent – similar to that scrutinised by the ECJ in cases *Banca Popolare* (ECJ, Case C-475/03 *Banca popolare di Cremona Soc. coop. arl v. Agenzia Entrate Ufficio Cremona* [2006] *ECR* I-9373) and *KÖGÁZ* (ECJ, Joined Cases C-283/06 to C-312/06 *KÖGÁZ rt and Others v. Zala Megyei Közigazgatási Hivatal Vezetője (C-283/06) and OTP Garancia Biztosító rt v. Vas Megyei Közigazgatási Hivatal (C-312/06)* [2007] *ECR* I-8463). The business community considered it to be a turnover tax which was not in line with the Sixth VAT Directive (Sixth Council Directive 77/388/EEC of 17 May 1977 on the harmonisation of the laws of the Member States relating to turnover taxes – the common system of value added tax: uniform basis of assessment, *OJ* 1977 L 145/1) and claimed that if the ECJ delivered negative judgment in the *Banca Popolare* case, they would launch actions on damages. Once the ECJ ruled that a regional tax introduced by Italy did not contravene EU law, these threats were not realised for some time. However, *Mechel Nemunas*, a company established in Lithuania brought an action against the state tax inspectorate and requested repayment of a sum which it paid to the state budget as temporary social tax in 2007. Its main argument was that the temporary social tax demonstrated features of a turnover tax within the meaning of First Council Directive 67/227/EEC (First Council Directive 67/227/EEC of 11 April 1967 on the harmonisation of legislation of Member States concerning turnover taxes, *OJ* 1967 No. 71/1301, English special edition: Series I Chapter 1967 p. 14) and Art. 33 of Directive 77/388/EEC and was therefore not allowed under EU law. The Supreme Administrative Court decided to stay proceedings and to ask the ECJ for a preliminary ruling on 18 March 2008. The ECJ rendered a reasoned order on 5 February 2009 (ECJ, Case C-119/08 *Mechel Nemunas v. Valstybinė mokesčių inspekcija prie Lietuvos Respublikos finansų ministerijos* [2009] *ECR* nyr).

[103] The case concerned the imposition of criminal liability by national law for the cultivation of fibred hemp. Criminal proceedings were initiated against a person who tried to cultivate fibred hemp in May 2006. The court of first instance (although not basing its decision on the ECJ practice (for instance Case C-462/01 *Criminal proceedings against Ulf Hammarsten* [2003] *ECR* I-781) and not referring the issue to the ECJ) handed down a decision on 18 December 2007 (case No. 1-61-128/2007). The Court acquitted the accused person on the ground that EU law did not prohibit the cultivation of fibred hemp and, on the contrary, even established aid schemes for its cultivation. Thus, it concluded that relevant provisions of national law were not compatible with EU law and decided to disregard them. The prosecution brought an appeal. Panevėžys District Court was not that courageous to disapply the relevant national rules by itself and decided to refer two questions to the ECJ (see the Order of 28 April 2008 in case No. 1A-114-145/2008). In a nutshell, it asked whether the prohibition to cultivate fibred hemp provided by national law was contrary to EU law, and, if the answer to that question was positive, whether it had a duty not to apply national provisions contravening EU law. Since answers to these questions were already clear under

The latter reference merits particular attention. It has its roots in a dispute concerning abduction and return of a child to the country of origin (Germany), which captured the attention of the Lithuanian public for more than two years. A divorce dispute between former spouses (Lithuanian and German citizens) involving a dispute concerning the rights of custody over their child produced dozens of legal proceedings both in Germany and Lithuania and involved interpretation and application of the Hague Convention on the Civil Aspects of International Child Abduction and Regulation 2201/2003/EC concerning jurisdiction and the recognition and enforcement of judgments in matrimonial matters and matters of parental responsibility.[104] When some of these cases reached the Supreme Court, it was confronted with questions concerning the balance of competence between courts of the country of origin and the country of enforcement, finality of a certificate issued by a court of country of origin under Article 42 of the Regulation, as well as conditions under which such a certificate could be issued. Accordingly, it decided to stay proceedings and ask the ECJ for a preliminary ruling.[105]

Attention should be paid to the fact that this was the first case ever decided by the ECJ using newly introduced urgent preliminary ruling procedure – so called PPU (the ECJ handed down the ruling in less than two months!). Surprisingly enough, it took the Supreme Court two orders to initiate the urgent procedure. At first, it adopted the order to refer the issue to the ECJ on 30 April 2008, but didn't ask to use the urgent procedure. Less than a month later, on 21 May 2008, it adopted the second order referring the same questions to the ECJ but this time requesting the use of the urgent procedure as well. Presumably, the Court might not have known about the existence of such a procedure, since it became available as of 1 March 2008. Once the ECJ handed down the ruling, the Supreme Court adopted two decisions (in different sets of civil proceedings: see the orders of the Supreme Court of Lithuania in cases No. 3K-3-403/2008 and No. 3K-3-126/2008 of 25 August 2008) in which it accepted and followed the ECJ's ruling. Both chambers of the Court extensively relied on the reasoning of the ECJ once reaching decisions in these cases. Thus, the Supreme Court left unchanged decisions adopted earlier by the Court of Appeal to reject the application to reopen the case concerning return of the child because of new circumstances and to reject the application concerning non-recognition of the decision of the German court which ordered the child's return. Furthermore, once the ECJ delivered the ruling, the European Commission started unofficial inquiries asking why the decision of the Court of Appeal, ordering the child's return, which was adopted on 15 March 2007, was not executed, although it was never repealed.

---

EU law, the ECJ decided to adopt a reasoned order and answered to both questions in positive (ECJ, Case C-207/08 *Criminal proceedings against Edgar Babanov* [2008] *ECR* I-108\*). After receiving the order from the ECJ, the Panevėžys District Court dismissed the appeal and left the decision of the first instance court unchanged.

[104] Council Regulation 2201/2003/EC of 27 November 2003 concerning jurisdiction and the recognition and enforcement of judgments in matrimonial matters and the matters of parental responsibility, repealing Regulation (EC) No 1347/2000, *OJ* 2003 L 338/1.

[105] ECJ, Case C-195/08PPU *Inga Rinau, loc. cit.* n. 46.

The question remains why Lithuanian courts have such a modest record in terms of the preliminary ruling procedure. It is difficult to provide an answer as to why such a practice exists. It is hard to find any rationale behind decisions not to refer, even though in some cases parties asked for that.[106] Interestingly enough, even the current President of the Supreme Court recognised that decisions of the Supreme Court 'are not very informative' about the reasons why the Court doesn't refer questions to the ECJ.[107] On the other hand, there are indications that several unsuccessful references from courts of new EU Member States might have some chilling effect.[108]

Finally, the issue of state liability for breaches of EC law should be mentioned. To date it remains purely theoretical, since national court practice doesn't exist in this area. Actually, the possibility to sue the state for damages caused by breaches of EC law was vividly debated in Lithuania at least once; however the ECJ judgments in *Banca Popolare di Cremona* and *KÖGÁZ and Others* extinguished these discussions for some time.[109] Given the above-mentioned reluctance of Lithuanian courts to use the preliminary ruling procedure, it might be speculated that there is a probability of court action at least in this area.


4.       CONCLUSIONS


Summing up, one could argue that after five years of membership in the EU, Lithuania remains one of those EU Member States where the general attitude to the integration process remains constantly high. Accession to the EU made a huge impact on core national constitutional principles, but these changes were reflected by a vast consti-tutional reform, which, in this author's opinion, secured a smooth transformation to a changed social and legal reality once Lithuania became an EU Member State. The atti-tude of both national political and judicial institutions to EU law is positive, although there remains plenty of room for improvement.

National political institutions so far treat EU issues as a priority. On the other hand, when it comes to the EU legislative process, problems regarding policy formation and priority setting at the national level should be highlighted. Moreover, the issue of boundaries of competence between the EU and the national level and problems with application of the subsidiarity principle surface from time to time.

Regarding practices of Lithuanian courts, an increasing impact of EU law in every sphere of their activities may be noted, whether in the Constitutional Court of Lithua-nia, courts of general competence or administrative courts. The Constitutional Court of

---

[106] See, in particular, the decision of the Supreme Court of 27 September 2004 in case No. 3K-3-461/2004. The Court simply stated that there is no need to refer the case to the ECJ. See also the decision of the Supreme Administrative Court of 9 September 2005 in case No. A5-878/2005.

[107] V. Greičius, 'Europos Sąjungos teisės taikymo Aukščiausiame Teisme problemos ir tendencijos' ['The Problems and Tendencies of Application of European Union Law by the Supreme Court'], 7(97) *Jurisprudencija* (2007) pp. 28-32.

[108] *Ibidem.*

[109] As mentioned above, decision of the ECJ in *Mechel Nemunas* declaring that temporary social tax was a turnover tax prohibited under EU law would certainly revive these discussions.

Lithuania went a long way in developing its practice reconciling the place of national constitutional law as "a higher law" in the national legal system with the specific needs of EU law. Although its attitude to EU law is not fully pro-European simply because it does not recognise the unconditional primacy of EU law over the Constitution of Lithuania as some national Constitutional Courts do, its practice so far demonstrates the Court's willingness to take the European dimension into account when it comes to the interpretation of the Constitution and to do its best to avoid possible conflicts. The practice of ordinary courts demonstrates their willingness to apply EU law as well. Lithuanian courts recognise specific principles of EU law (including the principle of primacy), and the penetration of EU law into national legal system increases constantly. Shortcomings of (non-/mis-) application of EU law at the national level are of a more practical nature (lack of knowledge, huge workload, etc.) and may not be treated as the expression of a negative attitude of Lithuanian courts to EU law in general. One of the more visible problems is the reluctance of Lithuanian courts to use the preliminary ruling procedure; however the situation is gradually improving.

*Chapter 8*

# THE APPLICATION OF EU LAW IN LATVIA

## Galina Zukova*

## 1.    INTRODUCTION

In 2007 the European Commission published a Communication 'A Europe of Results – Applying Community Law.'[1] In the opening paragraph the European Commission argued as follows:

> 'The European Union is founded in law, pursues many of its policies through legislation and is sustained by respect for the rule of law. Its success in achieving its many goals as set out in the Treaties and in legislation depends on the effective application of Community law in the Member States. Laws do not serve their full purpose unless they are properly applied and enforced. … Failure to rise to the challenge will weaken the foundations of the European Union. If laws are not being properly applied, European policy objectives risk not being attained and the freedoms guaranteed by the Treaties may only be partially realised.'

It is a trite observation that the success of the European Union project largely depends on the correct and effective implementation of EU law. This implementation takes place at different levels. However, the principal, and by far the most essential one is the very first – the domestic level. The quality of transposition and implementation of EU law in national legal orders, the application of the latter by state officials and the interpretation of EU law provided by the national judiciary, are the lakmus tests based on results of which the EU citizens form their opinion about the European Union.

---

* Associate Professor, Riga Graduate School of Law, Latvia; Of Counsel, 'Raidla, Lejins & Norcous.' My gratitude for comments on the earlier version of this paper goes to Prof. Kalvis Torgans (Judge at the Latvian Supreme Court), Kristine Kruma (Judge at the Latvian Constitutional Court), Esmeralda Balode-Buraka (Director of the ECJ Department, Latvian Ministry of Justice), Peter Gjortler (Acting Docent, Riga Graduate School of Law) and Jevgenijs Salims (Lejins, Torgans & Partners). I am grateful to my assistant Linda Germova (LL.M. candidate) for her valuable help in identifying the relevant case law for this article. The usual disclaimer applies.
[1] Communication from the Commission – A Europe of Results – Applying Community Law, COM (2007) 502 final, p. 2. In this regard see also Commission Communication Better Monitoring of the Application of Community Law, COM (2002) 725 final; Commission Communication A Strategic Review of Better Regulation in the European Union, COM (2006) 689 final.

This chapter offers an insight into application of EU law in Latvia.[2] The chapter covers two major areas of interest: the application of EU law by the Latvian judiciary and the participation of Latvia in proceedings before the European Court of Justice. The case law referred to throughout the chapter emanates primarily from the highest instance courts, given that the decisions of these courts, as a general rule, are more easily accessible. Furthermore, these are the last instance courts which set the exemplary practices for the lower instance courts. Given space constraints, the present work does not cover the implementation of EU law by other state institutions. In this respect, the application of EU law by the Competition Council would be particularly interesting.[3] For example, it is reported that so far the Competition Council has not been very active in taking decisions based on EU law, even though, as some argue, breaches of EU law are clearly evident.[4] One of the plausible explanations for this state of affairs is that, similarly to state aid practices contrary to EU law, 'Latvia constitutes a small market where in specific economic sectors there is very few or even just one major player, which of course receives the aid and there is no one to challenge that.'[5] An in-depth study of those practices, however, is left outside of the scope of this chapter.[6]

A short overview of the structure of the implementation process of EU law in Latvia and a brief explanation of the Latvian judicial system as well as the place of international law in the domestic legal order will precede the main parts of this chapter.

## 2. THE IMPLEMENTATION OF EU LAW INTO THE LATVIAN LEGAL ORDER

Shortly after regaining independence in 1990,[7] Latvia expressed a desire to join the family of the European Communities. The political momentum was there: the Berlin Wall fell down, the Soviet Union belonged to the past, and the United States and Western Europe were – at least *prima facie* – euphoric about the drive of Central and Eastern European countries towards democracy and market economy.

A number of instruments, binding and not, framed the process of gradual *rapprochement* of these emerging democracies to the European Union. In legal terms, Europe Agreements were of outmost importance.[8] They were concluded in the 1990s between the three European Communities, their Member States, on the one side, and countries

---

[2] See also D. Piqani, 'Constitutional Courts in Central and Eastern Europe and their Attitude towards European Integration', 1 *EJLS* (2007) pp. 1-22.

[3] See the official website of the Competition Council at http://www.kp.gov.lv.

[4] See E. Skibele and A. Vitols, 'Latvia', in P.F. Nemitz, ed., *The Effective Application of EU State Aid Procedures: The Role of National Law and Practice* (Alphen aan den Rijn, Kluwer Law International 2007) at p. 288.

[5] *Ibidem.*

[6] In this context, see also D.L. Lutere-Timmele, ed., *Eiropas Savienības tiesību piemērošana: rokasgrāmata praktizējošiem juristiem* [The Application of EU Law: Handbook for Practising Lawyers] (Rīga, Tiesu nama aģentūra 2007) at p. 221.

[7] See 4 May 1990 Declaration on the Restoration of Independence of the Republic of Latvia, adopted by the Supreme Council.

[8] For an academic commentary, see, *inter alia*, A. Mayhew, *Recreating Europe. The European Union's Policy towards Central and Eastern Europe* (Cambridge, Cambridge University Press 1999);

of Central and Eastern Europe, on the other side.[9] It is notable that the early Europe Agreements contained only unilateral declarations of the associated countries as to their EU aspirations. During the famous European Council summit in Copenhagen in 1993, the EU officially recognised the membership aspirations of those countries and its readiness to accept new members once the Copenhagen accession criteria are satisfied.[10] At the same time, the Europe Agreements served as the legal basis for the approximation of laws of the associated countries with *acquis communautaire*.[11]

The approximation process took place pursuant to a variety of documents adopted by the European Union as well as National Plans for Adoption of *Acquis* developed by the applicant countries. At the same time, the European Commission and the bilateral committees zealously oversaw the progress.[12]

Nowadays, as a Member State of the EU, Latvia is under a direct obligation to transpose relevant EU legislation, to give EU law effect and to apply it in the domestic legal environment. The Ministry of Justice is in charge of co-ordination of transposition effort. It is notable that it has taken a number of initiatives aimed at faster and more qualitative transposition process.[13]

In quantitative terms, Latvia is one of the leaders in transposition of EU legislation across the whole EU. When it comes to the internal market *acquis*, according to the data published by the European Commission in early 2009, Latvia is the eighth most successful implementer of EU directives with the transposition deficit of 0.5%. According to the European Commission, by the end of 2008, the transposition backlog amounted to only 5 directives.[14] Such hectic transposition, however, often translates into poor quality of domestic legislation, including partial transposition and scarce language.

It goes without saying that correct transposition and implementation of EU law depends both on the civil service and judiciary, as well as – to a great degree – on the invocation of EU norms by attorneys. It should be taken for granted that in the majority of cases, the national judiciary applies EU norms as already transposed into national legislation, and only in exceptional circumstances, a judge or a clerk will

---

A. Ott and K. Inglis, eds., *Handbook on European Enlargement. A Commentary on the Enlargement Process* (The Hague, T.M.C. Asser Press 2002). See also Chapter 1 in this volume.

[9] See, in relation to Latvia, Europe Agreement establishing an Association between the European Communities and their Member States, of the one part, and the Republic of Latvia, of the other part, *OJ* 1998 L 26/3.

[10] *Bull. EU* 6-1993, point 13.

[11] For an overview of relevant provisions, see, *inter alia*, A. Łazowski, 'Approximation of Laws', in Ott and Inglis, *loc. cit.* n. 8, pp. 631-640.

[12] See M. Maresceau, 'Pre-accession', in M. Cremona, *The Enlargement of the European Union* (Oxford, Oxford University Press 2003) pp. 9-42.

[13] See 'Koncepcija "Par Eiropas Savienības tiesību aktu pārņemšanas un ieviešanas kontroles sistēmu"' [A proposal to establish a control system on transposition and implementation of EU norms], approved by the Cabinet of Ministers on 17 November 2004, Latvijas Vēstnesis, 24 November 2004, 186 (3134), and amendments to this conception of 26 October 2006, Latvijas Vēstnesis, 27 October 2006, 172 (3540).

[14] See European Commission, Internal Market Scoreboard No. 18, December 2008, available at http://ec.europa.eu/internal_market/score/index_en.htm.

undertake a comparative analysis of a disputed norm with other available language versions. This is one of the reasons why the work on correct transposition of EU legal norms is so crucial.


3.    THE APPLICATION OF EU LAW IN DOMESTIC COURTS

3.1.    **Contextual observations**

As in any other new EU Member State, in Latvia the judiciary also received extensive training in EU law and EU matters generally. This training was carried out through different initiatives and with the help of different organisations, such as the TAIEX instrument of the European Commission,[15] the Latvian Judicial Training Centre,[16] the Latvian School of Public Administration[17] and the Continuing Legal Education Centre of the Riga Graduate School of Law.[18] Different areas of EU law have been the main focus in the curriculum programmes of all these institutions. A number of legal publications (but far from sufficient) explaining EU law in Latvian was released.[19]

However, there is a long way to go from theory to practice. Even though one could argue that basic principles on the application of EU law and its interrelationship with national law, such as direct effect or supremacy, are known and accepted as a matter of principle, still there are certain pitfalls in practical implementation by the Latvian judiciary. Even decisions of the Constitutional Court and of the Supreme Court[20] have not been developing in a completely consistent fashion. Still, as will be demonstrated, certain strands of reasoning are detectable.

Compared to previous years, the number of references to EU law and to jurisprudence of the ECJ steadily grows. This does not mean, however, that all judges warmly welcome

---

[15]   See http://taiex.ec.europa.eu.

[16]   See http://www.ltmc.lv. The Latvian Judicial Training Centre was set up in 1995 'with the aim of providing continuing legal education and training, as well as improving the level of professional knowledge and ethics for all judges, court employees, bailiffs and other legal professionals in Latvia.' Latvian Judicial Training Centre, Annual Report 2003, available at http://www.ltmc.lv/g_parskati/2003_annual_report.pdf.

[17]   See http://www.vas.gov.lv/en/?pg=55.

[18]   See http://www.rgsl.edu.lv.

[19]   See, e.g., Lutere-Timmele, *op. cit.* n. 6; B. Broka and S. Džohansens, *Juridiskā analīze un tekstu rakstīšana* [Legal Analysis and Writing] (Rīga, Tiesu nama aģentūra, Otrais papildinātais izdevums 2007); I. Alehno, ed., *Eiropas Savienības tiesību īstenošana Latvijā* [Enforcement of EU Law in Latvia] (Rīga, Latvijas Vēstnesis 2003); I. Alehno et al., eds., *Ievads Eiropas Savienības tiesībās: Tiesu prakse un komentāri* [Introduction to EU Law: Case-Law and Comments] (Rīga, Tiesu nama aģentūra, Otrais papildinātais izdevums 2004); S. Gatawis, ed., *Eiropas tiesības: Mācību līdzeklis* [European Law: Study Book] (Rīga, Latvijas Universitāte, EuroFaculty 2002); N. Reich, *Izprotot Eiropas Savienības tiesības* [Understanding EU Law] (Rīga, Tiesu nama aģentūra 2003).

[20]   The approach towards EU Law at the Senate of the Supreme Court depends on a department of that court. It is acknowledged that the Department of Administrative Cases quite often relies on EU Law, whereas the Department Civil Cases shows the strongest constraint in invoking EU rules.

such a development. A certain degree of reluctance comes as no surprise.[21] As was mentioned in a Latvian weekly legal publication, '[i]t is difficult to foresee how responsive Latvian courts will be against claims, which are based on directives' incidental horizontal or indirect effect. ... [T]his kind of legal argumentation, based on European law, could be unusual for the courts and as everything new slowly and with little enthusiasm acceptable.'[22]

For example, in one of the cases where a claimant based his claim on a directive which was not transposed by the prescribed deadline into the Latvian legal order, a judge ruled that:

> '[i]t should be noted that considering relief for securing a claim, there is no reason to apply the directive ... given that the directive is not introduced into the Latvian legislation and furthermore because the direct application of a directive is ruled out.'[23]

In the other case, decided in early 2005, the Supreme Court confused two European organisations, the Council of Europe and the European Union.[24] Ruling on excessive interest requested by one of the parties, the Supreme Court – at its own guise – referred to the Statute of the Council of Europe and to the Resolution (78)3 of the Committee of Ministers of the Council of Europe relating to penal clauses in civil law.[25] In continuation, the Court said that according to the established case law of the European Court of Justice, national courts are under an obligation to interpret national legislation in light of adopted recommendations, and, therefore, that the principle of indirect effect is applicable also to recommendations.[26] Thus, the Supreme Court first referred to the acts falling under Council of Europe *acquis*, and, second, applied to it the principle of EC law, as developed by the European Court of Justice.

Such lapses in legal reasoning are to a certain extent unavoidable at the stage when the domestic judiciary is learning how to apply EU law. However, it is also important to ensure the express identification of such lapses and their prompt correction by higher instances in the judicial structure.

The importance of correct interpretation and application of EU law by the judiciary cannot be overestimated. It is also imperative that courts – and the Member States –

---

[21] See, e.g., M. Papēde, 'Direktīvu piemērošana tiesās' [Application of Directives in Courts], *Jurista Vārds*, No. 7 (460), 13 February 2007: 'Latvian courts are averse to claims, which are based on application of provisions of directives' [author's translation]. See also Skibele and Vitols, *loc. cit.* n. 4, at pp. 283-289.

[22] E. Broks, 'Zaudējumu atlīdzināšana ceļu satiksmes negadījumos cietušajiem', *Jurista Vārds* No. 13 (416), 28 March 2006.

[23] Decision No. C-2452/17 of 2 January 2007 of the Riga District Court Civil Cases Department, as cited in Papēde, *loc. cit.* n. 21 [author's translation].

[24] Case SKC-48/2005 of the Senate of the Supreme Court [Lursoft database].

[25] Council of Europe, Committee of Ministers, Resolution (78)3 relating to penal clauses in civil law, text available at https://wcd.coe.int.

[26] For example, a reference to ECJ, Case C-322/88 *Salvatore Grimaldi v. Fonds des maladies professionnelles* [1989] *ECR* 4407.

know that the judicial practice which is contrary to EC law may be treated as a breach of EC law and thus lead to state liability.[27]

### 3.1.1.   *The Latvian judicial system*

Before looking at the application of EU law by Latvian courts, a few introductory remarks about the structure of the domestic judicial system seem to be necessary. The Law on Judicial Power[28] provides that 42 ordinary courts are divided into three tiers: District (city) Courts (35), Regional Courts (6) and the Supreme Court. The decisions of the lower courts can be appealed to the higher ranking courts. The Supreme Court Senate (most of the case law surveyed in this chapter emanates from the Senate), which is the highest judicial body in Latvia, acts as the court of cassation appeals (review of the legality of a lower court decision) in cases decided by the Supreme Court Chambers, by Regional Courts and by District (city) Courts.

The Constitutional Court of Latvia [*Latvijas Republikas Satversmes tiesa*] is not an appellate court, as its powers are limited to review of compliance of laws, by-laws and international treaties entered into by Latvia with the Constitution.[29]

In February 2004, a new branch of judiciary started its work – administrative courts. The administrative courts adjudicate complaints concerning the actions of state administration and officials, as well as matters arising from administrative legal relations.

### 3.1.2.   *European and international law in the Latvian legal system*

In the wake of Latvia's accession to the EU, a number of questions pertaining to the constitutionality of Latvian EU membership had to be resolved. The solution came in the shape of amendments to the Constitution [*Satversme*]. The Constitution, which was adopted in the times of the first independence period in 1922, resumed its force in 1993. There were heated debates whether the future Latvian membership in the European Union may affect Articles 1 and 2 of the Constitution. These provisions state that Latvia is an independent and democratic republic and that the sovereign power of the State of Latvia is vested in the people of Latvia. At the end of the day, it was decided that the Latvian EU membership does not put under threat these sacred for Latvia provisions,[30] even though debates in this respect still continue.[31]

---

[27] See ECJ, Case C-129/00 *Commission of the European Communities v. Italian Republic* [2003] *ECR* I-14637; Case C-224/01 *Gerhard Köbler v. Republik Österreich* [2003] *ECR* I-10239; Case C-173/03 *Traghetti del Mediterraneo SpA, in liquidation v. Repubblica italiana* [2006] *ECR* I-5177. See also Lutere-Timmele, *op. cit.* n. 6, at p. 67.

[28] 1993 Likums Par tiesu varu (last amendments in 2008).

[29] See information available at the website of the Court at http://www.satv.tiesa.gov.lv.

[30] See Presentation of the President of the Latvian Constitutional Court Prof. Dr. A. Endzins at the conference 'The Position of Constitutional Courts Following Integration into the European Union', Bled, Slovenia, 30 September-2 October 2004; materials of the conference available at http://www.us-rs.si/en/media/zbornik.pdf.

[31] See A. Albi, *EU Enlargement and the Constitutions of Central and Eastern Europe* (Cambridge, Cambridge University Press 2005) pp. 94-97; A. Ušacka, 'Latvia', in A.E. Kellermann, et al., eds., *The*

Against this background, Article 68 of the Constitution – revised before the EU accession – should be mentioned. Article 68 reads:

'All international agreements, which settle matters that may be decided by the legislative process, shall require ratification by the Saeima.

Upon entering into international agreements, Latvia, with the purpose of strengthening democracy, may delegate a part of its State institutional competencies to international institutions. International agreements in which a part of state institution competencies are delegated to international institutions may be ratified by the Saeima ...

Membership of Latvia in the European Union shall be decided by a national referendum, which is proposed by the Saeima.

Substantial changes in the terms regarding the membership of Latvia in the European Union shall be decided by a national referendum if such referendum is requested by at least one-half of the members of the Saeima.'

One should note that the Treaty of Lisbon[32] was ratified by the Latvian parliament (*Saeima*) in June 2008. No referendum was called. One of the often-heard explanations was that before the accession to the EU, the Constitutional Treaty had already been finalised and thus – by approving the EU membership – the sovereign (that is, the nation) implicitly also approved the Treaty establishing a Constitution for Europe.[33] Therefore, the procedure for ratification of the Lisbon Treaty – the successor of the Constitutional Treaty – was the same as the procedure which would have taken place had the Constitutional Treaty not been rejected by the French and Dutch population. This decision, of course, has to be judged in Latvia's political-constitutional and economic contexts, as well as against its full adherence to the democratic values.

The question of the place of EU law in the Latvian legal order has been answered within the usual matrix of place and role of public international law in the domestic legal order. As has been shown, this is first and foremost the Constitution (Art. 68), which provides basic rules about the status of international law in Latvia. In addition, pursuant to Article 13 of the 1994 Law on International Agreements,[34] where an international agreement approved by the *Saeima* provides for rules which differ from those laid down in Latvian legislation, the provisions of the international agreement are applicable. In the same vein, the Law on the Constitutional Court (Arts. 16(2) and 16(6)) states that national norms should comply with international agreements entered into by Latvia, whereas the latter should comply with the Constitution.[35]

---

*Impact of EU Accession on the Legal Orders of New EU Member States and (Pre-)Candidate Countries* (The Hague, T.M.C. Asser Press 2006) pp. 369-385. See also Chapter 3 in this volume.

[32] Treaty of Lisbon amending the Treaty on European Union and the Treaty establishing the European Community, *OJ* 2007 C 306/1.

[33] Treaty establishing a Constitution for Europe, *OJ* 2004 C 310/1.

[34] 13 January 1994. likums Par Latvijas Republikas starptautiskajiem līgumiem, published in Latvijas Vēstnesis, 26 January 1994, No. 11 (142) (with 2004 amendments).

[35] On interpretation, different from mainstream interpretation of place of international law in the Latvian legal system, see Dissenting Opinion of the Constitutional Court Justice Juris Jelāgins in case No. 2004-01-06, available at http://www.satv.tiesa.gov.lv/upload/2004-01-06_atsev.rtf, where the Justice, *inter*

According to the amendments to the Administrative Procedure Law,[36] which were adopted in 2004 shortly before Latvia joined the EU, 'the legal norms of the European Union (Community) shall be applied in accordance with their place in the hierarchy of legal force of external regulatory enactments. In applying the legal norms of the European Union (Community), institutions and courts shall take into account European Court of Justice case-law' (Art. 15(4) APL). Similar amendments of 2004 to the Civil Procedure Law[37] prescribe a legal duty of courts to adjudicate in civil matters 'in accordance with laws and other regulatory enactments, international agreements binding upon Latvia and the EU legal norms' (Art. 5(1) CPL). The principle of supremacy of EU law is embodied in Article 5(3) CPL, which stipulates, 'if the relevant issue is regulated by legal norms of the European Union, which are directly applicable in Latvia, the Latvian law shall apply insofar as the legal norms of the European Union allow it.' It is not quite clear, though, what the legislator had in mind by inserting the words 'which are directly applicable in Latvia' and whether 'direct applicability' is used (or not) as a synonym to 'direct effect.'[38] Do the words 'norms of the European Union, which are directly applicable in Latvia' mean that a certain portion of EU law is refused a status of 'supreme norms' to conflicting Latvian rules? It will be interesting to see how this provision will be interpreted by the domestic courts.

The rule of supremacy of international law over conflicting national provisions has been confirmed by the case law as well. Thus, in one of its cases, the Constitutional Court stressed that 'the person applying legal norms, also the court, when establishing discrepancy between the international legal norm and the national legal norm of Latvia, shall apply the international legal norm.'[39]

This embedment of the priority of international norms in national law and case law does not mean that there is unconditional acceptance of and submission to EU law in its entirety.[40] Some scholars do not exclude the possibility that one day the Constitutional Court may reach its own "Maastricht decision", referring to the famous decision of the German Constitutional Court. As Professor Endzins, former president of the Latvian Constitutional Court, wrote:

'[T]he higher force of the EU acts is not absolute. The EU is not a state; it has no sovereignty of its own. EU has only these competencies, which the Member States have delegated to it and only in the amount the EU has received. If the EU passes legal acts, which do not follow from the essence of the EU or which may endanger, e.g., the existence of the

---

*alia,* argued (para. 4) that 'The international agreement and the law by which it has been ratified may not be of differing legal force. There are of equal legal force.'

[36] Published in Latvijas Vēstnesis, 23 January 2004, No. 12 (2960).

[37] Published in Latvijas Vēstnesis, 23 April 2004, No. 64 (3012).

[38] On discussion on the scope of terms "direct effect" and "direct applicability", see Ch. Hilson and T. Downes, 'Making sense of rights: Community rights in EC law', 24 *ELRev.* (1999) pp. 121-138.

[39] Case 2004-01-06 of the Constitutional Court of Latvia, decision of 7 July 2004, available at http://www.satv.tiesa.gov.lv/upload/2004-01-06E.rtf, para. 6.

[40] See, e.g., presentation of the former President of the Latvian Constitutional Court Prof. Dr. A. Endzins, where it was voiced that 'even in case if the constitutionality of the process of accession is not challenged at the Constitutional Court, it sooner or later will have to solve the issue on the interaction of different EU acts with the Latvian legal norms', *loc. cit.* n. 30.

Latvian statehood or democracy, then the Republic of Latvia Satversme and not the above acts shall be applied. ... [T]*he national constitutional norms ... do not have and cannot have a lower legal force than the EU documents.*'⁴¹

Indeed, in the recent case decided by the Constitutional Court in January 2008, the Court explicitly stated the limits of EU law in Latvia. That is, Latvia is under an obligation to interpret domestic laws in a way that does not contradict the obligations taken *vis-à-vis* the EU, 'to the extent that these obligations do not encroach upon main principles of the Latvian Constitution [Satversme].'⁴² Against this background, it will be interesting to follow how the Latvian judiciary will apply the doctrine of supremacy of EU law.

### 3.2. Getting ready for EU membership: pre-accession case law

Even prior to Latvia's accession to the EU, domestic courts had referred to EU law and its principles, as well as to case law of the European Court of Justice. These references, however, were not – as they could not be – the basis for courts' rulings. In the words of the Supreme Court, at the pre-accession stage, Latvian courts could resort to ECJ case law only 'as a source of historical and systemic interpretation.'⁴³ A number of cases from the Constitutional Court of Latvia illustrate well this kind of mind-set and practice.

Thus, in 2003, in a case where the Constitutional Court was asked a question on the compatibility of the Latvian Election Law with the Constitution, the Court – on its own initiative – invoked the necessity to look at the compliance of the law with higher standards from the point of view of the state based on a rule of law, whereas the examples for the Court in this context were clearly the EU Member States.⁴⁴ The Court held:

> '6. ... In accordance with the Europe Agreement on the creation of association between the European Community and Member States [and Latvia] ... which in Latvia has taken effect on February 1, 1998, Latvia has expressed its will to become a Member State of the European Union. On December 13, 2002 in Copenhagen at the European Summit of the European Union Latvia received an official invitation to join the European Union. ... In conformity

---

⁴¹ *Ibidem.*

⁴² Case 2007-11-03 of the Constitutional Court of Latvia, decision of 17 January 2008, available at http://www.satv.tiesa.gov.lv/upload/2007-11-03_ostas%20lieta.htm, para. 25.4 [author's translation and emphasis]. For more on this case, see section 3.5 of this chapter.

⁴³ Case SKA-216/2004 of the Administrative Cases Department of the Senate of the Supreme Court, [Lursoft database], para. 10. In this case, the complainant submitted a cassation complaint against the decision of the administrative Regional Court, saying that the court applied ECJ case law as an applicable legal norm. The Supreme Court, however, disagreed with the complainant. See also Case SKA-222/2004 of the Administrative Cases Department of the Senate of the Supreme Court [Lursoft database], para. 5.5. (on the use of the trademark 'Niveja Dzintars', as registered by the Latvian company Dzintars and challenged by Beiersdorf AG, the owner of the NIVEA brand).

⁴⁴ Case No. 2002-18-01, judgment of the Constitutional Court of 5 March 2003, available at http://www.satv.tiesa.gov.lv/upload/2002-18-01E.rtf.

with the Association Agreement one of the fundamental assignments is gradual integration of Latvia into the European Union. And it – inter alia – is connected with implementation of adequate political reforms in Latvia. Thus – it means also legislative alignment. The legal norms of the European Union shall be approximated only with such national legal system, which meets the requirements of democratic states based on the rule of law.'

The Court's decision seems to suggest that as a state with EU aspirations, Latvia had to examine domestic laws not only within a tight timeframe that was available, but also from a broader perspective, that is, from the point of view of a country that was already based on the rule of law and not merely hoping to reach that stage in an undefined future.

In one of the cases decided in mid-2003, a complainant challenged a provision of the Civil Procedure Law, according to which natural persons could only proceed with cassation requests by themselves or when assisted by an attorney – thus excluding representatives of other legal professions, who were not members of the Latvian Bar.[45] It was argued that the contested provision was contrary to the Latvian Constitution. The Court referred to the Council Directive 2002/8/EC as an additional – but not a principal – basis for its argumentation.[46] The judges urged the Latvian legislature to bring domestic law in line with the EC Directive. They explained this urge in the following manner: unless such approximation takes place, the discrepancy will result in discrimination of Latvian citizens in comparison with citizens of other EU Member States, who are entitled to receive legal aid from representatives of different legal professions.[47] Such a discrimination of Latvia's own population seemed unacceptable to the Court.

Another judgment which merits attention was rendered shortly after the ruling discussed above.[48] The difference between two legal professions – legal representative [pārstāvis] and attorney [advokāts] – was at the heart of the matter. The Criminal Procedure Law (CPL) provided that only Latvian attorneys could plead in criminal cases (Art. 96 CPL). The claimant argued that the provision in question was in contradiction to Article 92 of the Latvian Constitution, which guarantees the right to timely, quality and affordable legal aid. The Constitutional Court ruled that it was incumbent on the legislature to take into account requirements of EU law, in order to secure that at the time of Latvian accession to the EU, domestic legal norms corresponded to EU acquis. The Court stressed the paramount importance of the freedom to provide services in the EU. In light of this, the challenged legislation would have created obstacles to that freedom of the internal market. Therefore, the Court advised the Latvian law-

---

[45] Case 2003-09-01 of the Constitutional Court of Latvia, decision of 27 June 2003, available at http://www.satv.tiesa.gov.lv.

[46] Council Directive 2002/8/EC of 27 January 2003 to improve access to justice in cross-border disputes by establishing minimum common rules relating to legal aid for such disputes, *OJ* 2003 L 26/41.

[47] *Ibidem,* para. 5.

[48] Case 2003-08-01 of the Constitutional Court of 6 October 2003, available at http://www.satv.tiesa.gov.lv.

maker to bring – at the earliest possibility – the legislation in question in compliance with relevant EC *acquis*.[49]

Following this historical path, one should also mention a dissenting opinion of three judges of the Latvian Constitutional Court presented in 2000. The case was about compliance of the Latvian electoral law with the CPHRs.[50] The following paragraph of the Opinion merits particular attention:

'When starting its talks about joining the European Union, Latvia has undertaken the obligation to observe the interpretation of legal norms, acknowledged by democratic states. To observe regulations expressed in Articles 69 and 70 of the June 12, 1995 Latvia-European Union Association Treaty [duty of approximation of the Latvian laws to the EU *acquis* (author's remark)], Latvia shall not only approximate the texts of its normative acts with the texts of legal norms of the European Union, but also adopt the Western legal theory, namely, the legal thinking. Only then the legislation, approximated on the content level, will function in the same way as in the European Union. Unified legal understanding in the European tradition and legal manner is one of the preconditions of functioning of the European Union.'

First, it is remarkable that even though the case did not deal directly with EU law as such, the judges *ex officio* addressed the question of impact of EU law on the Latvian legal order. Similarly to Case 2002-18-01[51] (referred to earlier in this chapter), the Court set up a high threshold for interpretation of EU law, meaning the interpretation of legal norms, as acknowledged by states which, first, are democratic, and, second, are based on the rule of law. Second, instead of referring directly to the concepts which were elaborated by the ECJ, the judges merely alluded to "Western legal thinking."[52] Though this was only a dissenting opinion, and, as such, was not a binding precedent, it demonstrated that there was a new trend – among some of the judges of the Constitutional Court – in the perception of EU-related implications on the Latvian legal theory. It demonstrates that even before the accession, there was a group of judges ready to transpose "Western legal thinking" to the Latvian legal theory.

---

[49] *Ibidem,* para. 6. See, e.g., Case 2002-21-01 of the Constitutional Court of Latvia, decision of 20 May 2003, available at http://www.satv.tiesa.gov.lv. In this case, the claimant challenged an age limit for academic professions. The Constitutional Court referred, *inter alia*, to Directive 2000/78/EC, which provides for prohibition of direct and non-direct discrimination in employment and occupation (Council Directive 2000/78/EC of 27 November 2000 establishing a general framework for equal treatment in employment and occupation, *OJ* 2000 L 303/16). However, the Court referred to the Directive as one of the examples of trends in EU Law, but did not use it as the prime basis for its argumentation. See also Case 2002-16-03 of the Constitutional Court of Latvia, decision of 24 December 2002, para. 1; Case 2003-12-01 of the Constitutional Court of Latvia, decision of 18 December 2003, para. 7; all available at http://www.satv.tiesa.gov.lv.

[50] Dissenting Opinions of the Constitutional Court justices A. Endziņš, J. Jelāgins and A. Ušacka in case No. 2000-03-01, http://www.satv.tiesa.gov.lv/Eng/Spriedumi/03-01(opinions).htm.

[51] *Loc. cit.* n. 44.

[52] A. Łazowski speaks about 'pro-European interpretation of domestic law'; see A. Łazowski, 'Approximation of Laws', in Ott and Inglis, eds., *op. cit.* n. 8, at p. 636. See also C. Hillion, 'Case C-162/00 Land Nordrhein-Westfalen v. Beata Pokrzeptowicz-Meyer', 40 *CMLRev.* (2003) pp. 465-491, at p. 486.

## 3.3.    The application of EU law and ECJ case law to pre-accession facts

### 3.3.1.    *The application of EU law to pre-accession facts*

In the years following Latvia's accession to the EU, case law – especially in higher courts – dealt mainly with facts which had taken place before the enlargement. However, that trend is naturally changing, and in the last few years, we have also witnessed the first wave of truly post-accession cases. However, in this domain case law is still scarce. This explains why the bulk of analysis that follows will cover post-accession cases with pre-accession factual background.

The main axiom is that EU law, at least in purely formal terms, did not apply to pre-accession facts. This finding, to some extent, is also supported by the case law of the European Court of Justice. In case C-302/04 *Ynos v. Varga*,[53] the ECJ concurred with the opinion of Hungary and the European Commission and ruled that:

> '[t]he Court has jurisdiction to interpret the Directive only as regards its application in a new Member State with effect from the date of that State's accession to the European Union.'[54]

The straight-forward application of this principle in Latvia can be illustrated by the following case. Mr. L. Zigurds was accused of illegal trafficking of sugar from Estonia to Latvia in 2002. The first instance court, which rendered a judgment in November 2004, found the perpetrator guilty as charged. It based the decision on customs legislation applicable at the time of deliberations. In fact, it was a piece of post-accession law, incorporating relevant EC customs *acquis*. On appeal, the Regional Court overruled the decision of the first instance court. The Regional Court held that the case at hand should have been analysed pursuant to law applicable at the time the facts had taken place. On a cassation appeal, the Supreme Court upheld the decision of the Regional Court. Hence, the Supreme Court endorsed the rule that EU law, which became binding upon Latvia's entry to the EU, did not apply retroactively.[55]

An example of the classical application of EU law can be illustrated by case *I.M. v. SIA Domenikss*.[56] The complainant argued that a provision of an employment contract she had concluded with her ex-employer in February 2003 was contrary to Article 39 EC. Pursuant to the contested clause, the plaintiff was not allowed to take up employment in the period of two years upon termination of the contract in any potentially competing company based in Latvia, Lithuania and Estonia. The Regional Court con-

---

[53] ECJ, Case C-302/04 *Ynos Kft. v. János Varga* [2006] *ECR* I-371. See also ECJ, Case C-261/05 *Lakép kft, Pár-Bau kft and Rottelma kft v. Komáron-Esztergom Megyei Közigazgatási Hivatal* [2006] *ECR* I-20; Case C-168/06 *Ceramika Paradyż sp. z oo v. Dyrektor Izby Skarbowej w Łodzi* [2007] *ECR* I-29. For a critical appraisal see, *inter alia*, N. Półtorak, 'Ratione temporis application of the preliminary rulings procedure', 45 *CMLRev.* (2008) pp. 1357-1381. See also Chapters 4 and 5 in this volume.

[54] ECJ, Case C-302/04 *Ynos Kft. v. János Varga, loc. cit.* n. 53, paras. 36-37.

[55] Case SKK-222/2005 of the Criminal Cases Department of the Senate of the Supreme Court [Lursoft database].

[56] As cited in SKC-6, decision of the Civil Cases Department of the Senate of the Supreme Court of 9 January 2008 [Lursoft database].

curred with I.M. and found, *inter alia*, that restrictions as to future employment in other EU Member States fell short of their compliance with Article 39 EC and the principle of free movement of workers laid down therein.

### 3.3.2. *The application of directives to pre-accession facts*

The landmark case on application of directives and domestic implementing measures to pre-accession facts is case SKC-87. The Supreme Court rendered the judgment in 2007.[57] The factual background of the case can be briefly summarised as follows. In 2002, a person died as a result of a traffic accident. An insurance company refused to pay insurance indemnity claiming that a person whose actions led to the accident was – at the given time – under the influence of alcohol. The Court of Appeal, which rendered its decision in 2005, relied on three EC directives on civil liability[58] as well as case law of the European Court of Justice.[59] The Supreme Court reversed the decision of the Court of Appeal. In its decision, the Supreme Court noted that the directives, on which the lower court based the decision, were implemented in the new Law on the Mandatory Insurance of the Drivers' Civil Liability. It entered into force only on 7 April 2007, several years after the accident had taken place. Accordingly, the Supreme Court held that the courts had the obligation to apply the law applicable at the time of the accident. In terms of reliance on EU law, the Supreme Court argued that 'the application of Community directives is admissible only after Latvia joined the European Union.'[60] Regrettably, the Supreme Court failed to elaborate on whether domestic courts were allowed to refer to ECJ case law on interpretation of the relevant directives in the period between the transposition of directives and Latvia's accession to the EU.

However, the practice of application of directives does not develop in a uniform manner. In an earlier case, decided in September 2004,[61] the facts of which had taken place in 2003, the Supreme Court found it appropriate to rely directly on Directive 89/665/EEC.[62] The judgment was rendered against the following factual background. A state authority – Latvian State Forests Authority – challenged a decision of the

[57] Case SKC-87, Civil Cases Department of the Senate of the Supreme Court [Lursoft database].

[58] Council Directive 72/166/EEC of 24 April 1972 on the approximation of the laws of Member States relating to insurance against civil liability in respect to the use of motor vehicles, and to the enforcement of the obligation to insure against such liability, *OJ English Special Edition*, Series I, Chapter (II) 1972 p. 360; Second Council Directive 84/5/EEC of 30 December 1983 on the approximation of the laws of the Member States relating to insurance against civil liability in respect to the use of motor vehicles, *OJ* 1984 L 8/17; Third Council Directive 90/232/EEC of 14 May 1990 on the approximation of the laws of the Member States relating to insurance against civil liability in respect to the use of motor vehicles, *OJ* 1990 L 129/33.

[59] ECJ, C-537/03 *Katja Candolin v. Vahinkovakuutusosakeyhtiö Pohjola & Jarno Ruokoranta* [2005] *ECR* I-5745.

[60] *Ibidem* [translation by the author].

[61] Case SKA-210/2004, Administrative Cases Department of the Senate of the Supreme Court [Lursoft database], para. 11.

[62] Council Directive 89/665/EEC of 21 December 1989 on the co-ordination of the laws, regulations and administrative provisions relating to the application of review procedures to the award of public supply and public works contracts, *OJ* 1989 L 395/33.

Procurement Monitoring Bureau (PMB, also a state authority). The Supreme Court based its decision exclusively on Article 8(2) of the Directive,[63] disregarding the fact that it was a pre-accession dispute and thus the applicability of the Directive could have been questioned. The Supreme Court did not inquire whether the version of the Latvian law in question (the Procurement Law), which had been in force when the facts giving rise to the dispute had taken place, had already contained provisions tailored to transpose the Directive. One more observation should be made. The Supreme Court merely cited the relevant provision of the Directive and, at the same time, did not find it important to clarify the renumbering of treaty provisions provided by the Treaty of Amsterdam.[64] Alas, the Supreme Court referred to Article 177 EEC, instead of Article 234 EC. This omission may be explained as a technical failure, but it is in some sense symbolic and a good example of the "easy-go" approach sometimes embarked upon by courts in the application of EU law.

In another case, decided in 2008, the Administrative Regional Court ruled that it could not apply the Sixth VAT Directive[65] to facts which had taken place before the accession and that the plaintiff accordingly could not directly rely on that Directive.[66] Interestingly enough, on a cassation appeal the applicant argued that it did not seek to rely directly on provisions of the Directive, but rather on writings of specialists, who already in the pre-accession period had argued that the Directive in question was binding upon Latvia.[67] To much regret, the court hearing the request for cassation, did not address this argument.

### 3.3.3.    The application of ECJ case law to pre-accession facts

The situation is not as straightforward with the application and reliance on ECJ case law to facts which had taken place in the pre-accession period. The following examples demonstrate how, over time, the Supreme Court changed and qualitatively developed the reasoning on application of ECJ jurisprudence. Thus, if in the first years after the accession, we see bold references to ECJ case law, without explanation what is the legal rationale for the Supreme Court to rely on ECJ case law, then in the last couple of years, the Supreme Court explains why it considers it possible and indeed important to invoke the jurisprudence of the European Court of Justice.

---

[63] Art. 8(2) reads '[w]here bodies responsible for review procedures are not judicial in character, written reasons for their decisions shall always be given. Furthermore, in such a case, provision must be made to guarantee procedures whereby any allegedly illegal measure taken by the review body or any alleged defect in the exercise of the powers conferred on it can be the subject of judicial review or review by another body which is a court or tribunal within the meaning of Article 177 of the EEC Treaty and independent of both the contracting authority and the review body.'

[64] Treaty of Amsterdam amending the Treaty on European Union, the Treaties establishing the European Communities and certain related acts, OJ 1997 C 340/1.

[65] Council Directive 77/388/EEC of 17 May 1977 on the harmonisation of the laws of the Member States relating to turnover taxes – Common system of value-added tax: uniform basis of assessment, OJ 1977 L 145/1.

[66] As cited in Case AA43-0154-08, Administrative Regional Court [Lursoft database], para. 5.15.

[67] Ibidem, para. 7.2.

In case SKA-195/2004[68] the Supreme Court relied on ECJ jurisprudence on the Sixth VAT Directive. The Directive itself had been transposed into the Latvian legal order before the accession. The fact that the events, which gave rise to the dispute, had taken place before Latvia joined the EU was of no significance to the Court.[69] A similar situation repeated in a decision of the Supreme Court in case SKA-0094-05.[70] This time the plaintiff – service provider SIA NEMO PARKS – requested a judicial review of a decision of the State Revenue Service (SRS) on the application of the VAT tax. The contested decision also imposed a fine for breach of the tax legislation. The alleged breach had taken place before the accession to the European Union. The Supreme Court – handling a cassation appeal – invoked ECJ case law in support of its findings. It held that pursuant to that case law, the application of 0% tax rate should be treated as an exception and thus should be interpreted in a narrow fashion.[71] However, the Supreme Court did not elaborate on the legal basis for relying on ECJ case law.

A decision of the Supreme Court in case SKA-0302-05 (also rendered in 2005) was a step forward. The Court again based its analysis on ECJ case law, but this time it hinted on the reasons for doing so. It held:

> '[W]hereas EU (Community) legal norms are not directly applicable in Latvia to the administrative acts issued before 1 May 2004, the decisions of the European Court of Justice should be used in the process of interpretation of norms transposed from the EU law into national law by means of historical and teleological interpretation.'[72]

A more sophisticated approach was taken by the Supreme Court in 2006. In case SKA-0083-06, the facts of which had taken place in 2002, the Senate affirmed the decision of a lower instance court to the extent that jurisprudence on the Sixth VAT Directive was applicable to the case at hand.[73] In contrast to the previous judgments, the Supreme Court provided a more extensive explanation for its decision. The Court argued that since the facts had taken place before the accession, Latvia had been – pursuant to the

---

[68] Case SKA-195/2004, Administrative Cases Department of the Senate of the Supreme Court [Lusoft database].

[69] *Ibidem*, para. 11.2.

[70] Case SKA-0094-05, Administrative Cases Department of the Senate of the Supreme Court [Lursoft database].

[71] *Ibidem*, paras. 10-11. See also Case SKA-0233-05, Administrative Cases Department of the Senate of the Supreme Court [Lusoft database], para.12. Although the case as such did not touch upon EU Law, still, the Court considered it appropriate to refer to the ECJ's judgment. In *Asmers* case (Case 2004-10-01 of the Constitutional Court of Latvia, decision of 17 January 2002), where the claimant argued that settlement of a dispute by the way of arbitration does not guarantee a 'fair trial', as the Latvian Constitution provides it (Art. 92). In its decision, the Constitutional Court invoked also the Latvian Consumer Protection Law, which partially incorporated the Council Directive 93/13/EC (Council Directive 93/13/EEC of 5 April 1993 on unfair terms in consumer contracts, *OJ* 1993 L 95/29) and its interpretation by the ECJ (see para. 9.3.2. of the judgment).

[72] Case SKA-0302-05, Administrative Cases Department of the Senate of the Supreme Court [Lursoft database], para. 11 [author's translation]. This case touched upon interpretation of the Latvian Procurement Law, which implements a number of EC directives in this area.

[73] Case SKA-0083-06, Administrative Cases Department of the Senate of the Supreme Court [Lursoft database].

EA Latvia – under an obligation to approximate its domestic laws with *acquis communautaire*. The 2002 amendments to the Latvian Law on Value Added Tax had been tailored to approximate the Latvian laws with the Sixth VAT Directive. This led the Supreme Court to the conclusion that in its interpretation of the Latvian law in question, it was entitled to rely on the ECJ's interpretation of the Sixth VAT Directive.[74]

A similar approach can be seen in another decision of the Supreme Court rendered in 2006. In case SKA-0129-06, the Court had to address an important competition law issue.[75] The facts dated back to 2003, when a private company filed an action against the Riga Stock Exchange (RSE), arguing that the RSE was a monopoly, which by imposing a relatively high membership fee, abused its dominant position. The submission was first made in 2003 to the Competition Council, which dismissed the claim. Following a judgment of the Administrative Regional Court, a cassation appeal was submitted to the Supreme Court. The latter upheld the contested decision and reasoned in the following way. First, it reiterated that the relevant provision of the Latvian Competition Law was analogous to Article 82(a) EC. Second, given the close resemblance of two provisions, the Court, in evaluating the legality of the challenged decision of the Competition Council, was entitled to rely on EU institutions' application of Article 82 EC. Third, the Supreme Court emphasised Latvia's obligation – based on the Europe Agreement – to approximate domestic law to that of the European Communities. This was particularly the case in the area of competition law (Art. 70 EA Latvia). Fourth, the Supreme Court turned attention to an annotation annexed to a Draft Competition Law, which made it clear that the aim of the bill was to fill in gaps in Latvian Competition Law and to bring it in line with *acquis communautaire*. Accordingly, held the Supreme Court, the lower court was correct to rely on the practice of the European Commission and of the European Court of Justice.[76]

In the same vein, the Supreme Court proceeded in 2006 in case SKA-149/2006, which is generally considered to be one of the most important competition cases ever in Latvia.[77] Kempmayer Media Limited (Kempmayer) challenged a decision of the Latvian Competition Council condemning Kempmayer's anti-competitive actions in the period preceding the accession to the European Union. The Supreme Court stressed that already before the accession, the Latvian competition law implemented the principles enshrined by Article 81 EC. Therefore, the relevant provisions of the domestic law had to be interpreted in the light of Article 81 EC. The following *dictum* of the Supreme Court is instructive:

'[D]eciding the cases, facts of which occurred before Latvia joined the European Union, the court, taking into account the [exercise of] approximation of Latvian legislation to the Community Law, *can* use ECJ's practice in the process of interpretation of national norms. In such cases, however, *this is the right of the court* [to rely on ECJ's case-law], *not a duty*.'[78]

---

[74] *Ibidem*, paras. 10-13.
[75] Case SKA-0129-06, Administrative Cases Department of the Senate of the Supreme Court [Lursoft database].
[76] *Ibidem*, paras. 9.1-9.2.
[77] Case SKA-149/2006, Administrative Cases Department of the Senate of the Supreme Court [Lursoft database].
[78] *Ibidem*, para. 11.1., author's translation [emphasis added].

The presented examples illustrate what seems to be an established approach of the Supreme Court to the relevance of ECJ case law in pre-accession cases. While EU law as such was not applicable before the enlargement, the case law of the ECJ, especially provisions approximating the Latvian legal order with EU law, could, nevertheless, be of relevance for the interpretation of domestic law.[79] This, accordingly, opened the possibility to the national courts to rely on ECJ case law in the interpretation of domestic norms worded similarly to EU provisions. Yet, it doesn't mean that Latvian courts always clarify the legal basis for their reliance on ECJ case law. The judgment of the Supreme Court in case SKA-162/2007 is a good illustration to this end.[80] It dealt with the liability for submission of false declaration on counterfeited goods in the pre-accession period. The Supreme Court reiterated its earlier finding that ECJ case law is applicable using both the historical and systemic methods of interpretation of legal norms.[81] The Supreme Court stressed great similarity between the facts of the case at hand and of the ECJ case, as invoked by one of the parties. The Supreme Court accordingly applied the test developed by the ECJ to its own decision.[82] However, a big similarity between the facts in two cases, where one took place in Latvia in the pre-accession period and the other gave rise to the ECJ judgment, hardly qualifies as a valid legal ground for full reliance on ECJ case law. With the same degree of success, the Supreme Court could have possibly relied on a decision of US or Australian courts. There were definitely much stronger arguments for the Supreme Court to call precisely upon ECJ jurisprudence, but – as already mentioned – they are non-existent in the judgment in question. The Supreme Court either assumes that these reasons are self-evident to the parties – which is a rather naïve presumption – or, by not elaborating on reasons for its approach, the Court is simply trying to expedite the proceedings. If this is the case, under no circumstances it is a legitimate justification for the scarcity of arguments employed by the Supreme Court.

### 3.4.    The interpretation of domestic law in light of directives during transposition periods

The question of interpretation of Latvian law in the light of an EC directive during the transposition period arose in two cases with very similar factual backgrounds. In both cases judgments were rendered by the Supreme Court in 2005.[83] Russian citizens, holders of the Latvian permanent residence permits issued in the 1990s and in the first years of this century, had their applications for renewal rejected. Arguably, the periods of

---

[79] See also A. Buka, 'Indivīda iespējas izmantot Eiropas Savienīabs tiesības' in Alehno, *op. cit.* n. 19, at p. 37.

[80] Case SKA-162/2007, Administrative Cases Department of the Senate of the Supreme Court [Lursoft database].

[81] Case SKA-216/2004, *loc. cit.* n. 43.

[82] SKA-162/2007, Administrative Cases Department of the Senate of the Supreme Court [Lursoft database], paras. 9-11.

[83] Case SKA-46/2005 and Case SKA-0024-05, Administrative Cases Department of the Senate of the Supreme Court [Lursoft database].

residence outside Latvia exceeded the time limit of four years established by the Latvian legislation. This fell under EC Directive 2003/109/EC dealing with the rights of third-country nationals who are long-term residents.[84] At the time the Directive was in force, however, the transposition period was still pending.[85] In both cases, the Supreme Court stressed that during a transposition period, domestic courts are entitled to apply such a directive for the purposes of interpretation of domestic law.[86] Therefore, the Supreme Court decided to refer to two provisions of the Directive in question. First, it referred to Article 9(5), which deals with the Member States' obligation to provide for a facilitated procedure for the reacquisition of long-term resident status. Second, the Supreme Court relied on Article 9(4), which releases the Member States from the obligation to grant long-term resident status after six years of absence from the territory of that state.[87] Interestingly enough, the Supreme Court – possibly due to the sensitivity of the situation[88] – held that upon the expiry of the transposition deadline, it will be up to the Office of Citizenship and Migration Affairs to answer the question whether claimants will be entitled to hold residence in similar cases.[89] In the meantime, the Directive was implemented by the Law on Long-term EC Resident Status in Latvia.[90] What is important, though, is that some organisations – for instance, the Latvian Centre for Human Rights – argue that the domestic law does not comply fully with the requirements of the Directive. It seems that especially Article 9(4) (cited above) of the Directive has not been duly transposed.[91] This point is rebutted by the Latvian Ministry of Interior – the drafter of the legislation. It remains to be seen whether such partial and controversial transposition will lead to further litigation. One could potentially consider state liability claims based on the Francovich line of case law.[92]

## 3.5. EU law as an inherent part of the Latvian legal order

The decision of the Constitutional Court of 17 January 2008 to a great extent can be seen as a turning point in the national jurisprudence on treatment of EU law by the Latvian courts.[93] The case, in which the plaintiff challenged as unconstitutional the

---

[84] Council Directive 2003/109/EC of 25 November 2003 concerning the status of third-country nationals who are long-term residents, *OJ* 2004 L 16/44.

[85] The Member States had the obligation to transpose the Directive before January 2006.

[86] Case SKA-46, para. 23, Case SKA-0024-05, para. 24.

[87] *Ibidem.*

[88] A considerable part of the population living in Latvia is of Russian origin and holds long-term or permanent resident status.

[89] *Ibidem.*

[90] 22 June 2006. likums 'Par Eiropas Kopienas pastāvīgā iedzīvotāja statusu Latvijas Republikā' (Latvijas Vēstnesis, 107 (3475), 07 July 2006.), in force since 21 July 2006.

[91] See Informatīva atsauce uz Eiropas Savienības direktīvu [Informative reference to the directive in elaborating the Draft Law].

[92] ECJ, Joined Cases C-6/90 & 9/90 *Andrea Francovich and Danila Bonifaci and others v. Italian Republic* [1991] *ECR* I-5357.

[93] Case 2007-11-03 of the Constitutional Court of Latvia, decision of 17 January 2008, available at http://www.satv.tiesa.gov.lv/upload/2007-11-03_ostas%20lieta.htm.

construction plans for the Riga free port territory (which comprises protected areas, known in Europe as *NATURA 2000* areas), at first sight did not promise invocation of any EU norms.[94] Despite this seeming irrelevance of EU law, the Constitutional Court broadly relied on EU law norms and principles and their interpretation by the European Court of Justice. The Constitutional Court referred to Latvia's official annotation to the Act of Accession,[95] whereby Latvia particularly stressed that upon joining the EU, the application of European Union law will have a major positive effect on the Latvian environment, where Latvia will take over the long-term experience and developed legislative practice in the field of protection of environment by the old EU Member States.[96] The Constitutional Court ruled:

> 'By ratifying the Treaty of Accession of Latvia to the European Union, the European Union law became an inherent part of the Latvian law. Therefore the EU legal acts and the interpretation by the European Court of Justice is to be taken into account in the process of application of domestic legislative acts.'[97]

The Constitutional Court particularly stressed the fact that the Latvian's obligation to protect its own environment is part of the common responsibility of all EU Member States as the Latvian environment is a constitutive part of the common European inheritance.[98] However, as was stressed earlier, the Court, nonetheless, did not miss the opportunity to emphasise the limits of EU law in Latvia. The Constitutional Court held that Latvia is under an obligation to interpret domestic laws in a way that does not contradict her obligations taken *vis-à-vis* the EU but only to the extent that these obligations do not encroach upon main principles of the Latvian Constitution.[99]

## 3.6.    Duty to rely on ECJ case law

The absolute duty of the domestic courts to rely on and to invoke ECJ jurisprudence was spelled out by the Supreme Court in case SKC-67/2007.[100] The plaintiff challenged different payments made to male and female employees providing the same kind of work for the same employer. The Supreme Court correctly said that the legal basis for the equal work and equal pay principle in the EU is Article 141 EC. It also reiterated the complainant's argument that Directive 75/117/EEC[101] and the relevant ECJ case law were equally important. The Supreme Court referred to Article 5(6) of the

---

[94] The norm relied upon by the claimant was Art. 115 of the Constitution [*Satversme*], which reads: 'The state protects everyone's right to live within a favourable environment by providing information about the status of the environment and taking care about its maintenance and improvement.'

[95] See http://www.mfa.gov.lv/lv/eu/3883/3749/4004/4005/#II-4.

[96] Para. 20.1. of the judgment.

[97] Para. 24.2. of the judgment [author's translation].

[98] Para. 25.4. of the judgment.

[99] *Ibidem* [author's emphasis].

[100] Case SKC-67/2007, Civil Cases Department of the Senate of the Supreme Court [Lursoft database].

[101] Council Directive 75/117/EEC of 10 February 1975 on the approximation of the laws of the Member States relating to the application of the principle of equal pay for men and women, *OJ* 1975 L 45/19.

Latvian Civil Procedure Law (CPL), which reads that '[i]n applying legal norms, the court shall take into account case law', and, in consequence, Article 220 EC, which sets up the ECJ's duty to 'ensure that in the interpretation and application of [EC] Treaty the law is observed.' Accordingly, in the words of the Supreme Court, the ECJ is vested with the obligation to ensure uniformity in application of legal norms. In the view of the Supreme Court, the Court of Appeal in the contested decision ignored the duty incumbent on it by virtue of Article 5(6) CPL and failed to take into consideration ECJ case law (as invoked by one of the parties). Thus, the Supreme Court basically affirmed the twofold nature of the duty of domestic courts to rely on ECJ jurisprudence; this duty stems both from the primary EU law (Art. 220 EC) as well as relevant Latvian law.[102]

### 3.7.    The application of general principles of EU law

Most of the case law referred to in previous sections of this chapter dealt with technical questions of application of EU law. Thus, the Latvian courts had to decide, among other things, from which point in time EU law was applicable in Latvia or how and whether to rely on ECJ case law. However, all these are relatively simple questions, covered in any introductory EU law course, and the answers to which can be found in basic EU law books. A more difficult and intellectually challenging task is the application of substantive EU rules, where it is essential to ensure the correct application not only of the letter but also of the spirit of the EC Treaty. That is why knowledge of substantive EU law and the principles according to which EU law works is so critical. Certain principles of law will be common to national law (including Latvian) and European Union law. In the end, EU law draws inspiration from constitutional traditions common to the EU Member States.

There are numerous instances when Latvian courts referred in their own judgments to principles of European Union law. For example, in one of its decisions in 2004, the Supreme Court briefly restated one of the EU principles as established by the ECJ, however, without explaining how it was relevant to the examination of the case. The Court held that in a case where it is not possible to draw a strict borderline between administrative acts and soft law not binding upon individuals, the court should employ the interpretation most favourable to individuals and by this token protect individuals' rights.[103] Unfortunately, the meaning of this reference remains unclear. In case 2005-12-0103,[104] the Constitutional Court stressed the importance of property rights in the EU legal order and, in order to support its argument, referred to the famous CFI judgment in case T-306/01 *Yusuf v. Council*.[105] In case 2005-13-0106, the Constitutional

---

[102] See Case AA-43-0305-07, Administrative Regional Court [Lursoft database], where the Court in its decision has extensively relied on ECJ jurisprudence, para. 21 of the decision.

[103] Case SKA–190/2004, Administrative Cases Department of the Senate of the Supreme Court [Lursoft database], para. 9.

[104] Case 2005-12-0103, Constitutional Court of Latvia, decision of 17 January 2002, available at http://www.satv.tiesa.gov.lv/?lang=1&mid=19, para. 21.4.

[105] CFI, Case T-306/01 *Ahmed Ali Yusuf and Al Barakaat International Foundation v. Council of the European Union and Commission of the European Communities* [2005] *ECR* II-3533.

Court was asked to rule on the unconstitutionality of the national provision which forbade former KGB collaborators to be elected to the Latvian Parliament or local municipalities.[106] The Constitutional Court referred to the Latvian obligations stemming from EU membership, including the duty to guarantee the right of EU citizens to stand as candidates and to be elected in local elections in other Member States in which they reside. In the already-mentioned Riga free port case, the Constitutional Court extensively elaborated on the precautionary principle in environmental law.[107]

One should bear in mind that some general principles of law are still a novelty to judiciaries of the new Member States. This is one of the reasons why the recently published 'Handbook for Latvian judges and lawyers'[108] covers different practical aspects of application of EU law and contains a separate chapter devoted solely to the general principles of EU law (including, *inter alia,* supremacy, direct effect, proportionality and state liability).[109] So far, these general principles of EU law have not been addressed or addressed at length in the case law of Latvian courts.

### 3.8.    The hierarchy of norms: international or European Union law?

As a consequence of the accession to the European Union, the question of the hierarchy of norms that is the relationship between public international law and EU law came up almost naturally. The question was whether Latvia should apply EU law if it was contrary to earlier international law obligations undertaken by Latvia, or the previous commitments were to take priority over conflicting EU law. A judgment of the Constitutional Court of 7 July 2004 illustrates this legal conundrum.[110] In this case, the plaintiff challenged a Latvian norm providing for an imposition of fines on carriers who facilitate entry of foreign citizens into Latvian territory without a valid document. This provision was allegedly in breach of the 1965 Convention on Facilitation of International Maritime Traffic, to which Latvia is a party. However, pursuant to the Council Directive 2001/51/EC,[111] the Member States of the European Union have the obligation to take the necessary measures to ensure that the penalties applicable to carriers under the provisions of the Schengen Implementing Convention are dissuasive, effective and proportionate (Art. 4). The Schengen Implementing Convention aims at third-country nationals travelling without valid documents, whereas the contested Latvian norm did not make a distinction between nationals of EU Member States and third-country nationals. The Constitutional Court started[112] by noting that after the accession to the

---

[106] Case 2005-13-0106, Constitutional Court of Latvia, decision of 15 June 2006, available at http://www.satv.tiesa.gov.lv/?lang=1&mid=19.

[107] *Loc. cit.* n. 93, para. 20.1.

[108] Lutere-Timmele, *op. cit.* n. 6.

[109] *Ibidem*, p. 33.

[110] Case 2004-01-06, Constitutional Court of Latvia, decision of 7 July 2004, available at http://www.satv.tiesa.gov.lv/upload/2004-01-06E.rtf.

[111] Council Directive 2001/51/EC of 28 June 2001 supplementing the provisions of Art. 26 of the Convention implementing the Schengen Agreement of 14 June 1985, *OJ* 2001 L 187/45.

[112] Case 2004-01-06, *loc. cit.* n. 110, para. 7.

EU, Latvia is bound by the provisions of the Treaty of Accession.[113] Furthermore, the Constitutional Court ruled that EU law is applicable in the internal relations among Member States. The Court then proceeded, relying on Article 307 EC and ECJ case law, that in a case where there is a contradiction between an earlier international obligation and an EU norm, a Member State is under an obligation to undertake all possible steps to mitigate such discrepancy. Accordingly, Latvia should take necessary measures to this end, even if it implies renegotiation of an earlier agreement.[114] By this means, the Constitutional Court reaffirmed the supreme status of EU law over Latvia's conflicting international obligations.

## 4.    LATVIA'S PARTICIPATION IN ECJ PROCEEDINGS

Having looked at the application of EU law by the Latvian courts, our next step is to explore how – and how successfully – does Latvia participate in proceedings before the European Court of Justice. It is fitting to note at the very outset, that thus far Latvia has not been a frequent guest in courtrooms in Luxembourg. It is only recently, in the very beginning of 2008, that Latvian domestic courts availed themselves of the possibility to submit requests for preliminary rulings to the ECJ.[115] As of 1 July 2009, Latvian courts submitted six requests for preliminary ruling to the ECJ.[116] Also, at the time of writing, no cases have been brought by the European Commission against Latvia, even though a number of formal notices initiating the administrative phase of the infraction procedure have been sent (see below).

Considering that many interests of the new Member States coincide, the Latvian position is to intervene in already-initiated proceedings, rather than to file separate actions. Especially active participation is occurring in cases involving common and sensitive issues for all new Member States, such as, for example, direct payments to milk and energy producers or the size of sugar stocks upon EU membership.[117] According to the prognosis of the Ministry of Justice, it will be not too long before Latvian public

---

[113] Treaty between the Kingdom of Belgium, the Kingdom of Denmark, the Federal Republic of Germany, the Hellenic Republic, the Kingdom of Spain, the French Republic, Ireland, the Italian Republic, the Grand Duchy of Luxembourg, the Kingdom of the Netherlands, the Republic of Austria, the Portuguese Republic, the Republic of Finland, the Kingdom of Sweden, the United Kingdom of Great Britain and Northern Ireland (Member States of the European Union) and the Czech Republic, the Republic of Estonia, the Republic of Cyprus, the Republic of Latvia, the Republic of Lithuania, the Republic of Hungary, the Republic of Malta, the Republic of Poland, the Republic of Slovenia, the Slovak Republic, concerning the accession of the Czech Republic, the Republic of Estonia, the Republic of Cyprus, the Republic of Latvia, the Republic of Lithuania, the Republic of Hungary, the Republic of Malta, the Republic of Poland, the Republic of Slovenia and the Slovak Republic to the European Union, *OJ* 2003 L 236/17.

[114] *Ibidem.*

[115] For the statistics see: Annual Report of the Court of Justice of the European Communities 2008, text available at http://curia.europa.eu/en/instit/presentationfr/index.htm.

[116] See further, section 4.3.2. in this chapter.

[117] See also Overview of the Latvian Participation in the ECJ Cases, for 2004-2005 (Pārskats par Latvijas Republikas dalību Eiropas Kopienu Tiesas lietās no 2004.gada 1.maija līdz 2005.gada 31.decembrim), Part I, available at http://www.tm.gov.lv/lv/daliba_es/ekt/Informativais%20zinojums_280206.doc.

institutions become more active in cases pending at the European Court of Justice. It is expected that this growth will go in hand with rising awareness and knowledge of the respective institutions about how to defend the interests of sectors/industries they represent, making their views known to the ECJ. Biggest involvement is expected in cases touching upon taxation matters.[118]

However, it would be misleading to assume that Latvia is a passive observer of the legal battles and debates taking place at the ECJ. It is quite to the contrary, as some of the examples below illustrate. Latvia participates quite actively and makes its opinion known in proceedings initiated against other EU Member States or on requests for preliminary rulings deriving from other countries' courts. The consolidated information about Latvian participation in the ECJ proceedings can be found in yearly overviews prepared by the Latvian Ministry of Justice.[119]

### 4.1. Article 226 EC proceedings: Latvia's participation in direct actions against other EU Member States

Article 226 EC empowers the European Commission to scrutinise Member States' compliance with EC law and submit actions to the European Court of Justice. As already noted, as of 1 July 2009, no single case against Latvia has reached the judicial stage; however several potential cases are pending at their preliminary administrative phase.[120] In order to prepare for potential litigation, the Latvian Cabinet of Ministers adopted in 2006 Rules on Preparation, Co-ordination and Adoption of the Latvian Position in the Framework of Procedures for Infringements of the EC Treaty.[121] The Rules prescribe the procedure for the reaction to the Commission's initiated infringement cases in line with Articles 226, 227 and 228 EC.

A number of actions were initiated against other new EU Member States, in which Latvia decided to present its position. For example, in 2007, Latvia requested participation as intervener in a case submitted by the European Commission against Poland.[122] The European Commission argued that Poland had failed to protect the natural habitat of wild fauna and fauna in one of the special protection areas and by this token had been in breach of EC law.[123] The alleged breach of Poland's obligations under EC law took place in the process of construction of a road, which bypasses the town of Augustów.

---

[118] Informatīvais ziņojums Pārskats par Latvijas Republikas dalību Eiropas Kopienu Tiesas lietās no 2006. gada 1. janvāra līdz 2006. gada 31. decembrim (Overview of the Latvian Participation in the ECJ Cases, 2006), Part I.

[119] See Overviews of the Latvian Participation in the ECJ Cases, for 2004-2005, 2006, 2007, 2008 available at http://www.tm.gov.lv/lv/daliba_es/ekt/lv_parstaviba.html.

[120] See Commission Staff Working Document accompanying the 25th Annual Report from the Commission on Monitoring application of Community Law (2007), SEC (2008) 2855.

[121] MK Noteikumi Nr.405 (2006.gada 16.maijs) Latvijas Republikas nostājas projekta Eiropas Kopienas dibināšanas līguma pārkāpuma procedūras ietvaros sagatavošanas, saskaņošanas un apstiprināšanas kārtība, Latvijas Vēstnesis. No. 92 (3460) 14 June 2006.

[122] Ordonnance du Président de la Cour, 30 janvier 2008 Intervention Dans l'affaire C-193/07, ayant pour objet un recours en manquement au titre de l'article 226 CE, introduit le 4 avril 2007, Commission des Communautés européennes contre République de Pologne, nyr.

[123] ECJ, Case C-193/07 Commission v. Poland, OJ 2007 C 199/14.

Latvia's interest in the case is explained by the fact that the contested road is meant to be part of the Via Baltica highway. A different location of the highway will not only extend the time span of the project but also will be detrimental to the construction of Via Baltica as such and possibly will result in major losses for the Latvian state. The strategic and financial interests of Latvia in the project justify the involvement in this case, which is still pending at the time of writing.[124]

## 4.2. Article 230 EC proceedings: Latvia's participation in actions brought against Community institutions

Article 230 EC entitles the Court of First Instance and the European Court of Justice (within their respective jurisdictions) to review the legality of acts adopted by the Community institutions in actions brought, *inter alia*, by the Member States. This right on the part of the EU Member States has been confirmed by the ECJ in case 294/83 *Les Verts*, where the ECJ held:

> '[T]he European Economic Community is a Community based on the rule of law, inasmuch as neither its Member States nor its institutions can avoid a review of the question whether the measures adopted by them are in conformity with the basic constitutional charter, the Treaty.'[125]

The participation of Latvia in this kind of case before the EU Courts is subject to 2005 Rules of the Cabinet of Ministers on Procedure for Elaboration and Adoption of Latvian Draft Position in the ECJ.[126] So far Latvia has used this possibility once, challenging the Commission's decision to reduce Latvia's gas emission quotas. This request for judicial review is discussed in the next section of this chapter.

### 4.2.1. *Case T-369/07 Latvia v. Commission of the European Communities*

On 26 September 2007, Latvia brought an action against the European Commission,[127] in which it challenged the decision amending the Latvian national plan for allocation of greenhouse gas emission allowances.[128] Similar cases were brought earlier the same

---

[124] See more, Chapter 9 in this volume.

[125] ECJ, Case 294/83 *Parti écologiste 'Les Verts' v. European Parliament* [1986] *ECR* 1339.

[126] MK Noteikumi Nr.989 (2005.gada 20.decembris) Kārtība, kādā tiek sagatavots un apstiprināts Latvijas Republikas nostājas projekts un nodrošināta Latvijas Republikas pārstāvība Eiropas Kopienu Tiesā, Latvijas Vēstnesis, No. 207 (3365) 24 December 2005.

[127] CFI, Case T-369/07 *Latvia v. Commission, OJ* 2007 C 269/66. See also Joëlle De Sépibus, 'Scarcity and Allocation of Allowances in the EU Emissions Trading Scheme – A Legal Analysis', 1 September 2007, *NCCR Trade Regulation Working Paper* No. 2007/32; Dr. Sebastian Oberthür et al., 'Abschätzung zur Änderung der Treibhausgas-Emissionen in den EU-Beitrittsstaaten zur Vorbereitung der Verhandlungen im Rahmen der Ausgestaltung des Kioto-Protokolls – Im Auftrag des Bundesministerium für Umwelt, Naturschutz und Reaktorsicherheit', Ecologic – Institut für Internationale und Europäische Umweltpolitik, G II 1 – 45134 – 18/6, March 2001, available at http://www.ecologic.de.

[128] Commission Decision C (2007) 3409, of 13 July 2007, on the amendment of the national plan for the allocation of greenhouse gas emission allowances notified by Latvia, not published in the Official Journal of the European Union.

year by some other new EU Member States,[129] in which Latvia submitted concurring opinions. Latvia argues that the European Commission has significantly restricted a country's sovereign rights in relation to energy, in particular, as regards Latvia's choice of energy sources and the supply of electrical energy. In Latvia's view, the Commission has infringed the principle of non-discrimination, in that the application of the method of calculation devised by it to determine the total volume of greenhouse gas emissions allowed disadvantages to the Member States with low total emissions. Although the European Commission increased the emission quotas for Latvia for the period 2008-2012, nevertheless, the new quota is 44.5% less than what Latvia had initially requested. In this context, it should be stressed that greenhouse gas emissions in the Baltic region are well below the limits set by the Kyoto Protocol. Still, the European Commission allocated to the majority of new EU Member States roughly half of the requested quotas, whereas, as a rule, the old Member States, who struggle with difficulties to comply with the requirements of the Kyoto Protocol, had their requests granted in roughly 90%.[130] Similar requests for judicial review have been submitted by other new Member States. It is highly probable that, given the great similarity of the claims, the cases will be joined. Arguably, this joined consideration of cases will be primarily in the interests of the new Member States, who will be in a stronger position to defend their cause. Possibly, the greenhouse emissions cases will be the most important cases after the *Laval* and *sugar stock* cases on juxtaposition of the positions of old Member States *versus* new Member States' positions.

### 4.2.2. Latvia's participation in actions brought by other Member States

Latvia took the side of Poland in the case where the latter challenged the Council decision, based on the Act of Accession, which provided for a different phasing-in system of direct payments for new Member States' farmers, therefore allegedly breaching the principles of equal treatment, non-discrimination and good faith.[131] The ECJ dismissed Poland's arguments in its judgment rendered at the end of 2007. Part of the Court's reasoning, which deals with the breach of the principle of equal treatment, is particularly weak and unconvincing and therefore, calls for special attention. The Court recalled the rule, according to which the principle of equal treatment requires that comparable situations must not be treated differently, and that different situations must not be

---

[129] See CFI, T-32/07 *Slovakia v. Commission, OJ* 2007 C 69/29; Case T-183/07 *Poland v. Commission, OJ* 2007 C 155/41; Case T-221/07 *Hungary v. Commission, OJ* 2007 C 199/41; Case T-194/07 *Czech Republic v. Commission OJ* 2007 C 199/38; Case T-263/07 *Estonia v. Commission, OJ* 2007 C 223/12; Case T-368/07 *Lithuania v. Commission, OJ* 2007 C 283/35; Case T-484/07 *Romania v. Commission, OJ* 2008 C 51/57.

[130] See also V. Dombrovskis, Eiropas Parlamenta deputāts, 'Ierobežot emisijas, nevis ekonomikas izaugsmi, Dienas bizness', 20 July 2007, available at http://www.jaunaislaiks.lv/news.php?id=80&news_id=520.

[131] ECJ, Case C-273/04 *Republic of Poland v. Council of the European Union* [2007] *ECR* I-8925.

treated in the same way unless such treatment is objectively justified.[132] From this the Court deduced:

> 'it is undisputed in the present case that the agricultural situation in the new Member States was radically different from that in the old Member States, which justified a gradual application of Community rules, in particular those rules relating to direct support schemes, in order not to disrupt the necessary on going restructuring in the agricultural sector of the new Member States.'[133]

The ECJ did not consider it necessary to equally invoke, for example, the principle of solidarity, which clearly is another pillar principle of European integration. This is not the first time or a unique situation when the ECJ overtly upholds the Community's political bargain; however, the argumentation employed in the present case is particularly unpersuasive and can be interpreted by the national administrations of the new Member States as an endorsement of practice to treat old and new Member States differently under the ECJ's endorsed aegis of different treatment of otherwise equal EU Member States.

Another instance where Latvia decided to support one of the EU newcomers is a pending action for annulment submitted by Cyprus against the European Commission, challenging a regulation which negatively affected the sugar sector in the new Member States.[134] In this case, Cyprus, *inter alia*, argues that the European Commission breached the principles of proportionality, non-retroactive legislation, equal treatment and the prohibition of discrimination. Arguably, the contested regulation leads to different treatment of undertakings in the new and old Member States when it comes to very similar, if not identical, situations. In another very similar case, which is also pending at the time of writing, Estonia challenged the Commission Regulation on the determination of surplus quantities of sugar in the new EU Member States.[135] Estonia argues that the European Commission breached a number of principles, including those of good faith, the right to property of undertakings and/or private households, proportionality and non-discrimination. According to the applicant, the calculation of excess sugar stocks laid down by the contested Regulation discriminates against Estonia as compared to the old Member States of the EU. Latvia shares both Cyprus's and Estonia's concerns, largely due to the defiance and dissatisfaction of farmers and the sugar industry with the new imposed regimes.

Of interest are also cases dealing with language policy in the EU. Language is one of the most important elements on which national identity is built and maintained. For the Baltic States, where the use of national languages was discouraged and oppressed during Soviet times, the guarantee of the possibility of unrestricted use of the language and promotion of it by all means is a major component of the nation's self-confidence

---

[132] *Ibidem*, para. 86.

[133] *Ibidem*, para. 87.

[134] CFI, Case T-300/05, *Cyprus v. Commission*, OJ 2005 C 271/19. See also Case T-316/05, *Cyprus v. Commission*, OJ 2005 C 271/23. Both cases were pending at the time of writing.

[135] CFI, Case T-324/05 *Estonia v. Commission*, OJ 2005 C 271/24.

exercise. As a result, it is not surprising that these states readily make submissions in the ECJ cases touching upon the language regime of the European Union.[136] Two cases, in which Latvia participated, should be mentioned in this context.

The first was case C-161/06 *Skoma-Lux*,[137] in which – in reply to a reference for a preliminary ruling submitted by a Czech court – the ECJ ruled that a Community regulation which at the time was not published in the Czech language remained unenforceable against individuals in that particular Member State. Otherwise, the application of such a piece of legislation would have run contrary to the principles of legal certainty and non-discrimination. These were also Latvia's arguments submitted to the ECJ in this case. The second case which merits attention was an action for annulment submitted by Italy against the European Commission.[138] Italy successfully challenged the procedure whereby vacancy notices for senior posts in the European institutions reserved for external candidates were published in the Official Journal of the European Union only in German, English and French. Latvia together with Spain supported Italy in this action. The main arguments submitted by Latvia were the breach of principles of legal certainty, non-discrimination and proportionality.[139]

### 4.3. Article 234 EC: preliminary ruling procedure

#### 4.3.1. *The legal framework*

The practical importance of the preliminary ruling procedure cannot be overestimated in the success story of European integration. It is a unique mechanism allowing domestic courts to address directly the European Court of Justice on interpretation of EU law. As argued by the ECJ itself: 'Article [234] is essential for the preservation of the Community character of the law established by the Treaty and has the object of ensuring that in all circumstances this law is the same in all States of the Community.'[140] The legal basis for different *alter egos* of the preliminary ruling procedure can be found in the Founding Treaties[141] as well as in some other legal acts.[142] Moreover, some of the Member States have domestic provisions governing the mechanics of the reference procedure. This is the case in Latvia, where – shortly before the accession to the EU – tailor-made provisions titled 'Assigning of Matters to the European Court of Justice'

---

[136] On treatment of use of language in the EU see, e.g., ECJ, Case C-379/87 *Anita Groener v. Minister for Education and the City of Dublin Vocational Educational Committee* [1989] *ECR* 3967.

[137] ECJ, Case C-161/06 *Skoma-Lux, s.r.o. pret Celní ředitelství Olomouc* [2006] *ECR* I-10841. See further, Chapters 4 and 5 in this volume.

[138] CFI, Case T-185/05 *Italian Republic v. Commission of the European Communities* [2008] *ECR* II-00000.

[139] Overview of the Latvian Participation in the ECJ Cases, for 2004-2005, Part III-2, *loc. cit.* n. 119.

[140] ECJ, Case 166/73, *Rheinmühlen-Düsseldorf v. Einfuhr- und Vorratsstelle für Getreide und Futtermittel*, [1974] *ECR* 33, para. 2.

[141] Art. 234 EC, Art. 68 EC, Art. 150 EAEC, Art. 35 TEU.

[142] For instance, First Protocol on the interpretation by the Court of Justice of the European Communities of the Convention on the law applicable to contractual obligations, *OJ* 1989 L 48/1.

had been added to the Civil Procedure Law (CPL) and to the Administrative Procedure Law (APL) (Art. 5*bis* and Art. 104*bis* respectively). Article 104*bis* APL reads:

> 'A court in the cases provided for by European Union (Community) legal norms, shall assign matters to the European Court of Justice regarding the interpretation or validity of European Union (Community) legal norms for the rendering of a preliminary ruling.'

Interestingly, the wording of both new provisions is not identical. Article 5*bis* CPL reads '[a] court in accordance with *European Union legal norms*' [author's emphasis]. Indeed, the latter provision refers only to EU law and not to Community law. It is not clear, however, what was the rationale behind the reference to the Community law after the EU law in the first-referred provision, and whether this difference can be explained by some high considerations or merely by the lack of coherent legislative process.

In addition, it should be noted that in 2007, the law on the recognition of the ECJ's jurisdiction according to Article 35 EU was adopted.[143] It allows Latvian courts of all instances to submit Third Pillar references to the European Court of Justice pursuant to Article 35 TEU.[144]

Last but not least, it is fitting to note that in order to foster the knowledge and understanding of the preliminary ruling procedure, the Latvian Ministry of Justice in 2006 produced a manual in Latvian on the preparation and submission of references for preliminary ruling.[145]

### 4.3.2. *References from Latvian courts*

As of 1 July 2009, six references for preliminary ruling have been submitted by Latvian courts.[146] Five of them originate from the Supreme Court and only one from a court of lower instance. Considering Latvia's five years of membership in the European Union, such a relatively modest number of references from lower instance courts – even in the case of a small country like Latvia – may seem quite surprising. One of the possible

---

[143] Law of 19 April 2007 'Par Eiropas Kopienu Tiesas jurisdikcijas atzīšanu saskaņā ar Līguma par Eiropas Savienību 35.panta nosacījumiem', Latvijas Vēstness, 5 May 2007, No. 72 (3648) [in force since 19 May 2007].

[144] As long as the Treaty of Lisbon is not in force, the jurisdiction of the European Court of Justice in these matters remains optional. At the time of writing, only 17 Member States recognised the jurisdiction of the ECJ. It is quite likely that, following the judgment of the Polish Constitutional Tribunal in case Kp 3/08, also Poland is going to accept the jurisdiction of the Court. See further, Chapter 9 in this volume. On the jurisdiction of the ECJ in the Third Pillar see, *inter alia*, S. Braum, A. Weyembergh, eds., *Le contrôle juridictionnel dans l'espace pénal européen* (Bruxelles, Editions de l'Université de Bruxelles 2009).

[145] Latvijas Republikas Tieslietu ministrija Informatīvais materiāls, 'Prejudicāls jautājums Eiropas Kopienu Tiesai', 2006 [Informative note by the Latvian Minsitry of Justice 'Reference for the preliminary ruling to the ECJ'], available at http://www.tm.gov.lv/lv/daliba_es/ekt/TM%20buklets.pdf.

[146] See, ECJ, Case C-93/08 *Schenker SIA v. Valsts ieņēmumu dienests* [2009] *ECR* nyr; Case C-16/08 *Schenker SIA v. Valsts ieņēmumu dienests* [2009] *ECR* nyr; Case C-472/08 *Alstom Power Hydro v. Valsts ieņēmumu dienests*, pending; Case C-199/09 *Schenker SIA v. Valsts ieņēmumu dienests*, pending; Case C-232/09 *Dita Danosa v. SIA "LKB Līkings"*, pending; ECJ, Case C-248/09 *SIA Pakora Pluss v. Valsts ieņēmumu dienests*, pending.

explanations for such a recourse and unwillingness of the Latvian courts to seize the ECJ might be procedural economy as judges are quite aware of consequences of long court proceedings.[147]

As of 1 July 2009, the European Court of Justice rendered judgments in two references from Latvia, that is, in cases C-93/08 *Schenker SIA v. Valsts ieņēmumu dienests*[148] and C-16/08 *Schenker SIA v. Valsts ieņēmumu dienests*.[149] It is noteworthy that in these two cases, parties are just the same; however, the subject matter of the dispute is different and references came from two different courts.

The reference in case C-93/08 *Schenker SIA v. Valsts ieņēmumu dienests* was submitted against the following factual and legal background. The plaintiff – Schenker SIA (a customs agent based in Latvia) – imported on its own name and on behalf of a consignee of goods a consignment of goods bearing the Nokia trademark. Riga Customs Office, suspecting the genuine nature of the imported goods, detained them pursuant to Article 9 of Regulation 1383/2003/EC on suspensive procedure of counterfeit and pirated goods.[150] The proprietor of the trademark – Nokia Corporation – reached an agreement with Rovens on the application of a simplified procedure for the destruction of goods in question. Shortly afterwards, the customs authorities drew up a certificate of administrative offence and imposed a penalty on Schenker SIA. A request for judicial review of that decision followed, and the case – having unsuccessfully passed the scrutiny of Administrative District Court and Regional Court – was appealed to the Supreme Court. Having raised doubts as to the interpretation of Article 11 of the Regulation and, in this context, the powers of customs authorities to impose a penalty, when the simplified procedure is employed by a right holder and an importer, the Supreme Court submitted a reference for a preliminary ruling. The European Court of Justice decided to proceed without an opinion of the Advocate General and almost exactly a year after the reference was submitted rendered its judgment. It held that initiation of the simplified procedure does not deprive national customs authorities from imposing a fine as in the case at hand.

The second judgment of the ECJ in a Latvian case (C-16/08 *Schenker SIA v. Valsts ieņēmumu dienests*) was one of those standard, very technical cases on the classification of goods in the Community Customs Tariff.[151] Upon importation of goods, the plaintiff filed a customs declaration and applied rate of import duty of 0%. Upon inspection of

---

[147] According to the official statistics, proceedings in the first instance courts take up to 3 months in approximately 50% of all civil cases and up to 45% of cases up to 12 months, appeal proceedings in civil cases in 50% of cases take up to 3 months, and in 35% of cases – up to 18 months (see http://www. tiesas.lv/files/statistika/2007/civillietas/civillietas_1_instance_ilgums.xls and http://www.tiesas.lv/index. php?id=2066); in administrative cases appeal procedure in almost 80 per cent of cases takes 6 up to 24 months (http://www.tiesas.lv/files/statistika/2007/admin/admin_apelacija_ilgums.xls).

[148] *Loc. cit.* n. 146.

[149] *Ibidem.*

[150] Council Regulation 1383/2003/EC of 22 July 2003 concerning customs action against goods suspected of infringing certain intellectual property rights and the measures to be taken against goods found to have infringed such rights, *OJ* 2003 L 196/7.

[151] Council Regulation (EEC) No 2658/87 of 23 July 1987 on the tariff and statistical nomenclature and on the Common Customs Tariff, *OJ* 1987 L 256/1.

customs authorities, this declaration was challenged, and a fine for an administrative infringement followed. The District Administrative Court rejected the request for judicial review; however, the Administrative Court of Appeal hearing the case in the second instance decided to seek assistance from the European Court of Justice. On 11 June 2009, the ECJ rendered the judgment and held that the classification suggested by the Latvian customs authorities was incorrect.

### 4.3.3.  *Requests to refer a question for preliminary ruling before Latvian courts*

The fact that Latvian courts are not frequent users of the preliminary ruling procedure does not mean that the possibility to refer a question to the ECJ is rarely discussed in courtrooms. Indeed, requests to address the ECJ on interpretation of EU law were raised on numerous instances by parties to legal proceedings. So far, generally such requests are refused. In one of the cases, the Supreme Court dismissed such a request as interpretation of the disputed provision, and in light of its compliance with EU law, was not a decisive factor in rendering decision in the case.[152] In another case, an appeal court (Riga District Court) similarly ruled that – contrary to the claimant's submission – the reference to the ECJ was unnecessary.[153] The District Court in Riga argued that, unlike the last instance courts, it was under no obligation to refer to the ECJ. Also, the legal issue at stake had been discussed at length in numerous previous judgments of the ECJ; therefore, there were no reasonable doubts as to the meaning of the term "transfer of undertaking". Another good example was already discussed in *Kempmayer* case.[154] It should be recalled that Kempmayer Media Limited (Kempmayer) challenged the decision of the Latvian Competition Council. In the course of litigation, formally a third party – Kempmayer Latvia – urged the first instance court, the appeal court and the Supreme Court to proceed with a reference for preliminary ruling. The courts were invited to ask the European Court of Justice if the Competition Council in the contested decision of June 2004 was empowered to apply to the facts that had taken place in the pre-accession period relevant provisions of the Europe Agreement, Decision 5/2001 of the EC-Latvia Association Council and Regulation 1/2003/EC.[155] The Supreme Court upheld the decision of the Court of Appeal that it was not "necessary" to refer to the ECJ for a preliminary ruling. The Supreme Court justified its decision in the fol-

---

[152]  SKA-34/2006, Administrative Cases Department of the Senate of the Supreme Court [Lursoft database]. In this case, the applicant argued that the decision taken by the interim deputy Minister of Justice was invalid, given that at the time when the decision was taken, the results of elections to the European Parliament were already announced, and the deputy minister was already an MEP. The Supreme Court dismissed the claim and demand to pose a preliminary question, saying that in the case at hand it was not essential to determine from which moment the person is considered to be elected to the EP and when s/he acquires an MEP status. See also Case SKA-210/2004, Administrative Cases Department of the Senate of the Supreme Court [Lursoft database].
[153]  As referred in Case SKC-134/2007, Civil Cases Department of the Senate of the Supreme Court [Lursoft database].
[154]  Case SKA-149/2006, Administrative Cases Department of the Senate of the Supreme Court [Lursoft database], *supra* n. 77.
[155]  Council Regulation (EC) No 1/2003 of 16 December 2002 on the implementation of the rules on competition laid down in Arts. 81 and 82 of the Treaty, *OJ* 2003 L 1/1.

lowing way.[156] First, the Supreme Court referred to the case 283/81 *CILFIT*, which provides guidelines to national courts of the last instance on the reference procedure.[157] The Supreme Court paid particular attention to the fact that even the last instance courts – including the Supreme Court itself – have a margin of discretion in assessing the need to refer. Second, as far as the Regulation 1/2003/EC was concerned, the Supreme Court had no difficulty in holding that it was applicable only as of 1 May 2004 (the date of entry into force of the Accession Treaty and the Regulation itself).[158] Third, the Supreme Court stressed the approximation of laws commitment based on EA Latvia (particularly applicable to competition law). At this stage, the Supreme Court invoked the controversial judgment of the ECJ in case C-302/04 *Ynos v. Janos Varga*,[159] where the ECJ held that it had no jurisdiction to give preliminary rulings with regard to the facts which had occurred in the pre-accession period.[160] Thus, said the Court, even if it were to send those questions, any such request would have been refused by the European Court of Justice.

In another case, decided one year later, the Supreme Court refused again to submit a reference to the ECJ. *Narvesen Baltija*, one of the leading Latvian retailers, requested the Supreme Court to pose a number of questions to the ECJ.[161] The Supreme Court held:

> '[T]he facts of the case had taken place before the accession of Latvia to the EU, and, accordingly, the dispute should be decided according to the Latvian legislation … therefore it is not necessary to go into substantive analysis of the necessity of the ECJ's opinion in the present circumstances.'[162]

This time, however, the Supreme Court did not refer to the *Ynos v. Varga* case but merely mimicked its decision in the *Kempmayer* case instead. The Supreme Court also pointed out, similarly to the *Kempmayer* case, that according to the Treaty of Accession, EU law was applicable in Latvia as of 1 May 2004. It referred then to the post-accession application of EU law, without explaining how relevant this observation was to the case at hand. It also noted that EA Latvia provided for approximation of the Latvian legislation to Community norms and that 'most of the national legal regulation was brought in line with European Community law before Latvia joined the EU.'[163] Here again it is difficult to disagree with the Supreme Court's argumentation. However, it is not clear how important it was for rendering the decision in this case. Indeed, as it follows from the facts, the party's claims rested on a provision of national law which had been tailored

---

[156] SKA-149/2006, paras. 9-12.
[157] ECJ, Case 283/81 *CILFIT and Lanificio di Gavardo SpA v. Ministry of Welfare* [1982] *ECR* 3415.
[158] SKA-149/2006, para. 9.3.
[159] ECJ, Case C-302/04 *Ynos kft v. János Varga* [2006] *ECR* I-371. See further, Chapters 4 and 12 in this volume. See also Półtorak, *loc. cit.* n. 53.
[160] SKA-149/2006, paras. 9.4.-9.5.
[161] SKA-45/2007, Administrative Cases Department of the Senate of the Supreme Court [Lursoft database].
[162] *Ibidem,* para. 12 [translation by the author].
[163] *Ibidem.*

in the pre-accession period to approximate Latvian law with an EC directive. The Supreme Court, by not including all this relevant information in the judgment, most probably presumed that its argumentation was already clear and did not call for further elucidation. Unfortunately, this was not the case. In its flawed analysis, unable to connect the above-cited assertion that EU law was applicable in Latvia only as of 1 May 2004, the Supreme Court abruptly referred to the ECJ's decision in the *Ynos v. Janos Varga* case, where 'in the similar circumstances' the ECJ found that it fell outside the ECJ's jurisdiction to interpret EU law if facts had taken place before EU accession of that particular Member State. These 'similar circumstances' are, nonetheless, not explained by the Supreme Court. As a result, although the decision of the Supreme Court is correct, the argumentation can hardly be called comprehensible.

### 4.3.4.    Latvia's participation in Article 234 proceedings before the ECJ

Two of the most controversial cases which came to the ECJ in connection with the fifth enlargement are *Laval*[164] and *Viking Line*[165] cases. Both cases are often seen as a victory of the new Member States over protectionist attitudes of the old EU Members.[166]

The importance of the *Laval* case, the decision in which came in December 2007, is evidenced by the fact that the case was deliberated in the Grand Chamber of the Court. The facts of the case will be summarised only briefly, given that the case was widely reported and commented. Thus, on initiative of the Swedish building and public works trade union, the work on the construction site (school) operated by the Latvian company Laval, bringing its construction workers from Latvia, was blockaded. As a result of the blockade, the company was forced to withdraw its workers, the contract with the municipality was rescinded and the company was declared bankrupt. The main contention of the Swedish trade union and of the Swedish government was that the actions of the Latvian company amounted to social dumping. The questions on interpretation of Articles 12 and 49 EC and the so-called posting-workers directive[167] were submitted to the ECJ by the Swedish court by means of Article 234 EC procedure.

---

[164] ECJ, Case C-341/05 *Laval un Partneri Ltd* v. *Svenska Byggnadsarbetareförbundet, Svenska Byggnadsarbetareförbundets avdelning 1, Byggettan and Svenska Elektrikerförbundet* [2007] *ECR* I-11767.

[165] ECJ, Case C-438/05 *International Transport Workers' Federation and Finnish Seamen's Union* v. *Viking Line ABP and OÜ Viking Line Eesti* [2007] *ECR* I-10779.

[166] Both judgments have created shockwaves in political and academic circles. See, *inter alia*, N. Reich, 'Free Movement v. Social Rights in an Enlarged Union – The Laval and Viking Cases Before the ECJ', 9 *GLJ* (2008) pp. 125-161; A.C.L. Davies, 'One Step Forward, Two Steps Back? The Viking and Laval Cases in the ECJ', 37 *ILJ* (2008) pp. 126-148; L. Azoulai, 'The Court of Justice and the social market economy: The emergence of an ideal and the conditions for its realization', 45 *CMLRev.* (2008) pp. 126-148; J. Malmberg, T. Sigeman, 'Industrial actions and EU economic freedoms: The autonomous collective bargaining model curtailed by the European Court of Justice', 45 *CMLRev.* (2008) pp. 1115-1146.

[167] Directive 96/71/EC of the European Parliament and of the Council of 16 December 1996 concerning the posting of workers in the framework of the provision of services , *OJ* 1997 L 18/1.

Latvia (alongside other new EU Member States, such as the Czech Republic, Estonia, Lithuania and Poland) took the side of the service provider, arguing that in the given circumstances, Sweden failed to ensure equal opportunities to provide services, which is one of the four basic EU internal market freedoms, and, therefore, the Swedish trade union's actions were contrary to Article 49 EC.

The Court condemned the Swedish actions. It agreed that the right to take collective actions constitutes a fundamental right, however this action taken against an undertaking established in another Member State, which posts workers in the framework of the transnational provision of services, does not escape its scrutiny in light of Community law.[168] The legitimate needs of social protection of workers have to be weighed against the market rules. Freedom to provide services can be restricted, but only if these restrictions pursue a legitimate objective compatible with the EC Treaty and are justified by reasons of public interest.[169] These conditions were not met at the case under consideration.

The collective actions, limiting the basic freedoms as guaranteed by the Treaty, came under scrutiny in another recent case, the so-called *Viking line* case. Running at financial loss on its Helsinki-Tallinn route due to Estonian competition, the company (Viking) decided to register its Rosella ship under the Estonian flag, which would give it some financial benefits. The trade union of seamen objected. In its judgment following Article 234 procedure, the Court ruled – similarly to its judgment in the *Laval* case – that the right to take a collective action is a fundamental right, which, however, is not absolute. This right is not paramount but should be reconciled with the freedom of establishment within the meaning of Article 43 EC.[170] Latvia, which submitted the observations to the Court, argued similarly to the *Laval* case, i.e., that the actions of the trade union, which created obstacles to one of the freedoms as set out by the EC Treaty, were discriminatory, disproportional to the sought objective and against the principle of mutual recognition.

## 5.    CONCLUSIONS

Five years have passed since Latvia became a member of the European Union. As such, it is perhaps too early to jump into conclusions on the application of EU law in the new members, but even so, some preliminary observations can be done already at this stage.

Latvian judges have undoubtedly been influenced by ECJ jurisprudence, and the impact of ECJ jurisprudence on the Latvian legal order is increasingly noticeable. However, the endorsement of most EU law concepts (foremost, the concepts of supremacy and direct effect of EU law) has still to find place in the jurisprudence of the Latvian courts. Some doctrinal foundations have been laid down. Practical embodiment of these doctrines in everyday judicial jurisprudence should turn into the next step. At

---

[168]  Judgment, para. 95.
[169]  Judgment, para. 101.
[170]  Judgment, see paras. 44, 69, 77, 79.

the same time, EU law has become a compulsory subject in the curriculum of law and economics faculties. This certainly will result (and already does) in broader and thorough application of EU law. One of the shortcomings of the present system is that by now in most of the cases, there are practicing attorneys who invoke EU law in protection of their clients' interests, whereas Latvian courts merely react to such invocations. This greatly mirrors the employment patterns in the legal field, where young graduates, who have recently passed EU law exams, prefer better-paid jobs in law firms, rather than clerking for a judge.

As far as Latvia's participation in ECJ proceedings is concerned, one can argue that Latvia actively submits views to the ECJ. Still until very recently, the Latvian judiciary showed self-restraint in submitting references for preliminary rulings. As awareness of European Union law grows, in parallel, the number of requests from parties to address the ECJ increases.

The only antidote to insufficient invocation and reliance on EU law before and by the Latvian judiciary is further promotion of the knowledge of EU law amongst practicing lawyers and judges and dissemination of local courts' decisions based on EU law and of ECJ case law among professionals. As the experience of old EU Member States shows, there will always be a certain healthy reluctance to give full effect to non-domestic norms. Still, as this chapter purported to show, the gradual acceptance of the primary status of EU law in the legal system of Latvia makes its way through initial constraints of aversion and suspicion.

*Chapter 9*

# POLAND: CONSTITUTIONAL DRAMA AND BUSINESS AS USUAL

Adam Łazowski* and Aleksandra Wentkowska**

## 1.     INTRODUCTION

Poland was in the group of ten countries that joined the European Union on 1 May 2004. The accession was considered to be a milestone in the contemporary history of the country and a final stage of its gradual *rapprochement* towards Europe. This had started with the fall of the Communist regime initiated by the creation of the Solidarity movement in the early 1980s.[1] As was the case of all other Central and Eastern European countries that managed to escape the dominance of the Soviet Union, this drive towards Europe led to membership in the Council of Europe, NATO and finally the European Union.[2] The purpose of this chapter is not to look at those historical events with the benefit of hindsight. To the contrary, we treat the date of accession as the opening of a new chapter in the history of the Polish legal order. It is neither desirable nor possible in the framework of this book to present every single legal aspect of Poland's membership in the EU. It is also not possible to consider all the EU-related judgments of Polish courts, including decisions of the Constitutional Tribunal. Therefore, when selecting material, the authors were governed by Cervantes's Law of Statistics – that by a small sample, one may judge the whole piece.[3] By selecting a number of legal developments, we shall argue that, apart from constitutional dramas of the European Arrest Warrant and the supremacy doctrine, EU law is functioning reasonably well in the Polish legal environment. However, business as usual does not equal an ultimate "success story"

---

* Reader in Law, School of Law, University of Westminster, London, United Kingdom.

** Lecturer in law, School of European Studies, Jagiellonian University, Kraków. The Regional Commissioner for Protection of Civil Rights in Poland. All opinions presented in this chapter are presented in private capacity only and shall not be attributed to the Polish Ombudsman's Office.

[1] With this in mind, the motto of this volume is quite symbolic. Indeed, Roger Gilmour of Pink Floyd played this well-known tune at his concert at the shipyard in Gdańsk, where the Solidarity trade union had been conceived.

[2] See further on the early attempts E. Piontek, 'Towards Membership of the European Union', 1-4 *DPC* (1994) pp. 5-15.

[3] H. Rawson, *The Unwritten Laws of Life. Unofficial Rules as Handed Down by Murphy and Other Sages* (Farnham, Carbolic Smoke Ball Co 2008) at p. 55.

*A. Łazowski (ed.), The Application of EU Law in the New Member States*
© 2010, T·M·C·ASSER PRESS, *The Hague, The Netherlands and the Authors*

and lack of uphill struggles. To the contrary, it denotes that Poland is like many other Member States of the European Union. Some of its courts are quite comfortable with EU law, some not necessarily yet on the right path. The same goes for public administration and political circles.[4] In this chapter, we shall endeavour to present examples that call for praise and those which may not – by any stretch of imagination – be considered as the finest hour of the Polish judiciary.

The starting point is the Polish Constitution of 1997.[5] Adopted with the view of potential membership in the European Union, it has been tested almost from the date of accession as to its compatibility with challenges the accession has brought. Although those matters are discussed elsewhere, such an introduction is pivotal as it will provide a systemic background to the analysis of the most fundamental judgments of the Constitutional Tribunal. This will lead to an overview of judgments of selected Polish courts. The selection made covers a wide range of courts. Arguably, administrative courts are the most advanced when it comes to the application of EC law on a daily basis. Problems start when one turns to courts of other branches of the judiciary. After initial shyness during the first two years of the membership in the European Union, Polish courts are clearly learning to talk and communicate with the European Court of Justice. It may not yet be a dialogue; however, with more than 15 references for preliminary ruling, the grounds have been laid. Analysis of those developments is provided in section 4 of this chapter. Last but not least, a brief overview of direct actions involving Poland as a plaintiff and a defendant is contained in the closing section.

## 2.      THE CONSTITUTIONAL FRAMEWORK

### 2.1.    Introduction

The history of the current Polish Constitution goes back to the mid-1990s when a decision had been made to replace an existing matrix of constitutional instruments (some reminiscent of the Stalinist post-World War II period) with a modern basic law reflecting the needs of the Polish society and taking into account its EU aspirations. At the time of the drafting, the application for Union membership had already been submitted, and Poland expected to commence accession negotiations on short notice. This was

---

[4] Polish politics are full of idiosyncrasies not easily understandable to the outside world. A good example is the quite considerable problems with the ratification of the Treaty of Lisbon. The President of the Republic played an important role in the negotiations and came back claiming the final arrangement to be a great success. Yet, when the Parliament adopted a bill authorising the ratification, the President signed the Act and locked the ratification documents safely in his drawer. It is expected that the procedures will be completed only if Ireland ratifies the Treaty of Lisbon. See Treaty of Lisbon amending the Treaty on European Union and the Treaty establishing the European Community, *OJ* 2007 C 306/1.

[5] Konstytucja Rzeczypospolitej Polskiej z dnia 2 kwietnia 1997 roku, Dz. U. 1997, Nr 78, Item 483. An English translation of the Constitution is available in A. Pol and W. Odrowąż-Sypniewski, eds., *Polish Constitutional Law. The Constitution and Selected Statutory Materials*, 2nd edn. (Warsaw, Chancellery of the Sejm 2000) at pp. 25-91. All of the quotes from the Constitution inserted throughout this contribution originate from this book unless stated otherwise.

one of the reasons why the drafters inserted into the new Constitution provisions on the application of international treaties and legal acts originating from international organisations.[6] They were tailored to facilitate the application of EU law upon accession.[7] The end result was a product of a political compromise, not always perfect and, at least in EU-related matters, not flexible enough to avoid constitutional battles and controversial choices. To give this argument merits, it is fitting to refer briefly – at this stage – to a recent decision of the Polish Constitutional Tribunal in case Kpt 2/08 (*re Participation in meetings of the European Council*).[8] It is up to Member States to decide who represents them at those so-called "European Summits."[9] Unfortunately, an idiosyncratic arrangement in the 1997 Polish Constitution makes it less than clear who takes the main responsibility for foreign policy. A conflict between the President and Prime Minister may have looked quite entertaining to the outside world;[10] however, it touched upon two crucial legal issues. First, who has the power. Second, whether the traditional division between foreign and domestic policy provided in the Constitution is redundant when it comes to EU membership. This is just a most recent example of challenges posed by the 1997 Polish Constitution in the wake of EU accession. The two well-known cases are Article 55 of the Constitution, which even after a revision triggered by the judgment of the Constitutional Tribunal, is contrary to EU law.[11] The second is the question of the relationship between the Polish Constitution and EU law. It is worth taking a quick look at the basics – provisions of the Constitution dealing with membership in international organisations as well as provisions on sources of law. This, as already indicated, will lead to the analysis of selected judgments of the Constitutional Tribunal provided in section 3 of this chapter.

---

[6] Interestingly enough, also at the time of drafting, the judicial milestones on the principle of supremacy had already been in place, making it very clear how it is perceived by the ECJ. Despite this, the national legislator had given supremacy to the Polish Constitution, thus potentially creating space for legal conflicts and, at the same time, leaving little flexibility for national courts. See further sections 2 and 3 in this chapter.

[7] One should note, however, that already before the accession, some had argued for a revision of the Constitution to make it more compatible with the EU integration endeavour. See, *inter alia*, K. Wójtowicz, 'Proposed Changes in the Polish Constitution of 1997 ahead of Poland's Accession to the European Union', 25 *PolYBIL* (2001) pp. 27-44.

[8] Constitutional Tribunal, 20 May 2009, Case Kpt 2/08 (*re Participation in meetings of the European Council*), nyr (on file with the Authors).

[9] Art. 4 EU reads 'The European Council shall bring together the Heads of State or Government of the Member States.' It is then a matter of national constitutional arrangement and, to a degree, political etiquette who represents a particular Member State. See further, J. Werts, *The European Council* (London, John Harper Publishing 2008).

[10] The conflict erupted in mid-2008 when suddenly the President of the Republic expressed a desire to participate in the session of the European Council. This led to a dispute about the use of the aircraft used by state officials and a bit of uncertainty as to the official representation at the Summit. The same scenario was repeated later that year and ultimately the Polish delegation arrived late for the meeting.

[11] See further, *inter alia*, A. Łazowski, 'From EU with Trust: the Potential and Limits of the Mutual Recognition in the Third Pillar from the Polish Perspective', in G. Vernimmen-Van Tiggelen, L. Surano, A. Weyembergh, eds., *The future of mutual recognition in criminal matters in the European Union/ L'avenir de la reconnaissance mutuelle en matière pénale dans l'Union européenne* (Bruxelles, Editions de l'Université de Bruxelles 2009) pp. 419-444.

## 2.2. Constitutional legal basis for membership in the European Union

Unlike constitutions of some old and new Member States, the Polish Constitution has no provisions explicitly mentioning membership in the European Union.[12] However, the process of integration, connected with the delegation of competences to EU institutions, has its basis in Art. 90 of the Constitution. In fact, a set of general rules on participation in international organisations served as one.[13] As Stanisław Biernat notes, this provision was 'deliberately formulated in a more general manner, so that it could be applied more broadly.'[14] However, it was bluntly clear already at the stage of drafting that it is an almost tailor-made provision for accession to the European Union.[15] The provision in question reads as follows:

'(1) The Republic of Poland may, by virtue of international agreements, delegate to an international organization or international institution the competence of organs of State authority in relation to certain matters.
(2) A statute, granting consent for ratification of an international agreement referred to in Paragraph (1), shall be passed by the *Sejm* by a two-thirds majority vote in the presence of at least half of the statutory number of Deputies, and by the Senate by a two-thirds majority vote in the presence of at least half of the statutory number of Senators.
(3) Granting of consent for ratification of such agreement may also be passed by a nationwide referendum in accordance with the provisions of Article 125.
(4) Any resolution in respect of the choice of procedure for granting consent to ratification shall be taken by the *Sejm* by an absolute majority vote taken in the presence of at least half of the statutory number of Deputies.'

This provision not only provides for the transfer of sovereign powers (although only in certain matters) to an international organisation but also provides for a special authorising procedure, which may, but does not have to, directly involve the nation. It leaves the *Sejm* (the lower chamber of the Parliament) the freedom to decide as to the method of giving the President the power to ratify such an international treaty. In the case of EU membership, a decision was made to hold an accession referendum. Its positive result permitted Aleksander Kwaśniewski – President of the Republic at the time – to ratify the Accession Treaty 2003.[16] It is fitting to note that the same procedure

---

[12] For a comparative analysis, see Chapter 3 in this volume.
[13] See further, *inter alia*, J. Barcz, 'Membership of Poland in the European Union in the Light of the Constitution of 2 April 1997. Constitutional Act of Integration', 23 *PolYBIL* (1997-98) pp. 21-34; S. Biernat, 'Constitutional Aspects of Poland's Future Membership in the European Union', 36 *Archiv des Völkerrechts* (1998) pp. 398-424; A. Łazowski, 'Poland', in A. Ott and K. Inglis, eds., *Handbook on European Enlargement. A Commentary on the Enlargement Process* (The Hague, TMC Asser Press 2002) pp. 299-307. For a comparative perspective, see also Chapter 3 in this volume.
[14] S. Biernat, 'Poland', in A.E. Kellermann, J. Czuczai, S. Blockmans, A. Albi, W. Douma, eds., *The Impact of EU Accession on the Legal Orders of New EU Member States and (Pre-)Candidate Countries. Hopes and Fears* (The Hague, T.M.C. Asser Press 2006) pp. 419-436, at p. 419.
[15] *Ibidem.*
[16] Treaty between the Kingdom of Belgium, the Kingdom of Denmark, the Federal Republic of Germany, the Hellenic Republic, the Kingdom of Spain, the French Republic, Ireland, the Italian Republic, the Grand Duchy of Luxembourg, the Kingdom of the Netherlands, the Republic of Austria, the Portuguese

was not employed for the ratification of the Treaty of Lisbon. That time, the Parliament adopted an Act authorising the President to ratify the Treaty.[17]

Prior to the accession, the focus of academic debate was on both elements of Article 90, that is, the transfer of sovereign powers and the *modus operandi* to be employed for that purpose. Considering the aim of this section of the chapter, our attention will turn to the first aspect of the authorising clause. The key question is what is meant by 'transfer of competences in certain matters.' The vagueness of this provision has been criticised in academic writing since, hypothetically, such transfer 'may concern the powers of all the categories of agencies of State authorities mentioned in Article 10 of the Constitution[18] and also to agencies of local government or others forms of self-government.'[19] Such interpretation leads to the conclusion that Poland is still able to execute its own competencies in the capacity of the so-called "reserved sphere" ("control gap"). According to Stanisław Biernat, some limits could be drawn out from general and introductory provisions, which determine the system of state,[20] basic rules,[21] the model of state[22] and general freedoms.[23] The interpretation of this provision has led to several controversies, including rather conservative conclusions of the Constitutional Tribunal in the *Accession Treaty* case discussed in section 3 of this chapter.

### 2.3. The status of international law in the domestic legal order: Article 91 of the Constitution

The 1997 Polish Constitution brought a number of crucial novelties to the constitutional landscape, including the first catalogue of sources of law as well as provisions

---

Republic, the Republic of Finland, the Kingdom of Sweden, the United Kingdom of Great Britain and Northern Ireland (Member States of the European Union) and the Czech Republic, the Republic of Estonia, the Republic of Cyprus, the Republic of Latvia, the Republic of Lithuania, the Republic of Hungary, the Republic of Malta, the Republic of Poland, the Republic of Slovenia, the Slovak Republic, concerning the accession of the Czech Republic, the Republic of Estonia, the Republic of Cyprus, the Republic of Latvia, the Republic of Lithuania, the Republic of Hungary, the Republic of Malta, the Republic of Poland, the Republic of Slovenia and the Slovak Republic to the European Union, *OJ* 2003 L 236/17.

[17] As noted earlier in this chapter, the President has decided to withhold ratification documents until Ireland holds the second referendum on the Treaty of Lisbon. At the time of writing, it was pencilled in for October 2009.

[18] Art. 10 provides that: '(1) The system of government of the Republic of Poland shall be based on the separation of and balance between the legislative, executive and judicial powers. (2) Legislative power shall be vested in the Sejm and the Senate, executive power shall be vested in the President of the Republic of Poland and the Council of Ministers, and the judicial power shall be vested in courts and tribunals.'

[19] Biernat, *loc. cit.* n. 13, at p. 402.

[20] 'Republic of Poland shall be the common good of all its citizens.' (Art. 1)

[21] 'The Republic of Poland shall be a democratic state ruled by law and implementing the principles of social justice.' (Art. 2)

[22] 'The Republic of Poland shall be a unitary State.' (Art. 3)

[23] 'The Republic of Poland shall safeguard the independence and integrity of its territory and ensure the freedoms and rights of persons and citizens, the security of the citizens, safeguard the national heritage and shall ensure the protection of the natural environment pursuant to the principles of sustainable development.' (Art. 5)

dealing explicitly with public international law and its position in the Polish legal order. It is necessary to look at Articles 8 and 9 of the Constitution, which provide as follows:

'Article 8
The Constitution shall be the supreme law of the Republic of Poland.
The provisions of the Constitution shall apply directly, unless the Constitution provides otherwise.

Article 9
The Republic of Poland shall respect international law binding upon it.'

Both provisions create fundamental rules underpinning the Polish legal order. First, as clear from Article 8, the accession of Poland to the European Union did not undermine the supremacy of the Constitution. At the same time, Article 9 set a general principle of respect to international law binding upon Poland. Reconciling the two provisions, taking into account European Court of Justice case law on the supremacy of EC law,[24] proved to be a major issue and, as explained in section 3 of this chapter, led to a controversial judgment of the Constitutional Tribunal. Clearly, the Constitution, as the supreme law of the land and an expression of the nation's will, would not lose its binding force or change its content because of an irreconcilable inconsistency with a provision of EC/EU law. In such a situation, the autonomous decision regarding the appropriate manner of resolving that inconsistency, including the expediency of a revision of the Constitution, belongs to the Polish constitutional legislator. This clearly is a message of the Constitutional Tribunal coming from the *Accession Treaty* judgment.[25] It is notable that the Polish Constitution has no provision even closely comparable to Article 2 of the Constitution of the Republic of Estonia Amendment Act. The latter, as explained in Chapter 6 of this volume, allowed the Estonian Supreme Court to extend the principle of supremacy of EC law to the Estonian Constitution. Without such a provision, the Constitutional Tribunal had no choice but to give supremacy to the Constitution under the terms of Article 8.

Although conflicts between national constitutions and EU law almost always create political and legal shockwaves, usually followed by waves of doctrinal debates, they do not – in general terms –affect in enormous proportions everyday application of EU law by national courts. Bearing this in mind, our attention will now turn to provisions of the Constitution that contain a closed catalogue of sources of law in the Polish legal order (Art. 87) and determine the relationship between EU law and national legal acts other than the Constitution (Art. 91). They read as follows:

---

[24] See ECJ, Case 11/70 *Internationale Handelsgesellschaft mbH v. Einfuhr- und Vorratsstelle für Getreide und Futtermittel* [1970] *ECR* 1125.
[25] Constitutional Tribunal, 11 May 2005, Case K 18/04 (*re Conformity of the Accession Treaty 2003 with the Polish Constitution*) OTK Z.U. 2005/5A/49; an English summary of the judgment is available at the Constitutional Tribunal website http://www.trybunal.gov.pl/eng/summaries/documents/K_18_04_GB.pdf.

'Article 87
1. The sources of universally binding law of the Republic of Poland shall be: the Constitution, statutes, ratified international agreements, and regulations.
2. Enactments of local law issued by the operation of organs shall be a source of universally binding law of the Republic of Poland in the territory of the organ issuing such enactments.

Article 91
1. After promulgation thereof in the Journal of Laws of the Republic of Poland (Dziennik Ustaw), a ratified international agreement shall constitute part of the domestic legal order and shall be applied directly, unless its application depends on the adoption of an act of Parliament.
2. An international agreement ratified upon prior consent granted by an act of Parliament shall have precedence over an act of Parliament if such an agreement cannot be reconciled with the provisions of such an act.
3. If an agreement, ratified by the Republic of Poland, establishing an international organization so provides, the laws established by it shall be applied directly and have precedence in the event of a conflict with acts of Parliament.'[26]

As seen in Article 87 of the Constitution, ratified international agreements are a source of law in the Polish legal order. Per Article 91(1) of the Constitution, such international treaties acquire that status once formally promulgated in the Polish official gazette [*Dziennik Ustaw*]. Such agreements are applied directly, unless their application depends on the enactment of an act of Parliament. Article 91(3) of the Constitution is absolutely crucial when it comes to the opening of the Polish legal order to EU law. Not only has it clarified that its scope extends to international agreements as such but also – if they constitute a founding treaty for an international organisation – to legislation adopted by it. Even more crucial is a clause defining the hierarchy between sources of national law (except for the Constitution, which is supreme under Article 8 of the Constitution) and law of such international organisation. The Constitution makes it clear that such law created by an international organisation shall be applied directly and have precedence in the event of a collision with acts of Parliament. Ratified international agreements that have become part of the domestic legal order shall not change into domestic law but shall remain, in their nature – and by virtue of their origin –acts of international law. The discussed proviso, especially paragraph 2, is supposed to fulfil a double function. On the one hand, it creates a *sui generis* "bond" between domestic and EU law, and, on the other hand, it defines the hierarchy of sources; in the same manner, it creates the basic mechanism for the elimination of potential conflicts with domestic legal acts. Consequently – where incompatibility between national and EC law is found, Article 91(3) of the Constitution constitutes the basis for the Constitutional Tribunal to adjudicate upon the loss of binding force of a Polish legal act. At the same time, it allows Polish courts to employ the *Simmenthal* mandate with-

---

[26] Translation by the authors.

out a major constitutional obstacle.[27] Selected examples provided in section 4 of this chapter shall illustrate the practical meaning of this provision.

## 3.   EU LAW IN THE JURISPRUDENCE OF THE POLISH CONSTITUTIONAL TRIBUNAL

### 3.1.   Introduction

The Constitutional Tribunal, similar to many Constitutional Courts in this part of Europe, plays a crucial role as the guardian of the national Constitution.[28] Created in 1985, it was meant to be for the Communist authority a facade of true democratic reforms. However, with the fall of Communism and multidimensional legal, economic and political transitions, the Constitutional Tribunal has become an inherent part of the legal landscape. Formally outside the judiciary, it plays an idiosyncratic role within the legal order. Pursuant to Article 188 of the Constitution:

'The Constitutional Tribunal shall adjudicate regarding the following matters:
1. the conformity of statutes and international agreements to the Constitution;
2. the conformity of a statute to ratified international agreements whose ratification required prior consent granted by statute;
3. the conformity of legal provisions issued by central State organs to the Constitution, ratified international agreements and statutes;
4. the conformity to the Constitution of the purposes or activities of political parties;
5. complaints concerning constitutional infringements ...'

In the period preceding the accession to the European Union, the Constitutional Tribunal rendered several judgments demonstrating its positive approach to EU law and the process of European integration as such.[29] For example, in 2000 it decided to take into account EU law as a source of inspiration.[30] In a judgment rendered in early 2003, the Constitutional Tribunal ruled that although EU law was not applicable prior to accession, nevertheless, it should have been taken into account.[31]

With membership in the European Union becoming a fact, the situation changed tremendously. EU law became binding on Poland and all its authorities, including the Constitutional Tribunal. However, it has maintained its own role as guardian of the

---

[27] ECJ, Case 106/77 *Amministrazione delle Finanze dello Stato v. Simmenthal SpA* [1978] *ECR* 629.
[28] See, *inter alia*, W. Sadurski, *Rights before Courts: a study of constitutional courts in postcommunist states of Central and Eastern Europe* (Dordrecht, Springer 2005).
[29] See further, S. Biernat, 'Die "europäische" Rechtsprechung polnischer Gerichte vor dem Beitritt zur Europäischen Union' in J. Masing and W. Erbguth, eds., *Die Bedeutung der Rechtsprechung im System der Rechtsquellen. Europarecht und nationales Recht* (Stuttgart-München et al., Richard Boorberg Verlag 2005) pp. 191-207.
[30] Constitutional Tribunal, 20 March 2000, Case K 27/99 (*re Conformity of Teachers Charter Act with the Constitution*), OTK Z.U. 2000/2/62.
[31] Constitutional Tribunal, 28 January 2003, Case K 2/02 (*re Conformity of Combating Alcoholism Act with the Constitution*), OTK Z.U. 2003/1A/4.

Constitution. This factor has to be taken into account in any analysis of Tribunal case law. Exactly a month after accession, the Constitutional Tribunal rendered its first EU law-related judgment. In case K 15/04, the Tribunal[32] was asked to verify conformity of the elections to the European Parliament Act with the Polish Constitution.[33] The case was submitted by a group of members of the *Sejm* who claimed that provisions of the Act giving voting rights to EU citizens who were not Polish nationals was contrary to Article 4(1) of the Constitution. The latter provides that the supreme power in the Republic of Poland is vested in the nation. The Tribunal dismissed all arguments submitted by the complainant as unfounded. This judgment was just a taste of what was to come in the following months and years.

During the first five years of Poland's membership in the European Union, the Constitutional Tribunal rendered a number of crucial judgments touching upon EU law in one way or another. Analysis of all of them would exceed the limits of this chapter and certainly deserves a separate study. The emerging picture is complex. On the one hand, some consider the Constitutional Tribunal to be following the steps of the *Bundesverfassungsgericht*; on the other hand, it has demonstrated its pro-EU face too. Definitely two of those judgments stand out: the judgment on the European Arrest Warrant[34] and the judgment on the conformity of the Accession Treaty 2003 with the Polish Constitution.[35] Due to their systemic importance they are analysed separately in two sections of the chapter that follow. However, before we turn to those fundamental decisions, a brief overview of a few other EU-related decisions seems fitting.[36]

The transfer of powers to the European Union by means of the Treaty of Accession 2003 has been far from a technical exercise only. It has changed tremendously the balance of powers between the Government and the Parliament.[37] Shortly before the enlargement, the Parliament adopted an Act on Cooperation between the Council of Ministers and the Parliament in EU matters.[38] Its adoption was preceded by intensive political and academic debate on the appropriate co-operation model. The key issue was how to find a balance between the ambitions of the Parliament and the fairly tight institutional arrangement provided in the Constitution. The division of powers between the *Sejm* and the *Senat* (upper chamber of the Polish Parliament) led to a constitutional conflict. A group of senators submitted a complaint to the Constitutional Tribunal

---

[32] Constitutional Tribunal, 31 May 2004, Case K 15/04 (*re Conformity of the Law on Elections to the European Parliament with the Constitution*), OTK Z.U. 2004/5A/47.

[33] Ustawa z dnia 23 stycznia 2004 r. – Ordynacja wyborcza do Parlamentu Europejskiego, Dz. U. 2004, Nr 25, Item 219.

[34] Constitutional Tribunal, 27 April 2005, Case P 1/05 (*re Conformity of provisions on EAW with the Constitution*), [2006] 1 C.M.L.R. 36.

[35] *Loc. cit.* n. 25.

[36] See also Constitutional Tribunal, 17 July 2007, Case P 16/06 (*re Conformity of legislation on agency contracts with the Constitution*) [2008] E.C.C. 18.

[37] See further, *inter alia*, A. Łazowski, 'The Polish parliament and EU affairs. An effective actor or an accidental hero?', in J. O'Brennan and T. Raunio, eds., *National Parliaments within the Enlarged European Union. From 'victims' of integration to competitive actors?* (London and New York, Routledge 2007) pp. 203-219.

[38] Ustawa z dnia 11 marca 2004 r. o współpracy Rady Ministrów z Sejmem i Senatem w sprawach związanych z członkostwem Rzeczypospolitej Polskiej w Unii Europejskiej, Dz. U. 2004, Nr 52, Item 515.

in which they questioned conformity of the Act with the Constitution. It was argued that the powers of the Senate were unjustifiably limited in EU matters. The Constitutional Tribunal agreed[39] with the applicant; therefore, the contested provisions had to be changed.[40] As we noted in the introductory part of this chapter, the Constitutional Tribunal was also asked to solve a competence conflict between the President and the Prime Minister on the participation in meetings of the European Council.[41] Although the decision may seem inconclusive at first sight, it definitely reflects a very unclear arrangement provided in the Constitution. The Constitutional Tribunal held that as a matter of principle, participation in meetings of the European Council falls under the competence of the Government; however, the President, when expressing a desire to this end, may participate as well. The Constitutional Tribunal emphasised that the President and the Government (including the Prime Minister) should be governed in their relations by the principle of co-operation laid down in the Constitution.

Already twice the Constitutional Tribunal dealt with the preliminary ruling procedure. Although it has not formally considered making a reference to the European Court of Justice,[42] it provided guidance to national courts on the procedure in its decision in 2006.[43] In a judgment of 2009, it ruled that an Act of Parliament on the Recognition of Jurisdiction of the European Court of Justice pursuant to Article 35 EU was in compliance with the Polish Constitution.[44] Both those judgments are discussed in section 5.2 of this chapter.

### 3.2.    The constitutional drama: European Arrest Warrant and supremacy of EC law on trial

#### 3.2.1.    *Case P 1/05 on the European Arrest Warrant*

Those previously discussed developments have not created shockwaves comparable to the two judgments discussed in this section of the chapter.[45] Following the chrono-

---

[39]   It is notable that three judges submitted dissenting opinions.

[40]   Ustawa z dnia 28 lipca 2005 r o zmianie ustawy o współpracy Rady Ministrów z Sejmem i Senatem w sprawach związanych z członkostwem Rzeczypospolitej Polskiej w Unii Europejskiej, Dz. U. 2005, Nr 160, Item 1342.

[41]   *Loc. cit.* n. 8.

[42]   Interestingly enough, as of 7 October 2009, former president of the Constitutional Tribunal Professor Marek Safjan became a judge of the European Court of Justice. See: Decision of the Representatives of the Governments of the Member States 2009/176/EC, Euratom of 25 February 2009 appointing Judges and Advocates-General to the Court of Justice of the European Communities, *OJ* 2009 L 63/13.

[43]   Constitutional Tribunal, 19 December 2006, Case P 37/05 (*re Division of jurisdiction between Constitutional Tribunal and European Court of Justice*) [2007] 3 C.M.L.R. 48. For an academic appraisal, see, *inter alia*, A. Łazowski, 'Poland. Constitutional Tribunal on the Preliminary Ruling Procedure. Decision of 19 December 2006', 4 *EUConst* (2008) pp. 187-197.

[44]   Constitutional Tribunal, 18 February 2009, Case Kp 3/08 (*re Conformity of the Act authorizing the President to Recognize the Jurisdiction of ECJ pursuant to Article 35 TEU with the Constitution*), nyr (on file with the authors).

[45]   See, *inter alia*, A. Nußberger, 'Poland: The Constitutional Tribunal on the implementation of the European Arrest Warrant', 6 *I·CON* (2008) pp. 162-170; A. Łazowski, 'Constitutional Tribunal on the Surrender of Polish Citizens Under the European Arrest Warrant. Decision of 27 April 2005', 1 *EuConst*

logical order of events, the judgment on the European Arrest Warrant will be considered first.[46] It should be noted that the Polish Constitutional Tribunal was not the only Constitutional Court to be asked to declare non- compliance of national implementing laws with a domestic constitution.[47] Similar challenges have been witnessed in Germany,[48] the Czech Republic[49] and Cyprus.[50]

The reference for adjudication on conformity of the Penal Procedure Code[51] with the Polish Constitution had been submitted by the Criminal Division of the Regional Court in Gdańsk. It had received a European Arrest Warrant requesting surrender of a Polish citizen to The Netherlands. Before authorising the surrender, the court wanted to clarify whether surrendering Polish citizens pursuant to the Penal Procedure Code was acceptable in the light of Article 55(1) of the Constitution. The latter prohibited extradition of Polish nationals. Unlike the Latvian or Bulgarian Constitutions, this prohibition was made without any exceptions.[52]

In order to provide the referring court with an answer, the Constitutional Tribunal had to address a very controversial question: whether surrender and extradition procedures were two sides of the same coin or whether they really were two different issues. The question was not new, and at that time, a considerable record of academic and political discourse had developed. The issue had been raised in Poland for the first time during the ratification of the Rome Statute of the International Criminal Court. At that time, the dominating school of thought had supported the treatment of the surrender procedure as something very different from classical extradition.[53] This idea had been followed during legislative works that had led to the transposition of the Framework Decision on the European Arrest Warrant.[54]

---

(2005) pp. 569-581; A. Wyrozumska, 'Some Comments on the Judgments of the Polish Constitutional Tribunal on the EU Accession Treaty and on the Implementation of the European Arrest Warrant', 27 *PolYBIL* (2004-2005) pp. 5-31; D. Leczykiewicz, 'Trybunal Konstytucyjny [Polish Constitutional Tribunal], Judgment of 27 April 2005, No. P 1/05', 43 *CMLRev.* (2006) pp. 1181-1192.

[46] Council Framework Decision 2002/584/JHA of 13 June 2002 on the European Arrest Warrant and the surrender procedures among Member States, *OJ* 2002 L 190/1. For an academic appraisal, see, *inter alia*, N. Keizer and Elies van Sliedregt, eds., *The European Arrest Warrant in Practice* (The Hague, T.M.C. Asser Press 2009).

[47] See, *inter alia*, E. Guild, ed., *Constitutional Challenges to the European Arrest Warrant* (Nijmegen, Wolf Legal Publishers 2006).

[48] Federal Constitutional Court of Germany, 18 July 2005, Case 2 BVR 2236/04 (*re Constitutionality of German Law Implementing the Framework Decision on a European Arrest Warrant*) [2006] 1 C.M.L.R. 16.

[49] Constitutional Court of the Czech Republic, 3 May 2006 (*re Constitutionality of Framework Decision on the European Arrest Warrant*) [2007] 3 C.M.L.R. 24.

[50] Supreme Court of Cyprus, 7 November 2005, Judgment in case *Attorney General of the Republic v. Konstantinou* [2007] 3 C.M.L.R. 42. See further, Chapters 3 and 15 in this volume.

[51] Kodeks postępowania karnego z dnia 6 czerwca 1997 r., Dz. U. 1997, Nr 89, Item 555 (as amended).

[52] Both countries have changed their Constitutions ahead of the accession in order to allow transposition of the EAW Framework Decision. See Chapter 3 in this volume.

[53] See further, Łazowski, *loc. cit.* n. 11, at pp. 422-426.

[54] Ustawa z dnia 18 marca 2004 r. o zmianie ustawy – Kodeks karny, ustawy – Kodeks postępowania karnego oraz ustawy – Kodeks wykroczeń, Dz. U. 2004, Nr 69, Item 626.

The Constitutional Tribunal held that the contested provisions were indeed contrary to Article 55(1) of the Constitution. It started with the analysis of framework decisions as sources of EU law. Surprisingly enough, the Tribunal refrained from presenting a clear view on the nature of those legal acts.[55] It merely concluded that academic opinions in this respect vary and allow treatment of framework decisions as *sui generis* pieces of EU legislation or, at the other extreme, as a very specific genre of international treaties. Rightly so, the Constitutional Tribunal concluded that Poland had the obligation to implement the Framework Decision in question on 1 May 2004 at the latest. Somehow forgetting about the obligation stemming from Article 34 EU, it argued that such an obligation comes only from Article 9 of the Constitution.[56]

This led the Constitutional Tribunal to the heart of the matter. It embarked on a thorough comparative analysis of the surrender and extradition procedures. Notwithstanding some important procedural differences between the two procedures, the Tribunal concluded that they constitute two sides of the same coin. In other words, it concluded that the surrender procedure is merely part of extradition and not a different process. To this end, the prohibition stemming from the Constitution was equally applicable to the extradition and surrender procedures. This point led to the conclusion that the contested provisions were contrary to the Constitution and had to be annulled.

There are a number of factors related to this judgment that deserve particular attention. The starting point shall be the application of the principle of indirect effect to Third Pillar legislation.[57] It has been argued that Article 55(1) of the Constitution deserves pro-European interpretation, facilitating surrender of nationals under the EAW surrender procedure. In this judgment, delivered shortly before the famous *Pupino* case,[58] the Constitutional Tribunal held that application of this principle to Third Pillar legislation shall not, as such, be excluded. However, considering the limitations set forth in ECJ case law, it would not be possible to invoke such interpretation to the provision at hand.[59]

Despite its final conclusion and the shockwaves the judgment produced, the Constitutional Tribunal clearly presented itself as supportive of the EU. A number of factors support such a conclusion. First, it decided to limit the temporal effects of the judgment and delay the annulment of the contested legislation by 18 months.[60] It made it clear that until the expiry of that period, national courts cannot refuse surrender of Polish nationals directly on the basis of Article 55(1) of the Constitution. It supported its argument by reference to Article 9 of the Polish Constitution, creating the obligation for state authorities to respect international law. More importantly, the Tribunal advo-

---

[55] For a comparative overview, see B. Kurcz and A. Łazowski, 'Two Sides of the Same Coin? Framework Decisions and Directives Compared', 25 *YEL* (2006) pp. 177-204.

[56] Para. 2.4. of the judgment.

[57] See, *inter alia*, M. Fletcher, 'Extending "indirect effect" to the Third Pillar: the significance of Pupino?', 30 *ELRev.* (2005) pp. 862-877; E. Spaventa, 'Opening Pandora's Box: Some Reflections on the Constitutional Effects of the Decision in Pupino', 3 *EUConst* (2007) pp. 5-24.

[58] ECJ, Case C-105/03 *Criminal proceedings against Maria Pupino* [2005] *ECR* I-5285.

[59] See, for instance, ECJ, Case 80/96 *Criminal Proceedings against Kolpinghuis Nijmegen BV* [1987] *ECR* I-3969.

[60] This is the maximum allowed under Art. 190(3) of the Polish Constitution.

cated the revision of the Polish Constitution in order to allow the complete transposition of the EAW Framework Decision. It held that revisions of national constitutions are a well-accepted method of securing effectiveness of EU law. To this end, the judges referred to modifications of the French, Spanish and German Constitutions.[61] It should be noted that in order to comply with this obligation, a revision of the Constitution was made in 2006. However, for political reasons only, it was amended in a way that is contrary to the EAW Framework Decision.[62] For the time being, Article 55 of the Constitution will have to remain in force in its current shape; however, the potential entry into force of the Treaty of Lisbon and the extension of the infraction procedure provided therein to the Police and Judicial Co-operation in Criminal Matters may potentially lead to an action against Poland at the European Court of Justice.

### 3.2.2.  *Case K 18/04 on the Accession Treaty 2003*

Further shockwaves were created by the judgment of the Constitutional Tribunal on the conformity of the Accession Treaty 2003 with the Constitution. As is often the case, this judgment is paradoxically a fundamental one given on the basis of substantially weak applications. Requests to review the Accession Treaty 2003 had been submitted by three groups of members of the Polish Parliament, who are generally known for their EU-phobic and not knowledge-based views on the European Union.[63] This is clearly reflected in their applications, which look more like populist political manifestos than documents containing legal argumentation necessary for an application to a Constitutional Court. All three groups argued that the Accession Treaty 2003 was contrary to the Polish Constitution, but their argumentation differed in parts.

The authors of the first application submitted that the principle of supremacy of EC law as established in ECJ case law is contrary to Article 8 of the Constitution. The latter, as explained above in section 2 of this chapter, gives supremacy to the Constitution itself. Moreover, the applicants claimed that the recognition of European Union law amounted to taking away sovereign powers from the nation and transferring them to external authorities. This, they argued, was contrary to Article 4(1) of the Constitution vesting the supreme power in the nation. The applicants added that all decisions of state authorities taken in breach of the Polish Constitution must be considered null and void. They claimed that the principle of supremacy leads to a gradual abolishment of sovereignty, and that membership equals an unlimited transfer of the state's competences, contrary to Article 90(1) of the Polish Constitution.[64] Their final argument dealt with the threats Union law poses for the status of real estate in the northern and western parts of Poland, i.e., in territories that had belonged to Germany before the Second World War.

---

[61]  Para. 5.7. of the judgment.

[62]  For a detailed analysis of this revision, see Łazowski, *loc. cit.* n. 11, at pp. 432-434.

[63]  Paradoxically, one of them became later a judge of the Constitutional Tribunal and was a judge *rapporteur* in a very pro-EU decision on the preliminary ruling procedure (discussed in section 5.2. of this chapter).

[64]  See section 2 of this chapter.

The second application followed the same school of thought. According to its authors, the sovereignty of the Polish nation disappeared as a result of membership in the European Union. The latter, as a supranational organisation, irreversibly takes away sovereign rights of states. The authors also argued that the principle of supremacy was contrary to Article 91(3) of the Constitution and was also in violation of Article 188 of the Constitution as it leads to a change in the jurisdiction of the Constitutional Tribunal. Furthermore, the applicants questioned the conformity of the principle of non-discrimination enshrined in Article 13(1) EC with Article 18 of the Constitution, which sets forth the principle of the protection of the family (understood as marriage between a man and a woman). Moreover, according to the applicants, membership has led to a revision of the Polish Constitution through the backdoor, i.e., without the use of the modification procedure spelled out in Article 235 of the Constitution. Finally, the conformity of the preliminary ruling procedure with the Polish Constitution was questioned.

The third application was the longest and most complex. First, the applicants submitted that the principle of supremacy was contrary to the Polish Constitution as it alienated powers of the nation to take sovereign and democratic decisions relating to Poland. Giving decision-making powers to the Council of the European Union results in EU law being adopted by an executive authority, hence, in an undemocratic fashion. Moreover, the powers of the Council reduce the powers of the Polish Parliament, thereby breaching the principle of division of powers among the executive, the legislature and the judiciary enshrined in the Constitution, and lead to 'despotism of the European Union and autocracy of the Council.' Article 308 EC was also questioned. Finally, the applicants submitted that Article 19(1) EC on electoral rights of Union citizens was contrary to Article 62(1) of the Constitution.

After analysing arguments submitted by the applicants, the Constitutional Tribunal held that the Accession Treaty 2003 was in conformity with the Polish Constitution.[65] Since analysis of the entire judgment goes beyond the scope of this chapter, we will only consider two key points related to the transfer of powers to the European Union and the principle of supremacy.[66]

The discussed judgment of the Constitutional Tribunal has ended an ongoing political and legal debate on the legality of Poland's accession to the European Union. In this respect, the Tribunal's judgment was, in legal terms, the second and final step; the first was the decision of the Supreme Court confirming the validity of the accession referendum.[67] The Tribunal made clear that the decision on membership was taken by the Polish authorities as well as the Polish nation in the accession referendum. The Tribunal concluded that the transfer of certain powers to the European Union was

---

[65] Since the applications had so much in common, the President of the Constitutional Tribunal decided to let the Tribunal consider them jointly. Moreover, the complexity and importance of the legal issues at stake resulted in the Constitutional Tribunal acting in a full court capacity.

[66] For an overview of those provisions, see section 2 of this chapter.

[67] Uchwała Sądu Najwyższego z dnia 16 lipca 2003 r. w przedmiocie ważności referendum ogólnokrajowego w sprawie wyrażenia zgody na ratyfikację Traktatu dotyczącego przystąpienia Rzeczypospolitej Polskiej do Unii Europejskiej, wyznaczonego na dzień 8 czerwca 2003 r., w którym głosowanie przeprowadzono w dniach 7 i 8 czerwca 2003 r.. Sygn. III SW 144/03, Dz. U. 2003, Nr 126, Item 1170, reported in [2003] *Euro.C.L.Y.* p. 825.

approved by the sovereign nation in accordance with procedures set forth by the Constitution. In order to address the concerns of the applicants, the Constitutional Tribunal engaged in a rudimentary explanation of the basic principles underpinning the European Communities and the European Union, including the principle of attributed powers as well as the role of Article 308 EC. It also clarified the Union's institutional structure, the role of the Council of the European Union and the European Parliament. The Tribunal made it clear that from the moment of accession, Polish authorities fully participate in the decision-making procedures of the European Union. Moreover, it stressed that both chambers of the Polish Parliament are engaged in EU-decision shaping under the terms of a tailor-made act of the Parliament (mentioned earlier in this chapter).

The Constitutional Tribunal took Articles 8 and 9 of the Constitution as an important point of reference for its analysis. According to the Tribunal, the joint analysis of both provisions proves that the Polish legislator had consciously envisaged a legal system composed of legal acts originating from different internal and external sources. As a result of accession to the EU, Polish and EU law co-exist. Such co-existence ought to be based on the principles of EU-friendly interpretation and co-operative co-application. Looking at the nature of the EU legal order, the Constitutional Tribunal concluded that EU legislation is not created by arbitrary actions of EU institutions but, to the contrary, is a product of the joint co-operation among Member States. The concept and model of EU law has produced a relatively new situation where national legal orders co-exist with EU legislation.

Looking at the principle of supremacy, the Constitutional Tribunal held that in cases of conflict between the Polish Constitution and EC law, under no circumstances may primacy be given to the latter. Such conflicts could lead neither to an annulment of a constitutional provision nor to its replacement by EC law. The judges added that under Article 8(1) of the Constitution, the Constitution remains the supreme law of the land. The *modus operandi* that shall be followed in case of such conflicts is suggested in the judgment. The Constitutional Court held that there are, in principle, three ways to proceed: a modification of the Polish Constitution, amendment of EU law or withdrawal from the EU. The Constitutional Tribunal acknowledged ECJ case law on the principle of supremacy. The judges argued that the ECJ's position is justified when aims and goals of the EC are taken into account. To this end, the principle of supremacy serves as a guarantor of the effectiveness of EC law. This factor does not determine decisions of Member States' authorities taken in cases of conflicts between domestic constitutions and EC law. However, the question must be asked whether this solution truly gives supremacy to the Polish Constitution. *Prima facie* it certainly looks so. However, the conclusion may be different when one looks at it from the perspective of the effects of such constitutional revisions. It is arguable that if they are inspired by conflicting provisions of EU law, they amount to indirect supremacy of EU law. In other words, national law concedes its place to EU law, although on its own terms. Even if one prefers this option to granting direct supremacy to EU law over domestic constitutions, the effects are the same – (indirect or direct) supremacy of EU law. In theory, of course, the other two scenarios presented by the Constitutional Tribunal are also possible. However, despite their intellectual attractiveness, both seem to be highly unrealistic in practical terms. In cases of a conflict between EU law and the Polish Constitution, it seems likely that Poland will not be politically capable of pushing forward an amendment to EU law necessary to accommodate its internal legal problems, nor it will have the political power and will to withdraw from the European Union. The revision of the Constitution following the judgment on the European Arrest Warrant proves this point. The Constitutional Tribunal itself has suggested a future revision of Article 227 of the Polish Constitution, which deals with the powers and tasks of the National Bank of Poland. The Article will have to be revised when Poland decides and is accepted to introduce the euro as its currency.

The Constitutional Tribunal also noted that neither Article 90 nor Article 91 of the Constitution may serve as the legal basis for a transfer of powers to the EU to an extent that adoption of legal acts contrary to the Polish Constitution would be allowed. To this end, the Tribunal explicitly referred to case law from the German Constitutional Tribunal and the Danish Supreme Court.[68] Moreover, in a rather unclear conclusion presented at the very end of the judgment, the Tribunal did not exclude the possibility of adjudication on conformity of secondary legislation with the Polish Constitution.[69] Undoubtedly, this issue will require further clarification, particularly in the light of the consistent ECJ case law on the powers of national courts to deal with validity of secondary legislation.[70]

## 4.     THE APPLICATION OF EU LAW BY POLISH COURTS

### 4.1.     Introduction

In the period preceding the accession to the European Union, a lot of warnings were made as to the ability of Polish courts to apply EU law. To approximate national law with *acquis communautaire* was a major effort; however, to apply such legislation in a manner consistent with EU law was considered an even bigger challenge to the national judiciary. Ewa Łętowska argued that the source of those barriers was to be found 'in the very way of Polish legal thinking.'[71] This acute observation reflected the reality of the Polish judiciary in the turbulent times of legal and economic transformation. Judges were suddenly exposed to a plethora of new legislation covering areas which previously had either not existed in the Polish legal order, or their practical role was marginal. Also, it became bluntly clear that the technical approach to application

---

[68] Para. 4.5 of the judgment.
[69] Para. 18.5 of the judgment.
[70] ECJ, Case 314/85 *Foto-Frost v. Hauptzollamt Lübeck-Ost* [1987] *ECR* 4199; Case C-461/03 *Gaston Schul Douane-expediteur BV v. Minister van Landbouw, Natuur en Voedselkwaliteit* [2005] *ECR* I-10513; Case C-344/04 *The Queen, on the application of International Air Transport Association and European Low Fares Airline Association v. Department for Transport* [2006] *ECR* I-403.
[71] E. Łętowska, 'The Barriers of Polish Legal Thinking in the Perspective of European Integration', 1 *YPES* (2007) pp. 55-72, at p. 55.

of law was officially made redundant, and a new, proactive approach based on robust judicial discourse was expected. This, as predicted, created a fair amount of resentment to the emerging "new world"; however, at the same time, good signs demonstrating a rapid change of approach were also emerging on the horizon. For instance, already in 1997, the Supreme Administrative Court referred to EC customs law to support its own interpretation of national law.[72] This was a rare example, but nevertheless, it demonstrated certain tendencies at the top of the judicial apex.[73] Five years after the accession, the general picture is positive, thus giving a lot of reasons for praise. At the same time, one can easily find examples of judgments giving grounds for concern. In this section of the chapter, we endeavour to strike a balance between those two extremes. The selection of judgments covers all branches of the judiciary, including civil, criminal and administrative courts.

It is only natural in a country the size of Poland, that judgments of domestic courts dealing with EU law can be calculated in hundreds, if not thousands. Unlike in the Czech Republic, the tide of EU law cases has flooded national courts. In hindsight, it is clear that the first to be exposed to such waves of cases were administrative courts. With dozens of tax and customs cases, judges of administrative courts were faced with the reality of being "European" judges almost as of the date of accession. They were also the first to test the functioning of the preliminary ruling machinery.[74] The wave of EU law-based cases shortly afterwards reached other branches of the judiciary, including criminal courts. In the latter, Third Pillar legislation is almost non-existent, but a plethora of cases dealing with the European Arrest Warrant exists. Paradoxically, the problem is not the lack of application of EU law in this respect but an excessive use of the surrender procedure.[75]

## 4.2. Pre-accession cases and application of EU law

As in other new Member States, the first wave of EU law-related litigation to reach Polish courts were cases where in substantive terms *acquis* was at stake; however, it was not applicable to facts that had taken place prior to accession. Even before the *Ynos* case,[76] the Polish courts took a strict approach, clearly delimiting the pre- and post-accession periods. In order to prove this argument, several judgments of the Supreme Administrative Court as well as the Supreme Court will be used.

---

[72] Supreme Administrative Court, 13 March 2000, Case V S.A. 1658/99, *S. v. Prezes Głównego Urzędu Cel*, ONSA 2001, Item 412 (interestingly enough, the full version of the judgment with its pro-EU law reasoning is only available electronically at http://orzeczenia.nsa.gov.pl/doc/E66633BAE4).

[73] See further, S. Biernat, '"European" Rulings of Polish Courts Prior to Accession to the European Union', 5 *The Polish Foreign Affairs Digest* (2005) pp. 127-149; M. Górka and C. Mik, 'Sądy polskie jako sądy Unii Europejskiej (na tle doświadczeń przedakcesyjnych)' [Polish courts as European Union courts (pre-accession experience)] 4 *Kwartalnik Prawa Publicznego* (2005) pp. 7-53. For a comparative look at the Czech, Slovak and Polish pre-accession experience, see Z. Kühn, 'Application of European law in Central European candidate countries', 28 *ELRev.* (2003) pp. 551-560.

[74] See section 5 in this chapter.

[75] See further, Łazowski, *loc. cit.* n. 11, at pp. 434-436.

[76] ECJ, Case C-302/04 *Ynos kft v. János Varga* [2006] *ECR* I-371.

To begin, one could refer to a judgment of the Supreme Administrative Court rendered in case I GSK 168/05 *S-P v. Dyrektor Izby Celnej w W.*[77] It is an example of a decision where the delimitation mentioned above is clearly made by a Polish court. The factual and legal background was as follows. Following an importation of pharmaceuticals from France, the plaintiff filed a customs declaration, which was accepted by customs authorities in late 1999. The customs value of the imported pharmaceuticals reflected the amount written down in the exporter's invoice dated 1 October 1999. A subsequent inspection by the customs authorities uncovered a contract between the exporter and the plaintiff on financial premiums. The pharmaceuticals covered by the customs declaration in question belonged to products to which fixed discounts applied. There was no doubt that the plaintiff's payments declared on the invoice were discount free. The court hearing the case in the first instance concluded that the complainant gained additional benefits by the application of the discount clause. The system of premiums reduced the transaction price specified in the invoice and in the customs declaration. In accordance with Polish customs law applicable at the time, the declared customs value should have been reduced. A national court seized with the request for judicial review rejected the plaintiff's argument based on a breach of the Polish Constitution as well as Articles 68-69 EA Poland.[78] The court emphasised that the contested decision was based on the Polish Customs law combined with Article VII of GATT. In its request for cassation appeal, the plaintiff requested a reference to the European Court of Justice on the interpretation of Articles 68 and 69 EA Poland, asking whether these provisions imposed the obligation to interpret the Polish law in accordance with the EC customs law. The Supreme Administrative Court held that the customs authorities properly verified the factual background. It rejected the plaintiff's argument that the financial premium (the discount) had no link to the price of imported pharmaceuticals. The terms of the contract clearly indicated the close link between the financial premiums available to the plaintiff and purchase of pharmaceuticals from the French contractor. By the same token, the financial premiums contributed to the reduction of the invoice price of purchased products. The Court held that neither the Polish Constitution nor Polish customs law were breached. The argument based on the breach of EA Poland was not accepted by the Court. Since the first instance court only scarcely covered the EU argumentation, the Court developed all links to EC law. The plaintiff wrongly relied on case C-224/97 *Erich Ciola v. Land Vorarlberg*,[79] as customs procedures had been completed and the goods imported long before the accession to the European Union. This precluded the application of EC law to the facts of the case. The application of cases 50/76 *Amsterdam Bulb BV v. Produktschap voor Siergewassen*[80] and C-118/00 *Gervais Larsy v. Institut national d'assurances sociales pour travailleurs indépendants (INASTI)* was also excluded. The Court rejected arguments as to the direct

---

[77] Supreme Administrative Court of Poland, 6 May 2005, Case I GSK 168/05, *S-P v. Dyrektor Izby Celnej w W.* (not reported, available at http://orzeczenia.nsa.gov.pl/doc/D122ECF2A6).

[78] Europe Agreement establishing an association between the European Communities and their Member States, of the one part, and the Republic of Poland, of the other part, *OJ* 1993 L 348/2.

[79] ECJ, Case C-224/97 *Erich Ciola v. Land Vorarlberg* [1999] *ECR* I-2515.

[80] ECJ, Case 50/76 *Amsterdam Bulb BV v. Produktschap voor Siergewassen* [1977] *ECR* 137.

effect of Article 68 EA Poland (based on the case C-63/99 *The Queen v. Secretary of State for the Home Department,* ex parte *Wiesław Głoszczuk and Elżbieta Głoszczuk*)[81] According to the Court, Article 68 EA Poland had no direct effect. Moreover, if such an argument would be acceptable, then it would have applied only to the Member States at the time (not Poland). The subsequent accession to the European Union did not extend the jurisdiction of the European Court of Justice; thus the Court rejected the request for the preliminary ruling. The accession did not mean that the ECJ has gained jurisdiction to handle preliminary rulings dealing with pre-accession cases. It is notable that this judgment had been rendered before the ECJ delivered a judgment in the *Ynos* case. Thus, the Supreme Administrative Court referred to earlier case law. It held that in accordance with case C-321/97 *Ulla-Brith Andersson and Susanne Wåkerås-Andersson v. Svenska staten,*[82] the ECJ has no jurisdiction to deal with requests for the preliminary ruling from third countries (which include the new Member States in the pre-accession phase). An argument to the contrary would have led to the extension of the EC legal system to the pre-accession phase, clearly not provided for by the EA Poland. A reference for the preliminary ruling on the application of Articles 68-69 EA Poland would go beyond the normative meaning of those provisions.

Another development that merits attention is a judgment of the Supreme Administrative Court rendered in case I FSK 117/05 *Przedsiębiorstwo Handlowo Usługowe D. v. Izba Skarbowa.*[83] It proves consistency in the approach of Polish administrative courts in such pre/post-accession cases. It was rendered against the following factual and legal background. The claimant made deductions in VAT tax reports for March, August, September and December of 1999. These submissions were partly rejected by the Polish tax authorities. This was due to several irregularities leading to discrepancies between tax estimates submitted by the applicant in VAT tax and invoices they were based on. The tax authorities argued that deductions were contrary to Polish VAT legislation. Since this decision was upheld by the Tax Chamber, the applicant requested judicial review. It argued, *inter alia,* that the tax authorities acted in breach of Polish law as well as Articles 17 and 19 of the Directive 77/388/EEC on VAT tax.[84] Voivod Administrative Court in Warsaw dismissed the complaint. It accepted arguments of the tax authorities proving the impossibility of verification of the invoices in question and amounts due. The Administrative Court considered the arguments based on case law of the Constitutional Tribunal to be irrelevant to the case at hand. The applicant submitted a request for cassation appeal to the Supreme Administrative Court. It requested annulment of the judgment and a reference for the preliminary ruling to the European

---

[81] ECJ, Case C-63/99 *The Queen v. Secretary of State for the Home Department,* ex parte *Wiesław Głoszczuk and Elżbieta Głoszczuk* [2001] *ECR* I-6369.

[82] ECJ, Case C-321/97 *Ulla-Brith Andersson and Susanne Wåkerås-Andersson v. Svenska staten* [1999] *ECR* I-2517.

[83] Supreme Administrative Court of Poland, 21 October 2005, Case I FSK 117/05, *Przedsiębiorstwo Handlowo Usługowe D. v. Izba Skarbowa,* (not reported, available at http://orzeczenia.nsa.gov.pl/doc/2C8B4A44A5).

[84] Sixth Council Directive 77/388/EEC of 17 May 1977 on the harmonisation of the laws of the Member States relating to turnover taxes – Common system of value added tax: uniform basis of assessment, *OJ* 1977 L 145/1.

Court of Justice on the interpretation of the Directive. The Supreme Court upheld the contested decision. It held that at the given time, Poland was not a member of the European Union; therefore EU law was not applicable. This meant that neither the Voivod Administrative Court nor the Supreme Administrative Court had a jurisdiction to proceed with a reference for the preliminary ruling to the European Court of Justice. It also confirmed that the contested decision of the tax authorities did not err in procedural or substantive Polish tax law.

During the period that falls under the category of post-accession cases with pre-accession factual background, one of the judgments that clearly stands out – due to a legal issue at stake – is a Supreme Administrative Court's decision in case III GSK 54/05 *TBC Plc Nottingham v. Urząd Patentowy*.[85] It is interesting as it touches upon the idiosyncratic relationship between EC law, TRIPS Agreement and the effects of both in the Polish legal order. The factual background was as follows. The applicant – TBC Plc (registered in Nottingham) – filed in December 1986 an application for registration of a patent to the Polish Patent Office. It was formally registered on 27 June 1989. According to Inventiveness Act 1972 (applicable at that time), the term of protection was 15 years from the date of registration.[86] In 2001, TBC Plc applied for the five-year prolongation of the term of protection. In its submission, the complainant relied on Article 33 of the TRIPS Agreement, which gives a minimum of 20 years patent protection. In its decision of February 2002, the Patent Office rejected the application. It argued that it had no legal basis for the prolongation in Polish law. Moreover, TRIPS was an international treaty, which required national implementing measures. Article 33 of the TRIPS Agreement provided for a minimum protection of 20 years; thus, it could not have any effects without domestic law. The Patent Office upheld its earlier decision on 30 July 2003. The complainant requested a judicial review of this decision. Voivod Administrative Court annulled both decisions of the Patent Office. It held that they lacked the legal basis. According to the Court, Article 33 of TRIPS was a self-executing norm that did not require domestic legislation giving it effect. Bearing in mind Article 31 of the Vienna Convention on the Law of Treaties 1969, the Administrative Court interpreted Article 33 of TRIPS as applicable to all existing patents benefiting from the protection under Polish jurisdiction. The Patent Office requested a cassation appeal. It submitted a number of procedural and substantive arguments undermining the decision of the first instance court. It confirmed its earlier approach to the legal effects of Article 33 of TRIPS and requested the Supreme Administrative Court to proceed with a reference for the preliminary ruling to the European Court of Justice. It referred to the ECJ's judgment in case C-245/02 *Anheuser-Busch Inc v. Budejovicky Budvar*.[87] The Supreme Administrative Court held it had no jurisdiction to submit a reference for the preliminary ruling to the European Court of

---

[85] Supreme Administrative Court of Poland, 8 February 2006, Case II GSK 54/05, *TBC Plc Nottingham v. Urząd Patentowy*, ONSAiWSA 2006, Nr 4, Item 96.

[86] Ustawa z dnia 19 października 1972 r. o wynalazczości, Dz. U. 1984, Nr 33, Item 177 (as amended).

[87] ECJ, Case C-245/02 *Anheuser-Busch Inc. v. Budějovický Budvar, národní podnik* [2004] *ECR* I-10989.

Justice as the facts of the case had taken place before the accession. To this end, it referred to the *Ynos* case.[88] It found Article 33 TRIPS to be a self-executing norm, which, in cases of conflicts with Polish legislation, takes primacy pursuant to Article 91 of the Polish Constitution 1997. The Supreme Administrative Court agreed that the first instance court erred in law in the evaluation of the legal basis for the contested decisions. It concluded that the prolongation of the patent protection was not *ex lege* but required an administrative decision. Since the Supreme Administrative Court had all the necessary facts, it decided not to return the case to the Voivod Administrative Court for further adjudication but to annul the contested decisions instead.

The Supreme Court has not been immune to such cases. Quite to the contrary, it has had to deal with similar types of problems itself. In a number of pre-accession cases, it refused to apply EU law; however, it used it as a source of inspiration and as a tool for the interpretation of Polish law. As an example, we will use case III PK 30/06 *Śliwiński v. Polskie Koleje Linii Hutniczej Szerokotorowej.*[89] The claimant, Jan Śliwinski, served as a legal advisor for the defendant between 1 October 2003 and 15 February 2004. Upon the expiry of a freelance contract between the parties, no further freelance or employment offers were made by the defendant. Mr. Śliwinski argued that the lack of the employment offer amounted to discrimination. In his claim to a first instance court, he requested an order guaranteeing an employment offer or award of damages. Polish courts hearing the case in the first instance and in the appeal dismissed those claims as unfounded. The evaluation of facts proved that there were no instances of discriminatory treatment. It was Mr. Śliwinski's poor performance that had led to the non-extension of the contract. In his request for cassation to the Supreme Court, Mr. Śliwinski submitted that the lower courts erred in the application of Polish employment law in relation to Article 3(1)(a) Directive 2000/78/EC on non-discrimination.[90] The applicant drew the Supreme Court's attention to discrepancies between Polish law and the Directive. The Supreme Court held that since the facts had taken place before the accession of Poland to the European Union, the Directive formally did not apply in this case. Nevertheless, national courts had the obligation to take EU law into account as part of the approximation process. The nature of cassation appeals limits the scope of review to legal issues only. Therefore, the Supreme Court upheld the decisions of the lower instance courts and held that discrimination had not taken place. It ruled, however, that Polish law must be read in the light of Article 10(1) of the Directive. According to Polish law, the burden of proof in discrimination cases lies in the hands of claimants. Discrimination is declared unless an employer is able objectively to justify its actions. However, the Supreme Court ruled that the provision in question had to be read as imposing the obligation on claimants to show the facts, on one hand, and the obligation to present counter arguments by defendants on the other. The burden of

---

[88] *Loc. cit.* n. 76.

[89] Supreme Court of Poland, 9 June 2006, Case III PK 30/06, *Jan Śliwiński v. Polskie Koleje Linia Hutnicza Szerokotorowa Sp. z o.o. w Zamościu*, not reported (available in Caselex database at http://www.caselex.com).

[90] Council Directive 2000/78/EC of 27 November 2000 establishing a general framework for equal treatment in employment and occupation, *OJ* 2000 L 303/16.

proof shifted to the latter to prove that discrimination did not take place. In order to support its interpretation, the Supreme Court referred to the Directive 97/80/EC on the burden of proof in sex discrimination cases[91] and relevant case law of the European Court of Justice.[92] This led the Supreme Court to the next point raised by the claimant, which was discrimination in access to the profession. Article 3(1)(a) of the Directive, published in the Polish edition of the Official Journal of the European Union, limits the scope of application of its provisions to the conditions on access to employment or self-employment. At the same time, the French and English versions of the Directive also include access to professions. By referring to the relevant case law of the ECJ, the Supreme Court clarified that in such cases, Polish courts shall have recourse to other language versions, primarily the French. In conclusion, the Supreme Court dismissed the cassation appeal as unfounded.

The three judgments of the Supreme Administrative Court clearly give merits to the argument made at the very outset. In a consistent fashion, the Court drew a line between pre- and post-accession periods. In cases where facts had taken place prior to the enlargement, EU law was not applicable; however it could have potentially served as a tool for interpretation of national law. Such pro-European interpretation was based on Article 68 EA Poland that served as the legal basis for the approximation of Polish law with *acquis communautaire*. Only as of the date of accession, were Polish courts bound by EU law with all legal consequences resulting from that. The Supreme Administrative Court rejected requests coming from parties to disputes to proceed with a reference for preliminary ruling. Even prior to the *Ynos* case, the Court resisted the temptation (if there was any) to engage in a dialogue with the European Court of Justice. The judgment of the Supreme Court adds additional flavours to the post-accession cases with pre-accession facts. Not only had the Supreme Court used EC law as a tool for interpretation for Polish law, but it also acknowledged teething problems with translation of *acquis* into Polish. This time, it was not the lack of availability of the Official Journal but the quality of translation as such. While those cases are interesting and played an important role in the first years upon the accession, they will slowly phase out for reasons which are self-explanatory. That is why this analysis will turn in the next section to cases where EU law was fully applicable.

4.3.    **The principles of supremacy, direct and indirect effect of EC law in operation**

A real test for the Polish courts started when the first truly and fully post-accession EU law-based cases reached courtrooms all over Poland. The question was how would national judges react to this new legal order. Would they pretend not to see it and let

---

[91] Council Directive 97/80/EC of 15 December 1997 on the burden of proof in cases of discrimination based on sex, *OJ* 2000 L 303/16.

[92] ECJ, Case C-196/02 *Vasiliki Nikoloudi v. Organismos Tilepikoinonion Ellados AE* [2005] *ECR* I-1789; Case 19/67 *Bestuur der Sociale Verzekeringsbank v. J.H. van der Vecht* [1967] *ECR* 345; Case 283/81 *Srl CILFIT and Lanificio di Gavardo SpA v. Ministry of Health* [1982] *ECR* 3415; Case C-236/97 *Skatteministeriet v. Aktieselskabet Forsikringsselskabet Codan* [1998] *ECR* I-8679.

the highest courts do the real job at the appeal stage? Would judges have the will and ability to become a part of this emerging "Brave New World"? One should recall that the Polish Constitution itself provided a legal framework for the supremacy and direct effect of EC legislation. Although pre-accession case law of ECJ was not officially available in Polish at that stage, a number of commercial publications appeared on the market carefully elaborating upon all tenets of EU law. Therefore, excuses for non-application of EU law were quite limited. It is notable that advice in this respect came also from the Constitutional Tribunal. In case P 37/05, it was faced with a reference from an administrative court as to the compatibility of Polish excise duty legislation with Article 90 EC.[93] When discussing the duties of national courts in the EU member-ship environment, it held:

> 'In the process of applying the law, judges shall completely be subject [to] the Constitution and statutes (art.178 para.1 of the Constitution). This principle is connected with the "conflicting norm", as expressed in art.91 para.2, imposing an obligation to refuse to apply statutes in the event of a conflict with an international agreement ratified by way of statute. The principle of precedence also applies to Community law (art.91 para.3 of the Constitution). Therefore – where no doubts arise regarding the contents of a Community law norm – a court ought to refuse to apply the statutory provision conflicting with Community law, and directly apply the provision of the latter (Community law) or, alternatively, if it is not possible to directly apply a Community law norm, the court should seek such interpretation of domestic law that it conforms to Community law. In the event of interpretational doubts regarding Community law, the national court should refer a question to the ECJ for a preliminary ruling to resolve the doubts.'[94]

This way, the Constitutional Tribunal made it clear what is the *modus operandi* that national judges should follow in cases of conflicts between Polish and EC law.

As was the case with some other new Member States, the first major problem encountered by public administration and national courts was delays with the publication of the Special Edition of the Official Journal in Polish.[95] Even before the judgment in the *Skoma-Lux* case, Polish courts had expressed doubts as to the application of such law in the Polish legal order. A judgment of the Voivod Administrative Court in Bydgoszcz in case I SA/Bd 275/05 *C. Sp. z o.o. v. Dyrektor Izby Celnej w T.*[96] is usually a point of reference in the academic writing.[97] The applicant requested annulment

---

[93] *Loc. cit.* n. 43.

[94] Para. 15 of the judgment.

[95] It is standard practice in the European Union that legislation pre-dating accession of new countries is published in the official languages of new Member States in special editions of the Official Journal of the European Union. Fifth and sixth enlargements were not an exception to that rule; however, unlike in previous enlargement rounds, delays were considerable. See M. Bobek, 'The Binding Force of Babel: The Enforcement of EC Law Unpublished in the Languages of the New Member States', 9 *CYELS* (2007) pp. 43-80. See also Chapter 5 in this volume.

[96] Voivod Administrative Court in Bydgoszcz, 20 July 2005, Case I SA/Bd 275/05 *C. Sp. z o.o. v. Dyrektor Izby Celnej w T.* (not reported, available at http://orzeczenia.nsa.gov.pl/doc/D3CA4CF9C4).

[97] See, *inter alia*, K. Lasiński-Sulecki and W. Morawski, 'Late publication of EC law in languages of new Member States and its effects: Obligations on individuals following the Court's judgment in Skoma-Lux', 45 *CMLRev.* (2008) pp. 705-725, at pp. 708-709.

of a decision of the customs authorities imposing payment of customs duty and VAT tax due on importation of goods. In the course of the procedure, the authorities relied on Commission Regulation 1972/2003/EC,[98] which, at the given time, was not yet formally published in the Special Edition of the Official Journal of the European Union. The Voivod Administrative Court quashed the contested decision and held that it had been adopted in breach of the principle of legal certainty. Similar judgments were rendered by other Polish courts.[99] Lack of publication was one thing; however, comparable problems have been created by poor quality of translated *acquis*. Judgment of the Supreme Administrative Court in case II GSK 452/08 *S.C.-B.R. v. Główny Inspektor Transportu Drogowego* may serve as a very good example in this respect.[100] The plaintiff challenged a decision of the road inspectorate imposing a penalty for breach of road transport rules provided in Council Regulation 3821/85/EEC.[101] One of the issues raised by the Voivod Administrative Court seized with the request for judicial review in the first instance and by the Supreme Administrative Court dealing with the appeal was a discrepancy between Polish and other language versions of the Regulation. According to the Polish version published in the Special Edition of the Official Journal of the European Union, the Regulation applied to 'vehicles used for the carriage of passengers on regular services where the route covered ... does not exceed 50 kilometres.' The Polish version was clearly illogical; the English version provided for the application of the Regulation 'where the route covered ... exceeds 50 kilometres.' Both courts agreed that as a matter of principle, a comparative analysis of language versions was necessary. However, it would have led to an imposition of obligations on the plaintiff on the basis of a legal act not available in the Polish language. This, according to both courts, would have been in breach of the principle of legal certainty.

As mentioned above, the first wave of cases reached administrative courts shortly upon accession to the European Union. A considerable number of them dealt with tax discrimination in importation of second-hand cars. This, as explained in section 5 of this chapter, led to the first reference from a Polish court to the European Court of Justice in the *Brzeziński* case.[102] An equally considerable number of disputes between companies and tax authorities dealt with VAT Act 2004 and its compliance with the Sixth VAT Directive. The Polish law in question had been adopted hastily in the last moment before the enlargement and clearly had not been the finest product of Polish legislature. Non-compliance with EC law was only one of the criticisms raised at the time. It was only a question of time when administrative courts would be faced with cases challenging the legality of tax decisions based on VAT Act 2004. Judgment of

---

[98] Commission Regulation 1972/2003/EC of 10 November 2003 on transitional measures to be adopted in respect of trade in agricultural products on account of the accession of the Czech Republic, Estonia, Cyprus, Latvia, Lithuania, Hungary, Malta, Poland, Slovenia and Slovakia, *OJ* 2003 L 293/3.

[99] See, *inter alia*, Lasiński-Sulecki and Morawski, *loc. cit.* n. 97, at p. 709.

[100] Supreme Administrative Court of Poland, 7 November 2008, Case II GSK 452/08 *S.C.-B.R. v. Główny Inspektor Transportu Drogowego* (not reported, available at http://orzeczenia.nsa.gov.pl/doc/1456D8773C).

[101] Council Regulation 3820/85/EEC of 20 December 1985 on the harmonisation of certain social legislation relating to road transport, *OJ* 1985 L 370/1.

[102] ECJ, Case C-313/05 *Maciej Brzeziński v. Dyrektor Izby Celnej w Warszawie* [2007] *ECR* I-513.

the Voivod Administrative Court in Warsaw in case III SA/Wa 2219/05 *General Electric*[103] was one of the first to demonstrate the real meaning of the principles of supremacy and direct effect.

On 24 November 2004, General Electric Polska requested reimbursement of VAT paid from June to September 2004. It provided a variety of technical services (including the construction of jet engines) for General Electric USA. In its application, the plaintiff argued that the supply of engineers' services for customers established outside the European Union constitutes a transaction covered by the rules set out in Article 9(2) (e) of the Council Directive 77/388/EEC. To this end, the services provided should have been considered as VAT non-chargeable in Poland. In its submission, the plaintiff argued that several provisions of VAT Act 2004 were not in conformity with the Directive as they restricted the application of Article 9(2)(e) to selected types of engineers' services only.[104] The services rendered by the plaintiff were not covered by the exception and were chargeable events under the Polish law. The request was rejected by the tax authorities, who argued that the Directive was properly implemented, and the services were not covered by the exception. Since the decision of the tax authorities was upheld by the Director of Tax Chamber, the plaintiff decided to proceed with judicial review. The Warsaw Administrative Court entertained the claim and annulled the contested decision. The judges confirmed the non-conformity of VAT Act 2004 with Article 9(2) (e) of the Directive. According to the Court, the latter provision was clear, precise and unconditional and, therefore, was capable of producing direct effect. The Court referred extensively to case law of the European Court of Justice on the direct effect of directives and on the supremacy of EC law.[105] In allowing the Directive to have direct effect, the Court relied on Article 91 of the Polish Constitution 1997, which – as explained in section 2 of this chapter – gives priority to EC law in the cases of conflicts with Polish legislation.

However plausible this decision was, it does not mean that the principles of supremacy and direct effect were easily received by national courts. Real litmus tests were dozens of cases dealing with discriminatory taxation of second-hand cars. Before the ECJ rendered its judgment in *Brzeziński*, case decisions of Polish administrative courts had been very inconclusive. The following litigation may serve as an excellent exam-

---

[103] Voivod Administrative Court in Warsaw, 12 October 2005, Case III SA/Wa 2219/05, *General Electric Polska v. Dyrektor Izby Skarbowej w Warszawie* (not reported, available at http://orzeczenia.nsa. gov.pl/doc/9626EF05C0).

[104] Ustawa z dnia 11 marca 2004 r. o podatku od towarów i usług, Dz. U. 2004, Nr 53, Item 545 (as amended).

[105] The Court referred to several evergreens, including Cases 26/62 *NV Algemene Transport- en Expeditie Onderneming van Gend & Loos v. Netherlands Inland Revenue Administration* [1963] *ECR* 1; Case 6/64 *Flaminio Costa v. E.N.E.L.* [1964] *ECR* 585; Case 41/74 *Yvonne van Duyn v. Home Office* [1974] *ECR* 1337; Case 148/78 *Criminal proceedings against Tullio Ratti* [1979] *ECR* 1629; Case 8/81 *Ursula Becker v. Finanzamt Münster-Innenstadt* [1982] *ECR* 53; Case 103/88 *Fratelli Costanzo SpA v. Comune di Milano* [1989] *ECR* 1839; Case 152/84 *M.H. Marshall v. Southampton and South-West Hampshire Area Health Authority (Teaching)* [1986] *ECR* 723; C-91/92 *Paola Faccini Dori v. Recreb Srl.* [1994] *ECR* I-3325.

ple. In case I SA/Łd 1059/04 *R.G. v. Dyrektor Izby Celnej w Ł.*,[106] the Voivod Administrative Court in Łòdź was seized with a request for judicial review of a decision of customs authorities imposing excise duty due on importation of such a vehicle. The importer paid the customs duty due and requested reimbursement on grounds of non-conformity of the Polish law with Article 90 EC. Before reaching the Voivod Administrative Court, the case had been dealt with by the Director of the Customs Chamber. While dismissing the request, it argued as follows:

> 'Evaluation of conformity of Community law with national law does not fall under the powers of the Director of Customs Chamber. Equally, it is not within its powers to interpret norms contained in Community Treaties and any potential discrepancies [between EC and national law] may only take place in co-operation with national authorities responsible for the functioning the tax system in Poland. Disputes relating to non compliance with Community law are within the jurisdiction of the European Court of Justice.'

However incorrect this approach is, it is far from being accidental in the practice of Polish tax and customs authorities. Judging from countless requests for judicial review entertained by Polish administrative courts, this mantra is a standard practice of administrative authorities. One cannot but agree with Michal Bobek who argues that while courts of the new Member States are adjusting to the requirements of membership, administrative authorities are lagging behind.[107] After looking at the merits of the case, the Administrative Court in Łòdź rendered a judgment demonstrating limited understanding of obligations resting on national authorities, including courts. By using procedural gimmicks, the Court upheld the contested decision. It held, *inter alia*, that the tax authorities had no powers to deal with matters of non-conformity of national law with EC legislation. The Supreme Administrative Court, dealing with an appeal in this case, annulled the contested judgment.[108] Acting with the benefit of the *Brzeziński* case (judgment of the ECJ was rendered in the meantime), the Court returned the case to the Administrative Court in Łòdź for further adjudication.

The previous example demonstrated a situation whereby a court of first instance erred in law and rendered a judgment subsequently quashed by the Supreme Administrative Court. However, the analysis of case law of first instance administrative courts demonstrates that quite often they are willing and able to refer to EC law in their decisions. The following decision of the Voivod Administrative Court in Wrocław in case I SA/Wr 1452/05 will be used to demonstrate this.[109] The factual background was as follows. The claimant, Jerzy S., ran a grocery store. In February 2005, he submitted a VAT declaration for May 2004. The Director of the Tax Office adopted a decision

---

[106] Voivod Administrative Court in Łòdź, 24 February 2005, Case I SA/Łd 1059/04 *R.G. v. Dyrektor Izby Celnej w Ł.* (not reported, available at http://orzeczenia.nsa.gov.pl/doc/E0403C7806).

[107] M. Bobek, 'Thou Shalt Have Two Masters; The Application of European Law by Administrative Authorities in the New Member Status', 1 *REAL* (2008) pp. 51-63.

[108] Supreme Administrative Court of Poland, 13 February 2007, Case I FSK 1206/05, *R.G. v. Dyrektor Izby Celnej w Ł.* (not reported, available at http://orzeczenia.nsa.gov.pl/doc/8A34558B9C).

[109] Voivod Administrative Court in Wrocław, 26 July 2006, Case I SA/Wr 1452/05, *Jerzy S. v. Naczelnik Urzędu Skarbowego* (not reported, available at http://orzeczenia.nsa.gov.pl/doc/C4BDDC2F02).

specifying the VAT tax due. The Director did not accept deductions made by the claimant. The Director held that the right to deduct VAT belongs only to registered VAT payers. Since Mr. S submitted his application for the registration only on 30 June 2004, he was not entitled to the deduction. The Director of the Tax Chamber upheld the decision of the Director. The claimant requested a judicial review of those decisions. His argumentation focused on the conformity of VAT Act 2004 with the Constitution and with the Council Directive 77/388/EEC on VAT tax. The Voivod Administrative Court started off by analysing Article 88(4) VAT Act 2004. The Court confirmed that the VAT registration was a *conditio sine qua non* for the establishment of the right to deduct VAT. At the same time, the Court noted that since the accession to the European Union, Polish authorities have the obligation to interpret VAT Act 2004 in the light of EC VAT legislation and the Directive in particular. The Court emphasised that the Polish legal system as well as the EU legal order function together in all Member States of the European Union. It referred to the principle of neutrality enshrined in the Directive. The analysis of Articles 17-20 of the Directive and case law of the European Court of Justice[110] led the Court to the conclusion that the decision of the tax authorities was contrary to the Directive. It argued that nothing in the Directive makes the right to deduct conditional upon an earlier registration for VAT purposes. To this end, Article 88(4) VAT Act 2004 should have been interpreted in the light of Articles 17-20 of the Directive. Moreover, the fact that the claimant submitted his tax reports with a delay did not preclude his right to the deduction. The contested decisions were thus repealed.

Case law of the Supreme Court also deals with fundamentals of the EC legal order. One of the first opportunities to elaborate on those matters was the case *Cz. Miś v. Samodzielny Publiczny Zakład Opieki Zdrowotnej im. Jędrzeja Śniadeckiego w Nowym Sączu.*[111] The facts of the case were as follows. The plaintiff requested an additional annual leave compensating for overtime work, including night shifts in the period starting from 1 May 2004. The defendant submitted that the claim should be dismissed and argued that the employment conditions had fully complied with the requirements set out in Public Health Units Act 1991.[112] The plaintiff in his claim relied on the Council Directive 93/104/EC on the working time.[113] On 22 November 2004, the District Court in Nowy Sącz dismissed the claim. The District Court concluded that the Public Health Authority could not be classified as an emanation of the state; therefore, the Directive could not have been relied upon by the plaintiff. According to the District Court, the

---

[110] ECJ, Case 268/83 *D.A. Rompelman and E.A. Rompelman-Van Deelen v. Minister van Financiën* [1985] *ECR* 655; Case 50/87 *Commission of the European Communities v. French Republic* [1988] *ECR* 4797; Case C-400/98 *Finanzamt Goslar v. Brigitte Breitsohl* [2000] *ECR* I-4321; Case C-33/03 *Commission of the European Communities v. United Kingdom of Great Britain and Northern Ireland* [2005] *ECR* I-1865.

[111] Supreme Court of Poland, 6 June 2006, Case I PK 263/05, *Cz. Miś v. Samodzielny Publiczny Zakład Opieki Zdrowotnej im. Jędrzeja Śniadeckiego w Nowym Sączu*, not reported (on file with the authors).

[112] Ustawa z dnia 30 sierpnia 1991 o zakładach opieki zdrowotnej, Dz. U. 1991, Nr 91, Item 408 (as amended).

[113] Council Directive 93/104/EC of 23 November 1993 concerning certain aspects of the organisation of working time, *OJ* 1993 L 307/18.

Directive did not apply in Poland during a five-year transitional period and, in the meantime, had been replaced by another piece of EC legislation.[114] On 31 May 2005, an appeal from this judgment was dismissed by the Regional Court. The Regional Court held that the first instance court erred in law as, according to case 152/84 *M.H. Marshall v. Southampton and South-West Hampshire Area Health Authority*, units of national health services constitute the emanation of state.[115] Moreover, it concluded that the Directive was not covered by transitional periods set out in the Accession Treaty 2003; therefore, it had an immediate effect in the Polish legal system as of 1 May 2004. In terms of substance, the Regional Court dismissed the claim for being unfounded. The plaintiff had received a financial compensation for the overtime work; however, the extension of annual leave was not granted. A request for cassation appeal was submitted to the Supreme Court. The Supreme Court held that the Regional Court erred in law by not correctly applying the Directives. Upon the accession to the European Union, Polish courts had the obligation to apply EU law and to take it into account in the interpretation of Polish implementing measures. The Supreme Court annulled the contested judgment and returned the case for further adjudication. It emphasised the ambiguities stemming from the Directives as well as derogations contained therein. It referred to Article 17 of the Directive, which allows Member States to provide derogations from the general rules on working time in hospitals and similar establishments. The Supreme Court asked the Regional Court to evaluate the facts of the case in light of the Directives.

One of the first instances where the Supreme Court directly applied a provision of an EC Regulation was case II CSK 178/06 *Sawicki v. Sawicka*.[116] The plaintiff – Roman Sawicki – submitted a suit for the termination of alimony, which had been granted to Renata Sawicka. The District Court in Skierniewice held it had no jurisdiction to consider the case. It based its decision on Article 9 of Council Regulation 1347/2000/EC on the jurisdiction and the recognition and enforcement of judgments in matrimonial matters and in matters of parental responsibility for children of both spouses.[117] Hearing the appeal, the Regional Court in Łódź annulled the decision of the first instance court; however, at the same time, it dismissed the claim. First, it held that the judgment was based on a wrong legal basis as Regulation 1347/2000/EC was no longer in force at the given time. Second, the Regional Court applied Article 5(2) of Regulation 44/2001/EC on jurisdiction and the recognition and enforcement of judgments in civil and commercial matters to the facts of the case.[118] This led to the conclusion that, since both parties had a legal residence in Spain, Polish courts had no jurisdiction to hear the case.

---

[114] Directive 2003/88/EC of the European Parliament and of the Council of 4 November 2003 concerning certain aspects of the organisation of working time, *OJ* 2003 L 299/9.

[115] *Loc. cit.* n. 105.

[116] Supreme Court of Poland, 16 November 2006, Case II CSK 178/06, *Sawicki v. Sawicka* [2008] *I.L.Pr.* 3.

[117] Council Regulation 1347/2000/EC of 29 May 2000 on jurisdiction and the recognition and enforcement of judgments in matrimonial matters and in matters of parental responsibility for children of both spouses, *OJ* 2000 L 299/9.

[118] Council Regulation 44/2001/EC of 22 December 2000 on jurisdiction and the recognition and enforcement of judgments in civil and commercial matters, *OJ* 2001 L 12/1.

On the contrary, the dispute fell into an exclusive jurisdiction of Spanish courts. The plaintiff submitted a cassation complaint to the Supreme Court. The question was whether Polish courts had jurisdiction to consider the case if both parties to a matrimonial dispute had a residence in Spain. The Supreme Court held as follows:

'Since May 1, 2004, the day of accession to the European Union, the application of Polish law and international treaties is excluded when a particular matter is regulated in an EC Regulation adopted by institutions of the European Community. In accordance with Art.249(2) of the EC Treaty, Regulations have general application; they are binding in their entirety and directly applicable in all Member States. The Regional Court in Łódź was right in concluding that the jurisdiction of courts in maintenance matters is regulated in Art.5(2) of EC Regulation 44/2001 on jurisdiction and the recognition and enforcement of judgments in civil and commercial matters. Bearing this provision in mind and the facts of the case, it leaves no doubt that the dispute falls under the jurisdiction of the Spanish courts. In accordance with Art.3(1) and (2) of the Regulation, persons domiciled in a Member State may be sued in the courts of another Member State only by virtue of the rules set out in sections 2 to 7 of Ch.II. In particular, rules of national jurisdiction shall not be applicable as against them. Arguments to the contrary submitted by the plaintiff suggesting that the choice of jurisdiction between the Polish and Spanish courts belong to the plaintiff, lack a legal basis.'[119]

The Supreme Court univocally held that the submission was manifestly inadmissible. Article 5(2) of Regulation 44/2001/EC was applicable to the facts of the case. It left no doubts that only Spanish courts had the jurisdiction to hear the case.

Another interesting development which merits attention in this part of the chapter is case I UK 182/07 *Zbigniew G. v. Zakład Ubezpieczeń Społecznych*.[120] This was one of the major gender discrimination cases, whereby the plaintiff claimed that Polish law provided for direct discrimination in access to retirement pensions. The plaintiff – a male orchestra conductor – at the age of 60 applied for a pension available for special professions at an earlier age. It should be noted that pursuant to general rules, the formal retirement age for male employees is 65. However, female orchestra conductors, pursuant to Polish law, were entitled to pensions at 55 as this profession was classified as employment in special conditions. Since the application was rejected, Zbigniew G. decided to proceed with the request for judicial review. The contested decision was upheld by the Regional Court and the Court of Appeal. Eventually, the plaintiff submitted a request for cassation appeal to the Supreme Court. The Supreme Court held that excluding male conductors from the right to pension at a lower age on the ground of sex constituted discrimination. The Supreme Court acting *ex officio* decided to assess the compatibility of the national law with the Directive. First, it concluded that the facts of the case were covered by Directive 79/7/EEC on the principle of equal treatment.[121] The Supreme Court held that the Directive applied to schemes providing protection

---

[119] Para. 6 of the judgment.
[120] Supreme Court of Poland, 4 January 2008, Case I UK 182/07 *Zbigniew G. v. Zakład Ubezpieczeń Społecznych* (not reported, available in Caselex database at http://www.caselex.com).
[121] Council Directive 79/7/EEC of 19 December 1978 on the progressive implementation of the principle of equal treatment for men and women in matters of social security, *OJ* 1979 L 6/24.

against the risk of old age. In that respect, the Supreme Court referred to the judgment of the European Court of Justice in case C-139/95 *Livia Balestra*.[122] Second, the Supreme Court confirmed that exclusion of male conductors in access to retirement pension on grounds of gender was contrary to the Directive, and, by the same token, the Polish law was contrary to this piece of legislation. Further, the Supreme Court held that Article 4(1) of the Directive was directly effective, and that individuals were entitled to rely on it in their claims. With a reference to case law of the ECJ, the Supreme Court made it clear that national courts – as long as the Polish law remained in force – were expected to apply the provisions on female conductors also to male representatives of the profession.[123]

## 4.4.    Polish courts and the Third Pillar of the European Union

### 4.4.1.  *Introduction*

Since the entry into force of the Treaty of Amsterdam, we have witnessed a proliferation of secondary legislation adopted within the Third Pillar of the European Union – Police and Judicial Co-operation in Criminal Matters.[124] Several framework decisions on carefully selected types of crimes have been adopted.[125] Moreover, a number of framework decisions embodying the principle of mutual recognition have enriched the legal landscape in this crucial area of EU law.[126] At the same time, unanimous decisions of the Council do not translate into robust transposition efforts at the domestic level.

---

[122] ECJ, Case C-139/95 *Livia Balestra v. Istituto Nazionale della Previdenza Sociale (INPS)* [1997] *ECR* I-549.

[123] ECJ, Case C-408/92 *Constance Christina Ellen Smith and others v. Avdel Systems Ltd.* [1994] *ECR* I-4435; Case C-442/00 *Ángel Rodríguez Caballero v. Fondo de Garantía Salarial (Fogasa)* [2002] *ECR* I-11915; Case C-81/05 *Anacleto Cordero Alonso v. Fondo de Garantía Salarial (Fogasa)* [2006] *ECR* I-07569; and Joined Cases C-231/06 to C-233/06, *Office national des pensions v. Emilienne Jonkman (C-231/06) and Hélène Vercheval (C-232/06) and Noëlle Permesaen v. Office national des pensions (C-233/06)* [2007] *ECR* I-5149.

[124] Treaty of Amsterdam amending the Treaty on European Union, the Treaties establishing the European Communities and certain related acts, *OJ* 1997 C 340/1.

[125] See, *inter alia*, Council Framework Decision 2002/629/JHA of 19 July 2002 on combating trafficking in human beings, *OJ* 2002 L 203/1. For an academic appraisal, see A. Weyembergh and V. Santamaria, eds., *The evaluation of European criminal law. The example of the Framework Decision on combatting trafficking in human beings* (Bruxelles, Editions de l'Université de Bruxelles 2009).

[126] Framework Decision 2003/577/JHA of 22 July 2003 on the execution in the European Union of orders freezing property or evidence, *OJ* 2003 L 196/45; Framework Decision 2005/214/JHA of 24 February 2005 on the application of the principle of mutual recognition to financial penalties, *OJ* 2005 L 76/16; Framework Decision 2006/783/JHA of 6 October 2006 on the application of the principle of mutual recognition to confiscation orders, *OJ* 2006 L 328/59; Framework Decision 2008/978/JHA of 18 December 2008 on the European evidence warrant for the purpose of obtaining objects, documents and data for use in proceedings in criminal matters, *OJ* 2008 L 350/72; Framework Decision 2008/909/JHA of 27 November 2008 on the application of the principle of mutual recognition to judgments in criminal matters imposing custodial sentences or measures involving deprivation of liberty for the purpose of their enforcement in the European Union, *OJ* 2008 L 327/27; Framework Decision 2008/947/JHA of 27 November 2008 on the application of the principle of mutual recognition to judgments and probation decisions with a view to the supervision of probation measures and alternative sanctions, *OJ* 2008 L 337/102.

Arguably, the Member States seem to be suffering from the "prisoners in paradise" syndrome.[127] On the one hand, they proceed with very ambitious legislative projects, while on the other hand, they fail to give EU legislation additional thrust making the *acquis* operational in the national legal orders. Failures and delays in transposition are seemingly one of the key features of the Third Pillar. Poland is – to much regret – not an exception in this respect. Lack of transposition of Framework Decision 2002/629/JHA on combating trafficking in human beings may serve as an excellent example. Although the transposition period expired on 1 August 2004, Poland still has not transposed Article 1 containing the definition of trafficking.

Considering the delays in transposition combined with a degree of uncertainty as to the rules on the application of Third Pillar *acquis* at the domestic level, it is hardly surprising that in general, EU secondary legislation in this area is quite often overlooked by national courts. The main exception, however, is the European Arrest Warrant, which has proved to be an extremely useful tool for both prosecutors and judges. As empirical research proves, Polish authorities are the most fond of the European Arrest Warrant among all Member States of the European Union. Poland regularly issues the highest amounts of European Arrest Warrants out of all twenty seven Member States of the European Union. Therefore, the volume of interesting case law is ever growing. It encapsulates practical challenges in the application of the EAW machinery as well as teething problems with the concept of mutual trust underpinning it. In order to give this argument merits, an overview of selected judgments is provided in the next section of this chapter.

### 4.4.2.   *European Arrest Warrant in case law of Polish courts*

Two judgments of the Supreme Court may serve as an excellent starting point. Both cases have been heavily publicised and elaborated on as they touched upon the fundamentals of the surrender system based on the European Arrest Warrant.

The first to be analysed is case I KZP 21/06 *Criminal proceedings against Adam G.*[128] The case dealt with a 17-year-old man of Polish nationality who was accused of committing a murder at the Brussels Central Train Station. Since the perpetrator managed to escape to Poland, the Belgian authorities requested surrender pursuant to the EAW provisions. This surrender request triggered a number of important questions regarding the scope of the EAW. Due to the age of the perpetrator and the wording of the EAW, it was not clear whether the request was covered by the EAW machinery. The question was whether the national Belgian procedure that could have been used in the given case fell under the EAW provisions. Before looking at the substance, in an interesting move, the Supreme Court expressed regret that it had no jurisdiction to make a reference for a preliminary ruling to the European Court of Justice. It held:

---

[127] See further, A. Łazowski, '"Prisoners in Paradise" Idiosyncrasies of Justice and Home Affairs Area', forthcoming.

[128] Polish Supreme Court, 20 July 2006, Judgment I KZP 21/06, *Criminal Proceedings against Adam G.* OSN Nr 6/2007.

'Unfortunately, a Polish court is deprived of the possibility of sending a reference for preliminary ruling to the European Court of Justice pursuant to Article 35 EU as Poland has thus
far not recognized the jurisdiction regarding instruments of the Third Pillar of the EU under
Article 35 (2) EU. Bearing in mind this normative factor, the Supreme Court has to take a
position on the matter by itself.'

Having analysed the merits of the case, the Supreme Court came to the following conclusions:

- the judicial authority of the executing state may refuse surrender, if it finds that the
  request was adopted in breach of conditions of issue;
- the decision whether the surrender of a person pursuant to the EAW machinery is
  admissible is based on legislation of the country of issue;
- surrender is possible, irrespective of the fact whether the criminal procedure against
  the person in question has already been initiated in the issuing Member State; yet
  surrender is only possible if the grounds for an EAW prove that initiation of criminal procedure is possible;
- since the surrender will facilitate criminal procedure in the issuing state, a Polish
  national should be returned if such procedure is not initiated therein.

These conclusions meant that the surrender was possible under the applicable legal
framework.

   This judgment was followed by equally publicised case I KZP 30/08 *Criminal proceedings against Jakub T.*[129] The factual background merits attention and may be summarised as follows. Jakub T. legally resided in the United Kingdom, where allegedly
he raped a 48-year-old woman. As he returned to Poland, the UK authorities issued a
European Arrest Warrant, requesting surrender for the purposes of prosecution and
sentencing. Pursuant to Article 607t § 1 of Penal Procedure Code 1997, the executing
court requested return of the perpetrator in order to serve the sentence. The English
court sentenced Jakub T. to life imprisonment, with a possibility of an earlier conditional release after 9 years. A Polish court confirmed the decision of the English judiciary and held itself to be bound by the decision of the English court. This decision was
challenged by the defendant as the maximum penalty for rape under Polish law is 12
to 15 years. The Court of Appeal decided to submit a reference to the Supreme Court
as to the interpretation of the Polish legislation. The Supreme Court, in its judgment of
3 March 2009, confirmed that Polish courts are bound by decisions of courts in other
Member States, both in terms of the sanction and potential early release. The basis for
the decision is the principle of mutual recognition considered by the Supreme Court as
the cornerstone of the Police and Judicial Co-peration in Criminal Matters. It extensively referred to EU legislation and practice, including the *Pupino* case and the very
recent Framework Decision 2008/909/JHA. It merits attention that apart from the

---

[129] Supreme Court of Poland, 3 March 2009, Case I KZP 30/08, *Criminal proceedings against Jakub
T.*, nyr (on file with the authors).

standard appeal, the defendant submitted a constitutional complaint to the Constitutional Tribunal (which was pending when this chapter was completed).

Having looked at the two landmark judgments of the Polish Supreme Court, we will take a few samples from case law of lower courts. The access to judgments of such courts is fairly limited; nevertheless, the selection provided may be considered as representative. In case II AK 577/04, the Court of Appeal in Warsaw was seized with a request for review of the decision of a Regional Court rejecting the submission for the adoption of the European Arrest Warrant.[130] According to the files of the case, the prosecutor submitted that the person covered by the prosecution was in a given time in Slovakia. The Regional Court rejected the request and concluded that the prosecutor did not manage to prove the person in question was in Slovakia. The Court of Appeal held that the appeal had merits and returned the case for repeated adjudication to the District Court. In order to issue a European Arrest Warrant, it was not necessary for the public prosecutor to prove high probability that a person in question resides in a particular Member State of the European Union. A decision of the Court of Appeal in Katowice in case II AKz 685/06 may serve as an example to prove the argument that Polish prosecutors and judges are fully aware of the principle of mutual recognition and legal consequences arising.[131] This Court held that issuing the EAW translates into the lack of need to verify the evidence which served as the basis for detention. However, decisions on surrender should not be automatic and should take into account circumstances surrounding the case. In the Order of 23 August 2006 adopted by the Court of Appeal in Katowice, it was held that any decisions on surrender must be governed by the principle of mutual recognition.[132] As a matter of principle, requests for surrender and detention should be entertained. This decision was delivered against the following factual and legal background. On 19 July 2006, the Regional Public Prosecutor in Katowice submitted to the Regional Court in Katowice a request for the execution of the European Arrest Warrant issued by the Public Prosecutor in Görlitz (German), supplemented by the request for the arrest of the person in question. Both requests were rejected by the Court. The Public Prosecutor submitted an appeal to the Court of Appeal in Katowice. The Court of Appeal annulled the contested judgment and returned the case for the repeated adjudication. It held that the original decision in part dealing with the request for surrender was under-argued and not really elaborated on. Moreover, several important documents regarding the case were submitted by the German authorities after the contested decision had been delivered. The Court of Appeal put a lot of emphasis on the principle of mutual trust. This led to the conclusion that, as a matter of principle, a decision requesting the arrest and surrender should not be verified, unless there were important factors justifying the verification. This was not the case with the request in question.

---

[130] Court of Appeal in Warsaw, 19 November 2004, Order II Akz 577/04, not reported (on file with the authors).
[131] Court of Appeal in Katowice, 25 October 2006, Order II Akz 685/06, not reported (on file with the authors).
[132] Court of Appeal in Katowice, 23 August 2006, Order II Akz 518/06, not reported (on file with the authors).

5.    IT IS IMPORTANT THAT WE KEEP TALKING:[133] POLISH COURTS
      AND THE PRELIMINARY RULING PROCEDURE

5.1.    **Introduction**

There is no doubt that the preliminary ruling procedure has played a crucial role in the
development of the EC/EU legal order. A clear signal of what was to come was definitely the Opinion of Advocate General Lagrange in the first preliminary ruling *Bosch*
case.[134] Since 1962, this direct communication channel between domestic courts and
the ECJ has facilitated a chain of extraordinary events giving an enormous thrust to the
enforcement of EC law at the domestic level. With the accession of ten new Member
States on 1 May 2004, one of the questions was whether national courts of the newcomers would be willing and able to engage in dialogue with the European Court of Justice.[135]
In the case of Poland, the first reference was submitted in the already-mentioned case
*Brzeziński*. This served as an ice-breaker and led to more than a dozen references submitted in the first five years of membership. As of 1 July 2009, the European Court of
Justice rendered judgments in ten cases referred by Polish courts and seven more were
pending. Five references were submitted by the Supreme Administrative Court,[136] one
by the Supreme Court,[137] seven by Voivod Administrative Courts,[138] one by a Regional
Court[139] and three by District Courts.[140] To analyse each and every reference would go

---

[133]  The title of this section borrows from M. Bobek. See M. Bobek, 'Learning to talk: Preliminary
rulings, the courts of the new Member States and the Court of Justice', 45 *CMLRev.* (2008) pp. 1611-1643.

[134]  ECJ, Case 13/61 *Kledingverkoopbedrijf de Geus en Uitdenbogerd v. Robert Bosch GmbH and
Maatschappij tot voortzetting van de zaken der Firma Willem van Rijn* [1962] *ECR* 45. See D. Thompson,
'The Bosch Case', 11 *ICLQ* (1962) pp. 721-737.

[135]  As noted in Chapter 1 in this volume, the ECJ has benefited itself with the arrival of ten new judges,
who have increased the capacity of the Court.

[136]  ECJ, Case C-502/07 *K-1 sp. z o.o. v. Dyrektor Izby Skarbowej w Bydgoszczy* [2009] *ECR* nyr. See
also pending Case C-441/08 *Elektrownia Pątnów II sp. z o.o. v. Dyrektor Izby Skarbowej w Poznaniu*,
*OJ* 2008 C 327/15; Case C-522/08 *Telekomunikacja Polska S.A., Warsaw, v. President of the Urząd
Komunikacji Elektronicznej*, *OJ* 2009 C 69/18; Case C-188/09 *Dyrektor Izby Skarbowej w Białymstoku v.
'Profaktor' Kulesza, Frankowski, Trzaska spółka jawna w Białymstoku*, *OJ* 2009 C 193/6; Case C-222/09
*Kronospan Mielec sp. z o.o. v. Dyrektor Izby Skarbowej w Rzeszowie*, *OJ* 2009 C 220/18.

[137]  Case C-99/09 *Polska Telefonia Cyfrowa sp. z o.o. v. Prezes Urzędu Komunikacji Elektronicznej*,
*OJ* 2009 C 129/6.

[138]  See ECJ, Case C-313/05 *Maciej Brzeziński v. Dyrektor Izby Celnej w Warszawie*, *loc. cit.* n. 102;
Case C-168/06 *Ceramika Paradyż sp. z o.o. v. Dyrektor Izby Skarbowej w Łodzi* [2007] *ECR* I-29*; Case
C-25/07 *Alicja Sosnowska v. Dyrektor Izby Skarbowej we Wrocławiu Ośrodek Zamiejscowy w Wałbrzychu*
[2008] *ECR* nyr; ECJ, Case C-426/07 *Dariusz Krawczyński v. Dyrektor Izby Celnej w Białymstoku* [2008]
*ECR* nyr; Case C-414/07 *Magoora sp. z o.o. v. Dyrektor Izby Skarbowej w Krakowie* [2008] *ECR* nyr; Case
C-544/07 *Uwe Rüffler v. Dyrektor Izby Skarbowej we Wrocławiu Ośrodek Zamiejscowy w Wałbrzychu*
[2009] *ECR* nyr. See also pending Case C-314/08 *Krzysztof Filipiak v. Dyrektor Izby Skarbowej w
Poznaniu*, *OJ* 2008 C 247/8.

[139]  ECJ, Case C-499/06 *Halina Nerkowska v. Zakład Ubezpieczeń Społecznych Oddział w Koszalinie*
[2008] *ECR* I-3993.

[140]  ECJ, Case C-134/07 *Piotr Kawala v. Gmina Miasta Jaworzna* [2007] *ECR* I-1073; Case C-344/08
*Criminal proceedings against Tomasz Rubach* [2009] *ECR* nyr. See also pending Case C-444/07 *MG
Probud Gdynia Sp. z o.o. v. Hauptzollamt Saarbrücken*, *OJ* 2007 C 283/23.

beyond the scope of this chapter; however an overview of a few cases is provided in section 5.4. Before that review, it is fitting to focus on decisions of the Constitutional Tribunal and the Supreme Court, which were not references as such but, nevertheless, provided guidance to national courts on the preliminary ruling procedure.

## 5.2. The Constitutional Tribunal and the preliminary ruling procedure

As indicated earlier in this chapter, the Constitutional Tribunal has thus far rendered two decisions touching upon the preliminary ruling procedure.[141] The first dealt with the division of jurisdiction between the Constitutional Tribunal and the European Court of Justice, the second with the recognition of jurisdiction of the ECJ pursuant to Article 35 EU.

In case P 37/05, the Constitutional Tribunal received an application for the constitutional review of Excise Duty Act 2004 with Article 90 EC prohibiting tax discrimination.[142] The reference was submitted by a Voivod Administrative Court in Olsztyn, which was seized with a request for judicial review of a decision imposing excise duty incumbent upon intra-Community importation of a second-hand vehicle. It is notable that the factual background of this case was equal to the one in the *Brzeziński* case that was pending at the ECJ at the time.[143] The Constitutional Tribunal began with three arguments for inadmissibility of the reference. This led to an in-depth analysis of the division of jurisdiction between national courts and the European Court of Justice. The point of departure was the prerequisite of uniform interpretation of EC law. The Constitutional Tribunal emphasised that adjudication on the substance of the request potentially could have led to divergent interpretation of EC law. The position of the ECJ as the guarantor of the application and uniform interpretation of EC law was emphasised. At the same time, the Constitutional Tribunal referred to Article 8 of the Constitution, which as explained in section 2 of this chapter, guarantees the supremacy of the Constitution. Therefore, the Tribunal made it clear that it would have the last word in cases with constitutional implications. It paid particular attention to different functions of the Constitutional Tribunal and the European Court of Justice. The second argument used by the Tribunal referred directly to the substance of the request. The judges rightly held that the question of the Voivod Court dealt with the interpretation of EC law, not the conformity of the Polish legislation with EC law and Polish Constitution. Finally, the Constitutional Tribunal argued that the reference itself dealt with the application of law, not general applicability. To this end, it fell outside the scope of the Tribunal's jurisdiction. It was emphasised that the referring court, if doubtful as to the interpretation of EC law, should set aside conflicting Polish law and adju-

---

[141] It should be noted that the Constitutional Tribunal has touched upon the preliminary ruling procedure also in its judgment in the Accession Treaty case. It held that Art. 234 EC was in compliance with the Polish Constitution. *Loc. cit.* n. 25.

[142] *Loc. cit.* n. 43.

[143] The Constitutional Tribunal rendered its decision on 19 December 2006, while the European Court of Justice delivered its judgment in *Brzeziński* case on 17 January 2007.

dicate directly on the basis of EC law. If a provision of the latter is not directly effective, the national court should proceed to interpret Polish law in accordance with EC legislation. Whenever there is a conflict between EC law and Polish legislation, national courts should adjudicate by themselves or submit a reference to the European Court of Justice. Although the conclusions as such are plausible, this decision received a fair amount of criticism for several loopholes left by the Tribunal. While it was meant to be an instruction to Polish courts, it failed to clarify the situation with Article 68 EC references or the lack of jurisdiction of Polish courts to refer questions pursuant to Article 35 TEU. It is not very clear whether the Tribunal would claim its jurisdiction in such cases. Also, there are a number of rather unfortunate statements, for example, on methods of approaching discrepancies between Polish and EC law.[144]

The second judgment was rendered by the Constitutional Tribunal on 18 February 2009 in case Kp 3/08.[145] The request was submitted by the President of the Republic, who prior to giving his seal of approval to this piece of legislation, wanted to have it clarified if an act of Parliament authorising the President to recognise the jurisdiction of the European Court of Justice pursuant to Article 35(2) TEU was in compliance with the Constitution.[146] A number of rather weak arguments were raised by the head of state. The main area of concern was the average duration of the preliminary ruling procedure and its compliance with Article 45 of the Constitution. The latter provides:

> 'Everyone shall have the right to a fair and public hearing of his case, without undue delay, before a competent, impartial and independent court.'

The applicant argued that the decision on the use of the urgent preliminary ruling procedure (tailor-made for the JHA questions) rests in the hands of the ECJ itself. Moreover, decisions of Polish courts on the employment of the preliminary ruling procedure are not subject to review and may lead to suspension of similar cases pending before Polish courts. Lack of comprehensive national legal framework on the reference procedure was also raised. All those arguments were dismissed by the Constitutional Tribunal as unfounded. The judges carefully explained all idiosyncrasies of the preliminary ruling procedure in the Third Pillar and its relationship with the general regime based on Article 234 EC. It is notable that the Tribunal referred to the judgment of the Supreme Court in case I KZP 21/06 *Criminal proceedings against Adam G.*,[147] where – as we explained earlier in this chapter – the Supreme Court expressed regret that it had no jurisdiction to refer in the given case. The Constitutional Tribunal used this argument to demonstrate a paradox that Polish courts will use judgments of the ECJ rendered in cases submitted by national courts of other Member States that recognised the jurisdiction, without being able to ask themselves. It is interesting to note that despite a clear

---

[144]  Para. 30 of the judgment.

[145]  *Loc. cit.* n. 44

[146]  Ustawa z dnia 10 lipca 2008 r. o upoważnieniu Prezydenta Rzeczypospolitej Polskiej do złożenia oświadczenia o uznaniu właściwości Trybunału Sprawiedliwości Wspólnot Europejskich na podstawie art. 35 ust. 2 Traktatu o Unii Europejskiej, Dz. U. 2009, Nr 33, Item 253.

[147]  *Loc. cit.* n. 128.

message from the Constitutional Tribunal, the head of state had not – as of 1 July 2009 – sent the notification on the recognition of jurisdiction. The Act itself only authorises the President to do so without imposing an obligation in this respect.

### 5.3. The Supreme Court and the preliminary ruling procedure: to refer or not to refer?

During the first five years of membership in the European Union, the Supreme Court of Poland rendered a number of very interesting judgments dealing, *inter alia*, with the preliminary ruling procedure before making its first reference in December 2008.[148] In this section of the chapter, we are going to take a closer look at two of those decisions.

The judgment in case II PK 17/06 *Grochowiak v. Fundusz Gwarantowanych Świadczeń Pracowniczych*[149] is a very good example of the *acte clair* doctrine employed by a national court from which there is no further remedy; therefore, such court is under an obligation to proceed with a reference pursuant to Article 234 EC.[150] The judgment was rendered against the following factual and legal background. A request for cassation of a judgment, dismissing the claim for the payment of outstanding salaries and severance pay, was submitted by the plaintiff. In its request Mr. Grochowiak submitted that the Regional Court-Labour and Social Insurance Court in Zielona Góra erred by strictly interpreting the term "date of insolvency of an employer", resulting in non-admissibility of the claimant's application. The argumentation of the claimant was based solely on Polish legislation. The Supreme Court had to consider if it had the jurisdiction to raise *ex-officio* issues of EC law. Also, it had to take into account the obligation to submit a request for the preliminary ruling and the application of the *acte claire* doctrine to the case. Under the terms of Polish law, the term "the date of insolvency of an employer" must be understood as the date when a decision of a court on bankruptcy becomes final. This, combined with very tight time limits restricting the workers' access to a guarantee institution, made the right to receive outstanding salaries and severance pay considerably limited. The Supreme Court clarified that the dispute at hand fell within the limits of EC law; therefore, it had to take into account the obligation stemming from Article 234 EC. Having looked at the existing case law of the ECJ, the Supreme Court held that the conditions for the application of the *acte claire* doctrine were met. Under the terms set out in joined cases 28/62, 29/62 and 30/62 *Da Costa*,[151] case 283/81 *CILFIT*,[152] case C-495/03 *Intermodal Transports*[153] and case C-461/03

---

[148] Supreme Court of Poland, 19 December 2008, Case III SK 27/08 *Polska Telefonia Cyfrowa v. Prezes Urzędu Komunikacji Elektronicznej*, nyr (on file with the authors).

[149] Supreme Court of Poland, 18 December 2006, Case II PK 17/06 *Grochowiak v. Fundusz Gwarantowanych Świadczeń Pracowniczych* [2008] 1 C.M.L.R. 41.

[150] See further, *inter alia*, M. Broberg, 'Acte clair revisited: Adapting the *acte clair* criteria to the demands of the times', 45 *CMLRev.* (2008) pp. 1383-1397.

[151] ECJ, Joined Cases 28/62, 29/62, 30/62 *Da Costa en Schaake NV, Jacob Meijer NV, Hoechst-Holland NV v. Netherlands Inland Revenue Administration* [1963] *ECR* 31.

[152] *Loc. cit.* n. 92.

[153] ECJ, Case C-495/03 *Intermodal Transports BV v. Staatssecretaris van Financiën* [2005] *ECR* I-8151.

*Gaston Schul Douane*,[154] the Supreme Court, as the court of last instance, was released from the obligation to refer as the existing judgments of the ECJ provided the necessary interpretation of the Directive 80/987/EEC. Since the claimant failed to raise EC-related issues in his request for cassation, it was necessary to verify if under the terms of procedural law, the Supreme Court had the jurisdiction to proceed *ex officio*. The Supreme Court referred to the ruling of the ECJ in joined cases C-430/93 and C-431/93 *van Schijndel*,[155] giving such right to the national court, subject to terms and limitations stemming from national law. Since the applicable law in question was a transposition measure for the Directive, the Supreme Court held it was within the limits of the cassation request to raise points of EC law *ex officio*.[156] The Supreme Court held that the original interpretation of the term "the date of insolvency of an employer", applied by the courts of first and second instance, was based solely on Polish law and, at the same time, was contrary to the Directive and case law of the ECJ. In cases C-373/95 *Maso*,[157] Joined cases C-94/95 and case C-95/95 *Bonifaci*,[158] case C-160/01 *Karin Mau*,[159] the ECJ held that the term in question should be interpreted as the day when an application for bankruptcy is filed.

---

[154] *Loc. cit.* n. 70.

[155] ECJ, Joined Cases C-430/93 and C-431/93 *Jeroen van Schijndel and Johannes Nicolaas Cornelis van Veen v. Stichting Pensioenfonds voor Fysiotherapeuten* [1995] *ECR* I-4705.

[156] The Supreme Court held as follows:

'At this stage we must return to the question whether the Supreme Court should consider provisions of European law if their breach wasn't listed in the submission for the cassation and there is no obligation to submit a reference on their interpretation to the European Court of Justice. As far as this is concerned, the Tribunal in the judgment of December 14, 1995 in Van Schijndel v Stichting Pensioenfonds voor Fysiotherapeuten (Joined Cases C-430/93 & C-431/93) [1995] E.C.R. I-4705; [1996] 1 C.M.L.R. 801 held that in proceedings concerning civil rights and obligations freely entered into by the parties, it is for the national court to apply Arts 3(f), 85, 86 and 90 of the Treaty even when the party with an interest in application of those provisions has not relied on them. Moreover, where domestic law allows such application by the national court; Community law does not require national courts to raise of their own motion an issue concerning the breach of provisions of Community law where examination of that issue would oblige them to abandon the passive role assigned to them by going beyond the ambit of the dispute defined by the parties themselves and relying on facts and circumstances other than those on which the party with an interest in application of those provisions bases his claim. This means that, as matter of principle, the Supreme Court has no obligation to consider potential breach of Community law, if a party failed to mention the breach as the basis for the cassation (Art. 398 Civil Procedure Code). However, there is such necessity, when there are no doubts that provisions of Community law regulate the same issue as national law and there is a possibility for their direct application or the necessity for the interpretation of domestic law in accordance with Community law. If a party submits argumentation based on the incorrect interpretation of domestic law then such point must be analysed taking into account provisions of Community law and their interpretation by the European Court of Justice. While considering the argumentation based on the incorrect application of domestic law one has to consider if such provision is not in conformity with a directly applicable provision of Community law. This does not amount to a step beyond the limits of the cassation as, in practical terms, the interpretation and application of a provision which was the basis for the cassation may require its interpretation (application) in the light of other provisions (of European law, in this case).' Para. 11 of the judgment.

[157] ECJ, Case C-373/95 *Federica Maso and others and Graziano Gazzetta and others v. Istituto nazionale della previdenza sociale (INPS) and Repubblica italiana* [1997] *ECR* I-4051.

[158] ECJ, Joined Cases C-94/95 and C-95/95 *Danila Bonifaci and others (C-94/95) and Wanda Berto and others (C-95/95) v. Istituto nazionale della previdenza sociale (INPS)* [1997] *ECR* I-3969.

[159] ECR, Case C-160/01 *Karen Mau v. Bundesanstalt für Arbeit* [2003] *ECR* I-4791.

In the decision in case III SK 23/07 *P v. Prezes Urzędu Komunikacji Elektronicznej*, the Supreme Court dealt with a cassation appeal submitted in course of a dispute between a company registered in Poland and a Polish regulatory authority. The dispute touched upon Polish law and EC Directive 2002/21 on electronic communications networks.[160] One of the issues raised was whether a court of appeal or the Supreme Court had the obligation to submit a reference to the European Court of Justice pursuant to Article 234 EC. The appellee argued that by not submitting a reference, the Court of Appeal acted in breach of Article 234(3) EC. The Supreme Court disagreed and held that it was the one with such an obligation. After careful examination of the applicable legal framework as well as case law of the European Court of Justice, it ruled that despite the limitations of the cassation appeal procedure, the Supreme Court may submit a reference should it be necessary in the first stage when it decides on the admissibility of an appeal. To this end, the Supreme Court supported the concrete theory developed in the academic writing and supported by the European Court of Justice in the *Lyckeskog* case.[161] The Supreme Court decided to employ the *acte clair* doctrine and rendered the judgment in the case without a reference to the ECJ.

### 5.4.    Knocking on heaven's door:[162] (the unfortunate) case C-168/06 *Ceramika Paradyż*

The decision of the European Court of Justice in case C-168/06 *Ceramika Paradyż*[163] will remain in law books as one of those unfortunate references where a national court dealing with a case with pre-accession factual background unsuccessfully sought the assistance of the European Court of Justice. In this very case, Voivod Administrative Court in Łódź was seized with a request for judicial review of a decision of tax authorities submitted by a Polish company *Ceramika Paradyż*. The plaintiff challenged the decision imposing payment of an additional amount of tax due for November 2003. On 6 March 2007, the ECJ rendered an order pursuant to Article 104 § 3 of Rules of Procedure[164] and held it had no jurisdiction in this case as the tax period covered by the dispute had been a pre-accession one. Thus, the Voivod Administrative Court in Łódź not only wasted almost twelve months waiting for the decision of the ECJ[165] but also, at the end of the day, had to adjudicate by itself.[166]

---

[160] Directive 2002/21/EC of the European Parliament and of the Council of 7 March 2002 on a common regulatory framework for electronic communications networks and services, *OJ* 2002 L 108/33.

[161] ECJ, Case C-99/00 *Criminal proceedings against Kenny Roland Lyckeskog* [2002] *ECR* I-4838.

[162] The term borrowed from T. Tridimas. See, T. Tridimas, 'Knocking on Heaven's Door: Fragmentation, efficiency and defiance in the preliminary reference procedure', 40 *CMLRev.* (2003) pp. 9-50.

[163] *Loc. cit.* n. 138.

[164] Rules of Procedure of the Court of Justice of the European Communities of 19 June 1991, *OJ* 1991 L 176/7 (as amended).

[165] The decision on the reference was made on 15 February 2006. It was received by the European Court of Justice on 20 March 2006 and its order was rendered on 6 March 2007.

[166] For a critique of this line of cases, including *Ceramika Paradyż* case, see N. Półtorak, 'Ratione *temporis* application of the preliminary rulings procedure', 45 *CMLRev.* (2008) pp. 1357-1381, at pp. 1372-1374. See also Chapters 4 and 5 in this volume.

## 5.5.    Breaking the ice: case C-313/05 *Brzeziński*

As we mentioned a number of times in this chapter, the judgment in the *Brzeziński* case proved to be a very crucial turning point, in terms of application of EC law in Poland and also as an ice- breaker in dialogue between Polish courts and the European Court of Justice. The factual background of the dispute was fairly straight-forward and not contested by the parties. The plaintiff – Mr. Maciej Brzeziński – had, shortly after the enlargement, imported a second-hand car from another Member State of the EU. Upon the importation, he was required to file a tax declaration and pay the excise duty due on the registration of the vehicle. Pursuant to a Polish law applicable at the time, the plaintiff had five days to file a simplified customs declaration and proceed with the payment.[167] Compliance with these requirements was *conditio sine qua non* for registration of a vehicle. The plaintiff complied with all the formalities and, having done that, decided to challenge the conformity of the Polish legislation with EC law and request reimbursement of the charge.[168] In his application for the review, the plaintiff relied on Articles 23, 25, 90 EC as well as on the case law on the principles of supremacy and direct effect. His application was rejected by the Director of Customs Office in Warsaw. The EU law-based argumentation was ignored as 'tax policy is a symbol of state sovereignty and part of the country's economic policy.'[169] As already argued in this chapter, this approach is unfortunately quite common among the Polish public administration. The contested decision was upheld by the Director of Customs Chamber. This was followed shortly by the request for judicial review, submitted by the plaintiff, to the Warsaw Administrative Court. In his application, Mr. Brzeziński relied extensively on EC law and submitted argumentation based jointly on Articles 25 and 90 EC. The bottom line for the suit was alleged tax discrimination of imported second-hand cars when compared with similar domestically purchased vehicles. The Court handling the case decided to suspend the procedure and submit a reference for the preliminary ruling to the European Court of Justice.[170] In the reference, the Court argued that the uneven practice of Polish authorities, including courts, begs for a clarification from the European Court of Justice. Notably, the referring court was unsure about the applicable law; therefore, the questions submitted to the ECJ dealt with the interpretation of Articles 25 and 90 EC as well as Council Directive 92/12/EC on the excise duty.[171] Moreover,

---

[167] Ustawa z dnia 23 stycznia 2004 r. o podatku akcyzowym, Dz. U. 2004, Nr 29, Item 257 (as amended).

[168] In a way, the applicant can be considered as "a man of principle" as most likely the costs of litigation exceeded the amount of the unduly levied tax (850 Polish Zlotys, which is the equivalent of approximately EUR 200). Certainly Mr. Brzeziński is neither the first nor the last "action hero" (the first one being Mr. Flaminio Costa, who had a huge role in the development of the principle of supremacy).

[169] Voivod Administrative Court in Warsaw, 6 March 2007, Case III SA/WA 254/07, *Maciej Brzeziński v. Dyrektor Izby Celnej w Warszawie* [2008] 3 C.M.L.R. 28, at p. 803.

[170] Postanowienie WSA w Warszawie z 22 maja 2005 r. o skierowaniu pytania prejudycjalnego w sprawie III SA/Wa 679/05, full text of the decision is available in Polish at http://www.nsa.gov.pl/ramki/main/1a.pdf.

[171] Council Directive 92/12/EEC of 25 February 1992 on the general arrangements for products subject to excise duty and on the holding, movement and monitoring of such products, *OJ* 1992 L 76/1.

the Warsaw Administrative Court expressed doubts as to the conformity of domestic procedural requirements with Article 28 EC. Finally, with the potential budgetary implications in mind, the referring court asked for the determination of temporal effects of the ruling.

Both Advocate General Sharpston and the European Court of Justice concluded that the measure in question was covered by Article 90 EC and thus was not a charge having equivalent effect to customs duty. Moreover, in the case of cars produced in Poland as well as imported cars before the expiry of the two-year period upon their production, there was no discrimination under the Excise Duty Act 2004. However, such discrimination was taking place in the case of imported second-hand cars that were two years old and older. The ECJ held that the formalities imposed by the Polish legislator were not covered by Article 28 EC. It also rejected the motion for temporal limitation of the effects of its judgment. It should be noted that the judgment of the ECJ was eagerly awaited not only by the referring court but also by almost all other administrative courts in Poland where similar cases were pending and, in some cases, suspended awaiting the result of the *Brzeziński* case. Although the conclusions of the ECJ were expected, the judgment received some criticism for a crucial substantive mistake made by the ECJ and a clear difference between the Polish and other language versions of the judgment. The original English version published on the website of the ECJ and reproduced in the Official Journal of the European Union read:

'The first paragraph of Article 90 EC is to be interpreted as meaning that it precludes an excise duty, in so far as the amount of the duty imposed on second-hand vehicles over two years old acquired in a Member State other than that which introduced such a duty exceeds the residual amount of the same duty incorporated into *the purchase price of similar vehicles* which had been previously registered in the Member State which introduced that duty.'[172] [emphasis added]

At the same time, the Polish version of the judgment received by the referring court and published in the Official Journal of the European Union mentioned a market value of a similar car. This issue was picked up by the Voivod Administrative Court in Warsaw, which made the reference. Since the language of the case was Polish, the judges decided to follow that version and rendered a judgment accordingly. Interestingly enough, the final version of the judgment published in the English version of the European Court Reports follows the market value approach used in the Polish text.

The judgment of the Voivod Administrative Court in the *Brzeziński* case was not appealed by either of the parties and became final. Not only did it allow (potentially) the plaintiff to recoup unduly levied duty, but it also opened a lot of doors to other importers of second-hand vehicles. *Brzeziński*-like judgments can be counted in the dozens and have become an important test for the effectiveness of EC law in Poland. This does not mean that reimbursements are proceeding smoothly. Arguably, tax authorities are still not fully aware of their obligations under EC law.

---

[172] *OJ* 2007 C 56/6.

### 5.6.     EU Citizenship in operation: case C-499/06 *Nerkowska*

The judgment of the ECJ in case C-499/06 *Nerkowska* merits attention for two main reasons.[173] It was the first reference for a preliminary ruling from a Polish non-administrative court. The Regional Court in Koszalin was seized with a request for judicial review of a decision of the local social assistance authority refusing a disability pension to a Polish national residing in Germany. By this token, it also touched upon the "fundamental status" of nationals of the Member States – the citizenship of the European Union. The factual and legal background was as follows. In 2002, the plaintiff applied for a special benefit available to victims of war, including atrocities attributable to the Communist regime. As a little girl she had been deported to Siberia where she had lost her parents; nevertheless, she had managed to return to Poland at the age of six. In 2002, the local social assistance authority confirmed she had been eligible for the benefit; however, as a result of her residence in Germany, the payment of the benefit had been suspended. A request for judicial review had been dismissed by Polish courts. Following Poland's accession to the European Union, Ms. Nerkowska submitted a fresh application for the benefit. Again, this application was rejected by the social assistance authorities, and, in turn, the applicant sought judicial review. The Regional Court in Koszalin expressed doubts as to the conformity of the Polish legislation at stake[174] with Article 18 EC and decided to proceed with a reference for preliminary ruling.

Advocate General Maduro as well as the European Court of Justice concluded that the Polish legislation was indeed precluded by Article 18 EC. This did not come as a surprise following an earlier judgment of the ECJ in the *Tas-Hagen* case.[175] The ECJ held that the applicant was an EU citizen and thus benefited from rights stemming from Article 18 EC. This in itself was quite symbolic. It was a clear sign that nationals of the new Member States might be covered by transitional periods when it comes to their access to labour markets in the old Member States under the terms of the Accession Treaty 2003; however, they became full-fledged citizens of the European Union as of 1 May 2004. The ECJ followed the well-known mantra:

> 'National legislation which places certain of the nationals of the Member State concerned at a disadvantage simply because they have exercised their freedom to move and to reside in another Member State is a restriction on the freedoms conferred by Article 18(1) EC on every citizen of the Union'[176]

It then held that the residence requirement imposed by Polish law was disproportionate to the objective pursued by the legislator – connection between a beneficiary and the

---

[173] *Loc. cit.* n. 139.

[174] Ustawa z dnia 29 Maja 1974 r. o zaopatrzeniu inwalidów wojennych i wojskowych oraz ich rodzin, Dz. U. 2002, Nr 9, Item 87 (as amended).

[175] ECJ, Case C-192/05 *K. Tas-Hagen and R.A. Tas v. Raadskamer WUBO van de Pensioen- en Uitkeringsraad* [2006] *ECR* I-10451.

[176] Para. 32 of the judgment.

society. The ECJ added that the same objective can be achieved by other means which will be less restrictive but equally effective. It was argued that:

'If medical or administrative checks make it necessary for the recipient of a benefit such as that at issue in the main proceedings to be in the territory of the Member State concerned, nothing precludes that Member State from requesting that the recipient go to that State for the purpose of undergoing such a check, including on pain of suspension of payment of the benefit if there is an unwarranted refusal on the part of the recipient.'[177]

The referring court followed the guidance of the European Court of Justice and annulled the contested decision in a judgment of 30 June 2008.[178] It held that the provisions of Polish law in question were contrary to Article 18 EC and thus could not serve as the legal basis for the suspension of such benefit available to victims of war.[179]


6.    DIRECT ACTIONS

During the five years of its membership in the European Union, Poland has been a frequent visitor in the EU courtrooms. Considerable delays in transposition of directives have led to numerous infraction cases reaching the judicial stage. In addition, Poland has submitted numerous actions for annulment, challenging the validity of several pieces of secondary legislation. In this section of the chapter, we shall present an overview of those direct actions.

    The number of infraction procedures usually corresponds to performance of a Member State in transposition of directives and adoption of national measures (should that prove necessary) giving effect to regulations. Therefore, one can conclude that five judgments of the European Court of Justice declaring Poland to be in breach of EC law is just the tip of the iceberg. Poland remains one of the worst performing countries in the Internal Market Scoreboards published by the European Commission. In mid-2009 with its 2.1% transposition deficit, it remains at the very bottom of the chart.[180]

    The first judgment where Poland was found to be in breach of EC law was rendered in case C-170/07 *Commission v. Poland.*[181] The European Commission questioned conformity of the Polish legislation on road traffic with EC law as far as it imposed an obligation of roadworthiness tests prior to the first registration of vehicles in Poland. Since new vehicles were exempted from that obligation, in practice only second-hand vehicles imported from other Member States were subject to such mandatory roadworthiness tests. The measures challenged by the European Commission could not be

---

[177] Para. 45 of the judgment.

[178] Regional Court in Koszalin, 30 June 2008, Case IV U 1660/06 *Halina Nerkowska v. Zakład Ubezpieczeń Społecznych*, not reported (on file with the authors).

[179] See also, ECJ Case C-221/07 *Krystyna Zablocka-Weyhermüller v. Land Baden-Württemberg* [2008] *ECR* nyr.

[180] See, European Commission, Internal Market Scoreboard No. 19, July 2009, at p. 12.

[181] ECJ, Case C-170/07 *Commission of the European Communities v. Republic of Poland* [2008] *ECR* nyr.

justified by any of the grounds listed in Article 30 EC or mandatory requirements developed in the case law of the European Court of Justice.

In chronological order, the next judgment rendered pursuant to Article 226 EC where Poland was found to be in breach of EC law was case C-227/07 *Commission v. Poland*.[182] This time Poland failed to transpose on time Article 4(1) of Directive 2002/19/EC.[183] This was followed by another straight-forward infraction in case C-492/07 *Commission v. Poland*.[184] The ECJ held that by not transposing properly Article 2 letter k of the Directive 2002/21/EC,[185] Poland breached EC law. In case C-475/07 *Commission v. Poland*,[186] the European Court of Justice held that by not transposing fully Directive 2003/96/EC,[187] Poland again failed to comply with obligations stemming from EC law. This was followed by cases C-143/08[188] and C-165/08,[189] whereby Poland was also declared to be in breach of EC law by failing to transpose on time and fully several directives (Directive 2006/73/EC[190] as well as – respectively – Directives 2001/18/ EC[191] and 2002/53/EC)[192] to national law.

Case C-193/07 *Commission v. Poland*, which was pending at the time of writing, merits particular attention.[193] The plaintiff argued that by failing to take appropriate measures to avoid deterioration in the habitats and significant disturbance to the species in the Special Protection Area *Puszcza Augustowska*, in the context of the approval procedures for the bypass around some cities, and by approving the project despite its adverse impact on the integrity of the area in question and by starting work on that

[182] ECJ, Case C-227/07 *Commission of the European Communities v. Republic of Poland* [2008] *ECR* nyr.

[183] Directive 2002/19/EC of the European Parliament and of the Council of 7 March 2002 on access to, and interconnection of, electronic communications networks and associated facilities (Access Directive), *OJ* 2002 L 108/7.

[184] ECJ, Case C-492/07 *Commission of the European Communities v. Republic of Poland* [2009] *ECR* nyr.

[185] Directive 2002/21/EC of the European Parliament and of the Council of 7 March 2002 on a common regulatory framework for electronic communications networks and services (Framework Directive), *OJ* 2002 L 108/33.

[186] ECJ, Case C-475/07 *Commission of the European Communities v. Republic of Poland* [2009] *ECR* nyr.

[187] Council Directive 2003/96/EC of 27 October 2003 restructuring the Community framework for the taxation of energy products and electricity, *OJ* 2003 L 283/51.

[188] ECJ, Case C-143/08 *Commission of the European Communities v. Republic of Poland* [2009] *ECR* nyr.

[189] ECJ, Case C-165/08 *Commission of the European Communities v. Republic of Poland* [2009] *ECR* nyr.

[190] Commission Directive 2006/73/EC of 10 August 2006 implementing Directive 2004/39/EC of the European Parliament and of the Council regarding organisational requirements and operating conditions for investment firms and defined terms for the purposes of that Directive, *OJ* 2006 L 241/36.

[191] Directive 2001/18/EC of the European Parliament and of the Council of 12 March 2001 on the deliberate release into the environment of genetically modified organisms and repealing Council Directive 90/220/EEC, *OJ* 2001 L 106/1.

[192] Council Directive 2002/53/EC of 13 June 2002 on the common catalogue of varieties of agricultural plant species, *OJ* 2002 L 193/1.

[193] Case C-193/07, Action brought on 5 April 2007 – *Commission of the European Communities v. Republic of Poland*, *OJ* 2007 C 199/14.

project, Poland failed to fulfil its obligations under Directive 92/43/EEC (Habitats Directive).[194] This piece of legislation aims to create a coherent European ecological network in order to promote the maintenance of or re-establishment to a suitable state of conservation of natural habitats and wild fauna and flora on the territory of the Member States. In order to achieve that objective, provision is made, *inter alia*, for the classification of special protection areas, where Member States shall take appropriate measures to avoid, by any of their acts, the deterioration of sites and significant disturbance to the species for which sites were classified. Poland is in the process of carrying out two road projects to bypass the towns of Augustów and Wasilków inside protected areas within the meaning of the Directive. The European Commission submitted in its action to the ECJ that Poland is in breach of the Habitats Directive with regard to two Special Protection Areas (SPAs) and in breach of the system of protection which follows from the case law with regard to a potential Site of Community Importance (SCI). In addition, Poland has proposed a compensatory measure for the ecological losses suffered because of the implementation of the project for a bypass around the town of *Augustów*, to be built on a potential SCI, which is likely to harm the ecological features of that site. The Commission takes the view that the project in question damages habitats, disturbs species for which the SPA was classified and does not constitute a measure liable to safeguard the interests of the potential SCI at a national level. According to the Commission, the project causes irreversible harm and will lead to deterioration of the unique and exceptional ecosystem of the valley of the *Rospuda* river in terms of its impact on birds, habitats and species in need of protection within the meaning of Habitats Directive. It must be noted that, at the time of the impact assessment of the *Augustów* bypass project on the Natura 2000 areas, the Polish authorities did not take into account appropriate alternative solutions. Therefore, the Polish authorities cannot rely on an overriding public interest in order to approve the project in question. Interestingly enough, the European Commission requested the ECJ to adopt interim measures, ordering Poland to suspend the work pending the infraction procedure. However, since Poland decided to suspend the construction on its own initiative, the request for interim measures was withdrawn.[195]

In the first years of EU membership, Poland brought several actions for annulment against the institutions of the European Communities. All of them proved to be unsuccessful. Since the majority of them have been discussed in Chapter 4 of this volume, we shall briefly refer to basics only. The first actions submitted pursuant to Article 230 EC dealt with measures adopted by EU institutions in the period preceding the entry into force of the Accession Treaty 2003. In case C-273/04 *Poland v. Council*,[196] the applicant challenged the legality of Council Decision 2004/281/EC.[197] One of the main

[194] Directive 79/409/EEC on the conservation of wild birds, *OJ* 1979 L 103/1.
[195] ECJ, Order in Case C-193/07 R-2 *Commission of the European Communities v. Republic of Poland*, not reported.
[196] ECJ, Case C-273/04 *Republic of Poland v. Council of the European Union* [2007] *ECR* I-8925.
[197] Council Decision of 22 March 2004 adapting the Act concerning the Conditions of Accession of the Czech Republic, the Republic of Estonia, the Republic of Cyprus, the Republic of Latvia, the Republic of Lithuania, the Republic of Hungary, the Republic of Malta, the Republic of Poland, the Republic of

issues considered by the plaintiff and defendant as well as Advocate General Maduro was the two months time limit to bring an action. If counted from the date of publication of the legislation in question Poland – as an Acceding Country – would have had to submit the action in the capacity of a non-privileged applicant under Article 230(4) EC. Thus it was argued that the time limits start to run for new Member States on their date of accession to the European Union. This crucial issue was – to much regret – only briefly elaborated on by the ECJ, which simply declared action admissible. In terms of substance, the Court held that there were no legitimate grounds to question the validity of the contested legislation.

A similar action was also submitted to the Court of First Instance where Poland sought annulment of the Commission Regulation 1972/2003/EC on trade in agricultural products.[198] It took the CFI five years to render a judgment in this case. All in all, it held that there were no grounds to annul the contested legislation.[199]

Poland has also challenged the legality of European Parliament and Council Directive 2005/36/EC on recognition of qualifications.[200] The action was clearly submitted for internal political reasons only, despite the fact that it was clear right from the start that it barely had merits.[201] The Directive itself merely repeated special rules provided in the Act on Conditions of Accession 2003;[202] therefore, the European Court of Justice dismissed the action as unfounded.

## 7.  CONCLUSIONS

In the title of this chapter, the authors argued that five years of Poland's membership in the European Union can be summarised as "constitutional drama" and business as usual. The selection of case law analysed in this chapter proves this argument. On the one hand, Poland has witnessed a series of shockwaves created by the judgments of the Constitutional Tribunal. On the other hand, as explained in section 3 of this chapter, the Tribunal presented its pro-European face, despite the very tight legal framework provided by the Polish Constitution. When it comes to national courts dealing with everyday litigation based on EU law, one can clearly see that this new legal order is

---

Slovenia and the Slovak Republic and the adjustments to the Treaties on which the European Union is founded, following the reform of the Common Agricultural Policy, *OJ* 2004 L 93/1.

[198] Commission Regulation 1972/2003/EC of 10 November 2003 on transitional measures to be adopted in respect of trade in agricultural products on account of the accession of the Czech Republic, Estonia, Cyprus, Latvia, Lithuania, Hungary, Malta, Poland, Slovenia and Slovakia, *OJ* 2003 L 293/3.

[199] CFI, Case T-257/04 *Republic of Poland v. Commission of the European Communities* [2009] *ECR* nyr.

[200] Directive 2005/36/EC of the European Parliament and of the Council of 7 September 2005 on the recognition of professional qualifications, *OJ* 2005 L 255/22.

[201] ECJ, Case C-460/05 *Republic of Poland v. European Parliament and Council of the European Union* [2007] *ECR* I-102.

[202] Act concerning the Conditions of Accession of the Czech Republic, the Republic of Estonia, the Republic of Cyprus, the Republic of Latvia, the Republic of Lithuania, the Republic of Hungary, the Republic of Malta, the Republic of Poland, the Republic of Slovenia and the Slovak Republic and the adjustments to the Treaties on which the European Union is founded, *OJ* 2003 L 236/33.

paving its way in national courtrooms. As in all new and old Member States, some judges are willing and able to follow EU law, and some still demonstrate a fair amount of resentment. Judging from countless cases challenging individual decisions of tax and customs authorities, we can see that EU law still remains an unknown world to some branches of public administration. Nevertheless, cases like *Brzeziński* play an extremely important role of ice-breakers. Not only do they indicate what EC law means in practice, but they also demonstrate the practical operation of basic tenets of EC law (supremacy, direct effect, etc.) and the usefulness of the preliminary ruling procedure. Polish courts are more and more willing to use this avenue to improve the interpretation and enforcement of EU law. The case law of the Supreme Court is very instructive in this respect. The judges seem to be employing the concept of *acte clair* carefully; however, when they can't reach a conclusion themselves, they are willing to engage in dialogue with the European Court of Justice. The same goes for the Supreme Administrative Court, which thus far has submitted five references for preliminary ruling. So, after all, it is business as usual.

*Chapter 10*

# WHAT ABOUT THAT "INCOMING TIDE"? THE APPLICATION OF EU LAW IN THE CZECH REPUBLIC

Michal Bobek* and Zdeněk Kühn**

## 1. INTRODUCTION

In one of his most famous decisions, Lord Denning, M.R. compared the effects of the Treaty establishing the European Economic Community and European Communities law generally within a national legal order to an incoming tide.[1] The Czech Republic joined the European Union on 1 May 2004. Nevertheless, five years after the accession, most of the Czech lands are rather dry, not much resembling anything like floods or tidal waves of EU law.

This chapter reflects the early experience with the new legal order in the Czech Republic. It first deals with the pre-accession phase and instances of the use of EU law in the Czech courts before the enlargement itself. Second, the post-accession case law of the Czech Constitutional Court is examined in order to identify any emerging constitutional doctrine *vis-à-vis* European Union law. Third, day-to-day judicial application of EU law is discussed, together with the practice of administrative authorities. Fourth, this chapter offers an overview of Czech references for preliminary ruling to the European Court of Justice and their domestic context. Finally, direct actions involving the Czech Republic as claimant (Art. 230 EC) or as defendant (Art. 226 EC) are examined against their domestic background and political context.[2]

---

* Michal Bobek is a Ph.D. researcher at the European University Institute, Department of Law, Florence, Italy.
** Zdeněk Kühn is a justice at the Supreme Administrative Court of the Czech Republic and associated professor of law at the Faculty of Law, Charles University, Prague.
[1] 'But when we come to matters with a European element, the Treaty is like an incoming tide. It flows into the estuaries and up the rivers. It cannot be held back.' Lord Denning MR in *H.P. Bulmer Ltd. and Another v. J. Bollinger S.A. and Others* [1974] Ch. 401, 418.
[2] The centre of gravity in this chapter is on the first years of membership, however a brief acknowledgment of legal developments in 2009 is also offered.

*A. Łazowski (ed.), The Application of EU Law in the New Member States*
© 2010, T·M·C·ASSER PRESS, *The Hague, The Netherlands and the Authors*

2.       OVERTURE: THE PRE-ACCESSION HARMONIOUS INTERPRETATION

2.1.     **The justification for the use of EU law before the accession and
         examples of its application**

As part of the first wave of fundamental changes in the Central and Eastern European
legal systems, major deficiencies of the communist legal systems were eliminated during the 1990s. A second wave of changes came soon thereafter. In anticipation of joining the European Union, the Czech Republic started to make its laws consistent with
the accumulated body of EU law. We must be cognisant of the fact that "Europeanisation"
has been the second major challenge in a single decade for the rapidly transforming
legal systems of post-communist states, the Czech Republic being no exception.

     The process of EU enlargement had a peculiar and multidimensional nature. In
purely legal terms, prior to the accession in 2004, EU law had not been formally binding for the acceding countries and their judiciaries. However, a generally framed obligation of gradual approximation with EU law rested on the EU candidates.[3] Consequently,
the application of EU law in the future Member States presented particularly interesting problems and challenges and called for the understanding of the sophisticated
concept of EU law's persuasive force. A rational choice in the pre-accession stage was
to apply EU law, not only considering the "limited law" of the texts of approximated
legislation, but also taking into account EU law in its full meaning. This included the
texts of EC directives, which had to be transposed into domestic law; their reasoning
and rationale, which would explain why a particular policy was regulated at the European
level; ECJ jurisprudence and, ideally, also case law of the EU Member States.

     One possible argument to support this ambitious claim was a broad understanding
of the obligation to approximate domestic law to that of the EU, covering adoption of
laws by domestic legislatures and application by national authorities, including courts
(often referred to as implementation). In Poland, for instance, the Constitutional Tribunal
referred to the EA Poland according to which Poland was 'obliged to use its best
endeavours to ensure that future legislation is compatible with Community legislation',
which resulted also in 'the obligation to interpret the existing legislation in such a way
as to ensure the greatest possible degree of such compatibility.'[4]

     The Czech courts and some public authorities followed a different track. Instead of
referring to the EA-Czech Republic, they simply highlighted the same set of basic
values and principles which underline both EU law and Czech law. 'Primary Community

---

[3] Art. 69 of the EA-Czech Republic read: 'The Contracting parties recognize that the major pre-
condition for the Czech Republic's economic integration into the Community is the approximation of
the Czech Republic's existing and future legislation to that of the Community. The Czech Republic shall
endeavour to ensure that its legislation will be gradually made compatible with that of the Community.'
(Europe Agreement establishing an association between the European Communities and their Member
States, of the one part, and the Czech Republic, of the other part, *OJ* 1994 L 360/2).

[4] Polish Constitutional Tribunal, case K 15/97 (*Re Gender Equality in the Civil Service*), OTK
19/1997, p. 380. English translation of the judgment available in 5 *E.Eur.Case Rep. of Const. L.* (1998)
p. 271, at p. 284. See also Z. Kühn, 'The Application of European Law in the New Member States: Several
(Early) Predictions', 6 *GLJ* (2005) pp. 563-582.

law is not foreign law for the Constitutional Court, but to a wide degree it penetrates into the Court's decision making – particularly in the form of general principles of European law', emphasised the Czech Constitutional Court (CCC) in a landmark pre-accession case.[5] Facing this justification, referring to arguments of EU law was desirable for the rationality and internal consistence and coherence of the Czech legal order.

A good example of a similar approach can be provided by the Czech Competition Authority, which took EU law into account in quite a few important cases decided well before the enlargement. This practice was approved by the Czech High Court in the *Skoda Auto* case. In that case, the appellant, one of the most important Czech companies, challenged a decision of the Competition Authority with the argument that EU law was not a binding source of law in the national legal system and that, therefore, it could not be taken into consideration in the interpretation of the domestic law. The High Court rejected this claim, emphasising the international links between national antitrust laws:

'The protection of free trade is specific in the way that national law is often not sufficient, and therefore is often enriched by the application of rules used in the countries with a long tradition of antitrust law (Germany, the United States). For that matter [the Czech antitrust law of 1991] received the basic ideas of the Treaty of Rome, particularly already mentioned articles 85, 86 and 92; this was from the perspective of harmonization of the legal systems of the European Communities and the Czech Republic an absolute necessity.'[6]

The High Court concluded that it was not an error of law for the public authority to interpret Czech antitrust law consistently with case law of the European Court of Justice and with Commission decisions. Seized on a constitutional complaint, the CCC affirmed the approach taken by the High Court, emphasising that both the EC Treaty and the EU Treaty derive from the same values and principles as the Czech constitutional law; therefore the interpretation of EC antitrust law by EU institutions is valuable for the interpretation of the corresponding Czech rules.[7] Both courts understood the difference between a source of law that is merely persuasive, a "may source" (interpretation consistent with EC law prior to accession) and a source that is directly or indirectly binding – a "must source" in a strict legal sense (which would be the case only if EU law had direct effect in an EU candidate country).[8]

---

[5] Czech Constitutional Court, Case Pl. ÚS 5/01, judgment of 16 October 2001 (*Milk Quota* case), published as no 410/2001 Coll.; English translation available at http://www.concourt.cz.

[6] High Court in Olomouc, decision of 14 November 1996, published in 5(9) *Právní rozhledy* (1997) p. 484.

[7] Czech Constitutional Court, judgment of 29 May 1997, *Skoda Auto* case, 8 *Sbírka nálezů a usnesení* [Collection of Judgments and Rulings of the Constitutional Court] p. 149.

[8] J. Wróblewski, *The judicial application of law* (Dordrecht, Kluwer Academic Publishers 1992) at p. 85. Wróblewski makes a distinction between a "must source" and a "may source" of legal interpretation. This conception of must and may sources is followed also by D.N. MacCornick and R.S. Summers (see D.N. MacCormick and R.S. Summers, eds., *Interpreting Precedents. A Comparative Study* (Aldershot, Darmouth 1997)). The inability to distinguish between the must and may sources is nicely illustrated in an analysis by V. Týč, who considers the decision of the CCC as though it accorded the EC Treaty direct effect (which is obviously absurd reading of the decision). See V. Týč, 'Czech Republic', in A. Ott and

## 2.2.    Examples of non-application and obstacles to the use of EU law prior to the accession

The cases mentioned above remained, however, only isolated instances of indirect use of EC law as persuasive authority in the Czech courts in the period before the accession. In most courts prior to 2004, however, deeply rooted legislative optimism and textual positivism produced an atmosphere where ordinary judges and lawyers generally over-emphasised the role of the legislature on the one hand, while they seriously under-stated their own role in that process on the other. Judicial logic appeared to be bipolar – a legislative text was either binding law or nullity. In systems where persuasive argu-ments are not recognised as relevant, a sensible harmonisation is not likely to succeed.

The Czech Supreme Court (CSC) is another good example substantiating this argu-ment. In its decision dealing with the validity of an agreement between a consumer and a distributor of expensive pottery, the consumer argued that the agreement was con-trary to the general clause on good morals, as the distributor sold him exceptionally expensive pottery under very harsh conditions. In his argumentation, the consumer referred to case law of Western European countries and to EC directives. By this token, the consumer urged the Czech courts to take these developments into account, as the Western European countries, in contrast to the Czech Republic, had long experience in dealing with consumer contracts. None of the three Czech courts dealing with the issue accepted this invitation to engage in a comparative analysis. The CSC based its final decision on quasi-liberal rhetoric of the freedom of contract, reminiscent more of the ideas governing European discourse in the mid-19th century than the 20th century discourse governed by the widely accepted necessity to protect a weaker party. It did not consider comparative arguments drawing upon EC law as potentially capable of filling the general clauses on good morals. Deciding as the court of final instance, it conceived of the defendant's arguments as arguments referring to binding sources. It opined:

> '[V]alidity of the agreement made between the parties on August 31, 1993 must be decided according to the then valid law, as both lower courts did. In contrast, laws and directives valid in the countries of the European Community are not applicable, as the Czech Republic was not (and still is not) a member of the Community, and that is why the Czech Republic is not bound by these laws. The binding force of the rules to which the appellant refers can-not be inferred from any provision of the [the Czech Association Agreement], as the court of appeal concluded. The question of harmonization of legal practice of the Czech Republic with legal practice of the European Community is gaining in, but this cannot change anything in the outcome of this case.'[9]

---

K. Inglis, eds., *Handbook on European Enlargement. A Commentary on the Enlargement Process* (The Hague, T.M.C. Asser Press 2002) pp. 229-237, at p. 231.

[9] Czech Supreme Court, Judgment of 12 December 2000, Case 25 Cdo 314/99, text available at http://www.nsoud.cz.

The line of cases relating to this issue did not end by 2004 and found its very interesting (and problematic) continuation in a recent judgment of the CCC.[10]

To sum up, textual positivism, with its severe "binding *vs.* non-binding" dichotomy, relegated the role of EU law in the pre-accession period to non-existence. There were only very few, rather exceptional instances, when Czech judges were ready to employ EU law as persuasive authority. To put it in blunt terms, EU law can only be relevant once it becomes binding. Since, obviously it had no binding effect on candidate countries, it remained beyond the view of the ordinary judiciary.

This "isolationist" practice of the Czech ordinary courts was criticised by a few exceptional ordinary judges[11] as well as by some politicians. In 2002, the Czech Minister of Justice (who in the meantime became the Chief Justice at the Constitutional Court) noted that only a few people were fully aware that ordinary judges have to deal with the bulk of international law, and that, after joining the EU, it would be up to them to ensure the priority of EU law over national law.[12]

3.    CONSTITUTIONAL POSITION *VIS-À-VIS* EU LAW UPON THE
      ACCESSION TO THE EUROPEAN UNION

In the first five years following accession to the European Union, the Czech Constitutional Court rendered seven landmark judgments. Six of these cases were initiated by members of the Czech Parliament pursuant to abstract constitutional review procedures. This chapter will take a closer look at four of them, demonstrating clearly the early approach of the Constitutional Court to EU law.[13]

In March 2006, the Czech Constitutional Court in the *Sugar Quota II* case[14] upheld EU sugar quotas against the framework of the Czech Constitution, although the opposition parliamentarians argued that the latter was in breach of the constitutional right

---

[10]  See further in this chapter.

[11]  See a commentary of Judge Filemon of the Regional Court in Brno: 'It would serve the development of specialized legal sub-branches of the copyright protection and the protection of industrial rights, if the Czech judiciary were more connected to "abroad" (following foreign up-to-date legal theory and case law) and overcame the "Czech" isolationist way of ignoring the importance of comparative law, as well as censorship of the editors of the collection of judicial judgments ... That is why we are attempting at least in the areas with applicable international treaties ... to use foreign commentaries and case law in original (e.g. from the Internet) or from the few available Czech translations.' A commentary of B. Filemon on a judgment no 11 Cms 231/96, in Jurisprudence, Vynutitelnost práva a právní praxe [The Enforceability of Law and Legal Practice], no 4-5/2000, p. 34.

[12]  See the interview with then Czech Minister of Justice, Mr. Rychetský (since 2004 Chief Justice of the Constitutional Court) in the Czech daily *Právo* of 25 September 2002, p. 1.

[13]  See also, Czech Constitutional Court, Judgment of 27 March 2008, Case Pl. ÚS 56/05; Judgment of 26 November 2008, Case Pl. ÚS 19/08 (*re Treaty of Lisbon*) and Judgment of 2 December 2008, Case Pl. ÚS 12/08 (*re supremacy of EC law*). Texts of all three judgments are available in English at http://www.concourt.cz.

[14]  Czech Constitutional Court, Judgment of 8 March 2006, Case Pl. ÚS 50/04 (*re Sugar Quota Case II*), no 154/2006 Coll. Text of this judgment is available in English at http://www.concourt.cz.

to engage in unrestrained business activities.[15] The Constitutional Court approved the European standard of fundamental rights protection. In May 2006, the Constitutional Court rejected the motion for annulment of domestic provisions transposing the Framework Decision on the European Arrest Warrant.[16] The parliamentarians of the conservative Civic Democratic Party challenged the possibility to surrender Czech citizens abroad under the EAW. This, according to the applicant, was contrary to Article 14(4) of the Czech Charter of Fundamental Rights. It provides that no citizen may be forced to leave his homeland. Moreover, taking into account rather poor drafting of the list of crimes to which the double criminality requirement does not apply, the complainant claimed that the legislation was contrary to the fundamental principle *nullum crimen sine lege.*[17] In January 2007, the Constitutional Court decided the issue of the national law regulating the prices of medicinal products for human use. Although a group of senators argued that there was a violation of the Czech Constitution because of the conflict with the corresponding EU law, the CCC rejected this argument; on the other hand, the CCC used EU law as a source of inspiration for the meaning of the national Constitution.[18]

3.1.    **The constitutional basis of opening the national legal system to EU law and the primacy of EU law**

The first delicate question with respect to the application of EU law in the Czech Republic after 1 May 2004 was whether there is any constitutional basis to apply EU law at all. The most probable reason for the silence of the Constitution with respect to EU law was the simple fact that parliamentarians were unwilling to deal with EU law and its primacy over national law expressly, fearing another step in the direction of losing national sovereignty.[19]

Despite some doubts relating to the fact that the Czech Constitution did not address the issue of EU membership and its law expressly, doctrinal consensus soon emerged that the Constitution is clear and provides enough support for EU law to be applied after 1 May 2004. The question was, however, which provision precisely "opens the gate." One opinion claimed that this is Article 10 of the Constitution, providing for international treaties being part of the Czech legal order; a competing opinion held that

---

[15] We might perhaps note that the CCC quashed a national implementing measure on procedural grounds (however, after finding that it was useless as the EC Regulation was able to be directly applicable).

[16] Council Framework Decision 2002/584/JHA of 13 June 2002 on the European arrest warrant and the surrender procedures between Member States, *OJ* 2002 L 190/1.

[17] Czech Constitutional Court, Judgment of 3 May 2006, Case Pl. ÚS 36/05 (*re European Arrest Warrant*), [2007] 3 C.M.L.R. 24.

[18] Czech Constitutional Court, Judgment of 16 January 2007, Case Pl. ÚS 36/05 (*re Medicinal Products for Human Use Case*), no 57/2007 Coll., no English translation available.

[19] The Czech Republic was not alone in this respect among EU newcomers. The similar situation could be found, for instance, in Hungary. See R. Uitz, 'EU Law and the Hungarian Constitutional Court: Lessons of the First Post-accession Encounter', in W. Sadurski and J. Ziller, eds., *Après Enlargement: Legal and Political Responses in Central and Eastern Europe* (Florence, European University Institute 2005) pp. 41-63.

the actual support for the application of Community law is provided by the competence clause of Article 10a which provides that certain powers of Czech Republic authorities may be transferred by treaty to an international organisation or institution (and which also incorporated EU law and thereby its effects as well).[20] Although the practical difference between both opinions was very limited, the latter opinion granted perhaps more leeway to situate EU law within the framework of the national legal system and enabled the CCC to serve as a "gatekeeper" of the application of EU law, which is entering the Czech legal system through the "bridge" of Article 10a.[21]

It was not until 8 March 2006 that the CCC explained in *Sugar Quota II* what is the basis for the application of EU law and what its primacy should be. The CCC openly chose the latter possibility. The Court reasoned that:

'Direct applicability in national law and precedence in application of a regulation follows from Community law doctrine itself, as it has emerged from the case-law of the ECJ (cf., for ex., decision 26/62 NV Algemene Transport- en Expeditie Orderneming Van Gend en Loos v. Nederlandse Administratie der Belastingen [1963] ECR 1; 6/64 Costa v. ENEL [1964] ECR 585). In contrast to international law, Community law itself determines and specifies the effects it has in the national law of the Member States.'

'If membership in the EC brings with it a certain limitation on the powers of the national organs in favour of Community organs, one of the manifestations of such limitation must necessarily also be a restriction on Member States' freedom to determine the effect of Community law in their national legal orders. ... In other words, the transfer of certain powers to the EC entails also the loss of the Czech Republic's freedom to designate the effects Community law has in national law and which effects are derived directly from Community law in fields in which such transfer occurred. Art. 10a of the Constitution of the Czech Republic thus operates in both directions: it forms the normative basis for the transfer of powers and is simultaneously that provision of the Czech Constitution which opens up the national legal order to the operation of Community law, including rules relating to its effects within the legal order of the Czech Republic.'[22]

### 3.2. The relationship between national constitutional law and EU law

Unlike the majority of constitutional systems in Europe, the Czech Constitution does not consist of one single constitutional text. Instead, the Czech Constitution is composed of a plethora of constitutional laws, which form the so-called "constitutional order" of

---

[20] The two conflicting opinions were offered by Jiří Malenovský (now a justice at the European Court of Justice), on the one hand, and Zdeněk Kühn and Jan Kysela, on the other. See J. Malenovský, 'Ve věci ústavního základu působení komunitárního práva uvnitř ČR nebylo řečeno poslední slovo' [No final word has been said in the matter of constitutional basis of functioning of EU law in the national legal system], 12 *Právní rozhledy* (2004) p. 227 and Z. Kühn and J. Kysela, 'Na základě čeho bude působit komunitární právo v českém právním řádu?' [What provides the basis for EU law in the Czech legal order ?], 12 *Právní rozhledy* (2004) p. 23.
[21] For this view (including references to German sources), see Z. Kühn, 'Rozšíření Evropské unie a vztahy šestadvaceti ústavních systémů' [EU Enlargement and the relations between 26 constitutional systems], 143 *Právník* (2004) pp. 745-786.
[22] *Loc. cit.* n. 14, part VI.B [emphasis added].

the Czech Republic. In addition to the list provided by the Constitution itself,[23] the CCC expanded the range of the Czech constitutional order also to the area of (unspecified and unlimited number of) international treaties on "human rights and fundamental freedoms." The judgment of the CCC announcing this opinion[24] soon became a target of frequent doctrinal criticism.[25] However, it could be fairly said that since 2002, what counts as constitutional law in the Czech Republic is open to the final say of the CCC.

Considering this creative case law, it is not surprising that the attempt to include EU law into the national constitutional order soon reached the CCC. The senators in an abstract constitutional review treated the conflict between the national law and EU law in the same manner as a conflict between the national law and the Czech Constitution, thus effectively making the entire body of EU law (or at least its substantial part) a part of the national constitutional order. They demanded to quash the national regulation on the prices of medicinal products for human use because of the alleged conflict between the national law and a corresponding EU directive.[26] In January 2007, the CCC, providing only little argument, rejected the thesis that EU law forms part of the Czech constitutional order. However, although the conflict between EU law and the national law, no matter how clear, cannot establish unconstitutionality of the national law, it can provide an important supportive argument to conclude that the law is in conflict with the national Constitution.[27]

The approach chosen by the CCC invited criticism. One of the authors of this chapter noted that, although the conclusion of the CCC can be accepted, the role of Community law in this case was far from a mere inspiration or any sort of supportive argument.[28] In fact, it was a conflict between national and EU law that was the crucial argument for annulling the national law (whereas argumentation by the national Constitution served as a charade to keep what the court said it was about to do, i.e., review the national law against its own Constitution). One might wonder what caused that the CCC decided to use EU law as a sort of "binding" constitutional argument. Perhaps the CCC intends to get back the power it has lost via a decentralised review of national law for its conflict with EU law. If combined with a sensible activity in individual cases, however, the logic which the CCC decided to follow can help the enforcement of EU law in the Czech Republic.

---

[23]  See Art. 112(1) of the Czech Constitution providing for the definition of the constitutional order.

[24]  Judgment of 25 June 2002, Case Pl. ÚS 36/01 (*re Bankruptcy Trustee Case*), no 403/2002 Coll. Translation in English available at http://www.concourt.cz.

[25]  See Z. Kühn and J. Kysela, 'Je ústavou vždy to, co Ústavní soud řekne, že ústava je? (Euronovela Ústavy ve světle překvapivého nálezu Ústavního soudu)' [Is the Constitution always what the Constitutional Court says it is? (Euro-amendment to the Constitution in light of the surprising decision of the Constitutional Court)], 10 *Časopis pro právní vědu a praxi* (2002) pp. 199-214.

[26]  Council Directive 89/105/EEC of 21 December 1988 relating to the transparency of measures regulating the prices of medicinal products for human use and their inclusion in the scope of national health insurance systems, *OJ 1989 L 40/8*.

[27]  *Loc. cit.* n. 18, para. 35.

[28]  See M. Bobek, 'Ústavní soud ČR a přezkum vnitrostátní implementace komunitárního práva: „*Poslouchej, co říkám a nekoukej, co dělám*"?' ['The Constitutional Court of the Czech Republic and the review of the national implementation of community law: "*Listen to what I am saying and do not look at what I am doing*"?'], 5 *Soudní rozhledy* (2007) pp. 173-180.

3.3.    **The constitutional duty to apply national law in a manner consistent with EU law**

In its reasoning in the *Sugar Quota II* case, the CCC re-emphasised the importance of the principle of interpretation of domestic law in a way consistent with EU law. In the Court's view, the principle acquired a new quality after the accession to the European Union:

> 'Although the Constitutional Court's referential framework has remained, even since 1 May 2004, the norms of the Czech Republic's constitutional order, the Constitutional Court cannot entirely overlook the impact of Community law on the formation, application, and interpretation of national law, all the more so in a field of law where the creation, operation, and aim of its provisions is immediately bound up with Community law. In other words, in this field, the Constitutional Court interprets constitutional law taking into account the principles arising from Community law.'[29]

This principle was even more stressed in the *EAW* case, where the CCC held:

> 'From Article 1 par. 2 of the Constitution, in conjunction with the principle of cooperation enshrined in Art. 10 of the EC Treaty, follows a constitutional principle according to which national legal enactments, including the Constitution, should whenever possible be interpreted in conformity with the process of European integration and the cooperation between European and Member State organs.'[30]

According to the *EAW* case, this principle is limited by the possible meaning of the constitutional text, which means that 'if the national methodology for the interpretation of constitutional law does not enable a relevant norm to be interpreted in harmony with European Law, it is solely within the Constituent Assembly's prerogative to amend the Constitution.' The second limit is implied by those essential attributes of a democratic law-based state which cannot be changed even by the Constituent Assembly.[31]

3.4.    **Constitutional review of EU law by the CCC**

Constitutional review of European Union legal acts seems to be excluded in the Czech Republic as a matter of principle. *Sugar Quota II* approved the current standard within the Community for the protection of fundamental rights, which is neither 'of a lower quality than the protection accorded in the Czech Republic', nor does the standard 'markedly diverge from the standard up till now provided in the domestic setting by the Constitutional Court'. The CCC emphasised that the delegation of part of the powers of national organs to the EU is conditional and 'may persist only so long as

---

[29] *Loc. cit.* n. 14 [emphasis added].

[30] *Loc. cit.* n. 17, para. 81 (the CCC referred to the decision of the Polish Constitutional Tribunal in case K 15/04 of 31 May 2004 and to the decision of the European Court of Justice in Case C-105/03 *Criminal proceedings against Maria Pupino* [2005] *ECR* I-5285).

[31] *Ibidem*, para. 82.

these powers are exercised in a manner that is compatible with the preservation of the foundations of state sovereignty of the Czech Republic', and should not threaten the basic principles of the Czech constitutional order which are not subject to revision (eternal law). If these conditions are threatened, the CCC would be 'called upon to protect constitutionalism'[32] and to exercise constitutional review. The CCC thus rephrased the famous Solange II decision of the German Federal Constitutional Tribunal.

Taking these premises into account, in the *Sugar Quota II* case, the CCC held as a matter of principle that it will refrain from reviewing EU law against the backdrop of the Czech Constitution. However, the crucial question of both the *Sugar Quota II* and the *EAW* cases was whether the Constitutional Court should review domestic laws which implement EU obligations. In *Sugar Quota II*, the CCC held that if 'the Community delegates powers back to the Members States for the purpose of implementing certain Community law acts, or if it leaves certain issues unregulated', respective rules take the form of national law, and as such, they must be in conformity with both EU law and the Czech Constitution. The domestic law implementing EC law (the CCC in its sweeping statement did not differentiate whether or not EU law gives the national legislature any discretion) is thus subject to full constitutional review, even though the principle of European-conform interpretation applies.[33]

The *EAW* case does not fit easily into this line of thought. While *Sugar Quota II* relies on full (though Euro-friendly) constitutional review of national acts implementing EU law, a few weeks later the *EAW* case stated:

> '[I]n areas where Community law applies exclusively, it is supreme, so that it cannot be contested by means of national law referential criteria, not even on the constitutional level. According to this doctrine the Constitutional Court would have no competence to decide on the constitutionality of a European Law norm, not even in the case that they are contained in legal enactments of the Czech Republic. Its competence to adjudge the constitutionality of Czech norms is, thus, restricted in the same respect. ... [W]here the delegation of authority leaves the member states no room for discretion ... the doctrine of primacy of Community law in principle does not permit the Constitutional Court to review such Czech norm in terms of its conformity with the constitutional order of the Czech Republic, naturally with the exception [of the alleged conflict with the very essence of the substantive law-based state].'[34]

Interestingly, this opinion was criticised as an unjustified "shift" by the Justice-Rapporteur of *Sugar Quota II*, who dissented in the *EAW* case.[35] Unfortunately, the CCC did not take pain to explain this obvious deviation.

---

[32] *Loc. cit.* n. 14, part VI.B.

[33] *Ibidem*, part VI.A.

[34] *Loc. cit.* n. 17, paras. 52 and 54.

[35] See the dissenting opinion of Justice Wagnerová in the *EAW* case: 'Today's majority opinion shifts this doctrine [announced in Sugar Quota II], formulated by the Constitutional Court not even two months previously ... In actuality, in the cited judgment the Constitutional Court declared that in the case that powers are re-delegated from EC (EU) organs to organs of the Czech Republic (this still concerns the First Pillar of the EU), the Constitutional Court will review legal norms resulting from that re-delegation from the perspective of the Czech constitutional order, in which case, however, it will interpret it with a

The doctrinal difference between *Sugar Quota II* and *EAW* cases, however, does not make a substantial difference in practice, because the CCC, despite its alleged self-restraint *vis-à-vis* the national laws implementing the EAW Framework Decision, did engage in a complete review of the law. The only way to reconcile the difference between what the CCC really did with what the Court had said it was about to do is to accept that all the arguments made by the petitioners were based on the 'eternal' constitutional core.[36] Interpreted in this way, the soft European constitutional supremacy claimed by the CCC has lost much of its weight and in fact is close to what M. Kumm calls 'Constitutionalism beyond the State' or Maduro's description of Constitutional Pluralism.[37]

### 3.5. Is there a consistent position of the CCC towards EU law?

In comparing Constitutional Courts, one should see them in their political context. While there are countries where political parties are almost united *vis-à-vis* European questions, many Central European countries are not. The detailed and frequently amended provision of Article 88 of the French Constitution regularly replies to the judgments of the French Constitutional Council in European matters. In contrast, amending the Czech Constitution in the face of a polarised political scene and the presence of strong Euro-sceptic parties effectively suggests roundabout pressure on the CCC to interpret its Constitution in a Euro-friendly manner and avoid the need for constitutional amendments. After all, as early as 2004, the Czech Parliament rejected the Government's attempt to amend the Czech Charter of Fundamental Rights and thus to confirm explicitly the possibility of extraditing nationals.[38] On the other hand, the Czech decision shows the dangers when the CCC pushes EU law hard against a passive legislature. One might wonder whether it would be ultimately helpful for democracy if problematic EU rules were justified by activist Constitutional Courts and by the technical language of law.[39]

The first three major decisions of the CCC on European Union law approved the hypothesis that the Constitutional Courts of the new EU Member States will not revolt

---

view toward the ECJ case law on those principles which are identical with the principles contained in the Czech constitutional order.'

[36] *Loc. cit.* n. 17, para. 53, the last sentence: '*In this matter, however, the petitioners asserted that, by adopting the European Arrest Warrant,* just such a conflict with the essential attributes of a democratic law-based state has come about' [emphasis added].

[37] M. Kumm, 'The Jurisprudence of Constitutional Conflict: Constitutional Supremacy in Europe before and after the Constitutional Treaty', 11 *ELJ* (2005) pp. 262-307; M.P. Maduro, 'Contrapunctual Law: Europe's Constitutional Pluralism in Action', in N. Walker, ed., *Sovereignty in Transition* (Oxford-Portland, Oregon, Hart Publishing 2003) pp. 501-537.

[38] *Loc. cit.* n. 17, para. 5.

[39] See in more detail, Z. Kühn, 'The European Arrest Warrant, Third Pillar Law and National Constitutional Resistence/Acceptance: The EAW Saga as Narrated by the Constitutional Judiciary in Poland, Germany, and the Czech Republic', 3 *CYELP* (2007) pp. 99-134. On the EAW saga before national Constitutional Courts generally, see also J. Komárek 'European Constitutionalism and the European Arrest Warrant: In Search of the Contrapunctual Principles' Limits', 44 *CMLRev.* (2007) pp. 9-40.

against principles of primacy and direct effect.[40] Interestingly, the CCC does not restrain itself to a strictly protectionist position of its German archetype. Like the German Federal Constitutional Tribunal, the CCC views its primary position as being an ultimate guardian of national sovereignty and constitutional traditions. In addition, the CCC gets inspired by EU law and does not hesitate to enrich the national Constitution through a more concrete content of EU law including the ECJ case law.

Unfortunately, the jurisprudence of the CCC is far from being settled and established. The CCC is lacking a consistent approach in answering the same questions. We have seen it on the example of reviewing national laws implementing EU law; in less than two months, the CCC answered this question in a strikingly different manner. There is also another rather surprising feature of EU-related cases of the CCC. Some of those cases are very long and barely offer a comprehensive analysis of the case law of the ECJ. The most striking example of this is the *Sugar Quota II* case, which covers many pages of a very long analysis of the ECJ case law. Thus, the case law relating to EU law is far from being final, and we might only wait for further developments.

## 4.   THE APPLICATION OF EUROPEAN UNION LAW AFTER THE ACCESSION BY CZECH COURTS AND ADMINISTRATIVE AUTHORITIES

With respect to the use of EU law in the reasoning of courts, at least three different types of EC law-related argument may be distinguished:

(i)   EC law is directly applicable, and it covers the area of law in question exclusively; i.e., a national court or administrative authority directly applies Community law, and there is no conflict with national rules.
(ii)   Directly applicable EC law enters into conflict with national legislation; the conflict should then be resolved by resorting to the principle of primacy of directly effective Community legislation over national law.
(iii)   Community law is not directly applicable but serves as a subsidiary argument for harmonious (conform) interpretation of national law with Community law. Conform interpretation is, of course, an extremely broad category, which may in practice involve anything between a very weak confirming argument based on Community law and a very strong "bending" of the domestic provision, thus bordering on the direct effect and the replacement of national rules by Community rules.

The application of EC law by the Czech courts in the first years following the accession could be summarised as swimming in a sea of harmonious interpretation with an occasional island or coastal rock of directly applied piece of Community legislation, without, however, any crash. The actual direct application of EC law has been so far limited, especially with respect to the higher courts. The reason for this fact is the normal delay with which cases enter the judicial domain. In 2004-2008, the higher courts (appellate and supreme) have mostly dealt with cases from the pre-accession

---

[40]   Further, see Kühn, *loc. cit.* n. 4.

period, when EC law was not directly applicable.[41] The use of EC law was thus most-ly limited to instance of self-imposed (i.e., not compulsory) harmonious interpretation, as there are only very few cases in which there was any directly applicable EC law at all.

## 4.1. Absence of direct conflicts before courts

As far as directly applicable EC law is concerned, i.e., the scenarios under points (i) and (ii), the distinctive feature of a few judicial decisions where EC law was directly applied is almost complete absence of any open conflicts, which would be solved by virtue of primacy of EC law. In the few cases where a potential conflict between EC law and national law was about to emerge, the case was considered to fall either within the Community exclusive area or it was tucked into some sort of conform inter-pretation with the meaning of the national law bent in order to efface the friction.

An example of this direct conflict avoidance could be the already above-described constitutional case of the European Arrest Warrant. Albeit the Czech Constitution is, as far as the extradition of its own nationals is concerned, worded similarly to the Polish or German ones, the CCC has preferred to considerably shift the meaning of the Constitution than to recognise a conflict between the EAW Framework Decision and the Czech Constitution.[42]

Obviously, the demarcation of the three categories mentioned above is very fuzzy. An example of a case on the borderline between an exclusive Community regulation and a conflict involving primacy issue was the case of Slovak asylum seekers before the Czech administrative courts. Shortly after the accession of Czech Republic and Slovakia to the European Union, there have been cases in which Slovak nationals (mostly Roma) applied for political asylum in the Czech Republic. An administrative authority – the Ministry of Interior – rejected these applications, directly applying the Protocol annexed to the EC Treaty,[43] and disregarded the provisions of the Czech Asylum Act.

Regional administrative courts, reviewing decisions of the Ministry in the first instance, were split on the direct application of the Protocol. Some[44] were of the opin-ion that the Protocol was to be directly applied and it had primacy over the provisions of national law; meaning there was no space for the simultaneous application of the Protocol and the Czech Asylum Act. Others believed that the Protocol provided just one additional instance of categories, where an asylum application under the Czech Asylum Act was to be rejected, with applicants coming from a safe third country.[45]

---

[41] Only the decisions of the two High Courts (the Supreme Court and the Supreme Administrative Court) and the Constitutional Court are published. Other courts publish their decisions very rarely and in a haphazard manner. This makes any comprehensive review of the case law of first instance courts virtually impossible.

[42] *Loc. cit.* n. 17.

[43] Protocol on asylum for nationals of Member States of the European Union, *OJ* 1997 C 340/103.

[44] E.g., judgment of the *Městský soud v Praze* [Municipal Court in Prague] of 20 June 2005, Case 7 A 7/2005, unpublished.

[45] E.g., judgment of the *Krajský soud v Ostravě* [Regional Court in Ostrava] of 6 April 2005, Case 65 Az 34/2004, unpublished.

The Supreme Administrative Court (SAC), which was eventually called to unify the practice of the regional administrative courts,[46] observed that it had no doubts that the Protocol was directly applicable EC law which, in the case of conflict, would have primacy over Czech law. However, the Protocol only states that the Member States shall be regarded as constituting safe countries of origin in respect to each other for all legal and practical purposes in relation to asylum matters. The Protocol does not, however, provide as to how this assumption should be realised at the national level. In this respect, the SAC emphasised the importance of the principle of national procedural autonomy. On the basis of these starting assumptions, the SAC announced a broader constitutional principle for the behaviour of administrative authorities. In applying EC law, national administrative authorities are servants to two masters: a Member State and the European Union. Should the need arise, under EC law they are also entitled to accord primacy to directly applicable EC law over national law. However, the SAC stressed that while doing so, national administrative authorities also have to respect the national legislative framework as much as possible. In the case in question, it was possible to observe the Community obligations within the framework of the Czech Asylum Act. The non-application of the national law was thus not necessary.

As far as the scenario described sub (ii) is concerned, that is the direct application of EC law taking precedence over national law, there appears to be so far only a few instances in which a Czech court set aside national legislation conflicting with EC law. A good example is a decision of the *Krajský soud v Ústí nad Labem* [Regional Court in Ústí nad Labem].[47] The case arose out of the incorrect transposition of the Council Directive 95/59/EC on taxes other than turnover taxes which affect the consumption of manufactured tobacco.[48] A vendor was fined by the Customs Authority for selling tobacco without the proper tax being paid on each package. The vendor defended himself by claiming that the tobacco was not tobacco designed for final consumption, and that he just repackaged the already-taxed tobacco into smaller bags for further sale; thus he was not producing final consumption tobacco which would be taxable under the Directive. The vendor pointed out that the definition of "producing" tobacco is different in the Directive and in the implementing Czech law. In such circumstances, it is the definition contained in the Directive which should prevail. The Regional Court agreed. Applying case law of the European Court of Justice,[49] it held that the relevant provision of the Directive was sufficiently clear and precise and that it was unconditional. It also observed that the transposition period already expired. Finally, the individual in question could derive rights from the Directive, and no obligation would be imposed on a third party. Under these conditions, the Court concluded that the Directive was directly effective. It annulled the administrative decision of the Customs Authority

---

[46] Judgment of the SAC of 19 July 2006, Case 3 Azs 259/2005, no 977/2006 Coll. SAC.

[47] Judgment of 19 July 2007, Case 15 Ca 184/2006, published as no 1359/2007 Coll. SAC.

[48] Council Directive 95/59/EC of 27 November 1995 on taxes other than turnover taxes which affect the consumption of manufactured tobacco, *OJ* 1995 L 291/40.

[49] The Regional Court referred in particular to the Case 41/74 *Yvonne van Duyn v. Home Office* [1974] *ECR* 1337.

for not having taken the Directive into account, i.e., not applying it directly and not setting aside the provision of Czech implementing law.

## 4.2. Direct effect and primacy before administrative authorities

The above-described case of the somewhat perhaps overzealous direct application of EC law by the Czech Ministry of Interior is an indication of a broader phenomenon. As was already mentioned above, the direct judicial application of EC law is "delayed" by the fact that EC law-related cases with full post-accession background came to higher courts (whose decisions are reported in their entirety) only years after the enlargement. This means that it was only in late 2007 that "Euro-cases" started to crystallise in the appellate courts in civil and commercial matters and before the Supreme Administrative Court in administrative matters.[50]

Administrative authorities have, on the other hand, been at the forefront of the direct application of EC law since the very first day of EU membership. In areas like customs, competition, agricultural policy or asylum, the respective administrative authorities started to apply EC law directly since "day one." It is thus not surprising that the first direct application of EC law with primacy being accorded to EC rules occurred not before the Czech courts, but in administrative proceedings before administrative authorities.[51]

The first example of non-application of national law because of its inconsistency with EC law is probably a decision of the Czech Competition Authority of 7 November 2005,[52] in which it set aside certain provisions of the Act amending the Act on the Protection of Competition,[53] which precluded it from conducting parallel inquiries into breaches of the competition law from the national as well as Community angles.[54] The direct application of EC law by the Competition Authority is perhaps not that surprising. Competition authorities in all Member States tend to be at the forefront of the application of EC law. The Czech Competition Authority is additionally staffed with

---

[50] In the Czech Republic, justice in civil, commercial and criminal cases is three-layered: first instance, appeal and cassation appeal, limited to points of law only, to the Supreme Court. The length of proceedings at any one of these layers is more than one year in average. The average length of procedure at administrative justice, composed of Regional Courts as courts of first instance and the Supreme Administrative Court as the highest jurisdiction, is also more than one year. One has, however, to count also in the two instances of administrative authorities, which precede the potential judicial review.

[51] It serves to be mindful that EC law accords the same powers (and duties) it grants to national courts, i.e., the power to disapply national law contrary to directly applicable EC law, also to national administrative authorities – cf., e.g., ECJ, Case C-198/01 *Consorzio Industrie Fiammiferi (CIF) v. Autorità Garante della Concorrenza e del Mercato* [2003] *ECR* I-8055, para. 49 or Case 103/88 *Fratelli Costanzo SpA v. Comune di Milano* [1989] *ECR* 1839, para. 31.

[52] File no. R 50/2004, accessible online at http://www2.compet.cz/ISU/2003/HS/pis26428.html.

[53] Zákon č. 340/2004 Sb., kterým se mění zákon č. 143/2001 Sb., *o ochraně hospodářské soutěže* [Law no 340/2004 Coll., amending the law no 143/2001 Coll., on the Protection of Competition].

[54] Further, see M. Petr, 'Přednostní aplikace komunitárního práva českými správními úřady' [Primacy in Application of Community Law before the Czech Administrative Authorities], 6 *Jurisprudence* (2006) pp. 14-16 or M. Petr and V. Vavříček, 'K paralelní aplikaci českého a komunitárního soutěžního práva' [On the Parallel Application of Czech and Community Law of Competition], 11 *Právní rozhledy* (2006) pp. 396-400.

younger lawyers, knowledgeable in EU law. For this reason, the second instance of setting aside a national regulation by administrative authorities is perhaps more unanticipated.

The Czech Agriculture and Food Inspection Authority is, *inter alia*, authorised to oversee and inspect products on the national wine market. In this capacity, the Authority openly refused to apply a piece of Czech legislation, which entered into force in July 2006 and which was in violation of an EC Regulation on the common organisation of the market in wine.[55] The Authority's correct decision is more praiseworthy than the law itself, and its adoption has been accompanied by populist rhetoric and intentional disregard for the EC legislation in the Chamber of Deputies of the Czech Parliament.[56]

### 4.3.    The practice of harmony in interpretation

The area of greatest judicial application of EC law in the first years following the accession has been the use of EC law in the form of harmonious or conform interpretation of national law with *acquis communautaire*. We are advisedly not referring to this phenomenon as "indirect effect", in order to avoid the confusion with the obligation of indirect effect (Euro-conform interpretation), imposed upon national courts by the case law of the European Court of Justice.[57]

The key difference in this respect was the fact that in the majority of cases in which harmonious interpretation of national law with EC law was used, the relevant facts had taken place before the Czech Republic became a member of the European Union. This meant that in these cases, even if they were being decided after 1 May 2004, an applicable (substantive) law was still domestic law as it had stood before the accession (more precisely in the moment when the material factual circumstances had occurred).

Moreover, in quite a few areas, the duty to harmonise (or, more precisely, to approximate) national law with EU law had been there well before the accession. The candidate states assumed this duty by virtue of the Europe Agreements (or, in the case of Malta and Cyprus, the Association Agreements).[58] In a great number of areas of law relating to the internal market, the necessary approximation steps were effectuated in the late 1990s and in years directly preceding the EU membership. In many areas, national law did not change on 1 May 2004 but already some months or even years before the accession.

Taking into account this normative reality, the Czech courts have formulated a doctrine of harmonious interpretation of approximated Czech law with EC law. In the case law of the Supreme Administrative Court, this approach was first articulated in

---

[55] Council Regulation 1493/1999/EC of 17 May 1999 on the common organisation of the market in wine, *OJ* 1999 L *179/1*.

[56] As Petr (*loc. cit.* n. 54) notes with reference to the minutes from the Chamber discussion on the bill, even the Member of the Parliament who introduced the amendments, which were incompatible with Community law, was well aware of that incompatibility.

[57] See, *inter alia*, S. Prechal, *Directives in EC Law*, 2nd edn. (Oxford, Oxford University Press 2005) pp. 180-215.

[58] See further, Chapter 1 in this volume.

2005. A leading case arose from a rather technical value-added tax (VAT) dispute. The complainant, an undertaking taxable under Czech law, reconstructed a glass-welding unit on a property located in Slovakia. The reconstruction contract between the complainant and the Slovak property owner was concluded at the incentive of a third party, a Czech undertaking, which acted as the property owner's agent. In the case before the Czech authorities, the complainant claimed deduction of VAT from a fee paid to the agent, as both parties to the agency agreement were incorporated under Czech law. The Czech Revenue Authority, however, refused to deduct VAT from the agency contract, claiming that the place of the taxable transaction was Slovakia, where the property was located.

The SAC observed that the issue in question had not been provided for in the Czech VAT Act 1992, which was in force at the time of the dispute. However, the Court went on to state that the Czech Republic's VAT system, introduced at the beginning of the 1990s, had been modelled on the EC VAT legislation, with an express approximation agenda. The rules of conflict for determination of a place of taxable transaction under the Czech VAT system were designed similarly to the EC ones. A comparison of relevant provisions of the Czech VAT Act and the Sixth VAT Directive[59] was, therefore, appropriate, also considering the fact that the Europe Agreement had already required the approximation of certain areas of Czech law – including indirect taxation – to EC standards. The SAC therefore affirmed the possibility of using EC law as an instrument for interpretation of approximated Czech legislation and applied the Sixth VAT Directive and ECJ case law. The Court made, however, this conform interpretation subject to two conditions:

(i) The interpreted national provision was adopted in view of approximating Czech law with the European model;
(ii) The Czech legislator did not demonstrate an express wish to deviate, as far as a particular provision is concerned, from the European model.[60]

A similar approach was also adopted in the case law of the Czech Supreme Court. After some initial resistance,[61] the CSC also noted that the European model is relevant for conform interpretation even in the pre-accession period. However, the CSC also held that conform interpretation has no place in the period prior to adoption of the national approximation legislation, i.e., in the period before the approximation itself started.[62]

---

[59] Sixth Council Directive 77/388/EEC of 17 May 1977 on the harmonisation of the laws of the Member States relating to turnover taxes – common system of value added tax: uniform basis of assessment, *OJ* 1977 L 145/1.

[60] Judgment of the SAC of 29 September 2005, Case 2 Afs 92/2005-45, no 741/2006 Coll. SAC. The holding has been accepted and applied in numerous other cases, e.g., judgment of 22 March 2007, Case 9 Afs 5/2007-70; judgment of 26 September 2007, Case 5 As 51/2006-287; judgment of 12 July 2007, Case 9 Afs 25/2007 -95; judgment of 31 January 2007, Case 3 As 41/2006-122; judgment of 31 January 2007, Case 7 As 50/2006-262. All decisions are accessible at http://www.nssoud.cz.

[61] Cf., the rather reluctant stance the CSC took to this matter in the period before 1 May 2004, discussed in section 2.2. of this chapter.

[62] Order of the CSC of 12 April 2006, Case 5 Tdo 290/2006, http://www.nsoud.cz. In this (criminal) matter, the CSC refused to draw any interpretative aid from European company directives as far as the

The harmonious interpretation in the case law of the Supreme Courts has two significant features. First, it is formulated rather in terms of the advisable and suitable, not as a general duty of conform interpretation. Second, the suitability is derived from national law and the decision of the national legislator to approximate national legal order with EC law. It is not framed as an obligation arising from EC law itself.

This line of authority has been perhaps somewhat overstretched by a recent decision of the CCC.[63] The case concerned the validity of a contract between the Zepter Company and an individual. In the 1990s, the Zepter Company was known for its rather dubious contracting practices, which on some occasions had been connected to a very particular interpretation of good morals (*bonos mores*).[64] The present dispute arose out of a contract concluded in 1995 between the litigants. The individual claimed that he had been induced into concluding the contract by deceit on the part of the company, and that some contractual terms were abusive. Civil law courts upheld the claims of the company, underlying the importance of contractual freedom and the absence of any commonly invoked reasons for voiding the contract.

The CCC disagreed. It held that the civil law courts had overemphasised the importance of free will in a similar contractual situation. The CCC furthermore held that the issue was substantively the same as a consumer contract, which is provided for in EC law.[65] The CCC made reference to the above-described doctrines of harmonious interpretation of approximated legislation. Those doctrines, which had been developed by both Supreme Courts, were adopted before accession. The CCC also noted that the facts of the case in question occurred in 1995, but the Czech approximation to the Community consumer protection directives was done only from January 2001. Irrespective of these facts, the CCC concluded that the civil courts were under the duty to interpret national legislation, even for that period, in conformity with EC law on that subject. The CCC found support for this conclusion in case law of the European Court of Justice, namely in cases *Marleasing*,[66] *Wagner Miret*[67] and *Faccini Dori*.[68]

Albeit one has full understanding of the substantive result the CCC aims at, it is submitted that in this particular decision, the CCC's use of harmonious interpretation might appear somewhat problematic. First and foremost, the CCC attempts to derive the duty of harmonious interpretation from EC law for the pre-accession period. However, there is no authority supporting this view; it cannot be derived from the

---

national definition of the notion of "insider trading" was concerned. Activities for which the criminal sanction was imposed had taken place in 1995, but the approximation of the Czech Commercial Code to relevant European directives was effectuated only in 2001.

[63]  Judgment of the CCC of 6 November 2007, Case II. ÚS 3/06, accessible at http://nalus.usoud.cz.

[64]  Judgment of the CCC of 30 November 2001, case no IV. ÚS 182/01, published in the Coll. CCC, Vol. 24, no 188, p. 401.

[65]  Council Directive 85/577/EEC of 20 December 1985 to protect the consumer in respect to contracts negotiated away from business premises, *OJ* 1985 L 372/31 and Council Directive 93/13/EEC of 5 April 1993 on unfair terms in consumer contracts, *OJ* 1993 L 95/29.

[66]  ECJ, Case C-106/89 *Marleasing SA v. La Comercial Internacional de Alimentacion* [1990] *ECR* I-4135

[67]  ECJ, Case C-334/92 *Teodoro Wagner Miret v. Fondo de Garantía Salarial* [1993] *ECR* I-6911.

[68]  ECJ, Case C-91/92 *Paola Faccini Dori v. Recreb Srl.* [1994] *ECR* I-3325.

cases the CCC is quoting, as these are concerned exclusively with duties Member States' courts have. The duty of harmonious interpretation could perhaps be derived from the Europe Agreements, if one were to interpret the duty to approximate certain areas of national law as to be binding even on national courts of candidate countries.[69] However, the European Court of Justice has addressed the issues of national application of association agreements only in respect to the old Member States,[70] never in respect to the new ones as it claims to have no jurisdiction to do so. Second, the duty of conform interpretation is being derived for the period before substantive rules themselves had been approximated. This appears to be also, from the temporal point of view, a rather problematic exercise.

At the same time, there is no problem in using EC law as a non-binding source of inspiration, which provides for common European roots and principles, which in turn help to shape contents of domestic undefined legal notions and general clauses, such as "good morals". However, such reasoning remains, similar to any other comparative reasoning, in the realm of persuasiveness, not the obligation to interpret in conformity. In this respect, the use of EC law was the same as the use of any comparative argument in a domestic judicial forum.[71]

As already mentioned, the first years of the Czech membership have been the time of self-imposed harmonious interpretation, in which courts have accepted the new legal order even for the period and the cases they were technically not obliged to do so. One may estimate that this practice of voluntary harmony in interpretation occurred in hundreds of cases before the courts; before both Supreme Courts, however, the number of cases runs only to tens.

There are a number of reasons for this openness to EC law arguments. First and foremost, the use of EC law in the new Member States did not start on 1 May 2004 (or 1 January 2007 in case of Bulgaria and Romania). EC law was *de facto* being applied already in the approximation period. Such judicial approximation to the "approximation parent" was not mandatory, but advisable. Second, in the 1990s and in the beginning of the new millennium, the legal orders of the then candidate countries suffered from great legislative instability. Key codes and laws were being constantly amended, the number of amendments soon amounting to a certain "deconstruction" of the legal orders.[72] In similar institutional settings, it would make sense to lean on the perhaps

---

[69] See Art. 69 EA Czech Republic. *Loc. cit.* n. 3.

[70] See, *inter alia*, ECJ, Case C-268/99 *Aldona Malgorzata Jany and Others v. Staatssecretaris van Justitie* [2001] *ECR* I-8615; Case C-63/99 *The Queen v. Secretary of State for the Home Department,* ex parte *Wieslaw Gloszczuk and Elzbieta Gloszczuk* [2001] *ECR* I-6369; Case C-257/99 *The Queen v. Secretary of State for the Home Department,* ex parte *Julius Barkoci and Marcel Malik* [2001] *ECR* I-6557.

[71] See, e.g., U. Drobnig and S. Van Erp, eds., *The Use of Comparative Law by Courts. XIVth International Coungress of Comparative Law, Athens 1997* (The Hague, London, Boston, Kluwer Law International 1999) or U. Uyterhoeven, *Richterliche Rechtsfindung und Rechtsvergleichung. Eine Vorstudie über die Rechtsvergleichung als Hilfsmittel der richterlichen Rechtsfindung im Privatrecht* (Bern, Verlag Stämpfli 1959). In Drobnig's classification, this type of use of comparative argument would fall into the "advisable" category.

[72] Term used by Justice P. Holländer when describing the legislative reality in 2001. In this context, the author used the example of the Czech Code of Civil Procedure, which, within one year, had undergone

not fully stable, but surely more stabilised, European legal order. Last, at some instances, the "voluntary" use of EC law helped to overcome problematic issues of temporal application of new legislation. Unlike the European Court of Justice, the Czech courts did not consider the difference between pre- and post-accession facts to be as sharp as the ECJ did in the case C-302/04 *Ynos*.[73]

In conclusion, the voluntary harmonious interpretation of national legislation in line with EC law was a reasonable step, which may have helped the Czech courts and administrative authorities to bridge the gap between zero direct application of EC law in the pre-accession period and its full application to cases with post-accession factual background.

5.    REFERENCES FOR PRELIMINARY RULING

As of 31 January 2008, there have been six requests for preliminary ruling submitted by the Czech courts.[74] It cannot be said that the Czech courts would disproportionately burden the ECJ; rather to the contrary. There is no use in entering the endless (and perhaps also somewhat fruitless) debate whether or not this amount of references is too low, too high or just about right. We will rather focus on structural (dis)incentives and a procedural framework under the Czech law for making references, on the references themselves and on known instances in which requests of various sorts and quality were submitted to the national courts, but no references were made.

5.1.    **The playground and incentives**

Shortly after the accession, the three major codes of judicial procedure were expressly amended to provide a legal framework for the submission of requests for preliminary ruling, thereby pre-empting a pre-accession debate whether or not, in the absence of specific national procedural provisions, requests could be made directly on the basis of Article 234 EC (or Art. 68 EC/Art. 35 EU). The minor amendments effectuated by the new provisions of § 109(1)(d) Code of Civil Justice and § 48(1)(e) Code of Administrative Justice only provided that a Czech judge has the power to stay proceedings provided s/he decides to submit a request for preliminary ruling. The new provision of § 9a Code of Criminal Justice is more "ambitious" in its scope. It provides not only for a possibility to stay proceedings, but it also contains a statement that all authorities involved in criminal proceedings (i.e., not only a criminal court, but also a prosecutor and police) are bound by decisions of the European Court of Justice.

---

18 direct and indirect amendments. P. Holländer, *Ústavněprávní argumentace* [Constitutional Legal Reasoning] (Prague, Linde Publishing 2003) at p. 11.

[73] ECJ, Case C-302/04 *Ynos kft v. János Varga* [2006] *ECR* I-371, see further, Chapters 4-5 in this volume.

[74] Two more requests were submitted later in 2008 and 2009; see Case C-233/08 *Milan Kyrian v. Celní úřad Tábor, OJ* 2008 C 209/26 and Case C-111/09 *Česká podnikatelská pojišt'ovna, a.s., Vienna Insurance Group v. Michal Bílas, OJ* 2009 C 141/25.

The Czech legislator was quite self-restrained as far as any detailed regulation regarding the actual form of submission of requests for preliminary rulings is concerned. It left the practice to the courts. The result is divergence. When submitting a request for preliminary ruling, a national court decides at least on two things: first, it decides on the submission of a question itself. Second, it stays the national proceedings. The court may furthermore issue other orders regarding the position of the parties, typically a preliminary order or an injunction. The question which arose in practice of the Czech courts and was also debated in academic writing[75] is whether or not these procedural decisions of national courts are all to be incorporated into one order (one decision of a court) or whether they should be contained in parallel documents; i.e., a court submitting a preliminary reference should issue separate orders. Some of the Czech courts which submitted references to the ECJ incorporated two types of orders into one decision, by which they stayed the national proceedings, and in addition submitted the request to the ECJ.[76] Others have issued two orders: one staying the proceedings and the other submitting the preliminary question.[77] Yet another solution within the sphere of administrative justice was to issue an order staying the procedure and then putting the question itself into a simple letter addressed to the ECJ.[78]

These matters are not only of an academic nature. They may not be significant for the ECJ itself,[79] but they are significant for the procedure before national courts. The key problem is potential appeals against decisions of first instance courts to submit requests for a preliminary ruling.[80] Under Czech law, an order of a court of first instance to stay proceedings can be reviewed on appeal. If an order to stay proceedings and to submit a request for a preliminary ruling were to be regarded as a single decision, then

---

[75] M. Bobek, et al., *Předběžná otázka v komunitárním právu* [Preliminary Ruling in Community Law] (Prague, Linde 2005) p. 172 et seq.; J. Grygar and E. Grygar, 'Česká procesní úprava ve vztahu k řízení o předběžné otázce před Soudním dvorem Evropských společenství' [Czech Procedural Framework in respect of the Preliminary Ruling Procedure before the Court of Justice of the European Communities], 8 *Právní rozhledy* (2005) pp. 276-283; D. Petrlík, 'Slučitelnost přezkumu rozhodnutí o předložení předběžné otázky Soudnímu dvoru ES s komunitárním právem' [The Compatibility of the Review of a Decision to Submit a Request for a Preliminary Ruling to the Court of Justice with Community Law], 18 *Právní rozhledy* (2005) pp. 673-679.

[76] Order of the *Obvodní soud pro Prahu 3* [District Court for Prague 3] of 24 November 2005, Case 18 C 140/2005-118, which became the reference in Case C-64/06 *Telefónica O2 Czech Republic, a.s. v. Czech On Line, a.s.* [2007] *ECR* I-4887.

[77] Orders of the *Okresní soud v Českém Krumlově* [District Court in Český Krumlov] of 28 November 2005, Case 6 C 296/2005-99 and 6 C 296/2005-101 respectively, which became Case C-437/05 *Vorel v. Nemocnice Český Krumlov* [2007] *ECR* I-331.

[78] Order and the letter of the *Krajský soud v Ostravě* [Regional Court in Ostrava] of 10 March 2006, case no. 22 Ca 69/2005, which later became the Case C-161/06, *Skoma-Lux, s.r.o. v. Celní ředitelství Olomouc* [2007] *ECR* I-10841.

[79] As the European Court of Justice highlights in its 'Information Note on References by National Courts for Preliminary Rulings', *OJ* 2005 C 143/01, point 20, it is quite benevolent as far as the procedural form of the reference is concerned. The Note contains a cross-reference to the domestic procedure with very few suggestions attached thereto.

[80] With respect to the situation in the old Member States, see D. O'Keeffe, 'Appeals Against an Order to Refer under Article 177 of EEC Treaty', 9 *ELRev.* (1984) pp. 87-104, or D. Anderson and M. Demetriou, *References to the European Court*, 2nd edn. (London, Sweet & Maxwell 2002) pp. 215-216.

a decision to submit a request for preliminary ruling would be reviewable by an appellate court. If they were two separate decisions of a first instance court, the review would be more indirect and problematic, but most likely still possible. This question has, however, not yet been posed, as none of the first requests for preliminary reference was appealed.

## 5.2.   Changing the established habits: incentives provided by the CCC for submitting request for preliminary rulings

Apart from the amendments of the codes of procedure, which smoothed the way for references from the Czech courts, an additional incentive for the courts to address the ECJ came from the CCC.

Under the Czech constitutional system, courts have the jurisdiction to refer questions of constitutionality of laws to the assessment of the CCC.[81] In Central and Eastern Europe, and above all, in former Czechoslovakia, one often hears that judges should not engage in constitutional reasoning, but rather apply law textually; that they are not able to take constitutional rights and values seriously and that the Constitutional Court is not a "court", but a special and unique body outside the judiciary. Under such conditions, centralised constitutional review presents a clear danger of being "over-centralised". If the central role of Constitutional Courts in the rule of law discourse is too emphasised, ordinary courts have a strong tendency to disappear from that story. Although Constitutional Courts are an important factor in remodelling the Central and Eastern European concept of law, their ultimate success depends on whether ordinary judges are included in the common enterprise of building a new idea of constitutionalism. The very nature of centralised post-communist Constitutional Courts is exclusive: they are the principal forum for constitutional arguments; they and only they can annul a legal act. Formal annulment through which a legal act loses its validity, unlike setting the law aside, matters in the post-communist legal system. Argumentation of Constitutional Courts must include ordinary courts, and they must be invited to engage in building the rule of law.[82] This is also an important argument for the genuine application of EC law.

This is why it is important to note that the CCC took the lead to show ordinary courts that it is their task to apply EU law directly and independently. The key decision came in a case involving so-called "golden shares", decided by the plenary CCC in 2006. In this case, a request to review constitutionality was made in September 2004 by the Regional Court in Hradec Králové, alleging that national law providing for the possibility of the existence of "golden shares" was incompatible with, first, the principle of equality of property, enshrined in Article 11 of the Charter of Fundamental Freedoms

---

[81] Art. 95(2) Constitution of the Czech Republic reads: 'If a court arrives at the conclusion that a law which is to be applied in decision-making is in contradiction with a constitutional act, it shall submit the matter to the Constitutional Court.'

[82] See Z. Kühn, 'Making Constitutionalism Horizontal: Three Different Central European Strategies', in A. Sajó and R. Uitz, eds., *The Constitution in Private Relations: Expanding Constitutionalism.* (Utrecht, Eleven International Publishing 2005) pp. 217-240.

of the Czech Republic, and, second with EC law, in particular with Article 42 of the Council Directive establishing the equality of share holders.[83]

The CCC rejected the application for procedural reasons.[84] It added, however, a significant *obiter dictum*, in which it observed that as far as the alleged incompatibility of Czech law with EC law was concerned, it was not the CCC's role to decide on the matter. Following the accession to the European Union, the CCC said, a national court, if necessary in co-operation with the European Court of Justice (by requesting a preliminary ruling), should adjudicate on the (in)compatibility of Czech law with EC law.

The message the CCC sent to the Czech courts of general jurisdiction was quite clear: matters of EC law are not to be submitted to us, but to the European Court of Justice. From the point of view of EC law, this is an obvious conclusion.[85] It might not, however, be that clear from the point of view of national courts and from the above-described Czech constitutional tradition. From this perspective, an early and unequivocal suggestion by the CCC to the courts of general jurisdiction might have helped them to realise their options and obligations under EC law.[86]

## 5.3.    The references

The first Czech request for a preliminary ruling – in case *Vorel*[87]– concerned payment for on-call duty by a hospital surgeon. All medical staff are required to serve a certain amount of on-call duty in emergency medical services. For most of this time, staff may not actually be working, but only waiting in "stand-by mode" for an emergency call. They must, however, be present at their workplace. The question which arose was how such "stand-by" work is to be remunerated: at a full rate or at a reduced rate?

This quite interesting reference demonstrated how important it is for national judges and lawyers to be informed about ongoing judicial business at the ECJ. The reference by the Czech court was made on 28 November 2005. Three days later, on

---

[83] Second Council Directive 77/91/EEC of 13 December 1976 on co-ordination of safeguards which, for the protection of the interests of members and others, are required by Member States of companies within the meaning of the second paragraph of Art. 58 of the Treaty, in respect to the formation of public limited liability companies and the maintenance and alteration of their capital, with a view to making such safeguards equivalent *OJ* 1977 L 26/1. For interpretation see ECJ, Case C-483/99 *Comission v. France (Elf-Acquitaine)* [2002] *ECR* I-4781; Case C-503/99 *Commission v. Belgium (SNTC)* [2002] *ECR* I-4809; Case C-98/01 *Commission v. United Kingdom (BAA)* [2003] *ECR* I-4641.

[84] Plenary Order of 21 February 2006, Case Pl. ÚS 19/04, published with a case note by M. Bobek in 5 *Soudní rozhledy* (2006) pp. 173-177.

[85] See notably ECJ, Case 106/77 *Amministrazione delle Finanze dello Stato v. Simmenthal SpA.* [1978] *ECR* 629, which in paragraphs 22 and 24 discusses the obligations of a national judge in cases of clash between the review of constitutionality and the review of compatibility of national law with EC law.

[86] Which it perhaps did, taking into account the positive reception of this decision by the legal practice – the decision actually won a prize for the "Judicial Decision of the Year 2006", which is awarded biennially by the *Vereinigung tschechisch-deutsch-slowakisch-österreichischer Juristen.* Interestingly, the case has never been published in the official reports of the CCC and came to be known to the public only via the case note referred to in footnote n. 84.

[87] *Loc. cit.* n. 77.

1 December 2005, the European Court of Justice rendered a judgment in a case, which concerned precisely the issue raised in *Vorel*.[88] The initial question in the *Vorel* case was thus later only summarily answered by the ECJ by a reasoned order, issued on the basis of Article 104(3) of the Rules of Procedure, with reference to the previous case law.

The second and the fourth references concerned telecommunications[89] and copyright law[90] respectively. The third reference was perhaps the most constitutionally significant one: it was submitted by the Krajský soud v Ostravě [Regional Court in Ostrava] and concerned the enforcement of EC legislation unpublished in the Czech language, in this particular case an EC regulation. The reference was submitted in the course of proceedings between Skoma-Lux s.r.o. (a company) and the Customs Authority, regarding a fine imposed on Skoma-Lux in respect to customs infringements which it was alleged to have committed between March and May 2004. One of the defences raised by the company in its request for the annulment of the fine was that the Customs Authority could not enforce against it the EC legislation which at the given time was not published in the Czech language in the Official Journal of the European Union. The background and context of the *Skoma-Lux* case has been analysed elsewhere.[91] The important constitutional message this litigation sends to the new Member States is perhaps that despite the linguistic problems in the enlarged European Union, the languages are still formally equal, and there is, at least residually, some protection afforded to the individuals speaking only the "smaller" languages.

The fifth request for a preliminary ruling came from the Arbitration Court attached to the Economic Chamber of the Czech Republic and the Agricultural Chamber of the Czech Republic.[92] The Czech Arbitration Court was appointed by the European Registry of Internet Domain Names in April 2005 to provide alternative dispute resolution for ".eu" domain name disputes. The reference was Czech only geographically, as it was submitted by the Arbitration Court residing in Prague. The internet domain dispute featured two German companies, with a German arbitrator and the question itself submitted in German. The Arbitration Court is a compulsory jurisdiction for ".eu" domain disputes and is regulated by law.[93] The submitted questions in themselves were quite

---

[88] ECJ, Case C-14/04 *Abdelkader Dellas and Others v. Premier ministre and Ministre des Affaires sociales, du Travail et de la Solidarité* [2005] *ECR* I-10253.

[89] More precisely the obligation of interconnection with other operators for a dominant operator on the internet access market. *Loc. cit.* n. 76.

[90] Case C-282/06 *Ochranný Svaz Autorský pro Práva k Dílům Hudebním (OSA) v. Miloslav Lev.* Following the decision of the ECJ in a similar Spanish case (Case C-306/05 *Sociedad General de Autores y Editores de España (SGAE) v. Rafael Hoteles SA* [2006] *ECR* I-11519) the Czech court withdrew its reference.

[91] M. Bobek, 'The Binding Force of Babel: The Enforcement of EC Law Unpublished in the Languages of the New Member States', 9 *CYELS* (2007) pp. 43-80. A shorter version of the argument is freely accessible as the *EUI LAW Working Papers* No. 2007/6 at http://cadmus.iue.it/dspace/handle/1814/6742. See also Chapters 4-5 in this volume.

[92] ECJ, Case C-126/07 *Reisebüro Bühler GmbH v. Dom.info e.K., OJ* 2007 C 117/8.

[93] Commission Regulation 874/2004/EC of 28 April 2004 laying down public policy rules concerning the implementation and functions of the ".eu" Top Level Domain and the principles governing registration (*OJ* 2004 L 162/40) and related Community legislation.

interesting, especially the first one, in which the Arbitration Court invited the European Court of Justice to re-examine some of its negative stance towards recognising arbitration courts as courts or tribunals within the meaning of Article 234 EC.[94] Unfortunately, the Arbitration Court withdrew its question in June 2007 due to a friendly settlement reached by the parties.[95]

The last reference in which the ECJ has rendered a judgment thus far was submitted in December 2007 by the Krajský soud v Ústí nad Labem [Regional Court in Ústí nad Labem], acting as the court of first instance in an administrative dispute. The question concerned the interpretation of the 6th VAT Directive and whether or not rental of an apartment and services related thereto are subject to VAT.[96]

All the above-mentioned references came from first instance courts, i.e., courts which may refer under Article 234(2) EC. The extent of the duty to refer from a court of last instance, enshrined in section 3 of Article 234 EC, has thus not yet been discussed.[97]

An intriguing issue is the position of the Czech Constitutional Court when it comes to its powers and/or duties under Article 234 EC, i.e., whether or not it would be a court or tribunal within the meaning of Article 234 EC. Unlike some of its Central and Eastern European counterparts,[98] the CCC has not taken any conclusive stance on this matter. In the constitutionally significant decision *Sugar Quota II*, the CCC expressly reserved this issue:

'The Constitutional Court is aware of the delicacy of the question as to whether the Constitutional Court can be considered a court in the sense of Art. 234 of the EC Treaty, or in which type of proceedings, and reserves to itself in the future the possibility of adopting an unequivocal answer, in other words, to refer a matter for the adjudication to the ECJ in individual types of proceedings.'[99]

---

[94] For a classical statement of the law on this point, see, e.g., ECJ, Case 102/81 *Nordsee Deutsche Hochseefischerei GmbH v. Reederei Mond Hochseefischerei Nordstern AG* [1982] *ECR* 1095 or Case 109/88 *Handels- og Kontorfunktionærernes Forbund i Danmark v. Dansk Arbejdsgiverforening, acting on behalf of Danfoss* [1989] *ECR* 3199. Further, see G. Bebr, 'Arbitration Tribunals and Article 177 of the EEC Treaty', 22 *CMLRev.* (1985) pp. 489-505 or P. Bonassies, 'Arbitrage et droit communautaire', in *L'Europe et le droit. Mélanges en hommage à Jean Boulouis* (Paris, Dalloz 1991) pp. 21-33.

[95] Order of the President of the Court of 8 October 2007 (reference for a preliminary ruling from the Arbitration Court attached to the Economic Chamber of the Czech Republic and Agricultural Chamber of the Czech Republic – Czech Republic) – *Reisebüro Bühler GmbH v. Dom.info e.K., Sebastian Dieterle*, *OJ* 2007 C 297/34.

[96] ECJ, Case C-572/07 *RLRE Tellmer Property v. Finanční ředitelství v Ústí nad Labem* [2009] *ECR* nyr.

[97] At least not by the courts themselves. It has been, however, discussed in the doctrine – see, e.g., M. Bobek, *Porušení povinnosti zahájit řízení o předběžné otázce podle článku 234 (3) SES* [*Violation of the Duty to Submit a Request for Preliminary Reference under Art. 234 (3) EC*] (Prague, C.H. Beck 2004) pp. 23-31.

[98] The Slovak, the Polish as well as the Austrian Constitutional Courts have expressly acknowledged that they felt to be courts within the meaning of Art. 234 EC. See, e.g., the various contributions on Poland, Germany and Austria in the volume *Řízení o předběžné otázce a národní soudy/Das Vorabentscheidungsverfahren und die nationalen Gerichte*, collection of contributions from the conference held at the CCC on 3 December 2004 in Brno (Prague, Constitutional Court of the Czech Republic and Linde Publishing 2005).

[99] Plenary decision of 8 March 2006, Case Pl. ÚS 50/04, published as no 154/2006 Coll.

Interestingly, two months prior to this statement, a chamber of three justices held in an individual constitutional complaint that:

> 'The Constitutional Court is not in this case the court of the last instance within the meaning of Art. 234 EC Treaty because its purpose is not to protect rights but to protect constitutionality ... and constitutional complaint is not a remedy against the decisions of the ordinary courts. The Constitutional Court could deal with the motion to refer preliminary reference only if the ordinary court whose decision cannot be appealed ... did not refer preliminary reference to the Court of Justice provided such a reference was demanded by one of the parties.'[100]

The CCC has repeatedly implicitly acknowledged that it considers itself to be a court within the meaning of Article 234 EC (similar logic can be found even in the case just mentioned). In quite a number of requests to submit a reference for preliminary ruling the CCC rejected the applications not because it had no power to submit (meaning it would not consider itself to be a court or tribunal for the purposes of Art. 234 EC), but because it held that the requests were unfounded. Arguably one does not need to assess the merits of an application (whether there are genuine grounds for making a reference) if one is incompetent to do so (a court does not consider itself having the power to refer). So far, however, an express recognition of the CCC that it would consider itself as a court within the meaning of Article 234 EC is lacking.[101] The delicacy of such a potential statement is underlined by the fact that once the CCC were to recognise that it indeed is a court for the purposes of preliminary ruling procedure, it would at the same time necessarily turn into a court of last instance with the obligation to refer.

## 5.4.    The less successful (?) attempts

Hidden and actually more intriguing cases are those which never made it to the European Court of Justice. The "success stories", i.e., the cases in which a request for a preliminary ruling was made, are counted in units; the "less successful" stories are to be counted in tens or perhaps already hundreds.

A substantive number of unsuccessful requests are rather spurious ways of protracting the proceedings or an argument of last resort. Cases of this type are typically only very distantly related or wholly unrelated to EU law. One prominent example of this type of attempt is a series of restitution cases,[102] in which the Supreme Court and later the Constitutional Court[103] rejected repeated requests for preliminary ruling. They were

---

[100] Judgment of 25 January 2006, Case II. ÚS 14/04, published as no 22 in Vol. 40, p. 169 Coll. CCC.

[101] However, this fact has already been recognised by some of the justices of the CCC writing extra-judicially – see, e.g., J. Mucha, 'The Presentation of the Czech Experiences', in *Proceedings of the International Conference 'The Position of the Constitutional Courts Following Integration into the European Union'*, Bled, Slovenia, 30 September–2 October 2004, pp. 163-170, at pp. 166-168.

[102] E.g., Order of the CSC of 28 April 2005, Case 28 Cdo 810/2005; Order of the Supreme Court of 3 August 2005, Case 28 Cdo 1347/2005; Order of the Supreme Court of 23 November 2005, Case 28 Cdo 2420/2005; all decisions available at http://www.nsoud.cz.

[103] Most importantly judgment of 25 January 2006, Case II. ÚS 14/04, published as no 22 in Vol. 40, p. 169 Coll. CCC and many other unpublished orders.

made by an unsuccessful claimant, a member of the pre-WWII Czech aristocracy, who argued that the Czech courts, including the Constitutional Court itself, deciding his restitution cases were biased and under political pressure. He suggested that a request for preliminary ruling be submitted regarding the interpretation of Article 6(1) EU, i.e., whether it was possible, in a particular case where alleged political interference with the independence of the courts has compromised their impartiality and independence, to transfer the case to courts in other Member States. These requests were rejected by both the Supreme and the Constitutional Court as manifestly unfounded.

Other examples of these attempts might include efforts to bring the question of court fees to the European Court of Justice,[104] suggestions that a request for a preliminary ruling should be made on the interpretation of a Council of Europe treaty[105] or "fishing expeditions" that just argue very broad issues of fair trial, considering the request for a preliminary ruling to be a sort of last instance appeal.[106]

There have perhaps also been instances in which a request for a preliminary ruling would have been appropriate. In respect to both Supreme Courts, i.e., the Supreme Court and the Supreme Administrative Court, the absence of any request for a preliminary ruling might be attributable to three factors. First, it is the ignorance of EU law angles in the pending cases. The "Euro-dimension" of a case is, in the vast majority of cases, dealt with when requested by parties and their representatives, very rarely by judges of their own motion. Second, the highest courts have already "discovered" the *acte clair* doctrine and the exceptions to the duty to refer provided in the *CILFIT* decision.[107] In a handful of cases, the CSC[108] as well as the SAC[109] rejected on these grounds motions for reference. Also the CCC referred to the *CILFIT* decision and the *acte clair* doctrine several times.[110]

However, so far the greatest dissuasion for making any reference to the European Court of Justice has been the *Ynos* decision.[111] The ECJ categorically stated that if the facts of a dispute in the main proceedings had occurred prior to the EU accession, the ECJ does not have jurisdiction to answer a request for preliminary ruling originating from a new Member State.[112]

---

[104] Order of 10 May 2007, Case IV.ÚS 887/07, and decisions in Cases IV.ÚS 416/05, I.ÚS 9/06, and II.ÚS 347/07, accessible at http://nalus.usoud.cz.

[105] Order of 25 July 2007, Case III. ÚS 868/06, http://nalus.usoud.cz.

[106] E.g., Order of 9 March 2007, Case III. ÚS 346/07, http://nalus.usoud.cz.

[107] ECJ, Case 283/81 *Srl CILFIT and Lanificio di Gavardo SpA v. Ministry of Health* [1982] *ECR* 3415.

[108] The Supreme Court referred to the *CILFIT* decision in over 15 cases – see, e.g., Cases 29 Odo 1128/2005; 29 Odo 1332/2005; 29 Odo 242/2006; 28 Cdo 2711/2005; 28 Cdo 1324/2006; 28 Cdo 2508/2005; 28 Cdo 2420/2005; 28 Cdo 372/2005; 28 Cdo 2882/2004; 28 Cdo 2348/2005; 28 Cdo 2102/2005; 28 Cdo 2051/2005; 28 Cdo 2020/2005; 28 Cdo 1347/2005, all accessible at http://www.nsoud.cz.

[109] The SAC used the *CILFIT* decision and the *acte clair* doctrine in more than 10 cases, e.g., Cases 5 Azs 56/2004; 6 As 44/2005; 6 As 55/2005; 4 As 36/2006; 6 As 24/2006; 5 As 53/2006; 6 As 57/2006; 4 As 70/2006; 1 As 39/2006, all accessible at www.nssoud.cz.

[110] Plenary decision of the CCC of 8 March 2006, Case Pl. ÚS 50/04, no 154/2006 Coll.; judgment of 25 January 2006, Case II. ÚS 14/04, published as no 22 in Vol. 40, p. 169 Coll. CCC.

[111] *Loc. cit.* n. 73.

[112] *Ibidem*, para. 37.

There is no point in repeating the critique to which one of the authors of this chapter subjected the *Ynos* decision elsewhere.[113] Clearly, in the practice of the Czech courts, the *Ynos* decision is used as a universal excuse to avoid discussing the possibility of requesting a preliminary ruling in cases with pre-accession factual background (even partial). From the substantive point of view, this does not make much sense – in most of cases, the Czech courts are already dealing with pure EU law, which had been transposed to the national legal order well before the accession pursuant to the approximation duty stemming from the EA Czech Republic. As was already discussed above, the Czech courts have opened themselves to Euro-conform interpretation even for the period before the accession. This means that they are in fact interpreting EC law, without, however, having the option of consulting the European Court of Justice.[114] Considering that Higher and Supreme Courts typically adjudicate on facts with a three-to-four-year delay, the first post-*Ynos* case from supreme jurisdictions could not have been expected before 2009.

The final and powerful disincentive for making preliminary references for a national judge is the duration of proceedings before the European Court of Justice. Albeit the ECJ claimed, in its latest Annual Report, an apparent victory in managing its workload,[115] the duration of a preliminary ruling procedure averages almost two years. National judges are under constant pressure to perform and finish a fixed amount of cases every month. From this perspective, it may appear advisable to render perhaps a not-so-perfect decision in a few months time than to strive for maybe a perfect one for years. Additionally, the ECJ has repeatedly rejected requests from the new Member States' courts to deal with submitted questions pursuant to the accelerated procedure.[116] Under these circumstances, it is hardly surprising that the duration of a preliminary ruling procedure often plays a decisive role in judicial deliberations as to whether or not to submit a request to the ECJ. There are areas of law in which the length of the procedure virtually excludes any request for a preliminary ruling. In other areas, the delay is still substantial: a preliminary ruling tends to be seriously considered only if there is a repetitive and major problem, amounting to a certain "structural" question.

---

[113] See M. Bobek, 'A New Legal Order, or a Non-existent one? Some (Early) Experience in the Application of EU Law in Central Europe', 2 *CYELP* (2006) pp. 265-298. See also the case note on the *Ynos* decision published in 3 *Soudní rozhledy* (2003) pp. 111-113.

[114] Some of the courts even openly regret that they have no jurisdiction to consult the European Court of Justice on specific issues. For instance, in an order dismissing the cassational appeal to the Supreme Court, the CSC, after having dealt in quite some detail with the interpretation of the Council Directive 77/91/EEC (Second Council Directive 77/91/EEC of 13 December 1976 on co-ordination of safeguards which, for the protection of the interests of members and others, are required by Member States of companies within the meaning of the second paragraph of Art. 58 of the Treaty, in respect of the formation of public limited liability companies and the maintenance and alteration of their capital, with a view to making such safeguards equivalent, *loc. cit.* n. 83), openly regretted that it cannot consult the ECJ whether or not its interpretation of the Directive is correct, as the facts of the case had taken place prior to the accession. See Order of 26 June 2007, Case 29 Odo 984/2005, available at http://www.nsoud.cz.

[115] Court of Justice Annual Report for 2008, available at http://curia.europa.eu/jcms/jcms/Jo2_7000/.

[116] See, for instance, Order of 3 April 2007, Case C-33/07 *Ministerul Administraţiei şi Internelor – Direcţia Generală de Paşapoarte Bucureşti v. Gheorghe Jipa*, unpublished, and Order of 8 November 2007, Case C-456/07 *Karol Mihal v. Daňový úrad Košice V*, unpublished. For analysis of both cases see Chapters 16 and 11 (respectively) in this volume.

## 6. INFRINGEMENTS AND DIRECT ACTIONS

Direct legal interchange between the European Union and the Czech Republic has been so far somewhat one-sided. On the one hand, the Czech Republic appears to be the uncontested champion amongst the new Member States as far as the amount of the launched infringement proceedings pursuant to Article 226 EC is concerned. On the other hand, there have been just few direct actions by the Czech Republic against the Community institutions.

### 6.1. Direct actions

In the first three years of EU membership, the Czech Republic did not bring, unlike Poland or some other new Member States, any action against the institutions of the European Communities. Only in 2007, it launched two proceedings for annulment against the European Commission: the first challenges the Czech national plan for the allocation of emissions allowances for greenhouse gases;[117] the second attacks the validity of the determination of surplus stocks of agricultural products other than sugar.[118] This was followed by a third request for annulment submitted in 2008.[119] This time the Czech Republic questioned the validity of the decision of the Commission of the European Communities of 7 August 2008 on offsetting the Commission's claims against its debts, BUG/C3 D(2008) 10.5-3956.

In two of these applications, the Czech Republic cannot be said to be the leading claimant. In the greenhouse allowances litigation, it followed, after a long national discussion, the example of Slovakia[120] and attacked the allegedly insufficient greenhouse gas quota allocated to the Czech Republic. The validity of the Commission's decision on the surplus stocks of agricultural products has been attacked by several other new Member States, including Poland, Slovakia and Lithuania.[121] Both actions were pending at the time of writing.

In most of the new Member States, the legal representation of the Member State has been entrusted to one specialised governmental agent and his/her cabinet, which represent the state before the European Court of Justice (and the Court of First Instance). The structure and the timing of the direct actions brought by the governments of (not only) the new Member States demonstrate not only that these representations are getting more and more experienced, but also that these states are starting to use their capital of being a repetitive player before the ECJ, and that they are also able to co-operate on their respective national levels and before the ECJ.[122]

---

[117] Case T-194/07 *Czech Republic v. Commission*, *OJ* 2007 C 199/38.

[118] Case T-248/07 *Czech Republic v. Commission*, *OJ* 2007 C 211/48.

[119] Case T-465/08 *Czech Republic v. Commission*, *OJ* 2008 C 327/39.

[120] Case T-32/07 *the Slovak Republic v. Commission*, *OJ* 2007 C 69/29.

[121] Case T-243/07 *Republic of Poland v. Commission of the European Communities*, *OJ* 2007 C 211/45; Case T-247/07 *the Slovak Republic v. Commission of the European Communities*, *OJ* 2007 C 211/47; Case T-262/07 *Republic of Lithuania v. Commission of the European Communities*, *OJ* 2007 C 211/53.

[122] Further, see M.-P.F. Granger, 'When governments go to Luxembourg... : the influence of governments on the Court of Justice', 29 *ELRev.* (2004) pp. 3-31. With respect to the Czech Republic, see

## 6.2.    Infringements proceedings

The Czech Republic is leading the informal "infringements league" amongst the new
Member States. As of January 2009, there have been hundreds of cases in which the
European Commission has inquired, formally or informally, about the status of implementation of a certain piece of Community legislation or certain administrative practice
of the Czech authorities. More than a hundred infringement proceedings under Article
226 EC have been launched, resulting so far in eight judgments by the European Court
of Justice against the Czech Republic.[123] All the infringement judgments are concerned
with a delay or no transposition of technical pieces of EC legislation and have often
not even been disputed by the Czech Government.

When compared to the other new Member States, the number of launched Czech
infringement procedures is high. The explanation why the number of infringement
proceedings against the other new Member States is limited to tens and, in respect of
the Czech Republic, it rises to hundreds, is a matter of controversy. A possible explanation, which borders on the bizarre, would be that the amount of infringements proceedings against the Czech Republic is a "sanction" for its efforts to run the implementation
and the notification process of directives correctly.

Already well before the accession, the Office of the Government of the Czech
Republic had established a specialised "Compatibility Department", which acted and
continues to act as the central supervision agency for the entire approximation and –
after the accession – the transposition and implementation process. The transposition
process itself was decentralised, i.e., carried out by respective line ministries and
other central authorities. However, all transposition information and notifications, which
were to be submitted to the European Commission, were first to be sent to the Office
of the Government, which would scrutinise them; only if the Office were satisfied,
would it pass them on to Brussels. Immediately after the enlargement, the Office established a stringent set of requirements on the precision and quality of notification documents. While enforcing these standards, the Office repeatedly returned to the respective
ministries notification documents which they had submitted and requested these to be
redrafted. This created substantive delays in the notification process and, already by
the end of 2004, amounted to about 145 launched infringement proceedings for the
failure to notify transposition measures.[124]

---

J. Komárek, 'Česká republika před Soudním dvorem ES' [The Czech Republic before the Court of Jus-
tice], 2 *Jurisprudence* (2006) p. 27.

[123] ECJ, Case C-203/06 *Commission of the European Communities v. Czech Republic* [2007] *ECR*
I-6; Case C-204/06 *Commission of the European Communities v. Czech Republic* [2007] *ECR* I-7; Case
C-115/07 *Commission of the European Communities v. Czech Republic* [2007] *ECR* I-126; Case C-117/07
*Commission of the European Communities v. Czech Republic* [2007] *ECR* I-127; Case C-114/07 *Commis-
sion of the European Communities v. Czech Republic* [2007] *ECR* I-147; Case C-60/07 *Commission of the
European Communities v. Czech Republic* [2007] *ECR* I-157; Case C-87/08 *Commission of the European
Communities v. Czech Republic* [2008] *ECR* nyr; Case C-41/08 *Commission of the European Communities
v. Czech Republic* [2008] *ECR* nyr.

[124] We are indebted to Mr. Martin Smolek, the Czech Agent for the Representation of the Czech Republic before the European Court of Justice, for this information.

The infringement spree is, of course, not without impact on the national political and legal level. Similarly to other Member States, politically unpopular measures tend to be, in the national political discourse, presented as decreed from Brussels. This trend may only be accelerated by the amount of infringement proceedings against the Czech Republic, especially if there is the vision that they may be followed, in the second stage, by penalties imposed by the European Court of Justice for non-compliance under Article 228 EC.[125]

The "Brussels wants it" argument as a conclusive argument to any debate, irrespective of whether EU law genuinely requires a particular measure, often empties the national political debate. It may equally harm the transparency and legitimacy of the legislative process. One example is fitting. An infringement procedure was about to be launched against the Czech Republic in respect to national legislation which partially limited and partially precluded the importation of second-hand cars from other Member States.[126] The problem was similar to issues raised in references for a preliminary ruling from Poland and Hungary.[127] In the Czech case, the problem was not, however, limited only to a registration tax. The Czech law on road traffic, which also contains conditions for the importation of second-hand cars, provided for a complete prohibition of importation of second-hand cars older than 8 years.[128] Some provisions of the law thus amounted to a measure having an effect equivalent to a quantitative restriction; others were quantitative restrictions as such; both were contrary to Article 28 EC. The law in question was promptly amended. It was done, however, in quite a peculiar way. The Minister of Transport at the time – Mr. Schling – used the fact that he was not only a minister of the Czech Government, but also a member of the lower chamber of Parliament (the Chamber of Deputies), and that the same law was being amended at that time in the lower chamber of the Czech Parliament in respect to other provisions. As a private member's initiative, the minister literally smuggled the necessary amendments, required by the European Commission, into the bill in the course of the second reading.

It is praiseworthy that the Czech Government is trying to react flexibly and to fulfil its obligations arising out of the Czech membership in the European Union. The question really is whether or not it should do so secretly and by circumventing the appropriate legislative procedures.[129]

---

[125] Following the famous rewriting of the s. 3 of the Art. 228 EC, which, after the ECJ's decision in Case C-304/02 *Commission of the European Communities v. French Republic* [2005] *ECR* I-6263 no longer reads "or"(disjunction), but "and" (conjunction), the awareness of potential sanctions is growing.

[126] Infringement procedure no. 2004/5151, reasoned opinion of the Commission of 4 July 2006.

[127] ECJ, Case C-313/05 *Maciej Brzeziński v. Dyrektor Izby Celnej w Warszawie* [2007] *ECR* I-513 and joined Cases C-290/05 and C-333/05 *Ákos Nádasdi v. Vám- és Pénzügyőrség Észak-Alföldi Regionális Parancsnoksága and Ilona Németh v. Vám- és Pénzügyőrség Dél-Alföldi Regionális Parancsnoksága* [2006] *ECR* I-10115.

[128] § 35 zákon č. 56/2001 Sb., *o podmínkách provozu na pozemních komunikacích* [Law no 56/2001 Coll., on the Conditions of the Road Traffic].

[129] If one looks into the Parliament papers, there is no justification whatsoever why the law is being amended in this way in the second reading. The amendments just "appeared" – contrast the original Government proposal for the bill (Chamber of Deputies print no. 1066/0 of 29 July 2005) with the amendments

What the number of infringement proceedings really says about the enforceability and compliance with EC law in a given Member State remains, eventually, an open question. One of the actions against the Czech Republic before the European Court of Justice[130] concerned the fact that the Czech Law on Merchant Shipping provided that the captain of any sea ship flying the Czech flag had to be a Czech national.[131] The Commission argued, grounding its argument in the wording of Article 39 EC as interpreted by the ECJ[132] that such a national provision hindered the free movement of workers (sea captains) and that it was not covered by the exception of public service and public authority. The argument of the Commission was probably correct. However, it was questionable how such action did contribute to the establishment of the Internal Market or the free movement of sea captains, considering that the Czech Republic is a land-locked country that since the mid-1990s has had no merchant fleet. There is currently not a single sea vessel that would be flying the Czech flag, and there appears to be no indications that this situation should change in the foreseeable future. [133]


7.      CONCLUSIONS

The purpose of this chapter was to present an overview of the domestic EU-related developments that followed the accession of the Czech Republic to the European Union on 1 May 2004. As argued in the introduction, the incoming tide defined years ago by Lord Denning hasn't exactly reached the Czech Republic in the first years of membership. The ever-growing number of EU-related cases is, nevertheless, a fact. For reasons which deserve no elaborate explanation, the first years were dominated by cases either fully based on the pre-accession environment or at least partly relating to it. During the first years, the Constitutional Court as well as two Supreme Courts of the country outlined (not always coherently) their approach to EU law and its position in the Czech legal order. Ordinary courts have had their first encounters with EU law, its methodology and new interpretation methods. They also managed to break the ice in the dialogue with the European Court of Justice. As demonstrated in the last part of the chapter, the Czech Republic has lost a number of infraction cases at the European Court of Justice; however all were rather straight forward accidents connected with transposition of directives.

made to the law in the second reading in the Chamber (Chamber of Deputies print no 1066/2 of 31 January 2006), both documents accessible at http://www.psp.cz.

[130] Case C-496/07 *Commission v. Czech Republic*, OJ 2008 C 37/3.

[131] § 24 s. 4 zákon č. 61/2000 Sb., *o námořní plavbě* [Law no 61/2000 Coll., on Merchant Shipping].

[132] ECJ, Case C-405/01 *Colegio de Oficiales de la Marina Mercante Espagnola v. Administración del Estado* [2003] *ECR* I-10391 and Case C-47/02 *Albert Anker, Klaas Ras and Albertus Snopek v. Bundesrepublik Deutschland* [2003] *ECR* I-10447.

[133] The case was eventually withdrawn by the European Commission in early 2009; see Case C-496/07 *Order of the President of the Seventh Chamber of the Court of 6 March 2009 – Commission of the European Communities v. Czech Republic*, not reported.

*Chapter 11*

# EUROPE YET TO COME: THE APPLICATION OF EU LAW IN SLOVAKIA

Michal Bobek* and Zdeněk Kühn**


## 1. INTRODUCTION

The application of EU law in Slovakia following the accession in 2004 poses a series of intriguing questions. Perhaps the most puzzling one lies in the comparison with its western neighbor – the Czech Republic. Why does the domestic application of EU law, its quantity as well as quality, differ in two countries, which, for about 80 years shared their legal history and most of the legal rules? Searching for some answers, this chapter first deals with the absence of argumentative use of EU law by Slovak courts prior to the fifth enlargement of the European Union. Second, the rather scarce post-accession constitutional case law is analysed. Third, the application of Community law in ordinary courts following the enlargement is assessed. Fourth, the chapter offers an overview of the up-to-date Slovak references for preliminary ruling within their national context. Finally, it outlines direct actions and infringements proceedings before the Court of First Instance and the European Court of Justice involving Slovakia or Slovak nationals/companies. We attempted to reflect the law as it stood in January 2009.


## 2. THE ABSENCE OF EUROPEAN UNION LAW ARGUMENTS PRIOR TO THE ACCESSION

One of the striking features of the domestic impact of EU law onto the national judicial process in Slovakia is the absence of any argumentative use of EU law prior to the accession. Slovak courts – including the Constitutional Court – appear to be trapped in a somewhat bipolar logic of binding/non-binding sources of law. The more subtle uses of legal reasoning and EC law as a persuasive authority or (comparative) interpretative aid are limited. If they are being used *de facto*, they do not find any reflection in the

---

\* Michal Bobek is a researcher at the European University Institute, Department of Law, Florence, Italy.

\*\* Zdeněk Kühn is a justice at the Supreme Administrative Court of the Czech Republic and associated professor of law at the Faculty of Law, Charles University, Prague.

*A. Łazowski (ed.), The Application of EU Law in the New Member States*
© *2010, T·M·C·ASSER PRESS, The Hague, The Netherlands and the Authors*

written form of the decision. It was perhaps this bipolar vision of the law as only binding or non-binding authority which prevented greater recourse to Community law in
cases with facts before the accession.[1] It is thus only after the accession in cases where
the factual background spreads from the pre- to post-accession period (or an ongoing
legal relationship is being modified after the accession), where any use of Community
law in the domestic forum has genuinely started.

In the period preceding the accession, Slovak courts had been consistent in adhering
only to binding sources of law, ignoring almost entirely persuasive arguments. A typical pre-accession example is the decision of the Slovak Supreme Court (SSC) of 25
August 1999. In that case, the SSC was invited by the parties to consider the fact that
the interpretation of law employed by lower courts was contrary to an EC directive
which served as the model for approximation in this field. The Court openly refused to
consider EU law as an argumentative tool to interpret domestic law in a Euro-friendly
way. The Court did not distinguish authoritative and persuasive arguments. In its world
of "limited law", only binding sources exist; anything else is not the law and cannot be
taken into consideration by a court. In the SSC's view, 'considering the current stage
of EU integration', an argument based upon an EC directive was not relevant.[2] The
same applies to the case law of the Slovak Constitutional Court (SCC). This court,
unlike its Czech counterpart, never referred to EU law which would serve as a persuasive argument in its reasoning.

3.     CONSTITUTIONAL BASIS FOR THE APPLICATION OF EUROPEAN
       UNION LAW AND THE SLOVAK CONSTITUTIONAL COURT

In contrast with the Czech Constitution, the Slovak Constitution explicitly deals with
the application of European Union law and its effects within the legal order. Article 7,
section 2 states:

> '[l]Legally binding acts of the European Communities and of the European Union shall have
> precedence over laws of the Slovak Republic. The transposition of legally binding acts which
> require implementation shall be realized through a law or a regulation of the Government
> according to Art. 120 para. 2.'

It seems that the Slovak doctrine generally interprets this provision as giving precedence
to EC and EU law over (ordinary) laws only, thus keeping the primacy of Slovak constitutional laws over the entire bulk of European Union law.[3]

---

[1] It seems that it is Slovakia which, in this respect, best fits some of the hypotheses of one of the authors of this chapter. See Z. Kühn, 'European Law in the Empires of Mechanical Jurisprudence: The Judicial Application of European Law in Central European Candidate Countries', 1 *CYELP* (2005) pp. 55-74.

[2] The decision was published as No. 76 of the Slovak official case reporter for 2000: *Zbierka stanovísk
Najvyššieho súdu a rozhodnutí súdov Slovenskej republiky* [Collection of Opinions of the Supreme Court
and courts of the Slovak Republic], Vol. 2000, No. 4, p. 55. As such, it might be considered an important
precedent (only a few judgments are published in the official case reporter of Slovakia).

[3] Cf., on this critically, V. Kunová, 'Účinok práva ES/EÚ na slovenský právny poriadok' [The effect of EC/EU law on the Slovak legal order] 11 *EMP* (2002) p. 28 (criticising that the amendment to the

Perhaps, this provision of the Slovak Constitution, providing expressly for the basis for the application of European Union law in Slovakia, contributed to the fact that the Slovak Constitutional Court (or the actors capable of initiating proceedings before the Court) so far felt only a limited need to explain the relation between the Slovak Constitution and EU law. In December 2008, there were just two cases which touched upon constitutional issues of EU law: the case of the ratification of the European Constitutional Treaty of 27 February 2008 and the case relating to positive measures as provided by the Slovak Anti-Discrimination Law of 18 October 2005.

However, the Slovak political actors, unlike litigants in ordinary lawsuits, soon proved that they are able to include their national judicial review in their political fights over "Europe". In the battle over the European Constitutional Treaty (ECT),[4] the parliamentary approval of the Treaty was immediately challenged before the Constitutional Court.

### 3.1.  The case of the European Constitutional Treaty

Unlike the Czech Constitution, the Slovak Constitution as amended in early 2001[5] includes a plethora of (perhaps somewhat conflicting) provisions on the European Union. Above all, the already mentioned new Article 7 was introduced, which is a complex provision that regulates accession to three different types of international organisations. It reads as follows:

'(1) The Slovak Republic may, by its own discretion, enter into a state formation with other states. A constitutional law, which shall be confirmed by a referendum, shall decide on the entry into a state formation, or on the secession from such formation.
(2) The Slovak Republic may, by an international treaty, which was ratified and promulgated in the way laid down by a law, or on the basis of such treaty, transfer the exercise of a part of its powers to the European Communities and the European Union. Legally binding acts of the European Communities and of the European Union shall have precedence over laws of the Slovak Republic. The transposition of legally binding acts which require implementation shall be realized through a law or a regulation of the Government according to Art. 120 para. 2.
(3) The Slovak Republic may for purpose of maintaining peace, security and democratic order, under conditions established by an international treaty, join an organization of mutual collective security.
[...]'[6]

First, the Constitution allows for entry into a "state formation" [*štátny zväzok*] with other states.[7] This is a term that is difficult to translate because it has no clear meaning.

---

Slovak Constitution did not take into account the fact that EC law takes precedence over constitutional law as well).

[4]  Treaty establishing a Constitution for Europe, *OJ* 2004 C 310/1.

[5]  See Constitutional Act No. 90/2001 Z.z. (*Zbierka zakonov*) [Official Gazette].

[6]  The translation is available at http://www.concourt.sk; however, for the purposes of this chapter, the translation has been modified by the authors.

[7]  On the historical background of that term, see Š. Šebesta in 'Diskusia' [Discussion], 87 *Právny obzor* (2004) p. 453.

In the summer of 1992, when the Constitution was drafted, its authors intentionally used this vague phrase rather than an established term of constitutional law, in order to provide some leeway for the Slovak politicians in negotiating some future state organisation for the then Czech and Slovak Federal Republic. Although Czechoslovakia was dissolved a few months later, the vague term itself remained. Entering into a "state formation with other states" requires approval by a super-majority of the Parliament and subsequent approval in a referendum.

Second, the Constitution specifically allows for the accession to the European Communities and the European Union. There is no mandatory referendum (though it can be held optionally), and any international treaty transferring powers to the EC/EU within the meaning of this clause must be approved by a three-fifths majority of the deputies.[8] This clause, including its optional referendum, was deployed upon Slovakia's accession to the European Union. Finally, Article 7 also allows for joining an organisation of mutual collective security.

After the ECT had been approved by the Slovak Parliament on 11 May 2005, thirteen Slovak citizens and members of the Slovak Conservative Institute,[9] a think-tank which includes several prominent former MPs who are close to the Slovak Christian Democratic Party, submitted a constitutional complaint against the decision of the legislature. Their main claim was that their basic right to participate in the administration of public affairs within the meaning of Article 30(1) of the Constitution would be violated if the Parliament were to decide that no referendum would be held on the Treaty. According to them, Article 7(1) which provides for a mandatory referendum, rather than Article 7(2) of the Slovak Constitution, should have been applied to the domestic ratification of the ECT.[10] That is because (in view of the applicants), by approving the Treaty, Slovakia actually agreed to join a "state formation with other states" within the meaning of Article 7(1).

On 14 July 2005, the Slovak Constitutional Court accepted the complaint for further proceedings and issued a preliminary ruling, preventing Slovak President Ivan Gašparovič from ratifying the Treaty. In his reply, the President responded that he would not be bound by the SCC's ruling and could therefore complete the ratification anyway. However, facing widespread criticism, he eventually complied with the SCC's preliminary ruling. The first public hearing took place on 18 January 2006, with the SCC deciding to postpone the case indefinitely. The Court's Chief Justice Mazák (who later became a Slovak Advocate General at the European Court of Justice) commented that '[t]his is a particularly complicated case. This issue has an international, European, as well as a national dimension.'[11]

Although one might have wondered whether or not the SCC would follow the German example and delay its decision until the final resolution of the issue of the ECT was no

---

[8]  See Art. 84(4) of the Slovak Constitution.
[9]  For basic information in English, see http://www.konzervativizmus.sk.
[10]  *Loc. cit.* n. 5.
[11]  'Citizens challenge EU treaty', *The Slovak Spectator* of 25 January 2006, available at http://euroustava.sk/en (last visited 28 February 2008).

longer necessary, the SCC finally reached its verdict on 27 February 2008.[12] Despite the EU's tendencies towards becoming a "state formation", the SCC reasoned, the European Union after the ECT would not become a "state formation". The SCC further held that the ECT made the current legal situation more precise when it specified what the valid rules of the European Union are. Ratifying the ECT cannot be viewed as joining a "state formation with other states". Moreover, the question of what is the legal nature of the European Union cannot be addressed by the authorities of the Slovak Republic independently of other states. The latter argument, however, does not seem very persuasive as the term of "state formation with other states" is part of the Slovak Constitution, and, as such, it must be interpreted by the authority empowered to interpret the Slovak Constitution, i.e., the SCC as the ultimate interpreter of the Constitution. Last but not least, because the ECT involves also the list of fundamental rights, holding a referendum on such an issue is expressly forbidden by the Slovak Constitution (see Art. 93 para. 3), noted the SCC.[13]

### 3.2.    The anti-discrimination law case

In its decision of 18 October 2005, the SCC reviewed a piece of national law which implemented the EC Race Equality Directive.[14] It held that positive action in favour of an underprivileged race or ethnicity, which was possible (albeit not compulsory) under Article 5 of the Directive,[15] was not compatible with the equality principle enshrined in the Slovak Constitution.[16] Although this case touched EU law only indirectly, it nicely illustrates some general misunderstandings which might be present in the relation between EU law and some legal systems of the new EU Member States.

The provision which was at stake was section 8(8) of the Slovak Anti-Discrimination Law (implementing the Directive), which reads as follows:

> 'In order to ensure equality of opportunities in practice and to fulfil the principle of equal treatment, it is possible to enact special affirmative measures to prevent certain disadvantages with respect to racial or ethnic origins.'

---

[12] The decision of 27 February 2008, case no II. ÚS 171/05, was not yet available by the time of completion of this section of the chapter, save for a short Press Release available in Slovak at http://www. concourt.sk. Both the Slovak as well as the Czech Constitutional Courts follow an unfortunate style when judgments are often published online months after the decisions (operative part) had been announced.

[13] For basic information on these proceedings in English, see http://euroustava.sk/en, which contains additional background materials. In more detail on this case (however, without analysing the decision of 2008 which did not exist at that time), see Z. Kühn, 'Ratification Without Debate and Debate Without Ratification: the European Constitution in Slovakia and the Czech Republic', in A. Albi and J. Ziller, eds., *The European Constitution and National Constitutions. Ratification and Beyond* (The Hague, Kluwer Law International 2007) pp. 157-170.

[14] Council Directive 2000/43/EC of 29 June 2000 implementing the principle of equal treatment between persons irrespective of racial or ethnic origin, *OJ* 2000 L 180/22.

[15] Art. 5 of the Directive reads: 'With a view to ensuring full equality in practice, the principle of equal treatment shall not prevent any Member State from maintaining or adopting specific measures to prevent or compensate for disadvantages linked to racial or ethnic origin.'

[16] See the decision (full court) of 18 October 2005, case no PL. ÚS 8/04-202, published as no 539/2005 Z.z., available in Slovak at http://www.concourt.sk.

The Government of the Slovak Republic, which challenged this particular provision of the law before the SCC, argued that the section dealing with affirmative measures is unconstitutional because it is discriminatory.

The divided SCC (of the then eleven justices, four justices dissented and another wrote a concurring opinion) upheld this view. The SCC annulled section 8(8) of the Anti-Discrimination Law for two reasons. First, it held that the statutory provision to apply affirmative measures, as provided by the law, is too broad and thus in conflict with the general concept that any deviation from the principle of non-discrimination should be narrowly drafted. Second, the SCC opined that the Slovak Constitution bans any positive action save those expressly enumerated by the Constitution itself (like special measures in employment in favour of women, minors and disabled).

However, in justifying its opinion, the SCC proved that it largely misses the current European discourse in the area of discrimination. For instance, the SCC was unable to distinguish between the concepts of formal and substantive equality:

'Adhering to the model of substantive idea of equality, it is necessary to say that it is not important which differences between people exist because people have equal value and that is why they deserve the same care and respect (Art. 12 para 1 of the Constitution). It has been the result of general values of human dignity, autonomy and equal value of every individual which form the basis for prohibiting unjust discrimination of human beings notwithstanding their position within the society. On the other hand, remedying unjust discrimination can never cause the situation when the prohibition of unjust discrimination transforms into the command to discriminate other people save those who are addressees and beneficiaries of measures remedying certain disadvantages or obstacles to the full realization of the principle of equality.'[17]

Last but not least, the case was perhaps the first example when the SCC tried to use case law of the European Court of Justice in order to further justify its reasoning. However, the way the SCC was doing it appears questionable. The SCC referred to two cases which – in the Court's opinion – supported its thesis that any derogation from the principle of non-discrimination must be narrowly tailored. However, neither of the cases cited deals with the issue of positive action (both cases related to the right of women to serve in armed forces);[18] moreover, in respect to one of the cases quoted, the SCC refers to paragraph 42 of the ECJ's decision – despite the fact that the case does not include so many paragraphs.[19]

The discussed case thus remains an example of a missed possibility of a Constitutional Court of a new Member State to participate in the European constitutional discourse. We are far from criticising the SCC for the result it reached. However, the way the SCC justified its opinion is unconvincing – the justification proper covers less than 4 pages (out of a total 23 pages of the entire reasoning, which covers mostly long recit-

---

[17] *Ibidem*, para. 16.

[18] ECJ, Case 222/84 *Johnston v. Chief Constable of the Royal Ulster Constabulary* [1986] *ECR* 1651 and Case C-285/98 *Tanja Kreil v. Bundesrepublik Deutschland* [2000] *ECR* I-69.

[19] The SCC referred to para. 42 in case *Tanja Kreil*. The decision is, however, composed of only 33 paragraphs.

als to the statements of the parties). Moreover, the Court used the established terms of legal philosophy in a haphazard and chaotic manner, apparently without proper understanding of those terms; this way of justification makes it almost impossible to understand the genuine motives behind the Court's judgment.

4.     THE APPLICATION OF EUROPEAN UNION LAW BY NATIONAL
       COURTS AFTER THE ACCESSION

As was already mentioned above in point 1, unlike, for instance, Czech or Polish courts, the Slovak higher courts have never formulated an overreaching doctrine of voluntary consistent interpretation of Slovak law with Community law for the period before the accession. After the accession, there have been some attempts to draw EC law into consideration before courts in cases with facts before the accession via the Slovak approximation obligation laid down in the EA Slovakia.[20] These remained, however, isolated instances. On the whole, the Slovak courts did not use, in the immediate post-accession period, EU law as an aid in interpretation of approximated national legislation.[21]

There are two exceptions to this general trend. First, there is a decision of the SSC of 13 November 2005,[22] in which the SSC reviewed a town planning decision. In doing so, it used Community law, especially the provisions of the Council Directive 85/337/ EEC on the assessment of the effects of certain public and private projects on the environment,[23] as a sort of confirming argument for the adopted interpretation of the corresponding Slovak legislation concerning the environmental impact assessment. The SSC's authority for using Community legislation as an interpretative aid was the EA Slovakia.

Similar reasoning was used in a VAT dispute for the 2002 taxation period, which was decided by the Slovak Supreme Court as the revision court of last instance in 2007.[24] Here the SSC referred to the Sixth VAT Directive,[25] which formed the inspiration for the 1995 Slovak VAT law. The SSC again referred to EA Slovakia and the approximation obligation contained therein (extending also to VAT matters). On the

---

[20] Europe Agreement establishing an association between the European Communities and their Member States, of the one part, and the Slovak Republic, of the other part, *OJ* 1994 L 359/2.

[21] To faithfully account for the practice of Slovak, especially higher courts, is, however, extremely difficult. The Supreme Court does not publish its decisions except for 80 selected decisions every year, which are selected internally by the Court and published in the (printed) official Collection of the Opinions of the Supreme Court and the Decisions of Slovak Courts; the vast majority of the decisions remains unpublished.

[22] Judgment of 13 September 2005, case no 1 Sž-o-KS 194/2004, unpublished.

[23] Council Directive 85/337/EEC of 27 June 1985 on the assessment of the effects of certain public and private projects on the environment, *OJ* 1985 L 175/40.

[24] Judgment of 17 May 2007, case no 2 SžoKS 90/2006, unpublished.

[25] Sixth Council Directive 77/388/EEC of 17 May 1977 on the harmonization of the laws of the Member States relating to turnover taxes – Common system of value added tax: uniform basis of assessment, *OJ* 1977 L 145/1.

other hand, the argument out of EC law formed only a supportive argument, which *de facto* confirmed the result reached by the Court on the basis of national legislation.

## 4.1.    The bottom-up emergence of European Union law in Slovak courts

Considering the situation described above, it can be said that by 2008, the application of EU law was limited to the courts of first instance or appellate courts. This was caused by the natural delay with which the post-accession cases appear in courts. Without any broader indirect use of EU law in Slovak courts in cases with facts before the accession, the post-accession cases with the facts after the accession tend to appear in the courts of first instance only after 2005; the genuine start of the "Euro" judicial business came in late 2006 and in 2007.

There are ample instances of direct application of regulations. In quantitative terms, the leading pieces of legislation directly applied by Slovak courts[26] are the Council Regulation 44/2001/EC on jurisdiction and the recognition and enforcement of judgments in civil and commercial matters;[27] Council Regulation 2913/92/EEC establishing the Community Customs Code;[28] Council Regulation 1348/2000/EC on the service in the Member States of judicial and extrajudicial documents in civil or commercial matters[29] and Council Regulation 1408/71/EEC on the application of social security schemes to employed persons and their families moving within the Community.[30] The direct application of these pieces of Community legislation is hardly surprising as similarly frequent use can be identified in other Member States as well.

After some hesitations,[31] lower Slovak courts also realised the potential (and obligation) of indirect application of Community law, especially the indirect effect of directives. The typical instances of conform interpretation include the Council Directive

---

[26] These decisions (currently dozens of first instance cases) can be located online at http://jaspi. justice.gov.sk.

[27] Council Regulation 44/2001/EC of 22 December 2000 on jurisdiction and the recognition and enforcement of judgments in civil and commercial matters, *OJ* 2001 L 12/1. The Regulation has been applied in dozens of cases, most of them concerning the other party located in the Czech Republic.

[28] Council Regulation 2913/92/EEC of 12 October 1992 establishing the Community Customs Code, *OJ* 1992 L 302/1.

[29] Council Regulation 1348/2000/EC of 29 May 2000 on the service in the Member States of judicial and extrajudicial documents in civil or commercial matters, *OJ* 2000 L 160/37.

[30] Regulation 1408/71/EEC of the Council of 14 June 1971 on the application of social security schemes to employed persons and their families moving within the Community, *OJ* 1971 L 149/2 (English Special Edition, Series I, Chapter 1971(II) p. 416).

[31] As an example, one may use a decision (first instance) of the *Okresný súd Bratislava II* [District Court for Bratislava II], judgment of 11 October 2005, case no 42Cb/67/2005, accessible at http://jaspi. justice.gov.sk. The Slovak court refused to take into (any) account Council Directive 86/653/EEC on commercial agents, which was invoked by the applicant (Council Directive 86/653/EEC of 18 December 1986 on the coordination of the laws of the Member States relating to self-employed commercial agents, *OJ* 1986 L 382/17). The Court held: 'The European Community Treaty provides for the binding force and the direct applicability, not necessitating any further implementation, only in the case of regulations and not in the case of directives. A non-transposed directive does not directly create any obligations. The invoked directive cannot thus be considered to be a legally binding act with any application on the territory of the Slovak Republic, as the directive cannot be found in the list of transposed measures.'

93/13/EEC of 5 April 1993 on unfair terms in consumer contracts;[32] Council Directive 2001/23/EC of 12 March 2001 on the approximation of the laws of the Member States relating to the safeguarding of employees' rights in the event of transfers of undertakings, businesses or parts of undertakings or businesses[33] or the Council Directive 90/314/ EEC of 13 June 1990 on package travel, package holidays and package tours.[34] These instances of indirect effect involve again only cases with facts posterior to the Slovak accession to the European Union.

So far, we were not able to identify any instances of according direct effect to directives or any situations in which Slovak courts were to resolve conflicts between Slovak law and Community law by letting the latter prevail over national law. A case which perhaps came the closest to this momentum was a recent decision of the Slovak Supreme Court, which concerned principles applicable to trademarks.[35] The case involved a Czech company which sought the registration of its trademark in the territory of Slovakia. The Slovak Trademark Law required that for a trademark of a foreign person to be registered, that person had first to prove that it was genuinely economically active in Slovakia and that it intended to really use its trademark there. The *Krajský súd v Banskej Bystrici* [Regional Court in Banská Bystrica] disagreed with this strict territoriality-based vision of the Slovak Trademark Law, an opinion which was upheld by the Supreme Court on appeal. The SSC noted that albeit the Slovak Trademark Law has not, following the accession to the European Union, been specifically amended, after the accession it must be interpreted taking into account the Slovak membership in the European Union. With references to the Community legislation[36] and the case law,[37] the SSC held that if the aim of the European Communities is to create the Internal Market, the Member States can no longer apply their national laws relating to the functioning of the Internal Market, such as copyright or trademark laws, on a strictly territorial basis. This meant in the particular case, that the Slovak Trademark Agency was no longer entitled to require, from a company registered in another Member State, the proof that

---

[32] Council Directive 93/13/EEC of 5 April 1993 on unfair terms in consumer contracts, *OJ* 1993 L 95/29. See, for instance, judgment of the *Okresný súd v Žiline* [District Court in Žilina] of 2 March 2007, case no 6C/174/2005 and also cases no 6C/174/2005, 6C/240/2007, 6C/252/2007, 6C/255/2007; judgments of the *Okresný súd Liptovský Mikuláš* [District Court in Liptovský Mikuláš] of 4 October 2007 and 30 October 2007, cases no 7C/148/2007 and 7C/168/2007; judgment of the *Krajský súd v Nitre* [Regional Court in Nitra] of 2 May 2007, case no 7Co/5/2007, all accessible at http://jaspi.justice.gov.sk.

[33] Council Directive 2001/23/EC of 12 March 2001 on the approximation of the laws of the Member States relating to the safeguarding of employees' rights in the event of transfers of undertakings, businesses or parts of undertakings or businesses, *OJ* 2001 L 82/16. See, *inter alia*, judgment of the *Krajský súd v Banskej Bystrici* [Regional Court in Banská Bystrica] of 30 November 2006, case no 12Co/259/2006, http://jaspi.justice.gov.sk.

[34] Council Directive 90/314/EEC of 13 June 1990 on package travel, package holidays and package tours, *OJ* 1990 L 158/59. See, *inter alia*, judgment of the *Krajský súd v Nitre* [Regional Court in Nitra] of 2 May 2007, case no 7Co/5/2007, http://jaspi.justice.gov.sk.

[35] Judgment of 19 April 2007, case no 4 SžkoKS 37/2006, unpublished.

[36] First Council Directive 89/104/EEC of 21 December 1988 to approximate the laws of the Member States relating to trade marks, *OJ* 1989 L 40/1.

[37] ECJ, Case C-218/01 *Henkel KGaA* [2004] *ECR* I-1725, Case C-245/02 *Anheuser-Busch Inc. v. Budějovický Budvar, národní podnik* [2004] *ECR* I-10989.

it was economically active in Slovakia. The fact that the company was economically active and duly registered in another Member State should have been sufficient.

## 4.2.    Potential explanations for the limited use of European Union law by Slovak courts

In contrast to the Czech Republic or Poland, the amount of judicial application of European Union law in Slovakia remains limited. This phenomenon can hardly be explained by any clear mathematical formulas. There are general problems, such as the inaccessibility of sources of law and secondary literature in Slovak. But these problems are shared with other Member States as well; they are the general characteristic of the last two waves of enlargement, where the amount of law and the lack of its translation complicated the situation in all new Member States.[38]

More detailed explanation can perhaps only be given in specified individual instances. As far as the highest judicial level is concerned, i.e., the Supreme Court and the Constitutional Court, one of the reasons for the moderate use of EU law in the reasoning may perhaps be simple technical limitations and time constraints. In all new Member States, judges had to take the shock of the new mass of EU law, including case law of the European Court of Justice. Some systems and some – especially supreme – courts have tried to facilitate the learning task of judges by establishing specialised European units or research departments within the courts, which could assist the judges in matters of EU law. For instance, the Czech, Polish or Lithuanian supreme administrative courts have established specialised research and documentation departments, staffed with (typically younger) lawyers or university lecturers skilled in European Union law and foreign languages. Other jurisdictions have tried to provide judges with legal assistants (law clerks), who could again assist the judge in matters of research and drafting decisions.

However, Slovak Supreme Court judges do not have any assistants and no support of a research and documentation service. The Constitutional Court judges are provided with advisors, but there is no European Union law unit or any research service. These may be small and technical things, but these are, at the same time, things that really matter. The likeliness of a judge independently launching an EU law expedition on her/his own, navigating in a system of law she/he never studied and typically in a language she/he does not well understand, is perhaps different from the likelihood of just asking a member of skilled support staff who is able and has the time to conduct such research.

It is perhaps also worth noting that Slovakia presents the most extreme variant of a centralised judicial review in the region. In most post-Communist countries, the previous Communist model of the judiciary's unconditional observance of the entire legal system (including various sub-statutory directives and regulations) seems to have been replaced by rigid adherence to centralised judicial review. The Slovak Constitution vests the exclusive competence to review any possible conflict among various legal

---

[38]    See Chapter 5 in this volume.

norms to the Constitutional Court: conflicts of statutes, or even sub-statutory decrees, with international treaties, of statutes with the Constitution, as well as of statutes with sub-statutory decrees, i.e., the issue of their legality.[39]

This centralisation of constitutional review meant that Slovak ordinary judges did not have the power to set aside a domestic law in conflict with general international law and must refer any such matter to the Constitutional Court. In fact, as Slovak judges operated within a completely centralised system of judicial review, they only acquired the power of judicial review on 1 May 2004, when they became part of the decentralised European judiciary and, thus, obliged to apply European Union law.[40]

Slovakia is an example of a constitutional regime in which too much emphasis is placed on the central role of Constitutional Courts in the construction of the rule of law. Under such conditions, the ordinary courts have a strong tendency to disappear from the scene. This is the current Slovak situation: any important legal issue is referred to the Constitutional Court, and ordinary courts are reduced to marginality. Although Constitutional Courts are an important factor in remoulding of the Central European concept of law and the judicial ideology of textual positivism, their ultimate success depends on ordinary judges joining in the common enterprise of building the rule of law and the new idea of constitutionalism.[41]

Finally, it is also clear that the genuine knowledge of EU law may vary considerably in the various new Member States. A rather anecdotic example may be provided in this respect: under Slovak law, there are legal experts who may be called to provide expert evidence before the national courts on EU law. These experts are registered with the Slovak Ministry of Justice.[42] The area of expertise for legal experts in EU law is classified as discipline "330000 – Foreign Law", branch "330300 – European law".[43] This means that for the purpose of legal expertise, European Union law in Slovakia is still considered to be "foreign law". One may only contrast this with the basic tenets established by the European Court of Justice, which not only considers the Community legal

---

[39] See Art. 125 para. 1(a) and Art. 144 para. 2 of the Slovak Constitution as amended in 2001; compare with Art. 95 para. 2 of the Czech Constitution until 2002 (and the subsequent reading of this Article by the Constitutional Court).

[40] In the Czech Republic and Poland, the judges have the power of statutory review, i.e., to decide whether a regulation is consistent with a statute. Accordingly, when judges find that a regulation is contrary to a statute, they have a duty not to apply the regulation. See Art. 95 para. 1 of the Czech Constitution and, for Poland, see L.L. Garlicki, 'The Experience of the Polish Constitutional Court', in W. Sadurski, ed., *Constitutional Justice, East and West. Democratic Legitimacy and Constitutional Courts in Post-Communist Europe in a Comparative Perspective* (Alphen aan den Rijn, Kluwer Law International 2002) pp. 265-282, at p. 274.

[41] See in more detail, Z. Kühn, 'Making Constitutionalism Horizontal: Three Different Central European Strategies', in A. Sajó and R. Uitz, eds., *The Constitution in Private Relations: Expanding Constitutionalism* (Utrecht, Eleven International Publishing 2005) pp. 217-240.

[42] Further, see Law no 382/2004 Coll., on legal experts, interpreters and translators [*č. 382/2004 Z.z., o znalcoch, tlmočníkoch a prekladateľoch*] and Regulation no. 490/2004 Coll., regulation carrying out the law no. 382/2004 Coll., on legal experts, interpreters and translators [*č. 490/2004 Z.z. vyhláška, ktorou sa vykonáva zákon č. 382/2004 Z.z. o znalcoch, tlmočníkoch a prekladateľoch*].

[43] Registry of the experts is accessible online at http://jaspi.justice.gov.sk/jaspiw1/htm_reg/jaspiw_maxi_regz_fr0.htm (last visited 28 February 2008).

system to be 'integrated into the legal systems of the Member States'[44] but also requires the courts of the Member States to apply Community law in the same way as they would apply national law.[45] This would, in the case of Slovakia, mean applying the entire body of EC law *ex officio*, i.e., by applying the principle that the judge knows the law.

As already mentioned, this is just an anecdotal example with little practical significance. The Slovak courts have already started applying EU law directly and on their own, some of them actually expressly recognising their duty to know EU law, which is imposed not only by virtue of EU law and the case law of the European Court of Justice but also by provisions of Slovak law.[46]

## 5. REFERENCES FOR PRELIMINARY RULING

In years 2004-2008, there were just two preliminary references from Slovak courts.[47] The first reference was submitted by the *Krajský súd v Prešove* [Regional Court in Prešov], the second by the *Najvyšší súd* [the Supreme Court].

The Slovak procedural framework for submitting requests for a preliminary reference to the Luxembourg court is, like in the Czech Republic, a "minimalist" one. Both codes of judicial procedure, i.e., the Code of Civil Procedure[48] and the Code of Criminal Procedure,[49] just include short provisions on the possibility for a presiding judge to stay national proceedings if he/she decides to make a reference. The form of a reference itself was left to the discretion of Slovak courts. Interestingly, in the two references submitted, the form has already diverged. The first reference by the Regional Court in Prešov was drafted as one single order, by which the national Court stayed the proceedings and submitted the question to the European Court of Justice. The second question by the Supreme Court was drafted as two separate orders of the Court: one order staying the national procedure, the other one submitting the question to the ECJ. Similarly, as in the case of the Czech Republic, this difference is of no significance to the ECJ; it might be, however, of importance later, once the issue of the possibility of domestic appeals against the orders making preliminary references arises.[50]

---

[44] See, e.g., ECJ, Joined Cases C-6/90 and C-9/90 *Andrea Francovich and Danila Bonifaci and others v. Italian Republic* [1991] *ECR* I-5357, para. 31.

[45] See, e.g., ECJ, Joined Cases C-430/93 and C-431/93 *Jeroen van Schijndel and Johannes Nicolaas Cornelis van Veen v. Stichting Pensioenfonds voor Fysiotherapeuten* [1995] *ECR* I-04705, para. 13.

[46] Apart from the constitutional level, the duty to know the applicable EU legislation can be inferred from the provision of § 121 of the Code of Civil Procedure [*Zákon č. 99/1963 Zb., Občiansky súdny poriadok*], which provides that before the court, the parties are not obliged to prove 'legally binding acts, which were published in the Official Journal of the European Communities and the Official Journal of the European Union.'

[47] As of 1 July 2009, Slovakia has not recognised the jurisdiction of the European Court of Justice to hear references submitted pursuant to Art. 35 EU.

[48] § 109(1)(c) of the Code of Civil Procedure [*Zákon č. 99/1963 Zb., Občiansky súdny poriadok*].

[49] § 7(3), § 241(3) and § 244(3) of the Code of Criminal Procedure [*Zákon č. 301/2005 Z.z., Trestný poriadok*].

[50] See further, Chapter 10 in this volume.

## 5.1. The references

The first Slovak reference concerned national legislation under which electrical installations may be placed on private land without the owners being entitled to compensation. In 1998, Mr. Koval'ský purchased a piece of land in the town of Prešov. There were two large steel cases located on the property. They contained electrical installations belonging to the town public transportation company. Under the legislation then in force, companies in the energy sector in Slovakia were entitled to construct and exploit electric lines and supporting pillars on any private property without any compensation to the proprietor. Mr. Koval'ský did not request the installations to be removed; he just requested to be compensated by the company for the use of his property.

His claims for compensation before civil courts were unsuccessful. The Regional Court in Prešov, however, submitted the question to the Slovak Constitutional Court for the review of constitutionality. The SCC twice rejected the application made by the Regional Court, refusing to deal with the issue. The Regional Court went on and, after the accession of Slovakia to the European Union, submitted the question as a request for preliminary ruling to the European Court of Justice. The three questions referred concerned the interpretation of Article 1 of the First Protocol to the Convention on the Protection of Human Rights and Fundamental Freedoms (right to property).[51] The European Court of Justice rejected the request for a preliminary ruling on 25 January 2007 as being manifestly outside its competence.[52]

The decision of the European Court of Justice was hardly surprising. *Koval'ský* belonged to the first, rather dubious wave of preliminary references from the new Member States. The case showed parallels to the Hungarian request for a preliminary reference in the *Vajnai*[53] case and, partially, also to their common predecessor, the first Austrian reference in the *Kremzow*[54] case. All these requests were made soon after the accession of the respective new Member State. All of them already had, at the moment of the accession, a rich procedural background on the national level. The retired judge Kremzow, who was sentenced to prison for murder, has spent his time filing appeals and requests for revision to all possible Austrian courts. Similarly, the Hungarian ban on the public display of the symbols of totalitarianism, which was the issue in the *Vajnai* litigation, has been repeatedly submitted to the Hungarian Constitutional Court. In all these cases, efforts were made to graft an EU dimension onto a domestic dispute and to have the European Court of Justice become the new forum for a battle already lost before national courts.

In the *Koval'ský* and *Vajnai* cases, there has been perhaps an additional motive, namely, to circumvent the prior negative decisions of the respective national Constitutional Courts. In Central and Eastern Europe, Constitutional Courts are powerful legal

---

[51] Notice with the formulation of the questions published in *OJ* 2006, C 249/2.
[52] ECJ, Case C-302/06 *František Koval'ský v. Mesto Prešov* [2007] *ECR* I-11.
[53] ECJ, Case C-328/04 *Criminal proceedings against Attila Vajnai* [2005] *ECR* I-8577.
[54] ECJ, Case C-299/95 *Friedrich Kremzow v. Republik Österreich* [1997] *ECR* I-2629.

and political players,[55] who may sometimes get into the conflict with courts of general jurisdiction, represented especially by the heads of the respective judicial corps, i.e., the Supreme Court and/or the Supreme Administrative Court. It remains to be seen whether or not these courts of general jurisdiction may be tempted to use the European Court of Justice as a sort of leverage against the decisions of national Constitutional Courts.

It is also true that the decision as to which question is within the competence of the European Court of Justice and which one is already beyond its jurisdiction is never clear cut. Is the request to be addressed "Mister" in criminal proceedings before national courts within or outside the competence of the European Court of Justice?[56] Is the national legislation regulating the stay of third-country nationals who are not EU citizens within or outside the scope of Community law?[57] What about a criminal (or administrative) penalty for drunken driving?[58]

The key factor in similar cases is obviously not the issue itself, but the way in which the request for a preliminary ruling is framed. Would the decision of the European Court of Justice perhaps be different if the submitting court were to ask whether the fact that the electric installations are placed on the property may shy away potential property buyers from other Member States and thus constitute a barrier to the freedom of establishment?[59] Alternatively, if Mr. Kovaľský decided to sell the property and move to another Member State, could the electric installations, which decrease the value of the property and thus make it difficult to sell it, not constitute a barrier to his free movement between the Member States?

---

[55] For a general introduction, see, e.g., R. Procházka, *Mission Accomplished: On Founding Constitutional Adjudication in Central Europe* (Budapest, Central European University Press 2002) or W. Sadurski, *Rights before courts: a study of constitutional courts in post-communist states of Central and Eastern Europe* (Dordrecht, Springer 2005).

[56] ECJ, Case C-291/96 *Criminal proceedings against Martino Grado and Shahid Bashir* [1997] *ECR* I-5531.

[57] ECJ, Joined Cases C-297/88 and C-197/89 *Massam Dzodzi v. Belgian State* [1990] *ECR* I-3763.

[58] ECJ, Case C-226/97 *Criminal proceedings against Johannes Martinus Lemmens* [1998] *ECR* I-3711.

[59] Somewhat artificial as this argument may sound, the views might be different if one considers, for instance, the case law of the European Court of Justice relating to so-called "golden shares." The owner of these golden shares is typically entitled to exercise special voting rights with respect to some key decisions in the administration of a company. In a series of direct actions (e.g., ECJ, Case C-483/99 *Commission of the European Communities v. French Republic* [2002] *ECR* I-4781; Case C-503/99 *Commission of the European Communities v. Kingdom of Belgium* [2002] *ECR* I-4809; Case C-98/01 *Commission of the European Communities v. United Kingdom* [2003] *ECR* I-4641), the ECJ came to the conclusion that golden shares are a barrier to the free movement of capital and the freedom of establishment. An investor from another Member State might be put off by the existence of golden shares in a company, as it would never be able to take it over. If golden shares are declared to be a barrier to freedom of establishment, why should a burden on a property, which may deter a potential buyer from another Member State from acquiring it, be considered any different?

The second Slovak request for a preliminary ruling was submitted by the Slovak Supreme Court.[60] It concerns whether or not under the Sixth VAT Directive[61] official bailiffs are liable to pay VAT or whether they can be exempted. Under Slovak law, the function of a bailiff is carried out by natural persons (individuals), but, at the same time, it is considered to be the exercise of public power.[62] Under the Sixth VAT Directive, state, regional and local government authorities and other bodies governed by public law are not considered taxable persons in respect to the activities or transactions in which they engage as public authorities.

The plaintiff in the original proceedings, Mr. Karol Mihal, is a bailiff in Košice, Slovakia. In July 2004, he applied to the local tax authority for his VAT registration to be cancelled, thus being exempted from the VAT. The tax authority refused to recognise him as a non-taxable person in respect to VAT, stating that only public bodies which were legal persons were exempted from VAT. Mr. Karol Mihal did not accept this interpretation of the term "public body" and initiated legal proceedings against the tax authority before the Slovak courts.

The Regional Court in Košice, acting as the administrative court of first instance, rejected the application.[63] It held that albeit bailiffs do exercise some public power, they are also members of a free profession and their aim is to make profit. The Regional Court considered the case law of the European Court of Justice, in particular the decision in case 235/85 *Commission v. the Netherlands*,[64] where the ECJ held that the Dutch public notaries and bailiffs were not to be exempted from the VAT duty under the Sixth VAT Directive. The SSC, seized on appeal, was not entirely sure about the interpretation adopted by the Regional Court and decided to submit the reference to the European Court of Justice. The SSC also requested the case to be dealt with under the accelerated procedure, which the European Court of Justice rejected by an Order of 8 November 2007. The ECJ observed that albeit the issue as to whether or not bailiffs are under the duty to pay the VAT may be of considerable financial significance for the Slovak Republic, the issue itself is not of extraordinary urgency.[65] The European Court of Justice considered the reference as a fairly straight-forward affair and thus rendered its decision in the form of a reasoned order based on Article 104, section 3 of the Rules of Procedure.[66] In the operative part it held as follows:

---

[60] Order of 24 May 2007, case no 1 Sžo KS/61/2005, unpublished.

[61] Sixth Council Directive 77/388/EEC of 17 May 1977 on the harmonisation of the laws of the Member States relating to turnover taxes – Common system of value added tax: uniform basis of assessment, *OJ* 1977 L 145/1.

[62] The SCC has repeatedly dealt with the status of bailiffs in national law, most significantly in a plenary decision of 10 January 2005, case no Pl. ÚS 49/03, published as no 125/2005 Z.z.

[63] Judgment of 9 March 2005, case no 4 S 40/04-25, unpublished.

[64] ECJ, Case 235/85 *Commission of the European Communities v. Kingdom of the Netherlands* [1987] *ECR* 1471.

[65] Order of the president of the Court of Justice of 8 November 2007 in Case C-456/07 *Karol Mihal v. Daňový úrad Košice V*, unpublished.

[66] ECJ, Case C-456/07 *Karol Mihal v. Daňový úrad Košice* [2008] *ECR* I-79.

'An activity exercised by a private individual, such as that of a bailiff, is not exempted from value added tax merely because it consists in engaging in acts falling within the rights and powers of a public authority. Even on the assumption that, in the exercise of his duties, a bailiff does carry out such acts, he does not, under legislation such as that at issue in the main proceedings, exercise his activity in the form of a body governed by public law, not being integrated into the organisation of the public administration, but in the form of an independent economic activity carried out in a self-employed capacity, and, consequently, he is not covered by the exemption provided for in the first subparagraph of Article 4(5) of Sixth Council Directive 77/388/EEC of 17 May 1977 on the harmonisation of the laws of the Member States relating to turnover taxes – Common system of value added tax: uniform basis of assessment.'

The European Court of Justice confirmed that activities of bailiffs were not subject to the exception provided in Article 4(5) of the Sixth VAT Directive.

## 5.2.    The absence of a reference

There appear to be very few instances in which a request to make a reference for a preliminary ruling is actually made before a Slovak court. The reasons for not referring to the European Court of Justice of course differ. Some of the reasons why not to refer, especially those put forward by the SSC, are rather singular. For instance, in a competition case (abuse of dominance), the SSC, while reviewing a decision of the Slovak Antitrust Authority, explained why it decided not to consider submitting a request for a preliminary ruling by stating:

'... in this particular case, the Slovak legal order allowed to sufficiently assess the case, moreover, the Slovak legal order is, as far as the legal issue in question is concerned, in conformity with EU law, which in turn means that there was no danger of conflict between EU law and the national law. It follows from the submissions of the claimant that he was above all concerned with the application of Art. 82 EC and not about its interpretation. The appellate court was therefore called to act.'[67]

In yet another decision, which concerned the review of a town planning decision, the SSC considered some provisions of the Council Directive 85/337/EEC on the assessment of the effects of certain public and private projects on the environment. When interpreting these provisions, the SSC was trying to delimit its competence in the area of interpretation of the said Directive, presumably with respect to a potential suggestion to submit a request for a preliminary reference on the issue. It stated:

'... The Supreme Court is aware of the fact that it is not competent to interpret unclear or otherwise disputable provisions of Community law, however, in the present case, the provisions in question are of a different sort.'[68]

---

[67] Judgment of 21 November 2005, case no 1 Sž-o-NS 87/2005, unpublished.
[68] Judgment of 13 September 2005, case no 1 Sž-o-KS 194/2004, unpublished.

These and other instances, perhaps together with the two requests for a preliminary ruling, which so far originated from Slovakia, would indicate that Slovak courts still have some leeway in seizing the potential and the purpose of request for a preliminary ruling to the European Court of Justice.

## 5.3.    The position of the Slovak Constitutional Court

In the Slovak judicial system, the Constitutional Court plays a key role. Not only may it review, if seized by a constitutional complaint, any final judicial decision, but it is also entitled to grant just satisfaction in cases of violation of basic rights or fundamental freedoms by administrative authorities or courts.[69] The position adopted by the SCC is thus instrumental for the judicial application of EU law in Slovakia and also for the approach courts of general jurisdiction might take to preliminary rulings.

So far, the SCC has showed itself open to EU law generally and to preliminary rulings in particular. Two issues are of importance in this respect. First, the SCC has openly acknowledged itself to be a court within the meaning of Article 234 EC. Second, the SCC appears to be ready to sanction the possible disregard of the duty to refer, imposed by Article 234(3) EC, by the Slovak courts of last instance.

The position of Constitutional Courts *vis-à-vis* preliminary rulings is often subject to controversy. The approach of the various Constitutional Courts varies considerably – from regarding itself to be outside the scope of Article 234 EC altogether,[70] through admitting to be a court in the meaning of Article 234 EC, but never referring one single question,[71] to recognising and actually referring questions to the European Court of Justice.[72]

The SCC appears to have accepted that it is a court within the meaning of Article 234 EC. Not only that, the SCC also recognised that it would be a court of last instance with a duty to refer. In the already discussed litigation concerning the domestic implementation of the Race Directive,[73] the SCC was seized by the Slovak Government to review the constitutionality of the facultative affirmative measures provided for in Article 5 of the Race Directive. In the course of this litigation, the Slovak Parliament (the National Council) suggested to the SCC to submit a request for a preliminary ruling on the proper interpretation of the relevant provisions of the Race Directive. The

---

[69] § 56 s. 4 and § 50 s. 3 of the Law no. 38/1993 Coll., on the Organisation of the Constitutional Court of the Slovak Republic [*Zákon č. 38/1993 Z.z. o organizácii Ústavného súdu Slovenskej republiky, o konaní pred ním a o postavení jeho sudcov*].

[70] For example Spain; see F. Mayer, 'The European Constitution and the Courts. Adjudicating European constitutional law in a multilevel system', *Jean Monnet Working Paper* 9/03.

[71] As is the case of the German Federal Constitutional Tribunal [*Bundesverfassungsgericht*] – see *BVerfGE* 52, 187 (201) – "*Vielleicht-Beschluss.*"

[72] Examples of this sort include Belgium (former *Cour d'Arbitrage*, recently renamed to *Cour constitutionnelle*), the Austrian Constitutional Court [*Verfassungsgerichtshof*], the Lithuanian Constitutional Court [*Lietuvos Respublikos Konstitucinis*], the Italian Constitutional Court [*Corte Costituzionale*].

[73] Finding of the SCC (full court) of 6 October 2005, case no PL. ÚS 8/04-202, published as no 539/2005 Coll. Discussed *supra*, text to nn. 15-18.

SCC refused, as far as the particular case in question was concerned.[74] However, the SCC generally accepted that it is a court in the meaning of Article 234(3) EC.[75] The SCC held that in the case in question, what the court was asked to do was to adjudicate on the compatibility of the Slovak implementing act with the Slovak Constitution. According to the view of the SCC, no issue of interpretation of Community law could thus arise in such a case.

This view is questionable. As is apparent from the case itself, one of the core issues was the notion of affirmative measures under Community law and the definition of equality. The content of these notions defines the (in)correctness of the domestic implementation of the Directive. Additionally, the SCC itself referred in its decision to the case law of the European Court of Justice,[76] thus indirectly admitting that it was interpreting some EC law. To maintain, under these circumstances, that no issue of interpretation of Community law could possibly arise in the particular case, is difficult.

Another significant decision of the SCC as far as preliminary rulings are concerned is the Order of 29 May 2007,[77] in which the SCC showed itself ready to supervise and, if necessary, to enforce the duty incumbent on the courts of last instance to refer requests for preliminary rulings to the European Court of Justice. The case came to the SCC as a constitutional complaint against a decision rendered by the Supreme Court. The claimant argued that his right to fair trial and the right to the lawful judge have been violated by the refusal by the SSC to submit a reference to the ECJ.

The SCC did not rule out the possibility that the violation of a duty to make a reference under Article 234(3) EC could amount to the breach of the right to lawful judge and to fair trial. In the particular case, however, the SCC observed, with a reference to the *Ynos* decision of the European Court of Justice,[78] that as the facts of the case had taken place before the accession of Slovakia to the European Union, the SSC could not have violated its duty to make a reference. Had it made the reference, it would have been declared inadmissible by the European Court of Justice.

It appears, nonetheless, that the SCC might be ready to adopt the German-Austrian model of the enforcement of the duty to make references to the European Court of

---

[74] Order of the SCC (full court) of 12 May 2005, case no PL ÚS 8/04-196, available at http://www.concourt.sk.

[75] This reading of the decision is supported by the views expressed by the then Chief Justice of the SCC, Mr. Jan Mazák, writing extra-judicially in: J. Mazák, 'Príspevok Ústavného súdu Slovenskej republiky pri uplatňování práv a plnení povinností na komunitárnej úrovni', 6 *EMP Jurisprudence* (2005) pp. 11-14. See also the same text published in English as 'The Constitutional Court of the Slovak Republic and its Contribution to the Enforcement of Rights and Obligations Created at the Community Level', in *EIF Working Paper Series – 1 Jahr EU Mitgliedschaft: Erste Bilanz aus der Sicht der slowakischen Höchstgerichte, Working Paper* No. 18 (Vienna, Austrian Academy of Science 2005).

[76] Finding of the SCC (full court) of 18 October 2005, case no PL. ÚS 8/04-202, no 539/2005 Coll., para. 18. The SCC referred to the ECJ, Case C-222/84 *Johnston v. Chief Constable of the Royal Ulster Constabulary* [1986] *ECR* 1651 and Case C-285/98 *Tanja Kreil v. Bundesrepublik Deutschland* [2000] *ECR* I-69.

[77] Order of the SCC of 29 May 2007, case no III. ÚS 151/07, available at http:// www.concourt.sk.

[78] ECJ, Case C-302/04 *Ynos kft v. János Varga* [2006] *ECR* I-371.

Justice via constitutional complaint.[79] From the practice of these systems, it seems that a Constitutional Court can enforce the duty to make a reference by the courts of general jurisdiction provided that two conditions are satisfied. First, there is a separate and concentrated review of constitutionality, which also allows for the review of last instance judicial decisions before the Constitutional Court. Second, the system knows the right to a lawful judge or has inferred it from more general rights, such as the right to fair trial, and is ready to consider the European Court of Justice to be, in proceedings before last instance courts, a lawful judge of its own.[80]

The Slovak constitutional system, together with the Czech, Austrian or German one, does fulfil these criteria. Should the SCC decide to follow this option, the incentive for courts of general jurisdiction to submit requests for preliminary rulings to the European Court of Justice would doubtless be stronger.

## 6. INFRINGEMENTS AND DIRECT ACTIONS

So far, there have been only two judgments rendered in infringement proceedings against Slovakia. In its decision of 8 February 2007,[81] the European Court of Justice held that Slovakia had failed to fulfil its obligation under the Treaty by not securing the interoperability of the trans-European high-speed rail system.[82] The failure to implement was not contested by Slovakia. The decision of the ECJ did not stir any controversy on the national level. In the second decision of 25 July 2008, the ECJ held that Slovakia was in breach of the EC Treaty.[83] The case concerned a failure on the part of Slovakia to ensure that that undertakings which operate public telephone networks make caller location information available to authorities handling emergencies for calls to the single European emergency call number 112.[84]

---

[79] For Germany, see, e.g., BVerfGE 82, 159 or BVerfGE of 9 January 2001, 1 BvR 1036/99 (=NJW 2001, 1267). Further, see, e.g., A. Vosskuhle, 'Zur verfassungsgerechtlichen Überprüfung der Pflicht der Fachgerichte, Rechtsfragen dem EuGH vorzulegen', *Juristische Zeitung* 18/2001. With respect to Austria, see the finding of the Austrian Constitutional Court of 11 December 1995, case no B 2300/95, WBl 1996, 24; finding of 30 September 1996, case no B 3067/95, WBl 1997, 86 and finding of 26 June 1997, case no B 3486/96, WBl 1997, 444. Further on Austria, see N. Solar, *Vorlagepflichtverletzung mitgliedstaatlicher Gerichte und ihre Sanierung* (Wien, Neuer Wissenschaftlicher Verlag 2004).

[80] For further details, see M. Bobek, '*Porušení povinnosti zahájit řízení o předběžné otázce podle čl. 234 (3) SES'* [Violation of the Duty to Make a Preliminary Reference under Art. 234(3) EC] (Prague, C.H. Beck 2004) p. 58.

[81] ECJ, Case C-114/06 *Commission of the European Communities v. the Slovak Republic* [2007] *ECR* I-18.

[82] As it was obliged to do by virtue of the Council Directive 96/48/EC of 23 July 1996 on the interoperability of the trans-European high-speed rail system, *OJ* 1996 L 235/6.

[83] ECJ, Case C-493/07 *Commission of the European Communities v. the Slovak Republic* [2008] *ECR* nyr.

[84] Obligations of transposition flowing from Directive 2002/22/EC of the European Parliament and of the Council of 7 March 2002, on universal service and users' rights relating to electronic communications networks and services (Universal Service Directive), *OJ* 2002 L 108/51.

Direct actions filed by Slovakia against the Community institutions are quite similar to those filed by the other new Member States. They concern, first, the validity of the Commission Decision C (2007) 1979 final of 4 May 2007 on the determination of surplus stocks of agricultural products other than sugar,[85] i.e., the validity of a measure that has been attacked by quite a few of the new Member States concerned.[86]

The second of the direct actions has a more intriguing background. It concerns, similar to the case of the Czech Republic,[87] the national plan for the allocation of greenhouse gas emission allowances submitted by Slovakia.[88] The Commission's refusal to accept the Slovak national allocation plan has, however, been attacked not only by the Slovak Government but also by the greatest Slovak $CO_2$ emitter – U.S. Steel Košice. The company is the only integrated steel producer in Slovakia. In its original national allocation plan, Slovakia intended to allocate an average of 41.3 million tonnes of $CO_2$ equivalent per year in total, of which approximately 12 million tonnes were allocated to U.S. Steel Košice. The Commission reduced this plan by one-fourth, cutting it down to about 31 million tonnes. The action for annulment brought by U.S. Steel Košice was declared inadmissible because of the lack of standing.[89] Considering the strict view of the European Court of Justice on standing for individual applicants, the producer was quite predictably not directly and individually concerned by the Commission's decision, despite the fact that, following the one-fourth cut decided by the Commission, its allocation quota would almost inevitably have to be reduced. It is notable that the European Court of Justice rejected an appeal as not admissible.[90]

A glance at the handful of other direct actions, submitted by Slovak companies,[91] demonstrates that so far, the access to the EU courts is an issue of big national industrial players. From these cases, the ongoing *Frucona v. Commission* litigation is an instructive example for realising the multilevel kind of litigation typical for the European legal environment. The case concerns the granting of illegal state aid to a Slovak company Frucona. The company produces agricultural products (canned fruit, vegetables and juices) and, until recently, also produced spirits. Following some financial difficulties, the company declared bankruptcy and applied for the protection of courts under the Slovak Bankruptcy Act. The protection was granted, and the company was allowed to restructure; in the course of the restructuring process, the Slovak State waived a tax

---

[85] Action brought on 11 July 2007, Case T-247/07 *the Slovak Republic v. Commission of the European Communities*, OJ 2007 C 211/47.

[86] Case T-243/07 *Republic of Poland v. Commission of the European Communities*, OJ 2007 C 211/45, Case T-248/07 *Czech Republic v. Commission of the European Communities*, OJ 2007 C 211/48; Case T-262/07 *Republic of Lithuania v. Commission of the European Communities*, OJ 2007 C 211/53.

[87] Case T-194/07 *Czech Republic v. Commission of the European Communities*, OJ 2007 C 199/38.

[88] Case T-32/07 *Slovak Republic v. Commission of the European Communities*, OJ 2007 C 69/29.

[89] CFI, Case T-27/07 *U.S. Steel Košice s.r.o. v. Commission of the European Communities* [2007] ECR II-128.

[90] ECJ, Case C-6/08P *U.S. Steel Košice s.r.o. v. Commission of the European Communities* [2008] ECR nyr.

[91] E.g., Case T-11/07 *Frucona Košice v. Commission*, OJ 2007 C 56/36. See also, CFI Case T-22/07 *US Steel Košice v. Commission of the European Communities* [2009] ECR nyr.

debt of 416.5 million Slovak kronas (approximately 10.4 million euros). The European Commission considered that this write-off of a tax debt amounted to state aid incompatible with the Common Market and requested its repayment.[92] On 21 November 2008, the European Commission brought an action to the European Court of Justice, arguing that by failing to execute this decision, Slovakia is in breach of Article 249 EC (the obligation to give EC decisions effect).[93]

The pending direct action before the Court of First Instance, by which Frucona seeks the annulment of the Commission's decision, is quite a predictable consequence of the Commission's decision. The more unexpected dimension of the litigation occurred on the national level before the Slovak courts. The *Krajký súd v Košiciach* [Regional Court in Košice] was the competent judicial body which, after the Slovak accession to the European Union, approved the proposed restructuring of the company (including the tax debt write-off).[94] The SSC, seized by an extraordinary complaint by the state attorney, refused to deal with the issue.[95] Under EC law, however, both courts were under an obligation to enforce the "standstill" provision, contained in Article 88(3) EC and to prevent the award of potential state aid or at least defer its payment to the moment after the European Commission has had the occasion to decide on its compatibility with the Internal Market.[96] However, neither of the deciding courts seemed to have been aware of the Community dimension to the dispute and the fact that they were supposed to apply EC state aid rules *ex officio*. On the other hand, following the Commission's decision declaring the state aid incompatible with the Common Market and requesting the Slovak Republic to secure its repayment,[97] it would appear that the Slovak courts would get a second chance for enforcing Community state aid rules on the national level.

## 7. CONCLUSIONS

This chapter demonstrates that arguably Europe has yet to come to Slovakia. The first five years of the membership in the European Union have been relatively calm, and the Slovak legal community avoided constitutional dramas comparable to some other new Member States. At the same time, the reasons for such quietness vary and spread from lack of preparedness on the side of the judiciary through initial limited access to *acquis* and case law in Slovakian to natural limits of a relatively small country with less than impressive numbers of litigation. A few examples of judgments presented in section

---

[92] Commission's Decision of 7 June 2006, C (2006) 2082 final, in state aid Case No C25/2005, available online in full-text at http://ec.europa.eu/comm/competition/state_aid/register/ii/.

[93] Case C-507/08 *Commission of the European Communities v. Slovak Republic*, OJ 2009 C 102/9.

[94] Order of the Regional Court in Košice of 20 July 2004, case no 3V 1/04, unpublished.

[95] Order of the SSC of 25 October 2004, case no 2 Obo 192/04, unpublished.

[96] As interpreted by the case law of the European Court of Justice – summary provided by the Commission Notice on co-operation between national courts and the Commission in the State aid field, OJ 1995 C 312/8.

[97] Arts. 1 and 2 of the Commission Decision of 7 April 2006 on State aid C 25/2005 (ex NN 21/2005) implemented by the Slovak Republic for FRUCONA Košice, a.s., OJ 2007 L 112/14.

4.1. give a bit of hope that EU law is slowly paving its way in the Slovak judiciary, and more robust enforcement is just a question of time. The same, hopefully, goes for the preliminary ruling procedure, which for the time being, has been employed in a very modest fashion by Slovak courts.

*Chapter 12*

# THE APPLICATION OF EU LAW IN HUNGARY: CHALLENGES AND EMERGING PRACTICES

Tamara Takács*

## 1.   INTRODUCTION

The requirements set for national courts to apply European Union law as "European courts" – going beyond their function to provide effectiveness to their national laws – translate into legal procedural consequences and a significant change to methodology, practices and attitudes. The challenges that Hungarian courts face in applying EU law indisputably resemble those of the other countries discussed in this volume. National particularities arise in the Member States on approaches, structural and operational solutions that national courts had employed in the preparation for EU membership and in the first years after the accession. The aim of the present chapter is to illustrate the response of Hungarian courts to the challenges that the application of EU law has brought. In addition, attention will be paid to general aspects of accommodating EU law in the Hungarian legal system, with particular regard to the approach of the Constitutional Court to the principle of supremacy of Community law. The interaction between national courts and the European Court of Justice will be analysed through the discussion of important aspects of the preliminary ruling procedure, which has been eagerly employed by Hungarian courts. Compliance with the obligation to implement EU law is one important prerequisite for its successful application; therefore, attention will be given to the implementation practices that characterise Hungary as a Member State. In this context, special attention will be paid to the infraction procedure. Finally, the interaction between the national level on the one hand, and the EU courts and indirectly the EU law-making machinery on the other hand, will be discussed through the actions for annulment submitted by Hungary as well as challenges submitted to the Court of First Instance by individuals.

## 2.   OVERVIEW OF THE HUNGARIAN JUDICIARY

The illustration of the practice of the Hungarian judiciary in the application of EU law requires an introduction to the legal, procedural and operative settings in which these

* Assistant Professor at the Europa Instituut, School of Law, University of Utrecht, The Netherlands.

*A. Łazowski (ed.), The Application of EU Law in the New Member States*
© *2010, T·M·C·Asser press, The Hague, The Netherlands and the Authors*

courts are functioning. This overview is necessary since the judiciary and its function to secure the rule of law were given primary attention in the overall political and constitutional reform that followed the change of political regime and constituted an important building block in the transition from communism to democracy. The position of the Constitutional Court deserves special attention as – being outside the judiciary structure – it plays a significantly different role from ordinary courts.

## 2.1.   The reform of the Hungarian judiciary following the fall of the Communist regime

The status of the judiciary during Communist times was, not surprisingly, dominantly linked to the executive branch. Consequently, the executive, under the competence of the Minister of Justice, had control and overview over the administration of all courts. Through supervision over the functioning of courts, the Minister of Justice had the competence to constantly guide and examine professional judicial activity, and this forceful interference significantly toned down the Supreme Court's responsibility of giving professional guidance to courts and judges.[1] In this manner, the separation of powers was greatly undermined.

The overall reform following the change of regime took a legal and political start with the amendment of the Constitution in October 1989. The Constitution granted the much-desired independence and impartiality of judges.[2] An additional and subsequent feature that served as a catalyst for the reform of the judiciary was the aspiration to bring Hungarian courts in line with "European" standards. To this end, attempts were made to adjust their operation to the practices established by the courts of the EU Member States. More importantly, preparatory work took place so that upon the accession, judges would apply and give effect to EU law. The role of the European Union in this process was to clarify standards for the membership. In 2002, the European Commission launched an Action Plan for each candidate's judiciary, accompanied by special financial assistance to reinforce its administrative and judicial capacity.[3]

Bearing in mind these principles, circumstances and aspirations, in 1997, the Hungarian Parliament adopted a comprehensive judicial reform package, introducing a considerable number of novelties. The subsequent amendments to the Civil and Criminal Procedure Codes fine-tuned these newly introduced guarantees. The reform added an additional layer to the structure of the court system and shaped it in the following way. The Local Courts and District Courts, with general jurisdiction, hear first instance cases.[4] The jurisdiction of the County Courts and the Metropolitan Court of Budapest coincide with the units of public administration; thus, these 20 courts act as

---

[1] 'The Judicial reform in Hungary', available at the Supreme Court's website at http://www.lb.hu.
[2] Art. 50(3) of Hungarian Constitution reads: 'Judges are independent and answer only to the law. Judges may not be members of political parties and may not engage in political activities.'
[3] 'Monitoring the EU Accession Process: Judicial Capacity', *Open Society Institute* (2002) p. 19.
[4] Art. 10(1) Act No. III of 1952 *Polgári perrendtartásról szóló törvény* [Civil Procedure Code].

first instance courts in specific types of cases[5] and, moreover, serve as courts of appeal for the decisions of Local or District Courts. The newly introduced (1 January 2005) Regional Courts of appeal function as appellate courts against decisions of Local or County Courts. The latter reform contributed to the reduction of the Supreme Court's workload.[6] The Supreme Court is at the apex of the judicial system. Per the Hungarian Constitution, it has the obligation to provide the unity and consistency of the legal system. The Supreme Court reviews decisions of the lower-level courts, adjudicates on petitions for review and adopts obligatory uniformity decisions applicable to the courts.[7]

As to the administration of the judicial system, the Hungarian Judicial Council and its Office were established to secure the impartiality that is required (as opposed to the dominance of the executive during the communist regime). The competence of the Judicial Council extends from personnel issues (appointing and dismissing the presidents and vice-presidents of County Courts and Regional Courts of appeals, making recommendations to the President of the Republic on the nomination or relief of judges, preliminary opinions on persons nominated for a president and vice-president of the Supreme Court) to monitoring the administrative activity of the presidents of courts (except that of the Supreme Court). It also includes preparation of the budget proposal regarding the chapter on courts as well as the implementation of this chapter with regard to previous years.[8]

Education and infrastructure constituted important prerequisites for successful application of EU law. Before accession, Government Resolutions No. 2282/1996. (X. 25.) and 2212/1998. (IX. 30.) targeted preparation of the judiciary for application of Community law, and the National Judicial Council devoted particular attention to this objective through programming and implementation of the training programmes. The training programmes, involving experts and trainers from "old" Member States, received positive evaluation in Annual Reports published by the European Commission.[9] Continual education and training of judges and judicial staff provided the opportunity for gradually catching up on the grey areas that were present with regard to knowledge of EU law and its effects on the national legal order. The idea of a specialised training institution first emerged in 2000 and was laid down in a Decision of the National Council of Justice, and the realisation of the idea (with significant assistance from the European

---

[5] In civil cases, when the legal issue exceeds 5 million forints and in copyright cases; in all administrative cases and in criminal cases of homicide, terrorism and trafficking in human beings.

[6] Act No. XXXVII of 2002 modifying Act No. LXVI of 1997 on the organisation and administration of courts [A bíróságok szervezetéről és igazgatásáról szóló törvény] and Act No. LXVII of 1997 on the status and remuneration of judges [A bírák jogállásáról és javadalmazásáról szóló törvény].

[7] Art. 47 of Constitution and Act No. LXVI of 1997 A bíróságok szervezetéről és igazgatásáról szóló törvény [Act on the Organisation and Administration of Courts].

[8] Act No. LXVI of 1997 A bíróságok szervezetéről és igazgatásáról szóló törvény [Act on the Organisation and Administration of Courts].

[9] Előterjesztés Az Országos Igazságszolgáltatási Tanács részére a bíróságok központi oktatási tervéről (2003. szeptember 1-től 2004. június 30-ig) [Report to the National Judicial Council regarding the central training plan of the judiciary (September 2003-June 2004) 28 024 /2003 OIT. p. 2. Cited by L. Kecskés, et al., Átvilágító tanulmány a magyar igazságszolgáltatás helyzetéről és az 1997. évi reformtörvények hatályosulásáról [Overview of the status of the Hungarian judiciary and the implications of the reforms adopted in 1997] (Pécs 2007) at p. 390.

Union reaching 1.78 million euros) finally led to the establishment of the Hungarian Academy of Judges.[10] The Hungarian Academy of Judges offers a wide-ranging selection of courses to judges and staff members of courts. It is a truly outstanding institution, gaining a well-deserved prestigious status ever since it started functioning in 2006 and is expected to become even more important once the planned e-learning is introduced as planned.[11] Modernising the work of courts with computers, databases and internet-access largely contributed to the effectiveness of adjudication and well-established functioning of the courts. In programmes of assistance provided by the EU, such as the PHARE programme, important steps were made to improve the serious lagging behind that courts were facing in this matter.

## 2.2.    The Constitutional Court's position in the national constitutional order

One of the major novelties in the political and constitutional order was the creation of the Constitutional Court. The Constitutional Court is the main body for safeguarding the Constitution; its tasks include reviewing the constitutionality of statutes and safe-guarding the constitutional order and fundamental rights guaranteed by the Constitution. The Hungarian Constitutional Court is not integrated in the judiciary and, therefore, is not regarded as a court functioning based on adversarial proceedings. This institutional separation between the Constitutional Court and the system of ordinary courts (including the Supreme Court) was laid down upon the establishment of the new Constitution in 1989 and has been confirmed ever since.[12] The Act on the Constitutional Court reinforces the division, while stipulating the roles and competences of the Constitutional Court. The Constitutional Court's role revolves around the interpretation of the Constitution and lies in the review of the constitutionality of laws as well as the protection of fundamental rights laid down in the Constitution and the constitutional order in general.[13] In terms of principles of constitutional law, the Constitutional Court is, therefore, regarded as an important actor in the system of checks and balances and carries out so-called "negative legislation" controlling the constitutionality of legal acts produced by the legislature.

---

[10] More information on the Academy of Judges is available at its homepage http://www.mba.birosag. hu.

[11] I. Lóránt, 'A Magyar Bíróképző Akadémia' [The Hungarian Academy of Judges], 11 *De Jure* (2006) pp. 20-21.

[12] Constitution Art. 45(1): 'In the Republic of Hungary justice is administered by the Supreme Court of the Republic of Hungary, the appeals courts, the Municipal Court of Budapest, the county courts and the local and labour courts.' For a confirmation provided by scholars, see A. Badó and J. Bóka, *Európa kapujában, Reform, Igazság, Szolgáltatás* [In the Gates of Europe. Reform, Justice, Service] (Miskolc, Bíbor Kiadó 2002) at p. 18.

[13] Constitution Art. 32/A(1): 'The Constitutional Court shall review the constitutionality of laws and attend to the duties assigned to its jurisdiction by law.' (2): The Constitutional Court shall annul any laws and other statutes that it finds to be unconstitutional.'

3. THE CONSTITUTIONAL AMENDMENT AS A PART OF THE PRE-ACCESSION PREPARATION AND AN APPRAISAL OF THE AUTHORISING ARTICLE

A constitutional amendment was widely considered in Hungary as an essential part of the preparation for EU membership. It was all the more important since the Constitution had not – until that point – contained any provisions on the country's membership in international organisations. In the late 1990s, at the governmental level, awareness and preparation increased gradually following initial attempts at a constitutional amendment.[14] In 2000, a proposal prepared by the Ministry of Justice was submitted to the government. This proposal provided the underlying framework for another document drafted by the Ministry of Justice in 2002 ('Theses on the amendment of the Constitution and the Act on Legislation in the light of the EU accession').[15] This document drew up general guidelines for the legal/constitutional adaptation, including the need for an authorising article in the Constitution. In academic circles, the need to establish such an authorising article in the Constitution was also emphasised.[16] In November 2002, a political agreement between parties represented in the Parliament outlined a general compromise on a constitutional amendment. However, to transform this political compromise into an act of Parliament proved to be very difficult. The reason for a particularly "painful" adoption procedure lays in the revision of the Hungarian Constitution, which required a two-thirds majority of 386 members of the Parliament. This requirement in itself would not seem to be an insurmountable obstacle, considering that the Hungarian Parliament is unicameral, and a national referendum was not required (unlike some countries where referenda for such purposes are inevitable). However, in the case of Hungary, one must look at the political reality. In fact, the underlying factors that caused an obstacle to the adoption of the constitutional amendment were fundamentally irreconcilable political forces within the Parliament. Finally, after debates, conciliation and constitutional drafts of varying quality in political and legal terms, the Parliament adopted the Act amending the Constitution.

---

[14] The first document AEB/1/2/1997 was prepared by the Parliamentary Committee charged with the preparation of the constitutional amendment and was dated 3 February 1997.

[15] *Tézisek az Európai Uniós csatlakozásunkkal összefüggésben az Alkotmány és a jogalkotási törvény módosításáról* [Theses on the amendment of the Constitution and the Act on Legislation in the light of the EU accession] IM/EUR/2002/TERVEZET/287/12, Budapest July 2002. See also N. Chronowski and J. Petrétei, 'Előkészületben az Európai Unióhoz való csatlakozással összefüggő alkotmánymódosítás' [In preparation for the constitutional amendment with regard to EU accession], 2 *JURA* (2002) pp. 115-124.

[16] Chronowski and Petrétei, *loc. cit.* n. 15. See also M. Ficsor, 'Megjegyzések az európai közösségi jog és a nemzeti alkotmány viszonyáról I-II' [Comments on the relationship between European Community Law and the national constitutions Part I and II], 8-9 *Magyar Jog* (1997) pp. 462-473 and pp. 526-534; N. Chronowski, *Integrálódó alkotmányjog* [Integrating constitutional law] (Pécs, Dialóg Campus 2005) at p. 175.

The amendment of the Constitution tackled multiple issues,[17] one of them being the introduction of a "Europe-clause". As far as the authorising article is concerned, the Act amending the Constitution inserted Article 2/A and provided:

'(1) By virtue of a treaty, the Republic of Hungary, in its capacity as a Member State of the European Union, may exercise certain constitutional powers jointly with other Member States to the extent necessary for the exercise of rights and fulfilment of obligations conferred by the treaties on the foundation of the European Union and the European Communities (hereinafter referred to as 'European Union'); these powers may be exercised independently and by way of the institutions of the European Union.
(2) The ratification and promulgation of the treaty referred to in subsection (1) shall be subject to a two-thirds majority vote of the Parliament.'[18]

In addition, Hungary's accession to the EU, as a general aim of foreign policy, was inserted amongst the state's aims in Article 6(4) of the Constitution,[19] stating that:

'the Republic of Hungary shall participate in establishing European unity for the accomplishment of freedom, welfare and safety of the European peoples.'

As can be seen from the wording of the Hungarian "Europe-clause" instead of a general reference to international organisations or a supranational organisation, the Hungarian Constitution now provides for the transfer of powers to the European Union, unmistakably demonstrating that the provision was inserted in order and with reference to the constitutional preparation for EU membership.[20] The Article furthermore contains an explicit reference to the European Union. The Article speaks about the aim and limit of the transfer of competences but does not provide for guarantees protecting the constitutional establishment in Hungary.[21] Furthermore, the provision remains silent on which obligations precisely stem from the membership. Here the drafters should have perhaps narrowed the scope of obligations by mentioning basic principles, (e.g.,

---

[17] The constitutional amendment touched upon the following issues: the transfer of competences Art. 2A(1), the position of the Hungarian National Bank Art. 32/D(1), the Government's participation in EU decision-making procedures Art. 35A(1), the Government's obligation to submit proposals on the EU decision-making agenda to the Parliament Art. 35A(2), the right to vote and to be elected in municipal elections and EP elections Arts. 70(2)-(4).

[18] The translation of the provision is taken from the website of the Hungarian Constitutional Court, which is available at http://www.mkab.hu.

[19] At the initiative of the Hungarian Democratic Forum, a small opposition party in this parliamentary cycle.

[20] Such an arrangement was also welcomed by J. Czuczai in 'Kritikai meglátások a kormánynak a Magyar Köztársaság Alkotmányáról szóló 1949.évi XX. Tv-nek az EU csatlakozást érintően szükséges módosításáról szóló T/1114 számú törvényjavaslatáról' [Critical observations on Bill proposal No. T/1114 on the amendment of the Hungarian Constitution with regard the EU accession], *Európa 2002* (2001) p. 2. See also J. Czuczai, 'Hungary', in A.E. Kellermann, J. Czuczai, S. Blockmans, A. Albi, W.Th. Douma, eds., *The Impact of EU Accession on the Legal Orders of New Member States and (Pre-) Candidate Countries. Hopes and Fears* (The Hague, T.M.C. Asser Press 2006) pp. 343-369, at p. 345.

[21] N. Chronowski, *Constitution and Constitutional Principles in the EU* (Pécs, Dialóg Campus 2005) at p. 130.

the application of Community law, the principle of loyal co-operation) to illustrate what kind of obligations they mean instead of such a generally worded definition.

In the Constitutional Court's jurisprudence, the interpretation of Article 2/A did not appear to add much during the first years of EU membership. In June 2006, the Constitutional Court regarded the Hungarian "Europe-clause" as one that:

'lays down the conditions and framework for Hungary's membership in the European Union and identifies the position of Community law within the Hungarian system of sources of law.'[22]

However, in reality, one can clearly see that the said provision does not contain specific reference to the relationship between EU law and national law. In 2008, progressive views were aired relating to the content of Article 2/A, and the Constitutional Court's interpretation provided a more elaborate position on its interpretation. This time the Court reaffirmed that Article 2/A essentially provides for the conditions and framework for Hungary's membership in the European Union and underscored that according to the provision:

'[T]he Hungarian Republic may enter an international treaty so as to exercise some of its constitutional powers jointly with other EU Member States or so that the joint exercise would be conducted by the institutions of the European Union.'

The progressive element in the decision focused on the limitations to the exercise of competences by the EU. The Court on this point emphasised that:

'[T]he exercise of competences can only be conducted to the extent which is necessary for the exercise of rights and fulfilment of obligations stemming from membership; and the extent of the jointly exercise-able constitutional competences is limited.'[23] [Author's translation]

## 4. SUPREMACY OF COMMUNITY LAW IN THE CONSTITUTIONAL COURT'S JURISPRUDENCE: BEFORE AND AFTER ACCESSION

Although the Constitutional Court is not part of the judiciary, its decisions in relation to the applicability of Community law in the national legal order have far-reaching consequences, *inter alia*, for national courts.

The first interpretative guidance on the pre-accession application of Community law was given by the Constitutional Court in late 1990s. It was binding not only for

---

[22] Constitutional Court Decision 1053/E/2005 AB határozat, 6 *ABK* 2006 p. 498. Available at the Constitutional Court's website at http://www.mkab.hu.hu/frisshat.htm. See also E. Vàrnay and A.F. Tatham, 'A New Step on the Long Way – How to Find a proper Place for Community Law in the Hungarian Legal Order?', 3 *MJIL* (2006) pp. 76-84.

[23] Constitutional Court Decision 61/B/2005 AB határozat. See N. Chronowski, 'Független állam – avagy a szuverenitás átértékelése' [Independent State- reconsidering sovereignty], presentation at the conference 'Egy független ország' held at the Eötvös Károly Intézet, 14 October 2008.

national courts but also national authorities in general. The details surrounding these interpretations also serve to illustrate the preliminary aspects of the Constitutional Court's approach to the relationship between Hungarian and EC legal orders.[24] In an early decision of 1997,[25] the Constitutional Court closely explored the Europe Agreement which provided the underlying legal framework for the pre-accession period and contained rules on the obligations leading up to the country's accession to the EU.[26] This decision primarily focused on the evergreen issue of the position of public international law in domestic law (thus, the dualism-monism dichotomy), and in our case, it applied to the Europe Agreement in the Hungarian legal order, expanding the analysis to the question of supremacy of EC law. This decision, as will be demonstrated, proved to be instrumental in defining, among other things, the Constitutional Court's position with regard to Community law and it revealed a similarity with the attitudes of German judges (due to the resemblance of the respective legal cultures and traditions).

The Constitutional Court carried out the analysis based on its competence for an *ex post* review of international agreements. As this decision primarily touched upon the issue of the position of international law in the domestic legal order, with particular emphasis on EC law, one should bear in mind the fact that the decision was rendered at a time when Community law, as well as EA Hungary, was regarded by the Constitutional Court as part of public international law.

The Court started off by explaining how its competence to review extends to the constitutionality of international agreements to which Hungary has agreed. By doing so, the Court referred to one of its previous decisions,[27] in which it had extensively interpreted Article 7(1) of the Constitutional Act, which describes the relationship between international law and domestic law. Article 7(1) provides that:

'The legal system of the Republic of Hungary accepts generally recognised principles of international law, and shall harmonise the country's domestic law with the obligations assumed under international law.'

This Article has been regarded as ambiguous and elusive, and while it does not regulate explicitly the position of international law, it indicates that the Hungarian system is dualist.[28] As the courts practically completely ignored international law as a source of law during the Communist times,[29] a clear-cut establishment of such a relationship

---

[24] N. Chronowski and T. Drinóczi, 'A Triangular Relationship between Public International Law, EC Law and National Law? A Case of Hungary' in J. Wouters, et al., eds., *The Europeanisation of International Law, The Status of International Law in the EU and its Member States* (The Hague, T.M.C. Asser Press 2008) pp. 161-185.

[25] Decision of the Constitutional Court No. 4/1997. (I.22.) ABH [Gazette of Decisions of the Hungarian Constitutional Court] 1997. 41.

[26] Europe Agreement establishing an association between the European Communities and their Member States, of the one part, and the Republic of Hungary, of the other part, *OJ* 1993 L 347/268.

[27] Decision of the Constitutional Court No. 53/1993 (X.13.).

[28] Chronowski and Drinóczi, *loc. cit.* n. 24.

[29] In a scholarly article published in the Hungarian Judges' Journal, Gábor Palásti reveals the passivity that the courts displayed to the application, exploration and consideration of such external laws in cases pending before them. See G. Palásti, 'Az Európai Unió jogának szupremáciája és a tagállamok jogszol-

would have been of the utmost importance in the run-up to accession, as was urged by scholars.[30] This is all the more so since the Constitutional Court has pointed out that it is the Constitution itself that transposes generally accepted principles of international law into the national legal order, and thus, it emphasised the dualist character. The Court argued that the synthesis required by Article 7 had to be achieved by taking into account three levels of norms and obligations: the Constitution itself, obligations under international law and obligations under domestic law. These three levels had to be examined with regard to each other. Therefore, the Court found that the analysis of an international obligation undertaken in the form of a treaty should be carried out – *a priori* or *ex post* – with the Constitution in the background as the highest in the hierarchy of norms. Thus, the Constitutional Court retained for itself the competence to constitutionally control norms that proclaim international agreements and set the Constitution as the point of reference.

This decision also explored the actual consequences of such *ex post* control of norms proclaiming international agreements and argued that the review can be applied to an international agreement which became part of a proclaiming norm. The Court ruled that if it finds an international agreement or a part thereof to be unconstitutional, a norm proclaiming such an agreement will be declared unconstitutional, but such a decision by the Court cannot release the country from international obligations it has undertaken under an agreement. Here, the Constitutional Court apparently took into account the principle of *pacta sunt servanda*, which was incorporated into the Vienna Convention on International Treaties in Articles 26-27 and 46 and is also a general principle of public international law.[31] The Court also pointed out that if it controls the conformity of an international treaty with domestic law, and there is incompatibility between the two, the Court will only give priority to an international treaty that has been transposed by a national measure if this transposing measure ranks higher in the hierarchy of norms than acts with which it is incompatible. Thus, public international law enjoys supremacy over domestic law, but as has been confirmed, it could never do so with regard to the Constitution.

The Constitutional Court then closely examined the nature of Community law and its relationship with domestic law. It referred to findings and reactions of other Constitutional Courts *vis-à-vis* the development of the Community's legal order. In this

---

gáltatása' [The supremacy of European law and the judiciary of Member States] 2-4 *Bírák Lapja* (1995) pp. 127-129, referred to by Badó and Bóka, see *loc. cit.* n. 12 at p. 50.

[30] J. Németh, 'Az európai integráció és a magyar Alkotmány' [European Integration and the Hungarian Constitution] in A. Bragyova, ed., *Nemzetközi jog az új Alkotmányban* [International law in the new Constitution] (Budapest, Economic and Legal Publishing House, Hungarian Academy of Sciences, Institute of State and Legal Science 1997) at p. 107; N. Chronowski: *Integrálódó alkotmányjog. Az Európai Unió és a Magyar Köztársaság alkotmányos rendszerének kapcsolata* [Constitutional law through integration. The relation between the European Union and the constitutional system of the Republic of Hungary] (Pécs, Dialóg 2004) at p. 85; T. Drinóczi, The Highs and Lows of International Law in the Hungarian System of Legal Sources, *"Adamante Notare" Essays in Honour of Professor Antal Ádám on the Occassion of his 75th Birthday* (Pécs, Dialóg 2005) pp. 469-488. See also Czuczai, *loc. cit.* n. 20, at pp. 343-368.

[31] M. Ficsor, 'Megjegyzések az európai közösségi jog és a nemzeti jog viszonyáról I' [Comments on the relationship between Community law and national law I.], *Magyar Jog,* pp. 462-473 at p. 463.

analysis, the Court devoted primary attention to findings of the German *Bundesverfas-sungsgericht*. The Constitutional Court clearly recognised the supremacy of EC law over domestic law, but emphasised that EC law is not given such priority with regard to the national Constitution.[32] So, the supremacy of EC law over sub-constitutional national law is accepted, but supremacy over the national Constitution is not. Therefore, the Constitutional Court retained the authority to review an international agreement which became domestic law via incorporation. On this point, the Hungarian justices referred to the German practice and especially to the decision on the constitutionality of the ratification of the Maastricht Treaty, arguing that Constitutional Courts cannot:

> 'relinquish fulfilling their function as the guardians of constitutionality, and that function includes every form of executing sovereignty based on the Basic Law; consequently, the Constitutional Court upholds its role with regard to reviewing the transfer of competences to the Community.'[33]

The Hungarian Constitutional Court also stated that as this decision was rendered before the accession to the European Union, thus neither the Constitutional Court nor other national authorities were obligated to recognise the supremacy of EC law.

This decision shows that the Constitutional Court, prior to accession and with regard to the position of other Constitutional Courts, recognised the underlying principles of supremacy and direct applicability. Nevertheless, it seemed to strive to maintain – following the example of *Bundesverfassungsgericht* – the right to oversee the transfer of competences and the exercise of transferred competences and to measure them against the national Constitution.

In another decision by the Constitutional Court (No. 30/1998) regarding the application of Community law raised with regard to the Europe Agreement, the dilemmas revolved around whether rights derived from an international treaty could be directly applicable, and, if so, how could individuals invoke these rights before courts. The Court referred to the second part of the same (previously analysed) claim that had been placed before it involving the Europe Agreement, in which the applicant directed the Court's attention to the fact that Article 62 EA Hungary ordered Hungarian competition authorities to apply certain Community criteria provided in the EC Treaty. Therefore, the Constitutional Court had to decide to what extent the provisions of EC Treaty on competition policy could be effective in the domestic legal system and whether to oblige national authorities to apply them prior to accession. To put it differently: could it be acceptable that the Europe Agreement referred to criteria provided by primary Community law and made it compulsory for national authorities to apply these criteria before EU law became applicable to Hungary?

In its decision, the Constitutional Court ruled that the Hungarian Parliament, by ratifying and proclaiming international agreements, should not amend the Constitution

---

[32] *Ibidem*, at p. 464.
[33] Constitutional Court Decision 4/1997 (I.22) ABH 1997, 51-52.

in a "disguised manner" by making an external legal order superior to it.[34] As Hungary was not a member of the European Union at that time, it would have been unconstitutional to transpose (incorporate) rules which had not been explicitly adopted by the Hungarian legislature. Thus, national authorities were not obliged to apply rules which had not been incorporated.[35] Therefore, the Hungarian Parliament could not agree to an international agreement that implied the transfer of competences exceeding what was confirmed for it by virtue of the Constitution. It was the national Constitution that should provide for the procedural rules of constitutionality for such a transfer.[36] The Constitutional Court here explicitly urged the insertion of an authorising article, with due consideration to the then already existing political aspiration of joining the EU and the preparation it entailed. Decision No. 30/1998 sees such an authorising article as a source of legitimacy for the exercise of competence by the Community *vis-à-vis* the national legal order. This would also bring the exercise of transferred competences into line with the guarantees laid down by Article 2(1) of the Constitution: an independent, democratic *Rechtstaat* and the sovereignty of the people. As the Constitutional Court put it:

'[I]t is a general guiding obligation that in the national jurisdiction all norms of public law applicable *vis-à-vis* domestic subjects of law emanate from democratic legitimacy and stem from the ultimate source of public authority.'[37]

In the present case, the fact that the Hungarian Parliament agreed to the Europe Agreement and ratified it does not imply the obligatory application of norms of an external legal order, as that would require legitimacy under the Constitution. This ruling puts the national Constitution in a primary position to provide legitimacy to the transfer of competences and limits the scope of a temporary application of EC law for a future Member State.

The relevant case law of the Constitutional Court rendered after Hungary's accession undoubtedly further raises many previously examined points. In particular, the review of an act implementing EU law and the question regarding the supremacy of Community law over national law and the national constitution was raised before the Constitutional Court practically immediately after Hungary joined the European Union. In its decision, the Constitutional Court further demonstrated the previously described "particular" attitude *vis-à-vis* EC law. In addition, the decision showed once again that the Hungarian Constitutional Court regards itself as the guardian of the Constitution and seems to largely identify its role as the guardian of national sovereignty, similar to the German

---

[34] Constitutional Court Decision No. 30/1998, (VI.25.) ABH Magyar Közlöny [Official Gazette] MK 1998/55.

[35] A. Harmathy, 'The Constitutional Court of the Republic of Hungary', in *The Position of Constitutional Courts Following the Integration Into the European Union, Conference Proceedings from Bled*, Slovenia, 30 September-2 October 2004, pp. 217-227, at p. 225. Text available at http://www.us-rs.si/media/zbornik.pdf.

[36] Decision of the Constitutional Court No. 30/1998, (VI.25.) ABH, Magyar Közlöny [Official Gazette] MK 1998/55.

[37] *Ibidem* [translation by the author].

*Bundesverfassungsericht,*[38] reserving for itself the authority to constitutionally review or control certain issues and to set limits on the competences of the ECJ.[39] The decision revolved around the constitutionality review of an Act of the Hungarian Parliament enacted on 5 April 2004, 'On measures concerning agricultural surplus stocks' (hereafter the Surplus Act).[40] This legislation was intended to implement Commission Regulation 1972/2003/EC on transitional measures to be adopted in respect to trade in agricultural products and Commission Regulation 60/2004/EC laying down transitional measures in the sugar sector.[41] The President of the Republic, instead of signing and promulgating the Act, sent it to the Constitutional Court for review as to its constitutionality. The Surplus Act was only scheduled to enter into force on 25 May 2004, while the obligations defined in the Surplus Act related to 1 May 2004, that is, the day of entry into force of the Accession Treaty.[42] The respective regulations stipulated that national law in question would enter into force on 1 May 2004, subject to the entry into force of the Treaty of Accession, and required the new Member States to develop and implement the relevant measures to be applicable as of 1 May 2004. The President claimed that the Surplus Act, with its entry into force on 25 May 2004, would have been retroactive and hence unconstitutional.[43]

The Constitutional Court agreed with this point and declared the implementing Surplus Act to be unconstitutional as it breached the principle of rule of law and violated legal certainty, which are both cornerstones of the Hungarian Constitution. They also were in breach of a principle of granting reasonable *vacatio legis* for measures imposing tax-related obligations. The decision thus referred to the principle that was established by the Constitutional Court and confirmed by the Constitution that Hungary

---

[38] As has been pointed out, references to the German Court as well as other traces and evidence of a similar legal heritage evidently demonstrated such an association as far as the Hungarian Court was concerned.

[39] Z. Kühn, 'The Application of European Law in the New Member States: Several (Early) Predictions', 6 *GLJ* (2005) pp. 563-582.

[40] Commission Regulation 1972/2003/EC of 10 November 2003 on transitional measures to be adopted in respect of trade in agricultural products on account of the accession of the Czech Republic, Estonia, Cyprus, Latvia, Lithuania, Hungary, Malta, Poland, Slovenia and Slovakia, *OJ* 2003 L 293/3.

[41] Commission Regulation 60/2004/EC of 14 January 2004 laying down transitional measures in the sugar sector by reason of the accession of the Czech Republic, Estonia, Cyprus, Latvia, Lithuania, Hungary, Malta, Poland, Slovenia and Slovakia, *OJ* 2004 L 9/8.

[42] Treaty between the Kingdom of Belgium, the Kingdom of Denmark, the Federal Republic of Germany, the Hellenic Republic, the Kingdom of Spain, the French Republic, Ireland, the Italian Republic, the Grand Duchy of Luxembourg, the Kingdom of the Netherlands, the Republic of Austria, the Portuguese Republic, the Republic of Finland, the Kingdom of Sweden, the United Kingdom of Great Britain and Northern Ireland (Member States of the European Union) and the Czech Republic, the Republic of Estonia, the Republic of Cyprus, the Republic of Latvia, the Republic of Lithuania, the Republic of Hungary, the Republic of Malta, the Republic of Poland, the Republic of Slovenia, the Slovak Republic, concerning the accession of the Czech Republic, the Republic of Estonia, the Republic of Cyprus, the Republic of Latvia, the Republic of Lithuania, the Republic of Hungary, the Republic of Malta, the Republic of Poland, the Republic of Slovenia and the Slovak Republic to the European Union , *OJ* 2003 L 236/17.

[43] A. Sajó, 'Learning Co-operative Constitutionalism the Hard Way: The Hungarian Constitutional Court Shying Away from EU Supremacy', 3 *ZSE* (2004) pp. 351-371, at p. 355. See also Czuczai, *loc. cit.* n. 20, pp. 343-368 and Chapter 3 in this volume.

is a state based on rule of law (*Rechtstaat*) where legal certainty is respected. The Hungarian Constitutional Court identified retroactive elements in the national provisions on surplus charges due on the basis of past stock averages, a matter and technique that was expressly authorised by the EC Regulations.[44] Thus, what was deemed to be in violation of legal certainty under the doctrines of the Hungarian Constitutional Court was expressly mandated by the EC Regulations. Consequently, the Constitutional Court held that the part of the Act which was actually aimed at implementing the EC Regulations was contrary to the Hungarian Constitution. The Court essentially found that the Parliamentary bill which introduced a legal obligation regarding agricultural surplus stocks gave too short a notice, thereby making it impossible for those affected to learn of their statutory duties in "due time".[45]

By this decision, the Constitutional Court essentially aimed to guarantee constitutional safeguards which had been achieved during the past century and which had been upgraded after the change in the regime, notably the fundamental right of legitimate expectations, non-retroactivity and the principle of the rule of law. In the decision, the Constitutional Court invalidated the Surplus Act by referring to national constitutional principles.

In its decision, the Court referred to transitional measures of previous enlargement rounds, relevant case law of the ECJ on this issue and even the fact that regulations are directly applicable in national legal orders. Nevertheless, the question of supremacy *per se* was not analysed by the Court.

5.      THE APPLICATION OF EUROPEAN UNION LAW BY ORDINARY
        COURTS: THE *SIMMENTHAL*-MANDATE AND OTHER
        CHALLENGES

The role of national courts to secure the application of EC law instead of a conflicting measure of national law is a primordial feature of the function of national judges in securing the uniform application and full effect of EC law. National courts of any rank are mandated to proceed with a compatibility check of national law with the relevant Community provision. This obligation has been reaffirmed by ECJ case law in the *Simmenthal* judgment[46] and reveals multiple questions with regard to legal and constitutional particularities of the Member States. Therefore, it is noteworthy to explore the status of the Hungarian courts with regard to the proper fulfilment of the so-called

---

[44] Sajó, *loc. cit.* n. 43, at p. 356.

[45] R. Uitz, 'EU Law and the Hungarian Constitutional Court, Lessons of the First Post-Accession Encounter', in W. Sadurski, et al., eds., *Après Enlargement, Legal and Political Responses in Central and Eastern Europe* RSCAS EUI 200, available at http://www.iue.it/LAW/Publications/WSJZApresEnlargement.shtml. See also A. Albi, 'Supremacy of EC Law in the New Member States Bringing Parliaments into the equation of 'Co-operative Constitutionalism', 3 *EuConst* (2007) pp. 25-67 at p. 49. Decision of the Constitutional Court No. 17/2004 (V.25.) ABH, Magyar Közlöny [Official Gazette] MK. 2004. 70.

[46] ECJ, Case 106/77 *Amministrazione delle Finanze dello Stato v. Simmenthal SpA* [1978] *ECR* 629.

"*Simmenthal*-mandate"[47] in order to highlight particular domestic difficulties that judges may face while aiming at applying the principle of the supremacy of EC law.

The ECJ case law in *Simmenthal* binds the Member States to ensure that:

> 'a national court, which is called upon, within the limits of its jurisdiction, to apply provisions of Community law is under a duty to give full effect to those provisions, if necessary refusing of its own motion to apply any conflicting provision of national legislation, even if adopted subsequently, and it is not necessary for the court to request or await the prior setting aside of such provisions by legislative or constitutional means.'[48]

Therefore, when it comes to the application of Community law, recourse to the Constitutional Court in case of incompatibility between Community law and national law is excluded by the *Simmenthal* mandate. Consequently, an obvious implication of national courts' *Simmenthal*-mandate is a significant change in the respective position of the judiciary *vis-à-vis* the legislature. A larger control by the judiciary over acts of the legislature puts the judiciary as a "watchdog" in a more restrictive position, in a position that was unperceivable in some countries and their constitutional structures just decades ago. Courts in every case have to give priority to Community law over incompatible norms enacted by national legislatures. Membership in the EU implies a modified set of checks and balances between the branches of the government.

In the Hungarian system, due to the lack of clarification on the relationship between national law and Community law and of the explicit reference to supremacy of the latter, there might be a risk that a national judge will be hesitant to review the compatibility of national law with Community law and to set aside the earlier should there be inconsistency as the *Simmenthal* mandate obliges it to do. However, in September 2008, the Constitutional Court interpreted its – otherwise extensive – review competence and explicitly rejected its competence to review the compatibility of domestic acts with EU law. The Constitutional Court pronounced that its review competences as laid down in Article 1 of the Act on the Constitutional Court do not authorise the Court to review conflicts between a national act of Parliament and EU law and recognised that the final arbiter on the issue should be the European Court of Justice.[49] Delineating the extent of its own review competences can be considered as a clear signal by the Constitutional Court towards the ordinary courts that the latter should do the compatibility check by their own powers. The Constitutional Court in this decision also attempted to clarify the relationship between national law and EC law (which is otherwise lacking from any Constitutional provision) and stated that:

> 'Article 2/A of the Constitution provides ... that Community law is applicable in the Hungarian legal order similarly to the law adopted by the Hungarian legislature.'

---

[47] The expression is borrowed from M. Claes, see further M. Claes, *The national courts' mandate in the European Constitution* (Oxford-Portland, Oregon, Hart Publishing 2006).

[48] *Loc. cit.* n. 46.

[49] Constitutional Court decision No. 61/B/2005 AB határozat, 29 September 2008, available at http://www.mkab.hu/hu/frisshat.htm.

Hopefully, this guidance will serve as a point of reference for national judges in the application of EC law enjoying supremacy over national acts.

When it comes to potential practical obstacles to the efficient application of EU law in Hungary, a stumbling block may be a previously mentioned characteristic, namely, that ordinary courts generally have had a rather limited outlook on any external sources of law, whether international law or even Community case law. From the moment of accession, this attitude had to be completely changed, and national judges must bear in mind and look up any Community legislation relevant to their case at hand. Such a tremendous challenge requires not only modification of the restricted attitude for an outlook regarding the sources of EU law, but also adequate infrastructural conditions: access to ECJ case law and EU legislation and knowledge of the legal system of the European Union. Another complicating factor is the fact that EC/EU law is heavily based on case law of the ECJ, laying down the fundamental lines for the notions and principles of EC/EU law. For practitioners, knowing how to apply the ECJ's interpretation is thus a challenge. As the Hungarian legal system is based on codes (i.e., textual application of law is in place), it is extremely important for judges and practitioners to get familiar with a legal system based on a mix of legislation and case law, with an emphasis on the legal principles developed by the ECJ. The preparation for fulfilling these challenges has to start in the course of legal education in order to train the next generations of lawyers as competent in EU law and its domestic implications.

As will be further explored, references for preliminary rulings submitted thus far by Hungarian courts to the ECJ reveal incentives that national courts are aware of and willing to utilise.

6.    THE APPLICATION OF EU LAW BY HIGHER COURTS: DIRECT EFFECT AND TEMPORAL LIMITATIONS

From the point of view of the national judiciary, the Supreme Court has rather firmly elaborated on fundamental EU law characteristics and the application of EU legislation in the national legal order. As explained further in this chapter, special attention has been paid by the Supreme Court to the direct effect of EC law and the possibility to invoke rights stemming from a non-transposed EC directive against national authorities. In addition, the Supreme Court has given equal attention to the temporal aspect of application of EC law in the Hungarian legal order.

### 6.1.    Individuals invoking rights stemming from an EC directive

The Supreme Court confirmed the direct effect of the Working-time Directive, which at the given time was not implemented correctly in the Hungarian legal system.[50] According to the applicable Hungarian legislation, half of the time that a doctor was

---

[50] Council Directive 93/104/EC of 23 November 1993 concerning certain aspects of the organisation of working time, *OJ* 1993 L 307/18.

required to spend on on-call duty at the hospital was remunerated with a lump sum as qualified working time. The claimant argued that the qualified remuneration should extend to the whole on-call duty period and invoked Articles 2(1) and 3 of the Directive. The Supreme Court referred to the interpretation of these articles by the ECJ provided in cases C-303/98 *SiMAP*,[51] C-151/02 *Jaeger*,[52] C-397/01 *Pfeiffer*.[53] The Supreme Court first considered Article 2/A(1)[54] of the Hungarian Constitution to have facilitated Community law to establish rights and obligations for individuals and also recalled that pursuant to Article 10 EC ("loyalty clause"), Hungary had undertaken the obligation to apply Community law in compliance with the interpretation given by the ECJ. In its judgment, the Supreme Court referred extensively to ECJ case law and employed the principle of direct effect. It held that individuals can invoke provisions of a directive *vis-à-vis* state authorities and authorities fulfilling public service related to the state, provided that provisions invoked are clear and unconditional, and their application has been established in practice. The Supreme Court referred to several judgments of the ECJ, including cases 80/86 *Kolpinghuis Nijmegen*[55] and C-253/96 *Kampelmann*.[56] Thus, the Supreme Court confirmed that the employees (in this case doctors in a hospital) could directly invoke provisions of the Directive in question, and by this token, the Court applied Article 2(1)-(2) of the Working-time Directive.[57]

6.2.    **Temporal limitation to the application of EC law: the relevance of pre-accession facts**

In an appeal procedure in an intellectual property case, the Supreme Court was faced with the question whether, under Article 234 EC, a national court was obliged to make reference to the ECJ although the established facts had taken place before Hungary's accession to the European Union. The Supreme Court held that Article 234 EC was applicable as of 1 May 2004, the date on which Hungary joined the European Union

---

[51] ECJ, Case C-303/98 *Sindicat de Médicos de Asistencia Pública (SiMAP) v. Conselleria de Sanidad y Consumo de la Generalidad Valenciana* [2000] *ECR* I-7963.

[52] ECJ, Case C-151/02 *Landeshaupstadt Kiel v. Norbert Jaeger* [2003] *ECR* I-8389, paras. 71, 75 and 103.

[53] ECJ, Joined Cases C-397/01 to C-403/01 *Bernhard Pfeiffer (C-397/01), Wilhelm Roith (C-398/01), Albert Süß (C-399/01), Michael Winter (C-400/01), Klaus Nestvogel (C-401/01), Roswitha Zeller (C-402/01) and Matthias Döbele (C-403/01) v. Deutsches Rotes Kreuz, Kreisverband Waldshut eV.* [2004] *ECR* I-8835, para. 93.

[54] '(1) By virtue of treaty, the Republic of Hungary, in its capacity as a Member State of the European Union, may exercise certain constitutional powers jointly with other Member States to the extent necessary in connection with the rights and obligations conferred by the treaties on the foundation of the European Union and the European Communities (hereinafter referred to as "European Union"); these powers may be exercised independently and by way of the institutions of the European Union.

(2) The ratification and promulgation of the treaty referred to in Subsection (1) shall be subject to a two-thirds majority vote of the Parliament.'

[55] ECJ, Case 80/86 *Criminal proceedings against Kolpinghuis Nijmegen BV* [1987] *ECR* 3969.

[56] ECJ, Case C-253/96 *Kampelmann and others v. Landschaftsverband Westfalen-Lippe and others* [1997] *ECR* 6907.

[57] Supreme Court Decision No. 10.921/2005, *Bírósági Határozatok Tára* [Digest of Court Decisions] BH 2006.34

and the Accession Treaty entered into force. Furthermore, the Supreme Court recalled the case law of the ECJ and case *Ynos Kft v. János Varga*, which established that in order to make a preliminary reference, the facts of the case should have occurred after a country's accession to EU.[58] The Supreme Court focused on the question whether the ECJ could have had the jurisdiction in the present case. The Supreme Court found that in the case pending before it, an attempt to establish a contractual patent license and its subsequent failure, and thus the facts establishing the claim for a compulsory license, had taken place prior to the accession. Bearing this in mind, the Supreme Court held that the ECJ had no jurisdiction under the preliminary procedure; *ergo*, the reference would not have been admissible. The Supreme Court confirmed that Hungarian courts could not submit references to the ECJ if, like in the given case, unsuccessful attempts at negotiations for a contractual patent license had taken place prior to the accession to the European Union.[59]

The application of Community law to pre-accession situations was the core issue in a competition case, in which the Fővárosi Ítélőtábla [Metropolitan Court of Appeal] explored the question on the applicability of Article 81 EC and Commission Regulation 2790/1999/EC on block exemptions on vertical agreements.[60] In this case, the Metropolitan Court of Appeal found that price negotiations carried out by bakeries in May 2002 led eventually to an increase of product prices in June 2002, which was against the competition rules. The Court furthermore stated that the national judge was not obliged to apply Article 81 EC and Commission Regulation 2790/1999/EC because the bakeries' unlawful conduct, as well as adoption of the Competition Authority's decision and initiation of the legal procedure, had preceded Hungary's accession to the EU. The Fővárosi Ítélőtábla thus confirmed, with relation to the pre-accession application of EC law, that Article 81 EC and Commission Regulation 2790/1999/EC were not applicable to conducts of undertakings if they had preceded Hungary's accession to the European Union.[61]

## 7. EC REGULATIONS IN THE HUNGARIAN LEGAL ORDER

The application of EC regulations imposes a particular challenge to national courts, because these are sources of EC law which are not transformed into national law (however, they may still need executive implementing measures at times) but are binding in full and require identification and obligatory application by a national judge. With regard to EC regulations, it is noteworthy to illustrate a rather unconventional approach and practice that constituted part of the legal preparation in the pre-accession period and which may have had implications for post-accession application of EC regulations.

---

[58] ECJ, Case C-302/04 *Ynos Kft v. János Varga* [2006] *ECR* I-371.

[59] Supreme Court Decision No. 24.516/2006/3 Civil Chamber, *Bírósági Határozatok Tára* [Digest of Court Decisions] 1/2006.

[60] Commission Regulation 2790/1999/EC of 22 December 1999 on the application of Art. 81(3) of the Treaty to categories of vertical agreements and concerted practices, *OJ* 1999 L 336/21.

[61] Metropolitan Court of Appeal Decision No. 27029/2006/4.

Approximation of national laws with EU law was an important aspect of the legal preparation for the accession. This also implied that national law had to be modified and adapted to EC regulations. This was all the more important because, as explained in the previous section, in the period preceding the accession, direct applicability of EC law (including regulations) was ruled out. This was not only due to the principle of EC law (direct applicability only takes effect when a country becomes a Member State), but also it was confirmed by the Constitutional Court in its decision regarding Article 62(2) EA Hungary (*re competition rules*).[62]

Thus, for example, in the areas of agriculture and competition policy, approximation was carried out practically by "implementing" EC regulations. When a country is a Member State of the European Union, such practice is considered to be contrary to Article 249 EC. However, agriculture and competition policies carry such economic significance and fundamental norms, which are prone to the requirement of legal certainty, that these regulations were taken *per se* into the national legal system regardless of and before the date of accession. In many cases, the EU even encouraged the incorporation of these regulations into national law.[63] However, since Hungary was not a Member State at this point, harmonisation of national law with regard to Community law and EC regulations translated into a technical transposition of EC regulations into national law. However, from the moment of accession, these national rules embedding EC regulations had to be repealed and removed from the national legal system. Moreover, if the previously implementing measure did not contain a clause providing for automatic repeal of these rules as of the date of accession,[64] a significant deregulating ("legislative-clearance") process was required, in order to comply with the underlying principle which prohibits the transposition of regulations.[65] Therefore, after accession, such "deregulating" obligations, coupled with thorough monitoring, implied that all national legislative measures bearing the same content as directly applicable EC regulations, as well as national legislative measures otherwise hindering the efficiency of a Community measure, had to be repealed.[66]

Consequently, national courts cannot anymore rely on (implementing) national legislation and must take into account EC regulations as directly applicable sources of law. This is a tremendous challenge and requires continual monitoring of EC legislation (including amendments) and the Official Journal of the European Union. The preliminary findings regarding domestic practice on the application of regulations reveal that

---

[62] See Constitutional Court Decision No. 30/1998 (IV. 25) *ABH* [Gazette of the Constitutional Court decisions] 1998 220.

[63] J. Fazekas, 'Jogharmonizációs feladatok a csatlakozás után' [The obligation of implementation of Community law after accession], 3 *Európai Tükör* 2004, pp. 18-29, at p. 21.

[64] "Automatic deregulation" was achieved by inserting an article into the final provisions of the harmonising act, stipulating that the act will be regarded as repealed as of 1 May 2004 – the day of accession.

[65] See well-established case law of the ECJ: Case 39/72 *Commission of the European Communities v. Italy* [1973] *ECR* 101, para. 17, Case 34/73 *Fratelli Variola Spa v. Amministrazione delle finanze dello Stato* [1973] *ECR* 981, para. 15.

[66] Joint Document Ministry of Justice and Ministry of Foreign Affairs from 2000 IM/EUR/2000/ Tervezet/228/8 Az Európai Unióhoz való csatlakozásnak a Magyar jogrendszert érintő egyes kérdései, [Selected issues on the Hungarian legal system in the light of EU Accession]. Text on file with the Author.

the free movement of goods, as one of the most pertinent implications of EU accession, has implied the application of EC regulations. Such was the case in an appeal procedure where the Supreme Court upheld a decision of a Regional Custom Office by applying Regulation 2913/92/EEC establishing the Community Customs Code.[67]

## 8.    THE PRELIMINARY RULING PROCEDURE IN HUNGARIAN LAW AND ITS APPLICATION BY NATIONAL COURTS

### 8.1.    Introduction

Engaging into a dialogue and co-operation with the European Court of Justice via the submission of a preliminary question renders national judges "Community judges" inasmuch as the interpretation and validity of the EU law is decided by the ECJ but is given effect by national judges at domestic level. The procedure not only establishes co-operative adjudication among the Community courts but also has equally contributed to the very development of underlying principles, notions primordial to the efficiency and uniform application of EU law. The actual engagement into such dialogue poses significant challenge to a national judge in a case where guidance on the validity and interpretation of EU law seems to be necessary to adjudicate in a given case.[68] The first and foremost challenge that requires adjustment from a national judge is the different approach to applicable laws. The obligations laid down in Article 10 EC and the fundamental principles of Community law, such as supremacy, direct effect and consistent interpretation, significantly extend the scope of attention of a national judge. Therefore, national judges should continually monitor EU legislation and ECJ jurisprudence in order to identify the relevance of EU law in their cases, identify the applicable rule of EU law or, if necessary, submit a preliminary reference to the European Court of Justice.[69] An additional challenge imposed on national judges is the obligatory use of interpretative precedence of the ECJ, as opposed to textual rules of worded legal definitions laid down in various codes of the national legal system.

Apart from such general aspects, the rules and practices related to preliminary references also imply various factors that deserve detailed attention when it comes to a country and its judges who are new to the co-operative adjudication between domestic courts and the European Court of Justice.

---

[67] Supreme Court Decision No. 35.198/2005, Public Administrative Chamber, *Bírósági Határozatok Tára* [Digest of Court Decisions] 1/2006.

[68] In accordance with the *Foto-Frost* doctrine, only the European Court of Justice (now also the Court of First Instance) has the jurisdiction to annul a piece of EC legislation. National courts have only the jurisdiction to confirm validity. See ECJ, Case 314/85 *Foto-Frost v. Hauptzollamt Lübeck-Ost* [1987] *ECR* 4199.

[69] The circumstances which exempt the national judge from such submission can be found in the *CILFIT* jurisprudence of the ECJ and will be illustrated in a subsequent section of this chapter with examples taken from Hungarian courts. See, ECJ, Case 283/81 *Srl CILFIT and Lanificio di Gavardo SpA v. Ministry of Health* [1982] *ECR* 3415.

## 8.2.    Provisions of Hungarian law on the preliminary ruling procedure

The procedure which should be followed by Hungarian courts when initiating preliminary reference is laid down in the amended Civil and Criminal Procedural Codes.
The amendment was adopted in Act No. XXX. of 2003, that is one year before the
accession to the European Union. The amended Civil Procedure Code in Article 155/A
reads as follows:

> 'a. The court may initiate preliminary procedure as is laid down in the founding treaties of
> the European Communities.
> b. The court decides on the submission of a preliminary question to the European Court of
> Justice with an order, and in the meantime suspends proceedings of the case. The court in its
> order formulates the question and – to the extent necessary for the answer – includes facts
> of the case and relevant national legislation. The court sends the Ministry of Justice the order,
> at the same time with the submission to the European Court of Justice.
> c. An appeal may be brought against a decision to make a reference for a preliminary ruling.
> An appeal cannot be brought against a decision dismissing a request for a reference for a
> preliminary ruling.'

The amendment in its Article 249/A states that:

> 'Appeal proceedings may also be brought against a decision made at second instance dismiss-
> ing a request for a reference for a preliminary ruling (Article 155/A).'

The Criminal Procedure Code was equally amended with regard to EU membership
and particularly the position of national judges putting forward preliminary questions
to the European Court of Justice in criminal cases. According to the newly inserted
Article 266(1) point c, the court suspends the proceedings *ex officio* or upon request,
if a preliminary question is put forward to the European Court of Justice. Similarly, the
decision on such initiative contains a question, facts of the case and relevant national
legislation as background. The Ministry of Justice receives a copy of an order initiating
a preliminary request in criminal cases as well.[70]
    It is fitting to note that Hungary was one of the first new Member States to recognise
the jurisdiction of the ECJ in respect to the preliminary ruling procedure in the third

---

[70] One year after accession, concerns were raised regarding these particular provision both in the
Civil Procedure and Criminal Procedure Codes, which require judges to forward requests for a preliminary ruling to the Ministry of Justice. According to J. Czuczai, the interaction with the executive in such
manner breaches the rule of law and separation of powers, the parties' fundamental rights to privacy and,
moreover, has no objective reasons regarding the process of preliminary proceedings. See J. Czuczai,
'A Pp. 155/A. §-a által szabályozott előzetes döntéshozatali kezdeményezése iránti eljárás a magyar
alkotmányosság rostáján' [Initiating prelimininary procedure according to Article 155/A of the Civil Procedural Code through the lens of constitutionality in Hungary], 9 *Magyar Jog* (2005) pp. 549-553.

pillar.[71] Initially it was reserved to the courts from which there is no further appeal;[72] however, subsequently Hungary extended the jurisdiction to all national courts.[73]

### 8.3. Preliminary ruling procedure in operation: a Hungarian perspective

#### 8.3.1. *National courts entitled to refer*

Within the previously illustrated underlying framework, additional issues might be of relevance, one of which is to determine which judicial organs (courts or tribunals) are entitled to make a reference for preliminary ruling. In line with Article 234 EC and the interpretative case law of the ECJ on the issue, one can tell that the situation in Hungary should be rather straightforward. One reason for this is that in the Hungarian judicial system, labour law cases, as well as administrative cases, ultimately belong to the jurisdiction of ordinary courts.[74] However, as it turned out very shortly after accession, a very specific issue was brought up by a Hungarian lower court in a case involving the status of courts maintaining commercial registers. The question related to their status under the preliminary ruling procedure when deciding upon the registration of undertakings and also to the status of courts of second instance dealing with review of decisions on registration. This led to the reference to the ECJ and its judgment in case C-210/06 *CARTESIO Oktató és Szolgáltató Bt.*[75] One of the pertinent issues referred to the ECJ was whether a court – such as the referring court – hearing an appeal against a decision of a lower court responsible for maintaining the commercial register, which rejected an application for amendment of information entered in that register, must be classified as a court or tribunal entitled to make a reference for a preliminary ruling under Article 234 EC. Moreover, neither a decision of a lower court nor the consideration by a referring court of appeal against that decision takes place in the context of *inter partes* proceedings. The ECJ found that a court hearing an appeal against a decision of a lower court responsible for maintaining a register, which rejected such application and which seeks annulment of such decision, which allegedly adversely affects the rights of the applicant, is called upon to give judgment in a dispute and is exercising a judicial function. Consequently, the ECJ held that the referring court is hearing a dispute and is exercising a judicial function, regardless of the fact that the proceedings

---

[71] Information concerning the declarations by the French Republic and the Republic of Hungary on their acceptance of the jurisdiction of the Court of Justice to give preliminary rulings on the acts referred to in Art. 35 of the Treaty on European Union, *OJ* 2005 L 327/19.

[72] Information concerning the declarations by the Republic of Hungary, the Republic of Latvia, the Republic of Lithuania and the Republic of Slovenia on their acceptance of the jurisdiction of the Court of Justice to give preliminary rulings on the acts referred to in Art. 35 of the Treaty on European Union, *OJ* 2008 L 70/23.

[73] This turned out to be a source of confusion. See, ECR, Case C-404/07 *György Katz v. István Roland Sós* [2008] *ECR* nyr.

[74] Badó and Bóka, *loc. cit.* n. 12, at p. 60.

[75] ECJ, Case C-210/06 *CARTESIO Oktató és Szolgáltató Bt* [2008] *ECR* nyr.

before that court are not *inter partes* and, hence, must be regarded as a court or tribunal for the purposes of Article 234 EC.[76]

Closely related, but raising another crucial legal issue, was the second question of the referring court in the *Cartesio* case. The referring court asked if the appeal court qualified as a court or tribunal which was entitled to make a reference for a preliminary ruling under Article 234 EC, or would that court be regarded as a court against whose decisions there was no judicial remedy, thus having an obligation to refer. According to Hungarian law, decisions delivered on appeal by the referring court may only be subject to an extraordinary appeal on a point of law before the Legfelsőbb Bíróság [the Supreme Court]. The purpose of this extraordinary appeal procedure is to ensure the consistency of case law, and, thus, the possibilities of bringing such appeals are limited, in particular, by the condition governing the admissibility of pleas, which is linked to the obligation to allege a breach of law. Under Hungarian law, an appeal on a point of law does not, in principle, suspend the enforcement of a decision delivered on appeal.[77] Cartesio claimed before the referring court that the court was required to make a reference to the ECJ for a preliminary ruling, since it fell to be classified as a court or tribunal against whose decisions there was no judicial remedy under national law.[78] In its answer, the ECJ referred to its decision in case C-99/00 *Lyckeskog*[79] and recalled that decisions of national appellate courts which can be challenged by parties before a Supreme Court are not decisions of courts from which there is no further remedy.[80] The ECJ thus reaffirmed that examination of merits of such challenges is conditional upon a leave to appeal granted by the Supreme Court and does not have the effect of depriving the parties of a judicial remedy. The referring court, whose decisions in disputes such as those in the main proceedings may be appealed on points of law, is a court from which there is a further remedy (thus with the right, not the obligation, to refer).[81]

### 8.3.2. *Appeals against decisions to refer*

Article 155/A(c) of the Civil Procedure Code merits attention. It allows for an appeal against national courts' orders initiating the preliminary ruling procedure. The Hungarian Supreme Court gave guidance on this matter in its decision 24.705/2005/2. It referred primarily to the *acte clair* doctrine and ruled that, taking into account the ECJ's decision in case 166/73 *Rheinmühlen-Düsseldorf*,[82] Article 234 EC does not exclude the possibility of an appeal from a decision regarding the submission of preliminary reference, when a decision on substance of a referring court can be challenged by an appeal to a higher court. Thus, in this case, the ECJ left it for the national legislature to provide

---

[76] The ECJ referred to several cases from its own jurisprudence, such as C-96/04 *Standesamt Stadt Niebüll* [2006] *ECR* I-3561 and Case C-182/00 *Lutz and Others* [2002] *ECR* I-547.

[77] *Ibidem*, para. 75.

[78] *Loc. cit.* n. 75, para. 68.

[79] ECJ, Case C-99/00 *Kenny Roland v. Lyckeskog* [2002] *ECR* I-4839, para. 19.

[80] *Ibidem*, para. 16.

[81] *Loc. cit.* n. 75, para. 76.

[82] ECJ, Case 166/73 *Rheinmühlen-Düsseldorf v. Einfuhr-und Vorratsstelle für Getreide und Futtermittel* [1974] *ECR* 33.

for a possibility to appeal decisions on references, when appeals are possible against decisions of referring courts on substance. The Supreme Court then investigated whether the answer would have been any different if the substantive judgment of the court in the present case could have only been challenged by an extraordinary appeal (see the *Cartesio* case in the previous section, explaining the particularities of this type of appeal). To explore this point, the Supreme Court turned to ECJ case law and the *Lyckeskog* case. The fact that examination of the merits of such appeals is subject to a prior declaration of admissibility by the Supreme Court does not have the effect of depriving the parties of a judicial remedy. Thus, in Hungary, the fact that the Civil Procedure Court allows for the possibility of appeal against the decision, submitting preliminary reference to the ECJ in case only an extraordinary appeal against its substantive judgment would be applicable, does not render the Hungarian laws incompatible with Community law.[83] Thus, this last passage clearly displays resemblance in the ECJ's reasoning in the *Cartesio* case and this earlier case decided by the Hungarian Supreme Court.

The reference in the *Cartesio* case touched upon another issue as well, namely, the actions of the appeal court during the preliminary procedure and their effects under Article 234 EC. Pursuant to the Hungarian law, a separate appeal may be brought against a decision requesting a preliminary ruling, although the main proceedings remain pending in their entirety before the referring court until the ECJ gives a ruling. The appellate court thus seized has, under the Hungarian law, power to vary that decision, to set aside the reference for a preliminary ruling and to order a court of lower instance to resume the proceedings. The question put forward to the ECJ was whether the right to submit a reference for a preliminary ruling is limited by the national measure that allows appeals against orders making a reference if, in the course of appeal proceedings, a national court of higher instance may amend an order, render a request for a preliminary ruling inoperative and order a court which issued a reference to resume the national proceedings which had been suspended. In its answer, the ECJ found that the jurisdiction of any national court or tribunal to make a reference to the ECJ is not limited by a national measure that permits an appellate court to vary the order for reference, to set aside a reference and to order a referring court to resume national proceedings.[84] The ECJ held:

'Where rules of national law apply which relate to the right of appeal against a decision making a reference for a preliminary ruling, and under those rules the main proceedings remain pending before the referring court in their entirety, the order for reference alone being the subject of a limited appeal, the second paragraph of Article 234 EC is to be interpreted as meaning that the jurisdiction conferred on any national court or tribunal by that provision of the Treaty to make a reference to the Court for a preliminary ruling cannot be called into question by the application of those rules, where they permit the appellate court to vary the

---

[83] Decision of the Supreme Court No. 24705/2005/2 Civil Law Chamber, *Bírósági Határozatok Tára* [Digest of Court Decisions] 2006.216.

[84] *Loc. cit.* n. 75.

402 CHAPTER 12

order for reference, to set aside the reference and to order the referring court to resume the domestic law proceedings.'[85]

In the course of other preliminary procedures, this very appeal against the reference turned out to be the cause for the suspension and later revocation of the procedure. In case C-447/06 *Vodafone Magyarország Mobil Távközlési Zrt. és társai v. Magyar Állam és társai*, the Fővárosi Bíróság [Metropolitan Court] put forward the preliminary questions, and two of the defendants in the meantime appealed against the order of the Fővárosi Bíróság initiating the preliminary procedure and asked for the suspension of the case at the ECJ. The President of the Court thus suspended the procedure until the result of the appeal procedure, and finally the Metropolitan Court informed the ECJ of the revocation of the preliminary questions at a later stage, and the case has been removed from the ECJ's register.[86]

### 8.3.3. *Challenging a decision not to refer*

The Supreme Court has taken a firm position on the application of the *acte clair* doctrine. It confirmed that a national court does not breach EU law by refusing to initiate a preliminary reference procedure if an EU measure in question is unambiguous for the national court and is not relevant for the legal proceedings pending before it.[87] In an appeal proceeding against a decision of the Metropolitan Court of Appeal [Fővárosi Ítélőtábla], the Supreme Court rejected an appeal of the applicant and upheld the decisions stating that the preliminary ruling procedure can only be initiated in case of questions which have particular relevance to solving a legal dispute at hand. The Supreme Court recalled a passage of the *CILFIT* case which required that, alongside the interpretation and validity question, another condition for preliminary proceedings, namely the necessity deemed by a national court for the determination of the legal proceedings pending before it.[88] In addition, the Supreme Court also referred to the *Hessische Knappschaft v. Maison Singer et Fils* case, which laid down that national courts may initiate the preliminary ruling procedure but may not be forced by the parties to do so.[89] The Supreme Court in its arguments also acknowledged that there was no need for a reference as an applicant's request would have been targeted at the interpretation of national law (in this very case, the question was whether national law was compatible with the general principles laid down by EC law) and not the interpretation of EU law as such. This reasoning has received criticism, taking into account that the ECJ often reformulates questions so that its interpretation of EU law may facilitate a national court's decision as to the conformity of domestic law with EU *acquis*.[90]

---

[85] *Loc. cit.* n. 75, para. 98.
[86] Order of the President of the Court of 17 April 2007, Case C-447/06 *Vodafone Magyarország Mobil Távközlési Zrt. és társai v. Magyar Állam és társai, OJ* 2007 C 96/29.
[87] Supreme Court decision, 30.120/2005, Economic Chamber, *Bírósági Határozatok Tára* [Digest of Court Decisions] 2006.18.
[88] *Loc. cit.* n. 69.
[89] ECJ, Case 44/65 *Hessische Knappschaft v. Maison Singer et Fils* [1965] *ECR* I-119.
[90] Kecskés, et al., *loc. cit.* n. 9, at p. 341.

In another case that merits attention, the Supreme Court upheld a decision of a court of appeal, which rejected a request for a reference (on similar grounds as in the case mentioned above). This time the Supreme Court recalled the same arguments based on the *CILFIT* judgment and, as in the above-mentioned decision, relied on case 44/65 *Hessische Knappschaft.* In addition, the Supreme Court also referred to the ECJ's ruling in case C-37/92 *José Vanacker and André Lesage v. SA Baudoux combustiles,*[91] confirming that the ECJ does not have the jurisdiction to interpret domestic law. Thus, the Supreme Court held that the dismissal of the motion for reference was not in breach of EC law and that the court of second instance had no obligation to proceed with a reference for preliminary ruling. The Court of Appeal was right to conclude that a reference was not necessary. It rightly found Article 3(4) and (5) of the Directive 68/151/EEC to be unambiguous (as transposed to Hungarian law by Article 10(1) of the Act on Registration of Companies) and, what is more important, the interpretation of the Directive was not needed for adjudication in the case at hand.[92]

These cases also include the question as to which court can be regarded as a court from which there is no further appeal, thus a court with the obligation to refer. The case law reveals that in neither case did the Supreme Court regard the appeal court to be such a court with the obligation to ask the assistance of the European Court of Justice.

### 8.4.    Legal issues in Hungarian references for preliminary ruling

Among the countries that joined the European Union in 2004, Hungarian judges were the most active – in the first years of membership – in submitting requests for a preliminary ruling.[93] The Hungarian Government was equally active in submitting (written) observations in preliminary proceedings, and so far has contributed in more than 13 cases of preliminary requests submitted by courts from other Member States, alongside more than 15 references for a preliminary ruling made by Hungarian courts.[94]

---

[91] ECJ, Case C-37/92 *José Vanacker and André Lesage v. SA Baudoux combustiles* [1993] *ECR* I-4947.

[92] Supreme Court decision No. 30.379/2006/3 Economic Law Chamber, *Bírósági Határozatok Tára* [Digest of Court Decisions] 2007.377.

[93] The Annual report of the ECJ for 2008 reveals the number of references for preliminary rulings from national courts. Amongst the "new" Member States, Hungary had put forward the most preliminary requests, in total 17; Poland came second with 14 preliminary requests. In both cases, further references have been submitted in the first six months of 2009. The 2008 Annual Report is available at http://curia.europa.eu/jcms/upload/docs/application/pdf/2009-03/ra08_en_cj_stat.pdf.

[94] See, *inter alia*, ECJ, Case C-475/03 *Banca popolare di Cremona Soc. coop. arl v. Agenzia Entrate Ufficio Cremona* [2006] *ECR* I-9373; Case C-292/04 *Wienand Meilicke, Heidi Christa Weyde and Marina Stöffler v. Finanzamt Bonn-Innenstadt* [2007] *ECR* I-1835; Case C-341/04 *Eurofood IFSC* [2006] *ECR* I-3813; Case C-168/05 *Elisa María Mostaza Claro v. Centro Móvil Milenium SL* [2006] *ECR* I-10421; Case C-437/05 *Jan Vorel v. Nemocnice Český Krumlov* [2007] *ECR* I-331; Case C-183/06 *RUMA GmbH v. Oberfinanzdirektion Nürnberg* [2007] *ECR* I-1559; Case C-199/06 *Centre d'exportation du livre français (CELF) and Ministre de la Culture et de la Communication v. Société internationale de diffusion et d'édition (SIDE)* [2008] *ECR* I-469; Case C-345/06 *Gottfried Heinrich* [2009] *ECR* nyr; Case C-393/06 *Ing. Aigner, Wasser-Wärme-Umwelt, GmbH v. Fernwärme Wien GmbH* [2008] *ECR* I-2339; Case C-455/06 *Heemskerk BV and Firma Schaap v. Productschap Vee en Vlees* [2008] *ECR* nyr; Case C-297/07 *Klaus Bourquain* [2008] *ECR* nyr; Case C-396/07 *Mirja Juuri v. Fazer Amica Oy* [2008] *ECR* nyr. A decision

## 8.4.1.  *Temporal limitation to the application of EC law*

As indicated, Hungarian courts and especially lower level courts can be regarded as quite active in putting forward questions to the European Court of Justice.[95] As early as 2004, the Szombathelyi Városi Bíróság [City Court of Szombathely] submitted a reference in the case *Ynos Kft v. János Varga* regarding the applicability of Directive 93/13/EEC.[96] The ECJ, however, declared the request inadmissible and found the lack of its jurisdiction, because the facts of the case had taken place before the country's accession to the European Union and, as such, ruled out the application of EC law to those legal situations.[97] As was seen in section 6.2. of this chapter, this judgment served on many occasions as a point of reference for national courts when deciding whether EC law should apply in the case pending before them and aided the decision in cases when the facts of the case were established before accession.[98] In his Opinion, Advocate General Tizzano elaborated extensively on the temporal limitations to the application of EC law and, as a consequence, the jurisdiction of the ECJ to rule on cases dealing with facts that had taken place before accession to the EU. This very issue also piqued the interest of other Member States who put forward (written) observations (amongst them a couple of "new" Member States).[99] However, in Hungary, some of the critics of the ECJ's judgment would have preferred to see the ECJ ruling on the substantive questions that had been raised and, as such, to contribute to the proper implementation of the Directive in question and to improve the relevant national regulatory framework.[100]

---

regarding the submission of (written) observations rests with the European Inter-Ministerial Coordination Committee. This Committee plays an important role in the co-ordination of EU policy in Hungary, and, *inter alia,* in the interministerial co-ordination and conciliation leading up to the establishment of national position to be presented in the EU decision-making process.

[95] See *loc. cit.* n. 93. The statistics provided in the 2008 Annual Report of the ECJ show that the Legfelsőbb Bíróság [Supreme Court], Szeged Ítélőtábla [Szeged Regional Court of Appeal], Fővárosi Ítélőtábla [Főváros Regional Court of Appeal] have so far submitted one reference each, while 14 requests have been submitted by other types of national courts.

[96] Council Directive 93/13/EEC of 5 April 1993 on unfair terms in consumer contracts, *OJ* 1993 L 95/29.

[97] ECJ, Case C-302/04 *Ynos Kft v. János Varga* [2006] *ECR* I-371.

[98] See Supreme Court decision No. 24.516/2006/3, where the Supreme Court found that the Hungarian courts could not submit a preliminary question to the European Court of Justice if attempts at negotiations for a contractual patent license occurred before Hungary's accession to the European Union, and the legal proceedings resulted from failed negotiations for the compulsory license; also in Decision No. 27.629/2006/4 of Metropolitan District Court: Art. 81 of EC and Commission Regulation 2790/1999/EC are not applicable to conducts of undertakings if they precede Hungary's accession to the European Union and the Supreme Court Decision No. 39.264/2005, Public Administrative Chamber, *Bírósági Határozatok Tára* [Digest of the Supreme Court] 1/2006 stating that Community tax rules are not applicable to fiscal years prior to accession.

[99] See Advocate General Tizzano's Opinion delivered on 22 September 2005 in Case C-302/04 *Ynos Kft. v. János Varga* [2006] *ECR* I-371.

[100] Z. Nemessányi, B. Kovács, 'Esélylatolgatások az első magyar döntéshozatali kérelem sorsáról (közösségi jogi és polgári jogi gondolatok)' [Contemplating the possible outcome of first Hungarian preliminary ruling request (matters of Community law and civil law)] available at http://www.jogiforum.hu/publikaciok/215.

On the same grounds, that is the lack of jurisdiction in cases with pre-accession factual background, the ECJ refused to deal with a reference submitted by the Komárom-Esztergom Megyei Bíróság [Komárom-Esztergom County Court] in the case C-261/05 *Lakép*.[101] The Hungarian court asked the ECJ to verify compatibility of the Hungarian so-called local business tax with the Sixth Council Directive 77/388/EEC on VAT.[102] However, as facts had taken place during a fiscal year predating the accession of Hungary to the European Union, the referring court had to render a judgment without the assistance of the ECJ.

### 8.4.2. *'Clearly no jurisdiction'*

In case C-328/04 *Attila Vajnai*,[103] the reference originated from Fővárosi Bíróság [Metropolitan Court]. The case dealt with the prosecution of *Attila Vajnai* who was accused of acting in breach of Article 269/B, first paragraph, of the Büntető Törvénykönyv [Hungarian Criminal Code]. The code provides that a person who uses or displays, in public, the symbol consisting of a five-pointed red star commits – where the conduct does not amount to a more serious criminal offence – a minor offence. In its reference, the Hungarian court wanted to verify if the provisions of Hungarian law were compatible with the fundamental EU law principle of non-discrimination. In addition, the Fővárosi Bíróság asked if Article 6 EU, according to which the Union is founded on the principles of liberty, democracy, respect for human rights and fundamental freedoms; Directive 2000/43/EC,[104] which also refers to fundamental freedoms; and Articles 10, 11 and 12 of the Charter of Fundamental Rights allow a person who wishes to express his political convictions through a symbol representing them to do so in any Member State.[105] The ECJ ruled that it had 'clearly no jurisdiction' to answer the question, and, indeed, the case would possibly have stood much more chance eventually in front of the European Court of Human Rights in Strasbourg. The Metropolitan Court's reference was mistaken not only because the reference to the Council Directive proved to be irrelevant, but invoking the provisions of the Charter of Fundamental Rights was equally redundant, since to that date it was a politically proclaimed but not legally binding document, one with which the ECJ should analyse compatibility.[106] It is worth mentioning that the case finally found its way to the European Court of Human Rights in Strasbourg, which rendered a judgment in July 2008 and found the violation of the

---

[101] ECJ, Case C-261/05 *Lakép v. Komárom-Esztergom Megyei Közigazgatási Hivatal* [2006] *ECR* I-20.
[102] Sixth Council Directive 77/388/EEC of 17 May 1977 on the harmonisation of the laws of the Member States relating to turnover taxes – Common system of value added tax: uniform basis of assessment, *OJ* 1977 L 145/1.
[103] ECJ, Case C-328/04 *Criminal proceedings against Attila Vajnai* [2005] *ECR* I-8577.
[104] Council Directive 2000/43/EC of 29 June 2000 implementing the principle of equal treatment between persons irrespective of racial or ethnic origin, *OJ* 2000 L 180/22.
[105] Charter of Fundamental Rights of the European Union, *OJ* 2000 C 364/1.
[106] A. Osztovics, 'Az első magyar előzetes döntéshozatali eljárás iránti kérelem' [The first Hungarian preliminary procedure request], 5 *Európai Jog* (2004) pp. 16-21.

freedom of expression enshrined in Article 10 ECHR by the Hungarian Criminal Code banning the display of the red star.[107]

### 8.4.3. Compatibility of national law with EC law

In joined cases C-290/05 *Nádasdi Ákos v. Vám-és Pénzügyőrség Észak-Alföli Regionális Parancsnoksága* put forward by the Hajdú-Bihar County Court [Hajdú-Bihar Megyei Bíróság] and C-333/05 *Németh Ilona v. Vám-és Pénzügyőrség Délalföldi Igazgatósága* initiated by the Bács-Kiskun County Court [Bács-Kiskun Megyei Bíróság], the ECJ examined the compatibility of the Hungarian registration duty on motor vehicles with Community law. The matter of the dispute was the so-called registration tax imposed on motor vehicles imported from other Member States, which ignored the value of a car, and an amount of tax to be paid was set by its technical features or of its environmental classification. After the cases were joined, the ECJ had to verify if the measure in question was a charge having equivalent effect to customs duty (caught by Arts. 23 and 25 EC), or if it was a discriminatory taxation, prohibited pursuant to Article 90 EC. Naturally, the ECJ also had to verify if EC law allowed or precluded such national legislation. The ECJ held that:

> '[A] tax such as that imposed in Hungary by Law No. CX of 2003 on registration duty (a regisztrációs adóról szóló 2003. évi CX. törvény), which does not apply to private motor vehicles by reason of the fact that they cross the frontier, does not constitute a customs duty on imports or a charge having equivalent effect within the meaning of Articles 23 EC and 25 EC.'[108]

However, the ECJ held that the registration tax was contrary to Article 90 EC, insofar as it imposed a higher amount of tax on used import cars than on used cars already registered in Hungary. As a result of these judgments, the Hungarian Parliament adopted Act No. CXXX of 2006[109] on the partial reimbursement of the excess amount of the paid registration taxes and amended the law relating to the registration procedure with Act No. CXXXI of 2006,[110] which adequately addressed devaluation as a factor of consideration during the registration process.

In joined cases C-283/06 *KÖGÁZ rt* and C-312/06 *OTP Garancia Biztosító rt*,[111] two Hungarian courts (Zala Megyei Bíróság and Legfelsőbb Bíróság, respectively)

---

[107] ECtHR, *Vajnai v. Hungary*, Case No. 33629/06.

[108] ECJ, Joined Cases C-290/05 and C-333/05 *Ákos Nádasdi v. Vám- és Pénzügyőrség Észak-Alföldi Regionális Parancsnoksága (C-290/05) and Ilona Németh v. Vám- és Pénzügyőrség Dél-Alföldi Regionális Parancsnoksága (C-333/05)* [2006] *ECR* I-10115.

[109] Act CXXX of 2006 *A regisztrációs adó részleges visszatérítésérő szóló törvény* [Act on the partial reimbursement of completed registration taxes].

[110] Act CXXXI of 2006 *Egyes pénzügyi tárgyú törvények módosításáról szóló törvény* [Act on the amendment of certain fiscal-related acts].

[111] ECJ, Joined Cases C-283/06 and C-312/06 *KÖGÁZ rt and Others v. Zala Megyei Közigazgatási Hivatal Vezetője (C-283/06) and OTP Garancia Biztosító rt v. Vas Megyei Közigazgatási Hivatal (C-312/06)* [2007] *ECR* I-8463.

approached the ECJ to evaluate the compatibility of Hungarian local business tax with the Sixth Council Directive 77/388/EEC on VAT. The distinctive feature between these cases and the previously mentioned cases *Ynos* and *Lakép* was the fact that this time, relevant facts took place after the accession to the European Union. The ECJ's ruling held that neither the Sixth Council Directive nor its amendment (Directive 91/680/EC)[112] must be interpreted as not precluding the maintenance of a tax with characteristics such as the Hungarian local business tax. This case thus did not require adjustment from the legislature on a very important national measure aiming primarily to provide municipalities with financial assets from local undertakings in the form of taxes. The judgment of the ECJ in these cases was rendered on 11 October 2007. Interestingly enough, on 10 April 2007 Zala Megyei Bíróság – the same court as in case C-283/06 *KÖGÁZ rt* – raised the issue again and requested a preliminary ruling on exactly the same legal issue. When judgments in cases C-283/06 *KÖGÁZ rt* and C-312/06 *OTP Garancia Biztosító rt* were rendered, the Registrar of the ECJ informed the referring court accordingly. In its response, the Zala Megyei Bíróság withdrew its reference, and thus the case was removed from the register.[113]

### 8.4.4. *The interpretation of right of establishment – the Cartesio case*

The previously mentioned *Cartesio* case raised an important substantive issue related to the freedom of establishment, alongside the analysed procedural matters.[114] Cartesio, a limited partnership incorporated under Hungarian law with an established seat in Hungary, transferred its seat to Italy but wished to retain its status as a company governed by Hungarian law. Under Hungarian law on the commercial register, a seat of a company governed by Hungarian law is a place where the central administration is situated. The court maintaining the commercial register rejected Cartesio's application for amendment of the entry regarding the company's seat, recalling that a company incorporated in Hungary may not transfer its seat abroad while continuing to be the subject of Hungarian law as the law governing its articles of association.[115] For such a transfer, it would be required that a company ceases to exist and then reincorporates itself in another country in accordance with the applicable laws of that country. The question of the referring court was whether Articles 43 and 48 EC are to be interpreted as precluding such legislation.[116] The ECJ pointed to the national legislation of sev-

---

[112] Council Directive 91/680/EEC of 16 December 1991 supplementing the common system of value added tax and amending Directive 77/388/EEC with a view to the abolition of fiscal frontiers, *OJ* 1991 L 376/1.

[113] Order of the President of the Court of 16 November 2007 (Reference for a preliminary ruling from the Zala Megyei Bíróság – Republic of Hungary) – *OTP Bank rt and Merlin Gerin Zala kft v. Zala Megyei Közigazgatási Hivatal*, Case C-195/07, *OJ* 2008 C 51/39.

[114] For an academic appraisal see, *inter alia*, A. Johnston, P. Syrpis, 'Regulatory competition in European company law after Cartesio', 34 *ELRev.* (2009) pp. 378-404.

[115] *Loc. cit.* n. 75, para. 102.

[116] *Ibidem*, para. 99.

eral Member States and referred to cases 81/87 *Daily Mail*[117] and C-208/00 *Übersee-ring*,[118] in which the ECJ confirmed a company's attachment to national legislation and affirmed the existing variety of national legislation. The Court inferred from *Überseering* that a Member State could restrict a company's right to retain the legal personality under its law when the centre of administration is transferred to a foreign country.[119] The ECJ thus considered that in the absence of uniform EC law, national law should resolve the question of whether the company has been established and thus enjoys the freedoms laid down in Article 43 EC. The ECJ recognised the Member State's power to define the connecting factor of a company to be regarded as incorporated under the law of a Member State as well as the possibility not to permit a company to retain that status once it breaks the connecting factor and moves its seat to another Member State.[120]

The Court concluded that Articles 43 and 48 EC did not preclude legislation of a Member State under which a company incorporated under the law of that Member State may not transfer its seat to another Member State whilst retaining its status as a company governed by the law of the Member State of incorporation. While the judgment of the ECJ had been anticipated eagerly, some commentators regard the final ruling as one that 'increases complexity of the rights to freedom of establishment'[121] and in the aftermath of the ruling, the reliance on the freedom of establishment remains to be essentially linked to the individual company laws of the Member States.'[122]

## 8.5.    References for preliminary ruling in the Third Pillar

As has been discussed in the general overview of national measures regarding preliminary ruling procedure, Hungary has accepted the jurisdiction of the European Court of Justice regarding measures falling under Article 35 EU. In Hungary, Third Pillar issues do not put courts of final instances in any privileged position as national courts of any level may submit references in this area. By the time of writing, the only reference in a Third Pillar matter was submitted by the Fővárosi Bíróság [Metropolitan Court]. It requested interpretation of the Council Framework Decision 2001/220/JHA of 15 March 2001 on the standing of victims in criminal proceedings.[123] The reference was made in criminal proceedings brought against Mr. Sós, who was being prosecuted for fraud by Mr. Katz, acting as substitute private prosecutor. The Fővárosi Bíróság was unsure as to what was meant by the concepts of a "real and appropriate" role for victims and the "possibility" they have "to be heard during proceedings and to supply

---

[117] ECJ, Case 81/87 *The Queen v. H.M. Treasury and Commissioners of Inland Revenue*, ex parte *Daily Mail and General Trust plc.* [1988] *ECR* 5483.

[118] ECJ, Case C-208/00 *Überseering BV and Nordic Construction Company Baumanagement GmbH (NCC)* [2002] *ECR* I-9919.

[119] *Loc. cit.* n. 75, para. 107.

[120] *Loc. cit.* n. 75, para. 110.

[121] C. Gerner-Beuerle and M. Schillig, 'The Mysteries of Freedom of Establishment after Cartesio', (11 February 2009), p. 11. available at SSRN http://ssrn.com/abstract=1340964.

[122] *Ibidem.*

[123] Council Framework Decision 2001/220/JHA of 15 March 2001 on the standing of victims in criminal proceedings, *OJ* 2001 L 82/1.

evidence", provided for in Articles 2 and 3 of the Framework Decision 2001/220/JHA respectively, and wondered whether they should include the possibility for a national court to hear a victim of crime as a witness for a substitute private prosecution. The ECJ held that Articles 2 and 3 of Council Framework Decision 2001/220/JHA should be interpreted as not obliging a national court to permit the victim to be heard as a witness in criminal proceedings instituted by a substitute private prosecution, such as in the main proceedings. However, in the absence of such a possibility, it must be possible for a victim to be permitted to give testimony which can be taken into account as evidence.[124]

## 9. INFRINGEMENT PROCEEDINGS AGAINST HUNGARY

### 9.1. The transposition record

By July 2009, when the Commission announced the 19th Scoreboard on the transposition of Internal Market directives, Hungary had a 0.6% deficit, not having transposed 10 directives out of more than 1,630 whose transposition deadline had passed.[125] One of the previous Scoreboards also revealed that Hungary shared the first place – together with Slovenia – for the shortest time required to resolve infringement proceedings, 10 months respectively, while the average was 12 months amongst the EU 10 (and 25 months in the EU 15).[126] The 2007 Scoreboard revealed that Hungary accomplished 21 out of the 25 practices that the Commission recommended in its recommendation on the transposition into national law of the directives affecting the Internal Market.[127] It is important to emphasise that the European Commission had not brought infringement actions to involve Hungary in the litigation phase before the European Court of Justice until January 2007.

Between 1 May 2004 and February 2008, the Commission initiated 153 procedures for failure to transpose EC law, and only 30 cases were still pending in February 2008; the 123 cases were solved and caught up with by the adoption of transposing measures. Out of the 30 cases in discussion between the Commission and the national level, 21 reached the official letter stage, another 9 reached the formal opinion stage and in none of the cases did the ECJ have to pronounce on an infringement case involving Hungary.

---

[124] *Loc. cit.* n. 73.

[125] Internal Market Scoreboard, July 2009, No. 19, available at http://ec.europa.eu/internal_market/score/docs/score19_en.pdf.

[126] Infringement cases closed or brought before the ECJ between 31/10/2005 and 31/10/2007: average time in months needed to either close an infringement case or bring it before the ECJ counted from the moment of the sending of the letter of formal notice. Internal Market Scoreboard: Member States back on track, Edition 16bis, European Commission, 14 February 2008. Available at http://ec.europa.eu/internal_market/score/docs/score16bis/score16bis_en.pdf.

[127] The practices that had not been established in Hungary by this point in time are the following: allocation of sufficient resources, avoiding gold-plating, fast-track procedure of adopting implementing measures, use of alternative legal instruments. See Internal Market Scoreboard: Best result ever, Edition 15 bis, European Commission, 1 February 2007. Text available at http://ec.europa.eu/internal_market/score/docs/score15bis/score15bis_en.pdf.

This, no doubt, shows Hungary's commitment to the Internal Market results and also the thorough legal work and successful co-ordination that lie behind the successful transposition-practice. According to the actual desk-officers responsible for transposition, the good result can be best attributed to various factors: the constant monitoring from the Commission, the discipline with which the administration approaches EU commitments, alongside the very short leeway the officers typically get to transpose a directive, which is in an increasing number of cases a word-by-word takeover.

For the purposes of enforcing substantial compliance between national law and Community law – thus caused by incorrect application of Community law – the Commission initiated 59 infringement procedures against Hungary between May 2004 and February 2008. Out of these, 33 cases were pending in February 2008 – 26 in the formal notice and 7 in reasoned opinion stages.[128]

In general, it can be said that the threat of initiating a Commission procedure does stimulate the national level to render its national legislation compatible with EC law. This is confirmed by the fact that even once the Commission signals potential breaches of implementation obligations, the national level responds quickly and aims to resolve the issue, as soon as the issue allows – depending on its political sensitivity, especially if a parliamentary act carries out the adoption and not a governmental or ministerial decree.

## 9.2.    Enforcing EC law: overview of infringement cases

Alongside the duly transposition of a directive, "substantial" compatibility of a national measure with Community law is also required for establishing compliance with Community law. Once the Commission finds a national measure to be incompatible with Community law, the Commission proceeds with a formal notice, followed by a reasoned opinion and ultimately pledging the issue before the ECJ so as to declare the national legislation incompatible with Community law. As of 1 July 2009, the European Commission submitted in total 5 actions for infringement to the European Court of Justice; however 4 of them were eventually dropped by the European Commission. In the next section two of those actions are elaborated on.

### 9.2.1.    *Cases C-30/07 Commission v. Hungary and C-148/07 Commission v. Hungary*

In January 2007, the Commission brought an action against Hungary to the European Court of Justice and sought the declaration that by failing to adopt the laws, regulations and administrative provisions necessary to implement Council Directive 2003/109/EC concerning the status of third-country nationals[129] who are long-term residents or by failing to inform the Commission thereof, Hungary failed to fulfil its obligations under

---

[128] J/5597 számú jelentés a Magyar Köztársaság európai uniós tagságával összefüggő kérdésekről és az európai integráció helyzetéről. [Report No. J/5597 on the isues related to Hungary's EU membership and the status of the European integration.] April 2008.
[129] Council Directive 2003/109/EC of 25 November 2003 concerning the status of third-country nationals who are long-term residents, *OJ* 2004 L 16/44.

that Directive.[130] The transposition period for this Directive expired in December 2006. The Hungarian Parliament adopted in December 2006 Act No. I of 2007 on the transit and residence of persons covered by the freedom of movement of residence[131] and Act No. II of 2007 on the transit and residence of third country nationals.[132] Both acts entered into force in July 2007. As a consequence, the Commission informed the ECJ that it revoked its action in October 2007. In November, the ECJ removed the case from the register.[133]

In case C-148/07 *Commission v. Hungary*,[134] the Commission sought the Court to declare that 'by failing to eliminate the restrictions to the provisions of cable television imposed by Article 115 (4) of Act No I of 1996 on Radio and television (the so-called Media Act), Hungary has failed to fulfil its obligations under the Commission Directive 2002/77/EC of 16 September 2002 on competition in the markets for electronic communications networks and services.'[135] In the case of the old Member States, the deadline for the transposition was set for 24 July 2003; however, for countries that joined the European Union on 1 May 2004, the deadline – pursuant to Articles 2 and 54 of the Act on Conditions of Accession 2003 – passed on 30 April 2004.[136] Since Hungary failed to comply with this requirement, the European Commission initiated the infraction procedure and submitted the case to the ECJ. The infringement procedure was triggered by the fact that the Commission found that Hungary had failed to transpose Article 2(3) of the Directive by restricting the right of cable television service providers to broadcast programmes in territories where coverage is no more than one- third of the population. Following the phase in which the Commission called upon the Government to secure compatibility, the Commission turned to the judicial stage of the infraction procedure. As the case was pending, the Hungarian Government exercised forceful actions to prepare and put forward the new bill and gain the necessary two-thirds majority of the voting deputies for the adoption of the Act. As a result, the new Act was adopted in July 2007, and Article 8(2) of Act No LXVII of 2007 repealed Article 115(4) of the Media Act, which brought the Hungarian laws entirely in line with the Commission Directive. As a result, the European Commission withdrew the action, and the ECJ removed the case from the register accordingly.[137]

---

[130] Case C-30/07 *Commission of the European Communities v. Republic of Hungary*, *OJ* 2007 C 69/8.

[131] Szabad mozgás és tartózkodás jogával rendelkező személyek beutazásáról ás tartózkodásáról szóló 2007. évi I. tv.

[132] Harmadik országbeli állampolgárok beutazásáról és tartózkodásáról szóló 2007. évi II. tv.

[133] Order of the President of the Eighth Chamber of the Court of 27 November 2007 – *Commission of the European Communities v. Republic of Hungary* (Case C-30/07), *OJ* 2008 C 51/38.

[134] Case C-148/07 *Commission of the European Communities v. Republic of Hungary*, *OJ* 2007 C 297/35.

[135] Commission Directive 2002/77/EC of 16 September 2002 on competition in the markets for electronic communications networks and services, *OJ* L 249/21.

[136] Act concerning the Conditions of Accession of the Czech Republic, the Republic of Estonia, the Republic of Cyprus, the Republic of Latvia, the Republic of Lithuania, the Republic of Hungary, the Republic of Malta, the Republic of Poland, the Republic of Slovenia and the Slovak Republic and the adjustments to the Treaties on which the European Union is founded, *OJ* 2003 L 236/33.

[137] Order of the President of the Court of 6 September 2007 – *Commission of the European Communities v. Republic of Hungary* (Case C-148/07), *OJ* 2007 C 297/35.

9.2.2.      *Letters of formal notice in the case of vehicle registration tax and*
            *"golden shares"*

The closer overview of the following two cases in which the Commission submitted
formal notices to Hungary regarding the vehicle registration tax and the golden-shares
issue might be of interest. The first issue is closely related to a previously analysed
reference for preliminary ruling, and the second issue is interesting due to its circumstances, the political-economic sensitivity and the corresponding interest at stake.

In October 2005, the Commission approached Hungary with a letter of formal notice
for information concerning the taxation rules that Hungary applied to the registration
of second-hand cars imported from other EU Member States. According to the
Commission, the way the rules were applied may have breached the EC Treaty provisions on equal treatment of domestic products and those of other Member States. Indeed,
the Commission's claim was similar to the one put forward by the individuals in the
joined cases C-290/05 *Nádasdi Ákos* and C-333/05 *Ilona Németh*. As explained earlier in this chapter, under the relevant Hungarian legislation, a car was subject to a
registration tax on its first entry for use in Hungary. This tax was applicable to new and
to second-hand cars alike, its level depending on engine capacity, type of fuel used and
emission standards, without taking into account the actual mechanical status of a vehicle. The ECJ, in the previously discussed cases, held that Article 90 EC required that
the imported second-hand vehicle's actual depreciation is taken into account by the
Member State in calculating registration tax. Otherwise, the tax imposed would exceed
the residual tax incorporated in the value of similar second-hand motor vehicles already
registered in the national territory.[138] Hungary also applied a surcharge of 25% on top
of the registration tax in the case of the intra-community acquisition of second-hand
cars, i.e., to all vehicles from other Member States other than those registered in Hungary
when new. In this respect, the Commission reminded that according to ECJ case law,
a criterion for charging higher taxation which, by definition, will never be fulfilled by
similar domestic products cannot be considered compatible with the prohibition on
discrimination laid down in Article 90 EC. Consequently, such a system has the effect
of excluding domestic products from heavier taxation.[139] As has been pointed out earlier, the infringement procedure was solved indirectly by adoption of national law
compatible with the EC Treaty (following the judgment of the ECJ in cases C-290/05
*Nádasdi Ákos* and C-333/05 *Ilona Németh*).

On another account, the Commission sent a letter of formal notice to the Hungarian
Government to signal incompatibility of the Hungarian practices of "golden-shares"
with EC law. The Hungarian regulatory framework relating to these golden shares

---

[138] ECJ, Case C-345/93 *Fazenda Pública and Ministério Público v. Américo João Nunes Tadeu* [1995]
*ECR* I-479; Case C-47/88 *Commission of the European Communities v. Kingdom of Denmark* [1990]
*ECR* I-4509; Case C-375/95 *Commission of the European Communities v. Hellenic Republic* [1997] *ECR*
I-5981.
[139] 'Car Taxation: infringement procedure against Hungary', IP/05/1279, Press Release from the Commission's website, published on 14 October 2005. Available at http://europa.eu/rapid/pressReleasesAction.
do?reference=IP/05/1279&format=HTML&aged=0&language=EN&guiLanguage=EN.

dated back to the lengthy process of privatisation and gained legal description in the privatisation framework law, Act No. XXXIX of 1995. These shares of particular status in rather primary businesses and companies provided for the state a status, a greater say, practically veto rights, upon the adoption of primordial business decisions, such as mergers, acquisitions, fusions or raising capital.[140] This law provided for a special say for the state in the functioning of the company, even though its shares as owner had been entirely or partially sold through the privatisation. The previously mentioned areas of decision making where the state retained a practical veto right were allowed and explained by serious economic interest of the country – to protect the interest of investors, while at the same time to prevent hostile takeovers.

In the Community legal order, the European Commission, in its role as guardian of the treaties and of the full effect and respect of European competition rules and the four freedoms securing the completion of the Internal Market, already in 1997 stipulated clearly its position in which it regards the wide-ranging practice of golden shares in the Member States as one that has potential to infringe upon the principle of free movement of capital.[141] Following this policy and the ECJ's ruling against Italy[142] consistently, the Commission in 2002 declared that these golden shares actually infringe Community law and the free flow of capital in the Internal Market and called upon a significant number of Member States to modify their regulatory framework for state-participation in these companies. Accordingly, Denmark, Portugal,[143] France,[144] Spain,[145] the UK[146] and the Netherlands[147] were forced to modify their laws. However, Belgium succeeded to justify in front of the European Court of Justice during the infringement procedure the necessity and the practice that the country had established and operated with regard

---

[140] The introduction of such special shares dates back to the economic reconstruction and privatisation process in the UK in the 1980s, when the M. Thatcher-Government aimed at maintaining the influence of the state regardless of its ownership rights within the company. Two modalities served such a goal: one kind of shares secured influence for the state in companies of particular economic importance, for an indefinite time; another type of shares served for the same aim for a definite time laid down in the company's constitution and mainly secured the smooth transition from public to private property. Generally speaking, the rationale behind these shares of special status was to protect the assets of the companies involved and to protect them from hostile takeovers, to get decision rights in the composition of management and reconstruction of the company.

[141] Communication of 19 July 1997 on certain legal aspects concerning intra-EU investment, *OJ* 1997 C 220/15.

[142] ECJ, Case C-58/99 *Commission of the European Communities v. Republic of Italy* [2000] *ECR* I-3811.

[143] ECJ, Case C-367/98 *Commission of the European Communities v. Republic of Portugal* [2002] *ECR* I-4731.

[144] ECJ, Case C-483/99 *Commission of the European Communities v. Republic of France* [2002] *ECR* I-4781.

[145] ECJ, Case C-462/00 *Commission of the European Communities v. Kingdom of Spain* [2003] *ECR* I-4581.

[146] ECJ, Case C-98/01 *Commission of the European Communities v. United Kingdom* [2003] *ECR* I-4641.

[147] ECJ, Case C-282/04 *Commission of the European Communities v. Kingdom of the Netherlands* [2006] *ECR* I-9141.

to golden-shares.[148] Thus, the "old" 15 were forcefully and consistently monitored, and the Commission allowed for exceptions only in case of significant public interest and with the stipulation that the state influence may not be discriminative and thus anti-competitive.[149] Obviously, the issue raised a particular challenge to the former socialist countries aspiring towards the EU, having experienced themselves the necessary, painful and lengthy process of economic reconstruction through privatisation just about a decade prior to acceding to the EU. In this process, based on the selling of former state-owned properties, the practice of golden-shares played an important role in granting certain control in privatised companies for the state. For example, in 2005, Poland had 49 companies where golden shares were active, the Czech Republic had 37, and Hungary came third in this ranking.[150]

With regard to the accession countries, and particularly Hungary, the Commission already at an early point, prior to accession, raised the issue to the Hungarian Government, reminding it to adopt legislation compatible with the *acquis communautaire*. The Government promised to pursue such expectations, and, consequently, a proposal was put forward even before the accession in spring 2004, which would have abolished the practice of golden shares with regard to eight companies and for the remaining ones would have allowed a more restricted interference from the state in the case of particular, well-defined situations. The preparation of this proposal was based on the observation that the EU leaves some room for manoeuvre for the Member States, if the latter can justify the national legislation.[151] However, the coalition partners in the Government could not come to a political agreement in the matter, which resulted in a premature death of the proposal without parliamentary debate. Thus, Hungary joined the European Union on 1 May 2004 with the conscious awareness of breach of Community law (most probably with the idea of gaining time and seeing what would turn out in other Member States), but the Commission did not turn a blind eye to such conduct. As a consequence, significant influence was secured for the state in companies of wide-ranging profile: pharmaceuticals, gas and electricity providers, power plants, telecom companies, an aircraft production company, Hungary's largest bank and companies specialising in the production of the so-called "hungaricum"-products, altogether 31 companies. The Commission subsequently initiated an infringement procedure with a formal letter against Hungary in December 2005, finding that the maintenance of golden shares is not justified either by strategic goals or public policy considerations. As a response to the subsequent formal notice by the Commission, the Government

---

[148] In Case C-503/99 *Commission v. Kingdom of Belgium* [2002] *ECR* I-4809, the European Court of Justice found that golden shares did not violate Arts. 56 and 43 EC *per se*, leaving hope for other Member States to bring along justifications for the practice of golden-shares.

[149] 'Mégis fénylik az aranyrészvény', [Golden-shares are still shining], *Jogi Fórum*, issue of 1 August 2007 available at http://www.jogiforum.hu/hirek/16366. The same source speaks of some 141 companies in the 15 Member States where the state's influence was secured via the golden shares.

[150] K. Facsinay, 'Vége az Aranyéletnek?' [Is golden life over?], *Heti Válasz Online*, 16 November 2006, available at: http://www.hetivalasz.hu.

[151] Such justification served France with regard to the monitoring of the defence industry; Germany maintained the production of Volkswagen and the UK the Rolls-Royce as industries of strategic importance, which may justify the interference of the state in companies.

bargained for extra time, claiming that due to the parliamentary elections,[152] more time was needed for the preparation of such reform. The Commission thus set a deadline to bring Hungarian legislation compatible with Community law until 20 October 2006. As an unavoidable reaction, the legislative machinery snapped into action, and the Ministry of Justice and Law Enforcement put forward a proposal. The adoption of the new Act required a two-thirds majority of the deputies present at the time of voting, which constituted the main obstacle for adoption. The Parliament finally adopted the new Act in April 2007, in which the golden shares of the state were rendered capital shares, and, as such, toned down the voting privilege that had been previously secured for the Government.[153] Consequently, the state may not interfere as owner, only as authority with regard to these companies.[154] The finally adopted, modified Act, which aimed to enter into force as of 20 July 2007, was then evaluated by the Commission's Competition DG, but the spokesperson of Commissioner Charlie McCreevy emphasised that only a 100% compatibility would be acceptable and would impede the pursuit of a procedure in front of the ECJ, to which the submissions had already been prepared by the Commission's services.[155]

Compared to other Member States, Hungary takes a relatively good place in the ranking in the initiated infringement procedures for not adequate implementation of Internal Market rules. In the Commission's overview from February 2006, only 6 other Member States triggered less attention from the Commission for the inadequate implementation of Internal Market rules.[156] Certainly, even in the infringement proceedings taken to the judicial phase, the Government's efforts subsequently prevented the threat of penalties for non-compliance with Community law. Clearly, the main issues for Hungary's late transposition revolve around domestical political particularities, as, for example, the lack of political agreements required for the adoption of laws in the Parliament, often demanding the support of a qualified majority of two-thirds of MPs present at the time of voting.

## 10.     DIRECT ACTIONS CHALLENGING EU SECONDARY LEGISLATION

### 10.1.   Challenging a Community act by the Hungarian Government

The Hungarian Government submitted the first direct action in 2006 challenging the validity of a Community act, a possibility offered to – among others – Member States

---

[152] The parliamentary elections were held in April 2006 and resulted in the reinforcement of the Socialist-Liberal coalition government.

[153] Replacing the explicit privileged decision-making rights (i.e., veto) with significantly weaker and indirect influence, which can be exerted via, for example, the delegation of members to the Board of Directory of the company by the state.

[154] Adopted by the Hungarian Parliament on 16 April 2007.

[155] Cs. Prókai, 'Brüsszel tovább vizsgáldik aranyészvény-ügyben' [Brussels keeps investigating the golden-shares case], *Bruxinfo*, 6 July, 2007, Article accessed at the website of the Pécs-Baranya Chamber of Commerce available at http://www.pbkik.hu.

[156] Malta 21, Slovakia 20, Lithuania 16, Latvia 12, Finland 12, Estonia 11.

as privileged applicants laid down in Article 230 EC. Challenging Commission
Regulation 1572/2006/EC, the so-called maize intervention Regulation, and seeking
the annulment of certain provisions therein were of particular interest to the country,
having a significant agriculture sector, and most of corn intervention stocks (approximately 93%) were located in Hungary. The said Regulation was also of particular
interest for Hungary in the course of legislative procedure. Within the Agriculture
Council, Hungary gained the support of other Member States[157] in going counter the
proposal, but the coalition resulted only in the postponement of adoption. In the European
Parliament rapporteur MEP was a Hungarian member from the European People's
Party. The shadow-rapporteur, appointed by the European Socialist faction, was also a
Hungarian MEP in the European Social Party group of the EP. The drafting process
within the EP contributed to a significant delay in the Council discussions, which later
served to be a good strategy for the countries opposing the proposal. The report prepared
by the rapporteur MEP rejected as a whole the Commission's proposal and was adopted in the Agricultural Committee of the EP, but it was eventually rejected in the final
plenary debate. The plenary finally approved a compromise, with a transitory period
aiming to phase out and to abolish the intervention system. The German Presidency in
the meantime already toned down the Commission's radical original initiative and
rather aimed at a compromise with transitory periods. A blocking-minority was formed
even against this toned-down construction with the lead of the French, proposing that
such reform should wait and integrate into the overall reform of the Common Agricultural
Policy to be expected in 2008-09. At a June 2007 meeting of the Agriculture Council,
the Regulation was adopted, gradually phasing out and setting ceilings for intervention
of maize, while finally abolishing it as of the 2009-10 marketing year. It is notable that
Hungary abstained from voting.[158] Thus, despite extremely forceful lobbying techniques,
a compromise was reached only with regard to the entry into force of the system envisaged by the Regulation. Following the adoption, the Hungarian Prime Minister put
forward a letter to Commission President Barroso highlighting the controversial aspects
of said Regulation and its potentially detrimental effects for Hungarian maize producers.[159] Finally, the Hungarian Government requested annulment of certain provisions
of the said Regulation relating to the criterion of specific weight of intervention maize,
claiming that they are detrimental to Hungarian maize producers and, as such, breached
the principles of legitimate expectations, legal certainty and proportionality. The
Hungarian Government also put forward a request for interim measures in the application of the provision of the Regulation, which was subsequently rejected,[160] but the
Court of First Instance did grant the applicant's request for an expedited procedure and
also referred the case to the Grand Chamber. The Hungarian Ministry of Justice and

---

[157] France, Italy, Slovakia and Austria were also opposing the proposal.

[158] See Press Release from the Agriculture Council meeting available at http://europa.eu/rapid/press
ReleasesAction.do?reference=IP/07/793&format=HTML&aged=0&language=EN&guiLanguage=en.

[159] The letter of Prime Minister Gyurcsány can be found at the website of the Ministry of Agriculture
(in Hungarian) at http://www.fvm.hu.

[160] Order of the President of the Court of First Instance of 16 February 2007, Case T-310/06R,
*OJ* 2007 C 95/42.

Law Enforcement worked closely with the Ministry of Agriculture on the submissions and regarded as an outstanding result the granting of expedited procedure as well as the final annulment of the provisions of the Regulation. Clearly, the said Regulation was in the limelight in domestic politics and particularly high on the priority list for the Government. As to the result of the proceedings in Luxembourg, the judgment of the CFI brought an important achievement for the Hungarian Government. The Court decided to annul said provisions of Commission Regulation (EC) No 1572/2006 of 18 October 2006 amending Regulation (EC) No 824/2000 establishing procedures for taking-over of cereals by intervention agencies and laying down methods of analysis for determining the quality of cereals relating to the criterion of specific weight for maize.[161]

Another direct action by the Government challenged the validity of Commission Decision of 16 April 2007 on the national plan for the allocation of greenhouse gas emission allowances notified by Hungary in accordance with Directive 2003/87/EC of the European Parliament and of the Council. The national plans for the allocation of greenhouse gas emission allowances were deemed rather contradictory in many other new Member States as well and implied a spectacularly quick reaction and submission of pleas after one another. Slovakia,[162] Latvia,[163] Lithuania,[164] Poland,[165] Estonia,[166] the Czech Republic[167] and Romania[168] submitted complaints against the Commission's decisions regarding their applicable national allocation plans. The Hungarian claim enlisted various grounds for annulment of the said Decision (such as lack of competence, manifest error of assessment, infringement of principle of fair co-operation and not adequate statement of reasons) in order to render the restrictive Community measure inapplicable in its form.[169] This particular issue reveals a rather sensitive point: the national allocation plans were adopted by the Commission Decision and were based on Directive 2003/87/EC, a measure that was adopted in a decision-making procedure in 2003 excluding the voting possibility for the new Member States (in which they could only participate as observers). Nevertheless, the said Commission Decision imposes restrictive and demanding obligations which the Member States are obligated to respect as Article 10 EC and the principle of loyal co-operation mandates them to do. The developments in Slovakia's case were particularly noteworthy. First, the Commission reconsidered the country's obligations upon the commencement of direct

---

[161] CFI, Case T-310/06 *Republic of Hungary v. Commission of the European Communities* [2007] *ECR* II-4619.

[162] Case T-32/07 *the Slovak Republic v. Commission of the European Communities*, *OJ* 2007 C 69/29.

[163] Case T-369/07 *Republic of Latvia v. Commission of the European Communities*, *OJ* 2007 C 269/66.

[164] Case T-368/07 *Republic of Lithuania v. Commission of the European Communities*, *OJ* 2007 C 283/35.

[165] Case T-183/07 *Republic of Poland v. Commission of the European Communities*, *OJ* 2007 C 155/41.

[166] Case T-263/07 *Republic of Estonia v. Commission of the European Communities*, *OJ* 2007 C 223/12.

[167] Case T-194/07 *Czech Republic v. Commission of the European Communities*, *OJ* 2007 C 199/38.

[168] Case T-483/07 *Romania v. Commission of the European Communities*, *OJ* 2008 C 51/56.

[169] Case T-221/07 *Republic of Hungary v. Commission of the European Communities*, *OJ* C 199/41.

action in front of the CFI. As a consequence, the Slovak authorities regarded this outcome as proving that the challenge had 'fulfilled its purpose and been successful';[170] therefore, the Slovak Government finally revoked its claim. At the time of writing the present study, the Hungarian case was still pending.

Alongside the cases of direct action initiated by Hungary, the Hungarian Government intervened in direct actions initiated by other Member States or Community institutions and put forward its positions in various instances.[171]

## 10.2.    Individuals challenging Community acts

Direct action against a Community regulation put forward by individuals and the challenge of proving individual concern for admissibility was taken by a Hungarian company, *CityLine Kft.*, and lodged at the CFI on 27 June 2007, asking the Court to declare Article 2 of Commission Regulation 375/2007/EC invalid. The Article deals with the continued operation of certain aircrafts registered by Member States. The said company claimed that the contested provision of the Regulation infringes the general principle of proportionality as well as legal certainty. With regard to the second ground, the applicant claimed that the Regulation requires registration of aircraft for its operation before Hungary's accession to the EU, and such requirement could not have been foreseeable by concerned persons, such as the claimant.[172] In May 2008, the applicant informed the CFI that it would withdraw its claims, and the case was removed from the register.[173]

Further references and claims based upon pre-accession situations were put forward by a Hungarian district heating supplier and electricity supplier against one of the Commission's decisions[174] to open formal investigation procedures into alleged new state aid in the form of power purchase agreements concluded between Hungarian electricity generators and the public Hungarian transmission operator. Based on the submission that the Commission only has jurisdiction over aid measures which are still applicable after the date of the country's accession to the EU, the applicant claimed that in the present case, the Commission lacked competence to take the decision, as the power purchase agreements were concluded prior to accession and were not still appli-

---

[170] Slovak Nap decision finalises 2008-12 EU ETS cap ENDS Europe DAILY 2445, 07/12/07.

[171] ECJ, Case C-304/02 *Commission of the European Communities v. French Republic* [2005] *ECR* I-6263; Case C-273/04 *Republic of Poland v. Council of the European Union* [2007] *ECR* I-8925; Case C-440/05 *Commission of the European Communities v. Council of the European Union* [2007] *ECR* I-9097; CFI, T-417/04 *Regione Autonoma Friuli-Venezia Giulia v. Commission of the European Communities* [2007] *ECR* II-641; Case T-418/04 *Confcooperative, Unione regionale della Cooperazione Fvg Federagricole and others v. Commission* [2007] *ECR* II-24; Case T-32/07 *the Slovak Republic v. Commission of the European Communities*, *OJ* 2007 C 69/29.

[172] Case T-237/07 *CityLine Hungary Kft. v. Commission of the European Communities*, *OJ* 2007 C 211/41.

[173] Order of the Court of First Instance of 9 July 2008 – *CityLine Hungary v. Commission* (Case T-237/07), *OJ* 2008 C 223/58.

[174] Decision of the European Commission to open the formal investigation procedure in Case State aid C41/2005 (ex NN 49/2005) Hungarian Stranded Costs of 9 November 2005.

cable after accession.[175] Certainly much anticipation revolves around the outcomes of the pending direct actions, the one submitted by the Government for its political weight and the other one for the consideration of individual concern and the claims based on pre-accession factors.

## 11.    CONCLUSIONS

This chapter reveals important challenges faced by the judiciary that has gone through a reconstruction after the change of political regime with the aim of establishing a functional state based on rule of law, just to face another challenge: to apply Community law consistently and in a self-started matter from the day of accession.

Law of the European Union takes a particular place in the interpretative decisions of the Constitutional Court. These decisions give guidance on the fundamental inter-relations between Community law and the national legal order from a constitutional point of view. Within the judiciary, the Supreme Court and ordinary courts, the application of Community law has increasingly gained attention and is gradually increasing in practice. The Supreme Court takes a special position with a consistent application of underlying doctrines (consistent interpretation, *acte clair* and direct effect) serving to guide national judges. As to preliminary procedures, the Hungarian courts are rather active in engaging in a dialogue with the ECJ. Despite one stumbling block in identifying which case would fit into the ECJ's jurisdiction for interpretation, the remaining references proved to be meaningful, illuminating crucial legal issues, and the outcome is applied consistently and identified successfully by the national judges in their practice.

As to the loyal co-operation that requires, *inter alia*, the proper implementation of EU law, Hungary shows good figures in transposition of directives and in case of late action, catching up with transposition. Matters of more serious action by the Commission arose in issue with sensitive political character, typically requiring wider political consensus and qualified majority voting in political parties within the Parliament for the adoption of the implementing act or amendment of the existing act breaching EU law. Every infringement procedure resulted in the Government's action to recuperate the breach of EU law before the ECJ would have imposed penalties for the conduct.

The Government also aims to guard national interest in matters where that has not been adequately inserted in the EU legislative measure upon its adoption. The overview illustrated that the Hungarian Government, in its claims challenging Community acts, puts forward a broad scope of grounds, conduct that has been so far rather successful. Direct actions put forward by individuals touch upon the issues of individual concern as well as pre-accession aspects, and the outcomes will certainly be of great interest for the individuals of other new Member States.

---

[175]  CFI, Case T-80/06 *Budapesti Erőmű v. Commission*, *OJ* 2006 C 108/25.

*Chapter 13*

# THE APPLICATION OF EU LAW IN SLOVENIA: TEETHING TROUBLES OF THE BLUE-EYED BOY

Saša Zagorc* and Samo Bardutzky**

## 1.     INTRODUCTION

Slovenia occasionally leaves the impression of a diligent student seated in the front row when it comes to issues of European integration. The public support for EU membership was very high and both the high turnout and percentage of votes for the accession at the March 2003 EU referendum are only equalled by the 1990 referendum on independence of the country. This allows us to conclude that both strategic goals enjoyed a similarly broad level of support on the part of citizens. A cause for the nation's pride was also that Slovenia was the first of the new Member States to join the Eurozone.

The Slovenian path for European integration has not been entirely free of obstacles. Those can hardly be traced to lack of will to fulfil the expectations and become an equal player in the Union; on the contrary, one could almost say that even blue-eyed boys have trouble teething.

The aim of this chapter is to take a close look at several issues regarding the attitude of Slovenian authorities, especially courts towards EU law and its relationship with the national legal order. The chapter will demonstrate that case law has developed in a fairly consistent fashion, without any substantial deviations from the well-established jurisprudence of the European Court of Justice.

Decisions of the Constitutional Court are analysed in a separate section, where matters regarding the application of the European Arrest Warrant, the principle of supremacy and application of EC regulations are also covered. Case law of the Supreme Court is dealt with in sections devoted to asylum and labour law (together with the jurisprudence of lower courts). We chose these two areas of law to depict the positive development of the recognition of EU law within the judiciary.

Some basic information on Slovenia's interventions in both preliminary ruling procedures and actions for annulment is elaborated on, primarily to shed some additional light on Slovenia's activity in the Luxembourg courtrooms.

\*   Assistant Professor, Faculty of Law, University of Ljubljana, Slovenia.
\*\* Researcher, Faculty of Law, University of Ljubljana, Slovenia.
Although the contribution is a result of mutual efforts, Saša Zagorc predominantly dealt with sections 1, 2 and 6, while Samo Bardutzky concentrated on sections 3, 4 and 5.

*A. Łazowski (ed.), The Application of EU Law in the New Member States*
© 2010, T·M·C·Asser press, *The Hague, The Netherlands and the Authors*

On several occasions, case law presented in this chapter may indicate a certain direction of development; however, it still remains too scarce for firm conclusions to be drawn. Accordingly, we refrained from generalisations that might, with the benefit of hindsight, turn out to be too hasty.

2.      DECISIONS OF THE CONSTITUTIONAL COURT ON THE
        APPLICATION OF EU LAW

2.1.    **Introduction**

The Constitutional Court has functioned in the Republic of Slovenia since 1963; however, it had not borne real significance until the Constitution of the Republic of Slovenia was adopted in 1991. It provided for a variety of new competencies of the Court.[1] As outlined in this chapter, decisions of the Constitutional Court regarding the relationship between European Union law and Slovenian law were a result of different proceedings before the Court. This included proceedings concerning constitutional complaint, assessment of constitutionality of international treaties in the process of ratification, assessment of constitutionality of laws and by-laws. Nowadays, the Constitutional Court is considered one of the "stronger" Constitutional Courts in Europe.[2] The Constitutional Court managed to further strengthen its position as the leading legal body and important political actor with some decisions that provoked enormous political consequences in Slovenia.[3] With this in mind, it is not surprising that the Slovenian academic circles were hardly waiting to see how the Constitutional Court would cope with the adjudication in matters of EU dimension. It has to be emphasised at the outset that the Constitutional Court has from 1994, i.e., the very beginning of the formal application of the European Convention on Human Rights in relation to Slovenia, extensively leaned its reasoning on jurisprudence of the European Court of Human Rights, particularly in the review of constitutional complaints.[4]

The role of the Constitutional Court and other courts in the Republic of Slovenia in the pre-accession period differs largely from the one after 1 May 2004. The approximation process in the pre-membership era was dominated mostly by the Government and

---

[1] Art. 160 *Ustava Republike Slovenije* [Constitution of the Republic of Slovenia], Ur. l. RS, št. 33/1991, 42/1997, 66/2000, 24/2003, 69/2004, 68/2006 (hereafter the Constitution).

[2] F. Testen, '160. člen (pristojnosti Ustavnega sodišča)' [Article 160 (Powers of the Constitutional Court)]', in L. Šturm, ed., *Komentar Ustave Republike Slovenije* [Commentary of the Constitution of the Republic of Slovenia] (Ljubljana, FPDEŠ 2002) p. 1090.

[3] E.g., decision of the Constitutional Court U-I-246/02 of 3 April 2003 regarding the issue of so-called erased persons; decision of the Constitutional Court U-12/97 of 8 October 1998 regarding the referendum on election systems for parliamentary elections.

[4] Up to 2005 the ECHR has been directly cited in more than 300 decisions of the Constitutional Court, and in approximately 80 cases, the Constitutional Court has referred to the case law of the ECrtHR. See also C. Ribičič, 'The European Dimension of the Decision-Making of the Constitutional Court of the Republic of Slovenia', in C. Ribičič, et al., *1 Jahr EU Mitgliedschaft: Erste Bilanz aus der Sicht der Slowenischen Höchstgerichte, Working paper* No. 19 (Vienna, Institut für Europäische Integrationsforschung 2005) pp. 8-9.

the National Assembly and was supported by immense media coverage. Article 70 EA Slovenia was the formal legal basis for the approximation of Slovenian law with that of the European Union.[5] The Constitutional Court thus, with the exception of several decisions, did not need to place itself on "the European approximation highway".

## 2.2. The pre-accession period

The first serious confrontation of the Constitutional Court with European Union matters occurred in the course of ratification of the EA Slovenia. According to Article 160(2) of the Constitution, the Constitutional Court issues opinions on the conformity of international treaties with the Constitution in the so-called *ex ante* review of constitutionality. It does so on the proposal of certain state authorities or a group of members of the Parliament, and such opinions bind the National Assembly. The Government requested such review in a reaction to speculations whether the provisions of EA Slovenia on acquisition of real estate by aliens were in conformity with the provision of Article 68 of the Constitution. Pursuant to the latter, the Slovenian real estate market had been highly inaccessible to foreign natural and legal persons until 1997. The Constitutional Court opined that the provision of EA Slovenia, which guaranteed equal treatment of foreigners and Slovenian nationals on the real estate market, was in conflict with the Constitution. Article 68(2) provided that foreigners were not allowed to acquire title to land except by inheritance (subject to reciprocity). Therefore, the National Assembly was not allowed to approve any such commitment under international law as it would be in clear conflict with the Constitution. The option available was to proceed with a formal amendment of the Constitution.[6] In other words, the Constitution could not be amended 'in a disguised way by ratification of treaties; the rule of law and legitimacy require the parliaments to respect the more stringent constitutional amendment.'[7] Reformulation of the provisions of the signed EA Slovenia in a way that the constitutional amendments would not be necessary was neither mentioned nor discussed in the opinion. The result of the opinion was the first amendment of the Constitution in 1997, which allowed the finalisation of ratification of the EA Slovenia. In the follow-up to the opinion, the Constitutional Court rejected or dismissed all petitions for subsequent review of the constitutionality of the ratified EA Slovenia.[8]

Notwithstanding a minor exposure in the pre-accession period, the Constitutional Court still managed to clearly indicate its "European policy", mainly by making references to the legislation of the European Union. One could argue that the Constitutional

---

[5] Europe Agreement establishing an association between the European Communities and their Member States, acting within the framework of the European Union, on the one part, and the Republic of Slovenia, on the other part, *OJ* 1999 L 51/3.

[6] See opinion of the Constitutional Court Rm-1/97 of 5 June 1997.

[7] See A. Albi, 'Supremacy of EC Law in the New Member States Bringing parliaments into the Equation of "Co-operative Constitutionalism"', 3 *EuConst* (2007) pp. 25-67.

[8] See M. Škrk, 'The Role of the Constitutional Court of the Republic of Slovenia Following Integration into the European Union', in A. Mavčič, ed., *International Conference The Position of Constitutional Courts Following Integration Into the European Union, Bled, Slovenia, 30 September – 2 October 2004* (Ljubljana, Ustavno sodišče Republike Slovenije 2005) p. 140.

Court, by doing this, only wanted to snatch any counter-argument from those who would oppose its argumentation.[9] In our opinion, this was not the case. Although the Constitutional Court could substantiate its viewpoints by sticking only to the interpretation of the Constitution, an EU-friendly approach of the Constitutional Court was perceived pretty early. In decision U-I-298/96, it based its reasoning on Council Directive 79/7/EEC on the principle of equal treatment for men and women.[10] With reference to this, it further set forth reasons that a gradual and progressive implementation does not contravene the constitutional principle of equality before the law.[11]

It is obvious that the Constitutional Court did not formally review the conformity of EU legal acts with the Constitution in the pre-accession period. However, the EA Slovenia and a huge amount of legislation, which was under the review of the Constitutional Court, were regarded as an implementation of *acquis communitaire* (due to the substantial amount of identical legal norms). By reviewing provisions of national law or international treaties in the process of ratification, the Constitutional Court could not abide the well-established concepts of EU law. That is why the principle of loyal interpretation comes as no surprise in the jurisprudence of the Constitutional Court, even in the pre-accession period. During this period, the application of loyal interpretation of national provisions in the light of EU law can be perceived as an additional tool to give more elaborate reasoning. Technically, this is visible by the use of certain adverbs (e.g., "also", "in addition", "finally", "beside that"). It would have been a problem though, if references to EU law had served as a crutch for the weak basic argumentation of (un)constitutionality of national provisions. This was not the case.

One of the competencies of the Constitutional Court involves the review of national laws with international agreements ratified by the National Assembly (Art. 153 of the Constitution). Since the Republic of Slovenia had concluded agreements with the European Communities/European Union and its Member States in the pre-accession period, these treaties were binding for the Constitutional Court. It, therefore, designated the scope of legal acts and documents on which individuals could rely when submitting requests for the assessment of conformity of laws with international agreements.[12]

---

[9] Such was namely practice of the Government, which quite often stressed the importance of accelerated passing of the "European legislation" in the National Assembly in order to avoid a thorough debate on important issues. See also Art. 142 *Poslovnik državnega zbora, uradno prečiščeno besedilo* [Rules of the Procedure of the National Assembly, consolidated version], Ur. l. RS, št. 92/07.

[10] Council Directive 79/7/EC of 19 December 1978 on the progressive implementation of the principle of equal treatment for men and women in matters of social security, *OJ* 1979 L 6/24.

[11] 'This goal [equality of sexes, authors' note] cannot be achieved by declaring equality and simply over the night. As asserted by the National Assembly and the Government, also the legislation of the European Union in the area of social security prescribes a gradual implementation of this principle. Council Directive 79/7/EEC of 19 December 1978 on the progressive implementation of the principle of equal treatment of men and women in matters of social security in its title demonstrates that the matter concerns the gradual introduction of the equality for men and women in determining conditions for the exercise of the rights arising under the statutory systems of social security.' Decision of the Constitutional Court U-I-298/96 of 11 November 1999.

[12] 'As the applicant does not assert eventual non-conformity of the contested act with the Europe Agreement establishing an association between the Republic of Slovenia of the one part, and the European

Two decisions need to be mentioned in connection with the effects of EU law *ratione temporis*. The question was which law applied in cases when material facts had taken place before the accession to the EU and possibly still produced legal effects after the accession.[13] In the decision of the Constitutional Court U-I-233/03, interesting notions of the principle of legality and the relationship between the EU and national legal orders were raised. Although the Constitutional Court rendered a decision after the accession to the EU, it referred to the validity of EU legislation in the pre-accession period. Besides that, the Constitutional Court did not find it necessary to answer whether EU law should have applied when a tax duty of petitioner still existed after the accession of Slovenia to the European Union. It set out that the tax duty originated from the pre-accession period. According to the Ministry of Finance, Germany and Italy did not refund VAT due for engine fuel to a taxable person with the registered office in Slovenia. Therefore, a material reciprocity was established by the certain Rules of the Ministry on 1 January 2003 in accordance with the Eighth Council Directive 79/1072/EC, which made the refund of VAT subject to reciprocity.[14] The Constitutional Court rejected assertions of the Ministry by pointing out that the legislation in the time of the validity of the Rules did not contain any legal grounds and did not set any framework for establishment of reciprocity by the Rules.[15] The Constitutional Court thus established that the provision of the Rules had independently and without a statutory ground defined rights and duties of taxable persons. Since the provision of the Rules was not in accordance with Article 120(2) of the Constitution – which states that administrative bodies perform their work independently within the framework and on the basis of the Constitution and laws – it was declared unconstitutional. It is obvious, although the Court did not explicitly address this issue in the decision, that it did not consider the Directive as binding law since the alleged duty to refund VAT had been established before the accession to the EU. Therefore, the Ministry could not base its decision to introduce reciprocity in the Rules solely on the Directive as long as the Republic of Slovenia had not been a member of the EU. It means that the principle of loyal interpretation to which national authorities are bound could not be applied in full scale in the pre-accession period. Nevertheless, national authorities could determine rights and duties of individuals in a way that they followed the purposes and goals of EU legislation even in the pre-accession period, save they meet all constitutional and other requirements in issuing legal acts. The Constitutional Court decision thus faith-

---

Communities and their Member States, acting within the framework of the European Union, including the final act, *or with any other agreement between the Republic of Slovenia and the European Union* [emphasis added], the Constitutional Court did not review the assertions', decision of the Constitutional Court U-I-141/97 of 22 November 2001.

[13] See R. Knez, '*Učinki prava ES ratione temporis*' [Effects of EC Law ratione temporis], 2 *Evro PP* (2004) pp. 9-11.

[14] Eighth Council Directive 79/1072/EEC of 6 December 1979 on the harmonisation of the laws of the Member States relating to turnover taxes – Arrangements for the refund of value added tax to taxable persons not established in the territory of the country, *OJ* 1979 L 331/11.

[15] Decision of the Constitutional Court U-I-233/03 of 24 March 2005.

fully follows the *Von Colson* like approach of applying the principle of loyal interpretation.[16]

In the second decision, the joined cases Up-328/04 and U-I-186/04, the Constitutional Court dealt with a case of bankruptcy that had occurred prior to accession to the European Union.[17] A referral was made by a German bank to the Council Regulation 1346/2000/EC on insolvency proceedings.[18] The petitioner argued that it should be informed of bankruptcy pursuant to the Regulation. The Constitutional Court did not accept the constitutional complaint and dismissed the petition to begin the review of constitutionality of the Slovenian bankruptcy law. It argued that prior to the accession to the EU, Slovenian courts had not been obliged to observe the Regulation, as Slovenia had not yet been a member of the European Union.[19] Although the bankruptcy case was still in the judicial proceedings after the accession, the Constitutional Court implicitly (since the decision did not refer to this) held that the phase of lodging claims, which had been disputed, ended before the accession to the EU. One can reproach the decision's awkwardly put reasoning that the provision of the Regulation on informing creditors is of a procedural (not substantive) nature, which is a correct remark, with an unintended misleading result, since the nature of the provision does not have an influence on validity of EU law in the pre-accession period.

## 2.3.    Post-accession decisions

Upon the accession to the EU, the Constitutional Court cannot abide the application of EU law on the grounds that it is not yet binding on Slovenia. Besides that, the Constitutional Court needs to apply EU law seriously and cautiously thenceforth, since it became an integral part of the European Union network of judicial bodies. It is not unusual that the Constitutional Court primarily deals with broader systemic issues and the relationship of EU and national law in contrast to the jurisprudence of ordinary courts, which decide in individual cases of application of EU law.

When it comes to questions of interpretation and validity of EU law, case law of the Constitutional Court relates to matters of factual suspension of implementation of EU law, limits of competence on assessment of conformity of national legislation with EU law and, predominantly, interpretation of national law in compliance with EU law, which – as a result – produces different legal effects for national legislation and national authorities.

So far, the most dramatic and substantial interweaving of the Constitutional Court jurisprudence and EU law happened in the so-called "Animal Feed Case".[20] At stake

---

[16] 'It is for the national court to interpret and apply the legislation adopted for the implementation of the Directive in conformity with the requirements of Community law, *in so far as it is given discretion to do so under national law*' [emphasis added]. ECJ, Case 14/83 *Von Colson and Kamann v. Land Nordrhein-Westfalen* [1984] *ECR* 1891, para. 28.

[17] Decision of the Constitutional Court Up-318/04 and U-I-186/04 of 8 July 2004.

[18] Council Regulation 1346/2000/EC of 29 May 2000 on insolvency proceedings, *OJ* 2000 L 160/1.

[19] See also Ribičič, *loc. cit.* n. 4, at pp. 10-11.

[20] Order of the Constitutional Court U-I-113/04 of 8 July 2004. Some refer to it as the "Jata Case", see M. Brkan, 'Zadeva Jata: Ustavno Sodišče in pravo EU' [Jata Case: The Constitutional Court and the EU Law], 25 *Pravna praksa* (2006) pp. 25-27.

was the request for a suspension of implementation (temporary injunction) of several provisions of Rules on the Quality, Labelling and Packing of Feedingstuffs in Circulation.[21] The Rules implemented provisions of Directive 2002/2/EC on feeding-stuffs issues. A temporary injunction may be ordered by the Constitutional Court; however, in that case, it acted according to the well-established case law of the ECJ on temporary injunctions. This was in order to satisfy the principle of effective judicial protection of individual's rights under Community law.[22] Instead of assessing only a criterion of difficulties to remedy harmful consequences,[23] a thorough assessment of four criteria established by the ECJ took place.[24] The duty of the Constitutional Court has been broadened in a way that it must demonstrate, in order to issue temporary injunctions, harmful effects while observing not only national scope but also the Community's one. However, such criteria do not worsen the actual position and pos-sibilities of petitioners to succeed with a request for interim relief. In this regard, the decision complies with newer case law of the ECJ.[25] The Constitutional Court sus-pended the implementation of the provisions of the Rules until the final decision of the ECJ on the validity of the Directive was rendered.

Yet, the Constitutional Court attitude towards the review of compliance of EU sec-ondary legislation with the Constitution is noticed in the short and flaccid remark, which other commentators completely overlooked.[26] Namely, the Constitutional Court does neither acquiesce in it nor exclude it from the future considerations. If the position of the Constitutional Court is firm, in the sense that the review of EU law is not in the scope of its competences, such a statement would not find its place in the issued tem-

---

[21] *Pravilnik o kakovosti, označevanju in pakiranju krme v prometu* [Rules on the Quality, Labelling and Packing of Feedingstuffs in Circulation], Ur. l. RS, št. 34/03.

[22] ECJ, Cases C-143/88 and C-92/89 *Zuckerfabrik Süderdithmarschen and Zuckerfabrik Soest* [1991] *ECR* I-451, para. 27; ECJ, Case C-465/93 *Atlanta Fruchthandelsgesellschaft mbH and others v. Bundesamt für Ernährung und Forstwirtschaft* [1995] *ECR* I-3761, para. 39.

[23] Art. 39(1) *Zakon o ustavnem sodišču, uradno prečiščeno besedilo* [Constitutional Court Act, con-solidated version], Ur. l. RS, št. 64/2007, provides: 'Until a final decision, the Constitutional Court may suspend in whole or in part the implementation of a law, other regulation, or general act issued for the exercise of public authority if difficult to remedy harmful consequences could result from the implementa-tion thereof.'

[24] The Constitutional Court needed to: 1. demonstrate serious doubts about the validity of the Direc-tive in terms of EU law; 2. refer the question of validity of the Directive to the ECJ if it had not already been brought before the ECJ by other authorities; 3. assess whether an urgency and a threat of serious and irreparable damage to the petitioner exists; 4. take into account the Community's interests. See J. Sladič, 'Spremembe v procesnem pravu in praksi slovenskih sodišč zaradi odločb Sodišča ES' [Changes in the procedural law and practice of Slovenian Courts due to the decisions of the ECJ], 33 *Podjetje in delo* (2007) pp. 1140-1141.

[25] The grant of interim relief must be necessary to ensure the full effectiveness of the judgment to be given on the existence of individual rights under Community law, provided that the criteria to grant interim relief are no less favourable than those applying to similar domestic actions and do not render practically impossible or excessively difficult the interim judicial protection of those rights, see ECJ, Case C-432/05 *Unibet (London) Ltd and Unibet (International) Ltd v. Justitiekanslern* [2007] *ECR* I-2271.

[26] 'As also the issue of the validity of the Directive, on which the Rules are based, is raised in the case at issue, the Constitutional Court did not need to address the issue whether and under which conditions the Constitutional Court could suspend the implementation of the Rules if there was only the issue of its con-formity with the Constitution'; see Order of the Constitutional Court U-I-113/04 of 8 July 2004, para. 8.

porary injunction order. Beside that, no statement on this issue was actually necessary for the decision. Two explanations are at hand why the wording was such. In our opinion, either the mysterious wording is a result of "judicial bargaining" to reach an agreement on the reasoning, or the affirmative approach towards the review of EU law with the Constitution may be expected in future considerations.

Once the ECJ rendered its judgment in case *ABNA and others*,[27] the Constitutional Court reinstated the suspended proceedings. In decision U-I-113/04, it repeated that the challenged Rules restate – in terms of substance – what was already determined in the Directive. By formally requiring annulment of the challenged provision of the Rules, the petitioners challenged provisions of the Directive which prescribe certain obligations concerning feedingstuffs. Since the ECJ established that – from the view of the principle of proportionality – there was no element that would affect the validity of the provision of the Directive, and that it did not violate fundamental rights, in particular the right to property and the right to freely carry out one's profession, the Constitutional Court made a comparison whether the scope and the substance of fundamental rights corresponded to the ones in the Constitution. It ascertained that human rights in Article 33 (right to private property), Article 60 (intellectual property rights), Article 67 (property) and Article 74 (free enterprise) of the Constitution did not ensure more rights than EU law. This conclusion of the Constitutional Court concerns only the case at issue and the specific circumstances of this case.[28] By stressing the individuality and concreteness of the case, the Constitutional Court suggests that the comparison cannot lead to any generalisation. Nevertheless, the opinion of academic circles alludes to the opposite that, in terms of substance, the protection of fundamental rights in the European Union, generally, at least equals the protection guaranteed by the Constitution.[29] The question is whether the Constitutional Court closed the doors to change its position in future decisions in cases of new and drastically altered circumstances. The Constitutional Court rests on the presumption that the position could eventually be challenged. However, from now on, the Constitutional Court will very probably not review the level of protection of fundamental rights on a case-to-case basis, unless parties will provide new facts or a review will concern the level of protection of those fundamental rights which has not been evaluated yet in relationship to EU law. Such a challengeable presumption of equivalence indicates that the initial burden of proof that the Constitution ensures a higher level of protection than EU law is now shifted completely on the petitioners' side.

Regarding the limits of its competence, the Constitutional Court still needs to give "free and basic lessons" to petitioners from time to time.[30] For instance, the Court

---

[27] ECJ, Joined Cases C-453/03, C-11/04, C-12/04 and C-194/04 *The Queen, on the application of ABNA Ltd and Others v. Secretary of State for Health and Food Standards Agency (C-453/03), Fratelli Martini & C. SpA and Cargill Srl v. Ministero delle Politiche Agricole e Forestali and Others (C-11/04), Ferrari Mangimi Srl and Associazione nazionale tra i produttori di alimenti zootecnici (Assalzoo) v. Ministero delle Politiche Agricole e Forestali and Others (C-12/04) and Nederlandse Vereniging Diervoederindustrie (Nevedi) v. Productschap Diervoeder (C-194/04)* [2005] *ECR* I-10423.

[28] Decision of the Constitutional Court U-I-113/04 of 7 February 2007.

[29] See Sladič, *loc. cit.* n. 24, at p. 1139.

[30] The "pedagogical" approach may originate in the predominance of university professors at the Constitutional Court throughout the 1990s and in the first half of the present decade.

stressed that it does not decide on conformity of laws with EC directives.[31] An act of EU law cannot be the sole legal ground on which the Constitutional Court would abrogate a Slovenian legal act, but it may serve as an additional interpretative tool in the reasoning of decisions of the Constitutional Court. The principle of loyal interpretation was emphasised with the name, its meaning and with references to the ECJ cases in the decision of the Constitutional Court U-I-321/02 early after the accession.[32]

When it comes to the interpretation of national law in light of EU law, the Constitutional Court firmly stands on the position that the matter at stake should be adjudicated solely by the application of national law only if no legal obligations for national authorities derive from EU law. In decision U-I-199/02, the Constitutional Court refused to follow the line of a petitioner's assertions that Directive 2004/25/EC on takeover bids[33] does not require abolition of a possibility of statutory limitations of voting rights in public limited companies. The Court agreed with the petitioner in general; yet it read the Directive in a way that the latter does not forbid such abolition as well. A possible abolition is a matter of national legislation.[34] Since EU law in the present case did not oblige national authorities to act in a manner compatible with it, the legislator was bound only by the constraints deriving from the Constitution (principle of proportionality, principle of legality, etc.).

In decision U-I-220/03, the Constitutional Court needed, among other issues, to review whether Article 224 of the Securities Market Act[35] – that gave a legal basis to withdraw the authorisation to conduct functions of a management board member of the Stock Exchange –lacked clarity and was vague insofar as it allowed an arbitrary action of state authorities, which would render it unconstitutional.[36] In *obiter dicta*, the Constitutional Court[37] explained that Council Directive 93/22/EEC on certain types of

---

[31] '[F]or this reason, the party cannot substantiate its assertions on non-conformity with the principle of proportionality with references to the Council Directive 2003/49/EC of 3.6.2003.' See Order of the Constitutional Court U-I-44/05 of 11 September 2007.

[32] 'And finally, the principle of loyal interpretation dictates such interpretation according to which the national law should be interpreted in the light of the Community law. From the jurisprudence of the European Court of Justice namely derives that the law of the European Community should be interpreted in a way that the time of a duty health service, in framework of which a doctor must be available at the working premises, reckons fully in the working time of the doctor.' See Decision of the Constitutional Court U-I-321/02 of 27 May 2004.

[33] Directive 2004/25/EC of the European Parliament and of the Council of 21 April 2004 on takeover bids, *OJ* 2004 L 142/12.

[34] Decision of the Constitutional Court U-I-199/02 of 21 October 2004.

[35] *Zakon o trgu vrednostnih papirjev* [Securities Market Act], Ur. l. RS, št. 56/1999, 52/2002, 108/2003, 117/2003, 16/2004, 86/2004. The Act was subsequently revised by another piece of legislation.

[36] 'The issue of lack of clarity and vagueness of the contested provision pops up in connection with the definition of a vague legal term repeated infringements. First, the question of interpretation of this term regarding the minimum number of infringements that has to be established in order to [fulfil the conditions for the withdrawal of authorisation, authors' note]. This dilemma can be resolved with the interpretation that there have to be … at least three reiterating infringements; if the legislator considers that two infringements would be enough, it should clearly prescribe so.' See decision of the Constitutional Court U-I-220/03, 13 October 2004.

[37] *Ibidem*.

investment services[38] mentioned the phrase "seriously and systematically infringes", which seems to be a more substantiated definition in comparison to the "repeated infringements" in the Slovenian legislation. Yet again, one gets an impression that the Constitutional Court did not hesitate to needlessly stick its nose into other institution's business. It called to attention that the transposition of the Directive had not been adequate. The competence of the Constitutional Court is to assess whether a provision of an act is in conformity with the Constitution. The issue of an appropriate transposition of directives can be challenged in other *fora;* that is why the Constitutional Court should refrain, as much as possible, from needless interpretation of EU law, especially in cases where the principle of loyal interpretation does not provide new arguments and viewpoints for a decision. Finally, as to the ruling of the Constitutional Court, the provision in question was declared unconstitutional as it did not protect management board members from arbitrary actions, since time-limits – in which infringements have to be committed – were not set.

In decision U-I-238/06,[39] the Constitutional Court instructed the legislator to take into consideration the judgment itself as well as provisions of the Council Directive 2005/85/EC on refugees (dealing, *inter alia*, with subsequent applications for asylum)[40] in order to rectify a discrepancy between the Asylum Act and the Constitution. It means that the correct transposition of EU law not only is the consequence of EU law but now may also derive from national law and authorities. The question was whether an asylum-seeker may submit in a subsequent application for asylum some new elements or findings relating to the examination of whether he/she qualifies as a refugee, regardless of the fact that they sprang up before or after the first decision of administrative authority had been issued. The Constitutional Court dismissed the assertions of the Government that the Directive allowed only the submission of findings that sprang up after the first decision had been issued. It resorted to teleological interpretation of Article 32(6) of the Directive, which implied that any, new or previous, evidence and findings may be reconsidered again in the subsequent application under certain conditions.[41] The provision of national legislation was declared unconstitutional as it violated the constitutional prohibition of torture that could have occurred in case of the *refoulement* without a proper assessment of newly submitted evidence and facts.

Finally, combined challenges of translation and transposition of EU law merit attention. In Decision U-I-293/04, the Constitutional Court dealt with interpretation of national law transposing Council Directive 87/102/EEC on consumer credits.[42]

---

[38] Council Directive 93/22/EEC of 10 May 1993 on investment services in the securities field, *OJ* 1993 L 141/27.

[39] Decision of the Constitutional Court U-I-238/06 of 7 December 2006.

[40] Council Directive 2005/85/EC of 1 December 2005 on minimum standards on procedures in Member States for granting and withdrawing refugee status, *OJ* 2005 L 326/13.

[41] 'Member States may decide to further examine the application only if the applicant concerned was, through no fault of his/her own, incapable of asserting the situations set forth in paragraphs 3, 4 and 5 of this Article in the previous procedure.'

[42] Council Directive 87/102/EEC of 22 December 1986 for the approximation of the laws, regulations and administrative provisions of the Member States concerning consumer credit, *OJ* 1987 L 42/48 (as amended).

Petitioners asserted that the protection of customers was guaranteed satisfactorily with the prohibition of usurious interest rates. Therefore, an obligation to respect the maximum annual percentage rate was, according to the petitioners, disproportional to their constitutional right of free economic activity. The Constitutional Court emphasised that the long-established definition of annual interest rate (in Slovenian, *letna obrestna mera*) in the Slovenian business practice cannot prevail over the clear and different definition of the equally named interest rate in the Directive. It accurately suggested – in *obiter dicta* – that the legislator should rather opt for a translation of the definition by its meaning and in accordance with the existing legal terminology in Slovenia (for example, *efektivna obrestna mera*), instead of the word-for-word translation.[43]

## 2.4. Supremacy unquestioned?

With the intention to give a better impression on the reception of principle of supremacy of EC law in the Slovenian legal system, one has to slightly turn back in the time to – in many ways – the unfortunate dissolution of Yugoslavia. Before many bloody battles occurred, a legal "battle" on several constitutional issues, one of them being the principle of supremacy of the federal Constitution and legislation over legal acts of federal states, had been going on between pro-federative, predominantly Serbian, and pro-confederative, mostly Slovenian, legal experts.[44] Despite nominally being a part of the federal state, the Slovenian Parliament adopted several constitutional amendments – the amendment XCVI being of the highest importance – that practically reversed the federal state, based on the principle of supremacy of federal law, into the confederation state.[45] While the consistency of legal argumentation of both sides can doubtlessly be contested in hindsight, the Slovenian authorities insisted in the said refit of the Yugoslav constitutional system, mainly by stressing the importance of the respect for human rights, fundamental freedoms and political pluralism as well. In the light of this experience, two comments can be made. First, the respect of human rights, which strongly underlines the valid Constitution, poses as *conditio sine qua non* for every sovereignty rearrangement on the territory of Slovenia. Second, one could interpret that the hardly won legal "battle" on the principle of the supremacy serves as proof of Slovenian unwillingness to accept the principle of supremacy in full scale. Yet, it seems that the pre-accession amendments of the Constitution took a slightly different direction.

The question how and to what extent to recognise the supremacy of EC/EU law was one of the hot issues in the pre-accession process of rearrangement of the constitutional framework. The "international law" clause in Article 8 of the Constitution was

---

[43] Decision of the Constitutional Court U-I-293/04, 6 October 2005.

[44] See C. Ribičič, *Ustavnopravni vidiki osamosvajanja Slovenije* [Constitutonal Aspects of Attainment of Slovenian Independence] (Ljubljana, Uradni list RS 1992) at pp. 27-30.

[45] *Amandma XCVI k Ustavi Republike Slovenije* [Amendment XCVI to the Constitution of the Republic of Slovenia], Ur. l. SRS, št. 35/1990, which stated that those provisions of the Constitution of the Socialist Federative Republic of Yugoslavia that conflict with the Constitution of the Republic of Slovenia should not be applied in the Republic of Slovenia. Beside that, a special constitutional act should have determined federal acts that were not to apply in the Republic of Slovenia.

deemed to be insufficient to allow the accession to the EU without a prior revision of the Constitution. With this in mind, the so-called European Articles (Arts. 3a, 47 and 68) were incorporated in the Constitution.[46] There were proposals not to incorporate the supremacy clause at all or, at least, to prescribe the framework for proceedings of the Constitutional Court in case of an alleged breach of basic constitutional principles by EU law in the constitutional text.[47] However, the end result of the constitutional revision seems to be one of the most EU-friendly definitions of the supremacy clause (taking into account the well-established jurisprudence of the ECJ on the supremacy of EC law).[48] Such provision divests the national authorities, particularly the Constitutional Court, with a possibility to oppose or even contravene EU law on constitutional grounds, leaving them only an option of a passive or negative approach.[49] Although the jurisprudence of the Constitutional Court momentarily indicates that it follows this approach, Ribičič interprets Article 3a of the Constitution in a way that leaves the door slightly open for future considerations of EU law (active approach).[50] This, a bit daring opinion is, according to his views, supported by the "Transfer of Powers" clause in Constitution Article 3a(1).[51] Such *Solange*-ish interpretation that implicitly imposes the feeling of moral superiority of the Slovenian constitutional values over their counterpart in the European context may elevate the importance of the Constitutional Court; however, it can be dethroned of its significance by at least three arguments. First, Article 3a(1) of the Constitution only regulates the entry and simultaneous transfer of sovereign rights and, with slight interpretational gymnastics, a potential withdrawal from an international organisation on the condition that such international organisation does not give a proper respect for the protection of democ-

---

[46] Constitution Art. 8 reads: 'Laws and regulations must comply with generally accepted principles of international law and with treaties that are binding on Slovenia. Ratified and published treaties shall be applied directly.'

[47] See P. Toškan, 'Evropski člen in ustavna zaščita temeljnih človekovih pravic' [The European Article and constitutional protection of basic human rights], 21 *Pravna praksa* (2002) pp. 4-7; I. Kristan, 'Dopolnilno (ločeno) mnenje' [Additional (separate) opinion], in M. Cerar, et al., eds., *Ustavne razprave 2001 – 2003* [Constitutional debates 2001-2003] (Ljubljana, Državni zbor Republike Slovenije 2004) pp. 172-174 and p. 219.

[48] Constitution Art. 3a(3) reads: 'Legal acts and decisions adopted within international organisations to which Slovenia has transferred the exercise of part of its sovereign rights shall be applied in Slovenia in accordance with the legal regulation of these organisations.'

[49] In general, Ribičič, a judge at the Constitutional Court, classifies the possible approaches of the Constitutional Court as (1) a negative or passive, where the Constitutional Court would more or less just follow European Union law and its interpretation by the ECJ; (2) neutral, the Constitutional Court would decide on (non)conformity between domestic legal acts, based on European Union law and the national constitution, but not to suggest the way to resolve the conflict; and (3) positive or active, where the Constitutional Court could decide on (non)conformity of European Union law to the national constitution. See C. Ribičič, 'Položaj slovenske ustave po vstopu v EU' [Position of the Slovenian Constitution after the accession to the EU], 25 *Pravna praksa* (2006) pp. II-VI (appendix).

[50] See Ribičič, *loc. cit.* n. 4, at pp. 5-7 and p. 14.

[51] Art. 3a(1) of the Constitution provides that 'Pursuant to a treaty ratified by the National Assembly … Slovenia may transfer the exercise of part of its sovereign rights to international organisations which are based on respect for human rights and fundamental freedoms, democracy and the principles of the rule of law.'

racy and human rights. However, it does not deal with individual cases where EU law contradicts the Constitution. Second, 'non-respect for human rights and fundamental freedoms, democracy and the principles of the rule of law' on the side of the EU institutions cannot be derived simply by taking into account the shortcomings of one legal act of the EU since only a serious and continual breach of the constitutional principles at the European level could legitimise eventual sanctions at the national level. The provision of the Constitution rests on the general observation of affairs at the EU level. For practical reasons, it should be emphasised that – taking into account the extensive caseload of the ECJ on protection of human rights – the Constitutional Court will find it hard to substantiate arguments that the EU does not respect human rights. Third, procedural norms were not established and a competence was given to the Constitutional Court in the Constitution for a review of EU law. Formation of a new competence of the Constitutional Court cannot rest only on the decision of the Constitutional Court itself, but on provisions of an act or the Constitution (Art. 160 Constitution), meaning that the Constitutional Court would preliminarily need to focus on this issue in order to, at least somehow, legitimise its intervention.

Nonetheless, a prominent judge notes that, by simply seeing the conflict between the Constitutional Court and EU law, one can miss the relevant point. Instead of sticking to the hierarchical-based relationship between the two legal systems, one has to observe the said relationship in the light of "a dynamic harmonisation" between EU law and constitutional law.'[52] The ECJ has even made "top-down" concessions in favour of national jurisdictions.[53] If the conflict between national law and EU law, even after all interpretative options have been exhausted, still persists, it should be resolved on a case-to-case basis.[54] Yet, irrespective of the fact that the idea of dynamic harmonisation of national and EU law faithfully resembles the trends of jurisprudence at the national and EU level, it still does not resolve the question of competence of a final say in an ongoing conflict between the Constitutional Court and the ECJ. Following the case-to-case approach means that the principle of legal certainty could be jeopardised.

As to the neutral approach, preliminary rulings procedure is a procedural reflection of the principle of supremacy of EC law. While most of material aspects of the principle of supremacy have already been raised, the question whether the Constitutional Court stands as one of the courts that are obliged to refer questions for preliminary ruling to the ECJ may offer several answers. In Slovenia, the Constitutional Court is the highest court regarding the protection of human rights and fundamental freedoms and the assessment of constitutionality of laws and bylaws. No legal remedies are provided in national law against decisions of the Constitutional Court. Article 234(3)

---

[52] B. Zalar, 'Prve izkušnje sodišča in sodnikovi pogledi na uporabo prava Evropske unije' [First Experiences of the Courts and Judge's Views on the Application of EU Law], 24 *Pravna praksa* (2005) pp. I-VIII (appendix).

[53] 'It is for the national court to determine whether in a case such as that in the main proceedings a person in K.B.'s situation can rely on Article 141 EC in order to gain recognition of her right to nominate her partner as the beneficiary of a survivor's pension.' See ECJ, Case C-17/01 *K.B. v. National Health Service Pensions Agency and Secretary of State for Health* [2004] *ECR* I-541.

[54] See Zalar, *loc. cit.* n. 52, at p. II.

EC (*mutatis mutandis* Art. 68 EC and Art. 35 EU) applies in cases where interpretation and, in case of secondary legislation also the validity, of EU law is raised before the Constitutional Court. The Constitutional Court must, if it considers that a decision on the question is necessary to enable it to give judgment, refer the question to the ECJ. It seems that the preliminary rulings system according to this interpretation is bullet-proof. Yet, it is really hard to imagine a simple case where the Constitutional Court would actually need an answer from the ECJ on validity or interpretation of acts of the EU institutions in order to render a judgment. However, the elaboration of reasons for this assertion goes beyond the scope of this chapter.[55]

With reference to this, one can argue that the classification of possible approaches of the Constitutional Court offered by Ribičič does not have legitimate grounds for several reasons. First, the active or positive approach of the Constitutional Court seems to be highly unlikely inasmuch as practice of the ECJ and other EU institutions will not lower the standards of protection of human rights. Second, the above-mentioned procedural issues of the constitutional review hinder the use of a neutral approach. Finally, the passive approach, i.e., the one the Constitutional Court followed so far, matches the most with Constitution Article 3a(3) that implemented the principle of supremacy into national law. The decision of the Constitutional Court on the constitutionality of an act by which the Framework Decision on the European Arrest Warrant was transposed into national law confirms these observations.[56]

As to the case law of the Constitutional Court, the principle of supremacy was fully accepted and exhaustively described in the already-mentioned decision U-186/04, in which the question of primacy of the EC Regulation over national provision was at stake.[57] Beside that, the Constitutional Court made a reference to the primary legislation of the EU concerning the direct effect of EC regulations and several judgments of the ECJ dealing with the principle of supremacy.[58] In the future, one can expect similar illustrative decisions of the Constitutional Court if a notion on the principle of supremacy of other acts of EU institutions will be needed for a clearer understanding of its position.

## 2.5.    European Arrest Warrant

Slovenia transposed the EAW Framework Decision by the Act on the European Arrest Warrant and Surrender Procedures in 2004 (a few months before the accession).[59] The

---

[55] See A. Alen and M. Melchior, 'The Relations Between the Constitutional Courts and the Other National Courts, Including the Interference in the Area of the Action of the European Courts', 23 *HRLJ* (2002) pp. 329-330.

[56] Council Framework Decision 2002/584/JHA of 13 June 2002 on the European arrest warrant and the surrender procedures between Member States, *OJ* 2002 L 190/1.

[57] Decision of the Constitutional Court Up-318/04 and U-I-186/04 of 8 July 2004, para. 10.

[58] 'In the event that a domestic legal norm is contrary to the legal norm of a regulation, the court in the concrete case must not apply the legal norm of the domestic law due to the principle of the supremacy or primacy of Community law. Thus it appears that the challenged regulation is not inconsistent with Article 22 Constitution merely because it does not cite the Regulation provisions.' See Decision of the Constitutional Court U-I-186/04, *loc. cit.* n. 17, para. 10.

[59] *Zakon o evropskem nalogu za prijetje in predajo* [Act on the European arrest warrant and surrender procedures], Ur. l. RS, št. 37/2004 (hereafter AEAW). AEAW was later repealed in 2007 by *Zakon o sode-*

Act had not raised any concern of Slovenian scholars until the German and Polish Constitutional Courts assessed the constitutionality of the transposed provisions concerning the EAW.[60] Early criticisms in Slovenia of the EAW Framework Decision coincided with the first procedure brought against the implementing Act.[61] The petitioner, who was supposed to be surrendered to Italy, challenged all provisions of the Act on grounds of an alleged non-conformity with several provisions of the Constitution. This included Article 25 (right to legal remedies); Article 2 (provision of the rule of law); Article 22 (equal protection of procedural rights) and Article 47 (extradition clause). The Constitutional Court rejected the request since the petitioner had not demonstrated legal interest anymore, as the surrender request had been executed as soon as the decision of the Slovenian court on the request had become final.[62] A laconic statement of the Constitutional Court that the eventual grant of the petition would not improve a petitioner's legal position was not well received by practitioners and scholars.[63] By formally rejecting the request, the Constitutional Court "washed its hands" like Pontius Pilate and avoided answering the question if the Slovenian legislation, which served as a legal foundation for the surrender procedure, was in conflict with the Constitution. In addition, since the reasoning of the order paid the decisive regard to *fait accompli*, the two-edged ruling of the order thus allowed the implementing state authorities to evade the constitutional control of their acts and actions with the immediate execution of the surrender. In our opinion, it is very likely that the Constitutional Court will have to withdraw from its initial stance. Nevertheless, due to the absence of any substantial conclusions in the order, we don't know yet if the Constitutional Court would indirectly interfere, like the German and Polish Constitutional Courts did, with the provisions of the EAW Framework Decision and national legislation.

In the order U-I-261/06, the Constitutional Court had a much easier task. The petitioner asserted that Article 47 of the Constitution allows the extradition and surrender of Slovenian citizens only to international organisations and not to other EU Member States.[64] The Constitutional Court did not accept the constitutional complaint since the

---

*lovanju v kazenskih zadevah z državami članicami Evropske unije* [Act on International Co-operation in Criminal Matters between the Member States of the European Union], Ur. l. RS, št. 102/2007.

[60] Cf. K. Šugman, 'Evropski nalog za prijetje' [European Arrest Warrant], 23 *Pravna praksa* (2004) pp. IV-VII (appendix).

[61] See B. Kovačič Mlinar, 'Je ZENPP v neskladju z Ustavo?' [Is AEAW in conflict with the Constitution?], in 25 *Pravna praksa* (2006) pp. 13-14.

[62] Order of the Constitutional Court U-I-14/06, 22 June 2006. The only judge that voted against the order was Professor Ciril Ribičič.

[63] See B. Kovačič Mlinar, 'Pomanjkanje poguma pri odločitvi o pobudi za oceno ustavnosti ZENPP' [Lack of Courage in the Rejection of the Request for the Assessment of Constitutionality of AEAW], in 25 *Pravna praksa* (2006) pp. 15-16; A. Erbežnik, 'Ustavno sodišče RS ter evropski nalog za prijetje in predajo ali "kdo se boji Virginije Woolf"' [The Constitutional Court RS and European Warrant for Arrest and Surrender or 'Who's Afraid of Virginia Woolf'], 27 *Pravna praksa* (2008) pp. II-VII.

[64] Art. 47 Constitution provides: 'No citizen of Slovenia may be extradited or surrendered unless such obligation to extradite or surrender arises from a treaty by which, in accordance with the provisions of the first paragraph of Article 3a, Slovenia has transferred the exercise of part of its sovereign rights to an international organisation.'

obviously incorrect interpretation of the Constitution on the side of the petitioner could not meet the requirements for ascertainment of breach of human rights.[65]

3.       JURISPRUDENCE IN THE FIELD OF ASYLUM LAW WITH REFERENCES TO EU LAW

Asylum law is one of those legal disciplines where the creativity of judiciary in the interpretation of law goes way above the average. From the judge's perspective, it is an eclectic mixture where application of provisions and principles of international law, EU law and national law is needed to eliminate the existent legal *lacunae* in domestic law.[66] Such is namely the case of the Slovenian asylum system, as is evident from the fact that several key definitions of asylum law, e.g., persecution, non-state actors, were not incorporated in the asylum legislation for a long time.[67] Until the recent shifts in the European and Slovenian legislation, conditions for granting asylum were determined only in Article 1 Geneva Convention on the Status of Refugees, 1952 (hereafter: GSR).[68]

In contrast to the reserved attitude of the Supreme Court to make a reference to EU law in judgments, the Administrative Court made numerous references, particularly in asylum law cases. The Administrative Court, which adjudicates in cases concerning decisions of the Government in asylum matters, applied the principle of loyal interpretation with EU law in a rather progressive manner.[69] As to the facts, the first instance governmental authority made a reference to Directive 2004/83/EC,[70] not only prior to the deadline for transposition but also before the Directive was published in the Official Journal of the European Union. As the Directive has more detailed definition in comparison to the GSR, the question was whether the government authority exceeded the limits of its competence as it strengthened its reasoning, among others, on the legal act which lacked the necessary prerequisite for its validity. The Administrative Court upheld the position of the government authority under the condition that the Directive at stake is, at least, adopted in the Council and does not leave a further possibility to politically influence the substance of the Directive. Further, the Directive in such circum-

---

[65]  Order of the Constitutional Court U-I-261/06 of 11 April 2006.

[66]  Professor Boštjan Zalar, judge at the Administrative Court, uses the term "multi-level constitutionalism". See B. Zalar, 'The Experiences and Challenges for Adjudication on Refugee Law in Slovenia', 18 *Int'l J. Refugee L.* (2005) pp. 118-181.

[67]  *Zakon o azilu, uradno prečiščeno besedilo* [Asylum Act, consolidated version], Ur. l. RS, št. 51/2006. The Asylum Act was repealed and replaced by *Zakon o mednarodni zaščiti* [International Protection Act], Ur. l. RS, št. 111/2007 which came into force on 4 January 2008.

[68]  Convention relating to the Status of Refugees of 28 July 1951, 189 *UNTS* p. 2545.

[69]  The practice of the Administrative Court does not differ much even in other fields of law. For instance, although the case concerning the market concentration did not have any European element, and it would normally be considered in accordance with the national law, the Administrative Court heavily relied on the Commission and the ECJ practice and case law in order to fill the gaps in the legislation. See judgment of the Administrative Court U 1286/2003 of 18 June 2004.

[70]  Council Directive 2004/83/EC of 29 April 2004 on minimum standards for the qualification and status of third country nationals or stateless persons as refugees or as persons who otherwise need international protection and the content of the protection granted, *OJ* 2004 L 304/12.

stances may serve only as an additional tool of interpretation of the valid legal acts, namely GSR.[71]

Beside that, the Administrative Court applied the principle of loyal interpretation of national law in the light of EU law in normal fashion in numerous cases, so that almost the whole European *corpus* of the asylum legislation has been weaved into the jurisprudence of the Administrative Court.[72]

It is worth mentioning that EU legislation in the field of asylum law often prescribes only the minimal standards which have to be transposed into national law. Therefore, it is quite possible that the transposition of directives in national law – to the extent that it would guarantee only the minimum EU standards – could infringe national constitutional standards. There are numerous cases where the Constitutional Court ruled that the provisions of the Asylum Act were not applied in conformity with the Constitution. For instance, irrespective of the fact that under Directive 2005/85/EC, state authorities are not required to inform the applicant for asylum about the main reason for the decision before the applicant receives the decision, the Constitutional Court, following the jurisprudence of the Administrative Court, decided that such action of the state authority is contrary to Article 22 of the Constitution that guarantees equal protection of procedural rights. The applicant should have had an option to express his views on these facts or findings prior to issuance of the decision.[73] Although the "minimal standard" approach in the EU legislation leaves the Member States with an option to or not to "maximise" the legal standards of addressees from the EU perspective, it does not necessarily satisfy the minimum constitutional standards in terms of protection of human rights. Therefore, the abrogation of national law that transposed the "minimal standards" of EU legislation on the grounds of its unconstitutionality could not necessarily infringe the principle of supremacy of EU law.

4.    JURISPRUDENCE IN THE FIELD OF LABOUR LAW WITH
      REFERENCES TO EU LAW

Under the Labour and Social Courts Act,[74] disputes concerning labour law are adjudicated by four first instance labour courts.[75] Appeals against the judgments of these courts are heard by the Higher Labour and Social Court in Ljubljana (*Višje delovno in socialno sodišče v Ljubljani,* VDSSL),[76] where the judicial panel for labour law is cur-

---

[71] Judgment and Order of the Administrative Court U 1534/2004 of 16 August 2004.

[72] See Zalar, *loc. cit.* n. 66, at pp. 158-165.

[73] Decision of the Administrative Court U 322/2005 of 9 March 2005; decision of the Constitutional Court Up-968/05 of 24 November 2005.

[74] *Zakon o delovnih in socialnih sodiščih* [Labour and Social Courts Act], Ur. l. RS, št. 2/2004, 10/2004 (herafter, ZDSS-1).

[75] Labour Courts at Celje, Maribor and Koper, competent for disputes from the respective judicial districts, and then the Labour and Social Court of Ljubljana that adjudicates labour law disputes in the judicial district of Ljubljana and disputes regarding social security law from the entire country (Art. 12 ZDSS-1).

[76] See Arts. 3 and 17 ZDSS-1.

rently seated by ten judges, and the judicial panel for social security law with six judges.[77] Cases are heard by senates, consisting of three judges. Appeals on points of law [*revizija*] against judgments of VDSSL are heard by the Supreme Court, where the judicial panel for labour and social security law is currently seated by five Supreme Court judges.[78] Cases are heard by senates, consisting of five judges.[79] Often characterised as "specialised courts" together with the Administrative Court of the Republic Slovenia (in comparison to "courts of general competence", i.e., Local and District Courts dealing with civil, criminal and commercial cases), labour courts as well as the procedural rules they apply boast some specific characteristics, such as procedural provisions *in favorem laboratoris* (e.g., on costs),[80] and participation in the judicial decision-making of assessors [*sodniki porotniki*], nominated by trade unions and employers' associations.[81]

In this specialised branch of the judiciary, a notable influence of EC law on judicial decisions can be observed when it comes to transfers of undertakings and businesses. References to Directive 23/2001/EC[82] indicate that labour courts were familiar with it and the transposition of its provisions into domestic law – i.e., Article 73 of the Employment Relations Act (hereafter: ZDR).[83] They also began using the Directive as an interpretative tool when applying domestic law to cases of transfer of undertakings. The judgments of the VDSSL began using the "retainment of identity" criterion from Article 1 of the Directive to supplement the laconic definition of transfer contained in Article 73(1) ZDR in 2005.[84] VDSSL used this criterion again in its judgment Pdp 1384/2004,[85] and its position was confirmed by the Supreme Court, stating that the Directive is not to be neglected as an interpretative tool, even though the transfer of the undertaking took place before the accession of Slovenia to the European Union.[86] In its judgment Pdp 954/2006, VDSSL declared a transaction to be a transfer of business in the sense of Article 73 ZDR, using the identity-retainment criterion and further applying criteria set in the case law of the European Court of Justice in cases *Spijkers*[87] (regarding the taking over of customers), *Schmidt*[88] and *Mercx and Neuhuys*.[89] In the

---

[77] Information available at http://www.sodisce.si/vdss/default.asp?id=62.

[78] Information available at http://www.sodisce.si/default.asp?id=22.

[79] Art. 38 *Zakon o pravdnem postopku, uradno prečiščeno besedilo* [Civil Procedure Act, consolidated version], Ur. l. RS, št. 73/2007 (hereafter: ZPP).

[80] Art. 38 ZDSS-1.

[81] Arts. 15 and 16 ZDSS-1.

[82] Council Directive 2001/23/EC of 12 March 2001 on the approximation of the laws of the Member States relating to the safeguarding of employees' rights in the event of transfers of undertakings, businesses or parts of undertakings or businesses, *OJ* 2001 L 82/16.

[83] *Zakon o delovnih razmerjih* [Employment Relations Act], Ur. l. RS, št. 42/2002, 46/2007, 103/2007.

[84] VDSSL, Judgment Pdp 1187/2004 of 11 May 2005, Judgment Pdp 1752/2003 of 3 October 2005.

[85] VDSSL, Judgment Pdp 1384/2004 of 9 February 2006.

[86] Judgment of the Supreme Court VIII Ips 178/2006 of 24 October 2006.

[87] ECJ, Case 24/85 *Jozef Maria Antonius Spijkers v. Gebroeders Benedik Abattoir CV and Alfred Benedik en Zonen BV.* [1986] *ECR* 1119.

[88] ECJ, Case C-392/92 *Schmidt v. Spar- und Leihkasse der früheren Amten Bordesholm, Kiel und Cromshage* [1994] *ECR* I-1311.

[89] ECJ, Joined Cases C-171/94 and C-172/94 *Albert Merckx and Patrick Neuhuys v. Ford Motors Company Belgium SA.* [1996] *ECR* I-1253.

beginning of 2007, the Supreme Court reversed the judgments of the first and second instance due to too narrow interpretation of Article 73(1) ZDR. The Supreme Court compared the abolition of an internal finance and accounting service within a company (factual background in VIII Ips 328/2006) to the dismissal of the person employed to clean the premises and entrusting an outside provider with this task (factual background of *Schmidt)* and applied the *Schmidt* criteria in its judgment.[90] Perhaps the label "landmark" does not best suit the decision of the Supreme Court, but it seems that it nevertheless sent a strong signal to the lower courts and encouraged them to use ECJ case law. In its judgment Pdp 833/2006, VDSSL upheld the judgment of the first instance court based on the *Mercx* rule that the Directive is applicable even in the absence of transfer of assets or direct contractual relations between the two undertakings concerned and reversed a first instance judgment for the same reason as in decision Pdp 1428/2006.[91] In its judgment Pdp 690/2006, VDSSL stated that 'it was correct to use Directive 2001/23/EC, the first instance court, however, interpreted it too narrowly', dubbing the decision in *Schmidt* 'notorious' and the position of ECJ "very clear".[92] Observing this style and phrasing from the aspect of "dialogue between judicial instances", this surely belongs to the most determinate among the pro-EC law messages ever transmitted within the Slovenian judiciary.

5.    THE PRELIMINARY RULING PROCEDURE IN NATIONAL LAW
      AND PRACTICE

5.1.    **Introduction**

Slovenian courts have so far not submitted a single request for a preliminary ruling to the European Court of Justice. However, national laws were amended shortly after the accession, establishing an abstract "platform" on which the request can be filed by courts, a platform that already provides for questions and dilemmas. Moreover, requests for preliminary rulings have been attempted by the National Review Commission for Reviewing Public Procurement Award Procedures. Slovenia has also intervened in several procedures of preliminary ruling before the ECJ.

5.2.    **The preliminary ruling procedure in national law**

On 17 June 2004, the National Assembly adopted the Act Amending the Courts Act, which came into force 20 July 2004. It regulates at the level of national law the mechanics of the preliminary ruling procedure. Article 113a is crucial; it reads:

'(1) When the decision of the court depends on a preliminary ruling concerning the interpretation or validity or interpretation of European Community Law, the court may issue a deci-

---

[90] Decision of the Supreme Court VIII Ips 328/2006 of 13 February 2007.
[91] VDSSL, Judgment Pdp 833/2006 of 26 April 2007; Decision Pdp 1428/2006 of 29 August 2007.
[92] VDSSL, Judgment Pdp 690/2006 of 10 May 2007.

sion with which it requests the Court of Justice of the European Communities for a preliminary ruling, pursuant to a treaty with which the Republic of Slovenia has transferred the exercise of part of its sovereign rights to the institutions of European Union.

(2) Where a decision of the Supreme Court or a decision of another court, against which there is no ordinary or extraordinary legal remedy depends on a preliminary ruling concerning the interpretation or validity or interpretation of European Community Law, the court must issue a decision with which it requests the Court of Justice of the European Communities for a preliminary ruling, pursuant to a treaty from the previous paragraph.

(3) The court stays the proceedings in cases, where requests from paragraphs 1 or 2 of this Article are filed until it receives the decision on a preliminary ruling. The court uses procedural provisions that apply to the case before it appropriately *(mutatis mutandis)* to stay the proceedings. There is no legal remedy, ordinary or extraordinary, against the decision of the court to stay the proceedings.

(4) Once preliminary ruling has been requested by the court, it may, using procedural provisions that apply to the case before it appropriately *(mutatis mutandis)*, until it receives the preliminary ruling, only conduct those procedural acts and make those decision that cannot be delayed, provided they do not depend on the questions concerning which the preliminary ruling was requested, or if they do not regulate legal relations terminally.

(5) If the court may no longer apply the provision due to which it requested a preliminary ruling and the question referred to the Court of Justice of the European Communities has not been ruled on yet, it must immediately withdraw the request for preliminary ruling unless there are statutory reasons for the proceedings to continue.

(6) The courts are bound by the preliminary ruling of the Court of Justice of the European Communities.

(7) A copy of the request for preliminary ruling and of the judgment of the Court of Justice of the European Communities is to be sent to the Supreme Court immediately.'[93]

The first two paragraphs of the above-mentioned Article basically only transpose the relevant provisions of Article 234 EC, giving the right to courts and establishing a duty for the Supreme Court and all courts of last instance to request the ECJ to give a preliminary ruling 'on interpretation or validity or interpretation of law of the European Community.' This literal translation of the Slovenian statutory text makes one guess whether this was not a rather clumsy attempt to shorten the wording of Article 234 EC and the distinction it makes with regard to primary and secondary law. The regulation of both the right and the duty of the Slovenian courts, however, explicitly refers to primary EC law, hopefully clarifying the confusion. In Zalar's view, the provisions of paragraphs 1 and 2 are redundant as they are a matter of EU law and even deceiving as they do not summarise the essential conditions for a request for a preliminary ruling as established in the jurisprudence of the ECJ.[94]

The provision of paragraph 3, pursuant to which the courts must stay proceedings if a preliminary ruling is requested, creates a situation similar to one where a court

---

[93] *Zakon o spremembah in dopolnitvah zakona o sodiščih* [Act amending the Courts Act], Ur. l. RS, št. 73/2004. The article has been translated by the authors informally and solely for the purpose of this volume. Another unofficial translation by Judge Andrej Kmecl is available in A. Kmecl, 'System of support to courts involved in the procedure for preliminary ruling (abstract)', in Ribičič, *op. cit.* n. 4, at pp. 29-30.

[94] See Zalar, *loc. cit.* n. 52, at p. IV (appendix).

deems a (domestic) statute which it should apply to be unconstitutional. In a case of a possibly unconstitutional statute, pursuant to Article 156 of the Constitution, a court must stay the proceedings and initiate proceedings before the Constitutional Court. It is also comparable to any situation where a decision of a court depends on a matter that must be preliminarily resolved by another court or state institution. According to Article 207 ZPP, time limits within which procedural actions must be conducted by parties cease to run when proceedings are stayed. A court itself cannot conduct any procedural actions, and procedural actions conducted by one party have no legal effect on the other party and gain legal effect only once the proceedings are resumed.

Paragraph 5 seems to be the most enigmatic one. The provision that "triggered" the request for a preliminary ruling and may now no longer be applied could, hypothetically, be either a provision of domestic law or a provision of secondary Community law. Should either a provision of secondary Community law be annulled by the ECJ or should a Slovenian statute be annulled by the Constitutional Court, it seems logical that a Slovenian court would in consequence withdraw its request. Moreover, it is unclear whether the word 'proceedings' in the phrase 'unless there are statutory reasons for the proceedings to continue' refers to the continuation of the main proceedings before the national court or to the preliminary ruling procedure. In case this phrase refers to main proceedings, the condition that proceedings continue will probably be fulfilled in every case as a court must decide regardless of the fact that the applicable law has changed. E.g., even if a Slovenian statute is annulled by the Constitutional Court during the course of proceedings, a court must ascertain what the law (in the sense of *praemissa maior*) in the given case is and apply it to facts of the case, so that statutory reasons for continuation of proceedings are given. If the phrase refers to the main proceedings, a Slovenian court does not have a choice but to insist on a request for a preliminary ruling even though it may not apply the provision that is the subject of the preliminary ruling. If the ambiguous phrase, however, refers to the preliminary ruling procedure, it is unclear and difficult to imagine what statutory reasons would call for the national court's perseverance regarding the request for preliminary ruling it filed.

The provision in paragraph 7 was inserted in the proposal of the Act Amending the Courts Act by the Government with the intention of guaranteeing the constitutional role of the Supreme Court as the highest court in the state.[95] The Supreme Court can observe the application of EU law in Slovenia by adopting a legal opinion of principle or a legal opinion, empowered by Article 110 of the Courts Act.[96] Legal opinions of principle and legal opinions regarding the application of EU law can be adopted in two situations: first, when a preliminary ruling has already been given, and the Supreme Court merely reminds the lower courts of the ECJ's interpretation of EU law, and second, when a preliminary ruling has not been given, but the Supreme Court holds either that there is

---

[95] *Predlog zakona o spremembah in dopolnitvah Zakona o sodiščih* [Proposal of the Act amending the Courts Act], Poročevalec Državnega zbora RS, št. 39/2004 p. 31.
[96] *Zakon o sodiščih, uradno prečiščeno besedilo* [Courts Act, consolidated version], Ur. l. RS, št. 94/2007 (hereafter: Courts Act).

no doubt regarding the correct interpretation or validity of EU law, or that there was no doubt that it was not necessary to apply EU law.[97]

The provision, if applied as envisaged in the proposal, veils some potential conflicts. Legal opinions of the Supreme Court are binding on panels of the Supreme Court (Art. 110(2) of the Courts Act), the only court in the country that is in every case the court of last instance in the sense of Article 234 EC and is therefore constantly under a duty to request a preliminary ruling, should it stumble upon questions of interpretation of EU law.

In the first situation mentioned in the law proposal, where the adoption of a legal opinion is envisaged as a reminder to lower courts of developments in ECJ case law, the instrument is redundant as all courts need to follow the jurisprudence of the ECJ on their own, and it is not the role of the Supreme Court to serve as a publication office of the ECJ. Much less is it its role to serve as an "editor" of "interesting" and "important" case law.

In the second situation, where the Supreme Court would adopt a legal opinion concerning a pending preliminary ruling case, it is unclear why the Supreme Court would find it necessary to express its opinion that the case is definitely such that EU law is not applicable when a lower court has found doubts regarding this issue and has requested the ECJ to rule on it. Would it ambitiously suggest to the ECJ the direction of its judgment, or suggest (or hint) to the lower court to consider a withdrawal of the request? Should a lower court, even though not legally bound by a legal opinion of the Supreme Court, convinced, however, by the Supreme Court's opinion, indeed withdrew the request, we would find ourselves in the situation where the only court bound by Article 234(3) EC has *a priori* precluded itself from requesting a preliminary ruling. Should a senate of judges of the Supreme Court, when deciding in the same case, realise that the question of interpretation of EU law is not as *claire* as it at first seemed, another Plenary Session of the Supreme Court would be needed to reverse the legal opinion of the Supreme Court and to ensure that the provisions of the Treaty are fully observed.

However, the provision is seen by Brus[98] and Kmecl[99] as a legal basis for establishing a database of cases where a preliminary ruling has been requested. Zalar claims it is redundant, as such a database could simply be created within regular court management without a specific statutory provision.[100]

## 5.3.    Slovenian courts and the preliminary ruling procedure

A few cases – that one can come across searching the case law database of the Slovenian judiciary – where it has been suggested by the parties that a preliminary ruling be

---

[97] Proposal of the Act amending the Courts Act, *loc. cit.* n. 95, at p. 31.

[98] M. Brus, 'Nationale Richter als Anwender des EU-Rechts – Bericht des Vertreters des OGH der Republik Slowenien', in C. Ribičič, *op. cit.* n. 4, at p. 23

[99] A. Kmecl, 'System of support to courts involved in the procedure for preliminary ruling (abstract)', in C. Ribičič, et al., *op. cit.* n. 4, at p. 30.

[100] Zalar, *loc. cit.* n. 52, at p. IV (appendix).

requested by the domestic court, show us that a modest catalogue of decisions regarding the request for a preliminary ruling is beginning to evolve.[101] The Supreme Court issued a separate decision *(sklep)*, no. III R 68/2004[102] after the judgment in that matter, namely case no. III Ips 50/2004-4 had already been rendered. It rejected a motion of one of the parties for a preliminary ruling. The filing of a request was suggested to the Court after the judgment had already been rendered, so it could not influence the decision of the Supreme Court in the case before it. The motion was therefore rejected.

Similarly, the motion to request a preliminary ruling on the question of legality of discrimination of foreign nationals regarding the denationalisation (restitution) of property confiscated after World War II was dismissed by the Supreme Court in case no. I Up 951/2005. Since the decision of the Court was solely on the admissibility of the remedy sought by one of the parties, therefore, substantial questions were not addressed in the judgment.[103]

In a criminal procedure before the Supreme Court, the defendant, accused of abuse of rights or position (Art. 244 of the Penal Code)[104] argued that his procedural rights were violated in the procedure before the Higher Court as the court did not request a preliminary ruling on the conformity of Article 244 of the Penal Code with EC law, pleading that the quoted article 'infringes upon the right to free entrepreneurship and private property.' In its judgment I Ips 378/06,[105] the Supreme Court opined that pursuant to Article 113a(1) of the Courts Act, it is the right, and not the duty, of the court to request a preliminary ruling if it finds it necessary. Only if the sovereign right of Slovenia to regulate the area of criminal law would be transferred to the institutions of the European Union, there would be an obligation for the court to request a preliminary ruling pursuant to Article 113(2) of the Courts Act.

In an administrative dispute in which three parties contested a decision on concentration (issued by the Competition Protection Office), the Administrative Court in its judgment U 1286/2003 first found that the assessment of concentration in question did not have a European dimension; therefore, national law, i.e., *Zakon o preprečevanju omejevanja konkurence* [Prevention of Restriction of Competition Act] had to be applied. The Court immediately added that the Prevention of Restriction of Competition Act took certain concepts from EC competition law, resulting in the Slovenian definition of concentration being almost identical to the EC definition. Therefore, for reasons of legal certainty, 'it is not unfounded' to interpret the Prevention of Restriction of Competition Act in accordance with EC law, jurisprudence of the ECJ and practice of the European Commission, 'to create a system of legal norms as just and comprehen-

---

[101] http://www.sodnapraksa.si.
[102] Decision of the Supreme Court III R 68/2004 of 21 December 2004.
[103] Judgment of the Supreme Court I Up 951/2005 of 28 September 2005.
[104] *Kazenski zakonik, uradno prečiščeno besedilo* [Penal Code, consolidated version], Ur. l. RS, št. 95/2004. Art. 244(1) Penal Code reads: 'Whoever, in the performance of an economic activity, abuses his position or acts beyond the limits of the rights inherent in his position or fails to perform any of his duties with a view to procuring an unlawful property benefit for himself or for a third person or to causing damage to the property of another, whereby such conduct does not constitute any other criminal offence, shall be sentenced to imprisonment for not more than five years.'
[105] Judgment of the Supreme Court I Ips 378/2006 of 22 June 2007.

sible as possible.' The Court backed its position with the Act on Conditions of Accession 2003.[106] The Court dismissed the motion, submitted by one of the parties, to request a preliminary ruling, stating that 'it did not address the issue of whether a preliminary ruling should be requested, as it found the essential parts of the contested decision to be illegal from the aspect of domestic law.'[107]

The few cases that dealt with motions for a request for preliminary ruling seem to be put forward by parties using the "Christmas tree approach", as yet another argument that is easily and without detailed argumentation included in their pleadings, even if the issues of the case are merely distantly related to EU law. Fear that pleas of EU law and motions for a request for preliminary ruling will become standard phrases, included in most lawsuits, appeals, etc., regardless of relevance and in the sense of "he who searches will find", as Zalar puts it,[108] is not an unfounded one. Nevertheless, courts seem to have dealt with these attempts patiently, and detailed reasoning regarding the court's decision on motions to request a preliminary ruling can hopefully lead to a responsible attitude of parties and of (lower) courts to this institution.

### 5.4. Requests for a preliminary ruling in the practice of the National Review Commission for Reviewing Public Procurement Award Procedures

Pursuant to Article 4 of the Auditing of Public Procurement Procedures Act,[109] National Review Commission for Reviewing Public Procurement Award Procedures [*Državna revizijska komisija za revizijo postopkov javnih naročil*] (NRC) ensures legal remedies to tenderers and monitors lawfulness of public awards procedures. It also acts as a review authority for offences that contravene the ZRPJN. It is an independent body; the chairperson and four members are appointed by the National Assembly for a five-year term with a possibility of re-election and limited grounds for an early relief (Art. 5 ZRPJN). The independence of the NRC is further guaranteed by provisions on funding (Art. 4 ZRPJN) and rules of procedure, adopted by the NRC and demanding consent of the National Assembly (Art. 7 ZRPJN). The only legal remedy against decisions of the NRC, which has the power to (partially or entirely) annul the contract award procedure, is a lawsuit for compensation before a court of general competence (and not an administrative dispute before the Administrative Court, which is the regular way of

---

[106] Act concerning the Conditions of Accession of the Czech Republic, the Republic of Estonia, the Republic of Cyprus, the Republic of Latvia, the Republic of Lithuania, the Republic of Hungary, the Republic of Malta, the Republic of Poland, the Republic of Slovenia and the Slovak Republic and the adjustments to the Treaties on which the European Union is founded, *OJ* 2003 L 236/33.

[107] See the description of this judgment in the context of "EU-friendliness", *loc. cit.* n. 69.

[108] B. Zalar, 'Der Einfluss des Europarechts auf die verwaltungsgerichtliche Rechtsprechung in Slowenien, oder: Werden (Verwaltungs-)Richter zu politischen Akteuren?', in R. Fritz, et al., eds., *Im Geiste der Demokratie und des sozialen Verständnisses* (Köln, Wolters Kluwer 2007) p. 262.

[109] *Zakon o reviziji postopkov javnega naročanja* [Auditing of Public Procurement Procedures Act], Ur. l. RS, št. 78/1999, 90/1999, 105/2002, 110/2002, 2/2004, 42/2004, 61/2005, 78/2006, 53/2007 (hereafter: ZRPJN).

judicial review of decisions of public administration).[110] Since the accession of Slovenia to the European Union, the NRC has systematically declared itself to be a court or tribunal within the meaning of Article 234(2) EC. This became a common feature in its annual reports,[111] presented to the National Assembly (Art. 32 ZRPJN) and in its decisions. The NRC requested a preliminary ruling in 2005 in its decision no. 018-390/2005.[112] The request regarded the interpretation of Article 1 Directive 93/37/EEC; it was, however, withdrawn before the ECJ decided on it as the audit claim was withdrawn by a party to the proceeding before the NRC. Similarly, in case no. 018-067/2005, the NRC informed in writing the parties to the proceedings that it intended to request a preliminary ruling from the ECJ. This information was followed by a withdrawal of the audit claim.[113] In two other cases that were decided in 2005, where the parties proposed that the NRC requests a preliminary ruling, these motions were dismissed as the case was either not decided on merits,[114] or the preliminary ruling would not have helped the NRC to decide the case.[115] In decisions issued in 2006 and 2007, where motions for a request for preliminary ruling were submitted by parties, the NRC rejected all of them, systematically taking the position, using almost exactly the same wording, that:

'... [T]he filing of a request for a preliminary ruling lies on the initiative of the court itself and that the parties to the proceeding have no direct influence on the decision of the court whether a request will be filed. ... The primary concern in the court's deliberation whether it is necessary to request a preliminary ruling is whether a question has been posed that requires the interpretation of the ECJ. ... When such a question has been posed, yet the decision on that question is not necessary for the court when deciding on the case, the court is relieved of its duty to request a preliminary ruling. The filing of such a request [lies] in the hands of the competent body and it is not a decision to be made by the parties to the proceeding.'[116]

---

[110] Art. 23(5) ZRPJN.
[111] *Letno poročilo 2006* [Annual Report 2006], available at http://www.dkom.si/util/bin.php?id=2007 021507523061, pp. 12-13.
*Letno poročilo 2005* [Annual Report 2005], available at http://www.dkom.si/util/bin.php?id=200602020 8302870, pp. 25-26.
*Letno poročilo 2004* [Annual Report 2004], available at http://www.dkom.si/util/bin.php?id=200502011 0042923, pp. 10-11.
[112] Decision 018-390/2005 *Holding Slovenske železnice, Javna agencija za železniški promet in Mestna občina Ljubljana* of 5 January 2005, available at http://www.dkom.si.
[113] Decision 018-067/2005 *Javna agencija za železniški promet RS* of 20 May 2005, available at http://www.dkom.si.
[114] Decision 018-232/2005 *Klinični center Ljubljana* of 11 August 2005, available at http://www.dkom.si.
[115] Decision 018-393/2005 *Klinični center Ljubljana* of 15 December 2005, available at http://www.dkom.si.
[116] Decision 018-069/2006 *Splošna bolnišnica Celje* of 7 March 2006, available at http://www.dkom.si. Decision 018-104/2006 *Banka Slovenije* of 31 March 2006, available at http://www.dkom.si. Decision 018-120/2007 *Republika Slovenija, Ministrstvo za javno upravo*, available at http://www.dkom. si.
Decision 018-042/2007 *Občina Piran*, available at http://www.dkom.si.

In all of the above-cited cases, the NRC simply added that it has concluded that a request for a preliminary ruling is not necessary in the concrete case before it, without further elaborating on the applicability, application or interpretation of EC law.

Undoubtedly, pursuant to Article 234(2) EC, the National Review Commission, as it is generally not a court of last instance, is not under duty to bring the matter before the ECJ, and the decision whether it shall do so remains in its hands. The reasoning of the Commission's decision not to request a preliminary ruling, however, remains questionable from the aspect of Community law, presupposing that the demand for notification of reasons as an element of the right to effective judicial protection (as seen in *Heylens*)[117] also encompasses the given situation.[118] Such reasoning can also be questionable from the aspect of constitutional provisions on the right to (effective) legal remedy (Art. 25 of the Constitution),[119] especially in light of the fact that judicial review of decisions of the NRC is only available through a compensatory lawsuit before a general civil court. Furthermore, such a practice of the NRC will probably discourage future parties to the proceedings before it to invoke EU law arguments, when they can reasonably expect that the NRC will deal with them in the same manner that it has in the above-stated cases.

## 5.5.    Interventions in preliminary ruling procedures initiated by courts from other Member States

Even though no preliminary rulings have yet been requested by Slovenian courts, Slovenia has, however, taken advantage of the opportunity to take part in the procedures before the ECJ by intervening in other preliminary ruling cases. Pursuant to Article 12 of the Rules on co-operation of national authorities with the Office of the State Attorney General of the Republic of Slovenia concerning the procedures before the Court of European Communities, the Court of First Instance and the European Commission [*Pravilnik o sodelovanju državnih organov z državnim pravobranilstvom Republike Slovenije glede postopkov pred Sodiščem Evropskih skupnosti, Sodiščem prve stopnje in Evropsko komisijo*][120] the Office of State Attorney General must forward notifications of requests for preliminary rulings, filed by courts from other Member States (that it receives from the ECJ) to competent ministries, government offices or to the Government Office for European Affairs without hesitation. In important cases, the Office of State Attorney General warns a relevant ministry that has been notified of the influence that

---

[117]  ECJ, Case 222/86 *UNECTEF v. Georges Heylens and others* [1987] *ECR* 4116.

[118]  See B. Bapuly, et al., *Pravo EU pred slovenskimi sodišči* [EU Law before the Slovenian courts] (Ljubljana, GV Založba 2005) p. 24.

[119]  See T. Jerovšek, '25. člen (pravica do pravnega sredstva)' [Article 25 (Right to Legal Remedies)], in L. Šturm, ed., *Komentar Ustave Republike Slovenije* [Commentary of the Constitution of the Republic of Slovenia] (Ljubljana, FPDEŠ 2002) p. 275.

[120]  *Pravilnik o sodelovanju državnih organov z državnim pravobranilstvom Republike Slovenije glede postopkov pred Sodiščem Evropskih skupnosti, Sodiščem prve stopnje in Evropsko komisijo* [Rules on co-operation of national authorities with the Office of the State Attorney General of the Republic of Slovenia concerning the procedures before the Court of European Communities, Court of First Instance and the European Commission], Ur. l. RS, št. 126/2004 (hereafter: Rules on co-operation).

the ruling of the ECJ may have on domestic legislation.[121] Pursuant to Articles 49j. and 49k. Rules of Procedure of the Government of the Republic of Slovenia,[122] the competent ministry or office must then prepare a position of the Republic of Slovenia, which has to be confirmed by the Government. The decision whether to intervene or not is made by the competent ministry or the Government depending on whether interests of the Republic of Slovenia have to be protected.[123] Final control over this decision, however, remains in the hands of the Government.

Slovenia has so far intervened in more than fifteen preliminary ruling cases, starting with 2 cases in 2005. Slovenian intervention in the case of C-140/05 *Amalija Valesko v. Zollamt Klagenfurt*[124] was very directly linked to Slovenian economic interests, as the issue of the case was quantitative restrictions imposed by Austria on the import of cigarettes from Slovenia in the transitional period that followed Slovenia's accession to the EU. The position that was also taken by Slovenia was rejected by the ECJ, which confirmed the legality of quantitative limitations that were stricter than general limitations considering import from third countries.[125] In the second case of a preliminary ruling where Slovenia intervened, C-2/05 *Rijksdienst voor Sociale Zekerheid v. Herbosch Kiere NV*,[126] Slovenia took the position that was eventually confirmed by the ECJ.[127]

In another case in which Slovenia intervened – case C-374/05 *Gintec International Import Export GmbH v. Verband Sozialer Wettbewerb eV* – the ECJ seems to have upheld those positions of Slovenia that can be identified from the text of the judgment.[128] In the majority of cases, intervention was proposed by the Slovenian Ministry of Justice.[129] Interestingly enough, three of five interventions in 2007 were suggested by the Ministry of Finance (as all three cases were connected to gambling law), while the other two cases were matters of social policy. In case C-426/05 *Tele 2 UTA*,[130] and in case C-175/06 *Tedesco*[131] (which was later removed from the register), Slovenia took

---

[121] L. Bembič, 'Vloga slovenskih organov v zvezi s postopki pred Sodiščem ES v Luksemburgu' [The role of Slovenian state organs with regards to procedures before the Court of Justice of the European Communities in Luxembourg], 32 *Podjetje in delo* (2006) p. 1096.

[122] *Poslovnik Vlade Republike Slovenije* [Rules of procedure of the Government of the Republic of Slovenia], Ur. l. RS, št. 43/2001, 23/2002, 54/2003, 103/2003, 114/2004, 26/2006, 21/2007.

[123] Bembič, *loc. cit.* n. 121, at p. 1096.

[124] ECJ, Case C-140/05 *Amalija Valesko v. Zollamt Klagenfurt* [2006] *ECR* I-10025.

[125] *Skupno letno poročilo Državnega pravobranilstva RS 2006* [Joint annual report of the Office of State Attorney General of the Republic of Slovenia 2006] p. 55, available at http://www.dp-rs.si/fileadmin/dp.gov.si/pageuploads/SKUPNO_LETNO_POROCILO_ZA_LETO_2006.pdf.

[126] ECJ, Case C-2/05 *Rijksdienst voor Sociale Zekerheid v. Herbosch Kiere NV* [2006] *ECR* I-1079.

[127] Joint annual report of the Office of State Attorney General of the Republic of Slovenia 2006, *loc. cit.* n. 125, at pp. 55-56.

[128] ECJ, Case C-374/05 *Gintec International Import Export GmbH v. Verband Sozialer Wettbewerb eV* [2007] *ECR* I-9517.

[129] Joint annual report of the Office of State Attorney General of the Republic of Slovenia 2006, *loc. cit.* n. 125, at pp. 51-53.

[130] ECJ, Case C-426/05 *Tele2 Telecommunication GmbH v. Telekom-Control-Kommission* [2008] *ECR* I-685.

[131] ECJ, Case C-175/06 *Alessandro Tedesco v. Tomasoni Fittings SrL, RWO Marine Equipment Ltd*, *OJ* 2007 C 315/31.

part in oral proceedings, which was mentioned by AG Trstenjak as a way of gaining experience in pleading before the Court that can also be used in other, e.g., infraction procedures.[132]

The dynamics of Slovenia's interventions in preliminary ruling procedures reassuringly depict a growing interest of the Slovenian Government and public administration in the influence of the ECJ on the shaping of policy in different fields. They also depict interesting oscillations with regard to the level of activity of different ministries, which could probably be traced back to reasons of organisational nature rather than policy reasons.

## 6.    INFRACTION PROCEDURES INITIATED BY THE EUROPEAN COMMISSION AND DIRECT ACTIONS

### 6.1.    Case C-267/07: the first or the last of the Mohicans?

The first infraction case against Slovenia that reached the judicial stage was submitted by the European Commission on 5 June 2007. The Commission claimed that Slovenia failed to adopt national law to comply with Directive 2004/50/EC of the European Parliament and of the Council[133] or, at any event, failed to communicate those measures to the Commission. Slovenia has therefore failed to fulfil its obligations under the Directive.[134] The case was therefore a matter of mere delay. On 23 July 2007, the Slovenian Government Communication Office issued a press release stating that the Railway Traffic Safety Act, the second of two pieces of legislation transposing the Directive was adopted, published in the Official Gazette on 10 July 2007 and came into force on 11 July 2007. On that day, the Ministry of Transport gave notice of compliance with Directive 2004/50/EC, and the statement of full transposition was conditionally confirmed in the Notification of National Execution Measures database on 19 July 2007. The press release also expressed the expectation of Slovenia that the Commission will withdraw the action as the objective of transposition was met by Slovenia.[135] This took place on 14 December 2007 when the case was formally removed from the ECJ's register.[136]

---

[132] V. Trstenjak, 'Slovenija prvič pred luksemburškim sodiščem: C-267/07. Prudenter facit, qui praecepto legis obtemperat' [Slovenia's first appearance before the court in Luxembourg: C-267/07. Prudenter facit, qui praecepto legis obtemperat], 26 *Pravna praksa* (2007) p. 3.

[133] Directive 2004/50/EC of the European Parliament and of the Council of 29 April 2004 amending Council Directive 96/48/EC on the interoperability of the trans-European high-speed rail system and Directive 2001/16/EC of the European Parliament and of the Council on the interoperability of the trans-European conventional rail system, *OJ* 2004 L 164/114.

[134] ECJ, application in Case C-267/07 *Commission of the European Communities v. Republic Slovenia*, *OJ* 2007 C 170/18.

[135] 'News from the Ministry of Transport on the court action brought against Slovenia by the European Commission', Press Release by the Government Communication Office (*Urad vlade za komuniciranje*), 23 July 2007, available at: http://www.ukom.gov.si/eng/.

[136] Order of the President of the Court of 14 December 2007 – *Commission of the European Communities v. Republic of Slovenia (Case C-267/07)*, *OJ* 2008 C 92/25.

## 6.2.    Case C-402/08: the first lost case

The first infraction case that led to a judgment of the ECJ was submitted by the European Commission on 18 September 2008. The European Commission argued that by failing to transpose Directive 2004/35/EC on environmental liability, Slovenia was in breach of EC law.[137] Again, this was a fairly straight-forward infraction, which this time led to a decision of the European Court of Justice. On 12 March 2009, it held that Slovenia did not comply with the requirements imposed by the Directive.[138]

## 6.3.    Cases C-440/05, C-414/04: (near) failures to intervene

Slovenia has not been very active when it comes to interventions in actions for annulment submitted pursuant to Article 230 EC. Case C-440/05 *Commission v. Council*[139] is an exception in this respect. The European Commission sought annulment of the Council Framework Decision 2005/667/JHA on criminal-law framework for the enforcement of the law against ship-source pollution.[140] The main argument of the Commission was that by virtue of the legal basis, the Framework Decision was adopted in breach of Article 47 TEU.[141] The main issue in the case was whether or not the provisions of Framework Decision 2005/667/JHA affected the Community's competence under Article 80(2) EC.[142] Considering the importance of cross-pillar battles, it did not come as a surprise that all twenty-five of the then Member States of the European Union intervened to support the Council, whereas the European Parliament intervened in support of the Commission. However, twenty-four Member States were granted leave to intervene on 25 April 2006, whereas the Republic of Slovenia intervened at a later point; therefore, it was only granted leave to intervene on 28 September 2006, and, as a consequence, it was only able to intervene at oral proceedings,[143] which, however, did not take place.[144] The ECJ found in favour of the applicant, annulling the contested Framework Decision and specifically stating that the arguments put forward by the intervening Member States were largely similar to those relied on by the Council.[145] It would be unreasonable to expect that the outcome of the proceedings would have been different if Slovenia intervened at an earlier point. The fact, however, that Slovenia was

---

[137] Directive 2004/35/CE of the European Parliament and of the Council of 21 April 2004 on environmental liability with regard to the prevention and remedying of environmental damage, *OJ* 2004 L 143/56.

[138] ECJ, Case C-402/08 *Commission of the European Communities v. Republic of Slovenia* [2009] *ECR* nyr.

[139] ECJ, Case C-440/05 *Commission of the European Communities v. Council of the European Union* [2007] *ECR* I-9097.

[140] Council Framework Decision 2005/667/JHA of 12 July 2005 to strengthen the criminal-law framework for the enforcement of the law against ship-source pollution, *OJ* 2005 L 255/164.

[141] *Loc. cit.* n. 139, para. 25.

[142] *Loc. cit.* n. 139, para. 54.

[143] ECJ, Case C-440/05 *Commission of the European Communities v. Council of the European Union*, Order of the President of the Court of 28 September 2006, not reported.

[144] Opinion of AG Mazák in Case C-440/05 *Commission of the European Communities v. Council of the European Union* [2007] *ECR* I-9097, para. 26

[145] *Loc. cit.* n. 139, para. 51.

the only Member State that almost failed to intervene, nevertheless, raises doubts regarding the functionality of the intervention system presented earlier in this chapter. Even more so, since Slovenia failed to intervene in another annulment case, namely C-414/04 *European Parliament v. Council of the European Union*.[146] The applicant sought the annulment of Council Regulation 1223/2004/EC amending Regulation (EC) No 1228/2003 regarding the date of application of certain provisions to Slovenia.[147] The issue was, again, one of legal basis.[148] As the outcome of the case was the annulment of the Regulation that Slovenia exclusively benefited from, it is surprising that Slovenia did not even attempt to intervene in support of the defendant. However, two Member States – Estonia and Poland – did, the former interested in the outcome of – at the time pending cases – regarding similar regulations regarding the date of application of certain provisions to it.[149]

7.      PUBLICATION OF EU LEGISLATION IN THE OFFICIAL JOURNAL IN SLOVENIAN LANGUAGE

When it comes to problems with application of EU law resulting from the late publication of the Official Journal of the EU in the Slovenian language, no judicial action has been demanded by individuals to remedy the situation. However, this does not mean that the issue of the late publication did not come to a certain extent onto the agenda of the Slovenian judiciary. In judgment U 1526/2004, the Administrative Court had to apply provisions of the Dublin II Regulation,[150] which was not published in the Slovenian language in the OJ at the material time. The question of compliance with the principle of legal certainty was raised. Since the Regulation had been adopted before the accession of Slovenia to the EU, the starting point was Article 2 of the Act on Conditions of Accession 2003, which speaks of the binding nature and direct applicability of the provisions of the original Treaties and the acts adopted by the institutions and the European Central Bank. However, this provision does not resolve the issue of a legitimate demand of individuals to have rights and duties vested upon them published in their language (being an official language of the EU) in order to be able to act in compliance with the legal rules. The Administrative Court relied on Article 58 Act on Conditions of Accession 2003. The Court held that the Dublin II Regulation was accessible in the EUR-lex database in the Slovenian language before the deliberation of the

---

[146] ECJ, Case C-414/04 *European Parliament v. Council of the European Union* [2006] *ECR* I-11279.

[147] Council Regulation 1223/2004/EC of 28 June 2004 amending Regulation (EC) No 1228/2003 of the European Parliament and of the Council as regards the date of application of certain provisions to Slovenia, *OJ* 2004 L 233/3

[148] *Loc. cit.* n. 139, para. 28.

[149] ECJ, Case C-413/04 *European Parliament v. Council of the European Communities* [2006] *ECR* I-11279.

[150] Council Regulation 343/2003/EC of 18 February 2003 establishing the criteria and mechanisms for determining the Member State responsible for examining an asylum application lodged in one of the Member States by a third-country national, *OJ* 2003 L 50/1.

Court and thus considered the Regulation as a valid legal act and applied it in the judgment.[151]


## 8.    CONCLUSIONS

Unlike the German experience, the Constitutional Court has not switched yet in the doctrinal approach to the relationship of European Union law and national law. The possibility cannot be excluded that the Court might take a different direction in the future. Besides the already described normative and dogmatic reasons, there are several practical ones for the consistent EU-friendly activity originating in the domestic sphere. First, an overload of cases pending before the Constitutional Court pushes it to take short-cuts while dealing with more complex cases (the EU-related cases certainly are such). Second, cases with EU significance are still scarce as they are probably still pending before the ordinary courts due to the unreasonably long-lasting judicial proceedings in Slovenia. Altogether, the Constitutional Court has been so far "a good pupil", a bit nerdy, in the class of the highest courts of the EU Member States. To be able to conclude this chapter with a definite position, the Constitutional Court would have first had to deliver a major substantial decision that would completely lift the veil from its doctrinal understanding of the relationship between the Constitution, the Constitutional Court and EU law.

At first sight, the jurisprudence of the Administrative Court may look satisfactory; nevertheless, it is the result of striving of individual judges, which is clearly indicated by the topics of administrative law where – in the judicial decisions – the interpretation of EU law took place. In Slovenia, asylum law allows judges to entangle EU law provisions, principles and standards into reasoning far more than in other fields of administrative law. This is due to the vagueness of legal provisions of the Geneva Convention relating to the Status of Refugees and the fact that the national legislation is not clear enough.

Similarly, the development of application of EU law in the field of labour law probably benefited from the concentration of appellate jurisdiction in small groups of judges dealing with labour law at the Higher Labour and Social Court of Ljubljana and at the Supreme Court, as it is easier to achieve uniformity of judicial practice in such a setting.

A relatively small number of decision-makers, concentration of competence for the entire territory of the country and specialisation in a relevant field of law seem to be the common denominator of the bodies, presented here as the main actors in the process of widening the use of EU law, including the Administrative Court, the Higher Labour and Social Court of Ljubljana, the National Review Commission and, to a certain extent, the Constitutional Court. The causal link between these characteristics and the progressiveness when it comes to "EU law awareness" is yet to be investigated. Even more

---

[151]  Judgment of the Administrative Court U 1526/2004 of 20 August 2004.

so, as the causes for the smaller extent of application of EU law by other authorities await analysis, that will probably only become possible in a couple of years' time.

The section on preliminary rulings and the analysis of interventions in both procedures of preliminary ruling and annulment actions may serve as (a part of) a lesson to be learned by the current candidate and pre-candidate countries not to take the legislative task of regulating the communication between national administration and judiciary and the European judiciary too lightly. Sometimes, indeed, provisions are better omitted than included.

*Chapter 14*

## MALTA AND EUROPEAN UNION LAW

Ivan Sammut*

1.      INTRODUCTION

The accession of Malta to the European Union followed an idiosyncratic political process that witnessed various twists and turns.[1] Before joining the EU, Malta had been associated with the European Community for more than 30 years. An association agreement was signed in 1970 and entered into force on 1 April 1971.[2] It provided for an ambitious plan of creating a customs union over a ten-year period (divided into two phases); however, due to political circumstances, this objective was never achieved under the association framework. A formal application for membership in the European Communities was submitted on 16 July 1990. *Avis* of the European Commission followed in 1993.[3] For several reasons – mainly economic – the opinion was negative. As explained in Chapter 1 of this volume, the membership application was frozen in 1996 as a result of changing domestic political climate and reactivated following parliamentary elections in 1998. A subsequent positive opinion of the European Commission permitted Malta to join the second group of countries negotiating the terms of accession and – following the negotiations – allowed it to become part of the "big bang" enlargement of 2004. It is a rule of thumb that membership in the European Union has far-reaching consequences for a national legal order of any Member State. Malta is no exception in this respect. Bearing this in mind, the author decided to devote this chapter to legal aspects of Maltese *rapprochement* to the European Union. The starting point is the Maltese Constitution, which contains very modest rules on membership in the European Union.[4] This is followed by an analysis of the European Union Act 2003, which – being modeled on the UK's European Communities Act 1972 – opened the Maltese legal order to EU law. The next section of this chapter looks at the practice of Maltese courts, including their reluctance to employ the preliminary ruling procedure.

---

* Department of European & Comparative Law, Faculty of Laws, University of Malta.
[1] For a detailed account, see, *inter alia*, R.C. Caruana, 'The accession of Malta to the EU', in G. Vassiliou, ed., *The Accession Story. The EU from 15 to 25 Countries* (Oxford, Oxford University Press 2007) pp. 259-296.
[2] Agreement establishing an association between the European Economic Community and Malta, *OJ* 1971 L 61/2.
[3] Commission Opinion on Malta's Application for Membership, COM (93) 312 final.
[4] See Chapter 3 in this volume.

*A. Łazowski (ed.), The Application of EU Law in the New Member States*
© 2010, T·M·C·Asser press, *The Hague, The Netherlands and the Authors*

Last but not least, infraction procedures invoked against Malta are discussed in section 5 of the chapter.


2.      THE EU LEGAL ORDER AND ITS CONSTITUTIONAL
        IMPLICATIONS FOR MALTESE LAW

2.1.    **The Constitution of the Republic of Malta**

A number of brief introductory comments on the Maltese Constitution are fitting at the very outset.[5] The Constitution serves as the basis of Maltese sovereignty, which was recognised internationally when Malta achieved independence in 1964. Prior to pre-accession reforms of fundamentals of the Maltese legal order, there had been no constitutional provisions dealing with international law and membership in the European Union. The approach of the Maltese legal order to international law is a textbook example of dualism: as long as an international treaty is not formally incorporated into the national law, it remains outside the ambit of Maltese law. Pursuant to the Ratification of Treaties Act 1983,[6] 'no provision of a treaty shall become, or be enforceable as, part of the law of Malta expect by or under an Act of Parliament.' This *modus operandi* was employed to incorporate the European Convention for the Protection of Human Rights and Fundamental Freedoms into Maltese law. In order to make ECHR domestically enforceable, the national Parliament had to enact the European Convention Act 1987[7] allowing individuals to plead on the basis of the ECHR as part of Maltese law. In this respect, the system is quite similar to the one from the United Kingdom. Bearing in mind the experience of the latter with opening – in the dualist environment – its domestic legal orders to EC/EU law, Malta employed a very similar *modus operandi*. On 16 July 2003, a tailor-made European Union Act 2003 was passed by the Maltese House of Representatives.[8] It entered into force on 1 May 2004 – the day of accession to the European Union. The Act facilitated the ratification of the Accession Treaty 2003[9] as

---

[5] See further, *inter alia*, P.G. Xuereb, 'Malta' in A.E. Kellermann, et al., eds., *The Impact of EU Accession on the Legal Orders of New EU Member States and (Pre-)Candidate Countries. Hope and Fears* (The Hague, T.M.C. Press 2006) pp. 409-417, at pp. 409-411.

[6] Ratification of Treaties Act; Act V of 1983; Chapter 304 of the Laws of Malta; text available at http://docs.justice.gov.mt/lom/legislation/english/leg/vol_6/chapt304.pdf.

[7] European Convention Act; Act XIV of 1987, as amended by Acts XXI of 2002, IX of 2006 and Legal Notice 424 of 2007; Chapter 319 of the Laws of Malta; text available at http://docs.justice.gov.mt/lom/legislation/english/leg/vol_7/chapt319.pdf.

[8] European Union Act; Act V of 2003, as amended by Act III of 2006 and Legal Notice 427 of 2007 Chapter 460 of the Laws of Malta. Text available at http://www.commonlii.org/mt/legis/consol_act/eua176.pdf.

[9] Treaty between the Kingdom of Belgium, the Kingdom of Denmark, the Federal Republic of Germany, the Hellenic Republic, the Kingdom of Spain, the French Republic, Ireland, the Italian Republic, the Grand Duchy of Luxembourg, the Kingdom of the Netherlands, the Republic of Austria, the Portuguese Republic, the Republic of Finland, the Kingdom of Sweden, the United Kingdom of Great Britain and Northern Ireland (Member States of the European Union) and the Czech Republic, the Republic of Estonia, the Republic of Cyprus, the Republic of Latvia, the Republic of Lithuania, the Republic of Hungary,

well as the opening of the domestic legal system to EU law and amendment of Article 65 of the Maltese Constitution. In the sections of the chapter that follow, all key provisions of the Act are analysed in details.

## 2.2. The European Union Act 2003

### 2.2.1. *Introductory remarks*

Initially, the acceptance of the principles of supremacy and direct effect of EC law in the Maltese legal order was considered to be problematic. This concern was based primarily on two factors: first, the dualistic approach to public international law inherent in the Maltese legal order and second, the supremacy of the Maltese Constitution laid down in Article 6. It reads:

> 'Subject to the provisions of sub-articles (7) and (9) of Article 47 and of Article 66 of this Constitution, if any other law is inconsistent with this Constitution, this Constitution shall prevail and the other law shall, to the extent of the inconsistency, be void.'

As a result of this clause, application of the doctrine of supremacy – as developed by the European Court of Justice in case 6/64 *Costa v. ENEL*[10] – could have been problematic. If the EC Treaty or any piece of EC secondary legislation were in conflict with ordinary Maltese law, it somehow could be accepted, but real trouble would have started if it were in conflict with the Maltese Constitution.

Malta was not alone in facing such problems at the time of accession. The acceptance of supremacy in the United Kingdom had been even more problematic. Since the UK's constitution is largely unwritten, it is even more difficult to amend it. The main problem is that the Parliament is deemed to be supreme under the doctrine of parliamentary sovereignty. This means that the Parliament has the power to do anything except bind itself in the future. Reconciling this principle with the *Costa v. ENEL* ruling had been one of the most complex constitutional issues that had had to be resolved prior to the accession. It merits attention that the United Kingdom also follows the dualistic approach to international law.

The UK, after signing and ratifying the Accession Treaty 1972,[11] decided to give internal legal effect to EC law by means of an Act of Parliament, that is, the European Communities Act 1972.[12] Malta followed the UK example by enacting the European Union Act 2003. As briefly explained in the previous section of this chapter, it was tailored to incorporate EU law into the Maltese legal order. This means that by the

---

the Republic of Malta, the Republic of Poland, the Republic of Slovenia, the Slovak Republic, concerning the accession of the Czech Republic, the Republic of Estonia, the Republic of Cyprus, the Republic of Latvia, the Republic of Lithuania, the Republic of Hungary, the Republic of Malta, the Republic of Poland, the Republic of Slovenia and the Slovak Republic to the European Union, *OJ* 2003 L 236/17.

[10] ECJ, Case 6/64 *Flaminio Costa v. ENEL* [1964] *ECR* 585.

[11] Treaty of Accession of the United Kingdom, Ireland and Denmark, *OJ* 1972 L 73/1.

[12] For an overview see, *inter alia*, G. Howe, 'The European Communities Act 1972', 49 *International Affairs* (1973) pp. 1-13.

power of the Act, the *acquis* became part of Maltese law. This solves problems posed by the dualistic approach to international treaties.

As far as supremacy is concerned, the issue remains more problematic. As already noted, in the United Kingdom, the Parliament is governed by the principle of sovereignty. This means that if the United Kingdom Parliament were to enact legislation conflicting with the EC Treaty, that national law would prevail. According to the doctrine of implied repeal, UK courts would be obliged to give effect to the latest expression of Parliament's legislative will and to treat an earlier act as having been implicitly repealed. As far as Malta is concerned, the problem would appear to be similar, though more limited, as a result of provisions of the national Constitution.

So what happens if an act of Parliament in the UK or the Maltese Constitution are in conflict with European Union law? With the conclusion of respective Accession Treaties, the United Kingdom as well as Malta – some thirty years later – have accepted an international obligation to comply with EU law. If national legislation were to conflict with EU law, this would mean that the respective Member State would be in breach of the obligations stemming from EU law. If this were to happen theoretically in the First Pillar, sanctions could range from a simple Article 226 EC procedure to political sanctions and to eventual exclusion from the European Union. However, this is unlikely ever to happen as the Member States are presumed to be acting in good faith, and, above all, the Founding Treaties do not provide for exclusion procedure. Membership in the European Union is voluntary, and although withdrawal from the European Union is not explicitly regulated in the current version of the Founding Treaties, a Member State could in theory withdraw from the European Union.[13] It is notable that the Treaty of Lisbon, following Article I-60 of the defunct Treaty establishing a Constitution for Europe,[14] provides such an exit clause.[15]

In practice it is highly unlikely that a Member State would ever be in a position where its basic law was in conflict with the general principles of EU law.[16] In fact, in case 44/79 *Hauer v. Land Rheinland-Pfatz,* the European Court of Justice argued that there is no rule of law that a particular right will be accepted as fundamental by the European Court if it is protected in the constitutions of some of the Member States, or even a majority of them.[17] If the right in question would be generally accepted throughout the European Union and would not prejudice fundamental Community aims, it is probable that the ECJ would, as a matter of policy, accept it as a fundamental right

---

[13] Greenland, which became part of the European Communities as part of Denmark in 1973, withdrew from the Community in 1985 after obtaining autonomy from Denmark and negotiating a withdrawal. See Treaty amending, with regard to Greenland, the Treaties establishing the European Communities, *OJ* 1985 L 29/1. For an academic appraisal see, *inter alia*, F. Weiss, 'Greenland's withdrawal from the European Communities', 10 *ELRev.* (1985) pp. 73-185.

[14] Treaty establishing a Constitution for Europe, *OJ* 2004 C 310/1.

[15] Treaty of Lisbon amending the Treaty on European Union and the Treaty establishing the European Community, *OJ* 2007 C 306/1.

[16] It is perfectly possible to have non-conformity between a provision of a national constitution and a substantive provision of EU law. See, in relation to conflicts between EU legislation on the European Arrest Warrant and constitutions of Poland and Cyprus, Chapters 9 and 15 (respectively) in this volume.

[17] ECJ, Case 44/79 *Liselotte Hauer v. Land Rheinland-Pfalz* [1979] *ECR* 3727.

under European Union law, even if it was constitutionally protected in a single Member State. If the right were a controversial one, it would probably be unlikely that the ECJ would seek to impose the will of the majority on those Member States who would consider such a right to be fundamental.

## 2.2.2. *The substance of the European Union Act 2003*

The main provision of the European Union Act 2003 – Article 4(1) reads:

> 'All such rights, powers, liabilities, obligations and restrictions from time to time created or arising by or under the Treaty, and all such remedies and procedures from time to time pro- vided for by or under the Treaty, that in accordance with the Treaty are without further enactment to be given legal effect or used in Malta, shall be recognised and available in Law, and be enforced, allowed and followed accordingly.'

This is merely a reproduction of Section 2(1) of the European Communities Act 1972, which proves that Malta attempts to adopt the UK's approach as regards the legal framework for the adoption of EU law. Section 2(2) of the European Communities Act 1972 provides for the implementation of Community obligations even when they are intended to replace national legislation and Acts of Parliament by means of Order in Council or statutory instrument rather than by primary legislation.

Article 3 of the European Union Act 2003 provides that as of 1 May 2004, the Accession Treaty 2003 and existing and future acts adopted by the European Union are binding on Malta and shall be part of the domestic law thereof under the conditions laid down in the Treaty. Any provision of any law which from the said date is incom- patible with Malta's obligations under the Treaty or which derogates from any right given to any person by or under the Treaty shall to the extent that such law is incompat- ible with such obligations or to the extent that it derogates from such rights be without effect and unenforceable. From here it emerges that the supremacy of EU law over Maltese law emanates from Article 3 of the European Union Act 2003. To what extent this would apply if there were a potential conflict with provisions of the Maltese Constitution is debatable. Parallelism can be drawn to the theoretical scenario of hav- ing the ECHR as incorporated into the Maltese law in conflict with the Maltese Constitution.[18] The same clout afforded to the ECHR by the Maltese court would prob- ably be afforded to the European Union Act. However, given the unique nature of EU law and the rights and obligations that entails, the fact that Malta voluntarily accepted to join the club should be enough to convince any Maltese court that should this theo- retical scenario happen in reality, as long as Malta wants to be part of the European Union, EU law is supreme and should prevail even if there were to be a conflict with the Constitution. The sharing of sovereignty is voluntary, and unlike a federation, if a country feels that it should no longer share its sovereignty with other Member States, then legally speaking, it should either opt out, or a withdrawal from the European Union should be negotiated. Unlike a federation, the EU does not compel Member States to

---

[18] Theoretical because in practice it is difficult, if not impossible, for such a scenario to happen.

stay in the Union by force and, in theory, a Member State does not give up any sovereignty but simply shares it with other Member States.

In order to give effect to the provisions of Article 3, the Prime Minister or/and any designated Minister or Authority may by order provide for the implementation of any obligation of Malta or enable any such obligation to be implemented, and any right enjoyed or to be enjoyed in Malta under or by virtue of the Treaty to be exercised. The same authorities shall also provide for the implementation of any necessary legislation for the purpose of dealing with matters arising out of or related to any such obligation or right or the coming into force, or the operation from time to time.

Article 4(1) of the European Union Act 2003 aims to make the concept of direct effect part of the Maltese legal system. It deems law which under the Founding Treaties is to be given immediate legal effect to be directly enforceable in Malta. Accordingly, Maltese courts, which on the orthodox domestic approach to international law may not directly enforce a provision of an international treaty or a measure passed thereunder, are directed by this provision to enforce any directly effective EC measure. There is no need for a fresh act of incorporation to enable Malta to enforce each provision of the EC Treaty or a regulation, directive or decision which – according to EC law – is capable of producing direct effect. Just as in the cases of France, Germany and Italy, the supremacy of EC law is recognised in Malta by virtue of a domestic legal process and legal theory – by means of an Act of Parliament.

The European Union Act 2003 also provides for any international treaty concluded by the European Union through its external relations powers. The procedure laid down in Article 4 provides that treaties and international conventions which Malta may accede to as a Member State of the European Union and treaties and international conventions which Malta is bound to ratify in its own name or on behalf of the European Community by virtue of its membership in the European Union, shall come into force one month following their being submitted to be discussed by the Standing Committee on Foreign and European Affairs. In addition, any financial obligations arising out of treaty obligations are to be charged against the consolidated fund.

As for the relationship between the Maltese courts and those of the European Union, the European Union Act provides that for the purposes of any proceeding before any court or other adjudicating authority in Malta, any question as to the meaning or effect of the Treaty, or as to the validity, meaning or effect of any instruments arising thereunder, shall be treated as a question of law. If the issue is not referred to the ECJ, it must be determined as such in accordance with the principles laid down by, and any relevant decision of, the ECJ or any court attached thereto. This allows the preliminary reference procedure under Articles 68 and 234 EC from the point of view of Maltese law. As for the judgments handed down by the EC courts, judicial notice is taken of the Treaty, of the Official Journal of the European Union and of any decision of, or expression of opinion by, the ECJ or any court attached thereto on any such question as aforesaid, and the Official Journal shall be admissible as evidence of any instrument or any other act thereby communicated by any of the Communities or of any institution of the European Union.[19]

---

[19] Art. 5 s. 2-3 European Union Act 2003.

## 2.3. The impact of the European Union Act 2003 on the Maltese Constitution

In order to facilitate the implementation of the European Union Act 2003, Act V of 2003 amended Article 65(1) of the Maltese Constitution as follows:

> 'Subject to the provisions of this Constitution, Parliament may make laws for the peace, order and good government of Malta in conformity with full respect for human rights, generally accepted principles of international law and Malta's international and regional obligations in particular those assumed by the treaty of accession to the European Union signed in Athens on the 16th April, 2003.'

In the above provision, the Constitution is complementing the European Union Act 2003 in ensuring that all legislation passed in Malta is in line with the EU legal order. The inclusion of this provision ensures that even in the fundamental law of the land, all legislation enacted in Malta has to be in line with EU legislation. This makes it easier for Maltese courts to give priority to EU law in cases of conflicting domestic legislation. However, it is worth mentioning that Article 65(1) is not entrenched in Article 66 of the Maltese Constitution. Article 66 provides for special procedures such as a two-thirds majority of the House of Representatives to amend certain parts of the Constitution. Article 65(1) is not included, and thus it can be amended like any other provision of the law. This makes it constitutionally possible for a government to amend the Constitution and to ensure that national law would be supreme over EU law in terms of the Maltese Constitution. However the very fact that a Constitutional amendment would be necessary would make it clear politically that the government of the day would like to withdraw from the European Union, and, therefore, national law cannot overrule EU accidentally. As already noted, a withdrawal from the European Union is technically possible as Malta is sharing its sovereignty with the other Member States and it has not lost it.

## 2.4. The European Union Act 2003 in practice

Maltese courts have not yet had enough opportunities to rule on how the EU legal order has been incorporated into the Maltese legal order. However, a look at some UK cases could offer some hint as to how Maltese courts should view the above. Initially, courts of the United Kingdom were hesitant in applying the above principles.[20] However, Lord Denning in *Shields v. E Coomes (Holdings) Ltd* seemed willing to accept the principle of supremacy of Community law, declaring that Parliament clearly intended, when it enacted the European Communities Act 1972, to abide by the principles of direct effect and supremacy.[21] As a consequence, in his view, national courts should resolve any ambiguity or inconsistency with EC law in national statutes so as to give primacy to EC law. He avoided the problem of implied repeal by giving such weight to the European

---

[20] See *Felixstowe Dock and Railway Company v. British Transport and Docks Board* [1976] 2 *C.M.L.R.* 655.

[21] *Shields v. E Coomes (Holdings) Ltd.* [1979] 1 *All ER* 456, at 461.

Communities Act 1972 and to Parliament's presumed intention in enacting it. Lord Denning argued that a UK court should not enforce a later conflicting act of Parliament if the domestic statute is ambiguous or if it is inconsistent with EC law. However, he did not expressly state that EC law should be given primacy. In Lord Denning's own words:

> 'In construing our statute, we are entitled to look to the EC Treaty as an aid to its construction; but not only as an aid but as an overriding force. If on close investigation it should appear that our legislation is deficient or is inconsistent with Community law by some oversight of our draftsmen then it is our bounded duty to give priority to Community law.

> Thus far I have assumed that our Parliament, whenever it passes legislation, intends to fulfil its obligations under the Treaty. If the time should come when our Parliament deliberately passes an Act with the intention of repudiating the Treaty or any provision in it or intentionally of acting inconsistently with it and says so in express terms then I should have thought that it would be the duty of our courts to follow the statute of our Parliament.'[22]

Here one can see a judicial reconciliation of the Parliamentary sovereignty with the supremacy of EC law. If a domestic provision of law appears to contravene the EC Treaty or any EC secondary legislation, this is presumed to be an accidental contravention, and in such circumstances, the domestic courts should give effect to the doctrine of direct effect of EC law if it is the case, and so EC law would prevail over conflicting domestic law. Such overriding is to be viewed as fulfilment of a true parliamentary intention that the European Communities Act 1972 should prevail in case of conflicting legislation. If it is clear that a domestic law should prevail, then it must do so.[23]

Lord Denning's overview gives a good idea of how EC law became accepted as a legal order working side by side with the English legal order. While his explanation is present, Lord Denning's words explain the position in a nutshell, and any further analysis on this point is beyond the scope of this chapter.[24]

Naturally Lord Denning's explanation can be extended to the Maltese legal order. If one were to apply his explanation to the Maltese system, it would mean as follows: if Parliament enacts any law that happens to conflict with the EU obligations, Maltese courts should ensure that the EC Treaty would prevail. However, given the fact that the ECJ has developed the doctrine of supremacy and of direct effect, we would dare to interpret European Union Act 2003 as prevailing over any Maltese legislation and the Maltese Constitution for two important reasons. The Act itself provides for the ECJ's judgments to prevail in case of conflict. This would also mean that if the ECJ says that its ruling should prevail over the Constitution, then that will be the case. Second, as long as there is the intention to remain in the European Union, there is no place for any domestic legislation to conflict with the *acquis*. If a Maltese Act of Parliament were to be enacted with the intention of conflicting with the *acquis*, then that cannot prevail as

---

[22]   *Macarthys Ltd v. Smith* [1979] 3 *All ER* 325, at 329.

[23]   For a more detailed debate on this issue, see, *inter alia*, T. Allan, 'Parliamentary Sovereignty: Lord Denning's Dexterous Revolution', 3 *OJLS* (1983) pp. 22-33.

[24]   T. Allan, *loc. cit.* n. 23 at p. 22.

long as Malta is a Member State of the European Union. Once an EU obligation is adopted at EU level and Malta does not negotiate any derogations or opt-outs, Europe is not *à la carte*; therefore, EU law prevails over any Maltese law. Does this mean that Malta has lost its sovereignty? The answer to such a provocative question is negative. It is sharing the sovereignty with other Member States, and in theory, there is always the choice to take all measures to be implemented or withdraw from the European Union. Malta has pooled some of its sovereignty, and as long as it remains pooled, the sovereignty is limited.

Could it be argued that the European Union Act 2003 modified fundamentals enshrined in the Maltese Constitution (apart from the revision of Article 65 as explained above)? This question has to be answered in the negative. First, nothing in the *acquis* is presumed to conflict with the Constitution. Second, the Founding Treaties, including the Treaty of Lisbon, do not provide for any requirement whatsoever in terms of the organisation of a Member State. A Member State is free to choose and maintain whatever form of government or legal system it prefers. Third, as far as fundamental rights are concerned, the ECJ confirmed many times that it draws inspiration from the constitutions of the Member States.[25] Thus the European Union Act 2003, by making EC law supreme over Maltese law, is in no way contravening the provisions of the Maltese Constitution. Any new human rights legislation is likely to be further protection, rather than a threat, to the basic rights as enshrined in the Maltese Constitution.

Foreseeable problems could be envisaged if "new human rights" are introduced at the European level which could conflict with principles of the majority of Maltese, such as the right for abortion or the right to divorce. As for the first case, this could never affect Malta against its will as it is provided for in the Accession Treaty.[26] As for the latter, it is not a constitutional right in Malta; therefore, if it were introduced as a right, Malta might be bound. However, if Malta were to provide against such a right in its Constitution, it is likely that European law would not force such right upon Malta as it is a general principle of EU law not to conflict with the basic rights enshrined in the Constitution of its Member States.[27] Thus conflict between the European Union Act and the Maltese Constitution is unlikely to exist both in theory and in practice.

Naturally Malta can amend its Constitution in a way to conflict with EU law. In this case, the Maltese courts should rule that EU law would prevail as long as the political intention is to stay in the European Union. Malta can get back its full sovereignty if it chooses to withdraw from the European Union.

## 3.    THE APPLICATION OF EU LAW IN MALTA

Malta started aligning itself with the *acquis* years before actual accession took place as a part of the pre-accession approximation exercise. However, following accession

---

[25] *Loc. cit.* n. 17.

[26] See Protocol No 7 on abortion in Malta, annexed to the Accession Treaty, *OJ* 2003 L 236/947.

[27] See ECJ, Case C-159/90 *The Society for the Protection of Unborn Children Ireland Ltd v. Stephen Grogan and others* [1991] *ECR* I-4685.

and entry into force of the European Union Act 2003, Maltese law is supposed to be in line with EU obligations. It is fitting to note that the Maltese legal order is a mixed system based on both common law and civil law principles. Mixed legal systems owe their *mixité* mostly to legal transplants, that is, the borrowing of legal institutions and rules by one country from another, often initiated by national courts. Reid and Zimmermann argue:[28]

> 'If, therefore, the establishment of an intellectual connection between civil law and common law is regarded as an important prerequisite for the emergence of a genuinely European legal scholarship, it should be of the greatest interest to see that such connection has already been established … in a number of mixed legal systems. Such systems provide a wealth of experience of how civil law and common law may be accommodated within one legal system.'

This statement is closely related to the idea that Scots law and the other mixed jurisdictions are an optimal mix of the best that both civil law and the common law can offer. Mixed legal systems present a mix of national mentality and European uniformity. Thus Malta, with a mixed legal system, is in a good position to adopt and integrate the workings of the EU legal order with that of the Maltese one. This reduces the possibility of legal irritants and, therefore, increases the success of the application of EU law.

EC regulations and directives are the most important legal instruments which have to be examined in order to see the effect of EC law on the Maltese legal order. Pursuant to Article 249 EC and Article 161 EAEC, regulations are binding upon all Member States and are directly applicable in all national legal orders. On the date of accession, all EC and Euratom regulations became binding in Malta unless they were covered by a transitional period guaranteed by the Accession Treaty 2003.[29] Basically, this means that EC regulations are to be considered as primary law, and they should not be transposed. They are the law. The Member States may need to modify their own law in order to comply with a regulation. This may be the case where a regulation has implications for different parts of national law. However, this does not alter the fact that a regulation itself has legal effect in the Member States independent of any national law, and that the Member States should not pass measures that conceal the nature of a Community regulation. In case national law is not amended, regulations would prevail. In the *Variola* case,[30] the ECJ was asked by a national court whether the provisions of a regulation could be introduced into the legal order of a Member State in such a way that the subject matter is brought under national law. The ECJ explained that by virtue of the obligations arising from the Treaty and assumed on ratification, the Member States are under a duty not to obstruct the direct applicability inherent in regulations and other rules of Community law.[31] The ECJ explains:

---

[28] K. Reid and R. Zimmermann, 'The Development of Legal Doctrine in a Mixed System', in K. Reid and R. Zimmermann, eds., *A History of Private Law in Scotland. Volume I* (Oxford, Oxford University Press 2000) pp. 1-13.

[29] This is the case with, *inter alia*, selected regulations dealing with agriculture. See Annex XI to Act on Conditions of Accession, *OJ* 2003 L 236/859.

[30] See ECJ, Case 34/73 *Variola v. Amministrazione delle Finanze* [1973] *ECR* 981.

[31] See para. 10 of the judgment.

'Member States are under an obligation not to introduce any measure which might affect the jurisdiction of the Court to pronounce on any question involving the interpretation of Community law or the validity of an act of the institutions of the Community, which means that no procedure is permissible whereby the Community nature of a legal rule is concealed from those subject to it.'[32]

As regulations – at least in general terms – require no transposition, there is no need to elaborate further in this section.[33] Analysis of transposition of directives proves to be a more effective way to gauge the reception of EU law by the Maltese legal order. As a general rule, there are a few possible scenarios. Directives are transposed either by an act of Parliament into primary legislation (for instance, company law directives[34] or VAT directives),[35] or by means of a legal notice, such as most of labour law directives,[36] or by a combination of both primary and secondary legislation. The choice of a legal act for transposition depends on a number of factors; however, the primary role is played by objectives of a particular directive. An act of Parliament is normally reserved for transposition of a directive which is either a framework law on which subsidiary legislation can be enacted, or it is a matter of high national importance. Being transposed through an act of Parliament would often mean that a national debate is held on the subject matter, and the law is adequately publicised; transposition by means of a legal notice is faster but is less publicised. However, it may be a better way of transposing EU law, particularly if a directive is technical and the transposition period is very short. Considering the number of directives adopted per annum, it would be impossible in practice to transpose every single directive by means of an act of Parliament. Such *modus operandi* would not guarantee timely transposition.

Malta has generally been on track in transposition of directives within the deadlines, and no major problems occurred. However, there have been cases where a directive or parts of a directive were not implemented, or the transposition was incorrect. This will be further elaborated upon in the next two sections of this chapter.

---

[32] See para. 11 of the judgment.

[33] One should note that there are a number of regulations which require domestic measures to give them effect. A good example is the Regulation on European Economic Interest Grouping (Council Regulation (EEC) No 2137/85 of 25 July 1985 on the European Economic Interest Grouping, *OJ* 1985 L 199/1). Such additional measures supplementing the Regulation were adopted in Malta by means of Subsidiary Legislation 386.08, Companies Act (European Economic Interest Grouping) Regulation. Text available at http://docs.justice.gov.mt/lom/Legislation/English/SubLeg/386/08.pdf.

[34] See Companies Act (Chapter 386 of the Laws of Malta) transposing, *inter alia*, so-called Prospectus Directive (Directive 2003/71/EC of the European Parliament and of the Council of 4 November 2003 on the prospectus to be published when securities are offered to the public or admitted to trading and amending Directive 2001/34/EC, *OJ* 2003 L 345/64). For the text of Maltese legislation, see http://docs.justice.gov.mt/lom/legislation/english/leg/vol_11/chapt386.pdf.

[35] See Value Added Tax Act (Chapter 406 of the Laws of Malta) transposing, *inter alia*, Directive 2006/112/EC (Council Directive 2006/112/EC of 28 November 2006 on the common system of value added tax, *OJ* 2006 L 347/1). For the text of the Maltese legislation, see http://docs.justice.gov.mt/lom/legislation/english/leg/vol_12/chapt406.pdf.

[36] Regulations 78 to 100 under Chapter 452 of the Laws of Malta.

## 4.    EUROPEAN UNION LAW IN MALTESE COURTS

### 4.1.    The application of EU law by Maltese courts

Following Malta's accession, EU law became directly applicable, but this did not result in having a lot of cases dealing with issues of EU law on accession. Lawyers somehow needed time to get accustomed to the idea that now EU law is not foreign law but local law as well. As a result, there were very few judgments dealing with issues of EU law in the first few years. However, the trend is slowly changing. The number of judgments dealing with EU law has increased and will continue to increase in the future. Numerous relevant examples of case law of the Maltese courts dealing with EU law concern the application of Regulation 44/2001/EC concerning the enforcement of judgments delivered by the courts of other Member States.[37]

One of the first cases in this regard was *Elwira Maria Opatecka v. Andrew Francis Ciantar* decided by the First Hall of the Civil Court on 30 June 2005 and upheld by the Court of Appeal on 27 June 2006.[38] The case was an order of maintenance by a Polish court against a Maltese citizen resident in Malta. The courts of both instances accepted the direct applicability of the above Regulation as part of Maltese law. This was one of the first cases whereby Maltese courts had an opportunity to accept the direct applicability of an EC regulation. As a result, the Maltese courts found no difficulties in enforcing the Polish judgment in Malta.

Another case in this regard is *Refalo v. Garden of Eden Limited.*[39] This case was about the enforcement of a judgment rendered by the Central London County Court on 14 December 2005. The judgment concerned a claim for damages due on a traffic accident which took place when the plaintiff was on holiday in Malta. The Court of Appeal upheld the judgment of the lower court ordering the enforcement of the English judgment in Malta. The court accepted that the English Court had jurisdiction over the case as the facts arose out of a package holiday contract signed in England. The court relied on Article 6 of the Regulation 44/2001/EC, which reads

> 'A person domiciled in a Member State may also be sued … where he is one of a number of defendants, in the courts of the place where any of them is domiciled, provided that the claims are so closely connected that it is expedient to hear and determine them together to avoid the risk of irreconcilable judgments resulting from separate proceedings.'

While the above cases prove that the Maltese highest court is ready to enforce EU law and enforce judgments from other EU Member States, the Court of Appeal ensures that this is only done after careful analysis that the case falls under Regulation 44/2001/EC.

---

[37] Council Regulation (EC) No 44/2001 of 22 December 2000 on jurisdiction and the recognition and enforcement of judgments in civil and commercial matters, *OJ* 2001 L 12/1.

[38] Application No. 303/2005 decided on 30 June 2005 and Civil Appeal 303/205/1 decided on 27 January 2006.

[39] Civil Appeal 305/2006/1 decided by the Court of Appeal on 13 March 2007.

In *GIE (PMU) v. Zeturf Ltd*,[40] the Court of Appeal revoked a judgment of the lower court enforcing a judgment of the Court of Appeal of Paris. The Maltese Court of Appeal refused to enforce the French judgment, arguing that the French court based its judgment on the grounds of public policy as interpreted by French law. The Maltese Court noted that the French provisions on which the judgment was based did not have an economic objective and were simply intended to protect French public policy. The Maltese Court rightly came to the conclusion that the French Court based its judgment on French public law rather than French private law in civil and commercial matters. Regulation 44/2001/EC specifically excludes the former; therefore, the court concluded that the Regulation was not applicable to the facts of the case. It is notable that the Court of Appeal did not entertain the request to proceed with a reference for preliminary ruling to the European Court of Justice.[41]

While the above case law centred on the application of EU law, there have also been instances where Maltese courts had to rule about which law should prevail in case of a conflict between EU law and domestic law. In *Sansone v. Comptroller of Industrial Property*, the Court of Appeal recognised the hierarchal superiority of an EC regulation over conflicting domestic law.[42] This judgment may serve as a proof that Maltese courts have no problems in accepting the supremacy of EC law.

However, there are examples of the opposite. Indeed, sometimes things go wrong, and Maltese courts make mistakes in the application of EU law. A typical example is the case of *Izola Bank Ltd v. Commissioner of VAT*.[43] This was a decision about a discrepancy between Chapter 406 of the Laws of Malta dealing with VAT law and Article 9 of the Sixth VAT Directive.[44] Following accession to the European Union, Malta failed to transpose the Directive fully by extending the VAT tax to an item previously not covered under Maltese law. The Court of Appeal, quoting the judgment of the ECJ in case C-106/89 *Marleasing*,[45] came to the conclusion that the concept of direct effect of directives as laid down by the ECJ in *Marleasing* was similar to that of an EC regulation. Referring to an earlier *Sansone* judgment delivered by the same Court, it ruled that the Directive was superior to the Maltese VAT law as it stood at the given time.

---

[40] Civil Appeal 92/2006/1 decided by the Court of Appeal on 3 January 2007.

[41] For more on this dispute, see J. Borg-Barthet, 'Online gambling and the further displacement of state regulation: a note on PMU v. Zeturf', 57 *ICLQ* (2008) pp. 417-426.

[42] Application 15/20 of 2005 Court of Appeal decided on 22 March 2006.

[43] Application 18/2006 Court of Appeal decided on 9 May 2007.

[44] Sixth Council Directive 77/388/EEC of 17 May 1977 on the harmonization of the laws of the Member States relating to turnover taxes – Common system of value added tax: uniform basis of assessment, *OJ* 1977 L 145/1.

[45] ECJ, Case C-106/89 *Marleasing SA v. La Comercial Internacionale de Alimetacion SA* [1990] *ECR* I-4135: The European Court of Justice held: 'In applying national law, whether the provisions in question were adopted before or after the directive, the national court called upon to interpret it is required to do so, as far as possible, in the light of the wording and the purpose of the directive in order to achieve the result pursued by the latter and thereby comply with the third paragraph of article 189 of the Treaty.' See also ECJ, Case C-456/98 *Centrosteel Srl v. Adipol GmbH* [2000] *ECR* I-6007; Joined Cases C-240/98 to C-244/98 *Océano Grupo Editorial SA v. Roció Murciano Quintero (C-240/98) and Salvat Editores SA v. José M. Sánchez Alcón Prades (C-241/98), José Luis Copano Badillo (C-242/98), Mohammed Berroane (C-243/98) and Emilio Viñas Feliú (C-244/98)* [2000] *ECR* I-4491.

Therefore, the taxpayer had to pay tax on the basis of the non-implemented Directive as opposed to the basis of the transposed legislation.

While the above is another proof that the Maltese courts have no problem in enforcing EU law as such, mistakes are also made. In the discussed case, the Maltese Court made a mistake by giving equal status to EC directives and regulations. While directives are capable of direct effect, this does not mean that they are directly applicable. In this case, the Maltese Court treated a directive as if it were directly applicable. Another mistake made by the Maltese Court was that it failed to follow the rules on direct effect of directives. The Court in question ignored – that is failed to refer and take into account – the case 148/78 *Ratti*.[46] It is a classic case, whereby the ECJ held that a Member State which did adopt implementing measures required by a directive may not rely on such directive *vis-à-vis* individuals because of its own failure to perform the obligation which the directive entails. This is a well-established principle, reiterated in other ECJ cases, such as *Faccini Dori*.[47] The ECJ maintained that its case law on direct effect of directives seeks to prevent the state from using its own failure to comply with Community law and thus depriving individuals of the benefit of the rights which directives may confer on them. Sacha Prechal argues that doctrine declared the so-called principle of estoppel to be the ultimate rationale of direct effect of directives.[48] The Maltese Court of Appeal in the *Izola Bank* case failed to recognise this.

## 4.2.    References for a preliminary ruling

While the application of EU law is generally satisfactory, surprisingly there have been very few attempts where Maltese courts felt the need to explore the possibility of making a preliminary reference under Article 234 EC or Article 68 EC.[49] In fact, during the first five years of membership, no questions were referred to the ECJ under the said procedure. The most important attempt worth mentioning from the period between 1 May 2004 and 1 May 2009 is the judgment passed by the Court of Appeal on 26 June 2007 in *GIE Pari Mutuel Urbain (PMU) v. Bell Med Ltd & Computer Aided Technologies Ltd*.[50] This case is about the enforcement of a judgment delivered by the French *Tribunal de Grande Instance* under the Brussels Regulation.[51] The dispute was about the applicability of the Brussels Regulation to the facts of the case. The Regulation applies to civil and commercial matters while the French court delivering the judgment was an administrative court.[52]

---

[46] ECJ, Case 148/78 *Criminal proceedings against Tullio Ratti* [1979] *ECR* 1629.

[47] Case C-91/92 *Paola Faccini Dori v. Recreb Srl.* [1994] *ECR* I-3325.

[48] S. Prechal, *Directives in EC Law* (Oxford, Oxford University Press 2004) p. 258.

[49] As of 1 July 2009, Malta did not recognise the jurisdiction of the European Court of Justice pursuant to Art. 35 TEU.

[50] Civil Appeal 224/2006/1 *GIE Pari Mutuel Urbain (PMU) v. Bell Med Ltd & Computer Aided Technologies Ltd* decided by the Court of Appeal on 26 June 2007 (text on file with the author).

[51] Council Regulation (EC) No 44/2001 of 22 December 2000 on jurisdiction and the recognition and enforcement of judgments in civil and commercial matters, *OJ* 2001 L 12/1.

[52] Art. 1.1 of the Regulation reads: 'This Regulation shall apply in civil and commercial matters whatever the nature of the court or tribunal. It shall not extend, in particular, to revenue, customs or administrative matters.'

In passing judgment, the Maltese Court of Appeal gave a well-studied analysis of why it should decline making a reference. The national court clearly accepted that regarding issues of interpretation of a Community law provision, the said Court is obliged to make a reference to the ECJ. Therefore, the Maltese Court of Appeal is stating clearly that it accepts its duty to make a reference if the conditions of Article 234 EC are satisfied. Regarding the interpretation of civil and commercial matters, the Court said there is much ECJ jurisprudence dealing with this issue. The Court made reference to authoritative textbooks as proof.[53] However, the Court went on to say that the dispute before it was not an issue of interpretation but rather an issue of application. While referring to Paul Craig and Graine de Bùrca,[54] the Court of Appeal acknowledged that the distinction between interpretation and application is meant to be one of the characteristic features of the division of authority between the ECJ and the national court; the former interprets EC law while the latter applies it. In this case, the national court felt that there was no need to seek a reference on this point.

The above judgment shows that the Maltese courts are ready to examine seriously EU law issues and will not hesitate to make a reference if it is needed. This was the case with Civil Court sized with a dispute between AJD Tuna Limited and Direttur tal-Agrikoltura u s-Sajd u Avukat Generali. The reference was submitted in June 2009[55] and deals with a regulation of the European Commission on the emergency procedures in the Mediterranean Sea.[56] It is pending at the time of writing.[57]

## 5.     ENFORCEMENT ACTIONS AGAINST MALTA

In exercising its function as guardian of the Treaties (Art. 211 EC), the European Commission ensures and monitors uniform application of EC law by Member States. After a relatively short honeymoon, in 2005 the European Commission started its first infringement proceedings against Malta. In 2005 alone, Malta received 55 formal notices, and the number increased to 77 in 2006.[58] The 2006 statistics do not provide a good impression of Malta in terms of implementation of EC law. During those two

---

[53] A. Layton and H. Mercer, *European Civil Practice Vol. 1*, 2nd edn. (London, Sweet & Maxwell 2004) pp. 336-349; A. Briggs and P. Rees,. *Civil Jurisdiction and Judgments*, 5th edn. (London LLP 2005) pp. 46-51.

[54] P. Craig and G. de Bùrca, *EU Law – Texts, Cases and Materials*, 3rd edn. (Oxford, Oxford University Press 2002) pp. 472-473.

[55] Text of the reference is available at http://docs.justice.gov.mt/SENTENZI2000_PDF/MALTA/CIVILI,%20PRIM%20AWLA/2009/2009-06-04_1210-2008_55464.PDF.

[56] Commission Regulation (EC) No 530/2008 of 12 June 2008 establishing emergency measures as regards purse seiners fishing for bluefin tuna in the Atlantic Ocean, east of longitude 45 °W, and in the Mediterranean Sea, *OJ* 2008 L 155/9.

[57] ECJ, Case C-221/09 *AJD Tuna Limited and Direttur tal-Agrikoltura u s-Sajd u Avukat Generali*, pending.

[58] Commission Staff Working Document: Annex to the 24th Annual Report from the Commission on Monitoring the application of Community Law (2006), SEC (2007) 975; Commission Staff Working Document accompanying the 25th Annual Report from the Commission on Monitoring application of Community Law (2007), SEC (2008) 2855.

468 CHAPTER 14

years, Malta was the worst of the ten new Member States in terms of reception of formal notices; out of the EU 25, Malta is surpassed only by Italy, a Member State with the highest number of formal notices, 126 in all, followed by Greece, Portugal and France respectively. Malta received 19 reasoned opinions in 2005 followed by 18 reasoned opinions in 2006.[59] In 2006 Malta's first infringements referrals to the ECJ appeared (one of them was later removed from the register).[60] There were three in all, making Malta the new Member State with the second highest number of referrals, exceeded by one by the Czech Republic and Poland.[61] Out of the 77 formal notices received in 2006, 58 related to the non-communication of the transposition measures for directives. Furthermore, 9 resulted in the non-conformity with a directive, while 3 resulted from a bad implementation of a directive. The final nine notices were received as a result of direct infringement of the EC Treaty.[62] In 2007, the Maltese Government received 69 formal notices as well as 25 reasoned opinions.[63] In the case of formal notices, 44 dealt with non-communication of transposition measures, 7 with non-conformity of domestic law with directives and 10 with bad application of directives. Reasoned opinions covered 13 instances of non-notification, 2 of non-conformity and 5 cases of bad application. Eight letters of formal notice and 5 reasoned opinions covered breaches of the Founding Treaties, regulations and decisions. Three cases were referred to the European Court of Justice.[64]

While most of the cases were settled at the administrative stage of the infraction procedure, several have reached the judicial stage. Still, one has to remember that an action can be withdrawn by the European Commission when a case is pending at the European Court of Justice. Action in case C-269/08 *Commission v. Republic of Malta* may serve as an excellent example. The action was submitted to the Court on 20 June 2008;[65] however following the transposition of Directive 2004/83/EC[66] into Maltese law,[67] the European Commission withdrew its application. Therefore, the President of

---

[59] Commission Staff Working Document: Annex to the 24th Annual Report from the Commission on Monitoring the application of Community Law (2006), *loc. cit.* n. 58 at p. 10.

[60] See Action brought on 10 March 2006 – *Commission of the European Communities v. Republic of Malta (Case C-136/06)*, *OJ* 2006 C 131/30; Action brought on 14 December 2006 – *Commission of the European Communities v. Republic of Malta (Case C-508/06)*, *OJ* 2007 C 56/15.

[61] Commission Staff Working Document: Annex to the 24th Annual Report from the Commission on Monitoring the application of Community Law (2006), *loc. cit.* n. 58 at p. 10.

[62] Commission Staff Working Document: Annex to the 24th Annual Report from the Commission on Monitoring the application of Community Law (2006), *loc. cit.* n. 58 at pp. 11-12.

[63] Commission Staff Working Document accompanying the 25th Annual Report from the Commission on Monitoring application of Community Law (2007), *loc. cit.* n. 58, p. 11.

[64] Action brought on 15 February 2007 – *Commission of the European Communities v. Republic of Malta* (Case C-87/07), *OJ* 2007 C 82/46; *Action brought on 13 February 2007 – Commission of the European Communities v. Republic of Malta* (Case C-79/07), *OJ* 2007 C 82/43; *Action brought on 20 December 2007 – Commission of the European Communities v. Republic of Malta* (Case C-563/07), *OJ* 2008 C 51/61.

[65] Action brought on 20 June 2008 – *Commission of the European Communities v. Republic of Malta* (Case C-269/08), *OJ* 2008 C 197/16.

[66] Council Directive 2004/83/EC of 29 April 2004 on minimum standards for the qualification and status of third country nationals or stateless persons as refugees or as persons who otherwise need international protection and the content of the protection granted, *OJ* 2004 L 304/12.

[67] An amendment to Refugees Act 2000 was adopted in 2008. See Refugees Act, Act XX of 2000, Chapter 420 of the Laws of Malta (as amended by Act VIII of 2004; Legal Notices 40 of 2005 and 426 of

the Chamber – to whom the case had been assigned – removed the case from the register.[68] It merits attention that in the course of 2007-2008, the European Commission withdrew all three actions submitted in 2007; consequentially, they were removed from the register of the European Court of Justice.[69]

The first judgment in an infraction case against Malta was rendered in case C-508/06 *Commission v. Republic of Malta*.[70] The ECJ held that by failing to communicate plans and outlines required by a Directive on disposal of chemicals Malta was in breach of EC law.[71] It is fitting to mention that numerous infringements against Malta concern environmental protection issues. Most of these, such as file no. 2007/4325 about Fort Cambridge, deal with the impact of major development projects on the environment. The most controversial infraction so far is pending case C-76/08 *Commission v. Republic of Malta*. The factual and legal background is as follows. The European Commission has submitted that Malta failed to comply with Article 9 of a Directive on conservation of wild birds.[72] Malta insists that it had negotiated a special derogation on spring hunting, while the plaintiff argues that any derogation has to be in line with Article 9 of the Directive with which Malta has allegedly failed to comply. This is a standard infringement proceeding; nevertheless, it is one of the few where the President of the ECJ entertained the Commission's request for interim measures. Pursuant to an Order of 24 April 2008, Malta shall refrain from adopting any measures applying the derogation laid down in Article 9 of the Directive for the 2008 spring migration of two species of birds.[73]

Other well-known infringements against Malta include file no. 2005/4534 about a car registration tax on second-hand cars infringing Article 90 EC. Malta has a very high registration tax on second-hand cars, which makes it very difficult to import second-hand cars from other EU Member States. The European Commission insists that this is discriminatory. Perhaps one of the most clear infringement proceedings against Malta is file no. 2005/4778 concerning departure tax on all air passengers starting their itinerary in Malta. The discrimination is clear as the same departure tax is not levied on Maltese domestic flights.

---

2007; and Act VII of 2008). Text available at http://docs.justice.gov.mt/lom/legislation/english/leg/vol_13/chapt420.pdf.

[68] ECJ, Case C-269/08 Order of the President of the Seventh Chamber of the Court of 5 February 2009, *OJ* 2009 C 141/65.

[69] Order of the President of the Seventh Chamber of the Court of 10 August 2007 – *Commission of the European Communities v. Republic of Malta* (Case C-87/07), *OJ* 2007 C 297/65; Order of the President of the Court of 8 August 2007 – *Commission of the European Communities v. Republic of Malta* (Case C-79/07), *OJ* 2007 C 297/65; Order of the President of the Fifth Chamber of the Court of 18 August 2008 – *Commission of the European Communities v. Republic of Malta* (Case C-563/07). *OJ* 2008 C 313/37.

[70] ECJ, Case C-508/06 *Commission of the European Communities v. Republic of Malta* [2007] *ECR* I-172.

[71] Council Directive 96/59/EC of 16 September 1996 on the disposal of polychlorinated biphenyls and polychlorinated terphenyls (PCB/PCT), *OJ* 1996 L 243/31.

[72] Council Directive 79/409/EEC of 2 April 1979 on the conservation of wild birds, *OJ* 1979 L 103/1.

[73] ECJ, Order of the President of the Court in Case C-76/08R *Commission of the European Communities v. Republic of Malta*, nyr.

## 6.      CONCLUSIONS

Much more needs to be done in integrating the EU legal order with the Maltese one, especially from the educational point of view. While most lawyers in the legal profession dealing with EU issues are adequately prepared, much more needs to be done in the civil service, particularly in those services that deal directly with EU matters, such as customs and tax authorities. Very often the main problem is not human resources as such, but rather that the bureaucratic structure in which the departments are set up would hinder the best use of available resources. Training is needed not only at the technocratic level but also at the level of the judiciary and of administrative tribunals. A major problem with the Maltese legal profession, particularly with the older generations, is that European Union law is considered similar to international law applicable in Malta rather than as a *sui generis* legal order operating in a juxtaposed position with the Maltese legal system. Another problem is a failure to comprehend fully the whole context of a European Union legal issue and thus to stop the analysis halfway through, as in the case *Izola Bank Ltd v. Commissioner of VAT*.[74] Finally, members of the judiciary should be more open to accepting that European Union law is now also domestic law, and they should not hesitate to refer to relevant treaty-based procedures if necessary.

If the above issues are addressed, Malta stands to be a good example of how EU law is integrated within the national legal system. The fact that the Court of Appeal in its superior jurisdiction as the highest civil court of the land would probably get the highest score among local Courts in applying European Union law could be taken as proof.

---

[74] Application 18/2006 Court of Appeal decided on 9 May 2007.

*Chapter 15*

# "BACK TO REALITY": THE IMPLICATIONS OF EU MEMBERSHIP IN THE CONSTITUTIONAL LEGAL ORDER OF CYPRUS

Stéphanie Laulhé Shaelou*

## 1.    INTRODUCTION

The process of integration of the new Member States following 2004 and 2007 enlargements is still unfolding, primarily due to the numerous measures contained in Accession Treaties 2003[1] and 2005[2] and arguably leading to differentiated integration. Differentiated or flexible integration with respect to the latest enlargements is characterised *a priori* by the fact that the new Member States, including Cyprus, have not fully participated – as of the date of accession – in all EU policies and/or could have been excluded from major policy areas while they were bound by the *acquis communautaire* (e.g., participation in Schengen zone or the Economic and Monetary Union).[3] The

*    Assistant Professor, Law Department, University of Nicosia. The author wishes to thank Dr. Constantinos Lycourgos for his assistance and very constructive comments on earlier drafts of this paper. The usual disclaimer applies.

[1]    Treaty between the Kingdom of Belgium, the Kingdom of Denmark, the Federal Republic of Germany, the Hellenic Republic, the Kingdom of Spain, the French Republic, Ireland, the Italian Republic, the Grand Duchy of Luxembourg, the Kingdom of the Netherlands, the Republic of Austria, the Portuguese Republic, the Republic of Finland, the Kingdom of Sweden, the United Kingdom of Great Britain and Northern Ireland (Member States of the European Union) and the Czech Republic, the Republic of Estonia, the Republic of Cyprus, the Republic of Latvia, the Republic of Lithuania, the Republic of Hungary, the Republic of Malta, the Republic of Poland, the Republic of Slovenia, the Slovak Republic, concerning the accession of the Czech Republic, the Republic of Estonia, the Republic of Cyprus, the Republic of Latvia, the Republic of Lithuania, the Republic of Hungary, the Republic of Malta, the Republic of Poland, the Republic of Slovenia and the Slovak Republic to the European Union, *OJ* 2003 L 236/17.

[2]    Treaty between the Kingdom of Belgium, the Czech Republic, the Kingdom of Denmark, the Federal Republic of Germany, the Republic of Estonia, the Hellenic Republic, the Kingdom of Spain, the French Republic, Ireland, the Italian Republic, the Republic of Cyprus, the Republic of Latvia, the Republic of Lithuania, the Grand Duchy of Luxembourg, the Republic of Hungary, the Republic of Malta, the Kingdom of the Netherlands, the Republic of Austria, the Republic of Poland, the Portuguese Republic, the Republic of Slovenia, the Slovak Republic, the Republic of Finland, the Kingdom of Sweden, the United Kingdom of Great Britain and Northern Ireland (Member States of the European Union) and the Republic of Bulgaria and Romania, concerning the accession of the Republic of Bulgaria and Romania to the European Union, *OJ* 2005 L 157/11.

[3]    Art. 2 of the Act on Conditions of Accession 2003.

*A. Łazowski (ed.), The Application of EU Law in the New Member States*
© 2010, T·M·C·Asser press, *The Hague, The Netherlands and the Authors*

situation of Cyprus seems somehow different to the extent that, in addition to this alleged regime of differentiated integration, its integration is singled out in two tailor-made protocols annexed to the Act on Conditions of Accession 2003,[4] potentially hindering further its integration into the EU.

It is clear that Cyprus stands on its own path of European integration. This is due to specific socio-legal and political factors, which ought to be taken into account if one wants to analyse the idiosyncrasies of Cyprus's *rapprochement* towards the EU.[5] On 1 May 2004, Cyprus acceded to the EU as a divided island. Although the process of accession was conducted – in theory – on behalf of the whole island and Cyprus joined as one country, the northern part of the island has been largely left out of the process due to the ongoing *de facto* division. The so-called areas of Cyprus falling "beyond the effective control" of the Government of the Republic of Cyprus (hereafter Areas) have been subject since then to a special regime based on the suspension of *acquis communautaire* provided by the Protocol 10,[6] even if initiatives to assist these Areas have been taken by the EU since accession.[7]

Even if it appears that EU membership may sometimes entail unique implications for Cyprus (resulting from its peculiar situation),[8] nevertheless, Cyprus is fully bound by the Accession Treaty 2003 – as are all other Member States that joined in 2004. As a result, many challenges associated with EU membership are common to all newcomers, especially with respect to the encounter of their national legal systems with the European Union legal order. In this chapter, the domestic legal systems of the new Member States will be the subject of a comparative analysis focusing on Cyprus as an alleged instance of furtherance of European integration in the field of European constitutional law.

---

[4] Protocol 3 on the Sovereign Base Areas of the United Kingdom of Great Britain and Northern Ireland in Cyprus, *OJ* 2003 L 236/940; Protocol No 10 on Cyprus, *OJ* 2003 L 236/955.

[5] For a detailed account of the allegedly differentiated regime of integration of Cyprus within the EU, see S. Laulhé Shaelou, *The EU and Cyprus: principles and strategies of full integration* (Leiden, Brill/Martinus Nijhoff Publishers 2009).

[6] For a legal review of its underlying mechanisms, see in Laulhé Shaelou, *op. cit.* n. 5, Chapters 5 and 7. See also S. Laulhé Shaelou, *The European Court of Justice and the Anastasiou saga: principles of Europeanisation through economic governance*, 18 *EBLR* (2007) pp. 619-639; N. Skoutaris, *The application of the acquis communautaire in the areas not under the effective control of the Republic of Cyprus: the Green Line Regulation*, 45 *CMLRev.* (2008) pp. 727-755.

[7] Protocol 3 on the Sovereign Base Areas of the United Kingdom of Great Britain and Northern Ireland in Cyprus falls beyond the scope of this chapter. For a legal appraisal see in Laulhé Shaelou, *op. cit.* n. 5, Chapter 4.

[8] See, *inter alia*, S. Laulhé Shaelou, 'Cyprus reunified under the Annan Plan: a hypothetical instance of "full" integration into the EU?', in S. Stavridis, ed., *Understanding and evaluating the EU: theoretical and empirical approaches* (Nicosia, Nicosia University Press 2009).

## 2.    THE APPLICATION OF THE PRINCIPLE OF SUPREMACY OF EC/EU LAW IN CYPRUS

### 2.1.    The Cypriot constitutional legal order

The origins of the Cypriot Constitution should be briefly explained. The Republic of Cyprus is a relatively "young" republic, since the island of Cyprus only gained the status of an independent and sovereign state in 1960 after the Zurich and London Agreements. The Agreements, reached between Greece and Turkey, looked on a plan for the establishment of an independent state. They comprised three treaties on the basis of which the Constitution of the newly created state was drafted. The three treaties were the Treaty of Guarantee,[9] the Treaty of Alliance[10] and the Treaty of Establishment,[11] which collectively provided, *inter alia*, a guarantee by Greece, Turkey and the UK for the independence, territorial integrity and security of the Republic; the establishment of Greek and Turkish military contingents in Cyprus and the preservation of two British sovereign military bases in Cyprus.[12]

The Treaty of Establishment is incorporated into the 1960 Cypriot Constitution. The Treaty of Guarantee and the Treaty of Alliance, which are annexed to the Constitution (Annexes I and II, respectively), have been given constitutional force by virtue of Article 181 of the Constitution. The Cypriot Constitution was described as standing 'as the centerpiece of an intricate network of international agreements and undertakings, delicately but inextricably interwoven with one another and with the Constitution itself.'[13] Papasavvas gives five attributes to the 1960 Constitution, namely 'imposed, rigid, complex, anti-democratic and dividing.'[14] Following the withdrawal of the Turkish Cypriots from the institutions of the Republic shortly after its creation, the Cypriot Government has continued acting on the basis of the "law of necessity." It is within this framework that the Republic of Cyprus is an actor in international law.

---

[9] Treaty of Guarantee between the Republic of Cyprus and Greece, the United Kingdom and Turkey of 16 August 1960.

[10] Treaty of Alliance between the Republic of Cyprus, Greece and Turkey of 16 August 1960.

[11] Treaty of Establishment of the Republic of Cyprus between the UK, Greece, Turkey and Cyprus of 16 August 1960.

[12] See S. Laulhé Shaelou, S. Stylianou, K. Anastasiou, 'Cyprus', in W. Faber and B. Lurger, eds., *National Reports on the transfer of movables in Europe*, Vol. 2 (Munich, Sellier-European Law Publishers 2009). See also A. James, 'The making of the Cyprus settlement 1958-60', 10 *Cyprus Review* (1998) pp. 11-32.

[13] A.S. De Smith, *The new Commonwealth and its Constitutions* (London, Stevens 1964) at p. 285.

[14] S. Papasavvas, *Justice constitutionnelle à Chypre* (Aix-en-Provence, Paris; Presses universitaires d'Aix-Marseille, Economica 1998) at p. 258.

## 2.2.    International legal agreements in the national legal order

### 2.2.1.    *Duty of compliance*

2.2.1.1. Initial legislative action in Cyprus in the context of EU accession

Cyprus is a monist country; therefore, international treaties to gain effect in the Cypriot legal order merely require ratification by relevant authorities of the Republic (pursuant to Art. 169 of the Constitution). It is fitting to note right at the outset that the Constitution remains the supreme law of the Republic.

Nevertheless, it is recognised that Community law, which is based on international treaties, is to form 'a distinct legal system which is capable of creating directly effective rights for those subject to it', which must be regarded as 'independent of national laws' and 'superior to them'.[15] To this end, there were voices recommending revision of the Constitution, pointing to the fact that Article 179 is not a basic provision of the Constitution. Therefore, it can be amended – despite the division of the island – under the procedure set out in Article 182 of the Constitution[16] (through the application of the law of necessity).[17] As a result, Article 169 of the Constitution (also a non-basic provision) would need to be amended as well.[18] The necessary amendments would reflect 'the actual accession of the Republic to the Union as well as the transfer of the exercise of national executive, legislative and treaty-making powers to the EU institutions, thus pre-empting the potential problems posed by Articles 54(1), 61(1), 136, 152 and 169 of the Constitution'[19] and thereby safeguarding the supremacy of Community law over the Constitution.

The express reference to EC law supremacy should have been decided by the House of Representatives on the basis of Articles 182(2) and (3) of the Constitution, but the Attorney General's office issued an opinion confirming that no amendment to the Constitution was necessary prior to the ratification of the Accession Treaty 2003.

---

[15] Case *Eracleous v. Municipality of Limassol*, No 5793, judgment of the Supreme Court, 14 December 1993. See N. Emiliou, 'Cyprus', in A.E. Kellermann, et al., eds., *The impact of EU accession on the legal orders of new EU member states and (pre-)candidate countries: hopes and fears* (The Hague, T.M.C. Asser Press 2006) pp. 303-311; see also F. Hoffmeister, *Legal aspects of the Cyprus Problem. Annan Plan and EU accession* (Leiden, Martinus Nijhoff Publishers 2006) at p. 205.

[16] Under Art. 182, basic articles of the Constitution cannot be amended while a two-thirds majority of both Greek Cypriot and Turkish Cypriot votes at the House of Representatives is necessary to amend the rest.

[17] See A. Markides, *The constitutional impact of Cyprus' accession to the EU* (speech, 21 May 2001, Nicosia) at p. 6; see also Emiliou, *loc. cit.* n. 15, at p. 307; *contra* K. Chrysostomides, *Issues under constitutional and international law in the path of Cyprus towards accession to the EU* (speech, 29-30 June 2001, Nicosia) at p. 5 as quoted in Hoffmeister, *op. cit.* n. 15, at p. 205 and p. 150.

[18] The example of the Irish Constitution, whereby the principle of Community law supremacy is incorporated into the Constitution, was brought forward in G. Bermann et al., *Opinion: implications of Membership in the EU for a constitutional settlement in Cyprus* of 29 March 2001 in A. Markides, ed., *Cyprus and EU membership: important legal documents* (Nicosia, PIO 2002) para. 44 and was said to provide a good precedent for Cyprus. See Emilou, *loc. cit.* n. 15, at p. 306.

[19] Emiliou, *loc. cit.* n. 15, at p. 307.

The House of Representatives therefore ratified the Treaty of Accession on the basis of Article 169 of the Constitution,[20] thereby creating in theory a principle of tacit acceptance of the supremacy of Community law or, at least, a principle of non-conflict between the two sets of legal norms.

The Cypriot courts have indicated in their case law that an international treaty, being inferior to the Constitution, is subject to judicial review to the extent that the constitutional provisions prevail in case of conflict.[21] As a result, the interpretation of the supremacy of Community law was left to the discretion of courts through judicial review; it was only a matter of time until the issue would be raised before the highest court of the country.

## 2.2.1.2. Judicial catalyst in the context of EU membership

The Supreme Court of Cyprus could only uphold the supremacy of the Cypriot Constitution over Community law on the first occasion provided by the challenge of the constitutionality of the European Arrest Warrant[22] under Cypriot law.[23] As the measure challenged in this case was national law transposing the EAW Framework Decision (a Third Pillar measure), this case seemed unlikely to shake the foundations of the principle of supremacy. Such an argument could be made given the intergovernmental nature of the Third Pillar, combined with the fact that the measure at stake did not even concern Community law rights and pursuant to Article 34 EU, could not produce direct effect.

It is notable that the EU Treaty in part devoted to the Third Pillar does not contain an equivalent of the fidelity clause spelled out in Article 10 EC. However, following the *Pupino* case,[24] it has been argued that 'the duty of loyalty owed by member states is freely exportable between EC and EU pillars under the current Treaty arrangements [and that] then presumably the cargo of developments that floats on the raft of Article 10 [EC] must come with it.'[25] If, indeed, the doctrine of supremacy extends to the Third Pillar in the name of effectiveness of EU law,[26] the traditional substantive principles of interpretation of Community law applicable during the judicial review process at the national level should also stand with respect to measures falling under the Third Pillar, including the competence of the ECJ to hear such references pursuant to Article 35

[20] Ratifying law No 35(III)/2003, *Official Gazette* No 3740, 25 July 2003.
[21] Emiliou, *loc. cit.* n. 15, at p. 307.
[22] Council Framework Decision 2002/584/JHA of 13 June 2002 on the European arrest warrant and the surrender procedures between member states, *OJ* 2002 L 190/1.
[23] *Attorney General of the Republic of Cyprus v. Costas Constantinou*, No 294/2005, 7 November 2005, [2007] 3 C.M.L.R. 42; see a case note by A. Tsadiras in 44 *CMLRev.* (2007) pp. 1515-1528. The case was brought before the Supreme Court on appeal lodged by the Attorney General of the Republic against a decision of the District Court of Limassol at first instance.
[24] ECJ, Case C-105/03 *Criminal proceedings against Maria Pupino* [2005] *ECR* I-5285.
[25] See M. Ross, 'Effectiveness in the European legal order(s): beyond supremacy to constitutional proportionality', 31 *ELRev.* (2006) pp. 476-498, at p. 483.
[26] See K. Lenaerts and T. Corthaut, 'Of birds and hedges: the role of primacy in invoking norms of EU law', 31 *ELRev.* (2006) pp. 287-315.

EU.[27] However, Cyprus – at that time – had not accepted the jurisdiction of the ECJ; thus, Cypriot courts had no jurisdiction to submit references dealing with Third Pillar matters.[28] Any attempt of judicial dialogue between the Supreme Court of Cyprus and the European Court of Justice in this case was therefore impossible.

Even if the Supreme Court could have formally had the possibility to send a reference to the ECJ (for the sake of the uniform interpretation and application of EU constitutional law), it would not have done so for several reasons. First of all, the issue of constitutionality at stake was internal to the national legal order. As in the other Member States, the Cypriot House of Representatives had to enact a law transposing the Framework Decision,[29] which is subject to the Constitution. Any dispute arising before the national courts should be based on this transposing law, which was ruled to be anticonstitutional, as Article 11 of the Cypriot Constitution does not provide for arrest with a view to the execution of a European Arrest Warrant. This appears clearly in all the judgments of the highest courts of Member States relating to the European Arrest Warrant,[30] including a few of the new Member States, where the constitutionality of national implementing measures was challenged and where controversial judgments were rendered by national Constitutional Courts.

In particular, the Polish Constitutional Court held in a judgment of 27 April 2005[31] that Article 607t(1) of the Code on Criminal Procedure was incompatible with Article 55(1) of the Polish Constitution 1997 to the extent that it authorised surrender of Polish nationals to other countries pursuant to the EAW procedure.[32] The Polish Constitution 1997 in force at the time prohibited extradition of Polish nationals (without exceptions). Hence, the Polish Constitutional Tribunal ruled that challenged measures were contrary to the Constitution. However, it decided to postpone the annulment by 18 months to allow the legislator to change the Constitution and not undermine the obligations resting on Poland as a Member State of the European Union. This decision was:

[27] '[J]urisdiction [under Art 35 EU] would be deprived of most of its useful effect if individuals were not entitled to invoke framework decisions in order to obtain a conforming interpretation of national law before the courts of the member states.' ECJ, Case C-105/03 *Pupino, loc. cit.* n. 24, para. 38.

[28] See para. 9 of the ECJ's Guidance on References by National Courts for Preliminary Rulings, *OJ* 2005 C 143/1.

[29] Law 133(1)/2004, *Official Gazette* No 3850, 30 April 2004.

[30] See, e.g., Case No 591/2005 of the Areios Pagos (Greek Supreme Court) 8 March 2005, where the Court ruled that the EAW did not violate any provision of the Greek Constitution; see also case *2 B v. R* No 2236/04 of the Federal Constitutional Court of Germany (2nd Chamber) 18 July 2005, where the Court rejected the EAW as it violated an article of the Basic Law (the provisions of the Act by virtue of which the EAW was incorporated into the legal system of Germany failed to take adequately into account the conditions and the requirements laid down in the article of the German Federal Constitution and, consequently, did not comply with it). For a legal review of the adoption of the Framework Decision in Member States, see S. Alegre and M. Leaf, 'Mutual recognition in European judicial co-operation: a step too far too soon? Case study – the EAW', 10 *ELJ* (2004) pp. 200-217.

[31] Judgment of 27 April 2005 in the case P 1/05 [Wyrok z dnia 27 kwietnia 2005 r. Sygn. akt P 1/05] OTK Z.U. 2005/4A, item 42, reported in [2006] 1 C.M.L.R. 36.

[32] See A. Łazowski, *Poland. Constitutional Tribunal on the Surrender of Polish Citizen under the European Arrest Warrant*, 1 *EuConst* (2005) pp. 569-581. See also Chapters 3 and 9 in this volume.

'in view of the constitutional obligation of Poland to observe international law and its duty to assure security and public order, which was enhanced by the surrender of indicted persons to other states ... and also the fact that Poland and other [m]ember [s]tates of the [EU] were bound by the community of principles of the political system, assuring proper administration of justice and trial before an independent court of law.'[33]

However, the Tribunal added:

'The obligation to interpret domestic law in a manner sympathetic to EU law (so as to comply with EU law) *has its limits* [emphasis added]. In particular, it stems from the jurisprudence of the [ECJ] that EU secondary legislation may not independently (in the absence of appropriate amendments in domestic legislation) worsen an individual's situation, especially as regards the sphere of criminal liability. It is beyond doubt that the surrender of a person prosecuted on the basis of an EAW, in order to conduct a criminal prosecution against them in respect of an act which, according to Polish law, does not constitute a criminal offence, must worsen the situation of the suspect.'[34]

Referring to the concept of EU citizenship as set out in particular in the EC Treaty, the Polish Court noted that this concept was not a sufficient premise from which to derive the existence of a limitation of the scope of Article 55(1) of the Constitution in favour of extradition to other Member States or the diminution of the guarantees provided by the Constitution concerning individual rights and freedoms.

Fundamental rights and the concept of EU citizenship were also referred to by the Czech Supreme Court but this time in favour of the constitutionality of the European Arrest Warrant in the national legal order. The Czech Constitutional Court decided on 3 May 2006 to dismiss an action for unconstitutionality brought by a group of members of Parliament contesting the law transposing the Framework Decision on the alleged ground that it authorised the surrender of Czech nationals and abolished the protection inherent in the double criminality rule with reference to the Czech Charter of Fundamental Rights.[35] The Court interpreted that the Charter was in its view never concerned with the extradition of Czech citizens for a limited period of time as envisaged in the European Arrest Warrant. It added that:

'if Czech citizens were to enjoy the advantages of EU citizenship, they had to accept certain responsibilities associated with international co-operation in the investigation and suppression of criminality.'[36]

Irrespective of the conclusions reached by the highest judicial authorities in the various Member States which arguably derive from and form part of national constitutional laws, the legality of this instrument of EU law at the supranational level has been con-

---

[33] *Loc. cit.* n. 31, para. 5.
[34] *Loc. cit.* n. 31, para. 8.
[35] Constitutional Court of the Czech Republic, 3 May 2006 (*Re Constitutionality of Framework Decision on the European Arrest Warrant*), [2007] 3 C.M.L.R. 24.
[36] *Ibidem.*

firmed by the ECJ, rejecting any idea of violation of human rights and of abuse of powers allegedly attributable to the legislator.[37] The review of the above national case law, however, clearly illustrates a certain degree of reluctance also among new Member States to accept the supremacy of EC/EU law unconditionally, in particular when fundamental rights of a national nature and/or with a particular meaning in the national system are involved.

This would appear to be in line with the ECJ case law regarding the Third Pillar and EU law more generally. The position of the ECJ on the issue of supremacy of EC law is very clear: it enjoys supremacy over national law,[38] including constitutional law, as the internal hierarchy of national law cannot jeopardise the need for uniformity of EC law.[39] Moreover, the duty of consistent interpretation imported from the First Pillar to the Third Pillar by the ECJ in case *Pupino* remains so far subject to the domestic court being able to interpret national law in accordance with framework decisions.[40] As a result, the main argument before the national courts in this series of cases relating to the European Arrest Warrant is not one of supremacy of EU law but one of conformity of the Framework Decision with national constitutions.[41] With respect to the latter, the Cypriot Supreme Court concluded that no provision in the Act promulgated by the House of Representatives could be interpreted 'in such a way so as to prevail and to be applied as regards the nationals of the Republic.'[42]

### 2.2.1.3. Legislative (re)action in the context of membership

Whatever the merits of this decision of the Cypriot Supreme Court may be, it did trigger legislative (re)action in Cyprus, which had been delayed thus far due mainly to political considerations surrounding the Cypriot Constitution. Certain amendments to the Cypriot Constitution were finally tabled before and voted by the House of Representatives with a clear objective to remove the potential conflict between EC/EU

---

[37] ECJ, Case C-303/05 *Advocaten voor de Wereld VZW v. Leden van de Ministerraad* [2007] *ECR* I-3633. See F. Geyer, case note, 4 *EuConst* (2008) pp. 149-161.

[38] ECJ, Case 6/64 *Flaminio Costa v. ENEL* [1964] *ECR* 585; Case 106/77 *Amministrazione delle Finanze dello Stato v. Simmenthal SpA.* [1978] *ECR* 629.

[39] ECJ, Case 11/70 *Internationale Handelsgesellschaft mbH v. Einfuhr- und Vorratsstelle für Getreide und Futtermittel* [1970] *ECR* 1125 (para. 3); Case C-473/93 *Commission of the European Communities v. Luxembourg* [1996] *ECR* I-3207 (para. 38). For a detailed review of the supremacy from the perspective of the Member States, see, e.g., D. Craig and G. de Búrca, *EU Law. Text, Cases and Materials*, 4th edn. (Oxford, Oxford University Press 2008) at pp. 353-377.

[40] The Court in *Pupino* did not address the issue of supremacy of EU law. P. Craig and G. de Búrca argue that 'this should not be taken as an implicit indication that measures enacted under the Third Pillar do not have primacy over national law. The ECJ was willing to apply principles such as loyal co-operation from the Community Pillar to the Third Pillar, and there is much in its reasoning that sits comfortably with the precepts underpinning the *Costa* case.' See Craig and de Búrca, *ibidem*, at p. 352.

[41] *Contra* para. 21 of the *Constantinou* judgment, *loc. cit.* n. 23, which reads as follows: 'Thus, the main issue concerning the present case that remains to be discussed is the submission put forward by the [AG], namely that the Act which incorporated the [EAW] into the legal system of our country ranks higher than the Constitution and, consequently, it must be applied.' See Tsadiras, *loc. cit.* n. 23, at pp. 1524-1526.

[42] *Loc. cit.* n. 23, para. 24.

law and Cypriot constitutional law.[43] To that intent, Article 1A was added, to the effect that the supremacy of *EU law* over the Constitution is *prima facie* established (unlike the Irish Constitution, which promotes the supremacy of *EC law* in a similar formula). Article 1A states:

'[n]o provision of this Constitution will be deemed to annul laws that are enacted, acts that are carried out or measures that are introduced by the Republic which are necessary by reason of its obligations as a Member State of the [EU] or prevent Regulations, Directives or other acts or binding legislative measures that are adopted by the [EU] or the [EC] or their institutions or their competent bodies on the basis of the [EC] Treaty or the [EU] from producing legal effect in the Republic.'[44]

In addition to Article 11 of the Constitution, which needed to be supplemented for the purpose of the European Arrest Warrant,[45] Articles 140,[46] 169[47] and 179[48] of the Constitution were also amended and/or supplemented in order to give full effect to new Article 1A of the Constitution. The precise "effect" of Article 1A nevertheless remains unclear.

In particular, while Article 179(1) refers to Article 1A, it does provide that the Constitution 'remains the supreme law of the Republic.'[49] No direct reference to the supremacy of EC/EU law is therefore made in the amendments, thereby avoiding addressing the very difficult question of what law prevails over the Constitution, i.e., EC law or EU law. Should it be EU law, then Cyprus – like Lithuania – would be considered at the forefront of European integration by recognising such supremacy even before the ECJ.[50] Should it be merely EC law, then the conflict between the European Arrest Warrant and the relevant provisions of the Constitution would have remained intact. The option was taken to deal with the supremacy issue only in an indirect way by providing that no provision of the Constitution could be an obstacle to Cyprus complying with its obligations as a Member State of the EU. Thus, without expressly providing so, Article 1A could set out the principle of supremacy not only of EC law

---

[43] Fifth Amendment to the Constitution Law 127(I)/2006, *Official Gazette* No 4090, 28 July 2006.

[44] Translation provided by the author; see also translation by Tsadiras, *loc. cit.* n. 23, at p. 1526.

[45] Art. 11(2)(f) was replaced with a new subpara. (f).

[46] The phrase 'deemed contrary to or in violation of the Law of the EC or of the EU' was inserted in paras. (1) and (3) of Art. 140.

[47] A new para. (4) was inserted, to the effect that the Republic of Cyprus commits to act upon all the provisions deriving from EC and EU law, including when they amend national law.

[48] Reference to Art. 1A was made in para. (1); para. (2) refers to the obligations on the Republic arising out of EU membership.

[49] It is clear from Art. 4 of Law 35(III)/2003 that the rights and obligations of the Republic arising out of the Treaty of Accession prevail against contrary national rules and regulations. With reference to the Cypriot Constitution and to the traditional debate relating to the perception of the supremacy doctrine in the Member States, the argument could be made also with respect to Cyprus that the supremacy accorded to EC/EU law would be placed 'under the authority of the national legal order', as opposed to deriving from the 'inherent nature of Community law' as promoted by the ECJ. For an overview of the debate, see, e.g., B. de Witte, 'Direct effect, supremacy and the nature of the legal order', in P. Craig and G. de Búrca, eds., *The evolution of EU law* (Oxford, Oxford University Press 1999) pp. 177-213.

[50] See Chapter 7 in this volume.

as per the ECJ's jurisprudence, but also of EU law,[51] possibly reflecting on the current "depillarisation" of the European Union by treating the Community and intergovernmental spheres "uniformly".[52] This very broad provision of Article 1A would appear to be justified primarily by the difficulty of amending the Cypriot Constitution in view of the doctrine of necessity.[53]

The legislative objective of removing the potential conflict between EC/EU law and the Constitution appears *a priori* achieved; it will however no doubt face the judicial scrutiny of the Cypriot courts through cases on the enforcement of EC and EU law rights in Cyprus. In the light of case law of the ECJ on the effectiveness of Community law, Cypriot courts should normally evaluate on the merits of each case whether national law, including the Constitution as amended, provides effective remedy and as a result allows for the full implementation and enforcement of EC and EU law rights in Cyprus.[54] It is quite clear that the doctrine of necessity still plays a key role in this exercise, as long as it remains in force.[55]

### 2.2.2.  *Duty of indirect interpretation*

The courts in Cyprus have long recognised the principle of indirect interpretation of national law in the light of international treaty provisions, at least as far as the treaties concerned show an intention of promoting the 'values and the protection of human rights.'[56] It seems that amendments made to the Cypriot Constitution expressly to introduce the European dimension clearly emphasise the fundamental rights associated with the concept of EU citizenship as well as other rights granted under EC/EU law, to

---

[51] L. Burgorgue-Larsen describes Art. 1A as a « véritable profession de foi juridique européenne » in 'Jurisprudence européenne comparée', 4 *Revue du Droit Public* (2006) p. 1099, at p. 1121.

[52] See Tsadiras, *loc. cit.* n. 23, at p. 1527.

[53] In constitutional law, "necessity" justifies acts done or proceedings taken under legislations passed in violation of a constitutional provision due to the occurrence of "necessitous" circumstances. The doctrine of necessity justifies the enforcement of an otherwise invalid and unlawful law. The beginnings of the application of the doctrine of necessity in constitutional law are traditionally presented as emanating from *A-G for Cyprus v. Mustafa Ibrahim & others* [(1964) *CLR* 195]. Mustafa was detained under the Administration of Justice (Miscellaneous Provisions) Law of 1964. This law had been passed in the Cyprus Parliament during a boycott of the Parliament by the Turkish minority, thereby denying Parliament a quorum. Mustafa challenged the constitutionality of his detention but the state argued that the boycott of Parliament constituted a "legislative paralysis" which justified the need to legislate in an amended form until the boycott of Parliament is terminated. This measure is therefore deemed temporary and shall continue 'so long as the necessitating conditions persist.' The court concluded that 'with the doctrine of necessity, in this well balanced form, I reach the conclusion that in the conditions prevailing at the material time, the enactment of the … Law was legally justified, notwithstanding the provisions of Articles … of the Constitution (214-215)'; see L. Marasinghe, 'Constitutionalism confused: the doctrine of necessity v. Kelsen's pure theory', *Daily News*, 5 May 2004, available at http://www.dailynews.lk/2004/05/05/fea01.html accessed on 27 February 2009.

[54] This section appears in an amended version in Laulhé Shaelou, *op. cit.* n. 5.

[55] The decision of the ECtHR in *Aziz v. Cyprus* [2005] 41 *EHRR* 11 should be mentioned in this respect. The ECtHR ruled that the doctrine of necessity in the case of Aziz had to be exercised in Cyprus in a manner that would not violate fundamental rights including the principle of equality.

[56] *Shipowners Union v. The Registrar of Trademarks* (1988) 3 *CLR* 457.

the extent that even the indirect interpretation of the national legislation in the light of EC/EU law is possible in case of uncertainty.

This was confirmed recently by the Supreme Court of Cyprus in *Nebojsa Micovic v. Republic of Cyprus through the Director of Migration Services*,[57] where Judge Nicolaides ruled on the basis of ECJ case law that a directive, for which the deadline for transposition into national law had not yet passed, was nevertheless capable of indirect effect in the national legal order. As a result, the Director of the Migration Services in Cyprus was ordered to interpret the relevant provisions of national law "in the spirit" and "in accordance with the objective" of Directive 2003/109/EC[58] with respect to the right of permanent residence in Cyprus of a citizen of the Former Republic of Yugoslavia.

In the joined cases of *Vera Joudine v. Republic of Cyprus through the Ministry of Interior, Migration Department* and *Jaroslav Joudine v. Republic of Cyprus through the Ministry of Interior, Migration Department*,[59] heard on appeal by the Supreme Court of Cyprus,[60] the Court reiterated the approach of Judge Nicolaides to the principle of indirect effect. This principle was, however, found irrelevant in these two cases as the applicants did not meet the necessary criteria to benefit indirectly from the provisions of Directive 2003/109/EC in national law. At the time of the rulings, the deadline for the implementation of the said Directive into national law had passed without the Republic of Cyprus taking appropriate measures to ensure its full implementation into Cypriot law.[61] However, the administrative decisions of the Migration Department challenged in these cases had, nevertheless, been taken before the expiry of the said deadline, therefore not entitling the parties potentially to rely on the direct effect of the Directive or on the Republic of Cyprus' failure to implement the said instrument of Community law into national law.

On the contrary, in *Cresencia Cabotaje Motilla v. Republic of Cyprus through the Ministry of Interior, Migration Department*,[62] another decision of the Migration Department rejecting the acquisition of the long-term resident status for a third-country national was challenged before the Supreme Court of Cyprus, this time following the expiry of the deadline for transposition of Directive 2003/109/EC into national law.[63] The Interior Minister's decision of rejection was based on Article 18Z(2) of the Aliens and Immigration Chapter 105 of the laws of Cyprus, as amended, on the ground that

---

[57] No 1012/2005, 18 November 2005.

[58] Council Directive 2003/109/EC of 25 November 2003 concerning the status of third-country nationals who are long-term residents, *OJ* 2004 L 16/44.

[59] No. 1632/2005 & 1633/05, 15 May 2006.

[60] No. 55/06, 28 July 2006.

[61] Directive 2003/109/EC as well as Directive 38/2004/EC, *inter alia*, were implemented belatedly into Cypriot law in early 2007 in Laws 8(I)/2007 and 7(I)/2007 respectively (*Official Gazette* No 4110, 9 February 2007).

[62] No 673/2006, 21 January 2008.

[63] Law No 8(I)/2007 transposes Directive 2003/109/EC and amends the Aliens and Immigration Law Cap 105 of the laws of Cyprus as a result. This law was enacted in February 2007, whereas the deadline for the implementation of the Directive expired in January 2006. The applicant was a female migrant who lived and worked lawfully as a housemaid in Cyprus for six years and applied to the Interior Minister as soon as the deadline for transposition expired.

the applicant's successive residence permits were 'limited as to their duration', and that the applicant was, therefore, excluded from the scope of the law. The applicant applied to the Supreme Court to have the decision set aside. The Court proceeded with the review of the case in accordance with the Directive and the Cypriot implementing legislation. The central issue concerned the way that Article 18Z(2)(c) of the implementing legislation transposed Article 3(2)(e) of the Directive and whether this transposition affected the essence of the Directive. This specific provision excluded from the scope of the implementing legislation applicants whose resident permits had been limited "in time", whereas the Directive merely excluded "formal" limitation, arguably relating to the nature of the status or the sector of employment of the person concerned. The Supreme Court by a majority decision of nine judges against four rejected the appeal on the ground that the fixed-term duration of the applicant's visas did fall under the exceptions of Article 18Z(2) of the implementing legislation, and that the addition of the phrase "as to its duration" did not deduct from the effectiveness of the Directive. The Court also ruled that the fixed-term nature of the residence visas granted to the applicant could not create a reasonable expectation 'that the person has put down root in the country', as per Recital 6 of the Directive's Preamble.[64]

On the other hand, the judges in the dissenting opinion stated that the said phrase fundamentally transformed the essence of the exception provided for in Article 3(2)(e) of the Directive. They recalled the ECJ's decision in case *Ratti*[65] establishing the principle that a Member State cannot rely on its own wrongdoing to frustrate the rights of individuals under a directive which it failed to implement. Pursuant to Article 4(1) of the Directive, Member States should grant long-term resident status to third-country nationals when they have been residing "legally and continuously" within its territory for five years immediately prior to the submission of the relevant application, with no further conditions being imposed regarding the issue, the nature or the duration of the residence permit. The Supreme Court identified the notion of "formal limitation" set out in Article 3(2)(e) of the Directive as having a specific meaning, common to the immigration policy of all Member States, formulated, in particular, during a conference of experts held in Brussels on 7-8 July 2005, although the Court recognised the exclusive competence of the ECJ to interpret the Directive as a Community instrument. The Supreme Court recalled, in particular, the recommendations of the summit that the implementation of the Directive does not require a residence permit but only the legality of the residence, and that any formal limitation on residence permits should remain an exception to be interpreted strictly (*ejusdem generis*) and in line with the examples given in Article 3(2)(e) of the Directive (seasonal workers, volunteers, posted workers, etc.). As a result, the fact that the residence permit is limited in time but is renewable does not make it fall under the exceptions as set out in the above Article, which are the only ones which can constitute by nature "formal limitations". Based on the above and

---

[64] See N. Trimikliniotis, *Cyprus Report 2007* (Network on the free movement of workers within the EU, Nicosia, 2009) 31-2; see also C. Demetriou and N. Trimikliniotis, *Cyprus update of the Data Collection Report on Ethnic and Racial Discrimination* (RAXEN National Data Collection Report 2007 – Cyprus, February 2008) pp. 16-22.
[65] ECJ, Case 148/78 *Pubblico Ministerio v. Tullio Ratti* [1979] *ECR* 1629.

on the principle of legitimate expectation, the dissenting judges found the drafting of the specific provision in the implementing law not only incorrect but also in violation of the substantive meaning of the Directive, hence leading to improper implementation.

It does not clearly appear from this case to what extent the Court considered the direct effect of the Directive and/or the liability of the Republic of Cyprus arising out of the late/improper transposition of the Directive into national law in order to reach its decision. The Court appears to have merely applied the Directive indirectly, in order to interpret the implementing legislation, which – although in existence at the time of the ruling – was enacted subsequently to the application made by the plaintiff, who could not, therefore, rely on provisions of national law when enforcing her rights initially, but only on rights deriving from Directive 2003/109/EC, provided the relevant provisions of the Directive would be found directly effective. The fundamental disagreement between the majority decision and the dissenting opinion of the Supreme Court judges did not appear to prompt any discussion as to the possibility of a reference to the ECJ under Article 234 EC so as to clarify the meaning of the relevant provision of the Directive. It is true that the interpretation of a directive in the national legal order is left to the discretion of the national courts.[66] However, the exercise of this discretion by the national courts also involves the possibility of making preliminary references to the ECJ regarding the interpretation of provision(s) of Community law including directives deemed relevant to the national proceedings at stake. When a court is the highest judicial body of the country acting at last instance, as in the present case, such a reference normally becomes *mandatory* under Article 234 EC, except as otherwise provided in the treaties. For matters falling under Title IV of Part Three of the EC Treaty on visa, asylum, immigration and other policies related to free movement of persons, such as the ones at stake in the *Motilla* case, Article 68 EC, however, clearly provides that a reference can only be brought by the final court or tribunal, at its own discretion.[67] It appears that the Supreme Court in this case did not find it necessary to refer to these provisions of the EC Treaty.

The decision of the Supreme Court to reject the application for judicial review in the *Motilla* case was ultimately justified by the geographical location, the small size and the limited population of Cyprus as underlying features of its immigration policy. As noted by Trimikliniotis, the vast majority of migrant workers are, 'as a matter of policy', issued fixed-term visas in Cyprus.[68] This decision could, therefore, have the effect of intentionally restricting in law and/or in fact the right to long-term residence provided by Directive 2003/109/EC. This approach was, nevertheless, confirmed by the Supreme Court in *Shahajan Mohamed Rawuttar v. Republic of Cyprus through the*

---

[66] With respect to the *positive* obligation on national courts of harmonious interpretation of national law in the light of directives, the Court recently clarified that 'where a directive is transposed belatedly, the general obligation owed by national courts to interpret domestic law in conformity with the directive exists only once the period for its transposition has expired.' See ECJ, Case C-212/04 *Konstantinos Adeneler et al v. Ellinikos Organismos Galaktos (ELOG)* [2006] *ECR* I-6057 (para. 116).

[67] See also para. 8 of the ECJ's Information Note on references from national courts for a preliminary ruling. *Loc. cit.* n. 28.

[68] Trimikliniotis, *loc. cit.* n. 64, *Cyprus Report,* at p. 32.

*Ministry of Interior, Migration Department*,[69] where Judge Erotocritou referred to the judgment reached by the Full Chamber of the Supreme Court in the *Motilla* case as a precedent where the relevant provisions of Community law had already been examined. It is interesting to note that Judge Erotocritou was a dissenting judge in the *Motilla* case.

Apart from litigation associated with the immigration policy of the Republic of Cyprus,[70] no other judgments have been issued by the Cypriot courts where the plaintiff or the applicant sought to rely on provisions of EC law and/or EU law before the national courts.[71] With respect to the public enforcement of Community law at the national level, mention should be made of the decision of the Supreme Court confirming the liability of the Republic of Cyprus as a single entity for obligations arising under Community law.[72]

As the legal profession becomes more aware of rights and liabilities arising under EU law and of the enforcement of individual rights, many more cases are expected to come before the courts in the years to come.

3.      PRINCIPLES OF JUDICIAL INTEGRATION IN CYPRUS:
        PRELIMINARY REFERENCES UNDER CYPRIOT LAW

3.1.    **National provisions on the preliminary ruling procedure**

As a result of the accession to the EU, the Courts of Justice Law of 1960 was amended to reflect the possibility for national courts to submit references for preliminary ruling to the ECJ. The Courts of Justice (Amendment) Law No 99(I)/2007[73] inserts a new paragraph (2A) in Article 25 of the 1960 Law[74] which provides that in the event that a first instance court decides to refer or not to refer to the ECJ in a given case on the basis,

---

[69] No 742/06, 24 September 2008.

[70] There is more litigation with respect to Directive 2003/109/EC, including, *inter alia*, cases *Imelda Bautista Balbin v. Republic of Cyprus through the Ministry of Interior, Migration Department*, No 857/2006, 16 September 2008 or *Sanka Manjula Kankani Gamage v. Republic of Cyprus through the Ministry of Interior, Migration Department*, No 61/2006, 11 November 2008, where the judges of the Supreme Court found the applicants for long-term residence outside the scope of the Directive due to the time factor (on or before the expiration of the deadline for implementation of the Directive), the status of the applicant (unlawful residence) and/or on under the *Motilla* jurisprudence.

[71] This chapter is deemed up to date as of February 2009.

[72] *President of the Republic v. House of Representatives*, No 1/2007, 15 February 2008, where the Supreme Court confirmed that the obligations arising from Community law were imposed on the Republic of Cyprus as a single entity within the meaning of ECJ, Case 77/69 *Commission of the European Communities v. Kingdom of Belgium* [1970] *ECR* 237, irrespective of which agency/authority of the state was responsible for the breach of Community law (in this instance, Art. 19 of Directive 2000/13/EC of the European Parliament and of the Council of 20 March 2000 on the approximation of the laws of the Member States relating to the labelling, presentation and advertising of foodstuffs, *OJ* 2000 L 109/29).

[73] *Official Gazette* No 4135, 18 July 2007.

[74] Para. (2A) of Art. 25 of the 1960 law was recently amended by Law 119(I)/2008 (*Official Gazette* No 4188, 31 December 2008) in order to submit to the jurisdiction of the ECJ under Art. 35 EU. A new Art. 34A was also added to the 1960 law for this purpose.

*inter alia*, of Article 234 EC, the decision can be appealed before the Supreme Court of Cyprus within a time limit of 15 days from the issuing of the decision by the lower court.

This effectively means that the Supreme Court can adopt an order not to initiate a preliminary reference on appeal of a decision of a lower court to refer to the ECJ and *vice versa*. However, Article 234 EC specifically provides that courts or tribunals which are not courts of last resort *may* request the ECJ to give a preliminary ruling at their own discretion.[75] This part of paragraph (2A) of Article 25 of the Courts of Justice Law, as amended, therefore appears *prima facie* contrary to Article 234 EC to the extent that it potentially violates the discretion of the lower courts to exercise their right to preliminary reference or not, as developed in the ECJ case law.

In case *Rheinmühlen-Düsseldorf*,[76] the ECJ clarified that a national court was not precluded from making a reference on a particular issue by the existence of a domestic rule of law which required that court to follow the judgment of a higher court on that issue. In the recent case of *Cartesio*,[77] the ECJ further developed the "widest" scope of the national courts' discretion under Article 234 EC, as initially interpreted in *Rheinmühlen-Düsseldorf*, in the event that the national court is subject to an order of *revocation* or of *amendment* of its preliminary reference by an appellate court, having implications on the resumption of the domestic proceedings. The Court recalls its established case law that in the case of a court against whose decision there is a judicial remedy under national law, Article 234 EC does not preclude decisions of such a court by which questions are referred to the ECJ for a preliminary ruling from a remaining subject to the remedies normally available under national law.[78] Such national remedies could also include the possibility of an appeal if this is permitted under national law.[79] Nevertheless, in the interests of clarity and legal certainty, the ECJ must abide by the

---

[75] Gordon argues that this discretion may be *qualified* in the case of particular questions of validity and direct effect of Community law instruments during the process of judicial review before the Administrative Court in particular, as a national court has no power to declare a Community act invalid. Relying on the ECJ case law, in particular the *Foto-Frost* case (ECJ, Case 314/85 *Foto-Frost v. Hauptzollamt Lübeck-Ost* [1987] *ECR* 4199) and the *British American Tobacco* case (ECJ, Case C-491/01 *The Queen v. Secretary of State for Health,* ex parte *British American Tobacco (Investments) Ltd and Imperial Tobacco Ltd.* [2002] *ECR* I-11453) as an illustration of this, Gordon writes that: '[w]hilst this does not prevent the Administrative Court, for example, from determining that the act is *valid*, it does raise an important point of principle as to whether, when such questions of validity are raised, the Administrative Court or other national court is, in practice, under a duty, as opposed to simply possessing a discretion, to request a preliminary ruling, since, it may be argued, a claimant loses the prospect of having a Community act such as a directive or regulation declared unlawful unless a reference is ordered.' See R. Gordon, *EC law in judicial review* (Oxford, Oxford University Press 2007) at pp. 128-129.

[76] ECJ, Joined Cases 146/73 and 166/73 *Rheinmühlen-Düsseldorf v. Einfuhr-und Vorratsstelle für Getreide und Futtermittel* [1974] *ECR* 33.

[77] ECJ, Case C-210/06 *CARTESIO Oktató és Szolgáltató bt.* [2008] *ECR* I-9641.

[78] *Loc. cit.* n. 76, para. 3.

[79] The Court on this point rejected Advocate General Warner's suggestion that the existence of a right to appeal 'constituted an improper fetter on the power of a national court to make a reference' and could render the preliminary ruling unnecessary in the (unlikely) situation that the appeal is allowed after the ruling has been made. T. Hartley argues that normally, an appeal will be decided before the case is heard by the ECJ and that the existence of a right of appeal could very well on the contrary 'prevent the European

decision to refer, which must have its full effect so long as it has not been *revoked*,[80] adding that the system of preliminary references is based on a dialogue between the courts, 'the initiation of which depends entirely on the national court's assessment as to whether a reference is appropriate and necessary.'[81] The ECJ continues that whereas Article 234 EC does not preclude a provision of national law allowing a *separate* appeal on a *point of law* against a decision making a reference while the main proceedings remain pending *in their entirety* before the referring court, and the appellate court has the power to vary the decision of the lower court to refer and to order this court to resume the domestic law proceedings, the outcome of this appeal "cannot limit" the jurisdiction referred by Article 234 EC on that court to make a reference at its discretion.[82] The Court held that:

> 'the autonomous jurisdiction which Article 234 EC confers on the referring court to make a reference to the Court would be called into question if – by varying the order for reference, by setting it aside and by ordering the referring court to resume the proceedings – the appellate court could prevent the referring court from exercising the right, conferred on it by the EC Treaty, to make a reference to the Court.'[83]

Thus, it would be for the referring court to:

> 'draw the proper inferences from a judgment delivered on an appeal against its decision to refer and, in particular, to come to a conclusion as to whether it is appropriate to *maintain* the reference for a preliminary ruling, or to *amend* it or to *withdraw* it.'[84]

It follows from this that the ECJ must in the interests of clarity and legal certainty abide by the decision to make a reference and give it its full effect, provided it has not been *revoked* or *amended* by the referring court.[85] Revocation or amendment are matters on which that court alone is able to make a decision, provided it can revoke its own order! Within this framework, the ECJ concluded that the discretion of the national courts deriving from Article 234(2) EC 'cannot be called into question' by the application of national rules permitting an appellate court to set aside a reference and to order the referring court to resume the domestic law proceedings.[86]

In Cyprus, the Supreme Court merely acts in its administrative capacity upon appeal against a decision of a lower court to refer or not to refer to the ECJ and does not pass judgment in this case. In view of the *Cartesio* case, one is entitled to wonder about the extent of the Supreme Court's review of the discretion of the lower instance judge to

---

Court from giving unnecessary judgments.' T.C. Hartley, *The Foundations of EC Law*, 5th edn. (Oxford, Oxford University Press 2003) at pp. 299-300.

[80] *Ibidem.*

[81] *Loc. cit.* n. 77, paras. 89-91 (with reference to ECJ, Case C-2/06 *Willy Kempter KG v. Hauptzollamt Hamburg-Jonas* [2008] *ECR* I-411, para. 42).

[82] *Loc. cit.* n. 77, paras. 92-93.

[83] *Loc. cit.* n. 77, para. 95.

[84] *Loc. cit.* n. 77, para. 96 [emphasis added].

[85] *Loc. cit.* n. 77, para. 97.

[86] *Loc. cit.* n. 77, para. 98.

refer or not to refer and/or about the extent of any review of legality involved in such an appeal. In any case, the responsibility of the application of any provisions of Community law to the factual situation underlying the main proceedings remains with the lower Cypriot court. Any possibility of confrontation of judicial opinions on the merits of the case, therefore, appears to be ruled out in this specific instance of appeal against a decision to refer or not to the ECJ.

Provisions granting a general right of appeal or a special right to appeal a decision of a lower court to refer (or not) to the ECJ exist in the domestic legislation of other Member States. As seen in the *Cartesio* case, Article 115/A of the Hungarian Law on civil procedure specifically provides for a right of appeal against a decision of a lower instance court to make a reference for a preliminary ruling. In the United Kingdom, there is a general right of appeal against any judgment or order deriving from section 16 of the Supreme Court Act 1981. Pursuant to Part 52.10 paragraph (2) of the Civil Procedure Rules (CPR), the Court of Appeal has the power, *inter alia*, to 'affirm, set aside or vary any order or judgment made or given by the lower court.' An order for a reference to the ECJ is an order made by the lower court and is therefore included in the powers of the Court of Appeal.[87] Under English law, references to the ECJ are governed by Part 68 of the CPR. Part 68(3) provides in paragraph (3) that a copy of the order will not normally be sent to the ECJ Registrar until '(a) the time for appealing against the order has expired; or (b) any application for permission to appeal has been refused, or any appeal has been determined.' Consequently, the concerns expressed by Advocate General Warner in *Rheinmühlen-Düsseldorf* are unlikely to arise in the case of references from English courts.[88]

In the recent case of *R (Horvath) v. Secretary of State for Environment, Food and Rural Affairs*,[89] the extent to which the Court of Appeal can review the correctness of a reference ordered by the High Court was addressed. In this case, an appeal brought by the Secretary of State regarding the decision of the High Court[90] to send two questions to the ECJ under Articles 234 EC and Part 68 of the CPR was permitted (only the second question was the subject of the appeal).[91] The Court of Appeal, however, dismissed the appeal on the disputed question due to the lack of complete confidence of the appeal judges that assistance from the ECJ was 'unnecessary', especially since the

---

[87] Special thanks to Prof. White of the Law Faculty of the University of Leicester for his private memo entitled 'References to the Luxembourg Court and English law' drafted for the purposes of the present chapter.

[88] See Hartley, *op. cit.* n. 79, at p. 300.

[89] [2007] *EWCA* Civ 620, CA (Civ Div), on Appeal from the Administrative Court The Hon. Mr. Justice Crane. This case concerned the execution of devolution arrangements in the UK when they concerned matters of Community law.

[90] *The Queen (on the application of Mark A B Horvath) v. The Secretary of State for the Environment, Food and Rural Affairs* [2006] *EWHC* 1833 (Admin), QBD (Admin).

[91] In granting permission to appeal, Buxton LJ wrote that the issue 'does not justify a reference' and that he was not persuaded that 'what is likely to be a very protracted inquiry, attracting intervention from other Member States, is necessary for the decision of a case that properly turns on the terms of one particular regulation.' As a result, the case proceeded and the appeal was presented at 'two levels', one of general principle and the other with respect to the wording of Art. 5(1) of the 2003 Council Regulation at stake. See *loc. cit.* n. 90, paras. 21-22.

judges presented different views as to why the High Court judge was right to make a reference. In reviewing the appeal, Lady Justice Arden clarified that this case was not an appeal 'against the weighing up by the judge of considerations relevant to the exercise of discretion, but an appeal on the point of law. If he was wrong on the view of Community law he took and the answer is clear, the appeal would be allowed without reference to any discretionary factor relevant to making a reference. The issue in this case, therefore, is whether the judge was *correct* in law and not whether he was perverse in the way he exercised his discretion.'[92] The issue of correctness of the reference, therefore, entailed a review of legality by the Court of Appeal, which did not appear to infringe the discretion of the High Court judge to order a preliminary reference.

In Cyprus, the legal effect of paragraph (2A) of Article 25 of the 1960 Law remains unclear since no such appeal has been brought before the Supreme Court, due mainly to the fact that so far only one preliminary reference has been sent by the Cypriot courts to the ECJ.[93] Following the *Cartesio* case, discussions are currently underway at the House of Representatives in Cyprus with a view to amending paragraph (2A), with respect to the right of appeal of a decision of a lower court to refer a preliminary reference to the ECJ (which would be abolished, to the effect that only the appeal of a decision not to refer would be possible, as it had originally been envisaged when para. (2A) was created). The right to decide to refer arguably lies at the heart of the widest discretion of the lower courts granted under Article 234(2) EC and as developed by the Court, as it could be argued that in case the lower court decides not to refer to the ECJ, there is always a possibility for such a reference to be made by the higher court. Arguments in favour of maintaining only the right of appeal for decisions not to refer or for no right of appeal at all (the latter arguably constituting the norm from a Community law perspective) could certainly be brought forward, as reflected in the legal traditions of Member States.[94]

In the meantime, the Supreme Court has issued procedural rules[95] pertaining to the exercise of preliminary references by the national courts under, *inter alia*, Article 234 EC, in accordance with Article 69(2) of the 1960 Law, as amended by law No 99(I)/2007. Section 4(c) of the Cypriot procedural rules reproduces Part 68.3 paragraph (3) of the English CPR regarding the transmission of the order to the ECJ, to the extent that the procedural rules are applicable in Cypriot law. Therefore, the registrar of the court will not send a copy of the order to the ECJ until '(i) the time for appealing against the order has expired; or (ii) any application for permission to appeal has been refused.'[96] Given

---

[92] *Loc. cit.* n. 90, para. 78 [emphasis added].

[93] *Nicosia Sewage Council v. Tenders Review Authority*, No 629/2006, 27 November 2008, see section 3.2.1.2 *infra*.

[94] For a detailed annual review of the constitutional legal traditions of the Member States pertaining, in particular, to the national mechanisms triggering Art. 234 EC, see L. Burgorgue-Larsen, *Jurisprudence européenne comparée* published annually in *Revue du Droit Public* from 2000 onwards; see, for instance, 4 *RDP* (2000) pp. 1081; 4 *RDP* (2005) pp. 1105 with respect to the practices of the Spanish, German and Austrian Constitutional Courts.

[95] No 1/2008, *Official Gazette* No 4076, 28 March 2008, App 2, Part I.

[96] There is, therefore, no provision in case an appeal has been determined, unlike in Part 68.3 para. (3) of the English CPR.

that the time for appealing under Cypriot law is currently fixed at 15 days from the date of the order by the lower court, there appears to be little or no risk that the ECJ's preliminary ruling will be deemed ultimately unnecessary by the Supreme Court, or worse, not followed by the lower court as a result of a decision of the Supreme Court against its decision to refer (assuming it is possible to ignore the legally binding effect of the preliminary ruling). Like Part 68.4 of the English CPR, the procedural rules also provide for the principle of stay of proceedings under section 5, 'unless the court orders otherwise.'

While the Cypriot procedural rules shed some light on certain procedural issues identified above, substantive issues relating to the powers of the Supreme Court in this specific instance of appeal remain outstanding. Pending any forthcoming amendment of paragraph (2A), the Supreme Court could follow an approach similar to the one of the English Court of Appeal involving the review of the correctness of the lower court's order to refer (or not to refer) to the ECJ. In the meantime, it has been suggested that since paragraph (2A) is likely to be found contrary to Community law, the Supreme Court could merely disregard it if and when needed.

## 3.2. Current practice of the preliminary ruling procedure by national courts

The practice of the courts in Cyprus regarding the exercise of their discretion to refer to the European Court of Justice remains – for the time being – very limited. This may be due, *inter alia*, to the uncertainty surrounding the procedure for preliminary ruling as identified above. At the supranational level, the ECJ has provided limited guidance emphasising the wide discretion vested in the national courts.[97] At the domestic level in Cyprus, the Supreme Court has started, although belatedly, building a body of case law providing some guidance for discretionary references by lower instance courts for matters falling under the First Pillar.[98]

### 3.2.1. *Competition law and procurement law under the EC Treaty*

### 3.2.1.1. Decision not to refer

In the joined cases of *Netmed NV v. Authority for the Protection of Competition* and *Multichoice (Cyprus) Public Company Ltd v. Authority for the Protection of Competition*,[99] the applicants sought before the Supreme Court acting at first instance the annulment of a decision taken by the Cypriot Commission for the Protection of Competition

---

[97] In Case C-338/95 *Wiener v. Hauptzollamt Emmerich* [1997] *ECR* I-6495, AG Jacobs in his Opinion of 10 July 1997 advised a 'greater measure of self-restraint' on the part of the national courts in exercising their discretion to request a preliminary ruling and apparently confirms the suggestion that there is no presumption in favour of referring (paras. 12-20). See Gordon, *op. cit.* n. 75, at pp. 124-125.

[98] As already explained, Cyprus has only recently submitted to the jurisdiction of the ECJ for matters falling under the Third Pillar. The Supreme Court has not yet referred to the ECJ under Art. 35 EU.

[99] No 1522/2006 & 1523/2006, 7 September 2007.

(CPC) in 2006,[100] which they considered violated, *inter alia*, the Cypriot Competition Law (law 207(I)/89 as amended). The applicants also argued that there was a violation of Article 81 EC and Regulation 1/2003/EC, to the extent that the Cypriot CPC refused to implement the said instruments of Community law on the ground that it was never appointed by the Republic of Cyprus as the official competition authority in accordance with Article 35 Regulation 1/2003/EC.[101] During the proceedings, the question of whether a preliminary reference should be made to the European Court of Justice in relation to, *inter alia*, the interpretation of Article 35 Regulation 1/2003/EC was raised by the applicants, and following the directions of the Court, a petition to that intent was made before the Court.[102]

Judge Photiou ruled against such a reference to the ECJ although he did admit that such an application could seem "logical" and "helpful".[103] As the case appears *prima facie* concerned with national law, his reasoning is based primarily on English case law,[104] mainly *Bulmer v. Bollinger*,[105] where Lord Denning referred to the term "necessary" appearing in Article 234 EC with reference to discretionary references as meaning, *inter alia*, that 'the outcome of the case must be dependent on the decision.'[106] Even if Judge Photiou chose to refer to guidelines issued by the ECJ for national courts on when to make a reference to introduce the notion of "necessity",[107] he did not give any further details on this, nor on the relevant ECJ case law,[108] and referred instead exclusively to the English jurisprudence which could be considered as a rather conservative interpretation of the concept of discretionary reference by national courts.[109] The case of *Bollinger*, in particular, has been found to conflict first with the general attitude of the ECJ, which has the leading role in Community matters, and also with specific guidelines laid down by the ECJ.[110] It should also be noted that since the *Bollinger*

---

[100] No 11.17.14/2006, 2 June 2006.

[101] Art. 35 Regulation 1/2003/EC provides that '[t]he Member States shall designate the competition authority or authorities responsible for the application of [Art] 81 and 82 of the Treaty in such a way that the provisions of this regulation are effectively complied with. The measures necessary to empower those authorities to apply those Articles shall be taken before 1 May 2004. The authorities designated may include courts.' See Council Regulation 1/2003/EC of 16 December 2002 on the implementation of the rules on competition laid down in Arts. 81 and 82 of the Treaty, *OJ* 2003 L 1/1.

[102] *Loc. cit.* n. 100, at p. 4.

[103] *Loc. cit.* n. 100, at p. 6.

[104] He refers in particular to *R v. International Stock Exchange of the UK and the Republic of Ireland Limited* ex parte *Else (1982) Limited and others* [1993] *QB* 53.

[105] *Bulmer v. Bollinger* [1974] 2 C.M.L.R. 91.

[106] *Loc. cit.* n. 100, at p. 5.

[107] To the extent, in particular, that the Court acknowledges the sovereignty of the national courts in determining why the interpretation sought is necessary to enable it to give judgment; see para. 14 of the Court's Guidance on References by National Courts for Preliminary Rulings, *loc. cit.* n. 28.

[108] The ECJ has expressed the view that the extent of the national courts' discretion is dependent on the correct interpretation of Art. 234 EC, and that it is the only body which is competent to make authoritative pronouncements on such an interpretation in the name of Community law effectiveness. See, e.g., ECJ, Joined Cases C-297/88 and C-197/89 *Massam Dzodzi v. Belgian State* [1990] *ECR* I-3763.

[109] For a detailed review of the question and related issues, see, e.g., F. Jacobs, 'When to refer to the European Court', 90 *LQR* (1974) pp. 486-493.

[110] See, e.g., Craig and de Búrca, *op. cit.* n. 39, at pp. 480-482.

case, the UK courts have softened their approach and have been found to be more "ready" to refer.[111] Justice Bingham summarises the "more modern approach" of the UK courts in the *Samex* case as follows:

> '[I]f the facts have been found and the Community law issue is critical to the court's final decision, the appropriate course is to refer the issue to the Court of Justice unless the national court can with *complete confidence*[112] resolve the issue itself. In considering whether it can … the national court must be fully mindful of the differences between national and Community legislation, of the pitfalls which face a national court venturing into what may be an unfamiliar field, of the need for uniform interpretation throughout the Community and of the great advantages enjoyed by the Court of Justice in construing Community instruments. If the national court has *any real doubt*,[113] it should obviously refer.'[114]

Judge Photiou concluded his reference to English case law by saying that the national courts should assess to what extent they can "with certainty" (as opposed to "complete confidence" in the *Samex* case) decide the matter themselves.[115] In this instance, Judge Photiou ruled that the court had all the necessary elements to reach a decision on its own on the basis of national competition law, especially since national law is similar to Community law in this case.[116] The decision was nevertheless appealed before the Supreme Court.[117]

Overall, the above decision could appear justified due to the fact that the area of law at stake is competition law, which is very much decentralised in the EU, even if the decision may present some deficiencies in its legal reasoning (in particular, it does not consider Community law to the extent it deserves so as to assist in the interpretation of the provisions of Art. 234 EC in the national legal order). As a result, the argument of the effectiveness of EC law and of its uniform application throughout the EU, allegedly in favour of such a reference to the ECJ, appears quite limited in this instance of implementation of competition law. Even if there may be doubt as to the degree of confidence of the Court in this case, it nevertheless seems to confirm that no reference to the ECJ was needed as there was sufficient certainty as to the issues which were at least clear and free from doubt, as required under the *acte clair* doctrine (not directly mentioned in this case).

In this instance of discretionary reference, no reference to the notion of *acte clair* as embodied in the *CILFIT* jurisprudence[118] of the ECJ is required, as may be the case

---

[111] See *Customs and Excise Commissioners v. ApS Samex* [1983] 1 *All* ER 1042. Also, the formulation of AG Jacobs in *Wiener* was approved by L.J. Chadwick in *Trinity Mirror plc v. Commissioners of Customs and Excise* [2001] *EWCA* Civ 65, para. 52, and was subsequently also endorsed by that court in *Professional Contractors' Group v. Commissioners of Inland Revenue* [2001] *EWCA* Civ 1945; see Gordon, *op. cit.* n. 75, at p. 125.

[112] [Emphasis added].

[113] [Emphasis added].

[114] See Craig and de Búrca, *op. cit.* n. 39, at p. 482.

[115] *Loc. cit.* n. 100, at p. 5.

[116] *Loc. cit.* n. 100, at p. 6.

[117] Appeal No. 152/2007.

[118] ECJ, Case 283/81 *CILFIT and Lanificio di Gavardo SpA v. Ministry of Health* [1982] *ECR* 3415.

for mandatory references, even if in practice, national courts considering points of Community law arising in domestic public law proceedings have shown a certain degree of caution in the exercise of their discretion.[119] In any case, the specific case mentioned above would not be pending before the Cypriot Supreme Court on appeal (the present appeal only concerns the possibility of a discretionary reference), but before the same court at first instance, which means that judicial remedies are still potentially available in national law and renders any consideration of mandatory reference under Article 234 EC irrelevant at present.

In the meantime, it should be noted that Judge Photiou had to annul his decision in this case,[120] relying on the precedent created by the Full Chamber of the Supreme Court in its judgment in *Telecommunications Authority v. Republic of Cyprus and Authority for the Protection of Competition* where the Court held that the wrongful composition of the Authority led to the annulment of the decision at stake.[121]

### 3.2.1.2.   Decision to refer

It was already pointed out that the first preliminary reference from the national courts in Cyprus was recently sent to the ECJ.[122] The question is whether Article 2(8) of Directive 89/665/EEC[123] recognises contracting authorities as having a right to judicial review of cancellation decisions by bodies responsible for review procedures which are not judicial bodies,[124] and is, therefore, important not only for the supremacy of Community law in Cyprus but also for the effectiveness of Community law overall. In order to decide to refer a preliminary question to the ECJ, Judge Erotocritou clarified that he was exercising his discretion to refer in his capacity as the lower instance judge (whose decision could be appealed to the Full Chamber of the Supreme Court), and that all conditions were met for such a reference, including its necessity so as to clarify the meaning of Community law.[125] He noted in particular that since such a preliminary question had never been put to the ECJ before, there was a need to refer so that the national court could render judgment in the case.[126] Relying on case *Rheinmühlen-Düsseldorf*, he stated that the existence of a previous decision of the Full Chamber of the Supreme Court of Cyprus on the same issue reached exclusively on the basis of

---

[119] See Gordon, *op. cit.* n. 75, at p. 125.

[120] *Netmed NV v. Authority for the Protection of Competition* and *Multichoice (Cyprus) Public Company Ltd v. Authority for the Protection of Competition*, No 1522/06 and 1523/06, 18 January 2008 (*ex tempore*).

[121] No 3902/07, 4 December 2007.

[122] Case C-570/08 Reference for a preliminary ruling from the Anotato Diskastirio Kiprou (Supreme Court of Cyprus) lodged on 22 December 2008 – *Nicosia Sewage Council v. Tenders Review Authority*, *OJ* 2009 C 55/13.

[123] Council Directive 89/665/EEC of 21 December 1989 on the co-ordination of the laws, regulations and administrative provisions relating to the application of review procedures to the award of public supply and public works contracts, *OJ* 1989 L 395/33.

[124] In Cyprus, the right of judicial review is granted exclusively to the Supreme Court of Cyprus under Art. 146 of the Cyprus Constitution.

[125] *Loc. cit.* n. 93.

[126] *Loc. cit.* n. 93, para. 22.

Article 146 of the Cyprus Constitution did not affect the exercise of his right to refer in the present case, since the Supreme Court had passed judgment without taking into consideration the relevant provisions of Community law, namely Directive 89/665/EEC (not argued by the parties).[127] In that respect, the present case had to be distinguished from the *Rawuttar* case,[128] where Judge Erotocritou himself exercised his discretion not to refer to the ECJ relying on the precedent created by the Supreme Court of Cyprus in the *Motilla* case,[129] where the relevant provisions of Community law had been considered, clarified and applied to the case.[130] Of course, it was not the only difference between these two types of cases. Cases *Rawuttar* and *Motilla* concerned the immigration policy of the Cypriot Government, which meant that any preliminary reference to the ECJ had to be considered within the framework of Article 68 EC.

### 3.2.2.   Title on visa, immigration and asylum under the EC Treaty: Article 68 EC

The facts in the *Rawuttar* case are similar to the facts in the *Motilla* case except for one important point: the title to lawful residence of the applicant had expired before the end of the deadline provided for the transposition of Directive 109/2003/EC into national law. The status of the applicant during the period running from the expiry of her work permit/right of residence up to the expiry of the deadline for transposition of the Directive into national law (at which point in time no transposing legislation had been enacted) was, therefore, at stake in this case, given the new legal environment created by the Directive. In this respect, the applicant's lawyer requested the judge to exercise his discretion to refer to the ECJ as it was a clear case of interpretation of Community law.

Referring to Article 8 of the Court's Guidance on References by National Courts for Preliminary Rulings, Judge Erotocritou expressly noted that for matters falling under Title IV EC Treaty, the right to refer to the ECJ is limited to final courts of law at their own discretion in accordance with Article 68 EC and concluded that the court did not satisfy these requirements in the present case. He then proceeded with the judicial review of the decision based on the principle of indirect effect and reached the conclusion that the applicant fell outside the scope of the Directive given the unlawfulness of her residence for a period of eleven days between the expiry of her residence permit and the expiry of the deadline for implementation of the Directive into national law.[131] He then added that even if the applicant had a lawful right of residence upon the expiry of the deadline for implementation of the Directive into national law, her application would have been subject to the precedent created by the Supreme Court in the

---

[127]  *Loc. cit.* n. 93, para. 23.
[128]  *Loc. cit.* n. 69.
[129]  *Loc. cit.* n. 62.
[130]  *Loc. cit.* n. 93, para. 24.
[131]  Judge Erotocritou referred to other cases of judicial review where similar decisions were reached by the Supreme Court, namely *Karapetyan v. Republic of Cyprus*, No 907/06, 1 July 2008; *Dmytriieva v. Republic of Cyprus*, No 1494/06, 11 June 2008; *Gamage v. Republic of Cyprus*, No 1358/06, 27 March 2008.

*Motilla* case, and, therefore, she would have fallen outside the scope of the Directive as transposed into Cypriot law.

With respect to the preliminary reference, Judge Erotocritou referred to the case of *Imelda Bautista Balbin v. Republic of Cyprus*,[132] where Judge Nicolaides issued a separate decision on the request by the parties' lawyers to make a preliminary reference to the ECJ in a similar situation (judicial review of an administrative decision). Judge Nicolaides noted that in accordance with Article 68 EC, he was under an obligation to reject the request as he was not acting as the court of last instance, despite being of the opinion that a reference to the ECJ would have been of assistance in the proper inter-pretation of the Directive. Instead, he had to abide by the decision of the Supreme Court in the *Motilla* case (Judge Nicolaides was yet another dissenting judge in that case) and set a further date for hearing of the case.

With respect to the relationship between Article 234 and 68 EC, Judge Nicolaides referred to ECJ case law in case C-555/03 *Magali Warbecq v. Ryanair Ltd*[133] and case C-51/03 *Nicoleta Maria Georgescu*,[134] where the ECJ gave a decision on these actions through an order taken on the basis of Article 92(1) of the Rules of Procedure. Since the instruments of Community law at stake in these actions fell under the special pre-liminary ruling regime of Article 68 EC, the Court confirmed that it had no jurisdiction to rule on preliminary questions referred by courts or tribunals against whose decisions there is a judicial remedy available under national law.[135]

The approach of the Supreme Court of Cyprus to the issue of preliminary refer-ences in the field of visas, immigration and asylum is unlikely to change until, and if, Article 68 EC is revised in the name of effective judicial protection.[136]

4. PRINCIPLES OF JUDICIAL INTEGRATION IN CYPRUS: THE APPLICATION OF COMMUNITY LAW, INFRACTIONS AND OTHER DIRECT ACTIONS BEFORE THE EU COURTS

### 4.1. The application of EC regulations in the Cypriot legal order

In Cyprus, the administration competent for the application of laws, including EC Regulations which are by nature directly applicable in their entirety, is decided by the

---

[132] No 857/06, 16 September 2008.
[133] ECJ, Case C-555/03 *Magali Warbecq v. Ryanair Ltd* [2004] *ECR* I-6041.
[134] ECJ, Case C-51/03 *Nicoleta Maria Georgescu* [2004] *ECR* I-3203.
[135] *Loc. cit.* n. 133, paras. 15-16; *loc. cit.* n. 134, paras. 32-33.
[136] See Commission's Communication to the EP, the Council, the EESC, the CoR and the ECJ, Ad-aptation of the provisions of Title IV of the EC Treaty relating to the jurisdiction of the Court of Justice with a view to ensuring more effective judicial protection, COM (2006) 346 final. It should be noted that the Treaty of Lisbon, if and when it enters into force, will abolish this special preliminary ruling regime (Treaty of Lisbon amending the Treaty on European Union and the Treaty establishing the European Com-munity, *OJ* 2007 C 306/1). For an academic appraisal see, *inter alia*, A. Łazowski, 'Towards the reform of the preliminary ruling procedure in JHA Area', in S. Braum and A. Weyembergh, eds., *Le contrôle juridic-tionnel dans l'espace pénal européen* (Bruxelles, Editions de l'Université de Bruxelles 2009) pp. 211-226.

Council of Ministers as per Article 54 of the Constitution. In the event that powers need to be granted to a specific administration in addition to competences in order to fully apply an EC regulation, a law giving effect to an EC regulation in the Cypriot domestic legal order will be required.[137] This law may take the form of a special law in certain predetermined areas, such as fishing, veterinary or phytosanitary matters, and is otherwise a law of general application for matters as set out in the Application of European Community Regulations and Decisions Law 78(I) of 2007.[138] As such, this law contains provisions on the competence and powers of the various authorities involved in the application of regulations and decisions in Cyprus not decided in a specific law. The competent authorities are defined in Article 4 of the law as being any ministry or independent authorities in the Republic appointed as such under the Constitution or under any piece of legislation, rule, practice or decisions of the relevant body in Cyprus.

The law grants to these competent authorities a series of powers usually required for the proper application of laws in the national legal order. In addition to these ordinary provisions of the law, a table containing a list of regulations is annexed thereto and can be amended by the Council of Ministers.[139] The table refers to a number of regulations whose application falls within the scope of Law 78(I)/2007 and sets out for each of them the competent authority as well as its powers regarding, in particular, the capacity to impose sanctions for the infringement of the regime established for the application of the said regulation under Cypriot law. This very detailed regime of application of regulations in the national legal order may appear quite unusual in comparison to the more general regime in place in the UK.[140] In addition, it may also be less practical as well as more controversial due to the fact that the competent authority can apply both administrative[141] and/or penal sanctions[142] for failure to comply with the appropriate regime under national law. The penalisation of the infractions under Law 78(I)/2007 prompted reactions at the Cypriot House of Representatives and led to the detailed setting out in the table of the types of infringements involved for each relevant provision of the regulations concerned by the law as well as the corresponding sanctions.

---

[137] Unlike other new Member States, problems of application of EC/EU law following the late publication of legal acts in the Official Journal of the European Union will not arise in Cyprus due to the fact that the Greek language is already one of the official languages of the EU since the accession of Greece in 1981. For analysis of those problems see, *inter alia*, Chapter 5 in this volume. See also K. Łasiński-Sułecki and W. Morawski, 'Late publication of EC law in languages of new member states and its effects: obligations on individuals following the court's judgment in Skoma-Lux', 45 *CMLRev.* (2008) pp. 705-725. On the consequences of non-publication see also ECJ, Case C-345/06 *Gottfried Heinrich* [2009] *ECR* nyr.

[138] *Official Gazette* No 4130, 29 June 2007. Art. 3 of the law provides that this law does not concern regulations or decisions whose application is the subject of specific laws.

[139] Art. 13 of the law, *ibidem*.

[140] See, e.g., J. Steiner, 'Direct applicability in EEC law – a chameleon concept', 98 *LQR* (1982) pp. 229-248.

[141] See Art. 7 of law 78(I)/2007.

[142] See Arts. 5 & 6, *ibidem*.

## 4.2.    Infractions and other direct actions before the EU courts

As seen above, there is no co-ordinated procedure of application and implementation of Community law in Cyprus, but rather a sectoral approach orchestrated by each competent ministry or independent authority. Therefore, procedural infractions to the application or implementation of EC/EU law are numerous and cannot be presented in a systematic manner in this chapter. For the purpose of clarity, this matter will be associated with the issue of direct actions before the EU courts giving rise to Member State and/or Community liability.

### 4.2.1.    Litigation relating to CAP

#### 4.2.1.1.    The sugar cases

The so-called sugar quota litigation before the courts in Cyprus, both at the supranational and national level, is a clear illustration of this relationship. The Republic of Cyprus was fined by the Commission 20 million Euro for the breach of its pre-accession obligations under the Treaty of Accession 2003 regarding sugar surpluses. Cyprus undertook, like all the new Member States, an obligation to prevent stockpiling of agricultural commodities in excess of usual imports immediately before and after joining the EU.[143] Following accession, the Commission adopted two EC Regulations specifically aimed at preventing speculation in the sugar market in the new Member States.[144] The European Commission argued that Cyprus, together with other new Member States, was in breach of the undertaken obligations.[145] The Cypriot Government has brought two legal actions before the CFI for annulment of the two Regulations.[146]

In its plea, the Cypriot Government claims first that the Commission lacked the power to adopt the contested Regulations under Article 41 of the Act on Conditions of Accession 2003.[147] Article 41 empowers the Commission to adopt transitional measures

---

[143]  Annex IV to Art. 22 of Act on Conditions of Accession 2003, Chapter 4, para. 2.

[144]  Commission Regulation 651/2005/EC of 28 April 2005 amending Regulation No 60/2004/EC laying down transitional measures in the sugar sector by reason of the accession of the 10 new member states, *OJ* 2005 L 108/3; Commission Regulation 832/2005/EC of 31 May 2005 on the determination of surplus quantities of sugar, isoglucose and fructose for the 10 new member states, *OJ* 2005 L 138/3.

[145]  With respect to delegation by the Community institutions to the Member States for the common organisation of the market in sugar, see ECJ, Case 23/75 *Rey Soda v. Cassa Conguaglio Zucchero* [1975] *ECR* 1279. See also Hartley, *op. cit.* n. 79, at pp. 123-124. Under the common organisation of the markets in the sugar sector, overall allocation is made to the Member States in the form of basic quotas, save in Greece and Finland where quotas were set directly for individual undertakings in the context of accession. It is then incumbent on the authorities of the Member States specifically to allocate the quotas to the respective undertakings; see Opinion of AG Kokott delivered on 26 October 2006 in Case C-441/05 *Roquette Frères v. Ministre de l'Agriculture, de l'Alimentation, de la Pêche et de la Ruralité* [2007] *ECR* I-1993.

[146]  Case T-300/05 *Republic of Cyprus v. Commission of the European Communities*, *OJ* 2005 C 271/19 and Case T-316/05 *Republic of Cyprus v. Commission of the European Communities*, *OJ* 2005 C 271/23. Latvia supports Cyprus in the first case and Estonia in the second one.

[147]  *Ibidem.*

if they are necessary to "facilitate" the transition from the "existing regime" in the new Member States to that resulting from the application of the CAP (as set out in the Treaty of Accession 2003).[148] But the Cypriot Government contends that the necessity of the measures was not established, that such measures should not *a priori* be a burden to the new Member States within the meaning of Article 41, nor should they have a retroactive effect (they concerned quantities which had already been accumulated before their entry into force). In this respect, the Cypriot Government questions the nature of acts based on Article 41 Act on Conditions of Accession 2003 as opposed to mechanisms usually found in previous Accession Treaties and argues that given that such acts provide for sanctions, they cannot have retroactive effect.[149] The Cypriot Government also claims that there is a breach of the principle of proportionality, as the European Commission failed to explain the grounds leading to the adoption of these measures rather than others.[150]

Finally, the Cypriot Government outlines the potential breach of the principle of equal treatment and non-discrimination by arguing that the contested Regulations provide for different treatment between undertakings of the new Member States and those of the old Member States in a similar, if not identical, situation. In this respect, the Cypriot Government outlines that it is especially the case for Cyprus, which had imported 95% of its sugar surplus from the rest of the EU. In that case, the old Member States should also take their share of the blame resulting in sanctions being imposed on them as well.[151]

---

[148] See in this respect, ECJ, Case C-179/00 *Gerald Weidacher (as administrator of the insolvent company Thakis Vertriebs- und Handels GmbH) v. Bundesminister für Land- und Forstwirtschaft* [2002] *ECR* I-501. In the context of Austria's accession, the ECJ rejected a claim based, *inter alia*, on the principles of legitimate expectations and of proportionality to review the validity of a Commission Regulation imposing fines on an olive oil importer as a result of the application of the provisions on CAP as embodied in the Act of Accession 1994, which led to the insolvency of the importer. The ECJ based its reasoning on the broad discretion enjoyed by the Community institutions, in particular the European Commission, when adopting measures for the implementation of CAP with a view to preventing the disruption of the proper functioning of the common organisation of the markets, while at the same time facilitating the transition of the new Member States to this organisation (paras. 19-22). See Act concerning the Conditions of Accession of the Kingdom of Norway, the Republic of Austria, the Republic of Finland and the Kingdom of Sweden and the adjustments to the Treaties on which the European Union is founded, *OJ* 1994 C 241/8.

[149] This may appear *prima facie* against the principle of legitimate expectations, but the ECJ clarified in the similar context arising in *Weidacher* that the principle, which may only be invoked as against the Community rules when the Community itself has previously created a situation potentially giving rise to a legitimate expectation, cannot apply in the event that the Community has not, "by act or omission" given a different impression, and the importer 'like any normally diligent economic operator', ought to have known, since in this case there had been publication in the *OJ* that under Article 149(1) of the Act of Accession 1994, the European Commission was empowered to adopt transitional measures facilitating the transition, and that such measures 'might, in some circumstances, have repercussions on surplus stocks' (paras. 30-35).

[150] With respect to the plea of breach of the principle of proportionality within the context of the broad discretion of the Commission arising out of the application of CAP, the Court rejected it in *Weidacher* on the ground that the Commission did not exceed the bounds of its discretion granted under the Act of Accession 1994 (paras. 26-29).

[151] See paras. 49-52 of *Weidacher* judgment, where the ECJ ruled that importers from Austria were not in a situation comparable to the operators in the twelve old (at the time) Member States with respect to imports from outside the Community (from Tunisia in that particular case).

Both actions are pending before the Court of First Instance. With respect to the procedure, the Commission argued in the first case, that the plea of illegality must be rejected as it falls outside the 2-month time limit to challenge the contested act in accordance with Article 230(5) EC. Regarding the admissibility of the action and in view of Article 58 of the Act on Conditions of Accession 2003,[152] the Cypriot Government reminds the Court that there was no possibility of judicial review before the EU Courts prior to the accession of Cyprus.

In the meantime, at the national level, legal proceedings have been brought before the Supreme Court of Cyprus by Cypriot importers challenging the validity of the decision of the Ministry of Trade, Industry and Tourism setting out surplus stocks for each undertaking importing sugar in Cyprus. The Ministry had charged importers with violating Law 40(I)/2005 implementing the provisions of Community law on the transitional measures regarding the trade of agricultural products on account of the accession of the Republic of Cyprus and other Member States to the EU.[153] The proceedings also challenged the decision of the Ministry to impose penalties on these importers as a result of their non-compliance with the first decision. Despite the delivery of a judgment by Judge Hadjihambis in one case,[154] it was decided that all these actions should be brought before the Full Chamber of the Supreme Court.[155] The proceedings are still pending.

### 4.2.1.2. Other agricultural products

More fines have been contemplated against the new Member States, including Cyprus, for stockpiling various agricultural produce and have given rise to litigation at the national and/or supranational level in several Member States.[156] In Cyprus, the Supreme

---

[152] Regarding the interpretation of Art. 58 of the Act on Conditions of Accession 2003, see ECJ, Case C-161/06 *Skoma Lux sro v. Celní ředitelství Olomouc* [2007] *ECR* I-10841.

[153] *Official Gazette* No 3981, 15 April 2005. Law 40(I)/2005 implements Commission Regulation 1972/2003/EC of 10 November 2003 on transitional measures to be adopted in respect of trade in agricultural products on account of the accession of the Czech Republic, Estonia, Cyprus, Latvia, Lithuania, Hungary, Malta, Poland, Slovenia and Slovakia, *OJ* 2003 L 293/3 (as amended) and Commission Regulation 60/2004/EC of 14 January 2004 laying down transitional measures in the sugar sector by reason of the accession of the Czech Republic, Estonia, Cyprus, Latvia, Lithuania, Hungary, Malta, Poland, Slovenia and Slovakia, *OJ* 2004 L 9/8.

[154] *Morphis Morphy & Associates Ltd v. Republic of Cyprus through the Ministry of Trade, Industry and Tourism*, No 1200/2005, 16 July 2007.

[155] A total of 52 actions were brought before the Supreme Court for judicial review. In a nutshell, the applicants are challenging the legality of Law 40(I)/2005, the constitutionality of the two decisions of the Ministry of Trade and/or the validity of Regulation 1972/2003/EC and/or other instruments of Community law. Judge Hadjihambis, in his judgment in the above decision, merely proceeded with a review of the mechanisms for evaluation of the surplus stocks of the importer and of the charges imposed on the importer, as contained in Law 40(I)/2005 in accordance with the relevant provisions of Community law (EC Regulations 1972/2003/EC, 60/2004/EC, 651/2005/EC and 832/2005/EC), and rejected the application for judicial review.

[156] For a review of the litigation in the new Member States, see A. Albi, 'Ironies in Human Rights protection in the EU: pre-accession conditionality and post-accession conundrums', 15 *ELJ* (2009) pp. 46-69, at pp. 52-57. For direct actions before the CFI with respect to the Regulation 1972/2003/EC (trade

Court has recently given judgment[157] on the application in Cyprus of Regulation 1972/2003/EC, as amended by Regulation 230/2004,[158] with respect to the calculation of the charge to be levied in the new Member States on holders of rice surplus stocks as set out in Commission Decision 2007/361/EC.[159]

In this case, Judge Hadjihambis addressed the issue of publication of the various instruments of Community law in Cyprus and of the way they were brought to the knowledge of the importers.[160] With respect to Regulation 1972/2003/EC (which was implemented into Law 40(I)/2005), Judge Hadjihambis noted that the competent authority, the Ministry of Trade, Industry and Tourism, arranged for an announcement to be placed in the local press shortly following the publication of the Regulation in the Official Journal of the EU. It was addressed to the rice importers and informed them of their obligations under the Regulation. This was followed by a letter to the importers, including the applicant, referring once more to the Regulation and to its various mechanisms and requesting the addressee to provide the necessary information for the purpose of the calculation of the surplus. Upon receipt of the information, the Ministry requested the assistance of the Customs Services since there were discrepancies between the official figures and the ones submitted. Judge Hadjihambis deemed satisfactory and in compliance with Community law the procedure and the methodology followed by the Ministry of Trade in order to determine the charge to be levied on the applicant, including the time frame for the publication of the obligations on the importers deriving from the application of Community law and the implementation of Regulation 1972/2003/EC itself into national law. As a result, he rejected the application for judicial review.[161]

---

in agricultural products), see CFI, Case T-257/04, *Republic of Poland v. Commission of the European Communities* [2009] *ECR* nyr. For direct actions before the CFI in the sugar sector, see also Case T-258/04, *Republic of Poland v. Commission of the European Communities, OJ* 2004 C 251/21 with respect to Regulation 60/2004/EC; and Case T-324/05, *Republic of Estonia v. Commission of the European Communities, OJ* 2005 C 271/48 with respect to Regulation 832/2005/EC. These actions present similar grounds of review as the actions brought by Cyprus. With respect to the sugar sector, Poland also argues breach of the principle of solidarity and good faith arising under Art. 10 EC between the Member States and the Community institutions, by imposing on Poland obligations 'with which it is in practice not possible to comply' and by refusing to co-operate 'with a view to overcoming difficulties which have arisen' (Case T-258/04). Estonia also focuses on the impact of the measures on private households through a breach of the right to property and of proportionality and a breach of the principle of sound administration.

[157] *Cooperative company ESEL-SKOLP Ltd v. Republic of Cyprus through the Ministry of Trade, Industry and Tourism,* No 1041/2007, 15 January 2009.

[158] Commission Regulation 230/2004/EC of 10 February 2004 amending Regulation (EC) No 1972/2003 on transitional measures to be adopted in respect to trade in agricultural products on account of the accession of the Czech Republic, Estonia, Cyprus, Latvia, Lithuania, Hungary, Malta, Poland, Slovenia and Slovakia, OJ 2004 L 39/13.

[159] Commission Decision 2007/361/EC of 4 May 2007 on the determination of surplus stocks of agricultural products other than sugar and the financial consequences of their elimination in relation to the accession of the Czech Republic, Estonia, Cyprus, Latvia, Lithuania, Hungary, Malta, Poland, Slovenia and Slovakia (notified under document number C(2007) 1979), *OJ* 2007 L 138/14.

[160] See in this respect, Case C-345/06, *Gottfried Heinrich, loc. cit.* n. 137, where the ECJ ruled that Member States must publish not only the national legislation at issue but also a Community regulation which forces Member States to take measures imposing obligations on individuals (para. 47).

[161] This section on the application of CAP in Cyprus appears in an amended version in Laulhé Shaelou, *op. cit.* n. 5.

It is argued that the legal proceedings arising both at the supranational and the national level in the new Member States reflect the normal and smooth application of the rules of the Accession Treaty 2003 to the new Member States. At the supranational level, they may, moreover, raise unusual difficulties in law, particularly in respect to the potential difference of treatment between the new and old Member States. However, this argument has been rejected by the EU Courts in respect to previous enlargements on the basis that the situation of the new and old Member States is not comparable.[162] The judgment of the Court of First Instance in the Case T-257/04 *Republic of Poland v. Commission of the European Communities* indicates that the line of jurisprudence known from the previous enlargement rounds is applicable *mutatis mutandis* to the fifth and sixth enlargements. At the national level, these proceedings raise constitutional issues relating to the protection of the fundamental rights of freedom of individuals, *inter alia*, to property, to trade, to non-discrimination or to legitimate expectations.[163]

### 4.2.2.  *Litigation arising out of the application of instruments of secondary legislation within the framework of Protocol 10*

This part will just present a brief overview of such litigation as, strictly speaking, it goes beyond the scope of this chapter.[164] The Financial Aid Regulation taken within the framework of Protocol 10[165] aims at providing financial assistance to the Turkish Cypriot community.[166] The assistance is geared towards the "economic integration of the island"[167] through the promotion of social and economic development, projects for the development and restructuring of infrastructures, bi-communal activities, information on the Union's political and legal order, the preparation of the harmonisation of the Turkish Cypriot "legal system" and implementation of the *acquis* (under TAIEX).[168] The aid programme is implemented by the European Commission in accordance with Article 53(1)(a) and (c) of Council Regulation 1605/2002/EC, Euratom on the financial regulation applicable to the general budget of the EC.[169]

Despite safeguard measures contained in the Regulation ensuring, *inter alia*, the lawfulness of the implementing powers, the Republic of Cyprus applied to the CFI for

---

[162] See ECJ, Joined Cases C-87/03 and C-100/03 *Kingdom of Spain v. Council of the European Union* [2006] *ECR* I-2915 (paras. 48-54).

[163] See Albi, *loc. cit.* n. 156, at pp. 55-57.

[164] For a more detailed analysis of the litigation within the framework of Protocol 10, see Laulhé Shaelou, *op. cit.* n. 5.

[165] Express reference is made to Art. 3, Protocol 10 in the Financial Aid Regulation. This provision triggers general and autonomous provisions of Community law. The Financial Aid Regulation was adopted on the basis of Art. 308 EC.

[166] Council Regulation 389/2006/EC of 27 February 2006 establishing an instrument of financial support for encouraging the economic development of the Turkish Cypriot community and amending Council Regulation (EC) No 2667/2000 on the European Agency for Reconstruction *OJ* 2006 L 65/5.

[167] Art. 1(1) Financial Aid Regulation.

[168] Arts. 1(1) and 2 Financial Aid Regulation.

[169] Council Regulation 1605/2002/EC, Euratom on the financial regulation applicable to the general budget of the EC, *OJ* 2002 L 248/1.

annulment of the operation of a number of procurement notices issued by the Commission for the encouragement of economic development in the northern part of Cyprus in the fields of energy, environment, agriculture, telecommunications, education and crop management and irrigation.[170] According to the Republic of Cyprus, the Commission's notices are unlawful both under EU law (abuse of powers/infringement of the relevant legal basis under the Financial Aid Regulation, violation of Art. 299 EC as amended by the Treaty of Accession 2003 and of Protocol 10, and/or non-publication in the Official Journal, and/or violation of the duty of sincere co-operation under Art. 10 EC) and under international law (mandatory rules and UNSC Resolutions 541(1983) and 550(1984) on Cyprus). All this justifies in the Republic of Cyprus' view the granting of interim relief through, *inter alia*, the suspension of the operation of the notices. The President of the CFI issued several orders[171] whereby he dismissed the applications for interim relief in these cases due to the absence of urgency and of manifest and serious breach of international and/or Community law by the Commission.[172] Nevertheless, he accepted that the conduct of the Commission was unlawful, and that it amounted to a violation of the sovereignty of the Republic (moral prejudice), which could be adequately remedied through annulment of the said instruments,[173] given the various socio-legal interests at stake.[174]

Following these orders, the cases were removed from the Court Register,[175] as Cyprus was officially satisfied with their outcome and did not wish to pursue the annulment of

---

[170]  Case T-54/08 *Republic of Cyprus v. Commission of the European Communities*, OJ 2008 C 79/34; Cases T-87/08 and T-88/08 *Republic of Cyprus v. Commission of the European Communities*, OJ 2008 C 142/27; Cases T-91/08, T-92/08 and T-93/08 *Republic of Cyprus v. Commission of the European Communities*, OJ 2008 C 142/29; Case T-119/08 *Republic of Cyprus v. Commission of the European Communities*, OJ 2008 C 142/29; and Case T-122/08 *Republic of Cyprus v. Commission of the European Communities*, OJ 2008 C 142/30.

[171]  CFI, Case T-54/08R, Order of the President of the CFI of 8 April 2008, *Republic of Cyprus v. Commission of the European Communities*; Joined Cases T-54/08 R, T-87/08 R, T-88/08 R, T-91/08 R, T-92/08 R and T-93/08 R, Order of the President of the CFI of 11 April 2008, *Republic of Cyprus v. Commission of the European Communities*; Case T-119/08 R, Order of the President of the CFI of 11 April 2008, *Republic of Cyprus v. Commission of the European Communities*; Case T-122/08 R, Order of the President of the CFI of 11 April 2008, *Republic of Cyprus v. Commission of the European Communities*, OJ 2008 C 171/38.

[172]  See Case T-54/08 R, *Republic of Cyprus v. Commission of the European Communities*, paras. 66-80 of the Order of the President of the CFI, 8 April 2008.

[173]  *Ibidem*, paras. 77-78.

[174]  "Cette solution est confirmée par la mise en balance des intérêts en cause. Ainsi que la Commission l'a relevé à juste titre ..., l'octroi des sursis à exécution sollicités porterait atteinte aux intérêts de tiers qui ne sont pas parties à la présente procédure et n'ont pas été entendus par le juge des référés. ... Tout retard dans la mise en œuvre des ces mesures risquerait de pérenniser le sous-développement structurel et économique des ces zones et les conditions de vie difficiles de leurs habitants, d'autant plus que l'aide communautaire vise, aux termes de l'article 2 du même règlement, la promotion du développement social et économique, notamment rural, le développement des infrastructures ainsi que le rapprochement entre la communauté chypriote turque et l'[UE]" (para. 79) *Ibidem*.

[175]  Order of the Court of First Instance of 29 April 2008 – *Republic of Cyprus v. Commission of the European Communities (Case T-54/08)*, OJ 2008 C 171/38; Order of the Court of First Instance of 16 June 2008 – *Republic of Cyprus v. Commission of the European Communities (Case T-87/08)*, OJ 2008 C 223/58; Order of the Court of First Instance of 16 June 2008 – *Republic of Cyprus v. Commission of the European Communities (Case T-88/08)*, OJ 2008 C 223/58; Order of the Court of First Instance of

these notices any further (there had been a change of government in the meantime; some of the calls were closed and/or had been unsuccessful anyway).


5.      CONCLUSIONS

The assumption as set out in the introductory part of this chapter that many of the challenges of EU membership are common to all the new Member States, especially with respect to the encounter of their national legal orders with the EU legal order, seems to be verified. Within this relationship, some issues have the potential perhaps to distinguish Cyprus from the other new Member States in a significant manner with respect, for instance, to the treatment of the supremacy of EC/EU law in the national legal order or the litigation arising out of the application of the regulatory regime deriving from Protocol 10.[176] Such differentiation could, however, be explained once more by the socio-legal and political context surrounding Cyprus' EU membership. Even in this particular context, it can be said that Cyprus actively participates to the development of the European constitutional legal order.

---

16 June 2008 – *Republic of Cyprus v. Commission of the European Communities (Case T-91/08), OJ* 2008 C 223/58; Order of the Court of First Instance of 16 June 2008 – *Republic of Cyprus v. Commission of the European Communities (Case T-92/08), OJ* 2008 C 223/59; Order of the Court of First Instance of 16 June 2008 – *Republic of Cyprus v. Commission of the European Communities (Case T-93/08), OJ* 2008 C 223/59; Order of the Court of First Instance of 16 June 2008 – *Republic of Cyprus v. Commission of the European Communities (Case T-119/08), OJ* 2008 C 223/59; Order of the Court of First Instance of 16 June 2008 – *Republic of Cyprus v. Commission of the European Communities (Case T-122/08), OJ* 2008 C 223/59.

[176] ECJ, Case C-420/07 *Meletios Apostolides v. David Charles and Linda Elizabeth Orams* [2009] *ECR* nyr. For a legal appraisal of the case and of the Opinion of Advocate General Kokott, see Laulhé Shaelou, *op. cit.* n. 5; see also S. Laulhé Shaelou, *Market Freedoms, EU fundamental rights and public order: views from Cyprus* (forthcoming).

*Chapter 16*

# THE APPLICATION OF EU LAW IN ROMANIA

## Kinga Tibori Szabó*

## 1.     INTRODUCTION

EU membership was the ultimate goal of Romanian politics after the 1989 regime change. At the time when the Trade and Cooperation Agreement[1] was signed, the Prime Minister Petre Roman was advocating for the liberalisation of the domestic market and for the initiation of comprehensive reforms vital for political and economic transition.[2] Nonetheless, the prospect of European integration proved not enough to speed up the transition process. Fourteen years later, in 2004, when ten new states joined the European Union, Romania was barely at the stage of concluding negotiations for accession. Finally, after 17 years, Romania joined the EU on 1 January 2007, together with Bulgaria. It is known as a highly debated, relatively unpopular and conditionality-toughened accession.

The purpose of this chapter is to offer a short description of the main steps in Romania's accession process and, specifically, to portray the most important implications of EU membership for Romania during 2007, the first year of membership. The study will also offer a succinct update of the most significant developments up to July 2009.

The analysis is divided into four main sections. Section 1 offers a short description of the application process and the Accession Treaty. Section 2 deals with the relationship between EU law and Romanian legislation, with emphasis on the Romanian Constitution and the way the principle of supremacy is incorporated into domestic legislation and applied by Romanian courts. The third section focuses on the special conditions attached to Romania's accession process, namely the JHA safeguard clause and the four benchmarks of the Commission's monitoring mechanism. Section 4 deals with the more traditional aspects of EU membership, namely, the Commission's infringe-

---

*   PhD researcher at the Amsterdam Center for International Law of the University of Amsterdam and a Dissertation Fellow at the T.M.C. Asser Institute in The Hague, The Netherlands.
    [1]   Agreement between the European Economic Community and the European Atomic Energy Community, of the one part, and Romania, of the other part, on trade and commercial and economic cooperation, *OJ* 1991 L 79/13.
    [2]   P. Roman, 'Nem elég hangoztatni a reformot' [It is not enough to only talk about reform], *Szabadság* (in Hungarian), 20 October 1990, p. 1.

*A. Łazowski (ed.), The Application of EU Law in the New Member States*
© 2010, T·M·C·ASSER PRESS, *The Hague, The Netherlands and the Authors*

ment procedures for 2007, Romania's direct actions before the European Court of Justice and some institutional aspects of membership. The conclusion attempts to offer a prognosis on the main issues that need to be addressed in the future by Romania as an EU member.

## 1.1.    Short summary of the application process

As early as 1990, Romania started diplomatic talks with the European Economic Community. The Trade and Cooperation Agreement was signed in Luxembourg on 22 October 1990 and entered into force on 1 May 1991.[3] This agreement was replaced in 1995 by the Europe Agreement, creating the basis for a 'regular political dialogue' with the intent to 'accompany and consolidate the rapprochement between the Community and Romania, support the political and economic changes underway in that country and contribute to the establishment of new links of solidarity and new forms of cooperation' (Art. 2).[4]

The formal application for membership was submitted on 22 June 1995, five years after the initiation of diplomatic talks. Following two years of further diplomatic dialogue, in July 1997, the Commission published its Opinion on Romania's application for membership in the European Union. In its conclusion, the Commission noted that Romania 'is on the way to satisfying the political criteria set by the European Council at Copenhagen', but that 'the economy needs a number of years of sustained structural reform' in order to become a functional market economy. Regarding Romania's administrative and legal capabilities as well as its capacity to take on the obligations of membership, the Commission observed many shortcomings at that time and set up a tentative list of goals to achieve. On the whole, the Opinion concluded that negotiations for accession should be opened as soon as Romania 'has made sufficient progress in satisfying the conditions of membership defined by the European Council in Copenhagen.'[5] Since 1998, the Commission has published yearly reports on the progress registered by Romania, assessing the failures and successes of the country on the basis of the political and economic criteria as well as the 31 negotiation chapters.

The official opening of negotiations took place at the Romania-EU intergovernmental conference in Brussels in February 2000. Two years later, the Presidency Conclusions of the 2002 Copenhagen European Council stipulated that 'the objective is to welcome Bulgaria and Romania as members of the European Union in 2007.'[6] In 2003, EU lead-

---

[3] *Loc. cit.* n. 1.

[4] Europe Agreement establishing an association between the European Economic Communities and their Member States, of the one part, and Romania, of the other part, *OJ* 1994 L 357/2.

[5] Agenda 2000 – Commission Opinion on Romania's Application for Membership of the European Union (hereafter 1997 Commission Opinion), DOC/97/18, Brussels, 15 July 1997, COM (97) 2003 final, pp. 111-114.

[6] Copenhagen European Council, 12 and 13 December 2002, Presidency Conclusions, Brussels, 29 January 2003, 15917/02, Point 14.

ers stated their determination to conclude negotiations with Romania in one year.[7] As a result, in December 2004, at the Brussels European Council, the two remaining negotiation chapters (competition policy and co-operation in the field of justice and home affairs) were closed.[8]

On 22 February 2005, the Commission delivered a favourable opinion regarding Romania's accession to the European Union. That opinion was followed by a legislative resolution in which the European Parliament gave its assent to the application of Romania to become a member of the EU.[9]

On 25 April 2005, in Luxembourg, Romania signed the Accession Treaty.[10] Three weeks later, on 17 May 2005, the two Chambers of the Romanian Parliament ratified the Treaty in a joint session.

In May 2006, the Commission published an Enlargement Package, in which it again assessed the overall progress registered by Romania and identified a number of important matters to address: four areas of major concern in agricultural policy and taxation and three "outstanding issues" that concerned the judiciary system, the fight against corruption and public administration.[11]

In its final monitoring report in September 2006, before the accession, the Commission observed that although further progress had been made in the justice system, 'a fully consistent interpretation and application of the law in all courts has not yet been ensured.' Similarly, regarding the fight against corruption, the Report concluded that progress had continued, but a clear political will was needed 'to demonstrate the sus-

---

[7] Brussels European Council, 12 and 13 December 2003, Presidency Conclusions, 5 February 2004, 5381/04, Point 36.

[8] Brussels European Council, 16 and 17 December 2004, Presidency Conclusions, Bulletin 20/12/2004, PE 352.185.

[9] Commission Opinion of 22 February 2005 on the Applications for Accession to the European Union by the Republic of Bulgaria and Romania, *OJ* 2005 L 157/3 followed by European Parliament legislative resolution on the application by Romania to become a member of the European Union (AA1/2/2005 – C6-0086/2005 – 2005/0902(AVC)) (Assent procedure), *OJ* 2005 L 157/7.

[10] Treaty between the Kingdom of Belgium, the Czech Republic, the Kingdom of Denmark, the Federal Republic of Germany, the Republic of Estonia, the Hellenic Republic, the Kingdom of Spain, the French Republic, Ireland, the Italian Republic, the Republic of Cyprus, the Republic of Latvia, the Republic of Lithuania, the Grand Duchy of Luxembourg, the Republic of Hungary, the Republic of Malta, the Kingdom of the Netherlands, the Republic of Austria, the Republic of Poland, the Portuguese Republic, the Republic of Slovenia, the Slovak Republic, the Republic of Finland, the Kingdom of Sweden, the United Kingdom of Great Britain and Northern Ireland (Member States of the European Union) and the Republic of Bulgaria and Romania, concerning the accession of the Republic of Bulgaria and Romania to the European Union, *OJ* 2005 L 157/11.

[11] Commission of the European Communities, May 2006 Monitoring Report, Romania, Brussels, 6 May 2006. The four areas of major concern were:
(1) fully operational paying agencies accredited for handling direct payments to farmers and operators, building on progress made, under the Common Agriculture Policy; (2) setting up a proper integrated administration and control system (IACS) in agriculture, building on progress made; (3) building up of rendering collection and treatment facilities in line with the *acquis* on TSE and animal by-products; (4) tax administration IT systems ready for inter-operability with those of the rest of the Union, to enable a correct collection of VAT throughout the EU internal market. For details on the three "outstanding issues" on judiciary, corruption and public administration, see pp. 12-13 of the Report.

tainability and irreversibility of the recent positive progress in fighting corruption.'[12] Consequently, in December 2006, the Commission set up a mechanism for the verification and assessment of Romania's progress. The Commission has delivered five progress reports since then: in June 2007, an interim report in February 2008, and other reports in July 2008, February 2009 and July 2009. The mechanism will be described in the following section, together with the content of the Accession Treaty.

## 1.2.    The Accession Treaty and associated legal instruments

The Treaty of Accession of Romania and Bulgaria to the European Union[13] was signed on 25 April 2005 in Neumünster Abbey, Luxembourg. At the signing ceremony, the Romanian President Traian Băsescu characterised the accession of Romania to the EU as 'the fulfilment of a dream, more than half a century old, that of overcoming all barriers and becoming part of the European community of values, prosperity and security.'[14] Such a statement accurately described how Romanians saw the prospect of being part of the European Union. Although the signing of the Accession Treaty was seen as a great momentum by Romania, the content of the documents supplementing the Treaty demonstrated that the sixth enlargement was far from being unproblematic.

The Treaty of Accession provided for the accession of Romania and Bulgaria to the European Union and set out the general conditions of membership. The Treaty was supplemented by a Protocol on Conditions for Accession[15] and an Act on Conditions for Accession.[16] The former was envisaged as the legal basis in the event of the entry into force of the EU Constitution, whereas the latter, identical to the Protocol, was set up to serve as an alternative legal basis in case the Constitution failed to enter into force.

For well-known reasons it is the Act on Conditions for Accession that serves as the legal foundation for Romania's membership in the EU. Judging by its content, the Act proves to be the "hardcore" of the accession basis. In its first part, the Act details the major principles regarding the binding nature of the Founding Treaties, the Schengen *acquis* and other acts adopted before accession as well as the rights and obligations of Romania in connection with various other agreements, such as third-country relations and specific trade policies. In the second part of the Act, the major institutional adjustments are described, and the third part makes reference to the acts that awaited adoption by Romania. The fourth part contains pre-accession and post-accession temporary provisions. The most important of such provisions are contained in Articles 36-38 of

---

[12] Communication from the Commission, Monitoring report on the state of preparedness for EU membership of Bulgaria and Romania, Brussels, COM (2006) 549 final.

[13] *Loc. cit.* n. 10.

[14] Speech by Traian Băsescu, President of Romania, on the occasion of the signing ceremony of Romania's EU Accession Treaty, 25 April 2005. Full text of the speech was accessed on 6 January 2008 at http://www.eu2005.lu/en/actualites/discours/2005/04/25basescu/index.html.

[15] Protocol concerning the conditions and arrangements for admission of the Republic of Bulgaria and Romania to the European Union, *OJ* 2005 L 157/29.

[16] Act concerning the Conditions of Accession of the Republic of Bulgaria and Romania and the adjustments to the Treaties on which the European Union is founded, *OJ* 2005 L 157/203.

the Act.[17] Article 36 provides for a general economic safeguard clause for and with regard to Romania, covering any economic sector or the economic situation of a given area. Article 37 contains an internal market safeguard clause, covering all those sectoral policies that involve economic activities with cross-border effects. Article 38 sets out the so-called JHA safeguard clause that covers mutual recognition in the area of criminal law and civil matters. All three clauses have already been stipulated in the 2003 Act on Conditions of Accession[18] (supplementing the 2003 Accession Treaty for the ten countries that joined the EU in 2004).[19] Nonetheless, for the assessment of Romania's and Bulgaria's progress, the Commission set up a special Cooperation and Verification Mechanism based on a number of benchmarks detailed in the September 2006 Report and in the annex to Decision 2006/928/EC:

1. Ensure a more transparent and efficient judicial process, notably by enhancing the capacity and accountability of the Superior Council of Magistracy. Report and monitor the impact of the new civil and penal procedures codes.
2. Establish, as foreseen, an integrity agency with responsibilities for verifying assets, incompatibilities and potential conflicts of interest and for issuing mandatory decisions on the basis of which dissuasive sanctions can be taken.
3. Building on progress already made, continue to conduct professional, non-partisan investigations into allegations of high-level corruption.
4. Take further measures to prevent and fight against corruption, in particular within the local government.[20]

Accordingly, the first benchmark requires Romania to continue its reform of the judicial system. The second calls for the establishment of an independent institution, competent to verify assets, incompatibilities and conflicts of interest in order to avoid high-level corruption. The third benchmark requires Romania to continue to conduct investigations

---

[17] Art. 39 contains another safeguard clause that allowed the Council to decide, on the basis of a Commission recommendation, to postpone the accession of Romania or Bulgaria by one year if certain conditions applied. This clause is now superseded.

[18] Act concerning the Conditions of Accession of the Czech Republic, the Republic of Estonia, the Republic of Cyprus, the Republic of Latvia, the Republic of Lithuania, the Republic of Hungary, the Republic of Malta, the Republic of Poland, the Republic of Slovenia and the Slovak Republic and the adjustments to the Treaties on which the European Union is founded, *OJ* 2003 L 236/33.

[19] Treaty between the Kingdom of Belgium, the Kingdom of Denmark, the Federal Republic of Germany, the Hellenic Republic, the Kingdom of Spain, the French Republic, Ireland, the Italian Republic, the Grand Duchy of Luxembourg, the Kingdom of the Netherlands, the Republic of Austria, the Portuguese Republic, the Republic of Finland, the Kingdom of Sweden, the United Kingdom of Great Britain and Northern Ireland (Member States of the European Union) and the Czech Republic, the Republic of Estonia, the Republic of Cyprus, the Republic of Latvia, the Republic of Lithuania, the Republic of Hungary, the Republic of Malta, the Republic of Poland, the Republic of Slovenia, the Slovak Republic, concerning the accession of the Czech Republic, the Republic of Estonia, the Republic of Cyprus, the Republic of Latvia, the Republic of Lithuania, the Republic of Hungary, the Republic of Malta, the Republic of Poland, the Republic of Slovenia and the Slovak Republic to the European Union, *OJ* 2003 L 236/17.

[20] Commission Decision of 13 December 2006 establishing a mechanism for co-operation and verification of progress in Romania to address specific benchmarks in the areas of judicial reform and the fight against corruption, *OJ* 2006 L 354/57.

into allegations of high-level corruption, the most important "pillar" in the fight against corruption by high public officials. The last benchmark calls for measures to prevent and fight local corruption, which is still very difficult to prevent, detect and punish.

Furthermore, Article 1 of the Decision requires Romania to submit by 31 March of each year, and for the first time, by 31 March 2007, a report to the Commission on the progress made in addressing each of the benchmarks. Moreover, in paragraph 2 of the same Article, the Commission is given the right to organise expert missions to Romania to gather and exchange information on the benchmarks. The Romanian authorities are bound to give the necessary support in such a context. In exchange, the Commission may, at any time, provide technical assistance.

Failure to comply with these criteria may trigger the Commission's decision to invoke one of the safeguard clauses. Since all benchmarks relate to the domain of justice and home affairs, the safeguard clause most likely to be invoked is the one in Article 38 of the Act, the JHA clause. As of July 2009, the Commission has not applied any of the safeguard clauses against Romania.

Before this chapter discusses the difficulties pertaining to each benchmark, emphasis will be placed on the relationship between EU law and Romanian legislation, before and after accession.

## 2.        THE APPLICATION OF THE PRINCIPLE OF SUPREMACY

### 2.1.    The 2003 revision of the Romanian Constitution

Pre-accession revision of laws started well before the first Progress Report in 1998. For instance, as early as 1996, the Romanian Parliament adopted a new Competition Act (several times amended since then) that was drafted in line with Articles 81 and 82 EC.[21] Reform of domestic legislation generally involved all political and economic sectors. The revision trend was later somewhat rationalised on the basis of the 31 negotiation chapters, with the Commission expressing its opinions on Romania's progress in the transposition of *acquis*.

One of the most important steps in that revision trend was the amendment of the Constitution. The seventh Constitution of Romania was adopted by referendum on 13 December 1991. That act was the first constitutional step in marking an end to Romania's communist regime. The Constitution of 1991 was amended in 2003, incorporating the principle of supremacy of EU Founding Treaties and mandatory legislation.[22] Accordingly, the second paragraph of Article 148 of the revised Constitution states that as a result of the accession, the provisions of the Founding Treaties of the European Union,

---

[21] Lege nr.21 din 10 aprilie 1996 – Legea concurenței [Law No. 21 of 10 April 1996 – Competition Act], published in *Monitorul Oficial* [Official Journal] No. 88 of 30 April 1996 and republished in *Monitorul Oficial* [Official Journal] No. 742 of 16 August 2005.

[22] Law No. 429 of 18 September 2003 on reform of the constitution. The law was approved by the national referendum of 18-19 October 2003, and came into force on 29 October 2003. The law was published in the *Monitorul Oficial* [Official Journal] No. 758 of 29 October 2003.

as well as the other mandatory Community acts, shall take precedence over conflicting provisions of national law, in compliance with provisions of the Accession Act. Furthermore, the Article also prescribes the binding nature of those acts that revise the Founding Treaties of the European Union. Paragraph 4 of the same Article designates the Romanian Parliament, the President of Romania, the Romanian Government and the Romanian judicial authority as guarantors of these obligations.

In view of the accession, the revision of the Constitution brought many other far-reaching amendments in the field of human rights, justice, economy and public finance. Concerning human rights, Article 16 of the Constitution, referring to 'Equality in Rights' was modified to guarantee equal opportunities for men and women to occupy public, civil, or military positions or dignities, provided that they have Romanian citizenship and that they reside in Romania. The fourth paragraph of the same Article provides that after Romania's accession to the EU, the Union's citizens who comply with requirements of the domestic electoral law have the right to elect and be elected to local public administration bodies. Regarding elections to the European Parliament, Article 38 of the revised Constitution states that after Romania's accession to the European Union, Romanian citizens shall have the right to elect and be elected to the European Parliament. The right of private property of land was for a long time denied to foreign citizens and stateless persons. The old version of Article 41 stipulated that aliens and stateless persons could not acquire the right of property of land. Nonetheless, with the 2003 revision, this was changed as well. Paragraph 2 of Article 44 now states that foreign citizens and stateless persons can acquire the right to private property of land, but only under the terms resulting from Romania's accession to the European Union and other international treaties Romania is party to, on a mutual basis. The same paragraph provides the right for foreign citizens and stateless persons to acquire the right to private property of land as a result of lawful inheritance.

Considerable changes have been made to the constitutional provisions detailing the powers and structure of the Superior Council of Magistracy. One of the major criticisms on behalf of the EU regarding justice and home affairs was the dependency of that Council on institutions of central administration. The amendments made envisaged remedying that problem by preventing certain members of the Council to vote in matters relating to the disciplinary liability of judges and public prosecutors.[23]

Regarding economy, the 1991 version of the Constitution only stipulated that Romania's economy is a free market economy. The 2003 revisions added in Article 135 that such an economy is based on the principles of free enterprise and competition, an addition that was necessary in view of the EU negotiations on Chapter 6 (competition policy). Also related to economy, paragraph 2, point (g) of the same Article provides

---

[23] Para. 2 of Art. 134 of the revised Constitution states that the Superior Council of Magistracy 'shall perform the role of a court of law, by means of its sections, as regards the disciplinary liability of judges and public prosecutors, based on the procedures set up by its organic law.' It is also stated that in such cases, three members of the Superior Council of Magistracy (the Minister of Justice, the President of the High Court of Cassation and Justice, and the general Public Prosecutor of the Public Prosecutor's Office attached to the High Court of Cassation and Justice) are not entitled to vote.

that the Romanian state must secure the implementation of regional development policies in compliance with the objectives of the European Union.

The 2003 revision also took into consideration the prospects of changing the national currency. Accordingly, paragraph 2 of Article 137 affirms that under the circumstances of Romania's accession to the EU, the circulation and replacement of the Leu by the Euro may be acknowledged by means of an organic law.

According to Duculescu and Adam, the constitutional reform has not entirely resolved the issues related to Romania's membership in the EU because, in some cases, the new constitutional provisions still require, in the short term, adoption of subsequent organic laws and other acts to transpose Community law. According to these authors, a reexamination of certain problems will be necessary in a second phase of the constitutional reform.[24] As a whole, the first revision phase engraved the principle of supremacy of EU law into Romanian legislation (Art. 148 para. 2) and brought a number of other amendments to ensure compliance with Community legislation. In the next section, the application of the principle of supremacy by the Romanian judiciary will be addressed.

## 2.2.    The Romanian judiciary and the principle of supremacy

### 2.2.1.    Pre-accession interpretation

Even before accession, explicit or implicit references to the supremacy of EU law and principles as well as to ECJ jurisprudence were made. Some lower courts explained modification of domestic law as a result of the 'harmonization of Romanian legislation with that of the European Union' or made reference to the Europe Agreement, by which Romania had assumed a number of obligations such as the 'legislative harmonization for ensuring the compatibility of national legislation with the acquis communitaire.'[25] The Romanian High Court of Cassation and Justice employed the same arguments by stating that interpretation of domestic laws has to be in concordance with Community legislation.[26]

A few judgments also made specific reference to EC directives or regulations. For instance, in Decision 2147/2003, the High Court reiterated the arguments of the lower court, showing that in the appealed judgment, specific reference was made to Council Directive 93/22/EEC on investment services in the securities field.[27] In another of its

---

[24] V. Duculescu and R. Adam, 'Romania', in A.E. Kellerman, et al., eds., *The Impact of EU Accession on the Legal Orders of New EU Member States and (Pre-)Candidate Countries* (The Hague, T.M.C. Asser Press 2006) pp. 113-141, at pp. 117-118.

[25] High Court of Cassation and Justice – Decision No. 2147 of 3 June 2003, quoting the lower court's judgment that formed the object of appeal. A similar quote of a lower court's judgment is made in Decision No. 1202 of 25 March 2003 regarding the compliance of domestic acts with *acquis communitaire*.

[26] See, for instance, Decision No. 2172 of 18 March 2005, Decision No. 4788 of 3 June 2005 and Decision No. 4380 of 4 May 2006 of the High Court of Cassation and Justice.

[27] Council Directive 93/22/EEC of 10 May 1993 on investment services in the securities field, *OJ* 1993 L 141/22. This Directive was repealed by Directive 2004/39/EC of the European Parliament and of the Council of 21 April 2004 on markets in financial instruments amending Council Directives 85/611/

decisions, the High Court quoted the appealed judgment of the lower court in which the challenged Governmental Decision was justified as transposing Council Directive 93/16/EEC[28] on the free movement of doctors and mutual recognition of their qualifications.[29]

## 2.2.2. The application of the supremacy principle after accession

Although the prevalence of Community law was often implicitly or explicitly stated before accession, the comprehensive interpretation and application of the principle of supremacy by the Romanian judiciary started in the first half of 2007. The High Court of Cassation and Justice emphasised several times the pre-eminence of EU law, mostly in its decisions regarding freedom of movement of Romanian citizens to other EU Member States.

These cases have as their object requests from the Romanian Ministry of Administration and Interior, addressed to the competent courts, to restrict the free movement of Romanian citizens on the territory of certain Member States for three years, on the basis of Articles 38-39 of Law 248/2005.[30] After the trial and appeal phase had passed, the cases ended up before the High Court as the highest appeal authority. In most of these cases, the question was raised whether restriction of free movement by a domestic act was compatible with Community legislation.

For instance, in Decision No. 4205 of 24 May 2007, the Court emphasised that Community law enjoys direct applicability, and domestic courts have to take that in consideration both at the trial phase and the appeal phase of the particular case. What is of special importance in this decision is the mentioning of the judgments of two lower courts (Dâmbovița Tribunal and Ploiesti Court of Appeal), both of which recognised the principle of supremacy of EC law. In its judgment, the Dâmbovița Tribunal held that after Romania's accession to the EU, the Community legal order must be recognised as having direct effect and enjoying supremacy over the domestic legal

---

EEC and 93/6/EEC and Directive 2000/12/EC of the European Parliament and of the Council and repealing Council Directive 93/22/EEC, *OJ* 2004 L 145/1.

[28] Council Directive 93/16/EEC of 5 April 1993 to facilitate the free movement of doctors and the mutual recognition of their diplomas, certificates and other evidence of formal qualifications, *OJ* 1993 L 165/1.

[29] High Court of Cassation and Justice – Decision No. 1110 of 4 April 2006.

[30] Legea 248/2005 privind regimul liberei circulatii a cetatenilor romani in strainatate [Law No. 248/2005 on the conditions for the free movement of Romanian citizens abroad], published in *Monitorul Oficial* [Official Journal], Part I No. 682 of 29 July 2005. Art. 38 of Law 248/2005 provides that the free movement abroad of a Romanian citizen can be restricted for up to three years, if that person has been returned to Romania on the basis of a readmission accord concluded between the Romanian Government and the other state, or if the activities undertaken or about to be undertaken by that person are capable of gravely endangering the interests of Romania or the bilateral relations between Romania and the other state. Art. 39 of the same law describes the procedure of imposing such a restriction on a Romanian citizen. Para. 1 of Art. 39 specifies that the measure is imposed by the Romanian Ministry of Administration and Interior – General Directorate for Passports, in case of readmitted persons, and by the Bucharest Tribunal, on the basis of a request filed by competent public institution, in case of persons whose activities endanger the interests of Romania. In the first case, the restriction must be validated by the competent court (para. 2 of Art. 39). The subsequent paragraphs describe the procedure for appeal against such a measure.

order. The Tribunal also emphasised that Article 18 EC, guaranteeing the freedom of movement of persons throughout the EU, creates rights that can be directly invoked by individuals before domestic courts.[31]

Similarly, in Decision No. 4206 of 24 May 2007, the High Court held that according to paragraphs 2 and 4 of Article 148 of the Romanian Constitution, as a result of Romania's accession to the EU, the provisions of the Founding Treaties and the other binding Community law acts have priority over contradictory domestic laws and that judicial authorities guarantee the fulfilment of the obligations stemming from the Accession Act. Consequently, the Court stated that national courts have the duty to interpret domestic law in the light of Community legislation, which, as shown, enjoys priority.[32]

Nevertheless, Article 18 EC was not interpreted as completely annulling Law 248/2005 governing freedom of movement of Romanian citizens. In Decision No. 2409 of 24 May 2007, the High Court showed that EU legislation does not render freedom of movement an absolute right, and that, according to Article 27 of Directive 2004/38/EC, freedom of movement and residence of Union citizens and their family members can be restricted, irrespective of nationality, on grounds of public policy, public security or public health.[33] The Court also held that, as long as the restrictions prescribed by Law 248/2005 are interpreted in the light of Article 27 of the Directive, the measures taken may be legal.[34]

A comprehensive decision, containing a short description of the freedom of movement and the consequences of Romania's accession to the EU for the internal legal order, was delivered by the High Court on 14 June 2007. In addition to the assertions detailed above, the Court also specified that a Romanian judge cannot refuse to apply domestic law for the sole reason that Community rules may be applicable. It is compulsory for domestic courts to identify the potential conflict hypotheses and to opt for either the domestic solution, compatible with EU law, or the directly applicable Community provisions, automatically integrated or transposed in national legislation.[35]

It thus becomes clear that the first major issue raising questions regarding the supremacy of EC law was the restriction of free movement of Romanian citizens. This matter also resulted in the first preliminary ruling request referred by a Romanian court to the European Court of Justice.

---

[31] High Court of Cassation and Justice – Decision No. 4205 of 24 May 2007.

[32] High Court of Cassation and Justice – Decision No. 4206 of 24 May 2007.

[33] Directive 2004/38/EC of the European Parliament and of the Council of 29 April 2004 on the right of citizens of the Union and their family members to move and reside freely within the territory of the Member States amending Regulation (EEC) No 1612/68 and repealing Directives 64/221/EEC, 68/360/EEC, 72/194/EEC, 73/148/EEC, 75/34/EEC, 75/35/EEC, 90/364/EEC, 90/365/EEC and 93/96/EEC, *OJ* 2004 L 158/77.

[34] High Court of Cassation and Justice – Decision No. 4209 of 24 May 2007.

[35] High Court of Cassation and Justice – Decision No. 4887 of 14 June 2007.

## 2.2.3. *Supremacy, free movement and reference for preliminary ruling*

Romania's first preliminary ruling reference was lodged on 24 January 2007, and, as said above, it concerned two provisions of Law 248/2005 on the free movement of persons (the *Jipa* case).[36] The question arose in connection with an order of the Ministry of Administration and Interior to restrict the free movement of a Romanian citizen (Mr. Jipa) on the territory of certain Member States for three years. According to Article 39 of Law 248/2005, such an order, after being issued by the Ministry, must be validated by a competent court. The Dâmbovița Tribunal, having to deliver a validating decision in the case, considered that in light of Romania's accession to the EU, the provisions of Law 248/2005 were not as clear and justifiable as before. Hence, the Tribunal lodged a reference for a preliminary ruling to the European Court of Justice, inquiring whether Article 18 EC must be interpreted as meaning that the relevant provisions of Law 248/2005 place obstacles in the way of the free movement of individuals. Furthermore, the reference also inquired whether a Member State may place a limitation on citizens' right of freedom of movement within the territory of another Member State. The last part of the reference dealt with Article 27 of Directive 2004/38/EEC, namely, with the restriction of grounds of "public policy" and "public security",[37] and whether the concept of "illegal residence" used in Romanian legislation falls within these terms so that a restriction on the freedom of movement of a citizen may be imposed, without that person's personal conduct being examined.

Approximately two months after the lodging, on 3 April 2007, the President of the Court delivered an order in which it rejected a request to handle the reference pursuant to the accelerated procedure. On 14 February 2008, the Advocate General delivered an opinion on the case. Accordingly, in the absence of valid justification, Article 18(1) EC precludes national legislation from placing restrictions on the right of Union citizens to leave their Member State of origin in order to travel to another Member State. Further, the Advocate General opined that the exercise of the right granted by Article 18(1) EC to leave one's own Member State to travel to another Member State may pose a genuine and sufficiently serious threat to the requirements of public policy affecting one of the fundamental interests of society. Nevertheless, the Member State of origin may not impose, on grounds of "public policy" or "public security" as provided by Article 27 of Directive 2004/38/EEC, restrictions on the freedom of movement of that person, unless there is a specific finding by that Member State justifying such restriction, adopted in compliance with the principle of proportionality and based exclusively on the personal conduct of the individual concerned.[38]

---

[36] ECJ, Case C-33/07 *Ministerul Administrației și Internelor – Direcția Generală de Pașapoarte București v. Gheorghe Jipa* [2008] *ECR* I-5157.

[37] Art. 27(1) of the Directive states: 'Subject to the provisions of this Chapter, Member States may restrict the freedom of movement and residence of Union citizens and their family members, irrespective of nationality, on grounds of public policy, public security or public health. These grounds shall not be invoked to serve economic ends.'

[38] Opinion of Advocate General Mazák delivered on 14 February 2008, Case C-33/07, *Ministerul Administrației și Internelor – Direcția Generală de Pașapoarte București v. Gheorghe Jipa,* Reference for a preliminary ruling from the Tribunalul Dâmbovița, paras. 38, 45 and 48.

The judgment in the *Jipa* case was rendered in July 2008. The ECJ held that, as a Romanian national, Mr. Jipa enjoyed the status of a citizen of the EU, and that the right of freedom of movement included both the right for citizens of the Union to enter a Member State other than the one of origin and the right to leave the state of origin. The ECJ noted that the right of free movement could be limited by other provisions of the Treaty and secondary legislation. Regarding the grounds of "public policy" or "public security", the ECJ held that Member States were essentially allowed to determine the relevant requirements, but such requirements had to be interpreted strictly. Accordingly, the scope of such restrictions could not be determined unilaterally by each Member State without any control by the Community institutions. The ECJ stated that such a restrictive measure 'cannot be based exclusively on reasons advanced by another Member State to justify a decision to remove a Community national from the territory of the latter State' (para. 25). Such reasons can, nevertheless, be taken into account in the context of the assessment which the competent national authorities undertake for the purpose of adopting the measure restricting freedom of movement. In any case, the personal conduct of the person whose freedom of movement is restricted must constitute 'a genuine, present and sufficiently serious threat to one of the fundamental interests of society' (para. 23).

Accordingly, the ECJ held in paragraph 26:

> '[I]n a situation such as that in the main proceedings, the fact that a citizen of the Union has been subject to a measure repatriating him from the territory of another Member State, where he was residing illegally, may be taken into account by his Member State of origin for the purpose of restricting that citizen's right of free movement only to the extent that his personal conduct constitutes a genuine, present and sufficiently serious threat to one of the fundamental interests of society.'

According to the ECJ, the situation in the *Jipa* case did not, however, seem to meet these requirements. Nevertheless, the Court asserted that it was up to the national court to make the necessary findings, on the basis of the matters of fact and law justifying, in the main proceedings, the request of the Minister for a restriction on Mr. Jipa's right to leave Romania (para. 28).

## 3.    THE SPECIAL ASPECTS OF ROMANIA'S ACCESSION

The closest-ever monitoring mechanism established to assess Romania's progress focuses on two major aspects: the judicial reform (the first benchmark) and the fight against corruption (the remaining three benchmarks). In October 2007, the Romanian Government published an Action Plan[39] to meet the requirements of the June 2007 report and to anticipate the findings of the February 2008 interim report. In the follow-

---

[39] Action Plan for Meeting the Benchmarks Established within the Co-operation and Verification Mechanism (hereafter Action Plan), October 2007.

ing sections, attention will be given to the progress of the judiciary reform and the fight against corruption, as well to the merits of the Action Plan.

## 3.1.    The need for a transparent and efficient judicial process

Although the Romanian judiciary has largely recognised the principle of supremacy and has vowed for the application of EU law on the basis of that principle, many serious concerns remain as to the capacity of the courts to cope with the more practical challenges of EU integration.

This capacity does not only concern administrative matters, but it also refers to the overall independence and impartiality of the Romanian judiciary system. The first of the four benchmarks identified by the Commission in 2006 concerns this problem. By requiring Romania to ensure 'a more transparent, and efficient judicial process notably by enhancing the capacity and accountability of the Superior Council of Magistracy', the Commission envisaged the completion of the long reform process the judiciary went through in the last decade.

### 3.1.1.    *Romanian court system*

Before this chapter highlights the major steps of the reform, a succinct description of the Romanian court system is necessary. Romania has a civil law system, based on the French model. There are four court levels in Romania: Local Courts [judecătorie], county Tribunals [tribunal], Courts of Appeal [curte de apel] and, at the highest level, the High Court of Cassation and Justice [Înalta Curte de Casație și Justiție]. Each of these courts has a prosecutor's office attached to it. The Constitutional Court of Romania examines laws before their promulgation by the President and laws constitutionally challenged before lower courts.

### 3.1.2.    *The long reform process of the judiciary system*

As early as 1998, the Commission observed the many shortcomings of the Romanian judiciary system. In its 1998 Progress Report, the Commission stated that 'judicial proceedings can take from 6 months to several years, particularly in commercial matters.' It further noted that:

> 'judicial decisions need to be more effectively enforced. Administrative weaknesses such as the lack of accessible case-studies and court verdicts affect the equitable application of law. Further efforts are also needed to improve the status and remuneration of judges and prosecutors, to attract and retain more qualified staff and to fill the current judicial vacancies. [...] These measures would help reinforce the independence of the judicial system and help safeguard it more effectively against possible corruption.'[40]

---

[40] Regular Report from the Commission on Romania's Progress towards Accession, 4 November 1998, (hereafter 1998 Report), p. 9.

Six years later, in 2004, the Commission saluted the improvements achieved. Accordingly, the 2004 Report concluded that the Romanian justice system underwent a number of structural changes. An order issued by the Minister of Justice in June 2004 required all courts of appeal to publish their annual jurisprudence bulletins, which was intended to create a more consistent application of the law across Romania. In June 2004, the Laws on the Superior Council of the Magistracy, on the Organisation of the Judiciary and on the Statute of Magistrates were adopted, i.e., the three-law package.[41]

One of the merits of the Law on the Organisation of the Judiciary was that it introduced new types of specialised courts next to the traditional civil, criminal, commercial, administrative and fiscal sections. Accordingly, specialised sections on first instance level (if needed) and on the tribunal and court of appeal levels have been created for cases involving minors and family disputes, labour disputes and social insurance, as well as, depending on the nature and number of cases, maritime and inland waterways sections or sections for other matters. Nevertheless, the Report also noted one of the major concerns regarding the judiciary, namely, the fact that an official survey found that a majority of judges had come under political pressure while exercising their official duties.[42]

A new package of 17 legal acts concerning reform in the fields of property and justice was put together in 2005. The reform brought changes to provisions regarding the careers of judges and prosecutors, to situations leading to the disciplinary liability and, *inter alia*, to the organisation of open competitions for appointment for top positions in the judiciary, as required by pre-accession standards. The reform package underwent several substantial amendments as a result of unconstitutionality rulings before it was adopted by the Parliament.[43]

In September 2006, the Commission acknowledged the achievements of the package reforms and outlined the steps that remained to be taken. It noted that progress continued in the reform of the justice system, especially in strengthening its administrative capacity, but that further efforts were needed to ensure a more consistent interpretation and application of the law in order to create legal certainty.

The June 2007 Report had an overall positive conclusion regarding the progress of the judicial reform. It reiterated that further efforts were needed to establish a coherent jurisprudence, to complete the staffing shortages and organisational reforms of the judicial systems. Moreover, it called for greater focus on the reform of the Civil Procedure Code and the Criminal Procedure Code, aimed at simplifying the judicial process, reducing the length of the procedures and the number of appeal procedures for certain categories of cases.

---

[41] Regular Report from the Commission on Romania's Progress towards Accession, 6 October 2004, (hereafter 2004 Report), p. 19. The three-law package consists of the Law on the Supreme Council of Magistrates (317/2004), the Law on the Statutes of Magistrates (303/2004) and the Law on the Judiciary (304/2004). All three laws have been several times amended since then.

[42] 2004 Report, p. 20.

[43] For details on the provisions found unconstitutional by the Constitutional Court and on the subsequent parliamentary amendments, see Duculescu and Adam, *loc. cit.* n. 24, at pp. 126-127.

The October 2007 Action Plan of the Romanian Government outlined an ambitious schedule to meet these requirements. The plan set the deadline for finalising the drafts of both codes for January 2008.[44] Moreover, it vowed to establish by December 2008 the obligation for all courts to permanently complete and update their web portals by publishing their jurisprudence. These updates would take place on on-going basis for the High Court of Cassation and Justice and twice per year for lower courts.[45] Regarding the necessary staffing of courts (judges and prosecutors), the plan promised that a minimum of 180 judge and prosecutor vacancies would be filled in 2008, and a minimum of 176 in 2009.[46]

The February 2008 Report voiced one major concern in respect to these engagements. It noted that the fast-paced *ad hoc* procedure of filling existing court vacancies was based only on interviews and previous work experience, without verification of the qualifications of the new magistrate and without ensuring training for the new magistrate.[47]

Most of these difficulties were still noted in the subsequent reports. The July 2009 Report saluted the adoption of the new Civil Code and Criminal Code but expressed concerns about the delays in the adoption of the Civil and Criminal Procedure Codes, necessary for the entry into force of the substantive codes.[48]

Staffing constraints of the judiciary were observed in the reports of July 2008, February 2009 and July 2009.[49] The February 2009 Report especially displayed a very sombre tone in relation to the capacity problems of the Romanian judiciary, and it pointed out that urgent measures were needed for its redress.[50]

Inconsistencies in jurisprudence were lamented in all reports. The July 2008 Report emphasised that even the High Court of Cassation and Justice failed to take the lead in unifying jurisprudence, by delivering inconsistent decisions regarding cases of high-level corruption.[51] The February 2009 Report reiterated the same concerns.[52] A few months later, the July 2009 Report acknowledged the positive impact of numerous decisions on appeals relating to the uniform interpretation and application of the law

---

[44] Action Plan, p. 11.

[45] Action Plan, p. 14.

[46] Action Plan, p. 22.

[47] Interim Report from the Commission to the European Parliament and the Council on Progress in Romania under the Co-operation and Verification Mechanism, 4 February 2008 (hereafter February 2008 Report), p. 3.

[48] Report from the Commission to the European Parliament and the Council, on Progress in Romania under the Co-Operation and Verification Mechanism, 22 July 2009 (hereafter July 2009 Report), p. 3.

[49] Report from the Commission to the European Parliament and the Council, on Progress in Romania under the Co-Operation and Verification Mechanism, 23 July 2008 (hereafter July 2008 Report); Report from the Commission to the European Parliament and the Council, on Progress in Romania under the Co-Operation and Verification Mechanism, 12 February 2009 (hereafter February 2009 Report).

[50] February 2009 Report, p. 4.

[51] July 2008 Report, p. 4.

[52] February 2009 Report, p. 4.

across the court system. At the same time, it voiced concerns over the 'cumbersome and questionable procedure' in accepting a certain interpretation of the law.[53]

The independence of the judiciary and the transparency of the judicial process have, of course, many implications for the accurate application and interpretation of EU law, for the enforcement of judicial decisions with domestic or international relevance and for the safe and secure execution of sentences of criminal courts. An unfortunate example of the weaknesses of the Romanian criminal justice system was the disappearance and subsequent departure from the country in July 2006 of defendant Omar Hayssam, accused of masterminding the kidnapping of three Romanian journalists in Iraq in 2005. Although Hayssam was later sentenced *in absentia* to 20 years imprisonment, the fact that his departure triggered the resignation of the General Prosecutor of Romania, together with the heads of the Romanian Intelligence Service, the Foreign Intelligence Service and the Directorate General for Intelligence and Internal Protection, showed the European Commission the lacunas of the judiciary system.

### 3.1.3.  *The principle of mutual recognition in civil and criminal matters*

A specifically important matter in relation to the remaining shortcomings of the judiciary system refers to the application of the principle of mutual recognition in civil and criminal matters. According to Article 38 of the Act on Conditions of Accession, the JHA safeguard clause can be invoked in situations where serious shortcomings or imminent risks appear in the transposition, implementation or application of the framework decisions or any other relevant commitments, instruments of co-operation and decisions relating to mutual recognition in civil and criminal matters.

The requirement to comply with the principle of mutual recognition is very closely linked with the necessity of Romania to execute European Arrest Warrants.[54]

### 3.1.3.1.  Romanian legislation regarding the European Arrest Warrant

Law No. 302/2004 on international judicial co-operation in criminal matters was adopted on 28 June 2004 and was amended and supplemented in 2006 and 2008.[55] Title III of Law 302/2004 specifically refers to the European Arrest Warrant. Article 77 defines the European Arrest Warrant as a judicial decision issued by the competent judicial authority of a Member State of the European Union, with a view to the arrest and surrender to another Member State of a requested person, for the purposes of conducting a criminal investigation or prosecution or executing a custodial sentence or

---

[53] Particularly, the procedure requires two-thirds of the 120 judges of the High Court having to participate in the decisions and agree to the reasoning (after having taken the decision); procedure, which – according to the Commission – causes delays and sometimes leads to unclear statements of reasons. July 2009 Report, p. 4.

[54] Council Framework Decision 2002/584/JHA of 13 June 2002 on the European arrest warrant and the surrender procedures between member states, *OJ* 2002 L 190/1.

[55] Law 302/2004 was published in *Monitorul Oficial* [Official Journal] No. 594 of 1 July 2004. The law was amended and supplemented by Law No. 224/2006 and one of its articles was abrogated by Government Emergency Ordinance No. 103/2006. The law was substantially amended by Law 222/2008.

detention order. The same paragraph identifies mutual recognition and confidence as main principles governing the execution of European Arrest Warrants. The drafting and phrasing of Title III closely follows the wording of the aforementioned Framework Decision.

The first Romanian citizen surrendered on the basis of a European Arrest Warrant was a 20-year-old woman suspected of being an accomplice to the murder of a Dutch citizen. The warrant was issued by a Dutch court in December 2006, and the suspect was handed over to officers of the International Center for Police Cooperation – National Interpol Bureau on 9 February 2007.[56]

### 3.1.3.2. The European Arrest Warrant and Romanian courts

The issuing of European Arrest Warrants has spurred a cascade of legal actions before both the Romanian Constitutional Court and the Romanian High Court of Cassation and Justice. In the following paragraphs, some of the most frequently raised issues will be discussed.

Legal actions before the Constitutional Court have taken the form of "unconstitutionality exceptions" and have characterised more than one Article of Law 302/2004 as breaching the Romanian Constitution. For instance, in Case No. 476/2007, the applicant claimed that Article 89 of Law 302/2004 is unconstitutional because, *inter alia*, it violates the constitutional provision guaranteeing the independence of the judiciary.[57] According to Article 89, upon the arrest of the requested person, the Romanian court will inform him or her of the existence of a European Arrest Warrant against him/her, its contents, the possibility for him/her to consent to being surrendered to the issuing Member State, as well as his/her procedural rights. Furthermore, the court will order the arrest of the requested person by means of a reasoned conclusion. In Case No. 476/2007, it was alleged that on the basis of such provisions, the Romanian magistrate plays a purely formal role because of the lack of any analysis and interpretation of the substantive content of the warrant. In response, the Court rejected the non-constitutionality exception and held that according to Law 302/2004, the Romanian judge only has to verify whether the procedural conditions for issuing the warrant have been met and cannot conclude on the legitimacy of the criminal prosecution or the execution of a custodial sentence or detention order. Otherwise, the principle of mutual recognition of criminal decisions would be violated. The Court also stated that Article 89 takes further the provisions of Law 302/2004 that secure the pre-eminence of international law concerning international judicial co-operation.[58]

---

[56] 'Primul cetatean roman predat in baza Mandatului European de Arestare' [First Romanian Citizen Surrendered on the Basis of a European Arrest Warrant], 12 February 2007, *EurActiv Press*, last accessed on 20 January 2008: http://www.euractiv.ro/uniunea-europeana/articles%7CdisplayArticle/articleID_9404/Primul-cetatean-roman-predat-in-baza-Mandatului-European-de-Arestare.html.

[57] Art. 124 para. 2 of the Romanian Constitution states that 'justice shall be one, impartial, and equal for all.'

[58] Constitutional Court Decision No. 400 of 24 April 2007 in Case No. 476/2007, published in *Monitorul Oficial* [Official Journal] No. 296 of 4 May 2007.

In another case before the Constitutional Court, the provisions of Article 79 of Law 302/2004 were challenged as unconstitutional. The applicant in Case No. 449/2007 claimed that Article 79, paragraph 1, letter (c) does not allow any inquiry as to the grounds on which provisional arrest has been ordered by the issuing authority and does not maintain that the warrant should be issued by a judge. In such way, the requested person does not have the right to be heard, is not considered a suspect and does not know the reasoning behind the arrest warrant. Accordingly, the constitutional right to defence and to free access to justice is being denied.[59] The Court responded to these claims by reiterating the pre-eminence of the principle of mutual recognition and by emphasising that in this case, the Romanian court is only the "executing judicial authority". Therefore, it does not have the right to conclude on the legitimacy of the grounds of the warrant. The Court added that Law 302/2004 is, in fact, implementing Framework Decision 2002/584/JHA, mentioned above, which is a specific measure implementing the principle of mutual recognition.[60]

The Romanian High Court of Cassation and Justice rendered judgments in line with the Constitutional Court's reasoning. In Decision No. 2862 of 28 May 2007, the High Court held that 'a European Arrest Warrant issued by the competent judicial authority of a European Union Member State is executed by the Romanian court on the basis of mutual recognition and confidence.'[61]

Apart from decisions regarding the pre-eminence of international law and the principle of mutual recognition, the High Court also decided about cases involving more technical details of executing European Arrest Warrants. For instance, in Decision No. 2492 of 8 May 2007, the High Court granted the appeal to the applicant on the basis of Article 87, paragraph 2 of Law 302/2004. Accordingly, a decision on the execution of a European Arrest Warrant, in which the executing court failed to request, in the case of the surrendered person receiving a penalty depriving him or her of freedom, that he or she be transferred to Romania to serve the penalty, may be deemed illegal.[62]

Furthermore, in Decision No. 4045 of 30 August 2007, the High Court emphasised that the objection of the requested person to surrender may be based only on an error regarding his or her identity or on the existence of grounds for non-execution of a European Arrest Warrant, as provided in Article 90 paragraph 6 of Law 302/2004. In this case, the applicant objected to his surrender on the basis that there was not enough information in the warrant regarding the crime committed and the characteristics of the suspect. The Court held that the discussion of such an objection would go against the well-established principle of mutual recognition, and, as long as the objection does not refer to an error of identity or to specific shortcomings in the execution of the mandate, the executing judicial authority has no reason to take into consideration the opposition.[63]

---

[59] Art. 24 of the Romanian Constitution guarantees everyone's right to defence and Art. 21 states that 'every person is entitled to bring cases before the courts for the defence of his legitimate rights, liberties and interests.'

[60] Constitutional Court Decision No. 419 of 3 May 2007 in Case No. 449/2007, published in *Monitorul Oficial* [Official Journal] No. 330 of 16 May 2007.

[61] High Court of Cassation and Justice – Decision No. 2862 of 28 May 2007.

[62] High Court of Cassation and Justice – Decision No. 2492 of 8 May 2007.

[63] High Court of Cassation and Justice – Decision No. 4045 of 30 August 2007.

## 3.2.    The fight against corruption

The remaining three benchmarks outline the necessary measures to be taken in order to establish an integrity agency (benchmark 2), to continue to conduct investigations into allegations of high-level corruption (benchmark 3) and to take further measures to prevent and fight against local corruption (benchmark 4).

### 3.2.1.    *The National Integrity Agency*

The second benchmark required the establishment of the National Integrity Agency designed to verify assets, incompatibilities and potential conflicts of interest of a large number of higher public and elected officials. Further, the Agency was envisaged to be able to issue mandatory decisions on the basis of which dissuasive sanctions could be taken. Law No. 144/2007 for the establishment, organisation and functioning of the National Integrity Agency (ANI) entered into force in May 2007.

Upon the adoption of the law by the Romanian Parliament, Transparency International (TI-Romania) issued a press release in which it appreciated that the final form of the adopted act responded to the key principles of anti-corruption public policy and could be correctly and efficiently implemented through the National Integrity Agency. TI-Romania also expressed its hope that the adoption of the act did not simply represent a political trophy for the central administration but a real engagement in preventing and combating corruption. In view of the continuing possibility of activation of the safeguard clause, TI drew attention to the fact that the adoption of the National Integrity Agency did not represent a complete fulfilment of the commitment assumed, and it encouraged the authorities in Bucharest to ensure that the Agency was effectively established with respect for the highest standards.[64]

The June 2007 Report concluded that substantial progress had been achieved regarding the second benchmark, saluting this way the entry into force of the law establishing the National Integrity Agency. According to the report, the Agency was expected to be operational by October 2007.[65]

The first competition for filling the vacancy of President of ANI was organised in September and October 2007. Since none of the registered candidates reached the minimum threshold of required points, it was decided that a new competition was to be organised in March 2008. According to a statement made by National Integrity Council member Mihai Șaptefrați, 'with some luck, by 1 April, All Fools' Day, ANI will have a new president.'[66]

---

[64]  Transparency International – Romania, National Report on Corruption, 2007, p. 45.

[65]  Report from the Commission to the European Parliament and the Council on Romania's progress on accompanying measures following Accession, 27 June 2007 (hereafter June 2007 Report), p. 12.

[66]  'Agenþia Naţională de Integritate ar putea avea un sef nou începând cu 1 aprilie' [The National Integrity Agency may have a new president by 1 April 2007], *Mediafax*, Bucharest, 14 January 2008. The National Integrity Council is a separate entity, autonomous and representative, with non-permanent activity that recommends, before the Romanian President, candidates for the Presidency and Vice-Presidency of the National Integrity Agency. Beside the Council, there is also a National Integrity Centre, an independent public advisory body on corruption, run in co-operation with civil society.

The significant delays in setting up a functioning ANI were noted in the February 2008 report, but no critical assessment was made. The Agency finally became functional in the second half of 2008, and, although the Commission considered that it was too early to assess its impact, all subsequent reports acknowledged the incipient positive bearing of the new body.[67]

### 3.2.2. Political willingness to fight corruption

The last two benchmarks refer to the fight against corruption. The third relates to high-level corruption, whereas the fourth to local corruption.

Romanian political analyst Alina Mungiu-Pippidi saw corruption as occasioned by the survival of a communist-era organisation and administration combined with the absence of any institutions of accountability. In her view, local corruption in Romania is the means by which the best-networked and the well-off manage to obtain what would be considered normal treatment elsewhere. Since accountability is missing, 'bribes are a supplementary tax paid to obtain normal public service, and, as such, bribery is a stark indicator of the lack of institutional performance.' Moreover, she observed an essential contradiction between the idea of an impartial, impersonal and fair (modern) bureaucracy and the communist power structure, which bred status groups such as the "nomenklatura",[68] enjoying political and economical monopolies. Status groups hinder the development of an open society and a free market because they create unpredictable patterns of distributing social and legal rights and allow success only for those who are acquainted with the 'patterns of authority generating the unwritten rules of the game.'[69]

Inheriting corruption as an essential element of the communist power structure, Romania still faces serious problems in fighting against it. In its 1997 Opinion on Romania's Application for Membership, the Commission noted that there was much to be done to root out corruption.[70] The 1998 Progress Report reiterated that and warned that the legal basis for the fight against corruption remained incomplete, and that there was a need for a clear definition of corruption in the Romanian Criminal Code.[71] Six years later, the prospects had not improved much. In its 2004 Report, the Commission concluded that surveys and assessments conducted by national and international organisations confirmed that corruption remained a serious and widespread problem in Romania, which affected almost all aspects of society. The Commission deplored the fact that there was no reduction in perceived levels of corruption, and the number of

---

[67] July 2008 Report, p. 5; February 2009 Report, p. 5; July 2009 Report, p. 3.

[68] "Nomenklatura" is a Russian word derived from the Latin *nomenclatura* (list of names) that denoted the select group, or class of people who held high-level positions within the bureaucracy of the Soviet Union and Eastern-European Communist states. This system was controlled by the national Communist Parties and the members of the "nomenklatura" were all members of the Communist Party.

[69] A. Mungiu-Pippidi, 'Culture of Corruption or Accountability Deficit?', 11/12 *East European Constitutional Review* (Fall 2002/Winter 2003) pp. 80-85, at pp. 81-82.

[70] 1997 Commission Opinion, p. 18.

[71] 1998 Report, p. 10.

successful prosecutions remained low, particularly for high-level corruption.[72] The September 2006 Report emphasised the need for clear political willingness of all political actors to demonstrate the sustainability and irreversibility of the positive progress in the fight against corruption, hinting this way at the lack of commitment in wiping out the remnants of the "nomenklatura" system embedded in Romanian society.[73] The September 2006 Report acknowledged some improvements in the fight against corruption. For instance, the Commission appreciated the more rigorous implementation of the anti-corruption laws and the increase in quantity and quality of serious non-partisan investigations into allegations of high-level corruption. Nonetheless, the overall progress registered was seen as lagging behind pre-accession expectations.

In its June 2007 Report, the Commission noted that progress in the judicial treatment of high-level corruption was still insufficient regarding the third benchmark, although some progress in the further prevention and fight against local corruption had been achieved regarding the fourth benchmark. The same assessment was made by the subsequent reports. The February 2009 Report declared that the pace of progress in dealing with such issues has not been maintained.[74] The July 2009 Report was somewhat more optimistic in its analysis, but it still emphasised that the kind of 'deep seated changes' that are needed 'can only come from within Romanian society.'[75]

### 3.2.2.1. Fighting high-level corruption: the National Anti-Corruption Directorate

According to the TI Global Corruption Barometer, in 2007, the Romanian population perceived political parties, the Parliament, the judiciary, medical services and police as the most corrupt with scores ranging from 3.9 to 3.7 (where 0 is "highly clean" and 5 is "highly corrupt").[76] Against this background, the Commission initiated the creation of a strong, independent system of organisations to tackle high-level corruption. The most important institution that "centralises" the fight against high-level corruption is the National Anti-Corruption Directorate (DNA).[77]

The precursor of DNA was the National Anticorruption Prosecutor's Office, set up in September 2002 as an independent prosecutor's office within the Public Ministry. As a result of substantial amendments in 2006, the Office was transformed into a structure with legal personality functioning within the Prosecutor's Office attached to the

---

[72] 2004 Report, p. 21.

[73] Communication from the Commission – Monitoring report on the state of preparedness for EU membership of Bulgaria and Romania, 26 September 2006 (hereafter September 2006 Report), p. 35.

[74] February 2009 Report, p. 2.

[75] July 2009 Report, p. 6.

[76] Transparency International, Global Corruption Barometer 2007 – The relevant survey results for Romania: http://www.transparency.org.ro/politici_si_studii/indici/bgc/2007/GCBsurveyRomania.pdf. The same survey showed relatively increasing scores in perceiving corruption in 2009, with the Parliament and political parties scoring 4.3 (where 1 was 'not at all corrupt' and 5 was 'highly corrupt'). Global Corruption Barometer 2009, p. 28: http://www.transparency.org/publications/publications/gcb2009.

[77] While the National Anticorruption Directorate is the leading institution in investigating and prosecuting high-level corruption cases, many other institutions have some form of responsibilities in this area. Most significantly after the DNA, the Directorate General for Anti-Corruption (DGA) within the Ministry of Administration and Interior is empowered to prevent and sanction corruption by officials of the Ministry.

High Court of Cassation and Justice and was renamed the National Anticorruption Directorate.[78] The Directorate's independence extends to its financing as well, in that it has its own budget and state-budget line. DNA is headed by the general prosecutor of the Prosecutor's Office attached to the High Court of Cassation and Justice, who carries out his duties through the chief prosecutor of DNA. The chief prosecutor of DNA, the two deputy chief prosecutors, as well as the prosecutor-chiefs of sections and their deputies are appointed by the President of Romania, at the proposal of the Minister of Justice, following the opinion of the Superior Council of the Magistracy. The Directorate has three operative sections that deal with corruption offences, crimes assimilated to corruption, crimes related to corruption and crimes against the financial interest of the European Communities.[79] The DNA also has a judicial section. The competences of DNA have been narrowed to only the highest corruption cases committed by perpetrators holding important public positions or where the bribe is over EUR 10,000 or the material damage exceeds EUR 200,000. In carrying out its activities, the DNA brings together prosecutors, police officers and specialists in economy, banking, finances, customs and IT. The Directorate also has 15 territorial offices.

The establishment of the DNA was acknowledged by the European Commission as a significant step in the fight against corruption in the October 2005 Report. Since then, the Commission several times praised the substantial work of the DNA, urging more support from the Government for its work. The September 2006 Progress Report showed that during 2005, approximately 770 files dealing with suspected corruption in the police were passed to the DNA (which amounts to a 133% increase compared to 2004), and more than 7,150 to other prosecutors. Therefore, the Commission concluded that in the fight against high-level corruption, the newly formed DNA had made more progress during the first seven months of its existence than had been made in the years before.[80]

In June 2007, the Commission reiterated its appraisal of the DNA, recognising its commitment and capacity to prosecute high-level corruption cases and acknowledging the professionalism of its investigating teams. The report showed that the number and profile of new investigations initiated by the DNA between September 2006 and June 2007 (84 indictments concerning 195 defendants) contributed to a good track record of non-partisan investigations into high-level corruption, thereby improving progress on benchmark 3.[81]

The October 2007 Action Plan of the Romanian Government set out numerous tasks for the fight against high-level corruption, including the drafting of a good practise

---

[78] Law No. 54/2006, published in *Monitorul Oficial* [Official Journal] No. 226 of 13 March 2006. Before this date, during October 2005 and March 2006, the Anticorruption Prosecutor's Office was organised as the 'National Anticorruption Department', an autonomous structure within the Prosecutor's Office attached to the High Court of Cassation and Justice.

[79] Corruption offences include active and passive bribery, trafficking in influence, obtaining of unlawful benefits, etc. Offences assimilated to corruption are the unlawful granting or use of credits or state subsidies, trafficking in influence or use of public function to obtain unlawful benefits, etc. Crimes related to corruption include money laundering, abuse in office and tax evasion.

[80] September 2006 Report, p. 35.

[81] June 2007 Report, p. 16.

guide in detecting fraudulent mechanisms and investigating serious corruption offences and economic macro-criminality and fraud with EU funds (deadline December 2009).[82] In the February 2008 Report, the Commission saluted the DNA's October 2007 request to start investigations on eight serving or former ministers, among whom was former Prime Minister Adrian Năstase.[83]

Notwithstanding such positive comments, the same report voiced concerns in relation to certain amendment proposals for the Criminal Procedure Code. Accordingly, the amendments would have brought significant changes to the legal framework for investigation and prosecution of criminal cases by stipulating, for instance, the temporal limitation of criminal investigations to six months, the illegality of search and interception/taping without prior information about the suspect and the characterisation of fraud below 9 million EUR as an offence punishable with maximum 5 years imprisonment. The report warned that, if promulgated, these amendments could seriously impair investigations not only into high-level corruption, but also into acts of terrorism and cross-border crime.[84] This problem was apparently solved by a decision of the Constitutional Court, which declared these amendments unconstitutional.[85]

Overall, the subsequent reports concluded that no convincing results have yet been demonstrated regarding the fight against high-level corruption. In particular, the February and July 2009 reports highlighted the negative track record of the Romanian Parliament in approving the opening of investigations in high-level corruption cases.[86] The steady progress of the DNA in investigating current and former ministers as well as other high-level officials was always acknowledged by the Commission, but the lack of commitment on behalf of the judiciary and the legislative is still considered a major hindrance.

### 3.2.2.2. Fighting local corruption

In 2005, a former Minister of Foreign Affairs Mihai Răzvan Ungureanu defined local corruption as a 'tool for survival' in a society torn by a communist power-structure.[87] In the 2007 Transparency International Global Corruption Index, Romania was the 69th with a score of 3.7 (where 10 is "highly clean" and 0 is "highly corrupt"), nevertheless showing improvement against its 2006 position, 84th with a score of 3.1.[88]

---

[82] Action Plan, p. 49.

[83] In January 2008, the Romanian President lifted the functional immunity of the incumbents. See Romanian Presidency Press Release, 16 January 2008. Most of these cases, however, have not yet reached a judicial phase.

[84] February 2008 Report, p. 5.

[85] Constitutional Court Decision No. 54 of 14 January 2009 in Case No. 2.042A/2008, published in *Monitorul Oficial* [Official Journal] No. 42 of 23 January 2009.

[86] February 2009 Report, p. 2; July 2009 Report, p. 5.

[87] 'România nu se poate schimba peste noapte' [Romania Cannot Change Overnight], Interview with Foreign Affairs Minister Mihai Răzvan Ungureanu, 17 April 2005, *Die Zeit*, website last accessed on 7 February 2008: http://www.mae.ro/index.php?unde=doc&id=26006.

[88] Transparency International, Global Corruption Perception Index 2007; In 2008, Romania was on the 70th place with a faintly improved corruption perception index of 3.8. (Transparency International,

The June 2007 Report noted that Romania has made progress with "flagship" projects to raise public awareness about corruption, such as the successful "Green Helpline" and the National Integrity Centre.[89] In addition, the Commission noted that Romania has organised a number of corruption awareness campaigns for the general public, the judiciary and public officials in different sectors of activity. What the Commission saw as a weakness was the lack of a comprehensive local anti-corruption strategy based on risk assessments targeting most vulnerable sectors and local administration.[90] Against this background, Victor Alistar, executive director of Transparency International in Romania, said the EU report was more positive than the reality, with less judicial progress made than the report implied.[91]

The October 2007 Action Plan vowed to tackle the existing problems by continuing to develop anti-corruption public awareness campaigns and by promoting the General Directorate for Anti-corruption within the Ministry of Interior and Administrative Reform. The most important goal regarding local corruption stipulated by the plan was the adoption, by March 2008, of a national anti-corruption strategy focused on the most vulnerable sectors and local public administration.[92]

The February 2008 Commission Report acknowledged that preparation work of the national anti-corruption strategy had started after several delays.[93] Finally, the new strategy was adopted in June 2008, and progress was acknowledged by the Commission.[94] Subsequent reports have emphasised the need for more preventive initiatives, such as awareness-raising campaigns aimed at the public and all levels of administration. In the Commission's opinion, 'a structural preventive effort' could yield more efficient results than a case-by-case approach in tackling local corruption.[95]

All in all, the five Commission reports issued in the last two-and-a-half years have asked for the de-politicisation of the fight against corruption, at both central and local levels. The efforts of the DNA and the Government in addressing the anti-corruption benchmarks have been constantly acknowledged by the Commission, whereas the approach of the judiciary (especially at the highest level) and the Parliament have been repeatedly criticised for inconsistency and lack of genuine commitment.

---

Global Corruption Perception Index 2008) http://www.transparency.org/news_room/in_focus/2008/cpi 2008/cpi_2008_table (last accessed 9 August 2009).

[89] See *supra* n. 64.
[90] June 2007 Report, p. 17.
[91] 'Bulgaria and Romania "plagued by corruption"', *The Independent – Europe,* 28 June 2007.
[92] Action Plan, pp. 58, 65, 68-69, 71 and 73.
[93] February 2008 Report, p. 6.
[94] July 2008 Report, p. 3.
[95] July 2009 Report, p. 6.

## 4.    TRADITIONAL ASPECTS OF MEMBERSHIP

After detailing the most significant "special conditions" of the 2007 enlargement, in the following sections, the chapter will discuss more traditional aspects of EU membership. First, the 2007 actions of the Commission against Romania – infringement procedures – will be presented. The section will only focus on the dynamics of the infringement procedures initiated in the first year of Romania's EU membership. Second, the actions of Romania against the Commission or other EU institutions will be discussed. Third, the institutional implications of accession will receive attention.

### 4.1.    Infringement procedures

Most of the infringement procedures started against Romania and closed by the end of 2008 concerned the non-communication of transposing measures of various directives. For instance, four cases were opened in April 2007 because Romania had not communicated to the Commission the transposing measures for four directives that were due, at the latest, by the date of accession to the European Union.[96] The European Commission decided to take the first step in the infringement procedure and sent a letter of formal notice on 20 April 2007. In the letter, Romanian authorities were reminded of the country's obligation to transpose the missing directives (in case that had not yet been done) and to communicate to the Commission the relevant national transposing measures. As a follow-up, a comprehensive list of the transposing measures adopted was communicated to the Commission at different dates between 24 April and 29 May 2007. An official reply to the letter of formal notice was sent by Romanian authorities on 21 June 2007, in which they reported about the progress made for each directive mentioned by the Commission. Since the transposing measures were communicated, the relevant non-communication infringement procedures were closed.

Another infringement procedure was launched against Romania in August 2007 for non-communication of national transposition measures of Directive 2005/29/EC (Unfair Commercial Practices).[97] The letter of formal notice was issued on 2 August 2007, and, as a result, in December 2007, the Romanian Parliament adopted Law No. 363/2007 for combating unfair commercial practices against consumers and for the harmonisation of legislation with Community law on the protection of consumers.[98] The Act entered into force on 31 December 2007.

---

[96]   See infringement procedures No. 2007/0511, 2007/0554, 2007/0576 and 2007/0646.

[97]   Directive 2005/29/EC of the European Parliament and of the Council of 11 May 2005 concerning unfair business-to-consumer commercial practices in the internal market and amending Council Directive 84/450/EEC, Directives 97/7/EC, 98/27/EC and 2002/65/EC of the European Parliament and of the Council and Regulation (EC) No 2006/2004 of the European Parliament and of the Council ('Unfair Commercial Practices Directive'), *OJ* 2005 L 149/22.

[98]   LEGE nr.363 din 21 decembrie 2007 privind combaterea practicilor incorecte ale comercianţilor în relaţia cu consumatorii şi armonizarea reglementărilor cu legislaţia europeană privind protecţia consumatorilor [Law No. 363 of 21 December 2007 for combating unfair commercial practices against consumers and for the harmonization of legislation with Community law on the protection of consumers], published in *Monitorul Oficial* [Official Journal] No. 899 of 28 December 2007.

In October and December 2007, approximately 150 infringement procedures against Romania were closed, most of them concerning non-communication of transposing measures for directives. Nonetheless, the end of 2007 found Romania with ten infringement procedures, which included four in the first phase (with letters of formal notice issued) and five in the second phase (reasoned opinions issued). The most important of these will be discussed below.

The most controversial infringement procedure commenced by the Commission referred to taxation of second-hand cars. In March 2007, the Commission decided to issue a letter of formal notice, in which it requested Romania to amend its car registration tax rules which discriminated against second-hand cars imported from other Member States. In the press release following the Commission formal letter of notice, it was specified that the ECJ has consistently held that a Member State is not prohibited from levying registration taxes on second-hand imported cars as long as those taxes are in conformity with Article 90 EC. In other words, a Member State cannot impose any internal taxation on the products of other Member States in excess of that imposed on similar domestic products. In the case of Romania, legislation on car registration tax failed to meet the standard of complete neutrality because, the car registration tax was levied only when the vehicle entered the Romanian market, the cars most heavily taxed were, by default, imported second-hand cars. For that reason, the European Commission considered that the Romanian legislation had to be changed to comply with the EC Treaty and accorded two months to Romania to take appropriate measures.[99]

The request of the Commission provoked intense debate in Romania, at the Government and Parliament level. The main opponent of the Commission's point of view was then Prime Minister Călin Popescu Tăriceanu, who repeatedly declared that Romania should not become 'the trash bin of Europe',[100] and that the purpose of the car registration tax is to restrict the import of unsafe, bad quality cars and to prevent Romania from excessively importing used cars.[101] Despite intensive discussions with the Commission, in which Romania constantly sustained the necessity of preventing the importing of used, bad quality cars, the Commission considered that no satisfactory arguments were given and decided to take the second step in the infringement procedure. Accordingly, at the end of November 2007, a reasoned opinion was issued, formally requesting Romania to change its legislation. In December 2007, Varujan Vosganioan, then Minister of Economy and Finances, affirmed that the registration tax would be changed in January 2008 by correlating the level of tax to the cars' market value.[102] In the Government Briefing of 9 January 2008, the Government spokesperson

---

[99] See Press Release of 21 March 2007, 'Car taxation: infringement procedure against Malta and Romania', Reference: IP/07/372.

[100] 'Guvernul nu renunţă la taxa de înmatriculare' [The government does not give up the car registration tax], 26 March 2007, *BBC Romanian*, website last accessed on 13 January 2008: http://www.bbc.co.uk/romanian/news/story/2007/03/070326_taxa_auto_tariceanu.shtml.

[101] 'Taxa de prima inmatriculare nu va disparea!' [The car registration tax will not disappear!], 20 March 2007, *Business.ROL.Ro*, website last accessed on 13 January 2008: http://business.rol.ro/content/view/38901/5/.

[102] 'Taxa auto se schimba in ianuarie' [The car tax will be changed in January], *Jurnalul National* [National Journal], 21 December 2007, p. 6.

announced that a draft proposal for adjusting the registration tax was sent to the European Commission, and that further measures would be taken on the basis of the response received.[103] The infringement procedure was finally closed in January 2009, when Romania changed the relevant legislation.

Three other infringement procedures, launched on 17 October 2007, were environment related. One of them concerned Romania's failure to designate any Special Protected Areas for migratory and vulnerable wild birds, thus violating the "Wild Birds Directive" (79/409/EEC) on the conservation of wild birds.[104] A reasoned opinion was issued by the European Commission in September 2008 concerning the same procedure. As of July 2009, the case had not yet been closed. Another procedure focused on climate change issues, and the letter of formal notice requested Romania to report information on climate change as required by Community law. The third environment-related procedure regarded the failure to implement Decision 280/2004/EC of the European Parliament and of the Council on a monitoring mechanism of greenhouse gas (GHG) emissions. Both latter procedures were closed in the first half of 2008.

On the same date, the Commission advanced to the second phase of issuing a reasoned opinion in four cases, two of them concerning the trade and distribution of toxic products.[105] Another reasoned opinion was issued to Romania and 21 other Member States for failure to inform the Commission of measures taken to implement a Directive providing for technical adaptations to EU rules on professional qualifications further to the accession of Bulgaria and Romania. The Directive updates, amongst others, all the qualifications which benefit from automatic recognition by completing them with the corresponding Bulgarian and Romanian qualifications. In its press release, the Commission warned that as long as the Directive is not fully transposed in the legislation of Member States, Romanian citizens risk lengthy bureaucratic procedures for recognition of qualifications for which this Community Act grants automatic recognition. This procedure was closed on 31 January 2008 as a result of Romania adopting the required transposing law.

A fourth reasoned opinion was issued to Romania and 7 other Member States for failure to notify national measures transposing Directive 2006/22/EC on minimum conditions for implementing new rules in the road transport sector on driving times and

---

[103] Government Briefing of 9 January 2008, Romanian Government Press Office (in English), website last accessed on 14 January 2008: http://www.guv.ro/engleza/presa/afis-doc.php?idpresa=8129&idrubrica presa=1&idrubricaprimm=&idtema=&tip=&pag=&dr=.

[104] Council Directive 79/409/EEC of 2 April 1979 on the conservation of wild birds, *OJ* 1979 L 103/1. See Press Release of 17 October 2007, 'Nature protection: Commission takes legal action against Romania for infringement of biodiversity legislation', Reference: IP/07/1508.

[105] Failure to apply the provisions of Council Directive 74/556/EEC of 4 June 1974 laying down detailed provisions concerning transitional measures relating to activities, trade in and distribution of toxic products and activities entailing the professional use of such products including activities of intermediaries and Council Directive 74/557/EEC of 4 June 1974 on the attainment of freedom of establishment and freedom to provide services in respect of activities of self-employed persons and of intermediaries engaging in the trade and distribution of toxic products.

rest periods and on the introduction of the digital tachograph.[106] Romania started using tachographs (tools for measuring rest periods and driving times) in July 2007. Initially, the use of tachographs should have started on 1 January 2007, but the Commission accorded Romania a transitional period until 1 August 2007. The Romanian Government adopted an ordinance for establishing an implementation framework regarding driving times and rest periods,[107] but without an Order of the Ministry of Transport on the application of the ordinance, implementation was not complete, and the Directive was not fully applicable. Immediately after the Commission sent its reasoned opinion on 17 October 2007, the Ministry of Transport issued an Order for the application of the Government Ordinance.[108] As a result, the Commission closed this infringement procedure.

At the same time, with the issuing of the reasoned opinion regarding car registration taxes, on 28 November 2007, the Commission sent a new letter of formal notice concerning the non-availability of caller location information for the single European emergency call number 112. In the letter, the Commission stated that Romania failed to ensure that telecom operators were able to provide emergency authorities with the caller location information for calls to 112 from land lines and mobile phones. In response, on 9 January 2008, the Romanian Government approved the memorandum submitted by the Ministry of Communications and Information Technology outlining measures to be taken by Romanian authorities for ensuring access to caller location data. Then-Minister of Communications Károly Borbély highlighted the importance of adopting as soon as possible a Government Emergency Ordinance to enforce the terms of the memorandum. The action plan was sent to the European Commission.[109] Nonetheless, the infringement procedure was only closed in January 2009, after more than a year delay in adopting the necessary measures.

To sum up, the first years of EU membership found Romania in constant need to address the incessant notices sent by the Commission as part of the infringement procedure. The Romanian Government was keen to show its co-operation for the swift closing of most of these procedures. That willingness has been maintained since then.

---

[106] Directive 2006/22/EC of the European Parliament and of the Council of 15 March 2006 on minimum conditions for the implementation of Council Regulations (EEC) No 3820/85 and (EEC) No 3821/85 concerning social legislation relating to road transport activities and repealing Council Directive 88/599/EEC, *OJ* 2006 L 102/35. Press Release of 17 October 2007, 'Road transport – enforcing social rules: Commission sends reasoned opinions to 8 Member States', Reference: IP/07/1532.

[107] Government Ordinance No. 37 for establishing an implementation framework for rules on driving times and rest periods and on the use of the activity registration machines was adopted on 7 August 2007 and published in the *Monitorul Oficial* [Official Journal] No. 565 of 16 August 2007.

[108] The Order of the Ministry of Transport was issued on 19 October 2007 and was published in the *Monitorul Oficial* [Official Journal] No. 721 of 25 October 2007.

[109] See Official Press Release of 9 January 2008 of the National Regulatory Authority for Communications and Information Technology, website last accessed on 14 January 2008: http://www.anrc.ro/desktopdefault.aspx?tabid=2922.

## 4.2.    Direct actions of Romania before the ECJ and the CFI

As of July 2009, several actions of Romania or on behalf of Romanian legal persons have been lodged before the EU courts.

The first direct action brought by a Romanian legal person for the annulment of a Community act concerned a registered Community trademark (CTM).[110] On 8 May 2007, the applicant, S.C. Gerovital Cosmetics S.A. (registered in Bucharest, Romania), brought an action against the Office for Harmonisation in the Internal Market (Trade Marks and Designs) and sought the annulment of a decision of that Office adopted on 27 February 2007. The decision upheld the earlier invalidation of Community trademark "GEROVITAL H3 Prof. Dr. Aslan", whose proprietor was the applicant. The invalidity of the figurative mark was declared by the Cancellation Division of OHIM on 23 December 2005. The applicant appealed the decision to the Board of Appeal of OHIM. In the decision sought for annulment, the Board decided to confirm the invalidation on the grounds that in 1999 the CTM in question was applied for in bad faith.[111] In the application for the Court of First Instance, S.C. Gerovital Cosmetics S.A. denied such contentions and argued that as a CTM proprietor, it was entitled to priority and exclusivity for registration purposes. In June 2008, however, the action for annulment was withdrawn, and the Court ordered that there was no longer any need to adjudicate on the action.[112]

The second action was filed by the Romanian Government for the annulment of the Commission decision regarding the carbon emission quota.[113] In October 2007, the Commission decided to cut Romania's emission quota for 2008-2012 by 20% and lower its 2007 ceiling by 10%, a quota that was criticised as too harsh by Romania. Even then-Minister for Environment and Durable Development Attila Korodi declared that in case 'the norms imposed by the Commission are respected, the Romanian industry would suffer insurmountable costs.'[114] As a result, in its 21 December 2007 meeting, the Romanian Government decided to start an action for the annulment of the relevant decision.[115] By early January 2008, seven other Member States – Poland, the Czech Republic, Slovakia, Latvia, Estonia, Lithuania and Hungary – had brought similar actions before the Court.[116]

---

[110] Case T-163/07, Action brought on 8 May 2007 – *SC Gerovital Cosmetics v. OHIM – SC Farmec (GEROVITAL H3 Prof. Dr. A. Aslan)*, *OJ* 2007 C 183/33.

[111] Decision of the Second Board of Appeal of 27 February 2007 in Case R 271/2006-2, Office for Harmonization in the Internal Market (Trade Marks and Designs).

[112] Case T-163/07, Order of the Court of First Instance of 27 October 2008 – *S.C. Gerovital Cosmetics v. OHIM – S.C. Farmec (GEROVITAL H3 Prof. Dr. A. Aslan) (Case T-163/07)*, *OJ* 2009 C 19/29.

[113] Commission Decision of 26 October 2007 concerning the national allocation plan for the period 2008 to 2012 for the allocation of greenhouse gas emission allowances notified by Romania in accordance with Directive 2003/87/EC of the European Parliament and of the Council, Brussels, 26 October 2007.

[114] 'Romania: Fighting for the "Right" to More Emissions', 15 January 2008, *Inter Press Service News Agency*, website last accessed on 2 February 2008: http://ipsnews.net/news.asp?idnews=40796.

[115] Press Release of the European Affairs Department of the Romanian Government (in Romanian), 22 December 2007, http://www.dae.gov.ro/index.php?pag=articol&pid=4&sid=35 (last accessed on 2 February 2008); See Cases T-483/07 and T-484/07, Actions brought on 22 December 2007 – *Romania v. Commission of the European Communities*.

[116] See Press Release, *loc. cit.* n. 114.

Three other cases were lodged before the Court in 2008 and in the first half of 2009, but all three were rendered inadmissible.[117]

## 4.3.    Institutional aspects

### 4.3.1.    *Romanian judges at the EU courts*

The nomination of candidates for the two judges at the EU courts (ECJ and CFI) had long been postponed by the Romanian Government due to mass-media allegations regarding the lack of transparency of the decision-making process.[118] The committee habilitated to choose the two candidates was composed of representatives of the Romanian Ministry of Justice, the Ministry of European Integration and the Ministry of Foreign Affairs. Finally, in November 2006, two Romanian judges were nominated for candidacy: Camelia Toader for the European Court of Justice and Valeriu M. Ciucă for the Court of First Instance. The Council of the European Union approved both nominations. The judges have been members of the respective EU courts since 12 January 2007.

### 4.3.2.    *The Romanian Commissioner*

The current Romanian Commissioner, Leonard Orban, received the portfolio of Multilingualism within the Commission. He was nominated by the Romanian Government only after the first nominee, Varujan Vosganian, withdrew his candidacy. An economist, Varujan Vosganian was criticized for lacking experience in European affairs and for having been an informant for the communist-era secret police, the Securitate. He denied the accusations several times. Romanian President Traian Basescu has said that Romania's intelligence agencies found no evidence in their archives that Vosganian had ever collaborated with the Securitate. Nevertheless, the nominee decided to withdraw his candidacy, declaring that although the accusations proved baseless, he did not wish to harm Romania's image.[119] Between January 2007 and December 2008, Varujan Vosganian served as Minister of Economy and Finance.

### 4.3.3.    *Elections to the European Parliament*

On 25 November 2007, Romania held its first elections to the European Parliament in line with the requirements set out by Article 24(2) of the Act. The elections were prepared by the adoption of Law No. 33/2007 regarding the organisation and procedure

---

[117] See Cases T-504/07, T-261/08 AJ and T-75/09 AJ.
[118] 'Cei doi judecători europeni desemnați de România' [The two European judges nominated by Romania], *BBC Romanian*, 10 November 2006.
[119] 'Romanian nominee withdraws candidacy for EU Commission', *The Associated Press, International Herald Tribune – Europe*, 28 October 2006, website last accessed on 2 February 2008: http://www.iht.com/articles/ap/2006/10/28/europe/EU_POL_Romania_EU_Commissioner.php.

of the elections to the European Parliament.[120] This law creates a general legislative framework for the EP elections based on the constitutional principle of universal, equal, direct, secret and freely expressed voting (Art. 1 para. 2 of Law 33/2007). The mandate of the Romanian EP representatives is set for five years. Romania accounts for one electoral district, and the voting system is based on party-list proportional representation. Regarding the candidate-lists, Article 12 of the law requires the representation of both genders, although without providing any details. Among the incompatibilities of a Romanian EP representative, the law lists senator or deputy in the Romanian Parliament, as well as member of the Romanian Government. Citizens of other Member States of the European Union who reside or live in Romania can request their inclusion in the special electoral lists in order to be able to vote. The law sets the electoral threshold at 5% of the total number of votes validly expressed on the national level. For independent candidates, the electoral threshold is any value larger than the national electoral coefficient.[121]

The first elections held for 35 representatives to the European Parliament ended on 25 November 2007 with the victory of one of the main opposition parties, the Democrats, with 28.81% of the valid votes. The other opposition party, the Social-Democrats, came second with 23.11% of the votes. The main governing party, the National Liberal Party, received 13.44% of the votes and became the third on the list. The Democratic Union of Hungarians in Romania, the main interest-group of the Hungarian minority, received 5.52% of the votes, and an independent candidate of the same minority, László Tőkés, received 3.44%. The Democrat Party and the Democratic Union of Hungarians joined the EEP-ED group with 16 members and 2 members, respectively. The National Liberal Party joined the Alliance for Liberals and Democrats of Europe with 6 members, whereas the Social-Democrats added 10 members to the Socialist Group. The independent candidate László Tőkés joined the EP as a non-attached member.

Two years later, in 2009, the Social-Democrat Party in alliance with the Conservative Party came first, with 31.07% of the valid votes and with 11 members elected to the EP. The governing Democrat-Liberal Party came second, with 29.71% of the valid votes and 10 members elected. The National Liberal Party (in opposition) came third with 14.52% of the valid votes and only 5 acquired seats. Compared to the 2007 EP elections, the Democratic Union of Hungarians in Romania registered a considerable success, with 8.92% of the valid votes and 3 seats gained in the Parliament. Finishing last, the Greater Romania Party, often characterised as right-wing extremist,[122] won 8.65% of the valid votes and secured three seats in the European Parliament.[123] One of

[120] Published in *Monitorul Oficial* [Official Journal], No. 28 of 16 January 2007. The Law was amended and completed by Government Emergency Ordinances No. 1/2007, 8/2007, 84/2007, 11/2009 and 55/2009.
[121] The national electoral coefficient is the absolute value of the total number of valid votes divided by the number of Romanian EP positions (Art. 20 para. 2 of Law 33/2007).
[122] 'Romania's far-right MEPs to stay home', http://euobserver.com/883/28277 (last accessed on 8 August 2009); 'Left-wing ahead in Romania's EU vote, far-right gains', http://www.eubusiness.com/news-eu/1244477019.77/ (last accessed on 8 August 2009).
[123] Official results of the Romanian EP elections, June 2009 – Alegeri Europarlamentare, http://www.alegeri.tv/alegeri-europarlamentare-2009 (last accessed on 8 August 2009).

the successful candidates of the Greater Romania Party is the controversial George "Gigi" Becali, a millionaire businessman and football-club owner, notorious for his flamboyant lifestyle and statements. Immediately after his election, George Becali was ordered by a court not to leave the country as he was charged with ordering his body-guards to capture and threaten three men who tried to steal his car.[124] In July 2009, however, the appeal judge annulled the order, and Becali was able to take up his mandate in the European Parliament.

5.      CONCLUSIONS

For Romania, 2007-2008 were years of intense efforts to keep up with the required pace of adjustments and reforms. The June 2007 and February 2008 EU Commission Monitoring Reports, although welcoming the specific achievements, kept a critical tone on the overall progress of Romania meeting the membership requirements.

As discussed, Romania registered good progress in its first benchmark (judicial reform) with certain important tasks remaining, but showed only "some" or "minimal" progress for the other three benchmarks, mainly because of incessant delays in the implementation of plans. In an interview given to the *Deutsche Welle*, Jonathan Scheele, former head of the European Commission Delegation in Romania, opined that the level of assumed commitments is beneath the pre-accession expectations.[125] That concern was also voiced in the subsequent reports of the European Commission.

The ungainly performance of Romania in its first EU membership years increased the fears – both on EU and domestic levels – that the country was not really prepared for being a member of the Union. The wariness of the European public was apparent before accession, with only 41 percent of the EU-25 population being in favour of Romania's accession to the EU. According to the Autumn 2006 Eurobarometer, 64% of the German, 53% of the Italian and 49% of the French interviewees declared their disagreement with the accession with Romania, while 70% of the Austrian and 51% of the Belgian interviewees were against further enlargement in general.[126] This negative attitude still persists in view of the troublesome progress rate of Romania in meeting EU requirements.

On the bright side, Romania proved to be considerably receptive in tackling the problems identified by the Commission through the infringement procedure. Replies by the Romanian Government were generally prompt, and most of the cases were closed at the early stages of the procedure. Further, the Romanian courts seem to have effec-

---

[124] 'Romania's far-right MEPs to stay home', http://euobserver.com/883/28277 (last accessed on 8 August 2009); 'Romanian judges bar populist MEP', http://news.bbc.co.uk/2/hi/europe/8092434.stm (last accessed on 8 August 2009).

[125] 'Jonathan Scheele: Nu există o viziune clară despre viitorul României în UE' [Jonathan Scheele: There is no clear vision on the future of Romania in the EU], *Deutsche Welle*, 25 January 2008, website last accessed on 3 February 2008: http://www.dw-world.de/dw/article/0,2144,3088711,00.html.

[126] Standard Eurobarometer 66, October-November 2006, website last accessed on 14 February 2008: http://ec.europa.eu/public_opinion/archives/eb/eb66/eb66_en.htm.

tively incorporated the principle of supremacy of EC law, and the European Arrest Warrant cases are proficiently handled by Romanian judges.

The greatest weakness of Romania as an EU member is, perhaps, its imprecision in addressing the new challenges. According to Scheele, quoted above, it is uncertain whether Romania has a clear vision – shared by the major part of its political actors – on the future of the country in the European Union. Still, the fact that no safeguard clauses have yet been employed shows that the progress registered by Romania – though slow – is seen as purposeful by decision-makers at the EU level.

*Chapter 17*

# LEARNING THE HARD WAY: BULGARIA AND EU LAW

Adam Łazowski* and Svetla Yosifova**

## 1.    INTRODUCTION

After almost two decades of an ever-developing relationship, Bulgaria joined the European Union on 1 January 2007. From the Bulgarian perspective, membership seemed to be a "dream come true" scenario. With the country's weak economy, unstable political system and considerable poverty, many Bulgarians regarded the accession as a magical panacea for all domestic problems.[1] Following the signature of the Accession Treaty 2005,[2] the political elites did all they could to demonstrate their commitment to the membership and at the same time to the fulfilment of the Copenhagen criteria. For the European Union, the accession of Bulgaria (together with Romania) was considered a real test for the absorption capacity. More than two years after the sixth enlargement, voices are heard that both countries were admitted too soon and at the time when neither of them complied with necessary criteria. Although fully aware of the challenges, the European Union decided not to activate the membership postponement clause available under the Accession Treaty 2005, but opted for a post-accession monitoring mechanism instead.[3] Apparently, the rationale behind this decision was correct. It was based on a premise that legal and political instruments available in the membership environment will be far more effective than largely political tools of the pre-accession phase. The experience thus far proves that neither

---

\* Reader in Law, School of Law, University of Westminster, London.

\*\*Lecturer in EU Law, De Haagse Hogeschool, The Hague, The Netherlands.

[1]    Arguably, this is still largely the case. See 'Bulgarian Rhapsody', *The Economist*, 14 May 2009.

[2]    Treaty between the Kingdom of Belgium, the Czech Republic, the Kingdom of Denmark, the Federal Republic of Germany, the Republic of Estonia, the Hellenic Republic, the Kingdom of Spain, the French Republic, Ireland, the Italian Republic, the Republic of Cyprus, the Republic of Latvia, the Republic of Lithuania, the Grand Duchy of Luxembourg, the Republic of Hungary, the Republic of Malta, the Kingdom of the Netherlands, the Republic of Austria, the Republic of Poland, the Portuguese Republic, the Republic of Slovenia, the Slovak Republic, the Republic of Finland, the Kingdom of Sweden, the United Kingdom of Great Britain and Northern Ireland (Member States of the European Union) and the Republic of Bulgaria and Romania, concerning the accession of the Republic of Bulgaria and Romania to the European Union, *OJ* 2005 L 157/11. For a legal appraisal, see, *inter alia*, A. Łazowski, 'And Then They Were Twenty-Seven… A Legal Appraisal of the Sixth Accession Treaty', 44 *CMLRev.* (2007) pp. 401-430.

[3]    See section 3.2. of this chapter.

legal, nor extraordinary political, mechanisms have been incentive enough. The case of Bulgaria is particularly daunting. Due to high levels of mismanagement and corruption the European Union had no choice but to suspend financial assistance to Bulgaria in late 2008. Also, as the recent Commission's report demonstrates, the performance in pursuing necessary reforms to combat corruption, organised crime and reform the judiciary is not very spectacular.[4] At the same time, one can see clear indications that there is light at the end of the tunnel. Bulgaria has a very positive record in transposition of EC directives and tops the Commission's charts.[5] EU law is slowly paving its way in Bulgarian courts, which – on a step by step basis – are getting used to this new legal order. With three references for preliminary ruling submitted by the end of June 2009, they are also learning their way of communicating with the European Court of Justice. Arguably then the bad experience can be – at least potentially – balanced out by a bit of good news. This is exactly what this chapter aims to achieve. Since two years of membership is a very short period of time, the experience is fairly limited; yet one can clearly see that, unfortunately, Bulgaria is learning the hard way. In order to understand idiosyncrasies of Bulgarian *rapprochement* towards Europe, it is fitting to present it from a multidimensional perspective. Therefore, the chapter starts with an overview of EC/EU relations with Bulgaria and proceeds to the Accession Treaty 2005. That part is followed by an analysis of the Bulgarian Constitution and multiple revisions which were introduced, *inter alia*, to meet requirements of EU membership. Case law of Bulgarian courts is presented in two separate sections. First, we will look at the pre-accession experience when EU legislation did not apply to Bulgaria, but had on occasion been used as an interpretation tool by domestic judiciary. This will lead to the first post-accession experiences, including the references for preliminary ruling submitted by Bulgarian courts.[6]

## 2. FROM ASSOCIATION TO MEMBERSHIP IN THE EUROPEAN UNION

### 2.1. Association with the European Communities

In the decades preceding the fall of the Iron Curtain, legal relations between the European Communities and Bulgaria were almost non-existent. The 1970s call of the EEC to set up a framework of general trade agreements with the countries of the Council of Mutual Economic Assistance (COMECON) remained unanswered or ignored.[7] The only inter-

---

[4] Report from the Commission to the European Parliament and the Council on Progress in Bulgaria under the Co-operation and Verification Mechanism, COM (2009) 402 final.

[5] According to the Scoreboard published by the European Commission in July 2009, Bulgaria has 0.3% transposition deficit, which gives it, alongside Romania, the third position out of 27 Member States. See European Commission, Internal Market Scoreboard No. 19, July 2009, at p. 13.

[6] Parts of this chapter draw from our earlier publication. See A. Łazowski and S. Yosifova, 'Bulgaria', in S. Blockmans and A. Łazowski, *The European Union and its Neighbours. A Legal Appraisal of the EU's Policies of Stabilisation, Partnership and Integration* (The Hague, T.M.C. Asser Press 2006) pp. 207-246.

[7] A. Mayhew, *Recreating Europe. The European Union's Policy towards Central and Eastern Europe* (Cambridge, Cambridge University Press 1998) at p. 7.

national treaties bridging the gap between the two sides were a few short-lived sectoral trade agreements concluded with some of them, including Bulgaria.[8] As was the case with all the countries of Central and Eastern Europe, the ice started to melt by the end of the 1980s.[9] Diplomatic relations between the EEC and Bulgaria were formally established on 9 August 1988. The conclusion of the first general bilateral trade agreement (the so-called first generation agreement) followed shortly afterwards.[10] With its entry into force on 1 November 1990, the parties received a proper legal framework for bilateral trade. Also, already in May 1990, a decision was made to extend the Phare programme beyond its initial borders and add Bulgaria to the list of beneficiaries.[11] As explained in Chapter 1 of this volume, the fall of the Communist dictatorships and the political and economic changes that rapidly started to emerge in the region forced the European Communities to adapt to this new geopolitical environment.[12] The trade agreements reached their limits in a very short amount of time and were soon replaced by Europe Agreements, marking a new type of association. The green light for the negotiations on the EA Bulgaria came from the European Council in April 1991.[13] In terms of its structure and contents, the agreement closely followed the earlier Europe Agreements signed with Poland, Hungary and Czechoslovakia (soon to be replaced by separate agreements with the Slovak and Czech Republics).[14] The EA Bulgaria was signed on 8 March 1993. Since it was a mixed agreement, it required ratification not only by the European Communities but also by its twelve Member States. The ratification procedure in Bulgaria was completed smoothly on 15 April 1993. In order to speed up the entry into force of the agreement's vital trade section, an additional interim

---

[8] See, *inter alia*, Agreement between the European Economic Community and the People's Republic of Bulgaria on trade in textile products, *OJ* 1982 L 330/2; Exchange of Letters between the European Economic Community and the People's Republic of Bulgaria on trade in the sheep meat and goat meat sector, *OJ* 1982 L 43/13; Agreement between the European Economic Community and the People's Republic of Bulgaria on trade in textile products, *OJ* 1986 L 293/2.

[9] See Chapter 1 in this volume and academic writing referred to therein.

[10] Agreement between the European Economic Community and the People's Republic of Bulgaria on trade and commercial and economic co-operation, *OJ* 1990 L 291/9. For an overview of the first generation agreements, see D. Horovitz, 'EC-Central/East European relations: New principles for a new era', 27 *CMLRev.* (1990) pp. 259-284, at pp. 267-272.

[11] Council Regulation (EEC) No 2698/90 of 17 September 1990 amending Regulation (EEC) No 3906/89 in order to extend economic aid to other countries of Central and Eastern Europe, *OJ* 1990 L 257/1.

[12] See, *inter alia*, Communication from the Commission to the Council, Implications of recent changes in central and eastern Europe for the Community's relations with the countries concerned, SEC (90) 111 final; Communication from the Commission to the Council and the Parliament, The development of Community's relations with the countries of central and eastern Europe, SEC (90) 196 final; Communication from the Commission, The development of Community's relations with the countries of central and eastern Europe, SEC (90) 717 final; Communication from the Commission to the Council and Parliament, Association agreements with countries of central and eastern Europe: a general outline, COM (90) 398 final.

[13] See Mayhew, *op. cit.* n. 7, at p. 21.

[14] For a comparative overview of the Europe Agreements, see, *inter alia*, A. Ott and K. Inglis, eds., *Handbook on European Enlargement. A Commentary on the Enlargement Process* (The Hague, T.M.C. Asser Press 2002).

agreement was concluded.[15] It entered into force on 31 December 1993. Upon the completion of the various ratification procedures, the EA Bulgaria became operational on 1 February 1995. It was signed for an indefinite period of time, with a ten-year transitional period envisaged by Article 7(1) EA Bulgaria. The Europe Agreement remained the key legal instrument connecting the parties until 1 January 2007 when Bulgaria joined the European Union. During the decade of its operation, the Europe Agreement was modified a number of times by means of additional protocols. Some of them were concluded to take account of the successive enlargements of the European Union.[16]

The objectives of the association were spelled out in general terms in Article 1 EA Bulgaria. Considering developments of the bilateral relationship, we suggest that this provision deserved a dynamic interpretation, bearing in mind the pre-accession reorientation of the Europe Agreement. The provision in question stated that the objectives of the association were:

- to provide an appropriate framework for the political dialogue between the Parties allowing the developments of close political relations,
- to establish gradually a free trade area between the Community and Bulgaria covering substantially all trade between them,
- to promote the expansion of trade and the harmonious economic relations between the Parties and so to foster the dynamic economic development and prosperity in Bulgaria,
- to provide a basis for economic, financial, cultural and social co-operation, as well as for the Community's assistance to Bulgaria,
- to support Bulgaria's efforts to develop its economy and to complete the transition into a market economy,
- to provide an appropriate framework for the gradual integration of Bulgaria into the Community,
- to set up institutions suitable to make the association effective.

It is questionable to what extent these broad and ambitious aims were achieved. It is even more questionable to what extent they could have been achieved without the prospect of membership on the horizon and the transformation of the Europe Agreement

---

[15] Interim Agreement on trade and trade-related matters between the European Economic Community and the European Steel and Coal Community, of the one part, and the Republic of Bulgaria, of the other part, OJ 1993 L 323/1.

[16] Protocol adjusting trade aspects of the Europe Agreement between the European Communities and their Member States, of the one part, and the Republic of Bulgaria, of the other part, to take account of the accession of the Republic of Austria, the Republic of Finland and the Kingdom of Sweden to the European Union and the outcome of the Uruguay Round negotiations on agriculture, including improvements to the existing preferential arrangements, OJ 1999 L 112/3; Additional Protocol to the Europe Agreement establishing an association between the European Communities and their Member States, of the one part, and the Republic of Bulgaria, of the other part, to take account of the accession of the Czech Republic, the Republic of Estonia, the Republic of Cyprus, the Republic of Latvia, the Republic of Lithuania, the Republic of Hungary, the Republic of Malta, the Republic of Poland, the Republic of Slovenia, and the Slovak Republic to the European Union, OJ 2005 L 155/5.

into the pre-accession vehicle. However, it is beyond any doubt that the agreement played an important role as a basic legal framework for the multidimensional bilateral relationship. One should particularly acknowledge its trade part, which had been the basis for the gradual creation of the free trade area. Also, the fifth *tiret* should not go unnoticed. It is quite astonishing to note that, on the one hand, the agreement had been envisaged as a framework for gradual integration,[17] while, on the other, the membership desire was only spelled out in a unilateral declaration. It read 'that Bulgaria's ultimate objective is to become a member of the Community, and that this association, in the view of the Parties, will help Bulgaria to achieve this objective.' It is also interesting to note that the latter provision was interpreted dynamically by the European Court of Justice. For example, in its judgment in case C-235/99 *The Queen and Secretary of State for the Home Department,* ex parte*: Eleanora Ivanova Kondova,*[18] the ECJ held that:

'[A]ccording to the 17th recital in its preamble and Article 1(2), the objective of the Association Agreement is to establish an association designed to promote the expansion of trade and harmonious economic relations between the Contracting Parties, in order to foster dynamic economic development and prosperity in the Republic of Bulgaria, with a view to facilitating its accession to the Community.'[19]

In institutional terms, the Europe Agreement proved to be a very good platform for the political dialogue, serving not only the association but also the implementation of the pre-accession strategy.

## 2.2.    Towards the membership in the European Union

Shortly after the fall of Communism, Bulgaria expressed a strong desire to join the European Communities. Already in December 1990, the Bulgarian Grand National Assembly had adopted a resolution placing membership on the list of priorities of Bulgarian foreign policy.[20] As explained in Chapter 1 of this volume, the first reaction of the Western European countries was far from enthusiastic. Against all odds, Bulgaria followed the other countries of the region and decided to treat the association as a step towards membership. As the Ratification of the Agreement progressed, the initial position of the European Communities changed, and it was ready to announce that the new democracies would have a chance to accede provided they fulfilled the membership criteria.[21] Following a Governmental Declaration of 14 April 1994, Bulgaria submitted

---

[17]  Moreover, Art. 2 EA Bulgaria was very clear in saying that the political dialogue conducted in the framework of the Europe Agreement 'will facilitate Bulgaria's full integration into the community of democratic nations and progressive rapprochement with the Community.'

[18]  ECJ, Case C-235/99 *The Queen and Secretary of State for the Home Department,* ex parte*: Eleanora Ivanova Kondova* [2001] *ECR* I-6427.

[19]  Para. 36 of the judgment.

[20]  Source: http://www.bulgaria.bg/Europe/EU/en/relationships/europeancommunity/default.htm.

[21]  See Ch. Hillion, 'The Copenhagen Criteria and Their Progeny', in Ch. Hillion, ed., *EU Enlargement. A Legal Approach* (Oxford and Portland Oregon, Hart Publishing 2004) pp. 1-22. See also Chapter 1 in this volume.

its formal application for membership on 14 December 1995. At the end of 1995, the European Council requested the European Commission to present its opinion on the membership applications that had by then been submitted by all the countries of Central and Eastern Europe. The batch of opinions was presented on 15 July 1997, together with a policy document entitled Agenda 2000. In the case of Bulgaria, the opinion was negative.[22] Although the political criteria were generally satisfied, the European Commission identified numerous shortcomings in the fulfilment of the economic criteria and in the approximation of laws.[23] Moreover, Bulgaria did not have the necessary institutional capacity. In its conclusions, the European Commission stated that:

> 'Bulgaria's progress in the creation of a market economy has been limited by the absence of a commitment to market-oriented economic policies. Early liberalisation of trade and prices was partially reversed, and price controls were not removed until this year. It is only since the crisis at the end of last year and the recent change of government that consensus about the desirability of economic reforms has began to develop.'[24]

Bearing this in mind, the European Commission expressed doubts as to Bulgaria's capability of coping with competitive market forces in the European Union. The approximation of laws proved to be yet another major problem. Bulgaria not only had a considerable backlog with regard to the transposition of the *acquis*, but also suffered from a very limited capacity to implement newly adopted legislation. As the Commission noted:

> '[T]he weakness of public administration is a major problem, putting in question both the rate and the quality of approximation of legislation.'[25]

In its final remarks, the European Commission argued that negotiations with Bulgaria could be opened as soon as the country made sufficient progress in its fulfilment of the Copenhagen criteria. This was considered to be the case two years later, and Bulgaria joined the group of negotiating countries following a decision by the Helsinki European Council in December 1999.[26] In the meantime, Bulgaria fell under the enhanced pre-accession strategy. The accession partnerships – the main policy instruments of this strategy – were based on Council Regulation 622/98/EC[27] and were updated regularly,[28]

---

[22] Commission Opinion on Bulgaria's Application for Membership of the European Union, DOC/97/11.

[23] See I. Shikova, 'Status and Tendencies in Bulgaria', in P.-Ch. Müller-Graff, ed., *East Central Europe and the European Union: From Europe Agreements to a Member Status* (Baden-Baden, Nomos 1997) p. 251.

[24] Commission Opinion on Bulgaria's Application for Membership of the European Union, DOC/97/11, at p. 119.

[25] *Ibidem*, at p. 120.

[26] Presidency Conclusions, Helsinki European Council of 10-11 December 1999, Bull. EU 12-1999.

[27] Council Regulation (EC) No 622/98 of 16 March 1998 on assistance to the applicant States in the framework of the pre-accession strategy, and in particular on the establishment of Accession Partnerships, *OJ* 1998 L 85/1.

[28] Council Decision 1999/857/EC of 6 December 1999 on the principles, priorities, intermediate objectives and conditions contained in the Accession Partnership with the Republic of Bulgaria, *OJ* 1999

allowing Bulgaria to respond with updates and adjustments of its own national plan for the adoption of the *acquis* (NPAA). An important role was also played by the European Commission's annual progress reports.[29] Shortly before the Copenhagen European Council in 2002, the European Commission also published roadmaps for Bulgaria and Romania.[30] The latter were tailored to support the pre-accession efforts of both countries to meet the remaining criteria for membership by identifying the tasks ahead and providing increased financial assistance.[31] Following screening and a political decision in December 1999, the negotiations started in February 2000. The negotiation framework and underlying principles were the same as for the first group of countries.[32] Since neither Bulgaria nor Romania managed to catch up with the other ten candidate countries, they could not participate in the "big bang" enlargement. The Presidency Conclusions from the Copenhagen European Council explicitly stated that:

> '[S]uccessful conclusion of accession negotiations with ten candidates lends new dynamism to the accession of Bulgaria and Romania as a part of the same inclusive and irreversible enlargement process.'[33]

Following their participation in the work of the European Convention, both countries were also invited to participate in the Intergovernmental Conference as observers. The accession negotiations were officially completed on 14 December 2004, and this was followed by the signature of the Accession Treaty on 25 April 2005. It entered into force on 1 January 2007. As already indicated, the Member States decided not to activate the postponement clause provided in the Accession Treaty 2005.[34]

---

L 335/48; Council Decision 2002/83/EC of 28 January 2002 on the principles, priorities, intermediate objectives and conditions contained in the Accession Partnership with Bulgaria, *OJ* 2002 L 44/1; Council Decision 2003/396/EC of 19 May 2003 on the principles, priorities, intermediate objectives and conditions contained in the Accession Partnership with Bulgaria, *OJ* 2003 L 145/1.

[29] 1998 Regular Report from the Commission on Bulgaria's progress towards accession, COM (1998) 707 final; 1999 Regular Report from the Commission on Bulgaria's progress towards accession, COM (1999) 501 final; 2000 Regular Report from the Commission on Bulgaria's progress towards accession, COM (2000) final; 2001 Regular Report on Bulgaria's progress towards accession, SEC (2001) 1744; 2002 Regular Report on Bulgaria's progress towards accession, COM (2002) 700 final; 2003 Regular Report on Bulgaria's progress towards accession, COM (2003) 676 final; 2004 Regular Report on Bulgaria's progress towards accession, COM (2004) 657 final.

[30] Communication from the Commission to the Council and the European Parliament – Roadmaps for Bulgaria and Romania, COM (2002) 624 final.

[31] *Ibidem*, at p. 2.

[32] See C. Banasiński, 'The Negotiations Decision-Making Machinery', 25 *PolYBIL* (2001) pp. 69-84.

[33] Presidency Conclusions, Copenhagen European Council of 12-13 December 2002, point 13.

[34] The Sixth Accession Treaty is the first to contain a clause giving the power to the European Union to delay the membership of a country with which an accession treaty has already been signed. Not only does it differentiate the two countries from the ones that have acceded in 2004, it also sets different standards for Bulgaria and Romania. The legal basis for the safeguard clause was Art. 4(2) of the Accession Treaty 2005 in conjunction with Art. 39 of the Act. The conditions for the delay of membership are spelled out in Art. 39(1) of the Act. The Council could have used the safeguard clause if there was 'clear evidence that the state of preparations or adoption and implementation of the *acquis* in Bulgaria or Romania was such that there was a serious risk of either of those states being manifestly unprepared to meet the requirements of membership by the date of accession of 1 January 2007 in a number of important areas. In order to

## 3. THE ACCESSION TREATY 2005

### 3.1. Introductory remarks

The Sixth Accession Treaty served as the legal basis for the accession of Bulgaria and Romania to the European Union. Since it is also analysed in Chapter 16 of this volume and since the majority of provisions apply *mutatis mutandis* to both Acceding Countries, this analysis is limited to issues relating specifically to Bulgaria. It will focus on two issues: first, on safeguard clauses provided in the Accession Treaty 2005 and second, on transitional periods suspending the application of EU law in relation to Bulgaria in certain areas.

### 3.2. Safeguard clauses

The Act on Conditions of Accession 2005 (hereafter the Act) provides three safeguard clauses that can be employed during the first three years of membership. However, introduction before the entry date but with the effect as of the date of accession has been made possible. Should it be necessary, the validity of measures adopted pursuant to Articles 37-38 of the Act may exceed the three-year period ('as long as the relevant commitments have not been fulfilled'). Any measures adopted by the Commission shall remain in force as long as necessary and must be lifted when a particular commitment is fulfilled. All are based on a model known from the fifth enlargement and arguably can be categorised as legal tools with a political touch. Articles 37 and 38 of the Act contain the internal market and JHA safeguard clauses (respectively). Both can be used by the European Commission on its own initiative or upon a motivated request of a Member State.

The conditions for the use of the safeguard clauses are spelled out in a very general fashion. Article 37 reads as follows:

'If Bulgaria or Romania has failed to implement commitments undertaken in the context of the accession negotiations, causing a serious breach of the functioning of the internal market, including any commitments in all sectoral policies which concern economic activities with cross-border effect, or an imminent risk of such breach the Commission may, until the end of a period of up to three years after accession, upon motivated request of a Member State or on its own initiative, take appropriate measures.'

---

adopt a decision in this respect, unanimity in the Council would have been required. Due to its relatively poor performance, a set of special arrangements had been prepared for Romania. In September 2006, the European Commission recommended the accession of both countries on 1 January 2007, subject to very strict scrutiny of both newcomers. The membership postponement safeguard clause wasn't used; however, it can be argued that its existence *per se* played an important political role. It served as a stick to discipline the forthcoming members in their last-minute pre-accession efforts. Had it been used, its potential benefits would have been rather limited. The postponement of membership by 12 months would have not saved the European Union from admitting the two countries struggling with their accession commitments.

The JHA safeguard clause may be invoked if there are 'serious shortcomings or any imminent risks' in transposition, implementation or application of First and Third Pillar measures relating to mutual recognition in civil and criminal matters. Measures adopted pursuant to either of the safeguard clauses must be proportional; moreover, the European Commission shall adapt measures which least disturb the functioning of the internal market. Under no circumstances, may the measures invoked constitute means of arbitrary discrimination or disguised restriction to trade.

The mere reading of Article 37 of the Act does not explain what measures adopted on its basis may amount to. Undoubtedly, this leaves a lot of discretion to the European Commission. Article 38 of the Act is more elaborate when it comes to the JHA safeguard clause. Such measures:

> 'may take the form of temporary suspension of the application of relevant provisions and decisions in the relations between Bulgaria and Romania and any other Member State or Member States.'

This, for instance, may apply to the European Arrest Warrant mechanism.

For the very first time, the European Commission invoked the internal market safeguard clause shortly before the sixth enlargement. Due to serious shortcomings in aviation safety, necessary measures against Bulgaria had been taken.[35] The administrative capacity of the Bulgarian Civil Aviation Authorities as well as its capability of fulfilling the safety oversight duties had been the matter of concern.[36] Under the terms of Regulation 1962/2006/EC, airworthiness and maintenance certificates issued by the Bulgarian authorities were not recognised in the EU. Moreover, air carriers having Bulgarian licences were not granted unlimited access to the EU aviation market and were treated as if they were third-country carriers.[37] Once the European Commission was satisfied with the progress made by Bulgaria, it lifted the restrictions imposed pursuant to the Regulation 1962/2006/EC.[38]

The Act provides also for the economic safeguard clause. Under the terms of Article 36, it can be invoked by Bulgaria and/or Romania as well as other Member States of the European Union when 'difficulties arise which are serious and liable to persist in any sector of the economy or which could bring about serious deterioration in the economic situation of a given area.' In such a case, any Member State may apply to the European Commission for an authorisation to take the necessary protective measures. They may involve derogations from the EC Treaty as well as the Accession Treaty 2005.

---

[35] Commission Regulation (EC) No 1962/2006 of 21 December 2006 on application of Article 37 of the Act of Accession of Bulgaria to the European Union, *OJ* 2006 L 408/8.

[36] In political terms, there is a bit of a paradox there since at the time when the Commission announced the application of the safeguard clause, one of its members (Commissioner Hübner) officially opened a new passenger terminal at the Sofia airport, in large part financed by the European Union. See Opening of new terminal for Sofia Airport co-financed by the EU, Press Release IP/06/1905.

[37] Arts. 1-2 of Regulation 1962/2006.

[38] Commission Regulation 875/2008/EC of 8 September 2008 repealing Regulation (EC) No 1962/2006, *OJ* 2008 L 240/3.

## 3.3.    Transitional periods

As in the case of previous enlargements, the acceding countries have an obligation to approximate their existing legislation to the *acquis communautaire*. Because no permanent opt-outs were available, the accession negotiations concentrated on transitional arrangements. In the case of Bulgaria, these are spelled out mainly in Annex VI to the Act.[39] The transitional periods relating to the free movement of workers were clearly inspired by the 2+3+2 model employed in the previous Accession Treaty.[40] The other temporal derogations relate to the free movement of services, the free movement of capital, agriculture, transport policy, taxation, social policy and employment, energy, telecommunications and information technologies, as well as the environment (air quality, waste management, water quality, industrial pollution and risk management).[41] It is impossible and in a way also pointless to discuss all of them. The rest of this analysis, therefore, is devoted to the areas of considerable sensitivity in the relations between Bulgaria and the European Union.

### 3.3.1.    *Free movement of workers*

The free movement of workers traditionally belongs to the areas of particular interest of acceding countries. In the perception of the general public, it is the key element that makes EU integration particularly attractive and renders the pre-accession effort worthwhile. As noted above, the Europe Agreements contained rather restrictive provisions in this respect, granting non-discriminatory treatment only to persons admitted legally to the labour markets of the Member States. This treatment remained in the hands of the legislators within the EU Member States. It did not come as a surprise that Bulgaria declared its readiness to apply the *acquis* upon accession[42] and did not request transitional periods.[43] It was the European Union that had an interest in imposing transitional arrangements, only gradually allowing Bulgarian nationals access to the labour

---

[39] Equally Annex VI to the Protocol.

[40] Treaty between the Kingdom of Belgium, the Kingdom of Denmark, the Federal Republic of Germany, the Hellenic Republic, the Kingdom of Spain, the French Republic, Ireland, the Italian Republic, the Grand Duchy of Luxembourg, the Kingdom of the Netherlands, the Republic of Austria, the Portuguese Republic, the Republic of Finland, the Kingdom of Sweden, the United Kingdom of Great Britain and Northern Ireland (Member States of the European Union) and the Czech Republic, the Republic of Estonia, the Republic of Cyprus, the Republic of Latvia, the Republic of Lithuania, the Republic of Hungary, the Republic of Malta, the Republic of Poland, the Republic of Slovenia, the Slovak Republic, concerning the accession of the Czech Republic, the Republic of Estonia, the Republic of Cyprus, the Republic of Latvia, the Republic of Lithuania, the Republic of Hungary, the Republic of Malta, the Republic of Poland, the Republic of Slovenia and the Slovak Republic to the European Union, *OJ* 2003 L 236/17.

[41] For a general overview, see Report on the Results of the Negotiations on the Accession of Bulgaria and Romania to the European Union, European Commission Doc. No. 5859/05.

[42] Details on Bulgarian legislation implementing the free movement of persons acquis is available at the official website of the Bulgarian Ministry of Labour and Social Policy, at: http://www.mlsp.government.bg/en/integration/euro/chapter-2/bg/index.htm.

[43] Intergovernmental Conference on the Accession of the Republic of Bulgaria to the European Union. Negotiating Position on Chapter 2: 'Freedoms of Movement of Persons', CONF-BG 37/01 and 23/02.

markets of its Member States. The negotiating position followed the 2+3+2 model, which was also applied to other countries of Central and Eastern Europe.[44] The relevant provisions of the Accession Treaty 2005 meet the European Union's position. It is important to note that the negotiations on Chapter 2 were opened in October 2001 and provisionally closed in June 2002. During this period, only fifteen EU Member States were engaged in the negotiations, although the future Accession Treaty was envisaged to be concluded by both the old and the new Member States.

As a general principle, the restrictions allowed under the Accession Treaty 2005 shall not result 'in conditions for access of Bulgarian nationals to the labour markets of the present Member States which are more restrictive than those prevailing on the date of signature of the Accession Treaty.'[45] By way of derogation from Articles 1-6 of Council Regulation 1612/68/EEC,[46] the Member States have been allowed to apply domestic law restricting access to their labour markets for an initial period of two years following Bulgaria's accession to the European Union. In fact, most of the old Member States decided to use this possibility and kept access to their labour markets quite restricted. The system was reviewed after two years.[47] However, most of the old Member States at that stage declared a desire to continue the application of the transitional periods for another three years. In the case of serious disturbances on the labour markets, or threats thereof, the Member States will be allowed to continue to apply restrictions for another two years. A notification to the Commission will be a *conditio sine qua non.*

The Accession Treaty 2005 allows Bulgaria to impose equivalent restrictions on the nationals of Member States that decide to make use of the transitional periods. Moreover, in the case of serious disturbances on the Bulgarian labour market, or serious threats thereof, Bulgaria may apply restrictions to Romanian nationals.[48] In such a case, the procedure envisaged in paragraph 7 of Annex VI to the Act is applicable.[49]

In order to placate serious concerns on the part of Germany and Austria, special derogations were allowed in relation to the free movement of selected types of services provided by companies established in Bulgaria.[50] In the case of Germany, the list includes construction services as well as industrial cleaning and the activities of inte-

---

[44] See M. Dougan, 'A Spectre is Haunting Europe… Free Movement of Persons and Eastern Enlargement', in Hillion, *op. cit.* n. 21, at pp. 111-141; A. Adinolfi, 'Free movement and access to work of citizens of the news Member States: the transitional measures', 42 *CMLRev.* (2005) pp. 469-498.

[45] Para. 14 of Annex VI to the Act.

[46] Regulation 1612/68/EEC of the Council of 15 October 1968 on freedom of movement for workers within the Community, *OJ* 1968 L 257/2 (English special edition).

[47] Communication from the Commission to the European Parliament, the Council, the European Economic and Social Committee and the Committee of the Regions – The impact of free movement of workers in the context of EU enlargement – Report on the first phase (1 January 2007-31 December 2008) of the transitional arrangements set out in the 2005 Accession Treaty and as requested according to the transitional arrangement set out in the 2003 Accession Treaty, COM (2008) 765.

[48] This possibility may be used provided that at least one of the existing Member States imposes restrictions towards Bulgaria.

[49] Under the same terms, Romania may impose restrictions towards Bulgarian nationals (see para. 1.11 of Annex VII to the Act).

[50] See also Joint declaration by the Federal Republic of Germany and the Republic of Austria on the free movement of workers: Bulgaria and Romania (Annexed to the Final Act).

rior decorators. The Austrian list is much longer, running from horticultural services to construction and security services. The restrictions can be maintained as long as both countries apply the derogations to Articles 1-6 of Council Regulation 1612/68/EC. Bulgaria is entitled to take equivalent measures, provided that the European Commission is informed.

The Accession Treaty 2005 also contains numerous provisions dealing with the status of Bulgarian workers employed in EU Member States prior to the accession. For example,

> 'Bulgarian workers legally working in a present Member State on the date of accession and admitted to the labour market of that Member State for an uninterrupted period of 12 months or longer will enjoy access to the labour market of that Member State but not to the labour market of other Member States applying national measures.'[51]

The Accession Treaty 2005 also provides for a special regime applicable to family members of Bulgarian workers. The main text of the Accession Treaty 2005 is supplemented by the Joint Declaration on the free movement of workers, in which EU Member States promise to make their best endeavours to grant increased access to their labour markets.[52]

### 3.3.2.    *Transitional periods – free movement of capital*

As in the case of some of the other new Member States, the acquisition of land belonged to the most sensitive areas of the negotiations. From the outset, Bulgaria requested a ten-year transitional period (counting from the day of accession).[53] The rationale for the request was clearly spelled out in Annex I of its negotiating position. The grounds were the following:

1.  The land market in the country is in the process of development;
2.  The price of land in Bulgaria is several times lower than the price of land in EU Member States;
3.  Due to the low income the Bulgarian citizens do not have yet the same possibilities as the citizens of the EU to acquire land;
4.  A uniform land cadastre and a property register are not completed yet. Their final completion and the availability of market information are basic prerequisites for further development of the land market;

---

[51]  Para.1.2 of Annex VI to the Act.

[52]  'The European Union stresses the strong elements of differentiation and flexibility in the arrangement for the free movement of workers. Member States shall endeavour to grant increased labour market access to Bulgarian nationals under national law, with a view to speeding up the approximation to the acquis. As a consequence, the employment opportunities in the European Union for Bulgarian nationals should improve substantially upon Bulgaria's accession. Moreover, the EU Member States will make best use of the proposed arrangement to move as quickly as possible to the full application of the acquis in the area of free movement of workers.'

[53]  Intergovernmental Conference on the Accession of the Republic of Bulgaria to the European Union. Negotiating Position on Chapter 4: 'Free Movement of Capital', CONF-BG 35/00.

5. After the completion of land restitution, a process of land consolidation is under way aimed at creation of economically viable farm structures.[54]

Another side of the problem was the Bulgarian Constitution, which, at that time, contained a prohibition of land ownership by foreigners. This was generally considered to be contrary to EU law.[55] Tanchev noted that, 'It is necessary that the subsisting ban on foreigners to acquire land under Article 22 of the Constitution be eliminated.'[56] The potential problem was also diplomatically acknowledged by the European Commission in its opinion on Bulgaria's membership application. It was noted that, 'While being compatible with the Europe Agreement, these restrictions hamper the free flow of capital.'[57] Since the amendments to the Bulgarian Constitution are discussed later in this chapter, it suffices to say at this stage that the necessary revision has taken place, and that the constitutional obstacle has been removed. The new version of Article 22 of the Constitution of Bulgaria entered into force at the moment of accession.[58]

The Accession Treaty 2005 provides for two transitional periods with regard to the acquisition of secondary residences and the acquisition of agricultural land, forests and forestry land. In the case of the former, Bulgaria may maintain the restrictions for five years from the date of accession. This applies to the acquisition of secondary residencies by nationals of the European Union or EFTA-EEA countries who are non-resident in Bulgaria, as well as legal persons formed in accordance with EU/EEA Member State law. The latter allows the maintenance of the restrictions that apply to nationals of EU/EFTA-EEA countries as well as legal persons established there for seven years following the date of accession. In the period following the signature of the Accession Treaty 2005, these categories of persons cannot be treated in 'a more restrictive way than a national of a third country.'[59] These restrictions do not apply to self-employed farmers who express a wish to establish themselves and reside in Bulgaria. The Accession Treaty 2005 provides for the initiation of a review procedure in the third year following the

---

[54] *Ibidem*, at pp. 4-5.

[55] See, *inter alia*, A. Albi, *EU Enlargement and the Constitutions of Central and Eastern Europe* (Cambridge, Cambridge University Press 2005) at p. 109; E. Tanchev, 'National Constitutions and EU Law: Adapting the 1991 Bulgarian Constitution in the Accession to the European Union', 6 *EPL* (2000) pp. 229-241.

[56] E. Tanchev, 'Constitutional amendments due to Bulgarian full EU membership', in A.E. Kellermann, J.W. de Zwaan and J. Czuczai, eds., *EU Enlargement. The Constitutional Impact at EU and National Level* (The Hague, T.M.C. Asser Press 2001) pp. 301-310, at p. 307.

[57] Commission Opinion on Bulgaria's Application for Membership of the European Union, DOC/97/11, at p. 47.

[58] The new version of Art. 22 of the Constitution of Bulgaria reads '(1) Foreigners and foreign legal persons may acquire property over land under the conditions ensuing from Bulgaria's accession to the European Union, or by virtue of an international treaty that has been ratified, published and entered into force for the Republic of Bulgaria, as well as through inheritance by operation of the law. (2) The law ratifying the international treaty referred to in paragraph 1 shall be adopted by a majority of two-thirds of all members of the Parliament. (3) The land regime shall be established by law.' The translation of the complete text of Bulgarian Constitution is available at the official website of the National Assembly of Bulgaria, at http://www.parliament.bg.

[59] Para. 3.2. of Annex VI to the Act.

date of accession. In the follow-up, the transitional periods may be shortened by a unanimous decision of the Council of the European Union.


4.      POST-ACCESSION MONITORING: CO-OPERATION AND
        VERIFICATION MECHANISM

4.1.    **Introduction**

The Accession Treaty 2005 itself provides for a one-stage procedure of invoking the safeguard clauses discussed in section 3.2. of this chapter. However, shortly before the sixth enlargement, the European Commission decided to develop a special political benchmarking mechanism to monitor implementation of necessary reforms by newcomers. This *par excellence* political mechanism was tailored to serve as a political tool allowing the European Commission to use a fair degree of pressure on Bulgarian and Romanian authorities. Before looking at the operation of the system, it is fitting to take a closer look at its legal basis and general aims.

To begin, the post-accession Co-operation and Verification Mechanism applies only to certain generally defined types of membership commitments. Namely, the scrutiny procedure extends to matters of respect for rule of law, reform of judiciary and fight against corruption. Due to limited competencies of the European Union in those areas, the European Commission has potentially little use of the traditional infraction procedure. However, those issues are of pivotal importance for the smooth functioning of Bulgaria (and Romania) as Member States of the European Union. Thus, those additional political mechanisms are quite crucial to secure ongoing monitoring. In terms of the methodology, they clearly reflect the pre-accession instruments that had been employed *vis-à-vis* the Central and Eastern European countries and are currently in operation in relations with the candidate and potential candidate states from the Western Balkans.

The Co-operation and Verification Mechanism is based on two decisions of the European Commission. Decision 2006/928/EC[60] deals with Romania and Decision 2006/929/EC with Bulgaria.[61] Both Decisions are based on Article 4(3) of the Accession Treaty 2005 and Articles 37-38 of the Act. They establish a benchmarking procedure allowing the verification of progress in the areas of judicial reform and the fight against corruption. Annexes to the Decisions set forth the lists of benchmarks to be addressed by the newcomers. The list of benchmarks for Bulgaria is bit longer than in the case of Romania and includes, *inter alia*:

---

[60] Commission Decision 2006/928/EC of 13 December 2006 establishing a mechanism for co-operation and verification of progress in Romania to address specific benchmarks in the areas of judicial reform and the fight against corruption, *OJ* 2006 L 354/56. See further, Chapter 16 in this volume.
[61] Commission Decision 2006/929/EC of 13 December 2006 establishing a mechanism for co-operation and verification of progress in Bulgaria to address specific benchmarks in the areas of judicial reform and the fight against corruption and organised crime, *OJ* 2006 L 354/58.

- continuing reforms of the judiciary,
- fight against corruption,
- fight against organised crime.[62]

Both newcomers have the obligation to report by 31 March of each year on the progress of necessary reforms. The European Commission shall provide the necessary technical assistance. It may also conduct fact-finding missions to Bulgaria and Romania. Failure to address the benchmarks may result in recourse to the safeguard clause; however, one has to remember that the latter remains available only until the end of 2009. The procedure set forth in both decisions does not preclude an immediate application of the safeguard clauses, should it prove necessary.[63]

The European Commission publishes reports on a biannual basis. They provide an overview of achievements and lists of tasks for the following periods. In the next section of this chapter, we shall take a brief look at the most recent report and its contents.

### 4.2. Co-operation and Verification Mechanism in operation: July 2009

On 22 July 2009, the European Commission published the latest series report on the progress (or, as some might argue, lack of progress) under the Co-operation and Verification Mechanism.[64] Indeed, despite the diplomatic language employed by the European Commission, one can clearly see relatively limited progress in meeting the well-known benchmarks. Some new momentum has been noticed, yet Bulgaria has failed to implement a robust policy for the fight against corruption and to adopt a comprehensive reform of the judiciary. The list of tasks for the next twelve months is impressive both in terms of the length and the seriousness of matters that need to be addressed. The state of affairs is profound enough to extend the application of this post-accession monitoring mechanism for at least one more year (going beyond the three-year period during which the safeguard clause mechanism is available). Unless the latter is activated before the end of 2009, the European Commission is going to lose quite a considerable weapon, which to the surprise of many, has not been used thus far.

The "to do list" is divided into two groups of tasks. The first one deals with the fight against organized crime and corruption. It requires several actions in order to:

'• develop an integrated strategy against organised crime and corruption;
- make the ad hoc structure of joint investigation teams on organised crime permanent;
- set up specialised structures for prosecuting and judging high level corruption and organised crime cases with appropriate functional and political independence;
- promote proactive ex-officio investigations of corruption by all administrative authorities with control functions;
- ensure effective implementation of the recent conflict of interest law through the development of implementing guidelines and a central reporting system;

---

[62] See Chapter 16 in this volume.
[63] See recitals 8 of both Decisions.
[64] *Loc. cit.* n. 4.

- on a horizontal level, monitor the impact of laws for the fight against corruption and organised crime and amend legislation where appropriate;
- improve the efficiency of the system to freeze/confiscate criminal assets;
- strengthen the capacity of the general inspectorate and of inspectorates to ministries and agencies and mandate them to act pro-actively in the identification and mitigation of vulnerable spots;
- strengthen the 28 regional anti-corruption councils in partnership with Civil Society;
- establish better administrative arrangements to safeguard whistle-blowers;
- monitor closely progress in the fight against corruption on central and local level through the inter-ministerial coordination group.'[65]

The list of tasks covering the reform of judiciary is equally long. Robust action is expected to:

'• proactively detect and analyse non-uniform application of law and stimulate further interpretative decisions by the Supreme Court;
- pursue urgently the draft concept paper for a full redraft of the Penal Code;
- consider a thorough reform of the Penal Procedures Code to simplify criminal proceedings and to reduce excessive formalism;
- implement urgently the recommendations of practitioners to improve practice under the existing Penal Procedures Code;
- implement all recommendations by the SJC regarding delays in important criminal cases and extend the monitoring systematically to all relevant cases
- monitor the use and impact of expedited procedures (lower penalty against confession) and plea bargaining;
- control the effective respect by all courts of the requirement to publish all judgements;
- ensure objective performance assessment of all magistrates and review the ordinance on rules and criteria for appointments by the SJC;
- analyse and address contradictory practice by the SJC in disciplinary proceedings;
- ensure a swift and effective follow up to the recommendations and findings of the inspectorate of the Supreme Judicial Council.'[66]

Not only are the contents of the tasks striking, but several other factors may also raise eyebrows and lead to fairly gloomy conclusions on the limits and potential of the Co-operation and Verification Mechanism. First, this list demonstrates clearly the limits of this *modus operandi*. One could reasonably argue that the soft political tools may be a driving force for several reforms, yet they fall short of achieving ambitious aims in countries suffering from profound fundamental problems in course of transition from communism to democratic governance.[67] This mechanism – in its post accession *alter ego* – has been in force for almost three years, and the list of tasks remains long and touches upon critical rule of law issues. Second, in legal terms, it remains a phenom-

---

[65] *Loc. cit.* n. 4, at p. 7.
[66] *Loc. cit.* n. 4, at pp. 7-8.
[67] For a comprehensive overview of EU's impact on the reform of the judiciary in Bulgaria, see D. Bozhilova, 'Measuring Success and Failure of EU-Europeanization in the Eastern Enlargement: Judicial Reform in Bulgaria', 9 *EJLR* (2007) pp. 285-319.

enon as most of the subject areas covered have limited formal legal basis in the Founding Treaties. In general, it is where the worlds of the European Union and Council of Europe collide. Nevertheless, since such matters affect the performance of countries like Bulgaria as Member States of the European Union, therefore, they remain of fundamental importance for the smooth functioning of the club. This, among other things, explains the need for the robust scrutiny in question. Third, Bulgaria serves as a very good example where the traditional approach to domestic constitutions and their immunity to pre-accession approximation become a bit redundant.[68] A number of times, Bulgaria has been invited by the European Commission to amend its basic law. One point was amendments necessary to meet the requirements stemming explicitly from EU *acquis* (*inter alia*, the voting rights of EU citizens); others have been revisions necessary to secure the independence of the judiciary and the rule of law. Bearing in mind their importance, the authors of this chapter devoted the next section to present them all.

5.      THE CONSTITUTION OF BULGARIA AND MEMBERSHIP OF THE
        EUROPEAN UNION

5.1.    **General remarks**

It is interesting to note that neither EA Bulgaria nor the Commission's White Paper imposed a direct obligation to change existing provisions of the Bulgarian Constitution.[69] However, this was the case with the accession partnerships and post-accession documents adopted under the Co-operation and Verification Mechanism, which, as already noted, called for the necessary revisions. Since its entry into force on 13 July 1991, the Constitution of Bulgaria[70] underwent four significant amendments. It is interesting to note that constitutional reform represents one of the few examples of joint and co-ordinated steps towards accession to the European Union, in which all political parties have taken part.

Before looking at the substance of those amendments, it is fitting to take a quick look at the revision *modus operandi*. The procedure for amending the Constitution adopted by the members of the Grand National Assembly addressed the apprehension of the "founding fathers" that passing acts of Parliament to amend the Constitution might be done in a fast and casual manner, which would be perilous for the young democratic traditions of the country. Each amendment of the Constitution starts under the procedure provided for in Chapter IX of the Constitution. The power to adopt the amendment act belongs to the National Assembly, i.e., the Bulgarian Parliament, with the exception of amendments within the powers of the Grand National Assembly. These include amendments affecting the territory of the country; changes in the form of state

---

[68]  See Chapter 3 in this volume.
[69]  Tanchev, *loc. cit.* n. 56, at pp. 229-241.
[70]  Конституция на Република България [Constitution of the Republic of Bulgaria], promulgated in State Gazette No. 56 of 13 July 1991.

and form of government; amendments to the provisions of Article 5, paragraphs 2 (direct applicability of the Constitution) and 4 (supremacy over domestic law of international treaties that have been ratified by the Parliament, promulgated in the State Gazette and are in force for Bulgaria), Article 57, paragraphs 1 (irrevocability of fundamental rights) and 3 (limitation of fundamental rights in wartime), and Chapter IX of the Constitution. The amendments are incorporated in an act of Parliament, which is passed under a procedure more complex than the ordinary legislative procedure. To begin with, the right of legislative initiative is limited to the President and one-quarter of all (or eighty) members of Parliament. The draft act is subjected to a debate at a session of the National Assembly, which is held no earlier than one month and no later than three months after its submission, thus providing a balance between two factors: having enough time for disseminating the draft act among the MPs and civil society and not allowing the parliamentary debate on the matter to get caught in a backlog. The draft act is passed by Parliament when it has successfully undergone three consecutive readings on three different working days and receives the support of three-quarters of all (or one hundred and eighty) members of Parliament.

## 5.2.    The first amendment

The debate on the first amendment of the Constitution[71] started as part of the judicial reform process in 2001-2002. The draft was presented in Parliament in July 2003 and was finally adopted in September 2003. The amendments to the Bulgarian Constitution introduced changes in three major areas that affect the status of the judiciary:

- immunity,
- appointment for life,
- term of office of administrative managers in the judiciary.

The amendments aimed to ensure integrity and unbiased judgments without compromising the independence of the judiciary. Immunity was limited to so-called functional immunity – criminal and civil non-liability for actions performed by members of the Bulgarian judiciary in their official capacity if not qualified as a premeditated offence. The legislator revised the provisions concerning the appointment for life of the members of the judiciary, extending to five the number of years of service required to achieve this status. Another amendment sets forth that members of the Bulgarian judiciary may be dismissed when they reach sixty-five years of age, previously upon retirement. The term of office of administrative managers was previously undetermined and was set at five years after the revision.

---

[71] Закон за изменение и допълнение на Конституцията на Република България [Act Amending and Supplementing the Constitution of Republic of Bulgaria], promulgated in State Gazette No. 85 of 26 September 2003.

## 5.3.    The second amendment

The second amendment of the Bulgarian Constitution[72] brought it into compliance with the provisions of the Treaty establishing the European Community and the Treaty on European Union, as well as – now defunct – the Treaty establishing a Constitution for Europe.[73] A new fundamental principle was laid down in Article 4(3): 'The Republic of Bulgaria shall participate in the establishment and development of the European Union', thus acknowledging that building up a united Europe is an ongoing task which involves all European states. Although the core of the public debate on the constitutional amendments was Article 22, which as already explained in the previous section of the chapter, governs the regime of land ownership in Bulgaria, the major changes are fourfold. They cover the lifting of the prohibition of land ownership by foreign persons, the lifting of the ban on extradition of Bulgarian citizens at the request of the competent authorities of EU Member States, the constitutional guarantees granted to citizens of the European Union to active and passive voting rights in local elections and elections to the European Parliament and the parliamentary majority needed to ratify the Accession Treaty.

## 5.4.    The third amendment

The third amendment[74] was adopted quite speedily[75] by the 40th National Assembly as the Bulgarian Government was already under strong pressure to continue with its commitment to the judicial system reform. The aim according to the draft was 'to improve the interaction between the legislative, executive and judiciary power and thus achieve better protection of the citizen's rights and fight crime and corruption.'[76]

One of the important changes[77] in the Constitution introduced by this amendment increases the grounds for criminal liability of the Bulgarian Members of Parliament (MPs). Generally, they have immunity from detention and prosecution, unless their immunity is withdrawn by the National Assembly or they are caught in flagranti. Previously, they could be detained and/or held criminally liable for serious public crimes (punishable by 5 or more years of imprisonment or life imprisonment).[78] After the amendment, the Members of Parliament can be prosecuted for all public crimes.

---

[72] Закон за изменение и допълнение на Конституцията на Република България [Act Amending and Supplementing the Constitution of Republic of Bulgaria], promulgated in State Gazette No. 18 of 25 February 2005.

[73] Доклад на временната комисия за подготовка на изменения в Конституцията на Република България [Report of the Ad hoc Commission on the Preparation of Amendments to the Bulgarian Constitution on the Draft Act to Amend and Supplement the Constitution of Bulgaria No. 454-01-137].

[74] Закон за изменение и допълнение на Конституцията на Република България [Act Amending and Supplementing the Constitution of Republic of Bulgaria], promulgated in State Gazette No. 27 of 31 March 2006.

[75] The Draft Act to Amend and Supplement the Constitution was submitted on 22 December 2005 and adopted on 30 March 2006.

[76] Ibidem.

[77] Art. 70 of the Constitution.

[78] Art. 93 Para. 7 of the Bulgarian Criminal Code.

Next, the institution of the ombudsman as an independent defender of the citizen's rights and freedoms is established.[79] The ombudsman's legal status, powers and duties are governed by the Ombudsman's Act.[80] One of the most important powers of the ombudsman is the right to bring proceedings for the unconstitutionality of secondary law or interpretation of the Constitution before the Constitutional Court.[81]

The rest of the amendment deals with the judiciary, in particular, with the right to draft the budget of the judiciary. This issue has been under ongoing debate for many years. Previously, the second amendment empowered the Minister of Justice to adopt the draft budget of the judiciary before it was submitted for voting to the Parliament. This amendment, however, was held unconstitutional as it encroached on the independence of the judiciary and 'violated the model of functioning of the powers provided for the Constitution.'[82] The new approach is to divide the power between the Minister of Justice and the Supreme Judiciary Council, which is an independent collective body consisting of members of the judiciary responsible, among others, for the appointment, promotions and dismissals in the judiciary.[83] In particular, the amendment empowers the Minister of Justice to propose the draft budget of the judiciary, which is then adopted by the Supreme Judiciary Council.

5.5.    **The fourth amendment**

The fourth amendment brought four groups of changes to the Constitution.[84] The first group is related to the abolition of compulsory military service (Arts. 9 and 59 of the Constitution). The second group aims to improve the efficiency and legitimacy in the functioning of the Bulgarian Parliament (Arts. 81 and 84 of the Constitution). The third group introduces changes in Chapter VI on the judiciary. The fourth group (Arts. 84 and 141 of the Constitution), empowers the municipal (local) authorities to determine the amounts of local taxes and charges in their bylaws. The establishing of the different types of local taxes and charges, as well as the republican ones, remains a prerogative of the National Assembly.

Of the above, the second and the third group deserve a closer look. One of the highly controversial changes is the abolition of the quorum for parliamentary sessions. Previously, a quorum of more than a half of all MPs was required for the entire duration of the sessions. After the amendment, the quorum is verified at the beginning of each session and prior to voting. According to the explanatory memorandum attached to the draft,[85] this aims to facilitate the functioning of the Parliament. But the question remains:

---

[79] Art. 90a of the Constitution.
[80] Закон за омбудсмана, [Ombudsman's Act], promulgated in State Gazette No. 48 of 2 May 2003.
[81] Art. 19 Para. 1 item 7 of the Ombudsman's Act.
[82] Judgment No. 7 of 13 September 2006 on case No. 6/2006.
[83] Art. 130 Para. 6 of the Constitution.
[84] Закон за изменение и допълнение на Конституцията на Република България [Act Amending and Supplementing the Constitution of Republic of Bulgaria], promulgated in State Gazette No. 12 of 06 February 2007.
[85] Проектозакон за изменение и допълнение на Конституцията на Република България [Draft Act Amending and Supplementing the Constitution of Republic of Bulgaria], No. 654-01-129, submitted 22 September 2006

is this not a clear recognition of the MPs absenteeism from parliamentary sessions and failure to deal with the problem by means other than merely revocation of the rule?

The amendments related to the judiciary are focused on strengthening the role of the Supreme Judiciary Council. An Inspectorate is established, to assist the Supreme Judiciary Council in the fact-finding related to its functions.

## 6.    PRE-ACCESSION APPROXIMATION OF LAWS AND CASE LAW OF BULGARIAN COURTS

### 6.1.    Introduction

The transposition and implementation of *acquis communautaire* is definitely a *conditio sine qua non* for EU membership.[86] In the pre-accession phase, the bulk of the effort rests on the shoulders of the legislature, which has an enormous task to approximate national law with the whole body of EU legislation. Bulgaria was no exception at all. The sources of law that were employed for that purpose varied. The Bulgarian legal order provides for the following sources, presented here in descending hierarchical order. At the top of hierarchy is the Constitution, followed by international treaties, acts of Parliament, acts of the Council of Ministers, acts of any of the ministers and acts of local government. Other sources include custom, the founding principles of law and justice.

The EU-related tasks of domestic courts are fairly limited in that period. Since EU law is not binding on candidate/acceding countries, the principles of supremacy and direct effect did not apply in Bulgaria prior to its accession to the European Union. However, a few examples of domestic case law demonstrate that Bulgarian courts considered themselves part of that process. To this end, in a few instances they took EU legislation into account while interpreting Bulgarian law. Although such cases were rare, nevertheless, they demonstrated the potential of this "Brave New World".

One of the few examples was a ruling of the Supreme Administrative Court that referred to the EA Bulgaria in case *'168 HOURS' EOOD v. the Competition Protection Commission*.[87] The claimant, a leading Bulgarian mass media company, submitted a motion for the judicial review of a decision in which the CPC imposed a penalty for a violation of Article 34(6) of the Competition Protection Act. In this case, the Court held:

---

[86] A formal legal basis for the approximation effort was Arts. 69-71 EA Bulgaria. The first of those provisions read 'The Parties recognise that an important condition for Bulgaria's economic integration into the Community is the approximation of Bulgaria's existing and future legislation to that of the Community. Bulgaria shall endeavour to ensure that its legislation will be gradually made compatible with that of the Community.' Considering the application for membership in the European Union, this proviso lost its best endeavors nature and should have been reinterpreted as an absolute obligation to approximate. See further, Łazowski and Yosifova, *loc. cit.* n. 6, at pp. 218-225.

[87] J-4420/30.07.1999 of the SAC on C-1257/1999.

'The concept of misleading advertising has been defined in the provisions of Article 2(3) of Council Directive 84/450/EEC.[88] The norms contained in the said Directive on protection against misleading advertising have been further developed in Directive 97/55/EC[89] of the European Parliament and the Council. Under the Competition Protection Act, the recommendations of the European Directives are fully taken into consideration by the Bulgarian legislator in the implementation of Articles 69-70 of the Europe Agreement … and in compliance with the undertaken obligation to approximate our legislation with that of the Community and to harmonise the measures granting administrative protection against misleading advertising and its prohibited effect on the consumers, competitors and the public interest.'

There is abundant case law of the Supreme Administrative Court in relation to the review of decisions of the Competition Protection Commission and, in particular, the review of penalties imposed under Article 34(6) of the Competition Protection Act. However, there are hardly any references to the case law of the Supreme Administrative Court and other Bulgarian courts. The main reason for this is that Bulgaria belongs to the family of civil law countries, and the case law of its courts is, therefore, not a source of law. This is the sole reason why the example of this judgment delivered in the late 1990s has not been taken forward by many Bulgarian courts.

Another interesting judgment[90] of the Supreme Administrative Court was delivered when a Bulgarian NGO seized the court with a claim regarding the compliance with Bulgarian legislation of a provision of an act of the Bulgarian Government,[91] which set forth the requirements for the photograph that should appear on the personal identification documents of Bulgarian citizens. Pursuant to this provision, a Bulgarian citizen was not allowed to use a photograph on which he or she wore a headscarf or hat on his or her identification document. The claimant maintained before the Court that this 'violated fundamental human rights and freedoms and facilitated indirect discrimination on the grounds of religion of those people whose traditional garments included wearing head or face scarves and hats.' The Court referred to Council Directive 2000/43/EC[92] and Council Directive 2000/78/EC[93] in order to substantiate its definition of the meaning of "indirect discrimination". It held that the limitation of fundamental human rights did not violate existing Bulgarian law or international legal instruments that are in force for Bulgaria, as the admissibility of this limitation of fundamental rights and freedoms was based on the priority of the public interest.

---

[88] Council Directive 84/450/EEC of 10 September 1984 relating to the approximation of the laws, regulations and administrative provisions of the Member States concerning misleading advertising, *OJ* 1984 L 250/17.

[89] Directive 97/55/EC of European Parliament and of the Council of 6 October 1997 amending Directive 84/450/EEC concerning misleading advertising so as to include comparative advertising, *OJ* 1997 L 290/18.

[90] J-11820/19.12.2002 of the SAC on C-7035/2002.

[91] Приложение No. 3 т.12 към Правилника за издаване на български документи за самоличност [Annex No. 3 i.12 to the Rules of Procedure for the issuance of Bulgarian identification documents].

[92] Council Directive 2000/43/EC of 29 June 2000 implementing the principle of equal treatment among persons irrespective of racial or ethnic origin, *OJ* 2000 L 180/22.

[93] Council Directive 2000/78/EC of 27 November 2000 establishing a general framework for equal treatment in employment and occupation, *OJ* 2000 L 303/16.

With regard to case law of the Constitutional Court, it is worth mentioning the judgment delivered in May 2005 on compliance with the Bulgarian Constitution of certain provisions of the Sea Spaces, Internal Waterways and Ports of Republic of Bulgaria Act.[94] By means of amendments to this Act, the Bulgarian Parliament tried to establish a new state-owned enterprise with the power to perform functions previously falling within the competences of the executive ports agency of the Ministry of Transport. Under the amendments, it was solely within the powers of the new enterprise to grant access to the Bulgarian ports, to collect port fees and decide on their disbursement, to implement port safety regulations, etc. The Court referred to – at the time – a draft Directive of the European Parliament and the Council on access to markets concerning the ports of the Member States.[95] In its judgment, the Court held that 'Art. 11(1) of the Draft Directive as an exception and subject to various limitations allows for the possibility that the managing body of the port may perform business activities, together with its state functions imposed by the national legislation.' The Court declared some of the provisions of the act of parliament unconstitutional. It held that 'Art. 11(1) of the Draft Directive [was] irrelevant with regard to the management model of the Bulgarian ports system', which was introduced by the Bulgarian Parliament by virtue of the amendments.

As argued above, those few examples from pre-accession case law demonstrate that already at that stage, there was a potential in Bulgarian courts to apply domestic law in a pro-EU fashion. Those examples were scarce; nevertheless, when viewed in hindsight, they were quite brave and promising moves.

7.     *APRES* ENLARGEMENT: THE APPLICATION OF EU LAW IN
       BULGARIA

7.1.   **Introduction**

Having briefly looked at the pre-accession case law of Bulgarian courts, we will turn the analysis to post-accession enforcement of EC law in national courts. A two-and-a-half-year period is relatively short and does not allow general conclusions of any kind. The first wave of truly post-accession cases is only now reaching Bulgarian courtrooms, and practice still remains scarce. However, the most recent examples presented in this section of the chapter demonstrate some early tendencies and practices. It is interesting to note that like all other new Member States that joined in 2004 and 2007, Bulgaria has seen challenges to EU legislation not available in Bulgarian by the time of accession, teething problems with post-accession cases based on pre-accession factual

---

[94] J-5/10.05.2005 of the CC on C-10/2004. For the Act, see Закон за морските пространства, вътрешните водни пътища и пристанищата на Република България, обн. ДВ бр. 24/2004 г. [Sea Spaces, Internal Waterways and Ports of the Republic of Bulgaria Act, promulgated in State Gazette No. 24 of 2004].

[95] Proposal for a Directive of the European Parliament and of the Council on market access to port services, COM (2004) 654 final.

background and first full-fledged post-accession EU law-based litigation. Samples of three categories of cases are presented in the sections of the chapter that follow. Before we turn there, a few words on the position of international law in the Bulgarian legal order seem necessary.

## 7.2.    The position of international law in the Bulgarian legal order

The Constitution of 1991 is the first to provide for the supremacy and direct effect of the Constitution and the primacy of international treaties over national law. Pursuant to Article 5(4) of the Constitution, all international treaties that have been ratified by the Parliament, promulgated in the State Gazette and are in force for Bulgaria become part of domestic law and have primacy over colliding provisions of national law. However, the Constitutional Court held that if a provision of the Constitution collides with a provision of an international treaty, the constitutional provision shall prevail. If any of the above prerequisites has not been fulfilled, the international treaty is in force for Bulgaria but does not become part of the legal order of the country and does not have primacy over conflicting national law. This creates a number of practical implications as not all international treaties ratified in the course of the last eighteen years have been duly promulgated in the State Gazette. In this regard, the Constitutional Tribunal ruled that in order to establish whether or not an international treaty has primacy over national law, it should be established whether at the time of the adoption of the treaty, there existed a statutory obligation to promulgate it. If such an obligation did not exist, then the treaty is part of the national law of Bulgaria. Nowadays, there is a trend towards promulgating the treaties that have not been promulgated at the time of their ratification for the sake of legal certainty. However, this belated promulgation may not remedy the lack of due and timely promulgation and does not have retroactive effect. Those provisions apply not only to traditional public international law but also to EU law.

## 7.3.    The immediate effect of EU law in Bulgaria and late publication of EU legislation in Bulgarian

The immediate effect of EU law in new Member States is thoroughly elaborated on in Chapter 4 of this volume; therefore, this section will repeat only some rudimentary points. Bulgaria, like all other newcomers became part of the European Union legal order on the date of accession. Article 2 of the Accession Treaty 2005 makes it clear that the *acquis* is binding on Bulgaria; moreover, according to Article 52 of the Act, Bulgaria is an addressee of EU legislation. The Act makes the necessary adaptations to the existing *acquis*. In relation to other measures omitted by the Act, the necessary legislation was adopted by the Council or the Commission shortly before the enlargement (according to the procedure set forth in Art. 56 of the Act).[96] Pursuant to Article

---

[96] See, for example, Council Regulation 1791/2006/EC of 20 November 2006 adapting certain Regulations and Decisions in the fields of free movement of goods, freedom of movement of persons, company law, competition policy, agriculture (including veterinary and phytosanitary legislation), transport policy, taxation, statistics, energy, environment, co-operation in the fields of justice and home affairs, customs

53, paragraph 1 of the Act, Bulgaria had the obligation to notify all national transposition measures to the European Commission by the date of accession, or at any later date specified in a piece of EU legislation. Should it prove necessary, the existing Member States also had the obligation to revise their national laws implementing directives in order to take account of the accession of the two countries.[97]

The extension of the EU legal system to Bulgaria implies that national courts and state administration had the obligation to ensure the effective application of EU law at the domestic level as of the date of accession. At the same time, Bulgarian courts have the jurisdiction to submit preliminary ruling references to the European Court of Justice with the exception of Third Pillar matters.[98] The effective application of EU law constitutes in itself a major challenge to the judiciary of any new Member State; Bulgaria is no exception. As mentioned many times in this volume, this is not only for purely internal reasons connected with the limitations of the judicial systems, but also due to considerable delays in the translation and publication of EU *acquis*.[99] The situation with the publication of the Special Edition of the Official Journal of the European Union in Bulgarian was equally problematic to the one experienced by the countries which joined the EU in 2004. In September 2006, the European Commission estimated that roughly 51% of the total number of pages was ready for publication in Bulgarian.[100] It was just a matter of time that the question of status of non-published legislation would be raised in Bulgarian courts. As of 11 December 2007, they could benefit from the judgment of the ECJ in case C-161/06 *Skoma-Lux*.[101] Although it had been rendered in the context of the fifth enlargement, the judgment can be applicable *mutatis mutandis* to the Bulgarian situation. Case law of the Bulgarian courts demonstrates that this is exactly the case. An analysis of the interpretative decision of the Supreme Administrative Court 3/06.06.2008 (General Assembly of the Colleges) is fitting at this stage.[102]

The factual and legal background to this interpretative decision is very complex. The case dealt with Bulgarian Value Added Tax Act 2006,[103] which in Article 3 specified that any person who carried out independent economic activity was subject to VAT,

---

union, external relations, Common Foreign and Security Policy and institutions, by reason of the accession of Bulgaria and Romania, *OJ* 2006 L 363/1; Council Directive 2006/110/EC of 20 November 2006 adapting Directives 95/57/EC and 2001/109/EC in the field of statistics, by reason of the accession of Bulgaria and Romania, *OJ* 2006 L 363/418; Decision 2006/881/CFSP of the Representatives of the Governments of the Member States meeting within the Council, of 30 November 2006 adapting Decision 96/409/CFSP on the establishment of an emergency travel document, in order to take account of the accession of Bulgaria and Romania to the European Union, *OJ* 2006 L 363/422.

[97] Art. 53 para. 2 of the Act.

[98] As of 1 July 2009 Bulgaria has not recognised the jurisdiction of the ECJ under Art. 35 EU.

[99] See, in particular, Chapter 5 in this volume.

[100] See Communication from the Commission. Monitoring Report on the state of preparedness for EU membership of Bulgaria and Romania, COM (2006) 549 final, at p. 32.

[101] ECJ, Case C-161/06 *Skoma Lux sro v. Celní ředitelství Olomouc* [2007] *ECR* I-10841.

[102] Under Bulgarian law, Arts. 124 and 125 of the Judiciary Act, State Gazette 64/2007 as amended, interpretative decisions are adopted by the two Supreme Courts (Supreme Administrative Court and Supreme Court of Cassation), where the interpretation and application of the law by the lower courts is divergent or incorrect, in order to ensure uniformity.

[103] Value Added Tax Act, State Gazette 63/2006, in force 1 January 2007 (as amended).

irrespective of purposes and results of that activity. It defined activities of private bail-iffs and public notaries as "independent economic activity". This was entirely in line with EC law, including case law of the ECJ.[104] In April 2007, the Constitutional Court found this provision unconstitutional due to a violation of the procedural requirements for its adoption by the National Assembly. Under Bulgarian law, if the Constitutional Court finds a provision unconstitutional, it is not applied as of the date of entry into force of a respective judgment. In order to reincorporate the problematic provision, the legislative procedure had to be repeated. This took place in December 2007, which was after the material facts in the case had taken place. Was the law to be interpreted broadly, as to include the private bailiffs and the notaries public among the VAT subjects, or was the law to be interpreted strictly?

The first view proved to be contrary to Article 60 of the Bulgarian Constitution, which stipulates that tax liability should be provided for in a law. Furthermore, anoth-er piece of Bulgarian law governed that criminal, administrative and disciplinary liabil-ity should not be established by interpretation. This view was advocated by the Bulgarian tax authorities. They argued that it followed from the ruling of the ECJ in case 235/85 *Commission v. Netherlands*.[105] The second view insisted on compliance with Article 60 of the Bulgarian Constitution and strict interpretation of the VAT Act. In essence, that view was based on case 152/84 *Marshall*[106] and advocated that the state could not plead the obligations of individuals, which are provided for in a non-implemented Directive. The SAC supported the second view. It held that the Sixth Directive had not been transposed into national law in the respective period and had not been published in the Bulgarian language in the Official Journal of the European Union. To support this argument, the Supreme Administrative Court referred to the *Skoma-Lux* case.

This decision has recently been confirmed by the Supreme Administrative Court (First Division) in case 6419/2009 *Customs Administration v. Kastel Export Ltd.*[107] It was rendered against the following factual background. Kastel Export Ltd imported goods of Chinese origin and, following the importation, an examination procedure was ordered by the customs authority pursuant to Article 84 of the Bulgarian Customs Act 1998 (giving effect to Art. 7(1) of the Community Customs Code).[108] The examina-tion led to the reclassification of the goods, and the customs authority levied a customs duty under the changed Taric number. It also imposed an additional anti-dumping duty. Those decisions were challenged by the importer before the Administrative Court. The Court found that the customs authority failed to specify the legal ground for imposing

---

[104] Council Directive 77/388/EEC of 17 May 1977 on the harmonisation of the laws of the Member States relating to turnover taxes – Common system of value-added tax: uniform basis of assessment, *OJ* 1977 L 145/1. See also ECJ, Case 235/85 *Commission of the European Communities v. Kingdom of the Netherlands* [1987] *ECR* 1471.

[105] *Ibidem.*

[106] ECJ, Case 152/84 *H.M. Marshall v. Southampton and South-West Hampshire Area Health Author-ity* [1986] *ECR* 723.

[107] J/18.5.2009 of the SAC on C-6419/2009 (available in Caselex database at http://www.caselex. com).

[108] Council Regulation 2913/92/EEC of 12 October 1992 establishing the Community Customs Code, *OJ* 1992 L 302/1.

the anti-dumping duty, and it also failed to state reasons for the decision in question. The Court *ex officio* took EC law on board. It found that Article 1(1) of the Regulation imposing a definitive anti-dumping duty on imports of steel ropes and cables originating in several countries (including China) imposed a definitive anti-dumping duty for goods of the kind imported by Kastel Export Ltd.[109] However, the Court observed that the publication of the Bulgarian version of this Regulation in the Official Journal of the European Union took place only upon the importation. This turned the Court to the analysis of Article 2 of the Accession Treaty 2005 (in combination with Art. 54 of the Act). The Court then referred to the principles of legal certainty and non-discrimination and the *Skoma-Lux* case. Based on these findings, the Administrative Court ruled that the definitive anti-dumping duty had to be revoked. The customs authority requested judicial review by the Supreme Administrative Court, which after a thorough examination upheld the judgment of the first instance court. It held that the import of the steel ropes had preceded the official translation and publication of the Bulgarian version of Regulation 1858/2005/EC in the Official Journal. Therefore, the Administrative Court had rightly concluded that the Regulation in question could have not been relied on *vis-à-vis* individuals. The Supreme Administrative Court emphasised that the official publication of Community acts was a *conditio sine qua non* for the application of the principles of supremacy and direct effect of Community law.

### 7.4.     Post-accession cases with pre-accession facts

As was the situation with other new Member States of the European Union, the first wave of cases to reach Bulgarian courts upon the accession were disputes with factual background locked in the pre-accession phase. The question that kept emerging in Bulgarian courtrooms was about the applicable law. The judgment of the Supreme Administrative Court in case 3302/2008 *Tourist Information and Registration Corp v. Customs Administration* is a very instructive example.[110] It was rendered against the following factual background. The Tourist Information and Registration Corporation (hereafter TIR Corp.), imported a Mercedes C200 car under the "transit" customs regime. The customs authority demanded proof of completion of the transit regime. However, in the absence of such proof, a customs duty was imposed pursuant to Bulgarian law. TIR Corp. was requested to pay the amount due on a voluntary basis. Failure to do so resulted in the adoption of a decision ordering the payment. TIR Corp. requested a review of the decision by the Director of the Regional Customs Directorate. It upheld the decision; therefore, the importer requested judicial review. Since the decision was upheld by the District Court, a further request for review was submitted to the Supreme Administrative Court. In its application, TIR Corp. referred to ECJ case law

---

[109] Council Regulation (EC) No 1858/2005 of 8 November 2005 imposing a definitive anti-dumping duty on imports of steel ropes and cables originating in the People's Republic of China, India, South Africa and Ukraine following an expiry review pursuant to Art. 11(2) of Regulation (EC) No 384/96, *OJ* 2005 L 299/1.

[110] J/24.3.2008 of the SAC on C-3302/2008 (available in Caselex database at http://www.caselex.com).

and argued that when required procedures are not adhered to, the ECJ favours appellants against the customs administration. The Supreme Administrative Court held that the customs administration was not bound by EU law at the time it made its decision. In its reasoning, the court referred to the *Gerlach* case,[111] where the ECJ provided a national court with the interpretation of relevant EC legislation on Community transit procedure.[112] However, this Regulation had not been applicable in Bulgaria prior to the accession. Therefore, the customs authorities were not obliged to apply EC law, nor were the courts obliged to reach their decisions based on the ECJ's decision. Since the facts had taken place before the accession and the litigation had been underway before the Republic of Bulgaria became an EU Member State, the decision had to be based on Bulgarian law applicable at the time. Accordingly, the Supreme Administrative Court held that the TIR Corp. was required to pay the customs duty as requested by the customs authorities.

This judgment of the Supreme Administrative Court of Bulgaria is hardly surprising, and, in fact, it mirrors case law of domestic courts from other new Member States. Also, it should be noted that it reflects fairly consistent case law of Bulgarian courts in such pre-accession cases. It merits attention that no Bulgarian court followed the footsteps of Hungarian and Polish courts, which tried to receive assistance of the ECJ in such cases.[113]

## 7.5. Supremacy and direct effect in operation

An overview of case law presented in this section demonstrates that the doctrines of supremacy and direct effect are slowly paving their way into Bulgarian courtrooms. Cases presented in this section of the chapter are a good illustration of this argument.[114]

The starting point is a very recent judgment of the Supreme Administrative Court rendered on 1 July 2009 in case 8768/2009 *Ministry of Interior v. Volodomir Filipenko*.[115] It was rendered against the following factual background. Volodimir Filipenko is a Ukrainian national with permanent leave to reside in Bulgaria. Filipenko was married to a Bulgarian citizen. His permit for permanent residence was withdrawn by the immigration authorities pursuant to the Bulgarian Foreigners Act 1998. According to the Act, permanent residence permits are withdrawn if foreigners spend less than 6 months in a previous year on Bulgarian soil. The decision in question was challenged by

---

[111] ECJ, Case C-44/06 *Gerlach & Co. mbH v. Hauptzollant Frankfurt (Oder)* [2007] *ECR* I-2071, paras. 33-39.

[112] Commission Regulation 1062/87/EEC of 27 March 1987 on provisions for the implementation of the Community transit procedure and for certain simplifications of that procedure, *OJ* 1987 L 107/1.

[113] ECJ, Case C-302/04 *Ynos kft v. János Varga* [2006] *ECR* I-371; Case C-261/05 *Lakép kft, Pár-Bau kft and Rottelma kft v. Komáron-Esztergom Megyei Közigazgatási Hivatal* [2006] *ECR* I-20; Case C-168/06 *Ceramika Paradyż sp. z oo v. Dyrektor Izby Skarbowej w Łodzi* [2007] *ECR* I-29. For critical assessment, see N. Półtorak, 'Ratione temporis application of the preliminary rulings procedure', 45 *CML-Rev.* (2008) pp. 1357-1381.

[114] The authors are grateful to Mr. Hristo Konstantinov (Apis) for his kind assistance and advice in the selection of case law presented in this section of the chapter.

[115] J/1.7.2009 of the SAC on C-8768/2009 (available in Caselex database at http://www.caselex.com).

Filipenko. In the request for judicial review, the plaintiff argued that his profession of a seaman did not allow him to stay the required minimum period in Bulgaria. Further complexity was added by the fact that Filipenko worked on a ship with UK registration. According to the plaintiff, he was entitled to rely on combined Articles 6 and 7 of Directive 2004/38/EC on EU citizens' right to move and reside freely.[116] The Administrative Court seized with the request for judicial review instead referred to Directive 2003/109/EC on the status of third-country nationals.[117] Pursuant to Article 9(1)(c) of that Directive, long-term residents are no longer entitled to reside after 12 months of absence. Having said this, the Court verified the conformity of Article 40(1) (6) of the Bulgaria Foreigners Act with the Directive. Since the Bulgarian law was not in compliance with the EC legislation, the Administrative Court held that in case of a conflict between Community and national legal rules, Community law had supremacy. Therefore, the decision of the Authority to withdraw Filipenko's permanent residence permit had to be set aside. This decision was challenged by the immigration authorities, who argued that the Foreigners Act was an imperative one, concerning the public order, and that it had no discretion to evaluate the merits of the case. The Supreme Administrative Court upheld the contested judgment. It confirmed the applicability of the Directive 2003/109/EC to Filipenko and the supremacy of Community law over national law. The Supreme Administrative Court challenged the argument submitted by the immigration authorities. It held that Community law had supremacy over national law, and it had to be applied not only by the courts but also by the state administration. Furthermore, the Court confirmed that as a seaman on ships sailing under the British flag, Filipenko had not actually left Community territory. The Supreme Administrative Court concluded that the Authority's decision to withdraw Filipenko's permit for permanent residence had to be set aside.

Also, the judgment of the Supreme Administrative Court in case 9083/2008 *Hild Bulgaria Ltd v. Consumer Protection Committee* merits attention. The appellant Hild Bulgaria Ltd (hereafter Hild) ran an advertising campaign in which it offered to buy homes from persons 65 years or older, indicating that it would make a lump sum payment and pay a lifetime rent, while these persons continued to live in their homes for the rest of their lives. The defendant – the Consumer Protection Committee – ordered Hild to discontinue airing its television commercial, stating that it amounted to misleading advertising under Article 33(2) of the Consumer Protection Act 2005. This piece of legislation prohibits such advertising. Hild requested judicial review of that decision by an administrative court; however, the decision was upheld. The Administrative Court in Sofia analysed the contract in question and held that it contained traces of misleading advertising (especially taking into account the receipients' target group). It is fitting

---

[116] Directive 2004/38/EC of the European Parliament and of the Council of 29 April 2004 on the right of citizens of the Union and their family members to move and reside freely within the territory of the Member States amending Regulation (EEC) No 1612/68 and repealing Directives 64/221/EEC, 68/360/EEC, 72/194/EEC, 73/148/EEC, 75/34/EEC, 75/35/EEC, 90/364/EEC, 90/365/EEC and 93/96/EEC, *OJ* 2004 L 158/77.

[117] Council Directive 2003/109/EC of 25 November 2003 concerning the status of third-country nationals who are long-term residents, *OJ* 2004 L 16/44.

to note that the Administrative Court referred to Article 153(1), (2) and (5) EC as well as to Directive 84/450/EEC on misleading advertising[118] and to Directive 2005/29/EC on unfair practicies.[119] Hild submitted an appeal to the Supreme Administrative Court. The Supreme Administrative Court considered that the dispute in question was not about the factual background of the case, but that an interpretation of the legal provisions was at stake. The key point was the interpretation of the term "misleading advertising" contained in the EC legislation and Bulgarian law implementing it. After a thorough analysis, the Court concluded that the words used in Hild's TV commercial did not mislead the consumers or harm their interests. The Supreme Administrative Court noted that Article 153 EC set out the general aim of the European Community; however, the vagueness of this provision precluded direct effect. The Court found that both Directives have been duly transposed to Bulgarian law (Consumer Protection Act 2005).[120]

Finally, it might be interesting to analyse the judgment of the Supreme Administrative Court in the case of *Rayko Raykov*.[121] The reasons for this are twofold. First, it is yet another example of application of EU law by a Bulgarian court. Second, the legal and factual background is quite similar to case *Jipa* from Romania, which led to the first reference from a Romanian court to the ECJ.[122] In the present case, the appellant Rayko Iliev Raykov challenged a decision of the Plovdiv Court of Appeal to allow a coercive measure imposed on him by the police. Under Bulgarian law, people who are convicted of intentional crimes but not reinstated into their rights,[123] may suffer certain restrictions on their freedom of movement abroad. They might not be allowed to leave the country, the authorities may refuse to issue passports and other identification documents to them and ones already issued may be reclaimed by the authorities. In November 2002, Mr. Raykov was sentenced to 17 years of imprisonment. In March 2008, a coercive measure was imposed by the chief of police in Plovdiv. From the appellate judgment, it is not clear what the crime that he committed was or what specifically did the coercive measure imply. Mr. Raykov argued that the Bulgarian law restricted his freedom of movement within the EU. He requested that the Supreme Administrative Court

---

[118] Council Directive 84/450/EEC of 10 September 1984 relating to the approximation of the laws, regulations and administrative provisions of the Member States concerning misleading advertising, *OJ* 1984 L 250/17.

[119] Directive 2005/29/EC of the European Parliament and of the Council of 11 May 2005 concerning unfair business-to-consumer commercial practices in the internal market and amending Council Directive 84/450/EEC, Directives 97/7/EC, 98/27/EC and 2002/65/EC of the European Parliament and of the Council and Regulation (EC) No 2006/2004 of the European Parliament and of the Council ('Unfair Commercial Practices Directive'), *OJ* 2005 L 149/22.

[120] Moreover, Art. 249(3) EC bound the Member States as to the result to be achieved, not to the means used to achieve those objectives. Therefore, the Court considered that those Directives could not have direct effect.

[121] J/16.12.2008 of the SAC on C-13983/2009 (available in Caselex database at http://www.caselex.com).

[122] ECJ, Case C-33/07 *Ministerul Administrației și Internelor – Direcția Generală de Pașapoarte București v. Gheorghe Jipa* [2008] *ECR* I-5157. See further, Chapter 16 in this volume.

[123] The term 'reinstated into rights' is used here in the sense of Arts. 86 to 88a of the Bulgarian Criminal Code.

make a preliminary reference to the ECJ under Article 234 EC. In particular, he wished to know whether Article 27 of Directive 2004/38[124] could be interpreted as allowing a national law restricting Bulgarian nationals' freedom of movement within the EU on grounds of a running imprisonment sentence.

The Supreme Administrative Court in a very brief decision did not find it necessary to make a reference to the ECJ under Article 234 EC. It held that the ECJ had already ruled on the issue at stake in its recent case *Jipa*. Specifically, it mentioned:

> '[T]he restriction on the freedom of movement on grounds of public policy or public security must be proportionate and must be based exclusively on the personal conduct of the individual concerned, and justifications that are isolated from the particulars of the case in question or that rely on considerations of general prevention cannot be accepted. ... [T]he personal conduct of that national must constitute a genuine, present and sufficiently serious threat to one of the fundamental interests of society and the restrictive measure envisaged be appropriate to ensure the achievement of the objective it pursues and not go beyond what is necessary to attain it.'

When applying the *Jipa* case, the Supreme Administrative Court supported its reasoning solely by referring to the fact of the appellant's long-term imprisonment sentence, which was enough for the SAC to define his personal conduct as a genuine, present and sufficiently serious threat to one of the fundamental interests of Bulgarian society. It held that the ban to leave Bulgaria was a proportionate measure.

All those judgments are definitely good examples demonstrating that EU law is slowly paving its way in Bulgaria. At the same time, the quality of judicial discourse is quite troublesome in places. The *Raykov* case merits closer attention in this respect. It is implied in the judgment that Mr. Raykov is serving a 17-year imprisonment sentence. His sentence became executable on 4 November 2002, that is, five years before Bulgaria joined the EU. He has never benefited from his right of free movement within the EU. If left to serve the full sentence, he will be out of prison in 2019. So the questions whether his freedom of movement within the EU was restricted seem rather theoretical. Next, it is not clear from the judgment what the implementation status of Article 27 Directive 2004/38/EC was. The SAC does not discuss this particular issue at all. It seems that it found the national law to be in conflict with the Directive; moreover it seems the Court found Article 27 to be directly effective. Without an in-depth analysis, the Court applied Article 27 of the Directive – as interpreted by the ECJ in case *Jipa* – to the facts of the case at stake and found that Mr. Raykov was indeed a felon sentenced to long-term imprisonment and banned him from leaving the country (and also reclaimed his passport). All of that was a proportionate coercive measure. Finally, the SAC applied the Directive without mentioning the fundamental status of

---

[124] Directive 2004/38/EC of the European Parliament and the Council on the right of citizens of the Union and their family members to move and reside freely within the territory of the Member States, has been transposed into Bulgarian law by means of the Act on entry, residence and leaving of the Republic of Bulgaria by EU citizens and their family members, State Gazette 80/2006, in force as of 1 January 2007.

the citizenship of the European Union, which lies at its heart of the case. The Court did not mention Articles 17 and 18 EC or corresponding case law.

## 8.    BULGARIAN COURTS AND THE PRELIMINARY RULING PROCEDURE

### 8.1.    Breaking the ice: case C-545/07 *Apis-Hristovich EOOD v. Lakorda AD*

As mentioned earlier in this chapter, as of the date of accession, Bulgarian courts have the jurisdiction to submit references for preliminary ruling pursuant to Article 234 EC and Article 68 EC. As Bulgaria has not yet recognised the jurisdiction of the ECJ under Article 35 TEU, no dialogue with the ECJ in matters of the Third Pillar is possible. The first reference from a Bulgarian court was submitted by *Sofiysky gradski sad* (Sofia City Court) on 19 November 2007 and dealt with interpretation of Directive 96/9/EC on the legal protection of databases.[125] The Bulgarian court was seized with a dispute between Apis-Hristovich EOOD and Lakorda AD regarding the *sui generis* right granted by the Directive and consequentially national implementing law.[126] Both companies market electronic databases for official legal data. The plaintiff argued that Lakorda AD illegally benefited from extraction and subsequent reutilisation of substantial parts of modules contained in its own databases. The question raised by the referring court deals with technicalities of such extraction (*inter alia*, the meaning of words "permanent transfer", "temporary transfer" as well as "extraction of substantial part"). Before looking at the substance of the reference, the European Court of Justice had to address the non-admissibility claim raised by Lakorda. Following well-established principles, the ECJ held that, subject to a few exceptions, when questions submitted concern the interpretation of Community law, it is – as a matter of principle – bound to give a ruling.[127] It was clearly so in the given case; thus, the ECJ rendered its judgment on 5 March 2009. It is notable that the ECJ decided to proceed without an opinion of the Advocate General. At the time of writing of this chapter, the final decision of the domestic court in this case was not yet available.[128]

### 8.2.    Subsequent references to the European Court of Justice

In a way, the *Apis-Hristovich* case has served as an ice breaker for other Bulgarian courts. Two more references for preliminary ruling have followed since the *Sofiysky gradski sad* made the first reference from Bulgaria. First, in early 2009, *Varhoven*

---

[125] Directive 96/9/EC of the European Parliament and of the Council of 11 March 1996 on the legal protection of databases, *OJ* 1996 L 77/20.

[126] *Sui generis* right is the right for the maker of a database which shows that there has been qualitatively and/or quantitatively a substantial investment in obtaining, verifying or presenting the contents to prevent extraction and/or reutilisation of the whole or of a substantial part, evaluated qualitatively and/or quantitatively, of the contents of that database.

[127] Para. 29 of the judgment.

[128] The authors are grateful to Mr. Hristo Konstantinov (Apis) for this information.

*administrativen Sad* (Supreme Administrative Court) submitted a set of questions on Articles 25 and 90 EC in relation to an allegedly discriminatory treatment of second-hand vehicles in Bulgaria.[129] Second, *Administrativen Sad Sofia* lodged in May 2009 a reference[130] on the interpretation of Council Regulation 1408/71/EEC.[131] Both cases are pending at the time of writing.

Following this brief overview, it is fitting to make a number of more general comments. Due to the secretive nature of the second and third references at this very early stage of the preliminary ruling procedure, some of those comments may look premature for those who will look at them with the benefit of hindsight. However, arguably, the Bulgarian courts are slowly getting familiar with the mechanics of the reference procedure and, what merits attention, have avoided mishaps comparable to the experience of Hungarian courts (discussed earlier in this volume). The *Apis-Hristovich* case may serve as a good example of a domestic litigation where the interpretation of EC secondary legislation plays a major role. Nuances of a very technical piece of legislation may indeed be a problem for even the most experienced national courts, let alone courts of the "Brave New World" coming to terms with EU law and its domestic enforcement.

9.      DIRECT ACTIONS

9.1.    **Infraction cases against Bulgaria**

As of 1 July 2009, no single case has been submitted to the European Court of Justice by the European Commission against Bulgaria pursuant to Article 226 EC. This, however, does not mean that the newest of the Member States has been on a membership honeymoon during the first years after accession. Quite to the contrary, a considerable number of infractions has already been launched but did not reach the judicial stage until mid-2009. The data available for 2007 shows that 107 cases were registered by the European Commission during that year. The majority of those were so-called non-communication cases,[132] most of which were dropped by the European Commission already in 2007 (out of 70 registered cases only 30 were subject to examination by the end of the year).[133] During the first year of membership in the European Union, Bulgaria received 80 formal notices and 2 reasoned opinions.[134] Since no case has yet been

---

[129] ECJ, Case C-2/09 *Peter Dimitrov Kalinchev v. Regionalna Mitnicheska Direktsia Plovdiv, OJ* 2009 C 55/19.

[130] ECJ, Case C-173/09 *Georgi Ivanov Elchinov v. National Health Insurance Fund, OJ* 2009 C 180/28.

[131] Regulation (EEC) No 1408/71 of the Council of 14 June 1971 on the application of social security schemes to employed persons and their families moving within the Community, *OJ* 1974 L 148/35 (amended).

[132] Non-communication cases are failures to notify national measures transposing directives.

[133] 25th Annual Report from the Commission on Monitoring the Application of Community Law (2007), Annex I Detection of infringement cases, COM (2008) 777, at p. 7.

[134] *Ibidem*, p. 10.

submitted to the European Court of Justice, it is very likely that most of those infractions have been resolved at the administrative stage.

## 9.2.    **Actions for annulment**

Bulgaria has thus far remained a very modest applicant in the EU courtrooms. The only two actions for annulment are still pending at the Court of First Instance at the time of writing and are very typical of a new Member State's challenges to the Commission's allocation of greenhouse emission allowances. In case T-500/07, Bulgaria has questioned the legality of the allocation for 2007 provided in Commission Decision C(2007) 5256 of 26 October 2007.[135] Case T-499/07 is the action for annulment of the allocation for 2008-2012 based on Commission Decision C(2007) 5255, also of 26 October 2007.[136] In both cases, Bulgaria submitted argumentation based on substantial procedural irregularities as well as infringement of the EC Treaty (including the principles of legal certainty and the principle of sound administration).

## 10.    CONCLUSIONS

The aim of this chapter was to present an overview of EU-related legal developments in Bulgaria. More than two years after the accession, Bulgaria remains a Member State that is learning the hard way how to participate in the club. At the same time, Bulgaria remains a big challenge for the EU itself, severely testing the potential and limits of its pre-accession conditionality and various benchmarking mechanisms. Alas, as demonstrated by regular reports of the European Commission, Bulgaria is still lagging behind with anti-corruption campaign and reform of judiciary. However, at the same time, some progress has been made. The overview presented in this chapter shows a growing volume of national case law which is based on EU law; moreover, Bulgarian courts have started to use the preliminary ruling procedure. Judicial discourse may not be up to the highest standards; yet practice usually makes a master. With more and more EU law-related cases reaching Bulgarian courts, the judiciary will hopefully gain confidence and experience with the new legal order. All in all, Bulgaria may be learning the hard way but certainly has a potential to become a full-fledged participant in the integration endeavor.

---

[135] Case T-500/07 *Republic of Bulgaria v. Commission of the European Communities*, OJ 2008 C 64/51.
[136] Case T-499/07 *Republic of Bulgaria v. Commission of the European Communities*, OJ 2008 C 64/50.

# CONCLUSIONS
## *Nowy Świat – Új világ – Nový Svět*

## Adam Łazowski*

This book gives a picture of a half full and half empty glass. This is not a black or white picture. There are plenty of shades of white, black and grey in-between. Depending on the point of view, we tend to see a glass that is half full or a glass that is half empty. Some of the authors (including the editor himself) see the results of the biggest EU enlargements as a successful endeavor. Despite all limitations and drawbacks, the overall balance sheet is seemingly positive. Bearing in mind the dramatic changes that have taken place in the past twenty years, one must argue that the recent enlargements have worked.

In 1995 Mirosław Wyrzykowski[1] wrote:

'The system transformations are brought about through legal means. Though historical experience shows that a revolution, meaning an interruption of the continuity of a legal system usually happens in the streets, the system transformation of Eastern Europe is being effected within the framework of law and by the law. We are watching a radical change in the political and legal systems being introduced through Parliament.'[2]

This acute observation reflected the state of affairs in the mid-1990s when the newly emerged democracies of Central and Eastern Europe were undergoing their first lesson of a multi-dimensional transformation from Huxley's "Brave New World" to democracy, political freedoms, independent judiciary and market economy. The transformation has proved to be turbulent, yet relatively peaceful,[3] as compared to the fall of Yugoslavia or some parts of the Soviet Union. In legal terms, this meant a radical change from a totalitarian system whereby a judge was generally considered to serve as a law enforcement officer and employ textual positivism (or binding *vs.* non binding

---

\* Reader in Law, School of Law, University of Westminster, London.

[1] Currently a judge at the Polish Constitutional Tribunal.

[2] M. Wyrzykowski, 'Selected Problems of System Transformation', in J. Aregger, J. Poczobut, M. Wyrzykowski, eds., *Rechtsfragen der Transformation in Polen* (Kraków, Wydawnictwo Baran i Suszczyński 1995) pp. 9-33, at p. 10.

[3] See, *inter alia*, A.L. Dimitrova, ed., *Driven to Change. The European Union's Enlargement Viewed from the East* (Manchester, Manchester University Press 2004).

*A. Łazowski (ed.), The Application of EU Law in the New Member States*
© 2010, T·M·C·ASSER PRESS, *The Hague, The Netherlands and the Authors*

dichotomy)[4] to an environment where national judiciaries operate in an ever-connected web of legal standards and are expected to be engaged in a judicial discourse. The process of transformation started twenty years ago, and, as proved in this volume, a lot has been achieved in a relatively short period. Naturally, it is not a success story in all possible respects, and to claim so would be an understatement of the decade. Yet, as argued in the introduction to this book, one can see this glass as half full rather than half empty. From such a perspective, we see a "Brave New World" within the meaning of those words. A brave, emerging new world in Central and Eastern Europe.

The fifth and sixth enlargements of the European Union have changed the integration endeavor completely. More than fifty years after the creation of the European Coal and Steel Community, Europe is enjoying – despite the current global recession – a period of peace and stability. This is largely attributable to the integration process that has turned traditional enemies into a ring of friends. Although criticism of the European Union is certainly *en vogue* these days, one cannot argue with the obvious fact that Europe – in the second part of the twentieth century and the first decade of the twenty-first century – has experienced an unprecedented period without a war of a massive scale. While old Member States tend to perceive EU integration as technocratic machinery for achievement of common goals, the newcomers have considered their *rapprochement* as the final chapter in the – far too long – history of the Iron Curtain. With twenty-seven Member States, the European Union has become an idiosyncratic polity spreading from the British Isles to the forests of northern Estonia or the Black Sea harbors in Bulgaria. Some argue that the enlargement policy has been the most successful external policy of the EU thus far. Some claim enlargement fatigue, post-accession blues and an unclear future for the EU. Seemingly, both of those opinions carry a bit of truth; neverthelesss, in 2009, the European Union simply works (for better or worse). As Chapter 1 demonstrates, no major decision-making paralysis has taken place, and the European Union has adjusted to the enlarged environment. It works despite the spectacular failure of the constitutional reform and unknown future of the Treaty of Lisbon.[5] The East has also brought new challenges to the West. External relations are a perfect laboratory for analysis of this change. With the EU borders moving eastwards, a new direct and rough at times neighbourhood has emerged. This is a major challenge not only to the European Union but also to the Member States, whose interests in particular regions do not always match or go together with visions of others. It is enough to mention relations with Turkey, Russia, Ukraine or the Western Balkans to start a long discussion on the peculiarities of the EU's external actions. Chapter 2 in this volume demonstrates clearly the complexities and challenges ahead for the EU in the aftermath of the fifth and sixth enlargements.

Although each and every newcomer had its own path to the European Union and had idiosyncratic experiences during the first five years of membership, a number of phenomena are appreciable best from a holistic perspective. The first of those is the

---

[4] See Chapter 10 in this volume.

[5] Treaty of Lisbon amending the Treaty on European Union and the Treaty establishing the European Community, *OJ* 2007 C 306/1.

constitutional change the accession brought. Unlike some of the old Member States, the newcomers, in one way or another, revised their constitutions prior or shortly after the accession to facilitate the transfer of sovereign powers and application of EU law at the domestic level. As Chapter 3 demonstrates, the breadth and style of those revisions varied. So did the approaches to the well-known conundrum of supremacy – EC/EU law *versus* national constitutions. In the first years of the enlarged European Union, we have witnessed Solange III saga in Hungary and Poland[6] as well as a very brave acceptance of supremacy of EU law over the national Constitution in Estonia.[7] Setting aside constitutional dramas, the real test for the effectiveness of EU law comes in national courts, which, at least theoretically, are faced on a daily basis with EU law-related litigation. As of the date of accession, the newcomers are addressees of EU law and are bound by it. This factor in itself – like any major change on a legal landscape – triggers a lot of intertemporal issues. Chapter 4 shows that the fifth and sixth enlargements of the European Union were not an exception. Traditional challenges associated with the application of new law were combined with the late publication of *acquis communautaire* in languages of the new Member States and the unwillingness of the European Court of Justice to assist national courts in post-accession cases with pre-accession factual background. The success of the European Union is quite often measured by the effectiveness of its unique legal order at the domestic level. Early predictions as to the ability of Central and Eastern European judges to apply the new legal order had been rather gloomy. All chapters contained in Part III of this book present a rather different view: after an initial warming up period, EU law is slowly paving its way in courtrooms from Tallinn to Sofia. As argued in Chapter 9, this looks like business as usual (which does not equal "great success"). Case law of domestic courts of the newcomers gives reasons for praise and reasons for concern. There is a plethora of examples demonstrating the ability to apply EU law and equally a plethora showing not the finest hour of national judiciaries. In a number of ways, it reflects the situation in some old Member States where judges are not always willing to take the challenge of EU law. In Chapter 5, M. Bobek looks at judges in the new Member States and the limits of the possible,[8] clearly showing the challenges waiting for EU law in the years to come.

The fifth and sixth enlargements of the European Union have triggered a new chapter in the years-long debate about the absorption capacity of the European Union. The accession of Bulgaria and Romania especially exposed weaknesses of the pre-accession conditionality employed *vis-à-vis* future Member States and forced the EU to revamp the existing framework for the Western Balkans and Turkey.[9] The final chapters of this

---

[6] See W. Sadurski, "'Solange, chapter 3': Constitutional Courts in Central Europe – Democracy – European Union', 14 *ELJ* (2008) pp. 1-35.

[7] Supreme Court of Estonia, 11 May 2006, Case 3-4-1-3-06 (*re Supremacy of EU Law*), available in English at http://www.nc.ee/?id=663.

[8] See also Z. Kühn, 'Worlds Apart: Western and Central European Judicial Culture at the Onset of the European Enlargement', 52 *AJCL* (2004) pp. 531-568.

[9] See, *inter alia*, S. Blockmans, 'Raising the Threshold for Further EU Enlargement: Process, Problems and Prospects', in A. Ott and E. Vos, eds., *Fifty Years of European Integration: Foundations and Perspectives* (The Hague, T.M.C. Asser Press 2009) pp. 203-220.

volume confirm that both newest members of the club are learning EU membership the hard way. Nevertheless, EU-related case law emerging from their domestic courts gives a bit of hope as to future developments.

It is twenty years since the Soviet empire started to crack and in a very short period of time fell apart like a castle made of sand. This historical event triggered an enormous legal change in Central and Eastern Europe. That historical perspective is absolutely crucial to understand the transformation these countries have gone through and to appreciate the effort that has been made. From that perspective, the glass looks half full, not half empty. The first years after the "big bang" enlargement of the European Union also demonstrated that the newcomers are slowly engaging in the ongoing EU law discourse. While the first examples of constitutional challenges might have looked a bit discouraging, judges of Constitutional and Supreme Courts are clearly passing the message as to their vision of united Europe. It may be a paradox; nevertheless, the beauty of the European Union is that the Latvian Constitutional Court renders more EU-friendly decision on the Lisbon Treaty than the *Bundesverfassungsgericht*.[10] This may be considered a sign of the value added by this new world (*Nowy Świat – Új világ – Nový Svět*) to the European Union. Arguably, it shows that the newcomers are willing and able to contribute in their own way to the ongoing existential dilemma of the European Union: *Quo Vadis?*

---

[10] Constitutional Court of Latvia, 4 April 2009, Case 2008-35-01 (*re Conformity of the Treaty of Lisbon with the Latvian Constitution*), available in English at http://www.satv.tiesa.gov.lv/upload/ judg_2008_35.htm; Constitutional Court of Germany, 30 June 2009, Case 2 BvE 2/08 (*re Conformity of the Treaty of Lisbon with the German Constitution*), available in English at http://www.bundesverfassungs-gericht.de/entscheidungen/es20090630_2bve000208en.html.

# ABOUT THE AUTHORS

**Anneli Albi** is a Senior Lecturer in European Law at the University of Kent (Canterbury, UK), which was recently ranked as a top six UK law school according to the UK's 2008 Research Assessment Exercise. She obtained her doctorate in 2003 from the European University Institute in Florence. Her doctoral thesis was published by Cambridge University Press as a book entitled *EU Enlargement and the Constitutions of Central and Eastern Europe* (2005). She recently completed the British Academy and European Commission funded project *The European Constitution and National Constitutions: Ratification and Beyond*, which led to a book published by Kluwer Law International (2006, co-edited with Prof. Jacques Ziller). Amongst a variety of consultancy work, she has lectured in EU law training seminars in South-East European countries, in the framework of the Netherlands Foreign Ministry funded MATRA Programme of the T.M.C. Asser Institute. She also serves as an expert in the European Commission's Gender Equality Network. Dr. Albi has frequently been invited to speak at conferences and to deliver guest lectures across Europe. Further details are available at http://www.kent.ac.uk/law.

**Samo Bardutzky** studied Law in Ljubljana and Greifswald. After graduating *cum laude* from the Faculty of Law of the University of Ljubljana in 2006, he completed his judicial traineeship at the Higher Courts of Ljubljana and Celje and passed the Slovenian State Law Examination in 2009. He has been employed as a Researcher in Constitutional Law at the Faculty of Law of the University of Ljubljana since 2007, where he also co-ordinates the Legal Clinic for Foreigners and Refugees project. In 2009, he was employed by the Ministry of Justice of the Republic of Slovenia to serve as a legal clerk to the group of experts preparing draft amendments to the Slovenian Constitution.

**Steven Blockmans** is a senior research fellow in EU law at the T.M.C. Asser Institute and the academic co-ordinator of the Centre for the Law of EU External Relations (CLEER). He is the author of *Tough Love: the European Union's Relations with the Western Balkans* (2007) and the (co-)editor of a number of volumes, among which are *The EU Constitution: the best way forward?* (2005, with Deirdre Curtin and Alfred Kellermann), *The EU and its Neighbours: a legal appraisal of the EU's policies of stabilisation, partnership and integration* (2006, with Adam Łazowski), *Reconciling the Deepening and Widening of the European Union* (2007, with Sacha Prechal), and *The European Union and Crisis Management: policy and legal aspects* (2008). Dr. Blockmans combines his academic research with consultancy activities carried out for the EU and the Dutch government. He frequently acts as a short-term expert in (potential) candidate countries to train judges, court staff and prosecutors in EU law. He served as a long-term expert in an EC project to Support the Ministry of European Integration of Albania in matters of legal approximation and the preparation of the administration for the next steps in the pre-accession process (2007-2009).

**Michal Bobek** is a PhD researcher at the European University Institute, Department of Law. He has qualified as a Czech judge, worked as a legal assistant (référendaire) for the Chief Justice and also served as the head of the Research and Documentation Department at the Supreme Administrative Court of the Czech Republic. B.A. (international studies, Charles University); M.A. (international relations, Charles University); M.A. (law, Charles University), Diploma (University of Cambridge); M. Jur. (University of Oxford; Jenkins Scholar and Visegrad Fellow); M. Res. (European University Institute); further non-degree studies at l'Institut d'etudes européennes, Université libre de Bruxelles (Erasmus/Socrates) and T.C. Beirne School of Law, University of Queensland, Australia (Sasakawa Fellow). President of the Czech Society for European and Comparative Law, co-founder and blogger at Jiné Právo. His areas of interest include various aspects of European Union law, comparative (public) law and legal theory. He extensively teaches and writes on EC law; his greatest mission (still to be accomplished) over the last few years following the 2004 EU Enlargement was to convince Czech and Slovak judges and legal practitioners at countless seminars and workshops that European law is a good thing.

**Irmantas Jarukaitis** is a lecturer at Vilnius University's Faculty of Law (Lithuania) and Deputy Director General of the European Law Department under the Ministry of Justice. Dr. Jarukaitis is an author and co-author of a number of books, articles and studies in the field of legal/constitutional issues concerning European integration and IT law (especially electronic communications). He participated in negotiations concerning Lithuania's accession to the EU. For a short period of time he worked at the European Commission, DG INFSO.

**Saulius Lukas Kalėda** holds Master's degrees from Vilnius University and the University of Bonn (ZEI), as well as a Doctoral degree in law from the Jagiellonian University in Cracow. His doctoral thesis on intertemporal and transitional aspects of the application of Community law in new Member States (*Przejecie prawa wspólnotowego przez nowe panstwo czlonkowskie: zagadnienia przejsciowe oraz miedzyczasowe*, Warszawa, WPiPG 2003) was awarded the prestigious prize of the "Panstwo i Prawo" Law Journal in Poland. Formerly an expert at the European Law Department of the Lithuanian Government and a lecturer at Vilnius University, since 2004 he has been working as a Legal Secretary at the EC Court of First Instance.

**Zdeněk Kühn** is an Associate Professor at Charles University Law School, where he teaches legal theory, criminal law and human rights. He is also a lecturer at the Judicial Academy of the Czech Republic, which further educates Czech judges, and has been the co-director of the international seminars *Constitutionalism: Europe and the United States in Comparative Perspective*, IUC Dubrovnik, since 2004. He graduated from the Charles University Law School in 1997 and received his PhD degree there in 2001. He holds a Master of Laws (LL.M.) and a Science Juridical Doctor (S.J.D.) degree from the University of Michigan Law School.

He has been awarded several prizes including the Bolzano Prize and the Hessel Yntema Prize, Berkeley, California, for the best article by a scholar under 40 (published in Vol. 52 of the American Journal of Comparative Law). In addition to publishing widely in the Czech Republic and abroad, Professor Kühn is also a legal practitioner (he passed the Bar Examination at the Czech Chamber of Advocates in 2000). He has served as a legal expert on Czech and Slovak law before US courts, for example in 2003 for the plaintiff in the case In Re: Assicurazioni Generali S.p.A. Holocaust Insurance Litigation (United States District Court Southern District of New York), one of the most important recent class action suits in the United States. In the autumn of 2007, he was appointed by the Czech government as an *ad hoc* justice at the European Court of Human Rights in Strasbourg in a highly profiled set of cases relating to rent control in the Czech Republic. In December 2007, he was appointed a Justice at the Supreme Administrative Court of the Czech Republic.

**Julia Laffranque** is a justice at the Supreme Court of Estonia. She sits in the administrative law and constitutional law chambers of the Supreme Court. Dr. Laffranque has a master's degree – LL.M. (Magistra legum) – from the Faculty of Law of the University of Münster, Germany and a PhD from the Faculty of Law of her home university (alma mater Tartuensis) – the University of Tartu, where she is also currently a lecturer (assistant professor) in European law. Dr. Laffranque is president of the Consultative Council of European Judges (a Council of Europe advisory body) and president of the Estonian Association of European Law (FIDE Estonia). She has served as an *ad hoc* judge at the European Court of Human Rights. From 1996-2004 she worked at the Estonian Ministry of Justice as an EU law expert, head of the EU and foreign relations division and later as a deputy secretary of state on legislative drafting. Dr. Laffranque has an Estonian White Star decoration and ordre national du mérite of the Republic of France.

She has studied at the Universities of Hamburg, Münster and Kiel in Germany as well as at the European University Institute in Florence and has undergone traineeships at the Legal Service of the European Commission, the Ministries of Justice of Sweden and France, the Federal Administrative Court of Germany and the Council of State of France. Dr. Laffranque is the author of the first Estonian law book on European Union law and institutions, and the co-author of a French-Estonian-French legal dictionary. She has presented papers at many conferences around Europe and in the USA, as well as published many articles in Estonian, English, German and French in different European and US legal journals.

**Adam Łazowski** is a Reader in Law at the School of Law at the University of Westminster (London). He obtained a Master's Degree in 1999 and a PhD in 2001 from the Faculty of Law of the University of Warsaw. Between 1999 and 2003, he lectured at the University of Warsaw. During the next two years, he worked as a senior researcher in European law at the T.M.C. Asser Institute (The Hague). Dr. Łazowski's scientific interests include the law of the European Union as well as public international law. His research has so far led to a number of books, articles, contributions to edited volumes and conference papers. In 2003, his monograph on non-judicial remedies in EU law received the first prize in a nationwide competition for the best book on EU law organised in Poland by the Foundation for the Promotion of European Law. Since 1999, Dr. Łazowski has actively participated in various EU law training programmes for practitioners in Poland, Bulgaria, Romania, Slovakia, Turkey and Estonia. In Estonia, he served as a mid-term expert in an EU-financed biannual project. In that capacity, he provided extensive training to national lawyers as well as co-writing a distance-learning course combined with a series of case studies aimed at Estonian judges. Over the past years Dr. Łazowski's teaching commitments have included the University of Warsaw (Poland), the University of Tartu (Estonia), Université Libre de Bruxelles (Belgium), the European Law Academy (ERA) in Trier (Germany), the University of Zagreb, the University of Luxembourg and the University of Basel. Further details are available at http://westminster.academia.edu/AdamLazowski.

**Ivan Sammut** graduated with a B.A. in Legal and European Studies from the University of Malta in 1999. In 2000 he was awarded the Diploma of Notary Public and graduated with the Degree of Doctor of Laws (LL.D) from the same University in 2002. The LL.D enabled him to be called to the Maltese Bar in 2003. In 2003 he was awarded an LL.M in European Legal Studies from the College of Europe in Bruges and in 2004 he obtained the degree of Magister Juris from the University of Malta. He is currently a PhD Candidate in European law at the University of London. Soon after being called to the Maltese Bar he joined a leading Maltese law firm for a few months after which we worked with the European Commission for two years. After leaving the European Commission in 2005, he joined the Faculty of Laws of the University of Malta as a full-time academic lecturer in EU law, in particular on the Internal Market and Private International law which are also his main research area.

**Stéphanie Laulhé Shaelou** holds a First Class LL.B. from the University of Paris, a B.A. in English and German for lawyers from the international language school I.S.I.T in Paris, an LL.M. in European and International Trade Law as well as a PhD in law from the University of Leicester. As an Assistant Professor at the University of Nicosia (Law Department), she specialises in EU law and wrote her PhD in the area of EU integration, EU external trade relations and the implementation of the Internal Market in Cyprus. She regularly participates in international conferences in her areas of research. Her publications include *The EU and Cyprus: strategies and principles of full integration* (Vol. 3, *Studies in EU External Relations*, Leiden, Brill/Martinus Nijhoff Publishers 2009); 'Cyprus', in W. Faber & B. Lurger, eds., *National Reports on the transfer of movables in Europe* (Vol. 2, *European Legal Studies*, Munich, Sellier-European law publishers 2009) (with S. Stylianou & K. Anastasiou); 'The European Court of Justice and the Anastasiou saga: principles of Europeanisation through economic governance', 18(3) *European Business Law Review* (2007) p. 619; 'Recent strategies towards the membership of Cyprus to the European Union: a case study on trade', 17(2) *The Cyprus Review* (2005) p. 103; 'Economic Aspects of Cyprus' Membership to the EU', *European Current Law* (July-August 1998) pp. 2-10.

**Kinga Tibori Szabó** is a PhD researcher at the Amsterdam Centre for International Law of the University of Amsterdam and a Dissertation Fellow at the T.M.C. Asser Institute in The Hague. Her PhD dissertation focuses on the right of self-defence in Public International Law. She is also a Legal Assistant for the Defence at the International Criminal Tribunal for the Former Yugoslavia. Her research interests focus on international criminal law, humanitarian law and military law. She received an MPhil degree in International Relations and European Studies from the Central European University (Budapest, Hungary) in 2006. She also obtained an LL.M. degree in international and European law from Utrecht University in 2004. She received her law degree from Babes-Bolyai University (Cluj Napoca, Romania). In 2005, Tibori Szabó worked as a Junior Legal Advisor on international and European law for the Legal Committee of the Romanian Senate. Since then, she has maintained an active interest in the progress of Romania as an EU member.

**Tamara Takács** is an Assistant Porfessor at the Europa Instituut of Utrecht University, School of Law, where she teaches courses on European Union law, international and European institutional law and international economic law. She wrote her PhD dissertation at Utrecht University School of Law and at the T.M.C. Asser Institute, The Hague. She received a Master's degree in European Union law (D.E.A en Droit Communautaire) from Université Nancy 2, Nancy, France in 2003. She obtained a law degree from the University of Pécs, Faculty of Law, Hungary, in 2002. Her research focuses on European institutional law, comparative constitutional law and EU external relations (EU enlargement, EU-WTO relations). Dr. Takács has delivered guest lectures at law schools in Hungary, the United States and Slovenia.

**Aleksandra Wentkowska** is a lecturer in law, Institute of European Studies, Jagiellonian University, Kraków. Dr. Wentkowska is also the Regional Commissioner for the Protection of Civil Rights in Poland and the Director of the Polish Ombudsman Office in Katowice. She is the author of more than 50 publications devoted to international and European law. She has been a guest lecturer at various Polish public institutions and universities in Slovenia, Turkey, Germany and Taiwan. She participated in a number of events and scholarships devoted to international law, including the Civic Education Project in Budapest (1997), The Hague Academy of International Law (1998), the European Institute in Florence (1999), the Summer School on the Comparative Interpretation of European Constitutional Jurisprudence at the University of Trento, Italy (2006). In 1996 and 1997 she attended Moot Court Competitions in Budapest and The Hague. In 2005-2006 she participated in the HESP Academic Fellowship Programme at the I. Franko University in Lviv as a non-resident international scholar. She is the founder of the Legal Students Association at the Silesian University, Journal *De Doctrina*

*Europea* and the chief editor of the *Humanitas Journal of European Studies*. She is a member of the ILA and FIDE.

**Svetla Yosifova** has been a lecturer in EU Law at The Hague University of Applied Sciences since 2007. She teaches EU economic and institutional law. Her research interests lie in the areas of enlargement, the internal market and competition law. Until September 2006, she had worked in Sofia, Bulgaria as a lawyer at PI Partners, a law firm associated with Ernst & Young. Her work involved assisting multinational companies in the set-up and regulatory compliance of their local branches, as well as legal due diligence projects. Prior to joining PI Partners in February 2005, she had worked on a judicial reform project under the EU PHARE Programme, which was implemented in Bulgaria by the British Council, the T.M.C. Asser Institute and the College of Europe. Svetla Yosifova holds an LL.M. in European Business Law from the University of Leiden (2007) and a Master's degree in Law from Sofia University St. Clement Ohridski, Bulgaria (2004). She was a MATRA scholar (The Hague Academy of International Law, 2005) and a Huygens scholar (University of Leiden, 2006).

**Saša Zagorc** is an Assistant Professor of Constitutional Law at the University of Ljubljana where he took his doctoral degree in 2008. He is a deputy member of the National Election Commission and a member of the Odysseus Network. He co-runs the Legal Clinic for Foreigners and Refugees at the University. He also serves as a legal expert for the Slovenian Football Association. He passed the State Law Examination in 2003. He has authored or co-authored several books and academic papers. Professionally, he deals with the status of state officials, parliamentary and election law, migration law and the European Union institutions

**Galina Zukova** is an Associate Professor at the Riga Graduate School of Law, Latvia where she teaches the settlement of disputes: private and public, international commercial arbitration and international economic law and WTO law. She is also a lecturer at the University of Latvia's Centre for European and Transition Studies, where she teaches the course Introduction to the European Union Law. Dr. Zukova obtained an LL.B from the University of Latvia and an LL.M in European Studies from the University of Exeter (UK). She has a PhD from the European University Institute in Florence. From October 2005 to November 2006, Dr. Zukova was a visiting scholar at the Yale Centre for International and Area Studies (Yale University). Prior to Latvia's accession to the EU, Dr. Zukova worked for the European Integration Bureau. Her latest experience includes work for the European Court of Justice, the Arbitration Court at the Latvian Chamber of Commerce and Industry and at one of the leading pan-Baltic law firms Raidla, Lejins & Norcous. In addition, Galina is among the founding members of the Society of International Economic Law (SIEL), which was established in 2008 in Geneva.

# INDEX